Architect's Legal Handbook
The Law for Architects

Ninth edition

Edited by
Anthony Speaight QC (Editor)

Consultant editor: His Honour Judge Gregory Stone QC

ELSEVIER

AMSTERDAM BOSTON HEIDELBERG LONDON NEW YORK OXFORD
PARIS SAN DIEGO SAN FRANCISCO SINGAPORE SYDNEY TOKYO

Architectural Press is an imprint of Elsevier

Architectural
Press

Architectural Press is an imprint of Elsevier
The Boulevard, Langford Lane, Kidlington, Oxford, OX5 1GB
30 Corporate Drive, Suite 400, Burlington, MA 01803, USA

First edition 1973 by the Architectural Press Ltd
Second edition 1978
Third edition 1982
Fourth edition 1985
Reprinted 1987
Reprinted 1989 by Butterworth Architecture
Fifth edition 1990
Sixth edition 1996
Reprinted 1997, 1998, 1999
Seventh edition 2000
Reprinted 2001, 2003 (twice)
Eighth edition 2004
Reprinted 2005, 2007, 2008 (twice)
Ninth edition 2010

British Library Cataloguing in Publication Data
A catalogue record for this book is available from the British Library

Library of Congress Cataloging-in-Publication Data
A catalog record for this book is available from the Library of Congress

ISBN: 978-1-85617-627-9

For information on all Architectural Press publications
visit our website at www.elsevierdirect.com

Printed and bound in the UK

10   9   8   7   6   5

**Working together to grow
libraries in developing countries**

www.elsevier.com | www.bookaid.org | www.sabre.org

ELSEVIER   BOOK AID
International   Sabre Foundation

Contents

Editor's Preface

The aim of this book remains to provide within the compass of a single volume a statement of the law relevant to an architect in practice.

No one lawyer could write with authority about so many different aspects of the law. Each chapter is contributed by an expert in the particular field. Our authors come from a range of backgrounds – barristers, solicitors and architects.

The book covers the law of the whole of Britain. In space terms the law of England and Wales occupies pride of place. But Scots law is also covered in respect of the many areas of law where it is different: I am grateful to Angus Stewart QC, of the Scots Bar, who has advised me as to Scottish authors. In a growing number of fields the law is the same throughout Britain by reason either of Westminster statutes or of EU directives.

At the risk of upsetting readers familiar with the order of chapters in recent editions, I have reordered the material into what I believe is a more logical arrangement:-

A. General principles of law.
B. The statutory framework: this part of the book encompasses the statutory authorities, construction, regulations, planning law, public procurement regulations, party wall legislation and health and safety law.
C. Building contracts: this covers procurement methods, the commonly used standard forms of building contract and Construction Act payment rules.
D. Building dispute resolution: this includes litigation, arbitration, adjudication and mediation.
E. The architect in practice: this part of the book focusses on architects' registration and professional conduct, architects' own contracts with clients and collateral warranties, and architects' liability in negligence; it also covers other aspects of the law relevant to an architect in practice such as copyright, employment law and insurance.

One of the changes over the years has been the decline in the popularity of the JCT forms. Once upon a time, any building contract of any formality would be likely to be on the conditions of one of the JCT family of forms. Partly as result of the complexity of JCT 1980 and its successors, other forms have come to be used, such as the Association of Consultant Architects' forms. Today the most important of these rival forms are those in the NEC family. At the same time new procurement methods – management contracting, design-and-build, and so on – have replaced the simplicity of the traditional arrangement. These changes are reflected by the inclusion in this book for the first time of a chapter on the topic of procurement methods, and by a chapter of its own being accorded to the NEC form. None of that prevents the May 2009 revision to JCT 2005 receiving detailed coverage.

While this new edition was in the course of preparation the government introduced into Parliament significant statutory changes by its Local Democracy, Economic Development and Construction Bill. It received royal assent in the final days of work on the revisions to this edition. I am grateful to the authors of chapters affected for so valiantly coping with the need to re-write parts of their text to incorporate changes made by the Act. However, these provisions are not expected to come into force until well after this book is published, so the old law will continue to be relevant for a little time to come.

The commencement of the UK Supreme Court in October 2009 provides a new focal point at the apex of our judicial system, whilst the ratification of the Lisbon Treaty may herald fresh changes from European institutions. Meanwhile architects may have more direct concern to study the 2010 ARB code.

Another change has been the growth of interest amongst architects in international work. Therefore, we have included two other new chapters to reflect this interest – one on the FIDIC form, and the other on arbitrations at the International Chamber of Commerce.

In fact, at the end of the task of assembling this ninth edition, I find that there are more new chapters, and more new authors, in this edition than in any of the previous revisions.

This book is not intended to turn architects into fully fledged legal advisers. What we hope is that it will identify for architects the legal issues affecting their work, and alert them to the circumstances in which legal advice is necessary. Unrealistic as many of us may consider the law's standard to be, the hard reality is that judges expect architects either to know a good deal of law themselves, or else regularly to call on legal advice. In *Rupert Morgan v Jervis* (2003) the Court of Appeal held that an architect might commit a negligent breach of duty if he failed to inform a client when a Construction Act withholding notice was needed.

It was a similar story in *West Faulkner Associates v London Borough of Newham* (1994). An architect's interpretation of 'regularly and diligently' in the JCT contract was different from that of the judges. The Court of Appeal said he would have been 'fireproof' if he had taken legal advice; but he had not, so he was not, and a heavy judgment against him for professional negligence was the result.

Anthony Speaight
4 Pump Court, Temple, London

Acknowledgements

Acknowledgement is given to the following bodies for permission to use sample documents and statutory publications:

Architects' Registration Council of the United Kingdom
British Property Federation
Building Employers's Confederation
Her Majesty's Stationery Office
Office for Official Publications of the European Communities
Royal Incorporation of Architects in Scotland
Royal Institute of British Architects
Scottish Building Contracts Committee

Extracts for the JCT documentation are reproduced by kind permission of the copyrights owners, The Joint Contracts Tribunal Limited, and the publishers, RIBA Publications.

The editors would also like to thank Anthony Lavers, Professor of Law of Oxford Brookes University for compiling the Bibliography.

Information provided in this document its provided 'as is' without warranty of any kind, either express or implied. Every effort has been made to ensure accuracy and conformance to standards accepted at the time of publication. The reader is advised to research other sources of information on these topics.

Contributors

Editor

Anthony Speaight QC – Barrister, in practice at 4 Pump Court, Temple, London. Bencher of Middle Temple. He is a co-author of *The Law of Defective Premises* and of *Butterworths Professional Negligence Service.* Anthony is a past member of the Council of the Society of Construction Law, past chairman of the Editorial Board of *Counsel, Journal of the Bar of England & Wales,* and past Chairman of the Bar Council's Access to the Bar Committee. He is a supervisor of dissertations at the King's College London Centre of Construction Law. He is an accredited Adjudicator and trained Mediator.

UK Contributors

Murray Armes, BA(Hons), DipArch, MA, MSc(Constr Law), RIBA, FCIArb – a Chartered Architect, adjudicator, expert witness and CEDR accredited mediator and a director of Probyn Miers Limited. He undertakes architectural consultancy in dispute resolution as an expert witness and adjudicator. He is on the adjudication panels of the Chartered Institute of Arbitrators and the Royal Institute of British Architects and is the Country Representative of the Dispute Resolution Board Foundation.

Graham Brown, ARB, RIBA, FCIArb – Architect, Arbitrator, Adjudicator and Mediator specialising in design, construction, and contract management and in construction industry disputes. Visiting lecturer at schools of architecture in the UK and overseas. Part 3 Examiner for Architects Registration Board and Architectural Association. Formerly director of Tindall Brown Architecture and Principal Lecturer in Law and Management and Director of Professional Training at Portsmouth School of Architecture.

James Cross, QC – read law at Magdalen College, Oxford and was called to the Bar in 1985. He was appointed a QC in 2006 having 'proved himself to be "absolutely first class"' (*Chambers UK*, 2007). James has an extensive and wide-ranging commercial practice with particular expertise in professional negligence (especially construction industry professionals), construction and engineering, insurance and product liability.

Dr Martin Dixon, MA PhD – Reader in the Law of Real Property, Fellow of Queens' College University of Cambridge, Visiting Professor of Law, City University, London. General Editor, *The Conveyancer & Property Lawyer.* Author (with C Harpum and S Bridge), Megarry & Wade, *The Law of Real Property.*

Ruth Downing – until September 2008 a Barrister in Devereux Chambers, a leading set of employment lawyers, now a Circuit Judge at Croydon Crown Court. After reading law at Cambridge between 1974 and 1977 she was called to the Bar at Grays' Inn and practised in both criminal and civil work before concentrating on employment law. She was a member of the Treasury Panel for employment work, specialising in discrimination cases. She appeared in a number of leading cases in disability and sex discrimination and latterly in a number of 'whistleblowing' cases.

Allen Dyer, BA Hons – practises from 4 Pump Court, a leading construction and commercial Chambers and specialises in construction, IT and professional negligence disputes. TECBAR-accredited Adjudicator and Past Secretary of TECBAR.

Tony Dymond – Partner, Herbert Smith LLP, Construction Projects and Engineering Group.

Richard Dyton, LLB, MSc, AKC – Solicitor, Partner at Simmons & Simmons; specialist advice to architects and engineers; negotiation and conclusion of international commercial agreements; author of *Eurolegislation in Building Maintenance and Preservation* (2nd edn) and *EC Legislation Affecting the Practice of UK Architects and Engineers.* Winner: Legal Business Construction Law Team of the Year: CTRL.

Martin Edwards, BSc(Hons)Arch, DipArch, RIBA, AAE, MIFireE – a Chartered Architect with 30 years' experience of private and public architectural practice, designing and administering hotel, office, exhibition, transportation, transmitting, industrial and housing projects. Principal in private practice 1992–2001. He joined Probyn Miers in 2003, contributing to expert reports on construction disputes up to £80 million. He has taken appointments as architect expert since 2005, specialising in fire safety issues.

Andrew Fraser-Urquhart, MA (Cantab) – called to the Bar in 1993, having previously been employed by the Bank of England. He practises from 4–5 Gray's Inn Square where he specialises in Town and Country Planning, Local Government and Judicial Review. He has extensive experience in both of planning inquiries and Local Plan work.

David Friedman, QC, MA (Oxon), BCL – specialises in litigation and arbitration concerning the construction industry and has been involved in most, if not all, types of construction disputes. He is a former Chairman of the Technology and Construction Bar Association and played a major part in drafting and administering the original TECBAR Adjudication scheme. He sits as an Arbitrator and has acted as an Adjudicator.

Jeremy Glover, (BA Hons), solicitor and accredited Adjudicator – joined Fenwick Elliott LLP over 10 years ago, becoming a partner in 2002. He specialises in construction, engineering and energy law both at home and abroad. Lead editor of *Building Contract Disputes: Practice and Precedents* and co-author of *Understanding the FIDIC Red Book: A Clause by Clause Commentary.*

Gordon Hall, BA (Law) LLB (Cape Town University); ACII; Advocate of the High Court of South Africa; Solicitor; Partner and Head of Construction Law at Radcliffes le Brasseur, London, specialising in Professional Appointment Documents and Warranties. Also qualified in Construction Insurance Law being an Associate of the Chartered Insurance Institute and a Chartered Insurance Practioner. Has previously worked in the Lloyd's and London Insurance markets.

James Leabeater, MA (Oxon) – Barrister practising from 4 Pump Court, Temple, London, in constructional, professional negligence and insurance law.

Sarah Lupton, MA, DipArch, LLM, RIBA, FCIArb – a partner in Lupton Stellakis and Reader in professional studies at Cardiff University. Lectures widely on subjects relating to construction law, and acts as adjudicator and expert witness in construction disputes. She is a member of a large number of industry and professional committees, and is also an elected member of the Architects Registration Board. Sarah is the author of many books, including a series on standard form building contracts, and is the editor of *Which Contract?* and *The Architect's Handbook of Practice Management.*

Stephen Mavroghenis – a partner at Howrey LLP in Brussels. In addition to advising governments and private entities on public procurement issues, he also advises on UK and EC competition law, including mergers and acquisitions, joint ventures, demergers, and public takeovers, cartel enforcement, dominance issues, state aid, and issues of compliance and competition governance.

Christopher Miers, BA, DipArch, MSc(Constr Law), RIBA, FCIArb, MAE – a Chartered Architect, Chartered Arbitrator and

a Director of Probyn Miers Limited, London, UK. He specialises in Dispute Resolution work in the construction industry in
the UK and internationally. Christopher is widely appointed as
an Arbitrator, Adjudicator, Mediator, dispute board member and
expert witness. He sits on JCT Council as a representative of the
RIBA. He is on the panel of mediators at the Centre for Effective
Dispute Resolution, Resolex and the RIBA, and as an Adjudicator
or Arbitrator he is also on the FIDIC President's List and the panels of the RIBA, RICS, ClArb, CEDR and CIOB.

Ann Minogue – a partner at Ashurst/LLP, specialising in construction law. She was involved in drafting construction documentation for many of the UK's major pioneering construction projects
of the 1980s. Ann is a past President of the British Council for
Offices (BCO), sits on the British Property Federation's (BPF)
construction committee and is a Member of the Strategic Forum
Olympic Task Group for London 2012.

Vincent Moran, MA (Cantab) – called to the Bar in 1991 and is a
member of Keating Chambers in London. He specialises in construction and professional negligence law. He is an editor of _Chitty on
Contracts_ (30th edition) and contributor to Keating on JCT Contracts.

Matthew Needham-Laing, RIBA, LLB, MSc, Architect, Solicitor
and TeCSA Adjudicator, Partner and head of the construction team
at solicitors Stevens & Bolton LLP – specialising in construction
and engineering law. Matthew advises employers, architects, contractors and sub-contractors in relation to the negotiation of construction and engineering contracts, appointments warranties and
acts for them in relation to disputes in adjudication, arbitration,
litigation and mediation.

Graham North, FRICS MClArb – a Chartered Building Surveyor
and Director of Anstey Home & Co, the leading Practice specializing in Party Wall and Rights of Light matters. He has updated
and edited _Anstey's Party Walls_ and _The Party Wall Surveyors
Manual_ by RICS books. In 2007 he was awarded the Michael
Barratt Memorial Medal by the RICS for his outstanding contribution to Party Wall matters.

Emelita Robbins, LLB – Senior Associate, Herbert Smith LLP,
Construction Projects and Engineering Group; Emelita specialises
in contentious construction, projects and engineering matters and
has a particular interest in PFI disputes. Emelita has been involved
in a number of large, legally complex and technical international
and domestic disputes and has experience of most forms of dispute resolution. Emelita is a regular contributor to industry and
legal publications.

John Salway – a Partner in Pinsent Masons' Construction and
Engineering Group. He advises clients on procurement, risk management, dispute avoidance and ADR. His practice includes drafting,
negotiating and advising on bespoke contracts and also project specific amendments to standard forms. He has particular experience of
negotiating and drafting amending provisions during the currency of
complex infrastructure projects. He joined Bechtel as Senior Counsel
in 2009. He has an LLB from Leicester University.

James Strachan, MA (Oxon) – a Barrister at Law practising
from 4–5 Gray's Inn Square, London, specialising in public and
administrative law, planning and environment, local government,
human rights and privacy. He was appointed to the A Panel of the
Attorney General's Counsel to the Crown in 2008 and the Welsh
Assembly's Government Panel of Counsel in 2009.

Clive Thorne – Partner and head of the Intellectual Property
Group at Arnold and Porter's London office. Co-author of
A User's Guide to Copyright and _A User's Guide to Design Law_.
He studied law at Cambridge and was admitted as a solicitor
in 1977. He is also admitted as a solicitor in Hong Kong and
as a Barrister and Solicitor in Australia. He is a Fellow of the
Chartered Institute of Arbitrators.

Melanie Willems, LLB (Hons), MSc Construction Law and
Arbitration – the head of International Arbitration at Howrey LLP,

a Washington DC-based US firm. Melanie works from the London
office, and her focus includes contentious construction and energy
matters, both domestically and internationally. Her experience
includes UK dispute resolution, international and domestic arbitration, and all forms of Alternative Dispute Resolution, including mediation and expert determination. She publishes and speaks
regularly on professional topics.

Scottish Contributors

Scottish Editor

Angus Stewart, QC, BA (Oxon), LIB (Edin), Advocate of the
Scottish Bar – formerly Standing Junior Counsel to the Department
of the Environment in Scotland, Keeper of the Advocates, Library,
Chair of the Scottish Council of Law Reporting, Chair of the
Faculty of Advocates Standing Committee on Human Rights, Senior
Advocate Depute, etc; his special professional interests include professional negligence, land law, health and safety, administrative law
and human rights; recent publications include articles on professional
negligence, health and safety, legal history and European law.

Scottish Contributors

Peter Anderson, LLB (Hons), currently Senior Litigation Partner
at Simpson & Marwick, Ediburgh. In 1992 became a Solicitor-
Advocate and in 2002 a Fellow of Royal Incorporation of
Architects in Scotland. In 1991 was appointed Royal Incorporation
of Architects in Scotland Legal Adviser. In 1994, he became a
Tribunal Judge for Criminal Injuries Compensation Appeal Panel
and Board; 2002 was appointed Chairman, Disciplinary Tribunal,
Institute of Chartered Accounts and in 2003 was appointed judge
in sheriff courts, Scotland.

Catherine Devaney, LLB Hons (Edin), DipLP, Advocate of the
Scottish Bar – professional interests include professional negligence,
land law, reparation and employement; she teaches on a part-time
basis on the Diploma in Legal Practice at the University of Edinburgh
and the Professional Competence Course for trainee solicitors.

Gordon Gibb, B Arch Dip Arch (Glas) LLM RIBA ARIAS
MCIArb – Director, Gibb Architects Ltd, Glasgow. Recipient of
Scottish Design Award 2005. Director of Professional Studies at
the Mackintosh School of Architecture. ARB Board vice chair, vice
chair of APSAA, co-author of Joint ARB/RIBA Part III Criteria,
RIBA Professional Examiner and Education Committee member,
APEAS Examination Committee member. Expert Witness with
over 20 years' court experience in contract and negligence claims.

Robert Howie, QC, LLB – Advocate.

James Murphie, Advocator – a graduate of the University of
Dundee, holding an LLB degree and a postgraduate Diploma in
Petroleum Law. He is admitted to the Scottish Bar, where he is a
practising member of the Murray Stable. James is an experienced
practitioner and academic specialising in employment law, European
Community law and criminal law. He is also a part-time tutor in EC
Law and EC Labour Law at the University of Abertay, Dundee.

Michael Upton – read Philosophy and Politics at Oxford
University and Law at Edinburgh University, and holds a Master's
degree in the law of the European Union from the European
University Institute at Fiesole. He was called to the Scots Bar in
1991 and practises in planning and commercial law. He has been
accredited as a Mediator by CEDR.

David O M Wedderburn OBE, Dip Arch, LLB, Dip LP, RIBA,
FRIAS, FClArb – a retired solicitor and architect with extensive
experience in private and public practice as an architect and in drafting and contentious construction law as a solicitor. He is a Member
of the Scottish Building Contract Commitee drafting commitee, and
a Member of the RIAS Contracts and Appointments Committee and
Chair of the Building Standards Advisory Committee and as such
was involved with the scoping, drafting, introduction and operation
of the new Building Standards System under the Building (Scotland)
Act 2003 and associated regulations.

Part A

General principles of law

1

Introduction to English law

ANTHONY SPEAIGHT QC

1 The importance of law

1.01 Every civilised human society has had a concept of law. The role of law within such a society is often expressed by the phrase 'the Rule of Law'. A distinguished academic lawyer, Professor Sir Neil MacCormick, recently explained the notion in this way:

> 'The Rule of Law is a signal virtue of civilised societies. ... This gives significant security for the independence and dignity of each citizen. Where the law prevails, you know where you are, and what you are able to do without getting yourself embroiled in civil litigation or in the criminal justice system.'
> (N MacCormick, *Rhetoric and the Rule of Law* (OUP, 2005))

The Rule of Law operates through the existence of many individual rules. In highly developed communities these rules have grown into a complex body of laws. Such laws are the subject of this book.

Architects and the law

1.02 It is an essential feature of the concept of the Rule of Law that its application should be universal: everybody must be subject to the law. It follows that the law must apply to an individual whether or not he is aware of the law. Hence the well-worn maxim that 'ignorance of the law is no excuse'.

1.03 This has a practical consequence for those who practise in any profession – in addition to the skills particular to that profession, they must also become acquainted with those parts of the law which are relevant to the work of their profession. Everyone who offers a service to others and claims expertise to do what he offers has a responsibility to society in general and to his clients in particular to know the law. That applies to architects, quite as much as to any other profession. Hence this book.

1.04 In the case of an architect, the relevant fields of law are notably those of contract, especially the standard forms of building contract, and the various statutory regulations, such as the Building Regulations, planning law, health and safety law, European procurement law, and the like. An architect will also want to know about the areas of law which affect him or her personally. When can he be sued? How can he sue for his fees? When is copyright in his drawings protected? How should he insure? What is the legal relationship between him and his employer, or between him and his employees? An architect is not expected to know all the law in these areas himself. But he is expected to ensure that his client does not suffer from the absence of his own legal knowledge. He is expected to know enough law to be aware of the circumstances in which specialist legal advice is needed. He should then advise his client to

obtain legal advice. Alternatively, he can himself instruct a barrister directly.

2 The legal systems of the United Kingdom

2.01 There are two principal legal systems in the Western world. One is the so-called civil law system, which prevails in most parts of continental Europe. It has its origins in Roman law and is today founded on written codes. The other is usually known as the common law system. This originated in England during the Middle Ages. Today it is the basis of law in Canada, Australia, New Zealand, Hong Kong, Singapore, and almost all former British territories. It is even the basis of law in the United States of America. The international character of English law is not often appreciated by non-lawyers, but is sufficiently alive for cases from other common law jurisdictions to guide English courts on those occasions, which are admittedly rare, when English case law is silent on a point. The courts of other common law countries more frequently follow English decisions. A Commonwealth Law Conference held every three years, at which the leading lawyers from remarkably diverse national backgrounds discuss legal issues together, serves to reinforce the bonds of the common law world.

2.02 Within the United Kingdom there are two traditions of law and three principal legal jurisdictions. English law prevails in the jurisdiction which is constituted by England and Wales. The English common law system is also the basis of the law in Northern Ireland, but Northern Ireland has its own statutory provisions and also its own courts. Scotland has not only its own courts, but also its own law and legal traditions. It had its own system at the time of the Union in 1707, and always retained them. Some aspects of Scots law are based on Roman law, and thus it reflects to some extent the features of the civil law system.

2.03 The one unifying feature of the legal system of the United Kingdom has been the House of Lords which was the supreme court of appeal for all three jurisdictions. It usually had twelve judges, of whom two were by tradition always Scots, and one has recently been from Northern Ireland. They were officially known as Lords of Appeal in Ordinary, and usually referred to as Law Lords. In October 2009 the judicial role of the House of Lords was taken over by a new UK Supreme Court. Apart from a change of name and a change of the building in which it sits, the new judicial body is currently undertaking judicial work in a manner similar to the House of Lords.

2.04 In consequence of this divergence between the legal traditions and laws of Scotland, on the one hand, and the other parts of the United Kingdom, on the other, throughout this book there will be separate sections discussing the particular features of Scots law.

3 Sources of English law

3.01 English law may be conveniently divided into two main parts – unwritten and written – and there are several branches of these.

Common law

3.02 Common law – the unwritten law – includes the early customary laws assembled and formulated by judges, with modifications of the old law of equity. Common law therefore means all other than enacted law, and rules derived solely from custom and precedent are rules of common law. It is the unwritten law of the land because there is no official codification of it.

Judicial precedent

3.03 The basis of all legal argument and decision in the English courts is the application of rules announced in earlier decisions and is called *stare decisis* (let the decision stand). From this has evolved the doctrine of judicial precedent, now a fundamental characteristic of common law.

3.04 An important contribution to the important position that the doctrine of judicial precedent holds today was made in 1865 by the creation of the Council of Law Reporting, which is responsible for issuing authoritative reports in which the judgments are revised by judges. Today judgments in many important cases are available free on the internet at http://www.bailii.org. A system of law based on previous cases requires well-authenticated records of decisions to be available to all courts and everyone required to advise on the law.

Authority of a judgment

3.05 Legally, the most important part of a judgment is that where the judge explains the principles on which he has based his decision. A judgment is an authoritative lecture on a branch of the law; it includes a *ratio decidendi* (the statement of grounds for the decision) and one or more *obiter dicta* (things said by the way, often not directly relevant to the matters at issue). It is the *ratio decidendi* that creates precedents for the future. Such precedents are binding on every court with jurisdiction inferior to the court that gave the decision; even courts of equal or superior jurisdiction seldom fail to follow an earlier decision. For many years even the House of Lords regarded itself as bound by its own decisions. In 1966 it announced that it would regard itself as free to depart from its previous decisions, and its is expected that the Supreme Court will feel likewise free. Nonetheless, House of Lords' departures from precedent were rare. One of the few occasions was the overruling of *Anns v Merton* [1978] AC 728 by *Murphy v Brentwood* [1991] AC 398 – a saga well known to architects, and described in Chapter 3 of this book.

Legislation

3.06 Legislation – the written or enacted law – comprises the statutes, Acts and edicts of the sovereign and his advisers. Although, historically, enacted law is more recent than common law because Parliament has been in existence only since the thirteenth century, legislation by Acts of Parliament takes precedence over all other sources of law and is absolutely binding on all courts while it remains on the statute books. If an Act of Parliament conflicts with a common law rule, it is presumed that Parliament was aware of the fact and that there was a deliberate intention that it should do so.

3.07 All legislation must derive its authority directly or indirectly from Parliament; the only exception being that in cases of national emergency the Crown can still legislate by Royal Proclamation. In its statutes, Parliament usually lays down general principles, and in most legislation Parliament delegates authority for carrying out the provisions of statutes to non-parliamentary bodies. Subordinate legislation is required which may take the form of Orders in Council (made by the Government of the day – in theory by the sovereign in Council), regulations, statutory instruments or orders made by Government departments, and the by-laws of statutory undertakings and local authorities.

3.08 The courts are required to interpret Acts in accord with the wording employed. They may not question or even discuss the validity of the enactment. Rules have been established to help them interpret ambiguities: there is a presumption that Parliament in legislative matters does not make mistakes, but in general this principle does not apply to statutory instruments unless the governing Act says anything to the contrary. The courts may decide whether rules or orders are made within the powers delegated to the authorised body ordered to make them, or whether they are *ultra vires* (outside the body's power). By-laws must not be only *intra vires* but also reasonable.

European Union law

3.09 Since 1 January 1973 there has been an additional source of law: that is, the law of the European Community. By accession treaty Her Majesty's Government undertook that the United Kingdom would accept the obligations of membership of the three original European Communities, that is, the Coal and Steel Community, the Economic Community and the Atomic Energy Community. That commitment was honoured by the enactment of the European Communities Act 1972. Section 2(1) of the 1972 Act provided that all directly applicable provisions of the treaties establishing the European Communities should become part of English law; so, too, would all existing and future Community secondary legislation. Since the terms of the treaties are in the main in very general terms, most detailed Community policy is embodied in secondary legislation. Most major decisions are taken in the form of 'directives', which require member states to achieve stated results but leave it to the member state to choose the form and method of implementation. Other Community decisions, known as 'regulations', have direct effect. In consequence, there is today an ever-growing corpus of European Union decisions incorporated into English law.

The European Convention on Human Rights

3.10 In 1950, a number of western European countries adopted a Convention for the Protection of Human Rights and Fundamental Freedoms (now invariably referred to as the European Convention on Human Rights). It was a symbolic response both to the horrors of Nazism in the recent past and to the curtailment of freedom in the communist states of eastern Europe. A novel feature of this Convention was the creation of a European Court of Human Rights Court in which individual citizens could present grievances against their Governments. For many years the Convention and the Court had no standing within the United Kingdom beyond the fact that the United Kingdom Government had by a treaty undertaken to accept them. Enthusiasts for the Convention saw it as potentially something which might play a role similar to that of the United States constitution. But this scenario faced a number of problems. First, the process of European integration has not, or at any rate has not yet, reached the point where United Kingdom domestic law is subject to a European federal law. Secondly, any form of entrenchment of fundamental rights in the United Kingdom is hard to reconcile with the democratic doctrine of the supremacy of Parliament, of which a facet is the principle that no Parliament can bind its successor. Eventually, a mechanism was adopted in the Human Rights Act 1998, whereby the Convention is accorded some standing in English law, without derogating from the supremacy of Parliament. This has been achieved by enacting that legislation should, so far as possible, be interpreted in accordance with Convention rights. If this is impossible, a court may make a declaration of incompatibility. Despite the interest which has been generated by the Human Rights Act, and the fact that it has been cited in a significant number of cases in recent years,

it has had little practical impact on the actual decisions of English courts: it has almost always been held, sometimes after prolonged argument, that existing English law is, in fact, compliant with Convention rights.

4 English legal history

The origins of the common law

4.01 One cannot understand some parts of English law, especially land law, without an awareness of its history. The seeds of custom and rules planted in Anglo–Saxon and earlier times have developed and grown gradually into a modern system of law. The Normans interfered little with common practices they found, and almost imperceptibly integrated them with their own mode of life. William I did not regard himself as a conqueror, but claimed to have come by invitation as the lawful successor of Edward the Confessor – whose laws he promised to re-establish and enforce.

4.02 The Domesday Book (1086), assembled mainly by itinerant judges for taxation purposes, provided William I with a comprehensive social and economic survey of his newly acquired lands. The feudal system in England was more universally applied than it was on the Continent – a result perhaps of the thoroughness of the Domesday survey. Consequently, in England, feudal law was not solely a law for the knights and bishops of the realm, nor of some parts of the country alone: it affected every person and every holding of land. It became part of the common law of England.

4.03 To the knowledge acquired from Domesday, the Normans applied their administrative skills; they established within the framework of the feudal system new rules for ownership of land, new obligations of loyalty to the administration under the Crown, and reorganised arrangements for control of the people and for hearing and judgment of their disputes. These were the true origins of our modern legal system.

4.04 Ultimate ownership of land in England is still, in theory, in the Crown. The lord as 'landowner' merely held an 'estate' or 'interest' in the land, directly or indirectly, as tenant from the king. A person holding an estate of the Crown could, in turn, grant it to another person, but the ownership still remained in the Crown. The tenant's 'interest' may have been of long or short duration and as varied as the kinds of services that might be given in return for the 'estate'. In other words, many different estates and interests in land existed. Tenure and estate are distinct. 'Tenure' refers to the relation of the landlord to his overlord, at its highest level to the king. 'Estate' refers to the duration of his interest in the land, and has nothing whatever to do with the common use of the word.

4.05 English law, as a result, has never used the concept of ownership of land but instead has concentrated on the fact of 'possession', mainly because ownership can refer to so many things and is ill fitted to anything so permanent and immovable as a piece of land. A man's title to land in England is based on his being able to prove that he has a better right to possession of it than anyone else who claims it.

4.06 In the reign of King Henry II (1154–1189) the 'king's justice' began to be administered not only in the King's Court where the sovereign usually sat in person and which accompanied him on his travels about the country, but also by justices given commissions of assize directing them to administer the royal justice systematically in local courts throughout the whole kingdom. In these courts it was their duty to hear civil actions which previously had been referred to the central administration at Westminster. It was these judges who created the common law. On completion of their circuits and their return to Westminster they discussed their experiences and judgments given in the light of local customs and systems of law. Thus a single system common to all was evolved; judge-made in the sense that it was brought together and stated authoritatively by judges, but it grew from the people in that it was drawn directly from their ancient customs and practices. To this day the year of Henry II's death, 1189, is regarded by the English common law as marking the start of legal history.

Equity

4.07 In the Middle Ages these common law courts failed to give redress in certain types of cases where redress was needed, either because the remedy the common law provided (i.e. damages) was unsuitable or because the law was defective in that no remedy existed. For instance, the common law did not recognise trusts and at that time there was no way of compelling a trustee to carry out his obligations. Therefore disappointed and disgruntled litigants exercised their rights of appeal to the king the – 'fountain of all justice'. In due course, the king, through his Chancellor (keeper of his conscience, because he was also a bishop and his confessor), set up a social Court of Chancery to deal with them.

4.08 During the early history of the Court of Chancery, equity had no binding rules. A Chancellor approached his task in a different manner from the common law judges; he gave judgment when he was satisfied in his own mind that a wrong had been done, and he would order that the wrong be made good. Thus the defendant could clear his own conscience at the same time. The remedy for refusal was invariably to be imprisoned until he came to see the error of his ways and agree with the court's ruling. It was not long before a set of general rules emerged in the Chancery Courts which hardened into law and became a regular part of the law of the land.

4.09 The consequence of the rules of equity becoming rigid was that the country had two parallel court systems, offering different remedies and applying different rules. The existence of separate courts administering the two different sets of rules led to serious delays and conflicts. By the end of the eighteenth century the courts and their procedures had reached an almost unbelievable state of confusion, mainly due to lack of coordination of the highly technical processes and overlapping jurisdiction. Charles Dickens describes without much exaggeration something of the troubles of a litigant in Chancery in the case of '*Jarndyce v Jarndyce*' (*Bleak House*).

Victorian reforms

4.10 Nineteenth-century England was dominated by a spirit of law reform, which extended from slavery to local government. The court system did not escape such reform. The climax came with the passing of the Judicature Acts of 1873 (and additional legislation in the years that followed) whereby the whole court system was thoroughly reorganised, and simplified, by the establishment of a single Supreme Court. The Act also brought to an end the separation of common law and equity; they were not amalgamated and their rules remained the same, but henceforth the rules of both systems were to be applied by all courts. If they were in conflict, equity was to prevail.

4.11 The main object of the Judicature Act 1873 was an attempt to solve the problems of delay and procedural confusion in the existing court system by setting up what was then called a Supreme Court. This consisted of two main parts:

1 The High Court of Justice, with three Divisions, all courts of Common Law and Equity. As a matter of convenience, cases concerned primarily with common law questions were heard in the Queen's Bench Division; those dealing with equitable problems in the Chancery Division; and the Probate, Divorce, and Admiralty Division dealt with the three classes indicated by its title.
2 The Court of Appeal – hearing appeals from decisions of the High Court and most appeals from County Courts.

Modern reforms

4.12 By the Courts Act 1971 there was a modest re-organisation of the divisions of the High Court. A Family Division was created to handle child cases as well as divorce and matrimonial property disputes, and the Crown Court was created in place of a confusing array of different criminal courts. During the last decades of the twentieth century the work of the County Courts was progressively extended, with the financial limit of their jurisdiction being progressively lifted.

4.13 By the Constitutional Reform Act 2005 a new UK Supreme Court has been established. It commenced operation on 1 October 2009. It took over the judicial work of the House of Lords. Whereas the present Law Lords were all peers with full membership of the upper chamber of Parliament, the judges of the new Supreme Court have no connection with the legislature. But individual judges are the same people: subject to any retirements, the existing Law Lords became the judges of the new court. Whereas the House of Lords sat in a committee room in the Palace of Westminster, the new court sits on the other side of Parliament Square in a building known as the Middlesex Guildhall, which until recently housed Crown Courts. The new Supreme Court will also hear challenges to the jurisdiction of the Scottish Parliament, Welsh Assembly and Northen Ireland Assembly – that is, cases raising questions as to whether those bodies' actions are within their devolved power.

4.14 Finally, mention should be made of a judicial body which in future will play no part in determining UK cases, but whose decisions are accorded the greatest respect in English courts. That is the Judicial Committee of the Privy Council. This body is composed, either wholly, or mostly, of the most senior UK judges, usually justices of the Supreme Court. Its work is to hear appeals from courts in various parts of the world, where the constitutions of the countries provide for a right of appeal to the Privy Council.

5 The scheme of this book

5.01 There are five main sections of the book:

1 In the first section the reader is offered the general principles of the law. This introductory chapter is immediately followed by chapters setting out the principles of the two areas of English law of the greatest importance to architects, namely contract and tort. A third area of basic English law of relevance to architects, namely land law, is also covered in an early chapter. There are separate chapters providing an introduction to Scots law and to Scots land law.
2 The second section is concerned with the statutory and regulatory framework. Statutory authorities are described. There follow chapters on statutory regulations in the fields of planning, construction regulations, and health and safety regulations.

EU regulations on public procurement and party wall law are also dealt with in this section.

3 The next main section of the book deals with what is almost certainly the legal subject of greatest day-to-day importance to architects, namely building contracts. This section begins with a general introduction. There is a full discussion on the most important of all standard forms, namely the JCT standard form (2005 edition). In the following chapters there is discussion of the NEC contract, nominated sub-contracting, and other standard forms; then collateral warranties from contractors and sub-contractors; then the international FIDIC form; and finally the payment rules imposed by the Housing Grants Regeneration and Construction Act and the Construction Act 2009.

4 The fourth section deals with dispute resolution. The normal method of resolving disputes in most spheres of activity is litigation. But in the construction world there are a number of alternatives which are frequently used. Most construction contracts contain an arbitration clause, by which the parties agree to be bound by the decision of a private dispute resolution mechanism: for many years arbitration was the most common mode of determining construction disputes. Today, however, the most common method is adjudication, which means a quick decision which is binding for only a temporary period. By legislation in 1996 a right to adjudication is now compulsory in almost all construction contracts. Such is the attraction of a quick decision that not only is adjudication today being used with great frequency, but hardly ever are adjudications' decisions being challenged in subsequent litigation of arbitration. Of growing popularity, too, is mediation, which refers to consensual meetings by parties with a neutral facilitator: the success rate in achieving a settlement at mediations is very high. Separate chapters deal with each of these methods of dispute resolution. This section is concluded by a chapter on international arbitration.

5 The final section of the book concerns the architect in practice. It begins with the law affecting the legal organisation of an architect's office. It covers the contracts which architects make with their own clients for the provision of their professional services, and contracts into which architects enter with non-clients in order to provide them with a cause of action against the architect if his professional work was faulty. The next chapter deals with the liability of architects when faulty professional services are alleged. That is followed by the chapter on professional indemnity insurance to cover architects against such risks. An architect's copyright in his own drawings is dealt with in the chapter on the distinct area of the law of copyright. The ever-changing field of employment law, which affects every architect who employs staff, is the subject of a separate chapter. The chapter on international work does not, by its very nature, deal with English or Scots law, and so in one sense ought not to be part of this book at all: but the information on the practices in other jurisdictions is invaluable to architects who undertake work abroad, and fits more logically here than anywhere else in this book. Finally, this section deals with architects' registration and professional conduct.

2

The English law of contract

ANTHONY SPEAIGHT QC

1 Introduction

1.01 The purpose of this chapter is to give an overview of the law of contract: to show both how it relates to other areas of the law, and to describe the general principles on which the English law of contract operates. Although most of the examples are from areas with which architects will be familiar, the principles they illustrate are for the most part general. Other sections of this book deal in detail with specific areas of the law of contract and their own special rules. The general rules described in this chapter may on occasion seem trite and hardly worth stating. Yet it is often with the most fundamental – and apparently simple – principles of law that the most difficult problems arise. Just as it is important to get the foundations of a building right, so also it is necessary to understand the basic rules of contract law, without which detailed knowledge of any particular standard form of contract is of little use. This chapter condenses into a few pages of material which if fully discussed would fill many long books. The treatment is necessarily selective and condensed.

2 Scope of the law of contract

2.01 The criminal law sets out limitations on people's behaviour, and punishes them when they do not conform to those rules. A criminal legal action is between the State (the Crown) and an individual. The civil law is quite different. It determines the rights and liabilities which exist between parties in particular circumstances. The parties to a civil action are known as 'claimant' (until recently the claimant was called 'plaintiff') and 'defendant' and the former claims a remedy for the acts or omissions of the latter. The difference, then, is that unlike criminal law (which is concerned with punishment) the civil law is about providing remedies – the law tries to put things 'back to rights' as best it can. The remedies available are various: the court may award 'damages' as a means of compensating the loss suffered by the claimant, or it may declare what the rights of the parties are, or, in certain circumstances, it will order a party to do or to refrain from doing something.

2.02 Two of the biggest areas of the civil law are contract and tort. In certain factual contexts they can overlap, and in recent years their overlap has caused the courts great problems, but they are conceptually distinct, and it is important to understand the distinction.

2.03 A claimant will sue a defendant in contract or tort when he objects to something the defendant has done or failed to do. Sometimes the claimant will not have spared a thought for the defendant – indeed, may very well not know the defendant – before the objectionable act or omission occurs. For example: the defendant carelessly runs the claimant over; the defendant's bonfire smoke ruins the claimant's washing; the defendant tramples across the claimant's field; the defendant writes a scurrilous article about the claimant in the local newspaper. All these wrongs are torts, indeed the label 'tort' is an archaic word for 'wrong'. Each of the torts listed above have particular labels, respectively negligence, nuisance, trespass and defamation. It is because the acts of the defendant have brought him into contact or proximity with the claimant the law of torts may impose a liability on the defendant. The law of torts is considered in Chapter 3.

2.04 On other occasions the claimant and defendant are parties to a contract, so that before the objectionable event occurs the parties have agreed what their legal obligations to one another shall be in certain defined circumstances. So, for instance, if the claimant engages the defendant plumber to install a new sink, and it leaks, or retains the defendant architect to design a house which falls down, or employs the defendant builder to build a house and it is not ready on time, the extent of the defendant's liability in a contract claim will depend on the terms and conditions of the contract between them. Of course, there may, in some circumstances, be an identical or similar liability in tort as well for the two are not mutually exclusive. But the conceptual distinction is quite clear.

3 What is a contract?

3.01 A contract is an agreement made between two or more persons which is binding in law, and is capable of being enforced by those persons in court or other tribunal (such as an arbitral tribunal). The people who made the contract are described as being party or 'privy' to it and they are said to enjoy 'privity of contract'. This expression means that the parties are drawn into a close legal relationship with each other which is governed by the agreement that they have made. That legal relationship creates rights and obligations between the parties and binds only between those who are privy to the contract, and not other people who are not parties (often described in law books as 'strangers' or by the misnomer 'third parties') even though those people may be affected by the contract directly or indirectly. The doctrine of privity of contract is examined in more detail later in this chapter. Usually the agreement will contain a promise or set of promises that each party has made to the other: this is known as a bilateral contract because each party promises to do something. For example, X promises to build a house for Y and Y promises to pay X for doing so. Sometimes only one party will make a promise to do something if the other party actually does something stipulated by the former. For example, X promises to pay £100 if Y completes and returns a marketing questionnaire to X. Such a contract is known as an unilateral contract because the promise is one-sided. Although X has promised to pay in the stipulated circumstances, Y is under no obligation to complete and return the marketing questionnaire but if he does the court or arbitral tribunal will recognise a binding agreement that X will pay him £100. In building projects during negotiations for the award of a formal contract one sometimes finds so-called letters of intent expressed in terms such as these: 'Please proceed with the works and if no formal contract is concluded we will pay you your costs and expenses that you have incurred.' It is often not appreciated that a letter in such terms can create a unilateral contract which the court will enforce, albeit not the formal contract which the parties had hoped to finalise. And although one often talks of a 'written' or 'formal' contract it is not really the piece of paper which itself is the contract – the piece of paper merely records what the terms of the contract are. For most types of contract there is no requirement for a written document at all and an oral contract is just as binding in law, although in practice when there is a dispute proving later what was orally agreed at the outset is more difficult. That difficulty is avoided if there is documentary evidence of what was agreed. Indeed, the usual (though not always the inflexible) rule is that the written document containing the agreed terms will be decisive evidence of the contract whatever the parties have said previously: this is sometimes called the 'four corners' rule.

Contracts under seal

3.02 There are some contracts which have to be made or evidenced in writing (such as contracts to transfer interests in land) and some contracts have to be made under seal. Either there is literally a wax seal at the end of the document where the parties sign, or there is some mark representing a seal. But any contract may be made under seal, and the seal provides the consideration for the contract (see below). The most important consequence, and often the reason why parties choose this method of contracting is that the limitation period for making a claim pursuant to a contract under seal is twelve years instead of the usual six (see paragraphs 14.01–14.02).

Basic requirements for establishing whether there is a contract

3.03 To test whether there is a contract the court or arbitral tribunal will look for three essential things: first, the intention of the parties to create legal relations, second, whether there was in fact agreement between the parties and third, whether there was consideration for the agreement. Each of these aspects requires further scrutiny.

4 Intention to create legal relations

4.01 'If you save me my seat I'll buy you a drink.' 'OK.' Such a casual exchange has all the appearances of a contract, but if the thirsty seat saver tried to claim his dues through a court he would probably be disappointed, for the law will not enforce a promise if the parties did not intend their promises to be legally binding. Bargains struck on terms that 'if you sell that car, I'll eat my hat' are not seriously considered to be legally binding. Similarly, one hears of people making a 'gentlemen's agreement' where honour dictates the actions between the parties along the lines of 'I'll see you right, if there is anything you need, it will be done'. However, a moral obligation is not enough.

5 Consideration

5.01 It is convenient to deal with consideration next. A simple one-way promise – 'I'll paint your ceiling' – without more is not a contract, because there is neither any element of bargain nor anything done in return. Again, a contingent promise such as 'I will pay you £100 if it rains on Tuesday' is not a contract. In such a case the person receiving the windfall of £100 did nothing to deserve or earn the money. It is important to distinguish this situation from a unilateral contract where there is a one-way promise but something is done in return. In the examples given above X completed and returned the marketing questionnaire; the builder proceeded to do the works while negotiations were ongoing. With the exception of

contracts under seal, English contract law demands that there must be consideration for the promise to be enforceable. Consideration is thus the other half of the bargain or, as lawyers used to say, the '*quid pro quo*', meaning 'something for something else'. In a unilateral contract the 'something else' is the performance by the party who wants to receive the promised benefit. In a bilateral contract often the promise of one party is exchanged for the promise of the other party. The court has defined consideration like this:

> 'An act or forbearance of one party, or the promise thereof, is the price for which the promise of the other is bought, and the promise thus given for value is enforceable.'
>
> (*Dunlop v Selfridge* [1951] AC 847 855)

5.02 There are a number of important and well-established rules about consideration. The rules, often expressed in rather antiquated language, are set out in the headings below but are best understood by giving some examples. Some, but not all, of these rules should now be considered with caution because the legal landscape has radically changed with the enactment of the Contracts (Rights of Third Parties) Act 1999. That Act made important changes to the doctrine of privity of contract, and consequently it will affect the closely related doctrine of consideration. The changes are discussed at paragraphs 12.05 onwards later in this chapter. However, the Act's provisions can be excluded if the parties so choose by the wording of their contract. It is the almost invariable practice for contracts in the construction industry, and in many other commercial fields, so to exclude the Act. Therefore, its practical effect is proving less than might have been expected.

1 Adequacy of consideration irrelevant

5.03 Although consideration must be given for value, this simply means that there must be some intrinsic value no matter how small: a peppercorn rent for a property, for instance, is good consideration. The value of the consideration can be quite disproportionate to the other half of the bargain which it supports. In *Midland Bank Trust Company v Green* [1980] Ch 590, a farm worth £40 000 was sold by a husband to his wife for just £500. £500 was good consideration. The court will not interfere with the level of consideration because to do so would be to adjudicate on the question of whether it was a good or bad deal for one of the parties. The commercial aspects of a contract, the bargain, is best left for the parties to decide.

2 Consideration must move from the promisee

5.04 If A (the promisor) promises B (the promisee) that he will build a wall on B's land and C will pay £1000 to A for doing so, there is no contract between A and B for the consideration of £1000 in return for the wall has not been given by B. B has done nothing to earn or deserve A's promise to build the wall so the court will not assist B in enforcing the promise. Another way of looking at this situation is to say that it is only when a party provides consideration that he is drawn into 'privity of contract'. It has been debated for centuries whether privity of contract and consideration are really the same thing or two sides of the same coin. At the very least it can be said that consideration is the touchstone for privity of contract for without consideration there can be no contract at all. Even if A and B had signed a piece of paper recording the 'agreement' between themselves, although they could say they are parties or privy to the arrangement, they do not enjoy privity of a (legally enforceable) contract. In the situation above, it might be that a contract was actually reached between A and C because each of them provided consideration which drew A and C into privity of contract. But the other essential requirements for a contract would need to be met before it could be said that there was a contract between them.

5.05 The effect of this rule is that if A does not build the wall, or does so but bodges the job, B has no right of recourse against A in contract. (He might, in certain circumstances, be able to sue A in tort if A bodged the building of the wall so that it collapsed and injured someone or if it damaged B's other property. This is no comfort to a peeved B who has no wall at all, or a badly built wall.) With the advent of the Contracts (Rights of Third Parties) Act 1999, however, so long as a contract exists between A and C, B would probably be able to sue A on the basis that a contract between A and C was for B's benefit even though B provided no consideration. B's position is, of course, not changed by the Act if no contract exists between A and C.

3 Consideration need not move to the promisor

5.06 On the other hand, if A promises to build the wall if B will pay £1000 to C (a local charity) and if B either pays C or promises A that he will pay C, B will have given consideration for A's promise. A contract will exist between A and B on these facts and B will be able to enforce A's promise. The difference between this situation and the former is that B has earned the right to enforce the agreement even though A does not directly benefit from B's consideration. C, however, is not a party to that contract and under the previous law C would have no right of recourse against B (or A) if B does not pay £1000 because C did not provide consideration. Now, C would be likely to use the 1999 Act to seek to enforce the contract by arguing that contractual promise to pay £1000 was for its benefit.

4 Consideration must not be past

5.07 The general rule (there are some ways around it) is that an act which has already been performed cannot provide consideration to support a contract subsequently entered into. Suppose A gives B £1000 at Christmas, and at Easter B agrees to build a wall for B 'in consideration of the £1000'. A cannot sue B if he does not build the wall, for there is no element of bargain, and no consideration supports the promise to build the wall. Also a past agreement to do something cannot usually be used as consideration for a new promise. However, in an unusual case, *Williams & Roffey Bros & Nicholls (Contractors) Ltd* [1990] 1 All ER 512, a main contractor had contracted to complete the building of some housing units by a certain time but it became clear that he was unlikely to do so because the sub-contractors were in financial difficulties and the main contractor was potentially exposed to liability for liquidated damages in his contract with the employer. The main contractor promised to pay the sub-contractors more money to ensure completion on time. The Court of Appeal held that that promise was enforceable because the main contractor's promise to pay more to ensure completion on time was supported by consideration from the sub-contractors. This was because the main contractor received the practical benefit of ensuring that he would not be penalised and that the work would continue (even though the sub-contractors were already contractually bound to do the work by that time).

5.08 As between the parties to a contract consideration rarely causes problems, because it is usually abundantly clear what the consideration is: very often in the contracts architects deal with, the consideration for providing works or services will be the fee to be paid for them. But on the rare occasions when consideration is lacking the consequences can be critical for the aggrieved party, who has no contract on which he can sue.

6 'Agreement'

6.01 The existence of agreement between the parties to a contract is in practice the most troublesome of the three essential ingredients.

6.02 The inverted commas around 'agreement' are intentional. The law of contract does not peer into the minds of contracting parties to see what they really intended to contract to do; it contents itself with taking an objective view and, on the basis of what the parties have said and done, and the surrounding context in which they did so, the courts decide what the parties should be taken to have intended. The court asks whether, in the eyes of the law, they should be considered to have been in agreement.

George Cruikshank.

6.03 To perform this somewhat artificial task the courts use a set formula of analytical framework which can be thought of as the recipe which must be followed by parties to a contract. The recipe is simple: offer and acceptance.

Offer

6.04 An offer is a promise, made by the offeror, to be bound by a contract if the offeree accepts the terms of the offer. The offer matures into a contract when it is accepted by the other party.

6.05 The offer can be made to just one person (the usual case) or it can be made to a group of people, or even to the world at large. The case of *Carlill v Carbolic Smoke Ball Company* [1892] 2 QB 484, [1893] 1 QB 256 is an example of an offer to all the world. The defendant company manufactured a device called a carbolic smoke ball, which was intended to prevent its users from catching flu. They advertised it with the promise that they would pay £100 to anybody who used the smoke ball three times a day as directed and still caught flu. The unfortunate claimant caught flu despite using the smoke ball, and not unnaturally felt she was entitled to the £100 offered. The Court of Appeal held that the company's advertisement constituted an offer to contract, and by purchasing the smoke ball the claimant had accepted the offer, so that a contract was created. Accordingly the claimant successfully extracted her £100 from the company.

6.06 Not all pre-contractual negotiations are offers to contract. In deals of any complexity there will often be a lot of exploratory negotiation before the shape of the final contract begins to emerge, and it is not until a late stage that there will be a formal offer to contract by one party to the other.

6.07 Easy to confuse with an offer to contract is an invitation to treat. An invitation to treat is an offer to consider accepting an offer to contract from the other party. Most advertisements 'offering' goods for sale, and also the goods lying on a supermarket shelf with their price labels, are merely invitations to treat. When the prospective purchaser proffers the appropriate sum to the cashier at the desk it is the customer who is making the offer, which can be accepted or rejected by the cashier. It will by now be obvious that the dividing line between an invitation to treat and an offer to contract can be very fine but the distinction is important.

Acceptance

6.08 The acceptance of the offer can be by word – written or oral – or by conduct and the acceptance must be communicated or made known to the offeror. Silence is not sufficient to accept an offer because neither assent nor dissent has been communicated by the offeree. The court is thus not able objectively to see whether there was an 'agreement': it will not peer into the offeree's mind.

6.09 An acceptance must be unequivocal and it must be a complete acceptance of every term of the offer. 'I accept your terms but only if I can have 42 days to pay instead of 28' will not be an acceptance, for it purports to vary the terms of the offer. It is a counter-offer, which itself will have to be accepted by the seller. And such a counter-offer will destroy the original offer which it rejects, and which can therefore no longer be accepted. In the old case of *Hyde v Wrench* [1840] 3 Beav 334, the defendant Wrench offered to sell some land to the plaintiff for £1000. On 8 June Hyde said he would pay £950. On 27 June Wrench refused to sell for £950 and on 29 June Hyde said he would pay £1000 after all. Wrench refused to sell. It was held that there was no contract. Hyde's counter-offer on 8 June had destroyed the initial offer of £1000 and by 29 June it was too late for Hyde to change his mind.

6.10 Sometimes an offer will specify a particular method of acceptance. For instance, A will ask B to signal his acceptance by signing a copy letter and returning it within 21 days. Ordinarily, B can only accept by complying with that method of acceptance. However, sometimes the court will decide that an equally effective method of acceptance will suffice if it is clear that both parties understood that there was acceptance and assumed there was a contract.

Revocation of offer and the postal rules

6.11 An offer can be withdrawn or revoked up until such time as it is accepted. An acceptance is, of course, final – otherwise people would constantly be pulling out of contracts because they had had afterthoughts. Since an offer can be both revoked by its maker and destroyed by a counter-offer, yet matures into a contract when it is accepted, it can be crucial to decide when these events occur.

6.12 An acceptance is generally effective when it is received by the offeror. But if the acceptance is made by posting a letter then the acceptance takes effect when the letter is posted. But revocation by post takes effect when the letter is received by the offeree. The working of these rules is neatly exemplified by the case of *Byrne v Van Tienhoven* [1880] 5 CPD 344. There the defendants made an offer to the claimants by letter on 1 October. The letter was received on 11 October and immediately accepted by telegram. Meanwhile, on 8 October the defendants had thought better of their offer and sent a letter revoking it. This second letter did not reach the claimants until 20 October. There was a binding contract because the acceptance took effect before the revocation. The result would have been the same even if the acceptance had been by letter and the letter had arrived with the defendants after 20 October.

Battle of the forms

6.13 These mostly Victorian rules about offer and acceptance may seem rather irrelevant to modern commercial transactions. But there is one context in which they regularly appear: the so-called 'battle of the forms' which takes place when two contracting parties both deal on their own standard terms of business, typically appearing on the reverse of their estimates, orders, invoices and other business stationery.

6.14 A vendor sends an estimate on his usual business form, with his standard terms and conditions on the reverse, and a note saying that all business is done on his standard terms. The purchaser sends back an order purporting to accept the estimate, but on the back of his acceptance are his standard terms, which are doubtless more favourable to him than the vendor's. The vendor sends the goods, and the purchaser pays for them. Is there a contract, and if there is, whose standard terms is it on?

6.15 The purchaser's 'acceptance' and order is not a true acceptance, because it does not accept all the terms of the vendor's offer, since it purports to substitute the purchaser's standard terms. So the purchaser's order is in legal terms a counter-offer, and this is accepted – in this example – by the vendor's action in sending the goods.

6.16 If there are long-drawn-out negotiations as to quantities, prices and so on, all on business stationery containing standard terms, the problems are compounded, and the result, best found by working backwards and identifying the last communication on standard terms, is rather artificial and is rather a matter of luck.

6.17 The courts have tried on occasion to substitute a rather less mechanical analysis of offer and acceptance, looking at the negotiations as a whole (see especially Lord Denning in *Butler Machine Tool Co. Ltd v Ex-Cell-O Corporation (England) Ltd* [1979] 1 WLR 401 at 405) but this approach has not found universal judicial acceptance, and it seems that whatever the artificiality of a strict analysis in terms of offer and acceptance it is difficult to find an alternative approach which is workable in all cases. However, in many construction and commercial cases in which protracted and complex negotiations result in a situation considered to be binding by the parties, pinpointing a defining moment when an offer and an acceptance was made ignores the modern commercial reality. In such cases, the court and arbitral tribunal tends to adopt an approach suitable to the needs of the business community and will look over the whole course of the negotiations to see whether the parties have agreed on all the essential terms. If they have the court or arbitral tribunal will usually find that there is a contract despite the difficulty of the legal analysis.

6.18 This topic leads on naturally to the next. Once it is established that a contract exists, what are its terms?

7 Terms of a contract

Express terms

7.01 The most obvious terms of a contract are those which the parties expressly agreed. In cases where there is an oral contract there may be conflicting evidence as to what actually was said and agreed, but with the written contracts with which architects will most often deal, construing the express terms is usually less problematic: just read the document evidencing the contract. The 'four corners rule' restricts attention to within the four corners of the document, and even if the written terms mis-state the intention of one of the parties – perhaps that party had not read the document carefully before signing it – he will be bound by what is recorded save in exceptional circumstances. This is another manifestation of the objective approach of English contract law discussed above.

7.02 It should be noted at this stage that things said or written prior to making a contract may affect the parties' legal obligations to one another even though they are not terms of the contract. This matter is discussed in the section on misrepresentation.

Implied terms

7.03 Implied terms are likely to catch out the unwary. There are three types of implied term: those implied by statute, those implied by custom, and those implied by the court.

Terms implied by the court

7.04 With unfortunate frequency, contracting parties discover, too late, that their contract has failed to provide for the events which have happened. One party will wish that the contract had included a term imposing liability on the other in the circumstances that have turned out, and will try to persuade the court that such a term should be implied into the contract, saying, in effect, that the court ought to read between the lines of the contract and find the term there. Obviously, one cannot have an implied term which is inconsistent with the express terms.

7.05 There are some particular terms in particular types of contract which the courts will, as a matter of course, imply into contracts of a particular kind. For instance, a contract for the lease of a furnished property will be taken to include a term that it will be reasonably fit for habitation at the commencement of the tenancy.

7.06 More frequently there will be no authority on the particular type of term which it is sought to imply. The courts have developed an approach to these problems, based on an early formulation in the case of *The Moorcock* [1889] 14 PD 64. There the owner of the ship *The Moorcock* had contracted with the defendants to discharge his ship at their jetty on the Thames. Both parties must have realised that the ship would ground at low tide; in the event it not only grounded but, settling on a ridge of hard ground, it was damaged. The plaintiff owners said that the defendants should be taken to have given a warranty that they would take reasonable care to ensure that the river bottom was safe for the vessel – and the Court of Appeal agreed. Bowen LJ explained: 'the law[raises] an implication from the presumed intention of the parties, with the object of giving to the transaction such efficacy as both parties must have intended it should have'.

This is called the 'business efficacy test', but it is clear that the term must be necessary for business efficacy, rather than be simply a term which makes better sense of the contract if it is included than if it is not. In *Shirlow v Southern Foundries* [1939] 2 KB 206 at 227, Mackinnon LJ expressed the test in terms of the 'officious bystander' which provides a readily memorable – if not always easy applicable – formulation of the rule:

'Prima facie, that which in any contract is left to be implied and need not be expressed is something which is so obvious it goes without saying; so that, if while the parties were making their bargain an officious bystander were to suggest some express provision for it in their agreement, they would testily suppress him with a common, "Oh, of course".'

The 'officious bystander test' is obviously difficult to pass. Both parties must have taken the term as 'obvious'. The ploy of trying to persuade a court that a term should be read into the contract in favour of one party is tried much more often than it succeeds. The moral for architects as for any other contracting party, is that the proper time to define contractual terms is before the contract is made, not after things have gone wrong.

7.07 Sometimes parties will argue for an implied term to fill in the gaps in an otherwise incomplete agreement or in situations where the parties have opposing arguments as to what was in fact agreed. In those situations the court is likely to say that there was no contract and it is not the court's role to make the contract for the parties.

Terms implied by custom

7.08 The custom of a particular type of business is relevant in construing the express terms of a contract and may on occasion be sufficient to imply into a contract a term which apparently is not there at all. In *Hutton v Warren* [1836] 1 M & W 466, a lease was held to include a term effecting the local custom that when the tenant's tenancy came to an end he would be entitled to a sum representing the seed and labour put into the arable land. There are other examples from the law of marine insurance, many of which are now crystallised in statute law, but

'An alleged custom can be incorporated into a contract only if there is nothing in the express or necessarily implied terms of the contract to prevent such inclusion and, further, that a custom will only be imported into a contract where it can be so imported consistently with the tenor of the document as a whole.'

(*London Export v Jubilee Coffee* [1958] 2 All ER 411, at 420)

The place of terms implied by custom in the modern law is small; but custom as a guide in construing terms of a contract continues to be of some importance.

Terms implied by statute

7.09 For architects there are two very important statutes which may automatically incorporate terms into their contracts: the Sale of Goods Act 1979 (SOGA) and the Supply of Goods and Services Act 1982 (SOGASA). The principal relevant sections of those Acts are fairly straightforward, but of course they have to be read in their context to see their precise effect (see Extracts 2.1 and 2.2).

Extract 2.1 Sale of Goods Act 1979, as amended by Sale and Supply of Goods Act 1994

14.(1) Except as provided in this section and section 15 below and subject to any other enactment, there is no implied condition or warranty about the quality or fitness for purpose of goods supplied under a contract of sale.

(2) Where the seller sells goods in the course of a business, there is an implied term that the goods supplied under the contract are of satisfactory quality.

(2A) For the purposes of this Act, goods are of satisfactory quality if they meet the standard that a reasonable person would regard as satisfactory, taking account of any description of the goods, the price (if relevant) and all the other relevant circumstances.

(2B) For the purposes of this Act, the quality of goods includes their state and condition and the following (among others) are in appropriate cases aspects of the quality of good –
  (a) fitness for all the purposes for which goods of the kind in question are commonly supplied,
  (b) appearance and finish,
  (c) freedom from minor defects,
  (d) safety, and
  (e) durability.

(2C) The term implied by subsection (2) above does not extend to any matter making the quality of goods unsatisfactory –
  (a) which is specifically drawn to the buyer's attention before the contract is made,
  (b) where the buyer examines the goods before the contract is made, which that examination ought to reveal, or
  (c) in the case of a contract for sale by sample, which would have been apparent on a reasonable examination of the sample.

(3) Where the seller sells goods in the course of a business and the buyer, expressly or by implication, makes known –
  (a) to the seller, or
  (b) where the purchase price or part of it is payable by instalments and the goods were previously sold by a credit-broker to the seller, to that credit-broker,
any particular purpose for which the goods supplied under the contract are reasonably fit for that purpose, whether or not that is a purpose for which such goods are commonly supplied, except where the circumstances show that the buyer does not rely, or that it is unreasonable for him to rely, on the skill or judgement of the seller or credit-broker.

Extract 2.2 Supply of Goods and Services Act 1982

12.(1) In this Act a 'contract for the supply of a service' means, subject to subsection (2) below, a contract under which a person 'the supplier' agrees to carry out a service.

(2) For the purposes of this Act, a contract of service or apprenticeship is not a contract for the supply of a service.

13. In a contract for the supply of a service where the supplier is acting in the course of a business, there is an implied term that the supplier will carry out the service with reasonable care and skill.

14.(1) Where, under a contract for the supply of a service by a supplier acting in the course of a business, the time for the service to be carried out is not fixed by the contract, left to be fixed in a manner agreed by the contract or determined by the course of dealing between the parties, there is an implied term that the supplier will carry out the service within a reasonable time.

(2) What is a reasonable time is a question of fact.

(Continued)

15.(1) Where, under a contract for the supply of a service, the consideration for the supply of a service is not determined by the contract, but left to be determined in a manner agreed by the contract or determined by the course of dealing between the parties, there is an implied term that the party contracting with the supplier will pay a reasonable charge.

(2) What is a reasonable charge is a question of fact.

7.10 The terms implied by SOGA and SOGASA can be excluded by express provision in the contract (SOGA, section 55 and SOGASA, section 16), although in both cases this is subject to the provisions of the Unfair Contract Terms Act 1977.

8 Exclusion clauses, UCTA and the Unfair Terms in Consumer Contracts Regulations 1999

8.01 A contracting party, particularly a contracting party with a dominant position relative to the other, may try to include in the contract terms which are extremely advantageous to him in the event that he is in breach of some principal obligation under the contract. The commonest way to do this is to exclude or limit his liability in certain circumstances. A carrier might, for example, offer to carry goods on terms including a clause that in the event of loss or damage to the goods being carried his liability should be limited to £100 per each kilo weight of the goods carried. The consignor of a parcel of expensive jewellery would be little assisted by a finding that the carrier was liable for their loss if the damages he could recover were limited to £100 per kilo.

Unfair Contracts Terms Act 1977

8.02 The Unfair Contracts Terms Act 1977 (UCTA) is quite different in ambit from what its title suggests. It should be understood from the outset that the Act is not concerned generally with the fairness of the contractual bargain or the contractual obligations that a party has agreed to. Broadly (although this is an over simplification) the Act is designed to do two things. First, the Act prevents or restricts a person from escaping liability (wholly or in part) for his negligence. Secondly, the Act prevents or restricts a person from escaping liability (wholly or in part) for breach of contract. The rules about which situations the Act covers are more complicated than that but a general summary of the relevant parts of the Act is set out below. Although this rather short Act is far from a model of clarity in the way that it is drafted and arranged, nevertheless it makes a hugely significant contribution to the law of contract and tort. UCTA does not apply to certain types of contract, in particular insurance contracts.

8.03 Section 2(1) of the Act makes it illegal for a person to exclude liability for death or personal injury as a result of his negligence. This section applies both in a contractual and a non-contractual context. For example, if a farmer sets up dangerous booby-traps on his land to dissuade burglars and puts up a notice saying that he will not be responsible for injuries caused to trespassers that notice will be ineffective by UCTA. In the contractual context, a coach operator who makes it a condition of travel that his liability for negligence to passengers is excluded will not escape liability if the coach has been negligently maintained resulting in a crash that injures the passengers. Contract clauses of this sort are becoming rarer but it is surprising how, even today some 25 years after the Act, one can find contracts which contain clauses that attempt to limit this type of liability.

8.04 Section 2(2) of the Act prevents a person from unreasonably excluding or restricting his liability for other loss and damage resulting from negligence (i.e. economic loss). Again, it applies both in a contractual and non-contractual context. It is of course possible, by using an appropriately worded clause, to exclude loss or damage caused by negligence if the test of 'reasonableness' in section 11 is satisfied. The test of reasonableness is that the term should be fair and reasonable having regard to the circumstances which were known, or ought to be known, to the parties when the contract was made. In practice, it is often difficult to satisfy this test. This section applies to all contracts, unlike the next major section of the Act.

8.05 Section 3 of the Act is one of the most important parts of the Act, which applies to ordinary (i.e. non-negligent) breaches of contract. However, it does not apply to all contracts. The situations to which it applies are these:-

(1) a contract where one of the parties is a consumer, that is to say, a person who is not acting in the course of business; or

(2) where the contract is made on one party's standard written terms of business. General standard forms of contract, such as JCT or ICE forms will not necessarily be a party's standard written terms. However, if a party regularly uses a particular form (perhaps with his own special amendments) those terms may be held to be his standard written terms, see *British Fermentation Products Ltd v Compair Reavell Ltd* – Technology and Construction Court (1999) 66 Constr LR 1; and *Pegler Ltd v Wang (UK) Ltd* [2000] BLR 218. UCTA was applied to the RIBA Architect's Standard Form of Agreement in *Moores v Yakely Associates Ltd* [1999] 62 Constr LR 76 where it was held that the Architect's limit of liability clause was reasonable, a decision which was subsequently affirmed in the Court of Appeal.

Section 3 provides that unless a party can prove that a contractual term was reasonable within the meaning of section 11 (see above), a party in breach of contract cannot exclude or restrict his liability for that breach of contract nor can a party claim to be entitled to render incomplete, significantly different, or defective performance of his obligations or, even worse, no performance at all.

8.06 Section 13 provides that a party is not permitted to make his liability or enforcement of his liability subject to onerous conditions or to restrict rights and remedies of the other party. This section only appears to apply in circumstances where sections 2 and 3 of the Act already apply.

8.07 In conclusion, where there is a one-off contract between two commercial enterprises, UCTA will not apply. There may be a growing practice in the future of litigants arguing that UCTA applies to standard forms, where it can be said that the other party has proposed the use of the form, particularly if there is evidence that the version used incorporates that other party's amendments. Nevertheless, it is probable that even if UCTA does apply, the terms of any standard term will satisfy the reasonableness test. The court is likely to say that experienced business men are the best judges of what is commercially fair. However, it is important to bear in mind that in a contractual chain, the party at the bottom may be a consumer who will be able to benefit from UCTA. This can mean that the contractor near the bottom of the chain will not be able to transfer onto the consumer the risk passed down from the top of the chain. The consumer obtains yet further protection from the Unfair Terms in Consumer Contracts Regulations.

Unfair Terms in Consumer Contracts Regulations 1999

8.08 These regulations replaced an earlier set of regulations introduced in 1994 to give effect to an EC directive on unfair terms in consumer contracts. Unlike UCTA, these regulations really are designed to examine whether or not clauses in the contract are unfair to the consumer. The 1999 regulations took effect on 1 October 1999 and apply to contracts made with consumers after that date. As is commonly the case with domestic legislation required by European law, the regulations use expressions and ideas that are unfamiliar or not well established in English law. Indeed, traditionally English law did not generally interfere with the bargain made by the parties to see if it was unfair. The modern era has been marked by a whole raft of Acts and regulations which were introduced to protect the consumer against the superior bargaining power of large commercial entities.

8.09 The regulations apply to contracts with consumers where the other party is a seller or supplier of goods or services: this is interpreted as broadly as possible so that a person will be a seller or supplier wherever that party is acting in the course of his trade profession or business. A consumer must be a natural person rather than a limited company. Certain contracts are excepted from the regulations, notably employment contracts.

8.10 The regulations only apply to terms which have not been individually negotiated between the parties. This upholds the principle that the bargain negotiated between the parties is a matter entirely for the parties. Consistent with that principle, the regulations will not apply to terms regarding the price or the subject matter of the contract provided that such terms are in plain intelligible language.

8.11 The regulations contain a non-exhaustive 'grey list' of terms which will generally be deemed to be unfair: most of these are the sort of clauses which common sense indicates are unfair to the consumer. Not surprisingly these include the same types of clauses which would fall foul of UCTA. Also included are clauses which impose penalties on consumers, which allow the other party to change the service or goods that it supplies, to interpret or change the terms of the contract at his discretion or to terminate the contract early. The regulations also give certain regulatory bodies, such as the Office of Fair Trading, the power to take legal action to prevent the use of such terms.

8.12 The full impact of the regulations remains to be seen. The regulations are likely to prove wider in scope than UCTA so far as consumer contracts are concerned. They have already been held to apply to strike out some onerous terms in mortgage lending agreements: see *Falco Finance Ltd v Gough* [1999] CCLR 16. They have also been used to strike out an arbitration agreement under the standard NHBC Buildmark Agreement in *Zealander v Laing Homes Ltd* (2000) 2 TCLR 724. In that case the home owner brought court proceedings against Laing Homes for breach of contract alleging that there were defects in the house. The defendant objected to the court's jurisdiction, contending that the dispute was required to go to arbitration. The court held that this arbitration clause only covered matters under the Buildmark agreement not all matters for which the claimant might claim against the defendant and this created a significant imbalance for the consumer because he would be put to the expense of using to separate proceedings to bring his claims and was financially disadvantaged compared with the defendant. Care must be taken, particularly when using standard terms of business, or a standard form contract, in agreements with a consumer to make sure that it will satisfy both the regulations and UCTA.

9 Standard term contracts

9.01 Many of the contracts with which architects are involved are standard form contracts. Chapter 17 deals at length with one such contract, the JCT Standard Form of Building Contract, and in other areas other standard form contracts are available. The use of such contracts has a number of advantages. A great deal of experience has gone into drafting these contracts so that many pitfalls of fuzzy or uncertain wording can be avoided. And where the words used are open to different interpretations it may well be that case law has definitively settled their meaning. In effect the user of a standard term contract enjoys the benefit of other people's earlier litigation in sorting out exactly what obligations the standard terms impose. The effects of well-litigated and well-established terms and conditions also have an impact on third parties. Insurers in particular will know where they stand in relation to a contract on familiar terms and therefore the extra premiums inevitable on uncertain risks can be avoided.

9.02 One potential problem with standard form contracts can be minimised if it is appreciated. Just as tinkering with a well-tuned

engine can have catastrophic consequences, so 'home-made' modifications of standard form contracts can have far-reaching effects. Many of the provisions and definitions used in standard form contracts interlink, and modifying one clause may have unforeseen and far-reaching ramifications. If parties to a standard form contract want to modify it because it does not seem to achieve exactly the cross-obligations they want to undertake, it is highly advisable to take specialist advice.

10 Misrepresentation

10.01 Pre-contractual negotiations often cover many subjects which are not dealt with by the terms (express or implied) of the eventual contract. In some circumstances things said or done before the contract is made can lead to liability.

Representations and misrepresentations

10.02 A representation is a statement of existing fact made by one party to the eventual contract (the misrepresentor) to the other (the misrepresentee) which induces the representee to enter into the contract. A misrepresentation is a representation which is false. Two elements of the definition need elaboration.

Statement of existing fact

10.03 The easiest way to grasp what is meant by a statement of existing fact is to see what is not included in the expression. A promise to do something in the future is not a representation – such a statement is essentially the stuff of which contracts are made, and the place for promises is therefore in the contract itself. An opinion which is honestly held and honestly expressed will not constitute an actionable misrepresentation. This is sometimes said to be because it is not a statement of fact and it is perhaps simplest to see this by realising that it does not make sense to talk of an opinion being false or untrue, so that in any event it cannot be a misrepresentation. But a statement of opinion 'I believe such and such . . .' can be a representation and can therefore be a misrepresentation if the representor does not actually hold the belief, because, as Bowen LJ explained:

> 'The state of a man's mind is as much a fact as the state of his digestion. It is true that it is very difficult to prove what the state of a man's mind at a particular time is, but if it can be ascertained it is as much a fact as anything else. A misrepresentation as to the state of a man's mind is, therefore, a statement of fact.'
> (*Edgington v Fitzmaurice* [1885] 29 Ch D 459 at 483)

10.04 A somewhat more surprising line of authority holds that 'mere puff' or sales-speak does not constitute a representation. Hence describing land as 'uncommonly rich water meadow' was held not to constitute a representation in *Scott v Hanson* [1829] 1 Russ & M 128. But the courts today are rather less indulgent to exaggerated sales talk and if it can be established that effusive description of a vendor's product is actually untrue it seems that the courts would today be more likely to hold that to be a misrepresentation than would their nineteenth-century predecessors.

10.05 Silence generally does not constitute a representation. A vendor is generally under no obligation to draw to the attention of his purchaser the defects in that which he is selling, and even tacit acquiescence in the purchaser's self-deception will not usually create any liability. However, there are cases in which silence can constitute a misrepresentation. If the representor makes some representation about a certain matter he must not leave out other aspects of the story so that what he says is misleading as a whole: so although a total non-disclosure may not be a misrepresentation, partial non-disclosure may be.

Reliance

10.06 To create any liability the representee must show that the misrepresentation induced him to enter into the contract – the misrepresentation must have been material. Therefore if the misrepresentee knew that the representation was false, or if he was not aware of the representation at all, or if he knew of it but it did not affect his judgement, then he will have no grounds for relief. But the misrepresentation need not be the only, nor even indeed the principal, reason why the misrepresentee entered into the contract.

The three types of misrepresentation

10.07 If the representor making the misrepresentation made it knowing it was untrue, or without believing it was true, or recklessly, not caring whether it was true or false, then it is termed a fraudulent misrepresentation. If, however, the representor made the false statement believing that it was true but had taken insufficient care to ensure that it was true, then it will be a negligent mis-statement. Finally, if the misrepresentor had taken reasonable care to ensure that it was true, and did believe that it was true, then it is merely an innocent misrepresentation.

Remedies for misrepresentation

10.08 This is a very difficult area of the law, and the finer details of the effects of the Misrepresentation Act 1967 are still not entirely clear. The summary which follows is extremely brief.

Principal remedy: rescission

10.09 The basic remedy for misrepresentation is rescission, which is the complete termination and undoing of the contract. The misrepresentee can in many circumstances oblige the misrepresentor to restore him to the position he would have been in had the contract never been made.

10.10 Rescission is not available if the misrepresentee has, with knowledge of the misrepresentation, affirmed the contract. A long lapse of time before the misrepresentee opts to rescind is often taken as affirmation. Rescission is not available if a third party has, since the contract was made, himself acquired for value an interest in the subject matter of the contract. Nor is it available, almost by definition, if it is impossible to restore the parties to the status quo before the contract was made.

10.11 The court now has a general power to grant damages in lieu of rescission (Misrepresentation Act 1967, section 2(2)), and may award damages to the victim of a negligent or innocent representation even where the misrepresentee would rather have the contract rescinded instead.

Damages

10.12 The victim of a fraudulent misrepresentation may sue for damages as well as claim rescission, and the measure of damages will be tortious.

10.13 The victim of a negligent misrepresentation may also recover damages (section 1) as well as rescission. It is not entirely clear how damages should be calculated.

10.14 In the case of an innocent misrepresentation there is no right to damages, but, as already explained, the court may in its discretion award damages in lieu of rescission.

The law of negligent mis-statement

10.15 Misrepresentation alone is complicated. The matter is compounded by the availability of damages for the tort of negligent mis-statement (rather than misrepresentation), which is discussed in Chapter 3. There will be many instances in which an actionable misrepresentation is also an actionable mis-statement.

11 Performance and breach

11.01 All the topics considered so far have been concerned with matters up to and including the creation of a contract – matters generally of greater interest to lawyers than to men of business or to architects. But both lawyers and architects have a close interest in whether or not a party fulfils its obligations under a contract and, if it does not, what can be done about it.

The right to sue on partial performance of a complete contract

11.02 Many contracts take the general form of A paying B to perform some work or to provide some service. It is unusual for the party performing the work or providing the service to do nothing at all; the usual case will be that much of the work is done according to the contract, but some part of the work remains incomplete, undone, or improperly performed. This situation needs to be considered from both sides. We begin with examining whether the incomplete performer can sue his paymaster if no money is forthcoming.

11.03 The general rule of contract law is that a party must perform precisely what he contracted to do. The consequence is that in order to make the other liable in any way under the contract all of that party's obligations must be performed. If the contract is divided up into clearly severable parts each will be treated for these purposes as a separate contract, and virtually all building contracts will of course make provision for stage payments. Nevertheless it is important to be aware of the general rule which applies to a contract where one lump sum is provided for all the works. Non-performance (as opposed to misperformance) of some part will disentitle the partial performer from payment.

11.04 An example is *Bolton v Mahadeva* [1972] 1 WLR 1009. There, the claimant agreed to install a hot water system for the defendant for a lump-sum payment of £560. The radiators emitted fumes and the system did not heat the house properly. Curing the defects would cost £174. The defendant was held not liable to pay the claimant anything.

11.05 There is an important exception to this rule, even for entire contracts. If the party performing the works has 'substantially performed' his obligations then he is entitled to the contract sum subject only to a counter-claim for those parts remaining unperformed. In *Hoenig v Isaacs* [1952] 2 All ER 176 there was a lump-sum contract for the decoration and furnishing of the defendant's flat for the price of £750. When the claimant left, one wardrobe door needed replacing and one shelf was too short, and would have to be remade. The Court of Appeal held that although 'near the border-line' on the facts, the claimant had substantially performed his contractual obligations and was therefore able to recover his £750, subject only to the deduction of £56, being the cost of the necessary repairs.

Remedies against the incomplete performer

11.06 The flip-side of the situation of suing on an incompletely performed contract is suing the incomplete performer. Obviously incomplete performance or misperformance gives to the other party, who has so far performed his obligations as they fall due, a right to damages to put him in the position he would have been in had the contract been performed. But in some circumstances another remedy will be available to the aggrieved party, for he will be able to hold himself absolved from any further performance of his obligations under the contract.

11.07 This right to treat the contract as at an end arises in three situations.

Breach of a contractual condition

11.08 The first situation is if the term which the non- or misperforming party has breached is a contractual condition rather than merely a warranty. It used to be thought that all contractual terms were either conditions or warranties. Whether a term was one or the other might be determined by statute, by precedent, or might have to be decided by the court by looking at the contract in the light of the surrounding circumstances. If the term was a condition then any breach of it, however minor, would allow the aggrieved party to treat the contract as at an end. The modern tendency is to adopt a more realistic approach and to escape from the strait-jacket dichotomy of conditions and warranties. In *Hong Kong Fir Shipping Co. Ltd v Kawasaki Kisen Kaisha Ltd* [1962] 2 QB 26, at 70 Lord Diplock explained that

> 'There are, however, many contractual terms of a more complex character which cannot be categorised as being "conditions" or "warranties" … Of such undertakings all that can be predicated is that some breaches will and others will not give rise to an event which will deprive the party in default of substantially the whole benefit which it was intended he should obtain from the contract; and the legal consequences of the breach of any such undertaking, unless provided for expressly in the contract, depend on the nature of the event to which the breach gives rise and do not follow automatically from a prior classification of the undertaking as a "condition" or "warranty".'

These terms which are neither conditions nor warranties have been unhelpfully named 'innominate terms' and although their existence decreases the importance of this first type of circumstance in which an aggrieved party can treat its contractual obligations as at an end, it is nevertheless still open for the contracting parties expressly to make a contractual term a condition, in which case any breach of it allows this remedy in addition to a claim for damages.

Repudiatory breach

11.09 If the breach 'goes to the root of the contract' or deprives the party of substantially the whole benefit the contract was intended to confer on him, then he will be entitled to treat the contract as at an end.

Renunciation

11.10 If one party evinces an intention not to continue to perform his side of the contract then the other party may again treat the contract as at an end.

Election

11.11 In all three of the circumstances described above the innocent party has a choice as to whether or not to treat himself as discharged. He may prefer to press for performance of the contract so far as the other party is able to perform it, and to restrict himself to his remedy in damages. But once made, the election cannot unilaterally be changed, unless the matter which gave rise to it is a continuing state of affairs which therefore continues to provide the remedy afresh.

11.12 The rule that the innocent party may, if he prefers, elect to press for performance following (for instance) a renunciation can have a bizarre result. In *White and Carter (Councils) v McGregor* [1962] AC 413 the claimant company supplied litter bins to local councils. The councils did not pay for the bins, but they allowed them to carry advertising, and the claimants made their money from the companies whose advertisements their bins carried. The defendant company agreed to hire space on the claimants' bins for 3 years. Later the same day they changed their mind and said that they were not going to be bound by the contract. The claimants could have accepted that renunciation, but, perhaps short of work and wanting to keep busy, opted to carry on with the contract, which they proceeded to do for the next 3 years. They sued successfully for the full contract price: there was no obligation on them to treat the contract as at an end and they were not obliged to sue for damages only.

12 Privity of contract

Privity of contract

12.01 As explained at the beginning of this chapter, the distinguishing feature of contract law is that it defines the rights and obligations of the two or more parties to the contract. That party

must have provided consideration in order to be able to enforce his rights or the obligations of the other party: without that consideration he will not have earned the right to the benefits of the contract. The issue of privity of contract really comes into sharp focus when the performance of the contract has not gone according to plan and a person wants to enforce the contract. Whether a person can sue or be sued in respect of a contract depends upon having privity of contract.

12.02 That rule has caused problems for third parties who stand to benefit by the contract, as in examples discussed above. In the construction industry there are often a number of complex contract chains where benefits extend to someone else at a different point in the chain. The industry is therefore prone to suffer the problems of deprived third parties who can see the benefits they are entitled to but cannot get at them because they depend upon enforcement by the parties to the contract. This can be frustrating for the third party, when the contracting parties do not take steps to secure the benefit either because the contracting party who can enforce the term is unwilling to rock the boat or cause confrontation with the other contracting party with whom he has (or hopes to have) a longstanding relationship, or because there is already some dispute between the third party and the contracting party who can enforce the benefit on his behalf, or, just as commonplace, because of general inefficiency or apathy. A typical example is where a main contractor has contracted with the employer to pass onto the subcontractor payments for the value of the work done or, from the other perspective, where an employer wants the sub-contract works to be finished but has no direct contract with them and can only badger the main contractor who has engaged the sub-contractors to insist on performance. Such problems become more acute when one of the contracting parties is incapacitated, usually through insolvency. What if the main contractor goes bust and is dissolved, leaving the employer with no recourse to the sub-contractors to secure completion of the sub-contract works? Or, similarly, how can the sub-contractor insist on being paid for work done ultimately for the employer, when he was depending upon the (now dissolved) main contractor to secure payment on his behalf?

12.03 Until the Contracts (Rights of Third Parties Act) 1999 the best a non-party could do was attempt to persuade one of the parties to sue the other on his behalf in order to be compensated for the non-party's lack of benefit. Obviously the party may not be willing to incur the cost or take the time and risk involved in suing the other party. Even if he did, the problem was that the party would normally be compensated only for his own loss – which in those circumstances would be no more than nominal – not the non-party's loss, which would be substantial.

12.04 The difficulties of a contracting party suing on behalf of the third party are discussed in the important House of Lords case of *Alfred McAlpine Construction Ltd v Panatown Ltd* [2001] 1 AC 518. In that case, a building contractor entered into a contract with the employer for the construction of an office block and car park. The site was actually owned by another company in the same group of companies as the employer, and the owner – rather than the employer – was ultimately going to benefit from the office block and car park. In addition to the contract with the employer, the building contractor also entered into a 'duty of care' deed with the owner of the site. By that deed (which was a contract in itself) the owner acquired a direct remedy against the contractor in respect of any failure by the contractor to exercise reasonable skill, care and attention to any matter within the scope of the contractor's responsibilities under the contract. Serious defects were found in the building and the employer served notice of arbitration claiming damages for defective work and delay. The contractor objected on the basis that that the employer, having suffered no loss, was not entitled to recover substantial damages under the contract. The arbitrator said that the employer could recover substantial damages, based upon one of the exceptions to the privity of contract rule. The High Court allowed the contractor's appeal against that decision and decided that the employer could not recover substantial damages. The Court of Appeal allowed the employer's appeal and the matter ended up in the House of Lords. Their Lordships held (by a 3:2 majority) that the employer was only entitled to nominal damages because it had suffered no loss itself. The House of Lords would not permit the employer to recover losses on behalf of the owner because the owner had a duty of care deed (a collateral contract) which provided him with a direct remedy against the contractor for the losses arising out of the contractor's defective performance. Interestingly, had the protaganists not set up that direct contractual framework by a duty of care deed for the owner, it is possible that the House of Lords might have been prepared to allow the employer to recover full damages (which he would then have to pass onto the owner) in order to fashion an effective remedy where otherwise none existed. If the situation were to arise now, the owner might be able to sue under the employer's contract by using the 1999 Act.

The Contracts (Rights of Third Parties) Act 1999

12.05 In order to resolve the privity problem for the third party stranger who benefits from a contract, Parliament introduced legislation – the Contracts (Rights of Third Parties) Act 1999 – to give that person a direct right to sue on that contract, although of course the stranger still cannot be sued on the contract. The Act is one of the most radical reforms to the law of contract since mediaeval times. Its effect is not to abolish privity of contract but to create a massive exception to the doctrine. The Act applies to all contracts made after 11 May 2000. The Act also applies to contracts made between 11 November 1999 and 11 May 2000 where the contract states that the Act is specifically to apply. However, it should be noted at the outset that the parties to the contract are free to exclude the Act.

12.06 By section 1 the third party will have a right to enforce a term in the contract made for his benefit if:

1 the term in the contract expressly says that he may enforce that term; or
2 if he is expressly identified in the contract by name, class or description (even if not in existence at the time the contract is made) and the term purports to confer a benefit on him.

An example of the first kind would be a contract term which says that X's next-door neighbours can claim compensation from the builder for any damage to their property while the works are carried out on X's land. An example of the second kind would be a contract term which says that compensation is payable by the builder to the next-door neighbours for any damage caused while the builder carries out works on X's land but does not specifically provide for the next-door neighbours to make a claim. A less clear-cut situation is where the builder has contracted not to cause a nuisance to X's neighbours while carrying out the works but says nothing about compensation or other remedy. It is in such a situation that the distinction between the law of contract and the law of tort seems to have become blurred.

12.07 It would appear that it is not only 'positive' rights that can be enforced by a third party (such as a claim to payment) but also a term which contains 'defensive' rights such as a limitation or exclusion clause (section 1(6) of the Act).

12.08 However, the statutory scheme only takes effect subject to the contract between the parties: the party's freedom of contract is preserved (except in the case of a subsequent variation to the contract where the original terms conferred a benefit on a third party which is enforceable by the statutory scheme see paragraph 12.10 below). For this reason a third party will not have the right to enforce a term of someone else's contract if on a proper interpretation of the contract, the contracting parties did not intend that term to be enforceable by the third party (see section 1(2) of the Act). What this means is that the term of the contract sought to be enforced cannot be viewed in isolation from the rest of the contract. It is thus possible to provide an express term conferring a benefit on a third party but precluding the third party from enforcing that benefit or simply to contract out of the statutory provisions altogether.

12.09 It is important to realise that the third party can only enforce the *term* which benefits the third party, not the whole contract. So a next-door neighbour who benefits from a compensation clause cannot enforce a term which obliges the builder to complete the work by a certain date where there has been delay because he is fed up with the duration of the works. However, it will no doubt be possible for the contract to provide that the whole terms of the contract should be for the benefit of the third party and should be enforceable by him.

12.10 In enforcing his right the third party will be able to enjoy all the remedies available to the contracting parties, although one notable exception seems to be the inability of the third party to invoke section 2(2) of the Unfair Contract Terms Act (see paragraph 8.04 above). It should be noted that the third party is not similarly prevented from relying upon the Unfair Terms in Consumer Contracts Regulations (see paragraph 8.08 and following). However, the third party will not be put in a better position than the contracting parties and so can only exercise his right in accordance with and subject to the terms and conditions of the contract. Where there are exclusions and limitations they will apply to the third party just as much as the contracting parties. And just as a contracting party has to mitigate his loss where the other party is in breach of contract, so too will a third party have to mitigate his loss. Also, the third party's right will be subject to any defence or set-off that the party against whom the term is enforced would have against the other contracting party. Additionally, the third party can also expect his right to be subject to counter-claims and set-offs which the other contracting party has against the third party under any separate relationship. For example, if C can sue B for the price of work done under the contract between A and B, B can counter-claim for damages suffered under a separate contract between C and B the previous year when C bodged that job. Of course, the rights of set-off will be subject to the express terms of the contract.

12.11 The Act also places restrictions on the contracting parties to preserve the third party's rights obtained under the statutory scheme. The restrictions apply where the third party has communicated his assent to the benefit/right to the person against whom the benefit/right would be enforced (called 'the promisor'), or if the promisor is aware that the third party has relied on the term, or where the promisor could reasonably have foreseen that the third party would rely upon and has in fact relied upon the term. The restriction upon the contracting parties in section 2, is to prevent the contracting parties from varying the contract terms, or cancelling the contract so as to extinguish or alter the third party's right without the third party's consent. But as has been said already, the statutory scheme is subject to the express terms of the contract and so the third party's consent is not necessary if the contract expressly provides so (but no doubt the court will require clear words dispensing with the need for the third party's consent). In the absence of an express term to this effect the third party's consent can only be waived by the court (not an arbitral tribunal) with or without conditions attached (e.g. the payment of compensation) where the court is satisfied that either

1 the third party's consent cannot be obtained because his whereabouts cannot reasonably be ascertained;
2 the third party is mentally incapable of giving his consent; or
3 it cannot reasonably be ascertained whether the third party in fact relied upon the term.

12.12 In order to avoid the problem of double liability, the court may reduce the award available to the third party in circumstances where one of the parties has already recovered a sum in respect of the third party's loss against the promisor. And of course the Act does not restrict in any way the ability of contracting parties to enforce the terms of the contract nor any other rights that the third party might have outside of the contract (such as a similar claim in tort).

12.13 Certain types of contract are excluded, such as contracts of employment, contracts for the carriage of goods, negotiable instruments or certain contracts under section 14 of the Companies Act 1985.

12.14 As has been mentioned, parties may, if they so choose, by the wording of their contract exclude this Act. In that case, the common law rules will continue to apply. The great majority of contracts in the construction industry, and, indeed, in many other commercial spheres, have routinely excluded the Act. Therefore, to date its impact in the construction field has been very small. But there are signs that this may be beginning to change. At the very least architects need to be aware of the Act's existence, so that they can make a conscious, and informed decision, at the time a contract is being made, as to whether they want third party rights under this Act to apply or not.

13 Agency

13.01 The law of agency has developed as a framework in which the doctrine of privity of contract is often applied, because a common problem is to determine exactly who the parties to a contract are. For A to act as an agent for P his principal is for A to act as P's representative. A's words or actions will create legal rights and liabilities for A who is therefore bound by what A does. It is just as if P had said or done those things himself. The agent's actions might have consequences for P in contract, or tort, or some other area of the law, but in this chapter it is naturally only with contractual liabilities that we are concerned. In general, if A, as P's agent, properly contracts with C, then the resulting contract is a contract between P and C. A is not privy to the contract, and can neither sue or be sued upon it.

13.02 There are two sets of legal obligations which are of interest. The first is those between the principal and his agent. That relationship of agency may, but need not, itself be the subject of a contract – the contract of agency. For instance, A may be rewarded by a percentage commission on any of P's business which he places with C. If A does not receive his commission he may wish to sue P, and he will do so under their contract of agency. That is a matter between P and A, and of no interest to C. It is governed by the rules for contracts of agency. These rules, just a specialized sub-set of the rules of contract generally, will not be further discussed here.

13.03 The second set of legal questions raised by an agency concerns how the relationship is created, whether and how it is that A's actions bind his principal, and whether A is ever left with any personal liability of his own. We begin by considering the first of these issues.

Creation of agency

13.04 There are three important ways in which an agency may be created.

1 By express appointment

This is, of course, the commonest way to create an agency. Generally, no formalities are necessary: the appointment may be oral or in writing. To take an example, the employees of a trading company are frequently expressly appointed by their contract of employment to act as the agents of the company and to place and receive orders on its behalf.

2 By estoppel

If P by his words or conduct leads C to believe that A is his agent, and C deals with A on that basis, A cannot escape the contract by saying that, in fact, A was not his agent. In these circumstances P will be stopped, or 'estopped', from making that assertion.

3 By ratification

If A, not in fact being P's agent, purports to contract with C on P's behalf, and P then discovers the contract, likes the look of it and ratifies and adopts it, then at law A is deemed to be P's agent for the purposes of that contract. The precise working of the rules of ratification are rather involved.

Authorisation

13.05 The effect of an agent's words or actions will depend crucially on whether or not he was authorised by his principal to say or do them. The agent's authority will usually be an actual authority, that is, an authority which he has expressly or impliedly been granted by his principal. But the scope of the agent's authority may, most importantly, be enlarged by the addition of his ostensible authority.

13.06 Ostensible authority is another manifestation of the operation of estoppel. If P represents to C that his agent A has an authority wider than, in fact, has been expressly or impliedly granted by P to A, and in reliance on that representation C contracts with P through A, then P will be stopped ('estopped') from denying that the scope of A's authority was wide enough to include the contract that has been made.

The liabilities of principal and agent

13.07 We now consider the liabilities of both principal and agent with the contracting third party C, and the discussion is divided into those cases in which the agent is authorised to enter into the transaction, and those in which he is not so authorised.

The agent acts within the scope of his authority

13.08 This division has three sub-divisions, depending on how much the contracting party C knows about the principal. The agent may tell C that P exists, and name him. Or he may tell C that he has a principal, but not name him. Or – still less communicative – he may not tell C that he has a principal at all, so that as far as C is concerned he is contracting with A direct.

1 Principal is named
This is in a sense the paradigm example of agency in action. A drops out of the picture altogether, the contract is between P and C and A can neither sue nor be sued on the P–C contract.

2 Existence of principal disclosed, but not his identity
The general rule is the same as in case 1.

3 Neither name nor existence of principal disclosed to C
This case is described as the case of the undisclosed principal. The rule here is somewhat counter-intuitive: both the agent and the principal may sue on the contract, and C may sue the agent, and, if and when he discovers his identity, the principal.

The agent acts outside the scope of his authority

13.09 The position as regards the principal is clear. The principal is not party to any contract, and can neither sue nor be sued upon it. This of course would have to be the case, for really in these circumstances there is no agency operating at all. But it is important to remember that ostensible authority may fix a principal with liability when the agent is acting outside his express or implied authority.

13.10 The position of the agent is more complex. We first consider the position of the agent as far as benefits under the contract are concerned – whether the agent can sue upon the contract. If the agent purported to contract as agent for a named principal, then the agent cannot sue on the contract. On the other hand, if the name of the principal is not disclosed the agent can sue upon the contract as if it were his own.

13.11 Turning now to the liability of an unauthorised agent to be sued by C, the position depends on what the agent thought was the true position between himself and P. If A knows all along that he does not have P's authority to enter into the contract, then C can sue A, although for the tort of deceit, rather than under the contract.

13.12 If, on the other hand, A genuinely thought that he was authorised by P to enter into the contract, he cannot be sued by P for deceit – after all, he has not been deceitful, merely mistaken. But C has an alternative means of enforcing his contract. A court will infer the existence of a collateral contract by A (as principal) with C, under which A warranted that he had P's authority to contract. This is a quite separate contract to the non-existent contract which C thought he was entering into with P, but from C's point of view it is just as good, for now C can sue A instead.

14 Limitation under the Limitation Act 1980

14.01 Armed with the information derived from this chapter a prospective claimant should have some idea of what his contract is, whether it has been breached, what he can do about it, and who he should sue. There is one more point to consider.

14.02 An action for breach of contract must generally be commenced within 6 years. Time begins to run – the 6 years starts – when the contract is breached. This may mean that the claimant can sue before any real physical damage has been experienced. Suppose the defendant is an architect who has, in breach of contract, designed foundations for a building which are inadequate, and it is clear that in 10 to 20 years' time the building will fall down if remedial works are not carried out. The claimant can sue straight away. Of course, although no physical damage has yet occurred there has been economic loss because the defendant has got out of the contract a building worth much less than what he paid for it, and it is obviously right that he should be able to sue straightaway.

14.03 The exception to this rule is that a claimant may sue on a contract contained in a deed up to 12 years after the contract was breached. It is for this reason that building contracts – which may take more than 6 years from inception to completion – are frequently made under deed.

14.04 The law on limitation periods is to be found in the Limitation Act 1980. The law on limitation periods for suing on a tort is different and more complicated, and is explained in Chapter 3.

3

The English law of tort

VINCENT MORAN

1 Introduction

1.01 The law of tort is concerned with conduct which causes harm to a party's personal, proprietary or financial interests. It is the law of wrongdoing. Its aim is to define obligations that should be imposed on members of society for the benefit of all. Its purpose is to compensate (or sometimes to prevent in the first place) interference with personal, proprietary or, occasionally, non-physical interests (such as a person's reputation or financial position). The law of tort therefore provides a system of loss distribution and regulates behaviour within society.

1.02 A general definition is difficult because it is impossible to fit the various separate torts that have been recognized by the common law into a single system of classification. The best that one can say is that torts are legally wrongful acts or omissions. However, to be actionable it is not enough that an act or omission as a matter of fact harms another person's interests in some way. The wrong must also interfere with some legal right of the complaining party.

1.03 The various categories of tortious rights provide the basis for assessing when actionable interference has occurred and when a legal remedy is available. But the law does not go so far as to protect parties against all forms of morally reprehensible behaviour, as Lord Atkin described in *Donoghue v Stevenson* [1932] AC 562 at 580:

> 'Acts or omissions which any moral code would censure cannot in a practical world be treated so as to give a right to every person injured by them to demand relief. In this way rules of law arise which limit the range of complaints and the extent of their remedy.'

1.04 Further, a factual situation may give rise to actions in a variety of overlapping torts. Also, the same circumstances may give rise to concurrent claims both in tort and contract (see generally Chapter 2). However, in contrast to the law of contract, which effectively seeks to enforce promises, the interests protected by tort are more diverse. Thus, contractual duties are agreed by the parties themselves, whereas tortious duties are imposed automatically by the general law. Contractual duties are therefore said to be owed *in personam* (i.e. to the other contracting party only, although there may be exceptions to this), whereas tortious duties may be owed *in rem* (to persons in general).

2 Negligence

2.01 The tort of negligence is concerned with the careless infliction of harm or damage. It has three essential elements, namely: (a) the existence of a legal duty of care; (b) a breach of that duty; and (c) consequential damage.

The legal duty to take care

2.02 The concept of the duty of care defines those persons to whom another may be liable for his negligent acts or omissions. The traditional approach to defining the situations that give rise to a duty of care was based upon a process of piecemeal extension by analogy with existing cases, rather than on the basis of a general principle. The first notable attempt to elicit a more principled approach occurred in the landmark case *of Donoghue v Stevenson* [1932] AC 562. There, the plaintiff, who was given a bottle of ginger beer by a friend, alleged that she had become ill after drinking it because of the presence of a decomposed snail in the bottle. As the plaintiff had no contractual relationship with the seller, since it was her friend who had purchased it from the shop, she attempted to sue the manufacturer of the beer bottle in tort.

2.03 The House of Lords held that a manufacturer of bottled ginger beer (or other articles) did owe the ultimate purchaser or consumer a legal duty to take reasonable care to ensure that it was free from a defect likely to cause injury to health. Therefore in principle the plaintiff had a cause of action against the ginger beer's manufacturer. However, the main significance of the case is contained in Lord Atkin's description of the general concept of the duty of care:

> 'The rule that you are to love your neighbour becomes in law, you must not injure your neighbour: and the lawyer's question, who is my neighbour? receives a restricted reply. You must take reasonable care to avoid acts or omissions which you can reasonably foresee would be likely to injure your neighbour. Who, then, in law is my neighbour? The answer seems to be – persons who are so closely affected by my act that I ought reasonably to have them in contemplation as being so affected when I am directing my mind to the acts or omissions which are called in question.'

2.04 What became known as Lord Atkin's 'neighbour' principle was initially criticised as being too broad, but in time it became accepted and remains today the central concept to an understanding of the tort of negligence. In the 1970s there was a more ambitious development of a general principle of liability in negligence. This was based on a 'two-stage test' derived from the decisions of the House of Lords in *Dorset Yacht Co Ltd v Home Office* [1970] AC 1004 and *Anns v Merton London Borough Council* [1978] AC 728. The first stage involved a consideration of whether there was a reasonable foreseeability of harm to the plaintiff. If so, there would be liability unless, under the second stage, there was some public policy reason to negate it. The piecemeal approach to the recognition of duty of care relationships was now very much in decline.

2.05 The 'two-stage' test represented a very wide application of Lord Atkin's dictum and it was at first applied with enthusiasm. However, increasingly, it appeared to many judicial eyes to herald an unwarranted potential extension of liability into situations previously not covered by the tort of negligence. As a result, there followed a steady retreat from the acceptance of a general principle of liability back to the traditional emphasis on existing case analogy and the incremental approach to the extension of liability situations. This has manifested itself in the development of a 'three-stage test' involving a consideration of (a) foreseeability of damage, (b) the relationship of neighbourhood or proximity between the parties, and (c) an assessment of whether the situation is one which in all the circumstances the court considers it fair and reasonable for the imposition of a legal duty.

2.06 Thus, in *Caparo Industries v Dickman* [1990] 2 AC 605 Lord Bridge described the judicial rejection since *Anns* of the ability of a general single principle to provide a practical test:

> '... the concepts of proximity and fairness ... are not susceptible of any such precise definition as would be necessary to give them utility as practical tests, but amount in effect to little more than convenient labels to attach to the features of different specific situations which, on a detailed examination of all the circumstances, the law recognises pragmatically as giving rise to a duty of care of a given scope. Whilst recognising, of course, the importance of the underlying general principles common to the whole field of negligence, I think the law has now moved in the direction of attaching greater significance to the more traditional categorisation of distinct and recognisable situations as guides to the existence, the scope and the limits of the varied duties of care which the law imposes'.

2.07 The *Anns* 'two-stage test' was further undermined by Lord Keith in the important decision of the House of Lords in *Murphy v Brentwood District Council* [1991] AC 398. In relation to the consideration of the duty of care in novel situations Lord Keith commented at p. 461:

> 'As regards the ingredients necessary to establish such a duty in novel situations, I consider that an incremental approach ... is to be preferred to the two-stage test.'

2.08 In *Henderson v Merrett Syndicates Ltd* [1995] 2 AC 145 the House of Lords emphasised the central importance of the concept of an 'assumption of responsibility' to the question of whether or not a duty of care in negligence is owed by one party to another. The relationship between this approach, the incremental approach and the three-stage test was explored by the House of Lords in *Customs & Excise Commissioners v Barclays Bank plc* [2007] 1 AC 181, where Lord Bingham considered the assumption of responsibility test to have primacy over the others and to be a sufficient, but not a necessary, condition for the existence of a duty of care. He also emphasised, however, the need to concentrate on the detailed circumstances of a particular case (rather than any supposed simplistic test) and in particular the relationship between the parties in their legal and factual context in order to determine this question (a point also emphasised by the Court of Appeal in the recent case of *Riyad Bank v Ahli Bank (UK) plc* [2006] EWCA Civ 780).

2.09 Further, in *South Australia Asset Management Corp v York Montague Ltd* [1997] AC 1 the House of Lords also emphasised the need to consider whether the scope of the duty of care (whether in contract or tort) is sufficient to embrace the kind of damage complained of in a particular case. The starting point in the assessment of damages should therefore be a consideration of whether the loss for which compensation was sought was of a kind or type for which the contract breaker or tortfeasor ought fairly to have accepted responsibility (a position re-emphasised by Lord Hoffmann in the recent decision of the House of Lords in the shipping case of *Transfield Shipping Inc v Mercator Shipping Inc* [2008] UKHL 48).

2.10 However, it should be noted that *Murphy v Brentwood* and most of the cases connected with this retreat from the recognition of a general principle of liability in negligence have been mainly concerned with the duty of care to avoid causing economic loss (for which see paragraph 2.21 below). In respect of non-economic loss situations, it is suggested that the *Anns v Merton* approach still provides a useful framework for the consideration of the existence of a legal duty of care. There should be little difficulty in considering whether such a duty exists where either damage to the person or property has been occasioned, although (at least conceptually) the approach to testing the existence of a duty of care in a given situation is not affected by the kind of harm sustained on the facts of the case under consideration (as explained by the House of Lords in *Marc Rich & Co v Bishop Rock Marine Co Ltd* [1996] AC 211).

Relationship to any duties existing in the law of contract

2.11 As well as emphasising the importance of the concept of an assumption of responsibility to defining the existence and scope of any duty of care in the tort of negligence, *Henderson v Merrett* also decided that concurrent duties of care in the tort of negligence may be owed by one party to another even if a contract already existed between them. Thus, even if an architect has a contract of retainer with his client, he will also owe the client a concurrent duty of care in the tort of negligence (but see the first instance decision in *Payne v John Setchell* – discussed below).

2.12 Although, generally, the nature of any tortious duty to take reasonable care against causing damage to the other party is likely to be co-terminous with the implied contractual duty to take reasonable care in the provision of services under their contract (see, for example, *Storey v Charles Church Developments Ltd* [1996] 12 Const LJ 206), the contents of the parties' contract may create stricter contractual duties than are owed in the general law of negligence, or, alternatively, the circumstances of the parties relationship may, in extreme situations, lead to the creation of wider tortious duties than have been created by the contract of retainer (see in the context of a surveyor's negligence action *Holt v Payne Skillington* [1995] 77 BLR 51 and in an engineering context *Kensington and Chelsea and Westminster AHA v Wettern Composites Ltd* (1984) 1 Con LR 114 and *Hart Investments Ltd v Fidler* [2007] EWHC 1058 (TCC)).

Breach of duty

2.13 In general, a person acts in breach of a duty of care when behaving carelessly. As Alderson J stated in *Blyth v Birmingham Waterworks Company* [1856] 11 Ex 781:

> 'Negligence is the omission to do something which a reasonable man, guided upon those considerations which ordinarily regulate the conduct of human affairs, would do, or doing something which a prudent and reasonable man would not do.'

2.14 The standard of care required, then, is that of the reasonable and prudent man: the elusive 'man on the Clapham omnibus'. It is not a counsel of perfection and mere error does not necessarily amount to negligence. The standard applied is objective in that it does not take account of an individual's particular weaknesses. However, where a person holds himself out as having a special skill or being a professional (such as an architect), the standard of care expected of him is higher than one would expect of a layman. He is under a duty to exercise the standard of care in his activities which could reasonably be expected from a competent member of that trade or profession, whatever his actual level of experience or qualification. In the case of architects (as with other professionals) the test is whether there is a responsible body of architects that could have acted as the architect being criticised has (see *Nye Saunders v Bristow* [1987] 37 BLR 92 per Stephen Brown LJ at 103), although this is not a rigid rule (see *Bolitho v City & Hackney HA* [1998] AC 232, HL) and not applicable where it is not necessary to consider professional expertise to decide the alleged acts of incompetence (see *Royal Brompton Hospital NHS Trust v Hammond (No.7)* (2001) 76 Con LR 148. In general, the duty owed by construction professionals is unaffected by the relative experience or inexperience of their clients (see *Gloucestershire Health Authority v Torpy* [1997] CILL 1281; but see *J Jarvis & Sons Ltd v Castle Wharf Developments Ltd* [2001] Lloyd's Rep PN 308). In contrast, however, there are also circumstances where the law accepts a lower standard of care from people, such as at times of emergency or dilemma (or, outside the field of professional negligence, generally in the level of care expected from children).

2.15 The value of the concept of 'reasonable care' lies in its flexibility. What will be considered by a court as 'reasonable' depends on the specific facts of a particular case and the attitude of the judge. Precedent is seldom cited or useful in this respect. However, in general the assessment of reasonableness involves a consideration of three main factors: (a) the degree of likelihood of harm, (b) the cost and practicability of measures to avoid it, and (c) the seriousness of the possible consequences. The application and balancing of these factors is best illustrated by reference to actual cases.

2.16 In *Brewer v Delo* [1967] 1 LIR 488, a case which involved a golfer hitting another player with a golf ball, it was held that the risk was so slight as to be unforeseeable and therefore the golfer had not acted negligently. Similarly, in *Bolton v Stone* [1951] AC 850 the occupiers of a cricket ground were held not to be liable for a cricket ball that had left the pitch and struck the plaintiff, because of the improbability of such an incident occurring. Finally, in *The Wagon Mound (No. 2)* [1967] 1 AC 617, crude oil escaped from a ship onto the surface of the water in Sydney Harbour. It subsequently caught fire and caused substantial damage to a wharf and two ships. However, notwithstanding expert evidence that the risk of the oil catching fire had been very small, it was held that the defendants were negligent in not taking steps to abate what was nevertheless a real risk and one which, if it occurred, was very likely to cause substantial damage.

Damage must be caused by the breach

2.17 In order to establish liability in negligence it is necessary to prove that the careless conduct has caused actual damage. There are three requirements in this process. The first is that, on the balance of probabilities, there must as a matter of fact be a connection between the negligent conduct and the damage (causation in fact). If there are competing causes of a claimant's loss he must establish as a minimum that the cause of which he complains materially contributed to his loss (see the decision of the House of Lords in *IBA v EMI and BICC* (1980) 14 BLR 1 at 37). The second is that the harm or damage caused is of a kind that was a foreseeable consequence of such conduct (causation in law). The third overarching requirement is that the breach of duty be the 'dominant and effective' cause of the loss. This latter test really represents the application of judicial common sense to cases which satisfy the first two requirements, but nevertheless involve losses which should not be recognised as caused as a matter of law by the relevant breach of duty under consideration.

2.18 Foreseeability of harm therefore plays a role in all three constituents of the tort of negligence: duty of care, breach and damage. In certain respects this makes a separate consideration of these individual constituents artificial. However, foreseeability of damage has a slightly different application when considering the causation of actionable damage. In assessing the existence and breach of a duty of care, it is the reasonable foreseeability of a risk of some damage that is being considered. Foreseeability of the occurrence of a particular kind of damage does not affect the existence of this duty or the assessment of carelessness, but it does dictate whether the damage that has been caused is actionable in law.

2.19 If the kind of damage actually caused was not foreseeable, there is no liability in negligence. However, as long as the kind of damage is reasonably foreseeable there will be potential liability even if the factual manner in which it was caused was extremely unusual and unforeseeable in itself. In *Hughes v Lord Advocate* [1963] AC 837 workmen left a manhole overnight covered by a tent and surrounded by paraffin lamps, but otherwise unguarded. The eight-year-old plaintiff ventured into the tent, fell down the manhole, dragged some of the lamps down with him and thereby caused an explosion which caused him to be severely burned. The House of Lords held that although the manner of the explosion was highly unusual, the source of the danger and kind of damage that materialised (i.e. burns from the lit paraffin) were reasonably foreseeable and therefore the workmen were liable.

2.20 As noted above, however, it is sometimes simplistic to view the law of causation as simply a consideration of the first two requirements outlined in paragraph 2.17 above. The courts may apply a less precise test of judicial common sense to distinguish between the effective cause of a loss from conduct which merely provides the occasion for it (as applied by the Court of Appeal in *Galoo v Bright Grahame Murray* [1994] 1 WLR 1360). Ultimately, this factor reflects the reality that judicial policy can play as important a role in deciding where responsibility for losses should fall (on the professional, his client or a third party) as any easily definable rules or principles of law.

Economic loss

(a) Introduction

2.21 Economic loss is a category of non-physical damage. It consists of financial losses (such as lost profits), as opposed to personal injury or physical damage to property (i.e. property other than, in the case of construction professionals, the property that is the subject of their services). Unfortunately, as well as being an area of the utmost practical importance for architects, the concept of a duty of care to prevent economic loss is also one of the more demanding aspects of the law of tort.

2.22 The tort of negligence originally developed in the late nineteenth and early twentieth centuries as a cause of action for a party who had been physically injured by the careless acts of another. It also quickly developed into a remedy for careless damage to property. However, the attempt from about the 1960s (associated with the developing concept of a general principle of liability in negligence described above) to extend its ambit to economic losses generally has been largely unsuccessful. Today, economic loss is not always irrecoverable in the tort of negligence, but it requires a claimant to prove the exceptional circumstances necessary in order to establish that a defendant owed him a duty not to cause such damage. This long-standing reluctance to recognise a duty of care to prevent economic loss has been largely based on what is referred to as the 'floodgates' argument – the concern that it would widen the potential scale of liability in tort to an indeterminable extent.

(b) Distinguishing consequential and pure economic loss

2.23 Although there is no general liability for economic loss which is disassociated from physical damage, economic loss consequential to damage to property is treated separately and is generally recoverable. The distinction between such 'consequential' economic loss and 'pure' economic loss is not always clear. Perhaps the best illustration is provided by the case *of Spartan Steel and Alloys Ltd v Martin & Co. (Contractors Ltd)* [1973] 1 QB 27. In this case the defendants negligently cut off an electricity cable which supplied the plaintiff's factory. As a result, some of the plaintiff's molten metal that was being worked upon at the factory was damaged, causing the plaintiff to make a smaller profit on its eventual sale. Production was also delayed generally at the factory and the plaintiff lost the opportunity to make profits on this lost production. It was held that although the economic loss caused by the general delay in production was not recoverable (being pure economic loss), the lost profit from the molten metal actually in production at the time of the power cut was recoverable as it was immediately consequential to the physical damage to the molten metal itself. This was because, economic loss immediately consequential to damage to property is recoverable in negligence.

(c) Liability for negligent statements

2.24 The first exception to the general rule of there being no duty to avoid causing pure economic loss was provided in the area of negligent mis-statement and the line of authorities following *Hedley Byrne & Co. Ltd v Heller & Partners* [1963] AC 465. In this seminal case, the defendants gave a favourable financial reference to the plaintiffs bankers in respect of one of the plaintiffs clients. The plaintiff relied on this incorrect reference and as a result suffered financial losses when the client became insolvent. The House of Lords held that a defendant would be liable for such negligent mis-statements if: (a) there was a 'special relationship' based upon an assumption of responsibility between the parties, (b) the defendant knew or ought to have known that the plaintiff was likely to rely upon his statement, and (c) in all the circumstances it was reasonable for the plaintiff so to rely on the defendant's statement.

2.25 In accordance with the retreat from an acceptance of a general principle of liability in negligence and, in particular, its extension to economic loss generally, the circumstances where the courts will now recognise the required 'special relationship' may have narrowed since the 1970s. In *Caparo v Dickman* [1990] 2 AC 605 the House of Lords held that auditors of a company's financial reports did not owe a duty of care to prospective share purchasers to avoid negligent mis-statements because, unlike a company's existing shareholders, the parties were not in a relationship of sufficient proximity. Liability for economic loss caused by negligent mis-statement was to be restricted to situations where the statement was given to a known recipient for a specific purpose of which the maker of the statement was aware.

2.26 This represented a narrow interpretation of the *Hedley Byrne* principle consistent with the revival of the incremental approach to liability discussed in paragraph 2.07 above. Although there is now authority for the need to emphasise a more flexible concept of 'assumption of responsibility' as the basis for potential liability (see paragraph 2.34 below), it is submitted that these restrictive criteria will probably continue to be applied by the courts.

2.27 Liability for negligent mis-statement may be of relevance to architects when giving their clients advice, for example in relation to cost estimates or which builders to use. In *Nye Saunders v Bristow* [1987] 37 BLR 92, although there was no allegation of defective work, the architect was found to be in breach of a *Hedley Byrne*-type duty by not advising his client as to the possible effect of inflation on his estimate for the cost of proposed works.

(d) Liability for negligent conduct

2.28 In contrast to the position with negligent statements, the attempt in a number of leading cases since the 1970s to extend liability for pure economic loss to negligent conduct has largely failed. The initial momentum for such an extension was provided by *Anns v Merton* which concerned structural damage in a building that had been caused by defective foundations. The House of Lords allowed the recovery in tort of the pure economic loss caused by the need to carry out repairs so that the property was no longer a threat to health and safety.

2.29 However, in its recent decisions in *Murphy v Brentwood District Council* [1991] 1 AC 398 and *Department of the Environment v Thomas Bates & Sons Ltd* [1991] 1 AC 499 the House of Lords has overruled *Anns v Merton*. The facts of *Murphy v Brentwood* also concerned a house which had been built on improper foundations, allegedly because of the Council's negligence in passing the building plans. It was held that the Council did not owe a duty in tort to the owner or purchaser of property in respect of the costs of remedying such defects in the property. The repair costs were held to be pure economic loss and irrecoverable, whether or not the defects amounted to a threat to health or safety.

2.30 There were two main reasons for the decision in *Murphy v Brentwood*. First, it was considered established law that in tort the manufacturer of a chattel owed no duty in respect of defects that did not cause personal injury or damage to other property. Thus, in *Donoghue v Stevenson* (see paragraphs 2.02 and 2.03 above) the defendant was not liable for the diminution in value of the bottle of ginger beer by reason of the presence of a decomposed snail in it. Mrs Donoghue could only recover damages against the manufacturer in respect of the physical harm caused to her by drinking it. Therefore, the defective house in *Murphy v Brentwood* was effectively considered analogous to the bottle of ginger beer in *Donoghue v Stevenson*: their Lordships held that it would be anomalous in principle if someone involved in the construction of a building should be in any different position from the manufacturer of bottled ginger beer or any other chattel.

2.31 The second main justification was that innovation in the law of consumer protection against defects in the quality of products should be left to Parliament, especially in the light of the remedies provided by the Defective Premises Act 1972 in the case of residential dwellings (for which see Section 3 below).

2.32 This latter justification is not very convincing since most decisions in this field, including *Donoghue v Stevenson* itself, can be viewed as essentially judicially created consumer-protection law in any case. However, it does illustrate the influence of judicial policy in the court's approach to the recognition of a duty of care in novel situations. Further, although *Murphy v Brentwood* has certainly simplified the law in this area, there remain recognised exceptions to the general rule against the existence of a duty of care to prevent economic loss in negligence.

(e) Exceptions to Murphy v Brentwood

2.33 First, the position in respect of economic loss consequential to physical damage and negligent mis-statements remains unaffected by the decision (see paragraph 2.23 above).

2.34 In addition, in *Murphy v Brentwood* their Lordships recognised that damage to a building caused by defects in a discrete part of it could in certain circumstances be recoverable in tort. Under the pre-*Murphy v Brentwood* 'complex structure theory' the individual parts of a building (such as the foundations, walls or roof) could be treated as distinct items of property. Therefore liability for damage caused to, say, the roof by a defect in the foundations could be justified by treating the building as a complex structure and depicting the damaged roof as a separate piece of damaged property. This analysis was proposed as a means of reconciling the post-*Anns v Merton* recognition of liability in negligence for defective premises with the established principle that there is no tortious liability for defective products.

2.35 In *Murphy v Brentwood* their Lordships rejected the complex structure theory and viewed the damaged house as a single piece of property (i.e. not a complex structure). However, they have left open the possibility of liability in the normal way where the item within a building that causes the damage is a distinct one (perhaps a faulty electrical fuse box which causes a fire) and is built or installed by a separate party from the builder. If damage is caused by such a 'non-integral' part of the building, it may be considered as damage caused to separate property (which under normal principles would be actionable damage in negligence). Therefore, in place of the complex structure analysis, their Lordships appear to have left a more restrictive 'non-integral piece of property' theory as a possible basis for continuing liability in tort for defective premises (see also *Jacob v Morton* [1994] 72 BLR 92 and *Bellefield Computer Services Ltd v E Turner & Sons Ltd* [2000] BLR 97 for an analysis of this exception).

2.36 This concept is illustrated by the case of *Nitrigin Eireann Teoranta v Inco Alloys* [1992] 1 All 854. The defendants had manufactured and supplied the plaintiff's factory with some alloy tubing in 1981 which had developed cracks by 1983. It was held that although the cracked tubing in 1983 constituted pure economic loss (because at this time there was no damage to other property), damage to the factory caused by an explosion in 1984 (itself caused by the continuing weakness in the tubing) did give rise to a cause of action in negligence. The structure of the factory surrounding the tubing was considered to be separate property and therefore this damage was not pure economic loss.

2.37 Two other bases for liability in negligence for defective premises have, in theory, survived the decision in *Murphy v Brentwood,* although their application in practice is extremely unlikely. First, Lord Bridge suggested that there may be a duty to prevent economic loss where the defective building is so close to its boundary that by reason of its defects the building might cause physical damage or injury to persons on neighbouring land or the highway. This approach was applied in *Morse v Barrett (Leeds) Ltd* (1993) 9 Const LJ. However, finding liability in these circumstances would appear to contradict the reasoning in the rest of their Lordships' judgments in *Murphy v Brentwood*. It is submitted that the better view is that the cost of repairing such defects would still be irrecoverable in negligence, as it amounts to pure economic loss. This was the approach taken by judge Hicks QC in *George Fischer Holding Ltd v Multi Design Consultants Ltd* (1998) 61 Con LR 85 at 109-11. However, until this point is clarified by future decisions it will remain a possible, if unlikely, basis for such liability.

2.38 Second, there is the anomalous case *of Junior Books v Veitchi & Co.* [1983] 1 AC 520 which the House of Lords could not bring itself to overrule in addition to *Anns v Merton*. In *Junior Books* the defendants were specialist floor sub-contractors who were engaged by main contractors to lay a floor in the factory of the plaintiff, with whom they had no formal contract. The floor subsequently cracked up and the plaintiff sued for the cost of relaying it. The House of Lords held that, on the particular facts of the case, there was such a close relationship between the parties that the defendants' duty to take care to the plaintiff extended to preventing economic loss caused by defects in their laying of the floor. This decision at first appears completely contradictory to the reasoning in *Murphy v Brentwood*, although some of their Lordships sought to explain it as a special application of the *Hedley Byrne* principle. One view is that *Junior Books* will continue to be considered as an anomalous case decided very much on its own facts, and not one that establishes as a matter of principle a further category of exceptions from the main decision in *Murphy v Brentwood.*

(f) The effect of Henderson v Merrett

2.39 However, an alternative interpretation is now possible in the light of Lord Goff's landmark speech in the decision of the House of Lords in *Henderson v Merrett Syndicates Ltd* [1994] 3WLR 761. Here, their Lordships unanimously held that a concurrent duty of care was owed in tort by managing agents to Lloyd's names notwithstanding the existence of a contractual relationship between them. The decision therefore established that concurrent duties in tort may exist between parties in a contractual relationship. However, of more significance in the present context are Lord Goff's comments on the ambit of the duty of care in tort under the *Hedley Byrne* principle.

2.40 In addition to characterising the basis of such liability as being the voluntary assumption of responsibility by one party to another, Lord Goff also interpreted the *Hedley Byrne* principle as applying to the provision of professional services generally, whether by words or actions. Thus, at p. 776 of his judgment he concludes:

'... the concept provides its own explanation why there is no problem in cases of this kind about liability for pure economic loss: for if a person assumes responsibility to another in respect of certain services, there is no reason why he should not be liable in damages for that other in respect of economic loss which flows from the negligent performance of those services. It follows that, once the case is identified as falling within the *Hedley Byrne* principle, there should be no need to embark upon any further enquiry whether it is "fair, just and reasonable" to impose liability for economic loss-a point which is, I consider, of some importance in the present case.'

2.41 This represented a major conceptual extension of the category of conduct in which the courts may recognise a duty to prevent causing economic loss. Although it is not as yet clear how the courts will apply Lord Goff's judgment in this respect (and in particular its relationship to the decision in *Murphy v Brentwood*), it is submitted that the courts will probably expressly recognise from now on liability for economic losses caused by the negligent actions of professionals if there is a *Hedley Byrne*-type special relationship with/assumption of responsibility toward the party suffering damage. Invariably, of course, this will be the case where there is a contractual relationship between an architect and his client.

2.42 However, the tension between the decisions in *Murphy v Brentwood* and *Henderson v Merrett* has become most clear in the case of liability in tort for defective building works. It is not easy to rationalise the apparent difference of approach in the authorities toward the builder who carries out as part of his services in constructing a wall a negligent design function (and who may well therefore be liable on *Hedley Byrne* principles) and a builder who does not carry out any design function (and who therefore would not normally be considered to be liable in tort for any defects in the wall itself on the basis *of Murphy v Brentwood*). In both situations the builder provides a service and could well be said to have assumed responsibility for the competency of his work in a *Henderson v Merrett* sense.

2.43 This apparent dichotomy between the law's approach to the liability of a simple builder compared with a design and building contractor or a construction professional has been grappled with at first instance in the decision in *Payne v John Setchell Ltd* [2002] BLR 48. Here it was held (rather surprisingly, it is suggested) that ordinarily both construction professionals (such as architects) and building contractors may only be under a duty of care in tort to take reasonable care against causing their contractual clients personal injury or damage to property *other than the building/item of work that is the subject matter of their services*. Thus, the dichotomy was resolved in this case by a finding that neither the contractor nor the construction professional should owe a duty of care in the ordinary course of events in respect of defects in quality to the product of their work or services.

2.44 It is suggested that this approach is probably wrong, as it appears to rest upon the assumption that *Murphy v Brentwood* is authority for the proposition that a building contractor can *never* owe his client a duty of care in tort in respect of the quality of his work. However, *Murphy v Brentwood* did not directly decide this point; rather, it dealt with the responsibility in tort of a local authority in respect of such defects. The better position in the light of *Henderson v Merrett* would appear to be that if a building contractor can be taken on the facts of a particular case to have assumed responsibility toward his client for his work a tortious duty in respect of the quality of that work may arise (for support for this proposition, see *Bellefield Computer Services Ltd v E Turner & Sons Ltd* [2000] BLR 96 per Schieman LJ at 102). The approach in *Payne v John Setchell* was not followed by Judge Toulmin CMG QC in *Ove Arup & Partners International Ltd v Mirah Asia-Pacific Construction (Hong Kong) (No. 2)* [2004] EWHC 1750 (TCC).

(g) Continuing evolution of the law

2.45 Finally, in the light of *Henderson v Merrett* it should be emphasised that *Murphy v Brentwood* does not shut off the possible recognition of new categories of relationships in which a non-contractual duty to avoid causing economic loss will be recognised. For example, in *Punjab National Bank v de Boinville* [1992] 1 WLR 1138 the Court of Appeal held that (a) the relationship between an insurance broker and his client was a recognised exceptional category of case where such a duty existed, and (b) it was, on the facts of the case, a justified extension of this category to hold that a broker owed a like duty to a non-client where the broker knew that the insurance policy was to be assigned to this person and that he had been involved in instructing the broker in the first place.

(h) Conclusion

2.46 In summary, as far as the particular position of professional architects is concerned the consequences of the landmark decisions in *Murphy v Brentwood* and *Henderson v Merrett* are probably as follows:

1   A duty of care in tort will be owed by an architect to his client in relation to economic losses of a similar nature and extent as that created by any contract between the parties.

2   Liability for economic loss claims by third parties (i.e. those not in a contractual relationship with the architect) for defective work (subject to the existence of a *Hedley Byrne* relationship or assumption of responsibility) has been eliminated.

3   However, potential *Donoghue v Stevenson*-type liability for damage caused to other property or the person as a result of such work remains: for example, if a piece of roofing falls off a building because of an architect's negligent design and breaks a person's leg or dents their car (whether or not that person is the owner of the building or a client).

4   The principle at 3 above extends to make an architect potentially liable to subsequent owners of a building in respect of damage caused to other property or the person by latent defects in the building attributable to his negligence (see *Baxall Securities Ltd v Sheard Walshaw Partnership* [2002] BLR 100; *Pearson Education Ltd v The Charter Partnership Ltd* [2007] EWCA Civ 130).

5   There will be a revival of interest in potential liability pursuant to the Defective Premises Act 1972 (see below).

6   Otherwise there will be a re-focusing of attention on possible *Hedley Byrne* relationships/assumption of responsibility as the only other effective basis for liability in tort for defective work to or related to the construction of buildings.

7   It is submitted that in practice the existence of a sufficiently proximate relationship to attract such liability between an architect and a client will rarely occur, outside contractual relationships (for a recent unsuccessful attempt at such in a construction project context, see the decision of Akenhead J in *Galliford Try Infrastructure Ltd v Mott McDonald Ltd* [2008] EWHC 1570 (TCC)).

8   An important factor to consider when analysing whether a duty of care in respect of economic loss exists between a construction professional and a non-client third party (say the contractor or a sub-contractor) are the terms of the contract between the professional and his client (see, for example, *Bellefield Computer Services Ltd v E Turner & Sons Ltd*) and the contractual matrix generally (see *Henderson v Merrett, Riyad Bank v Ahli Bank,* and *Galliford Try Infrastructure Ltd v Mott McDonald* above).

9   Where there is a relationship of proximity between an architect and his client or third party, the architect will owe a duty of care to prevent causing purely economic losses as a result of careless statements (via negligent designs, certification or advice) and, probably, his conduct and provision of his services in general.

10   An architect may also in appropriate circumstances owe his client or a third party a personal duty of care – distinct from the responsibility assumed by the firm or company for which he works (in the light of *Merrett v Babb* [2001] 3 WLR 1 which was a case where a surveyor was found to have owed his client a personal duty of care in respect of a valuation report prepared for mortgage purposes).

3   The Defective Premises Act 1972

3.01 Section 1 of the Act provides:

'1   A person taking on work for the provision of a dwelling (whether the dwelling is provided by the erection or by the conversion or enlargement of a building) owes a duty –
   (a) if the dwelling is provided to the order of any person, to that person; and

   (b) without prejudice to paragraph (a) above, to every person who acquires an interest (whether legal or equitable) in the dwelling;

to see that the work which he takes on is done in a workmanlike or, as the case may be, professional manner, with proper materials and so that as regards that work the dwelling will be fit for habitation when completed.'

3.02 All building professionals, including architects, can be 'persons taking on work' pursuant to the Act if the work undertaken is concerned with a dwelling. The duty created by the Act is owed to the person for whom the dwelling is provided, although the main purpose for the Act was to confer a right of action on subsequent owners of the dwelling which they would otherwise not have. Although not specified under the Act, the appropriate remedy for breach of its duty is damages. The duty cannot be avoided by exclusion clauses.

3.03 The person undertaking the work is liable not only for his own work, but also for the work of independent sub-contractors employed by him if they are engaged in the course of his business. The reference to a 'dwelling' implies that the Act is limited to property capable of being used as a residence. However, the Act does not apply to remedial work to an existing building. Further, liability under the Act is limited to a period of 6 years after the completion of the work concerned. This special limitation period provides a major restriction on the potential significance of the Act.

3.04 The Act appears to impose a dual statutory duty to ensure that (a) work is done in a workmanlike manner, and (b) as regards that work the dwelling will be fit for human habitation. It is unclear to what extent the latter requirement restricts liability under the Act for defective work. In *Thompson v Clive Alexander & Partners* [1993] 59 BLR 77 it was held that allegations of defective work alone on the part of an architect were not capable of amounting to a breach of the Act. It was held that the provision regarding fitness for habitation was the measure of the standard required in performance of the duty pursuant to section 1(1) and that trivial defects were not intended to be covered by the statute. There is authority to the contrary that suggests that the unfitness for habitation requirement adds nothing to the main one that the work is to be done properly. However, on its proper construction the Act probably does not cover every defective piece of work and something more than trivial defects are required to be in breach of it, although the precise ambit of the duty will have to await further litigation.

3.05 Notwithstanding these restrictions it is likely that liability under the Act will be of greater significance for architects and other building professionals in the future than it has been to date. There are two main reasons for this. First, although the decision in *Murphy v Brentwood* limited liability in negligence for pure economic loss caused to third parties by defective property, such pure economic loss is still recoverable under the Defective Premises Act 1972. Typically, claims against architects involve a large proportion of purely economic losses, therefore attention is likely to concentrate in the future on potential liability under the Act.

3.06 Second, the exception to liability created by section 2 of the Act which excludes certain approved building schemes from its provisions is likely to be of less significance in the future. This is because the last NHBC Vendor–Purchaser Insurance scheme to be approved by the Secretary of State as an 'approved scheme' under section 2 was in 1979. However, some time before 1988 the NHBC and the Secretary of State agreed that because of changes in the 1979 approved scheme it was no longer effective. No further scheme has been approved. Thus, there is potentially a large amount of post-1979 building work that will no longer be caught by section 2 and will now be subject to the Act's duties.

4   Nuisance

4.01 The tort of nuisance is concerned with the unjustified interference with a party's use of land. Whether activity which may as a matter of fact be a considerable nuisance to an individual is actionable in law depends, as in the case of the tort of negligence, on a consideration of all the circumstances of the case and the proof of consequential actionable damage. Although most nuisances arise out of a continuing state of affairs, an isolated occurrence can be sufficient if physical damage is caused.

4.02 There are two varieties of actionable nuisance; public and private. A public nuisance is one that inflicts damage, annoyance or inconvenience on a class of persons or persons generally. It is a criminal offence and only actionable in tort if an individual member of the public has suffered some particular kind of foreseeable damage to a greater extent than the public at large, or where some private right has also been interfered with. The House of Lords has recently confirmed the existence of the common law crime of a public nuisance in *R v Goldstein* [2006] 1 AC 459. Examples of public nuisances can include selling food unfit for human consumption, causing dangerous obstructions to the highway, and (by way of statutory nuisances) water and atmospheric pollution (see *East Dorset District Council v Eaglebeam* [2007] Env LR D9).

4.03 A private nuisance is an unlawful act which interferes with a party's use or enjoyment of land or of some right connected with it. Traditionally, interference with enjoyment of land in which the claimant had some kind of proprietary interest was one of the defining characteristics of a private nuisance. However, in *Khorasandjian v Bush* [1993] QB 727 a majority of the Court of Appeal granted an injunction against the defendant to prevent him telephoning the plaintiff at her mother's home (in which she was staying as a mere licensee with no proprietary interest). This decision may in time be seen as the precursor of a wider concept of actionable nuisance amounting to a general tort of harassment, and possibly the beginning of a tort of invasion of privacy. At present, however, it is submitted that the decision is best seen as a narrow extension of the availability of an action in private nuisance to interference with the enjoyment of premises at which the plaintiff lives, whether or not pursuant to a proprietary interest in the property itself. It is possible, however, that the requirement for a claimant to have a legal interest in land before making a claim in nuisance may have been further eroded by Article 8 of the Human Rights Act 1998 (see *McKenna v British Aluminium Ltd,* The Times 25 April 2002 and *Marcic v Thams Water Utilities Ltd* [2002] 2 All ER 55).

4.04 A private nuisance consists of a party doing some act which is not limited to his own land but affects another party's occupation of land, by either: (a) causing an encroachment onto the neighbouring land (for example, when trees overhang it or tree roots grow into the neighbouring land), (b) causing physical damage to the land or buildings (such as when there is an emission of smoke or other fumes which damage his neighbour's crops or property), or (c) causing an unreasonable interference with a neighbour's enjoyment of his land (such as causing too much noise or obnoxious smells to pass over it).

4.05 The actual or prospective infliction of damage is a necessary ingredient of an actionable nuisance. In a nuisance of the kind at 4.04(a), damage is presumed once the encroachment is proved. In (b) there must be proof of actual or prospective physical damage. Therefore in both these cases the requirement of damage is an objective test which does not involve a further examination of the surrounding circumstances. In nuisances of the kind at (c), however, there is no objective standard applied by the courts. Whether the acts complained of amount to the unreasonable use of land is a question of degree. The nuisance needs to amount to a material interference with the use of other land that an average man (with no particular susceptibilities or special interests) would consider unreasonable in all the circumstances of the particular case. The essence of this kind of nuisance is something coming onto or encroaching onto the claimant's land (see *Hunter v Canary Wharf Ltd* [1997] AC 655 and *Anglian Water Services v Crawshaw Robins & Co* [2001] BLR 173).

4.06 The duration and timing of the acts complained of is a relevant factor in this balancing of neighbours' interests. So too is the

character of the locality. In *Sturges v Bridgman* [1879] 11 ChD 852 at 856 Thesiger LJ put it as follows:

'... whether anything is a nuisance or not is a question to be determined, not merely by an abstract consideration of the thing itself, but in reference to its circumstances: what would be a nuisance in Belgrave Square would not necessarily be so in Bermondsey; and where a locality is devoted to a particular trade or manufacture carried on by the traders or manufacturers in a particular and established manner not constituting a public nuisance, judges ... would be justified in finding ... that the trade or manufacture so carried on in that locality is not a private or actionable wrong.'

4.07 The conduct of the defendant may also be a relevant factor. In *Hollywood Silver Fox Farm Ltd v Emmett* [1936] 2 KB 468 the defendant maliciously encouraged his son to fire shotguns on his own land but as near as possible to the plaintiff's adjoining property in order to disrupt his business of breeding silver foxes. Although the defendant was entitled to shoot on his own land, the court held that he was nevertheless creating a nuisance. The court held that the defendant's intention to alarm the plaintiff's foxes was a relevant factor in reaching this conclusion and specifically limited the injunction granted against the defendant to prevent the making of loud noises so as to alarm the plaintiff's foxes. Similarly, it is a nuisance if a person deliberately uses his land in a manner which he knows will cause an unreasonable interference with another's, whether or not he believes that he is entitled to do the act or has taken all reasonable steps (short of not doing the act itself) to prevent it amounting to a nuisance.

4.08 Traditionally, it was accepted that outside this kind of conduct nuisance had an uncertain overlap with the tort of negligence. There were some situations in which it involved negligent behaviour and others where this was not considered a requirement for liability. As Lord Reid rather confusingly put it in *The Wagon Mound (No. 2)*:

'It is quite true that negligence is not an essential element in nuisance. Nuisance is a term used to cover a wide variety of tortious acts or omissions and in many negligence in the narrow sense is not essential ... although negligence may not be necessary, fault of some kind is almost always necessary and fault generally involves foreseeability.'

4.09 Not surprisingly, a degree of confusion has been introduced by this distinction between negligence, on the one hand, and the requirement of some kind of fault, incorporating the concept of foreseeability, on the other. It is now established that liability in nuisance is not strict and that foreseeability of damage is a necessary ingredient (see *Leaky v National Trust* [1980] QB 485 and *Arscott v Coal Authority* [2005] Env LR 6, CA). However, the requirement of foreseeability of damage does not necessarily imply the need for negligent conduct, but may sometimes only be relevant to what kind of damage will be actionable. Further, the concept of 'fault' in nuisance is better viewed as unreasonable conduct (which is the essence of the tort) and may not always amount to negligent conduct (in the sense used in the tort of negligence), (see *Cambridge Water Co Ltd v Eastern Counties Leather plc* [1994] 2 AC 264 and *Jan de Nul (UK) v NV Royal Beige* [2000] 2 Lloyd's Rep 700).

4.10 Although, increasingly, the distinction between negligence and nuisance has become blurred (and in practice they have to a large extent become assimilated), they are not synonymous in principle. The following points should be emphasised: (a) where the nuisance is the interference with a natural right incidental to land ownership (such as the right to obtain water from a well) then liability is strict, (b) the act complained of may constitute the required 'unreasonable user' of land to constitute a nuisance without necessarily amounting to 'negligent' behaviour, (c) economic loss is generally recoverable in nuisance, (d) some kinds of damage recognised and protected in nuisance (such as creating an unreasonable noise or smell, or harassment such as in *Khorasandjian v Bush* above) would not amount to actionable damage in the tort of negligence, and (e) the remedy of an injunction is available to prevent an anticipated or continuing nuisance, but not to prevent someone acting negligently.

5 The rule in *Rylands v Fletcher*

5.01 An example of strict liability in tort (which does not require the proof of negligence or intent on the part of the wrongdoer) is the rule as stated by Blackburn J in *Rylands v Fletcher* [1866] LR 1 Ex 265 at 279:

> 'We think that the true rule of law is, that the person who for his own purposes brings on his land and collects and keeps there anything likely to do mischief if it escapes must keep it in at his peril, and, if he does not do so, is prima facie answerable for all the damage which is the natural consequence of its escape.'

5.02 In the House of Lords the rule was limited to apply only to the 'non-natural user' of land. The courts have failed to clarify precisely what non-natural user of land consists of and in what particular circumstances the rule should apply. However, it has been applied to water, fire, explosives, poison, and, in *Hale v Jennings Brothers* [1938] 1 All ER 579, to a seat becoming detached from a high-speed fairground roundabout. In general, the rule is applicable where a person brings onto his land something that is 'dangerous', in the sense that if the thing escapes from the land it would be likely to cause either personal or physical damage.

5.03 There are various specific defences available to *Rylands v Fletcher* liability, namely (a) that the escape of the dangerous thing was caused by an Act of God, (b) that it was caused by the independent act of a stranger (though not an independent contractor), or the claimant himself, (c) that the claimant has consented to the dangerous thing being kept on the defendant's land, and (d) that the dangerous thing has been stored pursuant to some statutory duty (in which case negligence must be established on the part of the defendant).

5.04 The tendency of the courts to adopt a very restrictive interpretation of what was considered as non-natural use of land and

therefore limited application *of Rylands v Fletcher* was considered in *Cambridge Water Co. Ltd v Eastern Counties Leather plc* [1994] 2 AC 264. In its first consideration of the rule for over half a century, the House of Lords took the view that the rule should be seen as no more than an extension of the law of nuisance to cases of isolated escapes from land.

5.05 Although the House of Lords considered that the concept of non-natural user had been unjustifiably extended by the courts, a restrictive interpretation of the rule was nevertheless confirmed as it found that foreseeability of harm of the relevant type was a prerequisite to liability under the rule (as in the case of nuisance). In an approach reminiscent of the House of Lords' attitude in *Murphy v Brentwood* to economic loss, the imposition of no-fault liability for all damage caused by operations of high risk was considered a more appropriate role for parliamentary, not judicial, intervention.

5.06 As in the case of nuisance it has been held that it is arguable that a claimant need not have a proprietary interest in the land affected to bring a claim under the rule in *Rylands v Fletcher* (see *McKenna v British Aluminium Ltd*, The Times 25 April 2002). However, unlike the tort of nuisance, pure economic losses are irrecoverable under this rule (see *Anglian Water Services v Crawshaw Robins & Co* [2001] BLR 173 at para 149).

5.07 In *Arscott v Coal Authority* the Court of Appeal confirmed that the rule in *Rylands v Fletcher* was still applicable (although the concept of natural/non-natural user should perhaps be replaced with one of 'reasonable user' as in nuisance) and the rule was applied in *LMS International Ltd v Styrene Packaging & Insulation Ltd* [2005] EWHC 2065 in a case involving the escape of fire.

6 Trespass

6.01 Trespass to the person involves an interference, however slight, with a person's right to the security of his body. It can be of three varieties: (a) a 'battery' which is caused by unlawful physical contact, (b) an 'assault' which is where the innocent party is

caused to fear the immediate infliction of such contact, and (c) 'false imprisonment' which involves the complete deprivation of liberty without proper cause for any period of time.

6.02 The tort of trespass to land involves any unjustifiable entry upon land in possession of another, however temporary or minor the intrusion. It is also a trespass to leave, place or throw anything onto another party's land, although if the material passes onto that party's land pursuant to the defendant exercising his own proprietary rights it is a nuisance. Unlike nuisance or negligence, trespass is actionable without proof of damage, although if consequential harm or losses are thereby caused damages, are recoverable. Ignorance of the law or the fact of trespass provides no defence for a trespasser.

6.03 As far as architects and building professionals are concerned, even the smallest infringements may be actionable. Thus, setting foot without permission on land adjoining the property where work is being conducted will constitute a trespass, as will allowing equipment or other material to rest against, hang over, fall upon or be thrown over adjoining land. However, it should be emphasised that trespass is only a civil wrong which involves no automatic criminal liability in the absence of aggravating circumstances (such as criminal damage).

7 Breach of statutory duty

7.01 Breach of a duty imposed by statute may lead to civil liability in tort. There is a vast array of statutory duties covering a wide variety of activities. In any particular case, however, in order to establish civil liability for breach of the statutory duty the claimant must prove: (a) that he is part of the class of persons intended to be protected by the statute, (b) that the loss or damage he has suffered is of a kind intended to be prevented under the statute, (c) that there is no express provision in the statute that civil liability is not created by a breach of its provisions, (d) that on the balance of probabilities his injury, loss or damage was caused by the breach of statutory duty, and (e) that there has been a breach of the relevant statutory duty by the defendant.

7.02 Some statutory duties are akin to the duty of care in the tort of negligence and are based upon what is considered to be reasonable behaviour in all the circumstances of the case. Others, notably in the field of health and safety in the workplace, impose strict liability for damage caused in certain circumstances. The Consumer Protection Act 1987, in response to an EEC directive, even extended statutory strict liability in certain circumstances into the field of defective domestic consumer products (the very area which gave birth to Lord Atkin's 'neighbour principle' in *Donoghue v Stevenson*).

7.03 As far as architects are concerned, the most important statutory duties are those imposed by the Defective Premises Act 1972 (which has been discussed above) and the Occupier's Liability Acts of 1957 and 1984. These impose duties on the occupiers of land (which an architect could be considered as if supervising a building project) in respect of consensual and non-consensual visitors to the land not unlike those owed at common law in the tort of negligence. There is probably no automatic civil liability, however, for breaches of the Building Act 1984 and its associated Building Regulations.

8 Inducing breach of contract/wrongful interference with contract

8.01 It is possible that in exercising a contract administration function (in certifying payments for example) an architect could be accused by a disappointed contractor (or conceivably an employer) of the tort of inducing a breach of contract or wrongful interference with contract.

8.02 In order to succeed in such an action a claimant would, however, have to establish more than just an error or a negligent error

in the certification process – it would need to be established that the architect had deliberately misapplied the relevant provisions of the building contract with the intention of depriving the contractor/ employer of a benefit to which they would otherwise have been entitled (see *Lubenham Fidelities & Investment Co Ltd v South Pembrokeshire District Council* [1986] 6 Con LR 85).

9 Limitation periods

9.01 To protect against the risk of stale claims being litigated as a matter of public policy, the law imposes time limits within which causes of action must be commenced if they are to remain actionable. The law aims to give claimants a reasonable opportunity to bring claims and defendants the assurance that the threat of liability will not be eternal and that any claim that they may have to face will not be so old as to prejudice the fairness of any proceedings. The two statutes that govern these time limits are the Limitation Act 1980 and the Latent Damage Act 1986.

9.02 Section 2 of the Limitation Act 1980 provides for tortious actions a prima facie limitation period of 6 years from the accrual of the cause of action. However, in personal injury cases the period is 3 years. Therefore when damage is an essential ingredient in liability (such as in negligence), time begins to run from the date that actionable damage occurs. If further damage occurs subsequently, then in respect of the additional damage time will run from this later date. If there is a trespass, libel or other act which in itself amounts to an actionable tort, time begins to run from the date of the act itself. In the cases of continuing torts (such as nuisance or trespass), therefore, the limitation period begins on each repetition of the wrong. In calculating whether the limitation period has expired, the date on which the cause of action accrues is normally excluded and the date on which the action is commenced is included.

9.03 However, these prima facie limitation periods may not be applicable in certain exceptional circumstances. In relation to personal injuries cases, section 33 of the Limitation Act 1980 provides the court with a general discretion to disapply the primary limitation period of 3 years if it considers it reasonable to do so. Further, section 32 provides that in a case where either: (a) there has been fraud by the defendant, or (b) any fact relevant to the claimant's cause of action has been deliberately concealed from him by the defendant, or (c) the action is for relief from the consequences of mistake, the limitation period shall not begin to run until the claimant has discovered this fraud, concealment or mistake, or until he could with reasonable diligence have done so. In building cases section 32 may become relevant where a party deliberately conceals negligent design or construction work by building over and hiding defects.

9.04 The common law rule that the cause of action in negligence accrues when damage is caused creates serious difficulties in construction cases. Often, damage which is caused in the process of building works is not discovered until some time after the building is completed. However, in *Pirelli General Cable Works v Oscar Faber* [1983] 2 AC 1 the House of Lords held that a cause of action for negligent advice by an engineer in connection with the design of a chimney accrued when damage, in the form of cracks in the chimney, first occurred. The fact that they may only become reasonably discoverable some time later was held not to be relevant. This approach left open the possibility of claimants becoming statute barred before they had a means of knowing that a cause of action actually existed.

9.05 The perceived injustice of this rule was addressed in the Latent Damage Act 1986. The Act modifies the limitation period for claims other than for personal injuries in the tort of negligence. The period should be either 6 years from the date that the cause of action accrued (on the basis of the *Pirelli* test for the time of damage) or, if this expires later, 3 years from the time the claimant knew certain material facts about the damage. This latter period is subject to a longstop provision expiring 15 years from the date of the negligent act or omission.

9.06 Regrettably, this has not entirely clarified matters. There remains the question of what constitutes damage in the first place. In *Pirelli* the House of Lords decided (save possibly in a case where a defect were so serious that the building was effectively predisposed to subsequent physical manifestation of damage) that there was actionable damage only when there were actual cracks in the chimney. The Court of Appeal has recently confirmed the correctness of this approach, at least in cases where there is some physical manifestation of the relevant damage, in *Abbott v Will Gannon & Smith Ltd* [2005] BLR 195. The difficulty with this proposition is reconciling it with the House of Lords' decision in *Murphy v Brentwood*. As we have seen, there it was held that damage of the kind which occurred in *Pirelli* was really economic loss, not physical damage, and therefore no longer recoverable. However, their Lordships also, rather confusingly, approved the previous decision in *Pirelli* which suggests that if there is liability in negligence for defectively constructed buildings (which could now probably only be pursuant to a *Hedley Byrne* relationship or one where damage is caused by a non-integral item in the building) the time for the accrual of the cause of action for limitation purposes starts at the time physical damage first occurs.

9.07 In practice, in defective building cases the courts have tended to apply this 'manifestation of physical damage' test for deciding when a cause of action in tort accrues. However, it is submitted that the post-*Murphy v Brentwood* characterisation of defective building work as economic loss (which logically may be present before there is any physical manifestation of it) is irreconcilable with the *Pirelli* test. Either such economic loss is suffered at the date on which the negligent service which caused it was relied upon (which would probably be an earlier date than the date of its physical manifestation) or it occurs at the date that the 'market' is able objectively to recognise and measure the financial scale of the loss suffered (which would suggest a later date for the accrual of the cause of action, namely the date of discoverability of the physical manifestation of defects by the market).

9.08 In *Invercargill City Council v Hamlin* [1996] AC 624 the Privy Council, in declining to follow the approach in *Pirelli,* held that the cause of action in negligence associated with the defective construction of foundations (similar to the facts of *Murphy v Brentwood*) accrued when the market value of the house fell as a result of the defects complained of, i.e. only once the market reflected the loss that had been suffered. In contrast, in an analogous case called *Bank of East Asia Ltd v Tsien Wui Marble Factory Ltd* the majority of the Hong Kong Court of Final Appeal endorsed the approach in *Pirelli*. In the result, this important area of the law is still in an unsatisfactorily unclear state.

10 Remedies

10.01 The principal remedies in tort are the provision of damages and the granting of an injunction. The general aim of an award of damages is to compensate the claimant for the damage and losses sustained as a result of the tort. In principle, damages are intended to put the claimant into the same position as he would have been in if the tort had not occurred. This restitutionary principle is inappropriate where personal injury has been caused, and so in these cases the courts apply a more general principle of what is fair and reasonable in all the circumstances. However, damages are recoverable only in respect of losses actually sustained and the claimant is under a duty to mitigate his losses by taking all reasonable steps to limit them.

10.02 In addition, a claimant may recover damages only in respect of losses that are reasonably foreseeable consequences of the defendant's tort (reasonable foreseeability has already been discussed in relation to the existence and breach of duty). Further, as

also referred to above, the law does not always recognise a duty of care to prevent certain kinds of loss (such as pure economic loss or nervous shock or embarrassment caused by an invasion of privacy). Thus, for all of these reasons it is not unusual for a claimant's actual losses suffered as a result of a tort to be greater than those that are compensated in law.

10.03 The remedy by way of injunction is aimed at preventing loss and damage, rather than compensating for it. It operates to prevent an anticipated tort or restrain the continuance of one (such as in the case of continuing torts like nuisance or trespass). An injunction will be available where the threatened tort is such that the claimant could not be compensated adequately in damages for its occurrence. Injunctions are of two varieties: first, 'prohibitive injunctions' which order a party not to do certain things that would otherwise constitute a legal wrong; second, 'mandatory injunctions' in which the court directs a defendant positively to do certain things to prevent a tort being committed or continued.

11 Apportionment of liability

11.01 More than one person can be responsible for the same damage. The claimant is under a duty in tort to take reasonable care of his own safety. If the claimant is the only cause of the damage, then he will not succeed in a tortious action against another person. If the claimant and one or more other persons are at fault, then damages are apportioned pursuant to the Law Reform (Contributory Negligence) Act 1945 according to the court's assessment of the relative degree of fault of the parties.

11.02 In assessing this relative responsibility the court considers both the causative potency of the parties' actions (i.e. how important was each party's role as a matter of fact to the ensuing damage) and their relative moral blameworthiness (for example, if one party to a road traffic accident is drunk at the time, he is likely to be apportioned more of the blame). Contributory negligence applies to liability in negligence, nuisance, the rule in *Rylands v Fletcher*, trespass, under the Occupier's Liability Acts and other breaches of statutory duty.

11.03 Further, section 1 of the Civil Liability (Contribution) Act 1978 provides:

> 'Subject to the following provisions of this section, any person liable in respect of any damage suffered by another person may recover contribution from any other person liable in respect of the same damage (whether jointly with him or otherwise).'

11.04 Thus, between themselves, defendants are also able to apportion blame and restrict their relative contribution to the claimant's damages. This may take the form of an apportionment of blame at the trial of the matter or the commencement of separate proceedings (called Part 20 proceedings) by a defendant against another party who is said to be jointly or wholly to blame. Of course if two or more persons are responsible for the claimant's damage, he may seek a remedy against either or both of them under the doctrine of joint and several liability.

12 Conclusion

12.01 The above has, no doubt, given some indication of the complex ever-changing nature of the law of tort and its relevance to the everyday activities of professional architects. Unfortunately, given the restrictions on space, this chapter is unavoidably limited in its scope and introductory by nature. The above is based upon the law as at June 2008.

4

English land law

MARTIN DIXON

1 Land law and conveyancing distinguished

1.01 This chapter is intended to give an impression of those aspects of land law that are relevant to architects, either in their professional capacity as designers of buildings for clients, as tenants of their offices or as prospective purchasers of land for redevelopment. At the outset, however, it is necessary to distinguish 'land law' as such from 'conveyancing'. Land law is concerned with the rights of a landowner in, or over, his own land and also with the rights that others may have over that land. The landowner's right of ownership of their land is often expressed by saying that they have an 'estate' in the land (i.e. a 'title' which may be either freehold or leasehold), while the rights of others in that land (or technically, in that 'estate') are often described by saying that they have 'proprietary interests' (or just 'interests') in it. By way of contrast, the law of conveyancing is concerned with the mechanics of the creation and transfer of estates and interests in and over land, usually, but not necessarily, pursuant to a contract between a seller and purchaser. Typically, an owner of an estate in land (being either 'the owner' under a freehold or lease) will transfer that estate to a purchaser, with the sale/purchase being subject to existing interests in the land and, possibly, creating new ones. An architect need not concern himself with the procedures and mechanics of conveyancing, for in the normal course of events such matters will be entrusted to a property professional such as a solicitor or licensed conveyancer. Indeed, because of the new regime of electronic conveyancing that began to be introduced in to England and Wales on 13 October 2003, wherein much of the conveyancing process will be conducted electronically without paper, it would be imprudent to attempt a conveyancing transaction without professional advice. Nevertheless, a certain amount must be said about title to land in England and Wales (being estates) and the methods that exist to protect other persons' property interests in that land.

1.02 Many of the concepts that underlie English land law are ancient and this is reflected in the curious terminology that is associated with the subject. However, the law was greatly simplified and restructured in 1925 by a series of important statutes. These, and later statutes building on them, form the foundation of modern land law and, generally, were designed to facilitate the easy transfer of land so that it could be used to its full economic potential. As part of this continuing development, a major reforming statute came into force on 13 October 2003. The Land Registration Act 2002 has replaced in full the Land Registration Act 1925. Although primarily designed to simply the conveyancing process, the Land Registration Act 2002 in due course will introduce electronic, paper free, conveyancing to England and Wales and should, in time, speed up the conveyancing process and reduce costs.

Necessarily, this reform of the conveyancing process has required some changes to the substantive principles of land law.

Title to land

1.03 Title to land in England and Wales is either 'unregistered' or 'registered', although the latter is now far more common and is the norm. With effect from 1 December 1990, all land (or more accurately, title to land) in England and Wales must be 'registered' consequent on a dealing with it, such as a transfer of ownership or a mortgage or the granting of certain leases. After this 'first registration', the title remains registered in all circumstances and for all future transactions. Thus, 'unregistered title' will disappear over time. The Land Registry estimates that virtually all transferable titles will be registered by 2012, but already all major urban areas consist substantially of 'registered title' and the Land Registration Act 2002 has greatly speeded up the process of first registration. In particular, owners of substantial parcels of land – such as local authorities – are being encouraged voluntarily to first register their land (that is, without there being any dealing with it) and many are taking advantage of lower fees and free assistance from the Land Registry. For the architect, as with others interested in the precise details of land ownership and the existence of obligations affecting land, the achievement of widespread registration of title greatly assists the development process.

1.04 For the moment, however, some land of unregistered title still exists. In unregistered conveyancing – being land where the title is *not* recorded on a register maintained by Her Majesty's Land Registry – the landowner will be either a freeholder or a leaseholder: i.e. have the equivalent of absolute ownership (freehold), or have such ownership for a precise amount of time under a lease from the freeholder (e.g. a 125-year residential lease of an apartment flat). On the sale of the freehold, or upon an assignment (sale or transfer) of a lease, the seller's proof of title is found in the title deeds to the property (which may be held by a lender if there is a mortgage) and the purchaser's solicitor will investigate these title deeds to satisfy himself on behalf of his client that the seller does indeed have title to the land. The purchaser's solicitor will investigate and verify all dealings with the land revealed by these deeds going back to the first valid conveyance of it more than 15 years old. That conveyance is known as 'the root of title' and is the proof of title required by the purchaser (Law of Property Act 1969, section 23). In addition, a physical inspection of the land is always desirable in order to discover any other person's interests in the land that might not be revealed by the title deeds: e.g. ancient rights of way, shared sewers, rights of light, etc. So, with unregistered land, the title of the vendor will be investigated (by documentary and physical inspection), a root of title produced

and, following a successful completion of the sale, the purchaser's solicitor will apply for 'first registration' of title. Thereafter, the land becomes and remains registered land.

1.05 Other persons' rights in unregistered land (i.e. interests) are either 'legal' or 'equitable' in character. This distinction was once of great significance and although it is now unnecessary to explain in detail why some rights are 'legal' and some 'equitable', its origins lay in the type of interest at issue and the manner in which the interest was first created. Fortunately, usually it will be readily apparent whether any given interest in the land is 'legal' or 'equitable'. The relevance of the distinction today lies in the effect that legal or equitable interests in unregistered land have when the title (the freehold or leasehold estate) to that land is transferred to another person, such as on sale. So, legal rights are 'binding on all the world', regardless of whether a purchaser of land (freehold or leasehold) knows of them or not. This means simply that a purchaser of the land (or any new owner) is bound to give effect to the interest. Most easements (such as a right of way or right to light) and most mortgages are legal rights and a purchaser of unregistered land cannot escape them by saying that he did not know of their existence, even if they were not discovered from the title deeds or inspection of the land. By contrast, equitable rights are binding on a purchaser only in certain circumstances, although they will always be binding on a person who received land by way of gift or under a will. The circumstances in which equitable interests over unregistered land will bind a purchaser are either:

1   Where the equitable interest over the land about to be purchased qualifies as a 'land charge' under the Land Charges Act 1972 *and* the interest is registered as a land charge in the appropriate manner. This system of registration is *entirely separate* from that pertaining to registered land. It means that if the equitable interest is a land charge (and this is defined in the Land Charges Act 1972) and is *not* registered, it cannot affect a purchaser of the land even if he knew about it, provided no fraud is involved.
2   Where the equitable interest over the land about to be purchased does not qualify as a land charge, the purchaser is bound only if he had 'notice' of the equitable interest. Such

notice may be 'actual' (as where the purchaser is told or sees that an equitable interest exists), 'constructive' (as where a reasonable purchaser would have realised from the available facts that such an interest existed: e.g. a path is visible) or 'imputed' (as where the purchaser's agent (i.e. solicitor) has actual or constructive notice). In the absence of such notice, the purchaser cannot be affected by the equitable interest and may use the land without regard to it. Note, however, that the number of equitable interests that depend on the 'doctrine of notice' for their validity against a purchaser is quite limited. Most equitable interests are land charges.

Land charges under the Land Charges Act 1972

1.06 As noted above, most equitable interests in unregistered land are registrable as land charges under the Land Charges Act 1972. This has nothing to do with registered land, although the registers are maintained by Her Majesty's Land Registry. Some of the most important of these registrable equitable interests from an architect's point of view are:

1   Estate contracts: i.e. contracts for the sale of land or of any interest in land, including contracts to grant leases, options to purchase land (i.e. a standing offer by a landowner to sell), and rights of pre-emption (i.e. rights of first refusal should a landowner decide to sell).
2   Restrictive covenants (being promises not to use the land for certain purposes, such as building, or trade or business and see paragraph 4.01 below), *except* those found in a lease (for which special rules exist) and those entered into before 1926 (to which the law of 'notice' applies).
3   Certain types of easement (such as rights of way or light), being those *not* originally created by a deed (a formal document) or those that endure only for the life of a given person. Note, however, that most easements are created by deed and are therefore 'legal' and are effective without registration.

Registration of these land charges ensures that the interest will be enforceable against all persons who come into possession or ownership of the unregistered land, regardless of any question of notice. If the interest is registrable but not actually registered, it will be void (i.e. unenforceable) against a purchaser of the land regardless of whether he knows of it. This will be so even if the sum paid by the purchaser is only a fraction of the true value of the property (*Midland Bank Trust Co. Ltd v Green* [1981] AC 513). Land charge registration suffers from a serious defect in that registration of the charge is not made against the land itself, but against the name of the landowner who created the charge, even if that was many years ago. Consequently, in order to search the Land Charges Register (to find any binding interests prior to a purchase), it is necessary to discover the names of all the persons who have owned the land. This is done by looking at the title deeds. However, it is only obligatory for the seller to provide the title deeds back to a good root of title: which may be only 15 years old. It is often impossible, therefore, to discover the names of all relevant landowners (i.e. going back to 1925 when land charge registration was introduced). Nevertheless, because registration of the land charge ensures that it is binding, a purchaser will still be bound by it, even though he could not have discovered it because he did not know the name against which to search! Under the Law of Property Act 1969, compensation is payable for any loss suffered in these cases. It is worth remembering that any person may search the Land Charges Register, and that an Official Certificate of Search is conclusive in favour of a purchaser, actual or intending and this will be useful in respect of potential development projects. There is, in addition, one clear advantage: a Certificate of Search is to be regarded as conclusive, thus if a Certificate of Search does not reveal a registered land charge, the purchaser will take free of it, provided that he searched against the correct name, even if the charge was actually registered. Note also, as mentioned above, that even an unregistered land charge (i.e. one that should have been registered but is not) is enforceable against someone who is not a purchaser. Thus, a person receiving the land by gift, or under a will, or even a squatter, is bound by all land charges – registered or not.

Registered land

1.07 Registered land is quite different from land of unregistered title and most titles are now of this type. In a relatively short time, registered land will be the only type of land that is commonly transferred by sale or gift or on death. It has many advantages over unregistered land in terms of certainty about estates and interests in the land and in respect of ease of transactions. The system is now governed by the Land Registration Act 2002.

1 The actual title (the estate) to the land is itself registered, eliminating the need for title deeds. Details of most (but not all) interests affecting the land will also appear on the Register, and such 'encumbrances' are registered against the title itself (identified by a unique title number) and not against the name of the landowner at the time the encumbrance was created. Transfer of the land is effected by registering the purchaser as the new 'registered proprietor'. Freeholds and very many (but not yet all) leaseholds may be registered as titles. As long as the land is registered, and the postcode or address is known, it is now possible for any person to do an on-line search of the land register for a nominal sum (www.landregisteronline.gov.uk) which will reveal the name of the owners, the existence of any mortgage and some (but not all) other interests affecting the land and often the price paid by the current owners.

2 The Register of Title is conclusive as to the nature of the title to the land and the doctrine of notice and the idea of land charges have no application. If for any reason the Register is not a true reflection of the title, it may, in certain limited circumstances, be 'altered' on application to the Registrar or the court, but the circumstances in which this is permitted are narrowly drawn. Any person suffering loss as a result of a qualifying alteration (called a 'rectification') may be entitled to compensation out of public funds. Note also, that because it is the Register of Title itself that is conclusive, if an erroneous Search Certificate is issued that fails to disclose an entry on the Register, a purchaser will still be bound by the interest protected by the entry, but will be entitled to compensation. Such errors are very rare.

3 An intending purchaser of registered land (including a person proposing to take a significant interest in the land, such as a bank lending on mortgage or a person paying for an option to purchase) will take the following steps:

(a) *Inspect the Register*. The Land Register is a public document and may be inspected by any person on payment of the appropriate fee. This may be done informally on line as noted above, but an Official Search should be obtained before any offer to purchase or lend is made or any contract signed. Usually, the property professional employed by the purchaser/transferee will obtain the Official Search. Of course, architects may identify owners of land for themselves even if the land is not yet up for sale (e.g. as having development potential) by means of the on-line search process.

(b) *Inspect the land itself*, because the Register is not conclusive on all matters. Certain rights – called 'interests that override' – may not appear on the Register but they are automatically binding on any transferee of the land (including a purchaser) by force of statute, irrespective of whether the purchaser knew about them. These include certain types of legal easements, legal leases of 7 years or less, local land charges (see paragraph 1.08 below) and the rights of persons (including squatters) in actual occupation of the land (provided the actual occupation is discoverable on a reasonable inspection of the land or the interest of the occupier is known of by the transferee). This last category can be a trap for the unwary, but much less so than was previously the case now that the Land Registration Act 2002 is in force. It means that a person may gain protection (i.e. may enforce their interest against a transferee) for most property rights (e.g. leases, shares of ownership) by virtue of being in 'discoverable actual occupation' of the land over which the right exists: *Williams & Glyn's Bank Ltd v Boland* [1981] AC 487. Consequently, a proper inspection of the land is vital and questions should be asked of any person who is, or appears to be, in occupation of the land. If necessary, the written consent of such persons to the proposed transaction should be obtained and this should be a matter of priority for the property professional engaged to manage the transaction.

Local land charges

1.08 Irrespective of whether the land is registered or unregistered, there are certain rights that are registrable quite separately in a register kept by all local authorities (e.g. District Councils and Unitary Authorities). These are 'local land charges' and they are regulated by the Local Land Charges Act 1975, which came into force in 1977. These charges are registered by reference to the land which they affect and not against the name of the landowner and should not be confused with land charges under the Land Charges Act 1972. Registration of a local land charge constitutes actual notice of it to all persons for all purposes. A local land charge is, however, enforceable even if not registered, but a purchaser of land burdened by an unregistered local land charge will be entitled to compensation from the local authority. Local land charges are numerous and of considerable practical importance. A search of the local land charges register held by the relevant local authority is vital before proceeding to deal with the land, either by way of purchase or development. They include:

1 Preservation instructions as to ancient monuments.
2 Lists of buildings of special architectural or historic interest.
3 Planning restrictions.
4 Drainage schemes.
5 Charges under the Public Health and Highway Acts.

1.09 As a matter of general good practice, an architect will be well advised to find out from the client what adverse rights (if any) affect the client's property before undertaking any scheme of work. It is particularly important that he discovers the existence of any easements, restrictive covenants or local land charges because these may constrict the architect in his plans. For example, the existence of a neighbour's right to light or right of way, or ability to enforce a building restriction (a restrictive covenant) can affect radically any plans for development, as might any local land charges registered against the land. If necessary, the client may have to engage the services of a property professional to make the relevant enquiries.

2 The extent and meaning of 'land' and intrusions upon it

2.01 'Land' in English law includes not only the soil but also:

1 Any buildings, parts of buildings, or similar structures.
2 Anything permanently attached to the soil (so-called 'fixtures' (see paragraph 5.03), which may include garden plants, green-houses, even garden statues).
3 Rights under the land. It has never been settled how far down the rights of a landowner extend, though it is commonly said that they extend to the centre of the earth. Certainly they go down as far as the limits of economic exploitation. A landowner is therefore entitled to the minerals under his land, although all gold, silver, coal and petroleum are vested in the Crown.
4 Rights above the land to such height as is necessary for the ordinary use and enjoyment of land and the structures upon it (*Baron Bernstein v Skyviews & General Ltd* [1978] QB 479 at 488). Thus, the flight of building cranes over a neighbouring property may be a trespass and this should be remembered when considering developments requiring such machinery.
5 Intangible rights such as easements (e.g. such as rights of way or rights to light), profits (such as a right to take fish or fruit from another's land) and restrictive covenants (rights to prevent activities on another's land).

Trespass

2.02 Any unjustifiable intrusion (i.e. without permission or without right) by one person upon 'land' in the possession of another is a trespass – a 'tort'. It is likewise a trespass to place anything on or in the land in the possession of another (e.g. by driving a nail into his wall, or propping a ladder against his house). It is a popular mis-conception that to be actionable as a tort, the trespass must involve damage to the claimant's property. Even if no damage is done, the court may restrain the trespass by injunction, binding immediately. See, for example, *Anchor Brewhouse Developments Ltd v Berkley House (Dockland Developments) Ltd* [1987] 2 EGLR 173, where the trespass arose out of building works on land adjacent to that of the claimant. Consequently, if construction work is likely to neces-sitate an incursion on to neighbouring land in some way – e.g. to erect scaffolding, inspect drains, or because a crane jib will swing over that land – then the client must come to an arrangement with the landowner, unless the client can prove some right to enter on the land (such as under the Access to Neighbouring Land Act 1992). Such permission will usually take the form of a 'contractual licence', being a temporary permission, often granted in return for a payment or other consideration (paragraph 2.04). But if a perma-nent incursion is contemplated – e.g. by the overhanging eaves of a building, the footings of a garage or the line of a boundary wall – it may be better to negotiate an easement (see paragraph 3.01).

2.03 In the absence of any easements, restrictive covenants or other binding agreements (e.g. a contract between landowner and neigh-bour), a person is generally free as a matter of private law to build anywhere on his own land. Necessarily, of course, there may be planning issues and other related matters that restrict this in practice. Note, however, that in some circumstances, the process of develop-ment may give rise to a claim by a neighbour in 'nuisance', such as where there is an unjustifiable interference with a neighbouring landowner's use and enjoyment of his own land through excessive noise or dust (see *Hunter v Canary Wharf Ltd* [1997] AC 655).

Licences

2.04 As noted above, a neighbour may give another person per-mission to use his land by means of a 'contractual licence' and it is convenient at this point to discuss licences generally. A licence is permission to do something that would otherwise be a trespass. For example, in the absence of an easement of way, a contractual licence permitting the passage and re-passage of construction traffic over neighbouring land might be required for some developments. There are several types of licence, of which only two need be con-sidered here. First, there is a 'bare licence', i.e. permission to enter land, given quite gratuitously without any counter-benefit for the landowner giving the permission. It is revocable at any time by the licensor/landowner and, on such revocation, the licensee becomes a trespasser, although he is entitled to a reasonable time to enable him to leave the land once notice of termination has expired. The second type of licence is the contractual licence mentioned above. This is a licence that is granted for some counter-benefit, usually a fee. Whether a contractual licence can be revoked depends upon the interpretation and meaning of the contract under which it was given. If a licence is either expressly or by necessary implication irrevoca-ble during its agreed duration (e.g. the erection of scaffolding on a neighbour's land for 6 months), the licensor will be unable to prevent the licensee from going on to the land for the purpose of the licence. Any attempted revocation of the licence can be prevented by the grant of an injunction or in appropriate circumstances, by a decree of spe-cific performance, that is an order forcing the licensor to permit the licensee to enter (*Verrall v Great Yarmouth Borough Council* [1981] QB 202). If a licence is silent as to the duration or terms on which it can be revoked, a court may supply such terms as is reasonable having regard to the circumstances in which the licence was granted (*Parker, the 9th Earl of Macclesfield v Hon Jocelyn Parker,* 2003).

Easements

2.05 If a landowner has an easement over adjacent land – such as a right of way – any interference with it by the owner of the burdened land (the 'servient' land) will not constitute a trespass but will be a 'nuisance'. However, not every interference with an easement will amount to a nuisance. If the easement is a positive one, being one which allows the person entitled to the benefit of it to do something on the burdened land (e.g. a right of way by foot or vehicle), the interference will constitute a nuisance only if it prevents the practi-cal and substantial enjoyment of the easement. If the easement is negative, being one which allows the person entitled to the benefit of it to prevent the use of the burdened land in a certain way (e.g. a right of light, being the prevention of building), the interference will be actionable only if it substantially interferes with the enjoyment of the right. (On positive and negative easements, see paragraph 3.03.)

Boundaries

2.06 A boundary has been defined as an imaginary line that marks the confines or line of division of two contiguous parcels of land (*Halsbury's Laws of England* (4th edn), vol. 4, paragraph 831). Boundaries are fixed in one of three ways: (a) by proven acts of the respective owners; (b) by statute or by orders of authorities hav-ing jurisdiction; or (c) in the absence of either of these, by legal presumption. Note, however, that as Lord Hoffmann said in *Alan Wibberley Building Ltd v Insley* (April 1999), '[b]oundary disputes are a particularly painful form of litigation. Feelings run high and disproportionate amounts of money are spent'. While it is true, there-fore, that the law on boundaries *should* be as clear as possible, the best approach is to agree matters such as the precise line of a bound-ary before development takes place and thus avoid resort to law.

1 Proved acts of the parties

(a) The parties may *expressly agree* on the boundaries. This is by far the best approach, particularly where new development is concerned. It is best to have the agreement formally drawn up by a solicitor or licensed conveyancer.
(b) The boundaries may be *defined by the title deeds*. These may in turn refer to a plan or to an Ordnance Survey map. As far as plans are concerned, the boundary lines are usually 'for the pur-poses of identification only' and, unless the context makes clear (as was the case in *Fisher v Winch* [1939] 1 KB 666), they do not purport to fix the exact boundary. Where the 'plan line' is for

purposes of identification only, topographical features and other evidence may be used to find the exact line. Likewise, Ordnance Survey maps do not purport to fix private boundaries and it is the practice of the Survey to draw the boundary line down the middle of a boundary feature (e.g. down the middle of a ditch) regardless of where the boundary line actually runs in law. If the title deeds do refer to an Ordnance Survey map, then that map will be conclusive in so far as it defines the *general* boundary. Again, however, unless the context makes clear, this may simply indicate the general line, not its precise course. In the case of registered land, the plans used by the Land Registry are based on the Ordnance Survey maps, but once again the boundaries on them are regarded as general and are not intended to be fixed precisely by the plan. A little-used procedure – unlikely to gain popularity even under the new law – exists by which the boundary of registered land may be defined exactly, and where this has been done the plan on the Register is definitive and is noted as such.

(c) A boundary of unregistered land may be *proved* by showing *12 or more years' undisturbed possession*. This may extend to possession of a boundary wall (*Prudential Assurance v Waterloo Real Estate* (1999)).

(d) A boundary of registered land may be *proved* by showing at least *10 years' undisturbed possession*, but such boundary is only conclusive when an application is made to the Land Registry and the register of title is amended accordingly. This may extend to possession of a boundary wall (*Prudential Assurance v Waterloo Real Estate* (1999)).

2 Orders of competent authorities

Establishment of boundaries by orders of authorities is now largely historical. Under the Enclosure Acts, the Tithe Acts, and certain Agricultural Acts, awards defining boundaries precisely could be made. These may still be relevant in some rural areas. Similarly, a boundary may be fixed by judicial decision, e.g. in an action for trespass or for the recovery of land.

3 Legal presumption

In the absence of clear definition by the above methods, certain rebuttable presumptions apply, being 'default' rules that will operate unless contrary evidence is available.

(a) *Hedges and ditches*. It is presumed that a person excavating a ditch will not dig into his neighbour's land, but that he will dig at the very edge of his own property, making a bank on his side of the ditch with the soil that he removes. On top of that bank a hedge is usually planted. He is, therefore, owner of both the hedge and the ditch. This presumption applies only where the ditch is known to be artificial, but it is readily applicable in cases of doubt, including cases where reference is made to a plan or Ordnance Survey map defining general boundaries (*Alan Wibberley Building Ltd v Insley* [1999]).

(b) *Fences*. It is said that there is a presumption that a wooden fence belongs to the owner of the land on whose side the posts are placed, on the basis that a landowner will use his land to the fullest extent (and display the better side of the fence to his neighbour!). Likewise, it is often said that nails are 'driven home'. These presumptions are, however, unsupported by authority and must be regarded as uncertain. Most modern plans mark the fence owned by the property in question by the indication of a 'T' on the plan.

(c) *Highways*. The boundary between lands separated by a highway or a private right of way is presumed to be the middle line of the highway or private right of way. There is no such presumption with railways. The bed of a railway will be the property of Network Rail, or its successors.

(d) *The seashore*. The boundary line between the seashore and the adjoining land is (unless usage to the contrary is proved) the line of the median high tide between the ordinary spring and neap tide (*Attorney General v Chambers* [1854] 4 De GM & G 206 at 218). Prima facie, the seashore belongs to the Crown.

(e) *Rivers and streams*. If a river or stream is tidal, the soil of the bed of the river or stream belongs to the Crown, or the Duchies of Cornwall or Lancaster, where appropriate. As a general rule, the boundary between the bed of a tidal stream and adjoining land is the line of medium high water mark. If the river or stream is non-tidal, it is assumed that adjoining owners own land to the middle of the flowing water, known as the 'thalweg' (although this may not be the middle of the river itself).

(f) *Walls*. If the division between two properties is a wall and the exact line of the boundary is not known, in determining the ownership of the wall, certain presumptions apply. Party walls outside London and Bristol (for the situation in London and Bristol, see Chapter 14) are subject to rights at common law. The usual, but by no means necessary, presumption is that the party wall is divided longitudinally into two strips, one belonging to each of the neighbouring owners, but where each half is subject to a right (an easement) of support in favour of the other. If one owner removes his building, he is obliged to waterproof the exposed party wall. (See Chapter 14 for the complicated procedures necessary when changes to party walls are contemplated in London.) Extensions to existing buildings can bear only on the half of the wall belonging to the owner of the building being extended, unless the consent of the adjoining owner is obtained. Note also that a former party wall can come under the exclusive ownership of one of the neighbours consequent upon the relevant period of undisturbed adverse possession, plus registration in the case of registered title.

3 Easements

3.01 Easements are rights that one owner of land may acquire over the land of another. They should be distinguished from other similar rights such as (i) profits, i.e. rights to take something from another's land, e.g. to cut grass or peat, or to shoot or fish; (ii) natural rights, e.g. rights of support of land (but not of buildings, which is a true easement); (iii) public rights, e.g. rights of way over a highway or rights of common; (iv) restrictive covenants (paragraph 4.01); and licences (paragraph 2.04).

3.02 The essentials of an easement are:

1 There must be a dominant and a servient tenement, where a 'tenement' is a plot of land held by a freeholder or leaseholder. The dominant tenement is the land benefited by the easement, the servient land is the land burdened. Note, therefore, it is impossible for someone occupying land as only a mere licensee to be party to the creation of an easement. Consequently, a developer seeking an easement over neighbouring land should ensure that they are dealing with the freehold owner. If the occupier is a tenant, any easement they grant is likely to last only for so long as their own tenancy and is unlikely to be permanent.

2 The easement must 'benefit' the dominant tenement to which it will become attached. So, although the two plots need not be contiguous or adjacent, they must be sufficiently close for the dominant tenement to be benefited by the easement. A landowner at one end of the village is unlikely to enjoy an easement of way over land at the other.

3 The two tenements must not be owned *and* occupied by the same person. Hence, a tenant can have an easement over land occupied by his landlord, because although both tenements are owned by the same person, they are not also occupied by him.

4 The easement claimed must be 'capable of forming the subject matter of a grant', i.e. of being created by deed. This means that the right alleged to be an easement must be sufficiently well defined, certain and limited in scope to qualify as an easement. So, although there are well-established categories of easements – rights of way, rights to light, rights of support – the list is not closed. New rights can become recognised as being capable of being 'granted', hence of being easements. Modern examples include the right to use a letterbox, the right to park a car on adjoining land and cross it with shopping trolleys, the right to locate a television aerial (and hence a satellite dish) on a neighbour's land, the right to display signs, the right to moor boats and the right to use paths in a park for pleasure and not simply for getting from one place to another. Against this,

certain rights cannot exist as easements: e.g. a right to a view; to privacy; to a general flow of air (as distinct to a flow through an air duct); to have a property protected from the weather and a general right to light (as opposed to as right through a defined aperture).

3.03 It is often said that easements may be either positive or negative, although there is no consequence in the distinction. A positive easement is one which enables the dominant owner to do some act upon the servient tenement, e.g. walk or drive along a right of way. A negative easement allows the dominant owner to prevent the servient owner from doing something on his land, e.g. a right to light, which restricts the servient owner's ability to build. Some easements do not readily fall into either category, e.g. a right of support for a building.

3.04 Easements may be acquired in a number of ways:

1   By *express grant or reservation*. A landowner may by deed (or written contract if the easement is to be equitable) expressly grant an easement over his land in favour of a neighbouring landowner. Equally, if a landowner is selling off part of his land, he may expressly grant an easement in the purchaser's favour (burdening the land he retains), or expressly reserve to himself an easement (burdening the land sold), in the documents that carry out the sale. Both express grant and reservation are common when a plot is divided into sub-plots and sold to different purchasers, as with a green-field housing development. The Land Registry is willing to offer advice to persons developing large estates as to the most effective way of expressly creating easements over the sub-plots as they are sold or leased.

2   By *implied reservation*. This occurs when the parties to a transaction concerning land (e.g. a sale or lease) have not expressly mentioned easements in the documents carrying out the transaction. So, if a landowner sells off part of his land and retains the rest, he may fail to reserve expressly any easements burdening the part sold (for the benefit of the part he retains). However, in two situations, easements may be implied in his favour – meaning that they will be treated as if they were deliberately *reserved* for the benefit of the land retained. These are easements of necessity and easements necessary to give effect to the common intentions of the parties. An easement of necessity in this context means an easement without which the vendor's retained land cannot be used at all. For example, if he retains land to which there is no access, an easement of necessity will be impliedly reserved over the land that he has sold for the benefit of the land he retains. An easement in the common intention of the parties means an easement which both parties accepted should exist as being required to put into effect a shared intention for the use of the land retained at the time of sale. Such an implied reservation can be difficult to prove, but a rare example is *Peckham* v *Ellison* (1999) concerning access via a rear pathway.

3   By implied grant. In similar fashion to the above, if a purchaser buys land from a seller (the seller again retaining certain land), and no easements are expressly *granted* to the purchaser for the benefit of the land sold, easements may be implied in favour of the land sold, burdening the land retained. This can occur in the following circumstances.
    (a) Easements of necessity, which in this context mean easements without which the purchaser cannot enjoy the land at all. An easement of necessity does not exist merely because it would be useful or convenient. The parties should, ideally, expressly create easements and implied easements of necessity are not a safety net for a failure to specify required easements.
    (b) Easements necessary to give effect to the common intentions of the parties: for example, where the shared intention of seller and purchaser is that a dwelling shall be built on the land sold, but no easements permitting access by construction traffic are expressly granted (*Stafford v Lee*). Again, however, it is always better to consider what easements are required and to have them expressly created.

    (c) Easements within the rule in *Wheeldon v Burrows* [1879] 12 ChD 31. This is best explained by an example. A landowner owns two adjacent plots, X and Y. He does certain things on plot Y for the benefit of X which would amount to an easement if X and Y were separately owned: e.g. he walks over plot Y, to get to plot X. This is called a 'quasi-easement'. When he sells off plot X, retaining plot Y, the purchaser of plot X will acquire an easement to do those acts over plot Y (walk across it) which the common owner had hitherto done, providing the quasi-easement was 'continuous and apparent', i.e. discernible on a careful inspection of the land; necessary for the reasonable enjoyment of plot X; and had been and was at the time of the grant used by the grantor for the benefit of plot X. Consequently, the seller finds his retained land burdened by an easement for the benefit of the land sold. Therefore, when selling land (but retaining part), a person should ensure that this rule is excluded.
    (d) Under the statutory 'general words' of section 62 of the Law of Property Act 1925. By virtue of this statutory provision, there will pass on every conveyance of land (meaning a transfer by deed or registered disposition only), unless a contrary intention is shown, all 'liberties, privileges, easements, rights and advantages whatsoever appertaining to or reputed to appertain to the land'. The somewhat unexpected and dramatic effect of this section is that it will convert merely permissive uses (i.e. licences) into full easements if a person sells land which, prior to the sale, was occupied by a person to whom he (the seller) gave some personal right over land he himself retained. Again, an example will make matters clearer. So, X, a freeholder, permits Y, a tenant of another part of X's land, to drive over that part of X's land that X himself occupies. X then sells and conveys to Y (or any other person) the land of which Y has hitherto been a leaseholder. On conveyance, Y acquires a full easement to drive over X's land (*International Tea Stores Co. v Hobbs* [1903] 2 Ch 165). Although section 62 has this effect only if the subsequent sale is by deed (or registered disposition) and, possibly, only if different people were occupying the two plots of land involved (but see a contrary view in *Platt v Crouch*, 2003), it is important to appreciate the unexpected effect that the section may have. It is imperative, therefore, for a seller of land to exclude the effect of section 62 LPA 1925 in any conveyance to which he is party – just in case. The same is true of the rule in *Wheeldon v Burrows*, above.

4   By prescription. Long use by a claimant of a 'right' over the defendant's land (*'nec vi, nec clam, nec precario'* – without force, secrecy, or permission) can give rise to an easement. An easement by prescription can only be claimed by one freehold owner against another and, with certain exceptions, 'user' must be shown to have been continuous over the relevant period. The rules concerning prescription are complicated (and unsatisfactory), but essentially there are three methods of acquiring easements by prescription: (a) at common law; (b) under the doctrine of 'lost modern grant'; and (c) under the Prescription Act 1832.
    (a) At common law an easement can be acquired by prescription only if it can be proved to have been used from time immemorial (which the law sets at 1189!). In fact, use for 20 years before the claim is made would normally be accepted. However, a claim can always be defeated by showing that the alleged right could not have existed since 1189. For example, there can be no prescriptive right to light under this head for a building that was constructed 'only' in 1585. Hence, 'pure' common law claims are rare.
    (b) The doctrine of lost modern grant was invented because of the ease with which it was possible to defeat a claim to prescription at common law. Where the origin of an alleged easement cannot otherwise be accounted for, then provided that there has been upwards of 20 years' use of the right, the court will presume that the right was lawfully granted and that the document making the grant has been lost. Of course, this is a complete fiction, but the presumption can be rebutted only by evidence that the existence of such a grant was impossible. The evidence necessary to persuade

a court to infer a 'lost' modern grant must be stronger than that required to prove common law prescription and it can be invoked only if common law prescription is for some reason excluded.

(c) The Prescription Act 1832 laid down time periods for prescription in general and for rights of light in particular (the latter are discussed in paragraph 3.08). The Act provides that uninterrupted use for 20 years before some action by the dominant owner for confirmation of an easement or by the servient owner for a declaration that a right does not exist, means that the claim cannot be defeated merely by showing that the claimed easement cannot have existed since 1189. The Act further provides that user without interruption for 40 years prior to a court action gives an absolute and unchallengeable easement. In both cases, user must be of right, i.e. *nec vi, nec clam, nec precario.* 'Interruption' is important because if a person wishes to establish an easement by prescription, he must not acquiesce in the interruption of his right for one year by the owner of the property over which he wishes to establish the easement. Any period during which the owner of the land over which the easement is claimed could not give consent to establishing an easement (e.g. because he was an infant or a lunatic) must be added to the 20-year period. This is part of the fiction that such rights are 'granted' by somebody, so cannot exist if there was nobody to grant them!

Extinguishment of easements

3.05 Apart from an express release by deed (i.e. deliberate agreement between the owners of the dominant and servient land), the most important method of extinguishing an easement is when the dominant and servient tenements come into the same ownership *and* possession. For example, acquisition and occupation by an owner of his neighbour's land, or consolidation of several plots into a development block, will extinguish all easements previously existing between them. Consequently, any subsequent development of the land that involves re-splitting the land into plots (either the same original plots or differently) may require new easements to be created expressly: e.g. as to water pipes, data cables, air ducts, rights of way and support etc.

Types of easement

3.06 As noted above, the 'list' of easements is not closed, and new types of easement will be required as the uses of land change and as construction methods develop. The following are examples of common types of easement:

1 *Rights of way.* A right of way, whether acquired expressly, impliedly, or by prescription, may be limited as to both frequency and type of use, e.g. a right obtained for passage by horse and cart in the nineteenth century will not extend to passage for many caravans if the dominant tenement has become a caravan park. It is a matter of construction of the easement (i.e. an interpretation of what it means) whether the easement gives a right to pass on foot or with vehicles or whether it includes the right to stop and park. A 'general' easement will usually encompass these rights on the basis that the grantor of the easement (he who first created it) cannot 'derogate from his grant' by claiming at a later date that some lesser use was intended. If some limitation to a general easement of way was intended, it should have been made clear at the time the easement was created.

2 *Rights of support.* Although the natural right of support for land by other land has been distinguished from an easement (paragraph 3.01), it is possible for one building to acquire an easement of support against another after a period of 20 years' prescriptive use (i.e. in the absence of any express grant of right). The only way of preventing this would be for the owner of the alleged supporting building to seek a declaration during the 20 years that the supported building has no right to support. It should be noted that where two detached buildings adjoin on separate plots, an easement cannot be acquired requiring

a person who removes his abutting wall to weatherproof the exposed flank wall of the remaining building (unless the wall is a party wall: paragraph 2.05).

3 *Rights of light.*

(a) To a considerable extent, the law relating to rights of light has been rendered of secondary importance by daylighting regulations under planning legislation and related planning controls (Chapter 11), but a knowledge of the law of easements is still required. There is no such thing as easement of light generally, but only in respect of some definite opening, such as a window or skylight. The owner of the dominant tenement has a right only to such amount of light as is necessary for 'ordinary purposes'. Many years' enjoyment of an exceptionally large amount of light does not prevent an adjoining owner from building so as to reduce light: for example, see *Ambler v Gordon* [1905] 1 KB 417 where an architect claimed that he had already enjoyed and needed more light for his studio than for ordinary office purposes but the court dismissed the claim. The decision about whether enough light is left for ordinary purposes after building work depends on observation and light measurement. The so-called '45° rule' from the centre of a window can do no more than help the judge make up his mind, although a reduction of more than 50% of previous light suggests that too much light has been denied. It should also be noted that if light could be obtained from an existing but blocked skylight, then this must be counted as an available alternative source in determining whether there is enough light for 'ordinary purposes'.

(b) Under the Prescription Act 1832, as amended by the Rights of Light Act 1959, it is provided that an absolute right of light can be obtained after 20 years' uninterrupted use (the 1959 Act provided a temporary extension of the period to 27 years due to the then abundance of bomb-damaged sites and the slow pace of redevelopment). The 1959 Act provides that a local land charge may be registered (see paragraph 1.09), indicating the presence of a theoretical wall of stated dimensions in such a position as would prevent an adjoining owner from claiming a prescriptive right of light. This useful provision avoids a landowner having to erect screens and hoardings (subject to planning permission: Chapter 11) to prevent a right of light being acquired over his land! Instead, he can register a local land charge that has the same effect as if the light had been blocked by a wall or screen, so preventing the neighbour's 20-year use.

4 Restrictive covenants

4.01 A restrictive covenant is a binding obligation that restricts an owner of servient land (burdened land) in his use and enjoyment of that land. The covenant must be made for the benefit of dominant land (benefited land) belonging to the covenantee, being the person who may enforce the covenant. Typical examples are covenants not to build above a given height or in a given place or a certain number of buildings, or covenants restricting the use of the land to given purposes: e.g. no trade or business permitted. Although to some extent superseded by planning controls, restrictive covenants still have a valuable role to play, particularly in preserving the character of housing estates and other homogenous developments. In particular, it is important to appreciate that the granting of planning permission does *not* remove any restrictive covenants. So, permission to build is meaningless if a neighbour has a covenant against building which he refuses to release. The essentials of a restrictive covenant are:

1 that it is in substance negative: a covenant that requires a landowner to spend money is *not* negative (e.g. a covenant to fence or repair is not negative);

2 that it is made between the covenantor (the person making the promise, whose land is burdened) and the covenantee (the person who can enforce the promise) for the benefit of the covenantee's land;

3   that the original parties intended the burden of the covenant to run with the covenantor's land so as to bind not only the covenantor but also his successors in title (e.g. purchasers from the original covenantor). Consequently, all subsequent owners of the burdened land can be prevented from carrying out the prohibited use.

4.02 A restrictive covenant is an equitable interest in land and therefore requires registration to be effective against all subsequent owners (unless the covenant is contained in a lease, for which different rules apply). If the land is unregistered, the covenant must be registered as a land charge. However, if – as is more likely – the burdened land is registered, a restrictive covenant must itself be registered by entering a Notice (usually an Agreed Notice) against the servient land on its Register of Title. These matters will usually be dealt with by the solicitor or property professional at the time the covenant was first created. If a restrictive covenant complies with the requirements listed in paragraph 4.01 and is properly protected by registration, it will bind the covenantor's successors in title. The rules on the passing of the benefit of restrictive covenants are complex and need not be considered here, save to say that it is very likely that a successor in ownership to the land benefited will be able to enforce the covenant against the person now owning the land burdened. In other words, restrictive covenants affect both burdened and benefited land long after they were first created. There is in consequence a procedure for their removal (see paragraph 4.04 below). The usual remedy for infringement of a restrictive covenant is an injunction to restrain further breaches, but the court may give damages either in addition to or in lieu of an injunction. A client who has the benefit of a restrictive covenant (i.e. the right to enforce it) must be aware that they might not, ultimately, be able to prevent the prohibited conduct if the court thinks that they can be adequately compensated in damages instead. Offers by the owner of the burdened land to 'buy out' the covenant are usually more generous that the court's award of damages.

4.03 Architects should request that their clients obtain confirmation that there are no restrictive covenants applying to a site that could affect the proposed design and use of a building or indeed whether a building can be constructed at all. An architect must proceed with caution as, for example, a simple covenant 'not to carry on any trade or business' on the land may effectively destroy a development, whether or not planning permission is required or has been given. Although the point has never been tested in court, an architect who continued to act for a client in designing a building that was known by both of them to contravene a restrictive covenant could be liable jointly with his client for the tort of conspiracy, i.e. of agreeing to do an unlawful act.

Discharge of restrictive covenants

4.04 Many restrictive covenants imposed in former years are no longer of real benefit to the owners of adjoining lands and may indeed be anti-social or in conflict with reasonable redevelopment proposals. Consequently, power is given to the Lands Tribunal by section 84 of the Law of Property Act 1925, as amended by section 28 of the Law of Property Act 1969, for the discharge or modification of any covenant if the Tribunal is satisfied that, among other things, changes in the neighbourhood make the covenant obsolete or that the restriction does not now secure practical advantages of substantial value to the person entitled to its benefit or is contrary to public policy (which may include planning policy). Compensation may be awarded to the person entitled to enforce the covenant if it is discharged or modified. However, it is not enough to secure the discharge or modification of a covenant that development would add amenity to the land or to the neighbourhood. Some reason why the private law rights of others should be overridden must be found and this may become more difficult to establish as human rights legislation (protecting private property) takes full effect.

5 Landlord and tenant

Landlord and tenant covenants

5.01 The vast majority of leases with which architects are concerned on behalf of their clients, particularly of trade and business premises, are the subject of formal agreements defining precisely the respective rights and obligations of the parties. Whether the architect's client is a tenant who wishes to rebuild, alter, or repair premises, or a landlord who requires evidence to recover damages from a tenant who has failed to observe a promise (covenant) for repair, regard must be had first to the express terms of the lease and the client's solicitor should be asked to advise on the meaning and extent of the terms. The following general remarks, except where otherwise stated, introduce the law only in so far as the lease itself does not make any express provision.

The doctrine of waste and repairing obligations

5.02 'Waste' consists of an act or omission that causes or is likely to cause a lasting alteration to the nature of the land or premises. A tenant of land for more than one year is, apart from statute and any terms of the lease, liable for 'voluntary waste' (any positive act such as pulling down or altering the premises) and 'permissive waste' (any omission, such as allowing the premises to fall into disrepair). In practice, however, the great majority of leases will contain clear repairing covenants going beyond these obligations. Normally, the landlord is responsible for external repairs and the tenant for internal repairs, although this may be different in very long leases. In any event, in respect of a lease of a dwelling house or flat for less than 7 years (excluding some leases granted to local authorities and other public sector bodies), the landlord is obliged to keep the exterior and general structure in repair and to keep in repair and working order all installations relating to heating and amenities: Housing Act 1985, section 11. Finally, there is a third type of waste: 'ameliorating waste', being some change that improves the value of the landlord's interest (his 'reversion'). The courts are very unlikely to restrain acts of ameliorating waste by the tenant precisely because they add value to the landlord's interest.

Fixtures

5.03 Prima facie, anything that is attached to the land becomes part of the land and therefore the property of the landowner. If, therefore, a tenant attaches something to land, it will presumptively become the property of the landlord. However, two questions arise. First, is the addition to the land in truth a 'fixture' in the sense that it has become part of the land or does it remain a 'chattel' – the personal property of the tenant? Second, even if it is a fixture, is it of a kind that for special reasons a tenant may remove at the end of the lease?

1   *Fixture or chattel?* In deciding whether something attached to the land is a fixture or a chattel, two matters are considered:
    (a) How is the thing attached to the land? If it is attached so that it can be removed readily without damaging the fabric of the land or the buildings on it, it may be regarded as a chattel and therefore as the property of the tenant. This is the 'degree of annexation' test. For example, something resting on the land by its own weight is likely to be a chattel: a usual garden ornament and even a temporary housing structure (e.g. a Portakabin) may fall into this category.
    (b) Why is the thing attached? This is the 'purpose of annexation' test and can override the 'degree' test. If the thing is attached to the land simply because it cannot otherwise be used or enjoyed as a chattel (e.g. a dentist's chair bolted to the floor or a tapestry fixed to a wall), then it remains a chattel. Conversely, if the thing is attached in order to improve the land permanently, then it is a fixture. So, a garden ornament forming part of an integrated garden design may well be a fixture as an object intended to form part of the land and which increases its value.

2 *Tenant's fixtures.* Even if the thing is a fixture, a tenant who has attached it may be able to remove it at the end of his lease under special rules. In the case of non-agricultural leases, the tenant may remove trade, domestic and ornamental fixtures before the expiry of the tenancy. He must make good any damage to the premises occasioned by the removal of the fixtures. If the lease is of agricultural land, the tenant can remove all fixtures that he has attached within 2 months of the lease expiring. The landlord has the option to purchase them if he wishes.

Alterations and improvements

5.04 In the absence of any term in the lease regulating the matter, the tenant should obtain the landlord's consent to do any alterations. This is because any alteration to the premises will constitute waste (voluntary or ameliorating) and are likely to be a breach of the terms of the lease. It is common for a lease to contain an express condition that no alterations shall be made without the landlord's consent, although in most cases such consent may not be unreasonably withheld where the alteration constitutes an improvement: Landlord and Tenant Act 1927, section 19. Whether a proposed alteration is 'an improvement' is a question of fact to be considered from the tenant's point of view. It should be noted that it is the tenant's responsibility to prove that the landlord's consent is being unreasonably withheld, that the landlord may object on aesthetic, artistic, and even sentimental grounds, and that although the above Act forbids the taking of any payment as a condition of giving consent, the landlord may reasonably require the tenant to pay the landlord's legal and other expenses (including architect's and surveyor's fees) plus a reasonable amount for any diminution in the value not only of the leased premises but also of any adjoining premises of the landlord.

Repairing covenants generally

5.05 Architects are frequently asked to prepare a 'schedule of dilapidations' at the start, during, or at the end of a lease. This will be used as a basis of assessing the extent of the repairing obligations of the parties under the lease. The importance of initial schedules is that in the absence of any covenant to do works as a condition of the grant of the lease, any repairing covenant must be interpreted with reference to the original condition of the premises. Thus, the original condition as detailed in the schedule is crucial. The extent of repairing obligations turns on the words used in the lease. For example, often the tenant's obligation is to 'repair, keep in repair and deliver the premises in repair at the end of the term' which encompasses an on-going obligation throughout the lease and an obligation to leave the premises in much the same condition as they were found. The actual meaning of 'repair' – or rather, what is a 'disrepair' so as to trigger the repairing obligation – can vary according to the circumstances of each case, including the length of the lease, purpose of the lease and location of the property. So, 'repair' may include the replacement or renewal of parts of a building but not renewal of the whole or substantially the whole of the premises. A common repairing obligation placed on tenants and found in leases of houses or flats is to 'keep and deliver up premises in good and tenantable repair' and (in the absence of a countervailing obligation of the landlord, such as in premises of low rent) the covenant can include an obligation to put the premises into repair (even if they were in disrepair by the omissions of another) as well as to keep them in repair. The quality of such repair must be such 'as having regard to the age, character and locality of the premises would make it reasonably fit for occupation by another reasonably minded tenant of the same class' (*Proudfoot v Hart* [1890] 25 QBD 42 at 55).

Exception to tenant's repairing obligations

5.06 The tenant is usually not liable for any damage that can be said to be a result of 'fair wear and tear' but it is the tenant's responsibility to prove that a bad state of repair is covered by the exception. In general terms, the phrase means that the tenant is

not responsible for damage resulting from exposure to the natural elements or reasonable use of the property. However, although not liable for direct damage due to fair wear and tear (e.g. a slate blown off a roof), the tenant could be liable for any consequential damage that then occurs (e.g. water damage to the interior). It is often the case, therefore, that tenants will carry out minor repairs for which they are not technically liable in order to prevent wider disrepair for which they would be liable.

Dilapidations

5.07 If asked to prepare a schedule of dilapidations, an architect should first find out from his client's solicitor the terms of the lease so that he is clear which portions of the building come within the repairing covenant. These are the only portions he need examine. As some tenant's fixtures are removable by the tenant, only dilapidations to landlord's fixtures need usually be catalogued. (Note, however, because of the difficulties of assessing ownership of fixtures, it is often wise to examine dilapidations on anything that is at all doubtful.) Estimates of the cost of making good dilapidations are often required. Unless an architect has much experience of this kind of work, it is advisable to involve a quantity surveyor or similar professional. When landlord and tenant cannot agree about the extent of the damage or the extent of responsibility for making them good, their dispute may have to be resolved in the courts or by arbitration. In such cases, the schedule of dilapidations becomes evidence, and it is therefore important that it is very clearly written. Where the parties agree to appoint an architect or surveyor to prepare a schedule of dilapidations, then, by analogy with the cases on valuations, if no reasons for the conclusions in the schedule are given and it was made honestly and in good faith, it cannot be set aside by the courts, even though it turns out to be mistaken: *Campbell v Edwards* [1976] 1 WLR 403. If reasons are given for the conclusions in the schedule and they are fundamentally erroneous, it may be set aside: *Burgess v Purchase & Sons (Farms) Ltd* [1983] Ch 216. When making an inspection for a schedule the possibility that matters might come to court should be borne in mind.

Consents

5.08 It must be emphasised that what has been stated is always subject to the express wording of the lease and also to the many statutory provisions for the protection of tenants of certain types of premises, particularly houses. Architects should remember that a client's tenancy may come at the end of a long line of underleases, and the consent of superior landlords may be required for any work that the client has requested. The client's solicitor should be consulted to determine the existence of any superior landlords.

Enforcement of repairing covenants

5.09 Under the Leasehold Property (Repairs) Act 1938, as extended by the Landlord and Tenant Act 1954, a landlord cannot forfeit the lease (i.e. force its early termination) or even begin an action for damages in respect of a tenant's failure to observe a repairing covenant unless he has first served on the tenant a notice under section 146 of the Law of Property Act 1925 clearly specifying the alleged breach of covenant. If the tenant serves a counter-notice within 28 days, the landlord cannot take any action without the consent of the court. Architects are frequently asked to produce a schedule of defects and dilapidations to accompany a section 146 notice (see also paragraph 5.06).

6 Surveys of property to be purchased

6.01 Architects are often asked to inspect property for clients who intend to purchase it or take a lease. A physical inspection of the property is required, bearing in mind the proposed use and taking into account all defects and dilapidations. Useful guides to technical points to be noted in such a survey are given in *Architectural Practice and Procedure* and in *Guide to Domestic Building Surveys.*

6.02 It is important to note that if defects are not observed and noted, the architect may be held to be negligent. For example, where a surveyor failed to report that the timbers of a house were badly affected by death-watch beetle and worm, he was held liable in negligence to the purchaser of that property (*Phillips v Ward* [1956] 1 WLR 471). The measure of damages in such a case is the difference between the market value of the property with the defect and the purchase price paid by the client. It is *not* the difference between the market value with the defect and the value of the property as it would have been if it had been as described (*Perry v Sidney Phillips & Son* [1982] 1 WLR 1297).

Hidden defects

6.03 It is often wise, particularly when investigating old property, to open up and inspect hidden portions of the building. If this is not done, the limitations of the investigation should be clearly pointed out to the client, and he should be asked to take a decision as to whether the expense of opening up is worthwhile. He must, of course, be informed of the probability or otherwise of, for example, rot or beetle infestation. If rot or similar is discovered and it was not mentioned in the survey and the architect did not recommend opening up to check, he is almost certainly negligent.

7 Mortgages

7.01 It is not proposed to discuss this subject in detail, but architects should remember that alteration to premises will alter the value of the mortgagee's (i.e. the lender's) security. For this reason, most mortgages contain covenants requiring the borrower to obtain the mortgagee's consent to any proposed works. As with leases, there may be several lenders who have advanced different amounts at different times and these will rank in order of their priority. The architect should ask the client whether the property is mortgaged and request him to obtain any necessary consents.

8 Business tenancies – architects' offices

8.01 This review of business tenancies can be in outline only, and it is written from the point of view of architects as tenants of office premises. Three preliminary matters of importance should be noted:

1 An architect should be careful if a lease includes an absolute right for the landlord to forfeit the lease (i.e. terminate it early) in the event of bankruptcy. It is difficult – if not impossible – to raise finance from institutional lenders on the security of such a lease because the value of the architect's interest in the land is precarious.
2 Care should be taken to check the wording of covenants concerning assignment (transfer of the lease to another) or sub-letting (creation of a sub-lease, with the architect becoming landlord of the occupier). The immediate lease offered to the architect and any superior lease (as where the architect's landlord is a tenant of the freeholder) should be inspected. Particularly, the architect should examine the circumstances in which the landlord can give or refuse his consent to assignment or underletting.
3 For leases granted on or after 1 January 1996, the Landlord and Tenant (Covenants) Act 1995 has introduced a new statutory code for the enforcement of leasehold covenants. This has a number of consequences and the architect should discuss this fully with his solicitor. In particular, the architect should note that if he takes an assignment of a lease from an existing tenant, he is likely to be taking on all the obligations of the original tenant. Secondly, if the architect assigns the lease, he is likely to be required to guarantee performance of the leasehold covenants by the person to whom he assigns. Thirdly, there are some circumstances where a landlord can make the giving of his consent to assignment dependent on the fulfilment of stringent conditions, even if these are not reasonable. For leases granted before 1 January 1996, different rules apply and enquiries should again be made of the solicitor handling the matter.

Protection of business tenants

8.02 Part II of the Landlord and Tenant Act 1954 (as amended by Part I of the Law of Property Act 1969 and the Regulatory Reform (Business Tenancies) (England and Wales) Order 2003), provides a substantial measure of protection to occupiers of business premises by providing in effect that the tenant may continue in occupancy indefinitely, unless the landlord satisfies the court that a new tenancy ought not to be granted for certain defined statutory reasons (paragraph 8.03). Note, however, that by following the correct procedure, the parties to an intended business lease can opt out of the protection provided by the Act *before* commencement of the tenancy. In that case, the lease is governed by ordinary principles and terminates after the original period has expired.

If the parties have not agreed to opt out of the Act, the tenant may apply for renewal of the lease by serving a notice on the landlord, which the landlord can oppose (after serving a counter-notice) by proving one of the recognised grounds. Similarly, a landlord may seek to terminate the tenancy at the end of the original lease (or thereafter) and prevent renewal by serving notice on the tenant (not more than 12 months or less than 6 months before the intended termination date), but the court may grant renewal unless one of the specified grounds are established without the tenant having to serve a notice requesting this. The court will settle the terms of any renewed tenancy.

8.03 There are a number of reasons that might prevent the grant of a new tenancy to the tenant; i.e. different circumstances that the landlord can rely on to recover the premises at the end of the original lease. The first three, if proved, conclusively prevent the tenant gaining a new tenancy, the latter four giving the court a discretion to deny a tenancy.

1 If, on termination of the existing tenancy, the landlord intends to demolish or reconstruct the premises and could not reasonably do so without possession of the whole, a new tenancy will be denied and the tenant must quit. Since the 1969 Act, this does not prevent a new tenancy of the whole or part of the premises if the landlord will be able to do the work without seriously 'interfering' with the tenant's business.
2 If the landlord proves that he intends to occupy the premises for his own business or as a residence a new tenancy will be denied. Since 1969 the landlord may successfully resist a new tenancy if he intends the premises to be occupied by a company in which he has a controlling interest.
3 If the landlord proves the premises are part of a larger holding for which he could obtain a substantially larger rent than for the individual parts, a new tenancy of the part will be denied.
4 If the tenant fails to keep the premises in repair, the court may deny a new tenancy.
5 If there are persistent delays in paying rent, the court may deny a new tenancy.
6 If there are breaches of covenant, the court may deny a new tenancy.
7 If the landlord is willing to provide suitable alternative accommodation on reasonable terms, the court may deny a new tenancy.

It should be noted, however, that their area of the law is likely to be reformed in the near future and so it will be necessary for the architect – as with all tenants of business premises – to such specialist advice.

Compensation

8.04 If the court cannot grant a new tenancy for any of the first three reasons above, the tenant will be entitled to compensation calculated under a formula set by the legislation.

New tenancy

8.05 If the landlord is unable to rely successfully on any of the above grounds, a new tenancy of the business premises can be granted. The court will fix the terms of the tenancy, including the rent and length, provided this does not exceed 15 years. The 15 year term can accommodate rent reviews at the current standard pattern of 3 or 5 years.

9 Estoppel

9.01 It will not usually be the case that the architect will have many dealings with his client's neighbours. Such matters will usually be dealt with by the client or his solicitor and this is by far the best option. However, circumstances may arise where the architect enters discussions about rights or interests affecting either his client's or the neighbour's land: e.g. discussions about the route of a new access way, the extent of overhanging eaves, drainage channels, etc. In such cases, the architect must take care not to make representations concerning his client's land that could later be held to be binding on his client: e.g. as to the route of the access. Although it is difficult to prove an 'estoppel' – i.e. that the architect has represented something about his client's land that the client is later held to – the architect should always make it clear that any agreement or offer with a neighbouring landowner is subject to written confirmation and should not be relied on by the neighbour until such confirmation is given. This is very important as the courts will enforce an estoppel against a person making such a representation and this can have serious consequences for the viability of the development.

5

Introduction to Scots law

CATHERINE DEVANEY

1 Scots law: a distinct legal system

1.01 Although the modern Scottish Parliament was not established until 1999, Scotland has always had a separate legal system independent of English law. Scots law was expressly preserved by the Treaty and Acts of Union in 1707, which gave rise to the United Kingdom. While it has not been immune to the influence of English law, which is part of the Common Law tradition, it has tended to have more in common with the legal traditions of continental Europe, known as the Civilian tradition.

1.02 Peculiar though it may seem to maintain separate systems of law within the relatively small geographical area of mainland Britain, the differences north and south of the border should not be underestimated. In some respects the differences of approach are fundamental; concepts that are second nature to a lawyer in Aberdeen can seem very alien to his contemporary in Birmingham (and vice versa). It is not simply the case that Scotland has its own set of procedural rules and a different court structure (which is discussed below). It has different roots and this means that the substance of the law is often different.

1.03 The differences are more apparent in some areas of law than others; in fields that are heavily statute based, such as intellectual property, there is often little practical difference. Often the ultimate answers to legal questions and the outcome of disputes will be similar, although the legal landscape might vary along the way. It would be both untenable and undesirable to have different legal systems within the United Kingdom that could produce widely differing practical results (although that is not to say it has never happened!).

2 Historical context

2.01 In mediaeval Scotland the religious courts, known as the canon courts, were influential. It is through the influence of canon law that Roman law came to be increasingly applied by the secular courts in the fourteenth century. Although it might seem odd to have turned to a legal system that was applied in the first six centuries AD, its comprehensive and analytical approach proved itself to have considerable utility and modern relevance. Many Scots lawyers also attended university on the continent and were there exposed to the influence of Civil Law.

2.02 While it might be said that in England the Common Law developed on a case-by-case basis, in Scotland there was a tendency to regard the law as a comprehensive and logical system. This is apparent in many works from the seventeenth and eighteenth centuries, whose authors are known as the Institutional Writers and which still have an authoritative status in Scots courts

and are not infrequently cited to this day. The Institutional Writers (such as Craig, Stair, Mackenzie, Forbes, Erskine and Bankton) found a language and a structure within the Roman law that they used and adapted.

2.03 Following the Act of Union in 1707 the UK Parliament passed legislation applicable to Scotland. Often, Scottish legislation was no more than an adapted version of the English model. Wide-ranging legislative reform specific to Scotland often had to compete for parliamentary time. Another effect of union was that a right of appeal developed to the Judicial Committee of the House of Lords, which often failed to recognise the differences that existed between the legal systems and tended historically to apply English law. Increasingly, English cases came to be cited in the Scottish courts and, although they were never binding, they were (and are) considered persuasive.

2.04 Over the centuries, Scotland has been influenced by both the Common Law and the Civil Law and it is because of this that it is known as a 'mixed legal system', like South Africa, Louisiana and Sri Lanka in that regard.

3 Modern context: devolution

3.01 Following devolution, the Scottish Parliament was officially opened on 1 July 1999 in Edinburgh. In terms of the Scotland Act 1998, the Scottish Parliament has the power to legislate on all matters except those specifically reserved to Westminster. This is not to say that Scots law is the same as English law where reserved matters are concerned; only that the power to legislate resides with the UK Parliament.

3.02 General reserved matters include the constitution, foreign affairs and defence. Specific reserved matters are more wide ranging. It is worth noting that these include a number of commercial matters, including business associations, employment law, insolvency and intellectual property. Regulation of the profession of architect is also a reserved matter.

3.03 Since 1999 a vast amount of new legislation has been passed and the opportunity has been taken to implement fundamental reform in certain areas, for example as regards the system of land tenure and the bankruptcy regime. There is now a greater degree of flexibility and parliamentary time within which to design Scottish solutions that are sensitive to and fit in with the broader scheme of Scots law.

3.04 The Scottish Parliament comprises 129 members (MSPs). A Government is formed which is known as the Scottish Executive.

This comprises MSPs in the capacity of Ministers and the offices of Lord Advocate and Solicitor General, led by the First Minister. Together they are known as the Scottish Ministers. Since May 2007, the Executive (now rebranded the Scottish Government) has been formed by the Scottish National Party.

3.05 Devolution has not altered the level of representation that Scotland has within the UK Parliament. MSPs and MPs now co-exist. This means that Scottish MPs still have an influence over legislation on purely English issues, while English MPs have no corresponding influence over Scottish devolved matters. This remains a vexed political issue and it remains to be seen whether devolution in Scotland will inevitably lead to complete independence or whether it will be matched by a system of regional devolution in England. Following the electoral victory of the Scottish National Party, it now seems inevitable that a referendum will be held on the question of Scotland's future within the union.

4 Scotland and European law

4.01 In 1973 Britain became a member of the European Economic Community. As a consequence, certain forms of European law became directly applicable in Scotland. Parts of the various European treaties, along with a type of legislation known as regulations, create legal rights and obligations that are directly enforceable in Scottish courts. European directives do not have the same effect and require implementation in the form of domestic legislation. Legislation must be interpreted in a way that is compatible with Community law and the courts cannot give effect to any provision that is contrary to it. The Scotland Act 1998 specifically provides that it is not competent for the Scottish Parliament to legislate in any way that is incompatible with Community law.

4.02 The European Court of Justice (the ECJ) in Luxembourg has the ultimate say in questions of interpretation of community law. It does not have a truly appellate function; rather, the domestic courts (at any level) can refer a question of interpretation to it. The Scottish courts are also bound to give effect to relevant decisions of the ECJ, which comprises judges from each member state. As a result, Scots law is once more exposed to the legal influences of continental Europe, which will no doubt bring further change and perhaps, an opportunity for a renaissance of Scotland's Civilian legal traditions. There was, for a time, discussion of a move towards a new European legal system along the lines of a comprehensive European Civil Code, although there seems to be little current appetite for such a move.

5 Scotland and human rights

5.01 One very important aspect of modern Scots law is human rights. The European Charter of Rights and Fundamental Freedoms was incorporated into domestic law by the Scotland Act 1998. The Scottish Ministers and, through the Lord Advocate, the prosecuting authorities cannot act in a way that is contrary to the rights set out in the Charter. This has resulted in a very large number of challenges being brought before the courts, particularly in the fields of immigration and criminal law. It has also had a wide-ranging impact on various aspects of private law. This is a rapidly expanding area of law which has radically altered the legal landscape in the last decade.

6 Categorisation of Scots law

6.01 Perhaps the principal division in the legal system is between public law and private law. Public law concerns the relationships between individuals and the state; it includes criminal law, immigration and all aspects of judicial review and administrative law. As well as the more traditional crimes, criminal law also comprises many statutory offences in the field of health and safety.

6.02 Private law concerns the relationships between individuals and other legal persons such as companies and partnerships. It is often referred to, by lawyers and layman alike, as 'civil law'. Private law, or civil law, has traditionally been subject to the three-fold classification of 'persons', 'things' and 'actions', following the taxonomy of Roman law. Specific branches of private law include contract; unjustified enrichment; delict; property; trusts; intellectual property; the law of agency and partnership; family law; company law; and bankruptcy/insolvency.

6.03 There is no distinction in Scots law between Law and Equity. General equitable concepts are recognised as part of the general law.

7 Sources of Scots law

Legislation

7.01 The primary source is legislation. Legislation is created by either the Scottish Parliament or the UK Parliament. Primary legislation takes the form of statutes; secondary legislation takes the form of statutory instruments and by-laws, issued by Ministers or local authorities pursuant to delegated authority. Legislation passed by the UK Parliament may apply in whole, in part or not at all to Scotland. If it applies solely to Scotland, or if it has been passed by the Scottish Parliament since 1999, this is denoted in the title, e.g. the Requirements of Writing (Scotland) Act 1995 and the Freedom of Information (Scotland) Act 2002. For statutes that are not wholly applicable, the scope can be found in the section of the statute called 'extent'. As discussed above, European Regulations have the same status as legislation. Copies of legislation can be ordered or downloaded from the website of the Office of Public Sector Information (www.opsi.gov.uk).

Case law

7.02 The decisions of certain courts are binding on other courts. This means that much of the law is effectively 'judge-made law'. To understand what the law is on a particular point it may be necessary to analyse previous decisions on the same point and extract from them the legal principle. English judgments are not binding in Scotland, with the exception of decisions of the House of Lords in Scottish appeals, although they have varying degrees of persuasiveness depending on how the judgment ranks within the English court system. As noted above, decisions of the ECJ are binding on Scottish courts at all levels. Decisions of the European Court of Human Rights in Strasbourg must be taken into account so far as relevant. Scottish decisions are reported in an official series called the *Session Cases* and also in *Scots Law Times* and various other legal reports. Unreported decisions since 1998 can be accessed through a database on the website of the Scottish Courts Service (www.scotcourts.gov.uk).

Authoritative writings

7.03 The works of the Institutional Writers (paragraph 2.02) are still binding in the courts today. Despite their vintage, it is not uncommon, when a question of legal novelty arises today, to find Stair or Erskine cited in court as the basis for a 'new' legal argument.

7.04 Roman law also exists as a persuasive source, even today; there are numerous instances where it has been cited in the last decade and it remains a resource for the more imaginative (or perhaps desperate!) lawyer searching for a basis for his argument.

8 The court structure

Criminal courts

8.01 The structure of the criminal court system is set out below. In criminal matters in Scotland the wrongdoer is known as the

LAST SITTING of the OLD COURT of SESSION 11 of JULY 1808
300

'accused'. The prosecuting authority is the Crown Office and Procurator Fiscal Service. All prosecutions are brought in the name of the Lord Advocate.

District Court

8.02 In very minor cases, criminal proceedings are brought in the district court before a lay magistrate: a Justice of the Peace. Every local authority previously had one or more district courts. These are in the process of a phased reorganisation and are being replaced by Justice of the Peace courts.

Sheriff Courts: criminal

8.03 Scotland is divided into six sheriffdoms (e.g. the Sheriffdom of Glasgow and Strathkelvin), each of which has a number of individual sheriff courts hearing both criminal and civil business. Criminal cases may be brought in the sheriff court in all matters with the exception of murder, rape and treason, although more serious assaults, culpable homicide and serious sexual assaults do not tend to be tried in the sheriff courts. Depending on the seriousness of the charges a trial may take place either before a single sheriff or before a sheriff sitting with a jury composed of 15 members of the public.

High Court of Justiciary

8.04 The most serious crimes are tried in the High Court of Justiciary. It has jurisdiction over crimes committed throughout the whole of Scotland. It sits permanently in Edinburgh, Glasgow and Aberdeen. It also sits on a temporary basis in other larger towns and cities. The High Court is presided over by Scotland's most senior judges: the Lord Justice-General and the Lord Justice-Clerk

(currently Lords Hamilton and Gill). Trials are conducted before a single judge sitting with a jury of 15.

Court of Criminal Appeal

8.05 When the High Court of Justiciary sits as an appeal court it is known as the Court of Criminal Appeal. Appeals are generally heard by a bench of three judges, although a larger bench (of five, seven or even nine) may be convened if an earlier judgment is to be departed from. There is no appeal to the House of Lords in criminal cases. However, if a question of human rights has arisen there can, in certain circumstances, be an appeal to the Judicial Committee of the Privy Council.

Civil courts

8.06 The structure of the civil court system is set out below. In Scotland, legal proceedings are referred to as 'actions' and the respective parties are known as the 'pursuer' and 'defender'. As a generality, actions are initiated by a document called an initial writ, or a summons, which is served upon the defender. Defenders are then obliged to lodge written defences if they wish to defend the action. The system dictates that parties' respective cases ought to be finalised in written form before any evidential hearing takes place in court; the scope of the written case then defines the parameters of the evidence that may ultimately be led. This is designed to ensure that parties have 'fair notice' of the case against them and that they cannot be ambushed. Once the cases are set down in writing, parties may wish to debate legal issues before a judge. However, if the legal issues are straightforward or if they cannot be resolved without leading evidence, a trial of the facts will be required. In civil cases this is called a 'proof', and it takes place before a single sheriff or judge. It is inevitable that as parties go through the process of refining their cases in writing, many actions settle without ever getting close to a court; others might settle at the very door of the court itself, on the morning of a proof.

Sheriff Courts: civil

8.07 The scope of actions that may be raised in the Sheriff Court is relatively wide ranging and, in particular, there is no financial limit on the value of claims that may be raised there. The only restriction is that claims worth less than £5,000 can be raised only in the sheriff court. There are rules which set out the circumstances in which a particular sheriffdom will have jurisdiction. Sheriffs are not bound by the decisions of other sheriffs. Appeals from the decision of a sheriff lie either to the sheriff principal (sitting as a single judge with an appellate function) or to the Inner House of the Court of Session (see paragraph 8.11).

Court of Session

8.08 The Court of Session is the supreme civil court in Scotland. It is permanently based in Edinburgh, in Parliament Square. It comprises around 30 judges at any one time, known as Lords Ordinary (the same judges that comprise the High Court of Justiciary), and is presided over by the Lord President and the Lord Justice-Clerk.

8.09 The Court of Session is divided into the Outer House, for first instance business, and the Inner House, where it hears appeals. In the Outer House, preliminary business, debates and proofs are usually heard by a single judge. Occasionally, jury trials can happen in civil cases, where a single judge will sit with a jury of 12 (unlike the criminal juries of 15) to determine disputed issues of fact. While civil jury trials have regained some popularity in recent years, they are still relatively rare; they occur largely in straightforward personal injury cases where the legal issues are not complex and the main question for the jury is the level of damages to award.

8.10 Much could be said about legal procedure generally, but for present purposes it is worthwhile noting that separate procedures exist for commercial actions and personal injuries actions respectively. Designated commercial judges now exist in the Outer House and their aims are to achieve speedy resolution of issues in a commercially responsive way, avoiding protracted litigation. The whole ethos of the commercial court is quite different from ordinary actions: the most striking visible sign of this is that advocates do not wear wigs and gowns.

8.11 Appeals in the Inner House are generally heard by a Bench of three judges, although a larger Bench can be convened.

Judicial Committee of the House of Lords

8.12 Appeals in civil matters lie ultimately to the Judicial Committee of the House of Lords. They are heard before a bench of five Law Lords. The Law Lords are predominantly English, although there is always at least one Scottish Law Lord, and business is generally arranged so that the Scottish judges can sit on Scottish appeals (although they are unlikely ever to form a majority).

The legal profession

8.13 A Scottish lawyer is either a solicitor, an advocate or a solicitor-advocate. Solicitors and solicitor-advocates are regulated by the Law Society of Scotland, whereas advocates are members of a different professional body, the Faculty of Advocates. In practical terms, solicitors deal directly with clients and carry out a variety of legal services, including direct representation in the sheriff court. Solicitors can become accredited specialists in twenty-four different areas of the law, including construction law, planning law and environmental law.

8.14 Only advocates and solicitor-advocates have rights of audience in the Court of Session, the High Court of Justiciary and

the House of Lords. When an advocate appears in court he is still required, for the time being at least, to wear the traditional court dress of wig and gown. Advocates are broadly equivalent to English barristers and traditionally specialise in the preparation of written pleadings, oral advocacy in the supreme courts and the provision of legal opinions.

8.15 Subject to certain exceptions, advocates must be instructed through a Scottish solicitor. This rule has been relaxed recently and certain professionals, including architects registered by the Architects' Registration Board and members of the Royal Institute of Chartered Surveyors and the Royal Town Planning Institute, can instruct an advocate directly.

9 Branches of Scots law

9.01 The following paragraphs are intended as a brief introduction to some of the main areas of private law with which architects may come into contact. Where relevant, these are dealt with in more detail in the chapters that follow.

Contract

9.02 A contract arises when two or more parties agree to be bound. It can exist only when there is consensus between the parties as to its essential terms and a mutual intention to be legally bound, which is referred to as *consensus in idem*. Contracts may be constituted verbally or in writing, but contracts for the creation, transfer, extinction or variation of an interest in land require to be in writing. The requirements for formal validity of written contracts are set out in the Requirements of Writing (Scotland) Act 1995.

9.03 There is no requirement in Scotland that a contract must include consideration. In other words, a party may undertake to perform an obligation gratuitously and still be bound under the law of contract.

9.04 A situation can become rapidly complex when a web of contracts and sub-contracts exists among a number of parties. For example, the building of a new house might involve contractual relationships among the client and the architect; the client and the main contractor; the main contractor and various sub-contractors. It is also possible in Scotland for a contract between A and B to confer enforceable rights on a third party, C, who is not party to the contract at all. This is known as *ius quaesitum tertio*. Accordingly, the English doctrine of privity of contract does not apply in Scotland.

9.05 If one party is in breach of his contractual obligations this may entitle the other party either to withhold performance or to declare that the contract is at an end and sue for damages. Legal advice should always be sought regarding the appropriate remedy.

9.06 General principles aside, particular types of contract have developed substantial bodies of law. Construction contracts are very much a speciality in their own right. Another particularly important contract is the employment contract, which is in a category of its own and is discussed further in Chapter 35.

Agency

9.07 The law of contract cannot be considered without reference to the principles of agency. Once a person is appointed as a party's agent, with authority to act on his principal's behalf, it is possible for the agent to enter into contracts on his principal's behalf. A partner in a firm is the agent both of the partnership and of his partners.

Partnership

9.08 A partnership in Scotland has separate legal personality, in the same way that a company does. It is defined as 'the relation which subsists between persons carrying on a business in common with a view to profit'. As such, it may sue and be sued in the firm name, although the partners may also be sued together in their capacity as individuals. Each partner is liable jointly and severally for the debts of the firm and any wrongful acts of his co-partners. The general law of partnership was codified in the Partnership Act 1890, although it is now possible to form a limited liability partnership under the Limited Liability Partnerships Act 2000.

Delict

9.09 Whereas the law of contract is concerned with obligations assumed voluntarily, the law of delict is concerned with the redress of legal wrongs which occur without justification. It is broadly equivalent to the English law of tort. It encompasses the law of negligence; in general terms, A will be liable to B if A owes a duty of care to B, has failed to exercise 'reasonable care' and B has suffered harm as a result. The law of delict also includes professional negligence; in order to succeed, a pursuer must prove that the professional said to have been negligent was guilty of such failure as no professional of ordinary skill would be guilty of if acting with ordinary care.

Property law

9.10 In this area the differences between Scotland and England are vast. Central to the law of property is a division between 'real' rights and 'personal' rights; a real right is a right directly in and to a piece of property which can be enforced against anyone who interferes with it, whereas a personal right is simply a right against an individual who, if he fails to perform, can be sued for damages. Ownership of land is a real right, as is the interest of a tenant under certain leases. In contrast to the law in England, ownership is absolute and the concept of a beneficial ownership has no place in Scots law. Moreover, there is no division in Scotland between leasehold and freehold property.

9.11 A sub-set of property law is intellectual property law, concerning copyright, designs, patents and trade marks. The differences between Scotland and England in this area are not so great and therefore no more will be said about them here.

10 Limitation of actions

10.01 The rules of limitation of actions in Scotland are contained in the Prescription and Limitation (Scotland) Act 1973. In very general terms, there is a 3-year limitation period in relation to actions for damages arising out of personal injuries and a 5-year limitation period for many other types of action, including contractual claims. The rules are not straightforward and legal advice should always be sought.

11 Choice of law

11.01 The question of whether Scots law will apply in any given situation is determined by private international law. Usually, in a contractual situation, parties will expressly provide which country's law applies to the contract and is to govern disputes.

12 Jurisdiction

12.01 The rules regarding when the Scottish courts will have jurisdiction are contained in the Civil Jurisdiction and Judgments Act 1982 and subsequent European regulations. Most commonly (but not exhaustively), unless parties have agreed otherwise, the Scottish courts will have jurisdiction if a defender is domiciled there; if the contract in question was to have been performed in Scotland; or if the harmful event in question occurred in Scotland.

6

Scots land law

CATHERINE DEVANEY

1 Introduction

l.01 When it comes to land law, the Scots and English legal systems are markedly different. This is true both at a conceptual level and as regards the way in which property is marketed and transferred. The landscape of Scots property law was itself altered dramatically by the coming into force of three pieces of legislation: the Abolition of Feudal Tenure (Scotland) Act 2000, the Title Conditions (Scotland) Act 2003 and the Tenements (Scotland) Act 2004. These were the product of a comprehensive programme of reform coordinated by the Scottish Law Commission. The aim was not to produce a complete codification; rather, the statutory innovations left parts of the common law largely intact and now coexist alongside it.

2 Rights: real and personal

2.01 Reference was made in Chapter 5 to the traditional distinction in Scots law between the laws of persons, things and actions. Property law is the law of 'things'. People hold rights in 'things', e.g. the right of ownership in a house. There are two categories of rights: real rights and personal rights. The real rights are finite in number. They include the ultimate right of ownership; a right in security (such as a standard security held by a bank); servitude (e.g. a right of access over another's land); and lease.

2.02 A real right is a right in and to the thing itself. A personal right is simply a right against another person to make him do something or refrain from doing something, e.g. the contractual right to payment of a debt. Whereas a real right can be enforced against any person who interferes with it, a personal right can be enforced only against one person or a defined class of people.

3 Classification of property

3.01 Property can be classified as corporeal or incorporeal. Corporeal things are tangible and have a physical presence, such as a field or a car. Incorporeal things are simply rights, e.g. the right of land ownership itself or a servitude right of access.

3.02 A further distinction is between heritable and moveable property, which roughly equates to the distinction between land and everything else that is not land. These distinctions give rise to a fourfold classification of property:

1 Corporeal heritable property, e.g. land and buildings.
2 Incorporeal heritable property, e.g. rights over land and buildings, such as leases or servitude rights (discussed further below).
3 Corporeal moveable property, e.g. a car or furniture.
4 Incorporeal moveable property, e.g. contractual right to receive payment of a debt.

3.03 These distinctions are important because there are different rules for transferring the different types of property. This chapter is concerned only with heritable property, i.e. the first two categories.

Accession: heritable and moveable property

3.04 It should be noted that corporeal moveable property can become heritable by the operation of the doctrine of accession. This occurs when a moveable thing (e.g. a central heating system, a fitted kitchen or heavy machinery) has become permanently attached to the land and 'accedes' to the land. The determining factor is the degree of physical connection. These items are often referred to as 'fixtures'. The sale of a house would therefore include fixtures (unless otherwise specified) but it will not include moveable items, such as curtains and furniture (unless otherwise specified).

3.05 The value of premises for rating or security purposes can often depend on what plant and machinery is counted as part of the heritable property.

4 Land ownership

4.01 As noted above, ownership is one of the real rights. This means that the rights of the owner transfer to his successors and can be enforced against anyone who interferes with the exercise of the right.

Abolition of feudal tenure

4.02 Historically, Scotland had a system of feudal land ownership, whereby all land was ultimately held by the Crown. The 'owner' of land at any given time was not the ultimate owner but a 'vassal' owning the *dominium utile,* while the feudal superior held the *dominium directum.* This often enabled the feudal superior to retain control over the use of the land, impose provisions relating to maintenance, retain rights of pre-emption, reversion or redemption and, in some cases, to extract annual payments known as feuduty. In many ways the system operated like a rudimentary (private) town planning system.

4.03 On 28 November 2004 this system was abolished by the Abolition of Feudal Tenure (Scotland) Act 2000. On that date every estate of *dominium utile* automatically became outright

ownership vested in the current proprietor. At the same time, all rights to extract feuduty were also abolished.

4.04 No more is said of the feudal system here; it is noted because the change was both radical and recent and many older deeds bear reference to it. Much of the utility of the feudal system lay in the mechanisms it provided for the private control and regulation of maintenance and development of properties. This has been preserved largely by reforming the law of real burdens.

Terminology: no freehold or leasehold

4.05 The distinction between freehold and leasehold (and commonhold) ownership has no place in the Scottish system. Certainly, land may be owned or it may be leased (often, in the commercial context, for long periods) but beyond that the terminology has little meaning in Scotland. In contrast to England, Scots law has long recognised the enforceability of positive covenants that run with the land and are enforceable against successive owners of property, e.g. maintenance covenants, in the form of real burdens. Accordingly, the necessity for leasehold ownership did not arise.

Shared ownership

4.06 It is possible for land to be held in common or jointly by two or more persons. Both types are known as *pro indiviso* ownership, meaning that the property is owned by both parties as an undivided whole. Common ownership frequently occurs when a husband and wife buy a house together. It also occurs in flatted properties or office blocks where the shared areas are in common ownership.

4.07 Subject to certain restrictions contained in the Matrimonial Homes (Family Protection) (Scotland) Act 1981, a *pro indiviso* owner is entitled to convey his own share of the property to a third party. Any *pro indiviso* owner is also entitled at any time to have the property physically divided or, if this is not possible, sold and the proceeds divided. Where parties cannot agree, an action for division and sale may be raised in court.

Divided ownership

4.08 A piece of land may be divided into what are known as separate tenements, which can be held by different owners. Salmon fishings are such a separate tenement, as are the rights to gather oysters or the rights to minerals. Since 2004, certain sporting rights (e.g. to shoot and hunt) previously held by feudal superiors have been preserved as separate tenements. These kinds of rights often have significant commercial value as they could effectively veto certain developments that are adverse to enjoyment of the rights.

5 Sale of land and buildings

5.01 The transfer of land is a two-stage process: the contractual stage and the conveyancing stage.

The contract: missives

5.02 A contract for the transfer of heritable property must be constituted in writing. An oral contract is not effective for this purpose. This usually involves the conclusion of missives, which take the form of a series of offers and qualified acceptances that flip back and forth between solicitors until the bargain is finally concluded. During this stage the purchaser's solicitor undertakes a full examination of the title and, as well as determining the extent of the property and considering issues such as building consent and planning permission, should flag up any title conditions or servitudes burdening (or benefiting) the property (discussed further below).

5.03 When newly built properties are sold off by a developer, the missives are generally in a form prescribed by the developer. These are notoriously weighted in favour of the seller and clients should be advised to take legal advice before agreeing to them.

5.04 When a building is less than ten years old the missives typically state that it is covered by a guarantee issued by the National House Builders' Council (NHBC). If a builder is not NHBC registered an architect may be asked to produce a certification of supervision, stating that it has been built in a proper and workmanlike manner, in accordance with building regulations and planning permission.

5.05 Conclusion of the contract does not mean that ownership passes. It means that the purchaser now has the right to insist upon delivery of a conveyance and the seller can insist on payment of the price.

The conveyance: disposition

5.06 The next stage is the granting of a disposition by the seller. The purpose of this is to convey the land from the seller to the purchaser. It must be probative, which usually means that it must be witnessed. However, since 2006 it has been possible for an electronic document authenticated by a digital signature to be effective for the transfer of an interest in land.

5.07 A form of personal guarantee known as warrandice will be either expressly included or implied in dispositions of heritable property. This is a personal guarantee of title by the seller (although it does not cover every risk and, in particular, is not a guarantee against defects in the condition of the property).

5.08 The real right of ownership is not actually transferred until the disposition is registered in the Land Register, even if consideration has been made. The Automated Registration of Title to Land (Electronic Communications) (Scotland) Order 2006 permits the electronic registration of transactions affecting land. Registration has always been pivotal in Scotland for the transfer of ownership. Accordingly, there is no equivalent to the English concept of 'beneficial ownership'.

6 Land registration

6.01 The Land Registration (Scotland) Act 1979 introduced a new system of land registration, superseding the Register of Sasines.

Every transfer of land is now registered on the Land Register, which is administered by the Keeper of the Registers and is fully accessible to the public. Every registered property has its own title sheet and title plan, which is part of a larger mapped index. A land certificate is issued, based on the title sheet. Entries on the title sheet are conclusive of the location and extent of property. Registration carries a guarantee that the position on the register is correct (although, exceptionally, the Keeper can register a title under exclusion of guarantee). It can be changed only by a formal process known as 'rectification', in very limited circumstances.

7 Title conditions: servitudes and real burdens

7.01 'Title condition' has a statutory meaning that was introduced by the Title Conditions (Scotland) Act 2003. The main examples of title conditions are servitudes and real burdens. These are the primary mechanisms for creating encumbrances on land; they serve many useful functions in regulating various issues, including use, maintenance, upkeep and access. It is important for purchasers and developers alike to be aware of the scope and extent of any encumbrances affecting a property. Architects and developers may wish to consider how prospective plans might be affected and whether it may become necessary to negotiate for variation or discharge of a real burden or servitude. It is best to address such matters at as early a stage as possible, to avoid any subsequent delay once a development is under way.

Nature: running with the land

7.02 Both servitudes and real burdens are 'real' in the sense that they run with the land. In essence, they are 'attached' to the lands that they respectively burden and benefit and, once constituted, apply to all successive proprietors indiscriminately. The defining feature is that they actually benefit the land itself and only inadvertently benefit the owners. In this way they differ from contractual rights, which do not extend beyond the original contracting parties.

Real burdens

Defined

7.03 A real burden is an encumbrance on land constituted in favour of the owner of other land in that person's capacity as owner of that other land. The encumbered land is known as the 'burdened property' and the other land as the 'benefited property'.

7.04 There are two principal kinds. An 'affirmative burden' imposes an obligation to do something, e.g. to maintain a road or build a boundary wall. A 'negative burden' is an obligation to refrain from doing something, e.g. building above a certain height or using the property for commercial purposes. A burden cannot provide the right to enter another property or make use of it, unless such a requirement is ancillary to another burden, e.g. a right to access a property to inspect maintenance work that is required by an affirmative burden. Subject to that limited exception, rights to do something on another property or access another property are now the domain of servitudes, not real burdens.

7.05 A check on the titles should reveal any real burdens which could affect design and legal advice should be sought in that regard.

Community burdens

7.06 Where properties in a common scheme, e.g. a housing estate or business park, are all subject to the same burdens which are mutually enforceable, these are called 'community burdens'. Where the property deeds are silent, the 2003 Act steps in to provide default rules for decisions to be taken by a majority for the carrying out of maintenance, enforcement, variation, discharge and the appointment of a manager.

Manager burdens

7.07 A manager burden is a real burden which makes provision for conferring on a specified person the power to act as a manager of related properties. This is typically utilised by developers, to deal with the initial years of a housing or other development.

Other types

7.08 Other special types of burden include conservation burdens; rural housing burdens; maritime burdens; economic development burdens; and health care burdens. In these circumstances there is no benefited property as such; rather, the burden is granted in favour of a conservation body, the Scottish Ministers, a rural housing body, a local authority, the Crown or a National Health Service Trust, as the case may be.

Creation

7.09 A real burden is created by a deed granted by the owner of the burdened property. This is usually a disposition or a deed of conditions. The deed must set out the terms of the burden and identify the benefited property. To take effect, it must be registered against both the benefited property and the burdened property.

7.10 Community burdens must define the community affected. They apply to all units within it.

7.11 The existence of any burden will always be evident from a search of the title of a burdened property. Determining what the benefited property is is not so simple, although the benefit of any new burdens created since 28 November 2004 will be evident from the Land Register.

7.12 The benefit of older burdens will not necessarily be apparent. When various properties were conveyed as part of a common scheme, or when a property was sub-divided, the deeds would often impose real burdens but remain silent as to the properties that were to benefit from them. This gave rise to complicated rules for the existence of implied enforcement rights. For common schemes, any such rights were extinguished by the 2003 Act and re-stated in a simplified form. Accordingly, many properties that were part of a common scheme may have enforcement rights that are not apparent on the face of the Land Register. Rights that arose by implication when a property was sub-divided will be extinguished in 2014; in the interim, affected parties can register a preservation notice.

Abolition and reallocation of feudal burdens

7.13 When the feudal system was abolished, all burdens enforceable by feudal superiors in that capacity were abolished. Of these it is worth noting the categories of 'facility conditions' and 'service conditions'. Facility conditions are typically concerned with the management and maintenance of common facilities such as private roads or boundary walls. Service conditions bind the owner of burdened property to permit services, such as water or electricity, to be supplied to the benefited property. Other burdens tended to preserve the amenity of neighbouring properties by regulating the use or development of the burdened property.

7.14 Feudal facility and service conditions, although no longer enforceable by the feudal superior, are now enforceable by all benefited proprietors.

7.15 Other burdens remain in existence only if the feudal superior 're-allotted' the benefit to a specified neighbouring property by statutory notice and registration in the Land Register.

Enforceable by whom?

7.16 A real burden is enforceable by an owner of the benefited property but also by certain lessees and the holder of a proper liferent, provided that person has an interest to enforce it.

The spouse or civil partner of any of these persons, provided they have occupancy rights within the meaning of the Matrimonial Homes (Family Protection) (Scotland) Act 198l, has an equal right to enforce them. Community burdens are enforceable by the majority of proprietors or, where appointed, by a manager on their behalf. The special types of burden noted above (paragraph 7.08) are enforceable by the relevant official body.

Enforceable against whom?

7.17 An affirmative real burden (i.e. an obligation to do something, e.g. maintain a stair) can be enforced only against the owner of the burdened property. Negative or ancillary burdens are different and can be enforced against not only the owner but also any tenant or any other person having use of the property.

Variation or discharge

7.18 Discharge is by registration of a deed of discharge, granted by the owner of the benefited property, in the Land Register. A separate procedure exists for termination of burdens over 100 years old, by the registration of a notice without objection. Where private agreement is not possible, the Lands Tribunal has the power to determine applications for variation or discharge of real burdens, as well as any question of validity, applicability, enforceability or interpretation. If an order is made, varying or discharging a real burden, it can order the applicant to pay compensation to the owner of the benefited property.

7.19 In relation to affirmative burdens, applications can be made only by the owner of the burdened property. As regards negative or ancillary burdens, applications can be made by the owner of the burdened property but also by the tenant or any person having use of the property. This gives rise to a potential disadvantage for developers who are faced with troublesome real burdens encumbering a prospective site. They are not in a position to make an application for variation or discharge, even when they have a concluded contract or option. Here the position differs from England because they must wait until they have obtained use of the site (for negative burdens) or obtained ownership (for affirmative burdens) or rely on the seller to make the application on their behalf. None of the options is satisfactory.

Servitudes
Defined

7.20 A servitude is an encumbrance on land or houses whereby the owner of the burdened property must allow certain use to be made of it by the owner of the benefited property. The closest parallel in England is the law of easements. A typical example is a servitude of pedestrian or vehicular access.

7.21 Where servitudes have been created otherwise than in a registered deed, there is a restricted number of recognised types. These include servitudes of building support, stillicide (eavesdrop), access, the taking of fuel (peat and turf) and the drawing or conducting of water. For servitudes created by deed, the categories are no longer closed. This paves the way for the recognition of new types of servitude, e.g. a servitude of parking. The restriction is that there must be some actual benefit to the neighbouring property, not simply a benefit to its owner personally.

7.22 The law now expressly recognises a servitude for the leading of pipes, cable or wire over or under land for any purpose.

Creation

7.23 Servitudes can be created by a deed which is registered against both the benefited and burdened properties in the Land Register. They can also be acquired by positive prescription through possession over a period of 20 years. It remains possible for servitudes to be created by implication when a piece of land is divided into different parts and sold. Accordingly, it is not always obvious from the Land Register whether a servitude exists.

Enforcement

7.24 As one of the real rights, a servitude is enforceable against anyone in the world who interferes with it. Parties should therefore be alive to the possibility that they may be interdicted along with the owner if they interfere with a servitude when undertaking preliminary work on a site they do not own.

Renunciation, prescription, variation and discharge

7.25 A servitude can be expressly renounced by the benefited proprietor. It can also be extinguished by negative prescription. This occurs if it is not used for a continuous period of twenty years.

7.26 As with real burdens, an application may be made to the Lands Tribunal for variation or discharge of a servitude by anyone against whom the servitude may be enforced. This is wider in effect than the corresponding provision for real burdens. It would include a developer who has a concluded contract or option but does not yet own the site (or indeed made any use of it).

8 Access rights

Private access

8.01 Within towns, the roads are adopted by local authorities and therefore problems ensuring access are less likely to arise. For rural properties, it is very important to check that a servitude of access exists. The difficulty is that it may not be apparent from the title sheet, as it may have been established by implication or prescription.

Public rights of way

8.02 A public right of way can exist as a footpath or road from one public place to another. It is established either by positive prescription (continuous use for 20 years) or by statutory creation.

Public right to roam

8.03 Very broad access rights for the public were created by the Land Reform (Scotland) Act 2003. The public now has the right to cross all land (subject to certain exceptions), although motorised vehicles cannot be used. Separate rights exist to access land for recreational, educational and other limited purposes. Exceptions include buildings, schools, land on which building work is being carried out, private gardens and golf courses. The Act imposes reciprocal duties on users and landowners to act responsibly.

9 Tenements

9.01 Many properties are made up of a number of different units sharing common areas such as the stair or lift. These include traditional tenements but also office buildings, new flatted developments and houses divided into flats. Unless the title deeds provide otherwise, the Tenements (Scotland) Act 2004 provides a default regime for determining who owns what and how the building is to be maintained and repaired.

Tenements

Common parts, the roof and the solum

9.02 By default, any shared 'close (entrance and passageway)', lift, path, outside stair, fire escape, rhone, pipe, flue, conduit, cable, tank, and chimney stack is owned in common by the flats that use it or are served by it. The roof is owned by the top flat. The solum and airspace is owned by the ground flat. The top flat is, however, allocated the part of the airspace extending to the highest point of the roof. This ensures that there is no difficulty with the installation of dormer windows.

9.03 There is a statutory prohibition on interfering with support, shelter or natural light for other flats. This replaces the old common law of common interest.

Repairs and maintenance

9.04 In many cases there will be a property management or factoring scheme. The Act provides a default management scheme which applies where the deeds do not provide otherwise.

9.05 There is a general definition of 'scheme property' which includes not only common property but all the potential 'big ticket items' which are owned individually: the roof, solum, foundations, external walls, gable walls and also any load-bearing walls. It provides a majority decision-making process whereby maintenance of these items can be arranged and the costs apportioned. The general rule is for equal division of costs. The scheme also provides for decisions to be taken about routine maintenance cleaning, painting and gardening. A manager may also be appointed and a common insurance policy arranged. Emergency repairs can be instructed by any owner and the costs are recoverable from the other owners.

9.06 Under the Civic Government (Scotland) Act 1982, councils also have power to light common stairs and passages and to require common areas to be kept clean and properly decorated. Fire authorities have power to deal with fire hazards in common areas.

10 Boundary walls and support

10.01 Where neighbouring properties, not forming part of a tenement, share a boundary wall, the respective parties each own their own half of the wall, up to the mid-point. They have reciprocal duties of support, founded on the doctrine of common interest. Each must therefore maintain his part of the wall to support the other.

10.02 Where walls are not shared there is no positive obligation to provide support to a neighbouring property. However, if something is done to undermine existing support, e.g. excavating in a way that threatens the foundations of a neighbour's property, then liability in damages can arise. Any proposed work that might threaten support could be interdicted.

11 Nuisance

11.01 The doctrine of nuisance is part of the law of delict that can provide a useful remedy in property disputes. The principle is that a person cannot interfere with his neighbour's comfortable enjoyment of his property. Nuisance will depend on the circumstances and the environment but can include loud noise or foul smells. If a nuisance has existed without challenge for a period of 20 years or more, it cannot be objected to.

12 Other restrictions on heritable property

12.01 Numerous other restrictions, both statutory and otherwise, may affect the owner of heritable property.

Statutory restrictions

12.02 The full ambit of statutory restrictions is beyond the scope of this chapter. Obvious examples are the Town and Country Planning Acts and the statutes and regulations governing compulsory purchase. A number of uses are not permitted except under licence (sale of alcohol, gaming, sex shops, tattooing and skin piercing etc).

12.03 The Public Health (Scotland) Acts prohibit the carrying on of a large number of activities, defined as statutory nuisances, on various kinds of properties. A proprietor is also subject to the building regulations administered by the appropriate local authority in respect of any building operations he may wish to carry out.

12.04 Under the Nature Conservation (Scotland) Act 2004 there are restrictions over certain uses and development of land that is designated as a Site of Special Scientific Interest or where a nature conservation order is in place. Various activities in relation to rivers and lochs, including the discharge of pollutants, are regulated by the Water Environment and Water Services (Scotland) Act 2003 and the Water Environment (Controlled Activities) (Scotland) Regulations 2005. Rights to enter property are conferred by the Housing (Scotland) Act 2006 in relation to maintenance, repair and the licensing of houses in multiple occupancy.

Right to buy

12.05 The Land Reform (Scotland) Act 2003 gave rural communities a right to buy land with which the community is connected. The community registers its interest in a register which is maintained by the Keeper of the Registers of Scotland. The right to buy is then activated when the land comes to be marketed or sold. Crofting communities were also given rights to buy certain land.

Repairs and maintenance

12.06 At present, under the Civic Government (Scotland) Act 1982 a local authority can go ahead and instruct repairs to property in the interests of health and safety or to prevent damage. It has the power to recoup costs. Under the Housing (Scotland) Act 1987 a local authority also has the power to serve repair notices on persons having control of property, to require certain repairs to be carried out when property is in a state of serious disrepair. These provisions are shortly to be repealed. A new system is due to come into force under the Housing (Scotland) Act 2006. This is to include powers for local authorities to designate Housing Renewal Areas and serve 'works notices' and 'maintenance notices'.

Occupiers' Liability (Scotland) Act 1960

12.07 The occupier of property is obliged to take reasonable care to see that persons entering his premises do not suffer injury because of the state of the premises. A failure which causes an accident can result in liability to pay damages.

13 Leases

13.01 A proprietor may lease his property to another in return for payment of rent. The law of leases is a specialised area and advice should be sought. Commercial leases, in particular, can be complex, for example in relation to rent review clauses. There are also numerous statutory provisions regulating leases, restricting rents and providing security of tenure. In the context of private residential tenancies, the Housing (Scotland) Act 2006 imposes a statutory code of landlords' repair and maintenance obligations. Separate frameworks exist for agricultural tenancies and crofting land respectively.

Part B

Statutory framework

7

Statutory authorities in England and Wales

JAMES STRACHAN

1 Local government

Introduction: relevant local government authorities

1.01 Local government in England and Wales, outside London, was completely reorganised on 1 April 1974, when the Local Government Act 1972 came into force. The pattern of local authorities, following this and subsequent local government legislation, is now simpler than it was before 1974, but Greater London (reorganised in 1965 by the London Government Act 1963) is administered differently, and there are also differences which exist between England and Wales. These three parts of the country should therefore now be considered separately.

1.02 Local government in England and Wales consists of administration by locally elected bodies constituted as corporations and subject to powers conferred and duties imposed by Parliament. Local authorities are subject to the direction, control and supervision of the Government, to the extent that Parliament has legislated for that direction, control and supervision in statute or in other legislation.

1.03 The Labour Government elected in 1997 carried out a reform of local government in England and Wales. The Local Government Act 2000 gave local authorities general powers to promote the well-being of their community; established executive and scrutiny arrangements within local government; modernised the laws relating to the conduct of members; and changed some of the local government election procedures, subject now to the Local Government Act 2003, which deals further with financial administration, and the Local Government and Public Involvement in Health Act 2007. The Government of Wales Act 1998 devolved certain powers from Westminster to the National Assembly for Wales. The Regional Development Agencies Act 1998 has created nine regional development agencies in England to promote sustainable economic development, and social and physical regeneration.

1.04 In London, the Local Government Act 1985 abolished the Greater London Council and redistributed its functions among the 32 London boroughs, the City of London and new specialised representative bodies (e.g. the London Fire and Civil Defence Authority). Housing became the responsibility of the boroughs and the City. The Greater London Authority Act 1999 established the Greater London Authority (GLA), which is composed of the London Assembly and the Mayor of London. The London Borough Councils and the Common Council of the City of London remain, although some of their responsibilities and functions have been affected by the creation of the GLA.

1.05 In England outside the London area, the country was divided among six metropolitan areas (West Midlands, Merseyside, Greater Manchester, West Yorkshire, South Yorkshire, and Tyne and Wear) and the 'ordinary' counties. Between 1974 and 1985 in the metropolitan areas there was a metropolitan county for each area, and a varying number of metropolitan districts, each with a council, within each county. Since 1985 the metropolitan counties have been abolished and their functions redistributed to the metropolitan districts and specialised representative bodies.

1.06 Outside the metropolitan areas the structure originally comprised 38 counties (each with a county council) and approximately 390 districts (each again with a council). However, following the recommendations of the former Local Government Commission, a number of the former county councils have been abolished in favour of new unitary authorities, which combine the functions of county and district councils. In other non-metropolitan counties, two tiers of government were retained, although in some cases large cities have been given unitary status with the county and district councils retaining their responsibilities for the remaining parts of the area. The Electoral Commission has the powers of the former Local Government Commission for England to review and make changes for effective and convenient local government under the Parties, Elections and Referendum Act 2000 and the Local Government and Public Involvement in Health Act 2007. The 2007 Act has enabled two-tier areas to propose a single unitary authority area, and a number of county councils have sought such change to create single unitary authorities, such as the Wiltshire Council in existence from 1 April 2009.

1.07 In addition, rural parishes which existed before 1974 have been allowed to continue, subject now to Part 4 of the Local Government and Public Involvement in Health Act 2007 (amending the Local Government Act 1972). Some of the pre-1974 district councils have been re-formed with parish council status. As an additional complication, district councils have been allowed to apply for a charter giving themselves the status of a borough, although this is solely a ceremonial matter. Some parishes have been allowed to call themselves 'towns' and have appointed 'town mayors', again with no real legal significance. The parishes ('communities' in Wales) have very few substantial functions, but may provide and maintain recreation grounds, bus shelters, and roadside seats. The Chairman and Vice-Chairman of a parish council must now be chosen from elected, as compared with appointed, councils. Eligible parish councils are now entitled to promote the economic, social or environmental well-being of their area, but do not need to produce a community strategy in order to do so. New parishes within an area, may arise as a result of community governance reviews.

1.08 In Wales there are no metropolitan areas. The former structure of 8 counties divided into 37 districts, with councils at each level, was abolished on 1 April 1996, since when all local administration has been undertaken by 22 new unitary authorities (11 counties and 11 county boroughs) under the Local Government (Wales) Act 1994. The Government of Wales Act 1998 provided for the devolution of certain powers from ministers to the National Assembly for Wales. In effect, the newly created Welsh Assembly has taken over the responsibilities that the Secretary of State for Wales previously exercised in Wales.

General characteristics of local authorities

1.09 The essential characteristic of every local authority under this complicated system is that it is governed by a council elected on a wide franchise at 4-year intervals. In districts, one-third of the councillors retire every year on three out of four years: but a non-metropolitan district may resolve that all their members shall retire together. In counties, all members retire together every fourth year. Some changes have been made to the system of election of councillors by the Local Government Act 2000 and now the Local Government and Public Involvement in Health Act 2007. Under this legislation district councils may be subject to schemes for whole-council elections, or elections by halves or thirds, and power is given to change the date of local elections to the date of a European Parliamentary general election. The term of office for an elected mayor is 4 years.

1.10 Local authorities are legal persons, capable of suing and being sued in the courts, entrusted by Parliament with a range of functions over a precisely limited geographical area. Each local authority is subject to the doctrine of *ultra vires*; i.e. it can perform only those functions within its powers conferred on it by Parliament, and only in such a manner as Parliament may have laid down. On the other hand, within the powers defined by Parliament, each local authority is its own master. In the two- or three-tier system there is no question of an appeal from the lower-rank authorities (the district or the parish) to the higher rank (the county council) or from the parish to the district. If the individual authority has acted within its statutory powers, its decision is final, except in cases precisely laid down by Parliament, where (as in many planning situations) there may be a right of appeal to a Minister of the central government (Chapter 11). If, however, a local authority has overstepped the limits of its legal powers, a private citizen who is aggrieved in consequence may apply to the courts for an order requiring the errant local authority to keep within its powers. Thus, a ratepayer at Fulham successfully obtained an order against the borough council, requiring the council to stop spending ratepayers' money on the provision of a service for washing clothes for members of the public, when the council had statutory powers to provide a service for washing only the bodies of members of the public (*Attorney General v Fulham BC* [1921] 1 Ch 440).

1.11 Local authorities have now been granted wide general powers under section 2 of Part I of the Local Government Act 2000. This enables every local authority to do anything which they consider likely to achieve the promotion or improvement of the economic, social or environmental well-being of their area. This is a significant enlargement of the powers of local authorities. It is coupled with the wider express powers under the Local Government Act 2003 of 'best value' local authorities, as established under the Local Government Act 1999, to charge for their services in many circumstances.

Human Rights

1.12 The enactment of the Human Rights Act 1998 has added a significant new dimension to the statutory duties of local authorities. The basic purpose of the Act is 'to give further effect to rights and freedoms guaranteed under the European Convention of Human Rights'. Of particular relevance to local authorities, the Act provides that it is unlawful for a public authority to act in a way which is incompatible with any Convention right.

Freedom of Information

1.13 Local authorities, like other public bodies, are now subject to the requirements of the Freedom of Information Act 2000 (FOIA) and the Environmental Information Regulations 2004 (SI 2004/339l) (EIR). This legislation gives important rights to the public to obtain information held by local authorities (subject to certain specified statutory exemptions) which may be particularly relevant to the local authority's decision-making in respect of development applications. Where a local authority refuses a request for information under the FOIA or the EIR, there is a right to pursue a comlaint with the Information Commissioner, and thereafter a right of appeal against an Information Commissioner's decision notice to the Information Tribunal. For further details of these rights, see: the Information Commissioner's website www.ico.gov.uk; and that of the Information Tribunal: www.informationtribunal.gov.uk.

Officers

1.14 All local authorities are alike in that they employ officers and other staff to carry out their instructions, while the elected members assembled in council make decisions as to what is to be done. Officers of the authority – chief executive, solicitor, treasurer, surveyor, architect, planning officer, and many others – play a large part in the decision-making process: they advise the council on the courses of action open to them, and also on the consequences of taking such actions. When a decision has been taken, it is then the duty of appropriate officers of the council to implement it: to notify persons concerned and to take any executive decisions or other action necessary to give effect to the main decision. It is sometimes said that the officers give advice and take action, while the council decides all matters of policy; although basically true (for statutes almost invariably confer the power to exercise discretion on the authority itself) this does not clarify what happens in practice. 'Policy' is incapable of precise definition. What is policy for some local authorities in some circumstances may be regarded as routine administration by other authorities in different circumstances.

Executive Arrangements and Committees

1.15 The Local Government Act 2000, as now amended by the Local Government and Public Involvement in Health Act 2007, required each local authority in England and Wales to adopt 'executive arrangements' in one of a number of specified forms. 'Executive arrangements' are arrangements made by the authority for, and in connection with, the creation and operation of an executive for the authority where certain of the authority's functions are the responsibility of the executive. Local authorities are required to put in place scrutiny and overview committees. A division has been created within each local authority between the making of decisions, and the granting of those decisions. The purpose of the reforms is 'to deliver greater efficiency, transparency and accountability of local authorities', ensuring that decisions are taken more quickly and efficiently than under the previous system, and that bodies responsible for decisions can be more readily identified by the public and held to account in public by overview and scrutiny committees.

1.16 The executive must take one of the four specified forms.

1 a directly elected mayor and cabinet executive of two or more councillors appointed by the mayor;
2 a leader of the council and cabinet executive of two or more councillors appointed by the leader;
3 a directly elected mayor and council manager executive who is an officer of the authority;
4 such other form as is prescribed by regulations.

Executive arrangements proposed by local authorities must be submitted to the Secretary of State.

1.17 The Local Government Act 2000 sets out the functions that are, and are not, to be the responsibility of the executive of the council. In particular, the functions of town and country planning;

licensing and registration; health and safety at work and by-laws are (among others) expressly stated not to be executive responsibilities. Such functions will generally continue to be dealt with by the system established under the Local Government Act 1972.

1.18 In practice this will mean decisions are normaly taken pursuant to committee system. Committees, consisting of named councillors, are usually considerably smaller in membership than the council as a whole and are entrusted with specified functions of the council. There are no general rules, but a council of, say, 48 members may place about 12 councillors on each of its committees. Recently there has been a tendency to streamline committee organisation, leaving more routine matters to the discretion of officers. Thus, every county council will generally have a planning committee and a finance committee, and most district councils will have a planning committee and licensing committee, although details will vary from authority to authority. Every matter requiring a council decision within the terms of reference of a particular committee is first brought before the committee. The committee then considers the matter and either recommends a certain decision to the council, or may itself make the decision. Whether the committee decides on behalf of the council depends on whether the council has delegated to the committee power to take the decision on its behalf, either in that particular matter, or in matters of that kind, or falling within a particular class.

1.19 Section 101 of the Local Government Act 1972 confers on all local authorities power to arrange for any of its functions (except levying a charge or raising a loan) to be discharged by a committee, a sub-committee, or an officer. However, this does not authorise the delegation of any function to a committee comprising only one member: *R v Secretary of State for the Environment, ex p. London Borough of Hillingdon* [1986] 2 All ER 273.

1.20 Proceedings in committee are normally held in public and tend to be informal. Officers attend, volunteer advice, and often take part in the discussion, although any decision is taken on the vote or assent of the councillors present. Council meetings and meetings of specified committees, such as the licensing committee, are more formal; the press and members of the public are entitled to be present, unless they have been excluded by special resolution of the council passed because of the intention to discuss exempted information, such as facts regarding individual council employees (Local Government (Access to Information) Act 1985); and proceedings are conducted in accordance with the council's standing orders. Officers do not speak at a council meeting unless their advice is expressly requested, and as much business consists of receipt of reports from committees, discussion tends to be confined to more controversial topics.

1.21 Because of the presence of the press and public, party politics tend to be more obvious at council meetings. Sometimes in committee, members from opposing political parties will agree, and members of a single party may disagree with one another. In recent years, however, there has been a tendency for authorities to be more closely organized on party political lines. When this occurs, 'group' meetings may be held preceding the committee meetings. Thus on important matters, decisions at committee meetings can be 'rubber stamps' of decisions already taken at the group meeting of the political party in power on the council. It has been held that it is legitimate, when deciding how to vote, for a councillor to have regard to party loyalty and party policy, provided they do not 'dominate so as to exclude other considerations or deprive the councillor of real choice: *R v Waltham Forest London Borough Council, ex p. Baxter* [1988] 1 QB 419. However, the Local Ombudsman's finding of maladministration where members of a planning committee were heavily influenced by party political loyalty, which was not material to the planning application before them, was upheld by the court: *R v Local Commissioner for Administration in the North and North East England, ex p. Liverpool City Council* (2000) 2 LGLR 603.

1.22 The law relating to the conduct of members was radically overhauled by the Local Government Act 2000. Part III of that Act creates a statutory scheme for ethical regulation of members. The Secretary of State has directed that all local authorities must develop their own codes of conduct, although the Secretary of State has produced a model code and the mandatory provisions of it must be included in the local authority's code. Each member is under a duty to comply with the authority's code. Ethical issues will be considered by the local authority's standards committee, but complaints about conduct of members may be made to the Standards Boards for England and Wales which will generally investigate complaints through local authority Ethical Standards Officers. However council members are no longer subject to the former surcharge provisions which rendered them potentially personally liable for Council decisions.

1.23 The law requires that councils must meet at least four times a year. Most councils arrange committee meetings in a cycle, monthly or perhaps every 6 weeks, so that each committee will normally meet at least once between council meetings.

Officers' powers

1.24 All discretionary powers are conferred on a local authority in the first instance, but decisions may also now be made pursuant to the Executive arrangements described above; and under section 101 of the Local Government Act 1972, every local authority has wide powers to delegate any of its discretionary decisions to any of its officers; a power which is often used, especially in planning. But there must always be a clear delegation before an officer can decide on behalf of the authority. Therefore, when an officer of a council who was asked for information as to the planning position in respect of a particular piece of land carelessly gave the wrong information, saying that planning permission was not required, it was held by the courts that the council were not bound by this statement. It could not be taken as the decision of the council, as the officer had no power to act on their behalf in that case: *Southend-on-Sea Corporation v Hodgson (Wickford) Ltd* [1961] 2 All ER 46. This decision is still good law in circumstances where powers have not been expressly delegated to the officer concerned (see e.g. *Western Fish Products Ltd v Penwith DC* [1979] 77 LGR 185 and now *R v East Sussex County Council, ex p. Reprotech (Pebsham) Ltd* [2002] UKHL 8; [2003] 1 WLR 348).

1.25 Local authorities do not stand outside the common law in respect of acts of negligence by their officers and employees. However, the House of Lords has held that a local authority is not generally liable in negligence to owners or occupiers of buildings for failings in the authority's enforcement of the Building Regulations concerning the defective construction of those buildings: *Murphy v Brentwood District Council* [1990] 2 All ER 908. Local planning authorities are also not liable for negligence in the grant of planning permission: see *Strable v Dartford Borough Council* [1984] JPL 329; and *Lam v Brennan* [1997] 3 PLR 22.

1.26 An alternative non-judicial method by which an aggrieved individual may seek redress against a local authority's actions or inaction is to make a complaint to the Local Government Ombudsman under the Local Government Act 1974 (as amended) (see www.lgo.org.uk). If the Local Ombudsman finds that a complainant has suffered injustice as a consequence of maladministration by the local authority, he may publish such a finding and recommend a suitable remedy (which can include financial compensation). The local authority are obliged to have regard to the report, but they cannot be compelled in law to implement the Local Ombudsman's recommendations to alleviate the injustice. In recent years approximately 40% of complaints to the Local Ombudsman have been about housing matters, and a further 25% have concerned planning functions. The Local Government Ombudsman can be contacted at PO Box 4771, Coventry CV4 OEH or on telephone numbers 0300 061 0614, 0845 602 1983 or by email: advice@lgo.org.uk.

There is a separate Public Services Ombudsman for Wales (www.ombudsman-wales.org.uk) which, in addition to investigating administration by local authorities, also covers complaints concerning the Health Service, the Welsh Administration and Social Housing.

Finding the right officer

1.27 Architects in the course of their professional business are obliged to have dealings with numerous local authority officials. Table 7.1 shows the purposes for which a permission, licence, or certificate may have to be obtained from the local authority identifying the officers initially responsible (see Chapters 9 and 11). But first of all it is essential to ascertain the authority in whose area the site lies.

Local government: distribution of planning functions

1.28 Within Greater London, the London Borough Council (or, as the case may be, the City of London) is both the local planning authority and the mineral planning authority. The London Mayor must prepare and publish a 'spatial development strategy' (SDS). He is empowered to direct the local planning authority of a London Borough Council to refuse an application for planning permission of a prescribed description in any particular. He must monitor the implementation of the SDS and monitor the UDP of each London Borough Council so that it is in accordance with the SDS. Similarly, within the metropolitan areas outside London, the metropolitan district councils fulfil both local planning and mineral planning functions.

1.29 For non-metropolitan areas where there is a unitary authority, those unitary authorities are the local planning authority for all purposes within its area.

Table 7.1 Responsibilities of local authority officers

Subject matter	Officer	Local authority
Planning	Planning officer or surveyor	DC
Building regulations	Building inspector or surveyor	DC
Development in a private street	Surveyor	CC
Surface water sewerage	Engineer	SU
Sewer connections	Engineer	SU
Blocked sewers	Engineer	SU
Housing grants; housing generally	Environmental health officer or (sometimes) surveyor	DC
Height of chimneys or other clean air matters	Environmental health officer	DC
Petroleum licensing; most other licensing	Petroleum inspector (often environmental health officer or surveyor)	CC or DC
Music and dancing licences	Licensing officer*	
Alcohol licences	Licensing officer*	
Late Night Refreshment licences	Licensing officer*	

Key: CC, county council; DC, district council; SU, sewerage undertaker

Notes

A company operating under the Water Act 1989, whose functions may be exercised by the district council under an arrangement with the sewerage undertaker.

London. In Greater London, in all cases (except for liquor licences) the responsible authority is the London Borough Council or the Common Council of the City.

Planning. In planning matters the authority given above should be contacted in the first instance, although the county council may ultimately make the decision.

Roads. In the counties highway functions are commonly administered by district or divisional surveyors, responsible to the county surveyor but stationed locally often at district council offices.

In the case of trunk and special roads (motorways) the highway authority is the Secretary of State for Transport, but the local county surveyor acts as his agent at local level. Maintenance of urban roads may be claimed by the DC.

Under the Local Government (Miscellaneous Provisions) Act 1982, several activities are made subject to licensing (e.g. acupuncture, tattooing, take away food shops, etc.). These provisions are administered by the district council.

*Under Licensing Act 2003.

1.30 For non-metropolitan areas where there is a two-tier local government structure, the vast majority of development control functions are vested in the districts.

1.31 In Wales, the local planning authority is the county council or the county borough council. All local planning authorities and the National Parks Authority within Wales are required to prepare and maintain unitary development plans for their areas.

1.32 Within the national parks, the functions formerly vested in the Planning Board in the Peak District and Lake District Parks, and elsewhere in the county planning authority, now vest in the National Parks authority for that area (section 4A, Town and Country Planning Act 1990). In relation to tree preservation and replacement (sections 198 to 201, 206 to 209, and 211 to 214) and the powers under section 215 (power to require proper maintenance of land) the district planning authority whose area includes that part of the Park has concurrent jurisdiction (section 4(2)).

1.33 Within the Norfolk and Suffolk Broads, the Broads Authority is the sole district planning authority for non-county matters (Town and Country Planning Act 1990, section 5).

1.34 Overlooking this general structure, the Secretary of State for Communities and Local Government has wide-ranging supervisory powers. There is a right of appeal to the Secretary of State from all adverse development control decisions and enforcement notices, although not from the issue of breach of condition notice. The Secretary of State may remove jurisdiction from the local planning authority in particular cases by calling a planning application in for determination (Town and Country Planning Act 1990, section 77). The Secretary of State also oversees the making and adoption of development plans, with powers to prevent adoption of such plans (although these powers are rarely exercised).

1.35 The plan-led system has been radically overhauled by the Planning and Compulsory Purchase Act 2004 under which the former system of local plans, structure plans, or unitary development plans for unitary authorities, and Regional Planning Guidance has been replaced by a new system of Local Development Frameworks and Regional Spatial Strategies.

1.36 The Regional Spatial Strategies are documents produced by each Regional Planning Body setting out a more strategic analysis of development requirements for the region. Local Development Frameworks are prepared by local planning authorities. They are described as a folder of documents, each of which provides more detail on the policy approach to development in the local authority area. They will normally include a Core Strategy, containing the general thrust of the development strategy for the area, and site allocation and development control policies. There will usually be separate development plan documents to deal with waste and mineral developments prepared by the relevant local authority (usually the County Council outside London or in metropolitan areas). More detail on the workings and formulation of local development frameworks is provided in the Government's planning policy statement PPS12: Local Spatial Planning.

Local government: other functions

1.37 Outside London, county councils are responsible for fire services, main and district highways, refuse disposal, and a few other functions. Outside the metropolitan areas county councils are also responsible for education and welfare services, which in the metropolitan areas are the responsibility of the district councils.

1.38 All district councils are responsible for housing, refuse collection, drainage, clean air and public health generally (but not sewerage and water supply), development control, parks and open spaces, and building controls, etc. A district council may also (by arrangement with the county council) undertake the maintenance of urban roads (other than trunk roads), bridleways, and footpaths within its district. Detailed provisions as to the tendering of services by local authorities are now set out in the Local Government Act 1999 and the Local Government Act 2003 in the creation of best value authorities.

1.39 From 1974 to 1989 the provision and maintenance of sewers and sewerage disposal, together with water supply and distribution and the prevention of river pollution, was the responsibility of special authorities: the ten regional water authorities (nine in England, one in Wales). Under the Water Act 1989 the water industry was privatised and as a consequence the sewerage functions of the former water authorities have passed to successor companies, which are in most instances also responsible for water supply, except in those areas where this was formerly the responsibility of statutory water companies which remain in existence. Water and sewerage undertakers are forbidden from causing river pollution, the prevention of which is now the responsibility of the Environment Agency. The successor companies are constituted under the regime of the Companies Acts and are appointed by the Secretary of State to act as water and/or sewerage undertakers.

2 Other statutory bodies

English Heritage

2.01 The Historic Buildings and Monuments Commission for England, more commonly known as 'English Heritage', was established under section 32 of the National Heritage Act 1983. It is an executive non-departmental public body sponsored by the Department of Culture, Media and Sport. As a body corporate, its members are appointed by the Secretary of State, and serve for a maximum of 5 years. Its functions include making grants in relation to historic buildings and conservation areas, acquiring historic buildings, acquiring or becoming the guardian of ancient monuments, and undertaking archaeological investigation and publishing the results. It may prosecute for offences under the Ancient Monuments and Archaeological Areas Act 1989 or under the Planning (Listed Buildings and Conservation Areas) Act 1990. Within Greater London, it has the power, concurrently with the London Boroughs, to take enforcement action against breaches of listed building control (Planning (Listed Buildings and Conservation Areas) Act 1990, section 45).

2.02 Its duties are, so far as practicable in exercising its functions: to secure the preservation of ancient monuments and historic buildings in England; to promote the preservation and enhancement of the character and appearance of conservation areas situated in England; and to promote the public's enjoyment and advance their knowledge of ancient monuments and historic buildings situated in England (section 33 of the National Heritage Act 1983).

2.03 English Heritage plays an important role in the listing of buildings. Although ultimate responsibility for deciding which buildings should (and should not) be listed rests with the Secretary of State, English Heritage may compile lists of buildings of special architectural or historic interest for the Secretary of State's approval, and must be consulted by him before he compiles, approves, adds to or modifies any such list (Planning (Listed Buildings and Conservation Areas) Act 1990, section 1).

2.04 English Heritage must be consulted by the planning authority on a range of applications, including: the demolition in whole or part, or the material alteration, of a listed building in Greater London; development likely to affect the site of a scheduled monument or development likely to affect any Grade I or Grade II registered garden or park of special historic interest: Article 10, the Town and Country Planning (General Development Procedure) Order 1995 (SI 1995/419).

2.05 English Heritage publishes a wide range of advice on the care of historic buildings, such as *The Repair of Historic Buildings: Advice on Principles and Methods*, and its guidance on *The Conversion of Historic Farm Buildings*. Early consultation with English Heritage will often be useful.

Natural England and the Countryside Council for Wales

2.06 Section 1 of the Natural Environment and Rural Communities Act 2006 established Natural England, an independent body replacing English Nature and the Countryside Agency. Nature conservation functions previously exercisable in respect of Wales by the Nature Conservancy Council were transferred to the Countryside Council for Wales (CCW) (section 128 of the Environmental Protection Act 1990).

2.07 These two bodies are responsible for the establishment, maintenance and management of nature reserves, the notification and protection of (SSSIs), the provision of advice for the Secretary of State or the Welsh Assembly on the development and implementation of policies for, or affecting, nature conservation in their areas, the provision of advice and the dissemination of knowledge about nature conservation in their areas, and the commissioning or support of research which is relevant to their functions. They also advise on any endangered animal or plant which should be added to, or removed from, the lists of protected species. The general purpose of Natural England is to ensure that the natural environment is conserved, enhanced and managed for the benefit of present and future generations.

2.08 Natural England or CCW must be consulted by planning authorities before permission is granted for development of land in a SSSI, or in any consultation area around a SSSI, or for development which is likely to affect a SSSI or major development in an area of particular natural sensitivity or interest which may be affected: Article 10, Town and Country Planning (General Development Procedure Order) 1995 (SI 1995/419). Consultation areas are defined by English Nature and may extend up to a maximum of 2 kilometres from the boundary of the SSSI.

The Environment Agency

2.09 The Environment Agency was established under the Environment Act 1995 as a body corporate, and has inherited functions previously carried out by; the National Rivers Authority; the Waste Regulation Authorities; HM Inspectorate of Pollution; and certain functions of the Secretary of State in relation to radioactive substances, 'special category effluent' and sludge. The Agency has functions with respect to pollution control, water resources, environmental duties with respect to sites of special interest and flood defence.

2.10 Its principal aim in discharging its functions, as set out in section 4 of the Environment Act 1995, is 'so to protect or enhance the environment, taken as a whole, as to make the contribution towards attaining the objective of achieving sustainable development', in which regard the Agency receives guidance from Ministers on the extent of the contribution the Agency is expected to make.

2.11 The Agency must be consulted by the planning authority on any application for development involving: mining operations; the carrying out of works or operations in the bed of, or within 20 metres of the top of a bank of, a main river which has been notified to the local planning authority by the Agency as a main river; culverting or controlling the flow of any river or stream; the refining or storage of mineral oils or derivatives; the deposit of refuse or waste; use of land as a cemetery; fish farming; (with certain minor exceptions) the retention, treatment or disposal of sewage, trade waste, slurry or sludge; and, other than for minor development, land in area within Flood Zones 2 or 3, or Flood Zone 1 if it has critical drainage problems and has been notified by the Agency; and land of more than 1 hectare: Town and Country Planning (General Development Procedure) Order 1995, Article 10.

2.12 The functions carried out by the Environment Agency are, largely mirrored by those carried out by the Scottish Environment Protection Agency for Scotland.

Sports Council for England

2.13 The Sports Council for England, known as 'Sport England', is the government agency responsible for developing a world-class community sport system in England. Sport England must be consulted by local planning authorities on an application for development which is likely to prejudice or lead to the loss of the use of land being used as a playing field, or is on land which has been used as a playing field at any time in five years before the making of the planning application where the land remains undeveloped, or on land which is allocated for playing field use, or involves replacement of a grass pitch with an artificial surface: see Town and Country Planning (General Development Procedure) Order 1995, Article 10.

Health and Safety Executive

2.14 The Health and Safety Executive (HSE) was established by section 10 of the Health and Safety at Work etc Act 1974. The HSE must be notified of development within an area which has been notified to the local planning authority by the HSE because of the presence within the vicinity of toxic highly reactive, explosive or inflammable substances, where the development involves residential accommodation, or more than $250\,m^2$ of retail space, or more than $500\,m^2$ of office space or more than $750\,m^2$ of industrial processes or it is likely to result in a material increase in the number of persons working within the notified area.

3 Statutory undertakers: connections to services

3.01 When starting to design a building for a client, any architect is obliged at an early stage to consider the availability of mains services and the rights of his client as landowner regarding the various statutory undertakers: sewer and highway authorities, water, gas, and electricity supply undertakings, and possibly the water undertaker if it is proposed to use a water course as a means of disposing of effluent from the building. The legal provisions regulating these matters are discussed below.

Sewers

3.02 Sewers are generally channels (artificial or natural) used for conveying effluent (i.e. waste liquids – clear water, surface water from covered surfaces, land or buildings, foul water, or trade effluent) from two or more buildings not within the same curtilage. Curtilage is normally in non-technical terms, equivalent to the natural boundaries of a particular building; thus the curtilage of an ordinary dwelling house would often include the garage, the garden and its appurtenances, and any outbuildings.) By contrast, a conduit which takes effluent from one building only or from a number of buildings all within the same curtilage, is in law a 'drain' (see the Public Health Act 1936, the Water Industry Act 1991 and the Building Act 1984). This distinction is important, as a landowner never has any legal right to let his effluent flow into a drain belonging to another person (even if that other person is a local authority) unless he has acquired such a right by at least 20 years' use or as the result of an agreement with the other person (Chapter 2). The same rule applies to a private sewer; but if the conduit to which he proposes to drain his effluent is a public sewer, he will have certain valuable rights to use it.

3.03 All public sewers are vested in (i.e. owned by) the sewerage undertakers. A sewer is a public sewer if it existed as a sewer (regardless of who constructed it) before 1 October 1937, or if it was constructed by a local authority after 1 October 1937 and before 1 April 1974, or by a water authority before 1 November 1989, or by a sewerage undertaker after 1 November 1989 and was not designed to serve only property belonging to a local authority (e.g. a council housing estate), or if it has been adopted as a public sewer since 1 October 1937 (see Water Act 1989 and Water Industry Act 1991).

Rights to connection

3.04 By section 106 of the Water Industry Act 1991, the owner or occupier of any premises in the area of a sewerage undertaker, or the owner of any private sewer which drains premises, has a right to cause his own drains or private sewer to communicate with the public sewers or public lateral drains (which satisfy sewer standards) of that undertaker and to discharge foul and surface water from his premises to it. Connecting sewers or drains from the premises to the public sewer must be constructed at the expense of the landowner concerned. Sometimes – but not often – the sewerage undertaker may itself construct 'laterals', or connecting drains leading from the main sewer to the boundary of the street to which house drains may be connected.

3.05 There are a few exceptions to this general rule:

1 No substance likely to injure the sewer or to interfere with the free flow of its contents, no chemical refuse or waste stream, or any petroleum spirit or calcium carbide, may be caused to flow into a public sewer (Water Industry Act 1991, section 111).

2 The general rule does not apply to trade effluents (section 106(2)(a)).

3 The general rule does not permit a communication directly with a storm-water overflow sewer (section 106(2)(c)).

4 Where separate public sewers are provided for foul and for surface water, foul water may not be discharged into a sewer provided for surface water, and surface water may not, without the consent of the sewerage undertaker, be discharged into a sewer provided for foul water (section 106(2)(b)). It is particularly important that an architect should know whether the undertaker's sewerage network is designed on the separate system, as he may in turn have to provide a separate drainage for the building he is designing.

Procedure

3.06 A person wishing to connect his sewer or drain to a public sewer must give the sewerage undertaker written notice of his proposal, and the undertaker may within 21 days of such notice refuse to permit him to make the communication if the mode of construction or condition of the drain or sewer is such that the making of the communication would be prejudicial to their sewerage system (section 106(4) of the Act), but they may not so refuse for any other reason. Any dispute with the undertaker under these provisions may be settled by way of an application to the local magistrates, or in some cases by a reference to arbitration.

3.07 Alternatively, where proposals have been served on the undertaker, the undertaker may within 14 days of service give notice that it intends to make the communication to the public sewer itself (section 107 of the Act). The private landowner is then obliged to permit the undertaker to do the work of making the house drains or sewer connect with the public sewer, and he has to bear the sewerage undertaker's reasonable expenses so incurred. The undertaker is not obliged to make the communication until his reasonable estimate of the cost has been paid, or security for such payment has been given.

3.08 When making the communication, the undertaker (or the private owner if he is allowed to do the work himself) has power as necessary to break open any street (section 107(6) of the Act).

Approval of drainage

3.09 The arrangements proposed to be made for the 'satisfactory provision' for drainage of a building must be approved by the district council or London Borough Council at the time when the building plans are considered under the Building Regulations (see Building Act 1984, section 21 and Chapter 9). Disposal of the effluent may be to a public sewer, or to a cesspool or private septic tank, and in the case of surface water, to a highway drain or a watercourse or to the sea. In this instance it should be noted that the powers remain with the district council and have not been transferred to the sewerage undertaker.

3.10 If there is no existing main sewer into which the property could be drained, the owner or occupier (usually with the owners, etc., of other premises) may requisition the sewerage undertaker to provide a public sewer, under section 98 of the Water Industry Act 1991. They must then satisfy conditions specified by the undertaker, the most important of which is likely to be that those requisitioning the sewer shall undertake to meet any 'relevant deficit' of the undertaker in consequence of constructing the sewer. This section applies only to sewers to be used for domestic purposes.

Highway drains

3.11 A landowner has no legal right to cause his drains (or sewers) to be connected with a highway drain, and this applies equally to surface water drains taking effluent from roads and paved surfaces on a private housing estate. Such drains may, in accordance with the statutory provisions outlined above, be connected with a public sewer, but if it is desired to connect with a drain or sewer provided for the drainage of a highway and vested in the highway authority, the consent of the highway authority must first be obtained. The highway authority will normally be the county council or unitary authority.

3.12 A public sewer may be used to take surface water from a highway, but that does not affect its status as a public sewer, nor does the fact that house drains may in the past have been connected (probably unlawfully) with a highway drain convert such highway drain into a public sewer (*Rickarby v New Forest RDC* [1910] 26 TLR 586). It is only to public sewers that drains or sewers may be connected as of right.

Rivers

3.13 If it is desired to discharge effluent into a watercourse the consent of the Environment Agency must be obtained for the making of a new or altered discharge of trade or sewage effluent under section 88(2) of the Water Resources Act 1991. Consents may be granted subject to conditions. The Secretary of State may direct particular applications for consent to be transmitted to him or her, and may cause an inquiry to be held into the application (Water Resources Act 1991, Schedule 10, as amended by Schedule 22 of the Environment Act 1995).

3.14 If a person causes or knowingly permits the discharge of any poisonous, noxious or polluting matter or any waste matter into a watercourse without the permission of the Environment Agency, he commits an offence under section 85 of the Water Resources Act 1991.

The sea

3.15 A private landowner has at common law no legal right to discharge his sewage or other polluting matter in to the sea; indeed, as the Crown originally owned the foreshore between high and low tides, he might not have any legal right to take his drain or sewer as far as the water. However, even if such a right can be acquired (and now the Crown's rights have in many cases been sold or leased to local authorities or private landowners) it seems that the discharge of sewage by means of a pipe into the sea is subject to the same control of the Environment Agency (see Water Resources Act 1991: and the definition of 'controlled waters' in section 104, which includes coastal waters and territorial waters).

3.16 There must also be no nuisance caused as a consequence, and no breach of any local by-law made by a sea fisheries committee prohibiting the discharge of matter detrimental to sea fish or sea fishing (Sea Fisheries Regulations Act 1966, section 5). If effluent discharging into the sea does cause a nuisance, any person harmed can take proceedings for an injunction and/or damages, as in *Foster v Warblington UDC* [1906] 1 KB 648, where guests at a banquet were poisoned from oysters taken from a bed which had been affected by sewage.

Trade effluents

3.17 In the case of a proposed discharge of 'trade effluent', the special controls of the Water Industry Act 1991, Chapter III, apply. 'Trade effluent' is defined in the Act of 1991 as meaning 'any liquid, either with or without particles of matter in suspension therein, which is wholly or in part produced by the course of any trade or industry carried on at trade premises, and, in relation to any trade premises, means any such liquid as aforesaid which is so produced in the course of any trade or industry carried on at those premises, but does not include domestic sewage' (1991 Act, section 141(1)). 'Trade premises' are defined as 'any premises used or intended to be used for carrying on any trade or industry' (including agriculture, horticulture, fish farming and scientific research) (Water Industry Act 1991, sections 141(1) and 141(2)).

3.18 Where it is intended to discharge trade effluent as defined above into a public sewer, consent must first be obtained from the sewerage undertaker (see Water Industry Act 1991, section 118). This is done by the owner or occupier of the premises serving on the undertaker a 'trade effluent notice' under section 119. This must specify (in writing) the nature or composition of the proposed effluent, the maximum quantity to be discharged in any one day, and the highest proposed rate of discharge of the effluent. From a date yet to be appointed, the legislation may be amended to include a requirement to identify the steps proposed to be taken in relation to the discharge for minimising the polluting effects on any controlled waters and the impact of the discharge on the sewerage services. This notice (for which there is no standard form) is then treated by the undertaker as an application for their consent to the proposed discharge. No effluent may then be discharged for a period of 2 months (or such less time as may be agreed by the undertaker).

3.19 A decision, when given by the undertaker, may be a refusal to permit the discharge or a consent. A consent may be given subject to conditions as to a number of matters 'including a payment by the occupier of the trade premises of charges for the reception and disposal of the effluent', as specified in section 121 of the Water Industry Act 1991. These conditions may be varied (not more frequently than once every two years) by direction given by the sewerage undertaker (section 124). The owner or occupier of trade premises has a right of appeal to the Water Services Regulation Authority against a refusal of consent to a discharge, against the conditions imposed in such a consent, or against a direction subsequently given varying the conditions (Water Industry Act 1991, sections 122 and 126). On appeal, the Authority may review all the conditions, whether or not they have been appealed against, and substitute for them any other set of conditions or annul any of the conditions (section 122(3)).

3.20 In practice, however, it is frequently desirable for an industrialist's professional advisers to discuss disposal of trade effluent with the officers of the sewerage undertaker, with a view to an agreement being entered into between the owner of the premises and the undertaker under section 129 of the Water Industry Act 1991. This will avoid the need to serve a trade effluent notice, and better terms can often be obtained by negotiation than by the more formal procedure of the trade effluent notice. The contents of any such agreement becomes public property, as a copy has to be kept at the sewerage undertaker's offices and made available for inspection and copying by any person (Water Industry Act 1991, section 196).

Water supply

3.21 The water supply authority will be the local water undertaker (a company appointed for a designated area of England and Wales by the Secretary of State (see Water Industry Act 1991, section 6), but where before 1989 supply was made by a statutory water company, this may remain in existence. The statutory water companies may have their own private Acts of Parliament regulating their affairs. Readers dealing in practice with a particular water undertaking should ascertain whether there are any local statutory variations.

Rights to connection: domestic premises

3.22 If the owner or occupier of premises which consist in the whole or any part of a building, or any premises on which any person is proposing to erect any building or part of a building, within the area served by a water undertaker wishes to have a supply for domestic purposes, he may serve a notice requiring the undertaker to connect a service pipe to those premises to provide a supply of water for domestic purposes (Water Industry Act 1991, section 45).

3.23 The obligation is to provide a *connection*. The undertaker is only required to lay that part of the service pipe serving the premises which leads from the main to the boundary of the street in which the main is laid or to the stopcock; the laying of the remainder is the responsibility of the owner or occupier. If the supply pipe passes through any property belonging to another owner, his consent must be obtained in the form of an express easement or a licence (Chapter 2). Any breaking up of streets must be effected by the undertakers and not by the owner requiring the supply.

3.24 Where a notice has been served under section 45, the undertaker is under a duty to make the connection. This must generally be done within 21 days of the service of the connection notice or, where it is necessary for the person serving the notice to lay any part of the service pipe himself, within 21 days of the date on which he gives notice stating that the pipe has been laid. Work carried out by the undertaker will be done at the expense of the person requesting the connection, and the undertaker may make it a condition of installation that a meter is installed, and may insist that the plumbing of the premises is compatible with such a meter (section 47).

3.25 Once a connection has been made, the undertaker is under a duty to provide a supply of water. The undertaker will have an excuse for not providing a supply if such failure is due to the carrying out of 'necessary works' (Water Industry Act 1991, section 60).

3.26 This assumes, of course, that the water main in the nearest street is within a reasonable distance from the house or other premises to be served. Where the main is not readily available, the owner of the premises may serve a requisition on the undertaker requiring them to extend their mains (Water Industry Act 1991, sections 41–43A). Where such a notice is served the water undertaker may require the owner to undertake to pay an annual sum, not exceeding the amount (if any) by which the water charges payable for the use during that year of that main are exceeded by the annual borrowing costs of a loan of the amount required for the provision of main. Such payments may be levied for a maximum of 12 years following the provision of the main (Water Industry Act 1991, section 42). Provided those conditions have been satisfied, the water undertaker must extend their main within a period of three months (Water Industry Act 1991, section 44).

Rights to connection: non-domestic premises

3.27 Owners or occupiers of premises requiring a supply of water for industrial or other (non-domestic) purposes or for premises not including the whole or any part of a building, must come to terms for a supply with the undertakers or, failing agreement, according to terms determined by the Director General of Water Services (Water Industry Act 1991, sections 55 and 56).

Gas supply

3.28 Following the privatisation of the gas industry in 1986, the privileges previously conferred on the British Gas Corporation have been abolished, and gas is now supplied by a number of different companies. Under the Gas Act 1995, the Gas and Electricity Markets Authority may grant licences: (1) to public gas transporters, authorising them to carry gas through pipes to any premises in their authorised area and to convey gas to any pipeline system operated by another transporter; (2) to gas interconnectors; and (3) to gas suppliers and shippers, authorising them to supply gas to specified premises. A person may not hold licences for both the public transport and the supply of gas (sections 6–7).

3.29 If the owner or occupier of premises requires a supply of gas for any purpose (not necessarily domestic), he may serve a notice on the public gas transporter for the area specifying the premises, and the day on which it is desired the service shall begin – and a reasonable time must be given (Gas Act 1986, section 10, as amended by the Gas Act 1995). The transporter must comply with such a request, but only if the premises are within 23 metres of any of their mains, not being a main used for a separate supply for industrial purposes or for conveying gas in bulk, or if they could be connected to any such main by a pipe supplied and laid by the owner or occupier of the premises.

Electricity supply

3.30 The Electricity Act 1989 provided for the privatising of the generation and supply of electricity. The Gas and Electricity Markets Authority is authorised to license persons to generate, transmit, distribute and supply electricity or participate in the operation of an electricity interconnector, in designated areas (1989 Act, section 6).

3.31 Under section 16 of the 1989 Act, a licensed electricity distributor for an area is under a duty to make or give a connection to premises where requested by the owner or occupier. The owner of occupier must serve a notice requiring the distributor to offer terms, specifying the premises, the date by which the connection should be made, and the maximum power which may be required. Where such a request necessitates the provision of electrical lines or plant by the public electricity supplier, the supplied may require any expenses reasonably incurred in providing the supply to be paid by the consumer requesting the supply (Act 1989, section 19). Any dispute arising out of the above obligations may be referred by either the consumer or supplier to the Authority for resolution (Act 1989, section 23).

Electronic Communications

3.32 The Telecommunications Act 1984 provided for the privatisation of British Telecommunications. Today consumers can obtain communication services from a wide variety of licensed operators. The terms for the provision of communications services depends upon: (1) the licence conditions regulating the particular communications company, as approved by Ofcom under the Communications Act 2003, the Telecommunications Act 1984 and the Wireless Telegraphy Act 2006, and (2) the standard contracts offered by the specific company supplying the service.

Construction of mains

3.33 All the utility undertakings have inherent powers to negotiate on terms with private landowners for the grant of easements or 'wayleaves' (Chapter 2) to enable them to place mains, cables, wires, apparatus, and so on over or under privately owned land. They also have powers to break open public streets for the purpose of constructing mains. Water and sewerage undertakers (Water Industry Act 1991, Schedule 6), gas transporters (Gas Act 1986, Schedule 3), electricity suppliers (Electricity Act 1989, Schedule 16) and licensed communications operators (Telecommunications Act 1984, Schedule 2, as amended by the Communications Act 2003, Schedule 3) all have statutory powers enabling them to place such mains and apparatus in private land, without the consent of the landowner or occupier concerned, on payment of proper compensation. Private persons have no such compulsory rights, although rights may be compulsorily acquired for an oil or other pipeline under the Pipelines Act 1962.

3.34 All the utility undertakers can also be authorised, without the consent of the landowner, to place their mains, apparatus, etc., on 'controlled land' (land forming part of a street or highway maintainable or prospectively maintainable at public expense) or in land between the boundary of such a highway and any improvement line prescribed for the street (New Roads and Street Works Act 1991, Part III).

4 Private streets

4.01 It is not within the scope of this chapter to describe the whole law governing the making up of a private street by county councils at the expense of the frontagers to such a street, but the special rules that regulate the construction of a building in a 'private street' are outlined.

Definition

4.02 A private street may or may not be a highway (i.e. any way, footpath, bridlepath, or carriageway over which members of the public have rights to pass and repass). The word 'private' does not mean that it is necessarily closed to the public (although it may be), but that the street has not been adopted by a highway authority, and therefore it is not maintainable by them on behalf of the public at the public expense. It must also be a 'street', an expression which has not been precisely defined, but which includes a cul-de-sac, lane, or passage (Highways Act 1980, section 331(1)). This does not mean, that every country road is a street; it has been said that

> 'what one has to find before one can determine that the highway in question is a street, is that the highway has become a street in the ordinary acceptation of that word, because by reason of the number of houses, their continuity and their proximity to one another, what would be a road or highway has been converted into a street'.
>
> (*Attorney General v Laird* [1925] 1 Ch 318 at p. 329)

Advance payments code

4.03 As a general principle, before a new building may be erected in a new street, the developer must either pay to the local authority or secure to their satisfaction (by means of a bond or mortgage, etc.), a sum equivalent to the estimated cost, apportioned to the extent of the frontage of the proposed building to the private street, of carrying out street works to such an extent that the street would be adopted by the highway authority (the advance payments code – Highways Act 1980, section 219). 'Street works' means sewering, levelling, paving, metalling, flagging, channelling, making good, and lighting. The standards required are not specified in the legislation, but clearly they must not be unreasonably stringent. In general, the standard prevailing for similar streets in the authority's district is required.

Section 38 of Highways Act 1980

4.04 The need to pay or give security in advance of the building work being started can be avoided if an agreement has been entered into with the local authority under section 38 of the Highways Act 1980, pursuant to an exception from the general principle contained in section 219(4)(d) of that Act.

4.05 Under section 38, the local authority may enter into an agreement with the developer of land on either side or both sides of a private street; the authority can agree to adopt the street as a highway maintainable at public expense when all the street works have been carried out to their satisfaction, and the developer agrees to carry them out within a stated time. If the works are not so carried out, the local authority can still use their statutory powers to carry out the works (or to complete them), at the expense of the frontagers; it is therefore customary for the developer to enter into a bond for his performance with a bank or an insurance company.

4.06 Such an agreement takes the street, or the part of the street to which the agreement relates, outside the operation of the above general principles. The developer can then sell building plots or completed houses 'free of road charges' to purchasers. Though the street may not have been made up at the time of purchase, the purchaser is protected, as the developer has agreed to make up the street; if he fails to carry out his promise, the local authority will be able to sue on the bond and recover sufficient to pay for street

works' expenses without having to charge them to the frontagers. If the authority should proceed against the frontagers, they in turn normally have a remedy against the developer and on the bond, but this may depend on the terms of their purchase.

4.07 The architect is not necessarily professionally concerned in such matters, but it is suggested that it is his duty to be aware of the potential expense to his client of building in an unmade private street, and he should advise his client to consult his solicitor in any difficult case, or where the exact legal position is not clear.

5 Grants

5.01 Circumstances in which a building owner is able to obtain a grant from the local authority (in this case, the district council) for some alteration or extension of his dwelling are considered below. All statutory provisions considered here concern dwelling-houses (or flats and so on), but it may be possible in development areas and enterprise zones (Local Government, Planning and Land Act 1980) to obtain grants for industrial development.

5.02 Up until July 2003, grants were available pursuant to the Housing Grants, Construction and Regeneration Act 1996. From 18 July 2003 that Act was substantively repealed and replaced by the Regulatory Reform (Housing Assistance) (England and Wales) Order 2002. The Government has published Circular guidance in Circular 05/2003 *Housing Renewal* which should be read by all architects when seeking to obtain grant money on behalf of their clients in connection with alteration or extension of dwellings, along with any relevant guidance or policy applicable to the relevant local authority area in question.

5.03 Under the Order, for the purpose of improving living conditions in their area, local authorities may provide direct or indirect assistance to a person for the purposes of enabling him:

(a) to acquire living accommodation;
(b) to adapt or improve living accommodation;
(c) to repair living accommodation;
(d) to demolish buildings comprising or including living accommodation;
(e) where buildings comprising or including living accommodation have been demolished, to construct buildings that comprise or include replacement living accommodation.

5.04 Assistance may be provided in any form and may be subject to conditions, including as to repayment or making a contribution towards the assisted work. Examples of possible conditions, such as to eligibility and payment are given in the guidance. Before imposing a condition as to repayment or contribution the authority must have regard to the ability of the person to make the repayment or contribution. The primary methods of assistance, will be grants or loans, although other forms of assistance, such as discounted materials, or access to a tool hire scheme, may also be provided. A mandatory grant remains available for the provision of facilities for a disabled person in a dwelling. Applicants must be 18 years old and are means tested. There is a maximum level of grant. For further information, see the terms of the above Order.

Agriculture

5.05 Under the Hill Farming Act 1946 and Livestock Rearing Act 1951, a grant may be obtained from the Minister of Agriculture, Fisheries and Food towards the cost of improving a dwelling as part of a scheme prepared with 'a view to the rehabilitation of livestock rearing land'.

Conversion of closets

5.06 A grant not exceeding half the cost may be claimed towards the expenditure incurred by the owners of a dwelling in converting an earth or pail closet to a WC, either pursuant to a notice served by the authority, or where it is proposed to undertake the work voluntarily. In the latter case the grant is payable at the local authority's discretion (Building Act 1984, section 66).

Clean air

5.07 Where a private dwelling (an expression which includes part of a house) is situated within a smoke control area, a grant may be claimed from the local authority amounting to 70% of the expenditure reasonably incurred in adapting any fireplace or fireplaces in the dwelling to enable them to burn only 'authorised fuels' such as gas, electricity, coke, or specially prepared solid fuels (Clean Air Act 1993, section 25 and Schedule 2). A similar grant may be obtainable for certain religious buildings (section 26).

Historic buildings

5.08 In the case of a building of historic or architectural interest, whether or not it is 'listed' as such (under section 1 of the Planning (Listed Buildings and Conservation Areas) Act 1990), a grant towards the cost of repair or maintenance may be obtained from the local authority under section 57 of the 1990 Act, but such grants are entirely discretionary and no amounts are specified in the legislation. Grants and loans are also available from English Heritage for the maintenance and repair of buildings of outstanding historical or architectural interest. The power to make such payments is found in section 3A of the Historic Buildings and Ancient Monuments Act 1953. Normally, the Commission only make payments for the maintenance and repair (excluding routine work) of outstanding Grade I or II buildings. The Commission do not normally make payments towards repair schemes costing less than £10,000. Further information on potential funds available in respect of historic buildings may be obtained from the Funds for Historic Buildings website: www.ffhb.org.uk. Where grants are given they are generally at the rate of 40% of approved expenditure. A similar scheme is administered in Wales.

Airport noise

5.09 Under the Civil Aviation Act 1982, section 79, a grant may be obtained from the manager of the aerodrome for a building 'near' an aerodrome towards the cost of insulating it, or any part of it, against noise attributable to the use of the aerodrome. The details of such grants are specified in schemes approved by the Secretary of State for Transport, and further particulars are obtainable from the Secretary of State or usually from the relevant airport operator.

Water supply

5.10 The local authority has a discretionary power to make a grant towards all or any part of the expenses incurred in the provision of a separate service pipe for the supply of water for any house which has a piped supply from a main, but which does not have a separate service pipe (Housing Act 1985, section 523).

6 Housing associations and societies

6.01 A housing association may be formed on a charitable basis for provision of houses for those in need, or for special groups of persons, such as the elderly or handicapped, in a specified area. Such an association may also be constituted by an industrial firm for housing its employees, or by a group of persons proposing to build its own homes by voluntary (or part voluntary) and co-operative labour. Frequently such associations are strictly housing societies having acquired corporate personality by registration with the Registrar of Friendly Societies. However, a housing association (which may be incorporated as a company under the Companies Acts, or by other means) which complies with the provisions of the Housing Acts (see definition in section 1 of the Housing Associations Act 1985) and, in particular, does not trade for profit, is entitled to be considered for certain benefits under the

Housing Acts. Tenants of a housing association who have occupied their homes for at least five years will have a right to purchase the dwelling under Part V of the Housing Act 1985.

Benefits

6.02 First, the association may be able to obtain 'assistance' from the local housing authority in whose area they propose to build. This may mean making arrangements so that the association can improve existing council-owned houses, or there is an acquisition of land by the local authority, which can then be sold or leased to the association for building houses; or, with the consent of the Secretary of State for the Environment, the authority may make grants or loans on mortgages (at favourable rates of interest – usually 0.25% above the ruling rate charged to local authorities by the Public Works Loan Board) to the association to enable them to build houses. They may be able to obtain a grant from the Housing Corporation (or in Wales a separate organisation called Housing for Wales, Part II of the Housing Act 1988) towards the expenses of forming and running the association (Housing Act 1988, section 50). Registered housing associations may also be able to obtain grants from the Secretary of State where the associations' activities have incurred a liability for income or corporation tax (Housing Act 1988, section 54).

Housing Corporation loans

6.03 These provisions depend on the goodwill of the local authority; a housing association cannot insist on being given assistance. As an alternative, an association may be able to get help by ways of loans for obtaining land and general advice from the Housing Corporation, a public body set up under the Housing Act 1964.

Setting up a housing association

6.04 In practice people proposing to form a housing society would be well advised to obtain advice from the Housing Corporation (Maple House, 149 Tottenham Court Rd, London W1P 0BN or telephone 0845 230 7000), and those proposing to set up an association should get in touch with the National Housing Federation (Lion Court, 25 Procter Street, London WC1V 6NY).

7 Special premises

7.01 If an architect is designing any kind of building, he must take into account the controls exercised under town and country planning legislation (Chapter 11) and under the Building Regulations (Chapter 9); and he must consider the question of sewerage and mains services and the other matters discussed in this chapter. But if his building is of a specialised kind, or is to be used for some specialised purpose, additional controls may have to be considered; the more usual types of special control are outlined below.

Premises for Sale & Supply of Alcohol

7.02 Premises for the retail sale of alcohol, such as a public house, restaurant or hotel, must be licensed by the local authority under the Licensing Act 2003. The suitability of the premises for the proposed use, including the ability to comply with relevant conditions, may be relevant. Applications will normally be granted unless the local authority raises an objection to the proposal. The licensing authority will advertise and consult upon applications, taking advice from the police, the officer of the local fire brigade, an environmental health officer, and the local planning authority. Each licensing authority is required to produce a statement of licensing policy which should be examined when making such applications. An appeal against an adverse decision of the licensing authority lies to the magistrates' court.

Theatres and cinemas

7.03 The Licensing Act 2003 also now covers the licensing of the provision of regulated entertainment including theatres and cinemas, whereas previously such controls were all contained in either the Theatre Act 1968 and the Cinemas Act 1985.

Hotels

7.04 Hotels are no longer under specific fire certificate obligations that previously existed under the Fire Precautions Act 1971. However hotels, as with other premises, are under a general duty to ensure, so far as reasonably practicable the safety of employees, and are under a general duty in relation to non-employees to take such fire precautions as may reasonably be required in the circumstances to ensure premises are safe. There is also a duty to carry out a risk assessment: see Regulatory Reform (Fire Safety) Order 2005 (SI 2005/1541).

Shops and offices

7.05 Shops, offices, and railway premises where persons other than close relatives of the employer are employed to work are subject to control by the district council, under the Offices, Shops and Railway Premises Act 1963, provided the time worked at the premises exceeds 21 hours a week (sections 1–3). This Act provides for such matters as cleanliness, temperature within rooms, ventilation, lighting, and the provision of WCs (if necessary for both sexes), washing accommodation, and so on. The standards specified are detailed, and the Act and regulations made thereunder should be referred to by architects designing such a building. See also the Workplace (Health, Safety and Welfare) Regulations 1992 (SI 1992/3004). Fire requirements are now governed by the Regulatory Reform (Fire Safety) Order 2005 (SI 2005/1541), under which there are general duties to take such fire precautions as may reasonably be required in the circumstances to ensure premises are safe.

Factories

7.06 The Factories Act 1961 imposes special control over certain specialised constructional matters in a factory (as defined in Factories Act 1961, section 175); there is no special control over plans (other than the normal controls of the planning legislation and the Building Regulations), but if the requirements of the Act are not met in a particular factory, the occupier or (in a tenement factory) the owner will be liable to be prosecuted for an offence. Many of these requirements relate to the use and fencing of machinery, keeping walls and floors clean, and so on, and as such they are not of direct concern to the architect.

7.07 The fire certificate legislation for factories, as with offices and shops, has now been changed by the Regulatory Reform (Fire Safety) Order 2005.

7.08 The effluent from a factory's sewers or drains may well be 'trade effluent' and will then be subject to the special control of the Water Industry Act 1991, Chapter III.

7.09 Under the Clean Air Act 1993 factories are subject to several constructional controls operating quite independently of the Building Regulations, but administered by the same local authorities (district councils). Thus any furnace installed in a building which will be used to burn pulverised fuel, or to burn any other solid matter at a rate of 45.4 kg per hour or more, or any liquid or gaseous matter at a rate of 366.4 kW or more, must be provided with plant for arresting emissions of grit and dust which has been approved by the local authority or has been installed with plans and specifications submitted to and approved by the local authority (Clean Air Act 1993, section 6).

7.10 Limits are set by regulations for the rates of emission of grit and dust, and there are certain exemptions from the provisions of section 5 (see the Clean Air (Emissions of Grit and Dust from Furnaces) Regulations 1971). In addition, a furnace of a type to which the section applies (section 14: see 1993 Act), may not be used in a building unless the height of the chimney serving the furnace has been approved by the local authority (1993 Act, section 15).

Petroleum

7.11 Any premises used for keeping petroleum spirit must be licensed by the county council; otherwise the occupier is guilty of an offence (Petroleum Consolidation Act 1928, section 1). The only exception is when the spirit is kept in separate vessels containing not more than 0.57 litre, with the total quantity not exceeding 15 litres. Detailed conditions are usually imposed when such a licence is granted, and these normally follow the model conditions recommended by the Home Office. Petroleum licences are usually renewable each year at a fee (section 2(2) and 4).

Food premises

7.12 If any part of the premises is used for a business involving food, the more stringent provisions of the Food Hygiene (England) Regulations 2006 (SI 2006/14) made under the European Communities Act 1972 and under the Food Safety Act 1990 must be observed. Premises used as a slaughterhouse or a knacker's yard for the slaughter of animals need to be licensed under the Slaughterhouses Act 1974.

Miscellaneous

7.13 Licences from the district council are also required for the use of premises as a shop for the sale of pet animals (Pet Animals Act 1951), for storage or sale of scrap metal (Scrap Metal Dealers Act 1964), for boarding cats and dogs (Animal Boarding Establishments Act 1963) or for guard dog kennels (Guard Dogs Act 1975), and for keeping a riding establishment (Riding Establishment Acts 1964 and 1970). Childrens Homes, Independent Hospitals and Care Homes must now be registered by the Secretary of State under the Care Standards Act 2000. In all these cases the suitability or otherwise of the premises for the particular purpose may be an issue in the grant or refusal of the licence.

7.14 Caravan sites used for human habitation also need a licence in addition to planning permission (Caravan Sites and Control of Development Act 1960, Part 1), and detailed conditions as to hygiene and sanitary requirements are customarily imposed. In many districts it will also be necessary to obtain a licence from the council if premises are to be used as a sex shop or for the practice of tattooing or acupuncture or electrolysis or ear-piercing (Local Government (Miscellaneous Provisions) Act 1982).

7.15 Premises serving late night refreshment, including take-away food shops, will require a licence from the local authority under the Licensing Act 2003.

*This chapter draws heavily on the chapter written for the first edition by Professor J. F. Garner.

8

Statutory authorities in Scotland

ROBIN FLETCHER

1 Introduction: government in Scotland

1.01 The Scotland Act 1998 devolves many central government functions to the Scottish Executive. Law-making for these functions is devolved to the Scottish Parliament. Regulation of the architectural profession is reserved to Westminster. Devolved matters relevant to architectural practice in Scotland include:

Local government
Housing
Land-use, planning and building control
Inland waterways
Liquor licensing
Environmental protection
Built heritage
Natural heritage
Road transport

The substantive law in devolved areas continues as before until altered by the Scottish Parliament. Functions previously exercised by the Secretary of State for Scotland in relation to matters now devolved, for example in relation to planning, are exercised by the Scottish Ministers.

Local authorities

1.02 The Local Government etc. (Scotland) Act 1994 created 32 single-tier, all-purpose, local government authorities in Scotland. Rockall is part of the Western Isles authority area. In general the new authorities inherit and exercise for their area all functions previously confided to regional, district and islands councils. Sewerage and water, however, have been reorganized and removed from local authority control (without, as yet, being privatized). At the same time as the 1994 Act abolished the strategically sized regional councils, it recognized in a variety of ways the need for inter-local authority cooperation: structure plans may extend to the district of more than one local authority; local authorities have power to make cooperative arrangements for education; there are only eight police authorities, six of which are joint boards comprising up to twelve local authorities; there are, similarly, eight fire brigades; there is a Strathclyde Passenger Transport Authority; and the Act generally encourages the formation of joint boards involving two or more councils for the more efficient discharge of other functions. Representative community councils with no statutory functions continue as previously.

1.03 Acts and proceedings of the Scottish Executive, the Scottish Parliament, local authorities, water and sewerage authorities and joint boards and other statutory authorities are subject to judicial review. This means, among other things, that there may be a remedy even where the specific legislation does not provide a right of appeal.

Local government officers and committees

1.04 Local councils are elected every three years. Councils have to choose a convener and may also choose a deputy convener. Councils appoint officials and staff to enable them to carry out their statutory functions. A chief social work officer and certain other officials have to be appointed. Otherwise councils have wide discretion in the matter of their internal organization. The top official, responsible for coordinating the various branches of the authority's activity, tends to be styled 'Chief Executive'. Departmental chiefs may be called 'directors', 'managers', 'heads', etc. From the architect's point of view the key officials will be in the departments, which go by many different names, responsible for planning and building control. Certain officials, such as the assessor/council tax registration officer and electoral registration officer, have specific statutory duties which they must perform regardless of any instructions from the authority.

1.05 Much of the work of local councils is delegated to committees. There is likely to be a committee for each service department, such as development, education or housing, with sub-committees for each departmental section. Policy may be left to the appropriate service committee in the area of its responsibility. In addition to standing committees such as these, the authority may also set up special committees from time to time to deal with particular problems as they arise.

1.06 In general, committees are composed of council members only. Employed officials are present at committee meetings to give advice when required, but without the right to vote.

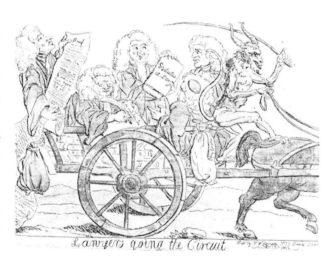

Lawyers going the Circuit

Scottish Water

1.07 The Water Industry (Scotland) Act 2002 provides for the establishment of a nationwide authority Scottish Water as successor to the three regional authorities which previously exercised water and sewerage functions under the 1994 Act. The property and functions of the existing authorities have now transferred to Scottish Water.

National Parks

1.08 Special considerations may apply to development within national parks designated in terms of orders made under the National Parks (Scotland) Act 2000. Various regulatory functions, including planning functions, may be devolved upon or transferred to national parks' authorities. Two national parks have been designated: Loch Lomond & the Trossachs and Grampians.

2 Connection to services

2.01 The 2002 Act is primarily concerned with organization and does not re-enact or spell out in detail the powers and functions which have been transferred from the old to the new authorities. The main local authority functions for present purposes are to be found in the Building (Scotland) Acts, the Sewerage (Scotland) Act 1968, the Town and Country Planning (Scotland) Acts, the Water (Scotland) Act 1980, the Civic Government (Scotland) Act 1982 and the Roads (Scotland) Act 1984. Under the Act of 1982 the Sheriff can authorize connections to services through other parts of a building in multiple ownership. The Water Environment and Water Services (Scotland) Act 2003 amends the 1968 and 1980 Acts to qualify the authority's duties to make provision by reference to ministerial directions as to 'reasonable cost' in specific cases. The Act changes the system for funding new connections and adds sustainable urban drainage (SUD) systems to Scottish Water's core functions as provider of sewerage services.

Sewers

2.02 The Sewerage (Scotland) Act 1968 as amended by the Local Government etc. (Scotland) Act 1994 and now by the 2000 and 2003 Acts details the powers and functions of sewerage authorities. The 1968 Act consolidated and simplified all previous legislation and introduced a statutory definition of 'drains' and 'sewers': drains are pipes within the curtilage of premises used for draining buildings and yards within the same curtilage; sewers are all pipes, except drains as defined, used for draining buildings and yards.

2.03 Public sewers are vested in sewerage authorities, as are various new sewers. Junctions to public sewers are also vested in sewerage authorities. If a private drain is connected to a public sewer, it is the sewerage authority's responsibility to maintain the junction. The 1994 Act makes new provision for the construction and maintenance of private sewers not connecting to the public system.

2.04 Sewerage authorities are obliged to provide public sewers as may be necessary for draining their area of domestic sewage, surface water and trade effluent. The authority has to take public sewers to such point as will enable owners of premises to connect their drains at reasonable cost. This is subject to the important proviso that the authority need itself do nothing which is not practicable at a reasonable cost. Nevertheless, the responsibility for providing sewers is clearly that of the sewerage authority, while the responsibility for installing drains in indvidual premises is that of the proprietor.

2.05 Sewerage authorities have powers to construct, close or alter sewers or sewage treatment works. Where they are not under an obligation to provide public sewers (i.e. where it is not practicable for them to do so at reasonable cost), they may enter into an agreement on construction and taking over of sewers and treatment works with any person they are satisfied is about to construct premises in their area. Where sewerage authorities come under the obligation to provide sewers, they may not enter into such agreements. The 1994 Act introduces more flexible arrangements for the construction of private sewers (including sewers to be connected to the public system) and gives sewerage authorities power, subject to the same safeguards which apply in relation to construction of public sewers, to authorize construction of private sewers on third parties' property. The 1994 Act also makes it easier to get the sewerage authority to empty a septic tank, with a right of appeal to the Sheriff in the event of refusal.

2.06 Where a new development is proposed with appropriate permissions the responsibility for providing sewers rests with the sewerage authority, although this does not apply in the case of an individual house where all that is necessary is a drain or private sewer to connect with the public system. The situation may arise where a delay by the authority holds up development. If a developer chooses to install sewers at his own expense, he will be able to recover from the authority only if, from the start, he adopts the correct procedure (*Lawrence Building Co. v Lanarkshire County Council* [1978] SC 30). In terms of amendments introduced by the Water Environment and Water Services (Scotland) Act 2003 Part 2, the vesting of private sewers, SUD systems and treatment works is dependent on compliance with such standards as may be laid down by statutory regulations.

Drains

2.07 Any owner of premises is entitled to connect his drains or private sewer to a public sewer and to allow his drains to empty into a public sewer on giving the sewerage authority 28 days' notice. However, the authority may refuse permission or grant it subject to conditions. A proprietor may connect his drains to a sewer in a different sewerage area, but he must first serve notice on both authorities. The Minister has powers to require the authority in whose area the premises are situated to pay for the service which the other authority is providing.

2.08 Where a notice regarding connection of a drain or sewer to a public sewer is served on a sewerage authority, the authority has powers to direct the manner in which the junction is to be constructed and to supervise construction. The authority has the same powers in relation to any new drain or private sewer if it appears likely that the drain or sewer will be wanted by it to form part of the public system. Authorities are bound to meet the extra cost arising from implementation of their instructions. To allow supervision, three days' notice of the start of work must be given to the authority.

2.09 A sewerage authority can also require defects in private drains and sewers to be remedied and may itself carry out the work if the proprietor fails to do so. Where the defect represents a health hazard, the authority is empowered to carry out emergency repairs on 48-hour notice. The cost of repairs carried out by the authority can be reovered from proprietors.

2.10 Sewage discharged into a public sewer must not be of such a nature as to cause damage to the sewer or, through mixture with other sewage, to cause a nuisance.

Trade effluent

2.11 The discharge of trade effluent into public sewers and other disposal and treatment of trade effluent is regulated by Part II of the 1968 Act as amended. New discharges can be made only with the consent of the sewerage authority. Application for consent is made by serving a trade effluent notice on the authority which must specify the nature of the effluent, the maximum daily quantity and the maximum hourly rate of discharge. The application has to be determined within three months. Consent may be granted subject to conditions. There is a right to appeal to the Minister. Sewerage authorities have power to treat and dispose of trade effluent by agreement with the occupiers of trade premises.

Scottish Environment Protection Agency (SEPA)

2.12 The Scottish Environment Protection Agency (SEPA) constituted by the Environment Act 1995 has assumed the functions of the River Purification Boards, HM Industrial Pollution Inspectorate and the waste and air pollution powers of local councils. SEPA has functions in relation to approving discharges of sewage and other effluent, the provision of septic tanks, etc. The Environment and Water Services (Scotland) Act 2003 implements the Community framework directive for action in the field of water policy 2000/60/EC. The Act sets out the duties of the Scottish Ministers and SEPA in relation to protection of the water environment.

Water supply

2.13 Substantive legislation on water supply is consolidated in the Water (Scotland) Act 1980 as amended by the Local Government etc. (Scotland) Act 1994 and now by the 2000 and 2003 Acts. In terms of the 1980 Act persons erecting new buildings of any type are obliged to make adequate provison to the satisfaction of the water authority for a supply of clean water for the domestic purposes of persons occupying or using the building. Water authorities may also require house owners to provide water supplies in, or if that be impracticable, immediately outside their houses.

2.14 Water authorities are under an obligation to provide supplies of wholesome water to every part of their areas where a supply is required for domestic purposes and can be provided at reasonable cost. They are obliged to lay main water pipes so that buildings where domestic supplies are required can be connected at a reasonable cost. When a question arises as to whether water can be supplied in this manner to any area at a reasonable cost, the Scottish Executive must decide, if requested to do so by ten or more local electors.

2.15 In terms of amendments introduced by the Water Environment and Water Services (Scotland) Act 2003 Part 2, the duty to lay supply pipes does not apply where there is an agreement with a third party to lay pipes; and third parties may be authorized by Scottish Water to lay mains and communication pipes under roads and on any land to connect to public mains. As a rule vesting takes place when a third party system connects with a public main but Scottish Water may determine that there shall be no vesting and that the duty of maintenance remains with the third party. Compliance with such standards as may be laid down by statutory regulations is a prerequisite of vesting. Vesting may be subject to conditions about costs on either side. Advance agreement is recommended.

2.16 Water authorities are also obliged to supply water on reasonable terms for non-domestic purposes, provided that to do so would not prejudice their ability to supply water for domestic purposes.

2.17 The procedure for obtaining a water supply for domestic purposes is regulated by the third schedule to the Water (Scotland) Act 1980 as amended. Broadly, the supply pipe is laid by the customer and then attached to the communication pipe by the water authority. The customer has to give 14 days' notice to the water authority and has to meet the expense of laying the supply pipe and obtain the appropriate consents but must not break open the street. The authority has to lay the communication pipe and connect it with the supply pipe and must also lay any part of the supply pipe which has to be laid in a street. The latter cost is recoverable from the customer.

2.18 The water authority may require a separate service pipe for each house supplied by them with water. The authority may serve notice on exisiting customers requiring provision of a separate service pipe. If the customer fails to comply the authority may execute the work and recover the cost.

Gas, electricity and telephones

2.19 On these topics reference should be made to Chapter 19, paragraph 3.28 to 3.32 as what is said there applies also in Scotland. The Gas Act 1986 applies with minor modifications in Scotland as in England. Likewise the Electricity Act 1989 applies with small modifications. Storage of liquid and gaseous fuel in tanks, cylinders for domestic use, etc. is regulated by the Scottish Building Regulations.

Construction of mains

2.20 Again the remarks on this topic in Chapter 19 (paragraphs 3.33 to 3.34) should be referred to. The authority for water and-sewerage authorities to lay mains is contained in the Water (Scotland) Act 1980 as amended.

3 Private streets and footpaths

3.01 The law on roads, streets and footpaths is consolidated in the Roads (Scotland) Act 1984 as amended by the Local Government etc. (Scotland) Act 1994, etc.

3.02 The 1984 Act defines roads as ways over which there is a public right of passage by any means, i.e. roads includes footpaths subject to a public right of passage. Public roads are roads entered by local councils in their 'list of public roads' and are roads which those authorities are bound to maintain. Private roads are roads which the authorities are not bound to maintain. The authorities can require frontagers to make up and maintain a private road. When a road has been properly made up, the council is bound to take it over and add it to the list of public roads if application is made by the requisite number of frontagers.

Footpaths

3.03 The above provisions apply to footpaths as well as vehicular routes. The authorities are also empowered to take over footpaths in new developments.

4 Grants

4.01 Local councils have power in terms Part XIII of the Housing (Scotland) Act 1987, as amended, to make payment of grants for improvement and repair of dwelling houses. Improvement grants are mandatory for provision of 'standard amenities'. Standard amenities include a water supply for washing and cooking, facilities for washing and bathing and a WC. The amenities must be for the exclusive use of the occupants of a dwelling house. Discretionary improvement grants are available for alteration and enlargement of dwellings and to make dwellings suitable for disabled occupation. The Housing (Scotland) Act 2001 amends the 1987 Act and extends eligibility for improvement grants to works including the provision of heating systems and insulation, replacement of unsafe electrical wiring, installation of mains powered smoke detectors and (in tenement properties) phone entry systems and fire-retardant entry doors for each house. The maximum approved expense for grant is £20,000.

Works such as lead piping replacement and installation of smoke alarms for the deaf may attract grant aid under this head. Repair grants are mandatory for dwelling houses within Housing Action Areas and where repairs notices have been served. Discretionary repair grants are subject to property value limits and needs assessments. Generally grant conditions have to be recorded or registered in the title or land registers.

4.02 In terms of section 233 of the 1987 Act assistance may be available to install separate service pipes to houses sharing the same water supply. Thermal insulation grants for roof space insulation, draughtproofing and insulation of water tanks and cylinders previously available from local councils in terms of Part XIII of the Housing (Scotland) Act 1987 are now administered by the Energy Action Grants Agency (EAGA) Scotland in terms of the Social Security Act 1990, section 15 and regulations made thereunder. From July 1999 grant aid in Scotland extends to wall insulation and heating systems controls. Comprehensive energy advice is available from the network of Energy Efficiency Advice Centres. Grants for means of escape from fire from houses in multiple occupation may be available in terms of section 249 of the 1987 Act. Environmental improvement grants for communal spaces are payable under section 251 of the 1987 Act as amended.

4.03 Various grants are available for improvement or rebuilding of agricultural workers' cottages. It is not proposed to examine these in detail. It should also be noted that special grants may be available in the Highlands, the Islands and in crofting areas for the erection, improvement or re-building of dwelling houses and other buildings under the Crofting Acts and regulations from 1955 onwards. Improvement and repair grants made in respect of croft houses are subject to special conditions in terms of section 256 of the Housing (Scotland) Act 1987.

4.04 Other grants are payable by various authorities. The Clean Air Acts and the Airport Authority Act apply in Scotland, and grants may be obtained where appropriate (Chapter 19, paragraphs 5.19 and 5.21).

5 Housing associations

5.01 The Scottish housing association scene was dominated from 1988 to 2001 by Scottish Homes, a body constituted by the Housing (Scotland) Act 1988. Under the Housing (Scotland) Act 2001 the functions of Scottish Homes have been transferred to the Scottish Ministers and the stock has either been transferred to local associations or to Scottish Ministers. Transferred functions include the duty to maintain a register of housing associations, promoting the formation of associations and exercising supervision and control over registered associatins. Housing associations with registered offices in England are subject to regulation under English law.

5.02 Housing associations as defined by the Housing Act 1985 as amended and satisfying the criteria for registration established from time to time may register. Registration brings associations under the supervision and control of the Scottish Ministers and confers the benefit of eligibility for the capital grants.

5.03 By virtue of sections 59 and 60 of the Housing Act 1988 as amended, local councils, with ministerial consent, are empowered to promote the formation and extension of housing associations and to give them assistance.

6 Special considerations

6.01 Special controls and regulatory regimes apply to a variety of premises, sites and structures. Some examples may be given.

Premises licensed for sale and consumption of alcohol

6.02 In terms of the Licensing (Scotland) Act 1976 as amended by the Local Government etc. (Scotland) Act 1994 liquor licensing is the function of licensing boards constituted by local councils. The suitability of premises is explicitly a matter for licensing boards in a number of important respects. Licenses may be refused on grounds related to the suitability of the premises, their location, character and condition. No reconstruction, extension or alteration of licensed premises which affects the public is permitted without licensing board approval. On any application for renewal the licensing board may require structural alterations to be made. Where a new licence is applied for, statutory certificates in relation to planning, building control and food hygiene must be presented. The board is also bound to consult with the fire authority.

Other licensed premises

6.03 In terms of the Betting, Gaming and Lotteries Act 1963, only premises licensed for that purpose may be used as betting offices.

In terms of the Gaming Act 1968 as amended, the licensing board may refuse a licence on the ground that the premises are unsuitable by reason of their lay-out, character, condition or location. Premises used for gaming, including bingo, have to be licensed. There is regulation of premises where gaming machines are placed by licensing and registration. In terms of the Theatres Act 1968 as amended, no premises may be used for the public performance of plays unless licensed by the local council. In terms of the Cinemas Act 1985 as amended, no premises may be used for showing films unless licensed by the local council. The Cinematograph (Safety) (Scotland) Regulations 1955 make detailed provision for the design and construction of cinemas. Premises may be licensed by local councils for public entertainment, indoor sports entertainment and late hours catering in terms of the Civic Government (Scotland) Act 1982 as amended. There is a licensing scheme for sex shops in terms of section 45 and Schedule 2 of the 1982 Act.

Sports grounds

6.04 Following the tragedy at Glasgow Rangers' Ibrox stadium in 1971 in which 66 people were killed and 140 were injured, the Safety of Sports Grounds Act 1975 was enacted. Local councils are responsible for issuing safety certificates for large sports stadia designated by the Minister in terms of the Act. The Fire Safety and Safety of Places of Sport Act 1987 extended regulation to all stands with covered accommodation for more than 500 spectators.

Nursing homes and residential establishments

6.05 Nursing homes have to be registered with the area health board in terms of the Nursing Homes Registration (Scotland) Act 1938 as amended. The board may refuse registration for reasons connected with situation, construction, state of repair of the premises, etc. Part IV of the Social Work (Scotland) Act 1968 as amended makes provision for registration of a variety of residential establishments including residential homes for the elderly and independent schools. The local council is the responsible authority. The council may refuse registration for reasons connected with situation, construction, state of repair of the premises, etc.

Workplaces

6.06 Health and safety legislation raises many design issues in relation to workplaces of all kinds. The traditional regime has been substantially replaced by regulation under the Health and Safety at Work Act 1974, much of it Europe-inspired and of wider application. A theme of the new regime is the emphasis on risk assessment. Having regard to the terms of the Workplace (Health, Safety and Welfare) Regulations 1992, although there is no duty laid directly on the designer, consideration should to be given to such things as ventilation, temperature, lighting, room dimensions, layout of workstations, design and materials of all surfaces, floors, window and doors, provision of washing and sanitary facilities. Where appropriate there has to be accommodation for storing clothing and changing. There have to be rest facilities for pregnant women and nursing mothers. Sections 42 and 43 of the Offices, Shops and Railways Premises Act 1963 continue in force in relation to the suitability of common parts of buildings in multiple occupation.

6.07 Particular health and safety regulations raise design issues in relation to particular kinds of premises, substances, operations or equipment. For example, the Manual Handling Operations Regulations 1992 direct attention to risk factors arising from the working environment; and the Health and Safety (Display Screen Equipment) Regulations 1992 set out minimum qualitative requirements for work stations in relation to space, lighting, reflections and glare, etc. The Health and Safety Commission should be able to advise of applicable regulations.

Building sites

6.08 Architects and engineers have to be aware of the raft of regulations designed to procure health and safety in relation to building and engineering sites and operations. Involvement in the design of permanent, temporary and protective works, the scheduling of works, the organization of working practices, etc. involves the potential for causing accidents and for liability, direct and indirect. Reference should be made to Chapter 28.

Fire precautions

6.09 All premises except private dwellings are, unless specifically exempted, subject to a process of fire certification by the local fire service in terms of the Fire Precautions Act 1971 as amended by the Fire Safety and Safety of Places of Sport Act 1987. Where there is excessive risk, use of premises may be prohibited or restricted by an order of the Sheriff made at the instance of the fire service. The Fire Precautions (Workplace) Regulations 1997 make provision for exit routes, emergency doors and signs. See Chapter 22.

Houses in multiple occupation

6.10 Houses let for multiple occupation by more than two unrelated persons have to be licensed by local authorities for compliance with fire, health and safety precautions in terms of the Civic Government (Scotland) Act 1982 and orders made thereunder.

9

Construction legislation in England and Wales

MARTIN EDWARDS AND MURRAY ARMES[*]

1 Building Acts and Regulations

1.01 Planning legislation is largely concerned with development policy and, in relation to the external appearance of a building, with safeguarding the amenity of neighbours and the general public (See Chapter 11). But obtaining planning permission is only the first legal hurdle. The architect is then faced with controls over the construction and design of buildings.

In England and Wales the basic framework of control is found in the Building Act 1984 and in the Building Regulations made under it. An important feature of the present system of building control is that there are two alternative means of control – one by local authorities operating under the Building Regulations 2000, and the other by a system of private certification which relies on 'approved inspectors' operating under the Building (Approved Inspectors etc.) Regulations 2000 (as amended).

In practice, most building work will be subject to control by the local authority, but there has been an increase in the number of approved inspectors, both individuals and corporate bodies who have been given licence to operate (see paragraph 3.03).

1.02 The Building Act 1984 applies in England and Wales, but does not extend to Scotland or to Northern Ireland. In Northern Ireland the Building Regulations (Northern Ireland) 2000 (as amended) applies (http://www.opsi.gov.uk/sr/sr2000/20000389.htm); for Scotland see Chapter 10. The Building Regulations 2000 are made under this Act (sections 1 and 2), which also contains provisions linked to the deposit of plans for Building Regulations purposes and provisions relating to existing buildings. Some sections of the Act have not been brought into force and others repealed.

There may also be additional provisions in local Acts and the local authority must say, if asked, whether a local Act applies in its area. For the additional provisions in Inner London, where some sections of the London Building Acts are still in force and may still apply (see section 6). For additional provisions in local Acts outside London, see section 7. Finally there may be relevant provisions in national Acts (see section 8).

2 The Building Regulations 2000

2.01 The Building Regulations 2000 (as amended) contain the detailed technical and procedural rules governing building control by local authorities. The Building (Approved Inspectors etc.) Regulations 2000 (as amended) set out the procedures to be adopted by an approved inspector (see section 3 of this chapter).

Technical requirements

2.02 The Building Regulations require that all 'building work' must be carried out in accordance with the requirements of Schedule 1, but there are important limitations on the requirements. Building Regulation 8 as amended states that nothing need be done other than the works necessary to secure reasonable standards of health and safety for persons in and about buildings, or matters connected with buildings. This limitation does not apply to Part E *(Resistance to the passage of sound)*, requirement H2 in Part H *(Drainage and waste disposal)* and J6 in Part J *(Combustion appliances and fuel storage systems)*, or to any of the requirements in Parts L *(Conservation of fuel and power)* and M *(Access to and use of buildings)*.

Part B (Fire Safety) makes reference to property protection, in addition to life safety, citing the Fire Protection Association (FPA) *Design Guide for the fire protection of buildings.* The RIBA and FPA have recently (2008) published a version of Building Regulations Approved Document B (Volume 2) 2006 *Buildings other than Dwellinghouses, incorporating Insurers' Requirements For Property Protection.* This contains a section relating to fire safety engineering solutions.

2.03 Checklist 21.1 sets out the requirements of Schedule 1 to the Building Regulations. Subject to certain exemptions (see section 4 of this chapter), all 'building work' must be carried out so that the relevant requirements of Schedule 1 are met.

There is an Approved Document (AD) for each part of the schedule, giving guidance to meeting the requirements. There are also two private sector ADs giving guidance to meeting the requirements relevant to *Timber intermediate floors for dwellings* 1991 (by TRADA) and to *Basements for dwellings* 2004 (Basement Information Centre).

Finally, there is an AD supporting Regulation 7 *(Materials and workmanship)* which now implements the Construction Products Directive (see section 9). Products bearing the CE mark may not be rejected if they are being used for their intended purpose and are not damaged. Note that the CE mark only underwrites the capability of a product to enable the works to meet the essential requirements of the Directive, reflecting the requirements of the Building Regulations, if the building is properly designed and built and its scope is therefore more limited than a European product standard. However, the mark does, in most cases, assert that the product is, subject to normal maintenance, capable of satisfying the essential requirements for an economically reasonable working life.

---

[*]In previous editions this chapter was contributed by Oliver Palmer. This is the first edition in which the chapter has been updated by Martin Edwards and Murray Armes.

Approved documents

2.04 The Building Regulations 2000 contain no technical detail, but they are supported by a series of Approved Documents. The status and use of these documents is laid down in sections 6 and 7 of the Building Act 1984. The purpose of the documents is to give practical guidance with respect to the requirements of any provision of the Building Regulations. The documents may be approved by the Secretary of State or by some other body designated by him. The current approved documents all refer to other non-statutory material, including British Standards and certificates issued by the British Board of Agrément. The documents are intended to give designers a considerable amount of flexibility. The details within the documents do not have to be followed if the requirements can be met in some other way.

2.05 Section 7 of the Building Act 1984 specifies the legal effect of the Approved Documents. Failure to comply with their recommendations does not involve civil or criminal liability, but they can be relied on by either party to any proceedings for alleged contravention of the Building Regulations. Thus if an architect proves that he has complied with the requirements of an Approved Document in any proceedings which are brought against him, he can rely on this as 'tending to negative liability'. Conversely, his failure to so comply may be relied on by the claimant as 'tending to establish liability', and the onus will be on the architect to establish that he has met the functional requirement in some other way.

In *Rickards v Kerrier District Council* [1987] CILL 345, in an appeal against enforcement proceedings under section 36 of the Building Act 1984, the High Court had to consider the application of section 6. The judge held that the burden of proving non-compliance with the Regulations was on the local authority, but if they established that the works did not comply with an Approved Document, then the evidential burden shifted to the appellant to show that the requirements of the Building Regulations had been met.

2.06 Space does not permit a detailed analysis of the technical content of the Approved Documents and readers should refer to one of the published guides to the Building Regulations. The guide should include the 2006 revisions to Part B *(Fire safety)*, Part F *(Ventilation)*, Part L *(Conservation of fuel and power)* and Part P *(Electrical safety – dwellings)*.

Procedural rules

2.07 Subject to a number of exemptions (see section 4) the requirements of Part II of the Building Regulations must be met where a person intends to carry out 'building work' or make a 'material change of use' which is subject to the control of the local authority, the procedural requirements of Part V (see paragraphs 2.16–2.18 below) must be met, and the work must comply with the relevant technical requirements of Schedule 1 of the regulations.

Building work is defined in Building Regulation 3 and the related requirements are set out in regulation 4.

A material change of use is defined in Building Regulation 5 and the related requirements are set out in regulation 6.

A local authority is defined in section 126 of the Building Act 1984 as a district council, a London Borough, the Inner and Middle Temples, the City of London and the Isles of Scilly.

The building work or the material change of use may be controlled by the local authority (see paragraph 2.16) or other than by the local authority e.g. by an Approved Inspector (see section 3).

2.08 The Building Regulations 2000 as amended are not a self-sufficient code and other legislation (and non-statutory documents) must be referred to (see sections 5–8).

Nature of approval

2.09 Before considering the procedural requirements in detail, several important matters must be emphasised: discretion of local authorities, breach of Building Regulations, enforcement and dispensation and relaxation of requirements (see paragraphs 2.10–2.15).

Discretion of local authority

2.10 Section 16 of the Building Act 1984 provides that the local authority must pass the plans of any proposed work unless they are defective, or show that the work would contravene any of the Building Regulations, or unless some other provision of the Act requires or authorises it to reject the plans. 'Plans' include drawings, specifications and information in any form (section 126 of the Act).

When considering whether the work does show a contravention it should be borne in mind that the Building Regulations require only compliance with the Requirements in Schedule 1, not the guidance in the relevant Approved Document (see paragraph 2.05).

Where the building notice procedure is followed (see paragraph 2.17) the local authority may specify in writing such plans as it requires to discharge its functions (Building Regulation 13(5)). Note that these plans will not be treated as having been deposited and they will not be passed or rejected.

Where the full plans procedure is followed (see paragraph 2.18) some local authorities may decline to 'register', i.e. accept, plans on the ground that they are defective (which here probably means incomplete) citing Building Regulation 14(3)(b), which requires the plans to show that the work would comply with the regulations. In practice, it is unlikely that plans can be sufficiently full for that purpose, but the local authority may be interpreting its function as requiring it to approve proposed work.

When Parliament introduced the procedure for depositing full plans, it stated that its purpose was to enable the depositor (and particularly builders before they started the work) to know whether what was being proposed showed a contravention; it follows that what the plans do not show will not elicit that information. It should be noted that the time limit for passing or rejecting the plans begins to run from the date they are deposited (not the date they are 'registered'), that if the plans are defective they can be passed subject to conditions (enabling the plans to be passed in stages) and that the work can be started within two days of the deposit.

The local authority, under its duty to enforce the Building Regulations, also has discretion to decide whether or not to inspect building work in progress and they must give proper consideration to the question. 'It is for the local authority, a public and elected body, to decide upon the scale of resources which it can make available to carry out its functions … – how many inspectors, with what expert qualifications, it should recruit, how often inspections are to be made, what tests it should carry out – must be for its decision' (per Lord Wilberforce in *Anns v London Borough of Merton* [1978] AC 728). This is without prejudice to the need for the person carrying out the work to give the notices required by Building Regulation 15. The judgment in *Anns v London Borough of Merton* was subsequently overruled by *Murphy v Brentwood District Council* (see paragraph 2.12 below), but not regarding the issue of inspection.

Breach of building regulations

2.11 Section 35 of the Building Act 1984 provides that a contravention of the Building Regulations is an offence. The position appears to be that the local authority can take enforcement action where an event to which a procedural regulation attaches a requirement has occurred, for example, if building work has started without a building notice being given or full plans deposited, or if a notice required by Building Regulation 15 has not been given.

However, where the building work contravenes a technical requirement the question arises whether an offence can be said to have been committed before the building work is complete. On the one hand the person carrying out the work will say that the offending work will be remedied before the building work, or perhaps the relevant stage of the work, is completed. On the other hand the Building Regulations require the 'building work' to comply and Building Regulation 15 requires notices to be given of the commencement and completion of certain stages of the work, at completion of the building work, and of completion before occupation if the building is to be occupied before completion. In some cases it also provides for notices to be given for remedial work to be carried out and requires notice of its completion to be given within a reasonable time. If the local authority intends to institute proceedings they are likely to be decided summarily, i.e. by the magistrates' court, when the authority must give notice of its intention within 6 months of the date of the alleged offence (see also paragraph 2.13).

2.12 A related matter is whether a breach of any duty imposed by the Building Regulations could give rise to a liability in damages. Section 38 of the Building Act 1984 (Civil liability) provides that a 'breach of duty imposed by Building Regulations, so far as it causes damage, is actionable' where 'damage' is defined as including death or injury (including any disease and any impairment of a person's physical or mental condition). However, the section has not been brought into force and meanwhile, unless and until it is, the position appears to be that as the duty on a local authority to enforce the Building Regulations is not absolute, a breach of the Building Regulations does not of itself, give rise to liability for damages. For example, a failure to reject plans is not actionable in the absence of negligence. The local authority's duties were reconsidered in the overruling case of *Murphy v Brentwood District Council* [1991] 1AC 398 where it was held that 'a local authority is not liable in tort for the negligent application of the Building Regulations, where the resulting defects are discovered before physical injury occurs.'

Enforcement

2.13 Section 36 of the Building Act provides that, without prejudice to its right to take proceedings under section 35, the local authority can by notice (a 'section 36 notice') require the offending work to be removed or corrected, but it has only 12 months from the date it was completed in which to do so, and cannot do so at all if the work is in accordance with plans which were passed or not rejected within the time limit. However, this does not prevent an application for an injunction (with the consent and in the name of the Attorney General) to remove or correct the work, but the court can order the local authority to pay the owner of the work such compensation as it thinks just.

2.14 The person on whom a section 36 notice is served has a right of appeal to the magistrates' court and an important procedure is provided by section 37 of the Building Act. Under section 37, the recipient of a section 36 notice may notify the local authority of his intention to obtain, from a 'suitably qualified person', a written report about the matter to which the section 36 notice relates. The expert's report is then submitted to the local authority and, in light of that report, the authority may withdraw the notice and pay the expenses reasonably incurred in obtaining the report which will relate to technical matters. If the local authority rejects the report, it can then be used as evidence in any appeal under section 40 of the Building Act, and if the appeal is successful the appellant would normally recover the costs of obtaining the report as well as his other costs: Building Act 1984, section 40(6).

Dispensations and relaxations

2.15 Section 8 of the Building Act conferred on the Secretary of State the power to dispense with or relax any Building Regulations requirement 'if he considers that the operation of (that) requirement would be unreasonable in relation to the particular case'. Sections 9 and 10 of the 1984 Act laid down the procedure for application for relaxation. It applies whether the *building notice or full plans* procedure has been followed. The power has since been delegated to local authorities (see Building Regulation 11).

If the local authority refuses the application; the applicant has a right to appeal to the Secretary of State within one month. If the local authority fails to give a decision within two months, section 39 of the Building Act 1984 provides that the application is deemed to be refused and the applicant may appeal forthwith. For more detailed information see *A Guide to Determinations and Appeals – Sections 16 (10) (a) and 39 of the Building Act 1984: An explanation of their purpose and how to proceed 2007*, published by Department for Communities and Local Government.

Nearly all the technical requirements of the Building Regulations are now in functional form to require that the level of provision is 'adequate', 'satisfactory' or 'reasonable' and it would not normally be acceptable to dispense with the whole requirement. The question which then arises is whether the proposal meets the requirement (in a few cases a 'nil' provision may do so) when an application for a determination is the proper course of action (see paragraph 2.19).

Control of building work by the local authorities

2.16 Unless the developer wishes to employ an approved inspector (see section 3) the general rule is that anyone intending to carry out 'building work' or make a 'material change of use' must give a building notice (Building Regulations 12 and 13 and paragraph 2.17) or submit full plans (Building Regulations 12 and 14 and paragraph 2.18). However, full plans must be deposited (Building Regulation 12) if the building is to be put to a 'relevant use', or the building to be erected will front onto a private street, or building work is to be carried out in relation to which Requirement H4 (building over sewers) of Schedule 1 imposes a requirement.

Whichever procedure is adopted the work may be inspected by the local authority's building control officer who may test any building work to establish whether it complies with regulation 7 or any applicable Requirements of Schedule 1 (Building Regulation 18 (testing of building work), as amended 2001) and who may also take such samples of materials to be used in the work as may be necessary to establish whether they comply with the provisions of the regulations (Building Regulation 19).

Building work is defined in regulation 3 to mean the erection or extension of a building, the provision or extension of a controlled service, the 'material alteration' of a building or controlled service, work required by Building Regulation 6 if a 'material change of use' occurs, the insertion of insulating material into a cavity wall and work involving underpinning. A *material change of use* is defined in Building Regulation 5 to mean one which would result in a relevant change of occupancy or remove exemption under Schedule 2.

A *material alteration* is defined in regulation 3(2) as one which would result in an existing building not meeting the requirements of Schedule 1, Parts A, B and M relating to structure, fire safety (except B2), and access and facilities for disabled persons either:

1 where previously it had; or
2 making it more unsatisfactory than it was before in respect of those particular requirements.

A *relevant use* is defined in Building Regulation 12(1) to mean a workplace to which Part II of the Fire Precautions (Workplace) Regulations 1997 apply or a use designated under the Fire Precautions Act 1971. This legislation has been revoked/repealed, and replaced by the Regulatory Reform (Fire Safety) Order 2005 (see paragraph 8.03). The building types regulated consisted of hotels, boarding houses, factories, offices, shops and railway premises. In practice, local authorities will continue to require a Full Plans submission for these building types.

The charges which may be made can vary between local authority districts, but only subject to the *Building (Local Authority Charges) Regulations 1998*.

Building notice procedure

2.17 The procedure is governed by section 16 of the Building Act 1984 and Building Regulations 12 and 13. It is not available if the building is (or is intended) to be erected and will front a private street, or includes building work for which Requirement H4 of Schedule 1 imposes a requirement (Building Regulation 12(1), (4) and (4A)).

There is no prescribed form, but the notice must be signed by or on behalf of the person intending to carry out the work and it must contain or be accompanied by the information listed in Building Regulation 13. The local authority is not required to accept or reject the notice and has no power to do so. However, the authority may ask for any plans and information it needs to enable it to discharge its building control functions and may specify a time limit for their provision. These plans will not be treated as having been deposited and the local authority has no power to pass or reject them. Information may also be required in connection with the linked powers under the Act (see section 5 of this chapter). Once the notice has been given with the required charge the work can start, provided the authority is given at least two days notice (Building Regulation 15(1)(a) and (b)).

A building notice ceases to have effect after three years if, within that period, the local authority gives formal notice to that effect and the work has not started (Building Regulation 13(7)).

Full plans procedure

2.18 The advantage of this procedure, if the developer wishes to adopt it (or the building notice procedure is not available, see paragraph 2.17), is that the local authority cannot take any action under section 36 of the Building Act 1984 if the work is carried out in conformity with the plans as passed.

The procedure is governed by section 16 of the Building Act and Building Regulation 12 (Giving of a building notice or deposit of plans) and 14 (Full plans). Again there is no prescribed form, but the deposited plans must be signed by or on behalf of the person intending to carry out the work and they must contain or be accompanied by the information listed in Building Regulation 14. Once the plans have been deposited (whether or not they have been passed or rejected) with the required charge the work can start, provided the authority is given at least 2 days' notice (Building Regulation 15(l)(a) and (b)). The charge which may be made is governed by the *Building (Local Authority Charges) Regulations 1998*.

The local authority must pass or reject the deposited plans within 5 weeks unless the period is extended, subject to the written agreement of the depositor and the local authority during the 5 week period, to take it to 2 months. Both times run from the date when the plans are deposited, with the appropriate charge. Where for any reason the authority has not given notice of passing or rejecting the plans within the time limit it must refund any plan charge paid.

If the local authority does reject the plans it must give its reasons and, ideally, it will do so in sufficient detail (and in sufficient time) for the depositor to make the necessary changes.

The deposit of the plans is of no effect after 3 years if, within that period, the local authority gives formal notice to that effect and the work has not started (section 32 of the Building Act).

Plans will usually be deposited with the local authority in whose area the intended work will be carried out. However, the individual local authorities co-ordinate their services regionally and nationally through the Local Authority Building Control (LABC). This runs a Partner Authority Scheme (PAS) which enables plans to be deposited with the local authority of your choice to be handled by LABC, together with the local authority in the area in which the intended work is to be carried out. It also runs the Local Authority National Type Approval Confederation (LANTAC) or LABC Type Approval scheme which enables standard designs to be approved for nationwide use. Details of these schemes are available on the LABC website http://www.labc.uk.com/site/index.php.

Applications for determination

2.19 If there is a dispute between a local authority and the person proposing to carry out the work as to whether the plans comply with the requirements of the regulations, section 16(10) of the Building Act 1984 provides for that person to apply to the Secretary of State for a determination. A fee of half the plans fee up to a maximum of £500 is payable for this service.

However, the application can only be made where *full plans* procedure has been followed, after the plans have been deposited and before the work to which the application relates has been started. For more detailed information, see *A Guide to Determinations and Appeals – Sections 16 (10) (a) and 39 of the*

Building Act 1984: An explanation of their purpose and how to proceed 2007, published by Department for Communities and Local Government.

Completion certificates

2.20 Local authorities will issue a completion certificate (see Building Regulation 17) where one is requested in accordance with Building Regulation 14(5).

Unauthorised building work

2.21 Where building work has been carried out without approval and notice was not given, the owner may apply for a regularisation certificate (Building Regulation 21). A regularisation certificate will be issued if the completed work complies with the Building Regulations.

Energy rating

2.22 Where a new dwelling is created by 'building work', or by a 'material change of use' in connection with which 'building work' is carried out, the energy rating of the dwelling must be calculated by a procedure approved by the Secretary of State and notified to the local authority (see regulation 16). The approved procedure is comparison of the Building CO_2 Emission Rate (BER) with the mandatory Target CO_2 Emission Rate (TER) using the Standard Assessment Procedure (SAP) 2005 for dwellings and the Simplified Building Energy Model (SBEM) or approved commercial software for buildings other than dwellings.

3 Control of building work other than by the local authority

3.01 Part II of the Building Act enables the person intending to carry out the work to appoint an approved inspector to take over from the local authority the responsibility for ensuring compliance with the Building Regulations.

It also enables approved public bodies to supervise their own work but to date only the Metropolitan Police Authority has been approved.

Approved inspectors

3.02 The procedures for ensuring compliance with the building regulations are governed by Part II of the Building Act 1984 and the Building (Approved Inspectors etc.) Regulations 2000 and amendments. Section 49 of the Building Act defines an approved inspector, authorised under the Building Act to carry out building control work in England and Wales, as a corporate body approved by the Secretary of State (or by a body designated by him for that purpose) or as an individual (not a firm) approved by a designated body.

The Secretary of State has designated the Construction Industry Council (CIC) as the body to receive all applications from corporate bodies and individuals for approved inspector status and for deciding on the applications. With one exception, approved inspectors are authorised to deal with all types of building other than new-build housing for sale. The exception is Building Control Services Ltd, a subsidiary of the National House Building Council (NHBC), which is authorised to deal with all types of building.

3.03 The CIC maintains the registers of all corporate and individual inspectors and the Association of Corporate Approved Inspectors holds a list of corporate approved inspectors. These lists are available on the respective websites. The approved inspector's charges are negotiable on a case-by-case basis.

4 Exemptions from control

4.01 There is a definition of a 'building' in section 121 (interpretation) of the Building Act 1984 and section 4(1) exempts certain

Table 9.1

Type of work	Person carrying out work
Installation of a heat -producing gas appliance.	A person approved under regulation 3 of the *Gas Safety (Installation and Use) Regulations 1998(c)*.
Installation of an oil-fired combustion appliance 45 KW maximum and oil storage tanks.	A person registered under the Oil Firing Registration Scheme and by the Petroleum Industry Limited.
Installation of a solid fuel combustion appliance 50 KW maximum.	A person registered under the registration scheme by HETAS Limited.
Installation of a replacement window, rooflight or door.	A person registered under the Fenestration Self-Assessment Scheme by Fensa Ltd.
Installation of fixed low or extra-low voltage electrical installations.	A person registered by EC Certification Limited, British Standards Institution, ELECSA Limited, NICEIC Certification Services Ltd, or NAPIT Certification Limited in respect of that type of work.
Installation of fixed low or extra-low voltage electrical installations as a necessary adjunct to or arising out of other work being carried out by the registered person.	A person registered by CORGI Services Limited, ELECSA Limited, NAPIT Certification Limited, NICEIC Certification Services Limited or Oil Firing Technical Association for the Petroleum Industry Ltd in respect of that type of electrical work.

types of buildings. The exemption for school buildings has been withdrawn in favour of the Building Regulations, though there are limited additional requirements in the Education (School Premises) Regulations 1999.

4.02 There is a narrower interpretation of a building in Building Regulation 2(1) and there are further exemptions in Building Regulation 9 (Exempt buildings and work), detailed in Schedule 2 to the Building Regulations:

I – Buildings controlled under other legislation; II – Buildings not frequented by people; III – Greenhouses and agricultural buildings; IV – Temporary buildings; V – Ancillary buildings; VI –Small detached buildings; VII – Extensions consisting of a conservatory, porch or carport. Even when the building or work is not exempt, there are limits on the application of some of the requirements in Schedule 1 (requirements). See Checklist 9.1 at the end of this chapter.

4.03 In addition to the exemptions from the technical requirements, there are exemptions from the procedural requirement to give a building notice or deposit full plans in Schedule 2A to Building Regulation 12(5), generally in small buildings (see Table 9.1):

5 Other controls under the Building Act 1984

5.01 Local authorities exercise a number of statutory public health functions in conjunction with the process of building control. These provisions are commonly called the 'linked powers' because their operation is linked with the authority's building control functions, both in checking deposited plans or considering a building notice, and under the private certification scheme. The most important of these linked powers are described below.

Building over sewers and drains

5.02 Section 99 of the Water Industry Act 1991 states that sewerage undertakers must keep a map showing the location of all public sewers and supply a copy to local authorities for public inspection. The map distinguishes among public sewers, those with respect to which a vesting declaration has been made but which has not yet taken effect, and those subject to an agreement as to future declaration. Where separate sewers are reserved for foul and surface water, this must be clearly shown. These four groups of sewers and drains are shown on the map.

5.03 Following the repeal of section 18 of the Building Act, this section is no longer a linked power. Instead, Requirement H4 (Building over sewers) of Schedule 1 to the Building Regulations now applies and Building Regulation 14(3)(aa) requires that, where full, plans have been deposited, particulars must be given of the precautions to be taken in building over a drain, sewer or disposal main shown on the map of sewers and Building Regulation 14A requires the local authority to consult the sewerage undertaker and 'to have regard to its views' (but not more).

New buildings and drains

5.04 Following the repeal of subsections 21(1) and (2) of the Building Act, this section is no longer a linked power. Instead Part H (drainage and waste disposal) of Schedule 1 of the Building Regulations now applies.

In *Chesterton RDC v Ralph Thompson, Ltd* [1947] KB 300, the High Court held that the local authority is not entitled to reject plans on the ground that the sewerage system, into which the drains lead, is unsatisfactory. What the local authority must consider is the drainage of the particular building only.

5.05 Under section 21(3) of the Building Act the local authority can determine the method of disposal from a drain – a connection to a sewer or discharge to a cesspool or some other place – provided that, in the case of a sewer, it satisfies certain conditions. A drain is defined as being used for the drainage of one or more buildings within the same curtilage and a sewer (which may be private or public) as being used for the drainage of buildings within two or more curtilages.

Under section 22 of the Building Act the local authority can determine whether a building shall be drained separately into a sewer or 'in combination' with two or more other buildings, by means of a private sewer discharging to the sewer, if it appears to the authority the buildings may be drained more economically or advantageously in this way. However, it can only do this when the relevant drains are first laid, not in respect of any building for whose drainage plans have previously been passed by it unless the owners agree.

Water supply

5.06 The effect of section 25 of the Building Act is that drawings of a house deposited with the local authority are to be rejected, unless 'there is put before (the local authority) a proposal which appears to it to be satisfactory for providing the occupants with a supply of wholesome water sufficient for their domestic purposes', and if possible the water is to be from a piped supply.

Fire safety

5.07 Section 24 of the Building Act, a linked power, required the local authority to reject plans if the entrances and exits of buildings where large numbers of the public were to be admitted were unsatisfactory, but it has been of no effect since 1992 when Building Regulations were made. Section 71 (Entrances, exits etc.) was repealed under the Regulatory Reform (Fire Safety) Order 2005 (see paragraph 8.03).

Height of chimneys

5.08 Section 73 of the Building Act enables the local authority, when a building ('the taller building') is being erected or raised to a height greater than an adjoining building, to require any chimney of the adjoining building within 6 feet of the taller building to be raised to the height of the taller building.

Section 16 of Clean Air Act 1993, a linked power, requires the local authority to reject plans unless it is satisfied that the height of any chemistry will be sufficient to prevent, as far as practicable, the smoke, grit, dust or gases from becoming prejudicial to health or a nuisance (see also paragraph 8.09).

Continuing requirements

5.09 Section 2 of the Building Act provides for Building Regulations to be made imposing continuing requirements on owners and occupiers of buildings, but none has yet been made.

6 Local legislation in Inner London

6.01 Inner London consists of the City of London and the twelve London Boroughs of Camden, Greenwich, Hackney, Hammersmith, Islington, Kensington and Chelsea, Lambeth, Lewisham, Southwark, Tower Hamlets, Wandsworth, and Westminster: London Government Act 1963, section 43.

6.02 Until 1986 the London Building Acts and Bye-laws formed a code of control which governed the design, construction and use of buildings in the area and differed from that which operated elsewhere. On 6 January 1986 the *Building (Inner London) Regulations 1985* came into effect, repealed the Bye-laws applied most of the national regulations and amended the London Building Acts. On 1 June 1987 the Building (Inner London) Regulations 1987 came into effect and applied the remaining national regulations.

The local authority, acting as the building control body and headed by the Chief Building Control Officer, is responsible for enforcing the building regulations. The sections of the London Building Acts which are still in force are usually administered by the local building control in the person of the chief officer acting as a District Surveyor. The more important of the remaining sections of the Act are summarized below (see paragraphs 6.03–6.05) but space does not permit a detailed examination of all the remaining sections which include special and temporary structures (sections 29 and 30) and dangerous and neglected structures (sections 60–70). For a full treatment, see the *Guide to Building Control in Inner London 1987* by P. H. Pitt.

Fire safety – precautions against fire

6.03 Section 20 of the London Building Act applies to:

(a) buildings of excess height – over 30 metres or over 25 metres if the area of the building exceeds 930 square metres; and
(b) buildings in excess cube – over 7100 cubic metres if used for trade (including warehouses and department stores) or manufacture.

Except in the case of a trade building which is properly sub-divided into divisions of less than 7100 cubic metres section 20 buildings require the consent of the local authority (a copy of the plans will be sent for comment to the London Fire and Civil Defence Authority). The consent will be subject to a schedule of requirements, which may include higher standards of fire resistance and the provision of automatic sprinklers, hose reels, dry risers, firemens' lifts, emergency lighting and escape routes. Full details will be required and approval must be obtained of all electrical installations, heating and ventilating systems, sprinkler installations, etc. Additional precautions can be required for 'special fire risk areas' (defined in section 20(2D)) such as any storey of a garage located in a basement or not properly ventilated.

Section 20(2) is amended by the Regulatory Reform (Fire Safety) Order 2005, so that 'maintenance' covers both interior and external maintenance.

Fire safety – uniting of buildings

6.04 Section 21 applies to buildings to which, if united, would not meet the continuing requirements of the Act.

The section requires the consent of the local authority to forming openings for access from one building to another without passing into the external air. The section also imposes limitations on forming openings in walls separating divisions of buildings of the warehouse class or used for trade purposes.

Temporary Buildings

6.05 Section 30 applies to consents for temporary buildings. Section 30(3) states that temporary buildings must not be used for the storage of inflammable materials or for the purpose of human habitation. Hoardings over seven feet in height are dealt with in Section 30(5) and any such structure which is in place for three years or more requires the approval of the district surveyor as to its structural stability. No temporary building shall infringe the requirements of Section 21 (see above).

Fire safety – means of escape

6.06 Part V/section 34 is repealed by the Regulatory Reform (Fire Safety) Order 2005 (FSO). Means of escape are now all dealt with by Building Regulations Part B1.

Sections 35(1) paragraphs (a), (b) and (d) are repealed by FSO and paragraph (c) is slightly modified. Section 35(5) is repealed, as are section 38 and section 42 (a), (b), (c) and (f).

Notice of Objection

6.07 Where a notice is given or plans deposited in respect of a building affected by the provisions of the Acts, and it discloses a contravention of the provisions, the district surveyor must serve Notice of Objection on the builder or owner or other person causing or directing the work. In effect this provides a *locus poenitentiae* (an opportunity for repentance).

However, an appeal may be made to the magistrates' court within 14 days after service of the notice: 1939 Act, section 39.

Notice of Irregularity

6.08 The district surveyor also has power to serve a Notice of Irregularity under section 88 of the 1939 Act. This can be served after the builder has completed the work. It was decided in *Coggin v Duff* [1907] 96 LT 670, that failure to give Notice of Objection is not a bar to proceedings under Notice of Irregularity. This notice will be served where work has been done and it is found that some contravention exists or that the work is so far advanced that the district surveyor cannot ascertain whether anything has been done in contravention. Its effect is to require the builder within 48 hours to amend any contravention or to open up as much of the work as may be necessary for the district surveyor to ascertain whether or not a contravention exists. The opening-up and rectification is done at the builder's or owner's expense. The notice cannot be served on the builder when he has completed the building, but there is power to serve notice on the owner, occupier, or other person directing the work.

6.09 The sanction behind a Notice of Irregularity is a fine. However, the district surveyor may apply to the magistrates' court for an order requiring the builder to comply within a stated time. Failure to obey an order of the court renders the builder liable to a daily fine: 1939 Act, section 148.

Powers of entry

6.10 The district surveyor and other authorised officers have wide powers of entry, inspection and examination to enable them to carry out their functions: e.g. section 142 of the London Building Acts (Amendment) Act 1939.

Appeals tribunals

6.11 Provision exists in the London Building Acts for special Tribunals of Appeal (one for each of the building control authorities) which hear appeals referred to them under the London

Building Acts: 1939 Act, section 109. The Tribunals have power to award costs and wide powers to order the production of documents, plans, specifications, and so on. A further appeal lies, by way of case stated, to the High Court: 1939 Act, section 116.

Dwelling houses on low-lying land

6.12 Part XII of the London Building Act 1930 prohibits the erection or rebuilding of dwelling houses on low-lying land without the consent of the appropriate Inner London Borough Council.

Party structures

6.13 Part VI of the 1939 Act has been repealed, subject to transitional provisions, by the Party Wall etc. Act 1996 which is applicable throughout England and Wales (see paragraph 8.21).

7 Local legislation outside Inner London

7.01 Although the Building Act 1984 and Building Regulations made under it were intended to provide a national code of building control, there are many provisions in local Acts which impose additional controls on the construction of buildings. The Regulatory Reform (Fire Safety) Order 2005 (FSO) has repealed many sections of these Local Acts which dealt with fire safety. See paragraph 8.3 below.

7.02 Section 90 of the Building Act provides that where (outside Inner London) a local Act imposes obligations or restrictions on the construction, nature or situation of buildings, the local authority shall keep a copy of those provisions at its offices for inspection by the public at all reasonable times free of charge.

The provisions of local Acts may include fire safety requirements relating to high buildings (over six storeys), large storage buildings (exceeding 7000 cubic metres), underground and multi-storey parking places, access for the fire service and means of escape. They may also include requirements relating to the separation of foul and rainwater drainage systems and the external storage of flammable materials. The authorities concerned are of the opinion that their local Act requirements are an essential part of the machinery of control and this list is not exhaustive. For a full treatment, see the *Guide to Building Control by Local Acts 1987* by P. H. Pitt.

7.03 Where an Approved Inspector is responsible for compliance with the building regulations the Building (Approved Inspectors etc.) Regulations 2000 and amendments require him to consult the Fire Authority where a local Act requires. The Building Act provides that local authority can reject the Approved Inspector's initial notice where the proposed work would 'contravene any local enactment which authorizes it to reject plans submitted in accordance with the Building Regulations'. However, the local authority is responsible for ensuring that the work complies with the local Act.

8 Other national legislation

8.01 Many general statutes contain further provisions affecting the construction of buildings, although this is not apparent from the titles of the Acts concerned. There are also numerous Statutory Instruments made under powers conferred by many of these Acts. In this section some statutory rules which affect the bulk of building developments will be considered. This list does not claim to be exhaustive, nor does it cover all the relevant sections. (Some provisions of statutes not discussed here are covered in Chapter 7).

8.02 Certain requirements are dealt with automatically on the deposit of drawings under the Building Regulations or, in some cases, at the same time as the application for planning permission. The following are some of the more important provisions which are relevant at that stage.

The responsibility for the enforcement of the various Acts will fall on a variety of different bodies. Some are departments of the local authority, but others are not when the building control body may be required to consult them. For the rest architect has no option but to negotiate.

The Regulatory Reform (Fire Safety) Order 2005 (FSO)

8.03 The FSO repeals or revokes much other legislation concerning fire safety, including the whole of the Fire Precautions Act 1971, the Smoke Detectors Act 1991, the Fire Certificate (Special Premises) Regulations 1976, the Fire Precautions (Workplace) Regulations 1997 and the Fire Precautions (Workplace) (Amendment) Regulations 1999. The FSO repeals parts of the Building Act 1984, the London Building Acts (Amendment) Act 1939, the Health and Safety at Work etc. Act 1974, the Safety of Sports Grounds Act 1975, the Fire Safety and Safety of Places of Sport Act 1987, and the Management of Health and Safety at Work Regulations 1999.

8.04 The FSO reforms the law relating to fire safety in non-domestic premises. In a coordinated revision of the Building Regulations, dwelling houses are now regulated by Volume 1 of Approved Document B (2006) and all other buildings by Volume 2. The FSO replaces fire certification under the Fire Precautions Act 1971 with a general duty to ensure, so far as is reasonably practicable, the safety of employees; a general duty, in relation to non-employees, to take such fire precautions as may reasonably be required in the circumstances to ensure that premises are safe; and a duty to carry out a risk assessment.

8.05 The person who must carry out the Fire Risk Assessment is the "Responsible Person", defined in article 3 of the FSO. The Responsible Person will be one of the following: an employer, if he controls the workplace; an occupier; an owner; any others that have a contract that gives them control over fire safety measures e.g. installer/maintainer of fire alarms. There may be more than one Responsible Person and they are obliged to cooperate with each other.

8.06 The Risk Assessment must take account of all the risks to which building occupants, and persons in the immediate vicinity of the premises, may be exposed. The Risk Assessment must be recorded and reviewed on a regular basis to keep it up to date. Article 18 of the FSO requires the Responsible Person to appoint one or more 'Competent Persons' to assist him in undertaking the fire prevention and fire protection measures, unless he or an employee has sufficient training and experience or knowledge. On new buildings, architects will be increasingly asked to carry out preliminary fire risk assessments, rather than leave these matters to a time close to occupation.

8.07 The FSO provides for the enforcement of the Order, for appeals, offences and connected matters. The enforcing authorities are:

The local Fire and Rescue authority for all except for the following specific cases:

The Health and Safety Executive for nuclear installations, ships and construction sites.
The Ministry of Defence fire service for premises occupied by armed forces.
The Local Authority for sports grounds and grandstands.
Her Majesty's Inspectorate for Crown Premises.

8.08 Article 27(1) of the FSO permits the inspector to do anything necessary for the purpose of carrying out the FSO. Articles 29, 30 and 31 provide for Alterations, Enforcement and Prohibition Notices. These notices are graduated in severity and that each of these notices is stiffer than the preceding notice:

The Alterations Notice requires the specified risk to be reduced or eliminated, but the Responsible Person can make a proposal of their own liking. There appears to be no provision for a time limit on the remedial works.

The Enforcement Notice has a deadline (not less than 28 days' notice) and may include directions as to the measures considered necessary to remedy the failure.

The Prohibition Notice prohibits or restricts the use of the premises until the specified matters have been remedied. It may also include direction as to the measures which will have to be taken to remedy the matters specified.

Article 32 relates to Offences and Penalties; articles 33 and 34 relate to Defence and article 35 relates to Appeals.

8.09 Construction sites are subject to Part 4 of the Construction (Design and Management) Regulations 2007 (which, broadly, incorporate the provisions of the Construction (Health, Safety and Welfare) Regulations 1996, which are now revoked. Work at height is now covered separately in the Work at Height Regulations 2005. The Health and Safety Executive (HSE) is responsible for enforcing these regulations (see also paragraph 8.20).

The Clean Air Act 1993

8.10 Among other things, this Act controls the height of chimneys on industrial premises, types of installation, and the treatment of offensive fumes from appliances. Sections 14 and 15 of the 1993 Act require the approval of the local authority for the height of a chimney serving a furnace, and approval may be granted subject to conditions as to the rate and/or quality of emissions from the chimney. There is a right of appeal to the Secretary of State.

8.11 Similarly, section 16 of the Act provides that in other cases the local authority must reject plans of buildings other than residences, shops, or offices unless the height of the chimney as shown on the drawings will so far on practicable, be sufficient to prevent fumes from being a nuisance or a health hazard. The factors to be considered are the purpose of the chimney, the position and description of nearby buildings, level of neighbouring ground, and other relevant matters. These provisions represent an important negative control. Again, there is a right of appeal to the Secretary of State.

Highways Act 1980

8.12 The Act contains several provisions of interest to architects. They include the construction of a new street (sections 186–196 of the Act), improvement lines (section 73), building lines (section 74), means of access (sections 124 and 184), building over highways (section 177) and precautions against accidents including the depositing and removal of a skip on a highway (sections 139, 140 and 168). Some may be enforced by the highway authority, others implemented by conditions attached to planning consents (see Chapter 11).

For provisions relating to a private street (one not adopted by the highway authority) and the procedures which enable a private street to be adopted under section 38 of the Act as a highway maintainable at the public expense (see Chapter 7, paragraph 4).

8.13 Section 73 requires the highway authority's consent, where an improvement line has been prescribed, to the erection of a building and the making of any permanent excavation in front of the improvement line. This may be granted with conditions. There is a right of appeal against a refusal of consent or its granting subject to conditions.

8.14 Section 74 requires the highway authority's consent to the erection of a new building (but not a boundary wall) in front of the building line. This may be granted with conditions or for a limited time.

8.15 Section 124 enables the Secretary of State, by order, to authorise the highway authority to stop up a private access to the highway if he considers that the access is likely to cause danger to, or interfere unnecessarily, with traffic on the highway. However, the order can only be made where no access to the premises from the highway is reasonably required or where another reasonably convenient means of access is available or will be provided. There is an objection procedure and compensation may be payable.

8.16 Sections 139 and 140 require precautions to be taken where a person is carrying out works in the street such as the planking and strutting of drainage works and shoring up any building adjoining a street. Stringent safety precautions must be observed in relation to builder's skips. They must not be placed on the highway without the authority's consent. This may be granted subject to conditions.

Section 168 provides that if, in the course of carrying out building work in or near the highway an accident gives rise to the risk of serious bodily injury to a person in the street, the owner of the land is guilty of an offence. Hoardings and scaffolding in or adjoining the highway require a licence from the highway authority.

8.17 Section 177 requires a license from the highway authority for the construction and subsequent alteration of buildings or parts of buildings over highways maintained at public expense. This may be granted subject to conditions and is registerable as a local land charge (see Chapter 4, paragraph 1.05).

8.18 Section 184 enables a building owner to initiate proposals to create a new means of access to his property to be constructed at his own expense for, for example, a vehicle crossing to a garage. In certain circumstance the authority may, on its initiative, construct the crossing at the owner's expense.

8.19 Sections 186–196 provide that when a new street is to be established an order will be made and, where Bye-laws are in force, they will prescribe the centre line and lines defining the minimum width. Any plans showing a contravention of the Bye-laws must be rejected.

Health and Safety at Work etc. Act 1974

8.20 The Act and the regulations made pursuant to it contain provisions relating to health and safety during the construction process and in the workplace and the design (which includes specification) should take account of these requirements (see also Chapter 15).

The Construction (Design and Management) Regulations 2007 'CDM Regulations' made under the Act require the architect to identify and eliminate or reduce risks during design and provide information about remaining risks which could arise during the construction or during the life of the building. Additionally, where the structure will be used as a workplace, architects need to take account of the Workplace (Health, Safety and Welfare) Regulations 1992. For projects notifiable under the CDM Regulations, the architect must check that the client is aware of its duties and that a CDM Coordinator has been appointed, and provide any information needed for the health and safety file. The HSE publishes an approved Code of Practice *Managing Health and Safety in Construction 2007*.

The Workplace (Health, Safety and Welfare) Regulations 1992 require employers to ensure, as far as is reasonably practicable, the health, safety and welfare of their employees at work. The regulations, which expand on these duties, include requirements for ventilation, lighting, sanitary conveniences, washing facilities, drinking water, etc. (see Chapter 15).

Much asbestos had been introduced in buildings before its use was banned. The Control of Asbestos Regulations 2006, which came into force on 6 April 2007, apply to non-domestic premises, also to the common residential rented premises. They require employers to manage the risk (removal is seen as the last resort) and clean their premises. This has implications, not least at the survey stage, for architects concerned with work which could damage or disturb asbestos already in a building.

Party wall etc. Act 1996

8.21 The Act, which came into force on 1 July 1996, drew on the sections of the London Building Act dealing with party walls, which it replaced. It applies to the whole of England and Wales (except the four Temples) to provide a national framework for preventing and resolving disputes between neighbouring owners in respect of party walls and similar matters. It deals with three main issues: construction of new walls on boundaries between adjoining owners' land (section 1); carrying out works to, or repair of a party wall and the rights of the owner (section 2); and excavation near to neighbouring buildings (section 6). See Chapter 14 for procedures.

Environment Acts 1995/1999

8.22 The Act is administered by the Environment Agency. Matters of concern to the Agency include contaminated land, flooding and the disposal of effluents.

Contaminated land may, on the advice of the Agency, be subject to planning conditions. It is also subject to Requirement C2 (dangerous and offensive substances) of Schedule 1 to the Building Regulations and such substances if 'found on or in the ground to be covered by the building', should be notified to the local authority's environmental officer who will advise. Radon may be a particular concern in specified areas.

Flooding may also, on the advice of the Agency, be subject to planning conditions to limit possible obstructions to flows (which may be contaminated by sewage). Flooding as such is not a matter for the Building Regulations, but Requirement C3 (subsoil drainage), requiring either drainage to be provided or measures to be taken (such as tanking) to prevent ground moisture entering the building or damaging its fabric, may be relevant.

Effluent disposal is unlikely to be subject to planning conditions (except perhaps in the case of major projects), but the consent of the Agency to outfalls is required (except for infiltration systems) and may be subject to conditions. Requirement H1(1)(c) (foul water drainage), H2(l)(b) (wastewater systems) and H3(3)(b) (rainwater drainage) of the Building Regulations may be relevant.

Clean Neighbourhoods and Environment Act 2005

8.23 Chapter 3, section 54 of the Act contains provisions for the preparation of plans for the management and disposal of site waste. The Regulations make provisions for the circumstances under which a plan must be prepared, the enforcement power to the local authority and the penalties for any offences.

Part 8 makes provisions for the establishment of the new Commission for Architecture and the Built Environment (CABE). The functions are the promotion of education and high standards in, and understanding and appreciation, of architecture and the design, management and maintenance of the built environment. The powers of the commission include the provision of advice and developing and reviewing projects (whether requested or not to do so), the provision of finance and the commissioning of works of art.

Section 94 of Part 8 gives the Secretary of State the power to provide financial assistance or a grant, or by any other means as the Secretary of State thinks fit, to any person or persons connected with the promotion of education or high standards in architecture and the design and management of the built environment.

Disability Discrimination Act 1995/2005 (DDA)

8.24 Part 3 of the Act comes into force on 1 October 2004 and enables a person who considers that, by reason of 'a physical or mental impairment which has a substantial and long-term adverse effect on (their) ability to carry out normal day-to-day activities', they suffer discrimination due to a physical feature of a building to take a provider of goods or services to court. The provider has three options – to remove the feature, alter the feature or avoid the feature – by providing a 'reasonable' means of avoiding the feature i.e. an alternative service.

The Disability Discrimination (Providers of Services) (Adjustment of Premises) Regulations 2001 made under the Act, provide that it is not reasonable for a provider to have to remove or alter a physical feature which satisfies a 'relevant design standard'. The Schedule to the Regulations provides that *Approved Document M* (access and facilities for disabled people) is, subject to conditions, a relevant standard.

The scope of the Act, which is overseen by the Disability Rights Commission, is wider than the scope of the building regulations and advice can be sought from the local authority's Access Officer or through the National Register of Access Consultants if an access audit is sought.

The Disability Discrimination Act 2005 makes substantial amendments to the original 1995 Act and arises out of the work of the Disability Rights Task Force established in 1997. Section 14 gives the Secretary of State the power to amend or repeal the small dwellings exemption contained in sections 23, 24B and 24H of the 1995 Act. Section 16 inserts a new Part 5B (Improvements to let dwelling houses) into the DDA. It applies when a lease requires landlord consent for the making of improvements, or prohibits making improvements at all. In the latter case, where the terms of the lease make it impossible or unreasonably difficult for a disabled person to enjoy the premises, the tenant could seek to have the lease adjusted. Section 18 sets out in detail and widens the definition of 'disability'.

Housing Act 1985/2004

8.25 The Act contains provisions relating to the fitness of dwellings, including houses in multiple occupation, and some environmental health authorities use their wide-ranging powers to seek to impose requirements which the building regulations have dropped (such as minimum ceiling heights and ventilated WC lobbies) or have chosen not to introduce (such as integrated smoke detection and alarm systems in blocks of purpose-built self-contained flats). The Act is enforced by environmental health officers and negotiation seems to be the best policy.

The Housing Act 2004, which replaces certain parts of the 1985 Act, was brought into force in November 2004 and it replaces the existing housing fitness standard with a Housing and Safety Rating System and the introduction of a scheme to license higher-risk Houses in Multiple Occupation. The Act also introduces the requirement for Home Information Packs to be produced by sellers or estate agents.

Special classes of building

8.26 The legislation dealt with so far is, in one sense, of general application. The architect dealing with the design and construction of specialised types of building may find that special controls apply. All these specialised provisions are extremely complex, and space does not permit any detailed examination of them. They range from premises (such as nursing homes and schools) to special risks (such as cinemas and the keeping of radio-active substances) (See Chapter 7.)

The Licensing Act 1993

8.27 The Act governs the operation of entertainment premises and premises where alcohol is sold. Application for a licence must be made to the local authority Licensing Committee, who will consult with

(a) the chief officer of police for any police area in which the premises are situated,
(b) the fire authority for any area in which the premises are situated,
(c) the enforcing authority within the meaning given by section 18 of the Health and Safety at Work etc. Act 1974 for any area in which the premises are situated,
(d) the local planning authority within the meaning given by the Town and Country Planning Act 1990 (c. 8) for any area in which the premises are situated,
(e) the local authority by which statutory functions are exercisable in any area in which the premises are situated in relation to minimising or preventing the risk of pollution of the environment or of harm to human health.

The licensing objectives are—

(a) the prevention of crime and disorder;
(b) public safety;
(c) the prevention of public nuisance; and
(d) the protection of children from harm.

The Licensing Authority may stipulate additional provisions for the welfare and safety of the staff and customers of the licensed premises. This may have a significant effect on the design of the premises and the architect should consult the licensing authority at an early stage in the design. See Chapter 7 for further detail.

9 Technical harmonisation and standards

The Construction Products Directive 89/106 EEC

9.01 A major barrier to the free movement of construction products within the European Community has been the differing national requirements relating to such matters as building safety, health, durability, energy economy and protection of the environment, which in turn directly influence national product standards, technical approvals and other technical specifications and provisions.

In order to overcome this problem, the Community has adopted the Construction Products Directive whose aim is to provide for the free movement, sale and use of construction products which are fit for their intended use and have such characteristics that structures in which they are incorporated meet certain essential requirements. Products, in so far as these essential requirements relate to them, which do not meet the appropriate standard may not be placed on the market (Article 2).

9.02 These essential requirements are similar in style to the functional requirements of the Building Regulations in force in England and Wales, but rather wider in scope. They relate to mechanical resistance and stability, safety in case of fire, hygiene, health and the environment, safety in use, protection against noise, and energy economy and heat retention. These requirements must, subject to normal maintenance, be satisfied for an economically reasonable working life and generally provide protection against events which are foreseeable.

The performance levels of products complying with these essential requirements may, however, vary according to geographical or climatic conditions or in ways of life, as well as different levels of protection that may prevail at national regional or local level and member states may decide which class of performance level they require to be observed within their territory.

9.03 Products will be presumed to be fit for their intended use if they bear the CE conformity mark as provided (or as provided for in Directive 93/68/EEC) showing that they comply with a European standard or a European technical approval or (when documents of this sort do not exist) relevant national standards or agreements recognised at Community level as meeting the essential requirements. If a manufacturer chooses to make a product which is not in conformity with these specifications, he has to prove that his product conforms to the essential requirements before he will be permitted to put it on the market. Conformity may be verified by third party certification.

9.04 European standards which will ensure that the essential requirements are met will be drawn up by a European standards body usually CEN or CENELEC. These will be published in the UK as identically worded British standards. European technical approvals will be issued by approved bodies designated for this purpose by the member states in accordance with guidelines prepared by the European body comprising the approved bodies from all the member states.

9.05 Member states are prohibited from interfering with the free movement of goods which satisfy the provisions of the directive and are to ensure that the use of such products is not impeded by any national rule or condition imposed by a public body, or private bodies acting as a public undertaking or acting as a public body on the basis of a monopoly position (Article 6). This would appear to include such bodies as the NHBC in their standard setting role.

9.06 The directive has been implemented in the UK by the Construction Products Regulations 1991 (SI 1991/1620), as amended by SI 1994/3051.

The implementation of the directive throughout the Community should greatly ease the task of the architect who is designing buildings in more than one member state as it means that he can now be sure that the products he specifies, so long as they comply with the directive, will comply with the regulations and requirements of every member state without his having to carry out a detailed check for that purpose.

Checklist 9.1: Technical requirements in Schedule 1 of the Building Regulations 2000, as amended by the Building (Amendments) Regulations 2001, 2002, 2002 (No. 2), 2003, 2004, 2004 (No. 3) and 2008.

The date of the current edition or amendment of the Approved Document is given after the title of each Part.

SCHEDULE 1-REQUIREMENTS	Regulations 4 and 6
Requirement	*Limits on application*

PART A: STRUCTURE (2004)

Loading
A1 (1) The building shall be constructed so that the combined dead, imposed and wind loads are sustained and transmitted by it to the ground –
(a) safely; and
(b) without causing such deflection or deformation of any part of the building, or such movement of the ground, as will impair the stability of any part of another building.

(2) In assessing whether a building complies with sub-paragraph (I) regard shall be had to the imposed and wind loads to which it is likely to be subjected in the ordinary course of its use for the purpose for which it is intended.

Ground movement
A2 The building shall be constructed so that ground movements caused by –
(a) swelling, shrinkage or freezing of the subsoil; or
(b) land slip or subsidence (other than subsidence arising from shrinkage), in so far as the risk can be reasonably foreseen, will not impair the stability of any part of the building.

Disproportionate collapse
A3 The building shall be constructed so that in the event of an accident, the building will not suffer collapse to an extent disproportionate to the cause.

PART B: FIRE SAFETY (2006)

Means of warning and escape
B1 The building shall be designed and constructed so that there are appropriate

Requirement B1 does not apply to any prison provided under

(Continued)

Checklist 9.1: (Continued)

provisions for the early warning of tire, and appropriate means of escape in case of fire from the building to a place of safety outside the building capable of being safely and effectively used at all material times.

Internal fire spread (linings)
B2 (1) To inhibit the spread of fire within the building, the internal linings shall –
(a) adequately resist the spread of flame over their surfaces; and
(b) have, if ignited, a rate of heat release or a rate of fire growth which is reasonable in the circumstances.
(2) In this paragraph, 'internal linings' mean the materials or products used in lining any partition, wall, ceiling or other internal structure.

Internal fire spread (structure)
B3 (1) The building shall be designed and constructed so that, in the event of fire, its stability will be maintained for a reasonable period.
(2) A wall common to two or more buildings shall be designed and constructed so that it adequately resists the spread of fire between those buildings. For the purposes of this sub-paragraph a house in a terrace and a semi-detached house are each to be treated as a separate building.
(3) Where reasonably necessary to inhibit the spread of fire within the building, measures shall be taken, to an extent appropriate to the size and intended use of the building, comprising either or both of the following:
a) sub-division of the building with fire-resisting construction;
b) installation of suitable automatic fire suppression systems.
(4) The building shall be designed and constructed so that the unseen spread of fire and smoke within concealed spaces in its structure and fabric is inhibited.

External fire spread
B4 (1) The external walls of the building shall adequately resist the spread of fire over the walls and from one building to another, having regard to the height, use and position of the building.
(2) The roof of the building shall adequately resist the spread of fire over the roof and from one building to another, having regard to the use and position of the building.

Access and facilities for the fire service
B5 (1) The building shall be designed and constructed so as to provide reasonable facilities to assist firefighters in the protection of life.
(2) Reasonable provision shall be made within the site of the building to enable fire appliances to gain access to the building.

section 33 of the Prisons Act 1952 (power to provide prisons. etc.)

Requirement B3 (3) does not apply to material alterations to any prison provided under Section 33 of the Prisons Act 1952.

Checklist 9.1: (Continued)

Checklist 9.1: (Continued)

PART C: SITE PREPARATION AND RESISTANCE TO MOISTURE (2004)

Preparation of site and resistance to contaminants
C1 (1) The ground to be covered by the building shall be reasonably free from any material that might damage the building or affect its stability, including vegetable matter, topsoil and pre-existing foundations.
(2) Reasonable precautions shall be taken to avoid danger to health and safety caused by contaminants on or in the ground covered, or to be covered by the building and any land associated with the building.
(3) Adequate sub-soil drainage shall be provided if it is needed to avoid –
(a) the passage of ground moisture to the interior of the building;
(b) damage to the building, including damage through the transport of water-borne contaminants to the foundations of the building.
(4) for the purpose of this requirement, "contaminant" means any substance which is or may become harmful to persons or buildings including substances, which are corrosive, explosive, flammable, radioactive or toxic.

Resistance to moisture
C2 The floors, walls and roof of the building shall adequately protect the building and people who use the building from harmful effects caused by:
a) ground moisture;
b) precipitation and wind-driven spray;
c) interstitial and surface condensation; and
d) spillage of water from or associated with sanitary fittings or fixed appliances.

PART D: TOXIC SUBSTANCES (2002)

Cavity insulation
D1 If insulating material is inserted into a cavity in a cavity wall reasonable precautions shall be taken to prevent the subsequent permeation of any toxic fumes from that material into any part of the building occupied by people.

PART E: RESISTANCE TO THE PASSAGE OF SOUND (2004)

Protection against sound from other parts of the building and adjoining buildings
E1 Dwelling-houses, flats and rooms for residential purposes shall be designed and constructed in such a way that they provide reasonable resistance to sound from other parts of the same building and from adjoining buildings.

(Continued)

Checklist 9.1: (Continued)

Protection against sound within a dwelling-house, etc.

E2 Dwelling-houses, flats and rooms for residential purposes shall be designed and constructed in such a way that –
(a) internal walls between a bedroom or a room containing a water closet, and other rooms; and
(b) internal floors, provide reasonable resistance to sound.

Requirement E2 does not apply to –
a) an internal wall which contains a door;
b) an internal wall which separates an en suite toilet from the associated bedroom; existing wall and floors in a building which is subject to a material change of use.

Reverberation in common internal parts of buildings containing flats or rooms for residential purposes

E3 The common internal parts of buildings which contain flats or rooms for residential purposes shall be designed and constructed in such a way as to prevent more reverberation around the common parts than is reasonable.

Requirement E3 only applies to corridors, stairwells, hallways and entrance halls which give access to the flat or room for residential purposes.

Acoustic conditions in schools

E4 (1) Each room or other space in a school building shall be designed and constructed in such a way that it has the acoustic conditions and the insulation against disturbance by noise appropriate to its intended use.
(2) For the purposes of this part – 'school' has the same meaning as in section 4 of the Education Act 1996[4] and 'school building' means any building forming a school or part of a school.

PART F: VENTILATION (2006)

Means of ventilation

F1 There shall be adequate means of ventilation provided for people in the building.

Requirement Fl does not apply to a building or space within a building –
(a) into which people do not normally go; or
(b) which is used solely for storage; or
(c) which is a garage used solely in connection with a single dwelling.

PART G: HYGIENE (2000)

Sanitary conveniences and washing facilities

G1 (1) Adequate sanitary conveniences shall be provided in rooms provided for that purpose, or in bathrooms. Any such room or bathroom shall be separated from places where food is prepared.
(2) Adequate washbasins shall be provided in –
(a) rooms containing water closets; or
(b) rooms or spaces adjacent to rooms containing water closets. Any such room or space shall be separated from places where food is prepared.
(3) There shall be a suitable installation for the provision of hot and cold water to washbasins provided in accordance with paragraph (2).

Checklist 9.1: (Continued)

(4) Sanitary conveniences and washbasins to which this paragraph applies shall be designed and installed so as to allow effective cleaning.

Bathrooms

G2 A bathroom shall be provided containing either a fixed bath or shower bath, and there shall be a suitable installation for the provision of hot and cold water to the bath or shower bath.

Requirement G2 applies only to dwellings.

Hot water storage

G3 A hot water storage system that has a hot water storage vessel which does not incorporate a vent pipe to the atmosphere shall be installed by a person competent to do so, and there shall be precautions –
(a) to prevent the temperature of stored water at any time exceeding 100°C;
(b) to ensure that the hot water discharged from safety devices is safely conveyed to where it is visible but will not cause danger to persons in or about the building.

Requirement G3 does not apply to –
a) a hot water storage system that has a storage vessel with a capacity of 15 litres or less.
b) a system providing space heating only
c) a system which heats or stores water for the purposes only of an industrial process

PART H: DRAINAGE AND WASTE DISPOSAL (2002)

Foul water drainage

H1 (1) An adequate system of drainage shall be provided to carry foul water from appliances within the building to one of the following, listed in order of priority –
(a) a public sewer; or, where that is not reasonably practicable,
(b) a private sewer communicating with a public sewer; or, where that is not reasonably practicable,
(c) either a septic tank which has an appropriate form of secondary treatment or another wastewater treatment system; or, where that is not reasonably practicable,
(d) a cesspool.
(2) In this part 'foul water' means waste water which comprises or includes –
(a) waste water from a sanitary convenience, bidet or appliance used for washing receptacles for foul waste; or
(b) water which has been used for food preparation, cooking or washing.

Requirement H1 does not apply to the diversion of water which has been used for personal washing or for the washing of clothes, linen, or other articles to collection systems for reuse.

Wastewater treatment systems and cesspools

H2 (1) Any septic tank and its form of secondary treatment, other wastewater treatment system or cesspool, shall be so sited and constructed that –
(a) it is not prejudicial to the health of any person;
(b) it will not contaminate any watercourse, underground water or water supply;
(c) there are adequate means for emptying and maintenance; and
(d) where relevant, it will function to a sufficient standard for the protection of health in the event of a power failure.

(Continued)

(2) Any septic tank, holding tank which is part of a wastewater treatment system or cesspool shall be –
(a) of adequate capacity;
(b) so constructed that it is impermeable to liquids; and
(c) adequately ventilated.
(3) Where a foul water drainage system from a building discharges to a septic tank, wastewater treatment system or cesspool, a durable notice shall be affixed in a suitable place in the building containing information on any continuing maintenance required to avoid risks to health.

Rainwater drainage
H3 (1) Adequate provision shall be made for rainwater to be carried from the roof of the building.
(2) Paved areas around the building shall be so constructed as to be adequately drained.

Requirement H3 (2) applies only to paved areas –
(a) which provide access to the building pursuant to paragraph M2 of Schedule 1 (access to and use of buildings);
(b) which provide access to or from a place of storage pursuant to paragraph H6 (2) of Schedule 1 (solid waste storage); or
(c) in any passage giving access to the building, where this is intended to be used in common by the occupiers of one or more other buildings.

(3) Rainwater from a system provided pursuant to sub-paragraphs (1) or (2) shall discharge to one of the following, listed in order of priority –
(a) an adequate soakaway or some other adequate system of infiltration system; or, where that is not reasonably practicable,
(b) a watercourse; or, where that is not reasonably practicable,
(c) a sewer.

Requirement H3(3) does not apply to the gathering of rainwater for reuse.

Building over sewers
H4 (1) The erection of extension of a building or work involving the underpinning of a building shall be carried out in a way that is not detrimental to the building or building extension or to the continued maintenance of the drain, sewer or disposal main.

(2) In this paragraph 'disposal main' means any pipe, tunnel or conduit used for the conveyance of effluent to or from a sewage disposal works, which is not a public sewer.

(3) In this paragraph and paragraph H5 'map of sewers' means any records kept by a sewerage undertaker under section 199 of the Water Industry Act 1991.

Requirement H4 only applies to work carried out –
(a) over a drain, sewer, or disposal main which is shown on any map of sewers; or
(b) on any site or in such a manner as may result in interference with the use of, or obstruction of the access of any person to, any drain, sewer or disposal main which is shown on any map of sewers.

Separate systems of drainage
H5 Any system for discharging water to a sewer which is provided pursuant to paragraph H3 shall be separate from that provided for the conveyance of foul water from the building.

Requirement H5 applies only to a system provided in connection with the erection or extension of a building where it is reasonably practicable for the system to discharge directly or indirectly to a sewer for the separate conveyance of surface water which is –
(a) shown on a map of sewers; or
(b) under construction either by the sewerage undertaker or by some other person (where the sewer is subject of an agreement to make a declaration of vesting pursuant to section 104 of the Water Industry Act 1991 (a)).

Solid waste storage
H6 (1) Adequate provision shall be made for storage of solid waste.
(2) Adequate means of access shall be provided –
(a) for people in the building to the place of storage; and
(b) from the place of storage to a collection point (where one has been specified by the waste collection authority under section 46 (household waste) or section 47 (commercial waste) of the Environmental Protection Act 1990 (b). or to a street (where no collection point has been specified).

PART J: COMBUSTION APPLIANCES AND FUEL STORAGE SYSTEMS (2002)

Air supply
J1 Combustion appliances shall be so installed that there is an adequate supply of air to them for combustion, to prevent overheating and for the efficient working of any flue.

Requirements J1, J2, and J3 apply only to fixed combustion appliances (including incinerators).

Discharge of products of combustion
J2 Combustion appliances shall have adequate provision for the discharge of products of combustion to the outside air.

Protection of the building
J3 Combustion appliances and flue-pipes shall be so installed, and fireplaces and chimneys shall be so constructed and installed, as to reduce to a reasonable level the risk of people suffering burns or the building catching fire in consequence of their use.

(Continued)

Checklist 9.1: (Continued)

Provision of information

J4 Where a hearth, fireplace, flue or chimney is provided or extended, a durable notice containing information on the performance capabilities of the hearth, fireplace, flue or chimney shall be affixed in a suitable place in the building for the purpose of enabling combustion appliances to be safely installed.

Protection of liquid fuel storage systems

J5 Liquid fuel storage systems and the pipes connecting them to combustion appliances shall be so constructed and separated from buildings and the boundary of the premises as to reduce to a reasonable level the risk of the fuel igniting in the event of fire in adjacent buildings or premises.

Requirement J5 applies only to –
(a) fixed oil storage tanks with capacities greater than 90 litres and connecting pipes; and
(b) fixed liquid petroleum gas storage installations with capacities greater than 150 litres and connecting pipes, which are located outside the building and which serve fixed combustion appliances (including incinerators) in the building.

Protection against pollution

J6 Oil storage tanks and the pipes connecting them to combustion appliances shall –
(a) be so constructed and protected as to reduce to a reasonable level the risk of the oil escaping and causing pollution; and
(b) have affixed in a prominent position a durable notice containing information on how to respond to an oil escape so as to reduce to a reasonable level the risk of pollution.

Requirement J6 applies only to fixed oil storage tanks with capacities of 3500 litres or less, and connecting pipes which are –
(a) located outside the building; and
(b) serve fixed combustion appliances (including incinerators) in a building used wholly or mainly as a private dwelling, but does not apply to buried systems.

PART K: PROTECTION FROM FALLING COLLISION AND IMPACT (2000)

Stairs, ladders, and ramps

K1 Stairs, ladders and ramps shall be so designed, constructed and installed as to be safe for people moving between different levels in or about the building.

Requirement K1 applies only to stairs, ladders and ramps which form part of the building.

Protection from falling

K2 (a) Any stairs, ramps, floors and balconies, and any roof to which people have access; and
(b) any light well, basement area or similar sunken area connected to a building, shall be provided with barriers where they are necessary to protect people in or about the building from falling.

Requirement K2 (a) applies only to stairs and ramps which form part of the building.

Vehicle barriers and loading bays

K3 (1) Vehicle ramps and any levels in a building to which vehicles have access, shall be provided with barriers where it is necessary to protect in or about the building.

(2) Vehicle loading bays shall be constructed in such a way, or be provided with such features as may be necessary to protect people in them from collision with vehicles.

Protection from collision with open windows, etc.

K4 Provision shall be made to prevent people moving in or about the building from collision with open windows, skylights or ventilators.

Requirement K4 does not apply to dwelling.

Protection against impact from and trapping by doors

K5 (1) Provision shall be made to prevent any door or gate –
(a) which slides or opens upwards, from falling onto any person; and
(b) which is powered, from trapping any person.
(2) Provision shall be made for powered doors and gates to be opened in the event of a power failure. Provision shall be made to ensure a clear view of the space on either side of a swing door or gate.

Requirement K5 does not apply to –
(a) dwellings; or
(b) any door or gate which is part of a lift.

PART L: CONSERVATION OF FUEL AND POWER (2006)

Conservation of fuel and power in new dwellings

L1A Reasonable provision shall be made for the conservation of fuel and power in buildings by:
(a) limiting the heat gains and losses:
(i) through thermal elements and other parts of the building fabric; and
(ii) from pipes, ducts and vessels used for space heating, space cooling and hot water services;
(b) providing and commissioning energy efficient fixed building services with effective controls; and
(c) providing to the owner sufficient information about the building, the fixed building services and their maintenance requirements so that the building can be operated in such a manner as to use no more fuel and power than is reasonable in the circumstances.

Conservation of fuel and power in existing dwellings

L1B Reasonable provision shall be made for the conservation of fuel and power in buildings by
(a) limiting the heat gains and losses:
(i) through thermal elements and other parts of the building fabric; and
(ii) from pipes, ducts and vessels used for space heating, space cooling and hot water services;

(Continued)

Checklist 9.1: (Continued)

(b) providing and commissioning energy efficient fixed building services with effective controls; and

(c) providing to the owner sufficient information about the building, the fixed building services and their maintenance requirements so that the building can be operated in such a manner as to use no more fuel and power than is reasonable in the circumstances.

Conservation of fuel and power in new buildings other than dwellings

L2A *as L1A.*

Conservation of fuel and power in existing buildings other than dwellings

L2B *as L2A.*

PART M: ACCESS TO AND USE OF BUILDINGS (2004)

Access and use

M1 Reasonable provision shall be made for people to
(a) gain access to; and
(b) use the building and its facilities

The requirements of this Part do not apply to –
(a) an extension of or material alteration of a dwelling; or
(b) any part of a building which is used solely to enable the building or any service or fitting in the building to be inspected, repaired or maintained.

Access to extensions to buildings other than dwellings

M2 Suitable independent access shall be provided to the extension where reasonably practicable.

Requirement M2 does not apply where suitable access to the extension is provided through the building that is extended.

Sanitary conveniences in extension to buildings other than dwellings

M3 If sanitary conveniences are provided in any building that is to be extended, reasonable provision shall be made within the extension for sanitary conveniences.

Requirement M3 does not apply where there is reasonable provision for sanitary conveniences elsewhere in the building, such that people occupied in, or otherwise having occasion to enter the extension, can gain access to and use those sanitary conveniences.

Sanitary conveniences in dwellings

M4 – (1) Reasonable provision shall be made in the entrance storey for sanitary conveniences, or where the entrance storey contains no habitable rooms, reasonable provision for sanitary conveniences shall be made in either the entrance storey or principal storey.

(2) In this paragraph 'entrance storey' means the storey which contains the principal entrance and 'principal storey' means the storey nearest to the entrance storey which contains a habitable room, or if there are two such storeys equally near, either such storey.

Checklist 9.1: (Continued)

PART N: GLAZING – SAFETY IN RELATION TO IMPACT, OPENING AND CLEANING (2000)

Protection against impact

N1 Glazing, with which people are likely to come into contact whilst moving in or about the building, shall –
(a) if broken on impact, break in a way which is unlikely to cause injury; or
(b) resist impact without breaking; or
(c) be shielded or protected from impact.

Manifestation of glazing

N2 Transparent glazing, with which people are likely to come into contact while moving in or about the building, shall incorporate features which make it apparent.

Requirement N2 does not apply to dwellings.

Safe opening and closing of windows, etc.

N3 Windows, skylights and ventilators which can be opened by people in or about the building shall be so constructed or equipped that they may be opened, closed or adjusted safely.

Requirement N3 does not apply to dwellings.

Safe access for cleaning windows etc.

N4 Provision shall be made for any windows, skylights or any transparent or translucent walls, ceilings or roofs to be safely accessible for cleaning.

Requirement N4 does not apply to –
(a) dwellings; or
(b) any transparent or translucent elements whose surface are not intended to be cleaned.

PART P: ELECTRICAL SAFETY (2006)

Design and installation

P1 Reasonable provision shall be made in the design and installation of electrical installations in order to protect persons operating, maintaining or altering the installations from fire or injury.

The requirements of this part apply only to electrical installations that are intended to operate at low or extra-low voltage and are:
(a) in or attached to a dwelling;
(b) in the common parts of a building serving one or more dwellings, but excluding power supplies to lifts;
(c) in a building that receives its electricity from a source located within or shared with a dwelling; or
(d) in a garden or in or on land associated with a building where the electricity is from a source located within or shared with a dwelling.

10

Building Regulations in Scotland

DAVID WEDDERBURN

1 Introduction

1.01 Building control and the new building standards system in Scotland are based on Building (Scotland) Act 2003. To understand Scottish practice, a knowledge of that Act is required, as well as of the Regulations made under it. The Building (Scotland) Regulations 2004 are only one part of the whole scene, although admittedly a very important part. Anyone trying to compare the Scottish building standards system and English building control must bear the above in mind, so that there is a comparison of like with like wherever possible.

1.02 This study is intended to describe the main provisions of the Building (Scotland) Act 2003 and procedures laid down under it, as well as the various Statutory Instruments associated with it. With regard to the Building Regulations themselves, it is obviously impossible to go into minute detail with interpretations, etc. The object of each of the Regulations has, therefore, been briefly stated and reference made to those provisions which have been amended in May 2007. This is because, except for some minor changes, when the new building standards system was introduced in May 2005 there was, wherever possible, a horizontal transposition of building standards from those applicable under the old system into the new system. The amendments introduced in May 2007 were, therefore, the first significant change to those standards.

Historical background

1.03 Building control is not new, and records of building law go back to the pre-Christian era. The first known are those found in the Mosaic Law of King Hammurabi of Persia *c.*2000 BC. Fire precautions which have always formed a major part of building codes were an accepted factor of Roman law and of English law from the twelfth century.

Dean of Guild Courts

1.04 In Scotland building control in royal burghs was exercised by Dean of Guild Courts where these existed. Originally, the Dean of Guild was the president of the merchants' guild, which was composed of traders who had acquired the freedom of a royal burgh. The post is an ancient one, e.g. in 1403 one Simon de Schele was appointed Dean of Guild and Keeper of the Kirk Work by Edinburgh Town Council. The Dean of Guild Court's original mercantile jurisdiction fell gradually into disuse to be replaced by a jurisdiction over such areas as markets, streets, and buildings. 'Questions of neighbourhood' were dealt with by Edinburgh Dean of Guild as early as 1584. Gradually the scope and nature of the powers of the Dean of Guild Courts became more precise until

during the last 150 years they were subjected to a process of statutory modification.

1.05 Not all burghs had Dean of Guild Courts, and it was not until 1947 that the Local Government (Scotland) Act required burghs without Dean of Guild Courts to appoint one. In other burghs, the functions of the Dean of Guild Courts were either carried out by magistrates or the town council itself. In counties, plans were usually approved by a sub-committee of the public health committee. There was no warrant procedure as in burghs.

By-laws

1.06 During the last 150 years, statutory requirements laid the foundation of specific and more widely applicable standards. The Burgh Police Act 1833 empowered burghs to adopt powers of paving, lighting, cleansing, watching, and supplying water. However, the building legislation content of the nineteenth-century Acts was not large and was related mainly to ruinous property and drainage, attention to the latter being attracted by the large-scale outbreaks of cholera at that time. In 1892 the Burgh Police Act introduced a detailed set of building rules which were repealed by the 1903 Burgh Police Act. This Act gave powers to burghs to make by-laws in respect of building and public health matters. Meanwhile in the counties, the Public Health (Scotland) Act 1897 had already given them the power to make similar by-laws.

1.07 By-laws made under these Acts, although limited in scope, remained the main form of building control until 1932 when the Department of Health for Scotland published model building by-laws for both burghs and countries. Local authorities could, if they wished, adopt these by-laws for application in their own area. However, many did not. The model by-laws were revised in 1934 and 1937, but, apart from a widening of scope, later editions did not differ much from the original 1932 version. A much more comprehensive review was carried out in 1954. Although many local authorities adopted the 1954 model by-laws, adoption was at the discretion of the local authority and many did not. (By 1957, 26 of the 33 counties, 127 of the 173 small burghs, 13 of the 20 large burghs, and none of the cities had adopted the model by-laws.) However, Edinburgh, Aberdeen, and Glasgow had local Acts which combined many of the requirements of old statutes and by-laws with local features.

1.08 The then existing legislation fell short of the requirements of a modern building code able to cope with the rapidly expanding building of post-war Scotland where new techniques and materials were rapidly being introduced. It was decided that the whole concept of building control should be reviewed, and to this end a committee under the chairmanship of C. W. G. Guest QC, later Lord Guest, was appointed by the Secretary of State.

1.09 The committee's terms of reference required that it examine the existing law pertaining to building and jurisdiction of the Dean of Guild Courts and make recommendations on the future form of a building control system for counties and burghs, which was to be flexible enough to take account of new techniques and materials.

1.10 The committee published its report in October 1957. Its main recommendation was that legislation was essential to enable a comprehensive building code to be set up in the form of national regulations to achieve uniformity throughout the country. The basic purpose of building control should be the protection of the public interest as regards health and safety. The law must ensure that occupants, neighbours, and passers-by are protected by preventing the erection of buildings that are liable to collapse or lead to unhealthy or insanitary conditions. It must also prevent individual and collective fire hazards.

1.11 The recommendations were accepted and led to the form of control established under the Building (Scotland) Act 1959 (as amended). For work carried out under building warrants issued before May 2005 this form of control still applies and reference should be made to the relevant chapter within the previous edition of this handbook for information on that form of control. This chapter will deal with the new system introduced from May 2005 under the Building (Scotland) Act 2003 and its subsidiary legislation.

2 Review of the new Building Standards system

Reasons for change

2.01 The previous Building Control system set up under the Building (Scotland) Act 1959 served Scotland well over the 41 years of its operation (and continues to do so for that small number of warrants still administered under that Act). However, present conditions are different from those in 1964, when the previous system first came into operation, and the need for change to the system has become clearer over recent years. There were a number of different problems with the old system but there were two which particularly necessitated a change.

Technical Standards

2.02 The first was that regulation 9 of the Building Standards Regulations made under the Building (Scotland) Regulations 1959 (as amended) stipulated that the requirements of regulations 10–33 (setting out the technical standards required for buildings) could be satisfied *only* by compliance with the standards set out in the relevant Technical Standards issued with the relevant Building Standards Regulations (issued in 16 parts: Parts A–S (with different parts dealing with different Regulations). This had two consequences. First, there was little flexibility for technical innovation or original design solutions, which led to an increasing need for individual and class relaxations. Secondly, because technical standards were a necessary part of the Regulations, they could only be changed by statutory instrument which, in addition to requiring parliamentary time, also required to be notified in draft to the European Commission and other member states, and were subject to an objection from those parties.

Construction Products Directive

2.03 The second problem also had its origins in European law. Under the Construction Products Directive, construction products for use in Scotland can no longer be specified in Technical Standards drafted in terms of British Standards and British technical requirements. This is considered under EU Law as a barrier to trade. Compliance with requirements of the Construction Products Directive created problems under the old system. The Scottish

Executive, in amendment 6 to the Building Standard (Scotland) Regulations 1990, addressed this problem by having two alternative Technical Standards, one using British Standards and the other using European Standards. However, amendment 6 was limited in its scope. It became clear at that stage that it would be very difficult to make all of the technical standards comply with the requirements of European law and research had already been initiated at that stage in preparation for a new Building (Scotland) Act and a new Building Standards system.

Reform process

2.04 The Scottish Executive, having decided that a new Building (Scotland) Act was necessary, took the opportunity to address a number of other problems. These related to: consistency of interpretation of the Building Regulations among local authorities; the need for continuing obligations to make certain physical requirements comply; the problem of unauthorised minor works; the problem of works carried out without a building warrant and/or without a completion certificate; the issue of Crown immunity; expansion of the objectives of the regulations; and the problem of defective as opposed to dangerous buildings.

2.05 Reform of the Building Standard system was initiated with a scoping study in the year 2000, a Green Paper in July 2001, the White Paper in March 2002 with Royal Assent to the Building (Scotland) Act 2003 in March 2003 and the Regulations produced in autumn of 2004 (the last regulations, on forms, being produced in 2005) and the system became operational, subject to two exceptions (building standards assessment and Crown immunity, which were to be introduced later), on May 2005.

New system

Statutory basis

2.06 The Act under which the new system is introduced is the Building (Scotland) Act 2003. A number of Regulations and Orders are introduced under the Act. These are set out at the end of this chapter. In addition, the Scottish Building Standards Agency was set up as an executive agency of the Scottish Executive in June of 2004 and was re-integrated into the Scottish Government in April 2007, as the Building Standards Division (BSD) of the Directorate for the Built Environment, where it acts on behalf of Scottish Ministers under the Act. In that capacity the BSD has issued: (1) Domestic and Non-Domestic Technical Handbooks which provide guidance as to compliance with the Building Regulations; (2) a Procedural Handbook (now in its 2nd edition) which provides advice on procedures under the Act and has a number of very useful flow charts covering most of the procedures arising under the Act and its regulations; (3) a Certification Handbook giving advice regarding the setting up of certification schemes under section 7(2) or individual applications under section 7(1) of the Act; (4) model forms to supplement those included in the Forms Regulations; (5) guidance on such matters as continuing requirements and staged warrants; and (6) directions on such matters as electrical installations and structural design together with other house keeping matters such as corrections and erratum to Handbooks and Forms.

2.07 The BSD also maintain an excellent website at www.sbsa. gov.uk which contains all of the above documents on line, most of which documents include interactive links within them to allow direct access to the documents referred to in them. The website also provides access to many other documents on related topics. BSD also produce an interactive CD-Rom which when used on a computer with access to the Internet provides links to other websites with such information as SAP ratings and their calculation. In addition, BSD issues e-newsletters at regular intervals, which provide subscribers with an update on the activities of BSD and related topics. Those wishing to receive these newsletters can register at the BSD website.

3 Outline of Building (Scotland) Act 2003

3.01 The Act is composed of 6 Parts, with 6 Schedules. The Parts consist of: Part 1 (Building Regulations: Sections 1–6) covering the making of building regulations, relaxations, guidance and assessments; Part 2 (Approval of Construction Work etc: Sections 7–24) covering building warrants their administration and those involved; Part 3 (Compliance and Enforcement: Sections 25–27), covering enforcement which is by the local authority; Part 4 (Defective and Dangerous Buildings: Sections 28–30) which provides local authorities with new powers in relation to defective buildings which bolster and partly replace the powers they already have under section 87 of the Civic Government (Scotland) Act 1982 (as amended) and reintroduces the powers it had under the 1959 Act in relation to dangerous buildings; Part 5 (General: Sections 31–56) covering miscellaneous matters including procedures, forms, fees, appeals, Crown application, penalties, corporate liability, civil liability and interpretation; and Part 6 (Supplementary: Sections 57–59) covering among other things commencement procedures.

Part 1 (Building Regulations) (Sections 1–6)

Scope of Regulations

3.02 The Act at section 1 has increased the purposes for which Building Regulations can be made to include 'furthering the achievement of sustainable development' and has added to the list of matters in relation which regulations can be made: suitability for use by disabled persons, security and reuse of building materials.

It should be emphasised that these are only matters, which may be, but do not have to be, covered. However such matters as sustainable development are being considered when drafting present regulations and the last amendments in May 2007 introduced concepts such as 'liveability', which relate to suitability for use by disabled persons. Reference should be made to paragraph 5(2) of Schedule 1 to the Act as to the subject matter of Building Regulations. In addition, those regulations which previously were covered in a separate set of regulations (Building Operations (Scotland) Regulations) have now been incorporated into the Building Regulations which therefore now include obligations relative to making completed demolition sites safe, protecting the works, clearing footpaths and securing unoccupied and partly completed buildings (regulations 10 (2), 13, 14 and 15). This means that where other parts of the Act require compliance with the Building Regulations or persons are required to certify such compliance these operational standards are covered along with the more expected building standards.

3.03 It was decided that since a new system was being introduced, where possible, the technical standards should not be changed. There was, therefore, at their introduction in May 2005, generally a horizontal transposition of standards from the old system to the new system. The only major change being the requirement for sprinkler systems in high-rise domestic buildings, dwellings, which form part of a sheltered housing complex, residential care buildings and enclosed shopping centres. However, in May 2007 amendments were introduced and it is those amended regulations which are covered in more detail later in this chapter.

Building Regulations

3.04 The Building Standards, which are set out in Schedule 5 to the Building Regulations and incorporated by regulation 9, are now drafted as expanded functional standards so that they should not need to be changed to accommodate technical or design innovations. The statutory requirement is to comply with these regulations. However one of the problems addressed under the new Act is that of unauthorised minor works. The old system required a building warrant for many small works for which, in practice, a warrant was never applied for or received. This caused problems in purifying missives in domestic conveyancing and could conceal dangerous works in amongst the harmless. The new system still requires a 'building warrant' before most works can be carried out, however the category of those works requiring to comply with the Building Regulations but not requiring a building warrant, which is set out in Schedule 3 to the Building Regulations, has been expanded. It should be noted, however, that while these works do not require a building warrant they do still require to comply with the Building Regulations. This could present problems in the sale and purchase of property where the missives require an undertaking regarding compliance with statutory requirements. Exhibition of a building warrant completion certificate (now to have been accepted by the verifier, more of which later) will only address those works, which were subject to a building warrant, and not other works, which did not need such a warrant.

Conversion

3.05 The old system of 'change of use' relied upon the grouping of buildings into different 'classes' to which the regulations applied to different degrees and therefore the need to change a building when it moved from one class to another to meet the requirements of the new class. Under the new system there are only two categories (Domestic and Non-Domestic), each with its own set of guidance. The new system has the concept of 'conversion' with those changes, which constitute conversion, being set out in Schedule 2 to the Building Regulations, and the regulations, which apply in relation to such conversions, being set out in Schedule 6 to the Building Regulations. However, Schedule 6 has two paragraphs. The first sets out those standards with which every 'conversion' must comply while the second sets out those standards which are to be met only so far as reasonably practicable as long as they are no worse than they were before the conversion.

Continuing requirements – Scottish Ministers

3.06 Under the old system it was found increasingly necessary, especially in relaxations from the Regulations, to use technical solutions, such as sprinkler systems or pressurised smoke control systems, whose efficacy relied upon their mechanical reliability. Under the old system the building warrant and completion certificate only certified (and then only to a certain extent) the condition of the system and its efficacy at completion of the works and could not control or check how it was maintained and tested over the years. The Act has therefore, at section 2, introduced a power to include such continuing obligations into the Building Regulations. This power has been used to introduce a new regulation (regulation 17) with continuing obligations in relation to the inspection of air-conditioning systems within buildings and the giving of advice in relation to them in order to implement, in Scotland, part of the European Directive on the Energy Performance of Buildings. This will be covered in more detail later.

Continuing requirements – Verifier

3.07 In addition the Act, at section 22, allows continuing requirements to be imposed with a Building Warrant or with the acceptance of a late submitted completion certificate (under section 17(4) of the Act) where necessary, to avoid the purposes of any provision of the Building Regulations being frustrated. For example acceptance of a moveable platform for cleaning widows could be made subject to a continuing requirement that adequate access and hard standing are provided and kept clear and properly maintained thereafter. The BSD has also issued guidance on staged warrants in which they suggest that for projects involving 'shell' and 'fit-out' works separate building warrants each with their own completion certificates could be issued but subject to a continuing requirement under the 'shell' building warrant that the building is not occupied or used until the 'fit-out' works are complete.

Technical Guidance

3.08 Because the Building Regulations are drafted in general terms, they provide no practical guidance as to how to comply with them. Under section 4 of the Act, Scottish Ministers, normally acting through the BSD, may issue guidance documents providing practical guidance on the requirements of the Building Regulations. This guidance may be withdrawn, fresh guidance may be issued, or the existing guidance revised by notice with no need for any parliamentary procedure or reference to the EU. This should allow such guidance to be changed quickly as the need arises. Under section 5 of the Act, failure to comply with the guidance does not, of itself, give rise to civil or criminal liability. It is sufficient for the applicant to show that his proposals meet the requirements of the Building Regulations, even if they adopt means which are different from those set out in the guidance. However, following the guidance can have its benefits as, under section 5 (2) of the Act proof of compliance with the guidance can be treated as tending to negative liability for a breach of the Building Regulations. This should be contrasted with the standing of approved codes of practice for Health and Safety Regulations made under the Health & Safety at Work Act 1974, where a breach of the relevant provision of the code can be used as proof of contravention of the relevant requirement or prohibition subject to proof of compliance by another means.

Technical Handbooks

3.09 The guidance is produced in two Technical Handbooks: one for domestic buildings and one for non-domestic buildings. The two Handbooks are organised into seven sections, the first section being a general interpretive section numbered '0' and providing guidance on the Building Regulations, except for regulation 9, and the following six sections numbered 1–6 corresponding to the six sections of Schedule 5 to the Building Regulations, incorporated into the Building Regulations by regulation 9, which set out the required building standards and which correspond with the six essential requirements of the Construction Products Directive (Structure; Fire; Environment; Safety; Noise; and Energy). This has meant that the contents of the different parts (A–S) of the old

Technical Standards have had to be re-arranged. There was, at Appendix C, to each of the original Handbooks a table cross-referencing the old sections with the new. However, as the new system is now over three years old and the original standards have been amended the present Handbooks do not have such an appendix. At the beginning of May 2007, in addition to the amendments to the different Regulations (set out in the rest of this chapter) and the updating of the two technical Handbooks mentioned above, a new handbook, *The Guide for Practitioners – Conversion of Traditional Buildings (Part 1: Principles and Practice & Part II: Application of the Building Standards)* prepared by Historic Scotland in conjunction with Scottish Building Standards Agency (now Building Standards Division), was issued by Scottish Ministers under section 4 (1) of the Act to come into effect under section 4(2) of the Act with the same status as the other two Technical Handbooks. Thus where building works, subject to the Building Regulations, are being carried out to historic buildings this guide can be used to give guidance, on a par with that in the Technical Handbooks, as to compliance with those Regulations. There is also a Technical Handbook, issued under section 4 of the Act, on conservatories, providing guidance on how to meet the Building Regulations for simple conservatories. In addition, BSD issues further guidance, which does not have the status of Technical Guidance but which is meant to assist in meeting the functional standards set out in regulation 9. For example, there are Accredited Construction Details (Scotland), which show one way, but not the only way, to address issues of air infiltration and heat-loss through junctions in the fabric of the building.

Relaxations

3.10 Provisions have still been retained, at section 3 of the Act, for the relaxation of any particular provision within the Building Regulations on the Scottish Ministers own initiative, in relation to a type of building, or upon an application from any person relative to a particular building. However, because the standards set by Building Regulations are drafted as functional standards, it is not expected that there will need to be many such relaxations.

Building Standards assessments

3.11 Section 6 introduces an obligation on local authorities, if requested by the owner of a building, to carry out a Building Standards assessment of that building. Assessing the extent to which: (i) the building complies with the Building Regulations applicable at the time of assessment; (ii) there is any unauthorised work to the building; (iii) any applicable continuing requirements relative to the building are being complied with; and (iv) the building has any defects which would entitle the authority to serve a defective building notice on the owner. This section has not yet been implemented.

Part 2 (Approval of Construction Work Etc) (Sections 7–24)

Verifiers and approved certifiers of design and of construction

The Act introduces three new persons: verifiers; approved certifiers of design; and approved certifiers of construction.

Verifiers

3.12 Verifiers have the duty to administer the granting of building warrants, amendments to those warrants, the staging of work under those warrants and the acceptance of completion certificates. Verifiers are appointed by Scottish Ministers under section 7(1)(a) of the Act. Scottish Ministers are to consider any potential verifier's qualifications; competence; accountability to the public; and impartiality before making any appointment (Part VI of the Procedure Regulations). At present, all 32 Scottish local authorities have been appointed as verifiers within their own areas for

6 years from May 2005 until 2011. Such appointment is subject to the provisions of section 7 of and Schedule 2 to the Act. Within Schedule 2 there is a provision (paragraph 9) prohibiting verifiers acting as such in relation to buildings in which they have an interest unless authorised to do so by a direction from Scottish Ministers. Such a direction was issued covering the first 3 years of the operation of the system. Under it local authorities, as verifiers, were able to act as verifiers in relation to works in which they had an interest, usually as owner. This authorisation expired in April 2008 but has been extended to April 2011 subject to the operation of a system of peer review within consortia of local authorities. At present there are six consortia, covering all of the main land local authorities (the island authorities have been exempted but are applying to join). The legislation is drafted so that verifiers need not necessarily be local authorities but at present there are no plans to involve any other bodies. Verifiers are subject to regular audit by Scottish Ministers, which is being carried out on their behalf by BSD, and the outcome of those audits can be viewed on BSD's website. It is intended that all of the verifiers will be audited, at least once, by the end of the first 6-year period. BSD also maintain a register of verifiers.

Certifiers

3.13 Section 7 also provides for Scottish Ministers appointing persons, or approving schemes entitling persons, to act as approved certifiers of design and as approved certifiers of construction. So far, only schemes have been approved, such schemes and the role of such certifiers of design and of construction in the building warrant procedures are discussed in more detail later in this chapter. Reference should be made to the Certification Handbook, available from the BSD website, if you should be considering setting up such a scheme, and to the links to the operating schemes, again available on the BSD website, should you be thinking of joining a scheme. These schemes are subject to audit by BSD, on behalf of Scottish Ministers, and operate their own internal audit both of certifiers and of the approved bodies who employ the certifiers. Scottish Ministers, through the BSD and their website, maintain a public register of approved certifiers of design and of construction which can be checked to ensure that a person holding themselves out as an approved certifier is approved and for what they are approved.

Views

3.14 As noted above, one of the problems, which the new Act was introduced to address, was the problem of different interpretations by different local authorities as to the meaning of the Regulations. This meant that persons building in different parts of Scotland could find that the same proposed construction could comply with the regulations in one part of Scotland and not in another. A power has therefore been given to Scottish Ministers, normally acting through the BSD, under section 12 of the Act, which allows them, at their discretion and at the expense of the verifier, to give a view as to the extent that any particular proposals comply with the Building Regulations. Such views will have to be taken into account when considering any application for a building warrant and the BSD is publishing those views of general application to encourage a consistent interpretation of the Building Regulations. Until the May 2007 amendments, most views were dealing with fire and means of escape but now with the changes to accessibility in May 2007 there have been a number of views on this subject. However, as the Building Regulations are legal documents, only the courts can give a definitive and binding interpretation as to what they mean.

Works requiring a building warrant

3.15 Under section 8 of the Act a building warrant is required for: construction or demolition; or the provision of services, fittings or equipment in or in connection with, a building to which the Building Regulations apply or to any conversion except for those works, mentioned above, which require to comply with the Building Regulations but do not require a building warrant.

Application for building warrant

3.16 The application for building warrant is submitted to the verifier who must grant a building warrant if, but only if, satisfied that the work, demolition or provision of services etc. will be carried out in accordance with the Building Regulations (including the building operations requirements mentioned above), that nothing in the drawings specifications etc. submitted with the application indicates that the works or services etc. when completed in accordance with those plans, specifications etc. will fail to comply with the Building Regulations or where the application is for a conversion that after the conversion is completed it will comply with the Building Regulations (but only to the extent set out in Schedule 6 to the Building Regulations).

Amendments to building warrants and staged building warrants

3.17 The new Act contains provisions on amendment to building warrants and for staged building warrants similar to those in the 1959 Act except that the provisions for staged building warrants in the new Procedures Regulations are much more flexible with no stipulation as to the stages (except for construction of foundations). This should allow verifiers and applicants to agree appropriate stages with further work beyond that stage being contingent upon an amendment to the building warrant incorporating the further stage of the works. In addition, a building warrant will not be granted for extensions or alterations to existing buildings where, in relation to compliance with the Building Regulations, the existing building complies but will not with the extension or alteration or where the existing building fails to comply but will fail to a greater degree with the extension or alteration.

Limited-life buildings

3.18 The Act has provisions, similar to those in the 1959 Act, relative to buildings with a limited life and also providing that any building warrant is granted subject to any conditions within it and subject to the works etc., which are the subject matter of the building warrant, being carried out in accordance with the Building Regulations. However the Act does, at section 14(6), create the specific statutory offence of occupying or using a building after the expiry of its limited life (other than for demolition) knowing the period has expired or without regard to as to whether it has expired or not. In addition to the powers of enforcement given under section 27 of the Act (Building Warrant Enforcement), the Act gives the local authority power to seek to prevent or restrain such actual or apprehended occupation or use by applying for an interdict.

Approved certifiers of design

3.19 In addition to submitting the plans specifications etc. to satisfy the verifier as to the matters noted above, the applicant can also, submit a certificate from an approved certifier of design. Such a certificate should certify that the part of the design for which the certifier is approved to certify and the proposed method of working both comply with the Building Regulations. The verifier must treat such a certificate, as conclusive evidence as to what it certifies and, other than satisfying themselves as to the validity and the scope of the certificate, the verifier need make no further enquiries. Anyone thinking of becoming an approved certifier should, however, note that it is a criminal offence knowingly or recklessly to issue such a certificate which is false or misleading in a material particular. The applicant also commits a criminal offence where they knowingly or recklessly make an application for a building warrant, which contains a statement, which is false or misleading in a material particular. It is therefore important, where advising applicants who are not technically expert, to ensure that they take expert advice before completing the application.

Approved certification schemes

3.20 Under Regulations made under the 1959 Act, as amended, chartered engineers could certify that their design complied with the building regulations and such certificates were accepted by the local authority as conclusive evidence of what they certified. This was the only such certificate accepted under the 1959 Act relative to building warrants. It was therefore decided that structural design should be the first area of design covered by a scheme for approved certifiers of design. The scheme is operated by SER Ltd (again there is a link to it on the BSD website). The Scheme covers all of Section 1 of Schedule 5 to the Building Regulations and therefore the certifier has to be in a position to be satisfied on all aspects of the structural design whenever and by whomsoever designed. This has been a problem in relation to staged works and in relation to contractor designed aspects of the works. The solution, in relation to staged warrants, is for the certificate to make clear which stage is covered and when the amendment for the next stage is applied for the accompanying certificate will not only certify the new work but will also confirm the effects of the new stage on the previous works, thus maintaining a certificate for all of the structural works. In relation to contractor designed structure, such as roof trusses or connection details, which at the time of the warrant application are not designed, the certificate is to include a performance specification for those items and when the detailed design is produced then the certifier is to confirm that it meets the performance specification (see model form Q). There have also been two new schemes relative to Section 6 (Energy) of Schedule 5 to the Building Regulations one for domestic buildings the other for non-domestic buildings. These will be covered later in this chapter.

Consequences of no building warrant or non-compliance with a building warrant

3.21 Under the 1959 Act it was an offence to conduct building operations or demolition or change of use to which the building regulations applied without a building warrant. However that Act did not make it explicit who was caught and what defences they might have. Under section 8 of the Act the situation is made clearer.

Offences under section 8

3.22 In relation to the carrying out of work, provision of services etc. conversion requiring a building warrant there are two offences: (1) carrying out such activity without a building warrant; or (2) where building warrant has been granted, carrying out such activity not in accordance with that building warrant: and there are three categories of potential offenders: (a) the person actually carrying out such activity ('person carrying out the activity'); (b) the person on whose behalf such activity is carried out ('person instructing the activity'); and (c) the owner of the building within which, or in relation to which, such activity is carried out where they are not already a person in category (a) or (b) above ('owner').

Section 8 defences

3.23 Each of these persons has different statutory defences to the two different offences. Where the activity is being carried out without a building warrant: (i) the person carrying out the activity has a defence where, before the activity commenced, the person instructing the activity or the owner gave him reasonable cause to believe that a building warrant had been granted for such activity; and (ii) the owner has a defence where, whilst the activity is being carried out, he did not know, and had no reasonable cause to know, that the activity was being carried out. In such circumstances the person instructing the activity has no statutory defence.

3.24 Where a building warrant has been obtained for the activity but the activity is being carried out not in accordance with that building warrant, the person instructing the activity and the owner, where appropriate, each has a defence where, at the time of the alleged offence, they did not know and had no reasonable cause to know that the activity was being carried out not in accordance with the building warrant. In such circumstances the person carrying out the activity has no statutory defence.

Consequences

3.25 In future, therefore, any person instructed to carry out an activity for which a building warrant is required should, before starting, require confirmation from the person instructing such activity or the owner of the building, in relation to which such activity is instructed, as appropriate, that a building warrant covering the proposed activity is in place. The person instructed to carry out such activity should also have a copy of the building warrant and associated plans, specifications and documents and should insist that, in carrying out the proposed activity, he should not be required to breach either the building warrant or the Building Regulations. The building contract documents should, therefore, not conflict with building warrant plans, specifications and documents.

3.26 The person instructing the activity and the owner, where appropriate, will need to ensure that, where the proposed activity requires a building warrant, one is obtained and that they have procedures in place, in relation to the implementation of the building warrant, where they might have reasonable cause to suspect that the implementation may not be in accordance with the building warrant, to ensure that such implementation is in accordance with the building warrant. In this regard you should note that, where the owner of the building, in relation to which such activity is to be carried, is not the applicant for the building warrant, the verifier is required to notify them of the issue of the building warrant.

3.27 The owner of such a building should, therefore, have procedures in place to ensure that a building warrant is obtained for any activities requiring such a warrant and both the person instructing such activity and the owner of the building should have procedures to ensure that it is being carried out in accordance with that building warrant.

Liability of applicant

3.28 As already noted, the applicant for a building warrant also commits an offence where they knowingly or recklessly make a statement, in their application, which is false or misleading in a material particular. The Act does not stipulate who can make the application but the model form A of the model forms includes a declaration *"1. That the work will be carried out in accordance with building regulations, and in accordance with the details supplied above and with any necessary accompanying information (including annexes to this application, drawings, and specifications), (see note 6 [this covers matters relating to building operations]) 2. I am/we* are the owner of the building/That the owner of the building is aware of this application* 3. [Where the warrant involves a specified conversion] That after conversion the building as converted will comply with building regulations*"*. The applicant will therefore need to be in a position, contractually, to ensure that the works are carried out in accordance with the declaration and, where they are not technically competent, will need to receive undertakings, from those acting for them who are, that the above declaration is being implemented. Finally there is a further consequence of carrying out works without a building warrant which will be dealt with in more detail later when discussing the completion certificate.

Completion certificate

3.29 Under the new Act there is no longer an application for a completion certificate. Instead the 'relevant person' must submit a completion certificate when the work or the conversion, in respect of which the building warrant was granted, is complete. The certificate may be signed by the 'relevant person' or their duly authorised agent but remains the relevant person's certificate even if signed by their agent. That certificate must certify that the works were carried out, or conversion was made, in accordance with the building warrant and the works or services, fittings or equipment which are, or the converted building which is, the subject of the building warrant comply or complies with the Building Regulations. The verifier can either accept or reject that certificate and must accept it if, after reasonable enquiry, it is satisfied as to the matters certified in it.

'Relevant person' under section 17

3.30 The 'relevant person' is one of three different persons: (1) the person carrying out the work for themselves, as where, for example, it is the tenant where he does the work himself; or (2) the person for whom the work is carried out where it is carried out by others, as where, for example, it is the tenant where he gets a builder to do the work for him; or (3) the owner but only where the owner does not fall within categories (1) or (2) above and where neither (1) or (2) above, submit the certificate. The completion certificate is only effective once the verifier has accepted it. Thus where no one has submitted a completion certificate the owner can be obliged to submit it.

Approved certifiers of construction

3.31 The relevant person can submit with the completion certificate, certificates from approved certifiers of construction certifying that the specified construction complies with the Building Regulations. These certificates are treated, by the verifier, as conclusive evidence of what they certify. At present there is only one scheme (the Scheme for Certification of Construction (Electrical Installations to BS 7671)), which is operated by both SELECT and by NICEIC through Scottish Building Services Certification. This scheme was introduced to cover a similar aspect of construction as was covered by the electrical compliance certificates issued under the 1959 Act (details on BSD website, as is the register of approved certifiers (both of design and of construction)).

Offences under sections 19 and 20

3.32 The relevant person submitting the completion certificate and any certifiers of construction issuing certificates of construction are guilty of an offence if they, knowingly or recklessly, submit or issue, as appropriate, such a certificate which is false or misleading in a material particular. In relation to the completion certificate, this means that, where the 'relevant person' has insufficient knowledge or understanding of how building warrant works were carried out, it would be advisable for that relevant person to consult with those who do before submitting the completion certificate.

Unauthorised occupation or use

3.33 The new Act, like the 1959 Act, makes it an offence to occupy or use any building, except for construction, which is the subject of a building warrant, except where it is only for alteration, without an accepted completion certificate or without consent from the verifier for the temporary occupation or use of the building. The offence is committed where the above noted exceptions do not apply and the person, knowingly or without regard to whether a completion certificate has been accepted, occupies or uses the building. Under the Act, in addition to committing an offence, it is now possible for the local authority, should they so wish, to apply to a court for an interdict to restrain or prevent such actual or apprehended occupation or use.

Unauthorised works and 'letters of comfort'

3.34 One of the problems which the new Act sought to solve was that of works for which there was no building warrant or, where there was a building warrant, no completion certificate. Such works cause problems especially in the sale and purchase of domestic dwellings. Under the 1959 Act there was no statutory solution where the works had been carried out so long ago that a building warrant could not be applied for. In such circumstances a non-statutory solution emerged, whereby some local authority would examine such works, for a fee, and if they complied with or did not breach, to a material extent, the building regulations, they gave an undertaking that no proceedings for enforcement of compliance with the Building Regulations (under section 10 of the 1959 Act where there is no warrant) would be taken by the local authority. Such an undertaking has often been referred to as a 'letter of comfort' and has been relied upon in the past to purify conditions within missives of sale.

Building Standards assessments and completion certificates for works without a building warrant

3.35 The new Act introduces a new right, in section 6 of the Act, for the owner of a building, requiring the local authority to carry out a 'Building Standards assessment' of a building if so requested by the owner. This obligation has not yet been brought into force. However, even though Building Standards assessments are not yet available, sections 15 and 17(4) of the Act do apply. Under section 15, a building warrant can be applied for at any time before a completion certificate has been accepted, notwithstanding that it is an offence to start work without a building warrant. However the Building Regulations applicable to any building warrant are those applicable at the time of application for the building warrant even if the works were carried out earlier. In addition, under regulation 7(2) of the Procedure Regulations the verifier is entitled, in such circumstances, to require the works to be opened up to establish that they have been built in accordance with the plans submitted. Under section 17(4), where works or a conversion requiring a building warrant have been carried out without a building warrant then the 'relevant person' must submit a completion certificate which can only be accepted if the verifier is, after reasonable enquiry, satisfied as to the matters certified. Such a certificate certifies compliance with the Building Regulations and where it is submitted under section 17(4), where there is no preceding building warrant, the applicable Building Regulations are those applicable at the time the completion certificate is submitted. In addition, any such late submission of a completion certificate with no preceding building warrant attracts, under the Fees Regulations, a 125% building warrant fee. It should also be noted that, under section 41 of the Act, where a completion certificate is submitted under section 17 of the Act (or a building warrant is applied for, or building works are carried out pursuant to, a building warrant), the verifier may require materials tests to be made which could include tests of combinations of materials or of the whole building and under regulation 46 of the Procedure Regulations may require the exposure of concealed parts of the structure to establish compliance with the Building Regulations.

Building Standards Register

3.36 Section 24 of the Act requires local authorities to keep a Building Standards Register covering its own geographical area. This register is in two parts. Part I contains the basic data on any building warrants relative to a particular works or conversion including any applications and amendments for warrant, any completion certificates submitted and their acceptance or rejection, and any energy performance certificates and notices issued relative to those works or conversion (including any issued under the Housing (Scotland) Act 2006). Part II contains the relevant documents. Building Standards assessments, when introduced, will not be recorded on the register but if any enforcement notices are issued as a result of any assessment they will. The register is public with Part I being in electronic form but access to some of the documents lodged in Part II may be restricted where there are issues of security or privacy.

Part 3 (Compliance and Enforcement) (Sections 25–27)

3.37 Verifiers mainly administer the provisions within Part 2 of the Act, while the main body responsible for implementing the provisions in Part 3 is the local authority.

Building regulations compliance notice

3.38 Building warrants, completion certificates and the other provisions in Part 2 of the Act relating to the approval of building works are concerned with actual building works (new or alterations) or conversions but not with existing buildings (except where they are affected by such works or conversions).

3.39 Under section 25 Scottish Ministers can, where they consider buildings of any description, to which the Building Regulations apply, ought to comply with a provision of those regulations, direct all or particular local authorities or a particular local authority to secure that such buildings comply with that provision but only for certain specified purposes. Those purposes fall into three main categories, which, in general terms, are: (i) health, safety, welfare and convenience; (ii) furthering the conservation of fuel and power; and (iii) furthering the achievement of sustainable development. It is, however, the local authority, on the direction of Scottish Ministers, who serves the notice (known as a 'building regulations compliance notice') on the owners of the specified buildings. The notice must specify the provision of the regulations to be met, the date after which the building should comply, any particular steps to be taken and the date on which the notice takes effect. Any work carried out under such a notice must still comply with the provisions of Part 2 of the Act (Building Warrant granted and Completion Certificate accepted) but the local authority can vary the date by which the building must comply, where a building warrant is applied for before that date. If, by that date, the owner has not complied with the notice, the owner is guilty of an offence and the local authority can carry out the work necessary to make the building comply. The local authority does not need a warrant for such work but must register a completion certificate in the buildings register (which will show up on a search). The local authority may withdraw the notice or waive or relax any of its requirements but this does not preclude the issue of a further notice.

3.40 The increasing concern regarding 'greenhouse gases' and the need to conserve energy resources has put the spotlight onto existing building as it is realised that we can make significant energy savings and could reduce CO_2 emissions if we improved the thermal performance of our existing buildings. It is in this context that it is interesting to note the provisions and powers contained in section 25 of the Act. This section is to be used to enforce the display of energy performance certificates (EPCs) in public buildings as required under the Energy Performance of Buildings Directive. Implementation of this directive in Scotland is covered in more detail later in this chapter. In addition the Climate Change (Scotland) Act 2009 contains further powers regarding changes to existing buildings. These will be covered later in this chapter.

Continuing requirement and building warrant enforcement notices

3.41 The local authority can, under section 26 of the Act, serve a 'continuing requirements enforcement notice' requiring an owner to comply with continuing requirements imposed by the verifier under section 22 of the Act or by the Building Regulations under section 2 of the Act. Failure to comply with such a notice is an offence and the local authority may carry out such work as is necessary to comply with the notice and recover the reasonably incurred expenses of such work from the owner.

3.42 The local authority can also under section 27 of the Act serve a 'building warrant enforcement notice' requiring the relevant person (in this case: (i) the person doing the work for themselves; or (ii) the person for whom the work is being done; or (iii) the owner, where not (i) or (ii) and where (i) or (ii) cannot be found or no longer have an interest in the building) to obtain a building warrant (where the work is being carried out) or to submit a completion certificate (where it has been completed without a building warrant) and, where the works have not been carried out in accordance with a building warrant, to secure compliance with, or obtain an appropriate amendment to, the building warrant. Failure to comply with such a notice is an offence and the local authority may carry out such work as is necessary to comply with the notice and recover the reasonably incurred expenses of such work from the owner.

3.43 It is therefore important when purchasing property to check that all the relevant building warrants are in place and that completion certificates have been submitted and accepted in relation to all building warrants as a failure to do so could leave the new owner with an obligation to pay the building warrant fee + 25% and to meet the standards of the Building Regulations applicable at the time of submission of the completion certificate (and not when the works were carried out). In addition, until that completion certificate is accepted, they could be prevented from occupying or using the building. It is also important to note that all of the above notices are either served on the owners of the relevant buildings or, in relation to the building warrant enforcement notice, on the relevant person, who is likely to be the owner. Finally it should be noted that the local authority can carry out such works as is necessary to comply with such a notice, including demolition of the works, and recover the costs, less any proceeds from the sale of the materials arising from the demolition, from the person on whom the notice was served. Therefore if you are, or are advising, a prospective purchaser of a building you should check that there are not any such notices outstanding on that building.

Part 4 (Defective and Dangerous Buildings) (Sections 28–30)

Defective buildings

3.44 Under the 1959 Act, although there was provision, in section 11 of that Act, for requiring a building to comply with certain building standards, there was no provision for the rectification of buildings in disrepair and the local authorities could only take action against dangerous building (see section 13 of the 1959 Act). Section 87 of the Civic Government (Scotland) Act 1982 did contain powers to require the rectification of buildings, not dangerous, needing repair. These powers have now been transferred into the Act and expanded as section 28. This empowers the local authority to serve a notice (a 'defective building notice') on owners requiring them to rectify specified defects. Such defects being those, which require rectification in order to bring the building into a reasonable state of repair having regard to its age, type and location.

Dangerous buildings

3.45 Sections 29 and 30 contain similar provisions to those contained in the 1959 Act and deal with buildings which constitute a danger to persons in or about them or to the public generally in relation to which the local authority can issue notices ('dangerous building notices').

3.46 The provisions in Part 4 go into detail regarding action to be taken to bring defective buildings up to the required standard and to make dangerous buildings safe, the powers of local authorities to carry out emergency work to dangerous buildings and to recover the cost from the owner and with regard to purchasing such buildings where owners cannot be found, and the selling of materials from buildings demolished by the local authority.

Part 5 (General) (Sections 31–56)

3.47 This part of the Act covers a number of administrative details and should be referred to if it is required to check whether the powers contained in the Act have been properly used or to make use of provisions within the Act. For example, any notices served by a local authority need to comply with section 37 and any appeals under the Act need to comply with the provisions in section 47. In addition, where scheduled monuments or listed buildings are involved section 35 sets out special procedures which are to be followed. It should be noted that, while Section 31 sets up the Building Standards Advisory Committee, which is a continuation of that set up under the 1959 Act, to advise Scottish Ministers on matters relating to the Act, there are proposals from Scottish Ministers to abolish this committee, but these will have to await primary legislation and until this happens the committee will continue to discharge its statutory functions. The following provisions within this part should also be noted.

Entry, inspection and tests (Sections 39–41)

3.48 These sections give the local authority powers to enter buildings and carry out inspections and tests relative to Part 3 (Compliance and Enforcement) and Part 4 (Defective and Dangerous Buildings) and allow, at section 41, Scottish Ministers to require the testing of materials by those applying to them for a relaxation. The same section allows verifiers to require those applying to them for a building warrant or carrying out work under a building warrant or submitting a completion certificate, to carry out a materials test. It is these powers which allow the verifier to require such tests as sound tests. It should be noted that these tests are to be carried out at the expense of the applicant. Powers to require testing, arising under this section, are included in the Procedure Regulations (regulation 61).

Appeals (Section 47)

3.49 In addition to setting out those decisions or notices which can be appealed to the sheriff within 21 days of the date of the decision or notice (such appeal being final), this section also provides that certain decisions are deemed to have been made if they are not made within certain time limits. Those time limits are specified in the Procedure Regulations (regulation 60). Where the verifier has not made a 'first report' (see Procedure Regulations later in this chapter) on a building warrant, or amendment to warrant, application within three months, or where the verifier has, but has not made a decision on the application within 9 months of that report, or such longer period as is agreed between the verifier and the applicant (or the owner), then the application is deemed to have been refused (subject to any periods required for considering relaxations or making consultations being disregarded). Where the verifier has not made a decision on an application to extend the period for demolition of a 'limited-life' building within one month of that application then it is deemed to have been refused and where a completion certificate has not been accepted or rejected within 14 days of its submission, or such longer period as agreed between the verifier and applicant, then it is deemed to be rejected. Except that where the completion certificate is submitted for work requiring a building warrant but carried out without such a warrant (see section 17(4) of the Act), as the certificate must be accompanied with the same drawings and information as if it were a building warrant application, the time limits in relation to a building warrant application apply.

Offences and liability (Sections 48–51)

3.50 These sections cover statutory offences by persons and corporate bodies, criminal liability of trustees and civil liability. Section 48 sets the level of fines on summary conviction for an offence under the Act (not exceeding level 5 on the standard scale (at present £5000:

see section 225 of the Criminal Procedure (Scotland) Act 1995, as amended, for the current value)), it should be noted that offences under sections 14(6), 21(5) and 43(1), which all relate to illegal occupation of premises, can be subject to indictment, with an unlimited fine on conviction. Section 49 extends liability for offences committed by corporate bodies, local authorities, Scottish partnerships and unincorporated bodies from those bodies to include those persons within those bodies in positions of authority and control who consent or connive in the offence or where such offences are attributable to their neglect. Section 50 provides specific defences for trustees etc.

3.51 The Act is much clearer than the 1959 Act as to what actions constitute offences. These are statutory offences giving rise to criminal liability and penalties. However, the Act, at section 51, includes for civil liability. These are specific statutory provisions and expressly do not exclude delictual liability (that is common law non statutory or contractual liability) arising due to breach of a duty of care or negligence. The statutory civil liability arises where there is a breach of a duty imposed by the Building Regulations which causes damage except in so far as the regulations provide otherwise and subject to any defences provided within those regulations. 'Damage' is defined to include death or physical injury.

3.52 However, the definition is silent as to whether it includes financial loss, what is often referred to as 'pure economic loss', as opposed to financial recompense for physical damage both to person (death or injury) and to buildings. It is therefore not clear how wide such damages will extend. It should be noted that while the 1959 Act had, at section 19A, provision for civil liability it was never brought into force and so this statutory civil liability is a new provision and we must wait to see how it is interpreted and applied in the courts.

Crown rights – removal of Crown immunity

The commencement of Section 53 of the Building (Scotland) Act 2003 to remove Crown immunity from building regulations came into force on 1 May 2009. This was effected by *The Building (Scotland) Act 2003 (Commencement No.2 and Transitional Provisions) Order 2009* which includes transitional provisions to allow work that had already started or is subject to contract to retain Crown immunity for a limited period. Under these transitional arrangements a building warrant *will not* be required when: (1) work starts before 1 May 2009; *or* (2) a contract is in place before 1 May 2009 and work starts before 1 November 2009; *and* (3) In both of the above cases, work is completed before 1 May 2012. However a building warrant *will* be required when: (1) a contract *is not in place* before 1 May 2009 and work starts on or after 1 May 2009; *or* (2) a contract *is in place* before 1 May 2009 but work starts on or after 1 November 2009 *or* (3) at the outset of the project the work is not anticipated to be completed by 1 May 2012.

However exemptions have been introduced. A Section 104 Order under the Scotland Act 1998 to deal with reserved matters *(The Building (Scotland) Act 2003 (Exemptions for Defence and National Security) Order 2009)* introduces exemption from the Building (Scotland) Act and Scottish building standards system for buildings used or to be used for defence or national security purposes. In addition *The Building (Scotland) Amendment Regulations 2009* amends the Building Regulations to include within Schedule 3 additional work types that do not require a building warrant. These are works to: the Scottish Parliament; Her Majesty's private estate; and prisons or buildings where persons may be legally detained (such as police or court cells or secure mental institutions) where work does not increase floor area by more than 100m².

There are also amendments to the Procedure Regulations *(The Building (Procedure) (Scotland) Amendment Regulations 2009)*. These Regulations: (i) amend the interpretation of 'fire authority' to recognise the different enforcing authorities for Crown buildings; (ii) amend Regulation 58 to reference specific Crown buildings being a prison, a building where a person may be lawfully detained or lawfully held in custody, the Scottish Parliament or a building owned by Her Majesty in her private capacity; and (iii) widen the public access to all documents on the Building Standards Register except those that the local authority are satisfied would raise genuine security concerns.

In addition the Scottish Government have produced Procedural Guidance for Crown Buildings which is available to download from the Building Standards Division's website at www.sbsa.gov.uk/pdfs/Procedural_Guidance_Crown_Buildings.pdf and the required amendments to the procedural handbook at www.sbsa.gov.uk/proced_legislation/ProcHB_updpgs_may09.pdf

Interpretation

3.54 Section 55 covers the meaning of 'building' and section 56 covers most of the other definitions. Whenever in doubt as to the meaning of a word used in the Act you should first check these two sections, as they can often provide the answer.

Part 6 Supplementary (Sections 57–59)

3.55 This part principally deals with modification of enactments and commencement and the short title (Building (Scotland) Act 2003).

Schedules

3.56 These relate to matters in regard of which regulations may be made, verifiers and certifiers, procedure regulations, powers of entry, inspection and testing, evacuation of buildings and modifation of enactments.

4 Commencement orders

4.01 There have only been two commencement orders so far. The first is the Building (Scotland) Act 2003 (Commencement No. 1, Transitional Provisions and Savings) Order 2004. Under this, except for two sections, the Act came into force for all purposes on 1 May 2005. The commencement order provides that work carried out under warrants applied for before 1 May 2005 will be administered and carried out under the regulations in force immediately before 1 May 2005 but that such warrants are to be valid for a maximum of 5 years. Thus there may be work carried out under building warrants granted and administered under the 1959 Act until 2010 (provided, of course, that the warrant's validity, which under the 1959 Act is, without extension, 3 years, is extended to at least that date). The two sections not coming into force on 1 May 2005 were section 6 and section 53. Section 53 was commenced on 1 May 2009 and the transitional arrangements are covered in the preceding paragraph. Section 6 still has to come into force.

5 Building (Procedure) (Scotland) Regulations and subsequent amendment (2007)

5.01 The Procedure Regulations were laid before the Scottish Parliament on 1 October 2004 and came into force on 1 May 2005 except for certain regulations setting up the certification and verification system which came into force on 4 November 2004. These regulations are still in force, but have been subject to two amendments, the Building (Procedure) (Scotland) Amendment Regulations 2007 which came into force on 1 May 2007 and the Building (Procedure) (Scotland) Amendment Regulations 2009 which came into force on 1 May 2009. The principal changes introduced by the 2007 Amendments are in relation to: the implementation of the Energy Performance of Buildings Directive; the submission of a single completion certificates relative to multiple existing buildings in the same ownership; and extending the types of persons allowed access to information on the building standards register. The principle changes introduced by the 2009 Amendments are covered in paragraph 3.53 above.

Interpretation

5.02 Part I of the Procedure Regulations deals with citation, commencement and interpretation and includes a provision allowing the submission of documents by electronic transmission, where the recipient has, in advance, accepted such transmission. Thus, where the verifier or local authority has made provision for such electronic transmission, building warrant applications can be made electronically.

Applications for warrant

5.03 Part II of the Procedure Regulations deals with applications for warrant. The following is a précis of the new arrangements. The applicant, whose identity is not restricted, must lodge the application with the verifier in writing or, where the verifier allows electronic transmission, in electronic form, on the appropriate form which, in the case of an application for building warrant, is not one of the statutory forms. However the BSD provides 'Model Forms' (available on their website) which should, normally be the basis for any form produced by the verifier. It can be signed by the applicant or, on behalf of the applicant, by his agent (or, where it is an electronic submission, authenticated by an electronic signature). The application should be accompanied by the principal plans specified in Schedule 2 to the Procedure Regulations and, where the submission is not in electronic form, a copy of each of the plans together with the appropriate fees. The plans to be to such scale as the verifier may require. If a direction relaxing any regulation has already been given by Scottish Ministers, this should accompany the application. The model form application for building warrant now has a question regarding security matters as the 2009 amendments to the Regulations provide for the restriction of access to such information as referred to in 'Note 4' in the Model Form A.

5.04 There is an alternative to giving the verifier all of the detailed information referred to above. An approved certifier of design can provide a certificate saying that particular aspects of the work will comply with the Building Regulations. Such a certificate, once it is proved to be valid, is conclusive evidence as to what it certifies and no further enquiry by the verifier is necessary. The certificate must be issued by an approved certifier of design employed by an approved body operating under an approved scheme. The current scheme providers, in relation to design, are SER Ltd under whose scheme compliance of building structures with section 1 (structure) of Schedule 5 to the Building Regulations is certified, BRE Certification Ltd under whose scheme compliance of non-domestic buildings with section 6 (energy) of Schedule 5 to the Building Regulations is certified and RIAS Services Ltd under whose scheme compliance of domestic buildings with section 6 (energy) of Schedule 5 to the Building Regulations is certified. The information on the certificate should match that on the building warrant application form in respect of the location of the project, the description of the works and, where there is a staged warrant, the description of the stage of work applicable. The applicant must also provide enough information in respect of the certified work to assist in any site inspections the verifier may wish to make. The submission of such a certificate with the application entitles the applicant to a reduction in the fee properly payable (reference should be made to the Fees Regulations for details).

5.05 When the application is received, the verifier shall forthwith consider the application. However where the application is submitted without the specified plans, except where it is an application for a staged warrant or the verifier is satisfied that the plans submitted sufficiently describe the proposed works, the verifier must advise the applicant of the specified plans still required and accept the application on condition that the applicant submits the missing plans within 42 days of the applicant's receipt of that advice. This provision allows application to be made without all the details, with such details being submitted 42 days later, with the applicable regulations being those in force at the date of application. In addition a warrant is valid for 3 years from the date it is granted such validity being subject to further extension, at the discretion of the verifier, if applied for before the expiry of the warrant. This has allowed warrants to be applied for immediately prior to the coming into force of more onerous regulations with very little detail in the application and for the works under that warrant not to be built for many years thereafter when the regulations current at that time may be very different to those under which the warrant is granted.

5.06 This problem of work being carried out under out of date regulations was recognised by the Sullivan Committee (more of whom later) who, in their report, recommended that there should be "consideration of the duration of warrants and examination of the possibility of requiring a substantial start to be made on site within a fixed period of the date of granting the warrant" (Second recommendation in Chapter 6 (Process)). However, it should be noted that any extension to the duration of a warrant allowed under regulation 19, if granted by the verifier, can, if the verifier sees fit, be subject to any work carried out during the further period of validity being compliant with the Building Regulations applicable at the time the extension is granted (regulation 19(5)). In addition where a warrant relates to multiple subjects the verifier may require that separate applications are made in respect of such multiple subjects as the verifier thinks fit (regulation 19(6)).

5.07 The verifier shall: if the application complies with the requirements of the Procedure Regulations and satisfies the matters set out in section 9 of the Act grant the building warrant; or, within three months of receipt of the application, send a report to the applicant or the applicant's agent, identifying what further information is required and anything which is not in accordance with section 9(1) of the Act (the 'first report'); or, after giving the applicant or agent 14 days notice of any grounds for refusal and an opportunity to be heard, refuse the application. Such application or its refusal being sent to the local authority for registration in the building standards register.

5.08 Part II contains further provisions in relation, amongst other things, to: staged warrants; warrants for conversions; late applications under section 15 of the Act; consultation; demolition (where period for demolition must be stated); and limited life buildings (including the requirement that it must be demolished and removed from the site before the expiry of that limited life).

5.09 Part III covers reference to Scottish Ministers for views under section 12 of the Act. Parts IV and V cover applications to Scottish Ministers for a direction under section 3(2)(a) or 3(2)(b) of the Act to relax, or dispense with, a particular provisions of the Building Regulations or to vary such a direction under section 3(4)(c). Part VI sets out the qualities to be considered when appointing a verifier.

5.10 Part VII covers procedures relative to certification of design and of construction. Any scheme will need to comply with these requirements. However these requirements are mainly relevant to the scheme providers and members of the scheme should refer to the scheme itself for their obligations as any scheme must comply otherwise it will not be approved. However, the requirements relative to the promotion of good practice regulation 36(3) and the requirements regarding the maintenance of records in regulation 37 should be noted.

5.11 Part VIII covers the procedures in relation to completion certificates. The completion certificate is to be submitted in prescibed form (Form 5, 6 or 7, as appropriate, in the Schedule to the Forms Regulations). The regulations set out what should be covered in the submission and what should accompany the form. You should note that the 2007 Amendment Regulations introduce the requirement to submit an energy performance certificate where required under the Building Regulations and permits the submission of a single completion certificate for multiple dwellings where the work is to existing dwellings in the same ownership (such as work for a local authority or social landlord). The regulations make further provisions, which have been covered earlier in this chapter, regarding completion certificates for works carried out without a building warrant.

5.12 Parts IX and X cover notices by local authorities and general procedures for local authorities and verifiers. Part IX requires local authorities to enter in the building standards register any notices issued by them under Parts 3 (Compliance and Enforcement) and 4 (Defective and Dangerous Buildings) of the Act, including any waiver or relaxation of any requirement contained in those notices or any withdrawal or the quashing of such notices. The building standards register can therefore be a useful source of information on an existing building. Part X covers procedures to be followed by verifiers and local authorities relative to a number of matters. Some of these, such as deemed determination, have already been mentioned in the commentary on the appropriate parts of the Act. However, regulation 57, which is amended by the 2007 Amendment to the Procedure Regulations, should be noted. This lists what should be included in Parts I and II of the Building Standards Register and is a useful check list of information most of which should be available for public inspection (parts of Part II may be restricted). Part I should include: list of applications, submissions and decisions; particulars of energy performance certificates, certificates from approved certifiers and of notices issued under Parts 2 and 3 of the Act; and particulars of all other documents submitted to the local authority for registration on the Building Standards Register. Part I should be available in electronic form on line and therefore should be freely available. However the information in Part II, which includes drawings, specifications and other technical information, may be restricted, for privacy or security reasons the 2009 Amendments to the Procedure Regulations have amended regulation 58 to make further provisions regarding security, and if a copy of any of the available documents is requested, the local authority is entitled to charge for such provision (regulation 8 of the Fees Regulations).

6 Building (Forms) (Scotland) Regulations 2005 and subsequent amendments (2006 and 2007)

6.01 Section 36 of the Building (Scotland) Act 2003 gives Scottish Ministers power to make Regulations prescribing the form and content of any application, warrant, certificate, notice or document authorised or required to be used under or for the purposes of the Act. Where such a form is used it must be used in the form set out in the Forms Regulations or in a form as close to it as circumstances permit. The Forms Regulations contain, in a schedule, 16 prescribed forms which include notes as to their completion. However these forms do not cover all circumstances where forms may be needed and BSD have published a number of 'Model Forms' (available on the BSD website), which cover a number of circumstances not covered by the statutory forms. These forms are intended for use by verifiers and local authorities to assist in composing their forms covering the same subject. They therefore give an indication of the general information to be expected but anyone needing to use such a form should check with the relevant verifier or local authority as to actual forms required to be used.

6.02 If you are checking the statutory forms in the Forms Regulations you should note the amendments to the fifth and sixth paragraphs of the declaration in Form 5 and to the third and fourth paragraphs of the declaration in Form 6 of the 2006 Amended Forms Regulations introduced by the 2007 Forms Regulations Amendment. This change introduces the requirement to submit an EPC for each building where the building regulations apply.

7 The Building (Fees) (Scotland) Regulations 2004 and subsequent amendment (2007 and 2008)

7.01 These Regulations set the fees charged by verifiers for building warrant submissions, including submissions after work has already started and for submissions of completion certificates without any building warrant (where a surcharge applies). They also set out the discounts available when parts of a submission for a building warrant are covered by a certificate from an approved certifier of design (as such design does not need to be checked by the verifier) and the discounts available when a completion certificate is submitted with one or more certificates from approved certifiers of construction. The verifier is to be informed of the proposed use of such certificates, when the building warrant application is made. Where such certificates are not, in fact, submitted the fee otherwise applicable will become due. There is a zero fee for work to improve the suitability of a dwelling for use by a disabled occupant (such work is already required for most non-domestic buildings under the Disability Discrimination Act). The fees are set out in a table in the schedule to the Fees Regulations and are based on the estimated value of the work (which is an estimate of the commercial cost or, where there are special circumstances such as self-build, what would be the cost on a commercial basis). However the cost is only of that work subject to the Building Regulations and does not include such items as decorating or floor coverings not required to comply with the Building Regulations.

8 Building (Scotland) Regulations 2004 and subsequent amendments (2006, 2007, 2008 and 2009)

8.01 The Regulations, as amended, consist of 17 regulations. Regulation 2 provides the definitions to a number of terms used in the regulations. Careful note should be taken of the definitions of 'domestic', 'residential' and 'dwelling'. Whilst the actual definitions should be examined, in general terms a 'domestic building' is equivalent to a 'dwelling' plus common areas, a 'dwelling' is residential accommodation for a family or less than 6 persons living together as a single household and a 'residential building' is a building, other than a 'domestic building' having sleeping accommodation. These definitions apply only to the Building Regulations (although they can be shared by the Act and other regulations under the Act) and care should be taken when using similar terms in different legislation (thus houses subject to licensing, under other legislation, as Houses in Multiple Occupation (covered later in this chapter) can be classified as either domestic or non-domestic principally depending on the number of occupants).

8.02 Regulation 3 provides for certain types of building, services, fittings and equipment, as set out in Schedule 1 to the Regulations, to be exempt from regulations 8–12, subject to the exceptions stated in the schedule. Schedule 2 to the Regulations sets out what changes in occupation or use of a building constitute conversion and Schedule 6 sets out the extent to which, in a conversion, particular standards require to be complied with.

8.03 Regulation 5 and Schedule 3 to the regulations set out the work which, while it does require to meet the standards set out in regulations 8–12, does not, subject to the exceptions and conditions, require a building warrant. It was noted in the research leading up to the new Act that a large number of minor works are being carried out without a building warrant. This provision is therefore wider in scope than its predecessor. However, it should be noted that even though this work does not require a building warrant it still requires to comply with the Building Regulations. This work, as it does not require a building warrant or a completion certificate, will not feature on the building standards register. Thus a search against the register will not reveal its existence.

8.04 Regulation 8(1) requires all work carried out to meet the standards set out in regulations 9–12 to be 'carried out in a technically proper and workmanlike manner, and materials must be durable and fit for their intended purpose'. Regulation 8(2) requires materials, services, fittings and equipment used to meet such standards to be, so far as reasonably practicable, sufficiently accessible to enable any necessary maintenance or repair work to be carried out. It should be noted that this fitness for purpose

standard applies only to work required to comply with the building standards but that breach of this regulation could give rise to civil liability under section 51 of the Act.

8.05 Regulation 9 and Schedule 5 are the heart of the Building Standards system as they set out what must be achieved in building work. The standards are set out in full in Sections 1–6 of Schedule 5 to the Regulations with associated guidance on compliance in sections 1–6 of the Technical Handbooks (both Domestic and Non-Domestic versions). The sections relate directly to the 'Essential Requirements' of the Construction Products Directive. Schedule 5 and the 66 expanded functional standards (arranged within six sections) will be covered later in this chapter.

8.06 Regulations 10, 13, 14 and 15 contain provisions regarding demolition, protective works, clearing of footpaths and the securing of unoccupied and partly completed building, which were previously contained in separate Buildings Operation Regulations. By bringing these regulations within the Building Regulations, compliance with them becomes an obligation under the building warrant and is included in the completion certificate.

8.07 The amendment regulations of 2006 introduced a new regulation 17. This regulation, on continuing requirements was introduced to implement the terms of Article 9 of the Energy Performance of Buildings Directive regarding the inspection of air-conditioning systems.

The following paragraphs give a brief description of the expanded functional standards as amended in 2006, 2007, 2008 and 2009 and brought into force in May 2009. (Amendment 2008 makes only a definitional change to Schedule 5 and Amendment 2009 mainly amends Schedule 3). However, this is only meant to guide readers to the appropriate part of the regulations and the relevant Technical Handbooks which should be consulted for more detailed information and guidance.

8.08 Schedule 5 to the Building Regulations

This schedule contains the expanded functional standards. That is, the standards describe the functions a building should perform, such as, in Fire, 'providing resistance to the spread of fire,' and are an expanded and more detailed form of the previous building standards regulations. They are arranged into 6 sections: 1 (Structure); 2 (Fire); 3 (Environment); 4 (Safety); 5 (Noise) and 6 (Energy) corresponding with the six essential requirements of the Construction Products Directive (1: Mechanical Resistance & Stability; 2: Safety in case of Fire; 3: Hygiene, Health and the Environment; 4: Safety in Use; 5: Protection against Noise; 6: Energy, Economy and Heat Retention). Each of the standards includes, where appropriate, limitations on the standards contained in them. Two Technical Handbooks (regularly updated) have been provided by Scottish Ministers giving guidance on how to comply with these regulations. One handbook for where the buildings are domestic and one for where they are non-domestic. The Regulations define a 'domestic building' as a dwelling or dwellings and any common areas associated with the dwelling, while 'dwelling' is defined as a unit of residential accommodation occupied: by an individual or individuals living together as a family; or by not more than six individuals living together as a single household. Following such guidance is not mandatory but compliance with the applicable requirements set out in this Schedule 5 (subject to any relaxation) is mandatory.

Section 1: Structure (Standards 1.1 and 1.2)
1.1 Structure

Every building to be designed and constructed so that the applied loadings, taking account of the ground, will not lead to collapse of the whole or part of the building, deformations rendering the building unfit for the intended purpose, unsafe or causing damage to other parts of, or fittings in, the building or impairment to the stability of any part of another building.

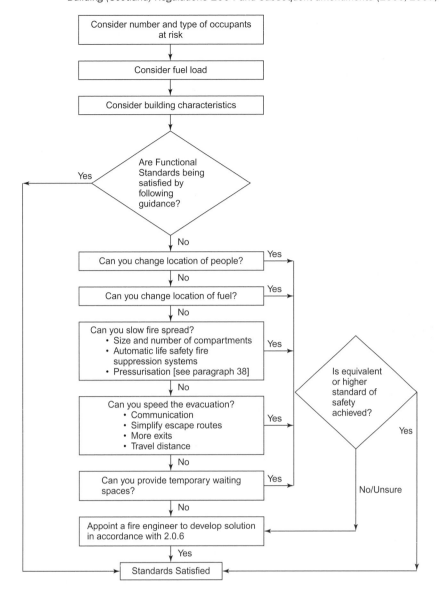

MEANS OF ESCAPE FROM FIRE
Flowchart for assessing appropriate method for compliance with Standards taken from Building Standards Division of the Directorate of the Built Environment of the Scottish Governments consultation on proposed changes to the Means of Escape.

An escape route and circulation area should have a clear headroom of at least 2 metres (Headroom Guidance 2.98)

Every building must be accessible to five appliances and five service personnel (Standard 2.12)

1.2 Disproportionate collapse

Every building to be designed and constructed so that, in the event of damage occuring to any part of the structure of the building, the extent of any resultant collapse will not be disproportionate to the original cause.

Comments

The main changes introduced by the 2007 Amendments were the revision of the guidance on disproportionate collapse and on stone masonry, new guidance on the nature of the ground and stability of other buildings and the replacement of the Small Buildings Guide (which dated back to before the new system) with a Small Buildings Structural Guidance, introduced as Annex l.A; B; C; D; E; and F providing structural guidance to designers of small domestic buildings. This section (Standards 1.1 and 1.2) is covered by the certification scheme operated by SER Limited, discussed earlier in this chapter, under which approved certifiers of design can certify that particular applications for building warrant comply with this section of Schedule 5 to the building regulations. Under this scheme the certifier must certify compliance of all of the design with the requirements of section 1 (structure).

Section 2: Fire (Standards 2.1–2.15)

In relation to these standards every building is to be designed and constructed so that, in the event of an outbreak of fire within that building, the requirements set out below, against each of these standards, are met (with Standards 2.12, 2.13 and 2.14 applying to every building). Each standard being subject to the limitations stated.

Comments

In relation to fire, these standards should be read along with the provisions of Part 3 of the Fire (Scotland) Act 2005 and any regulations and guidance issued under that Act (see later in this chapter for a brief overview). There are no major changes introduced by the 2007 Amendments but amendments to the provisions for means of escape and associated standards and guidance are at present under review and new standards are programmed for introduction in the spring 2010.

2.1 Compartmentation

Fire and smoke are to be inhibited from spreading from the compartment of origin until occupants have had time to leave and any fire containment measures initiated.

Limitation

Not applicable to domestic buildings.

2.2 Separation

Where a building is divided into more than one area of different occupation it must inhibit fire and smoke from spreading from the area of occupation where the fire originated.

2.3 Structural protection

The load-bearing capacity of the building must continue to function until all occupants have escaped or been assisted to escape from the building and any fire containment measures have been initiated.

2.4 Cavities

The unseen spread of fire and smoke within concealed spaces in its structure and fabric is to be inhibited.

2.5 Internal linings

The development of fire and smoke from the surfaces of the walls and ceilings within the area of origin is to be inhibited.

2.6 Spread to neighbouring buildings

The spread of fire to neighbouring buildings is to be inhibited.

2.7 Spread on external walls

The spread of fire on the external walls of the building is to be inhibited both where the fire originates within the building and where it originates from an external source.

2.8 Spread from neighbouring buildings

Where the fire originates in a neighbouring building the spread of fire to the building is to be inhibited.

2.9 Escape

The occupants, once alerted to the outbreak of fire, are to be provided with the opportunity to escape from the building before being affected by fire or smoke.

2.10 Escape lighting

Illumination is to be provided to assist in escape.

2.11 Communication

The occupants are to be alerted to the outbreak of fire.

Limitation

Only applies to a dwelling, residential building or enclosed shopping centre.

2.12 Fire Service access

Every building to be accessible for fire appliances and fire service personnel.

2.13 Fire Service water supply

Every building to be provided with a water supply for use by the fire service.

Limitation

Not applicable to domestic buildings.

2.14 Fire Service facilities

Every building to be designed and constructed to provide facilities to assist fire-fighting and rescue operations.

2.15 Automatic life safety fire suppression systems

Fire and smoke to be inhibited from spreading through the building by the operation of an automatic life safety fire suppression system.

Limitation

Only applies to enclosed shopping centres, residential care buildings, high rise domestic buildings or whole or part of sheltered housing complex.

Section 3: Environment (Standards 3.1–3.26)

In Standards 3.1–3.4 and 3.10–3.26 every building (every dwelling in the case of Standard 3.11) must be designed and constructed in such a way that specific requirements are met, as set out below, in brief, (subject to the limitations). Standards 3.5–3.9 deal with drainage as detailed below.

Comments

The main changes are to Standards 3.11 and 3.12 and relate to 'live-ability' and 'lifetime homes' and issues of sustainability and convenience. There now needs to be provision, on one level, of an enhanced apartment and kitchen and an accessible toilet, which taken with improved circulation spaces (under Standard 4.2) will assist in creating homes that can be lived in even when mobility is impaired. Thus, promoting both sustainability and lifetime homes (which have been an aspiration ever since Parker Morris). A requirement for a space for drying clothes has also been re-introduced to assist in sustainability.

3.1 Site preparation – harmful and dangerous substances

There is not to be danger to the building nor threat to health of people in or around the building due to presence of harmful or dangerous substances.

Limitation

Not applicable to removal of unsuitable materials (topsoils etc) on site of temporary (under 5-year intended life) non dwellings.

3.2 Site preparation – protection from radon gas

There is not to be a threat to the health of people in or around the building due to emission and containment of radon gas;

3.3 Flooding and ground water

There is not to be a threat to the building or the health of the occupants due to flooding and the accumulation of ground water.

3.4 Moisture from ground

There is not to be a threat to the building or the health of the occupants due to moisture penetration from the ground.

3.5 Existing drains

No building to be constructed over an existing active drain.

Limitation

Not applicable where not reasonably practicable to re-route existing drain.

3.6 Surface water drainage

Every building and hard surface within the curtilage of a building to be designed and constructed with a surface water system which has facilities for separation and removal of silt, grit and pollutants and ensures disposal of surface water without threatening the building and the health and safety of people in and around the building.

3.7 Wastewater drainage

Every wastewater drainage system serving a building to be designed and constructed to ensure removal of wastewater from building without threatening health and safety of people in and around the building and: (a) provide facilities for separation and removal of oil, fat, grease and volatile substances; (b) where reasonably practicable, discharge to be to public sewer or public wastewater treatment plant and where not, to a private wastewater treatment plant or septic tank.

Limitation

Facilities for separation and removal of oil, fat, grease and volatile substances not required for dwellings.

3.8 Private wastewater treatment systems – treatment plants

Every private wastewater treatment plant or septic tank serving a building must be designed and constructed to ensure the safe temporary storage and treatment of wastewater prior to discharge.

3.9 Private wastewater treatment systems – infiltration systems

Every private wastewater treatment system serving a building must be designed and constructed so that the disposal of wastewater to ground is safe and is not a threat to the health of people in and around the building.

3.10 Precipitation

There is not to be a threat to the building or the health of occupants from moisture due to precipitation penetrating to inner face of the building.

Limitation

Not applicable where effects of moisture penetration from outside no more harmful than effects from building use.

3.11 Facilities in dwelling

The size of any apartments or kitchen to ensure the welfare and convenience of all occupants and visitors and an accessible space is provided to allow safe, convenient and sustainable drying of washing.

Limitation

This standard only applies to dwellings.

3.12 Sanitary facilities

Sanitary facilities to be provided for all occupants of, and visitors to, the building allowing convenient use with no threat to the health and safety of occupants or visitors.

3.13 Heating

The building to be capable of being heated and maintain heat at temperature levels that will not threaten the health of the occupants.

Limitation

This standard only applies to dwellings.

3.14 Ventilation

The air quality within the building is not to be a threat to the health of the occupants or to the capacity of the building to resist moisture, decay or infestation.

3.15 Condensation

There is not to be a threat to the building or the health of the occupants due to moisture caused by surface or interstitial condensation.

Limitation

This standard only applies to dwellings.

3.16 Natural lighting

Natural lighting to be provided to ensure that the health of occupants is not threatened.

Limitation

This standard only applies to dwellings.

3.17 Combustion appliances – safe operation

Each fixed combustion appliance installation is to operate safely.

3.18 Combustion appliances – protection from products of combustion

Any component part of each fixed combustion appliance installation shall withstand heat generated from its operation without any structural change impairing the stability or performance of the installation.

3.19 Combustion appliances – relationship to combustible materials

Any component part of each fixed combustion appliance installation not to cause damage to the building in which it is installed by radiated, convected or conducted heat or from hot embers expelled from the appliance.

3.20 Combustion appliances – removal of products of combustion

The products of combustion to be carried safely to the external air without harm to the health of any person through leakage, spillage, or exhaust and not to permit the re-entry of dangerous gases from the combustion process of fuels into the building.

3.21 Combustion appliances – air for combustion

Every fixed combustion appliance installation to receive air for combustion and the chimney to operate so that the health of persons within the building is not threatened by the build-up of dangerous gases as a result of incomplete combustion.

3.22 Combustion appliances – air for cooling

Every fixed combustion appliance installation to receive air for cooling so that it will operate safely without threatening the health and safety of persons within the building.

3.23 Fuel storage – protection from fire

Every oil storage installation, incorporating oil storage tanks used solely to serve a fixed combustion appliance installation providing space heating or cooking facilities in a building, or each container for the storage of woody biomass fuel, to inhibit fire from spreading to the tank, or to the container, and its contents from within, or beyond, the boundary.

Limitation

This standard does not apply to portable containers.

3.24 Fuel storage – containment

The volume of every woody biomas fuel storage to be such as to minimise the number of delivery journeys and every oil storage installation, incorporating oil storage tanks used solely to serve a fixed combustion appliance installation providing space heating or cooking facilities in a building, to reduce the risk of oil escaping from the installation, contain any oil spillage likely to contaminate any water supply, groundwater, watercourse, drain or sewer, and permit any spill to be disposed of safely.

Limitation

This standard does not apply to portable containers.

3.25 Solid waste storage

Accommodation for solid waste storage provided which permits access for storage and for the removal of its contents and does not threaten the health of people in or around the building or contaminate any water supply, ground or surface water.

Limitation

This standard applies only to a dwelling.

3.26 Dungsteads and farm effluent tanks

There not to be a threat to the health and safety of people from the construction or location of dungsteads or effluent tanks.

Section 4: Safety
The standards in this section require every building to be designed and constructed so that the requirements set out below are met.

Comments

Standards 4.1 and 4.2 provide enhanced access relative to buildings and within buildings both domestic and non-domestic.

4.1 Access to buildings

All occupants and visitors to be provided with safe, convenient and unassisted means of access to the building.

Limitation

No need for wheelchair access to the entrance of a single house where not practicable to do so or to a common entrance of a domestic building, without a lift, where no dwelling entered off that entrance storey.

4.2 Access within buildings

In non-domestic buildings safe, unassisted and convenient access to be provided throughout, in residential buildings wheelchair access also to be provided to a proportion of bedrooms, in domestic buildings safe and convenient access to be provided within common areas and to each dwelling and in dwellings safe and convenient means of access to be provided throughout and unassited access to, and throughout, at least one level.

Limitation

No need for wheelchair access to bedrooms not on entrance storey in non-domestic building without lift or to dwellings on upper storeys of a building without a lift.

4.3 Stairs and ramps

Every level to be reached safely by stairs or ramp.

4.4 Pedestrian protective barriers

Every sudden change of level that is accessible in, or around, the building is guarded by pedestrian protective barriers.

Limitation

Standard does not apply where guarding would obstruct the use of the area so guarded.

4.5 Electrical safety

The electrical installation not to threaten the health & safety in, or around, the building or to become a source of fire.

Limitation

Not applicable for installations for buildings covered by Mines and Quarries Act 1954, Factories Act 1961 or for works of undertakers covered by the Electricity Act 1989.

Comments

The only current scheme for approved certifiers of construction relates to the certification of the installation and commissioning of electrical installations to BS 7671 complying with the Building Regulations. There are two scheme providers for this scheme

(SELECT and NICEIC) and the scheme is described in more detail elsewhere in this chapter.

4.6 Electrical fixtures

Electric lighting points and socket outlets provided to ensure health, safety and convenience of occupants of, and visitors to, the building.

Limitation

Standard applies only to domestic buildings where electricity is available.

4.7 Aids to communications

Every building to have aids to assist those with hearing impairment.

Limitation

This standard does not apply to domestic buildings.

4.8 Danger from accidents

People in and around building to be protected from injury caused by fixed glazing, projections or moving elements on the building, fixed glazing not to be vulnerable to breakage where there is possibility of impact by people in or around the building, both faces of windows and rooflights to be cleanable without threat to cleaner of severe injury from a fall, safe and secure access to roof and safe operation of manual controls for ventilation and electrical fixtures.

Limitation

Provision of safe and secure access to roof does not apply for domestic buildings.

4.9 Danger from heat

Protection to be provided for people in, or around, the building from the danger of severe burns or scalds from the discharge of steam or hot water.

4.10 Fixed seating

Where there is fixed seating for an audience or spectators, a number of level spaces for wheelchairs to be provided proportionate to the potential audience olr spectators.

Limitation

This standard does not apply to domestic buildings.

4.11 Liquified petroleum gas storage

Every liquified petroleum gas storage installation, used solely to serve a combustion appliance providing space or water heating or cooking, to be protected from fire spreading to any liquified petroleum gas container and not to permit the contents of any such container to form explosive gas pockets in the vicinity of any container.

Limitation

Not applicable to such storage used with portable appliances.

4.12 Vehicle protective barriers

Every building accessible to vehicular traffic to have every change in level guarded.

Sections 5: Noise
5.1 Resisting sound transmission to dwellings using appropriate constructions

Every building must be designed and constructed in such a way that each wall and floor separating one dwelling from another or one dwelling from another part of the building or one dwelling from a building other than a dwelling, will limit the transmission of noise to the dwelling to a level that will not threaten the health of the occupants of the dwelling or inconvenience them in the course of normal domestic activities provided the noise source is not in excess of that from normal domestic activities.

Limitation

Not to apply to fully detached houses, roofs or walkways with access solely for maintenance, or solely for the use, of the residents of the dwelling below.

Section 6: Energy

Comment

The main changes to this section arise due to the implementation of the Energy Performance of Buildings Directive. This is covered in more detail later on in this chapter.

6.1 Carbon dioxide emissions

Energy performance to be calculated with methodology which is asset based, conforms with Energy Performance of Buildings Directive and uses UK climate data and that energy performance is capable of reducing CO_2 emissions.

Limitation

Not to apply to alterations & extensions, conversions, stand alone buildings (non domestic and ancillary to domestic) of less than $50\,m^2$, not heated (other than for frost protection) or cooled buildings, or buildings with intended life of under 2 years.

6.2 Building insulation envelope

Insulation envelope to be provided to reduce heat loss.

Limitation

Not to apply to non-domestic buidings, communal parts of domestic buildings; and buildings ancillary to dwellings (other than conservatories) which are not heated (other than for frost protection).

6.3 Heating system

The installed heating and hot water service systems to be energy efficient and capable of being controlled for optimum energy efficiency.

Limitation

Not to apply to buildings where fuel or power is not used for controlling internal environment temperature or heating is provided only for frost protection or to secondary heating in domestic buildings provided by individual solid fuel or oil fired stoves or open fires, gas or electric fires or room heaters (excluding electric storage or panel heaters).

6.4 Insulation of pipes, ducts and vessels

Temperature loss from heated pipes, ducts and vessels and temperature gain to cooled pipes and ducts to be resisted.

Limitation

Not to apply to buildings not using fuel or power for heating or cooling of internal environment or water services, unheated parts or whole buildings (other than for frost protection), pipes, ducts or vessels forming part of an isolated industrial or commercial process and cooled pipes or ducts in domestic buildings.

6.5 Artificial and display lighting

The artificial or display lighting installed is energy efficient and capable of being controlled to achieve optimum energy efficiency.

Limitation

Not to apply to process and emergency lighting, communal areas of domestic buildings or alterations in dwellings.

6.6 Mechanical ventilation and air conditioning

The form and fabric of the building to minimise use of mechanical ventilation or cooling systems for cooling and, in non-domestic buildings, installed ventilation and cooling systems are energy efficient and capable of being controlled to achieve optimum energy efficiency.

Limitation

Not to apply to buildings not using fuel or power for ventilating or cooling internal environment.

6.7 Commissioning building services

Energy supply systems and building services, which use fuel or power for heating, lighting, ventilation and cooling the internal environment and for heating water, to be commissioned to achieve optimum energy efficiency.

Limitation

Not to apply to major power plants serving National Grid, process and emergency lighting components, heating solely for frost protection or energy supply systems used solely for industrial and commercial processes, leisure and emergency use within a building.

6.8 Written information

Occupiers of the building to be provided with written information by the owner on operation and maintenance of building services and energy supply systems and, where any air-conditioning system is subject to regulation 17 (Continuing requirements relative inspection and provision of advice relative to air-conditioning systems), stating a time based interval for inspection of the system.

Limitation

Not to apply to major power plants servicing the National Grid, buildings not using fuel or power for heating, lighting, ventilating and cooling the internal environment and heating the water supply services, the process and emergency lighting components of a building, heating solely for frost protection, lighting, ventilation and cooling systems in domestic building and energy systems used solely for industrial and commercial processes, leisure use and emergency use within a building.

6.9 Energy performance certificates

An energy performance certificate (EPC) for the building to be affixed to the building. The EPC to be defined in The Energy Performance of Buildings (Scotland) Regulations as amended. The energy performance certificate to be displayed in a prominent place within the building.

Limitation

Not to apply to buildings not using fuel or power for controlling temperature of internal environment or non-domesitc buildings and stand alone buildings ancillary to dwellings of less than $50\,m^2$ area or conversions, alterations and extensions with an area of less than $50\,m^2$ or buildings with intended life of less than 2 years. The obligation to prominantly display the EPC to apply only to buildings, which can be visited by the public, of floor area over $1000\,m^2$ occupied by public authorities and institutions providing public services.

6.10 Metering

Each part of a building designed for different occupation to be fitted with fuel consumption meters.

Limitation

Not to apply to domestic buildings, communal areas of buildings in different occupation or district or block heating systems (where each of the parts designed for different occupation are fitted with heat meters) or heating fired by solid fuel or biomass.

Technical Handbooks

8.09 There are two Technical Handbooks, one covering domestic buildings (as defined in the building regulations) and one non-domestic buildings (that is all buildings which are not domestic). There is also the *The Guide for Practitioners – Conversion of Traditional Building*, issued by Historic Scotland, and guidance on conservatories produced by BSD which have already been mentioned. The Technical Handbooks, the *Guide for Practitioners* and the guidance on Conservatories, are issued by Scottish Ministers under section 4(4) of the Act to provide practical guidance with regard to the requirements of the building regulations and their status is as set out in sections 4 and 5 of the Act, as discussed above. There is not space here to review the contents of the guidance, but it is available in three forms, on the website of the Building Standards Division (formerly the Scottish Building Standards Agency), on a single CD-ROM and on paper in two loose leaf A4 binders. With both the website and the CD-ROM (when the user is connected to the internet) being interactive and containing links to other sources of information. The intention is, where possible, to have all the information necessary to comply with the standards either within the Technical Handbooks or in documents directly available from the internet via web links within the text on the website or within the CD-ROM. Some information, such as that from British Standards, is not available in this way (mainly due to copyright issues) and must be obtained from other sources.

8.10 The introductory sections to the Handbooks and to each section are especially useful and should be studied before launching into the particular standard upon which guidance is sought. At the beginning of each Handbook there is a section '0', which covers the Building Regulations themselves (rather than the standards set out in Schedule 5 to the Regulations) and provides valuable explanations as to their import and effect. In addition each of the six sections (setting out the standards relevant to that particular subject (equivalent to the CPD Essential Requirements)) starts off with an introduction, which normally consists of four parts. This introduction normally starts with the background to these particular standards followed by the aims, which these standards are attempting to achieve. There then follows a list of the latest changes, which allows the reader to see what amendments to the guidance there have been (it should be noted that the Handbooks can be changed without there having been an amendment of the regulations) and then there is normally a list of relevant legislation. It should be noted that where the website, or the CD-ROM (on a computer connected to the internet), is used the legislation and a large number of the references to further guidance and documentation have hypertext links giving direct access to those documents allowing them to be examined and copied.

8.11 There are, in addition to the guidance, three appendices. The first appendix (Appendix A) contains defined terms, including those from the Act and from the building regulations (which are in inverted commas) and the second (Appendix B) which contains a useful note on the Construction Products Directive and guidance on how British Standards, British Standards Codes of Practice, European Standards or Internation Standards are to be used in the Technical Standards. Appendix B also includes a list of such standards together with a list of legislation and other publications referred to in the technical handbooks. Such references include a note of the sections within the technical handbooks where they are to be found. The final appendix is an index (Appendix C) showing where, within the handbooks, any particular subject matter can be found.

Related legislation

8.12 As noted above, Appendix B to the technical handbooks provides a comprehensive list of all of the legislation referred to in the guidance (it should be noted that some of this may be out of date and in such circumstances reference can be made to the original or the current legislation at the users discretion). However, there are a number of statutes which are more relevant than the others and the more important of those are listed below with a brief note on their relevance.

9 Other national legislation affecting building

It is important to remember that, while a building warrant and planning consent are normally required before most construction work, they are not necessarily the only statutory consents required. There is a wide range of statute covering construction, some requiring licences, others requiring only compliance and some only relevant when the construction is operated for a particular purpose. It is therefore important to understand to what use any particular construction is to be put as it is not much use constructing a building which complies with the building regulations if it cannot be put to the use for which it was designed. The following list of legislation (although not completely exhaustive) applies in Scotland, and the comments under each heading may give guidance regarding the Scottish scene.

Legislation relevant to the Building Regulations

The following legislation is mentioned in the Technical Handbooks as relevant to the standards set out in the appropriate section of Schedule 5 to the Building Regulations. The web version and the CD-ROM version, when read on a computer connected to the internet, both have hypertext links to copies of the relevant legislation.

9.01 Section 1 – Structure

- **Safety of Sports Grounds Act 1975** and **Fire Safety and Safety of Places of Sport Act 1987.** When designing or verifying sports grounds, reference should be made to the Guide to Safety at Sports Grounds (fourth edition 1997) (often referred to as the 'Green Book'). The guide has no statutory force but many of its recommendations will be given force of law at individual grounds by their inclusion in safety certificates issued under the Safety of Sports Grounds Act 1975 or the Fire Safety and Safety of Places of Sport Act 1987. The guide covers the management of such sports facilities as well as the physical arrangements recommended. It also covers other matters such as safe means of escape and provides general design advice on the design of the facilities. However as noted below in 'Section 2 – Fire', any guidance regarding 'fire safety' (including safe means of escape in the event of fire) is superseded by the relevant guidance issued under the Fire (Scotland) Act 2005 and its regulations.
- **Civic Government (Scotland) Act.** This Act has a number of provisions requiring licenses for premises which are relevant to building standards. These licenses are operated under a general licensing system operated under Part 1 and Schedule 1 of this Act. This system provides wide discretion to the licensing authority. Therefore where premises are to be put to a use, which requires such a licence it will be prudent to consult with the licensing authority regarding the physical arrangements and provisions within the premises to see if they are such that a licence

could be granted. It should, however, be remembered that, being a discretionary grant, it cannot be promised in advance and it also depends upon other factors such as the management of the premises and the identity of those managing. Paragraph 5(3)(c) of Schedule 1 to this Act sets out the criteria for considering whether or not premises are appropriate. These include: (i) the location, character or condition of the premises; (ii) the nature and extent of the proposed activity; (iii) the kind of persons likely to use the premises; (iv) the possibility of undue public nuisance; or (v) public order or public safety. Matters relevant to the Building Regulations could arise relative to 'public safety'. It should also be remembered that under section 71 of the Fire (Scotland) Act 2005 the requirements of that Act, relative to fire safety, override any provisions within such a license

- **Section 41.** Under this section a 'Public Entertainment Licence' (PEL) is required for the use of any premises as a place of public entertainment (being a place to which members of the public are admitted, on payment of money or money's worth, for entertainment or recreation). Those premises covered by other legislation (principally the above noted Sports Ground and Places of Sport Acts, the Theatres Act, 1968, the Cinemas Act 1985, the Licensing (Scotland) Act 2005) and premises used for educational or religious purposes are not subject to a PEL. Section 41A has been added requiring licences for indoor sports events.
- **Section 44.** This makes provision regarding Houses in Multiple Occupation. See below for the relevant Order made under this section.

Part VIII, Buildings etc. (Section 87–109)
This covers various requirements as to maintenance and repair of buildings, installation of lighting, fire precautions in common stairs. In particular:

- **Section 87** relates to repairs to buildings where it is necessary in the interests of health or safety or to prevent damage to any property. However this section has been amended by the Building (Scotland) Act 2003 and its provisions are to a large extent accommodated within section 28 of that Act.
- **Section 88** relates to the installation of pipes through a neighbouring property and the procedure to be followed where consent of the neighbouring owner has been withheld or refused.
- **Section 89** requires that the use of a raised structure for seating or standing accommodation has been approved by the local authority. Certain raised structures are exempt from this, including any structure that has been granted a building warrant.

9.02 Section 2 – Fire

It is important to be aware that there is other legislation, apart from building regulations, imposing requirements for means of escape in case of fire and other fire safety measures. It is therefore recommended that consultation with those responsible for administering such legislation takes place before the application for building warrant is finalised. Any necessary fire safety measures requiring additional building work can then be included in the application.

Fire (Scotland) Act 2005

9.02.01 Part 3 (principally sections 57, 58 and 59(2)) of the Fire (Scotland) Act 2005, together with the Fire Safety (Scotland) Regulations 2006 made under that Act, set up a fire safety regime for non-domestic premises in Scotland (non-domestic includes, under this Act, Houses in Multiple Occupation even if they come within the definition of domestic building or dwelling under the Building Regulations). This regime replaces that previously operated under the Fire Precautions Act 1971 (with some minor exceptions – see Fire (Scotland) Act 2005 (Consequential Modifications and Savings) Order 2006) and replaces a system of 'fire certificates' with a system of risk assessment by the persons in control of premises and the implementation by them of appropriate fire safety measures.

9.02.02 The fire safety measures which are required to be taken under this Act (set out in Schedule 2 to this Act), include measures also covered by the Building Regulations (such as: measures to reduce the risk of fire and spread of fire; means of escape from, and means of fighting fires in, relevant premises; and means of detecting, and giving warning of, fire in relevant premises). Under the Fire Precautions Act 1971 (now revoked) there was provision, in section 14, that the requirements imposed under that Act in relation to means of escape, for buildings subject to the Building Standards (Scotland) Regulations, should not exceed the requirements of those Regulations. This ensured, for means of escape at least, that the standards imposed by fire safety legislation did not conflict with the relevant building standards. The Fire Safety Regulations do not have any equivalent provision.

9.02.03 The Fire Safety Regulations are written in the same type of general terms as the Building Regulations although they are not the same. The standards set out in Schedule 5 to the Building Regulations provide very general requirements. The details of how such requirements can be met are set out in the relevant provisions within the technical handbooks. The Fire Safety Regulations provide much more specific detail. However they also leave further detail to a number of guides one being a general guide the others covering a number of building types:

- care homes;
- offices, shops and similar premises;
- factories and storage premises;
- educational and day care for children premises;
- small premises providing sleeping accommodation;
- medium and large premises providing sleeping accommodation;
- transport premises;
- places of entertainment and assembly (this supersedes the 'Green Guide' relative to fire safety); and
- healthcare premises.

These guides also include generalizations relative to the technical requirements for the layout and construction of relevant premises but they do include 'Technical Annexes' which are stated to contain benchmarks against which existing provision can be compared. It should be remembered, that a building need only comply with the Fire Safety Regulations, once it is put into use and therefore all buildings constructed in accordance with the Building Regulations are treated as existing buildings when assessing if the provisions within them comply with the Fire Safety Regulations.

9.02.04 Where existing fire safety measures fall below these benchmarks, the guide recommends that consideration should be given during the fire safety risk assessment to assess whether this poses a risk, which requires action. Where this is the case then upgrading may remove or reduce the risk.

The guide states that most of the benchmarks in the Technical Annexes are a modification of the standards, in the Building Regulations and associated technical handbooks, that apply to new buildings. It should however be remembered that these are only benchmarks contained in an annex to guidance relative to general provisions within the Fire Safety Regulations and that such benchmarks, guidance and regulations will, in most circumstances, be assessed by the local fire authority whilst compliance or not with the Building Regulations will be assessed by the relevant verifier (unless covered by a certificate from an approved certifier of design). There is therefore potential for conflicting opinions as to compliant design.

9.02.05 Under the Fire (Scotland) Act 2005 the duties imposed apply only to employers, to persons in control of relevant premises (to the extent of their control) or the owners of relevant premises (in certain circumstances) or persons with contractual obligations in relation to maintenance or repair or fire safety of relevant premises or, to a certain extent, to employees. These duties, which in turn impose standards, do not, therefore, apply to the relevant premises in themselves, but only to the extent that they are used by the

persons named above. They can therefore not be imposed until the premises come into use. In addition, these duties can include such matters as the manner in which the premises are managed and operated which is not normally covered in the Building Regulations. However there is no system of certification by the fire authority and it is up to the operators themselves to carry out the relevant risk assessment and take such measures as they consider necessary.

9.02.06 Note should be taken of section 70 and 71 of this Act. Section 70 of the Fire (Scotland) Act 2005 restricts the application of Part 1 of the Health and Safety at Work etc Act 1974 and any regulations or orders made under it in relation to general fire safety. There are exceptions; first, where a single enforcing authority enforces both pieces of legislation (to avoid duplication) and secondly, in respect of sites where the Control of Major Accident Hazards Regulations 1999 (COMAH) apply (where the HSE and HSC need to be the authority). Section 71 of this Act makes of no effect, any terms, conditions or restrictions imposed under a license of premises, to the extent that they relate to matters covered by the requirements and prohibitions of Part 3 of the Fire (Scotland) Act 2005. This means that conditions within, for example, Public Entertainment Licences, to the extent that they deal with fire safety are of no effect and the provisions in the new Fire Safety Regime, with its risk assessments etc., apply instead. There are many specialised uses, such as theatres, cinemas and premises with a liquor licence, where the licence conditions include matters relating to fire safety and section 71 will equally apply in relation to such licences.

Health and Safety at Work etc. Act 1974

9.02.07 This Act is a general purpose Act giving powers to make specific regulations under section 15, referred to as 'health and safety regulations'. Section 16 provides for the issuing of 'approved codes of practice'. Section 17 provides that breach of a provision of an approved code of practice raises the presumption of breach of the regulation to which that provision refers subject to evidence of compliance by other means. The term 'relevant statutory provisions', which is a term used in a number of health and safety regulations, is defined in this Act as, Part I of this Act, the health and safety regulations (referred to above) and the existing statutory provisions (a number of existing statutes set out in Schedule 1 to this Act). It should be noted that under section 11 of the Interpretation Act 1978, unless expressly provided otherwise, definitions within an Act are operative within subordinate legislation (which would include regulations made under this Act). While most of the provisions relating to health and safety are implemented through 'health and safety regulations' there are some provisions of this Act itself, which are relevant to the design and construction of buildings.

9.02.08 Sections 2, 3 and 4 contain general duties respectively: of employers to their employees; of employers and self-employed to others; and of those responsible for premises to others. Those duties, undertaken by an employer, include ensuring, so far as reasonably practicable, the health, safety and welfare of all employees. In addition each employer or self-employed person shall conduct their undertaking so that, as far as is reasonably practicable, there is not put at risk the health and safety of those not in their employment who may be affected by those undertakings. Those in control of premises, including their access and egress and any plant or substance therein, to the extent that they are in control, are to ensure, so far as is reasonably practicable, that such premises are safe and that the health and safety of persons using those premises is not to put at risk.

9.02.09 While most of these general duties are covered by specific health and safety regulations (such as those discussed below) these general duties can be used where the enforcing authority (usually the Health and Safety Executive but, in some circumstances, the local authority within whose jurisdiction the unsafe practice is being perpetrated) is aware of a dangerous practice but cannot bring it within the provisions of a specific health and safety regulation. It should be remembered that these powers apply only to unsafe use and therefore premises can be designed and built and breach only occurs when the operator attempts to bring them into use. Thus, in one case, the local authority, as enforcing authority, considered premises, which complied with building regulations and had a completion certificate, as unsafe. Costly alterations were, therefore, required before they could be used for the purpose for which they were designed.

Construction (Design and Management) Regulations 2007

9.02.10 These Regulations, which implement Council Directive 92/57/EEC, are made under the Health and Safety at Work etc. Act 1974. These Regulations combine the Construction (Design and Management) Regulations 1994 (as amended by amendment regulations 2000) and the Construction (Health, Safety and Welfare) Regulations 1996 as well as amending those regulations. The key aim is to integrate health and safety into the management of the project and to encourage everyone involved to work together to: improve the planning and management of the projects from the very start; identify hazards early on, so they can be eliminated or reduced at the design or planning stage and the remaining risks properly managed; target effort where it can do most good in terms of health and safety; and discourage unnecessary bureaucracy. The Regulations are divided into five parts: (1) interpretation and application; (2) general management duties applicable to all construction projects, including those which are non-notifiable; (3) additional management duties for those projects over the notifiable threshold (lasting over 30 days or involving over 500 person days' construction work); (4) duty, to provide physical safeguards needed to prevent danger on construction sites, imposed on contractors and all who control construction sites, to the extent they exercise such control; and (5) issues of civil liability, transitional provisions and amendments and revocations of other legislation.

The Health and Safety (Safety Signs and Signals) Regulations 1996

9.02.11 These regulations impose requirements in relation to fire exit and directional signs. In addition, the Fire Safety Regulations require emergency routes and exits to be indicated by signs. Advice on fire safety signs is given in the HSE publication, 'Safety signs and signals: Guidance on Regulations – The Health and Safety (Safety Signs and Signals) Regulations 1996'. Guidance is also available in BS 5499: Part 1: 2002, and BS 5499: Part 4: 2000 on graphical symbols, fire safety signs and escape route signing.

Houses in Multiple Occupation (HMO)

9.02.12 Under the Civic Government (Scotland) Act 1982 (Licensing of Houses in Multiple Occupation) Order 2000, is made under section 44 of the Civic Government (Scotland) Act 1982, it is mandatory for all local authorities to operate an HMO Licensing Scheme and for all owners of an HMO to be licensed under such a scheme. An HMO is essentially shared accommodation for three or more persons, for which this is their only or principal residence, not being members of the same, or of one or other, of two, families (families can include same-sex couples). Guidance is provided in the publication 'Mandatory Licensing of Houses in Multiple Occupation: Guidance for Licensing Authorities, 2004' which includes information on the licensing scheme and benchmark standards. HMOs which require a licence are also subject to Part 3 of the Fire (Scotland) Act 2005 'Nursing homes' as so defined under the Nursing Homes Registration (Scotland) Act 1938, private hospitals under the Mental Health (Scotland) Act 1984, boarding schools, Monasteries, convents and similar religious communities are all exempt because they are either covered by other legislation or because of their spiritual nature. The licensable activity is the provision of such accommodation. Such a licence is granted subject to conditions. Where the accommodation is new then they should be built to comply with the Building Regulations. The domestic Technical Handbook should be used for HMOs that are dwellings and the non-domestic Technical Handbook should be used for all other HMOs. Where the accommodation is in existing premises the guidance provides minimum benchmark standards

which include detailed provisions on space requirements, fire protection and means of escape amongst other things.

Regulation of Care (Scotland) Act 2001

9.02.13 The Scottish Commission for the Regulation of Care is responsible for regulating a diverse range of care services some of which are provided in non-domestic buildings (e.g. care homes, nurseries, independent hospitals, hospices, residential schools, secure accommodation) and some in domestic buildings (e.g. child minding, supported accommodation, adult placement services). The services are inspected by the Commission against national care standards issued by Scottish Ministers some of which include physical standards for the premises. Where the applicant for a building warrant intends to use or provide such a service, they should consult the Commission for advice.

9.03 Section 3 – Environment

Listed below are some pieces of legislation that may be relevant to the matters covered in this particular section. Some of this legislation will affect the type of equipment that can be installed and some, the persons who can install it. Whilst other provisions impose obligations on any developer, in addition to those in the Building Regulations, relative to the environment.

Gas Safety (Installations and Use) Regulations 1998

9.03.01 These Regulations require that any person who installs, services, maintains, removes, or repairs gas fittings must be competent. It covers, not only materials, workmanship, safety precautions and testing of gas fittings but also the safe installation of all aspects of gas-fired appliance installations.

Gas Appliance (Safety) Regulations 1995

9.03.02 These Regulations cover all aspects of gas appliances and fittings and sets safe standards to satisfy the essential requirements set by the EU. It sets procedures and duties for demonstrating attestation of conformity.

Workplace (Health, Safety and Welfare) Regulations 1992

9.03.03 These Regulations, which implement Council Directive 89/654, are made under the Health and Safety at Work etc. Act 1974. The Regulations apply to the workplace therefore they are only enforceable once a building is occupied as a workplace. However, they contain many requirements regarding the physical building conditions and environment. It is therefore sensible to ensure that buildings capable of complying with these regulations are initially constructed so that further work is not required after obtaining acceptance of a completion certificate. The regulations include provisions regarding the physical environment of the workplace, which, although in different terms from those in the Building Regulations, cover similar requirements. These include: Ventilation (reg. 6); Temperature in indoor workplace (reg. 7); Lighting (reg. 8); Room dimensions and space (reg. 10); Conditions of floor and traffic routes (reg. 12); Prevention of falls and falling objects (reg. 13); Provision of windows and transparent or translucent doors, gates and walls (reg. 14); Provision of windows, skylights and ventilators (reg. 15); Ability to clean windows, etc safely (reg. 16); Organization etc of traffic routes (reg. 17); Suitably constructed doors and gates (reg. 18); Escalators and moving walkways (reg. 19); Suitable sanitary conveniences (reg. 20); Suitable washing facilities (reg. 21); adequate supply of drinking water (reg. 22); Suitable accommodation for personal and work clothing, as appropriate (reg. 23); Suitable facilities for changing clothing, as appropriate (reg. 24); Suitable facilities for rest and eating meals (reg. 25).

Control of Pollution Act 1974

9.03.04 This Act covers, among others, duties and powers of the local authority to control and dispose of solid waste.

Clean Air Act 1993

9.03.05 This Act control emissions from domestic premises and from certain industrial processes which fall outwith the provisions of the Environmental Protection Act. Sections 14 and 15 of this Act provide a new control for the heights of chimneys serving furnaces. The situation, therefore, is that special application must be made to the local authority for chimney height approval for furnace chimneys. The height of non-furnace chimneys is dealt with under the Building Regulations without need for special application. Constructional details of all chimneys are of course subject to local authority approval.

Environment Act 1995

9.03.06 This Act covers, among others, duties and powers of the Scottish Environment Protection Agency.

Environmental Protection Act 1990

9.03.07 This Act covers, among others, management and enforcement of the collection, disposal and treatment of waste, control of hazardous substances, oil pollution and nature conservation. Part IIA covers contaminated land.

The Groundwater Regulations 1998

9.03.08 These regulations were introduced to prevent pollution of groundwater and to manage groundwater resources in a sustainable way.

The Ionising Radiation Regulations 1999

9.03.09 These regulations cover, among others, general principles and procedures, the arrangements for the management of radiation protection and the duties of employers.

Water Byelaws 2004

9.03.10 These by-laws, made under section 70 of the Water (Scotland) Act 1980, apply to any water fitting installed or used in buildings where Scottish Water supplies water, other than where specifically exempted. They include requirements for water fittings, notification, and consent, before starting work in relation to particular operations unless work by approved contractor and the issue of certificates by approved contractors.

Sewerage (Scotland) Act 1968

9.03.11 This Act covers, among others things, duties and powers of the local authority to provide, construct and maintain public sewers and rights of connection and discharge. Drains are defined as being 'within the curtilage of those premises used solely for or in connection with the drainage of one building or of any buildings or yards appurtenant to buildings within the same curtilage' and are, in general, to be the resposibility of the owner. Public sewers include all sewers, pipes or drains used for drainage of buildings and yards which are not 'drains' as defined in this Act and which are vested in Scottish Water. Under section 12 of this Act, and subject to the conditions of this section, an owner has a right to connect to a Scottish Water sewer or sewage treatment works. The owner of any premises who proposes to connect his drains or sewers to a public sewer or works of Scottish Water, or who is altering his drain or sewer in such a way as to interfere with those of Scottish Water, must, however, give 28 days' notice to the Scottish Water, who may or may not give permission for the work to proceed. The authority can give conditional approval, and the owner has right of appeal against any decision.

Powers are given in this Act to require defects in drains or sewage treatment works to be remedied. Scottish Water has the power to take over private sewage treatment works, including septic tanks. Other powers include rights to discharge trade effluents into public sewers, emptying of septic tanks, provision of temporary sanitary conveniences, etc.

The Water Environment (Controlled Activities) (Scotland) Regulations 2005 (CAR Regulations 2005)

9.03.12 These regulations give Ministers the power to introduce controls over a range of activities that have an adverse impact upon the water environment.

The Water Environment (Oil Storage) (Scotland) Regulations 2006 (Oil Storage Regulations 2006)

9.03.13 These Regulations were introduced to help reduce the incidence of oil pollution particularly from inadequate storage.

Roads (Scotland) Act 1984

9.03.14 Where a development includes roads and footpaths together with their associated lighting then consideration will need to be taken as to building them to an adoptable standard and then having them adopted by the roads authorities. In addition, where an alteration is to be made to an existing public road consent will also need to be applied for. Section 21 of this Act provides for construction consents to be granted by the roads authority to others constructing roads and under section 16 the developer can apply for such roads to be adopted by the Roads Authority. In addition, under section 18 paths associated with a development can also be taken over by the Roads Authority. In addition consents may be required under section 58 regarding temporary occupation of, and deposit of materials on, a public road in the course of construction or under section 85 regarding the use of builders' skips occupying part of a public road. The obligation to obtain these consents is usually passed to the builder under any building contract.

9.04 Section 4 – Safety

Listed below are some pieces of legislation that may be relevant to the issues of safety covered in the standards set out in this section of Schedule 5 to the Building Regulations. The principal Act relative to health and safety is the Health and Safety at Work etc. Act 1974, which is discussed in more detail earlier in this chapter.

Factories Act 1961 and Offices, Shops and Railway Premises Act 1963

9.04.01 The majority of the parts of these Acts, relevant to building standards for new buildings, are repealed by the Workplace (Health, Safety and Welfare) Regulations 1992, which have equivalent provisions.

Electricity Safety, Quality and Continuity Regulations 2002

9.04.02 These Regulations define the duties of any party supplying electricity to premises with regard to matters such as supply, equipment, protection and provision of earthing.

The Electricity at Work Regulations 1989

9.04.03 These Regulations define the duties of an employer to ensure and maintain a safe working environment with respect to any electrical installation within a building.

The Work at Height Regulations 2005

9.04.04 These Regulations apply to all work at height where there is a risk of a fall liable to cause personal injury. They place duties on employers, the self-employed, and any person who controls the work of others, such as facilities managers or building owners who may contract others to work at height.

Disability Discrimination Act 1995, as amended

9.04.05 This Act sets out measures intended to end discrimination against people with disabilities in the areas of employment, access to goods, facilities and services, in the management, buying or renting of land or property, in education and in public transport. Part III of this Act places a duty on those providing goods, facilities or services to the public and those selling, letting or managing premises not to discriminate against disabled people in certain circumstances. These duties were introduced in three stages, the last being 1 October 2004. Under section 21 there is an obligation on service providers to make reasonable adjustments for disabled people. The duty to make reasonable adjustments comprises a series of duties falling into three main areas: (i) changing practices, policies and procedures; (ii) providing auxiliary aids and services; and (iii) overcoming a physical feature so as not to discriminate against disabled people. From 1 October 2004 there has been an obligation, where a physical feature makes it impossible or unreasonably difficult for disabled people to make use of services to: (i) remove the feature; or (ii) Alter it; or (iii) Avoid it; or (iv) Provide services by alternative methods.

9.04.06 This can mean that physical alterations or adaptations need to be made to the building within which the services are being provided. In order to avoid having to change or remove features recently made to assist access to, and use of facilities within, buildings under section 21 of this Act, the Disability Discrimination (providers of Services)(Adjustment of Premises) Regulations 2001 as amended by the 2005 Amendment Regulations, introduce special provisions. Under these provisions such features need not be removed if they are built to the 'relevant design standards'. Those standards, in Scotland, to be, where provided on or after 30 June 1994 and before 1 May 2005, the technical standards applicable under the Building Standards (Scotland) Regulations 1990 current at the time the features were provided and, where provided on or after 1 May 2005, the non-domestic technical handbook applicable under the Building (Scotland) Regulations 2004. However in either case those standards are not satisfactory if over 10 years have elapsed since the feature was completed or, in large projects, the project was completed. Therefore works assisting access to or use of a building, which are under 10 years old, as long as they meet the building standards applicable at the time of construction, need not be changed.

9.05 Section 5 – Noise

Designers and specifiers should consider the health and safety implications of using mass to limit sound transmission.

Manual Handling Operations Regulations 1992

9.05.01 Buildings should be designed to avoid repetitive manual handling of excessively heavy blocks and boards. HSE advises on the assessment of manual handling operations.

Consultation on Section 5: Noise

9.05.02 This section is to be revised and the proposed changes are outlined in the current consultation on a review of standards and guidance in the technical handbooks on Section 5: Noise available on the BSD website (www.sbsa.gov.uk). The relevant law or pieces of legislation mentioned in that consultation are:

Common law of nuisance

9.05.03 The common law of nuisance recognises that an occupant has the right to the free and absolute use of the property, but only to the extent that such use does not discomfort or annoy a neighbour.

Civic Government (Scotland) Act 1982

9.05.04 Part IV sets out a range of public nuisance offences.

Environmental Protection Act 1990

9.05.05 Environmental Protection Act 1990 as it relates to noise, states that 'any premises in such a state as to be prejudicial to health or a nuisance ranks as a statutory nuisance'.

Human Rights Act 1998

9.05.06 Human Rights Act 1998: (as it relates to noise) Article 8 guarantees the right to respect for private and family life.

Antisocial Behaviour etc. (Scotland) Act 2004

9.05.07 Antisocial Behaviour etc. (Scotland) Act 2004 empowers the local authority to serve a warning notice in relation to noise which exceeds the permitted level.

Noise Act 1996

9.05.08 Noise Act 1996 (as amended by the Antisocial Behaviour Act 2003) makes similar provisions to the Antisocial Behaviour (Scotland) Act 2004 in relation to noise from dwellings during night hours.

9.06 Section 6 – Energy

The main legislation relative to energy which impacts upon the Building Regulations is European Directive 2002/91/EC on the energy performance of buildings. This has been implemented in Scotland principally through the building standards system but other legislation is also involved, as set out below.

Implementation of the Energy Performance of Building Directive (EPBD)

9.06.01 The EPBD was required to be implemented within EU member states by 4 January 2006. Although energy is generally a UK matter, building legislation and the promotion of energy efficiency is a devolved matter. Much of EPBD impacts on how energy standards are set for, and applied to, new and existing buildings, as well as introducing certification and inspection processes. It was therefore decided to implement the EPBD principally through the new building standards system (one of the objectives of which is 'conservation of fuel and power' – section 1(1)(b) of the Act). The new building standards system already includes enforcement powers and provisions regarding not only maintenance but also other continuing obligations which would be needed to implement EPBD and the requirements for setting energy standards and for energy certification build on what already exists in Scotland.

9.06.02 Scotland was in a position to implement Articles 3, 4, 5 and 6 of EPBD on 4 January 2006, but a decision was made to align implementation with England and Wales in the spring of 2006. Article 15.2 allows for the implementation of Articles 7, 8 and 9 to be delayed for 3 years (up until 4 January 2009) and Scottish Ministers made use of this derogation to implement these further articles over the following 3 years. Article 3, 4, 5 and 6 were initially complied with through the original standards of 2005 (which were transferred from the last amendment to the Building Standards (Scotland) Regulations 1990) these standards were upgraded in the amendments to the Building Regulations in the spring of 2007.

Article 3

9.06.03 Article 3 requires the adoption of a methodology for the energy performance of buildings. We have had such a methodology for domestic building 'The Government's Standard Assessment Procedure for Energy Ratings of Dwelling' – for some time, the latest edition being 'SAP 2005', and a similar energy rating methodology for non-domestic buildings has been developed 'Simplified Building Energy Model' (known as 'SBEM'). Both of these methodologies have been developed by BRE for UK use, and SBEM allows use of a Scottish climate data site instead of one that is general to the UK. The output of these tools gives a CO_2 emission indicator which is consistent with the Government's message on reduction of CO_2 emissions.

Article 4

9.06.04 Article 4 requires the setting of energy performance require-ments (based on the methodologies set up under Article 3). The Scottish Energy Standards had last been updated in 2002 under the 6th amendment to the Building Standards (Scotland) Regulations 1990 and require, under EPBD, to be reviewed every 5 years. New Energy Standards and guidance were therefore introduced with the Building Regulations Amendments of May 2007. It should be noted that Article 4 has certain exemptions, most of these are simi-lar to those within the Building Regulations, however Article 4 does exempt 'buildings used as places of worship and for religious activities' which is not an exemption included in Schedule 1 to the Building Regulations. However, EPBD only permits such exemp-tions and does not require them.

Article 5

9.06.05 Article 5 requires all new building to meet the energy performance requirements introduced pursuant to Article 4. The Building (Scotland) Act 2003 and associated Procedure Regulations already require this and the amendments to the Energy standards introduced in May 2007 are also be subject to this legislation.

The second paragraph of Article 5 requires the Building Regulations to take decentralised low-carbon and zero-carbon energy-generating technologies into consideration (where techni-cally, environmentally and economically feasible) for new build-ings which are over $1000\,m^2$ in floor area. Examples of these technologies are:

● solar water heating;
● micro-wind turbines;
● heat pumps; and
● Combined Heat and Power (CHP).

Such technologies are taken into consideration in the May 2007 amendments and are being further considered pursuant to the Sullivan Report (covered later).

Article 6

9.06.06 Article 6 requires minimum energy standards to be applied to large buildings when they are renovated. This is already the case under the current Building Regulations when alterations to exist-ing building takes place and although 'renovation' under EPBD is not defined it does imply more than mere repair or maintenance. Where alteration work is done the new components and systems must meet Building Regulations. The May 2007 Amendments upgrade the energy requirements under the Building Regulations and as before, these new standards will apply to alterations to existing buildings as well as new build.

Articles 7, 8 and 9

As noted above, Scottish Ministers used the option in Article 152 to delay implementation of Articles 7 (Energy Performance Certificates), 8 (Inspection of Boilers) and 9 (Inspection of Air-Conditioning Systems) for up to 3 years and implemented these provisions prior to 4 January 2009.

Article 7

9.06.07 Article 7 requires energy performance certificates ('EPCs') to be produced (and updated not later than every 10 years) for a building when it is: (1) constructed; (2) sold; or (3) rented: such certificates to be made available to the owner, pro-spective buyer or tenant. Such certificates are to include reference values such as current legal standards and benchmarks (so that the energy performance of different buildings can be compared) and to be accompanied by recommendations for cost-effective improvements of energy performance. However such certificates are to be for information only and their effect in any legal pro-ceedings to be decided in accordance with Scottish legal rules.

9.06.08 The Article also requires such certificates (regardless of whether or not the building is being or has just been constructed sold or rented) to be prominently displayed and visible to the pub-lic in all buildings (with a useful floor area over $1000\,m^2$) occupied by public authorities or institutions providing public services to a large number of persons (and frequently visited by such persons).

9.06.09 The timetable for the implementation of Article 7 is as follows:

● Such certificates have been required for new construction from May 2007 at the same time as the new energy standards under section 6 of Schedule 5 to the Building Regulations were introduced.
● In relation to sale, it was decided to produce the EPC (together with an Energy Report) as part of the 'Home Report' to be avail-able, on request, to every prospective purchaser (consisting of the Energy Report (with EPC) the Single Survey and a Property Questionnaire) which was introduced from 1 December 2008 under the Housing (Scotland) Act 2006. Strictly speaking, the EPC was introduced under the Energy Performance of Buildings (Scotland) Regulations 2008 which came into force on 4 January 2009 and which are discussed later.
● Finally, those EPCs required for rented properties are also introduced under the Energy Performance of Buildings (Scotland) Regulations 2008 which came into force on 4 January 2009 (the last date allowed under the derogation) to give social landlords time to carry out all of the energy ratings necessary to produce the relevant EPCs.

Article 10

9.06.10 Article 10 requires that EPCs are provided independently by qualified and/or accredited experts. In relation to new build, the present procedure for application to a verifier for a building warrant and the submission of a completion certificate, with the appraisal of that application and acceptance of that completion certificate by the verifier is sufficient to satisfy the requirements of Article 10.

9.06.11 In relation to existing buildings, BSD has entered into pro-tocols with the Chartered Institution of Building Services Engineers, Scotland (CIBSE Scotland), the Association of Building Engineers (ABE), the Energy Institute (EI), the Royal Institution of Chartered Surveyors (RICS), the Heating and Ventilation Contractors Association (HVCA), the Building Research Establishment (BRE), National Energy Services (NES) and Elmhurst to deliver services in relation to energy performance certificates.

Enforcement of the EPC requirement

9.06.12 This does not present a problem for new construction, which will be subject to the requirement to apply for a build-ing warrant and show compliance with the Building Regulations (including Standard 6.9 in Schedule 5 to the Building Regulations relative to EPCs) although as noted below, from 4 January 2009, whilst it is necessary to affix an EPC to a new building (subject to certain exceptions) and display it in certain public buildings to comply with the Building Regulations, it is not be necessary to obtain a building warrant to do so. In relation to existing build-ings, the obligation to produce an EPC when selling or rent-ing buildings will principally be enforced through the Energy Performance of Buildings (Scotland) Regulations 2008, which are discussed in more detail later.

Article 8

9.06.13 This Article has two alternatives. Either a procedure for regular inspections of boilers or the provision of advice to boiler users on replacement or other modifications to heating systems and on alternative solutions such as efficiency and boiler size assess-ments. If the latter alternative is chosen it needs to have an impact which is equivalent to that of the former approach. The Scottish Ministers have opted for the 'provision of advice' alternative.

However this does not fit with the normal requirements of Building Standards. The BSD has therefore engaged the Energy Saving Trust to deliver this requirement. However, the advice produced is available for down loading from the BSD website. By adopting this alternative Scottish Ministers, through BSD, will have to report to the Commission on its equivalent impact.

Article 9

9.06.14 Article 9 requires regular inspection of air-conditioning systems over 12 kW, an inspection report and an assessment of the systems capacity with recommendations for improvements or replacement. A new continuing requirement Building Regulation (regulation 17) was introduced with the amendment to the Building Regulations in May 2007. These continuing requirements are introduced under section 2 of the Act (providing for continuing requirements) to ensure that the inspections are continued on an ongoing basis. Section 26 of the Act can also be used to enforce such continuing requirements. It is proposed that implementation of Article 9 will be phased through use of a series of relaxation directions. BSD is proposing to enter into a protocol with the appropriate experts relative to those experts carrying out the required inspections.

Energy Performance of Buildings (Scotland) Regulations 2008 as amended by The Energy Performance of Buildings (Scotland) Amendment Regulations 2008

9.06.15 These regulations were made under section 2(2) of the European Communities Act 1972, laid before the Scottish Parliament on 18 September 2008 and came into force on 4 January 2009. The Amendment Regulations were laid before the Scottish Parliament on 26 November 2008 and came into force on 31 December 2008 (before the regulations they were amending came into force). These amendments were introduced to provide transitional arrangements for the period up to 31 March 2009 in relation to penalties applicable for the late provision of an EPC. The Energy Performance of Building Directive (2002/9I/EC) has primarily been implemented through the Building (Scotland) Act 2003 and regulations made under it, as described earlier. However where existing buildings are either sold or rented the directive requires the production of an energy performance certificate and this obligation is not easily dealt with under the Act and its regulations and so these regulations have been made to implement these requirements. These regulations do not apply for temporary buildings (planned use of 2 years or less) or workshops and non-residential agricultural buildings with low energy demand and stand-alone buildings of area less than 50 m^2, which are not dwellings. Where a building is sold or let the regulations oblige owners of that building to make available to prospective purchasers or prospective tenants (as defined in the regulations) a copy of a valid energy performance certificate (regulation 5). This regulation does not apply at any time before the construction of the building has been completed. The form and content of the EPC, the approved method for assessment of energy performance and the definition of those organisations approved to issue EPCs, are all set out in the regulations. The regulations also provide for the display of EPCs in public buildings (as defined in the Regulations).

9.06.16 The Regulations do exceed the requirements of the Energy Performance of Buildings Directive in one respect. The Regulations require one or more registers of EPCs each maintained by a keeper, such EPCs to be kept on the register for at least 10 years. Where a member of an approved organisation issues an EPC they must ensure that it is sent, with associated data, to the relevant register before being given to the person requesting it.

9.06.17 The Regulations go on to regulate access to the registers and provide that every local authority is an enforcement authority under the regulations with powers to require the production by owners of EPCs (regulation 16) and to issue penalty charge notices, subject to certain conditions being met, where it believes an owner has breached regulation 5 (regulation 17). There are statutory defences for owners who breach regulation 5 (regulation 18), provisions for review of the penalty charge notices (regulation

19) and appeals to the sheriff (regulation 20). Finally, there are provisions for recovery of penalty charges, service of documents and offences relating to enforcement officers (appointed by the enforcement authorities).

Building (Scotland) Amendment Regulations 2008

9.06.18 These amendment regulations are made under sections 1 and 8(8) of the Building (Scotland) Act 2003, were laid before the Scottish Parliament on 18 September 2008 and come into force on 4 January 2009. They amend the Building (Scotland) Regulations 2004 by inserting a definition of 'energy performance certificate' which is the definition in the Energy Performance of Buildings (Scotland) Regulations 2008 with a consequential amendment to Standard 6.9 of Schedule 5 to the Building (Scotland) Regulations 2004. They also amend Schedule 3 to those regulations (the schedule which sets out certain types of work which must comply with the building regulations but do not require a warrant) to include work, which involves affixing an EPC to a building. Therefore from 4 January 2009 it was not be necessary to obtain a building warrant for the affixing of an EPC to a building.

Building (Scotland) Amendment Regulations 2009

9.06.19 These amendment Regulations, which are made under sections 1 and 8(8) of the Building (Scotland) Act 2003, were laid before the Scottish Parliament on 23 March 2009 and came into force on 1 May 2009. They amend the Building (Scotland) Regulations 2004 by amending Schedules 1 and 3. The first amendment is to restrict the exemption of paved areas from regulations 8–12 to areas of 50 m^2 or below with paved areas between 50 and 200 m^2 being subject to compliance with regulations 8–12 but not requiring a building warrant. The second amendment is to make certain work done to: prisons and other places of detention; the Scottish Parliament; and property owned by Her Majesty in her own capacity: to not require a building warrant (but still be required to comply with the building regulations).

10 Scotland Act 1998

10.01 This major piece of constitutional legislation set up a devolved Scottish Parliament within the UK. The Parliament came into being in May 1999. Under this Act every matter is devolved to the Scottish Parliament except for those matters listed in this Act as 'reserved matters'. In relation to the built environment, the relevant reserved matters are: energy (however implementation of EPBD and other energy conservation matters are being implemented on a devolved basis) and health and safety; The setting up, maintaining and administration, of a building standards system is a devolved matter as is the implementation of the EPBD in Scotland. This has allowed the Scottish Executive (and now the Scottish Government) to introduce a new Building (Scotland) Act, through the Scottish Parliament, and a new building standards system and to implement EPBD in a manner suited to Scotland.

11 Proposed changes for building standards

A Low Carbon Building Standards Strategy for Scotland – The Sullivan Report

11.01 The Scottish Government in August 2007 set up an expert panel to recommend measures to improve the energy performance of houses and buildings in Scotland. The panel was chaired by Lynne Sullivan and the report produced by the panel is therefore normally referred to as the 'Sullivan Report'. Membership included the heads of the building regulatory systems from Norway, Austria and Denmark, together with designers, developers, contractors, regulators, researchers and energy specialists, some of whom are members of BSAC.

11.02 The panel produced a number of recommendations, most of which are being implemented under the building standards system, overseen by BSD and with the advice of BSAC, and its working parties. The panel's recommendations for standards for new buildings were:

- net zero carbon buildings by 2016/17, if practicable;
- intermediate stages of 2010 (low carbon) and 2013 (very low carbon);
- 2010 changes to deliver carbon savings, beyond 2007 level, of 50% for non-domestic & 30% for domestic;
- 2013 changes to deliver carbon savings, beyond 2007 levels, of 75% for non-domestic & 60% for domestic;
- backstop U-Values and air-tightness standards to match Nordic standards in 2010 but with consideration of social and financial impact of need for whole house ventilation and heat recovery in domestic buildings;
- ambition of total-life zero carbon buildings (including embodied energy) by 2030.

With the panel's recommendation for existing buildings being that consideration should be made for developing practical standards for existing buildings (aligned with the EPCs)

11.03 To implement these recommendations the panel proposed nine work streams to be followed and funded by the Scottish Government. Those nine work streams each to consist of a number of linked recommendations:

- **Performance in Practice:**
  - Four recommendations on research, into and monitoring of, the performance of buildings (and their occupants), and of installed equipment, designed for low or zero, carbon or low or zero, energy use.
- **Raising Standards**
  - Adoption of the carbon reduction target standards set out above but with account also taken of energy consumption (carbon reduction alone could allow poorly insulated or heated buildings).
  - Consideration of inclusion of energy performance of built in 'white goods' for new dwellings and IT equipment for non-domestic buildings and the energy performance of such items as escalators and the role of 'smart meters'.
  - Consideration of a requirement for consequential improvements (where work carried out to existing buildings) and associated issues of unfairness and of compliance.
  - New public building should be built to future energy standards.
  - Training in new technologies, new products and new standards by construction industry should be supported by Scottish Government.
  - Consideration of embodied energy, once Construction Products Directive allows it.
- **Existing Non-domestic Buildings**
  - Legislation requiring owners of non-domestic buildings to make carbon and energy assessments, to be checked by local, or other public, authorities, and a programme for upgrading. Guidance to be provided for assessment and ways of encouraging upgrading to be considered.
  - Rating on EPCs should be significant factor for Scottish Government building procurement.
- **Existing Domestic Buildings**
  - Considering measures and targets to reduce carbon emissions from existing stock and incentives to encourage improvements with existing carbon and energy efficiency programmes continued but more carbon focused.
  - Building Regulations and BSD to continue providing standards and guidance, for work on existing buildings with advice from BSD on energy and CO_2 saving, and sustainability only if necessary.
- **Low and Zero Carbon Technology (LZCT) Equipment**
  - Requirement, in Scottish Planning Policy No. 6 (SPP 6), for on-site LZCT equipment to be reviewed and probably removed when 'very low carbon' for building standards are

introduced in 2013 with energy standards only being set at a national level under Building Regulations.
  - Consideration of split of responsibilities, planning and building standards, for local energy generation.
  - Research ways to encourage large-scale low-carbon CHP for new and existing buildings.
  - Guidance for safe and productive installations (for designers, installers and general public).
  - Examination of Building Regulations and guidance relative to low-carbon equipment.
  - Encouragement of approved certifiers of construction relative to LZCT.
- **Process**
  - Publish future standards in advance (2010 in 2008 and 2013 in 2010) with zero or reduced fees for using future standards.
  - Consideration of warrant duration (at present 3 years) possibility of requiring substantial start within fixed date from grant of warrant.
- **Compliance**
  - Consideration of what constitutes 'reasonable enquiry' (under section 18 of the Act.
  - Consideration of role of 'air tightness testing' and 'thermal imaging'.
  - Research into gap between 'as designed' and 'as built' and 'as managed' energy performance.
  - Consideration of funding verification work at completion certificate stage.
  - Encouragement of more schemes for certifiers of construction (only one so far).
- **Energy Performance of Buildings Directive**
  - Primary legislation sought to allow Scottish Ministers to extend provision and type of EPCs.
  - National electronic database for collecting information relative to non-domestic EPCs.
- **Costings**
  - Research cost impact on new build of 2010 energy and sustainability standards with life cycle analysis.
  - Cost-benefit analysis: of building warrant incentives (reduced or zero fees) for improved energy standards; of use of energy standards compliance tests; and of measures to improve energy performance of existing buildings.
  - Research analysing cost projections for new technologies and techniques.
  - Costing research to be carried out with industry with attention to full cost of development and potential impact on construction practice.
  - Opportunities to learn from international partners.

All of these work streams are being progressed at the moment, with some more advanced than others. This is a work in progress and reference should be made to the BSD website in order to obtain updates on where implementation of these recommendations has reached and how they are being implemented.

Climate Change (Scotland) Act 2009

The provisions in this Act set a long-term target to reduce Scotland's emissions of Kyoto Protocol greenhouse gases by at least 80% by the year 2050. This long-term target is supported by a 2020 interim target and a framework of annual targets intended to drive the policies necessary for achieving the long-term target. Many of the policy measures required to meet these targets will not require legislation to implement, but certain climate change mitigation and adaptation policies have been identified which do require legislation and this Act contains provisions in Part 5 to allow these to be taken forward.

The chapter of Part 5 relevant to Building Standards is chapter 3; this contains a range of provisions relating to energy efficiency. These include -

- production by the Scottish Ministers of a plan for the promotion and improvement of energy efficiency;

- production by the Scottish Ministers of a plan for promoting of the use of heat from renewable sources;
- the making of regulations regarding the assessment and improvement of the energy performance of non-domestic buildings and living accommodation;
- a duty on local authorities to establish energy efficiency discount schemes using the council tax system;
- provisions enabling the Scottish Ministers to make regulations in respect of non-domestic rates discounts related to energy efficiency;
- a 'climate change burden' that can be added to a property's title deeds to specify the mitigation or adaptation standards that must be met when the burdened property is developed;
- provision on Tenement Management Schemes;
- provisions on permitted development rights for the installation, alteration or replacement of microgeneration equipment in domestic and non-domestic buildings; and
- changes to the Town and Country Planning (Scotland) Act 1997 so that development plans contain policies for reducing the greenhouse gas emissions of new buildings by the installation of low and zero carbon technologies.

The main provisions, which could affect the building standards of existing buildings are sections 63 and 64. Section 63 requires Scottish Ministers, by regulations, to: (1) provide for the assessment of the energy performance of non-domestic buildings (buildings other than dwellings or a yard, garden, outbuilding or any common areas associated with a dwelling) including the greenhouse gas emissions associated with such buildings; and (2) requires the owners of such buildings to take steps, identified in those assessments, to improve their energy performance and reduce greenhouse gas emissions. The section makes further provision regarding the scope and content of such regulations (including the form that any recommendations should take and the way, and timescale within which, persons must take steps to comply with those recommendations) and the authority or authorities required to enforce such regulations. Scottish Ministers are required to publish a report, within 12 months of this section coming into force, setting out how they intend to reduce emissions from non-domestic buildings, the form of the required recommendations and what steps will be required for compliance and when. Section 64 has similar provisions regarding 'living accommodation' (being a dwelling of over 50m^2 including common areas). As at October 2009 neither of these sections has been brought into force.

Once brought into force these sections require the assessment of existing buildings to produce recommendations for the improvement of their energy performance and the reduction of greenhouse gas emissions and the implementation of those recommendations.

12 General

12.01 The following points may be useful to persons wishing to design and build in Scotland for the first time:

1 Scots law differs from that of the rest of the UK (see Scottish chapters in this handbook).
2 The granting of building warrants and their administration is carried out by the relevant verifier (who, at present, is the local authority within whose jurisdiction the works are to be carried out) but the enforcement of compliance with those warrants and with the Building Regulations is exercised by local authorities.
3 Warrant must be obtained from the verifier before any building (including alterations and extensions) can begin, and it is separate from planning permission. A fee related to the estimated value of the job is usually payable in accordance with the scale laid down in the table of fees set out in the Fees Regulations.
4 Ensure that the latest amendments to the Building Regulations and the Technical Handbooks are available as well as a copy of the Regulations themselves, the Procedure Regulations, and the correct forms (both those in the Forms Regulations and the 'Model Forms') all of which are available at the Building

Standards Division's website but the appropriate forms to use will normally be those provided by the relevant verifier.
5 Relaxation of the Building Regulations is the responsibility of Scottish Ministers. The Building Regulations are not prescriptive but are drafted as functional standards and therefore there should be less need for relaxation of them.
6 If problems occur, consult the building standards surveyor of the appropriate authority, but remember that although that officer will normally give advice, they are not there to design or redesign, draw or redraw plans. However where there is a genuine doubt on the part of both the applicant and the verifier as to the compliance of any particular application with the Building Regulations then the views of Scottish Ministers, referred to above, can be sought.
7 Check carefully the requirements of the sewerage authority where appropriate.
8 Check carefully whether a class relaxation has been issued in respect of a new building product.
9 Check carefully to what use, the building you are designing, altering or converting, is to be put. Different activities are subject to different regulatory controls and licences. It is no use obtaining planning consent and an accepted completion certificate and complying with the requirements of the Building Regulations if the building cannot be put to the use for which it was commissioned because the fabric and form/or of the building does not allow the legal operation of that building for that use.

Building Standards Division E – newsletter and website

12.02 The most important thing to remember about the Scottish Building Standards system is the Building Standards Division website (www.sbsa.gov.uk) which you should have as one of your 'favourites' and the BSD e-newsletter to which you should subscribe and which will keep you up to date on changes to the Scottish Building Standards system.

13 Building standards in Scotland: current legislation

Building Acts

Building (Scotland) Act 2003 (asp 8)

Building (Scotland) Act 2003 (Commencement No. 1, Transitional Provisions and Savings) Order 2004 (SSI 2004/404)

Building (Scotland) Act 2003 (Commencement No. 2 Transitional Provisions) Order 2009 (SSI 2009/150) Building (Scotland) Act 2003 (Exceptions for Defence and National Security) Order 2009 (SSI 2009/822)

Building Regulations

Building (Scotland) Regulations 2004 (SSI 2004/406)

Building Standards Advisory Committee (Scotland) Regulations 2004 (SSI 2004/506)

Building (Scotland) Amendment Regulations 2006 (SSI 2006/406)

Building (Scotland) Amendment Regulations 2007 (SSI 2007/168)

Building (Scotland) Amendment Regulations 2008 (SSI 2008/310)

Building (Scotland) Amendment Regulations 2009 (SSI 2009/119)

Building Procedure Regulations

Building (Procedure) (Scotland) Regulations 2004 (SSI 2004/428)

Building (Procedure) (Scotland) Amendment Regulations 2007 (SSI 2007/167)

Building (Procedure) (Scotland) Amendment Regulations 2009 (SSI 2009/117)

Building Fees Regulations

Building (Fees) (Scotland) Regulations 2004 (SSI 2004/508)

Building (Fees) (Scotland) Amendment Regulations 2007 (SSI 2007/169)

Building (Fees) (Scotland) Amendment Regulations 2008 (SSI 2008/397)

Building Forms Regulations

Building (Forms) (Scotland) Regulations 2005 (SSI 2005/172)

Building (Forms) (Scotland) Amendment Regulations 2006 (SSI 2006/163)

Building (Forms) (Scotland) Amendment Regulations 2007 (SSI 2007/168)

Energy Performance of Buildings Regulations

Energy Performance of Buildings (Scotland) Regulations 2008 (SSI 2008/309) (made under section 2(2) of European Communities Act 1972 16.9.08; in force 4.1.09)

Energy Performance of Buildings (Scotland) Amendment Regulations 2008 (SSI 2008/389)

11

Planning law in England and Wales

ANDREW FRASER-URQUHART[*]

Note

Throughout this chapter the following abbreviations are used:
TP = The Town and Country Planning Act 1990;
The 1990 Act = The Town and Country Planning Act 1990, except in Section 5 of this chapter where it means the Planning (Listed Buildings and Conservation Areas) Act 1990.

1 Introduction

1.01 Town and country planning control over the development of all land (including buildings) in England and Wales is an administrative process deriving from the Town and Country Planning Act 1947. See Chapter 12 for the position in Scotland. It has operated since 1 July 1948 and was brought about (to mention no other matter) for the simple reason that in England and Wales there is a limited amount of land for an increasing number of people who wish to live and work upon it and who, increasingly, call for more space both for working and for leisure. Thus the pressure on a limited amount of land is great and is getting greater.

1.02 By way of the most basic introduction, activity which falls within the definition of 'development' requires planning permission. Unless the 'development' in question falls into a defined class for which that permission is deemed to be granted, the way in which planning permission is obtained in England and Wales is described as 'plan-led'. For each area there is something known as the development plan (which, confusingly enough, does not consist of a single document or plan but instead an interlocking series of documents and plans). By law, applications for planning permission must be decided in accordance with that development plan 'unless material considerations indicate otherwise'. 'Material considerations' can consist of any matter which properly relates to the desirability, in land use terms, of permitting a particular development. They may, for example, consist of statements of central government planning policy. Equally, they might consist of the fact that a development which would be contrary to the development plan would nevertheless bring about some particular benefit in terms of, say, the improvement of the environment or the creation of jobs or any such matter arising out of the use of the land for a particular purpose. The essential exercise in planning judgement is to properly assess the weight to be given to all these different factors when arriving at the fundamental judgement as to whether or not planning permission ought to be granted.

The Main Acts

1.03 Following major reforms in 2004, there are now two principal Acts on the subject. The first is the Town and Country Planning Act 1990 ('the 1990 Act'). It contains 337 sections (although some are now only to be referred to as part of the transitional process to the procedure in the 2004 Act) and 17 Schedules and came into operation on 24 August 1990. Associated with this principal Act are three further Acts related to planning, namely the Planning (Listed Buildings and Conservation Areas) Act 1990, the Planning (Hazardous Substances) Act 1990 and the Planning (Consequential Provisions) Act 1990. These four Acts are defined (TP, section 336(l)) as 'the Planning Acts'.

The reader should also be aware that, as well as the major changes brought about in 2004, the Planning and Compensation Act 1991 also amended in 1990 Act. It is therefore imperative to consult an appropriate looseleaf or online resource to see the 1990 Act as it currently stands, rather than the original Queen's Printer's version.

After a very long gestation period from 1997, in 2004 Parliament enacted the Planning and Compulsory Purchase Act 2004. This introduced major reforms into the system of 'development plans' but left broadly unchanged the fundamental principles by which the content of those development plans bears upon the decision about whether or not to grant planning permission for any particular development.

1.04 Planning control over land development is rooted in central government policy. Accordingly, attention is drawn to the various statements of that policy. These used to be known as Planning Policy Guidance Notes (PPG) but are in process of being replaced by Planning Policy Statements (PPS). The reader will find a mix of PPGs and PPSs in force at any particular time, as the process of replacement proceeds. These documents are some of the most important 'material considerations' which can affect the decision as to a grant of planning permission.

These documents are issued by the central government Department responsible for town and country planning from time to time (currently the Department of Communities and Local Government). The following notes have application at the time of writing:

2005/PPS1	Delivering Sustainable Development
1995/PPG2	Green Belts (superseding Green Belts, 1988)
2007/PPS3	Housing
1992/PPG4	Industrial and Commercial Development and Small Firms (revised)
1992/PPG5	Simplified Planning Zones (revised)
2005/PPS6	Planning for Town Centres

[*]The assistance of Miss Denise Condon and Mrs Jennie Thelen in the preparation of this chapter is gratefully acknowledged.

2004/PPS7	Sustainable Development in Rural Areas
2001/PPG8	Telecommunications (revised)
2005/PPS9	Biodiversity and Geological Conservation
2005/PPS10	Planning for Sustainable Waste Management
2004/PPS11	Regional Spatial Strategies
2008/PPS12	Local Spatial Planning
2001/PPG13	Transport
1990/PPG14	Development on Unstable Land
1994/PPG15	Planning and the Historic Environment
1990/PPG16	Archaeology and Planning
2002/PPG17	Planning for Open Space, Sport and Recreation
1991/PPG18	Enforcing Planning Control
1992/PPG19	Outdoor Advertisement Control
1992/PPG20	Coastal Planning
1992/PPG21	Tourism
2004/PPS22	Renewable Energy
2004/PPS23	Planning and Pollution Control
1994/PPG24	Planning and Noise
2006/PPS 25	Development and Flood Risk

More detailed guidance and advice to local planning authorities is contained in a series of Departmental Circulars and, increasingly, by Parliamentary Statements by Ministers. There also exist a series of Regional Planning Guidance Notes, which, as their name suggests, provide guidance on a regional basis. It is no exaggeration to say that there is a morass of guidance, much of which can be seen as in a state of flux, due to an ongoing process of revision as central government policy evolves.

In Wales, central government advice is provided by a series of Technical Advice Notes (Wales) which are broadly equivalent to the PPGs/PPSs.

Planning control process

1.05 As noted above, the planning control process is a two-part process involving, on the one hand, the making of development plans (that is, blueprints for the future) that seek to show what the state of affairs will be when all foreseeable development (or non-development) in the area covered by the plan has been achieved. The other prong of the process is the day-to-day control over the carrying out of development through the medium of a grant or a refusal of planning permission for development. All this is a highly simplified statement of the entire complicated and sophisticated process of town planning control as it functions today.

1.06 In the ultimate analysis, all this control is done by the minister for town and country planning by whatever name he or she may be known. At the moment 'he' is known as the Secretary of State for Communities and Local Government, but this does not alter the fact that, one minister of the Crown is, by law, rendered responsible ultimately for the way in which all town planning control is carried out in England and Wales. For his actions he is answerable to Parliament. Thus the control is exercised, in the ultimate analysis, in accordance with the town and country planning policies of the central government for the time being in power at Westminster.

1.07 In this chapter no attention is given to the first prong of the process, namely the making, approving, and bringing into operation of development plans. The 2004 Act was primarily aimed at improving the system by which this came about. The architect must, however, be able to identify which of the suite of local authority documents are those known as 'Development Plan Documents'. As the name suggests, those are the documents

which form at least part of the development plan. The architect must also be able to identify any policies which are 'saved' for the time being from the old system of county structure plans and local plans. It is also imperative to identify the 'emerging' policy documents which may carry considerable weight in the planning process even though they have not completed the complicated formal statutory process of adoption. Fortunately, this information is usually readily available from either the planning department of the relevant local authority or from its website.

It is assumed for the purpose of this chapter that all the requisite development plan documents and saved policies have been identified and are in operation. Accordingly, attention in succeeding paragraphs is given to the day-to-day process of development control through the medium of grants or refusals of planning permission for development.

1.08 Moreover, it should be made clear at the start that this chapter is written primarily for the guidance of architects; it is deliberately slanted in the direction of architects. An effort has been made to pick out from the surging cauldron of town planning controls some of the more important controls and particularly those that would affect an architect seeking to organise development on behalf of a client. Thus the chapter does not purport to deal with control over advertisements, caravans, mineral workings or hazardous substances.

1.09 Accordingly, there will be found in succeeding paragraphs a brief statement on local planning authorities (paragraph 2.09) and what they can do when faced with an application for planning permission for development (paragraph 4.11). Development itself is treated in some detail (paragraph 3.01) though, maybe, not in all the detail into which the expression breaks up once it is investigated. The method of making planning applications is dealt with, as are the consequences of a refusal or a grant of permission subject to conditions (paragraph 4.04). Special reference is made to buildings of special architectural or historic interest (paragraph 5.01) because these are matters which, although standing outside the main stream of town planning control, are nevertheless highly important matters to a developer and to any architect advising him.

There is a brief reference (paragraph 6.01) to the special concepts in the planning field of urban development areas and corporations, and of simplified planning zones. There is reference to the enforcement of planning control over the development of land (paragraph 7.01) or, in other words, there is a statement on what happens if a person does indeed carry out development without getting the appropriate planning permission in advance.

1.10 The length of this chapter has been limited. This means that it has not been possible in every instance to put in all the qualifications, exceptions, reservations, and so forth which, in a more categorical statement, would necessarily be appended to the general statements set out in the paragraphs which follow.

2 Local planning authorities; or who is to deal with planning applications?

2.01 The first thing an architect seeking to carry out development must do is to inspect the site of the proposed development. It is most important nowadays to discover:

1 whether it is a cleared site; or
2 whether it contains a building and, if it does, whether that building is a building of special architectural or historic interest (see paragraph 5.01).

2.02 Second, the architect must consider carefully the definition of 'development' in the 1990 Act (section 55) and the possible effect of the Town and Country Planning (Use Classes) Order 1987. Many building operations and changes of use do not constitute development by virtue of the definitions and provisions of this section and the 1987 Order. If they do not, then nothing in the town planning Acts applies to them. 'Development' is defined in paragraph 3.01. Copies of the Town and Country

Planning (Use Classes) Order 1987 (SI 1987 No. 764) and its two amending orders of 1992 (SI 1992 Nos 610 and 657) are available from The Stationery Office or online at http://www.opsi.gov.uk.

2.03 Third, the architect must examine closely the type of development which is sought to be carried out. Is it development which can be dealt with in the normal run of planning control, or will it be subject to some additional control over and above the normal run? It certainly will be if it happens to be development of land occupied by a building of special architectural or historic interest (paragraph 5.01) which has been listed by the Secretary of State.

2.04 Fourth, the architect must investigate generally the Town and Country Planning (General Permitted Development) Order 1995 (SI. 1995 No. 418). It will be necessary to do this sort of investigation in order to ascertain whether the development is 'permitted development' under the Order because, if it is, it gets automatic planning permission and there is no need to make any application to a local planning authority (see paragraph 4.02).

2.05 When considering the T & CP (General Permitted Development) Order 1995, the architect must satisfy himself whether the site for the development does, or does not:

1 Comprise so-called 'Article 1(4) land' (as defined in Article 1(4) of the T & CP (General Permitted Development) Order 1995
2 Comprise 'Article 1(5) land' (as defined in Article 1(5) of the Town and Country Planning (General Permitted Development) Order 1995), which land includes land within:
 (a) A national park declared under the National Parks and Access to the Countryside Act 1949
 (b) An area of outstanding natural beauty (AONB) declared under the same Act of 1949
 (c) An area designated as a conservation area under section 69 of the Planning (Listed Buildings in Conservation Areas) Act 1990
 (d) An area specified for the purposes of the Wildlife and Countryside Act 1981, section 41(3) and
 (e) The Broads as defined in the Norfolk and Suffolk Broads Act 1988.
3 Comprise 'Article 1(6) land' (as defined in Article 1(6) of the Order) which land includes:
 (a) Land in a National Park
 (b) In the Norfolk and Suffolk Broads (as defined above) and
 (c) In land outside a national park but within an area (specified in Article 1(6)) as set out in schedule 1, Part 3, of the aforesaid 1995 Order.

If the development site is on 'Article 1(4) land' or on 'Article 1(5) land' or on 'Article 1(6) land' then the amount of 'permitted development' (see paragraph 2.06) allowed on the site is constricted by the said 1995 Order. Copies of the Town and Country Planning (General Permitted Development) Order 1995 are obtainable from The Stationery Office (see paragraph 2.02). Any such land falls within what are nowadays called 'sensitive areas' and the relaxation of development control brought about by the General Development (Amendment) Order 1981 was denied to them – and is still denied to them by the Town and Country Planning (General Permitted Development) Order 1995.

2.06 Fifth, the architect must ascertain whether the development site is in an Urban Development Area (see paragraph 6.02); in an Enterprise Zone (see paragraph 6.10); or in a Simplified Planning Zone (see paragraph 6.14). If the site is in any one of these areas or zones, then the normal constraints of development control (e.g. the need to obtain, from a local planning authority, planning permission for development (see paragraph 2.10)) are relaxed (see paragraphs 6.01, 6.11 and 6.14).

2.07 All these are preliminary matters about which the architect should become fully informed at the outset. In this chapter it will be assumed, for the moment, that the architect is dealing with a cleared site (or, at least, a site not containing anything in the nature of a special building), and that the development he wishes to carry out is development that can be dealt with under the general run of town planning control and does not attract any additional, i.e. special, control. (The special control over development which is going to occupy the site of an existing building of architectural or historic interest is dealt with later.) For the moment it is assumed that the development which the architect is considering is straightforward building development not subject to any special form of control, but only to general town planning control under the Town and Country Planning Act 1990.

Which authority?

2.08 This being the case, the next thing which the architect must consider is the local government authority to whom the application for planning permission is to be made. It must be made to the local planning authority.

2.09 The local government system in England and Wales was completely reorganised as from 1 April 1974 under the provision of the Local Government Act 1972. It was further reorganized as from 1 April 1986 by the Local Government Act 1985 which abolished the Greater London Council and the six metropolitan county councils (but not the metropolitan counties themselves) of Greater Manchester, Merseyside, South Yorkshire, Tyne and Wear, West Midlands, and West Yorkshire respectively. The most recent change was the introduction in the mid-1990s of a series of 'unitary' authorities which took the functions of both district and county council in their areas.

2.10 After all the foregoing reorganisations the system (outside Greater London) provided for local government to be discharged either at three separate tiers, namely:

1 by 34 non-metropolitan county councils popularly called 'shire' county councils;
2 by 264 district councils (36 metropolitan district councils if they happen to be in a metropolitan county and 238 'shire' district councils if they happen to be in a 'shire' county) some of which have borough status; and
3 by parish councils;
or by one of the 47 Unitary Authorities.

2.11 In Greater London local government is carried out by each of the 32 London borough councils plus the Corporation of the City of London. These authorities are the local planning authority for their borough but the Greater London Authority has the right to be consulted on major applications and has the right in certain circumstances to direct that planning permission be refused on such major applications in the event the application conflicts with the mayor's strategic policies.

2.12 The county councils and the district councils and the unitary councils are all local planning authorities and thus current nomenclature speaks of the 'county planning authority', the 'district planning authority' and the 'unitary planning authority'. A purchaser or a developer of land must, at the very start, ascertain which is the local planning authority for the purpose of whatever he wishes to do.

2.13 All applications for planning permission will go to the district planning authority or the unitary planning authority except (in the area of a shire district council) when the application relates to a 'County matter' (see TP, Schedule 1, paragraph 1) in which event the application is to be made to the shire county council (see paragraph 2.14).

2.14 The instances of 'county matters' when, in a shire county, the application for planning permission goes in the first place not to the district planning authority but to the county planning authority, are (TP, Schedule 1, paragraph 1):

1 Applications relating to mineral mining, working, and development (including the construction of cement works) (TP, Schedule 1, paragraph 1(1) (a) – (h) inclusive)

2 Applications relating to development straddling the boundary of a national park (TP, Schedule 1, paragraph 1(1) (i)) and
3 Applications in England relating to waste disposal matters (TP, Schedule 1, paragraph 1(1) (j)) and Town and Country Planning (Prescription of County Matters) Regulations 1980 (SI 1980 No. 2010) which does not apply to Greater London.

2.15 Parish councils are not local planning authorities but, even so, have the right (if they have claimed it) to be consulted by the district council about planning applications for development falling within the area of the parish council (TP, Schedule 1, paragraph 8).

2.16 In Greater London the 32 London boroughs (each for its own borough) with the Common Council (for the City of London) are all local planning authorities (1990 Act, section 1(2)).

3 The meaning of 'development'

3.01 The question as to whether that which the architect seeks to carry out is or is not development is a potentially difficult one. The meaning of 'development' is defined in the Town and Country Planning Act 1990, section 55, and it is a question of taking the relevant provisions of this Act, working carefully through them, and then applying the appropriate parts of these provisions to the matter in hand to ascertain if that which it is sought to do is, in law as well as in fact, development.

3.02 Putting the matter quite briefly, development consists of:

1 The carrying out of operations (that is to say, building, mining, engineering or other operations), or
2 The making of any material change in the use of land (including buildings on land).

It will be seen that the big cleavage in the definition is between the carrying out of operations, on the one hand, and the making of a material change of use, on the other.

What is an operation?

3.03 If the definition of what constitutes development is important, it may be said that the definition of what does not constitute development is equally important. Section 55 of the 1990 Act contains quite a list of operations and uses which do not amount to development. If that which the architect seeks to do falls within this particular list, then he need worry no more about the 1990 Act or any part of it. In particular, purely internal works or works which do not materially affect the external appearance of a building are not development. (Remembering of course that this exception most definitely does not apply to Listed Buildings!).

What is a change of use?

3.04 The list of specific exceptions in section 55 of the 1990 Act must be read with the Town and Country Planning (Use Classes) Order 1987, which contains 11 classes of use. If that which the architect seeks to do is, in fact, a material change of use, then if the existing use is any one of those specified in the 1987 Order, and if the change of use will still leave the use within the same use-class, the proposed change of use will not, in law, constitute development. In short, a use may switch around without planning permission, provided its total manoeuvring does not take it out of its use-class as set out in the 1987 Order.

3.05 However, since the case of *City of London Corporation v Secretary of State for the Environment and Watling Street Properties Ltd* (1971) 23 P and CR 169, it is clear that, on granting planning permission, a local planning authority may impose such conditions as would prevent any future change of use, notwithstanding that any such change would not constitute development of land by virtue of the provisions of the Use Classes Order 1987 and section 55(2)(f) of the 1990 Act. In effect, the local planning authority may remove from a developer the right to make a change of use even if that change of use would not normally (because of the Use Classes Order) need planning permission.

3.06 For the purpose of removing all doubt, section 55(3) of the 1990 Act specifically states that merely using a single dwelling house as two or more separate dwelling houses does involve making a material change of use and it is 'development' needing planning permission before it can take place. Thus the architect may carry out, at ground level or above, internal building operations (not affecting the exterior elevations) on a single house in order to adapt it for use as two houses. Such building operations will not need planning permission. However, when it comes to inaugurating the use of the former single house as two houses, this change of use will call for planning permission which may or may not be granted.

3.07 If the architect has any doubts as to whether that which he seeks to do is or is not 'development', he can apply (1990 Act, section 192) to the local planning authority for a certificate of lawfulness relating to any proposed use or development of land. Such a certificate relating to any existing use or development can be made under section 191 of the 1990 Act. In either case there is a right of appeal to the Secretary of State for Communities and Local Government (hereinafter referred to as 'the Secretary of State') against the decision of the authority (TP, section 195).

4 Control of development in general

4.01 Once the architect is satisfied that that which he seeks to do is indeed development, but is not an Enterprise Zone (see paragraphs 6.09 to 6.11 of this chapter) nor a Simplified Planning Zone (see paragraphs 6.12 to 6.15 of this chapter), he must next ascertain whether it falls within the privileged category of 'permitted development'. For this he will have to investigate the Town and Country Planning (General Permitted Development) Order 1995.

Permitted development

4.02 The 1995 Order carries no less than 84 separate classes of development which are categorized as permitted development, that is, they comprise development for which a grant of planning permission is automatically given by virtue of the General Permitted Development Order 1995 itself (TP, sections 58, 59 and 60). If development falls within any one of these 84 classes of permitted development there is no need to make any application to any local planning authority for planning permission for the development. If the development is not permitted development, then a formal application must be made (TP, sections 58 and 62).

4.03 It is to be stressed that the General Permitted Development Order of 1995 is a most important document, particularly for smaller scale development where the architect may find himself advising without the benefit of a specialist planning consultant or solicitor. The 111 classes of permitted development are spread across 33 Parts – Part 1 to Part 40 respectively – as set out in Schedule 2 to the Order as follows:

Permitted Development Order 1995

Part	Class	Permitted development
1	A	Development within the curtilage of a dwelling house. The enlargement, improvement or other alteration of a dwelling house
1	B	The enlargement of a dwelling house consisting of an addition or alteration to its roof
1	C	Any other addition to the roof of a dwelling house
1	D	The erection or construction of a porch outside any external door of a dwelling house
1	E	The provision within the curtilage of a dwelling house, of any building or enclosure, swimming or other pool required for a purpose incidental to the enjoyment of the dwelling house, or the maintenance, improvement or other alteration of such a building or enclosure
1	F	The provision within the curtilage of a dwelling house of a hard surface for any purpose incidental to the enjoyment of the dwelling house
1	G	The erection or provision within the curtilage of a dwelling house of a container for the storage of oil for domestic heating
1	H	The installation, alteration or replacement of a satellite antenna on a dwelling house or within the curtilage of a dwelling house
2	A to C	Minor operations
3	A to G	Changes of use
4	A to B	Temporary buildings and uses
5	A to B	Caravan sites
6	A to C	Agricultural buildings and operations
7	A	Forestry buildings and operations
8	A to D	Industrial and warehouse development
9	A	Repairs to unadopted streets and private ways
10	A	Repairs to services
11	A	Development under local or private Acts or Orders
12	A to B	Development by local authorities
13	A	Development by local highway authorities
14	A	Development by drainage bodies
15	A	Development by the National Rivers Authority
16	A	Development by or on behalf of sewerage undertakers
17	A to J	Development by statutory undertakers
18	A to I	Aviation development
19	A to C	Development ancillary to mining operations
20	A to E	Coal mining development by the Coal Authority Licensed Operators
21	A to B	Waste tipping at a mine
22	A to B	Mineral exploration
23	A to B	Removal of material from mineral-working deposits
24	A	Development by telecommunications code system operators
25	A to B	Other telecommunications development
26	A	Development by the Historic Buildings and Monuments Commission for England
27	A	Use by members of certain recreational organisations
28	A	Development at amusement parks
29	A	Driver information systems
30	A	Toll road facilities
31	A to B	Demolition of buildings
32	A	Schools, Colleges, Universities and Hospitals
33	A	Closed circuit television cameras
34	A – D	Development by the Crown
35	A – H	Aviation development by the Crown
36	A – D	Crown Railways, Dockyards and Lighthouses
37	A	Emergency Development by the Crown
38	A – C	Development for National Security Purposes
39	A	Temporary Protection of Poultry and Other Captive Birds
40	A – F	Installation of Domestic Microgeneration Equipment

Other than permitted development – the planning application

4.04 If the proposed development does not fall within any of the 84 classes of 'permitted development' above mentioned, then a formal application for planning permission will need to be made (TP, section 57). Sections 58 and 62 of the Town and Country Planning Act 1990 require an application for planning permission for development to be made in accordance with the Town and Country Planning (Applications) Regulations 1988 (SI 1988 No. 1812) and the Town and Country Planning (General Development Procedure) Order 1995 to each of which reference must be made. The requisite form on which the application is lodged can be obtained from the local planning authority.

4.05 When making an application for planning permission for development reference must further be made to the Town and Country Planning (Environmental Impact Assessment) Regulations 1999. These regulations provide in broad terms that if a development is likely to have significant environmental impacts (a term which includes such matters as the effect on the landscape, or on air quality or on ecology) the planning application cannot be decided until the local planning authority has received and assessed so-called 'Environmental Information'. This must include an Environmental Statement, prepared by the developer which sets out the nature of the development, the effect it is likely to have and the measures which are proposed to deal with such effects.

A failure to comply with these regulations (which are detailed and complex) will render any planning permission liable to be quashed by the High Court on an application for judicial review. Such a legal challenge is an obvious tactic for person opposed to a development. While the regulations are most likely to be 'in play' in a large development when the architect may well be part of a team advising the developer, even a smaller-scale development with particular effects may trigger the application of the regulations. Furthermore the architect will need to be aware of the effects of the Habitats Regulations SI 1994 No. 2716 (as amended) which impose particular controls on development which have a significant effect on the habitat of particular protected species.

4.06 Although the application for planning permission will formally be made to a local planning authority it will often be the case that a good deal of 'negotiation' relating to the application will take place between the applicant's architect and officers of the local planning authority.

4.07 Recent case law from the House of Lords (see *R v East Sussex County Council ex p. Reprotech (Pebsham) Ltd* [2002] UKLR 8) makes plain, however, that it is almost impossible for the discussions with a planning authority during such negotiations to be binding on the local planning authority when the formal decision comes to be made. Nevertheless, such discussions are a sensible, if not essential, part of the process and can save a good deal of time and money.

4.08 Once that process has been undertaken, a formal application for planning permission can be made, on a form provided by the local planning authority. It is now required that the application be accompanied by a 'Design and Access Statement'. This is a document in which the architect is likely to take the primary responsibility and which must set out, in some reasonable detail, the basis on which the architect has formed his views as to the type of design appropriate to the area and the nature of the design and access proposed.

4.09 Fees are payable to local planning authorities in respect of applications for planning permission, applications for approval of matters reserved in an outline planning permission, or applications for consent to display advertisements. The amount of the fees is set out in Schedule 1, Part II and Schedule 2 to the Town and Country Planning (Fees for Applications and Deemed Applications) Regulations 1989 (SI 1989 No. 193) as amended

several times. The reader will not be surprised to learn that each of the amendments has led to a progressive increase in the fees.

4.10 A reduced planning fee is payable, in certain circumstances, where an application is made for a scheme which has been slightly altered from a scheme for which permission was refused, when the alterations are made in order to overcome the problems which led to the refusal.

Deciding the planning application

4.11 As to what should be the attitude of a local planning authority when faced with an application for planning permission, attention should be paid to Planning Policy Statement 1 (PPS1) dated 2005, entitled 'Delivering Sustainable Development', and an accompanying statement of general principles. These are most important documents, both for the developer (and those advising him) as well as for the local planning authority.

4.12 PPS1 states the general principles underlying the entire system of control over land development and deals in particular with the important section 38(6) of the 2004 Act which is in the following terms: 'Where in making any determination under the Planning Acts, regard is to be had to the development plan, the determination shall be made in accordance with the plan unless material considerations indicate otherwise.'

4.13 Put simply, section 38(6) means that if the proposed development is in accordance with the development plan (policies in the relevant Development Plan Documents generally the Local Plan and Structure Plan read together or the Unitary Development Plan) a presumption in favour of granting planning permission would exist. If it was not in accordance with the development plan, then good reasons would need to be shown as to why the development should be permitted. Thus, if a developer sought to put houses on a site allocated in the development plan for housing, there would need to be significant reasons as to why permission should not be granted. If, on the other hand, the site for this proposed housing was allocated in the development plan for employment uses, then there would need to be good countervailing reasons as to why it should be permitted. These good reasons are described in the statutory language as 'material considerations'.

4.14 Material considerations might, for example, include the fact that a particular development, while contrary to the development plan, would generate considerable employment opportunities or would cause the removal of what was previously an 'eyesore'. Further, while the development plan for the purposes of section 54A is only the plan which has been formally adopted, if a later, revised, plan is at an advanced stage of the statutory consultation process, the provisions of that forthcoming development plan would be a material consideration. The provisions of PPGs and Department of Environment Circulars are also material.

4.15 If the application for planning permission is refused, or is granted subject to conditions unacceptable to the applicant for planning permission, there is a right of appeal to the Secretary of State within 6 months of the authority's decision (TP, sections 78 and 79). Before deciding the appeal the Secretary of State must, if either the applicant for planning permission or the local planning authority so requests, afford each of them an opportunity of being heard by a person appointed by the Secretary of State – an inspector. Such an opportunity to put the case will take the form of either written representations, an informal hearing or a public local inquiry. Neither party can demand a public local inquiry although the Secretary of State (it is entirely a matter for him) frequently decides to hold such an inquiry. Procedure at such an inquiry is dealt with in the Town and Country Planning (Inquiries Procedure) Rules 2000 (SI 2000 No 1624).

4.16 Under section 79 of and Schedule 6 to the 1990 Act, it is open to the Secretary of State to empower his inspector holding a local inquiry not only to hold the inquiry but to determine the appeal. The majority of smaller appeals are determined in this manner. The procedure at such appeals is found in the Town and Country Planning Appeals (Determination by Inspectors) (Inquiries Procedure) Rules 2000 (SI 2000 No. 1625).

In either case, the public inquiry is a formal, legalistic, process. It is most usual to use specialist advocates to present the case. Evidence is presented in the form of a 'proof of evidence' from each witness, with the rules requiring that proofs be exchanged, usually 4 weeks before the inquiry. Witnesses are subject to cross-examination and detailed submissions will be made to the Inspector in the last stages of the inquiry.

4.17 For cases of lesser complexity, the matter may be dealt with by an informal hearing. In such cases, each party prepares a written statement of its case and attaches any relevant documents. There is then a hearing before the inspector which takes the form of a round-table discussion. Such hearings do not have the formality of public inquiries and it is not unreasonable to suggest that the degree of scrutiny of a case is less than that which is achieved by a full public inquiry. However the savings in costs to be achieved if this route is pursued can be considerable and the choice of appeal method (the parties being allowed to express a preference but not to have the final decision as to method of appeal, which rests with the Secretary of State) can be a difficult and important one.

4.18 For the smallest cases, there is the written representations process. As the name suggests, the process involves the submission of written statements to the Inspector who will consider them and, having inspected the site, come to his decision. This is dealt with in the Town and Country Planning (Appeals) (Written Representations Procedure) Regulations 2000 (SI 2000 No. 1628).

4.19 In any planning appeal the Secretary of State may (if he can be persuaded) award costs to the appellant against the local planning authority (see DoE Circular 8/93) or vice versa. Costs can only be awarded where there has been 'unreasonable' behaviour by a party.

4.20 As an alternative to the consideration of planning applications by the local planning authority, the Secretary of State has power under TP, section 77 to 'call in' the application, with the result that the Secretary of State himself makes the decision. This power is generally only used for the most major developments which would have effects outside the area of the local planning authority where the development would take place. Where a decision is 'called in' a public inquiry is held, so the Secretary of State when deciding has the benefit of advice from his Inspector. The Heathrow Terminal 5 Inquiry gives an indication of the scale and length which such Inquiries can reach. However, it must be noted that despite the length and complexity of these inquiries, and the considerable resources which the parties necessarily spend on them, the Inspector's report is not binding upon the Secretary of State. It is not at all uncommon for the Secretary of State to disagree with the conclusions the Inspector reaches and to go against his recommendations.

Following the determination of the Secretary of State there is a further appeal under section 288 of the 1990 Act. However, such an appeal can only be made on point of law and the courts are hostile to challenges which simply seek to undermine the planning judgement made by the Secretary of State (or her Inspector). Those contemplating bringing such an appeal are well advised to take specialist legal advice as to the possibility of success as, once the High Court is reached, the normal rule is that 'costs follow the events' and an unsuccessful litigant will be likely to pay not only his own legal costs but those of the Secretary of State in defending her decision. Furthermore, a strictly applied deadline of 6 weeks from the date of the Secretary of State's decision letter ensures that those wishing to challenge a decision in the High Court must move quickly to begin the procedure.

Outline permission

4.21 If the architect knows exactly what he wants to do by way of building operations he will be able to put in a complete detailed application for planning permission. But it may be that he wants in the first place to 'test the temperature of the water', that is, to see what are his chances of getting planning permission at all for, say, a block of offices 20 storeys high. If he wishes to do this, then he can save time, trouble, and expense by putting in an application (TP, section 92) for outline planning permission so that the principle of having a block of offices 20 storeys high may be tested. If it is approved, then it will be necessary for the architect later on, within the period (if any) specified in the grant of outline planning permission and before he begins any development, to put in detailed plans and specifications for the approval of the local planning authority, these being what are called 'reserved matters', that is, matters reserved, at the stage when the local authority is granting the planning application in outline, for later and further consideration.

4.22 An outline application should make it clear that it is an application in outline and nothing more. Thus any plans and drawings which accompany it should be clearly marked as being by way of illustration only. At the stage of applying for outline permission, the architect should not fetter himself as to the styling of development. All he wants at the outline stage is to know whether or not he can, under any circumstances at all, have planning permission to do the sort of thing he wishes to do. If he gets that permission, then he must return, in due course, to the local planning authority with detailed plans and specifications so that the authority may consider these detailed matters.

4.23 If the outline application for planning permission is refused, there is a right of appeal against that refusal to the Secretary of State within 6 months. Similarly, if the outline application is granted but, later on, the local authority refuses to approve reserved matters, that is, refuses approval of detailed plans and specifications, then again there is an appeal against such refusal to the Secretary of State (see paragraph 4.16).

4.24 It will be seen that for an applicant who does not own land and who wonders how much he ought to pay for it, the making of an outline application to test the position *vis-à-vis* the local planning authority is a useful arrangement. It is not necessary for the applicant to go into details and incur the expense thereby involved. All he wants to know before he makes his bid for the land is whether, if he is able to buy the land, he will then be able to develop it in anything like the manner he has in mind. To get to know this, all that he need do is make an outline planning application.

4.25 Sadly, this effective and convenient procedure is increasingly constricted, particularly in larger schemes, by the operation of the Environmental Assessment Regulations considered at paragraph 4.05 above. The difficulty lies in the fact that if an application is too 'outline', the environmental impact may be impossible to properly assess. How, for example, can the impact on the landscape of a development be properly assessed when that development has not been designed? In the case of *R v Rochdale MBC ex p. Tew* [1999] 3 PLR 74, an outline application for a proposed mixed use residential and business park, where the submitted plan was 'illustrative only' and did not even define which areas would be business premises and which would be housing, was granted outline permission. The level of the detail on the plan was thought to be quite sufficient for an outline application. The planning permission was, however, quashed on an application for judicial review because the plan was insufficiently detailed to be a proper foundation for the Environmental Assessment.

4.26 The common solution to this problem is the 'Masterplan'; a plan is drawn up which, while leaving some flexibility in matters of detailed design, shows definitely the location of internal roads, the location and density of different types of development and the main design features. The developer can then offer to submit himself to a condition on his outline planning permission that the development will be in accordance with the Masterplan. The

Environmental impact of the scheme set out in the Masterplan can then be properly assessed and a lawful outline permission can be granted.

Notices re planning applications

4.27 Notice of the making of any application for planning permission to develop land must be given to the owner of the land and to any tenant of an agricultural holding any part of which is comprised in the land (TP, section 65; T and CP (General Development Procedure) Order 1995, Articles 6, 8 and Schedule 2, Parts 1 and 2). Any application for planning permission must be accompanied by a certificate indicating the giving of notice to owners and agricultural tenants. If the appropriate certificate is not included with the planning application, then the local planning authority 'shall not entertain' the application (TP, section 65 (5)).

General publicity

4.28 In addition to the foregoing personal or private publicity deriving from the notices referred to in the previous paragraph, there must be what can be called general publicity by newspaper advertisement for all planning applications (TP, section 65; T and CP (General Development Procedure) Order 1995, Article 8). Thus the owners and occupiers of neighbouring land will be informed, provided they keep a sharp eye open for newspaper planning advertisements, of any application to carry out development so that they may give their views and opinions to the local planning authority before a decision is arrived at. Such views and opinions must be considered by the local planning authority (TP, section 71).

Site notices

4.29 Moreover, a site notice, exhibited on the site where the development is to take place, may have to be given (T and CP (General Development Procedure) Order 1995, Article 8). Those instances in which a site notice may have to be posted are referred to in the 1990 Act, section 65 and Article 8 of the (General Development Procedure) Order 1995 and (so far as listed buildings and conservation areas are concerned) in the Planning (Listed Buildings and Conservation Areas) Act 1990, sections 67 and 73 and the Planning (Listed Buildings and Conservation Areas) Regulations 1990 (SI 1990 No. 1519).

Local authority procedure

4.30 On receipt of an application for planning permission, the local planning authority must consider the matter and, generally speaking, give a decision within eight weeks unless an extension of time is agreed (T & CP (General Development Procedure) Order 1995, Articles 20 and 21). In the event that the authority classifies the development as 'major development', a period of 13 weeks is applicable. The decision as to whether or not to so classify an application is one for the discretion of the local planning authority. The authority will probably need to consult the appropriate county council (Article 11) and may also have to consult any parish council within whose area the proposed development is going to take place (Article 13).

The authority may grant the application, may refuse it, or may grant it subject to conditions (TP, 1990 section 70). Whatever it does, the authority must state its reasons for having so decided (Development Procedure Order 1995, Article 22). Where the decision is to grant planning permission, only summary reasons need to be given. If, however, permission is refused, full reasons for refusal must be provided. This is to enable the unsuccessful applicants to challenge the decision of the local planning authority if the applicant decides to appeal to the Secretary of State, as he may do within a period of 6 months (TP, section 78; Development Procedure Order 1995, Articles 22 and 23) or to allow those who might be aggrieved by the grant of planning permission to consider whether further legal action (by way of an application for judicial review) should be pursued.

If no decision is given within the appropriate period, the applicant may appeal (again, within 6 months) to the Secretary of State as if he had been faced with a refusal (TP, section 78; Development Procedure Order 1995, Article 23). This is known as an appeal on the grounds of 'non-determination'. In such a case, which usually arises in circumstances where the local planning authority knows it intends to refuse the application but has not properly formulated its reasons for doing so, the local planning authority will subsequently formulate 'putative' reasons for refusal. The subsequent appeal will usually consist of an examination of those putative reasons for refusal.

Conservation areas

4.31 If the site of the development is within a conservation area designated under the Planning (Listed Buildings and Conservation Areas) Act 1990, sections 69 and 70, then the local planning authority, in considering the application, will have to pay attention to sections 71, 72, 74 and 75 of that Act and to any directions given to them by the Secretary of State as to the manner in which they should consider applications for development within areas of special architectural or historic interest. Development in a conservation area must 'preserve or enhance' the appearance of the Conservation Area and detailed design will invariably be expected from the architect to demonstrate that this condition is complied with.

Conditions

4.32 The local planning authority in granting planning permission may attach such conditions as it thinks fit (TP 1990, section 70); but this does not mean that it can attach any conditions it likes; not at all. The conditions must be fit, that is to say, fit, meet, and proper from a town planning point of view, because the legislation under which all this control functions is town planning legislation.

4.33 A local planning authority in attaching conditions must ensure that the conditions fairly and reasonably relate to the development. The authority is not at liberty to use its powers for an ulterior object, however desirable that object may seem to be in the public interest. If it mistakes or misuses its power, however bona fide, the court can interfere by the making of an injunction – per Lord Denning in *Pyx Granite Co. Ltd v Ministry of Housing and Local Government* [1958] 1 QB 554, CA.

4.34 Suppose one of the conditions attached to a grant is improper and thereby unlawful; does this invalidate the entire planning permission or can the unlawful condition be severed from the rest, leaving the planning permission intact but shorn of the improper condition? There have been several cases on this particularly difficult point, and the most authoritative guidance was offered in *Kent County Council v Kingsway Investments (Kent) Ltd* [1971] AC 72. It would appear from the decisions of the courts that the question of whether or not a planning permission is to be held wholly bad and of no effect, by reason of the invalidity of some condition attached to it, is a matter which should be decided on the basis of common sense and with particular inquiry as to whether the valid condition is fundamental or trivial.

4.35 The views of the Secretary of State on attaching conditions to a grant of planning permission are set out at length in the interesting and instructive DoE Circular 1/85 to which reference can be made with advantage (see the Bibliography at the end of the book).

4.36 The Annex to DoE Circular 1/85 (above mentioned) refers to this matter of the imposition of planning conditions the object of which is to secure some sort of a planning gain for the local planning authority (see paragraphs 20–21 and 63 of the Annex). The Annex sets out six tests to ascertain whether a planning condition is (as it should be) 'fair, reasonable and practical'. The six tests are (paragraph 11):

1 Necessity of the condition
2 Relevance of the condition to planning

3 Relevance of the condition to the development to be permitted
4 Enforceability of the condition
5 Precision of the condition and
6 Reasonableness of the condition in all other respects.

The Annex puts each of these six tests to close scrutiny which should certainly be read in full in the Annex itself. To take but one example (relating to test (1) about the necessity for a planning condition being imposed at all), the Annex, paragraph 12, declares:

'Test of need'

'12. In considering whether a particular condition is necessary, authorities should ask themselves whether planning permission would have to be refused if that condition were not to be imposed. If it would not, then the condition needs special and precise justification. The argument that a condition will do no harm is no justification for its imposition: as a matter of policy, a condition ought not to be imposed unless there is a definite need for it.'

4.37 One particularly important type of condition is the so-called *Grampian* condition. This provides that certain things may not happen (such as the commencement of the development of the occupation of the first dwelling in it) may not occur until certain other steps have been undertaken (for example the construction of a new road junction). Such conditions are entirely lawful but the Secretary of State in Circular 1/85 has made clear that such a condition should not be imposed if there is no reasonable prospect of it being complied with during the lifetime of the permission (now three years).

Section 106 agreements

4.38 TP, section 106 provides that a developer may enter into either a unilateral undertaking or an agreement with the local planning authority (both referred to as a 'planning obligation') so as to offer some planning benefit as part of a package involving the grant of a planning permission. Most unusually in English law, a section 106 undertaking or agreement binds both the current *and any future* owner of the land. A typical example of a section 106 obligation is that a developer might offer, as part of a package which led to grant of planning permission for a supermarket, to pay for the upgrading of the road junction giving access to the site of the new supermarket.

4.39 The Secretary of State has offered guidance as to the proper use of section 106 agreements (see Department of the Environment Circular 05/05). The central principle is that planning permission cannot be 'bought' by means of a section 106 obligation. Instead, the benefits to be conferred by means of the section 106 obligation must be related to the development being proposed. Usually, a section 106 obligation is used to provide benefits which overcome a problem caused by the development, which problem would, without mitigation, provide a reason to refuse planning permission.

Other controls

4.40 It should be remembered that obtaining planning permission for development may not necessarily be the end of the matter. Certain specialised forms of development, e.g. development relating to the display of advertisements (TP, 1990 sections 220–225 and the T and CP Control of Advertisement Regulations 1992 (SI 1992 No. 666)) or to the creation of caravan sites (Caravan Sites and the Control of Development Act 1960, Part I), are subject to additional control over and above the general run of town planning control.

4.41 Moreover, the architect must never forget that town planning control is a control which functions entirely without prejudice to the long-established control of building operations through the medium of building by-laws created under a code of law relating to public health and dating back to the Public Health Act 1875 and even before. Irrespective of town planning control, such detailed matters as the thickness of walls, the opening of exit doors in public places in an outward and not an inward direction, the provision of means of escape in case of fire – all these are matters which are entirely separate from the sort of control over development which is discussed in this chapter. (For such matters, see Chapter 9.)

Duration of permission

4.42 Nowadays, any developer obtaining planning permission must remember that, unless the permission itself specifies otherwise, permission will last for only 3 years. Permissions which last for 3 years are those which were secured by applications made after 24 August 2005. Permissions are secured by applications made before this date will have a time limit of 5 years. This is to prevent, among other things, an accumulation in the records of local planning authorities of quantities of planning permissions granted from time to time over a long period of years and never acted upon. This had been going on for a long time, but was brought to an end by provisions in the Town and Country Planning Act 1968, now sections 91 to 96 of the 1990 Act.

4.43 If that which is obtained is an outline planning permission granted between 1 April 1969 and 24 August 2005, the submission of detailed plans and specifications for the reserved matters necessary to bring the outline permission to full fruition must be done not later than 3 years from the grant, while the development itself must be begun within 5 years of the grant or within two years of the final approval of any reserved matter, which ever of these two periods happens to be the longer. The outline planning permission is granted up to 24 August 2005, the requirement is that development must be begun within 2 years of the final approval of any reserved matter.

Starting development

4.44 When is a project of development to be regarded as having been begun? This is an important question. The 1990 Act provides the complete answer in section 56 by providing that a project of development is begun on the earliest date on which a material operation in connection with the development is started. A 'material operation' will include, among other things, the digging of a trench which is to contain the foundations of a building. Thus, only a trivial amount of labour needs to be spent in order to ensure that development has been begun and that a town planning permission has been embarked upon.

Abandoning development

4.45 A ticklish question has always been: can a planning permission be lost through non-use? Can it be abandoned? In *Pioneer Aggregates (UK) Ltd v Secretary of State for the Environment* [1985] AC 132, a decision of the House of Lords, it was held that there was no legal principle that a planning permission could be abandoned by the act of a party entitled to the benefit of the permission.

Completion notices

4.46 Having begun his development, a developer cannot unduly delay the completion of the development. If he is dilatory it is open to the local planning authority to serve him with 'a completion notice' requiring the completion of his development within a certain period (TP, sections 94 and 96). A completion notice will declare that the relevant planning permission will cease to have effect on such date as may be specified in the notice but this date may not be earlier than 12 months from the date of the notice. A completion notice will not take effect unless and until it is confirmed by the Secretary of State, who may substitute a longer period for completion. Any person served with a completion notice may demand to be given an opportunity of being heard by an inspector appointed by the Secretary of State. Of course, a local planning authority, having served a completion notice, may for good and sufficient reason be prevailed upon to withdraw it; the law authorises such withdrawal.

Revoking or modifying planning permission

4.47 It should be remembered that a planning permission once given ensures a right to develop for the benefit of all persons for the time being interested in the land, subject to any limitation of time contained in the grant of planning permission itself or imported into the matter by the 1990 Act, as mentioned in paragraph 4.34. This, however, is subject to the right of a local planning authority to revoke or modify a planning permission by means of an order made by the authority and confirmed by the Secretary of State (TP, sections 97–100 and 102–104). Before confirming the order the Secretary of State must afford the owner and the occupier of the land affected by the order an opportunity of being heard by the Secretary of State's inspector. There are certain revoking or modifying orders which, being unopposed and unlikely to give rise to claims for compensation, can be made by the local planning authority without need for confirmation by the Secretary of State.

4.48 If the local planning authority wish to make a revocation or modifying order they must remember to do so before buildings authorised by the planning permission in question have been started. If they fail to do so, the revocation or modification may not affect so much of the building operations as have already been carried out. Compensation may become payable on the revocation or modification of a previously granted planning permission (TP, sections 115, 117 and 118).

5 Buildings of special architectural or historical interest – listed buildings

Listing

5.01 Lists of special buildings are compiled under section 1 of the 1990 Act by the Secretary of State or the Historic Buildings and Monuments Commission for England (established under the National Heritage Act 1983). Once a building is listed it is no longer possible for a local authority to make (as hitherto) a building preservation order for it; in lieu the 1990 Act provides a different kind of protection (see further, paragraphs 5.07 and 5.8).

5.02 The owner of such a special building need not be consulted before it is listed; he is merely told what has occurred. However, the statutory list of special buildings must be kept open by the Secretary of State for free public inspection. Similarly, a local authority must also keep open for free public inspection any portion of the list which relates to their area.

5.03 To damage a listed building is to commit a criminal offence punishable with a fine up to level 3 on the Standard Scale (currently £1000) and a daily penalty of up to one-tenth of that scale (1990 Act, section 59) (see further, paragraph 5.11).

5.04 A local authority may carry out works urgently necessary for the preservation of an unoccupied listed building after giving the owner seven days' notice (the 1990 Act, sections 54, 55, 60 and 76). A local authority may make a loan or a grant towards preserving buildings of special historic interest (whether listed or not) under section 59 of the 1990 Act.

5.05 In deciding whether to list a building or not, the Secretary of State may now take into account not only the building itself, but also its relationship to other buildings and the desirability of preserving features associated with the building but not actually forming part of the building. Thus, it is not solely the building which is to be considered but the entire setting of the building (the 1990 Act, section 1).

5.06 When speaking of a building it must be remembered that the law is so framed as to give protection to any object or structure fixed to a building or forming part of the land on which the building stands and comprised within the curtilage of the building

(1990 Act, section 1 and see *Watts v the Secretary of State for the Environment* [1991] JPL 718).

Listed building consent

5.07 There is no provision for the owner of a special building to appeal against the listing of his building. Once the building is listed, the whole of the protective provisions of Part I of the 1990 Act automatically swing into operation. The consequence of this is that while (as already explained in paragraph 4.04) it is necessary to get planning permission for any kind of development, if the site of the development happens to be occupied in whole or in part by a listed building, then the development simply cannot take place unless an additional form of consent, known as 'listed building consent', is first obtained (the 1990 Act, sections 16, 17 and 19).

5.08 Listed building consent must be obtained in order to demolish, alter, or extend a listed building (the 1990 Act, sections 7, 8 and 9). It may be granted (like a planning permission) with or without conditions. The application for listed building consent is made to the local planning authority, and the procedure is given in sections 10 to 16 of the 1990 Act and in the Planning (Listed Buildings and Conservation Areas) Regulations 1990 (SI 1990 No. 1519). A grant of listed building consent will last for only 3 years, following the general reduction in the duration of permissions brought about by the 2004 Act. If planning permission for development has been granted, or if an application for planning permission has been duly made, and if there is a building (unlisted) on the site, the developer may, since 13 November 1980, apply to the Secretary of State for a certificate that the Secretary will not list any such building for at least 5 years (the 1990 Act, section 6 and see *Amalgamated Investment and Property Co. Ltd v John Walker and Sons Ltd* [1976] 3 all ER 509 SA). This is a most useful provision when the architect feels that a building standing on the development site is potentially a 'listable' building.

5.09 In deciding whether or not to grant listed building consent with respect to a special building, the local planning authority must pay 'special regard' to the desirability of preserving the building or its setting and of preserving any features of special architectural or historic interest which the building possesses (the 1990 Act, sections 16 and 72). Notwithstanding this, it must be remembered that the grant of planning permission is one thing and the grant of listed building consent is another. Merely because planning permission is granted for development, it does not follow that listed building consent will be given to remove some obstructive listed building to allow such development to go forward. The planning permission, once granted, will (as explained in paragraph 4.42) last, generally speaking, for 5 years. During that time views and opinions about a listed building may change; views and opinions about architecture do tend to fluctuate. During the first years of the planning permission it may be impossible to get the requisite listed building consent to demolish some obstructive listed building. Later on, different opinions about preservation may prevail or pressure to carry out development may become stronger. Thus, different considerations in the view of the authors apply when a local planning authority is considering whether it should grant planning permission for development and when it is considering whether it should grant listed building consent for the demolition of a listed building in order to allow planned development to go forward.

5.10 If listed building consent is refused, there is a right of appeal to the Secretary of State after the style of the appeal against refusal of planning permission (the 1990 Act, sections 20 and 21 and the Planning (Listed Buildings and Conservation Areas) Regulations 1990 (SI 1990 No. 1519)).

5.11 It is an offence to demolish, alter, or extend a listed building so as to affect its character as a building of special architectural or historic interest, without first getting listed building consent (the 1990 Act, sections 7 to 9; see also *Britain's Heritage v Secretary of State and Others* (the *Peter Palumbo* case) [1991] 1WLR

153). It is also an offence to fail to comply with any conditions attached to such consent. The penalty for each of these offences is (on summary conviction) a fine of £20 000 or imprisonment for 6 months or both, and on conviction on indictment, a fine of unlimited amount or imprisonment for 2 years or both. It is, however, a defence to prove that any works carried out on a listed building were urgently necessary in the interests of safety or health, or for the preservation of the building and that notice in writing of the need for the works was given to the district planning authority as soon as was reasonably practicable (the 1990 Act, section 9).

5.12 If the owner is faced with a refusal of listed building consent and can demonstrate that in its present state his listed building has become incapable of reasonable beneficial use, then he may serve a listed building purchase notice on the local planning authority requiring the authority to purchase the building (the 1990 Act, sections 32 to 36 and the Planning (Listed Buildings and Conservation Areas) Regulations 1990 (SI 1990 No.1519)).

Listed building enforcement notices

5.13 If unauthorised works to a listed building are carried out, then the local planning authority, in addition to taking proceeding for the commission of a criminal offence, may serve a 'listed building enforcement notice' upon the owner, requiring full reinstatement of the listed building (the 1990 Act, section 38). There is a right of appeal against the notice to the Secretary of State (the 1990 Act, sections 39 to 41, 64 and 65 and T and CP (Enforcement Notices and Appeals) Regulations 2002 (SI 2002 No. 2682)). Penalties are provided in the case of non-compliance with the terms of the listed building enforcement notice. The guilty person is liable to a fine of £20 000 on summary conviction and of unlimited amount on conviction on indictment (the 1990 Act, section 43). These penalties are recoverable from the owner of the land who is in breach of the notice and this may include a subsequent owner. So the purchaser of a listed building must be careful to ascertain before he buys whether there are any listed building enforcement notices outstanding in respect of the building.

5.14 A local authority is authorised to acquire compulsorily any listed building which is not properly preserved (the 1990 Act, sections 49 to 50). This power may not be exercised until at least 2 months after the service on the owner of the building of a repairs notice specifying the work considered necessary for the proper preservation of the building. An owner faced with the possibility of having his listed building compulsorily acquired from him cannot appeal to the Secretary of State, but curiously enough, he can, within 28 days, appeal to the local magistrates' court to stay the proceedings under the compulsory purchase order. If the court is satisfied that reasonable steps have been taken for properly preserving the building then the court may order accordingly. Against the order of the magistrates there is a further appeal to the Crown Court.

5.15 If a listed building is compulsorily acquired, then the compensation to be paid to the owner will, in general, disregard the depressive effect of the fact that the building has been listed. On the other hand, if it is established that the building has been allowed deliberately to fall into disrepair for the purpose of justifying the redevelopment of the site, then the 1990 Act provides for the payment of what is called 'minimum compensation'. This means that the compensation will be assessed at a price which disregards any profit which might have accrued to the owner from the redevelopment of the site. Against any direction in a compulsory purchase order providing for the payment of this minimum compensation there is a right of appeal and, again, this is to the local magistrates' court, with a further appeal to the Crown Court (the 1990 Act, section 50).

Building preservation notices

5.16 Are there any means today of protecting a building which is not a listed building, but which appears to the local planning authority to be of special architectural or historic interest? The answer is yes. Although the district planning authority can no longer make a building preservation order, it can serve on the owner of the building a building preservation notice which gives temporary protection for 6 months, during which time the building is protected just as if it were listed (the 1990 Act, section 3). The object of this is to give time for consideration by the local planning authority and the Secretary of State, or indeed by anybody else, as to whether the building should in fact be listed. If, at the end of 6 months, the Secretary of State will not make any such listing, then the building preservation notice automatically ceases, and the local planning authority may not serve a further building preservation notice within the next 12 months. Moreover, compensation may become payable to the owner of the building for loss or damage caused by the service of the building preservation notice which failed to be followed by the listing of the building.

5.17 Certain buildings of undoubted architectural and historic interest do not come within the protection of listing at all. These are:

1 Ecclesiastical buildings in use for church purposes (but not the parsonage house, which is capable of being listed)
2 A building included in the Schedule of monuments compiled and maintained by the Secretary of State under ancient monuments legislation.

Buildings in conservation areas

5.18 In addition to the special protection given to listed buildings as described above, the 1990 Act, section 74 gives protection to all buildings if they happen to be in a conservation area designated under section 69 of the 1990 Act.

6 Urban Development Corporations; Simplified Planning Zones

Urban development areas and corporations

6.01 The Secretary of State is empowered to designate an area of land as an 'urban development area' and to establish an Urban Development Corporation to encourage re-development. An Urban Development Corporation is a limited life body tasked with a broad remit to secure the regeneration of their area. The rationale behind Urban Development Corporations was originally articulated on 14 November 1980 by the then Minister for Local Government and Environmental Services, Mr Tom King, MP, who declared 'We shall shortly be bringing forward Orders under powers in the [Local Government, Planning and Land] Act to set up Urban Development Corporations as single-minded agencies to spearhead the regeneration of the London and Merseyside docklands and to introduce the bold new experiment of enterprise zones, where business can be freed from such detailed planning controls'. In the 1980s Urban Development Corporations were established for Trafford (Manchester), The Black Country, Teesside, Tyne and Wear, Cardiff Bay, Leeds, Bristol, Sheffield and Wolverhampton.

6.02 These Urban Development Corporations were all wound upon in the mid-1990s. However, in February 2003 the government re-endorsed the idea of Urban Development Corporations to drive development. Since that time, Urban Development Corporations have been established in the Thurrock Thames Gateway, East London and West Northamptonshire.

6.03 The statutory objectives of the Urban Development Corporations include:

- bringing land and buildings into effective use;
- encouraging the development of existing and new industry and commerce;

- creating an attractive environment; and
- ensuring that housing and social facilities are available to encourage people to live and work in the area.

Urban Development Corporations are empowered to deal with matters of land assembly and disposal, planning, housing and industrial promotion.

6.04 An Urban Development Corporation is not an elected body. It is appointed by the Secretary of State and comprises a chairman and a deputy chairman, together with not fewer than five, nor more than eleven, other members as the Secretary of State may see fit to appoint. In making these appointments the Secretary of State must consult such local government authorities as appear to him to be concerned with the regeneration of the urban development area, and he must have regard to the desirability of appointing persons having special knowledge of the locality where the area is situated.

6.05 Urban Development Corporations have a term set for 7 to 10 years, with a review after 5 years, and are funded by the Department of Communities and Local Government. Urban Development Corporations may by order made by the Secretary of State (and subject to annulment by either House of Parliament) become the local planning authority for its own area thereby taking over all the planning control duties of any local government planning authority functioning within the urban development area. Historically, extensive planning powers were bestowed on Urban Development Corporations. However, the planning powers of the new Urban Development Corporations are intentionally not as broad as the first generation of Urban Development Corporations; second generation Urban Development Corporations do not have powers in relation to determining the overall level of development or the location and distribution of development. Rather, these Urban Development Corporations have been invested with development control powers for strategic planning applications in support of their objectives and purposes. Domestic and routine applications will be left to the local authority.

6.06 It will be observed that, each time an Urban Development Corporation is established, there is bound to be a consequential diminution of the planning control powers of any local government planning authority functioning within the urban development area over whose regeneration it is the responsibility of the Urban Development Corporation to preside. Accordingly, it will not be surprising to find that the establishment of any Urban Development Corporation, and the demarcation of the boundaries of any urban development area, are matters which will be eyed critically by any local government authority out of whose area the urban development area is to be carved. On this it may be mentioned that the London borough of Southwark petitioned the House of Lords to have the boundaries of the London Dockland Development Corporation redrawn. The petition failed.

6.07 The trend to delegate planning powers to Urban Development Corporations seems to be on the wane; in recent years Corporations in, for example, Sheffield and Leeds have had the transfer of planning powers to them revoked.

Simplified Planning Zones (SPZs)

6.08 By the enactment of the Housing and Planning Act 1986, Part II, Simplified Planning Zones were created. Simplified Planning Zones are now dealt with in the Town and Country Planning Act 1990, sections 82 to 87 and 94 and Schedule 1, paragraph 9 and Schedule 7, and in the Town and Country Planning (Simplified Planning Zones) Regulations 1992 (SI 1992 No. 2414). Simplified Planning Zones will be established by local planning authorities by means of a new system of Simplified Planning Zone Schemes (it is the word 'Scheme' which is the really important part of this expression) each of which will specify types of development permitted in a zone. A developer will be able to carry out such development without making an application for planning permission and paying the requisite fee.

7 Enforcement of planning control

7.01 The enforcement of planning control is dealt with in sections 171A to 196C of the Town and Country Planning Act 1990. Important new enforcement powers were added to the original 1990 Act by the Planning and Compensation Act 1991.

Time limits

7.02 If development consisting of building or other operations is carried out without planning permission and if the authorities allow 4 years to elapse without doing anything about the matter (i.e. without taking action by issuing an enforcement notice, as to which see paragraphs 7.06 to 7.08 below), then such development becomes validated automatically for town planning purposes and no enforcement action can be taken thereafter. It may be said at once that nothing in the 1990 Act interferes with this state of affairs so far as building development is concerned.

7.03 However, so far as development involving only a change of use of land is concerned, the equivalent time limit is 10 years from the date at which the change of use occurred. In order to take advantage of this time limit a developer must be able to demonstrate that the unlawful use has gone on continuously for over 10 years before the date of issue of any enforcement notice.

Certificates of lawful use

7.04 Until the Planning and Compensation Act 1991 development in respect of which the time limit for enforcement had expired was regarded as being 'established' but was not regarded as lawful. This bizarre situation led to great difficulty in assessing the lawfulness of development on land where there had previously been an 'established' but not 'lawful' use and was swept away by TP 1990, section 191 (as inserted into the 1990 Act by the 1991 Act). Henceforth, all development in respect of which the time limit for enforcement has expired is lawful.

7.05 A developer may now apply under TP, section 1991 for a 'certificate of lawful use or development'. This is obtained from the local planning authority, and there is a right of appeal to the Secretary of State if one is refused. The certificate makes it clear that the use in question, though originally instituted without planning permission, is now lawful and immune from enforcement action.

Enforcement Notices

7.06 Enforcement action is by way of Enforcement Notice served by the local planning authority upon the owner and occupier of the land to which it relates (see generally TP 1990, Part VII and T and CP (Enforcement) (Inquiries Procedure) Rules 2000 (SI 2000 No 2686)). Briefly, the notice must state exactly what the alleged breach of planning control is and the steps required to remedy the breach. There is an appeal to the Secretary of State against the notice, and the appeal must now state not only the grounds of the appeal but the facts on which it is based. The penalty for non-compliance with an Enforcement Notice is, on summary conviction, a fine of £20 000 or on conviction on indictment, a fine of unlimited amount (TP, section 179).

7.07 Architects should note that a local planning authority is never obliged to serve an Enforcement Notice whenever there has been a breach of planning control. The authority always has a discretion which it must be expected to exercise reasonably, as must any public authority holding discretionary powers. What the authority have to consider is whether, notwithstanding the breach of planning control, it is expedient to take enforcement action, and on this the authority must have regard not only to the provisions of the relevant development plan but also to 'any other material considerations'.

7.08 Should an Enforcement Notice be served, the land owner or occupier has the right to appeal on a number of grounds, including on the basis that planning permission should be granted for whatever is going on on the land. It may also be claimed that the development (whether it be operational development or a material change of use) has become, due to the expiry of the time limits referred to above, immune from enforcement action. Finally, it may be suggested that the steps which the notice requires to be taken are excessive or that the period allowed for compliance is too short. The appeal will be determined by the Secretary of State following an inquiry and there is a right of appeal to the High Court on point of law under section 289 of the 1990 Act. That right is not, however, unfettered: the landowner/occupier must show at a preliminary hearing that there is an arguable case that the Secretary of State has made an error of law before permission to bring the appeal will be granted.

Stop Notices

7.09 The legal pitfalls associated with an Enforcement Notice have, in the past, sometimes led a developer to 'spin out' the appeal procedure while getting on in the meantime with his building development. There is an appeal to the High Court on a point of law from the Secretary of State's decision in an enforcement notice appeal, and there are further appeals (on points of law) to the Court of Appeal and to the House of Lords. This is still the position, but the 1990 Act prevents a building developer from continuing his building operations while the protracted appeals procedure is working itself out. There is no longer the possibility of (quite lawfully) finishing the building before the appeal to, and in, the House of Lords is concluded. The Stop Notice procedure prevents this from happening (TP, section 187).

7.10 Once an Enforcement Notice has been served, the local authority may follow it with a Stop Notice which brings all building operations or changes of use to a halt under a penalty, for breach of the notice, of £20 000 on summary conviction or of a fine of unlimited amount on conviction on indictment (TP, section 187).

7.11 A Stop Notice may also be served following an enforcement notice which relates, not to building or other operations, but to any material change in the use of land (TP 1990, section 183). If a Stop Notice is so served, it must be served within 12 months of the change of use occurring. But a Stop Notice on a change of use can never be served when the change of use is change of use of a building into use as a dwelling house (TP, section 183(4)).

7.12 There is no appeal against a stop notice. Such a notice is dependent entirely on the enforcement notice with which it is associated. If, on appeal, the Enforcement Notice fails, so does the Stop Notice. In this instance, compensation is payable under the 1990 Act in certain (but not all) cases for loss or damage arising from the Stop Notice (TP, section 186). Thus a local authority will be inclined to think twice before serving a Stop Notice.

Temporary Stop Notices

7.13 Local authorities may also issue temporary Stop Notices where there is a breach of planning control and it is 'expedient' that the breach is stopped immediately (TP, section 171E). Temporary Stop Notices have effect from the time they are displayed on the land in question, however they are only effective for, at most, 28 days (TP, section 17IE). A temporary Stop Notice cannot prohibit the use of a building as a dwelling house or an activity which has been carried out for 4 years prior to the notice (TP, section 17IF). A local authority cannot issue a second or subsequent temporary Stop Notice; rather, he must take enforcement action (TP, section 17IF). Temporary Stop Notices are subject to similar enforcement and compensation provisions as Stop Notices (TP, sections 171G to H).

Injunctions

7.14 TP, section 187B enables local planning authorities to seek injunctions in respect of actual or apprehended breaches of planning control. The use of injunctions by local planning authorities is on the increase and developers tempted by the apparent slowness of the statutory enforcement proceedings to step outside the law should beware. It is for the local planning authority, not the court, to determine whether it is necessary or expedient to restrain an actual or apprehended breach of planning control. An injunction can be sought irrespective of whether the local planning authority has exercised any of its other enforcement powers and irrespective of whether there are, for example, pending applications for planning permission. The court's consideration will simply be limited to an assessment of whether the circumstances of the case are such that only an injunction will actually be effective to stop the breach of planning control taking place.

Guidance

7.15 Department of the Environment Circular 10/97 and its nine Annexes give much useful guidance on the subject of Enforcement Notices, Stop Notices and injunctions to enforce planning control over land development.

12

Planning law in Scotland

MICHAEL UPTON

1 Introduction

1.01 The principal statutes in respect of town and country planning in Scotland are the Town and Country Planning (Scotland) Act 1997 ('the 1997 Act') and the Planning etc. (Scotland) Act 2006. The section numbers given below are from the 1997 Act unless otherwise stated. The Planning (Listed Buildings and Conservation Areas) (Scotland) Act 1997 is also important. There are a considerable number of statutory instruments dealing with planning matters. These are regulations or Orders made by the Scottish Ministers under powers granted by provisions in the principal Acts or other Acts. These cover a wide variety of matters including procedure for making applications, for dealing with planning applications, fees for applications, permitted development (i.e. development granted planning permission by the terms of the order and not requiring an application for planning permission), development by planning authorities, appeals and inquiries procedure, tree-preservation orders, specification of classes or use not involving development and enforcement of planning control.

1.02 By virtue of the Scotland Act 1998, town and country planning is a matter on which the Scottish Parliament has power to legislate. Orders and regulations are made by the Scottish Ministers. References in pre-1998 legislation to Ministers of the Crown, such as the Secretary of State are now to be read so as to include Scottish Ministers. Reference will be made here to the Scottish Ministers rather than the Secretary of State as in the original measure.

1.03 The legislation governing planning in Scotland is presently undergoing significant changes, as the 2006 is brought into force and regulations made and to be made under it are the subject of consultation and implementation. This process will not be completed until 2010, whereafter the legal position on certain matters will require to be reviewed by the interested practitioner. Those matters are described in Section 9 below. In the interim, regard should be had to the fact that not all of the new laws have been published and brought into force, and that this is a continuing process.

1.04 Following consultation with the Scottish Parliament, a National Planning Framework is to be published by the Ministers (1997 Act Part 1A, as amended) and revised quinquennially, stating what developments they consider to be priorities and designating certain matters as national developments, with the Ministers' reasons for considering them to be necessary. The Framework is to inform the content of subordinate plans and planning measures (see, e.g., section 8).

1.05 Government or Scottish Executive policy on planning was formerly found in National Planning Policy Guidelines (NPPG), many of which have been replaced by Scottish Planning Policies (SPPs). SPPs and NPPGs are being consolidated into a single Scottish Planning Policy (SPP), Parts 1 and 2 of which were published in October 2008, and Part 3 of which is to be published in 2009. Apart from the 2008 SPP itself the most significant individual policies are SPP2, Economic Development; SPP3, Planning for Homes; SPP4, Planning for Minerals; SPP6, Renewable Energy; SPP7, Planning and Flooding; SPP8, Town Centres and Retailing; SPP10, Planning for Waste Management; SPP15, Planning for Rural Development; SPP17, Planning for Transport; and SPP21, Green Belts.

1.06 The Scottish Executive also publishes advice in circulars and planning advice notes (PANs). Important circulars include 12/1996 on Planning Agreements; 32/1996 on Local Plan Inquiries, 4/1997, 15/1998 and 20/1998, 1/2005, 1/2006 and 5/2007 on Notification of Applications; 4/1998 on the Use of Conditions in Planning Permissions; 17/1998 on Planning and Compulsory Purchase Order Inquires and Hearings; 4/1999 on Planning Enforcement; 10/1999 on Planning and Noise; 1/2000 on Planning Appeals Determined By Written Submissions; 1/2003, 2/2004 and 8/2007 on Environmental Impact Assessments; 1/2004 and 2/2007 on Fees; 4/200 on Houses in Multiple Occupation; 3/2007 on the 2006 Act; and 3/2008 on Strategic Development Plan Areas. Important Notes include PAN 37, Structure Planning; PAN 40, Development Control; PAN 41, Development Plan Departures; PAN 44, 67 and 72 on Housing; PAN 45, Renewable Energy; PAN 48, Planning Application Forms; PAN 54, Planning Enforcement; PAN 56, Planning for Noise; PAN 58, Environmental Impact Assessment; PAN 59, Improving Town Centres; PAN 74, Affordable Housing; PAN 75, Planning for Transport; PAN 79, Water and Drainage; and PAN 81, Community Engagement – Planning with People.

1.07 There are specific differences in the statutory provisions applicable to Scotland and England. However, those differences aside, Scots planning law and procedure is generally similar to and often identical with that of England. To that extent, Chapter 11 may be commended to the Scots reader. More detailed information and treatment in respect of Scottish planning law may be found in Rowan Robinson et al, *Scottish Planning Law & Procedure* (2001, W. Green & Son), and the more concise texts, McAllister & McMaster, *Scottish Planning Law* (2nd edn, 1999, Butterworths) and Collar, *Planning Law* (2nd edn, 1994, W. Green & Son). The principal statutes, statutory instruments and official guidance together with articles on selected planning topics are published in loose-leaf format in the *Scottish Planning Encyclopaedia* (4 volumes, regularly updated, W. Green & Son). Similar material although less extensive in terms of statutory coverage and excluding articles is found in the *Scottish Planning Sourcebook* (3 volumes, updated to 2002, Hillside Publishing, Dundee).

2 General

2.01 Whether a proposed development requires planning permission depends on whether it is 'development' in terms of the definition in section 26 (see Section 4 of this chapter). However, certain changes of use do not constitute development by virtue of the provisions of the Town and Country Planning (Use Classes) (Scotland) Order 1997 (S.I. No. 3061) as amended. Certain classes of development are automatically permitted by the General Permitted Development (Scotland) Order 1992 (S.I. No. 223) as amended. The Scottish Ministers or the planning authority may direct that development within any class in the Order, with the exception of certain mineral operations, should not be carried out without planning permission. There are certain other exceptions and qualifications (see Article 4 of the Order).

2.02 In relation to buildings which are listed as being of special architectural or historical interest, particular provisions of the Planning (Listed Buildings and Conservation Areas) (Scotland) Act 1997 (as amended by the 2006 Act) apply. In addition, under the same Act special provisions apply to proposals for development of buildings or land within a conservation area designated as such by the planning authority or the Ministers. For demolition of a building in such an area a consent known as conservation area consent is needed.

2.03 If the site of the proposed development is within what is known as a Simplified Planning Zone then the relevant Simplified Planning Zone scheme provides planning permission for development in accord with it without the need for application.

3 The planning authority

3.01 A system of unitary local authorities has been in place in Scotland since 1996. Planning permission ('permission') is sought from the local authority as the planning authority ('the authority').

3.02 It is possible for the Scottish Ministers to designate what is termed an 'Enterprise Zone' and the relevant Order may provide that the Enterprise Zone Authority shall be the planning authority for the zone for such purposes of the Planning Acts and in relation to such kinds of development as may be specified.

3.03 The Scottish Ministers retain power to give directions requiring applications to be referred to them for determination. This is the power to 'call in' an application (section 46).

3.04 While informal negotiation frequently takes place between the applicant's representatives and planning officers with a view to arriving at details for a proposal which the officers would find acceptable and recommend for approval to the planning committee, ordinarily comments or opinions expressed by an officer do not bind the authority, unless the officer was exercising delegated powers or, possibly, that the statement was about a matter on which the authority had represented that the officer had power to make a binding decision.

3.05 Fees payable in respect of various applications are found in the Town and Country Planning (Fees for Applications and Deemed Applications) (Scotland) Regulations 2004 (S.I. No. 219), as amended by the Town and Country Planning (Fees for Applications and Deemed Applications) (Scotland) (Amendment) Regulations 2007 (S.I. No. 253). The latest scale of fees was published in Circular 2/2007.

4 Development

4.01 Section 26(1) defines 'development' as the carrying out of building engineering mining or the operations in and over or under land or the making of any material change in the use of any building or land.

202

4.02 Building operations include demolition rebuilding and structural alteration and additions (section 26(4)). Section 26(2) sets out operations which do not involve development. These include works affecting only the interior of the building and which do not materially affect the exterior and the use of buildings or land within the curtilage of a dwelling house for a purpose incidental to the enjoyment of the dwelling house. The use as two or more separate dwelling houses of a building previously used as a single dwelling house involves a material change in the use of the building and each part of it (section 26(3)). The operation of a marine fish farm after a prescribed date (generally, 1 April 2010) is also 'development' (section 26AA; Town and Country Planning (Prescribed Date) (Scotland) Regulations 2007 (S.S.I. No. 123).

4.03 In relation to change of use, the Town and Country Planning (Use Classes) (Scotland) Order 1997 (S.I. No. 3061) specifies 11 classes of use under these headings: Class 1, Shops; Class 2, Financial, professional and other services; Class 3, Food and drink; Class 4, Business; Class 5, General industrial; Class 6, Storage or distribution; Class 7, Hotels and hostels; Class 8, Residential institutions; Class 9, Houses; Class 10, Non-residential institutions; Class 11, Assembly and leisure. A change of use which does not involve a change from one class to another is not development. For instance, a change from retailing goods in a building to using it as a travel agency is not development requiring permission for both activities come within Class 1, Shops. Incidental uses do not require permission merely because they fall within a different class. The statutory classification of uses is not exhaustive; an activity may fall outwith any of the eleven classes.

4.04 In cases of doubt it is possible to apply for a certificate of lawfulness of an existing or proposed use or development (sections 150 and 151) and there is provision for an appeal to the Scottish Ministers against a refusal or failure to give a decision.

5 Control of development

5.01 Permitted development is, development which is granted permission automatically by virtue of the Town and Country Planning (General Permitted Development (Scotland)) Order 1992 (S.I. No. 223) as amended (see section 31), which provides for 71 classes of development covered by 24 Parts (Schedule 1). The Parts indicate general descriptions of groups of classes. Part 1, for instance, covers development within the curtilage of a dwelling house; Part 2, minor operations; Part 3, changes of use; Part 6, agricultural buildings and operations; Part 8, industrial and warehouse operations, and so on. A full explanation of 'permitted development' is found in Article 3. The Order does not authorise development contrary to a condition imposed by a permission granted otherwise than by the Order. Directions restricting permitted development may be issued (Article 4). Where a proposed development does not fall within the classes of permitted development, an application for permission requires to be made (sections 32 and 33). Detailed procedure is set out in the Town and Country Planning (General Development Procedure) (Scotland) Order 1992 (S.I. No. 224) ('the GDPO').

5.02 In relation to *determination* of a planning application the authority must have regard to the provisions of the development plan and to any other material considerations (section 37(2)). Section 25 provides that a determination shall be made in accordance with the development plan unless material considerations indicate otherwise. There is accordingly a presumption that the development plan will govern the decision. Where a proposal is in accordance with the development plan, the principle of development should be 'taken as established' (SPP, para.28). Under the 1997 Act the development plan was the approved structure plan and adopted local plan. As the 2006 Act's amendments to Part 2 of the 1997 Act come into force, structure plans and local plans will be replaced. For four regions around Aberdeen, Dundee, Edinburgh and Glasgow respectively, planning authorities are grouped into strategic development plan authorities ('SDPAs') which are obliged to prepare such plans (1997 Act, Part 2, as amended); the Aberdeen City and Shire SDPA; the Dundee, Perth, Angus and North Fife SDPA ('TAYplan'), the Edinburgh and South-East Scotland SDPA and the Glasgow and Clyde Valley SDPA. It is expected that the four plans will all have been submitted to the Ministers by 2012. The Ministers may approve, modify or reject the plans (section 13). The development plan will comprise the strategic development plan, in those areas, and the local development plan outwith those areas. When the 2006 Act's enactment of a new Part 2 of the 1997 Act comes into force, it will provide that where, in making any determination under the planning statutes, regard is to be had to the development plan, unless material considerations indicate otherwise, the determination shall be made in accordance with the development plan, and, where the decision concerns a national development, in accordance with any relevant statement in the National Planning Framework (section 25, as amended).

5.03 Material considerations are not defined and extend to all matters relating to the use and development of the land which the law does not regard as irrelevant. What is 'material' depends on the nature and circumstance of the what is proposed. It will generally include government policy and guidance, such as found in SPPs, relevant public representations, consultation responses, the effect on the natural and man-made environment, including the design and the external appearance. A replacement local plan, particularly if it is at an advanced stage of preparation even though it has not yet been adopted is also relevant.

5.04 Where permission is sought in respect of subjects in a conservation area, special attention must be paid to the desirability of preserving or enhancing the area's character or appearance (section 64 of the Town and Country Planning (Listed Buildings and Conservation Areas) (Scotland) Act 1997).

5.05 Refusal of an application is subject to a right of *appeal* to the Scottish Ministers within six months of the decision (section 47(1)). Appeal may also be taken against what is termed a deemed refusal, namely where an application has not been determined within two months of receipt (section 47(2)). The Ministers' obligation to determine appeals is ordinarily delegated to officials known as reporters although they may recall for their own determination particular cases. Appeals by statutory undertakers are reserved for determination by the Ministers. Appeals may be dealt with by the holding of a public inquiry or, in the vast majority of

cases, by way of written submissions. Procedural rules govern appeals determined by public inquiry and written submissions: the Town and Country Planning Appeals (Determination by Appointed Person) (Inquiries Procedure) (Scotland) Rules 1997 (S.I. N0. 750), and the Town and Country Planning (Inquiries Procedure (Scotland) Rules 1997 (S.I. No. 796), both as amended.

5.06 An application for permission may contain full details and plans of the development. Alternatively, what is termed 'Outline planning permission' may be sought, where permission for the principle of development is requested, with reservation for subsequent approval by the authority of matters identified in the application as 'reserved matters' (section 59(1)). 'Reserved matters' are defined in the GDPO as those in respect of which details have not been given in the application and concern the siting, design or external appearance of the development, the means of access, or the landscaping of the site (Article 2). By imposing a condition, the authority may also reserve other matters for its subsequent approval (*Inverclyde District Council v Inverkip Building Co. Ltd* 1983 SLT 563). Where approval is sought purely for the principle of development, drawings and illustrations submitted should be marked as indicative only. The right or appeal applies both to refusal of outline permission and to subsequent refusal of a reserved matter.

5.07 The GDPO requires notification of applications to the owners of the land to be developed and neighbouring land, and agricultural tenants (paragraphs 8 and 9). Generally, neighbouring land is land which is conterminous with or within four metres of the boundary of the land to be developed, but only if any part of the land is within ninety metres of any part of the site of the proposed development itself. The applicant must submit with the application a certificate that he has given the requisite notice with details, or that he has been unable to do so. In cases where he has been unable to notify neighbours or in cases of 'bad neighbour' development (Schedule 7 to the Order) then the authority must publish a newspaper advertisement of the application (the cost of which is to be paid for by applicant) (Article 12).

5.08 An application must be made on a form obtainable from the authority. It must describe the development (Articles 3 and 4, GDPO). In the case of an outline application there must be a plan sufficient to identify the relevant land. In relation to any other application such other plans and drawings as may be necessary to describe the development must be submitted. It is essential that the description of the proposed development in the application accurately describes the development, failing which, even although the nature of the application may be clear from the plans, any grant of permission may be challenged by, e.g. an owner of neighbouring land to whom erroneous notification was given (*Cumming v Secretary of State for Scotland* 1993 SLT 228).

5.09 The GDPO also provides (in Article 15) who must be consulted before any grant of permission. This depends on the nature of the development and whether there are implications for the body concerned. The list includes the roads authority, the Scottish Ministers, the water and sewerage authority, Scottish Natural Heritage, the Scottish Environmental Protection Agency and the Health and Safety Executive. The Ministers may issue directions about consultations.

5.10 An application may be granted refused or granted subject to such conditions as the authority thinks fit (section 37(1)). In the case or refusal or conditional grant the reasons for the decision must be given (Article 22(1)(a) of the GDPO). As noted earlier, a refusal may be appealed as may a conditional grant if the applicant objects to a condition.

5.11 The power to impose *conditions* is found not only in section 37(1) referred to above but also in section 41(1) which allows the imposition of conditions regulating the development or use of any land under the applicant's control (whether or not it is part of the application site) or requiring that works be carried out there if expedient for the purposes of or in connection with the authorised development. Conditions may also provide for the removal of buildings or works authorised by the permission. Conditions may be imposed which depend on the actions of a third party. The applicant cannot lawfully be required to secure that such action is taken, but a condition can require that no development shall proceed until the specified action has been taken.

5.12 A planning condition must have a planning purpose, fairly and reasonably relate to the permitted development and not be so unreasonable that no planning authority could have imposed it. Guidance is given in the Circular 4/1998 on the Use of Planning Conditions, which states that a condition should only be imposed where it is necessary, relevant to planning, relevant to the proposed development, enforceable, precise and reasonable. A condition should not qualify the permission so as to make it substantially different in character from what was sought. A condition requiring any consideration for the grant of permission cannot be imposed without statutory authority.

5.13 In an appeal against a condition, it may be deleted or modified. A more onerous condition may be imposed by the reporter, or he may refuse permission, although the appeal is only against the imposition of the condition (section 47(1)). Where a reporter's decision is appealed to the Court of Session, the court has no power to sever an invalid condition from the rest of the permission; if a condition is held to be invalid, the entire permission falls (*BAA v Secretary of State for Scotland* 1979 SC 200).

5.14 Section 75 provides that an authority may enter into an *agreement* with any person interested in land in their area for the purpose of restricting or regulating the development or use of the land. Such an agreement may include necessary or expedient incidental and financial provisions; for instance, the applicant may agree to make payment in respect of the cost of providing, infrastructure required by the development. Guidance on the scope of section 75 agreements is found in the Circular 12/1996. In contrast to the position in England, there is no provision for an applicant to enter a unilateral undertaking.

5.15 While a grant of planning permission authorises the particular development to be carried out, it will often be necessary to apply separately for a building warrant from the local authority.

5.16 A permission has a duration of 5 years unless the grant specifies otherwise. That means that development must be begun not later than the expiration of 5 years or the appropriate period beginning with the date of the permission (section 58). Section 27 sets out detailed provisions for the purpose of determining when development is taken to have begun, which is generally on the earliest date on which any material operation comprised in the development is started. That includes any construction work in the course of erection of a building, any demolition work and, commonly, the digging of a trench for the foundations of the buildings: Any one of the specified operations suffices to begin the development (*City of Glasgow DC v Secretary of State for Scotland* 1993 SLT 268).

5.17 Where outline permission has been given, application for approval of reserved matters must be made within 3 years of the date of the outline permission (subject to certain qualifications) and the development itself must be begun (as explained above) within 5 years of the permission or within 2 years of the approval of the last reserved matter (section 59).

5.18 While there is no rule that a permission can be abandoned by the actings of a party entitled to its benefit, its implementation may be rendered physically impossible by another development.

5.19 Where permission is subject to a condition that development must begin before the expiry of a particular period, the development has been begun but not completed within that period, and the authority considers that it will not begin within a reasonable period if time, it may serve a completion notice stating that the permission will cease to have effect at the end of a stated period

of not less than 1 year (section 61). The authority may withdraw a notice. The notice must be confirmed by the Ministers before it takes effect. If it takes effect, then at the end of the period the permission becomes invalid (section 62).

5.20 Section 65 empowers an authority to revoke or modify a permission if it appears expedient to do so. The authority must have regard to the development plan and other material considerations. The power may be exercised before the operations have been completed, or the use has been changed, as the case may be. In relation to operations, the revocation does not affect what has already been carried out. Procedure is dealt with in sections 66 and 67. The authority may also make an order requiring discontinuance of use or alteration or removal of buildings or works (section 71). Compensation may be payable (sections 76 and 83).

6 Listed Buildings

6.01 The statutory provisions in respect of buildings of special architectural and historical interest are found in the Town and Country Planning (Listed Buildings and Conservation Area) (Scotland) Act 1997 (the 'Listed Buildings Act'). Lists of such buildings are compiled by the Scottish Ministers. Any object or structure fixed to a Listed Building and any object or structure within its curtilage which though not fixed to it forms part of the land and has done so since before 1 July 1948 is treated as part of the building. The desirability of preserving such objects or structures on the ground of architectural or historical interest may be taken into account in considering whether to list a building. Similarly, in deciding whether to list a building the Ministers may have regard not only to the building itself but also any respect in which its exterior contributes to the architectural or historic interest of any group of buildings of which it forms part. There is no right of appeal against listing, although the owner, tenant and occupier must be advised.

6.02 A Listed Building may not be demolished, altered or extended in any manner which would affect its character as a building of special architectural or historic interest without written consent ('Listed Building consent') (section 6). Conditions may be attached (section 7). A Listed Building may not be demolished within 3 months of notice of the proposal being given to the Royal Commission on the Ancient & Historical Monuments of Scotland, following the grant of Listed Building consent (section 7(2)). Listed Building consent is required in addition to any necessary planning permission. Applications for consent are made to the planning authority (section 9). Procedure is set out in sections 9 to 16 of the Listed Buildings Act and the Town and Country Planning (Listed Buildings and Buildings in Conservation Areas) (Scotland) Regulations 1987 (S.I. No. 1529), as amended. The Ministers may call an application in for determination by them. Listed Building consent is granted on condition that works permitted by it shall begin within a specified period. If none is specified the works must commence within 5 years of the grant of consent (section l6). Listed Building consent may be granted subject to conditions; e.g., requiring the preservation of particular features of the building, the remedying of damage caused by the works, and re-construction following execution of the works using, where practicable, original materials with interior alterations as specified (sections 14(1) and 15(1)). Specified details may also be reserved for subsequent approval (section 15(2)).

6.03 In reaching a decision on an application for consent the authority or the Ministers must have special regard to the desirability of preserving the building or its setting or any features of special architectural or historic interest which it possesses (section 14(2)). Accordingly, these are considerations which should be addressed when the development is formulated. These are, of course, different considerations from those which apply to an application for planning permission for an unlisted building, but in an application to develop a Listed Building or its setting, the same requirement applies; special regard is to be had to the desirability of preserving the building or its setting (section 59).

6.04 There is a right of appeal against a refusal of consent or a grant subject to conditions. Where consent is refused but the building and land cannot reasonably be used beneficially in their existing state, a Listed Building Purchase Notice may be served on the authority requiring them to purchase it (section 28). It is an offence to execute or cause to be executed any works for the demolition of a listed building or for its alteration or execution in a manner which would affect its character as a building of special architectural or historic interest unless there is Listed Building consent for those works (section 8). Failure to comply with a condition under such a consent is also an offence and punishable by fine or imprisonment.

Defences are provided in section 8(3) where works are urgently necessary in the interests of health and safety, or for preservation of the building although there are then specific criteria which require to be met.

6.05 The authority may serve a Listed Building Enforcement Notice where works have been or are being executed to a listed building in contravention of section 8 (see section 34). It is an offence not to comply with such a notice (section 39). Where after the period for compliance specified has elapsed, a required step has not been taken, the person who is 'for the time being owner of the land' is guilty of an offence. Defences are available, including not having been served with the notice or not being aware of its existence (section 39(4)). There is a right of appeal against a notice (section 35).

6.06 The planning authority or the Ministers may use a compulsory purchase order to acquire a listed building in need of repair, after service of a repairs notice (section 42). Where reasonable steps have been taken for properly preserving the building the sheriff may halt the compulsory purchase. Compensation provisions are found in sections 44 and 45.

6.07 There are provisions enabling the authority to protect a building which is not listed but which appears to them to be of special architectural or historic interest and to be in danger of demolition or alteration in such a way as to affect its character as a building of such interest. They may serve a Building Preservation Notice on the owner (section 3). It remains in force for 6 months. The effect is that the building is protected as if it were listed. During that period the Ministers can consider whether to list it. If at the end of the period they do not do so, then the notice ceases and no further notice can be served for 12 months.

7 Enterprise Zones, Simplified Planning Zones and Business Improvement Districts

7.01 The Ministers may by order under Schedule 32 to the Local Government Planning and Land Act 1980 designate an Enterprise Zone. This has the effect of granting permission for development of any class specified in the scheme (1997 Act, section 55). Planning permission so granted will be subject to the conditions, if any, specified in the scheme. The Enterprise Zone Authority may direct that any such permission shall not apply to a specified development or to specified classes of development either generally or within a specified area.

7.02 In a Simplified Planning Zone the adoption or approval of such a scheme has the effect of granting permission for development specified in the scheme or for development of any class so specified. Such a permission may be unconditional or subject to conditions specified in the scheme (section 49). The planning authority has the power to make or alter such schemes. The types of conditions which may be specified are set out in section 51. Such a scheme has effect for a period of 10 years. A planning authority shall not include in a scheme development which requires environmental assessment or is likely to affect a European site (regulation 20 of

the Town and Country Planning (Simplified Planning Zones) (Scotland) Regulations 1995 (S.I. No. 2043)). Certain specified descriptions of land may not be included in such a zone.

7.03 An authority may make an arrangement for an area to be a Business Improvement District for up to 5 years, so that projects specified in the arrangements may take place for the benefit of the district or of people who live or work there, by means of financial contributions authorised under Part 9 of the 2006 Act (2006 Act, sections 33 to 49). The creation of a district is to be approved by a ballot of eligible local tenants, owners and non-domestic rate-payers (2006 Act, sections 38 to 39).

8 Enforcement of planning control

8.01 The relevant provisions are found in Part VI of the 1997 Act (sections 123 to 158) and Part IV of the 2006 Act (sections 25 to 27). Where there has been a breach of planning control, i.e. development without planning permission or breach of a condition, then, if the development consists of building or other operations, no enforcement action may be taken after the end of 4 years from the substantial completion of the operations. In the case of a change of use the period is 10 years, beginning with the date of the breach. It is possible, as noted earlier, to apply for a certificate of lawfulness of an existing or proposed use or development (sections 150 and 151).

8.02 Before enforcement action is taken, where it appears to the authority that there may have been a breach of planning control, it may serve on the owner or occupier or any person using the land or carrying out operations on it a Planning Contravention Notice requiring the giving of information about operations on and use of the land (section 125). Non-compliance with such a notice is a criminal offence (section 126).

8.03 Where it appears to the authority that there has been a breach of planning control it may serve an Enforcement Notice on the owner or occupier of the land (section 126). The notice must specify the matters considered to be a breach of planning control and the step required to remedy the breach or any consequent injury to amenity. It should also specify a period for compliance (section 128). An appeal may be made against such a notice (sections 130 to 133).

8.04 Where the authority considers it expedient that any activity specified in an enforcement notice as one which it requires to cease should do so before the expiry of the period for compliance, it may upon serving the Enforcement Notice or afterwards serve a Stop Notice prohibiting the activity (section 140). Such a notice may not be served where the enforcement notice has taken effect. A stop notice cannot prohibit the use of any building as a dwelling house nor any activity which has been carried out for a period of more than 4 years ending with the service of the notice. There is no right of appeal against a Stop Notice. It stands or falls with the relative Enforcement Notice.

8.05 An authority may, where a condition attaching to a planning permission has not been complied with, serve a Breach of Condition Notice on any person carrying out the development or on any person having control of the land (section 145). The notice requires that the conditions specified be complied with. The notice should specify the steps to be taken or the activities which should cease to secure compliance. The period for compliance must be not less than 28 days.

8.06 Finally, an authority may seek to restrain or prevent a breach of planning control by applying to the court for an interdict (section 146).

8.07 Official guidance on enforcement matters is found in Circular 4/1999 on Planning Enforcement and in PAN 54 on the same topic.

9 The implementation of the 2006 Act

9.01 The Scottish Executive intends to bring into force further provisions of the 2006 Act, and regulations to be made under it, in 2009 and 2010. These will relate to, *inter alia*, strategic development plan and local development plan preparation procedures and contents; permitted development rights, householder' permitted development rights, 'micro-generation permitted development rights'; the handling of planning applications and pre-application consultations; appeals procedures, local review bodies, schemes of delegation and examination procedures; regulations on a hierarchy into which developments are to be discriminated in order to apply different procedures to different classes of applications, 'good-neighbour agreements'; enforcement powers, fixed penalty fines, site notices, notices anent initiation and completion, and temporary Stop Notices; Tree Preservation Orders; and fees. Foremost in importance among the new measures will be the Town and Country Planning (Development Management Procedure) (Scotland) Regulations 2008 (S.S.I. No. 432), which are to be brought into force in 2009.

13

Public procurement under European Union law

STEPHEN MAVROGHENIS

1 The European Union and its institutions

Introduction

1.01 The opening up of the Single European Market has had and continues to have a profound effect on every sector of the UK construction industry. Building material producers have easier access to more than 492 million people living in the European Union (EU) (a market which is a 60% larger than the USA, and triple the Japanese). Building products and practices are being standardised, building contractors have greater opportunities to tender for public sector projects throughout the EU and architects, surveyors and other professionals are able to practise with greater ease in the EU. In addition, the growing tendency of the EU to insist on higher standards of protection for the consumer and for the environment is placing greater burdens on those working in the building industry who are affected by these matters.

1.02 The Single European Market provides an opportunity for the UK construction industry but it also poses a threat. UK suppliers, contractors and professionals are being exposed to increased competition in the UK from their competitors in the rest of the EU and it is anticipated that this threat will be at its most formidable in respect of the largest and most profitable contracts where economies of scale justify the effort involved in competing away from the home market.

1.03 If the UK construction industry is to compete successfully in this new environment it must have an understanding of those EU measures which affect it and ensure that its interests are taken into account when legislation is being drafted and standards are being agreed. A basic knowledge of the EU institutions and how they work is essential if this is to be achieved.

2 The founding treaties

2.01 The 27 European countries which form the EU act and cooperate together within a complex legal framework. This comprises the European Communities (ECs), legal and institutional arrangements under which the EU member states accept the sovereignty of the Community institutions, notably in all aspects of economic activity including agriculture and transport, environmental issues and increasingly also in social matters, and arrangements for inter-governmental cooperation and development of policies in wider spheres, including foreign policy, defence and criminal justice. The ECs are founded on three treaties. The European Coal and Steel Community (ECSC) was set up by the treaty of Paris in 1951 and has now expired. The two other ECs were established by the Treaties of Rome signed on 25 March 1957. The first treaty

established the European Atomic Energy Community (Euratom), and the second, and by far the most important, is the founding treaty of the EC, formerly the European Economic Community.

2.02 The initial objectives of the EC were the establishment of a customs union with free movement of goods between member states, the dismantling of quotas and barriers to trade of all kinds and the free movement of people, services and capital. The original EC Treaty also provided for the adoption of common policies on agriculture, transport and competition. It looked forward to the harmonization of laws and technical standards to facilitate its fundamental objectives and to the creation of a social fund and an Investment Bank.

The Single European Act (SEA) and the amending treaties

2.03 By 1982 it was recognised that the progress towards the completion of a European Market without physical technical or fiscal barriers had been unacceptably slow and the European Council in that year pledged itself to the completion of this internal market as a high priority. In 1985 the Commission published its White Paper entitled 'Completing the Internal Market' in which it set out proposals for some 300 legislative measures which it considered would have to be adopted in order to achieve this aim. At the same time the member states agreed to amend parts of the Treaty of Rome so as to extend their scope and to facilitate the implementation of the legislative programme. The result was the Single European Act which came into force on 1 July 1987. The principal objective of the SEA was the removal by 31 December 1992 of all the remaining barriers within the EC to the free movement of goods, services, persons and capital. It introduced for the first time a system of qualified majority voting in the Council so that proposed legislation cannot so easily be blocked. The Act also provides for further technological development, the strengthening of economic and social ties and the improvement of the environment and working conditions throughout the Community.

The EC Treaty was further amended on 1 November 1993 when the Treaty on European Union (the Maastricht Treaty) entered into force. That Treaty marked a further step in the process of European integration and for the first time established that the new Community is both an economic and political entity in which its citizens are the possessors of enforceable Community rights. The Maastricht Treaty also laid the foundation for European Monetary Union and the adoption of a single European currency by the majority of the EU Member States (currently excluding the UK). The Treaty of Amsterdam, which entered into force in May 1999, made further amendments to the EC Treaty and the Treaty on EU, notably in relation to external policy, the fundamental rights of Community citizens and cooperation in the areas of justice and

home affairs. It also rationalised the texts of the Treaty of Rome and the Maastricht Treaty with the result that virtually every provision has been renumbered. Finally, the Treaty of Nice, which entered into force on 1 February 2003, made further amendments to the EC Treaty and the Treaty on EU, notably extending the use of qualified majority voting and making changes to the institutions to accommodate enlargement.

The reshaping of the EU institutions is still under way. The objective of this process is to adapt the legal and institutional framework which has evolved over the course of more than 50 years to the requirements of an enlarged and more wide reaching EU, in particular by creating stronger, partially elected, central institutions as well as increasing the role of the elected Parliament. After the failure of the Treaty establishing a Constitution for Europe, the Treaty of Lisbon, also known as the Reform Treaty, was signed on 13 December 2007. Ratification by member states was completed in November 2009.

The member states

2.04 The founding member states were Belgium, France, (West) Germany, Italy, Luxembourg and the Netherlands. Denmark, Ireland and the UK became members in 1973. Greece entered the Community in 1981 and Portugal and Spain in 1986. Sweden, Finland and Austria joined in January 1995. Ten new member states joined the EU on 1 May 2004. They are: Cyprus, the Czech Republic, Estonia, Hungary, Latvia, Lithuania, Malta, Poland, the Slovak Republic and Slovenia. They were followed by Bulgaria and Romania in January 2007. Current accession candidates are: Croatia, the Former Yugoslav Republic of Macedonia and Turkey.

The Community institutions and legislation

2.05 Each of the founding Treaties provided that the tasks entrusted to the ECSC, EC and Euratom should be carried out by four institutions: the Council, the Commission, the European Parliament and the Court of Justice. The Parliament and the Court of Justice were from the start common to all three communities and from 1967 this

was also true of the Council and the Commission. The Treaty on EC confirmed the roles of the institutions in all areas of EU activity. The Council is assisted by a Committee of Permanent Representatives (COREPER) made up of representatives of the various member states and for EC and Euratom matters. The Council and the Commission are assisted by an Economic and Social Committee and a Committee of the Regions acting in an advisory capacity.

The Commission

2.06 The Commission, whose headquarters are in Brussels, is currently composed of one representative from each member state and consists of 27 members prior to the Lisbon Treaty changes. Members of the Commission are appointed for 5 years. The Commission, as well as its President, are nominated by the member states after approval by the Parliament.

The Commission is supported by a staff of some 32,000 officials, a quarter of whom are involved in translation made necessary by the use of twenty-three official languages. The staff is mainly divided between a number of directorates-general, each with a separate share of responsibility. Commission decisions, however, are taken following the principle of collegiality. The Commission is the official guardian of the Treaties and ensures that the EC rules and principles they contain are respected. It is responsible for proposing to the Council measures likely to advance the development of EC policies. Once a measure has been adopted it is the Commission's task to ensure that it is implemented throughout the Community. It has wide investigative powers, in particular within the field of competition law. It may initiate proceedings on its own motion, or as a result of a complaint by a third party. It can impose fines on individuals or companies found to be in breach of EC Rules and these frequently run into millions of pounds. An appeal against a Commission decision lies to the Court of First Instance and to the European Court of Justice. In addition the Commission can take a member state before the European Court of Justice if it fails to respect its obligations.

The members of the Commission act only in the interest of the EC. During their term of office they must remain independent of the governments of the member states and of the Council. They are subject to the supervision of the European Parliament which is the only body that can force them to resign collectively.

The Council

2.07 The Council is made up of representatives of the governments of the member states. Each government normally sends one of its ministers. The Council meets in nine different formation, dealing with different matters: General Affairs and External Relations, Economic and Financial Affairs, Competitiveness, Cooperation in the fields of Justice and Home Affairs (JHA), Employment, Social Policy, Health and Consumer Affairs, Transport, Telecommunications and Energy, Agriculture and Fisheries, Environment and finally Education, Youth and Culture. National ministers are thus sent to Council meetings according to their field of competence. The Presidency of the Council is held for a term of six months by each member state in turn. The Council is, with the Parliament, the EC's principal legislative body and makes all the main policy decisions.

For some issues (such as taxation, and certain social matters) the Council must act unanimously in order to adopt new legislation. But the Council may now act in a wide range of matters by qualified or absolute majority. Under the qualified majority system the member states are allocated a block of votes according to their size, economic significance and the arrangements negotiated on their accession to the Treaties. The current rules require a minimum of 255 out of the total of 345 votes for a qualified majority. These votes must represent at least a majority of members states as well as 62% of the total population of the Union. The groundwork for the Council's response to Commission proposals is carried out by officials of the member states, coordinated within the COREPER.

EC legislation

2.08 Measures adopted by Community institutions have the force of law, and take precedence over the national laws. In some cases these measures have direct effect throughout the EC. In others the member states must first implement them by way of national legislation.

These measures may be:

1 Regulations, in which case they apply directly.
2 Directives which lay down compulsory objectives to be achieved by a certain date but leave to member states how they are to be implemented into national law. In certain defined circumstances when a member state has failed to implement a directive in due time, a citizen can rely directly on the directive as against the state.
3 Decisions, which are binding only on the member states, companies or individuals to whom they are addressed.

Community institutions also adopt resolutions or communications which are declarations of intent and do not have legal force.

Where a national measure implements a directive or even where that measure merely covers the same legislative field as a directive (e.g. because the national measure preceded the coming into force of the directive) the national measure must be construed as far as possible so as to give effect to the purpose of the underlying directive. In such cases therefore it is almost always necessary to look at both the directive and the relevant national measure before the true legal position can be established.

The European Court of Justice and the European Court of First Instance

2.09 The European Court of Justice ('ECJ'), which sits in Luxembourg, consists of 27 judges, one per member state, assisted by eight advocates-general. They are appointed for a renewable term of 6 years by mutual consent of the member states and are entirely independent. The ECJ has sole authority to interpret the Treaties. It can quash any measures adopted by the Community institutions or declare acts of national governments incompatible with EC law. An application for this purpose may be made by an EC institution, a member state, or an individual. The ECJ also gives judgment when requested to do so by a national court or a national competition authority on a question of EC law.

Judgments of the Court are binding on all national courts.

The Court of First Instance ('CFI') hears cases principally relating to acts of Community institutions or against a failure to act on the part of those institutions. These cases can be brought by individuals and member states. The CFI consists of 27 judges (one from each member state). The judges are appointed by agreement of the member state governments for a renewable term of 6 years. Unlike the ECJ, the CFI does not have permanent advocates-general. An appeal on points of law can be brought before the European Court of Justice against decisions of the CFI.

The European Parliament

2.10 The Parliament which principally meets in Brussels, Belgium but holds plenary sessions in Strasbourg, France currently consists of 785 members elected from the member states broadly in proportion to their size. Elections take place every 5 years. The Parliament has an important part to play in three areas:

1 It adopts and controls the EC budget.
2 It shares responsibility with the Council for the adoption of EC legislation.
3 It supervises activities of the EC institutions. It has the power to question and criticise the Commission's proposals and activities in debate. It can exert influence through its budgetary power and has the power to dismiss the Commission by a two-thirds majority.

2.11 As from June 2009, the maximum possible number of members of the Parliament is 736. The members of Parliament sit in Europe-wide political groupings rather than national blocks.

3 Public procurement

Introduction

Applicable EC framework

3.01 The opening up of procurement by government bodies and by utilities to EC-wide competition has been recognised by the member states as a key component in the creation of the internal European market. This huge sector of the economy has been estimated by the Commission to represent more than £1.2 billion. Although there are a number of directly effective Treaty provisions which must be taken into account in the award of public authority contracts these are insufficient to ensure that such contracts are opened up to Community-wide tendering. The EC has consequently adopted a number of specific measures whose purpose is to supplement the Treaty provisions by applying detailed rules to the award of contracts over a certain value by public bodies and utilities.

Equivalent objectives have been pursued at an international level under the auspices of the World Trade Organisation through the 1994 Agreement on Government Procurement (the 'GPA'). There are currently 12 signatories to the GPA including the USA and the EC. EC rules have been amended to take full account of these international obligations and to extend appropriate rights to contractors from GPA signatory countries.

The principal specific measures currently in force in the EC (as at December 2008) are:

● the 'Public Sector' Directive 2004/18/EC, which applies to the award of public works contracts, public supply contracts and public service contracts, incorporated into UK law by the Public Contracts Regulations 2006 SI 2006/5;
● the Utilities Directive 2004/17/EC, which applies procurement procedures to entities operating in the water, energy, transport

and postal services sectors, incorporated into UK law by the Utilities Contracts Regulations 2006 SI 2006/6;

- the 'Defence and Security' Directive 2009/81/EC, which applies to the award of services, supply, and works procurement contracts in the fields of defence and security;
- the Compliance Directive 89/665/EEC, which sets out the remedies that must be made available to those injured by a breach of the Public Sector Directive, incorporated into UK law by the Public Contracts Regulations 2006 SI 2006/5;
- the Remedies Directive 92/13/EEC, which introduced equivalent remedies for breach of the Utilities Directive, incorporated into UK law by the Utilities Contracts Regulations 2006 SI 2006/6;
- The Form Regulation 1564/2005/EC, which establishes standard forms for the publication of notices for public procurement procedures.

3.02 The Public Sector Directive (which in 2004 replaced the Public Services Directive 92/50/EC, the Public Suppliers Directive 93/36/EC and the Public Works Directive 93/37/EC) has not only simplified and modernised procurement legislation, but also seeks to increase flexibility and in some respects standardise the procedural rules applicable to all kinds of public sector contracts.

The Utilities Directive applies to the award of works, supplies and service contracts by public and private entities operating in defined sectors (the telecommunications sector has now been recognised as fully competitive and is excluded from its ambit).

Directive 2007/66/EC of the European Parliament and of the Council of 11 December 2007 amending the Remedies and Compliance Directives was formally adopted on 11 December 2007. It aims to increase the protection of tenderers against breaches of the law by contracting authorities when they award public contracts by introducing a mandatory standstill period of 10 days before a contract authority can conclude a public contract.

The Directive must be implemented by member states by 20 December 2009. It has not yet been implemented in the UK.

The Public Sector Directive and the Public Contracts Regulations 2006

3.03 The Public Sector Directive and therefore the Public Contracts Regulations have three principal aims in respect of the contracts to which they apply:

1 EC-wide advertising of contracts above a certain value threshold so that contractors in every member state have an equal opportunity of expressing their interest in tendering for them.
2 The prohibition of technical specifications in the contract documents which favour particular contractors.
3 The application of objective criteria in procedures leading to the award, and in the award itself.

In addition, the Regulations make available through the courts certain remedies (including damages) to contractors which suffer or risk suffering loss as a result of a breach of the Regulations or any related Community obligation.

As part of the objective of modernising the procurement rules there is an added objective of promoting and facilitating electronic purchasing systems and the use of electronic communications in procurement.

Contracts to which the Regulations apply

3.04 The Regulations apply whenever a contracting authority seeks offers in relation to a proposed public supply, works, and/ or services contract other than a public contract expressly covered by the Utilities Contracts Regulations, regardless of whether a contract is awarded or not. Special rules apply for certain types of services defined in the annexes (such as hotels and restaurants, legal service or personnel placement). Architectural services are not covered by these exceptions. Special rules for public works concessions have also been retained.

Meaning of 'contracting authority'

3.05 Under the Public Sector Directive, 'contracting authorities' means the State, regional or local authorities, bodies governed by public law, associations formed by one or several of such authorities or one or several of such bodies governed by public law.

Under the Public Contracts Regulations, contracting authorities include the state and state-controlled bodies, local authorities and certain bodies governed by public law. A list of 'contracting authorities' is set out in Regulation 3. Contracting authorities can also purchase work, goods or services from or through a central purchasing body.

Types of public contracts

3.06 Under the Public Sector Directive, a distinction is made between works, supply and service contracts although all three are defined as sub-categories of public contracts. The Public Contracts Regulations maintains a similar distinction and relevant annexes listing the activities covered by each type of contract ensure that each definition is mutually exclusive. In all cases therefore it will be important to establish at the outset whether a public contract is a 'works', 'supply' or 'services' contract.

Public works contract

3.07 A 'public works contract' means a contract, in writing, for consideration (whatever the nature of the consideration) for the carrying out of a work or works for a contracting authority or under which a contracting authority engages a person to procure by any means the carrying out for the contracting authority of a work corresponding to specified requirements.

The 'works' referred to are any of the activities listed in Schedule 2 to the Regulations. The schedule sets out a variety of building and civil engineering activities (e.g. 'construction of flats, office blocks, hospitals and other buildings both residential and non-residential') broken down into tasks (e.g. 'erection of and dismantling of scaffolding') carried out in the course of those activities. A 'work' is a larger concept and is defined as the outcome of any works which is sufficient of itself to fulfil an economic and technical function. Thus a 'work' would include the construction of an airport; it would also include the construction of its runways or of a terminal as both these are capable of fulfilling an economic and technical function but it would not include the associated drainage or electrical work as these are merely ancillary and cannot of themselves fulfil an economic and technical function. In some cases a contract may be for both works and services and/or for supplies of goods. There was no specific provision in the previous Directive dealing with this situation. However, in *Gestion Hotelera v Communidad Autonoma de Canarias* (Case 331/92, 1994 ECR) the Court of Justice held that where works are incidental to the main object of the award (in this case, refurbishment of a hotel and casino as an adjunct to a casino concession) the award should not be characterised as a public works contract. This principle is reflected in the Public Sector Directive.

In *R v Rhondda Cynon Taff Borough Council ex parte Kathro* (judgment of High Court Queen's Bench Division 6 July 2001) the judge indicated that the use of both a relative value and a principal purpose test might be legitimate. This case concerned a project being taken forward under the private finance initiative (PFI). PFI projects can raise particularly difficult classification issues since they frequently involve both major infrastructure works and provisions of services over a long period. It follows that, for example, a property management contract which incidentally includes a requirement from time to time to carry out some works is a services and not a works contract. A contract specifically for building maintenance or repair is on the other hand a works contract and the higher threshold will apply (see below).

Public supply contract

3.08 A 'public supply contract' means a contract, in writing, for consideration (whatever the nature of the consideration) for the purchase of goods by a contracting authority (whether or not the consideration is given in instalments and whether or not the purchase is conditional upon the occurrence of a particular event), or for the hire of goods by a contracting authority (both where the contracting authority becomes the owner of the goods after the end of the period of hire and where it does not).

A supply contract can imply the siting or installation of goods, but where under such a contract services are also to be provided, the contract shall only be a public supply contract where the value of the consideration attributable to the goods and any siting or installation of the goods is equal to or greater than the value attributable to the services.

Public services contract

3.09 A 'public services contract' means a contract, in writing, for consideration (whatever the nature of the consideration) under which a contracting authority engages a person to provide services but does not include a public works contract or a public supply contract.

Unlike works and supply contracts, the extent of the application of the Public Contracts Regulations to services contracts depends upon the type of services contract concerned. The Regulations adopt a two-tier approach. Certain services listed in Part A of Schedule 3 to the Regulations are subject to the Regulations in full, while others listed in Part B of Schedule 3 are subject at present only to the regulations relating to technical specifications in contract documents (regulation 9), contract award notice (regulation 31), certain reporting responsibilities (regulations 40(2) and 41), and publication of notices (regulation 42). Both Part A and Part B services are subject to Part 1 (General) and Part 9 (applications to the court) of the Regulations. Part A comprises sixteen categories of service of which 'architectural and related services' and 'property management services' are included (see paragraph 3.43 below). Other services fall into Part B.

Where services specified in both Parts A and B of Schedule 3 are to be provided under a single contract, then the contract shall be treated as a Part A services contract if the value of the consideration attributable to the services specified in Part A is greater than that attributable to those specified in Part B. Conversely, the contract shall be treated as a Part B services contract if the value of the consideration attributable to the services specified in Part B is equal to or greater than that attributable to those specified in Part A.

In order to establish which services fall into which Part it will usually be necessary to check the full CPC (Customs Procedure Code) reference rather than rely on the abbreviated lists set out in the Schedule. For example, 'legal services' appear under Category 21 of Part B, but where legal services take the form of 'research and experimental development services on law' they will fall into Category 8 of Part A (research and development services) as provided for in CPC Reference 85203.

The Regulations only apply when a contracting authority 'seeks offers in relation to a proposed public services contract'. They impose obligations only in relation to service providers that are nationals of and established in a member state, or in certain other relevant states including GPA signatory states but they do not require any preference to be given to offers from them. They do, however, prohibit treating non-EC service providers more favourably than EC service providers.

Furthermore, the Regulations only apply when a contracting authority seeks offers from service providers which are not part of the same legal entity as itself, but they do not require a contracting authority to seek outside offers unless it chooses to do so. If it does do so it must treat any in-house offer on the same basis as the outside offers for the purpose of evaluating the bids. If the outside bid is successful the fact that the contract award procedure has been conducted does not mean that a contract has to be awarded. The contracting authority can choose not to accept the outside offer, but it should be made clear from the outset that it reserves the right not to award the contract.

Borderline cases

3.10 A contract for both goods and services will be considered to be a public services contract if the value of the consideration attributable to those services exceeds that of the goods covered by the contract. A contract for services which also includes incidental works is also considered to be a public services contract.

Contracts excluded from the operation of the Regulations

Contracts related to certain utilities

3.11 The Public Contracts Regulations do not apply to the seeking of offers in relation to a proposed public works, services or supply contract by a contracting authority for the purpose of carrying out certain activities in the water, transport, postal, or energy sectors. Contracting authorities awarding contracts in the exercise of activities in the specified excluded sectors will be covered by the Utilities Contracts Regulations. The excluded sectors are initially the operation of networks and associated activities relating to provision of water, energy, inland transport and reserved postal services. Public contracts awarded by bodies providing telecommunications networks or services are now excluded from the rules altogether when they are for the principal purpose of a telecommunications activity.

Secret contracts, contracts involving state security and contracts carried out pursuant to international agreements

3.12 In addition the Regulations do not apply to a public sector contract which are classified by the Government as secret or where the carrying out of the contract must be accompanied by special security measures approved by law or when the protection of the basic interests of the security of the UK require it. Certain contracts carried out pursuant to international agreements are also exempt.

Contracts below certain value thresholds

3.13 Most importantly of all, the Regulations do not apply to the seeking of offers in relation to a proposed public contract where the estimated value of the contract (net of VAT) at the relevant time does not exceed specified thresholds. These thresholds are regularly revised. The 2008–09 thresholds are as follows:

- For public works contracts, subsidised public works contracts and public works concessions contracts, **5,150,000 euros (£3 497 313)**.
- For supply and services contracts when the concerned authority is a GPA authority (effectively central Government bodies), **133,000 euros (£90 319)**.
- For supply and services contracts when the concerned authority is a local authority, **206,000 euros (£139 893)**.

The 'relevant time' is the date on which the contract notice was sent to the *Official Journal of the European Union* (the '*Official Journal*'). This date generally corresponds to the time when the contracting authority forms the intention to seek offers in relation to the contract.

The 'estimated value' is the sum which the contracting authority expects to pay under the contract. In determining the estimated value contracting authorities must, where appropriate, take account of:

- any form of options;
- any renewal of the contract;
- any prize or payment awarded by the contracting authority to the economic operator;
- the premium payable and other forms of remuneration for insurance services;
- fees, commission, interest or other forms of remuneration payable for banking and other financial services; and
- fees, commission or other forms of remuneration payable for design services.

Where a contracting authority has a single requirement for goods or services or for the carrying out of a work or works and a number of contracts have been entered into, or are to be entered into, to fulfil that requirement, the estimated value is the aggregate of the sums which the contracting authority expects to pay under all the contracts. Exceptionally, where one or more of the contracts is for less than 80,000 euros (£54 327) for supply or services contracts or one million euros (£679 090) for public works contracts, such contracts need not be aggregated so long as in total they represent less than 20% of the total cost of the work. Thus for example where a contracting authority seeks offers in relation to site clearance at an estimated cost of one million euros for the purpose of constructing a hospital at an estimated cost of 20 million euros, the Regulations will apply both to the site clearance contract and the construction contract. If the cost of the site clearance was only 900 000 euros (and there were no other contracts which together with that one aggregated to four million Euros or more) the contracting authority would not be required to comply with the Regulations in respect of that contract.

The estimated value of a public services contract which does not indicate a total price is:

- the aggregate of the value of the consideration which the contracting authority expects to be payable under the contract if the term of the contract is fixed for 48 months or less; or
- the value of the consideration which the contracting authority expects to be payable in respect of each month of the period multiplied by 48 if the term of the contract is fixed for more than 48 months, or over an indefinite period.

Where a contracting authority intends to provide any goods to the person awarded a public works contract for the purpose of carrying out that contract, the value of these must be taken into account when calculating the estimated value of the contract.

In relation to public works concession contracts the 'estimated value' is the payment that the contracting authority would expect to make for the carrying out of the work (taking into account any goods supplied by them) if it did not propose to grant a concession.

A contracting authority must not enter into separate contracts with the intention of avoiding the application of the Regulations to those contracts.

Rules governing technical specifications

3.14 Detailed rules as to the technical specifications which are permitted in public contracts are set out in the Regulations. The purpose behind these rules is to avoid any discrimination against contractors that might be at a disadvantage if technical specifications were required which could only be met, or met more easily, by a national contractor.

Technical specifications for the purpose of the Regulations are those which apply to:

- the services to be provided under a public services contract and the materials and goods used in or for it;
- the goods to be purchased or hired under a public supply contract; or
- the work or works to be carried out under a public works contract and the materials and goods used in or for it.

Subject to certain exceptions, reference to technical specifications must be made in the following order of preference:

- British standards transposing European standards;
- European technical approvals;
- common technical specifications;
- international standards; and/or
- other technical reference systems established by the European standardisation bodies.

The Commission has issued policy guidelines on what is meant by this obligation to refer to European standards. In the absence of such standards, it is possible to make reference to British national technical specifications.

Where reference to specific European, international or national standards is included a tender cannot be rejected on the grounds that it does not comply with that standard if the tenderer proves that its offer satisfies in an equivalent manner the technical requirements defined by the specification in question. Similarly tenderers will be able to rely on appropriate national or European standards to show that they satisfy performance or functional requirements.

When a contracting authority lays down environmental requirements, it may make reference to international, European, or national standards, such as 'eco labels'.

Rules governing the procedures leading to the award of a public works contract

3.15 The principal requirement of the Regulations is that in seeking offers in relation to a public works contract from contractors or potential contractors that are nationals of and established in a member state, a contracting authority must use one of the following procedures:

- **The open procedure** whereby any interested person may submit a tender;
- **The restricted procedure** whereby only those persons selected by the contracting authority may submit tenders;
- **The negotiated procedure** whereby the contracting authority negotiates the terms of the contract with one or more persons selected by it.
- **Competitive dialogue procedure**, whereby the contracting authority discusses with selected tenderers in order to define a specification against which the tenderers will tender. This new procedure is available where a contracting authority considers that use of the open or restricted procedures will not allow the award of the contract because it is not objectively able to define the technical specifications capable of satisfying its needs or objectives with sufficient precision to conduct an open or restricted procedure and/or because it is not able to specify the legal and/or financial make-up of a project. The new procedure is intended for use particularly for complex projects (for example where Public/Private Partnerships are involved) and it is not possible at the outset to determine how the project should be structured or what solution will best meet the contracting authority's objective. It is likely that the Commission will expect contracting authorities to look to the competitive dialogue procedure to provide flexibility in circumstances in which they might previously have sought to use the negotiated procedure.

The Regulations lay down provisions for making the choice of procedure. The negotiated procedure may only be used in a limited number of circumstances. The competitive dialogue may be used only in case of a particularly complex contract that is when the contracting authority is not able to establish technical specification or the financial and legal make-up of a project.

Special rules apply in relation to a public housing scheme works contract and public works concessions.

Advertising the intention to seek offers by means of a prior information notice

3.16 The contracting authority must publicise its intention to seek offers in relation to a public contract as soon as possible after the beginning of the financial year in the case of public supply or public services contract or after the decision authorising the contract in the case of a public works contract. Contracting authorities can either send a notice to the Commission in the forms prescribed by the Form Regulation, or publish a prior information notice on an electronic 'buyer profile' database accessible via the Internet.

The notice must contain the following information:

- the public supply contract, the public services contract or the framework agreements, which the contracting authority expects to award or conclude during the period of 12 months beginning with the date of the notice; and

- the public works contracts, or the framework agreements, for the carrying out of works which the contracting authority expects to award or conclude.

The obligation to publish a prior information notice applies only to supply and services contracts which exceed 750,000 euros (£509 317) and to works contracts which exceed 5 150 000 euros (£3 497 313). In the context of an open or restricted procedure, the contracting authority can set shorter time limits for the receipt of tenders when it publishes a prior information notice.

The contracting authority must do this again at the start of the procedure leading to the award once this has been selected (the 'contract notice'), although the latter requirement is dispensed with in certain circumstances when the negotiated procedure is used. The form of the advertisement and the information which it must contain in relation to the proposed contract is specified in Annex II to the Form Regulation.

Selection of contract award procedure

3.17 Usually a contracting authority must either use the open procedure or the restricted procedure, at its choice. The negotiated procedure may only be used in the exceptional circumstances specified in the Regulations.

When a contracting authority has already published a prior information notice, the negotiated procedure may be used in the following circumstances:

1 Where the use of the open procedure, the restricted procedure or competitive dialogue was discontinued because of 'irregular' or 'unacceptable' tenders. However, the negotiated procedure may only then be used if the proposed terms of the contract are substantially unaltered from the proposed terms of the contract in relation to which offers were sought using the previous procedure. A tender will be 'unacceptable' if the operator has committed a fraud or offence listed in regulation 23 (see below), or fails to meet the requirements of economic and financial standing or of technical or professional ability.

The Regulations (and the Directive) do not make clear in what circumstances a contracting authority would be entitled to discontinue the open or restricted procedure in the circumstances defined above. The correct approach is probably that they would be entitled to do so where there remains insufficient valid tenders for there to be any real competition and after irregular or unacceptable tenders have been excluded. It will be noted below that absence of tenders is a separate ground for justifying use of the negotiated procedure.

2 When the public contract is entered purely for the purpose of research, experiment or development, but this exception will not apply if the contract is carried out to establish commercial viability or to recover research and development costs.

Once the experiment or trial has proved successful, this exception will cease to apply, and if the contracting authority then decides to enter into further contracts it must comply with the Regulations if the contract is one which falls within their provisions.

3 Exceptionally, in the case of a public works contract, the nature of the work or works to be carried out is such, or the risks attaching thereto are such, as not to permit overall pricing.

4 In the case of a public services contract, when the nature of the services to be provided, in particular in the case of services specified in category 6 of Part A of Schedule 3 and intellectual services, such as services involving the design of work or works, is such that specifications cannot be established with sufficient precision to permit the award of the contract using the open procedure or the restricted procedure.

When the contracting authority has not published a prior information notice, the negotiated procedure may be used in the following circumstances:

1 In the absence of tenders or of appropriate tenders in response to an invitation to tender by the contracting authority using the open or restricted procedure. However, again this exception may not be relied upon unless the proposed terms of the contract are substantially unaltered from the proposed terms of the contract in relation to which offers were sought using the previous procedure.

2 When for technical or artistic reasons, or for reasons connected with the protection of exclusive rights, the project may only be carried out by a particular person. It might be argued by a disappointed contractor which had been excluded for technical reasons that given enough time he could have acquired the expertise and/or machinery to qualify technically but the exception can probably be relied upon where for technical reasons only one contractor can carry out the works within the time required by the contracting authority for their completion so long as this is reasonable. However, the European Court in Case 57/94, *Commission v Italian Republic,* stressed that the derogation must be interpreted strictly and that a contracting authority relying on technical reasons must show that the technical reasons make it absolutely essential that the contract is awarded to a particular person.

3 When for reasons of extreme urgency brought about by events unforeseeable by and not attributable to the contracting authority, the time limits specified in the Regulations relating to the various contract award procedures cannot be met.

4 In the case of a public supply contract, when the goods to be purchased or hired under the contract are to be manufactured solely for the purpose of research, experiment, study or development but not when the goods are to be purchased or hired with the aim of ensuring profitability or to recover research and development costs.

5 In the case of a public supply contract, when the goods to be purchased or hired under the contract are required by the contracting authority as a partial replacement for, or in addition to, existing goods or an installation and when the recourse to another supplier other than the supplier would result in incompatibilities or create disproportionate technical difficulties.

6 For the purchase or hire of goods quoted and purchased on a commodity market.

7 In order to take advantage of particularly advantageous terms for the purchase of goods in a closing down sale or in a sale brought about because a supplier is subject to a procedure for bankruptcy.

8 In the case of a public services contract, when the rules of a design contest require the contract to be awarded to the successful contestant or to one of the successful contestants, provided that all successful contestants are invited to negotiate the contract.

9 When a contracting authority asks a provider which has entered into a public works contract with the contracting authority to carry out additional works which through unforeseen circumstances were not included in the project initially considered or in the original public works contract and either (a) such works cannot for technical or economic reasons be carried out separately from the works carried out under the original public works contract without great inconvenience to the contracting authority, or (b) such works can be carried out separately from the works carried out under the original public works contract but are strictly necessary to the later stages of the contract. However, this exception may not be relied upon where the aggregate value of the consideration to be given under contracts for the additional works exceeds 50% of the value of the consideration payable under the original contract.

The value of the consideration must be taken to include the estimated value of any goods which the contracting authority provided to the person awarded the contract for the purposes of carrying out the contract.

10 When a contracting authority wishes a provider which has entered into a public works contract with that contracting authority to carry out new works which are a repetition of works carried out under the original contract and which are in accordance with the project for the purpose of which the first contract was entered into. However, that exception may only be relied upon if the contract notice relating to the original contract

stated that a public works contract for new works which would be a repetition of the works carried out under the original contract may be awarded using the negotiated procedure and unless the procedure for the award of the new contract is commenced within 3 years of the original contract being entered into.

In accordance with principles of Community law each of the above exceptions must be interpreted strictly.

The open procedure

3.18 In this procedure, any interested economic operator may submit a tender. The contracting authority must publicise its intention to seek offers in relation to the public contract by sending to the *Official Journal* a notice in the form prescribed by Annex II to the Form Regulation (the 'contract notice') inviting tenders and containing specified information in relation to the contract.

There are strict minimum time limits laid down for the receipt of tenders. A contracting authority must allow at least 52 calendar days after the despatch of the contract notice for tenderers to submit their tenders. This time-limit can be reduced by 7 calendar days when the contract notice is transmitted electronically and by another 5 calendar days when all contractual documents are available online. Time-limits can be further reduced when a prior information notice has been issued.

The contracting authority may only exclude a tender from the evaluation of offers if the contractor may be treated as ineligible on grounds specified in regulation 23 (see below) or if a contractor fails to satisfy minimum standards of economic and financial standing and technical capacity required of contractors by the contracting authority. These minimum levels must be specified in the contract notice and must be related to and proportionate to the subject matter of the contract.

The restricted procedure

Selecting those invited to tender

3.19 When using the restricted procedure the contracting authority must, as with the open procedure, publish a contract notice as soon as possible after forming the intention to seek offers. The contract notice must be in the form prescribed by Annex II to the Form Regulation. There are strict minimum time limits for receipt of requests to be selected to tender.

This procedure also includes minimum time limits for the receipt of tenders. A contracting authority must allow at least 37 calendar days after the despatch of the contract notice for tenderers to submit their offers. This time-limit can be reduced by 7 calendar days when the contract notice is transmitted electronically. Shorter time-limits can also be imposed in case of urgency.

The contracting authority may exclude a contractor from the selection of those invited to tender only if the contractor may be treated as ineligible on a ground permitted by the Regulations or if the contractor fails to satisfy the minimum standards of economic and financial standing and technical capacity required by the contracting authority. These minimum levels must be specified in the contract notice and must be related to and proportionate to the subject-matter of the contract.

Having excluded any contractors as above, the contracting authority must select the contractors they intend to invite to tender solely on the basis of the contractor's past record, his economic standing and his technical capacity, following the criteria laid down by regulation 25. In making the selection and in issuing invitations the contracting authority must not discriminate between contractors on the grounds of their nationality or the member state in which they are established. The contracting authority may, however, limit the number of economic operators which it intends to invite to tender. The number invited must be not fewer than five. The number must be specified in the contract notice and in any event the number must be sufficient to ensure genuine competition. Contracting authorities are also required to indicate in the contract notice the objective and non-discriminatory criteria they intend to use to select those to be invited to tender.

The invitation to tender

3.20 The invitation to tender must be sent in writing simultaneously to each contractor selected to tender, and must be accompanied by the contract documents or contain the address from which they may be requested. The invitation to tender must include all necessary information on delays, content of tenders, and criteria for the award. The Regulations lay down minimum time limit of 40 calendar days for the receipt of tenders. Shorter periods are allowed in case of urgency, when a prior information notice has been issued or when contract documents are available electronically.

The negotiated procedure

Selecting those invited to tender

3.21 where the negotiated procedure is used without the publication a prior information notice (see above), contracting authorities are not required to follow any procedural rules other than those relating to the exclusion of contractors on the ground of ineligibility and relating to their selection to negotiate. However, where a contracting authority uses the negotiated procedure after the publication of a prior information notice then the following rules apply in addition:

1 The contracting authority must publicise its intention to seek offers in relation to the public works contract by publishing a contract notice in the *Official Journal* in the form prescribed and containing all necessary information.
2 The date fixed as the last date for the receipt of requests to be selected to negotiate must be specified in the contract notice. A contracting authority must allow at least 37 calendar days after the despatch of the contract notice for contractors to submit their requests to be selected to negotiate. This time-limit can be reduced by 7 calendar days when the contract notice is transmitted electronically. Shorter time-limits can also be imposed in case of urgency.
3 Where there is a sufficient number of providers which are suitable to be selected to negotiate the contract, the number must be not less than three. The selection of contractors must be made following objective and non-discriminatory criteria.

The contracting authority may provide for the procedure to take place in stages, with the number of tenders to be negotiated being reduced by application of the award criteria along the way. This reflects standard practice in the UK. In these circumstances, the contracting authority must ensure that the number of tenderers invited to negotiate the contract at the final stage are sufficient to ensure genuine competition to the extent that there are a sufficient number of tenderers to do so.

The invitation to tender

3.22 The invitation to tender must be sent in writing simultaneously to each contractor selected to tender, and must be accompanied by the contract documents or contain the address from which they may be requested. The invitation to tender must include all necessary information on delays, content offenders and criteria for the award.

The competitive dialogue procedure

3.23 Under the competitive dialogue procedure, as under the restricted procedure, the contracting authority must publish a contract notice in the same prescribed form, setting out the contracting authority's needs and requirements (which are to be defined either in the notice or in a descriptive document). The notice will identify the objective and non-discriminatory criteria to be applied to select candidates. A minimum of three candidates must be invited to participate. The number of candidates must be sufficient to ensure genuine competition. The date fixed as the last date for the receipt of requests to be selected to negotiate must be specified in the contract notice. A contracting authority must allow at least 37 calendar days after the despatch of the contract notice for contractors to submit their requests to participate in the competitive dialogue procedure. This time-limit can be reduced by 7 calendar days when the contract notice is transmitted electronically.

The dialogue phase of the procedure will be opened with selected candidates on the basis of the requirements set out in the contract notice or descriptive document. The aim of the dialogue will be to identify and define the means best suited in order to satisfy the contracting authority's needs. All aspects of the contract can be discussed with chosen candidates during the dialogue phase. The contracting authority must ensure equality of treatment among tenderers, particularly in the way in which information is provided. To this end, the contracting authority must send invitations in writing simultaneously to each candidate selected to participate in the dialogue. An invitation must include all contractual documents and information, including the relative weighting of criteria for the award of the contract. The contracting authority may provide for the procedure to take place in stages, with the number of tenders or solutions being reduced by application of the award criteria along the way. This can only occur however if it has been identified as a possibility in the contract notice or descriptive document.

When a solution which is capable of meeting the authority's need has been identified the authority will declare that the dialogue is concluded and invite tenderers to submit final tenders on the basis of the solution or solutions which have emerged from the dialogue.

Selection of contractors

Criteria for rejection of contractors

3.24 Detailed rules are laid down in the Regulations as to the only criteria on which applicants to tender and tenderers may be excluded from the tendering process. These relate to the contractor's financial solvency and business and fiscal probity. In addition, a contractor may be excluded as ineligible where he is not registered on the professional or trade register of the member state in which he is established. Special provisions apply in relation to contractors established in member states where such registers do not exist in order to enable them to satisfy this condition. Furthermore, contracting authorities have an obligation to disqualify tenderers convicted of:

- conspiracy relating to the participation in a criminal organisation;
- corruption;
- bribery;
- fraud;
- money laundering.

Tenderers must also be excluded when they have been convicted of equivalent offences in other EU member states.

The contracting authority may require a contractor to provide such information as it considers it needs to satisfy itself that none of the exclusionary criteria apply, but it must accept as conclusive that the contractor does not fall within any of the grounds relating to financial solvency or fiscal probity, an extract from a judicial record or a certificate issued by a competent authority (whichever is appropriate) to this effect. In member states such as the UK where such documentary evidence is not available, provision is made for the evidence to be provided by binding declaration. Special rules apply to contractors registered on official lists of approved contractors, services providers or suppliers in any EU member state.

Where a tender is submitted by a consortium of undertakings, the contracting authority can not treat it as ineligible on the grounds that the consortium has not formed a legal entity for the purposes of tendering for, or negotiating, the contract. However, where a contracting authority awards the contract to a consortium, it may require it to form a legal entity for the performance of the contract.

If a service provider is required to adopt a given legal form in accordance to the provisions of a law in the UK, a service provider established in another EU member state can not be treated as ineligible if under the law of that member state it is authorised to provide such services.

Information as to economic and financial standing

3.25 Subject to a similar provision relating to the situation where the contractor is registered on an official list of recognised contractors, under the Regulations the contracting authority, in assessing whether a contractor meets any minimum standards of economic and financial standing, may take into account the following information: bank statements, existence of a relevant professional risk indemnity insurance, published accounts, and turnover of the three previous financial years. The contracting authority may require a contractor to provide such information as it considers it needs to make the assessment or selection.

Where the information specified is not appropriate in a particular case, a contracting authority may require a contractor to provide other information to demonstrate the contractor's economic and financial standing. Where a contractor is unable for a valid reason to provide the information which the contracting authority has required, the contracting authority must accept such other information provided by the contractor as the contracting authority considers appropriate. The information required must be specified in the contract notice.

An operator may also rely on the capacities of the corporate group to which it belongs in establishing its economic and financial standing.

Information as to technical capacity

3.26 Subject to a similar provision relating to the situation where the contractor is registered on an official list of recognised contractors, the contracting authority, in assessing whether a contractor meets any minimum standards of technical capacity, may under the Regulations take into account the following information: technical ability, past record, availability of technical services or technicians, measures to ensure quality, research facilities, professional qualifications of the contractor or its employees, environment management measures, number of staff, available equipment, potential sub-contractors, certification of quality control agencies, and a certificate attesting conformity to quality assurance standards.

The contracting authority may require a contractor to provide such of that information as it considers it needs to make the assessment or selection. The information required must be specified in the contract notice.

Limits on the information which may be required or taken into account

3.27 The contracting authority may also require a tenderer to provide supplementary information. However, this information must relate to the matters specified in the Regulations. It should be noted that the mandatory nature of the Regulations as regards information which may be required and/or taken into account by a contracting authority when assessing a contractor's economic and financial standing and technical capacity is not reflected in the Public Sector Directive. Based on the preceding Works Directive, the European Court has held in respect of the provision concerning economic and financial standing that 'it can be seen from the very wording of that Article and in particular the second paragraph thereof that the list of references mentioned therein is not exhaustive' and that consequently a contracting authority is entitled to require a contractor to furnish a statement of the total value of the works it has in hand as a reference within the meaning of that Article. This rationale applies equally to the current Public Sector Directive. The list of references which may be required to establish technical capacity on the other hand is exhaustive and a contracting authority may not *require* a contractor to furnish further information on that topic. However there would appear to be nothing to prevent a contracting authority from *taking into account* other information relevant to technical capacity which the contracting authority has acquired by other means. That appears to have been the view taken by the English High Court in *GBM v Greenwich BC* [1993] 92 LG R21 where in relation to a public works contract, it was held that a contracting authority was entitled to take into account when assessing a contractor's technical capacity, any independent knowledge it might have regarding a contractor's compliance with health and safety legislation when carrying out other contracts. Indeed it would seem remarkable if a contracting authority were to be prohibited from taking into account for example, the technical performance of a contractor experienced by it during other dealings with that contractor. A contracting authority may require a contractor to provide information supplementing the information supplied in accordance with the Regulations or to clarify that information, provided that the information required is in respect of matters permitted by the Regulations.

A contracting authority must comply with such requirements as to the confidentiality of information provided to it by a supplier as the supplier may reasonably request.

The award of the public works contract

The basis for the award

3.28 The contracting authority must award the public works contract on the basis either the tender (including in-house bids) which offers the lowest price or the one which is the most 'economically advantageous' (i.e. best value for money). In *R. v Portsmouth City Council* [1997] the Court of Appeal, applying a European Court decision, confirmed that where no criteria had been specified a contract must be awarded on the basis of lowest price.

A contracting authority must use criteria which are relevant to the particular project to determine whether an offer is the most economically advantageous. These criteria can include quality, price, technical merit, aesthetic and functional characteristics, environmental characteristics, running costs, cost effectiveness, after sales service, technical assistance, delivery date, delivery period, and period for completion. The list is not exhaustive, but it is clear from the examples given that only objective criteria which are uniformly applicable to all bidders may be used. A contracting authority must state the weighting it gives to each criteria either in the contract notice or in the contract documents or, in the case of a competitive dialogue procedure, in the descriptive document. Criteria not mentioned in the contract notice or the contract or descriptive documents may not be used.

Contract award notice

3.29 A contracting authority which has awarded a public contract or concluded a framework agreement must, not later than 48 calendar days after the award of the contract or conclusion of the procedure, send to the *Official Journal* a notice in the form of the contract award notice contained in Annex III to the Form Regulation including the information therein specified.

Contract performance conditions

3.30 A contracting authority may stipulate conditions relating to the performance of a public contract, provided that those conditions are indicated in the contract notice and/or the contract documents. These conditions may include social and environmental considerations.

A distinction must be made between a contractual condition requiring the successful contractor to cooperate with some policy objective of the contracting authority, and the criteria for the selection of contractors or for the award of the contract. Thus a condition attached to the award of a public contract, under which the contractor is required to engage a given number of long-term unemployed, is compatible with the Directive and therefore the Regulations. It is not relevant to the assessment of the contractor's economic, financial or technical capacity to carry out the work,

provide the service, or supply the goods, nor does it form part of the criteria applied by the contracting authority to decide to whom to award the contract. Such conditions must, however, be compatible with the EC Treaty, particularly with those provisions on freedom to provide services, freedom of establishment and non-discrimination on the grounds of nationality. They must also be mentioned in the contract notice. Thus it would be a breach of the EC Treaty if it appeared on the facts that the condition could only be fulfilled by national firms or it would be more difficult for tenderers coming from other member states to fulfil that condition. Even a request for information from tenderers (as opposed to the insertion of a contractual term) can in certain circumstances be in breach of the rules if such request would reasonably lead the tenderer to believe that discrimination on local or national grounds is likely to occur.

When a contracting authority awards a public contract on the basis of the offer which is most economically advantageous it may take account of tenders which offer variations on the requirements specified in the contract documents if they meet the minimum requirements and the contracting authority has stated in the contract notice that tenders including variations will be considered and has indicated these minimum requirements in the contract documents.

Post-tender negotiations

3.31 It should also be stressed that in open and restricted procedures all negotiations with tenderers on fundamental aspects of the contract and in particular on prices are not permitted, although discussion with tenderers may be held for the purposes of clarifying or supplementing the content of their tenders or the requirements of the contracting authority, provided this does not involve unfairness to their competitors.

Under the competitive dialogue procedure discussion may be held to establish a specification and project structure but, once the dialogue is concluded, tenderers must bid their firm, final price and no discussion on other fundamental terms is permitted.

Abnormally low tenders

3.32 If an offer for a public contract is or appears to be abnormally low the contracting authority may reject that offer but only if it has requested in writing an explanation of the offer or of those parts which it considers contribute to the offer being abnormally low and has:

- requested in writing an explanation of the offer or of those parts which it considers contribute to the offer being abnormally low;
- taken account of the evidence provided in response to a request in writing; and
- subsequently verified the offer or parts of the offer being abnormally low with the tenderer.

Thus a contracting authority may not automatically reject a tender because it fails to satisfy some predetermined mathematical criterion adopted in relation to the public contract concerned. In every case, the contractor must be given an opportunity for explanation and thereafter the examination procedure specified must be followed.

If a contracting authority which rejects an abnormally low tender is awarding the contract on the basis of the offer which offers the lowest price, it must send a report justifying the rejection to the Office of Government Commerce for onward transmission to the Commission.

Where a contracting authority establishes that a tender is abnormally low because the tenderer has obtained state aid, the offer may be rejected on that ground alone only after:

- consultation with the tenderer; and
- the tenderer is unable to demonstrate, within a reasonable time limit fixed by the contracting authority, that the aid was granted in a way which is compatible with the EC Treaty.

The contracting authority's obligations once the contract has been awarded

3.33 It may be a matter of considerable importance to allow disappointed tenderers to know the outcome of a contract award procedure, not least to establish whether there may be grounds on which to challenge the award. The Regulations therefore impose a series of obligation upon contracting authorities.

First, the authority must not later than 48 calendar days after the award of the contract, send to the *Official Journal* a notice, in the form of the contract award notice contained in Annex III to the Form Regulation. The information required may be omitted in a particular case where to publish such information would impede law enforcement, would otherwise be contrary to the public interest, would prejudice the legitimate commercial interests of any person or might prejudice fair competition between contractors.

Secondly, the contracting authority must as soon as possible after the award of the contract, inform tenderers which submitted an offer, applied to be included amongst the tenderers to be selected to tender for or to negotiate the contract, or applied to be party to a framework agreement, of its decision in relation to the award of the contract or the conclusion of the framework agreement. Furthermore, the contracting authority must allow a period of at least 10 calendar days to elapse between the date of despatch of the contract award notice and the date on which the contracting authority proposes to enter into the contract or to conclude the framework agreement. This standstill provision reflects the ECJ's judgments in *Alcatel Austria and others* C-81/98 [1999] ECR 1-7671, and *Commission v. Austria* C-212/02 [2004] (unpublished), and is intended to afford unsuccessful tenderers the opportunity to effectively challenge the contract award. This 10 day standstill period has been memorialised in Directive 2007/66/EC which was adopted on 11 December 2007. The new Directive requires public authorities to wait a certain number of days, known as a 'standstill period', before concluding a public contract. By doing so, rejected tenderers are afforded an opportunity to commence an effective review procedure at a time when unfair decisions can still be rectified. If the standstill period has not been respected by a public authority, the Directive requires national courts to render the contract 'ineffective'. The Directive must be implemented by Member States by 20 December 2009. The UK has not yet implemented the Directive.

If, by midnight at the end of the second working day after the despatch of the contract notice, a contracting authority receives a request in writing from a tenderer asking for reasons why it was unsuccessful, the contracting authority must inform that tenderer of the characteristics and relative advantages of the successful tender. This information must be transmitted to the tenderer at least 3 working days prior to the end of the 10 calendar day period.

Thirdly, in all other cases, the authority must within 15 calendar days of the date on which it receives a request from any unsuccessful tenderer inform that tenderer why he was unsuccessful and if the tenderer was unsuccessful as a result of the evaluation of offers it must also tell him the name of the person awarded the contract. The Regulations also impose a requirement to tell any tenderer which submitted an admissible tender the characteristics and advantages of the successful tender, subject to the same considerations of confidentiality as apply to publication of a notice.

A contracting authority must also as soon as possible after the decision has been made, inform a tenderer which submitted an offer, or applied to be included amongst the tenderers to be selected to tender to negotiate a contract, or to be admitted to a dynamic purchasing system, (see below), of its decision to abandon or to recommence a contract award procedure in respect of which a contract notice has been published.

A contracting authority must in addition prepare a record in respect of each public contract awarded containing specified information. This record must be available for transmission to the Commission if requested.

Framework agreements

3.34 The Regulations also allow a contracting authority to enter into framework agreements by which it can award to the same operator a series of specific contracts, following terms that are already determined in the framework agreement. Specific contracts should not include terms that are substantially amended from the terms laid down in the framework agreement. A framework agreement can include several operators, but in that case there must be at least three of them. Moreover, when the framework agreement does not lay down all the terms of specific contracts, competition between tenderers for the framework agreement must be re-opened. Save exceptional circumstances, the contracting authority must not conclude a framework agreement for a period which exceeds 4 years.

Dynamic purchasing systems

3.35 A 'dynamic purchasing system' is a completely electronic system of limited duration which is established by a contracting authority to purchase commonly used goods, work or works, or services, and is open throughout its duration for the admission of tenderers. Tenderers must:

- satisfy the selection criteria specified by the contracting authority; and
- submit an indicative tender to the contracting authority or person operating the system on its behalf which complies with the specification required by the contracting authority or person.

When establishing a dynamic purchasing system, the contracting authority must send to the *Official Journal* a notice in the prescribed form and give information on the nature of the goods, work or works or services intended to be purchased and on technical aspects of the purchasing system. The contracting authority must admit to the dynamic purchasing system all tenderers which satisfy the selection criteria and have submitted an indicative tender which complies with the specification.

When the contracting authority intends to award a contract it must send to the *Official Journal* a notice in the form of a simplified contract notice on a dynamic purchasing system inviting candidates to submit an indicative tender. A contracting authority must allow at least 15 calendar days after the despatch of the contract notice for contractors to submit their indicative tenders. The contracting authority must then invite all tenderers admitted to the dynamic purchasing system to submit a tender for each contract. The contracting authority must award the contract to the tenderer which submits the tender that best meets the award criteria specified in the contract notice for the establishment of the dynamic purchasing system.

Save exceptional circumstances, the contracting authority should not operate a dynamic purchasing system for more than 4 years.

Electronic auctions

3.36 An electronic auction is a repetitive electronic process for the presentation of prices to be revised downwards, or of new and improved values of quantifiable elements of tenders, including price. An electronic auction is therefore a system that ranks offers using automatic evaluation methods and allows tenderers to compete by transmitting better prices or improved features of their offer. At the end of the process, the contract will be awarded to the best offer, based on the pre-programmed criteria. Electronic auctions must take place after an initial evaluation of tenders.

An electronic auction can be used in the open procedure, the restricted procedure, and under certain circumstances, the negotiated procedure, framework agreements or dynamic purchasing systems. An electronic auction may only be held when the contract specification can be precisely established. Electronic auctions can be based on price alone, or on the values of quantifiable elements of tenders indicated in the contract specification. The intention of the contracting authority to hold an electronic auction must be stated in the contract notice. Contract specifications must include all necessary information regarding quantifiable elements of tenders.

When it decides to set up an electronic auction, a contracting authority must make an initial evaluation of the tenders in accordance with the award criteria specified and then invite all tenderers which have submitted admissible tenders to submit new prices or new values in the electronic auction. Invitations must contain all necessary technical and practical elements of the electronic auctions, as well as the mathematical formula used to determine automatic re-ranking of tenders. The auction must start at least two days after the invitation to participate is sent.

During all phases of the electronic auction, tenderers must be able to ascertain their relative rankings in the auction at any time. However, the contracting authority must not disclose the identity of any tenderer participating in the auction. The electronic auction can close at a defined date, after all phases have lapsed, or when no further offers are received. Finally, the contract must be awarded according to the results of the auction.

Design contests

3.37 A design contest is a competition, particularly in the fields of planning, architecture, civil engineering, and data processing:

- which is conducted by or on behalf of a contracting authority and in which that contracting authority invites tenderers to submit plans and designs;
- under the rules of which the plans or designs entered will be judged by a jury;
- under which prizes may or may not be awarded; and
- which enables a contracting authority to acquire the use or ownership of plans or designs selected by the jury.

The Regulations apply to design contests whether they are organised as part of a procedure leading to the award of a public contract. The thresholds for the application of these provisions are the following:

- when the concerned authority is a 'Schedule 1 authority' (effectively central Government bodies), 133 100 euros (£90 319);
- for supply and services contracts when the concerned authority is a local authority, 206 000 euros (£139 893); and
- for public contracts concerning telecommunications services, research and development, and Part B services, 206 000 euros (£139 893).

These thresholds take into account the aggregated value of all payments received by the operator. They are therefore the same whether the winner is awarded a prize, a public contract, or a combination of both.

The Regulations also exclude a series of contracts from the application of rules on design contests (utilities, telecommunications networks, contracts classified as secret or contracts based on international agreements).

Where a design contest is caught by the Regulations the following provisions apply:

- the contracting authority must publicise its intention to hold a contest by sending to the *Official Journal* a notice in the form set out in Annex XII to the Form Regulation;
- the rules of the contest must be made available to all service providers wishing to participate; the number of service providers invited to participate may be restricted but the contracting authority must ensure that the selection is made on the basis of clear and non-discriminatory criteria. The number participating must be sufficient to ensure that there is adequate competition;
- the participants' proposals must be submitted anonymously to a jury composed of individuals who are independent of the participants. Where the participants are required to possess a qualification at least one-third of the jury must also possess that qualification or its equivalent;
- the jury must make its decision independently and solely on the basis of the criteria set out in the published notice. The jury must not be informed of the authorship of the proposals; and
- no later than 48 calendar days after the jury has made its selection the contracting authority must publicise the result in the *Official Journal* using the prescribed form set out in Annex XIII to the Form Regulation.

Subsidised public works contracts and public services contracts

3.38 Where a contracting authority undertakes to contribute more than half of the cost of certain specified public works contracts which will be or have been entered into by another body (other than another contracting authority), the contracting authority must make it a condition of making such contribution that other body complies with the Regulations in relation to the contract as if it were a contracting authority, and must ensure that that body does so or recover the contribution. The contracts to which this provision applies are those which are for carrying out any of the activities specified in Schedule 2 to the Regulations (civil engineering, construction of roads, bridges, railways, etc.) or for the carrying out of building works for hospitals, facilities intended for sports recreation and leisure, school and university buildings or buildings for administrative purposes, as well as services connected to these types of activities,

Subsidised housing scheme works contracts

3.39 For the purpose of seeking offers in relation to a subsidised housing scheme works contract where the size and complexity of the scheme and the estimated duration of the works involved require the planning of the scheme to be based from the outset on a close collaboration of a team comprising representatives of the contracting authority, experts and the contractor, the contracting authority may, subject as below, depart from the provisions of the Regulations in so far as it is necessary to do so to select the contractor which is most suitable for integration into the team. The contracting authority must in any event comply with the provisions relating to equal treatment of contractors, prior information notices, contract award notices, publication of notices, confidentiality and time-limits. The contracting authority must in addition include in the contract notice a job description which is as accurate as possible so as to enable contractors to form a valid idea of the scheme and of the minimum standards relating to the business or professional status, the economic and financial standing and the technical capacity which the person awarded the contract will be expected to fill.

Public works concession contracts

3.40 The Regulations lay down special rules which apply to public works concession contracts. A public works concession contract is defined in the Regulations as 'a public works contract under which the consideration given by the contracting authority consists of or includes the grant of a right to exploit the work or works to be carried out under the contract'.

When a contracting authority seeks offers in relation to a public works concession contract, it can request tenderers to specify their intention to sub-contract to other economic operators. The contracting authority may also require the concessionaire to sub-contract some or all of the work or works to be carried out. A percentage can be specified.

If the concessionaire is not itself a contracting authority, it must nevertheless still launch a call for tender and respect certain provisions of the Regulations regarding publicity, supply of information, and selection of contractors.

Obligations relating to taxes, environmental protection, employment protection and working conditions

3.41 A contracting authority may include in the contract documents relating to a public works contract or to a public services contract information as to where a contractor or services provider may obtain information about obligations relating to taxes, environmental protection, and employment protection and working conditions which will apply to the works to be carried out under the contract.

When the contracting authority provides this information, it must request contractors or services providers to indicate that they have taken account of these obligations in preparing their tender or in negotiating the contract.

The Utilities Directive and the Utilities Contracts Regulations 2006

3.42 The Utilities Regulations 2006 apply similar rules to those contained in the Public Contracts Regulations to certain contracts for works, supplies or services entered into by entities operating in the water, energy and transport sectors. The entities affected are specified in Schedule 1 and in the Regulations are called utilities.

Certain contracts listed in Regulation 6 are excluded from the application of the Regulations. This exemption applies in particular when the contract is not for the purpose of carrying out an activity specified in the part of Schedule 1 in which the utility concerned is specified, or when the contract is for the purpose of carrying out an activity outside the territory of the Community. Contracts for resale, secret contracts, contracts connected with international agreements, contracts for the purchase of water and contracts for the purchase of energy or of fuel for the production of energy are also excluded.

Certain contracts awarded by utilities operating in the energy sector may be exempt from the detailed rules of the Regulations. In this case the utility must comply with the principles of non-discrimination and competitive procurement in seeking offers in relation to them.

Moreover, these Regulations do not apply when the concerned activity is directly exposed to competition in markets to which access is unrestricted.

The Utilities Regulations do not apply to contracts below certain thresholds. These thresholds are:

- 422 000 euros for a supply contract or a services contract (£279 785);
- 5 278 000 euros for a works contract (£3 497 313).

Like the Public Contracts Regulations, the principal requirement of the Utilities Regulations is that in seeking offers in relation to a works, supply or services contract, a utility must use either the open procedure, the restricted procedure or the negotiated procedure. However, the Utilities Regulations in accordance with the Utilities Directive has adopted a more flexible approach to the choice of procedure. So long as the utility makes a 'call for competition' as defined in the Regulations any of the three procedures may be used. In certain specified circumstances no call for competition needs to be made.

The Utilities Regulations do not include the competitive dialogue procedure.

As with the Public Contracts Regulations, a utility is required to publicise the contracts which it expects to award in the *Official Journal* at least once a year and again when it starts the procedure leading to the award. This latter requirement is dispensed with in certain cases.

The Utilities Regulations allow the operation of a system of qualification of providers, from which a utility may select suppliers or contractors to tender for or to negotiate a contract without advertisement at the start of the award procedure. In this case the existence of the qualification system must be advertised.

Similar to the Public Contracts Regulations, the Utilities Regulations lay down minimum time limits in relation to responses by potential providers to invitations to tender, to be selected to tender for or to negotiate the contract, and for obtaining the relevant documents. The Regulations also indicate the matters to which the utility may have regard to in excluding tenders from providers that are regarded as ineligible or in selecting providers to tender for or to negotiate the contract, and as before they require that the utility award a contract on the basis either of the offer (including in-house bids) which offers the lowest price or the one which is the most economically advantageous. In addition the Regulations lay down similar rules in relation to technical specifications to publicising their awards and to the keeping of records and to reporting.

Under the Regulations, a utility is permitted to advertise an arrangement which establishes the terms under which providers will enter into contracts with it over a period of time (called in the Regulations 'framework arrangements') in which case it does not need to advertise the supply and works contracts made under it.

Secondly a utility may, and in other limited circumstances must, reject an offer for a supply contract if more than 50% of the value of the goods are goods which originate in states with which the Community has not concluded an agreement ensuring comparable and effective access to markets for undertakings in member states. The Utilities Directive and the Utilities Regulations also take account of the GPA in order to grant tenderers established from GPA countries equivalent rights as those established in EU member states.

The Regulations also introduce provisions related to dynamic purchasing systems, electronic auctions, and design contests.

Remedies for breach of the Community rules governing procurement

3.43 The Public Contracts Regulations and the Utilities Regulations provide economic operators (i.e. those which are established in an EU member state or in a state party to the European Economic Area Agreement) and GPA operators. with a right to obtain redress by way of court action, when they suffer or risks suffering loss or damage as a result of a breach of the relevant Regulations or the breach of any Community obligation in respect of a contract to which the Regulations apply. The term 'economic operator' includes providers of architectural or related services (see paragraph 3.09 above). The remedies available and the procedure by which they may be obtained are very similar in respect of each of the Regulations. In this way the Regulations implement the 'Remedies' Directive and the 'Compliance' Directive already referred to.

The obligation on contracting authorities and utilities to comply with the provisions of the Regulations (other than certain provisions relating to reporting and the supply of information) and with enforceable Community obligations in respect of contracts falling within the Regulations, is conceived under the Regulations as a duty owed to providers the breach whereof gives rise to an action for breach of statutory duty.

A similar duty is placed upon a public works concessionaire to comply with the obligations placed upon it by regulation 37(3) of the Public Contracts Regulations and where such a duty is imposed the term 'contractor' includes thy person who sought or who seeks or who would have wished to be the person to whom a contract to which regulation 37(3) applies is awarded and who is a national of and established in a member state.

A breach of the duty referred to is not a criminal offence but is actionable by any provider who in consequence 'suffers or risks suffering loss or damage'. Proceedings brought in England and Wales and in Northern Ireland must be brought before the High Court, and in Scotland, before the Court of Session. However, proceedings under the Regulations may not be brought unless:

1 the provider bringing the proceedings has informed the contracting authority (including a concessionaire), or utility of the breach or apprehended breach of the duty referred to and of his intention to bring proceedings under the Regulations in respect of it; and

2 they are brought promptly and in any event within three months from the date when grounds for the bringing of the proceedings first arose unless the court considers that there is good reason for extending the period within which proceedings may be brought.

In proceedings brought under each of the Regulations the court may, without prejudice to any other powers it may have:

1 by interim order suspend the procedure leading to the award of the contract or the procedure leading to the determination of a design contest, or suspend the implementation of any decision or action taken by the contracting authority or concessionaire, as the case may be, in the course of following such a procedure; and

2 order the setting aside of that decision or action or order the contracting authority or utility to amend any document, award damages to a contractor or supplier which has suffered loss or damage

as a consequence of the breach, or do both of those things, in all instances if satisfied that a decision or action taken by a contracting authority or utility was in breach of the duty referred to.

However, in proceedings brought under each of the Regulations, the court can only award damages if the contract in relation to which the breach occurred has already been signed. The court cannot therefore set aside a contract which has been entered into in breach of the Regulations. It is uncertain however whether such a contract in English law is unenforceable as between the parties to it on the grounds of public policy. It is submitted that where both parties are aware of the breach at the time of entering into the contract (e.g. where the proposed contract was not advertised) public policy requires that the contract should be unenforceable by both parties. Where only one party is in breach without the other party's knowledge (e.g. where a contracting authority without justification selects a contractor that has not submitted the lowest tender) then the contract should only be unenforceable by the party in breach.

The newly adopted Directive 2007/66/EC provides that contracts entered into without any prior competitive tendering or in breach of the standstill obligation must be declared 'ineffective'. The Directive leaves it to the member states to determine the exact legal consequences of a declaration of ineffectiveness (see paragraph 3.33 above). The Directive must be implemented by member states by 20 December 2009 and has not yet been implemented in the UK.

In the English courts any interim order under (1) above will be by way of interlocutory injunction which it is anticipated will be granted or refused on the familiar principles laid down by the House of Lords in *American Cyanamid Co. v Ethicon Ltd* [1975] AC 396. These principles may be summarised as follows:

1 the plaintiff must establish that he has a good arguable claim to the right he seeks to protect;
2 the court must not attempt to decide the claim on the affidavits; it is enough if the plaintiff shows that there is a serious question to be tried; and
3 if the plaintiff satisfies these tests the grant or refusal of an injunction is a matter for the court's discretion on the balance of convenience including that of the public where this is affected.

Although the exercise of discretion applies to many factors (of which the question whether damages would be a sufficient remedy is arguably the most important), in public procurement cases the question of the public interest is often likely to be decisive against the grant of the injunction. This fact is expressly recognized by both Remedies Directives which provide that:

'The member states may provide that when considering whether to order interim measures the body responsible may take into account the probable consequences of the measures for all interests likely to be harmed, as well as the public interest, and may decide not to grant such measures where their negative consequences could exceed their benefits. A decision not to grant interim measures shall not prejudice any other claim of the person seeking these measures.' (Article 2(4) of both Directives)

No such provision appears in the Regulations no doubt because it was considered that the practice of the courts when granting or refusing interlocutory injunctions was entirely consistent with the discretion given by the Remedies directive in this respect.

Even where the public interest element is not decisive the usual requirement that the plaintiff undertake to pay the defendant's damages caused by the injunction should it prove to have been wrongly granted will often dissuade a plaintiff from pursuing this remedy in public procurement cases where such damages are likely to be heavy. It has been suggested that because there is an obligation under EU law for member states to provide an effective remedy for breach of rights arising under Community law the strict conditions which usually apply to injunctions, including the requirement for an undertaking to pay the defendant's damages, should not apply. However, this approach has not to date been applied in the English courts.

A provider may wish to have set aside a decision to reject his bid made on the basis of criteria not permitted by the Regulations, or a decision to exclude his bid as abnormally low where he has not been given an opportunity to give an explanation. Equally a provider may require that a contract document be amended so as to exclude a specification not permitted by the Regulations.

It will be noted that Regulations do not specify how damages are to be assessed. In Community law it is left to national laws to provide the remedies required in order to ensure that Community rights are protected. Until the first cases go through the courts it is uncertain how such damages will be assessed.

In the case of the Utilities Regulations alone the task of recovering certain damages is eased by regulation 45(8) which provides that:

'Where, in proceedings under this regulation, the Court is satisfied that an economic operator would have had a real chance of being awarded a contract or winning a design contest if that chance had not been adversely affected by a breach of the duty owed to it by the utility in accordance with paragraphs (1) or (2) the economic operator shall be entitled to damages amounting to its costs in preparing its tender and in participating in the procedure leading to the award of the contract or its costs of participating in the procedure leading to the determination of the design contest.'

Regulation 45(9) of the Utilities Regulations makes it clear that the limitation in available remedies does not affect a claim by a provider that has suffered other loss or damage or that is entitled to relief other than damages.

To what standard the plaintiff will have to prove that he had a 'real chance' (identical words are used in Article 2(7) of the Remedies Directive) of being awarded the contract is as yet unclear but it is submitted that this will be something less than on the balance of probabilities.

Defence Procurement

3.44 Before the existence of specific EC legislation in the defence sector, member states frequently justified exemptions from the EC public procurement rules on the basis of their defence and security interests under Article 296 EC Treaty. On 21 August 2009, the EC Directive 2009/81/EC entered into force, which provides a general framework for defence procurement. The Directive not only applies to the procurement of arms, munitions, war materials, but also for works and services for specifically military purposes or sensitive works and sensitive services. Contracts for architectural services must be awarded in accordance with the Directive. The Directive contains a number of features to reflect the specific needs of procurement in defence and security markets, in particular: (i) the negotiated procedure can be used as a standard procedure (albeit the publication of a tender notice is required); (ii) candidates can be required to put in place measures to ensure the protection sensitive information; and (ii) member states can request guarantees to ensure that armed forces are delivered in time especially in times of crisis or conflict. Member states have until 21 August 2011 to implement the Directive.

The role of the architect in relation to the procurement regulations

3.45 It is to be noted that the obligations imposed by the procurement Regulations are placed on the 'contracting authority' or utility concerned. However an architect employed by such a body may be under a contractual duty to carry out those obligations as its agent and liable to indemnify it where a breach of that duty results in loss. This could occur, for example where the contract award is delayed, or where the authority or utility is compelled to pay damages as the result of an infringement.

On the other hand architects who wish to tender for public authority (and utility) contracts for architectural services will be able to take advantage of the provisions of the Public Sector Directive to ensure equal treatment with other EC architects. It should be borne in mind that the Public Sector Directive applies throughout the Community and that therefore a UK architect can as much take advantage of its provisions in another member state as architects from other member states can take advantage of it in the UK.

Public works contracts and Article 28 EC

3.53 Even where a public procurement contract falls outside the provisions of the relevant Directive, architects will still have to take care that they do not specify in such a manner as will render any public authority employer in breach of Article 28 EC.

Article 28 provides that:

'Quantitative restrictions on imports and all measures having equivalent effect shall, without prejudice to the following provisions be prohibited between Member States.'

In Case 45/87 *Commission v Ireland,* the Dundalk Urban District Council (a public body for whose acts the Irish Government are responsible), permitted the inclusion in the contract specification for a drinking water supply scheme of a clause providing that certain pipes should be certified as complying with an Irish standard and consequently refusing to consider without adequate justification a tender providing for such pipes manufactured to an alternative standard providing equivalent guarantees of safety, performance and reliability. The contract fell outside the provisions of the Works directive because it concerned the distribution of drinking water. Nevertheless, the Court held that Ireland had acted in breach of Article 28 EC. Only one undertaking was capable of producing pipes to the required standard and that undertaking was situated in Ireland. Consequently, the inclusion of that specification had the effect of restricting the supply of the pipes needed to Irish manufacturers alone and was a quantitative restriction on imports or a measure having equivalent effect. The breach of Article 28 could have been avoided if the specification had included the words 'or equivalent'.

14

Party walls

GRAHAM NORTH

1 The Party Wall etc. Act 1996

1.01 The Party Wall etc. Act 1996 came into force in 1997 and extended the party wall legislation previously applying to London and set out in Part VI of the London Building Acts (Amendment) Act 1939 to the rest of England and Wales.

1.02 The Act sets out a procedure for serving notices that must be followed if one is carrying out the following works:

Section 1 Building along the line of junction of the boundary which is not currently built on other than to the extent of a boundary wall (not being the wall of a building).

Section 2 Carrying out works to a party structure/party wall/ party floor/party fence wall, such as underpinning, demolishing and rebuilding, raising, removing chimney breasts, cutting into install beams, injecting a damp-proof course, columns, etc.

Section 6 (a) Excavating or excavating to construct new foundations within 3 metres of an adjoining building and to a greater depth than the foundations of that adjoining building or structure (Figure 14.1).
(b) If one is excavating or excavating to construct foundations within 6 metres of an adjoining building or structure and to a depth which would intersect a 45° line drawn downwards from next door's footings (Figure 14.2).

1.03 Before the Act was passed, a party wall outside of London was defined as being severed vertically through its centre. One could carry out works to one's own half of the wall but not to the neighbour's side unless consent was given. In some cases, this provided difficulties if the party wall required underpinning or had to be raised for its full thickness.

2 Definitions

2.01 The Party Wall etc. Act now gives two definitions for a party wall:

1 *Section 20(a)*: A wall which forms part of a building and stands on lands of different owners to a greater extent than the projection of any artificially formed support on which the wall rests.
2 *Section 20(b)*: So much of a wall not being a wall referred to in section 20(a) above as separate buildings belonging to different owners.

Figures 14.3 and 14.4 illustrate these definitions.

2.02 A **party structure** can be a party wall, party floor, partition or other structure separating buildings or parts of buildings approached solely by separate staircases or separate entrances. A **party fence wall** is a wall which does not form part of a building but stands astride the boundary.

3 Notices

3.01 The Act sets out the steps which must be followed if one is intending to carry out any of the works referred to above. This involves the service of notice, commonly known as a Party Structure Notice, Line of Junction Notice or a Foundation Notice and the notice must state:

- The name and address of the building owner.
- The nature and particulars of the proposed works.
- The date on which the proposed works will begin.

In respect of a Foundation Notice, it must also be accompanied by plans and sections showing:

- The site and depth of any excavation the building owner proposes to make.
- If he proposes to erect a building or structure, its site.

A Line of Junction Notice must describe the intended wall.

3.02 A Party Structure Notice must be served at least 2 months before the works are due to start, and in respect of a Foundation and Line of Junction Notice, 1 month before. Works to which these notices relate cannot start even after these periods if an award is yet to be agreed and published to the owners. Notices must be re-served after 12 months if an award has not been agreed within this time.

A notice is served on any owner who has an interest in their property of greater than 12 months. A building owner must be someone who has an interest in the land and is 'desirous of exercising rights' under the Act. A building owner can also be someone who has contracted to purchase an interest in the land or signed an agreement for a lease as long as this is for greater than 12 months.

It is vitally important that any notice served contains the correct information. Failure to include these details on the notice will render the notice invalid. Thereafter, any matter or award agreed by the surveyors following the service of a defective notice will also be invalid.

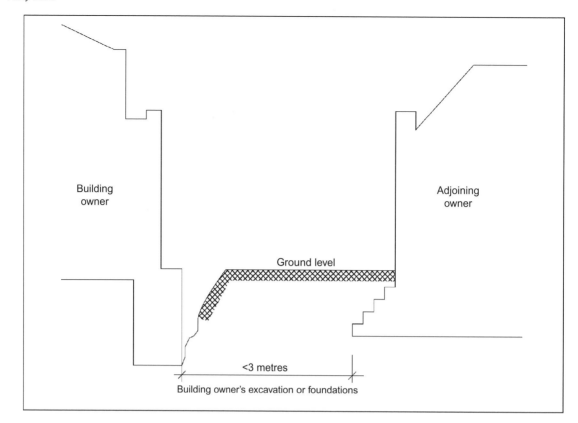

Figure 14.1 For a 3-metre notice.

3.03 An adjoining owner has 14 days in which to dissent or consent to the works described in the notice otherwise he will be deemed to have dissented by default. Thereafter, a *dispute* arises and surveyors must be appointed to settle the matter by an award.

The parties can agree to the appointment of one surveyor, known as the 'agreed surveyor', a role which the surveyor can fulfil because of his statutory responsibility to act impartially. Alternatively, the adjoining owner can appoint their own surveyor. If there is no agreed surveyor but a surveyor appointed for each of the building and adjoining owners, then their first duty is to select a third surveyor who will adjudicate on any matter in dispute between the surveyors and in some instances between the owners.

3.04 If an adjoining owner fails to respond to a notice, then a written request must be made to him, either by the building owner or his surveyor if he has due authority, to appoint a surveyor within 10 days. If the adjoining owner ignores this request, then the building owner is in a position to appoint a surveyor for the adjoining owner.

4 The surveyors

4.01 The surveyor can be any person who is not a party to the matter. No specific qualifications are required but it is important to ensure that if such an appointment is accepted, one has the knowledge and experience required. The appointment is personal to the individual.

4.02 It is the surveyors' duty in their award to determine the right for the works to be carried out, the time and manner of executing this work and any other matter arising out of or incidental to the dispute, including the costs of making the award.

4.03 If the surveyors are unable to agree, then an approach can be made to the third surveyor who will make his decision in the form of an award. Submissions to the third surveyor are normally in writing once the third surveyor has confirmed he is able to accept the appointment.

Information sent to the third surveyor should include copies of each surveyor's letter of appointment from the owner, copies of the notices and evidence that the third surveyor has been selected. An outline of the matters in dispute should be given along with supporting arguments.

4.04 One of the most important aspects of the award will be the Schedule of Condition taken of the adjoining property or land. This is normally in a written form and can be supplemented with photographs.

If the adjoining owner's surveyor fails to respond within 10 days to a written request from the building owner's surveyor or does not act *effectively* then the building owners surveyor can proceed *ex parte* and this will be as effectual as if he had been the agreed surveyor.

5 The award

5.01 Once the award is agreed, it is published to the owners who have 14 days in which to appeal against the award in the country court if they feel it has been made improperly or incorrectly.

The Act does not say that once the award is published to the owners that the building owner must wait 14 days before his works can start, although some awards will make that a condition. If an adjoining owner wishes to appeal against an award and in the meantime the building owner's works commence, then the adjoining owner must lodge an appeal and also obtain an injunction to prevent the works from proceeding further. Legal advice must be sought at this stage.

The surveyors decide who pays the fees for agreeing the award and any other costs arising from it. In the majority of cases, it is the building owner who will bear the fees for the surveyors appointed because the works will be for his benefit.

If there are works which are necessary to a party wall on account of defect or want of repair, then the costs of such works will be defrayed by the building owner and the adjoining owner with regard to the use which each of the owners make of the structure or wall concerned and the cause of the defect.

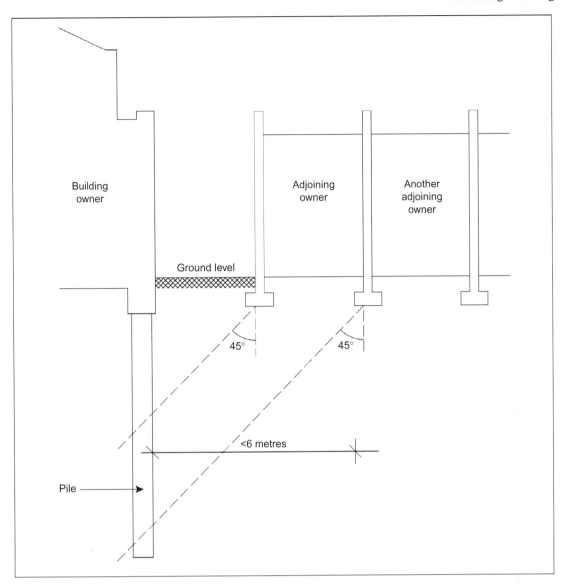

Figure 14.2 For a 6-metre notice.

6 The building owner's rights

6.01 Section 8 grants a building owner, his servants, agents and workmen the right to enter the land of an adjoining owner for the purpose of executing any works under this Act. This could include the erection of scaffolding over the adjoining owner's land and buildings, although details of the access will be agreed by the surveyors beforehand.

If an adjoining owner fails to give such access to the building owner, or to the surveyors if they need to carry out an inspection, to take a Schedule of Condition for example, then that owner would be guilty of an offence and liable on summary conviction to a fine imposed by the courts.

6.02 The Act does not permit a building owner to install *special foundations* on an adjoining owner's land unless the adjoining owner's consent is obtained. Special foundations are defined as foundations *in which assemblage of beam or rods is employed for the purpose of distributing any load*.

This type of foundation is becoming more common where basements are being excavated and the party walls are underpinned.

If a building owner proposes to reduce the height of a party wall or party fence wall to no less than 2 metres in height, an adjoining owner can serve a counter-notice and insist that the wall is left at a greater height but the adjoining owner must bear the costs of the work necessary to achieve this. A building owner upon whom a counter-notice has been served must comply with the requirements

of the counter-notice unless the works required would be injurious to him, cause him unnecessary inconvenience or delay in the execution of the works pursuant to the notice which he had served.

The Act also permits a building owner to chase into an adjoining owner's wall to install a flashing or other weatherprooitng of a wall erected against the adjoining owner's wall (section 2(2)(j)).

6.03 In the event of damage being caused to the adjoining owner's land or property, an adjoining owner can either insist that the building owner makes good that damage or he can request payment in lieu. The amount of any money to be paid to the adjoining owner in this situation is to be determined by the surveyors.

As far as the award is concerned, it is the building owner who is responsible for making good or paying for the damage, not the contractor. It is for the surveyors to determine what damage has been caused and the extent of remedial work necessary.

A building owner is not permitted to exercise any rights conferred upon him *in such a manner or at such time as to cause unnecessary inconvenience* to any adjoining owner or occupier (section 7(1)). It is incumbent upon a building owner to ensure that he takes all reasonable measures to minimise any inconvenience to an adjoining owner.

6.04 It is vitally important that the procedures are followed. Failure to do so can lead to legal action from adjoining owner and subsequent delays to the works. The case of *Louis v Sadiq* [1997] 1 EGLR 137 is an example where works to a party wall started without the procedures being followed (this case was under the

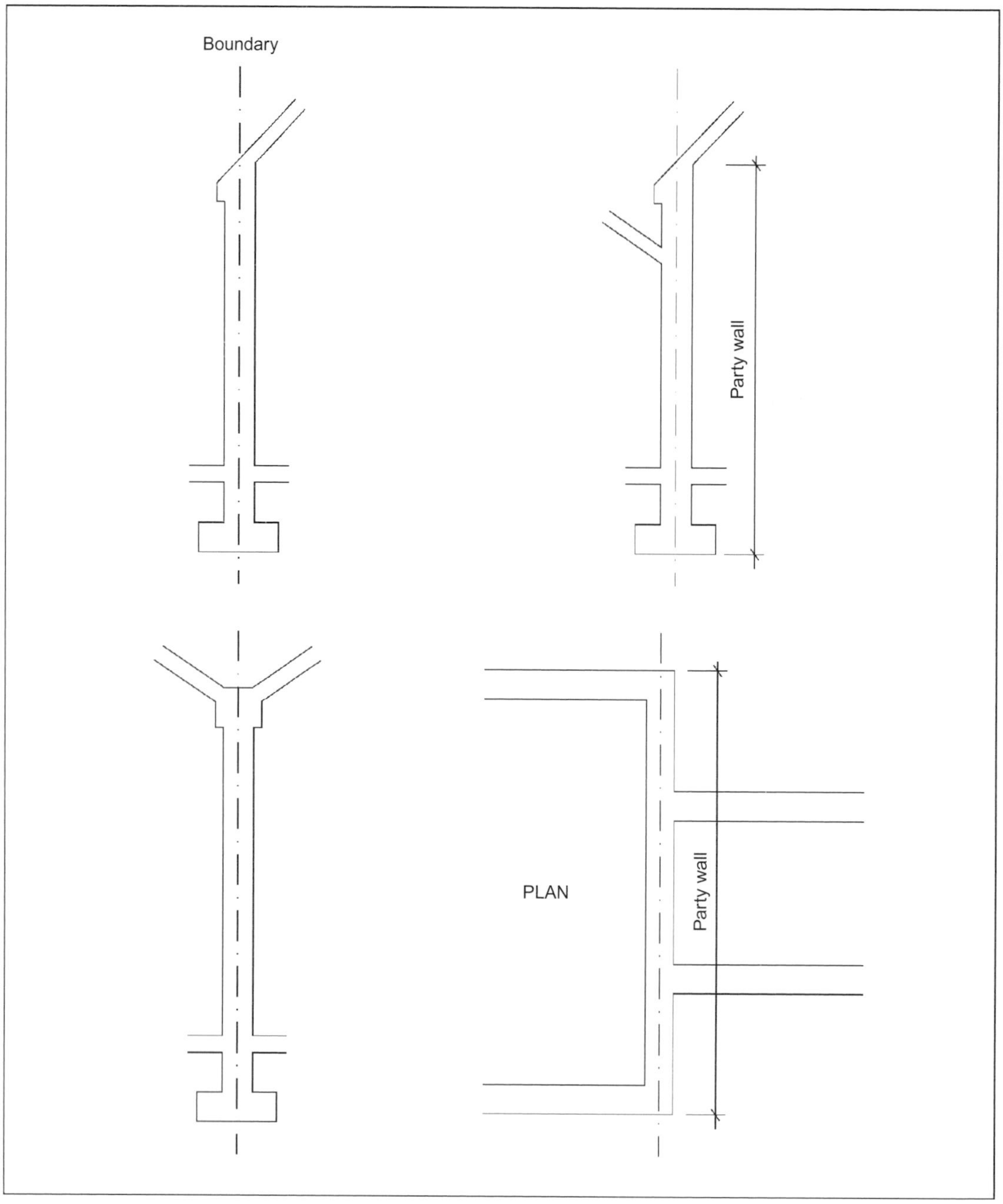

Figure 14.3 Party wall as defined by Section 20(a).

1939 Act) and the court took a dim view of the building owner's failure to observe the legislation.

6.05 Where an adjoining owner may be vulnerable if the building owner does not honour his obligations, for example, if a party wall is to be demolished and rebuilt but the building owner disappears prior to reconstruction, the adjoining owner can request security for expenses. The request for such security must be in writing and made before the works commence. The amount of security will vary depending upon the extent of the works which may be necessary if the adjoining owner has to complete them. However, the security requested should not be so much that to provide the money a building owner would be prohibited from commencing the works.

Security for expenses is usually provided as a financial deposit in an account from which the money can only be released upon the signatures of two of the three surveyors appointed. If there is no requirement to use the security then the money is released to the building owner with any interest which may have accrued.

6.06 The standard forms for notices, awards, letters of appointment, etc. are in various publications including the *RICS Guidance Note*, the *RIBA Guidance Note* and the *Party Wall Act Explained*, published by the Pyramus and Thisbe Club.

7 Boundary structures in Scotland[*]

7.01 'Party wall' is not a term of art in Scotland. The Party Wall etc. Act 1996 does not extend to Scotland. North of the border, the common law, property titles and local by-laws regulate mutual boundary wall questions and other questions about 'joint ownership', 'common ownership' and 'common interest'. The common law developed an elaborate doctrine of 'common interest', notably in relation to flats in different ownership within the same tenement building, which has now been codified by the Tenements (Scotland) Act 2004. Proprietors now have a statutory duty to maintain their own parts of the building so as to ensure that they continue to provide support and shelter their properties within the tenement, e.g. to maintain walls, partitions, floors and ceilings and

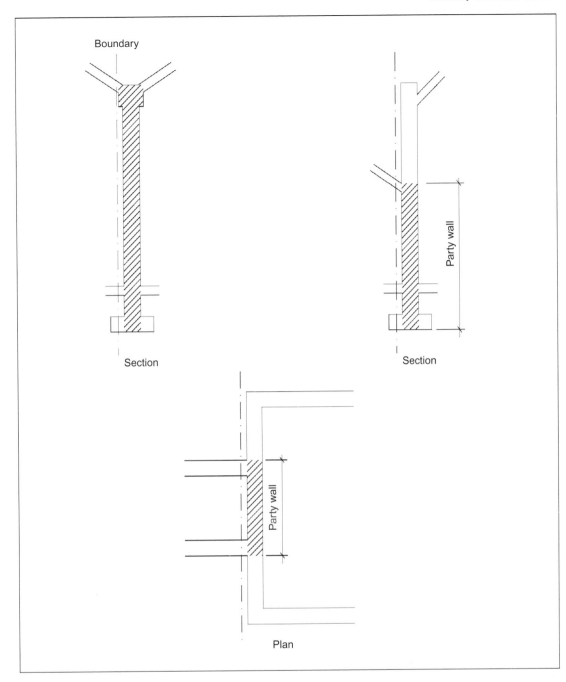

Figure 14.4 Party wall as defined by Section 20(b).

to carry out repairs. The Tenements (Scotland) Act 2004 also now provides a default management scheme for the maintenance of many parts of a tenement building, including external walls, gable walls and load-bearing walls. Where neighbouring properties, not forming part of a tenement, share a boundary wall the general rule is that each owns half of the wall up to its mid-point. Each owner has an obligation at common law, based on common interest, not to undermine the support of the other half. Where it is proposed to carry out works on or adjacent to boundary structures or adjoining property and, in the case of buildings in multiple ownership, where it is proposed to carry out operations which may affect the stability of the building or interface with services, legal advice should be taken. The same applies where there is a question about maintenance or repairs to the common parts of a building or a development of several buildings.

*This section was written by Catherine Devaney.

15

Health and safety law affecting architects

RICHARD DYTON

1 Introduction

1.01 Health and safety is a major matter of debate between architects, employers and contractors. The most significant legislation ever to affect the construction industry was implemented by the Construction Design and Management ('CDM') Regulations 1994. These were replaced by the Construction (Design and Management) Regulations 2007 (the 'CDM Regulations 2007') which aimed to clarify and improve the regulations which they superseded, and came into force on 6 April 2007. The legislation is complex and gives rise to additional costs in compliance.

The introduction of CDM legislation has seen a string of prosecutions by the Health and Safety Executive (the 'HSE', which is the enforcement arm of the Health and Safety Commission), together with the publication of formal amendments to the standard forms of contract by the Joint Contracts Tribunal ('JCT') and the Institution of Civil Engineers ('ICE'). Subsequent amendments have been published by both organisations to reflect the changes arising from the 2007 Regulations. These prosecutions and publications gave meat to the bones of the Regulations by showing the type of incident that would be prosecuted and the effect of health and safety issues on the normal contractual relationship. In terms of the prosecutions, the HSE followed the spirit of the legislation and focused upon the 'client' as target, but at the same time held the designer responsible, in some cases, for failing to warn the client adequately of his responsibilities. The case law highlights the increasing importance of architects being familiar with and adhering to health and safety legislation. In terms of the amendments to the standard forms of contract, these have increased the grounds for extensions of time and loss and expense for the contractor arising from the performance of the office-holders for health and safety purposes: the CDM coordinator and the principal contractor.

Also of significance are the Control of Asbestos Regulations ('CoAR') 2006, which replaced the Control of Asbestos at Work Regulations 2002. The CoAR impose a duty in relation to 'non-domestic premises' to manage asbestos risk, and are discussed in greater detail later in the chapter.

The scope of this chapter is to consider the structure of the existing legislation and, more importantly, to provide a practical guide to the obligations of the architect under the CDM Regulations in the context of the various stages within the project plan. The architect's existing and future obligations under the CoAR will also be explained. This should enable architects to advise clients how to minimise their exposure and so avoid prosecution.

2 Existing health and safety position

Health and Safety at Work Act 1974

2.01 The Health and Safety at Work Act 1974 ('HSW Act') enacted a system progressively to replace the older law which had grown up piecemeal and which addressed only certain types of workplaces or processes (such as under the Factories Act 1961 and the Offices, Shops and Railway Premises Act 1963). The old system had left other workplaces uncovered by the legislation and the HSW Act provided the framework for a system of regulations applying generally to all workplaces, employers and employees. It also extended to many self-employed persons and to others such as manufacturers, designers and importers of articles to be used at work. Examples of the regulations which were brought in under the new policy were those covering the protection of eyes (Protection of Eyes Regulations 1974), noise (Noise at Work Regulations 1989), the use of lead (Control of Lead at Work Regulations 1980), the use of asbestos (Control of Asbestos at Work Regulations 1987), the control of industrial major hazards (Control of Industrial Major Accident Hazard Regulations 1984), and the control of substances hazardous to health (Control of Substances Hazardous to Health Regulations 1988). Many of these original regulations have now been either revoked or amended and other regulations exist in their place. The existing regulations are considered in more detail below.

Structure of the Act

2.02 The structure of the HSW Act is that sections 2–4 and 6 place general duties on employers, the self-employed, persons otherwise in control of premises and designers, manufacturers, importers or suppliers of articles for use at work. The duties are normally qualified by the phrase 'reasonably practicable'. Section 6 refers to the duties of designers together with those who manufacture and import or supply an article for use at work. The general obligation is:

'To ensure, so far as is reasonably practicable, that the article is so designed and constructed that it will be safe and without risks to health at all times when it is being set, used, cleaned or maintained by person at work.'

The structure of the HSW Act is, therefore, divided into general obligations under the Act itself and more specific obligations under the existing body of regulations.

Buildings and construction sites

2.03 The HSE has, in a number of cases, applied the general obligation in relation to buildings and construction sites. Prosecutions of high-profile clients since the introduction of the CDM Regulations has completed the principle together with the imprisonment of one demolition contractor for flagrantly disregarding the asbestos regulations.

Liability under the Act and Regulations

2.04 Breaches of the HSW Act or of the regulations brought in by it (the 'HSW Regulations') give rise to criminal liabilities which may lead to sentences of unlimited fines and/or a maximum term of imprisonment not exceeding 2 years. The policy of the HSE in enforcing the HSW Regulations has been to prosecute and fine an organisation rather than an individual, although there is nothing in law to prevent an individual being prosecuted and, ultimately, imprisoned. However, the HSE's enforcement policy emphasises the importance of prevention over prosecution. Codes of practice are regularly issued with the relevant HSW Regulations, and these are used to flesh out the Regulations concerned. Breach of the codes is not, in itself, breach of the HSW Regulations but the codes are admissible in criminal and, indeed, in civil proceedings to determine whether or not there has been a breach of the HSW Regulations. Compliance with the relevant code raises the (rebuttable) presumption that the HSW Regulations themselves have been complied with.

In the context of civil liability, there are two potential limbs: first, the tort of breach of statutory duty which is a 'strict' liability in the sense that it is not qualified by what is reasonable in the context of the profession at large (although the statutory duties in the Regulations themselves are usually qualified by statements such as 'so far as is reasonably practicable'); and, second, the tort of negligence which arises from common standards becoming established in the profession of which the reasonable architect is deemed to have knowledge and breach of which thereby renders the architect liable.

Breach of the provisions of the HSW Act does not itself give rise to a civil action for breach of statutory duty. However, if there is a breach of the HSW Regulations this may enable a claimant to cite the breach as a basis for a civil claim, depending upon whether the specific HSW Regulations allow such a claim and whether the claimant's interest is intended to be protected by the Regulations. Under the CDM Regulations, for example, breach of regulation 16 which provides that the construction phase of any project cannot commence until a compliant construction phase plan has been prepared (by the principal contractor), gives rise to civil liability without the need to prove negligence or breach of contract.

Inevitably, the influence of the Regulations will affect the law of negligence in setting specific legal standards in the context of health and safety. A failure to meet those standards may represent a breach of duty in negligence, even if the matter in question is not specifically covered by the Regulations. Therefore, liability is not restricted merely to claims based upon breach of statutory duty but also, indirectly, in the tort of negligence. In addition, the requirement for employers to carry out risk assessments is likely to be of significance when considering questions of foreseeability at common law.

Relevant regulations

2.05 There are a large number of health and safety regulations in addition to the CDM and CoAR Regulations which, while not necessarily specific to the construction industry, affect the work of architects. Many of these regulations apply to the duties of employers in the workplace. As such, the architect must have a general knowledge of these when designing such workplaces in order to avoid risks to the health of employees and generally to allow them to be safe. These regulations are, briefly, as follows.

Workplace (Health, Safety and Welfare) Regulations 1992

2.06 These Regulations extend the duties of employers into areas not previously the subject of specific statutory provisions, such as hospitals, schools, universities, hotels and court houses. The Regulations require that the workplace, equipment, devices and system shall be maintained in an efficient state, in efficient working order and in good repair. Specifically, the Regulations specify suitable provision for the ventilation, temperature, lighting, cleanliness and removal of waste materials, sufficient working area and suitable work station provision. There are a number of provisions relating to the condition of floors, windows, skylights, doors, gates, escalators, sanitary conveniences and washing facilities. Where the workplace is a building, the regulations now require the workplace to be appropriately stable and solid for the use to which it is to be put. See Chapter 9.

Personal Protective Equipment at Work Regulations 1992

2.07 The employer's obligations relate to the suitability of protective clothing to be worn by employees. In June 2003, in the case of *Fytche v Wincanton Logistics plc*, the court held that regulation 7(1) of these Regulations imposed an absolute duty on employers to make sure protective equipment was kept in good condition. However, that duty only applied to risks against which the equipment was supposed to protect the employee. In this case, steel toe-capped boots were provided to the employee to protect his feet from falling objects. A tiny hole in the boots caused the employee to sustain frostbite but the employer was not liable for this injury as the boots were not intended to protect the employee from that type of harm.

Manual Handling Operations Regulations 1992

2.08 This imposes obligations on an employer to avoid a manual handling operation where there is a risk of injury from such an operation. The employer's duty is to take steps to reduce the risk of injury to the lowest level reasonably practicable. Regulation 4(1)(b) imposes the requirement to reduce the risk of injury to the lowest level practicable. It also requires an employer to make an assessment of the manual handling to be carried out and provide information to the employee as to the type of load to be lifted. The case of *Swain v Denso Marston* (2000) held that these three requirements should not be read conjunctively so that breach of any of them could be enough to make the employer liable. A further case stated that, in assessing whether a task involved a risk of injury and in assessing whether it was 'reasonably practicable' for an employer to avoid his employees being subjected to that risk, it was necessary to look at the particular activity in context (*Koonjul v Thameslink Healthcare Services NHS Trust*).

In determining whether the manual handling operations involve a risk of injury and in determining appropriate steps to reduce the risk, regard must be had to such things as the employee's suitability to the tasks he is carrying out, the employee's clothing, the results of any risk assessment that has been carried out under the Management of Health and Safety at Work Regulations 1999 and the employee's knowledge and training.

The importance of an employer giving careful consideration to the type of tasks it will be asking its employees to carry out is clear. It is not enough to consider the tasks in their own right. The employer will have to address the individual employee's suitability to a task which is an onerous burden for the employer.

Health and Safety (Display Screen Equipment) Regulations 1992

2.09 The employer must ensure that all display screen equipment which may be used for the purposes of the employer business meets the requirements set out in the Regulations. The employer is under an obligation to make an assessment of the relevant risks to health and safety from the operation and reduce the risks to the 'lowest extent reasonably practicable'. It requires employers to plan the activities of their 'users' so that there are periodic interruptions in their work on the display screen equipment. There must be appropriate eye and eyesight tests for the employees.

Provision and Use of Work Equipment Regulations 1998

2.10 'Work equipment' is defined broadly, to include anything from a pair of scissors to a steel rolling mill. There is an obligation on the employer and (with the revised Regulations) on others having 'control' of work equipment to ensure that work equipment is used only for the operations for which and under conditions for which it is suitable. If the equipment has a health risk, the employer (or relevant person) must restrict its use and maintenance to specific persons.

Lifting Operations and Lifting Equipment Regulations 1998

2.11 The Regulations impose duties on employers, self-employed persons and certain people having control of lifting equipment to ensure that the equipment is strong, stable, positioned and installed correctly, examined, inspected, marked and organised and in respect of which records are held.

2.12 The client, who may also be an employer, will rely upon the architect to advise him whether and what assessments are required and the hazards which must be identified in the workplace. He will also rely upon the architect to advise him how to avoid any such hazards and thereby to avoid any potential liability under the Regulations. If the client is a developer who has only a short-term interest in the building, then collateral warranties may be granted to a purchaser or tenant who is to occupy the building or a unit of the building. If the purchaser or tenant is an employer and is found subsequently to be in breach of the Regulations it is arguable that unless the architect has, at least, advised on compliance with the Regulations and how best to design in order to ensure compliance, then an indemnity and or damages could be sought. Such an indemnity could be in respect of the defence costs associated with a criminal prosecution or in respect of compensation paid out to employees.

Management of Health and Safety at Work Regulations 1999

2.13 The basic obligation under these Regulations requires employers to carry out a 'suitable and sufficient' assessment of the risks to the health and safety of his employees to which they are exposed while at work. The assessment must also consider the risks to the health and safety of other people not in his employment but arising out of his business. The purpose of the assessment is to identify measures the employer needs to take to comply with law. From 27 October 2003 these Regulations enabled employees to bring civil claims against their employers where they are in breach of duties imposed by these Regulations. It will remain the case that it is not possible for non-employees to bring such civil claims. This right to bring civil claims will mean that a breach of the Regulations by architects, as employers, can give rise to civil liability without the need to prove negligence or even a breach of contract.

Control of Asbestos Regulations 2006

2.14 The CoAR replace the Control of Asbestos at Work Regulations 2002, the Asbestos (Licensing) Regulations 1983 and the Asbestos (Prohibitions) Regulations 1992, and came into force on 13 November 2006. These Regulations impose duties on persons with obligations in relation to non-domestic property, such as freehold owners, leaseholders and landlords. The client and architect must be fully aware of the duties these regulations impose. Even if the client is aware of his responsibilities he may turn to the architect for advice on the practical implications of the Regulations and how they can be complied with.

The Regulations impose a duty to manage asbestos in non-domestic premises, which is of considerable significance in construction and building maintenance. It goes further than the duty imposed by the CDM Regulations 2007 (which requires the provision of information to the CDM coordinator during the course of a project so that the presence of asbestos can be taken into account). The CoAR requires those people having control of non-domestic premises (the 'dutyholders') to make an assessment as to whether asbestos is likely to be present. The circumstances in which an architect will fall within the definition of a dutyholder is not clear. An architect will have 'control of non-domestic premises' in far more limited circumstances than, for example, the client. An architect will be a dutyholder in respect of the premises he operates from if there is, 'by virtue of a contract or tenancy, an obligation of any extent in relation to the maintenance or repair' of the premises. It is advisable for an architect expressly to avoid this role where possible.

If there is doubt as to the presence of asbestos, the dutyholder must work from the presumption that it is present, before making a 'suitable and sufficient assessment' of its presence. In making such an assessment, the dutyholder may need physically to inspect the building as well as examine building plans.

3 Construction (Design and Management) Regulations (CDM)

Background

3.01 The impetus for the CDM Regulations was the increasingly high level of fatal and non-fatal injuries to those working in the construction industry. Between 1 April 2006 and 31 March 2007 there were 77 fatal injuries to workers in construction in the U.K. In 1989 and 1990 the European Council of Ministers agreed to a Framework Directive on health and safety together with five other directives. The Temporary or Mobile Construction Sites Directive (Council Directive 92/57/EC) is a further directive under the Framework Directive and its aim is to limit accidents and injuries to construction workers. Construction sites were specifically excluded from the scope of the Workplace Directive and, hence, this separate measure covers a wide range of construction activities and requires separate implementing legislation in the UK.

Effect of the Regulations

3.02 Subject to very few exceptions, the Regulations relate to all aspects of construction and affect all those concerned in the construction process. Projects excluded from the regulations for CDM coordinators and principal contractors (not designers) are:

1 projects which are not expected to employ more than five persons on site at any one time; and
2 projects which will be no longer than 30 days or will involve no more than 500 person days of construction work.

Projects not excluded are known as 'notifiable' projects.

The CDM Regulations dramatically changed the previous allocations of responsibility for health and safety between contractors, clients and consultants. No longer is the contractor solely responsible for health and safety on site. The Regulations created two new roles within construction projects, namely the CDM coordinator (formerly the planning supervisor under the CDM Regulations 1994) and the principal contractor. They also impose specific obligations on designers to consider matters of safety in the execution of their designs and in the subsequent maintenance of the completed structure in subsequent years. The CDM Regulations 2007 have also widened the duties imposed on designers. The term 'designer' has been considered in the courts and has been refined by the revised Regulations. Consequently, it is now more important than ever for architects to know and understand the Regulations and what compliance entails. The CDM Regulations 2007 provide for notification of construction projects to the HSE together with a detailed consideration of all variations and financial considerations on safety throughout the duration of the project.

The CDM Regulations 2007 contain transitional provisions all of which have now passed. Supplementing the amended Regulations is a Revised Approved Code of Practice ('ACoP') called 'Managing Health and Safety in Construction'. The ACoP is published by the HSE and it gives practical examples of how the Regulations are intended to bite. Parts of the ACoP (those parts in bold type) have special legal status; if an architect is prosecuted for breaching health and safety law and it is proved that he has not complied with the parts of the ACoP with the special status, then he will be held to be at fault unless he can show compliance with the law in some other way. Compliance with the ACoP effectively gives rise to a presumption of compliance with the law.

In order to assess the effect of the revised Regulations and ACoP upon architects, it is simpler to consider the impact they have at the various stages in a normal project plan.

Appointment of CDM coordinator

3.03 Where a project is notifiable, the client has an obligation to appoint a CDM coordinator (previously known as the 'planning supervisor' under the CDM Regulations 1994) who has responsibility for the health and safety aspects of the planning phase. The CMD coordinator must monitor the health and safety aspects of the design, advise the client on the adequacy of resource provision for the project, verify that changes to the proposals contained in the tender by the principal contractor, take account of health and safety matters and prepare a health and safety file (basically a maintenance manual with health and safety matters specifically noted). It is expected that the lead designer would normally be appointed by the client as the CDM coordinator in the majority of projects. The CDM coordinator's appointment must be in writing, and the CDM coordinator has a duty under the CDM Regulations 2007 to notify the HSE of his appointment. The effect on the architect where the project is notifiable is therefore twofold: to advise the client of his health and safety responsibilities (and specifically his obligation to appoint a CDM coordinator) and to assess and report to the client on the additional costs which the health and safety obligations will involve. Under the 1994 CDM Regulations the CDM coordinator (or planning supervisor as it was then known) was responsible for preparation of the health and safety plan setting out the overall arrangements for the safe operation of the project. This was renamed the 'construction phase plan' under the CDM Regulations 2007, and is now the responsibility of the principal contractor.

Scheme and detailed design

3.04 The CDM Regulations have two broad effects on the architect at this stage: the imposition of specific design obligations in relation to the safety of those who will be building, maintaining or repairing the structure; and the responsibility (if appointed) of the role of CDM coordinator for a range of health and safety functions.

Designer

3.05 The definition of 'designer' has been considered by the courts and consequently refined by the amended regulations. In the case of *R v Wurth* (2000) it was determined that the regulation which imposes requirements on designers only applied to the actual preparation of designs. To own, arrange to have prepared, or to approve a design did not amount to having 'prepared a design'. As a result of this case the Regulations were amended to ensure that in future 'designer' will include a designer's employee or other person who prepares a design for him. The definition will not, however, extend to an employer who supplies his employee to a designer. The amendment means that an architect must carefully monitor and supervise those people in his employ who are carrying out design work, as he will be held responsible for their errors.

The ACoP contains a large amount of guidance on the regulation which relates to designers. It clarifies the roles and responsibilities of designers and emphasises the importance of managing health and safety for the life of the project and beyond. It also includes key areas of the Management of Health and Safety at Work Regulations 1999 for ease of reference. Architects must also bear in mind that if they sub-contract design work they also have a duty under regulations 8 and 9 as to the competence of such sub-contractors. Architects should keep a copy of the ACoP close at hand because, as well as general guidance, it includes specific practical examples which will be of considerable assistance.

The designer's obligation is basically to design in such a way as to prevent construction workers from being exposed to risks to their health and safety. What this means in practice is not entirely clear, since construction is inherently risky, with hazards arising from a large number of potential sources, including feature of design, sequencing, coordination, methods of work, weather and lack of operative discipline or training. However, it is clear that designers will be under a duty to design in such a way as to reduce hazards by adhering to good practice (especially that described in the ACoP) taking into account the normal health and safety considerations in relation to hazards identified in current trade literature, and identifying hazards that are exceptional in the circumstances of the particular project and sequencing operations.

Risk analyses and hazard management are already conducted by those responsible for problematic designs (particularly in civil engineering projects) such as large atria, deep excavations or box girder bridges. However, since there are now a large number of construction activities which will be covered ranging from renovations and repair to demolition, and from excavation to maintenance, decoration and cleaning work, the impact on the UK architect is substantial.

Since the designer must integrate his designs with those of specialist sub-contractors, he must give much greater thought to ways of eliminating, reducing or at least controlling hazards, not just in the original design but also if and when variations are instructed during the contract. Specific examples are how heavy loads can be installed (e.g. beams in section) so as to avoid manual handling by construction workers of excessive loads. Other examples which raise obvious problems relate to the duty to design to avoid health and safety problems for those who maintain or clean the structure. Thus, the cleaning of windows or glass atria must be considered at the design stage, as must also the re-pointing of brickwork and the replacement of roof linings in years to come.

The designer also has an obligation to consider the requirements set out in the Workplace (Health, Safety and Welfare) Regulations 1992 (see paragraph 2.06). Regulation 11 of the CDM Regulations 2007 prohibits the designer from commencing work on a project until the client is aware of the requirements under those regulations, while where project is notifiable, the designer may not start any detailed design work on the project unless and until the CDM coordinator has been appointed (regulation 18).

CDM coordinator

3.06 Whether or not the architect is appointed as the CDM coordinator, he must be aware of this role and, if he is not so appointed, must work closely with the CDM coordinator to enable him to carry out his various duties. The first prosecution under the CDM Regulations (in 1996) was of an architectural practice, Taylor Young, who was convicted for failing to advise the client that a CDM coordinator needed to be appointed. The CDM coordinator's duties are set out in regulation 20 of the CDM Regulations 2007 and, briefly, are as follows:

1 Ensuring that designers have complied with their design obligations in relation to health and safety issues. This means a prompting and coordinating duty to ensure that the designs of the entire professional team have considered all the health and safety angles.
2 Liaising with the principal contractor regarding the information required to prepare the construction phase plan.
3 Compiling a health and safety file, focusing particularly on health and safety aspects of materials used together with design implications that will affect those who will be maintaining and cleaning the structure.

Production information and tender action

3.07 In any tender action, even if not appointed as the CDM coordinator, the architect will have a duty to consider a contractor's health and safety record and advise the client accordingly. The architect will be involved in contractor pre-selection, with one criterion being health and safety competence. Contractors will be requested to explain and justify their responses to health and safety requirements. A case on this particular area has highlighted the potential impact of the regulations, *General Building & Maintenance v Greenwich Borough Council,* The Times 9 March 1993. This case concerns public-sector work where Greenwich Borough Council invited tenders for repair and maintenance work on a stock of 34 000 dwellings. The estimated annual value of the contract was £12 million. The EC Public Procurement Regime therefore applied and when the local housing authority considered the 104 applications from contractors, it took into account their health and safety records as one of the factors used to short-list those to be invited to tender. One of the contractors who was rejected, General Building and Maintenance, alleged that the housing authority was in breach of the Public Procurement Rules in excluding them since there was no specific wording which allowed the authority to consider and exclude a contractor on the basis of its health and safety record. The judge, however, applied a purposive interpretation to the Rules and held that since the Treaty of Rome expressly stated the need to promote improved working conditions and prevent occupational accidents and diseases, it would be 'incomprehensible' to conclude that consideration of health and safety issues was forbidden by the Rules.

In the light of this case, UK architects should be aware of the high priority given to health and safety issues by public clients and, so it appears, by the courts as well.

It is the duty of the client under regulation 4(1) to appoint a 'competent' principal contractor. The client will rely largely upon his professional adviser in this respect, and if no enquiries are made as to the health and safety record, it may constitute breach of the Regulations. In addition, the client must ensure that there are adequate resources in terms of time and financial provision to give effect to health and safety measures. Architects must carefully consider these points when assessing tender documents before recommending merely the lowest tender bid. The specific duties of the principal contractor are to prepare and manage the construction phase plan to facilitate the carrying out of the project without risk to health and safety, as far as is reasonably possible. There is also a duty of consultation with the CDM coordinator, and of cooperation and consultation with workers.

Operations on site and completion

3.08 If the roles of CDM coordinator and architect are to be performed by the same person or firm (as is likely in the majority of cases) it is not difficult to conclude that the level of supervision required of the architect will be affected by his knowledge of the level of experience of the contractor and the risks and hazards identified in the health and safety plan. Thus, for instance, even if an experienced contractor is engaged it could be argued that the architect must be present on site to supervise at times of identified hazard. Failure to supervise at these times may constitute breach of appointment or, worse, may bring criminal sanctions following prosecution by the HSE. The Regulations do not, however, require the architect to dictate construction methods or to exercise a health and safety supervisory function over contractors as they carry out construction work. Thus, it is not intended that designers, for instance, should be required to prepare method statements or otherwise intrude into the contractor's domain.

Nevertheless, given that the nature of the architect's normal inspection duty and duty to warn of health and safety problems is dependent upon the circumstances of each project, the laying down of specific obligations by the Regulations is bound to have an effect upon that duty.

If a variation is requested, the architect's duty again is affected since, in relation to health and safety, the architect's role as designer means that he must consider the implications of variations and inform the CDM coordinator of any impact on health and safety. If the architect is appointed as the CDM coordinator for the project then he must discuss with the principal contractor as to how the variation could affect the health and safety plan and he must also advise the client on the adequacy of revised sums and time allowed to give effect to health and safety measures.

4 Relevant EU legislation

4.01 EC legislation on health and safety affects the construction industry's operation on site, in the design of buildings and civil engineering works and in the use of plant. In the UK existing legislation such as the Health and Safety at Work etc. Act 1974 already meets many of the requirements of the European directives.

Additional regulations under the 1974 Act have or will be issued to cover the remaining requirements as they come into force.

4.02 The fundamental directive is the Safety and Health of Workers at Work Directive 89/391/EC under which the Management of Health and Safety at Work Regulations 1992 (SI 1992 No. 2051) were implemented in the UK. The directive sets out the responsibilities of employers and employees for safety and health at work and provides for further directives covering specific areas. Directives made under that framework directive which are of particular relevance to the construction industry are:

1 **Safety and Health for the Workplace Directive 89/654/EC** The directive lays down minimum safety and health requirements relating to the design structure and maintenance of buildings.
2 **Use of Work Equipment Directive 89/655/EC** The directive which has been implemented in the UK by the Provision and Use of Work Equipment Regulations 1992 (SI 1992 No. 2932) requires employers to provide for the safe use and maintenance of 'work equipment' (defined as any machine, apparatus, tool or installation at work) and sets out minimum safety and health requirements relating to training and safe operating procedures.
3 **Use of Personal Protective Equipment Directive 89/656/EC and 89/686/EC** These directives have been implemented in the UK by the Personal Protective Equipment at Work Regulations 1992 (SI 1992 No. 2966) and the Personal Protective Equipment (EC Directive) Regulations 1992 (SI 1992 No. 3139). They set out minimum health and safety requirements for the use by workers of PPE in the workplace and set minimum standards designed to ensure the health and safety of users of PPE.
4 **Mobile Machinery and Lifting Equipment Directive 91/368/EC** The directive which was required to be in force by 1 January 1993 extends the scope of the Machinery Directive 89/392/EC laying down essential safety requirements for mobile machinery and lifting equipment such as dumpers and cranes used on construction sites. Both directives have been implemented in the UK by SI 1992 No. 2932, referred to above.
5 **The Construction Sites Directive 92/57/EC** This is the directive implementing the CDM Regulations, and lays down minimum safety and health requirements for temporary or mobile construction sites (defined as any construction site at which building or civil engineering works are carried out). It places particular responsibilities on 'project supervisors' who are 'any person responsible for the design and/or execution and/or supervision of the execution of a project acting on behalf of a client' (Article 2(d)) and would therefore include architects. Those responsibilities include:
   (a) Appointing one or more safety coordinators for safety and health matters for any construction site on which more than one contractor is present (Article 3(1)). The proper carrying out of the coordinators' duties is the responsibility of the project supervisor.
   (b) Ensuring that prior to the setting up of a construction site a 'safety and health plan' is drawn up in accordance with requirements set out in the directive (Article 3(2)).
   (c) In the case of construction sites on which work is scheduled to last longer than 30 working days and on which more than 20 workers are occupied simultaneously or on which the volume of work is scheduled to exceed 500 person days, communicating a 'prior notice' drawn up in accordance with the directive, to the competent authority (Article 3(3)).
   (d) Taking account of the general principles of prevention concerning safety and health contained in directive 89/391/EC (above) during the various stages of designing and preparing the project, in particular:
      (i) When architectural technical and/or organisational aspects are being decided, in order to plan the various items or stages of work which are to take place simultaneously or in succession.

(ii) When estimating the period required for completing such work or work stages. Account must also be taken each time this appears necessary of all safety and health plans drawn up or adjusted in accordance with requirements of the directive (Article 4).

Product Liability Directive 85/374/EEC and the Consumer Protection Act 1987

4.03 The Product Liability Directive 85/374, which was adopted on 25 July 1985, was required to be implemented throughout the EC by 30 July 1988. It has been implemented into UK law by the Consumer Protection Act 1987, Part I.

4.04 The directive introduces into every member state a system of strict liability (i.e. without the need to prove negligence) for death, personal injury and damage to private property resulting from defective products put into circulation after the date when the national law came into force (in the UK this is 1 March 1988). A 'product' is very widely defined under the Act (section 1(2)) as:

'any goods or electricity and . . . includes a product which is comprised in another product, whether by virtue of being a component part or raw material or otherwise'.

Goods are defined (section 45) as:

'substances, growing crops and things comprised in land by virtue of being attached to it . . .

It is clear therefore, that building products are covered by the Act and at first sight it might appear that buildings themselves and/or parts of buildings such as roofs or foundations are also covered.

4.05 However, by section 46(3) of the Act it is provided that:

'subject to subsection (4) below the performance of any contract by the erection of any building or structure on any land or by carrying out of any other building works shall be treated for the purpose of the Act as a supply of goods in so far as it involves the provision of any goods to any person by means of their incorporation into the building, structure or works'.

4.06 Subsection 4 provides in so far as is relevant:

'References in this Act to supplying goods shall not include references to supplying goods comprised in land where the supply is affected by the creation or disposal of an interest in land.'

In the case, therefore, of a builder building under a contract and who does not own the land on which he builds he may be liable as 'supplier' or 'producer' (see below) in respect of defective products supplied or produced by him and incorporated into the building whether by way of construction, alteration or repair and will not be liable as producer of the defective building itself or of its immovable parts such as foundations.

In the case of a speculative builder, however, who builds on his own land and then effects the supply of that building by the creation or disposal of an interest in land (e.g. by sale of the freehold or lease) the Act appears to leave him liable as *producer* of the defective building while exempting him from any liability as supplier of any defective product comprised within the building. It is submitted that that is not the case.

4.07 By section 1(1) of the Act it is provided that the Act must be construed to give effect to the directive.

It is clear from the Recitals and from Article 2 that the directive does not apply to 'immovables' and that buildings and probably parts of buildings fall within that term. It is submitted therefore that when the Act is properly construed to give effect to the directive it must follow that a speculative builder cannot be liable under it as producer of a defective house.

Similarly, neither in Article 3(6) (which renders a supplier of a defective product liable if he fails to identify its producer within a reasonable time) nor anywhere else in the directive is any exemption from liability accorded *to the supplier* where the supply is effected by the creation or disposal of an interest in land. It is submitted therefore that no distinction should be made between the liability of a speculative builder and a contract builder under the Act and indeed it is difficult to see in logic why there should be any.

4.08 The Act places primary liability on the 'producer' of the product who will normally be the manufacturer but may also be the product's importer into the EC where it has been manufactured outside the EC. Secondary liability is placed on the supplier of the goods in question where that supplier fails to identify within a reasonable time the person who sold the goods to him.

It may be a matter of importance therefore to know who in a given case is the 'producer' or 'supplier' of a building product for the purpose of the Act. There is as yet no authority on the matter but the following is put forward as a tentative answer:

1   **Where the building is erected by a speculative builder** The builder alone will be the 'supplier' in the first instance of the products incorporated into the building and may therefore be liable as such under the Act (i.e. where he fails to identify his supplier within a reasonable time). **H**e may also be liable as 'producer' of a product where he has given that product its 'essential characteristics' (see section 1(2)) (an example of such a product would be concrete where this is mixed by the contractor), or where he has imported that product into the EC.
2   **When the building is erected under a contract with the building owner** The contract builder's liability as 'producer' and 'supplier' of the building products he incorporates into the building he erects will normally be no different from that of the speculative builder. However, circumstances may arise, whether by express agreement or otherwise, where the contractor acts as agent for the building owner or his architect in the 'production' or 'supply' of the product in question. In that case the building owner or the architect would be liable as 'producer' or 'supplier' under the Act in the same way as the contractor would have been. Such cases outside express contract are, however, likely to be rare. In *Young & Marten Ltd v McManuschilds* [1986] AC 454, HL, it was held that even where a product was specified that could only be purchased from one source, the contractor purchasing it was liable to the building owner for breach of implied warranty of merchantable quality where the product proved to be defective. It was implicit in that decision that the contractor was not acting as the building owner's agent in making the purchase.

4.09 Even where the builder is not acting as the building owner's agent, he may well wish in future to seek an indemnity from the building owner in respect of any liability he may incur under the Act, particularly in respect of any latent defects in products specified by the architect. Similarly, the building owner will no doubt seek an indemnity in respect of such liability from his architect.

4.10 Where the builder has no choice in the product he purchases and where the exercise of reasonable skill and care on his part in the selection of that product is ineffective in ensuring that the product is of merchantable quality (as might well be the case where there is a design defect) it would seem reasonable that ultimate liability under the Act (when this cannot be passed on to the others) should fall on the architect who has chosen the product and who has had the best chance of assessing that product's quality. Such indemnity provisions may well become a common feature of building and architectural service contracts in the future.

5 Summary and practical considerations

5.01 As already indicated, there are three principal areas of potential liability for the architect in failing to comply with obligations relating to health and safety:

1   criminal prosecution with potentially unlimited fines, notably under new corporate manslaughter provisions;

2 civil action based on breach of statutory duty (in limited circumstances) or based upon the tort of negligence for injured workers; and

3 contractual claims where Regulations are incorporated into the appointment or referred to in a collateral warranty.

The following procedures should be considered by architects in order to take account of the potential liabilities in the following ways:

1 Seek to acquire the necessary information and training by way of professional courses and by absorbing the limited literature on the subject. In this respect the HSE have issued a number of publications, for example '*Managing for Health in Construction*', whilst a number of other publications available are written specifically from the designer's standpoint. The new ACoP is likely to be the most useful and up-to-date guidance document available to architects. Regular guidance notes are also published.

2 Review design management procedures. At the end of concept and scheme design, during detailed design and immediately before tender documents are prepared, architects are specifically building in 'breaks' to formally and systematically review whether health and safety matters have been considered as part of the design to reduce or control hazards. Those firms who are quality assured have less difficulty in introducing these reviews, since they would normally be part of a QA system which would allow them to trace records to confirm that the review has been carried out.

3 Liaise with professional indemnity insurers. Liability both as a designer and CDM coordinator (if this role were to be accepted) will be affected by the Regulations and so architects have found it necessary to check with their insurers whether their new potential liability would be covered. Generally (although every policy is subject to its own terms and conditions), insurers have confirmed that the liability would be insured provided the architect does not accept any general duty above that of reasonable skill, care and diligence. It seems unlikely that any criminal penalty received by an architect would be covered by insurance, although the defence costs of the architect may be covered in some cases, either in the general wording, or by way of specific endorsement.

4 Architects should avoid incorporating, without qualification, the Regulations or the Codes of Practice into their appointment. The consequence of this would be that any breach of the Regulations or Code would incur contractual claims for damages with the breach forming the ground for the action. If incorporation becomes unavoidable then any duty to comply with the Regulations or Code should be qualified by 'reasonable skill and care'. This is particularly important if collateral warranties are to be issued to funds, tenants or purchasers who may seek to claim an indemnity from the architect if held liable for damages in respect of personal injury to workers. These types of claims may well be limited by the extent to which such damage could have been reasonably foreseeable at the time of entering into the warranty.

5 If architects are to provide indicative designs for temporary work, where they foresee problems, then those designs should only comprise ideas to be adopted, if appropriate, by a contractor who is then responsible for their sufficiency and implementation. In addition, if site visits result in an architect noting serious infringements of the Regulations or Code then any report to the principal contractor or ultimately the Health and Safety Executive must be qualified to the extent that such professional inspections do not attract liability which is properly the responsibility of others. This should be recorded in correspondence at the time.

6 The Health and Safety Commission has set national targets for improving health and safety performance generally by 2010. Of relevance to architects and the construction industry generally will be its targets relating to the reduction of falls from height. Specifically in relation to the construction industry, targets relating to the reduction of fatal and major injuries and work-related ill health. These targets recognise the need to 'radically' improve health and safety performance in the industry.

7 Careful consideration should also be given to the Control of Asbestos Regulations 2006 and its ACoP, given the duty of cooperation in regulation 4(2) which is likely to extend to architects.

6 Health and safety law in Scotland*

6.01 The Health and Safety at Work Act 1974, and the aforementioned regulations, are all applicable to Scotland. Part III of the Health and Safety at Work Act 1974 amends the Building (Scotland) Act 1959. It should be noted that, in criminal matters, there is no appeal from a Scottish court to the House of Lords. Therefore, as the Health and Safety at Work Act 1974 is essentially enforced by means of criminal prosecution, there is scope for different interpretation and application of its provisions by the courts in Scotland. Even in civil court cases, where an appeal does lie to the House of Lords, as a result of the separate appellate structure occasionally the interpretation of substantive law can be different until matters are finally resolved by the supreme appellate forum.

Although there is provision in very rare circumstances for private prosecution, with these exceptions all prosecutions in Scotland are undertaken by the Crown. In health and safety prosecutions the Crown is advised by the Health and Safety Executive. The distinction between the Crown and the Health and Safety Executive in Scotland was emphasised in the case of *HM Advocate v Shell UK Ltd* 2003 SLT 1296. The Health and Safety Executive had carried out investigations in January 2001 and, on 19 December 2001, informed the respondents by letter that a report had been sent to the procurator fiscal. The respondents were not notified that they were to be prosecuted until the indictment containing the allegation was served on 4 March 2003. The question before the High Court of Justiciary was whether there had been unreasonable delay in commencing proceedings and whether the respondents' rights in terms of Article 6(1) of the European Convention on Human Rights had been breached thereby. The respondents argued that the appropriate starting point of the period which fell to be considered was the serving of the Executive's letter. The High Court held that the date of service of the indictment was the appropriate starting date for the period and that, accordingly, there had been no unreasonable delay. The court stated: 'The Executive is not a law enforcement service and has no power to institute or determine upon prosecution. In these circumstances, it is difficult to see how it could be characterised as an authority having the competence to notify a suspect that it is alleged that he has committed a criminal offence.'

On occasions, if supported by an authoritative expert witness, the High Court will be prepared to accept as evidence codes of practice not approved in terms of section 16 of the Health and Safety at Work Act 1974. In February 1996, the High Court on Appeal held that a sheriff was right to give effect to the British Standard Code of Practice of the Safe Use of Cranes after it had been spoken to by an inspector in the context of a criminal prosecution following the death of an employee at work.

6.02 In the context of civil liability, many regulations create statutory delicts and also assist in raising standards in industry; even regulations which do not create such statutory delicts, by raising standards, help create a common law delict if said standards are not reached. Scottish courts have been happy to consider the corresponding European directive, but have been cautious about giving weight to guidance issued by the Health and Safety Executive. From time to time, questions relating to the interpretation of UK regulations arise, which may require the court to look behind these to the terms of the original EC directive which the regulations seek to implement. In the recent Scottish case of *Spencer-Franks v Kellog Brown & Root Ltd* 2008 SLT 875 the House of Lords, on appeal, overturned the decision of the Inner House of the Court

---

*This section was written by Jim Murphie.

of Session where the latter had adopted a narrow, literal interpretation of the term 'work equipment' in terms of the UK Work Equipment Regulations. Lord Hoffmann, in allowing the pursuer's appeal, referred the House to the stated purpose of the EC Framework Directive 89/391/EEC and the subsequent Equipment Directive. As EC law is the higher law, UK implementing regulations must be interpreted in such a way as to give effect to the principles of the directive — if necessary, by adopting a purposive rather than literal approach.

One area of potential difficulty is the interaction between criminal prosecutions for breaches of the 1974 Act and civil claims for damages which involve a statutory health and safety element in the form of specific regulations. It is competent to plead, as evidence, a defender's criminal conviction under the Health and Safety at Work Act 1974 in the context of a civil court claim for damages. An example of this arose recently in the case *Slessor v Vetco Gray UK Ltd* 2007 SLT 400. The defenders maintained that, although they had pled guilty to failures to instruct employees properly and to have a safe system of work, this was not relevant to the civil case as the alleged breaches of the Provision and Use of Work Equipment Regulations 1998 related to the suitability of work equipment. Ultimately, the judge did not require to decide this matter in granting decree to the pursuer as, in her view, the Regulations were clearly breached notwithstanding the criminal conviction. Nevertheless, the case illustrates that the distinctions, and the interplay, between civil and criminal procedure require to be borne in mind in relation to civil claims which involve a statutory health and safety element.

The relationship between civil and criminal liability for health and safety breaches was recently brought into sharp focus in the European Court of Justice in *Case C-12 7/05 Commission v United Kingdom (2007 IRLR 720)* (See Murphie J., *In Defence of the Employer's Defence?* Scottish Law Gazette, 2007 vol 75 (6) 208). The Commission alleged that the UK had failed to transpose correctly Article 5(1) of the Framework Directive Health and Safety 89/391/EEC into national law. Article 5(1) provides that *'the employer shall have a duty to ensure the safety and health of workers in every aspect related to the work'*. This provision is qualified by Article 5(4) which provides that *'where occurrences are due to unusual and unforeseeable circumstances, beyond the employer's control, or to exceptional events, the consequences of which could not have been avoided despite the exercise of all*

due care'. The alleged failure of the UK related specifically to the 'so far as is reasonably practicable' defence provided by section 2(1) of the Health and Safety at Work Act 1974. One of the Commission's principal complaints was that the provision of this defence apparently diluted employers' liability for their employees' injury or damage under civil law, in breach of the directive's aims. However, the UK Government's response was that criminal law and procedure had been specifically selected in order to give optimum effect to the Directive's aims. The UK pointed out that the 1974 Act was a criminal law statute, and that it did not affect the civil obligations of employers or employees, either under statute or at common law.

Site Waste Management Plans (SWMP) Regulations 2008

And finally . . . architects should be aware of a recently established scheme which follows very closely the model of the CDM Regulations: namely the Site Waste Management Plans Regulations 2008. These have an indirect relationship to health and safety (certainly in respect of low level hazardous waste) but are primarily intended to make construction activities far more efficient when it comes to dealing with waste on site. Under the SWMP Regulations (which came into force in England – note not Wales or Scotland – in April 2008) the client is again responsible for appointing a principal contractor to monitor and co-ordinate a site waste management plan. The plan itself must be in place *before* construction takes place and if this and certain other express requirements are not complied with the Environment Agency will prosecute and the criminal offence is punishable by a fine. The regulations apply only for construction activities costing over £300,000 and there are more detailed requirements for those which cost over £500,000. The requirement for the plan: detailing the activities to minimise waste, the types and quantities of waste (eg excavation/demolition), and the destination for that waste, together with the person dealing with it, is an onerous task and architects will be asked to advise on those aspects. The principal contractor must confirm within 3 months of completion that the plan has been monitored and up-dated throughout the course of the project and it must be retained for at least two years following completion.

Part C

Building contracts

16

Introduction to procurement methods in construction

JOHN SALWAY

1 Introduction

1.01 Selecting the most appropriate procurement strategy for a construction project of any significant size is unlikely to be as straightforward as many might think. The aim should be to provide a suitable contractual framework which at the very least takes into account the *complexity* of the project, the *expertise* of the procuring party and the *commercial drivers* behind the project. But, of course, there is a huge range of construction projects and, as a result, many different ways of procuring construction works and services have developed.

2 Complexity

2.01 Construction projects range from the very small and simple (e.g. those where sole traders carry out relatively straightforward extension works for a residential occupiers); to the very large and complicated (e.g. huge, complex, state-sponsored, infrastructure projects involving multiple parties which utilise innovative design and advanced engineering). The former can often be procured using a simple contract; the latter most certainly cannot and are more likely to be procured using a great many inter-related contracts providing for the roles and responsibilities of the parties involved.

2.02 Where the project is large, complicated or requiring innovation, there is likely to be a commensurate increase in the complexity of the procurement. There are likely to be more interested parties, including funders, client, tenants, multiple specialist contractors and consultants, all of whose positions will need to be taken into account in the contractual matrix. In such circumstances it is inevitable that the procurement method will need to be sophisticated enough to provide for multiple, often competing, interests.

2.03 Providing for the risks inherent because of the complexities of the project will also be required. For example, there will be specific risks in the construction of a rail system under a city centre, e.g. risks such as those associated with different ground conditions, access to the sites, land acquisition and obtaining planning consents. In the process engineering sector there are likely to be demanding performance specifications to meet and liabilities associated with not being able to meet such specifications. Therefore on a project of any significant size or complexity the many issues and risks will be given to various parties to manage and bear responsibility for. All these roles will need to be described and the interactions and interfaces between the parties provided for in the project contracts.

3 Clients' expertise

3.01 Construction projects often feature experienced clients whose business is very much about construction, e.g. government departments or major developers. However, at the other end of the spectrum, construction projects are frequently procured by 'one-off procurers' with no previous experience, e.g. major sports clubs developing new stadia. The relative level of the client's experience will be an important factor in the selection of the procurement approach. As well as experience, the paying party's attitude to risk and the level of responsibility it wishes to retain will be relevant to the suitability of any procurement method. This attitude to risk is often directly related to the client's expertise. For example, an experienced client may be prepared to take a more 'hands on' approach to a project and carry more of the risk, with the aim of reducing the price to be paid. Certain procurement methods lend themselves to such an approach better than others. Similarly, there are other approaches which can be adopted to insulate an inexperienced or risk averse client from responsibility and risk.

3.02 While a professional client experienced in construction projects may be willing to take on more responsibility, a 'one-off' client is likely to look for a contractual arrangement which places as much responsibility and risk with the delivery team as possible. There are many different procurement models which can achieve this to a greater or lesser extent, and the final choice of route won't be governed by this consideration alone – many other factors will come into play.

3.03 A further relevant question will be whether even the experienced client has the internal resources to manage the project or whether a third party will need to be appointed to perform the management function on the client's behalf. A client who wishes to retain control of the project will have to be prepared to allocate the time or in-house expertise to manage the project. It may be more appropriate for a client that does not have the necessary expertise or resources to relinquish a degree of control and appoint an experienced professional to perform the traditional client role. Among all these questions, one thing is for sure: management of a construction project will be key to its success and a failure to recognise this will have a significant impact.

4 Commercial drivers

4.01 One also needs to consider the commercial drivers of a project and the fact that most clients and other stakeholders will want a high-quality project completed as quickly and cheaply as possible. Sadly, however, this 'holy trinity' of high quality, high speed and low price are fundamentally incompatible. Procurement in construction is often therefore about finding the right balance between these objectives. A decision has to be taken as to the prioritisation and balance of this trinity. Questions need to be put and answers sought. More often than not, in the commercial world, the answers come from a cold, financial calculation: does it make financial sense to pay more for a construction if it means an earlier completion date and therefore an earlier income stream? Does it follow that paying more for a state-of-the-art design means that higher rents can be commanded as a result? These sorts of commercial drivers will have an impact on the chosen procurement method. Some procurement methods are better suited to getting a project to an early start on site and therefore an earlier finish, while others are designed to engage all parties together to ensure a high-quality product – perhaps at the expense of speed.

4.02 It can be seen, then, that the question of which procurement method should be chosen is often a complicated equation involving the consideration of such things as the size and complexity of the project, the client's experience and attitude towards risk, and the tension between the three client objectives of high quality, speed to completion and low price. When one factors in the plethora of other relevant considerations, it is not surprising that the choice of procurement route is seldom an easy one to make. Nor is it surprising that history is littered with examples of where the procurement choice made for a project turned out to be the wrong one, resulting in it being a painful experience for at least some of the participants.

5 Other factors affecting choice of procurement method

Design responsibility

5.01 The question of who is to take responsibility for the design of the project is fundamental. The 'traditional' approach to construction is to engage an architect to design a building and then appoint a building contractor to construct in accordance with the architect's completed design. Where a project is to be designed by an architect in this way, the contractor can be brought on board at a later stage and then merely employed to build to the specification or employer's requirements. The works are therefore designed as the first stage, and thereafter the client tenders for contractors to carry out the works according to the design. This arrangement can be perceived to have advantages for the client, most notably in terms of control of costs. It ought to be easier for contractors to price works accurately if their tender is based on a completed design. However, the result is that there are several points of responsibility and a need to manage the relationship between the professional team and the building contractor. This is sometimes viewed as placing an onerous burden on the client and there may be a risk of responsibilities for build issues 'falling between the cracks' and remaining with the client.

5.02 The other extreme is to hand the entire design and build obligation to a contractor who is then engaged to carry out the works to accord with a relatively brief statement of the employer's requirements. In reality, most building contracts today represent a 'hybrid' of the two approaches whereby an architect is initially employed to work up the design of the project on the client's behalf and the contractor is then required to develop the design or to design discrete, specialist parts of it, before the architect's appointment is transferred to the design and build contractor who then takes on responsibility for the whole of the design and build. The theory here is that the contractor has a far clearer picture of what he is required to build than with the traditional approach, before becoming solely responsible to the client for doing so.

Funding

5.03 The impact and influence of funders on the choice of procurement route should not be underestimated and it is usually prudent to get the funder's views as early as possible.

5.04 The client's objectives will be numerous and competing, whereas a funder's only real concerns are the protection of his financial stake and the return on his investment. A funder is likely therefore to want the security of knowing that the design will be complete at an early stage so that variations to the works are going to be limited and therefore initial pricing is more accurate. He will also be looking to have direct contracts with key participants in the design and construction of the project, and rights to step into the shoes of the client in circumstances where there may be uncertainty as to the client's ability to complete the procurement of the project in question. This will inevitably add layers of complexity to a procurement as the funder's rights vis à vis the project participants need to be enshrined in direct agreements and other security instruments.

Ability to change design

5.05 The question of whether and the extent to which the design should be allowed to change during the construction phase is an important factor in choosing the correct procurement route because of the consequential impact this is likely to have on cost and time to completion. Where the design is not complete before the construction works are commenced, clearly, a procurement route that is flexible enough to allow for changes to the design is required. The same is true where the nature of the site may determine whether design changes are required as the project progresses. For example, works to existing buildings often uncover features that were not known at the original design stage and which will result in necessary changes to the design.

How important is a fixed price?

5.06 The importance to the client of obtaining a fixed price from the contractor will depend on the client's ability to pay for any price increases and/or a funder's willingness or otherwise to back a project where the price is uncertain. Other factors (such as completion by a certain date) may take priority, in which case the client may be prepared to pay more to achieve this.

5.07 For price certainty, a client should be looking to issue a tender package which specifies the works in terms of quality and quantity at tender stage. However, in practice, while most clients require some element of price certainty, it must be recognised that unless the scope of works is very accurately defined and the risks of the project are minimal and predictable, it is unlikely to be the case that any price is absolutely guaranteed. It is more likely to be the case that a tight specification allows the selection of a procurement route which provides for the price to alter only pursuant to the operation of very limited, specific provisions of the contract.

5.08 It may also be the case that scope and risks are far from clear at the outset, in which case a client is going to have to accept that he is likely to have to pay the outturn cost plus margin. For example, this may be the case where urgent work, such as repairs after fire or water damage, are required and where the scope of the work cannot be ascertained until the work has been commenced.

How important is time for completion?

5.09 For some clients, an early completion is key, e.g. where the financial gains to be had are greater, the earlier the project is completed. In such circumstances the contract may provide that the contractor is incentivised to work efficiently either by 'carrot' or 'stick', or both, i.e. by way of bonus payments for early completion and/or damages for late completion.

6 Procurement options

Traditional

6.01 The traditional procurement route, as its name suggests, was, until relatively recent times, the most widely used in the UK. As touched on above, at its most basic the traditional route is where the client appoints an architect to carry out the design. Once the design is complete, the client tenders for a contractor to carry out the works and appoints the other members of the professional team. The main contractor will then often sub-contract the works, particularly specialist works. The client will have a direct contractual relationship with the main contractor and all of the professionals. The client will usually enter into direct contractual relationships with key sub-contractors under separate collateral warranties or direct agreements to provide it with direct rights against those sub-contractors.

6.02 This method can be suitable for all clients, experienced or otherwise. As the design is fixed at an early stage it gives the client some degree of certainty as to price. Tenders are priced on a fixed design and can therefore be required to be lump sum/fixed price.

6.03 It is also the case that because the contractor is working to a completed design this should lead to a greater chance of the contractor being able to complete to time. It is also suggested that the employer and the architect should be able to work closely together to arrive at designs which mirror the client's precise requirements which can then be implemented by a contractor closely supervised by the architect, thereby resulting in better quality. This is perhaps rather simplistic, however, as it is often the case in complex projects that the early involvement of the contractor and the specialists is desirable in order to benefit from their expertise to consider 'buildability' and other issues with design.

6.04 Disadvantages with traditional procurement include the fact that work will not start on site until the design is finalised and this potentially increases the length of time taken from inception of the project through to completion. Another potential issue is that there is no single point of responsibility for the client when issues arise. The two-stage process can mean that the lines of responsibility can become blurred. This is particularly so where the contractor undertakes elements of the design. The lack of communication and the fact that the design team and the construction team approach the project from a different professional perspective can also hinder smooth running of the project. This is because the contractor is arguably not on board sufficiently early to advise on the buildability of the architect's design. There can be arguments from the construction team that the design is not adequate or complete and therefore the contractor may say he has been prevented from completing the works as required. In the event of a dispute it may be difficult to determine which party, designer or contractor, is responsible.

Design and build

6.05 As mentioned above in design and build contracts the contractor carries out (or is at least responsible for) both the design and the construction works. As a result, an increasing number of large contracting firms have developed their own internal design capability.

6.06 Commonly the client will have prepared a basic design or outline specification (or appointed an architect to do so) and this will be given to the contractor to develop. The client will put together the employer's requirements setting out the basic design requirements and the contractor will prepare the contractor's proposals incorporating those requirements. In the building contract the contractor will take responsibility for the design and for ensuring it meets the client's requirements. Often the client will appoint the professional team and these appointments will be novated to the contractor once it is on board.

6.07 While the administrative burden of novating the professionals and providing warranties from the professionals back to the client is seen as a disadvantage of this procurement route, it does mean that the contractor becomes the client's single point of responsibility to the client in respect of the design and the construction, while the contractor has a direct contractual route to the professionals

should he need to pass down liability for any negligence on their part. Thus the client's recourse in the event of any defect in either the design or the works will be against the contractor. It is then up to the contractor to recover further down the contractual chain where appropriate. The client will also have the benefit of collateral warranties in its favour from the professionals in case it is in need of a direct relationship, e.g. where the contractor becomes insolvent.

6.08 Some have said that contractors approach design from a different perspective from an architect, putting cost above aesthetics and as a result design and build projects are largely uninspiring. In defiance of this view design and build has grown in popularity as a procurement route since it was originally used in the 1980s by the public sector. It is undeniably suitable for projects where aesthetics are not an issue and has been found to work well on repeat projects.

Two-stage tendering

6.09 This approach is used where the time from inception to completion needs to be short – something which is a major downfall of the traditional route. While there are a variety of ways of going about this it usually involves appointing at the first stage through a competitive tender a preferred contractor. The tender usually requires certain deliverables, e.g. including a construction programme and method statement, preliminaries prices and overheads and profit margins. There may also be required lump sums for pre-construction services and design fees.

6.10 The second stage is a negotiation over time between the employer and the preferred contractor as the scope becomes clearer, with a view to arriving at fixed prices for the works. The element of competition is meant to be maintained by the fact that the other original first-stage tenderers remain willing and able to step in to pick up the main second-stage works packages.

6.11 The theory is that the design process can overlap with the construction works meaning that the construction phase should be shorter. The involvement of the contractor at an early stage also ought to result in a better understanding of the project among the parties. The contractor is available during the design stage to advise on buildability of the architect's design. However, given that the tenderers are narrowed down (usually to one) following the first stage, there is less competition during the second stage and this may mean that the client does not achieve the best price.

Construction management

6.12 In the construction management procurement route the client contracts with all the parties directly, including with the construction manager. The construction manager manages the project on the client's behalf and his role includes overseeing the placement of contracts between the client and the other professionals and the contractor(s) for the provision of works and services.

6.13 The construction manager administers the appointments and the trade contracts for the client. His only role is this management role. He does not carry out any of the other services, and is therefore only responsible to the client for the performance of the construction management services, for which he is likely to charge a fee. If there is a problem with any of the other works and services then the client needs to look to his other direct contracts, albeit it is likely to be one of the construction manager's services to assist the client in the conduct of any disputes.

6.14 Some advantages of this method are said to be speed as design and works can move forward in parallel and flexibility allowing the construction manager to drive up quality for the client. On the flip side there is inherent uncertainty as to time for completion and price, and there may also be difficulties for the client in identifying the responsible party where the project goes awry.

Management contracting

6.15 With management contracting the client appoints the designers. The management contractor then lets the works to various works contractors. The management contractor is paid a fixed fee plus the prime cost of his on-site management staff and of the works contractors. It enables a quick start on site as the design need not be particularly detailed when the management contractor is engaged. It also tends to promote a speedy completion as the management contractor should be able to effect very good supervision and management of the works on site and the contract may contain incentives to him to secure early completion. This advantage is derived from the fact that the contractor is involved from an early stage, working with the design team and developing the programme.

6.16 The management contractor's relationship with the client is that of a consultant rather than a contractor. While letting works packages as and when required by the programme can speed up the process, the price is subject to adjustment until all packages have been let, meaning price certainty for the client can come at a late stage.

Partnering/framework agreements

6.17 Under a framework agreement the client engages a supplier that it intends to appoint in connection with a number of projects over a period of time. The framework agreement sets out the principle terms and conditions and then the client can simply call off each project without the need to re-tender. The call-off of each project may be no more than a simple purchase order as the detail is already agreed in the framework. There is usually no guarantee as to the volume of work and no obligation to instruct any works whatsoever.

6.18 As well as reducing tendering costs, the purpose of framework arrangements is to encourage construction teams to stay together from project to project and make the most of what they have learned from working together on a number of similar projects.

6.19 The framework agreement approach typically promotes 'partnering' and collaboration by including provisions designed to encourage the parties to work together in a manner requiring openness and a spirit of mutual trust and respect. This idea rather obviously only works well where all parties buy into the ethos.

PFI/PPP

6.20 Public Private Partnerships (PPP) is a programme where private-sector resources are used to deliver services that were traditionally provided by the public sector. In 1992 the UK Government introduced the Private Finance Initiative (PFI) to encourage private-sector businesses to engage in the finance and management of public infrastructure. PFI has been used to procure a large number of projects across a range of sectors, including the transport, energy and health sectors.

6.21 There are certain advantages of using the private sector in the construction of public infrastructure. As governments face pressure to control their spending, PFI enables private-sector money to be utilised to ensure successfully funded developments. Involving private-sector management skills is also perceived to increase the likelihood of discipline, efficiency and innovation in a project. The usual PFI structure involves the provision of the capital asset by the private sector in return for a long-term operating and maintenance contract for the public sector, usually for 25 or 30 years.

6.22 The awarding authority, typically a government body, is the party who owns the site at which the project will take place and who will therefore seek to procure works and services from the private sector. In a typical project, a company formed solely for the purpose of the project, called a special purchase vehicle (SPV) will contract with the authority. The SPV will be a 'shell' company with few assets of its own owned by several parties which may include the contractor. The SPV will sub-contract the construction

works for the project to a contractor. For ongoing services, the SPV will sub-contract to a facilities management contractor. A lender will provide capital for the project through the construction phase and on completion the authority will pay unitary charges for use of the completed infrastructure.

6.23 The authority and the SPV will enter into a project agreement which will set out details of the project, the SPV's obligations and objectives and which party takes on the various risks associated with the project. The building contract between the SPV and contractor will mirror certain provisions of the project agreement so that liability for construction works will be passed from the SPV to the building contractor. Similarly, the operating agreement will pass liability for the operation of the project to the facilities management contractor and will also mirror related provisions of the project contract. There will be several documents relating to financing the project. The project will usually be financed by way of a loan governed by a facility agreement between the SPV and the lender setting out the terms and conditions.

7 Some pricing mechanisms

Lump sum/fixed price

7.01 In a lump-sum or fixed price contract, the price is determined before the works start on site and the agreed amount is written into the contract. This is subject to change only where there are variations instructed or where events occur which are at the client's risk and which give rise to a right to additional payment. It is an approach which is suitable where the scope of works is well developed at the time of contracting.

Measurement contracts

7.02 A measurement contract might be selected by a client who needs an early start on site at the expense of price certainty. In such contracts the contractor usually gives rates and prices for labour and materials against an indicative bill of quantities in order to give an indication of the likely final price for the client. However, the price ultimately paid is assessed by measuring the amount of the actual work done on the basis of the rates provided and agreed.

7.03 In extreme circumstances a measurement contract may be based on drawings and schedules of rates where there is not sufficient time to prepare even an approximate bill of quantities. This exposes the client to the risk of price uncertainty and for that reason is rarely recommended.

7.04 In recent times measurement contracts have been developed to include **target cost** mechanisms where contractors are incentivised by cost-saving sharing provisions to drive down costs below targets and also by sharing cost overruns where targets are exceeded.

Cost reimbursable/prime cost

7.05 This type of contract is again used mainly where a quick start on site is required and the design is not sufficiently developed to allow the contractor to price the works. The contractor will be paid the prime cost or actual cost of labour, plant and materials. The contractor is also paid an additional fee for carrying out the works. This can be a fixed percentage fee tendered by the contractor which is applied to the actual cost or a variable fee. A variable fee will usually be some form of target fee where the contractor benefits from keeping the prime cost down, thereby discouraging inefficiency.

8 Which contract?

8.01 The decision as to which procurement route to use will naturally lead to a decision as to which contract to select. While professional appointments, warranties and other related contracts are often bespoke documents, the building contract itself is usually based on one of the industry standard forms of which there are many including those in the Joint Contracts Tribunal (JCT) and the New Engineering Contract (NEC) suites, the two suites of contract most often used in the UK. Each drafting body issues traditional, design and build, framework, construction management and management contracting editions with numerous different pricing approaches.

8.02 There is a tendency in the industry for parties to favour a particular form, or at least a particular edition of that form. This is not entirely unreasonable as it is crucial that the parties understand the contract they are using and how it operates. If a decision is taken to switch forms without any education, the reality on site may well be that the contract will be administered incorrectly. It is, however, sensible to consider carefully which form of contract will best meet the competing considerations that will be relevant to the project. For example, it would be wholly inappropriate to propose the use of the NEC Option A contract (which is a fixed-price contract by reference to an activity schedule) where the parties have never used the NEC contract before, a prompt start on site is of the utmost importance and the scope of works is far from clear.

9 Conclusion

9.01 Often a client or contractor will favour a particular form of contract. A decision will be taken about which form is used and the parties work backwards from that to determine the procurement route. While familiarity with a contract form has its advantages, it is fundamental to the success of a project that the parties take a step back and ask some basic questions about what the client is trying to achieve.

9.02 A failure to recognise the significance to the client of a demanding specification or completing on time or keeping to the budget can mean that the contract chosen does not adequately provide a mechanism for achieving those objectives.

9.03 A design and build contract, for example, will mean that there is a single point of responsibility for both the design and the constructions of the works which may be considered to be a good thing until the client who requires flexibility for late design changes realises that he has little scope for varying the works except at great cost. Similarly, the traditional procurement route may allow the contractor to price accurately but this is very likely to increase the time from inception to completion of the project. This isn't necessarily going to be a good thing for a developer with tenants waiting to take occupation.

9.04 Time spent considering the options and in making the right choice of procurement route is likely to save time and cost in the long run. It might even lead to a procurement tool being selected that gives a better chance of the project being of high quality.

17

The JCT Standard Form of Building Contract, 2005 edition

ALLEN DYER*

The text discussed in this chapter is that of the Standard Building Contract With Quantities 2005 edition, which is for the first time suitable for use by both private and local authority employers. Amendment 1 was issued in April 2007, and incorporated in Revision 1 published in June 2007. Revision 2 was published in May 2009; the principal changes it makes relate to:

1 Simplification of the payment provisions, in particular payments following practical completion.
2 The introduction of additional provisions which reflect the Achieving Excellence in Construction principles adopted by the Office of Government Commerce; this has resulted in the addition of the Seventh and Eighth Recitals to the Articles of Agreement (the existing Recitals being renumbered) and the inclusion of Supplemental Provisions in Schedule 8 of the Contract.
3 New provisions acknowledging the increasing importance of sustainability in construction projects.

This chapter is a commentary on the text of the Standard Building Contract following Revision 2, which is also the text of the contract clauses which are here set out in full. Many fewer clauses have been included than in previous editions, concentrating upon those considered to be of particular relevance to architects.

The current edition is the product of a significant exercise in re-ordering the 1998 edition of the contract, with a beneficial effect on the logic of its layout. Although the commentary below remains relevant to the 1998 edition, most of its clauses are now to be found in different locations within the 2005 edition. Considerable care should, of course, be taken to ensure that the wording of the clause is identical when considering any case law applying to earlier editions.

1 Articles of Agreement

1.01 The first part of the form, which contains the Articles of Agreement, has four elements: the front page, the Recitals, the Articles and the Contract Particulars. Their purpose is to establish the fundamental terms of the contract. The front page, when completed, identifies the parties and the date upon which the contract is made. The Recitals (the twelve statements commencing with the word 'Whereas') record the nature of the intended works, identify the documents in which those works are described (the Bills of Quantities and Contract Drawings) and provide for the Activity

*In early editions this chapter was written by the late Donald Keating QC, who gave permission for his text to be used as the basis for the chapter in subsequent editions.

Schedule and the Information Release Schedule as options after their introduction as contractual documents in the 1998 edition. They also, for the first time, provide for a Contractor's Designed Portion of the intended works if applicable.

It is important that the particular set of drawings which are intended to comprise the Contract Drawings are properly identified, and, where there is a Contractor's Designed Portion, that the documents comprising the Employer's Requirements and the Contractor's Proposals are also properly identified and are checked for inconsistencies. Last minute changes often occur and care should be taken to ensure that the documentation is correct when the contract is executed.

1.02 The Articles state shortly the substance of the parties' agreement. Articles 1 and 2 define the basic contractual obligations of the parties. The contractor agrees to carry out and complete the works in compliance with the Contract Documents (defined in clause 1.1 as the Contract Drawings, the Contract Bills, the Articles of Agreement, the Conditions and (where applicable) the Employer's Requirements, the Contractor's Proposals and the Contractor's Designed Portion Analysis). The employer, in consideration, agrees to pay the contractor the Contract Sum at the times and in the manner specified in the conditions. These Articles provide the bedrock for the remainder of the contract: they identify the contract as a lump-sum contract, with the contractor being paid in accordance with the issue of Architect's Certificates (see clauses 4.9 to 4.15).

1.03 Article 3 identifies the Architect or Contract Administrator. The inclusion of the latter term is new, but its use would not appear to introduce any substantial difference. In this chapter the term 'the Architect' will be used to describe both functions. Article 4 identifies the Quantity Surveyor, and Articles 5 and 6 the CDM Co-ordinator and Principal Contractor for the purposes of the CDM Regulations, if they are other than the Architect and the contractor.

1.04 Clause 3.5.1 requires that if either the Architect/Contract Administrator or the Quantity Surveyor cease to hold their contractual post, the employer comes under a duty to appoint another, and, if he fails to do so, he will be in breach of contract. The employer is required to nominate a replacement as soon as reasonably practicable and in any event within 21 days. The contractor normally has a right to object to the nominee within 7 days. If he chooses to do so a contractual dispute resolution procedure applies. Any replacement Architect is bound by final decisions of his predecessor.

1.05 Articles 7, 8 and 9 contain dispute resolution procedures. Under Article 7 either party has the right to refer any dispute or

difference arising under the contract to adjudication, to which the rules of the statutory Scheme for Construction Contracts will apply (with certain variations). This is a change from the 1998 edition, which required the parties and the adjudicator to execute the JCT Adjudication Agreement.

1.06 Paragraph 8 of the Supplemental Provisions which are found in Schedule 8 to the Conditions, and which incorporate the Achieving Excellence in Construction principles, provides an alternative dispute resolution procedure of direct, good faith negotiations between senior executives of each party who are named in the Contract Particulars. This procedure is, as it must be, subject to either party's right to refer any dispute to adjudication at any time.

1.07 The arbitration agreement is contained in Article 8, if the parties elect to apply it, in which case they must make a positive election in the Contract Particulars. The application of the arbitration procedure is subject to the unfettered right to refer to adjudication. If applied, disputes arising out of or in connection with the contract may be referred to arbitration in accordance with clauses 9.3 to 9.8 of the 2005 edition of the CIMAR rules, subject to certain exceptions. The wording of the arbitration clause has been widened to encompass disputes '*arising out of or in connection*

with the contract' following the decision of the House of Lords in *Fiona Trust v Privalov* [2007] UKHL 40.

1.08 The main exception is that matters in connection with the enforcement of decisions of an adjudicator cannot be referred to arbitration. Disputes under or in respect of the Construction Industry Scheme or VAT are also excluded from the arbitration provisions. The object of these exclusions is clear: statute provides alternative methods of resolving disputes relating to these matters.

1.09 If legal proceedings are brought against a party, that party may apply to stay those proceedings insofar as their subject-matter is covered by a valid arbitration clause. It must make the application before taking any step in the proceedings to answer the substantive claim, but should first acknowledge service of those proceedings. The court *must* then stay the proceedings – it has no discretion (see section 9(4) of the Arbitration Act 1996).

1.10 Article 9 provides for the English courts otherwise to have jurisdiction over any dispute or difference between the parties arising out of or in connection with the contract. This marks a change from the 1998 edition, in which arbitration was the default provision.

Contract Particulars

1.11 There follow the Contract Particulars, which were entitled 'Appendix' in the 1998 edition and there followed rather than preceded the contractual conditions. The Contract Particulars are divided into two – Part 1: General and Part 2: Third Party Rights and Collateral Warranties. Part 2 is new, and, in conjunction with Section 7 of and Schedule 5 to the Conditions, enables the grant of third party rights to named or identified purchasers, tenants and funders, as did the JCT Collateral Warranty forms used with the 1998 edition.

1.12 Architects should ensure that the Contract Particulars are carefully completed. It is not unknown for this to be overlooked. Care should be taken to follow the format and instructions. In *Temloc v Errill Properties* (1987) 39 BLR 30 an entry of the word 'nil' was made in respect of liquidated damages. Did this mean that there were to be no damages for delay payable at all, no matter how late was completion? Or did it mean that damages for delay were not to be at a pre-agreed rate, but were left to be assessed, if they arose, on normal common law principles, namely to compensate for any actual loss which could be proved? The Court of Appeal held that it meant that there were to be no damages for delay at all. Obviously, parties should try to avoid creating uncertainties of this character.

1.13 The Articles conclude with a space for the appropriate attestation clause under hand or as a deed. If the contract is to be executed by an individual as a deed, following the Law of Property (Miscellaneous Provisions) Act 1989 there is no longer any requirement that it be executed under seal (although the use of a seal will not invalidate it). The instrument must make it clear on its face that it is intended to be a deed and must be signed by the individual in the presence of a witness who attests the signature (or if it is signed at the individual's direction in his presence it must be attested by two witnesses). Further, the instrument must be delivered as a deed by the signatory or by a person authorised to do so on his behalf. If the contract is to be executed by a company, the Companies Act 1989 provides that a document executed by a company which makes it clear on its face that it is intended to be a deed has effect upon delivery as a deed, and it is presumed to be delivered upon execution unless a contrary intention is proved. A document may be executed by a company by affixing its seal but, irrespective of whether or not the company has a seal, a document signed by a director and the secretary of the company or by two directors or by a single director whose signature is attested by a witness, and expressed to be executed by the company, has the same effect as if executed under the common seal of the company.

1.14 In deciding whether the agreement should be made as a deed or not, the key factor is that if it is made as a deed, the limitation period for bringing actions is 12 years from the date of the breach of contract (see section 8 of the Limitation Act 1980); otherwise it is 6 years (see section 5 of the Limitation Act 1980).

Conditions

2 Section 1: Definitions and Interpretation

2.01 The purpose of this section is to provide a list of definitions of the main terms used in the contract (clause 1.1), and a number of interpretation clauses (clauses 1.2 to 1.12). All listed definitions commence with capital letters and are of general application throughout the contract, whereas particular definitions applicable only to a particular section or clause are found in those particular locations. The following interpretation clauses are of particular significance.

2.02 Clause 1.6 excludes the effect of the Contracts (Rights of Third Parties) Act 1999, but the exclusion is now limited because of the inclusion of rights for purchasers, tenants and funders provided for by clauses 7A and 7B.

2.03 Clause 1.7 requires all notices and communications referred to in the contract to be in writing, and encourages the parties to agree a communications protocol as soon as possible to provide for their effective transmission. This is particularly important where there is a Contractor's Designed Portion. Key notices (relating to termination and to the grant of third party rights) are required to be hand delivered or sent by recorded or special delivery post. In the absence of a communications protocol all other notices may be given or served by 'any effective means' to a specified address, or to the last known principal business address or to the registered or principal office of a company.

2.04 Clauses 1.09 and 1.10 are significant clauses which concern the effect as between employer and contractor of interim and final certificates issued by the Architect: see paragraphs 5.19 to 5.21 below.

2.05 Clause 1.11 is a new clause included to make it clear, to adjudicators in particular, that the failure to issue a certificate creates a dispute or difference just as much as the issue of the certificate itself.

3 Section 2: Carrying out the Works

3.01 Section 2 contains a series of important clauses relating to the performance of the works, and is a combination of clauses collected together from different parts of the 1998 edition and new clauses.

The position of the Architect

3.02 The Architect is the employer's agent, with authority to exercise those powers conferred on him by the contract. As such, he is both entitled and obliged to protect the employer's interests. Formerly the courts took the view that, because of the grave disadvantages which would be suffered by the contractor if the Architect failed to certify properly or otherwise exercise in a proper manner duties given to him by the contract, the Architect was to some extent in an independent 'quasi-judicial' position, and immune from actions for negligence by either party when performing functions requiring the exercise of his independent professional judgement and the application of his mind fairly and impartially between the parties. However in *Sutcliffe v Thackrah* [1974] AC 727, it was held that an architect was liable to his employer for negligently over-certifying in interim certificates, and the House of Lords said that the Architect enjoyed no such 'quasi-judicial' immunity.

3.03 In *Pacific Associates v Baxter* [1990] QB 993, the Court of Appeal held that an engineer (and by analogy an architect) could not be sued by the contractor for negligently issuing a certificate for the contractor's payment. The decision turned on the fact that the contractor could challenge the certificate (by going to arbitration). If there is no challenge mechanism (which there is in the JCT family of contracts) there might exist the possibility that an architect may be liable to a contractor for negligent under-certification.

Similarly it is likely that an employer will not be under a duty to ensure that the Architect discharges his duties correctly. In *Hiap Hong & Co Pte Ltd v Hong Huat Development Co (Pte) Ltd* [2001] 17 Const LJ 530 the Singapore Court of Appeal held that the Architect was under a duty to act independently. He was not subject to the instructions of either employer or contractor and had to reach his own decisions. He was not an agent of the owners. The control exercised over the Architect by the owner was limited to acts that were performed by the Architect on the owner's behalf but this did not include the Architect's certification duties: see also *Scheldebouw BV v St James' Homes Ltd* [2006] BLR 113.

3.04 The Architect must at all times seek to perform as exactly as possible his duties under the contract. Thus, for example, it is wrong to permit a contractor to carry out work to a standard lower

Materials, goods and workmanship

2.3 .1 All materials and goods for the Works, excluding any CDP Works, shall, so far as procurable, be of the kinds and standards described in the Contract Bills. Materials and goods for any CDP Works shall, so far as procurable, be of the kinds and standards described in the Employer's Requirements or, if not there specifically described, as described in the Contractor's Proposals or documents referred to in clause 2.9.4. The Contractor shall not substitute any materials or goods so described without the Architect/Contract Administrator's consent, which shall not be unreasonably delayed or withheld but shall not relieve the Contractor of his other obligations.

.2 Workmanship for the Works, excluding any CDP Works, shall be of the standards described in the Contract Bills. Workmanship for any CDP Works shall be of the standards described in the Employer's Requirements or, if not there specifically described, as described in the Contractor's Proposals.

.3 Where and to the extent that approval of the quality of materials or goods or of the standards of workmanship is a matter for the Architect/Contract Administrator's opinion, such quality and standards shall be to his reasonable satisfaction. To the extent that the quality of materials and goods or standards of workmanship are neither described in the manner referred to in clause 2.3.1 or 2.3.2 nor stated to be a matter for such opinion or satisfaction, they shall in the case of the Contractor's Designed Portion be of a standard appropriate to it and shall in any other case be of a standard appropriate to the Works.

.4 The Contractor shall upon the request of the Architect/Contract Administrator provide him with reasonable proof that the materials and goods used comply with this clause 2.3.

than that required by the contract, because the Architect discovers that the contractor has tendered low. It is also wrong to insist on a standard of work higher than the contract standard because the employer demands it. Architects are reminded that quite apart from what the courts have explained as their role under the building contract, the RIBA Code of Professional Conduct requires all members and students of the RIBA to act impartially in all matters of dispute between the building owner and the contractor, and to interpret the conditions of the building contract with entire fairness as between the parties.

3.05 This duty to act fairly is often extremely difficult for an employer client to appreciate, but is essential to the correct functioning of the contract. The foregoing does not mean that the Architect may not consult with the employer on matters within the sphere of his independent duty, but obliges the Architect when he comes to make his decision to make up his own mind, doing his best to decide in accordance with the contract terms, interpreted against the background of the circumstances prevailing at the time of entering into the contract. He should then certify or give his decision accordingly whether or not he thinks it will please the employer. It is in this way that the Architect must act in an independent manner.

Liability for design

3.06 It is thought that provided the contractor carries out the work strictly in accordance with the contract documents, he is not responsible if the works prove to be unsuitable for the purpose which the employer or architect had in mind. The Architect is responsible for the integration of the design of any Contractor's Designed Portion of the works with the design of the works as a whole, and may direct the contractor to that effect (clause 2.2.2). It is not otherwise the Architect's function to direct the contractor in the way he shall carry out the works, save where the Conditions expressly give him this power, for example his power to issue instructions requiring a variation: see Section 5.

3.07 Under clause 2.3.1 the Architect must give written consent, not to be unreasonably delayed or withheld, to the substitution of any specifically described materials or goods by the contractor.

3.08 Clause 2.3.3 provides that where and to the extent that approval of the quality of materials or of the standards of workmanship is a matter for the opinion of the Architect, such quality and standards shall be to his reasonable satisfaction. It may be that the Architect can, and perhaps should, take account of the price of the works in deciding whether or not he is reasonably satisfied: *Cotton v Wallis* [1955] 1 WLR 1168. Under clause 1.9.1 the final certificate is conclusive evidence that the quality of materials or standard of workmanship are to the reasonable satisfaction of the Architect, where they are expressly required to be so (thus negating the effect of *Crown Estates v John Mowlem & Co. Ltd* [1994] 10 Const LJ 311 (CA), which was decided on previous wording).

Possession of the site

3.09 Clauses 2.4 to 2.6, which are concerned with possession and use of the site, should be read in conjunction with clauses 2.26 to 2.28 (Adjustment of Completion Date), 2.30 to 2.32 (Practical Completion, Lateness and Liquidated Damages) and clauses 4.23 to 4.26 (Loss and Expense).

3.10 If possession of the site cannot be given on the date for possession, the employer is in serious breach of contract and the contractor is entitled to claim damages. Giving possession is a matter of fact. It was held in *Whittal Builders v Chester Le Street DC* (1988) 40 BLR 82 that giving possession in stages was a breach of this term, but the 2005 edition allows possession to be given in sections if the parties agree. They may also agree that the employer can delay the giving of possession by up to 6 weeks (clause 2.5), without affecting his right to recover liquidated damages.

3.11 Once the contractor has possession of the site, he is deemed to retain it for the purpose of works insurance until practical completion. If the employer takes partial possession (pursuant to clause 2.33) then practical completion is deemed to have occurred in respect of that part. The employer is not otherwise entitled to take possession of any part of the works.

3.12 The employer may however, with the contractor's consent, use or occupy the site of the works before practical completion without taking possession of it (clause 2.6), as long as he notifies the works' insurers and receives confirmation that the insurance will not be prejudiced.

3.13 Clause 2.7 governs the position where the employer wishes to carry out certain work himself (or by persons employed, engaged or authorised by him) while the contractor is engaged on the works. Where this work is described in the bills the contractor is obliged to permit the employer to carry the work out, but where it is not, the contractor is required to give his consent, which must not be unreasonably delayed or withheld. For the meaning of 'work not forming part of this Contract', see *Henry Boot Construction Ltd v Central Lancashire New Town Development Corporation* (1981) 15 BLR 1.

Supply of Documents, Setting Out etc.

Contract Documents

2.8　.1　The Contract Documents shall remain in the custody of the Employer and shall be available at all reasonable times for inspection by the Contractor.

　　.2　Immediately after the execution of this Contract the Architect/Contract Administrator, without charge to the Contractor, shall (unless previously provided) provide him with:

　　　　.1　one copy, certified on behalf of the Employer, of the Contract Documents;
　　　　.2　two further copies of the Contract Drawings; and
　　　　.3　two copies of the unpriced bills of quantities.

　　.3　The Contractor shall keep upon the site and available to the Architect/Contract Administrator or his representative at all reasonable times a copy of each of the following documents, namely: the Contract Drawings; the unpriced bills of quantities; the CDP Documents (where applicable); the descriptive schedules or similar documents referred to in clause 2.9.1.1; the master programme referred to in clause 2.9.1.2; and the drawings and details referred to in clauses 2.10 and 2.12.

　　.4　None of the documents referred to in this clause 2.8 or provided or released to the Contractor in accordance with clauses 2.9 to 2.12 shall be used by the Contractor for any purpose other than this Contract, and the Employer, the Architect/Contract Administrator and the Quantity Surveyor shall not divulge or use except for the purposes of this Contract any of the rates or prices in the Contract Bills.

Construction information and Contractor's master programme

2.9　.1　As soon as possible after the execution of this Contract, if not previously provided:

　　　　.1　the Architect/Contract Administrator, without charge to the Contractor, shall provide him with any descriptive schedules or similar documents necessary for use in carrying out the Works (excluding any CDP Works), together with any pre-construction information required for the purposes of regulation 10 of the CDM Regulations; and
　　　　.2　the Contractor shall without charge provide the Architect/Contract Administrator with his master programme for the execution of the Works identifying, where required in the Contract Particulars, the critical paths and/or providing such other details as are specified in the Contract Documents.

　　.2　Within 14 days of any decision by the Architect/Contract Administrator under clause 2.28.1 or of agreement of any Pre-agreed Adjustment, the Contractor shall provide him with an amendment or revision of the master programme that takes account of that decision or agreement, with the details referred to in clause 2.9.1.2.

　　.3　Nothing in the descriptive schedules or similar documents, or in the master programme or any amendment or revision of it, shall however impose any obligation beyond those imposed by the Contract Documents.

　　.4　In relation to any CDP Works, the Contractor, in addition to complying with regulations 11, 12 and 18 of the CDM Regulations, shall without charge provide the Architect/Contract Administrator with copies of:

　　　　.1　such Contractor's Design Documents, and (if requested) related calculations and information, as are reasonably necessary to explain or amplify the Contractor's Proposals; and

.2   all levels and setting out dimensions which the Contractor prepares or uses for the purposes of carrying out and completing the Contractor's Designed Portion.

.5   The Contractor's Design Documents and other information referred to in clause 2.9.4.1 shall be provided to the Architect/Contract Administrator as and when necessary from time to time in accordance with the Contractor's Design Submission Procedure set out in Schedule 1 or as otherwise stated in the Contract Documents, and the Contractor shall not commence any work to which such a document relates before that procedure has been complied with.

Levels and setting out of the Works

2.10 The Architect/Contract Administrator shall determine any levels required for the execution of the Works and, subject to clause 2.9.4.2, shall provide the Contractor by way of accurately dimensioned drawings with such information as shall enable the Contractor to set out the Works. The Contractor shall be responsible for, and shall at no cost to the Employer amend, any errors arising from his own inaccurate setting out. With the Employer's consent, the Architect/Contract Administrator may instruct that such errors shall not be amended and an appropriate deduction shall be made from the Contract Sum for those that are not required to be amended.

Information Release Schedule

2.11 Except to the extent that the Architect/Contract Administrator is prevented by an act or default of the Contractor or of any of the Contractor's Persons, he shall ensure that the information referred to in the Information Release Schedule is released at the time stated in that schedule. The Employer and the Contractor may agree to vary any such time, such agreement not to be unreasonably withheld.

Further drawings, details and instructions

2.12 .1   Where not included in the Information Release Schedule, the Architect/Contract Administrator shall from time to time, without charge to the Contractor, provide him with such further drawings or details as are reasonably necessary to explain and amplify the Contract Drawings and shall issue such instructions (including those for or in regard to the expenditure of Provisional Sums) as are necessary to enable the Contractor to carry out and complete the Works in accordance with this Contract.

.2   The further drawings, details and instructions shall be provided or given at the time it is reasonably necessary for the Contractor to receive them, having regard to the progress of the Works, or, if in the Architect/Contract Administrator's opinion practical completion of the Works or relevant Section is likely to be achieved before the relevant Completion Date, having regard to that Completion Date.

.3   Where the Contractor has reason to believe that the Architect/Contract Administrator is not aware of the time by which the Contractor needs to receive such further drawings, details or instructions, he shall, so far as reasonably practicable, notify the Architect/Contract Administrator sufficiently in advance as to enable the Architect/Contract Administrator to comply with this clause 2.12.

Administration of the contract

3.14 Clauses 2.8 to 2.12 are concerned with matters of contract administration, namely the custody and issue of the contract and other documents. The Architect is closely involved in these matters, and is from the execution of the contract obliged to provide or release a series of documents and schedules to the contractor. Clauses 2.9.1.2 and 2.9.2 in particular should be noted: these clauses require the contractor to supply the Architect with his master programme for the execution of the works and to update it to take account of extensions of time granted under clause 2.28.1. This master programme does not, however, impose any obligation beyond those imposed by the contract documents (clause 2.9.3).

3.15 By clause 2.10, the Architect must determine the ground level information required to set out the works, and provide drawings

containing that information to the contractor. Unless the Architect, with the employer's consent, instructs that any errors arising from inaccurate setting out by the contractor are not to be amended, the contractor must amend them at his own cost. If the Architect does instruct that the errors need not be amended, an appropriate deduction in respect of the errors is to be made from the contract sum.

3.16 By clause 2.11 where, at the time of the contract, the employer has provided the contractor with an Information Release Schedule (see the fifth recital to the Articles of Agreement), the Architect is required to provide information to the contractor in accordance with the dates set out in the schedule, subject to a proviso that the employer and contractor may agree to vary those times. If all the information required by the contractor is not

Notice of discrepancies etc.

2.15 If the Contractor becomes aware of any such departure, error, omission or inadequacy as is referred to in clause 2.14 or any other discrepancy or divergence in or between any of the following documents, namely:

- .1   the Contract Drawings;
- .2   the Contract Bills;
- .3   any instruction issued by the Architect/Contract Administrator under these Conditions;
- .4   any drawings or documents issued by the Architect/Contract Administrator under any of clauses 2.9 to 2.12; and
- .5   (where applicable) the CDP Documents,

he shall immediately give notice with appropriate details to the Architect/Contract Administrator, who shall issue instructions in that regard.

Discrepancies in CDP Documents

2.16 .1   Where the discrepancy or divergence to be notified under clause 2.15 is within or between the CDP Documents other than the Employer's Requirements, the Contractor shall send with his notice, or as soon thereafter as is reasonably practicable, a statement setting out his proposed amendments to remove it. The Architect/Contract Administrator shall not be obliged to issue instructions until he receives that statement, but, when issued, the Contractor shall comply with those instructions and, to the extent that they relate to the removal of that discrepancy or divergence, there shall be no addition to the Contract Sum.

.2   Where the discrepancy is within the Employer's Requirements (including any Variation of them issued under clause 3.14) the Contractor's Proposals shall prevail (subject to compliance with Statutory Requirements), without any adjustment of the Contract Sum. Where the Contractor's Proposals do not deal with such a discrepancy, the Contractor shall notify the Architect/Contract Administrator of his proposed amendment to deal with it and the Architect/Contract Administrator shall either agree the proposed amendment or decide how the discrepancy shall be dealt with; that agreement or decision shall be notified to the Contractor and treated as a Variation.

Divergences from Statutory Requirements

2.17 .1   If the Contractor or Architect/Contract Administrator becomes aware of any divergence between the Statutory Requirements and any of the documents referred to in clause 2.15, he shall immediately give the other notice specifying the divergence and, where it is between the Statutory Requirements and any of the CDP Documents, the Contractor shall notify the Architect/Contract Administrator of his proposed amendment for removing it.

.2   Within 7 days of becoming aware of such divergence (or, where applicable, within 14 days of receipt of the Contractor's proposed amendment), the Architect/Contract Administrator shall issue instructions in that regard, in relation to which:

.1   in the case of a divergence between the Statutory Requirements and any of the CDP Documents, the Contractor shall comply at no cost to the Employer unless after the Base Date there is a change in the Statutory Requirements which necessitates an alteration or modification to the Contractor's Designed Portion, in which event such alteration or modification shall be treated as an instruction requiring a Variation of the Employer's Requirements; and

.2   in any other case, if and insofar as those instructions require the Works to be varied, they shall be treated as instructions requiring a Variation.

.3   Provided the Contractor is not in breach of clause 2.17.1, the Contractor shall not be liable under this Contract if the Works (other than the CDP Works) do not comply with the Statutory Requirements to the extent that the non-compliance results from the Contractor having carried out work in accordance with the documents referred to in clauses 2.15.1 to 2.15.4 (other than an instruction for a Variation in respect of the Contractor's Designed Portion).

covered by the Information Release Schedule then the Architect is required, by clause 2.12, to provide such information, by way of further drawings, details and instuctions, when it is reasonably necessary to do so. The Architect is obliged to act with reasonable diligence and to use reasonable care and skill in the provision of such information: *London Borough of Merton v Leach* (1985) 32 BLR 51.

3.17 Clauses 2.13 to 2.20 deal with errors, discrepancies and divergences in and between the contract and related documents, and require the contractor to report a number of such occurrences to the Architect, who is required to issue instructions to resolve the difficulty. In general, the cost involved is borne by the party responsible for the preparation of the document in question.

3.18 Under clause 2.13 (unless otherwise expressly stated in respect of any specified item or items), the contract bills are to have been prepared in accordance with the principles of the Standard Method of Measurement (SMM). If they have not been so prepared, this constitutes an error which must be corrected (clause 2.14.1). By virtue of clause 2.14.3 the correction is to be treated as though it was a variation required by the Architect. SMM expressly requires contract bills fully and accurately to describe the work. For example, if in carrying out work it becomes clear that excavation of rock is necessary and that the bills should have stated that excavation would be required, it seems that the contractor will become entitled to extra payment for all such excavation (see *Bryant & Son Ltd v Birmingham Hospital Saturday Fund* [1938] 1 All ER 503).

3.19 By clause 2.17, the contractor is required to give written notice to the Architect of any divergence he finds between the statutory requirements and the documents referred to in clause 2.15. The Architect is required to issue instructions in relation to the divergence, and this instruction will be treated as an instruction requiring a variation under clause 3.14. It is probably also the contractor's implied duty to bring to the Architect's attention any obvious errors in the Architect's design of which the contractor has actual knowledge.

3.20 Clauses 2.24 and 2.25, which deal with unfixed materials and goods on and off site, should be read in conjunction with clauses 4.16 and 4.17. The position as to materials and goods intended for the works is as follows:

1 As soon as materials or goods are delivered to or placed on or adjacent to the works, they must not be removed without the Architect's consent (clause 2.24).
2 Provided that the materials or goods have not been prematurely delivered to site and are adequately protected against weather and other casualties the Architect is bound to certify them for payment (clause 4.16.1.2).
3 As soon as materials or goods are paid for, property in them passes to the employer (clause 2.24).
4 As soon as materials or goods are incorporated into the works, property in them passes to the owner of the land by operation of law, whether the goods are paid for or not.
5 Pre-fabricated materials or goods which are off site may be certified for payment provided they were contained in a list annexed to the contract bills and certain conditions have been met by the contractor (clause 4.17).
6 If off site materials are certified and paid for, property in them passes to the employer (clause 2.25).

Adjustment of Completion Date

3.21 Clauses 2.26 to 2.29 make provision for extensions of time to be given to the contractor through delay caused by 'Relevant Events' as defined in clause 2.29. When it becomes reasonably apparent that the progress of any section of the works is being or is likely to be delayed from any cause whatever, the contractor is

---

Adjustment of Completion Date

Related definitions and interpretation

2.26 In clauses 2.27 to 2.29 and, so far as relevant, in the other clauses of these Conditions:

.1   any reference to delay or extension of time includes any further delay or further extension of time;

.2   'Pre-agreed Adjustment' means the fixing of a revised Completion Date for the Works or a Section by the Confirmed Acceptance of a Variation Quotation or an Acceleration Quotation;

.3   'Relevant Omission' means the omission of any work or obligation through an instruction for a Variation under clause 3.14 or through an instruction under clause 3.16 in regard to a Provisional Sum for defined work.

Notice by Contractor of delay to progress

2.27 .1   If and whenever it becomes reasonably apparent that the progress of the Works or any Section is being or is likely to be delayed the Contractor shall forthwith give notice to the Architect/ Contract Administrator of the material circumstances, including the cause or causes of the delay, and shall identify in the notice any event which in his opinion is a Relevant Event.

.2   In respect of each event identified in the notice the Contractor shall, if practicable in such notice or otherwise in writing as soon as possible thereafter, give particulars of its expected effects, including an estimate of any expected delay in the completion of the Works or any Section beyond the relevant Completion Date.

.3   The Contractor shall forthwith notify the Architect/Contract Administrator of any material change in the estimated delay or in any other particulars and supply such further information as the Architect/Contract Administrator may at any time reasonably require.

Fixing Completion Date

2.28 .1   If, in the Architect/Contract Administrator's opinion, on receiving a notice and particulars under clause 2.27:

    .1   any of the events which are stated to be a cause of delay is a Relevant Event; and
    .2   completion of the Works or of any Section is likely to be delayed thereby beyond the relevant Completion Date,

    then, save where these Conditions expressly provide otherwise, the Architect/Contract Administrator shall give an extension of time by fixing such later date as the Completion Date for the Works or Section as he then estimates to be fair and reasonable.

.2   Whether or not an extension is given, the Architect/Contract Administrator shall notify the Contractor of his decision in respect of any notice under clause 2.27 as soon as is reasonably practicable and in any event within 12 weeks of receipt of the required particulars. Where the period from receipt to the Completion Date is less than 12 weeks, he shall endeavour to do so prior to the Completion Date.

.3   The Architect/Contract Administrator shall in his decision state:

    .1   the extension of time that he has attributed to each Relevant Event; and
    .2   (in the case of a decision under clause 2.28.4 or 2.28.5) the reduction in time that he has attributed to each Relevant Omission.

.4   After the first fixing of a later Completion Date in respect of the Works or a Section, either under clause 2.28.1 or by a Pre-agreed Adjustment, but subject to clauses 2.28.6.3 and 2.28.6.4, the Architect/Contract Administrator may by notice to the Contractor, giving the details referred to in clause 2.28.3, fix a Completion Date for the Works or that Section earlier than that previously so fixed if in his opinion the fixing of such earlier Completion Date is fair and reasonable, having regard to any Relevant Omissions for which instructions have been issued after the last occasion on which a new Completion Date was fixed for the Works or for that Section.

.5   After the Completion Date for the Works or for a Section, if this occurs before the date of practical completion, the Architect/Contract Administrator may, and not later than the expiry of 12 weeks after the date of practical completion shall, by notice to the Contractor, giving the details referred to in clause 2.28.3:

    .1   fix a Completion Date for the Works or for the Section later than that previously fixed if in his opinion that is fair and reasonable having regard to any Relevant Events, whether on reviewing a previous decision or otherwise and whether or not the Relevant Event has been specifically notified by the Contractor under clause 2.27.1; or
    .2   subject to clauses 2.28.6.3 and 2.28.6.4, fix a Completion Date earlier than that previously fixed if in his opinion that is fair and reasonable having regard to any instructions for Relevant Omissions issued after the last occasion on which a new Completion Date was fixed for the Works or Section; or
    .3   confirm the Completion Date previously fixed.

.6   Provided always that:

    .1   the Contractor shall constantly use his best endeavours to prevent delay in the progress of the Works or any Section, however caused, and to prevent the completion of the Works or Section being delayed or further delayed beyond the relevant Completion Date;
    .2   in the event of any delay the Contractor shall do all that may reasonably be required to the satisfaction of the Architect/Contract Administrator to proceed with the Works or Section;
    .3   no decision of the Architect/Contract Administrator under clause 2.28.4 or 2.28.5.2 shall fix a Completion Date for the Works or any Section earlier than the relevant Date for Completion; and
    .4   no decision under clause 2.28.4 or 2.28.5.2 shall alter the length of any Pre-agreed Adjustment except in the case of a Variation Quotation where the relevant Variation is itself the subject of a Relevant Omission.

Relevant Events

2.29 The following are the Relevant Events referred to in clauses 2.27 and 2.28:

.1   Variations and any other matters or instructions which under these Conditions are to be treated as, or as requiring, a Variation;

.2   Architect/Contract Administrator's instructions:

.1   under any of clauses 2.15, 3.15, 3.16 (excluding an instruction for expenditure of a Provisional Sum for defined work), 3.22.2 or 5.3.2; or

.2   for the opening up for inspection or testing of any work, materials or goods under clause 3.17 or 3.18.4 (including making good), unless the inspection or test shows that the work, materials or goods are not in accordance with this Contract;

.3   deferment of the giving of possession of the site or any Section under clause 2.5;

.4   the execution of work for which an Approximate Quantity is not a reasonably accurate forecast of the quantity of work required;

.5   suspension by the Contractor under clause 4.14 of the performance of his obligations under this Contract;

.6   any impediment, prevention or default, whether by act or omission, by the Employer, the Architect/Contract Administrator, the Quantity Surveyor or any of the Employer's Persons, except to the extent caused or contributed to by any default, whether by act or omission, of the Contractor or of any of the Contractor's Persons;

.7   the carrying out by a Statutory Undertaker of work in pursuance of its statutory obligations in relation to the Works, or the failure to carry out such work;

.8   exceptionally adverse weather conditions;

.9   loss or damage occasioned by any of the Specified Perils;

.10   civil commotion or the use or threat of terrorism and/or the activities of the relevant authorities in dealing with such event or threat;

.11   strike, lock-out or local combination of workmen affecting any of the trades employed upon the Works or any of the trades engaged in the preparation, manufacture or transportation of any of the goods or materials required for the Works or any persons engaged in the preparation of the design for the Contractor's Designed Portion;

.12   the exercise after the Base Date by the United Kingdom Government of any statutory power which directly affects the execution of the Works;

.13   force majeure.

obliged to give notice forthwith to the Architect of the material circumstances identifying (clause 2.27.1):

1   The cause or causes of the delay.
2   Any event which is in his opinion a 'Relevant Event'.

Note that the provision is both forward and backward looking.

3.22 Clause 2.27.2 requires the contractor to give particulars of the expected effects of the event causing delay, and an estimate of the extent of delay in completion of any section of the works beyond the completion date, resulting from that particular event (whether or not the delay will be concurrent with a delay resulting from any other relevant event). This information should be included in the notice where possible, alternatively it should be given in writing as soon as possible after the issue of the notice.

3.23 It is clear that the contractor is required to give full particulars and details of the delay, even if the delay is the contractor's own fault. Obviously, more than one notice under these clauses may be served during the currency of the contract.

3.24 It was held in *Balfour Beatty Building Ltd v Chestermount Properties Ltd* (1993) 62 BLR 1 that where the works are delayed as a result of the contractor's fault, so that the original completion date has passed, the Architect still has power on the happening of a Relevant Event to re-fix the completion date. The appropriate way to do this is to take the original completion date and add the number of days which the Architect regards as fair and reasonable in all the circumstances, even if the effect of this is that the new completion date has already passed before the happening of the Relevant Event. It would be wrong in principle to re-fix the completion date by starting at the date of the Relevant Event and adding days to that date.

Architect's action

3.25 On receipt of the contractor's notice, particulars and estimate, the Architect must first decide whether the contractor is entitled to an extension of time in principle (i.e. whether the delay is caused by a Relevant Event as defined by clause 2.29) and secondly, whether the occurrence of the Relevant Event will in fact cause delay beyond the completion date. Having decided these two points, the Architect grants an extension of time if he thinks that it is fair and reasonable to do so, by fixing a new completion date which is notified to the contractor in writing. His notice must state the extension of time which he has attributed to each Relevant Event.

3.26 In making his decision the Architect must consider a number of different matters, including the effect of other causes of delay, whether they are or are not Relevant Events, and action taken by the contractor both to prevent delay and in the event of delay: clause 2.28.6.

3.27 The Architect must either issue a new completion date or notify the contractor of his decision not to do so, as soon as is reasonably practicable and in any event within 12 weeks of receipt of the required particulars, or (where there are fewer than 12 weeks to completion) no later than the completion date (using his best endeavours).

3.28 Under clause 2.28.4 if the Architect has already exercised his power to grant an extension, he may fix a completion date which is earlier than the previously extended completion date if he thinks it fair and reasonable to do so, having regard to variations requiring the omission of work which have been issued after the last occasion on which an extension of time was granted. This is, however, subject to the proviso that (under Clause 2.28.6.3) no completion date can be fixed earlier than the date for completion stated in the Contract Particulars. Thus the Architect is entitled to reduce a previously granted extension of time if work is subsequently ordered to be omitted, thereby reducing the amount of the contractor's commitments and justifying an earlier completion date, but he cannot rewrite the contract. RIBA Publications Ltd publishes a form of 'Notification of Revision to Completion Date'.

Duty of Architect to review after practical completion

3.29 When practical completion has occurred, provision is made for the Architect finally to review the position as regards extensions of time. He must do this within 12 weeks after practical completion (clause 2.28.5). He may fix a later completion date than that previously fixed and in so doing take into account all Relevant Events whether or not specifically notified by the contractor. It is also open to him to fix an earlier completion date, having regard to omissions which have occurred since the last occasion when an extension of time was granted. Alternatively, he may simply confirm the previously fixed completion date. It is important for the Architect to carry out an overall review with knowledge of all the relevant facts and with time to make a careful assessment of the contractor's entitlement.

Relevant events

3.30 The first six of the Relevant Events are also Relevant Matters falling within clauses 4.23 and 4.24, which entitle the contractor to claim the reimbursement of direct loss and expense incurred by him. Hence notices of delay and applications for reimbursement are likely to be combined in the case of these Relevant Events/ Matters. Only some of the Relevant Events require any comment.

Clause 2.29.5

3.31 Clause 4.14 allows the contractor to suspend performance of the works if the employer fails to pay him in full (pursuant to the contract and subject to the giving of withholding notices). This suspension is not to be construed as a failure to proceed diligently with the works, but entitles the contractor to an extension of time.

Clause 2.29.6

3.32 This sub-clause is intended to assimilate a number of acts of prevention or events of delay committed by the employer or by his agents which were specified in clause 25 of the 1998 edition. They are only to be effective to the extent that the contractor or his agents have not caused or contributed to them.

Clause 2.29.7

3.33 This sub-clause covers delay caused by statutory undertakers in performing their statutory obligations, usually the laying of gas, water and electricity mains. Where the contractor has no choice but to employ these statutory undertakers, it is thought unjust that he should be penalised for their delay. This sub-clause does not apply where such an undertaking is carrying out work extending beyond its statutory obligations as sub-contractors to the employer (see *Henry Boot Construction Limited v Central Lancashire New Town Development Corporation* (1981) 15 BLR 1).

Clause 2.29.8

3.34 Exceptionally adverse weather conditions require quite unusual severity: it will frequently be necessary to establish this with the aid of weather charts covering a considerable period. Note that the definition includes exceptional extremes of heat and dryness, as well as the more normal British weather; such extremes can, of course, have a serious effect on progress.

Clause 2.29.9

3.35 Loss from specified perils (defined in clause 6.8): these contingencies are very wide, and in some instances may be due to an act of negligence on the part of the contractor, at any rate in their underlying causes.

Clause 2.29.12

3.36 This clause will tend to reduce the scope of the immediately following *'force majeure'* Relevant Event.

Clause 2.29.13

3.37 The meaning of the term 'force majeure' is difficult to state exactly, but very broadly the words extend to special circumstances quite outside the control of the contractor, proceeding from a cause which is unforeseeable but inevitable. Such happenings will not by their very nature have been dealt with elsewhere in the contract. The effect of inundations and epidemics are examples of events which are probably within this clause. Financial difficulties experienced by the contractor are equally clearly not within this definition. Because of the specific inclusion of specified perils and government interference earlier in the Relevant Events it is probable that *'force majeure'* requires to be given a restrictive definition in these Conditions.

Practical Completion, Lateness and Liquidated Damages

3.38 Clause 2.30 provides for the issue of a certificate of practical completion when, in the opinion of the Architect, practical completion of the works or of a section of the works has been achieved and the contractor has sufficiently complied with clauses 2.40 (as-built contractor's design drawings) and 3.23.4 (health and safety file information). The certificate signifies that all the necessary construction work has been done without any obvious defects, but does not exclude the existence of latent defects.

3.39 Clause 2.31 obliges the Architect to issue a certificate of non-completion in the relevant circumstances, whether or not the employer intends to deduct (or call for the payment of) liquidated damages.

3.40 Clause 2.32 gives the employer the right to deduct or claim liquidated and ascertained damages at the rate stated in the Contract Particulars. The issue of a certificate under clause 2.31 is a condition precedent to the employer's right to deduct liquidated damages (see *Ramac Construction v Lesser* [1975] 2 Lloyd's Reports 430).

3.41 The certificate is, it seems, required in order to ensure that the Architect has properly considered any contractor's notices of delay given under clause 2.27 and has granted all extensions of time to

Practical Completion, Lateness and Liquidated Damages

Practical completion and certificates

2.30 When in the Architect/Contract Administrator's opinion practical completion of the Works or a Section is achieved and the Contractor has complied sufficiently with clauses 2.40 and 3.23.4, then:

.1   in the case of the Works, the Architect/Contract Administrator shall forthwith issue a certificate to that effect ('the Practical Completion Certificate');

.2   in the case of a Section, he shall forthwith issue a certificate of practical completion of that Section (a 'Section Completion Certificate');

and practical completion of the Works or the Section shall be deemed for all the purposes of this Contract to have taken place on the date stated in that certificate.

Non-Completion Certificates

2.31 If the Contractor fails to complete the Works or a Section by the relevant Completion Date, the Architect/Contract Administrator shall issue a certificate to that effect (a 'Non-Completion Certificate'). If a new Completion Date is fixed after the issue of such a certificate, such fixing shall cancel that certificate and the Architect/Contract Administrator shall where necessary issue a further certificate.

Payment or allowance of liquidated damages

2.32 .1   Provided:

.1   the Architect/Contract Administrator has issued a Non-Completion Certificate for the Works or a Section; and

.2   the Employer has notified the Contractor before the date of the Final Certificate that he may require payment of, or may withhold or deduct, liquidated damages,

the Employer may, not later than 5 days before the final date for payment of the debt due under the Final Certificate, give notice to the Contractor in the terms set out in clause 2.32.2.

---

which the contractor is entitled. Under clause 2.28 provision is made for reassessment of the need for extension of time throughout the contract period. Clause 2.32.3 provides for the situation where, after liquidated damages have been deducted, a later completion date is fixed under clause 2.28.5.1. In such circumstances, the employer would be obliged to pay or repay to the contractor amounts in respect of the period up to such later completion date. Clause 2.32.3 does not state whether the employer must pay interest on any damages repaid and it is unclear at present what is the correct interpretation of the clause in this respect.

3.42 Clause 2.32 provides two methods by which the employer may recover liquidated damages that are due: either as a debt (clause 2.32.2.1) or by deduction from monies due to the contractor (clause 2.32.2.2). The latter method now requires notice to be given to the contractor (under clause 4.13.4 or clause 4.15.4), to ensure compliance with section 111 of the Housing Grants, Construction and Regeneration Act 1996.

Meaning of practical completion

3.43 The term 'practical completion' is not defined in the contract, but it has been said (by Lord Dilhorne in *Westminster City Council v Jarvis Limited* [1970] 1 All ER 943 at 948) that it does not mean the stage when the work 'was almost but not entirely finished', but 'the completion of all the construction work that has to be done'. Such completion is subject to defects which may thereafter appear and require action under clause 2.38. In the same case in the Court of Appeal, Salmon LJ said: 'I take these words

to mean completion for all practical purposes, i.e. for the purpose of allowing [the employer] to take possession of the works and use them as intended. If "completion" in Clause 21 [Clause 2.4 of the 2005 Form] means completion down to the last detail, however trivial and unimportant, then Clause 22 [Clause 2.32 of the 2005 Form] would be a penalty clause and as such unenforceable'. Neither explanation is binding as to the meaning of the words for the purposes of considering whether the contractor has reached the stage of practical completion. However, it is suggested that the Architect can issue his certificate despite very minor defects (applying the *de minimis* principle: *HW Nevill (Sunblest) Limited v Wm Press & Son Limited* (1982) 20 BLR 78) if:

1   He is reasonably satisfied that the works accord with the contract and

2   There is adequate retention and

3   The employer will not suffer loss due to disturbance or otherwise and

4   He obtains a written acknowledgement of the existence of any defects and an undertaking from the contractor to put them right. If the defects are other than trivial, the views of the employer should first be obtained.

It goes without saying that the Architect must exercise the above discretion with extreme care.

Form of certificate

3.44 This is not prescribed by the contract, but it should be clear and definite. The RIBA issues suitable forms.

Defects

Shedules of defects and instructions

2.38 If any defects, shrinkages or other faults in the Works or a Section appear within the relevant Rectification Period due to materials, goods or workmanship not in accordance with this Contract or any failure of the Contractor to comply with his obligations in respect of the Contractor's Designed Portion:

> .1 such defects, shrinkages and other faults shall be specified by the Architect/Contract Administrator in a schedule of defects which he shall deliver to the Contractor as an instruction not later than 14 days after the expiry of that Rectification Period; and
>
> .2 notwithstanding clause 2.38.1, the Architect/Contract Administrator may whenever he considers it necessary issue instructions requiring any such defect, shrinkage or other fault to be made good, provided no instructions under this clause 2.38.2 shall be issued after delivery of a schedule of defects or more than 14 days after the expiry of the relevant Rectification Period.

Within a reasonable time after receipt of such schedule or instructions, the defects, shrinkages and other faults shall at no cost to the Employer be made good by the Contractor unless the Architect/Contract Administrator with the Employer's consent shall otherwise instruct. If he does so otherwise instruct, an appropriate deduction shall be made from the Contract Sum in respect of the defects, shrinkages or other faults not made good.

Certificate of Making Good

2.39 When in the Architect/Contract Administrator's opinion the defects, shrinkages or other faults in the Works or a Section which he has required to be made good under clause 2.38 have been made good, he shall issue a certificate to that effect (a 'Certificate of Making Good'), and completion of that making good shall for the purposes of this Contract be deemed to have taken place on the date stated in that certificate.

Effect of certificate of practical completion

3.45 The practical completion certificate has the following important effects:

1 It marks the date when the employer re-takes possession of the site (subject to clauses 2.6 and 2.33).
2 It fixes the commencement of the Rectification Period (as stated in the Contract Particulars).
3 It fixes the commencement of the period for the final adjustment of the contract sum (clause 4.5).
4 It gives rise to the right of release of the first half of the retention percentage (clause 4.20.3).
5 It marks the time for release of the contractor's obligation to insure under Schedule 3 Option A where this applies.
6 It marks the end of the contractor's liability for liquidated damages under clause 2.32.

3.46 The employer's remedies for defective work are not limited to that contained in clause 2.38 (requiring the contractor to make good defects). He may additionally sue for damages for breach of contract: *HW Nevill (Sun Blest) Ltd v Wm Press & Son Ltd* (1982) 20 BLR 78.

Procedure

3.47 The requisite clause 4.13.4 or clause 4.15.4 notice should set out the amount that is proposed to be withheld and the ground or grounds for withholding payment. Under the 1963 JCT Form it has been held that no certificate under clause 22 of that form (the equivalent clause to clause 2.32) could be issued after the issue of the final certificate (*Fairweather v Asden Securities* (1980) 12 BLR 40). It is thought that the position is the same under the 2005 Form.

Advantage of liquidated damages

3.48 If there is no provision for liquidated damages, ascertainment of the damage suffered by reason of non-completion can involve the parties in long and costly proceedings. Where the parties have made and agreed a genuine pre-estimate of damages, such proceedings are avoided. The rate agreed, described here as 'liquidated damages', will be given effect to by the courts without enquiring into the actual loss suffered.

Liquidated damages and penalties distinguished

3.49 In circumstances where the liquidated damages are construed as a penalty, the contractor can have the agreed rate of liquidated damages set aside and make the employer prove and be limited to his actual loss. It is therefore extremely important that liquidated damages should be stated in the Contract Particulars in such a way that they cannot be construed as being a penalty. This is particularly likely to happen, as it did in *Bramall & Ogden Ltd v Sheffield City Council* (1985) 29 BLR 73, where the liquidated damages provision is sectional, but sectional completion is not required by the contract.

Delay partly employer's fault

3.50 At common law an employer who was partly responsible for delay could not rely on a liquidated damages clause. However, under clause 2.28 extensions of time may be granted in respect of Relevant Events which include delay caused by the employer's fault, and, provided such extensions are properly granted, the right to liquidated damages is preserved.

3.51 Failure to grant proper extensions of time in respect of such Relevant Events as arise through the employer's fault will disentitle him from claiming liquidated damages. In *Percy Bilton Ltd v Greater London Council* [1982] 2 All ER 63 (HL), it was held that delay caused by the bankruptcy of a nominated sub-contractor (for which no provision for extension is made by clause 2.28) did not arise through any fault of the employer, so he was not disentitled from claiming liquidated damages.

Partial possession by employer

3.52 Clauses 2.33 to 2.37 bring forward clauses previously found in clause 18 of the 1998 edition. They provide for the situation where, before the works are completed, the employer with the contractor's consent takes possession of part or parts of the works. They include provisions as to practical completion, defects, insurance, and retention percentage for application to each part analogous to those which apply to the whole, and for proportionate reduction of any liquidated damages payable. The appropriate Contract Particulars entry (referring to clause 2.32.2) must be completed so as to allow the proper operation of clause 2.37, otherwise liquidated damages will not be enforceable. In *Bramall & Ogden Ltd v Sheffield City Council* (1985) 29 BLR 73 (a case on JCT 63), the Appendix had been completed so as to allow a sum in damages for each uncompleted dwelling. This was held to be inconsistent with Clause 16(e) (equivalent to clause 2.37). If possession is given in sections, the Architect must apply clauses 2.33 to 2.37 and has no power, without the parties' consent, to issue a certificate of practical completion for an average date of completion.

Duty to complete in sections

3.53 Clause 2.33 does not impose any duty to complete in sections. Equally, if the contractor is delayed and therefore subject to the deduction of liquidated damages, he is not entitled to any contra-credit for having completed some of the work before the contractual completion date, although an employer's unreasonable refusal of an offer of partial possession might limit his entitlement to recover liquidated damages. If sectional completion is required, the provisions of the Contract Particulars for Sectional Completion must be completed.

Defects

3.54 The Contract Particulars require a Rectification Period to be stated. In default, the contract specifies the period to be 6 months. If any defects, shrinkages or faults (due to materials or workmanship not in accordance with the contract, or any failure by the contractor to comply with his obligations in respect of the Contractor's Designed Portion) appear within this period, the Architect should list these in a schedule of defects. This must be delivered to the contractor no later than 14 days after the end of the Rectification Period. The contractor must then, within a reasonable time, make good these defects at his own cost. An alternative procedure is to allow the defects to remain and make a deduction from the contract sum. This must be the subject of an architect's instruction made with the consent of the employer.

3.55 The Architect also has power before issuing the comprehensive schedule of defects to issue instructions requiring the contractor to make good particular defects (clause 2.38.2). In practice the Architect may wish to leave the delivery of a schedule of defects as late as possible, using the clause 2.38.2 procedure until then.

3.56 After all such defects, shrinkages or faults have been made good, the Architect should issue a Certificate of Making Good: clause 2.39. Its issue acts as a trigger for the issue of the final Interim Certificate (clause 4.9.2), the Final Certificate timetable (clause 4.15.2) and the final release of Retention (clause 4.20.3).

Meaning of defects

3.57 For the contractor's obligation as to standards of workmanship, materials, and goods, see clauses 2.1 and 2.3. Defects are, generally, work, materials and goods which are not in conformity with the contract documents. They do not include a failure by the Architect to design the works, for example.

3.58 It is, in general, no excuse for a contractor to say that the Architect or the Clerk of Works ought to have observed bad work during site inspections.

Architect's remedies

3.59 A notice under clause 3.11 can be given for non-compliance with an instruction to make good defects. If the notice is not complied with, others can be employed to do the necessary work and the cost deducted from the Retention Percentage. Further, until defects have been made good, the Architect need not and should not issue his Certificate of Making Good. The second half of the Retention Percentage will not be released, and issue of the Final Certificate, with the protection it usually affords to the contractor (see clause 1.10), may be delayed. The power of determination under clause 8.4 is not designed to be exercised after practical completion, and the remedies set out above ought to be sufficient to make it unnecessary to attempt to rely on clause 8.4.

Irremediable breach

3.60 The Architect may require a defect to be remedied in an instruction or in the schedule, but then find on representation by the contractor that it cannot be remedied except at a cost which is unreasonable in comparison with the loss to the employer and the nature of the defect. If the employer consents, the Architect may issue the Certificate of Making Good under clause 2.39, having made an 'appropriate' deduction from the Contract Sum by the amount certified for payment in respect of the works not properly carried out (clause 2.38). This deduction will usually be the amount by which the works are reduced in value by reason of the unremedied defect.

Defects appearing after the expiry of the defects liability period

3.61 If defects appear after the issue of the Certificate under clause 2.39, the Architect can no longer issue instructions under clause 2.38, but the appearance of the defects is the disclosure of a breach of contract by the contractor. The employer is entitled to damages, and the Architect should adjust any further certificate to reflect the effect on the value of the works. In accordance with common law rules as to mitigation of damages, the contractor, if it is reasonable to do so, should be given the opportunity of rectifying the defects. A Final Certificate should not be issued if the defects remain unremedied (see clause 1.10).

4 Section 3: Control of the Works

4.01 The scope of this section extends over a number of different matters, the most important of which for present purposes are Access and Representatives (clauses 3.1 to 3.6) and Architect/Contract Administrator's Instructions (clauses 3.10 to 3.21).

Access and Representatives

4.02 In the absence of express provision doubts might arise as to the Architect's right of access to the site, since the contractor is entitled as against the employer to free and uninterrupted possession of the site during the progress of the works. Therefore clause 3.1 reserves to the Architect and his authorised representative a right of access to the works. There is a similar right of access in relation to workshops and other places in the possession of the contractor or a sub-contractor where work is being prepared for incorporation in the works. This right is subject to such reasonable restrictions by the contractor and sub-contractor as are necessary to protect any proprietary right in the work for the contract. The provisions relating to sub-contractors do not, of course, directly

Section 3 Control of the Works

Access and Representatives

Access for Architect/Contract Administrator

3.1 The Architect/Contract Administrator and any person authorised by him shall at all reasonable times have access to the Works and to the workshops or other premises of the Contractor where work is being prepared for this Contract. When work is to be prepared in workshops or other premises of a sub-contractor the Contractor shall by a term in the sub-contract secure so far as possible a similar right of access to those workshops or premises for the Architect/Contract Administrator and any person authorised by him and shall do all things reasonably necessary to make that right effective. Access under this clause 3.1 may be subject to such reasonable restrictions as are necessary to protect proprietary rights.

Clerk of works

3.4 The Employer shall be entitled to appoint a clerk of works whose duty shall be to act solely as inspector on behalf of the Employer under the Architect/Contract Administrator's directions and the Contractor shall afford every reasonable facility for the performance of that duty. If any direction is given to the Contractor by the clerk of works, it shall be of no effect unless given in regard to a matter in respect of which the Architect/Contract Administrator is expressly empowered by these Conditions to issue instructions and unless confirmed in writing by the Architect/Contract Administrator within 2 working days of the direction being given. Any direction so given and confirmed shall, as from the date of issue of that confirmation, be deemed an instruction of the Architect/Contract Administrator.

affect the obligations of the sub-contractors, but the contractor would be liable in damages to the employer if the employer could establish damage flowing from failure by the contractor to ensure that the appropriate terms were included in the sub-contracts.

4.03 The person-in-charge on site is the contractor's agent to receive instructions. To avoid confusion he should be named.

4.04 The note to clause 3.3 makes it clear that, in order to avoid any risk of confusion between the different roles of individuals involved in the contract, neither the Architect/Contract Administrator nor the Quantity Surveyor should be appointed as the Employer's representative.

4.05 The clerk of works is to act 'solely as inspector'. He is not the Architect's agent to give instructions, and it will be a source of confusion and dispute if he purports to do so. If the clerk of works gives 'directions' they are to be of no effect unless converted into Architect's Instructions by the Architect within two working days. Such directions can lead to uncertainty on the part of the contractor. It is suggested that the clerk of works should be discouraged from giving directions in ordinary circumstances. However, if directions are to be given, the problems will be minimized if they are in writing and the Architect immediately confirms, amends or rejects them. If the clerk of works gives 'directions' in regard to a matter in respect of which the Architect is not empowered to issue instructions, and the contractor follows that direction, it may be that the Architect can sanction that 'direction' under clause 3.14.4.

4.06 In *Kensington and Chelsea and Westminster Area Health Authority v Wettern Composites* (1986) 31 BLR 57 it was held that the employer was responsible for the contributory negligence of the clerk of works, because the clerk of works was his employee. Responsibility for his acts was not borne by the Architect, even though he was acting under the direction and control of the Architect.

4.07 Clause 3.5 is a new provision designed to ensure continuity in the contractual posts of Architect/Contract Administrator and Quantity Surveyor. The clause protects the contractor from the whims of the employer in that:

1 The employer is obliged to give the contractor notice of the identity of any replacement.
2 The contractor may object to the nominated replacement, which objection may be accepted by the employer or decided by an adjudicator.
3 The replacement is bound to follow any certificate, opinion, decision, approval or instruction given or expressed by his predecessor, except and insofar as that predecessor would have been able to disregard or overrule it.

4.08 Clause 3.6 restates the contractor's primary and entire responsibility for carrying out the works in accordance with the contractual Conditions, unaffected by any supervision or inspection by the Architect or clerk of works or by the issue by the Architect of any certificate, whether in respect of an interim payment or otherwise.

Sub-contracting

4.09 The increasingly complicated provisions for nominations of sub-contractors and suppliers which developed through previous editions of the JCT forms have all disappeared from the 2005 edition, reflecting the minimal extent of their use in recent years. The only involvement of the employer in the selection of sub-contractors is through the listing process contained in clause 3.8. The Architect's only involvement in the process is the giving of consent to sub-contracting of the whole or part of the works (clause 3.7.1), which consent is not be unreasonably delayed or withheld.

Architect/Contract Administrator's instructions

4.10 Clauses 3.10 to 3.13 govern the Architect's authority to give instructions and the contractor's duty, subject to certain conditions, to comply with those instructions. Clauses 3.14 to 3.16 specify the Architect's authority to vary or postpone the works, and clauses 3.17 to 3.21 his authority to control work, workmanship, goods or materials which are found to be not in accordance with the contract. The wording of clauses 3.14 to 3.21 is clear, and those clauses do not here call for separate comment.

4.11 The contractor must comply with the Architect's instructions. Failure to do so gives rise to the employer's right under clause 3.11 to have work carried out by others, and in some circumstances can result in the employer having the right to determine the contractor's employment (see clause 8.4.1.3).

Architect/Contract Administrator's instructions

Compliance with instructions

3.10 The Contractor shall forthwith comply with all instructions issued to him by the Architect/Contract Administrator in regard to any matter in respect of which the Architect/Contract Administrator is expressly empowered by these Conditions to issue instructions, save that:

- .1 where an instruction requires a Variation of the type referred to in clause 5.1.2, the Contractor need not comply to the extent that he notifies a reasonable objection to it to the Architect/Contract Administrator;
- .2 where an instruction for a Variation is given which pursuant to clause 5.3.1 requires the Contractor to provide a Variation Quotation, the Variation shall not be carried out until the Architect/Contract Administrator has in relation to it issued either a Confirmed Acceptance or a further instruction under clause 5.3.2;
- .3 in the Contractor's opinion compliance with any direction under clause 2.2.2 or any instruction issued by the Architect/Contract Administrator injuriously affects the efficacy of the design of the Contractor's Designed Portion (including the obligations of the Contractor to comply with regulations 11, 12 and 18 of the CDM Regulations), he shall within 7 days of receipt of the direction or instruction give notice to the Architect/Contract Administrator specifying the injurious effect, and the direction or instruction shall not take effect unless confirmed by the Architect/Contract Administrator.

Non-compliance with instructions

3.11 Subject to clause 3.10, if within 7 days after receipt of a notice from the Architect/Contract Administrator requiring compliance with an instruction the Contractor does not comply, the Employer may employ and pay other persons to execute any work whatsoever which may be necessary to give effect to that instruction. The Contractor shall be liable for all additional costs incurred by the Employer in connection with such employment and an appropriate deduction shall be made from the Contract Sum.

Instructions other than in writing

3.12 .1 Where the Architect/Contract Administrator issues an instruction otherwise than in writing, it shall be of no immediate effect but the Contractor shall confirm it in writing to the Architect/Contract Administrator within 7 days, and, if he does not dissent by notice to the Contractor within 7 days from receipt of the Contractor's confirmation, it shall take effect as from the expiry of the latter 7 day period.

- .2 If within 7 days of giving an instruction otherwise than in writing the Architect/Contract Administrator confirms it in writing, the Contractor shall not be obliged to confirm it and it shall take effect as from the date of the Architect/Contract Administrator's confirmation.

- .3 If neither the Contractor nor the Architect/Contract Administrator confirms such an instruction in the manner and time stated but the Contractor nevertheless complies with it, the Architect/Contract Administrator may at any time prior to the issue of the Final Certificate confirm it with retrospective effect.

Provisions empowering instructions

3.13 On receipt of an instruction or purported instruction the Contractor may request the Architect/Contract Administrator to notify him which provision of these Conditions empowers its issue and the Architect/Contract Administrator shall forthwith comply with the request. If the Contractor thereafter complies with that instruction with neither Party then having invoked any dispute resolution procedure under this Contract to establish the Architect/Contract Administrator's powers in that regard, the instruction shall be deemed to have been duly given under the specified provision.

Instructions requiring Variations

3.14 .1 The Architect/Contract Administrator may issue instructions requiring a Variation.

.2 Any instruction of the type referred to in clause 5.1.2 shall be subject to the Contractor's right of reasonable objection set out in clause 3.10.1.

.3 In respect of the Contractor's Designed Portion, any instruction requiring a Variation shall be an alteration to or modification of the Employer's Requirements.

.4 The Architect/Contract Administrator may sanction in writing any Variation made by the Contractor otherwise than pursuant to an instruction.

.5 No Variation required by the Architect/Contract Administrator or subsequently sanctioned by him shall vitiate this Contract.

Postponement of work

3.15 The Architect/Contract Administrator may issue instructions in regard to the postponement of any work to be executed under this Contract.

Instructions on Provisional Sums

3.16 The Architect/Contract Administrator shall issue instructions in regard to the expenditure of Provisional Sums included in the Contract Bills or in the Employer's Requirements.

Inspection – tests

3.17 The Architect/Contract Administrator may issue instructions requiring the Contractor to open up for inspection any work covered up or to arrange for or carry out any test of any materials or goods (whether or not already incorporated in the Works) or of any executed work. The cost of such opening up or testing (including the cost of making good) shall be added to the Contract Sum unless provided for in the Contract Bills or unless the inspection or test shows that the materials, goods or work are not in accordance with this Contract.

Work not in accordance with the Contract

3.18 If any work, materials or goods are not in accordance with this Contract the Architect/Contract Administrator, in addition to his other powers, may:

.1 issue instructions in regard to the removal from the site of all or any of such work, materials or goods;

.2 after consultation with the Contractor and with the agreement of the Employer, allow all or any of such work, materials or goods to remain (except those which are part of the Contractor's Designed Portion), in which event he shall notify the Contractor to that effect but that shall not be construed as a Variation and an appropriate deduction shall be made from the Contract Sum;

.3 after consultation with the Contractor, issue such instructions requiring a Variation as are reasonably necessary as a consequence of any instruction under clause 3.18.1 and/or of any notification under clause 3.18.2 (but to the extent that such instructions are reasonably necessary, no addition shall be made to the Contract Sum and no extension of time shall be given); and/or

.4 having due regard to the Code of Practice set out in Schedule 4, issue such instructions under clause 3.17 to open up for inspection or to test as are reasonable in all the circumstances to establish to the reasonable satisfaction of the Architect/Contract Administrator the likelihood or extent, as appropriate to the circumstances, of any further similar non-compliance. To the extent that such instructions are reasonable, whatever the results of the opening up, no addition shall be made to the Contract Sum but clauses 2.28 and 2.29.2.2 shall apply unless the inspection or test shows that the work, materials or goods are not in accordance with this Contract.

Workmanship not in accordance with the Contract

3.19 Where there is any failure to comply with clause 2.1 in regard to the carrying out of work in a proper and workmanlike manner and/or in accordance with the Construction Phase Plan, the Architect/ Contract Administrator, in addition to his other powers, may, after consultation with the Contractor, issue such instructions (whether requiring a Variation or otherwise) as are in consequence reasonably necessary. To the extent that such instructions are reasonably necessary, no addition shall be made to the Contract Sum and no extension of time shall be given.

Executed work

3.20 In respect of any materials, goods or workmanship, as comprised in executed work, which under clause 2.3 are to be to the reasonable satisfaction of the Architect/Contract Administrator, the Architect/Contract Administrator, if he is dissatisfied, shall give the reasons for such dissatisfaction to the Contractor within a reasonable time from the execution of the unsatisfactory work.

Exclusion of persons from the Works

3.21 The Architect/Contract Administrator may (but shall not unreasonably or vexatiously) issue instructions requiring the exclusion from the site of any person employed thereon.

Power to issue instructions

4.12 The Architect, by clause 3.10, can only issue instructions where express power is given to him to do so. In some instances the employer's consent is required. The most important powers for the issue of instructions relate to:

1   Clause 2.10 (levels).
2   Clause 2.15 (discrepancies in documents).
3   Clause 2.16 (discrepancies in CDP documents).
4   Clause 2.17 (divergence between statutory requirements and documents).
5   Clause 2.38.1 (defects, shrinkages or other faults).
6   Clause 2.38.2 (rectification of defects).
7   Clause 3.4 (instructions to clerk of works).
8   Clause 3.14.1 (variations) – subject to right of reasonable objection in clause 3.14.2.
9   Clause 3.15 (postponement of work).
10 Clause 3.16 (instructions on provisional sums).
11 Clause 3.17 (opening up and tests).
12 Clause 3.18.1 (removal of work, materials and goods).
13 Clause 3.18.3 (variation instructions following clauses 3.18.1 and 3.18.2).
14 Clause 3.18.4 (inspections and tests).
15 Clause 3.19 (failure to comply with clause 2.1).
16 Clause 3.21 (exclusions of persons from the works).
17 Clause 3.22 (antiquities).

4.13 The Architect will not usually be able to vary the works simply to have them carried out by a different contractor (see *Commissioner for Main Roads v Reed & Stuart Pty* (1974) 12 BLR 55). In principle, in the absence of an architect's instruction, the contractor is not entitled to extra payment for any increased costs due to variations (although by clause 3.14.4 the Architect may sanction in writing any variation made by the contractor otherwise than pursuant to an instruction). Merely permitting the contractor to alter the proposed method of construction at the contractor's request does not ordinarily amount to a variation, although such permission may amount to a variation in the design or quality – or both – of the works (see *Simplex Concrete Piles v Borough of St Pancras* (1980) 14 BLR 80).

4.14 If the contractor does not comply with any instructions properly given by the Architect, the Architect may give written notice to the contractor to comply. If compliance is not achieved within 7 days, clause 3.11 allows the employer to employ others to carry out and complete the works. The employer may obtain an interim injunction to prevent the contractor from refusing access to the site for persons whom the employer has employed to carry out works necessary in respect of an instruction with which the contractor has not complied: *Bath and North East Somerset District Council v Mowlem plc* [2004][1] BLR 153.

4.15 Under clause 3.13 the contractor may request the Architect to specify in writing the provision of the Conditions which empowers the issue of an instruction. If the Architect specifies a provision and the contractor then obeys the instruction, the instruction is deemed to be empowered by the provision in the contract specified in the Architect's answer. If the contractor is not satisfied with the Architect's answer, the matter may be referred to adjudication or arbitration during the progress of the works.

Form of instructions

4.16 By clause 1.7.1 all instructions are to be in writing, but note the elaborate provisions in clauses 3.12.1 to 3.12.3 for confirmation in writing if the Architect in fact issues an oral instruction. Instructions should be given in clear terms. The RIBA publishes a common form for the giving of instructions, which should be used.

Site meeting minutes

4.17 Sometimes the Architect and the contractor expressly agree that site meeting minutes are to operate as the confirmation of oral instructions contemplated by clause 3.12.2. If there is no express agreement as to the status of the minute, in each case it must be decided whether in fact it was intended that the minutes should act as written confirmation of the instructions. Significant factors to take into account would be the authorship of the minutes and whether they are accepted by all parties as a true record of the meeting.

---

[1]BLR changed its form of citation from 1999 when it was acquired by Lloyd's of London Press.

5 Section 4: Payment

Clauses 4.1 to 4.5: Contract Sum and Adjustments

5.01 Unless there is a case for rectification the parties are bound by any errors incorporated into the contract sum. Rectification is available either where the document fails to record the mutual intentions of the parties or where it fails to record accurately the intention of one party only, where the other with knowledge of the first party's error has nevertheless stood by and allowed him to sign the agreement (see *Bates v Wyndhams* [1981] 1 All ER 1077).

5.02 Clause 4.3 provides a detailed guide as to how the contract sum is to be adjusted by way of variation agreements, deductions and additions so as to produce the final account. Clause 4.5 provides a timetable for the production of the final account by way of provision by the contractor of all necessary material within 6 months of the date of issue of the Practical Completion Certificate, and for the production of a final account within 3 months thereafter. Subject to the Architect's decision on matters of principle, the final account will be prepared by the quantity surveyor. In *Tameside Metropolitan Borough Council v Barlow Securities Group Services Ltd* [2001] BLR 113 the Court of Appeal held that it was a pre-condition of the Architect's duty to provide a final account that the contractor should provide him with all the necessary documentation to do so pursuant to the requirements of (the predecessor of) clause 4.5.1.

5.03 Clause 4.4 provides for adjustments to the Contract Sum to be included in interim certificates as soon as their amount has been ascertained.

Issue of Interim Certificates

4.9 .1 The Architect/Contract Administrator shall issue Interim Certificates in accordance with clause 4.9.2, each stating the amount due to the Contractor from the Employer, to what the amount relates and the basis on which the amount has been calculated.

.2 Interim Certificates shall be issued on the dates provided for in the Contract Particulars up to the date of practical completion of the Works or the date within one month thereafter. Interim Certificates shall thereafter be issued on the same date at intervals of 2 months (unless otherwise agreed) and upon whichever is the later of the expiry of the Rectification Period or the issue of the Certificate of Making Good (or, where there are Sections, the last such period or certificate).

Amounts due in Interim Certificates

4.10 Subject to any agreement between the Parties as to stage payments, the amount stated as due in an Interim Certificate shall be the Gross Valuation pursuant to clause 4.16 less the aggregate of:

.1 any amount which may be deducted and retained by the Employer as provided in clauses 4.18 to 4.20 ('the Retention');

.2 the cumulative total of the amounts of any advance payment that have then become due for reimbursement to the Employer in accordance with the terms stated in the Contract Particulars for clause 4.8; and

.3 the amount stated as due in previous Interim Certificates.

Interim valuations

4.11 Interim valuations shall be made by the Quantity Surveyor whenever the Architect/Contract Administrator considers them necessary for ascertaining the amount to be stated as due in an Interim Certificate, except where Fluctuations Option C (*formula adjustment*) applies[45], when an interim valuation shall be made before the issue of each Interim Certificate.

Application by Contractor

4.12 Without affecting the Architect/Contract Administrator's obligation to issue Interim Certificates, the Contractor, not later than 7 days before the date for issue of an Interim Certificate, may submit to the Quantity Surveyor an application setting out what the Contractor considers to be the amount of the Gross Valuation. If the Contractor submits such an application, the Quantity Surveyor shall make an interim valuation. If the Quantity Surveyor disagrees with the amount shown in the application, he shall at the time of making the valuation submit to the Contractor a statement, which shall be in similar detail to the application and shall identify the disagreement.

Interim Certificates – payment

4.13 .1 The final date for payment pursuant to an Interim Certificate shall be 14 days from the date of issue of that Interim Certificate.

.2 Notwithstanding his fiduciary interest in the Retention as stated in clause 4-18, the Employer is entitled to exercise any rights under this Contract of withholding or deduction from sums due or to become due to the Contractor against any amount due under an Interim Certificate, whether or not any Retention is included in that Interim Certificate under clause 4.20.

.3 Not later than 5 days after the date of issue of an Interim Certificate the Employer shall give a notice to the Contractor which shall, in respect of the amount stated as due in that Interim Certificate, specify the amount of the payment proposed to be made, to what the amount relates and the basis on which the amount has been calculated.

.4 Not later than 5 days before the final date for payment the Employer may give a notice to the Contractor which shall specify any amount proposed to be withheld or deducted from the amount due, the ground or grounds for such withholding or deduction and the amount of withholding or deduction attributable to each ground.

.5 Subject to any notice given under clause 4.13.4, the Employer shall no later than the final date for payment pay the Contractor the amount specified in the notice given under clause 4.13.3 or, in the absence of a notice under clause 4.13.3, the amount stated as due in the Interim Certificate.

.6 If the Employer fails properly to pay the amount, or any part of it, due to the Contractor under these Conditions by the final date for its payment, the Employer shall, in addition to the amount not properly paid, pay the Contractor simple interest at the Interest Rate for the period until payment is made. Interest under this clause 4.13 shall be a debt due to the Contractor by the Employer.

.7 Where there is a failure to issue an Interim Certificate either on time or at all, the Contractor's entitlement to interest shall commence on and be calculated from and including the day immediately following the date that would have been the final date for payment had that certificate been issued on time.

.8 Acceptance of a payment of interest under this clause 4.13 shall not in any circumstances be construed as a waiver of the Contractor's right to proper payment of the principal amount due, to suspend performance under clause 4.14 or to terminate his employment under section 8.

Contractor's right of suspension

4.14 Without affecting the Contractor's other rights and remedies, if the Employer, subject to any notice issued pursuant to clause 4.13.4, fails to pay the Contractor in full (including any VAT properly chargeable in respect of such payment) by the final date for payment as required by these Conditions and the failure continues for 7 days after the Contractor has given notice to the Employer, with a copy to the Architect/Contract Administrator, of his intention to suspend the performance of his obligations under this Contract and the ground or grounds on which it is intended to suspend performance, the Contractor may suspend such performance until payment is made in full.

Final Certificate – issue and payment[46]

4.15 .1 The Architect/Contract Administrator shall issue the Final Certificate not later than 2 months after whichever of the following occurs last:

    .1 the end of the Rectification Period in respect of the Works or (where there are Sections) the last such period to expire;

    .2 the date of issue of the Certificate of Making Good under clause 2.39 or (where there are Sections) the last such certificate to be issued; or

    .3 the date on which the Architect/Contract Administrator sends to the Contractor copies of the statement and of any ascertainment to be prepared under clause 4.5.2.

.2 The Final Certificate shall state:

    .1 the Contract Sum adjusted as necessary in accordance with clause 4.3; and

    .2 the sum of the amounts already stated as due in Interim Certificates plus the amount of any advance payment paid pursuant to clause 4.8;

and the difference (if any) between the two sums shall (without affecting the rights of the Contractor in respect of any Interim Certificate not paid in full by the Employer by its final date for payment) be expressed in the Final Certificate as a balance due to the Contractor from the Employer or to the Employer from the Contractor, as the case may be. The Final Certificate shall state the basis on which that amount has been calculated.

.3 Not later than 5 days after the date of issue of the Final Certificate the Party by whom the balance is stated to be payable ('the paying Party') shall give a notice to the other Party which shall, in respect of the balance stated as due, specify the amount of the payment proposed to be made, to what the amount relates and the basis on which the amount has been calculated.

.4 The final date for payment of the balance shall be 28 days from the date of issue of the Final Certificate. Not later than 5 days before the final date for payment the paying Party may give a notice to the other Party which shall specify any amount proposed to be withheld or deducted from any balance due to the other Party, the ground or grounds for such withholding or deduction and the amount of withholding or deduction attributable to each ground.

.5 Where the paying Party does not give a notice pursuant to clause 4.15.3 he shall, subject to any notice given under clause 4.15.4, pay the other Party any balance stated as due to the other Party in the Final Certificate.

.6 If the paying Party fails properly to pay the balance, or any part of it, by the final date for its payment, he shall in addition to the amount not properly paid pay to the other Party simple interest at the Interest Rate for the period until payment is made.

.7 Where there is a failure to issue the Final Certificate either on time or at all, the provisions of clause 4.13.7 shall correspondingly apply in respect of interest on any balance due to the Contractor.

.8 Acceptance of a payment of interest under this clause 4.15 shall not in any circumstances be construed as a waiver of any right to proper payment of the balance.

.9 The balance due and any interest under this clause 4.15 shall be a debt due by the paying Party to the other Party.

Gross Valuation

Ascertainment

4.16 The Gross Valuation shall be the total of the amounts referred to in clauses 4.16.1 and 4.16.2 less the total of the amounts referred to in clause 4.16.3, applied up to and including a date not more than 7 days before the date of the Interim Certificate.

.1 The total values of the following which are subject to Retention shall be included:

.1 work properly executed by the Contractor (including work so executed for which a value has been agreed pursuant to clause 5.2.1 or which has been valued under the Valuation Rules and work for which there is a Confirmed Acceptance of a Variation Quotation), together, where applicable, with any adjustment of that value under Fluctuations Option C or by Confirmed Acceptance of an Acceleration Quotation, but excluding any amounts referred to in clause 4.16.2.3. Where there is an Activity Schedule, the value of the work in each activity to which it relates shall be a proportion of the price stated for the work in that activity equal to the proportion of the work in that activity that has then been properly executed;

.2 Site Materials, provided that their value shall only be included if they are adequately protected against weather and other casualties and they are not on the Works prematurely; and

.3 Listed Items (if any), when their value is to be included under clause 4.17.

.2 The following which are not subject to Retention shall be included:

.1 any amounts to be included in Interim Certificates in accordance with clause 4.4 as a result of payments made or costs incurred by the Contractor under clause 2.6.2, 2.21, 2.23, 3.17 or 6.5 or paragraph A.5.1, B.2.1.2 or C.3.1 of Schedule 3;

.2 any amounts ascertained under clause 4.23;

.3 any amounts in respect of any restoration, replacement or repair of loss or damage and removal and disposal of debris under paragraph B.3.5 or C.4.5.2 of Schedule 3 or clause 6.10.4.2; and

.4 any amount payable to the Contractor under Fluctuations Option A or B, if applicable.

.3 The following shall be deducted:

.1 any amounts deductible under clause 2.10, 2.38, 3.11 or 3.18.2; and

.2 any amount allowable by the Contractor to the Employer under Fluctuations Option A or B, if applicable.

Clauses 4.6 to 4.15: Certificates and Payments

5.04 When Value Added Tax was introduced the Joint Contracts Tribunal decided that the Contract Sum should be exclusive of VAT. A separate document was issued by the JCT originally entitled 'supplemental VAT Agreement'. The general intention was that the contractor should be entitled to recover from the employer, as an additional sum, such VAT as he might have to pay to HM Customs and Excise on his supply of goods and services to the employer. The agreement also provided a machinery for dealing with difficulties which might arise. The subsequent document, entitled 'Supplemental Provisions (the VAT Agreement)' has disappeared from the 2005 edition, in recognition of the fact that most building work today attracts VAT.

5.05 Clause 4.6.1 states that the Contract Sum is exclusive of VAT and requires the employer to pay the VAT properly chargeable in respect of any payment made under the contract. Clause 4.6.2 caters for the situation where the supply of goods and services to the employer becomes exempt after the date of tender.

5.06 Tax is a complicated subject, and one wholly outside the scope of this chapter. On any point of difficulty architects should take advice from an accountant, a solicitor or a barrister specializing in tax matters.

Certificates

5.07 The Architect is under a duty to issue interim certificates at monthly intervals following the date specified in the Contract Particulars, stating the amount due to the contractor and (in accordance with section 110 of the Housing Grants, Construction and Regeneration Act 1996) to what the amount relates and the basis on which it was calculated. If he certifies an excessive amount, he may be liable to the employer in damages (see *Sutcliffe v Thackrah* [1974] AC 727). The Conditions now provide (clause 4.9.2) that following practical completion the interval between interim certificates extends to two months, until and including the later of the expiry of the Rectification Period and the issue of the Certificate of Making Good.

5.08 The issue of the certificate is a condition precedent to the contractor's right to payment: *Henry Boot Ltd v Alstom Combined Cycles Ltd* [2005] 1 WLR 3850. In the event, however, of non-issue of a certificate, the new clause 1.11 provides that a failure to issue an interim certificate on time or at all creates a dispute or difference so enabling an adjudicator to review the position and decide that the contractor is entitled to receive an interim payment as if the certificate had been issued.

5.09 Certificates are finally payable within 14 days of issue: clause 4.13.1. Interest, at 5% above current Bank of England base rate, is due in the event of late payment (clause 4.13.6). Clause 4.13.3 requires the employer, within 5 days of the issue of an interim certificate, to give the contractor a payment-notice, that is, a notice of the amount that he proposes to pay, to what it relates and its basis of calculation. This is a statutory requirement of HGCRA 1996, section 110(2). However, clause 4.13.5 in effect allows him simply to pay the total amount due under the interim certificate without giving the payment-notice. This may avoid unnecessary administration where there is no objection to the total certified. If, however, the employer proposes to deduct or withhold any amount he must provide a payment-notice.

5.10 Under clause 4.13.4, the employer is entitled, in the exercise of a right under the contract, to make a deduction from interim certificates, including retention money included in such certificates, by means of a withholding-notice as required by HGCRA 1996 section 111. A withholding-notice is a mandatory condition of the right to withhold or deduct: *Morgan Building Services (LLC) Ltd v Jervis* [2004] BLR 18. The clause states that the employer may, not later than 5 days before final payment becomes due, give (written) notice to the contractor of any payment that he proposes to withhold, and the ground or grounds for withholding, and of the amount to be withheld under each ground. If a payment-notice has been issued under clause 4.13.3, covering the matters otherwise required by clause 4.13.4 (i.e. reasons for and amount of deductions), it can double as a withholding-notice and a separate notice under clause 4.13.4 would be superfluous. Only if the payment-notice is insufficient, or if new matters have arisen, will a separate withholding-notice be required under clause 4.13.4.

5.11 The contract does not cover the position if defects appear within the last five days before payment (i.e. after the time for issue of a withholding-notice). It is not clear whether there could be a valid ground for holding up the payment or whether the Architect would have to take the defects into account in the following certificate. Given the statutory requirement for a withholding-notice, it is more likely that the latter would be the appropriate course.

5.12 Clause 4.11 provides that interim valuations may be carried out by the Quantity Surveyor, although the Architect should ensure that the Quantity Surveyor adopts the correct principles when making such valuations. If Fluctuations Option C applies the Quantity Surveyor must make an interim valuation before the issue of each interim certificate.

5.13 The contractor is permitted to submit an application to the Quantity Surveyor stating what he considers to be the gross valuation of the works (clause 4.12). It should be noted that the Architect must issue interim certificates irrespective of whether there has been any such application, but that, if one is made, the Quantity Surveyor is obliged to make an interim valuation.

5.14 Under clause 4.14 the contractor is entitled to suspend the performance of *all* his obligations under the contract in the event of non-payment by the employer (and not just the obligation to perform the works), after the contractor has given written notice to the employer and the Architect of his intention to do so. Thus, for example, the contractor may suspend his insurance cover. The implications of so doing should be brought to the employer's attention.

Amounts due in interim certificates

5.15 Clause 4.10 has considerably simplified the ascertainment of the amount due in any interim certificate. It is to be the Gross Valuation (as ascertained pursuant to clause 4.16) less the aggregate of:

1   The amount of any retention (see clauses 4.18 to 4.20).
2   The cumulative total of the amounts of any advance payment reimbursement (see clause 4.8).
3   The amounts stated as due in previous interim certificates.

Changes to the payment regime

5.16 The Local Democracy, Economic Development and Construction Act 2009 received the Royal Assent on 12th November 2009. This marks the conclusion of the lengthy process of review of sections 104 to 117 of the Housing Grants, Construction and Regeneration Act 1996 which began in 2004. The majority of the draft sections of the proposed legislation have been in the public arena since July 2008, although two further government amendments were introduced in October 2009.

5.17 The passage of the Act will be followed by a further consultation upon the necessary consequent changes to the Scheme for Construction Contracts, so that part 8 of the Act, which contains the amendments to the Housing Grants, Construction and Regeneration Act 1996, may not come into force until late 2010 at the earliest. The new payment regime will only apply to contracts entered into after the coming into force of part 8 of the Act, so that the existing regime is set to continue for some time. However the amendments to the existing regime are considerable and will require changes to be made to the standard forms of contract, including the JCT suite of contracts. It would be as well for architects to begin to familiarise themselves with the effects of the amendments as soon as possible.

5.18 The principal changes to the statutory payment regime are designed to address the problems which have been encountered with the existing regime since 1996 as revealed by the case law on the subject and are as follows:

1 The regime will apply to all construction contracts whether oral or written or a combination of the two. The relevant provisions of the Scheme will apply if the contract is non-compliant with the statute.
2 The regime will be based on the giving of payment notices not later than five days after any contractual payment becomes due. These may be given by the payer or by a specified person on his behalf (likely to be the certifier in JCT contracts), or, if they fail to do so, by the payee. Payment notices must be given even if the sum due is zero.
3 The sum notified must be paid on or before the final date for payment unless the payer or the specified person gives a pay less notice to the payee specifying the lesser sum considered to be payable and the basis of calculation of that sum.
4 The payee's right to suspend performance in the event of non-payment may be exercised in respect of some only or all of his contractual obligations, and he may recover reasonable costs and expenses incurred as a result of the suspension. Furthermore he will be entitled to an extension of time not only for the period of suspension but for any consequential delay resulting from the suspension.

5.19 A fuller discussion of the legislative amendments can be found at paragraphs 9.01 to 9.20 of Chapter 22 of this book.

Final certificate

5.20 The responsibility for issuing this certificate is a heavy one, and the Architect should not issue it unless he is satisfied that the contract has been fully complied with. He must re-consider the whole of the contractor's performance under the contract and his right to payment notwithstanding the inclusion or otherwise of sums in interim certificates. The final certificate must be issued within 2 months of the latest of the following events (clause 4.15.1):

1 The end of the Rectification Period.
2 The issue of the Certificate of Making Good under clause 2.39.
3 The date upon which the Architect sent to the contractor a copy of any statement and ascertainment to which clause 4.5.2.2 refers (final adjustment of Contract Sum).

In each case where the contract provides for work sections the reference is to the last such event.

5.21 The form of the final certificate is governed by clause 4.15.2. Note that the final certificate may show a balance in favour of the employer if monies have been over-paid in earlier certificates. It is not necessary to hold back payment from earlier certificates merely to keep something in reserve for the purposes of the final certificate, although it is often considered prudent. RIBA Publications Ltd publishes a form of Final Certificate.

5.22 Again (see paragraphs 5.09 and 5.10 above) the contract contains detailed notice provisions which the employer is required to follow if he wishes to withhold any sums from the final payment (clauses 4.15.3 and 4.15.4). There is a right to interest, at 5% above current Bank of England base rate, in the event of late payment (clause 4.15.6).

Effect of final certificate

5.23 The final certificate is not merely the last certificate; it is, if properly issued in accordance with the contract, a document of considerable legal importance. Subject to certain qualifications, it is conclusive evidence of the following matters:

1 Where the quality of materials or goods or the standards of workmanship are expressly stated to be for the approval of the Architect, they are to his reasonable satisfaction, but not that the materials or goods or workmanship comply with any other contractual requirement (clause 1.9.1.1).
2 All the terms of the contract which require an adjustment to be made of the contract sum have been complied with (clause 1.9.1.2).
3 All and only such extensions of time as are due under clause 2.28 have been given (clause 1.9.1.3).
4 The reimbursement of direct loss and/or expense, if any, to the contractor pursuant to clause 4.23 is in final settlement of all claims arising out of the occurrence of the Relevant Matters referred to in clause 4.24 (clause 1.9.1.4).

5.24 In summary, the qualifications are:

1 Where proceedings of any sort have been commenced by either party before the issue of the final certificate, the conclusiveness of the certificate becomes subject to any decision, award, judgment or settlement of such proceedings or settlement of matters in issue in such proceedings (clause 1.9.2).
2 Where proceedings of any sort are commenced by either party within 28 days after its issue, the final certificate is then conclusive save only in respect of the matters to which the proceedings relate (clause 1.9.3).
3 Fraud (clause 1.9.1).
4 Accidental inclusion or exclusion of items or arithmetical error (clause 1.9.1.2).

5.25 Clause 1.9.4 provides that, where the parties receive an adjudicator's decision after the issue of the Final Certificate, if one of the parties wishes the subject matter of the decision to be litigated or arbitrated, that party may commence proceedings within 28 days of that decision. It does not mention the evidential effect of the Final Certificate. It is probably intended to mean that the Final Certificate (as confirmed or amended by the adjudicator's decision) does not have conclusive effect provided that legal or arbitration proceedings are commenced within 28 days after the adjudicator's decision.

Gross Valuation and interim certificates

5.26 The amount to be included in interim certificates is defined by clauses 4.16 and 4.17. Clauses 4.16.1 and 4.16.2 deal with matters which are and are not subject to retention respectively. The principal item in clause 4.16.1.1 is the total value of work properly executed by the contractor. This means that the amounts certified should take into account adjustments for variation, price fluctuations, and defects. RIBA Publications Ltd publishes forms of interim certificate and direction, and a statement of retention. Clause 4.16.1.1 includes provisions for where a Variation Quotation (formerly a Price Statement) is accepted, and further that the prices to be used in the valuation should be ascertained from a priced Activity Schedule (if one is used).

5.27 Clause 4.16.1.2 requires the total value of unincorporated materials and goods to be included in interim certificates, subject to certain conditions. By clause 2.24 where such materials and goods have been paid for, by inclusion of their value in an interim certificate, property in them passes to the employer.

5.28 Clause 4.16.2 deals with materials which are not subject to retention. Broadly, retention is to be deducted where the contractor had some responsibility for the matters in question, so that the employer's interests have to be protected by making the deduction. There will be no retention in instances where the employer's interests do not require such protection: thus, for example, ascertained additions to the Contract Sum are not subject to retention (see clause 4.16.2.1) nor are amounts of direct loss and/or expense payable to the contractor and included in interim certificates (see clause 4.16.2.2).

5.29 Clause 4.16.3 provides for there to be deducted from the Gross Valuation sums which are deductible from the Contract Sum by reason of contractor defects, omissions or errors.

Valuation of off-site materials

5.30 Clause 4.17 deals with certification in respect of prefabricated goods and materials not on site. If goods and materials are not on site, the employer has less protection in the event of the contractor's insolvency, and in certain other circumstances, than if they are on site. If the employer wishes to pay for goods before their delivery to site, he must list those goods and annex the list to the Contract Bills ('the Listed Items'). The contractor must then fulfil certain conditions if he desires to be paid for those goods in interim valuations:

1   The contractor must provide reasonable proof to the Architect that the property in the items has vested in him, so that upon payment property in them can pass to the employer.
2   The contractor must also provide reasonable proof that the items are insured against Specified Perils for the period from the transfer of property to the contractor until their delivery to the works.
3   If the items are off-site, they must be set apart or visibly and individually marked, identifying the employer and their destination as the works.
4   If the goods are 'uniquely identified Listed Items' (e.g. a boiler from a specified supplier), the contractor must provide a bond in favour of the employer from a surety if required to do so in the Contract Particulars.
5   If the goods are 'Listed Items which are not uniquely identified' (e.g. a quantity of bricks) the contractor must in any event provide a bond from a surety.

Retention

5.31 The purpose of retention is to provide the employer with security for the contractor's due performance of his obligations in relation to the quality of the work. The percentage of retention is now 3%, unless the parties have agreed a lesser rate for work or sections of work which have not reached practical completion (clause 4.20.2.1), and half that on work which has reached practical completion (clause 4.20.3). When the Certificate of Making Good is issued, it has the effect of releasing the retention in respect of the works, or that part of them to which that certificate relates.

Rules on treatment of retention

5.32 The retention rules are contained in clauses 4.18 and 4.20. They provide a precise regime for the treatment of retention monies, but complications can arise when the employer does not pay retention monies into a separate bank account, whether because the contractor does not request it or because his request is ignored. Complications can also be experienced where sub-contractors have interests in part of the retention monies.

5.33 Under clause 4.18.1, the employer holds the retention monies as fiduciary on trust for the contractor. In *Wales Construction Ltd v Franthom Property Ltd* (1991) 53 BLR 23, the Court of Appeal held that (the equivalent of) clause 4.18.1 had the effect of requiring the employer to place the retention monies in a separate bank account if required to do so, and clause 4.18.3 makes this an express requirement except where the employer is a local authority. The intention is that the retention money should be set aside as a separate fund to be used only for the purpose of providing the employer with security against the making good of defects, and the purpose of making the employer a trustee is to protect the retention money against his liquidation. It is not available for the employer to use as working capital.

5.34 If, however, no actual separate fund is set up, in the event of the employer's liquidation there will be no effective trust, and therefore the contractor will have to prove for his retention monies along with the employer's general creditors (*MacJordan Construction Ltd v Brookmount Erostin Ltd* (1991) 53 BLR 1), so it is important to ensure that the exercise of setting up a separate fund is carried out. If the employer fails to do this the court will grant a mandatory injunction enforcing the obligation before liquidation, but the Court of Appeal considered that it would be unlikely to do so after liquidation, as to do so might constitute a preference under the Insolvency Act 1986. If the case involved a solvent employer but an insolvent contractor, and the employer had failed in his contractual obligation to set the retention monies aside, the court would treat the fund as having been set aside, so as to prevent the employer from relying on his own breach of contract. However, the court will not grant an injunction compelling the employer to set aside the retention money in a separate fund, where the employer has a claim against the contractor for a greater amount which is deductible from the retention monies (see clause 4.13.2 and *Henry Boot Building Ltd v The Croydon Hotel and Leisure Co Ltd*) (1985) 36 BLR 41).

5.35 Where clause 4.19 is applied by the Contract Particulars, it entitles the contractor to provide a Retention Bond from a surety approved by the employer in order to procure the release to him of monies that would otherwise be retained by the employer.

Fluctuations

Clauses 4.21 and 4.22

5.36 Clause 4.21 identifies three different bases, namely those set out in Options A, B and C of Schedule 7, by reference to which fluctuations are to be calculated. JCT Practice Note 17 (Series 1) gives guidance on the choice of fluctuations provisions. The Contract Particulars provide that Option A shall apply where no Fluctuations Option is selected. VAT is excluded from each of the Options.

5.37 Option A allows fluctuations in prices arising from changes in rates of contribution, levy, or tax payable by the contractor. These cover such matters as national insurance contributions and Industrial Training Board levies. Apart from changes in tax rates, no other price changes are taken into account where the parties contract on the basis that fluctuations are to be governed by Option A.

5.38 Options A and B both provide for the addition of a percentage increase, which must be specified in the Contract Particulars, to cover increases in head office or administrative costs. NJCC Procedure Note 7 contains information about the relevant clauses (A12 and B13). In both Options A and B notification in writing by the contractor to the Architect is a condition precedent of any payment being made to the contractor, and such notice must be given within a reasonable time after the occurrence of the event in question.

5.39 Options B and C both provide for what are known as 'full' fluctuations entitling the contractor to recover extra costs of labour, transport and materials as from a date specified in the contract.

5.40 Under Option C, adjustment of prices takes place in accordance with the Formula Rules issued by the JCT, using those current at the date of tender. Monthly bulletins are issued by the JCT giving details of price changes, and the contract sum falls to be adjusted in accordance with these.

Fluctuations where contractor is guilty of delay

5.41 In principle, the contractor is not entitled to price increases under the fluctuations clauses where these price increases arise during a period after the contractual completion date: this provides an added incentive to the contractor to meet the completion date. This is subject, however, to no amendments or deletions having been made to clauses 2.26 to 2.29 of the Conditions, and to the Architect having, in respect of every written notification by the contractor under clause 2.28, fixed or confirmed in writing a completion date in accordance with that clause (see paragraphs A9, B10 and C6). It is therefore incumbent on the Architect to ensure that clause 2.28 is properly administered, and that no amendments have been made to clauses 2.26 to 2.29, or alternatively that the appropriate parts of the selected fluctuations option are amended so as to delete the provision removing the 'freeze' on fluctuations if clauses 2.26 to 2.29 are amended.

Loss and Expense

Matters materially affecting regular progress

4.23 If in the execution of this Contract the Contractor incurs or is likely to incur direct loss and/or expense for which he would not be reimbursed by a payment under any other provision in these Conditions due to a deferment of giving possession of the site or relevant part of it under clause 2.5 or because the regular progress of the Works or of any part of them has been or is likely to be materially affected by any of the Relevant Matters, the Contractor may make an application to the Architect/Contract Administrator. If the Contractor makes such application, save where these Conditions provide that there shall be no addition to the Contract Sum or otherwise exclude the operation of this clause, then, if and as soon as the Architect/Contract Administrator is of the opinion that the regular progress has been or is likely to be materially affected as stated in the application or that direct loss and/or expense has been or is likely to be incurred due to such deferment, the Architect/Contract Administrator shall ascertain, or instruct the Quantity Surveyor to ascertain, the amount of the loss and/or expense which has been or is being incurred; provided always that the Contractor shall:

.1 make his application as soon as it has become, or should reasonably have become, apparent to him that the regular progress has been or is likely to be affected;

.2 in support of his application submit to the Architect/Contract Administrator upon request such information as should reasonably enable the Architect/Contract Administrator to form an opinion; and

.3 upon request submit to the Architect/Contract Administrator or to the Quantity Surveyor such details of the loss and/or expense as are reasonably necessary for such ascertainment.

Relevant Matters

4.24 The following are the Relevant Matters:

.1 Variations (excluding those where loss and/or expense is included in the Confirmed Acceptance of a Variation Quotation but including any other matters or instructions which under these Conditions are to be treated as, or as requiring, a Variation);

.2 Architect/Contract Administrator's instructions:

.1 under clause 3.15 or 3.16 (excluding an instruction for expenditure of a Provisional Sum for defined work);

.2 for the opening up for inspection or testing of any work, materials or goods under clause 3.17 (including making good), unless the cost is provided for in the Contract Bills or unless the inspection or test shows that the work, materials or goods are not in accordance with this Contract;

.3 in relation to any discrepancy or divergence referred to in clause 2.15;

.3 compliance with clause 3.22.1 or with Architect/Contract Administrator's instructions under clause 3.22.2;

.4 suspension by the Contractor under clause 4.14 of the performance of his obligations under this Contract, provided the suspension was not frivolous or vexatious;

.5 the execution of work for which an Approximate Quantity is not a reasonably accurate forecast of the quantity of work required;

.6 any impediment, prevention or default, whether by act or omission, by the Employer, the Architect/Contract Administrator, the Quantity Surveyor or any of the Employer's Persons, except to the extent caused or contributed to by any default, whether by act or omission, of the Contractor or of any of the Contractor's Persons.

Amounts ascertained – addition to Contract Sum

4.25 Any amounts form time to time ascertained under clause 4.23 shall be added to the Contract Sum.

Reservation of Contractor's rights and remedies

4.26 The provisions of clauses 4.23 to 4.25 are without prejudice to any other rights and remedies which the Contractor may posses

Clauses 4.23 to 4.26: Loss and expense caused by matters materially affecting regular progress of the works

Nature of Clauses 4.23 to 4.26

5.42 Clause 4.23 entitles the contractor to claim direct loss and/or expense arising as a result of the regular progress of the works (or part of them) being materially affected by any of the list of matters contained in clause 4.24 or by deferment of possession under clause 2.5. This is a carefully restricted list of circumstances under which the contractor may obtain payment, but since 2002 the list has included a 'catch-all' clause (clause 4.24.6) to the effect that any impediment, prevention or default by the employer (or his agents) will entitle the contractor to claim under the clause, except to the extent that the contractor (or his agents) have contributed to the default. By clause 4.26 the provisions of clauses 4.23 to 4.25 are without prejudice to any other rights and remedies which the contractor may possess, and therefore the provisions of clause 4.23 do not preclude any claim by the contractor for damages for breach of contract, negligence, misrepresentation, etc. Thus the contractor may pursue a claim for damages, even if a claim under clause 4.23 fails (*Fairclough v Vale of Belvoir Superstore* (1991) 56 BLR 74), or may even make a claim under clause 42.3 in order to obtain prompt reimbursement, and later claim damages for breach of contract, taking into account the amount awarded under clause 4.23 (*London Borough of Merton v Leach* (1985) 32 BLR 51 at 108).

5.43 The word 'direct' means damages which flow naturally from the breach without other intervening cause and independently of special circumstances (*Saint Line Ltd v Richardson* [1940] p4060 2 KB 99) and excludes claims for consequential loss (*Cawoods v Croudace* [1978] 2 Lloyd's Reports 55). It thus includes damages arising in the ordinary course of things, as in the first limb of *Hadley v Baxendale* (1859) 9 Ex. 3421. In general the computation of the amount of direct loss and/or expense should follow the lines for computation for ordinary damages for breach of contract, although a claim under clause 4.23 is not a claim for breach of contract as such: see *Wraight Ltd v PH & T (Holdings) Ltd* (1980) 13 BLR 26. In *F. G. Minter v Welsh HTSO* (1980) 13 BLR 1 the Court of Appeal held that under the 1963 JCT Form Clause 24(1) the contractor could claim as part of his direct loss and/or expense the amount of finance charges he incurred in respect of the amount of such loss and expense.

5.44 The word 'ascertain' means 'to find out for certain' rather than 'to make a general assessment' (*McAlpine v Property and Land Contractors* Ltd (1995) 76 BLR 59), but there is room for the exercise of judgment in the ascertainment of loss and expense (*How Engineering Services Ltd v Lindner Ceilings Ltd* (1999) 64 Con LR 67). It is not necessary to attempt too fine a distinction between what amounts are to be regarded as 'loss' and 'expense' respectively (*McAlpine v Property and Land Contractors Ltd* (1995 76 BLR 59).

5.45 All that is required under clause 4.23 is that direct loss/expense arises because 'regular progress of the works' is 'materially affected' or because giving possession of the site has been deferred under clause 2.5. There is no requirement that progress be delayed, nor that the whole of the works be affected. It could apply, for example, where the contractor is obliged to bring extra operatives on site, or where there is a loss of productivity of a certain trade.

5.46 It should be noted that any possible overlap between the operation of clause 4.23 and clauses 5.1 to 5.10 (Variations) is precluded by clause 5.10.2.

Notice

5.47 Clause 4.23 requires the contractor to make an application in writing to the Architect stating that he has incurred or is likely to incur such loss and expense. Once a notice has been given, the loss and expense must be ascertained from time to time by the Architect or quantity surveyor. Due to the wording of the current clause, only one such notice need now be given (reversing the position under the previous JCT Form). Under clause 4.23.1 the application must be made as soon as it has become or should reasonably have become apparent to the contractor that regular progress is being affected. The contractor must submit information in support of his application (clause 4.23.2), and must on request supply a breakdown of the loss and/or expense (see clause 4.23.3). It is thought that the requirement of a notice is a condition precedent to the contractor's rights under this clause.

Claims generally

5.48 The term 'claim' has no exact meaning, but for present purposes it may be considered to be any claim for payment by the contractor other than in respect of the original contract price. Any such claims fall under one of the following categories:

1 A right to payment arising under a clause of the contract.
2 A claim for damages for breach of contract.
3 Any other claim arising under neither 1 nor 2.

5.49 If a claim comes within 1, the Architect must follow whatever procedure the contract prescribes, according to the clause relied on by the contractor. The Architect need not consult the employer, although he may do so if he thinks it desirable. If the claim falls within 2, the Architect has no formal role under the contract in relation to it. He should consult the employer and should not include in a certificate any sum in respect of such a claim without the employer's agreement, as the contract gives him no power to certify in respect of a contractual claim for damages. Other, non-contractual, claims may be made, such as a claim for damages in tort, a restitutionary claim, or a claim to an ex gratia payment. In relation to these the Architect should only act as directed by the employer.

6 Section 5: Variations

6.01 The clauses in this section have been substantially re-organised and simplified in the 2005 edition. Clauses 5.1 to 5.10 are concerned with:

1 defining what constitutes a variation (clauses 5.1 to 5.5);
2 laying down the rules for valuing variations (clauses 5.6 to 5.10).

They should be read in conjunction with clauses 3.14 and 3.16, which respectively give the Architect power to issue instructions requiring a variation (subject to the contractor's right of reasonable objection set out in clause 3.10.1), and require the Architect to issue instructions in regard to the expenditure of provisional sums.

Definition of variation

6.02 Clause 5.1 defines the word 'Variation' in wide terms. Not only does it include alterations in the design, quality or quantity of the work itself (clause 5.1.1), but also, by clause 5.1.2, the imposition by the employer of, or alterations or omissions of, obligations or restrictions in relation to such matters as site access, working space, working hours and work sequence. Disputes frequently arise between employer and contractor as to whether work constitutes a variation and such disputes were frequently referred to arbitration. The Architect's decision as to what constitutes and does not constitute a variation will be subject to the adjudication process.

Limits on the Architect's powers

6.03 Despite the apparent breadth of the Architect's powers to order variations, it is generally thought that he cannot order variations of such extent or nature as to alter the nature of the works as originally contemplated. Nor is he entitled to include work wholly outside the scope of the original contract within a variation instruction (*Blue Circle Industries PLC v Holland Dredging Co (UK) Ltd* (1987) 37 BLR 40). The Architect's powers are limited to those given by the Conditions, which he has no power to vary or waive. Thus he cannot without the contractor's agreement require work that is the subject matter of a prime cost sum to be carried out by the contractor, and cannot omit work in order to have it carried out by another contractor (*Commissioner for Main Roads v Reed & Stuart Pty* (1980) 12 BLR 55; *Amec Building Ltd v Cadmus Investments Co Ltd* (1996) 51 Con LR 105 at 125–128). Nor can he instruct variations after practical completion.

Prime costs, provisional sums and approximate quantities

6.04 Prime cost sums are pre-estimates of expenditure which it is known will be incurred when the contract is entered into. Where work can be described but the quantity of work required cannot be accurately determined, an estimate of the quantity is to be given. This is identified as an approximate quantity. A provisional sum represents a sum which is included to meet unforeseen contingencies (which may not arise). More detailed definitions of these terms are set out in SMM. An instruction to expend a provisional sum is valued in the same way as a variation (clause 5.2.1.3).

Valuation rules

6.05 Clause 5.2 sets out the method for valuing all:

1 variations, whether instructed or sanctioned by the Architect or treated as such by the Conditions;
2 work executed in accordance with an instruction as to the expenditure of provisional sums;
3 work for which an approximate quantity has been included in the contract bills.

6.06 There are in effect four methods by which variations may be valued:

1 The value may be agreed at any stage by the employer and contractor.
2 Absent such agreement, the value is to be determined by the quantity surveyor in accordance with the rules contained in clauses 5.6 to 5.10.
3 As an alternative, employer and contractor may agree a different method of valuation.
4 In any event, a different method applies to variation instructions in respect of which a Variation Quotation has been formally accepted by the Architect (see clause 5.2.2): see paragraphs 6.18 to 6.24 below.

6.07 The rules set out in clauses 5.6 to 5.10 cover seven different situations:

1 The execution of additional or substituted work which can properly be valued by measurement (clauses 5.6.1.1 to 5.6.1.3).
2 The execution of work for which an approximate quantity is included in the Contract Bills, provided that the work has not been altered or modified other than in quantity (clauses 5.6.1.4 and 5.6.1.5).
3 The omission of work set out in the Contract Bills (clause 5.6.2).
4 The execution of additional or sustituted work which cannot properly be valued by measurement (clause 5.7).
5 Valuations relating to the Contractor's Designed Portion (clause 5.8).
6 Variations effecting a substantial change in the conditions under which other work is executed (clause 5.9).
7 Finally a residual provision for a fair valuation (clause 5.10).

6.08 Rule 1 governs three different scenarios relating to the similarity or dissimilarity of additional or substituted work to work originally set out in the Contract Bills:

1 The rates and prices set out in the Contract Bills determine the valuation where the additional or substituted work:
   (a) is of similar character to and
   (b) is executed under similar conditions as and
   (c) does not significantly change the quantity of the work set out in the Contract Bills.

2 The rates and prices set out in the Contract Bills form the basis for determining the valuation, with a fair allowance for difference in conditions or quantity, where (a) above remains true but either (b) or (c) do not.
3 The work is to be valued at fair rates and prices where it is of dissimilar character to work set out in the Contract Bills. This rule of valuation (clause 5.6.1.3) is in practice probably the most difficult to apply. It is necessary to decide first, whether it applies and then, if it does, how to apply it. It seems that one must look at the position at the time of acceptance of the tender and consider the character of the work then priced and the conditions under which the parties must have contemplated that it would be carried out. If the character of the various works or the conditions under which they were to be carried out differ, then this rule applies. The following, it is thought, may be examples of its application: material changes in quantities; winter instead of summer working; wet instead of dry; high instead of low; confined working space instead of ample working space. If it does apply, it is necessary to look at its effect, which must vary according to circumstances. In some cases a 'fair valuation' may result in no or very little change from bill rates. Indeed, the wording of this subclause is so wide that the payment of less than bill rates might be justified. Note, however, that a claim under clause 5.6.1.3 must be sharply differentiated from a claim for loss and expense.

6.09 Rule 2: in the case of Approximate Quantities, there are two alternatives:

1 The rate or price for the Approximate Quantity determines the valuation where the Approximate Quantity is a reasonably accurate forecast of the quantity of work required (clause 5.6.1.4).
2 Where that is not so, the rate or price for the Approximate Quantity forms the basis for determining the valuation, with a fair allowance for the difference in quantity (clause 5.6.1.5).

6.10 Measurement of variations under Rules 1 and 2 above is to be carried out in accordance with SMM, with allowance to be made for any percentage or lump sum adjustments in the Contract Bills, and preliminary items are also subject to adjustment (clause 5.6.3). Preliminary items defined by SMM consist broadly of overhead items which the contractor will incur, such as plant, site establishment, etc.

6.11 Rule 3: where work is omitted from the Contract Bills, the valuation of the omission is to be determined by the rates and prices for such work in the Contract Bills, except where it is CDP work, in which case clause 5.8 is applicable (clause 5.6.2).

6.12 Rule 4: where additional or substituted work is incapable of valuation by measurement, clause 5.7 requires it to be valued at daywork rates. Subject to any special agreement, the quantity surveyor must carry out the valuation in accordance with the rules laid down in clause 5.7, but the Architect is not bound to follow the quantity surveyor's valuation. The responsibility for valuation rests ultimately with the Architect, who may in a particular case take the view that the quantity surveyor has failed to apply the rules laid down correctly in principle. He may, for example, consider that varied work should have been valued at bill rates, whereas the quantity surveyor has valued it at 'fair' rates. At least in matters relating to certification the Architect is not bound to accept the quantity surveyor's opinions or valuation (*R B Burden Ltd v Swansea Corporation* compliance; [1957] 3 All ER 243). Note that the quantity surveyor has no authority to vary the terms of the contract; his function is confined to measuring and quantifying (*John Laing Construction Ltd v County and District Properties* (1982) 23 BLR 1).

6.13 Rule 5 is a new provision for the valuation of CDP work (clause 5.8), which imports the provisions of a number of the other valuation clauses into such a valuation.

6.14 Rule 6 deals with what might be termed indirect variations, where a variation which directly affects one aspect of the work also has indirect effect upon another aspect. For example, the Architect may require work to be carried out in a different sequence from that envisaged, resulting in certain finishing trades being obliged to work in parts of the building which are not fully watertight. In such circumstances the contractor would be entitled to be paid as if the indirectly-affected work were itself the subject of a variation (clause 5.9).

6.15 Rule 7 provides a 'fall back' method of valuing a variation to produce a fair result where none of the other methods can be applied, by simply providing for a fair valuation (clause 5.10).

6.16 Clause 5.10.2 excludes additional payment under the Valuation Rules for items which the contractor would be able to claim as loss and/or expense under any other provision of the contract. The policy of the 2005 JCT Form is, save in the case of Variation Quotations, to divorce claims for variations from claims for loss and expense.

Errors in the bills

6.17 The contractor may have made errors in pricing his tender on the basis of the bills of quantities, either by totalling figures incorrectly or by inserting a rate for a particular item which is manifestly excessive or too low. The parties are precluded from disputing the total contract sum by the wording of clause 4.2. Where a particular item is priced manifestly too low, contractors sometimes argue that, if work the subject of the uneconomic rate becomes the subject of variation, it should be valued at an economic rate and not at the bill rate. In the absence of any claim for rectification being sustainable it is thought that the bill rate should prevail and it is probable that the Architect would be in breach of his duty to his employer were he to agree to adopt the economic rate without the employer's express agreement.

Clause 5.3: Variation instruction – contractor's Variation Quotation

6.18 Clause 5.3 provides an alternative to the traditional method of valuing in accordance with the other valuation rules in Section 5. It is for the Architect in the first instance to decide whether he wishes clause 5.3 to be applied. If so he must specify this in his instruction. If he does the clause 5.3 method will apply, unless within 7 days the contractor states in writing that he disagrees with the application of clause 5.3 to the instruction. If the contractor does that, then, provided the Architect issues a further instruction for the variation to be carried out, it will be valued in accordance with the rules in clauses 5.6 to 5.10.

6.19 At the heart of the clause 5.3 method of valuation is what is called a 'Variation Quotation', which is a quotation to be provided by the contractor. Much of the detail of the operation of this method of valuation, which was previously to be found in clause 13A of the 1998 edition, has been removed into Schedule 2 of the 2005 Form. The commentary at paragraphs 6.21 to 6.25 below is therefore upon the provisions of Schedule 2.

6.20 Architects should not seek to employ the Variation Quotation procedure in the following situations, to which it is inappropriately suited because of its complexity and because of the amount of time required to operate it:

- a variation instruction which requires virtually immediate compliance;
- a variation which amounts to a minor amendment or correction to information in the contract documents.

6.21 If the valuation system is to work properly the Architect's variation instruction must give the contractor sufficient information upon the basis of which to provide a quotation. The note in Schedule 2 suggests that the information should be in a similar format to that provided at tender stage. If the contractor considers that the information provided is insufficient, then he has the right within 7 days to request further information: paragraph 1.1. The contractor

is allowed 21 days from receipt of the instruction or the further information in which to provide the quotation: paragraph 3.1.

6.22 The Variation Quotation must not merely provide a price for the variation. It must give the value of the entire adjustment to the contract sum, including the effect on any other work, any adjustment to the time required for completion of the works, any sum by way of 'direct loss and expense' under clause 4.23 and a fee for preparing the quotation: paragraph 1.2.

6.23 On receipt of the quotation the employer must choose whether or not to accept it. If he decides to accept it, the Architect must do so on his behalf within 7 days by giving the contractor an instruction to that effect referred to as a 'Confirmed Acceptance' containing specified information: paragraph 4.

6.24 The alternative course is for the employer not to accept the quotation. This may happen for two different reasons. One is simply that the employer considers the contractor's price to be excessive. In that case the Architect must instruct that the variation is to be carried out in any event and to be valued in accordance with the normal valuation rules: paragraph 5.1.1. The other reason is that, having seen the cost or delay implications, the employer decides that he does not want to have the varied work carried out after all. In that case the Architect should instruct the contractor that the varied work is not to be carried out: paragraph 5.1.2. Whatever the reason for the non-acceptance of the quotation, the contractor is entitled to be paid a fair and reasonable fee for preparing it: paragraph 5.2.

6.25 Revision 2 has introduced a new provision for an Acceleration Quotation into Schedule 2 by way of paragraph 2. This applies where the employer wished to investigate the possibility of achieving practical completion before the Completion Date for the works or for any section. The Architect will then invite proposals from the contractor in that regard, and the contractor may either provide an Acceleration Quotation setting out the details required by paragraph 2.1.1 or explain why it would be impracticable to accelerate the Completion Date. The provisions for submission, acceptance and non-acceptance are the same as those for a Variation Quotation.

Deemed variation

6.26 This term is frequently used to denote an occurrence which entitles (or is alleged to entitle) the contractor to extra payments even though the requirements of clause 5 have not been complied with. There are two principal occurrences which often give rise to a deemed variation:

1 The bills of quantities are inaccurate and fail to record correctly the quantity of work actually required, in which circumstance the contractor is entitled to extra payment under clause 2.14.1, which provides for such errors to be corrected, and clause 2.14.3, which provides for such correction to be treated as a variation.
2 Misstatements or inaccuracies in the bills of quantities may constitute an actionable misrepresentation for which the contractor is entitled to damages under the Misrepresentation Act 1967.

7 Section 6: Injury, Damage and Insurance

Contractor's liability under clauses 6.1 to 6.6 in respect of personal injury and injury or damage to property

7.01 Clause 6.1 requires the contradictor to indemnify the employer against liability, claims, losses and expenses, etc. arising from the death of or personal injury to any person occasioned in the carrying out of the works. However to the extent that the death or injury is due to any act or neglect of the employer or of the employer's persons there will be an apportionment of liability between employer and contractor.

7.02 Clause 6.2 deals with damage to property other than the works themselves. It requires the contractor to indemnify the employer against liability etc. arising from damage to property, real or personal, occasioned by the carrying out of the works. It differs from clause 6.1 in that the onus is implicitly on the employer to show that the injury or damage was due to negligence, breach of statutory duty, omission or default on the part of the contractor or the contractor's persons.

7.03 In clause 6.2 'property real or personal' excludes the works, work executed or site materials before the issue of the Practical Completion Certificate or the determination of the contractor's employment if earlier (clause 6.3). In a case of sectional completion (clause 6.3.2) or partial possession by the employer (clause 6.3.3) the completed section or part falls within the definition 'property real or personal'.

7.04 If Option C applies (insurance of existing structures), then the indemnity also excludes loss or damage to any property caused by a Specified Peril which is required to be insured under that clause. The decision in *Ossory Road (Skelmersdale) Limited v Balfour Beatty Building Limited* [1993] CILL 882 confirmed that where the contractor negligently damaged an existing structure, and such damage was caused by a Specified Peril (fire), the contractor would not be liable to the employer for loss or damage suffered by, or for third party claims against, the employer. This approach was affirmed by the Court of Appeal in *Scottish & Newcastle Plc v GD Construction (St Albans) Ltd* [2003] BLR 131, which held that the effect of requiring the employer to take out joint names insurance with the contractor, was that the parties allocated to the employer the risk of loss or damage by a fire caused by the negligence of a sub-contractor. The employer must look to his insurers for reimbursement: see also *Co-operative Retail Services Ltd v Taylor Young Partnership & Others* [2002] BLR 272.

7.05 Clause 6.9.1 provides protection for sub-contractors from liability to the employer for loss or damage to the works or a relevant section by one of the Specified Perils, in the form either of their recognition as a co-insured in the Joint Names Policy required by that clause, or by the inclusion in such policy of a waiver by the insurer of any right of subrogation against sub-contractors: see *The Board of Trustees of the Tate Gallery v Duffy Construction Ltd* [2007] BLR 216.

7.06 In addition to his liability under clause 6.2, the contractor must, as an incident of his duty to complete, make good damage to the works. This would apply, for example, to damage caused by vandalism or theft occurring before practical completion (provided it was not caused by the employer's negligence or default and was not within the risks accepted by the employer where Options B or C are selected). The contractor's plant, equipment, and unfixed goods and materials are at his risk. Goods and materials when certified remain at his risk.

Clauses 6.4 to 6.6: Insurance against personal injury or property damage

7.07 Clause 6.4.1 requires the contractor to take out and maintain insurance in respect of claims arising under clauses 6.1 and 6.2 (see above).

7.08 Clause 6.4.2 obligates the contractor, when required to do so by the employer, to provide proof to the Architect of the continuing existence of such insurance. If the contractor fails to take out such insurance the employer may do so and recover the cost of so doing from the contractor (clause 6.4.3).

7.09 Clause 6.5.1 obligates the contractor, if instructed to do so by the Architect, to take out insurance in the names of contractor and employer in respect of liability, loss, claims, etc. for damage to property caused by collapse, subsidence, heave, vibration, weakening or removal of support or lowering of ground water arising out of the actual execution of the works. This is subject to a number of exceptions, which include damage caused by the contractor's own negligence, design errors, injury for which the employer should insure (under Option C if applicable) and inevitable damage which is a reasonably foreseeable consequence of undertaking the work. If such insurance is taken out the contractor should send the policy and and premium receipts to the Architect for deposit with the employer (clause 6.5.2).

7.10 The amount spent by the contractor in taking out or maintaining the clause 6.5.1 insurance is added to the contract sum (clause 6.5.3).

Clauses 6.7 to 6.10: Insurance of the works

7.11 These clauses provide for all-risks insurance of the works. There are three alternatives, one of which may be stated in the Contract Particulars to apply. Two are to be used for new works: Options A or B. Option A requires the contractor to take out the policy; Option B the employer. Option C relates to works to existing buildings. It requires the employer to take out a joint names insurance policy covering the existing structures and the new works. Sub-contractors are entitled to the benefit of the insurance (clause 6.9.1).

Clauses 6.11 to 6.16: CDP insurance and the Joint Fire Code

7.12 Clause 6.11 requires the contractor, where there is a Contractor's Designed Portion of the contract, to take out and maintain professional indemnity insurance in an amount and for a period (normally 6 years from practical completion) which the parties have agreed and stated in the Contract Particulars. The contractor must produce evidence of such insurance to the Architect when the employer reasonably requests him to do so (clause 6.11.3).

7.13 The parties may decide that the Joint Fire Code (the 'Joint Code of Practice on the Protection from Fire of Construction Sites and Buildings Undergoing Renovation') applies. If so, clause 6.14 places a duty upon each of the contractor and employer to comply with the same, and to ensure the compliance of those for whom they are responsible. In the event of a breach of the Code the relevant insurers may specify the remedial measures to be carried out, and the contractor is obliged to carry them out, if necessary under an instruction from the Architect by way of a variation. If the contractor fails to carry out the necssary works the employer may pay others to carry them out and may deduct the cost from the contract sum (clause 6.15.2).

8 Section 7: Assignment, Third Party Rights and Collateral Warranties

8.01 Clause 7.1 prevents either party from assigning the contract or any rights under it except:

(a) with the other's written consent or
(b) to allow the employer, on or after practical completion of the works or of a section, to grant a limited right to bring proceedings in the employer's name to enforce any of the contract terms made for the employer's benefit (clause 7.2). The parties must have stated in the Contract Particulars that clause 7.2 applies, so as to cater for employers who wish to transfer an interest in the subject matter of the contract on achieving practical completion.

8.02 At law, a party may assign the benefit of a contract on giving notice of the assignment to the other party, but may not assign the burden without the other party's consent. This clause prohibits either party making *any* assignment without the written consent of the other save as stated. The rationale behind this is to ensure that the original contracting parties are not brought into direct contractual relations with third parties with whom they may not wish to contract. The House of Lords held in *Linden Garden Trust Ltd v Lenesta Sludge Disposals Ltd* [1993] 3 All ER 417 that any purported assignment would be invalid under this clause, and therefore not effective to transfer any rights of action under the contract. This is emphasised by the fact that clause 1.6 expressly excludes the effect of the Contracts (Rights of Third Parties) Act 1999 save as is permitted by clauses 7A and 7B.

8.03 The remainder of Section 7 covers the grant of Third Party Rights and the giving of collateral warranties, which are of importance as between employer and contractor but do not justify commentary in this chapter.

9   Section 8: Termination

9.01 Section 8 revises and re-orders all the termination provisions which were previously to be found in clauses 27 and 28 of the 1998 edition. The general clauses (clauses 8.1 to 8.3) define the meaning of insolvency for the purpose of the Conditions, cover the giving of notice of termination, and set the termination provisions apart from any other contractual rights and remedies of either party, e.g. termination for repudiatory conduct by the other party. Clause 8.3.2 provides for the reinstatement of the contractor's employment if the parties so agree, irrespective of the grounds of termination.

9.02 The basis of the section is that the contractor's employment may be terminated by either party either because of a specified default by or the insolvency of the other or because the whole or substantially the whole of the works are suspended for specified reasons beyond the control of either party for a continuous period which is stated in the Contract particulars or, in default, is 2 months. In addition the employer is entitled to terminate the contractor's employment because of an offence of corruption committed by the contractor.

Clauses 8.4 to 8.8: Termination by employer

9.03 These clauses make provision for the following possibilities:

1   Discretionary termination by the employer in event of certain defaults by the contractor, including insolvency.
2   Automatic suspension of the works and accounting provisions in the event of insolvency.
3   The consequences following termination by the employer of the contractor's employment.

Termination on notice

9.04 The employer is entitled to terminate the contractor's employment in the circumstances specified in clause 8.4, subject to the giving of the notices required by the clause by the Architect. Notices must, by virtue of clause 8.2.3, be in writing and be given by actual, special or recorded signed for delivery. Normally there must be two notices, a notice of default or defaults by the Architect and a notice of termination by the employer, although clause 8.4.1.3 (refusal or neglect to comply with a written notice/instruction) requires a total of three notices. Revision 2 has extended the period in which the termination notice may be given to 21 days.

9.05 It was held in *West Faulkner Associates v London Borough of Newham* (1995) 74 BLR 1, a case on the JCT 63 clause which is in similar terms to clause 8.4.1.2, that 'regularly and diligently' meant that a contractor must perform his duties in such a way as to achieve his contractual obligations. The clause requires a contractor to plan work, to lead and manage his workforce, to provide sufficient and proper materials and to employ competent tradesmen so that the works are fully carried out to an acceptable standard and that all time, sequence and other provisions of the contractor are fulfilled. The Architect will be in breach of contract if he fails to serve a notice under the clause if an ordinarily competent architect would have done so in the same circumstances.

9.06 At common law a party is entitled to treat a contract as repudiated and therefore at an end if the other party so conducts himself as to show no intention to carry on with the contract

(see *Universal Cargo Carriers v Citati* [1957] 2 QB 401). The purpose of clause 8.4 is to confer on the employer additional and alternative rights by which he may determine the contractor's employment, without having to prove that the contractor has repudiated the contract. However, having regard to clause 8.2.1 (which requires that notice should not be given unreasonably or vexatiously), there is sometimes uncertainty as to whether the circumstances which exist justify determination of the contractor's employment (see *J M Hill & Sons Ltd v London Borough of Camden* (1982) 18 BLR 31, CA and *John Jarvis Limited v Rockdale Housing Association Ltd* (1986) 36 BLR 48, CA, on the corresponding provisions in clause 8.9.

9.07 Under clause 8.6 the employer is entitled to determine the contractor's employment on discovery of corrupt practices by the contractor, and in this case there is no requirement for an architect's notice of default.

Insolvency

9.08 The 1998 edition provided for automatic termination of the contractor's employment in the event of his insolvency. This is no longer so. If the contractor makes any proposal, gives notice of any meeting or becomes the subject of any proceedings or appointment relating to any of the matters referred to within the definitions of insolvency contained in clause 8.1, he must immediately inform the employer in writing (clause 8.5.2). The employer then has a right under clause 8.5.1 to determine the employment of the contractor by notice. Whether or not he chooses to do so, clause 8.5.3 sets out certain automatic consequences of the insolvency:

1   The employer's obligation to make any further payment or release of retention ceases to apply and is replaced by the taking of an account.
2   The contractor's obligation to carry out the works (and the design of the CDP) is suspended.
3   The employer is entitled to protect the site, the works and site materials.

In any event, the insolvent contractor's representatives have a statutory right to disclaim the contract if it is unprofitable, which is likely to be the case.

Rights of parties after termination by the employer

9.09 Clause 8.7 governs the rights of the parties after termination by the employer. Briefly, the position is that:

1   The employer is entitled to have the work completed by others and to take possession of the site and to use all contractor's equipment and materials on site (subject to obtaining necessary third party consents e.g. from those who have hired equipment to the contractor) (clause 8.7.1).
2   The employer is entitled to request and to take an assignment of contracts for the supply of materials and of sub-contracts, although such assignments may not be effective where the contractor is insolvent (clause 8.7.2.3).
3   The contractor is obliged on receiving written notice from the Architect (but not before) to remove all temporary buildings, plant, tools, equipment, goods and materials belonging to him or those for whom he is responsible (clause 8.7.2.1).

9.10 Typically, the employer will obtain a new contractor to carry out and complete the work. Under clause 8.7.3, the employer is not bound to make any further payments to the contractor whose employment has been terminated. Upon completion of the works and making good defects an account will be taken, normally by the Architect but otherwise by the employer (clause 8.7.4), which is in effect a final account as between employer and contractor. If the employer has in fact got the work completed for less than he would have had to pay the contractor, the contractor is in principle entitled to be paid the difference, but if (as is far more likely) the work has cost more than the contractor would have charged, the contractor is obliged to pay the difference to the employer. In addition the Architect must certify the amount of direct loss and/or damage caused to the employer for which the contractor is liable, whether caused by the termination or otherwise, and this will be taken into account (clause 8.7.4.1). This wider wording than in the 1998 edition allows a full account to be taken.

Clauses 8.9 to 8.10: Termination by contractor

9.11 These clauses, which should be compared with clauses 8.4 and 8.5, entitle the contractor to determine his own employment in certain circumstances. Clause 8.9.1.1 provides for determination for non-payment of amounts properly due on a certificate (or the VAT thereon); clause 8.9.1.2 deals with interference with or obstruction of the issue of certificates; clause 8.9.1.3 deals with failure to comply with clause 7.1 (prohibition against assigning without consent). Clause 8.9.2 deals with suspension of the work for a period in excess of that which the parties have agreed. The procedure is in two stages: first, a notice of specified default/s or suspension event/s from the contractor, then, if the default or event continues or is repeated, a notice of determination.

Clause 8.9.1.1: Non-payment of certificates

9.12 If the employer intends to withhold payment from the contractor he must give the requisite notice under clause 4.13.4, otherwise he must pay the amount properly due under any certificate. Thus it is likely that the employer is entitled to exercise any contractual right of deduction or set off to which he is contractually entitled (see for example clause 2.32) before arriving at the sum 'properly due'. The contractor's remedy in such a case is to refer to adjudication; if he terminates the contract he risks a finding that he was not entitled to do so.

Clause 8.9.1.2: Obstruction of certificates

9.13 Interference with or obstruction of the issue of certificates by the employer includes preventing the Architect from performing his duties, directing the Architect as to the amount for which he is to give his certificate, or as to the decision which he should reach, in respect of matters which are within the sphere of the Architect's independent duty.

9.14 This clause relates to suspension of the works for the continuous period the length of which has been agreed and included in the Contract Particulars. Care must be taken to ensure that the periods in the Contract Particulars are reasonably sufficient. The contractor must be careful not to give notice of a specified suspension event when one of those for whose actions or omissions he is responsible has been negligent or in default.

9.15 In *John Jarvis Ltd v Rockdale Housing Association Ltd* (1986) 36 BLR 48, the Court of Appeal held that notice under the previous clause 28.1.3 (now 8.9.2) was not given 'unreasonably or vexatiously' unless a reasonable contractor in the same circumstances would have thought it unreasonable or vexatious to give the notice.

Clause 8.10: Insolvency of employer

9.16 Clause 8.10.2 provides that the employer must inform the contractor immediately in writing if he makes any proposal, gives notice of any meeting or becomes the subject of any proceedings or appointment relating to any of the matters referred to within the definitions of insolvency contained in clause 8.1. The contractor has the right to terminate his employment by notice in the event of the employer's insolvency (see clause 8.10.1), and his obligations to carry out and complete the works (and CDP design) are in any event suspended.

Clause 8.11: Termination by either party

9.17 Either party may before practical completion terminate the contractor's employment, where the works have been suspended for the relevant continuous period agreed and stated in the Contract Particulars, by reason of one of the events specified in clause 8.11.1. These are events which are not the fault of either party. If in fact loss or damage to the works occasioned by a Specified Peril has been caused by the negligence of the contractor or one of those for whom he is responsible, he is disentitled from giving such notice. This includes the negligence of sub-contractors. Again, care should be taken to ensure that the periods provided in the Contract Particulars are reasonably sufficient.

Clause 8.12: Rights of parties after determination

9.18 Clause 8.12 governs the rights of the parties after termination under clauses 8.9 to 8.11 (and two other circumstances). In summary:

1 The contractor is to remove his temporary buildings, plant, etc. from the site with all reasonable dispatch and ensure that his sub-contractors do the same (clause 8.12.2.1).
2 If there is a Contractor's Designed Portion the contractor must provide the employer with `copies of the relevant documents (see clause 8.12.2.2).
3 The contractual payment and retention provisions cease to apply (see clause 8.12.1).
4 The contractor is to prepare (or to provide the documents necessary for the employer to prepare) a final account as between contractor and employer, including the amounts referred to in clause 8.12.3.
5 The employer shall pay the amount properly due to the contractor (assuming that it is likely that there will be such a balance in such circumstances) within 28 days of the submission of the account (see clause 8.12.5).

10 Section 9: Settlement of Disputes

10.1 Section 9 must be read in conjunction with Articles 7, 8 and 9. For the first time in the 2005 edition the dispute resolution procedures of the JCT form provide four separate but overlapping methods of dispute resolution:

1 Mediation (clause 9.1).
2 Adjudication (Article 7 and clause 9.2).
3 Arbitration (Article 8 and clauses 9.3 to 9.8).
4 Litigation (Article 9).

To these must be added the good faith negotiations between senior executives available under paragraph 6 of Schedule 8 if selected to apply in the Contract Particulars.

10.02 The key recent developments have been the growth in popularity of mediation and the mandatory imposition of the Housing Grants, Construction and Regeneration Act 1996 into almost all construction contracts, which allows for adjudication so as to enable disputes arising during the course of the contract to be provisionally determined, pending final review by the courts or in arbitration. It has been extremely successful; whilst there have been a significant number of decisions of the Technology and Construction Court concerning adjudication enforcement, they represent a tiny minority of the disputes referred to adjudication, and such evidence as exists suggests that very few adjudicators' decisions are reconsidered in substantive litigation or arbitration.

10.03 The overruling of *Northern Regional Health Authority v Derek Crouch Construction Co Ltd* [1984] QB 644 by the House of Lords in *Beaufort Developments Ltd v Gilbert-Ash (Northern Ireland) Ltd* (1998) 88 BLR 1 has allowed parties to challenge decisions and interim certificates of the Architect in other than arbitral proceedings. The parties now have a genuine tactical choice as to whether to litigate or arbitrate.

10.04 The full scope of the adjudication, arbitration and litigation processes are dealt with elsewhere in this book. The following text is an overview of these complementary and developing areas.

Article 7 and Clause 9.2: Adjudication

10.05 Article 7 gives the parties the substantive right to refer 'any dispute or difference arising under this Contract' to adjudication. This can exclude certain disputes, e.g. whether a contract exists at all or was induced by misrepresentation or fraud. Clause 9.2 now provides that the procedural rules governing a dispute referred to adjudication shall be those of the Scheme for Construction Contracts instead of (as previously) those of the JCT Adjudication Agreement. Clause 9.2.1 allows the parties to select the identity of the adjudicator and/or the nominating body, and clause 9.2.2 provides for a specialist adjudicator (or independent expert) in a dispute concerning an instruction to open up or test work not in accordance with the contract.

Article 8 and Clauses 9.3 to 9.8: Arbitration

10.06 The parties have to make a positive choice whether or not to include the arbitration provisions as part of their agreement, otherwise litigation will be their preferred method of final dispute resolution. Note the broad scope of the dispute or difference which may be referred to arbitration as opposed to adjudication:

> *'any dispute or difference between the Parties of any kind whatsoever arising out of or in connection with this Contract . . .'*

Article 8 provides that this excludes adjudication enforcement disputes and one other (minor) category of dispute. The Court of Appeal has held that the words 'arising in connection with this Contract' are wide enough to cover claims for rectification and misrepresentation (*Ashville Investments Ltd v Elmer Contractors Ltd* (1987) 37 BLR 55). The Scottish Court of Session has held that a similarly-worded clause is sufficiently wide to allow an arbitrator to entertain a *quantum meruit* claim.

10.07 The arbitration is to be conducted in accordance with the JCT 2005 edition of the CIMAR rules, although the parties can agree to include any subsequent amendments.

10.08 Clause 9.5 sets out some of the powers of the arbitrator, which are:

1 To rectify the contract so as to reflect the true agreement made by the parties.
2 To direct measurements and valuations that he thinks desirable in order to determine the rights of the parties.
3 To ascertain and award any sum that he thinks should have been included in any certificate.
4 To open up, review and revise any certificate, decision, opinion, requirement or notice (subject to clause 1.10 which concerns the effect of the final certificate).
5 To determine all matters in dispute submitted to him.

10.09 The award of the arbitrator is final and binding on the parties (clause 9.6) subject to applications for determination of questions of law (clause 9.7.2) and rights of appeal on questions of law (clause 9.7.2) under sections 45(2)(a) and 69(2)(a) of the Arbitration Act 1996.

Article 9: Litigation

10.10 The parties have an unfettered choice under the contract to dispense with arbitration altogether, and apply straight to the courts. This is a tactical decision to be made by the parties at a very early stage in the contractual process. Litigation has certain advantages over arbitration:

1 Cases are heard by judges with considerable experience of construction litigation, usually in the Technology and Construction Court.
2 Judges have a full range of preliminary remedies available to them, e.g. the power to grant injunctions.
3 Questions of law and fact may be appealed directly to the Court of Appeal.
4 Apart from standard Court fees no further fees are payable.
5 Co-defendants and third parties may be joined in the same action.

10.11 Against this arbitration offers flexibility in the way that the matters are to be decided and (unless there is an appeal to the court) privacy. However, architects should be slow to advise their clients to litigate before exploring other avenues of dispute resolution. In *Paul Thomas Construction Ltd v Hyland* [2002] 18 Const LJ 345 the claimant started proceedings after refusing to participate in adjudication and generally not co-operating. Indemnity costs were awarded against the claimant.

11 The Schedules

11.01 The Schedules to the 2005 form comprise the following:

1 Contractor's Design Submission Procedure: this is new to the 2005 form. It follows clause 2.9.3 of the Conditions and provides for the submission to the Architect of copies of the Contractor's Designed Portion for the purpose of his marking it as either in accordance with or not in accordance with the Contract.
2 Variation and Acceleration Quotation Procedures: these follow clause 5.3 and have been considered in paragraphs 6.18 to 6.25 above.
3 Insurance Options: these have been considered in paragraph 7.11 above.
4 Code of Practice: this sets out a procedure to assist in the fair and reasonable operation of clause 3.18.4 i.e. where the Architect issues an instruction for the opening up for inspection or testing of work which is considered not to be in accordance with the contract. It sets out fifteen criteria for the Architect to consider in issuing instructions pursuant to that clause.
5 Third Party Rights: this is new to the 2005 form and follows clauses 7A and 7B of the Conditions. It confers certain rights as against the contractor on named or identified Purchasers, Tenants and Funders.
6 Forms of Bonds in respect of advance payment (clause 4.8), Listed Items (clause 4.17) and the Retention Bond (clause 4.19).
7 Fluctuations Options: Options A, B and C have been considered in paragraphs 5.32.to 5.36 above.
8 Schedule 8 has been introduced by Revision 2 and is designed, in conjunction with Recital 8, to incorporate the Achieving Excellence in Construction principles into the form.

18

The NEC Engineering and Construction Contract and related architects' forms

GORDON HALL

1 Introduction

1.01 In our previous edition of this book (Chapter 10, paragraph 16) we included the 'NEC' as a subsection of the chapter entitled 'Other Standard Forms'. Since then, the NEC form of contracts (or as it is fondly referred to – 'the family of contracts' has undergone further revision on 14 July 2005 and the revised suite of documents are now known collectively as the 'NEC3'. The forms have been updated and others added including a Framework Contract ('FC') for the appointment of service suppliers. The NEC3 is also in much wider use. For example it is the preferred agreement for Consultants appointed by the Olympic Delivery Authority (ODA) in respect of the Stratford, London, Olympic site. More and more architects have been presented with the NEC as a form of Consultant's Appointment for them to sign and as indicated below the Royal Institute of British Architects (RIBA) has now produced its own 'Concise Agreement for the Appointment of an Architect' (C-CON-07-A and D-CON-07-A) and the Standard Conditions of Appointment for an Architect (CA-S-07-A) in response to the industry's general wish for a more 'uniform' concise and user friendly form of Consultant's appointment. However it is arguable that the Agreement now produced by the RIBA whilst to a large extent meeting those desired objectives does not in any way mirror the collaborative intent which is behind the NEC3.

1.02 There is, arguably, no form of 'standard' appointment document, in the writer's experience, which has caused as such misgiving and uncertainty among the Architectural profession as the NEC3. This is undoubtedly due to its complexity in that even lawyers need to 'tread warily' when interpreting the NEC3 terms and conditions. It is also far removed from the architect's 'favourite' namely the Standard Form of Appointment (SFA/99) which has now been withdrawn from general use by the RIBA in favour of its new forms of Appointment. It is interesting for construction lawyers to note that in practice architects still employ the SFA/99 form as an Agreement of choice, although, in time, the profession may be persuaded to totally embrace the new RIBA forms and the NEC3.

1.03 It is not the purpose of this chapter to analyse in great detail the terms and conditions of the NEC family of Agreements. This sort of 'exercise' warrants a book in itself. The reader is referred to our previous (8th) edition regarding the background to and evolution of this contract whilst those requiring specific commentary on detail are referred to the excellent commentary entitled the 'NEC3 Engineering and Construction Contract' which was published in its second edition by Brian Eggleston in 2006. This chapter will, instead, deal with the NEC3 including the 2006 updates and will, furthermore, compare the NEC3 to the standard form of architects appointment (SFA 1999 Rev 2004) and the new RIBA forms of appointment. It will highlight those clauses which are worthy of

particular consideration in all three forms of appointment and, furthermore, highlight those issues which may be of concern from the point of view of any architect's professional indemnity insurance policy.

2 NEC3 Professional Services Contract June 2005 (as further amended in June 2006)

2.01 This contract, like its predecessor published in June 1998, is divided into a 'schedule of options' and 'core clauses'. It seems to us that it is counter-productive to compare changes since 2004 and it would be more helpful to the practitioner to review the new agreement 'as it stands'.

2.02 The agreement commences with a 'schedule of options'. It should be noted that under options W1 and W2 the parties must select a dispute resolution option which may be in either (W1) the appointment of an adjudicator under the *NEC form of adjudicator's appointment* unless the Housing Grants Construction and Regeneration Act 1996 applies or the Adjudication procedure when the Housing Grants Construction and Regeneration Act 1996 applies. Under both options the reader should carefully note that under W1 (10) and W2 (11) '*the adjudicator's decision is binding on the parties unless and until revised by the tribunal and is enforceable as a matter of contractual obligation between the parties and not as an arbitral award. The adjudicator's decision is final and binding if neither party has notified the other within the time required by this contract that he is dissatisfied with a matter decided by the adjudicator and intends to refer the matter to the tribunal*' (our underlining). Most London market professional indemnity Insurance policy wordings provide that an insured may *not 'agree to accept any decision of an adjudicator as "final and binding" unless and until insurers have given their consent'*. It goes without saying that particular attention must be given to the time limit set out in the adjudication table (page 29) within which to take action.

Option X2 – Changes in the Law

This is an interesting provision which provides that a 'change in the law of the project' is a 'compensation event' if it occurs after the contract date. From the architect's perspective the effect of a change in the law is to reduce the total time charged if the prices are reduced.

Option X7 – Delayed Damages

Another interesting provision which survives the 1998 edition and which is more suited to the position of a contractor than a consultant involving as it does an agreement to pay liquidated damages

209

at a rate stated in the Contract Data. This type of provision does not appear in any other consultant appointment document including SFA/99 or its predecessor SFA/92 or indeed the 'new' RIBA Forms.

Option X8 – Collateral Warranty Agreement

Under X8.1 '*the consultant enters into the collateral warranty agreements*'. This clause may be criticised through its lack of precision. It is therefore vital that the Contract Data clearly identifies the specific requirement in each case.

Option X9 – Transfer of Rights

Option clause X9.1 provides '*the Employer owns the Consultant's rights over material prepared for this contract by the Consultant except as stated otherwise in the Scope. The Consultant obtains other rights for the Employer as stated in the Scope and obtains from a Sub-consultant equivalent rights for the Employer over the material prepared by the Sub-Consultant. The Consultant provides to the Employer the documents which transfer these rights to the Employer*'.

This attempt to remove all 'legalese' raises the real possibility of confusion. What is clear is that the rights to all ownership of copyright material produced by the consultant vest in the client. The practitioner should also note that any material which comes into the consultant's possession ('obtains other rights for the employer') becomes vested in the employer. There is no indemnity provision in favour of the Consultant and the following should be carefully considered as an amendment '*the consultant will not be liable for any misuse, variation or the use of material prepared contrary to the purpose for which it was originally intended in relation to this project*'.

Option X11 – Termination by the Employer

X11.2 provides a formula for termination for reasons 'outside' the terms of the contract and can be 5% of the difference between:

- The forecast of the final total of the Prices in the absence of termination and
- The title of the other amounts and costs included in the amount due on termination.

Option X18 – Limitation of Liability

A welcome clause limiting the liability of the architect in respect of indirect or consequential losses, defects and liability in general in that claims are limited unless notified to the consultant before the end of the liability date.

Option Y (UK) 3: The Contracts (Rights of Third Parties) Act 1999

This provides that a '*person or organisation who is not one of the parties may enforce a term of this contract under the Contracts (Rights of Third Parties) Act 1999 only if the term and the person or organisation or as stated in the contract data*'.

The importance of this provision is that it extends rights to particular 'classes' which are stated in the contract data. The Contracts (Rights of Third Parties) Act 1999 extends rights to those third parties *in general* provided that they can establish that the contract was made 'for their benefit'. One can say, therefore, that the NEC3 makes provision for Collateral warranties (subject to the concern expressed above regarding the wording of the clause in question) and a form of 'quasi-collateral warranty' in favour of third parties provided that they are included in the contract data.

Option Z Additional Conditions of Contract

This is self-explanatory and, briefly, will cover additional conditions (amendments) to the contract.

Core Clauses

10.1 '*The employer and the consultant shall act as stated in the contract and in a spirit of mutual trust and cooperation*'. It is submitted that this is a statement of intent and unless there is evidence of bad faith unlikely to create legal obligations.

11.2 (1) '*The accepted Programme is the programme identified in the contract data or is the latest Programme accepted by the employer. The latest Programme accepted by the employer supersedes previous accepted programmes*'. This highlights (see later) the importance of accurately completing the 'contract data'.

11.2 (2) '*Completion is when the consultant has*

- *Done all the work which the scope states he is to do by the completion date and*
- *Corrected defects which would have prevented the employer from using the services and others from doing their work*'.

This is another example of a clause which is more appropriate in a contractor's contract as opposed to an architect.

Clause 11.2 (5) '*A defect of the services which is not in accordance with the scope or the applicable law*' – again, a sub-clause which is more appropriate to a contractor than an architect.

11.2 (9) '*To provide the services and means to do the work necessary to complete the services in accordance with this contract and <u>all incidental work, services and actions which the contract requires</u>*' (our underlining). We anticipate that those words which are underlined will inevitably be amended by architects, in practice in all likelihood at the behest of Insurers, since not to do so would 'open the way' for the employer to argue that the architect is required to do works beyond the agreed Services if, in the employer's view, they are 'incidental work services and actions which the contract requires'.

Interpretation of the law

12.2 '*This contract is governed by the law of the contract.*' This wording obviously reflects the fact that the NEC3 is intended to be used outside the United Kingdom. However, architects are advised, if the contract is in the United Kingdom to slightly amend this clause to read '*This contract is governed by (specifying the particular United Kingdom entity where the contract took place)*'.

12.4 '*This contract is the entire agreement between the parties.*' This is imprecise and should, it is suggested, read '*This contract represents the entire agreement reached between the parties and supersedes all earlier contracts, whether oral or written or any representations made before this contract was signed*'.

Acceptance

14.1 '*The employer's acceptance of a communication from the consultant or of his work does not change the consultant's responsibility to provide the service.*' Again, we anticipate that this clause will be amended by the architect, in practice, since there seems to be no apparent good reason why an employer, having accepted, for example, a notice of change to a design (through a communication from the consultant) should continue to hold the consultant responsible for this change.

3 The parties' main responsibilities

The Consultant's Obligations

21.2 '*The consultant's obligation is to use the skill and care normally used by professionals providing services similar to the services*'. Insurers cover the 'reasonable skill and care' of professionals and, as such, this clause should be amended to read '*the reasonable skill and care normally used by professionals …*'.

Time

31.3 '*Within two weeks of the consultant submitting a programme to him for acceptance the employer either accepts the programme or notifies the consultant of his reasons for not accepting it. Their reason for not accepting a programme is that*

● *The consultant's plans which it shows are not practicable.*
● *It does not show the information which this contract requires.*
● *It does not represent the consultant's plans realistically or*
● *It does not comply with the Scope'.*

It is implicit in this clause that if the employer does not respond within the two weeks acceptance period, then the programme is accepted.

Instructions to stop or not to start work

33.1 'The employer may instruct the consultant to stop or not to start any work and may later instruct him that he may re-start or start it'. This raises the 'nightmare' prospect of 'stop start' construction. There is no period of notice comprised within this clause (e.g. 14 days) and raises the danger of an architect being left with potentially costly mobilisation charges if, for example, it is a major project and the architect has had to hire additional staff and invest. We anticipate that architects will seek to amend or modify this clause, in practice.

4 Quality

This, again, is yet another clause which is more appropriate to contractors than architects.

Correcting defects

Clause 41.1 provides that '*until the defects date, the employer notifies the consultant of each Defect as soon as he finds it and the consultant notifies the employer of each Defect as soon as he finds it*'. The difficulty in this clause is the wording 'as soon as he finds it' in that it does imply that the architect has a positive duty to actually go out and 'find it'. This would impose a duty of supervision on the architect. This clause should be amended to read '*And the consultant notifies the employer of each Defect if and when he finds it*'. Finally, the clause provides '*the employer's rights in respect of a defect which the employer has not found or notified by the defects date are not affected*'. This makes architects liable for latent defects in the works and will obviously be carefully considered by architects and their insurers before agreeing to it.

41.2 entitles the '*employer (to assess) the cost to him of having the Defect rectified by other people and the Consultant pays this amount*'. This clause entitling the Employer to simply make up its own mind on remedial costs is most unlikely to be acceptable to insurers.

5 Payment

50.1 '*The consultant assesses the amount due and submits an invoice at each assessment date. The consultant assesses in consultation with the employer the date of the first assessment and at the end of each assessment interval until eight weeks after the defects date and at completion of the whole of the services*'. The invoice detail laid down in NEC3 is unsurprising, being details sufficient to identify the services carried out in the Scope, how the amount has been assessed, changes in the amount due since the previous invoice, expenses and VAT. Each payment is made three weeks after receipt of the invoice (unless a different period is stated in the Contract Data). If the employer does not accept the assessment he notifies the consultant before the payment becomes due. The consultant either corrects the invoice to the sum agreed by the employer or provides further information. Alternatively, the employer (in the case of dispute) notifies the consultant of his reasons and pays that sum which the employer considers to be payable interest is calculated on a daily basis on sums outstanding and compounded annually.

6 Compensation events

60.1 provides 12 different 'compensation events'. Those which could particularly affect the architect are:

(4) The employer gives an instruction to stop or not to start any work or to change a key date.
(5) The employer or others do not work within the time shown on the accepted programme or within the conditions stated in the Scope.
(6) The employer fails to reply to a communication from a consultant within the period required by this contract.
(7) The employer changes a decision which he has previously communicated to the consultant.
(8) The employer withholds an acceptance (other than acceptance of a quotation for acceleration) for reasons not stated in the contract.
(10) A breach of contract by the employer.
(11) An event which stops the consultant completing the services or stops the consultant completing those services by the date shown in the accepted programme and which neither party could prevent or an experienced consultant 'would have judged that the contract date to have such a small chance of occurring that it would have been unreasonable for him to have allowed for it' (this does raise a possibility of dispute as to what is or is not 'a small chance of occurring').
(12) The consultant corrects a defect for which he is not liable under the contract (a matter of concern to a consultant if, for example, the defect involves an element of design by another consultant or a specialist design subcontractor).

Clause 64 provides the formula for the employer assessing a 'compensation event'.

7 Rights of material

The parties' use of a material

We 'touched' on this issue of copyright earlier so far as the Option Clauses were concerned and clause 70.1 confirms that the '*employer has the right to use the material provided by the consultant for the purpose stated in the Scope*'.

70.2 makes clear that the '*consultant has the right to use material provided by the employer only to provide the services*'. The material is to be returned to the employer on completion of the services.

There is no provision as in the 'older' traditional architect's Appointment for the protection of the Architect's moral rights (i.e. to be accorded recognition for their work and for the work not to be subjected to derogatory treatment) as laid down in part IV of the Copyright Designs and Patents Act 1988.

70.3 '*The parties do not disclose information obtained in connection with the services except where necessary to carry out their duties under this contract*'.

This raises obvious difficulties as there will be circumstances in which an architect, unhappily, may need to involve his insurers especially if criticism is levelled against him during the progress of a project; he or she may similarly need to consult solicitors or counsel and if there is a dispute which leads to litigation the circumstances of the project may be aired in 'open court'. This clause will, therefore, require amendment.

70 .4 '*The consultant may use the material provided by him under this contract for other work unless stated otherwise in the Scope.*'

Publicity

71.1 does go some way to entitling the consultant to publicise the services but 'only with the employer's written agreement'. This clause could very simply be included in clause 70.3 by insertion of the words, '*unless with the employer's written agreement after the word "informations"' in line 1.*

8 Indemnity, insurance and liability

80.1 '*The consultant indemnifies the employer against claims, proceedings, compensation and costs payable arising out of an infringement by the consultant of the rights of others except an infringement which arose out of the use by the consultant of things provided by the employer*'. It is suggested that this clause should read '*The consultant indemnifies the employer against legal liability for claims, proceedings, compensation and costs payable arising out of an infringement of the rights of others by the consultant under this agreement to the extent that this is provided for under option X18, except where an infringement arose out of the use by the consultant of matter provided by the Employer.*'

Insurance cover

The 'Insurance Table' provides for '*liability of the consultant for all claims made against him arising out of his failure to use the skill and care normally used by professionals providing services similar to the services*'. The amount is limited to the amount stated in the contract data. This clause requires slight amendment to bring it into 'line' with most if not all professional indemnity policies and this should therefore read '*the liability of the consultant for claims made against him arising out of his failure to use the reasonable care expected of any reasonably competent professional providing services equivalent to the services under this agreement.*'

Please note that for the purposes of clause 82.1 the 'cap' on liability specifically excludes the following:

● Delayed damages.
● Consultant's share if option C (target contract) applies.
● An infringement by the consultant of the rights of others (e.g. breach of copyright).
● Loss or damage to third party property.
● Death of or bodily injury to a person other than an employee of the consultant.

It is pleasing to note that by clause 82.2 the consultant additionally has the benefit of a 'net liability' clause but unfortunately the existing wording leads to an unhappy result. The whole purpose of a 'net liability' clause is to '*limit that proportion of the consultant's liability to that which is just and equitable and on the basis that all other consultants, sub-consultants, contractors and sub-contractors have either paid or are deemed to have paid their full contribution towards the claim and without reference to the consultant*'. The wording of clause 82.2 in its existing form can be read to mean that the consultant's liability to the employer is limited to that proportion or employer losses for which the consultant is responsible (i.e. the consultant's total liability) under the contract if other consultants etc are unable to contribute.

9 Termination

Clause 90 sets out the grounds of termination and clause 90.2 provides that the consultant may terminate the services by notifying the employer if the employer has not paid an amount due to the consultant within 8 weeks of the issue of a notice by the consultant to the employer that payment is overdue. On the other hand,

the employer by virtue of clause 90.3 may terminate the consultant's obligation (apparently without any 8 weeks' notice) if:

● the employer no longer requires the services; or
● the consultant has substantially failed to comply with his obligations and has not put the default right within 4 weeks of a notification by the employer.

Under clause 90.4 the project may be stopped if an event occurs which stops the consultant completing the services or stops the consultant from doing so on the Accepted programme and this is forecast to delay completion by more than 13 weeks and which neither party could prevent and an 'experienced consultant' would have judged at the contract date to have such a 'small chance of occurring that it would have been unreasonable for him to have allowed for it'.

Contract data

Great care must be taken in completing the data in full as the pre-amble to Part 1 (page 42) states '*completion of the data in full, according to the Options chosen, is essential to create a complete contract*'.

Clause 8 **Indemnity, Insurance and Liability** needs amending. The words 'reasonable' should be inserted before 'skill and care' in line 2 under the heading 'event'. Furthermore, under the heading 'cover' insurers simply do not cover '*each claim, without limit to the number of claims*'. London Market Insurers cover '*each and every claim or series of claims attributable to or arising from the same original cause or source*'. If, for example, a Practice has £5 million cover on this basis then if 'each and every claim or series of claims was attributable to a single source' then the policy of limit of indemnity would be exhausted if the claims all came from that same source and exceeded £5 million.

Part 2 – Data provided by the consultant

Here, again, this section needs to be completed very carefully by the consultant.

One of the glaring omissions (see below) of the NEC3 when compared to, say, SFA/99 (Schedule 2) is there is no schedule of services equivalent to the RIBA stages of services. (Stages A to L). Care must be taken in identifying accurately those services which the architect intends to perform under the contract and it would be advisable in our view to retain the industry accepted traditional RIBA 'work stages' in identifying those services.

Comparison with SFA/99 (REV 2004) Standard Form of Architects Appointment

4.1 The SFA/99 like the NEC3 has a 'net liability' clause in clause 7.3. Like NEC3 it seeks to limit liability (clause 7.2) but has the advantage of limiting such liability to the **lesser of the sums** '*stated in the Memorandum of Agreement or the net contribution*'.

4.2 Copyright (clause 6.1) remains with the architect who additionally positively asserts the architect's moral rights to be identified as the author of the work comprising the project. The Architect always retains ownership of the copyright material but gives the employer/beneficiary, instead, '*a licence to copy and use (the copyright material) and to allow all other consultants and contractors involved in the project to similarly use and copy the drawings, documents and bespoke software produced by the architect in performing the services, but only for purposes relating to the project on the site or part of the site to which the design relates*'. An advantage it has over NEC3 is that it is specifically provided in clause 6.2.1 that '*the architect shall not be liable if the material is modified other than by or with the consent of the architect or used for any purpose other than that for which it was prepared or used for any unauthorised purpose*'.

4.3 Clause 6.3 entitles the architect to have the right to publish photographs of the project (with the consent of the client which consent shall not be unreasonably withheld) before publication of any other information about the project unless reasonably necessary for the performance of the services.

4.4 There is a time limit on the bringing of claims under NEC3 (unless such claims involve those relating to latent damage) to those brought during the currency of the works. Under SFA/99 by contrast the time limit on any action or proceedings is stipulated in the Memorandum of Agreement, being the date of the last services performed under the agreement or if earlier, the date of practical completion of the construction of the project. On this basis, and assuming that the agreement is not under 'seal' then the time limit would be 12 years whilst if this was a 'simple contract' such time limit would be 6 years, either from the date of practical completion or, if later, the date of the 'last services performed under the agreement'.

Clause 7.5 Third Party Agreements

Here SFA/99 specifically provides that any third party agreements (collateral warranties) are those which are 'set out in an annexe to this agreement'. NEC3 (as previously indicated) states this provision in vague terms. The rights of third parties under the *Contracts (Rights of Third Parties) Act* is specifically excluded under SFA/99 clause 7.6 unlike the NEC3 which extends quasi-third party rights as an alternative to collateral warranties (see above).

Suspension and determination

The grounds for suspension and determination under SFA/99 are broadly in line with NEC3 except that under SFA/99 the client is required to give 7 clear days notice of suspension of the contract which, if it exceeds 6 months, entitles the architect to request written instructions as to whether or not to proceed. If these have not been received within 30 days of the date of such request then the architect has a right to treat performance of any service or obligations as having been determined.

Adjudication England and Wales

Under SFA/99 Clause 9.2 adjudication under section 108 of the *Housing Grants Construction and Regeneration Act 1996* is dealt with under procedures set out in the model adjudication procedures published by the Construction Industry Council (CIC) current at the date of the reference. Under clause 9.3 where the adjudication is held in respect of a Scottish contract, then the parties may refer the matter to 'some independent and third person appointed pursuant to the provisions of the Memorandum of Agreement'.

Clause 9.5 provides for arbitration both in England and Wales and Scotland but provided always that the client or the architect may litigate (in England and Wales) any claim for a remedy which does not exceed £5,000 (Small Claims limit) or such other sum as provided by statute pursuant to section 91 of the *Arbitration Act 1996*. The CIMAR arbitration rules current at the date of the reference apply.

Where Scotland is concerned the Scottish Arbitration Code for use in Domestic and International Arbitration 1999 (the Arbitration Code) prepared by the Scottish Council for International Arbitration, the Chartered Institute of Arbitrators (Scottish Branch) and the Scottish Building Contract Committee apply.

5. The Concise Conditions of Appointment for an Architect (Published by the RIBA)

In 2007 the Royal Institution of British Architects (RIBA) published the 'Concise Agreement for the Appointment of an Architect' (C-CON-07-A) and a 'Domestic Project Agreement for the Appointment of an Architect' (D-CON-07-A). The former is referred to as the 'Green Book'; the latter the 'Red Book'. Both versions are intended to replace SFA/99 (Rev 2004) which has now been withdrawn. However, as stated at the beginning of this chapter, SFA/99 still continues to be used by many architects.

Both the Green and Red Books contain helpful notes on the 'use and completion of the concise agreement'. The Green Book notes include alternative forms of service schedules for use in a particular situation e.g. CDM coordinator's services (SS-CDM-07); interior design services (SS-ID-07); project management services (SS-PM-07).

Fees and expenses can be recorded using component SS-FE-08.

The intention behind these new publications is to simplify the form of appointment and, like NEC3, set it out in easy to read, 'user friendly' terms. The salient terms are analysed as follows:

CA-C-07-A Precise Conditions of Appointment (Commercial Contracts)

Clause 1.1 – in contrast to NEC3 uses the words '*exercises reasonable skill and care and diligence in accordance with the normal standards of the architect's profession in performing the services…*'

1.2 – the architect:

'*Performs the services so far as reasonably practicable in accordance with the client's requirements without undue delay*'.

4.2 – preserves (except in the case of employees, sub-consultants or agents of the architect) the exclusion of any rights under the Contracts (Rights of Third Parties) Act 1999.

Fees and expenses

Clauses 5.1 to 5.10 are more precise than under NEC3 regarding the terms on which fees are calculated, the payment of fees in the event of suspension or termination and the requirement of the architect to keep records and make these available on request.

Copyright and use of information

6.1 – here, in contract to NEC3, the architect '*owns the copyright in the original work and the drawings and documents produced in performing the services and generally asserts the architect's moral rights to be identified as the author of such works*'. The client is granted, instead, a '*licence to copy and use and allow other persons providing services to the project to copy and use such drawings and documents only for purposes related to the Project providing that all fees and./or other amounts due are paid in accordance with (conditions 5.4 and 5.7). The architect is not liable for any use of the drawings and documents other than for the purpose for which they were prepared*'. This is, from the architect's viewpoint, far superior to the NEC3 provisions in both protecting the architect's rights in the copyright material as well as providing an indemnity against misuse or variation of such drawings and documents. It also contains a provision which is not found in either NEC3 or the 'old' SFA/99 namely that '*no part of any design by the Architect may be registered by the client without the written consent of the Architect*'.

6.2 – here '*neither the client nor the architect may disclose confidential information unless necessary for the proper performance of the services or if it is already material in the public domain or disclosure is required by law or through any dispute arising out of or in connection with the agreement*'. It also provides that the architect and client must both take reasonable steps to ensure confidentiality is observed by any sub-consultants of the architect or the employees or agents of the client.

Architect's liability

7.1 – like SFA/99 actions or proceedings arising out of or in connection with this agreement is (apparently) limited to expiry of the period stated in the letter of appointment either from the date of practical completion or the date of the last service rendered under the agreement whichever is earlier. The agreement contains a 'net liability' clause which partly 'mirrors' the equivalent clause 7.5 in SFA/99 but is far more extensive than NEC3.

There is provision for a notice of termination on the part of the client by giving no less than 14 days' notice in writing stating the reasons (clause 8.3) whilst it may be terminated immediately by notice from either party in the event of the commission of an act of bankruptcy or if the architect becomes unable to provide the services through death or incapacity. Upon termination (clause 8.5) a copy of the material not previously provided to the client (i.e. copyright material) is delivered to the client '*on demand... subject to terms of the licence under section 6.1 (having been satisfied) i.e. that fees have been paid other amounts due under condition 5.5 and 5.7 plus reasonable copying charges are paid*'.

Clause 9.1 provides that any dispute or difference arising out of this agreement, if the matter is suitable, should be submitted for Mediation. This provision is not contained in either SFA/99 or NEC3.

Under clauses 9.2 and 9.3 there is provision for adjudication and the details of any nomination are included in the Letter of Appointment. The appropriate adjudication procedures which are provided for under the 'model letter' of appointment are the 'Scheme for Construction Contract Regulations 1998'.

Arbitration is provided as an alternative to adjudication, where appropriate, under clause 9.4 and there is a further provision in clause 9.5 where the client or the architect may litigate any claim that does not exceed £5,000 or such sum as is provided by statute pursuant to section 91 of the Arbitration Act 1996. This is also provided for under corresponding section of NEC3.

Clause 9.7 'Common Law Rights' – do not exclude any rights of common law in equity except where expressly stated to do so.

Clause 9.8 – Duration.

This states that the provisions of the Agreement continue to bind the client and the architect 'as long as necessary to give effect to their respective rights and obligations'. This clause should in our view be amended because it is arguable that if the clause remains it will extend the rights of each party beyond those timescales which are laid down under the Limitation Acts 1980 (as amended).

Another criticism is that the Conditions of Appointment does not have an 'entire contract clause' which should read '*This agreement supersedes all earlier contracts or agreements whether written or oral or any representation and constitute, together with the letter of appointment dated ...a copy of which is appended hereto, and represent the entire agreement reached between the parties*'.

ML-C-07 Model Letter

The model letter has been drafted on the basis of 'filling in the blanks' in each particular section. The advantage of using the model letter is that an architect has a 'checklist' of matters which ought to be covered in a letter of appointment at the outset and can merely add to or vary any parts of the model letter which are inappropriate for any particular project. The disadvantage is, however, that no two projects are the same. It is inevitable that there will be situations in which the 'model letter' may require significant amendment including additions to cater for a particular project.

Domestic Project Agreement for the Appointment of an Architect (D-CON-07-A) 'Red Book'

The 'Red Book' like the 'Green Book' comes in a 'pack' with the 'architect's copy' and the Client's copy of the 'services for a small

project'; useful notes on use and completion of the documents and '*conditions of appointment for an architect domestic project*'. It also contains notes addressed to the client entitled 'Working with an Architect for your Home' and a 'model letter'. We will not repeat our comments on the 'model letter' which we have stated above except to say that the model letter and the conditions of appointment will always be tested by the courts as to whether or not they satisfy the test of being 'reasonable' under the Unfair Contract Terms Act 1977 in that the contracts apply to a domestic or private consumer.

The conditions of appointment are set out, very simply, but limit liability for six years after practical completion of the construction of the project or the date of the last services performed under the agreement whichever is the earlier. Under clause 7.2 the client does not hold, *inter alia*, sub-consultants of the architects liable in respect of any negligence, default or other liability arising from performance of the services. On this basis, collateral warranties are not covered from any sub-consultant even though they may be of considerable importance to a home owner wishing to secure funding or a mortgage or 'sell a property on'.

There is no exclusion of the Contracts (Rights of Third Parties) Act 1999 and, therefore, an employer would be able to offer this alternative (to collateral warranties). However Architects and their solicitors may well wish to provide for traditional Collateral Warranties by amendment to the conditions.

There is no provision for compulsory insurance but this is covered under clause (8) of the model letter. The latter models cover in most respects, the model letter for commercial projects.

Standard Conditions of Appointment of an Architect (CA-S-07-A) ('Blue Book')

Clause A2 – Obligations and Authority of the Architect

Duty of Care – A2.1.1 – '*the architect exercises reasonable skill care and diligence in conformity with the normal standards of the Architect's profession in performing the services including any specified roles and discharging all the obligations under this clause A2*'. This is in line with the old SFA/99.

Legal Advice A3.9 '*The Client procures such legal advice and provides such information and evidence as required for the resolution of any dispute between the client and any other parties providing work or services in connection with the Project*'. This is an innovation and is not found in either the 'old' SFA/99 or the NEC3. It is a useful provision which apparently entitles the Architect to require legal advice on issues where, experience has shown, the Architect has often had to turn to his own solicitors to provide him with advice (e.g. on Certificates or withholding payments to Contractors).

A5 – Payment. This section largely restates clauses 5.4, 5.5 and 5.6 of SFA/99 red with Schedule 3 of the 'old' agreement. It also provides for a pro rata payment for fees and disbursements.

Other innovations involve a payment deadline (clause A5.12) being imposed on fees rendered namely 28 days from the date of issue and instalments are calculated on the estimated percentage of completion of the services or stages or other services or any other specified method. *The Architect issues accounts showing the build up of any accrued instalments of the fees and other amounts due less those paid as a basis of calculating the amount due* (A5.12). Any sums due and remaining unpaid after 28 days *attract simple interest at 5% over the Bank of England's base rate on the date the payment becomes overdue (A5.13)* and this applies in addition to interest in respect of any amounts awarded to an Architect in an adjudication, arbitration or legal proceedings.

A5.16 the Client (or the Architect) '*pays to the other party all costs reasonably incurred including costs of time spent by principals,* *employees and advisors in recovering payments properly due for successfully resisting or defending a claim brought by the other'.* Again this raises an interesting practical proposition which is – does the agreement to meet costs as contained in A5.16 override the court's inherent jurisdiction to award costs which may or may not be the full costs incurred? All legal costs at trial are liable to be assessed by the court and does this clause inhibit the discretion of the courts in applying the normal rules of costs assessment in awarding costs?

A6 – Copyright and use of Information

This clause follows it's predecessor in protecting ownership of the original work produced by the Architect and the right of the Architect to be identified as the author of such work. Under A6.1.2 *'no part of any design by the Architect may be registered by the client without the consent of the Architect in writing'.* There is provision **for a licence to be granted** to the Client under clause A6.2.

Time Limit for Action for Proceedings – A7.1 *'any action or proceedings have to be commenced before the expiry of the period stated in the agreement from practical completion or the date of the last service performed under the agreement whichever is the earlier'.* This raises an interesting point – what is the position where the damage that is conplained of is latent damage and only appears some time after the *'date of practical completion or the date of the last service'*? This clause will in all likelihood

be the subject of a request for an amendment by a client to something along the lines of the traditional liability period of 6 or 12 years from the date of certificate of practical completion or the date of the last service performed by the Architect, whichever is the later.

Limits of Liability and Net Contribution clauses appear in A7.21 and A7.3 which limit the architect's liability to the lesser of either the architect's 'net contribution' or the sum stated in the agreement, whichever is the lesser.

No set-off B1.2 – there is no right to set off amounts which right the client would be entitled to exercise by law.

There is no provision for the procurement of collateral warranty agreements from the Architect unless this is specified in the project data. Furthermore, the Agreement excludes rights of third parties under the Contracts (Rights of Third Parties) Act 1999 and as such particular care will need to be exercised by both Architects and employer's regarding third party rights which are intended to be given under any project to avoid unnecessary disputes at a later stage since collateral warranties or third party rights cannot be claimed by an employer unless there was clear provision for those rights in the agreement once it has been signed.

Like its companions, the 'Green' and 'Red' Books, this contract is written in a 'user friendly and straightforward fashion' but is not 'collaborative' in approach like the NEC3 contract.

19

Other standard forms of building contract

GORDON HALL

1 Introduction

1.01 This chapter discusses standard forms of building contract other than the Joint Contracts Tribunal (JCT) 2005 Standard Form of Contract (see Chapter 17) and the NEC contract (Chapter 18). As well as the JCT family of forms there are a number of standard forms issued by other bodies such as the Association of Consultant Architects (ACA), the Royal Institution of British Architects (RIBA) and the Institution of Civil Engineers (ICE). All of these forms are regularly amended, sometimes several times a year: it is sometimes difficult for ordinary practitioners involved in the construction industry to keep up with the issue of the various supplementary amendments. Fortunately there was a general overhaul of most of the standard forms to incorporate all existing updates when they were re-issued in 1998, brought about by the need to incorporate the adjudication and payment provisions required by the Housing Grants, Construction and Regeneration Act 1996. Since then, however, the amendments have continued to flow. There have been five general amendments since then which affect the JCT suite of Forms, including a general revision of Forms WCD98, IFC98, MC98 and NSC98 and NW98 to accommodate the following:

- amendment 1: Construction Industry Scheme (CIS) (June 1999);
- amendment 2: Sundry Amendments (January 2000);
- amendment 3: Terrorism Cover/Joint Fire Cost/CIS (January 2001);
- amendment 4: Extension of Time/Loss and Expense/Advance Payment (January 2002);
- amendment 5: Construction Skills Certification Scheme (July 2003).

Of particular interest is the fact that amendment 2 (in the light of what follows) was necessary because it sought to actually exclude the operation of the Contract (Rights of Third Parties) Act 1999. The present situation is that the JCT is actively promoting the use of Third Party Agreements under the Act. It also introduced some interesting new forms.

1.02 In 2005 the JCT issued a completely new 'family' of contracts. It is generally agreed by most commentators that although there are changes to a certain degree, these mostly go to the form of presentation and not of substance. This chapter seeks, however, to address the material changes to the Forms with some reference to the previous 1998 editions which we analysed in some detail in the 8th edition of this work.

1.03 It is beyond the scope of this book to provide a commentary on every standard form or to set out the amendments which have been made. It is interesting to note that many practitioners continue to use the more popular '98 forms' such as WCD98 and MW98 despite 2005 new editions being available. The reader is therefore invited to take into account our previous analysis of the 98 forms in the previous edition of this book in conjunction with what follows.

2 JCT Documents for entering into Nominated Sub-contracts

2.01 These forms, which have a very long 'history', going back to the JCT 1963 standard form and the 1980 Form for Nominated Sub-contracts, have been discontinued. Nominated Sub-contractors were catered for in the JCT 1998 contracts but are not now in the JCT 2005 suite. They are now provided for under Section 4 (below).

3 Nominated Sub-contract Conditions (NSC/C1998 edition)

3.01 These only now exist in the 'old' JCT98 form.

4 JCT Standard Form of Domestic Sub-contract 2002 (DSC)

4.01 This form of agreement had been replaced by:

(a) **The standard Building Sub-contract Agreement/Conditions (SBC/SUB/A and SBC/SUB/C)** which also replaces the domestic Sub-contract Agreement incorporating Sectional Completion Supplement (DSC/A/SC) and JCT98 Sub-contract Conditions 2002 edition (SDC/C) and Domestic Conditions Incorporating Sub-contract Sectional Completion (DSC/C/SC).

(b) **Standard Building Contract with Sub-contractor's Design Agreement/Conditions (SBC SUB/D/A and SBC SUB/D/C)** – replaces the 'old' domestic sub-contract Agreement incorporating design Portion (DSC/A/DB), Domestic Subcontract Agreement Incorporating Sub-contractors Design Portion (DSC/C/SDP) and Domestic Sub-Contract Conditions Incorporating Sub-contractor's Design Portion and Sectional Completion (DSC/C/DPSC).

The most important aspects of these changes are (i) that both (a) and (b) can be used with the standard forms of main contract and follow their form and conditions. For this reason aspects relating to CDM, VAT and insurance are not heavily detailed but appear in a much more shortened form.

Design matters

4.02 There is clarification of the sub-contractor's design responsibility with reference to the Contractor's Requirements and the following is noteworthy:

(i) The sub-contractor's design is limited to that of the appropriate consultant professional – usually architect, engineer etc. – under the main contract;

(ii) The sub-contractor is not liable for any inadequacy of any design which is contained in the Employer's Requirements. It merely has to notify the Main Contractor if any design deficiency comes to the sub-contractor's attention.

Payment

4.03 Payments are made upon the basis of interim certificates and Contractor's applications. Payment notices are to be in accordance with the HGCRA provisions.

JCT Short form of sub-contract (short sub 2005)

4.04 This form is suitable for small 'package contracts' or works of a small content.

JCT Sub-sub-contract (sub-sub 2005)

4.05 Almost exactly the same as the short form. There is a slightly extended (31 days) final payment date compared to the 28 days in the short form. It is little used.

Generic sub-contracts

4.06 JCT has issued a generic form of sub-contract which is suitable to be used in conjunction with the MW2005 forms. Since this is intended to be used 'on the back of' a range of JCT main contracts, care must be taken to ensure that they are 'back to back' with the main contract.

5 JCT Intermediate Form of Building Contract (IC 2005)

5.01 This replaced the IFC 98 form.

Changes:

5.02 (i) IFC 98 fluctuations supplement (including amendments 1–5) is now incorporated within IC 2005.

(ii) SCS/IFC sectional completion supplement (including amendments 1–5) are now incorporated within IC 2005.

(iii) NAM/T form of tender and agreement (including amendments 1–5) is now replaced by Intermediate Named sub-contract Tender and Agreement.

(iv) Sub-contract conditions (NAM/SC) replaced by Intermediate Named sub-contract Conditions.

Types of intermediate building contract

Intermediate Contract IC, revision 1, 2007 with attestation update – used where there are works of a simple content and/or non-complex works.

5.03 – Works are designed by an Employer/where works involve administration by architect/contract administrator when the Employer must provide appropriate drawings/specifications/bills of quantities to clearly set out the scope of works required.

– It is a more detailed form than the Minor Works Contract and can be used in a situation where works are to be carried out in sections but it is unsuitable where a portion of the works is to be designed by the Contractor.

– This form also covers works of a comparatively simple form and content and also where the works are to be carried out in sections.

– It is not however appropriate to be used as a Design and Build Contract.

Intermediate sub-contract agreement (rev 1) 2007 with attestation update

5.04 Used where:

– The sub-contractor or main contract works are to be carried out in sections.

– Where main contract is IC with Contractor's design but where the sub-contractor is not required to undertake design.

– Where sub-contractor works are based on an adjusted contract sum (e.g. variations or by re-measurement).

– It is unsuitable: where the sub-contractor has part of the design responsibility (it is preferable to use the intermediate sub-contract with sub-contractor's design, IC SUB/D).

Intermediate sub-contract conditions revision 1 2007 (IC SUB/C)

5.05 When used: where the main Contractor is engaged in an IFC and where no design input is required by the sub-contractor. Also where the sub-contractor works are to be carried out in sections; are to be carried out on the basis of an adjusted subcontract or by complete re-measurement.

Unsuitable: where sub-contractor has responsibility for elements of design or where it is 'named' in the main contract.

Intermediate sub-contract with sub-contractor's design agreement rev 1 2007 (IC SUB/D/A)

5.06 When used; where the main Contractor is engaged under IC with Contractor's design and where some or all of the design is to be carried out by the sub-contractor. It is also suitable for sectional completion and/or where the contract sum is adjustable (e.g. variations).

It is unsuitable where no sub-contractor design element (use intermediate sub-contract ICSub instead).

Intermediate sub-contract with sub-contractor's design conditions rev 1 2007 (IC SUB/D/C)

5.07 When used: where main contract IC with Contractor's design and where all or some of the design is to be carried out by the sub-contractor.

Unsuitable: where no sub-contractor design element is involved (use intermediate sub-contract IC/SUB) instead.

Intermediate named sub-contract tender and agreement, revision 1 2007 (IC SUB/NAM)

5.08 Used in conjunction with IC or IC with Contractor's design and where there is a 'named' sub-contractor whether or not with a design responsibility.

Can also be used where sectional works are involved and where the contract sum is adjusted (e.g. variations).

Unsuitable where sub-contractor is not 'named' in the main contract or where the works comprise a sub-contractor designed portion.

Intermediate named sub-contractor conditions revision 1 2007 (IC SUB NAM/C)

5.09 Used where main contract is IC or IC with Contractor's design and where sub-contractor is 'named' to carry out work (whether works are designed or not).

It is suitable for sectional completion work or where there is an adjusted contract sum (variations).

Unsuitable: where sub-contractor is not named or sub-contractor work forms Contractor's designed portion.

Intermediate named sub-contractor/employer agreement, revision 1 2007 (IC SUB/NAM/E)

5.10 Used where there is a contract between a named sub-contractor and an Employer and where the main contract is IC or IC with Contractor's design and where a sub-contractor is 'named' in main contract to carry out the design of sub-contractor works under an IC SUB/NAM/A (intermediate named sub-contract agreement).

It is unsuitable for any works forming the Contractor's designed portion.

6 JCT Minor Works (MWO5) Agreement – replacing MW98

6.01 This earlier form of this popular agreement (MW98) states that the form is generally suitable for works up to the value of £70 000 based on 1992 prices. Given inflation over the years it is more generally in use nowadays involving works of £100 000–£150 000 in value. It is in very wide use together with its companion form of Minor Works Building Contract with Contractor's Design and both forms have been re-issued in 2005. It is particularly appropriate for a situation whereby the works are comparatively modest in content and value and where the contract is to be administered by an architect. Medium-priced domestic contracts immediately come to mind.

It is unsuitable as a design and build contract or where the works are complex or exceed £150 000. It is also inappropriate where there is a necessity to involve a range of consultants and sub-contractors.

Main changes to the MW98

6.02 This is in line with the purpose underlying the launch of the 2005 suite of documents this being a rewording and rearrangement of clauses and sections for the purposes of simpler accessibility and clarity of language and understanding. A definition section has also been added. The dispute resolution clause in the old edition has now been substituted to provide for legal proceedings at first instance unless (Article 7 read with Schedule 1) Arbitration is specified at the outset as a means of resolving matters.

A section entitled 'Contract Particulars' has been added to the front of the new edition, again for clarity.

7 HOC 2005 (Formerly JCT Building Contract for a Home Owner/Occupier 2002)

7.01 This can be described as a 'consumer' contract which is drafted in simple and easily understood language and which is appropriate for small works such as extensions and alterations to homes or where the works are to be carried out for an agreed lump sum and where, ideally, the works are to be overseen by an architect or contract administrator. Since it is a form of domestic contract it falls outside the provisions of the Housing Grants Construction and Regeneration Act 1996 but the contract does provide for the right of Adjudication to resolve any disputes with the Contractor.

Since it is a 'consumer contract' as defined in the Unfair Contract Terms Act 1977 the homeowner Employer would be entitled to the benefits of that Act and with particular reference to the question of whether or not any terms and conditions in the agreement pass the 'test of reasonableness' under the Act.

Consultant agreement for a home owner/occupier appointing a consultant in relaton to building work (HO/CA)

7.02 This form is used in conjunction and is intended to be an adjunct to HOC 2005 and is used to engage a consultant to provide services such as the preparation of a design or detailed specification and to obtain the appropriate building regulation approvals and planning consents. As with HOC2005, it is intended to be a simple, easily understood, agreement with accompanying rights under the Unfair Contract Terms Act 1977. It similarly provides for adjudication notwithstanding the fact that it is a 'domestic contract' and therefore outside the terms of the HCCRA 1996.

8 JCT Conditions of Contract for Building Works of a Jobbing Character (previously JA/C/T90 now RM 2006 and called JCT Repair and Maintenance Contract (Commercial))

8.01 RM 2006 represents a complete replacement of the obscure and very rarely used JA/C/90 which might even have been described as a contract to carry out works which are even smaller than those envisaged under MW98 (now MW05). The intention behind this agreement was to cover small jobs for organisations such as local authorities (e.g. maintenance on a stock of houses or flats). It does not envisage the use of an architect or contract administrator and the JCT suggests that it may be appropriate for works up to £10 000 (at 1990 prices).

8.02 The contract comprises in its present form an invitation to tender (with contract particulars), conditions and the Contractor's tender. The Employer's requirements are contained within the contract particulars and covers commencement and completion. Any drawings are attached and returned with the tender. The Employer is entitled to tender through either a fixed price, hourly rates or other rates (including day work rates) and payment can be by a single sum or by instalments.

8.03 It is unsuitable where the works comprise regular maintenance or where the works are to be carried out for a homeowner or occupier. The contract comprises an invitation to tender (with contract particulars), the Contractor's tender and conditions. The Employer signs the form of acceptance of tender to which is attached the drawings. The advantage of using this form of agreement is that the Employer can do so on the basis of a fixed price or hourly rate while payment methods can be either by payment in full or by instalments. Insurance for public liability and Employer's liability rests with the Contractor who also has a responsibility to insure the works under a suitable Contractor's all risks (CAR) form of insurance.

9 JCT Standard Form of Measured Contract 1998 (MTC98) now replaced with MTC 2006

9.01 The reason behind the issue of MTC 2006 was to provide contract simplification both in terms of language and presentation and this involves simplification and redrafting of various clauses.

Major changes

9.02 – The provision of a section entitled 'Contract Particulars' which appears at the front of the agreement and replaces the appendix in the old edition
   – The incorporation of the statutory scheme for construction contracts and the consequent omission of the JCT adjudication procedure
   – 'Prime Cost' has been replaced by a schedule of rates and charges. This is accompanied by a requirement that the national schedule of rates should be extended to the particular category of work, e.g. electrical services, mechanical and electrical etc.
   – 'A' of MTC98, the addition of a percentage or reduction against selected rates, has been renamed the 'Adjustment

Percentage' to provide for an addition to cover overheads on plant materials and sub-contractors.

The Form is designed for the use of large Employer organisations such as local authorities who employ building Contractors on small jobs. It is especially appropriate where the Employer wishes to enter into an umbrella contract with a Building Contractor to cover a series of small jobs rather than a separate RM 2006 contract for each individual job. It creates a framework for subsequent orders and as such is unlike any other contract in that it does not involve an obligation by the Employer to order an item of works at all. The Contractor is obliged to carry out any order which is given. The 'Contract Particulars' are unusually important in this form of agreement since these will identify the location of the works ordered, the period over which the works will be ordered (usually a year) and also an indication (although not a guarantee) as to the contract value. It mentions the type of works which may be ordered under the contract.

10 DB2005 (previously JCT Standard Form of Building Contract) with Contractor's Design 1998 (WCD98)

10.01 In the 1970s the concept emerged of a contract under which a package deal of both design and build would be provided. The notion was supplied by an NEDO report 'Construction for Industrial Recovery'. Originally it was intended that it would be used by local authorities for public housing projects. In fact it has been used in practice for commercial light industrial building and by developers of offices and shops. In 1981 the JCT published its design and build form which was known as CD81. There were twelve subsequent amendments all of which have been incorporated, together with some corrections into the 1998 form (CD98). During the JCT 'revamp' of contract forms in 2005, WCD98 was replaced with DB2005.

The principal changes to the previous agreement and/or the analysis of sections are:

Section 1 – definition and interpretation section is now provided.
Section 2 – carrying out the works – (which combines the Contractor's Obligations with other provisions relating to materials goods and workmanship) – possession – supply of documents – discrepancies and divergences – fees royalties and patent rights – unused materials and goods – adjustment of completion date – practical completion; delay and liquidated damages – partial possession by Employer – defects – Contractor's design documents.
Section 3 – Control of the Works.
Section 4 – payment and covers matters which were previously dealt with under clause 30 of WCD98.
Section 5 – changes – now includes a definition of changes sets out the basis for valuation.
Section 6 – injury damage and insurance – covers the previous clauses 20-22 ofWCD98.
Section 7 – assignment – covers third party rights and collateral warranty agreements; also the parties' rights of assignment.
Section 8 – termination – provides a shortened version of clauses 27, 28 and 28A of WCD98.
Section 9 – settlement of disputes. This provides for adjudication and arbitration along the lines of WCD98 (clauses 39A and 39B) and introduces, for the first time, a new provision for the parties to mediate.
Supplements under the previous WCD98 form – have now been brought into the contract conditions (i.e. Contractor's design portions and modifications – sectional completion).

Schedules

10.02 There is a greater use of schedules. Under WCD98 there are for example three alternative means of insuring the works under clauses 22A, 22B and 22C. Under DB2005 the schedules are incorporated by reference to the contract conditions – for example clause 6.7 states *'Insurance options A, B and C are set out in schedule 3. The insurance options that apply to this contract are those that are stated in the contract particulars'*. The schedules cover the following:

Schedule 1 – Contractor's design submission procedure
Schedule 2 – supplemental provisions-this covers what was previously dealt with under WCD98 except for the submission of drawings to the Employer.
Schedule 3 – insurance options
Schedule 4 – code of practice for opening up and testing which reads equivalent to WCD98.
Schedule 5 – Third Party Rights
Schedule 6 – Bonds
Schedule 7 – fluctuation options equivalent to those which were previously covered by clauses 36, 37 and 38 of WCD98.
Appendix 1 of WCD98 has now been superseded by the 'Contract Particulars'. There is also considerable use of 'default provisions'. By way of example, if there is no specific amount inserted in the Contract Particulars in relation to the professional indemnity insurance amount which is required in relation to clause 6.11 then none is required. The contract particulars are divided into part 1 (general) and equate to the 'old' Appendix 1 of WCD98 and part 2 which covers Third Party Rights.

However, the principle objectives of WCD98 and its principles remain. The following are worthy of mentions:

Article 1 – the contract documents have been defined as the articles of Agreement, Conditions, Employer's Requirements, Contractor's Proposals and Contract Sum Analysis. The reader will note that the important absentee in this definition is 'drawings' and an appropriate amendment will need to be made in this regard.
Article 8 – unlike the previous form, arbitration applies only if it is stated in the Contract Particulars to apply. If arbitration is not included then litigation automatically applies.

Design submission procedure

10.03 This concept was introduced by DB2005 and the Contractor may not be paid for any work unless it has complied with the design submission procedure and/or the requirements which are set out in the contract documents (clause 2.8). In this regard, documents are to be marked 'A', 'B' or 'C'. If 'A', the Contractor can proceed with the works; if 'B', the documents have to be resubmitted to the Employer for comment but the Contractor can proceed; where documents are marked 'C' the Contractor may not proceed. If documents are not returned by the Employer within 14 days they are deemed to be in category 'A'.

Professional indemnity insurance

10.04 This is dealt with under clause 6.11 to cover the Contractor's design liability from the stage of Practical Completion as set out in the Contract Particulars. It is vitally important that the Contract Particulars accurately reflect the insurance requirements and the period when cover should be maintained. This especially in view of the default provisions under the contract if a particular sum or period of requisite cover is not stated. In the absence of any stated period within which the insurance is to be maintained it is deemed to be for 6 years.

Design liability

10.05 Clause 2.11 – the Contractor is not responsible for the content of the Employer's Requirements or the checking of the adequacy of the design contained within the Employer's Requirement. This followed the decision in *Cooperative Insurance Society Ltd v Henry Boot Scotland Ltd (2002)*. In these circumstances, any correction of the Employer's Requirements will constitute a change under the contract. It is anticipated that this particular clause will, in practice, be suitably amended.

Copyright

10.06 Clause 2.38.2 states '*Subject to all monies due and payable under this contract to the Contractor having been paid . . . the Employer is granted an irrevocable royalty–free licence to use the Contractor's design documents to complete the works*'. It is highly likely that this clause will also be amended in practice to remove what is tantamount to the exercise of a right of a lien by the Contractor on the drawings (i.e. by removing the words 'Subject to all monies due . . . having been paid'.

Adjustment of completion date

10.07 'Pre-agreed Adjustment' means a revised completion date having been agreed for sectional work or for provisional sum works. 'Relevant Omission' means the omission of work by way of an instruction received for a change.

Extension of time

10.08 Clauses 2.2.3 to 2.2.6 now include 'relevant events' (clause 2.2.6).

Defects

10.09 The defects liability period is now known as the 'Rectification Period'.

Changes to pricing

10.10 Alternative A – the Contractor's price statement under WCD98 has now been removed as a method of valuing changes.

Injury, damage and insurance

10.11 This is much the same as under WCD98, with the exception of the deletion of clause 22D (insurance for Employer's loss of liquidated damages).

Third party rights and collateral warranties

10.12 The following alternatives are offered under DB2005:

(i) the Contractor offers third party rights under the Contracts (Rights of Third Parties) Act 1999 to a funder and/or purchase or tenant;

(ii) the Contractor gives collateral warranties to a funder for purchaser/tenant.

There is also provision for the Contractor to procure either third party rights or collateral warranties from its own sub-contractors.

Settlements of disputes

10.13 Under DB2005 there is provision for mediation as an alternative form of dispute resolution. DB2005 now advances the Statutory Scheme for Construction Contracts as the appropriate adjudication procedure.

11 JCT 1998 Contractor's designed Portion Supplement 1998 (was CDPS98) now contained within the SPC suite of contracts

SPC/AQ – Standard building contract with approximate quantities rev 1 2007

11.01 For larger works designed and/or detailed by the Employer and the drawings are to be provided by the Employer with approximate quantities. It is suitable for use where an Architect/Contract Administrator is appointed. It is also appropriate where the works are to be carried out in sections and/or where a particular part is to be designed by the Contractor.

Standard building contract with approximate quantities without contractor's design (SBC/AQ/XD)

11.02 This is appropriate where the Employer provides the Contractor with drawings and approximate bills of quantities. Appropriate for sectional work. Not suitable where the Contractor is to design a discrete part, when the SBC/Q should be used instead.

Standard building contract with quantities revision 1 2007 (SBC/Q)

11.03 Used for larger works designed or detailed by the Employer with the latter to provide the Contractor with drawings and bills of quantities. Suitable for larger works involving the Architect or Contract Administrator. Appropriate where Contractor designs discrete parts (designed portion) or where work is to be carried out in sections.

Standard building contract with quantities but without contractor's design

11.04 For larger works as above but not suitable where the Contractor has a designed portion.

Standard building contract without quantities revision 1 2007 (SBC/XQ)

11.05 Used for larger works which are designed or detailed by or for the Employer who provides the Contractor with drawings and a specification and where the works do not require a detailed bill of quantities. Suitable where works are administered by Architect or Contract Administrator and where the Contractor is to produce a part of the works (Contractor's Designed Portion) and/or the works are to be carried out in sections.

Standard building contract without quantities or contractor's design rev 1 2007 (SBC/XQ/XD)

11.06 Where the portion or work to be carried out in sections but inappropriate where Contractor has a design responsibility.

Standard building sub-contract agreement rev 1 2007

11.07 Used where main contract is a standard form of building contract (with or without quantities or approximate quantities) and where sub-contractor has no design input.

Standard building sub-contract conditions rev 1 2007 (SBC SUB/C)

11.08 Used where main contract is standard building contract (with or without quantities or approximate quantities) and for sub-contractor works not involving design. Unsuitable where sub-contractor has any design responsibility for part of the works.

Standard building sub-contract with sub-contractor's design agreement rev 2007 with attestation update (SBC SUB/D/A)

11.09 Used where main contract is standard building contract (with or without quantities or approximate quantities and where the contract has a designed portion and sub-contractor is to carry out design of part of the sub-contract works. Unsuitable if no sub-contractor design involved.

Standard building sub-contract with sub-contractor design conditions (rev 1 2007) (SBC SUB/D/C)

11.10 For use when main contract is standard form (with or without quantities or approximate quantities) where Contractor designs discrete part of the works and sub-contractor is to design part of the sub-contracted works. Unsuitable where no sub-contractor design input.

12 JCT Major project Form 2003 (MPF) now MP2005

12.01 The previous (8th) edition of this book dealt at some considerable length with the MPF form. Its successor, the 'JCT major projects form' – of February 2007 as with JCT 05 – DB, IC and MWD provides that the Contractor *'shall not be responsible for the contents of the Employer's Requirements or the adequacy of the design contained within the Requirements'*.

12.02 The Contractor's warranty as to design continues to be one of *'the skill and care to be expected of a professional designer appropriately qualified and competent in the discipline to which such design relates and experienced in carrying out work of a similar scope, nature and size to the project'*. What seems clear, therefore, is that the Contractor undertakes to use reasonable skill and care in respect of any design which is its responsibility.

12.03 In three areas there is an exception to the basic warranty of 'reasonable skill and care', namely; that the design will be in accordance with statutory provisions, and that it will comply with any performance specification which is set out in the Employer's Requirements and that the Materials will conform to Ove Arup's *Guide to Good Practice in the Choice of Construction Materials* (1997).

12.04 In keeping with other parts of the 2005 suite, there is an extension of third party rights to include rights under the Contracts (Rights of Third Parties) Act 1999 as an alternative to the provision of collateral warranty agreements. The third party rights under the Act are extended to funders, purchasers and tenants. The definition of beneficiaries in these categories is however very widely stated – i.e. does it include, for example, the tenant of the entire building or individual tenants? This is bound to raise concerns on the part of Insurers as well as Practitioners as to what precisely they are being asked to cover. Furthermore, the third party rights in favour of purchasers and tenants only cover the 'reasonable cost of repair, renewal and/or reinstatement of any part of the project to the extent that a purchaser or tenant incurs such costs and/or a purchaser or tenant is or becomes liable either directly or by way of financial contribution for such costs.' This 'wording' which is found in the British Property Federation (BPF 3rd edition, 2005) Collateral Warranty in favour of purchasers or tenants was inevitably amended in practice since in its existing form it does not cover any consequential losses over and above the costs of repair. It remains to be seen whether or not a Third Party rights Agreement will follow the same trend.

13 JCT Standard Form of Management Contract 1998 edition (MC98) now the JCT Management Building Contract 2008

13.01 The reader is referred to our analysis of the previous form of management contract which is to be found in the 8th edition (page 182 *et seq*). The previous form MC98 underwent a further revision during the overhaul of the entire 1998 suite and further revisions of the contract are contained in the latest 2008 edition which was in fact the 2005 edition subsequently corrected and which was published in February 2008.

13.02 The key changes in the latest contract include:

– the option for possession and completion of the project by sections;
– the extension of third party rights and collateral warranties to purchasers, tenants and funders;
– a new provision which introduces a Notice to Proceed after the pre-construction stage.

13.03 It contains Contract Particulars which are divided into two parts namely Part 1 – General and Part 2 – Third Party Rights and Collateral Warranties. Part 1 provides for the first time that the construction industry scheme (CIS) as referred to in the fifth recital and clause 4.4 is now the designated adjudication procedure.

13.04 Article 11 read with clauses 9 and 11 provide for the first time that where arbitration is not specifically designated, then legal proceedings will decide any issue.

13.05 Clause 1.1 article 11 provided for the first time for key personnel to be set out in the Contract Particulars.

13.06 The 'defects liability period' is now replaced with reference to the 'rectification period'.

13.07 Clause 6.11 should be particularly noted. This provides that where professional indemnity insurance is not stated in a particular sum, insurance under this clause shall not be required. If no time period is stated then a period of 1 year is implied.

Termination by employer

13.08 It should be noted that under clause 8.4 the Employer is entitled to terminate this contract at will by notice in writing to the management Contractor.

Once a notice to proceed is issued the management Contractor is responsible to supervise and carry out the works which will be undertaken by works Contractors who may or may not have a design role. This is covered under the fifth to seventh recitals of the agreement. The management Contractor will be responsible to ensure that any such design works meet the contractual requirements. He is liable to the Employer to the extent that he is able to recover damages in respect of any such works from the works Contractor and to the extent that there is any shortfall the Employer will cover the same.

Payment

13.09 This is under the following bases: prime cost and management fee. Prime cost will, of course, cover amounts paid to the works Contractors, materials, plant etc to which is added a management fee. These costs will invariably be arrived at through negotiation however it is idle to deny that any formula involving a combination of prime cost and a Management Fee may be an unattractive 'package' to any Employer.

Advantages

13.10 Management contracting is an attractive choice for a property developer for whom interest charges are a major commercial consideration since this is a matter of procurement which tends to allow the quickest start to the workforce. It has been found by many developers to offer the best prospect of a speedy completion. It provides stronger management of the works than any other: since the management Contractor has no responsibility for any hands-on construction he has nothing to distract him from using his experience of running construction projects to drive the project forward to an efficient and fast completion. The arrangement is attractive to management Contractors because they assume virtually no financial risk.

Disadvantages

13.11 The Employer does not have any certainty as to the ultimate cost of the project. The Employer is heavily dependent upon the Contractor's ability to 'performs and deliver'.

14 GC/Works/1 (1998 edition)

14.01 The reader is referred to our analysis in the 8th edition at paragraph 14.01 *et seq*. There have been no further amendments to this contract.

15 JCT 2005 Framework Agreement

15.01 The basis of framework agreements are to provide a general 'umbrella' in which various work programmmes may be carried out and they are generally used where there are requirements for larger public-sector or private-sector or involvement (such as schools and hospitals).

The JCT 2005 framework agreement is a new form and is suitable where it is intended that there should be a participation of parties involved in a particular ongoing programme (e.g. the Building Schools for the Future 'BSF' projects).

The Framework agreement envisages a direct contractual arrangement between the Employer and what is described as the 'Service Provider' and seeks to bring other members of the 'team' into identical arrangements on the same terms. The intention is to create a number of separate but uniform agreements ideally on the same terms and conditions to promote a working environment of 'mutual cooperation and participation' with a view to achieving 'framework objectives' (nine in all) aimed at quality of delivery of services and performance. These are:

- achieving health and safety objectives;
- team working and consideration of others;
- greater predictability of costs and programme;
- improvements in quality productivity and value for money;
- improvements in environmental performance and sustainability and reductions in environmental impact;
- 'right first time', with zero defects;
- the avoidance of all disputes;
- employer satisfaction with product and services;
- enhancement of service provider's reputation and commercial opportunity.

The 'Framework Particulars' refer to performance indicators with a view to monitoring the progress in achieving the nine framework objectives. There are 'best practice' provisions included with a view to encouraging cooperation, trust and mutual respect to achieve the framework objectives. They also include performance indicators used to monitor success of the service provider in achieving the framework objectives.

The JCT forms which apply to the Framework Agreement are as follows:

Framework Agreement (FA2005)

For use where the parties wish to be bound by the terms of the framework agreement.

Framework Agreement (Non Binding) FA/N2005

15.02 For use where the parties do not elect to be bound by the framework agreement. It is intended, instead, to create an environment in which the parties cooperate with a view to achieving objectives.

Arrangement of Binding Framework Agreement

15.03 The Framework Agreement (Binding) is set out in 28 clauses together with particulars. The clauses are as follows:

1 Definitions
2 Interpretation
3 Supplemental underlying contracts
4 The role of the framework agreement
5 The framework objectives
6 Legal status of framework agreement
7 Contracts (Rights of Third Parties) Act 1999
8 Applicable law and jurisdiction
9 Organisational structure and decision making
10 Collaborative working
11 The service providers supply chain
12 Sharing of information and know how
13 Communications protocol
14 Confidentiality
15 Risk assessment and risk allocation
16 Health and safety
17 Sustainable development and environmental considerations
18 Value engineering
19 Change control procedures
20 Early warning
21 Team approach to problem solving
22 Performance indicators
23 Termination
24 Settlement of disputes
25 Mediation
26 Adjudication
27 Arbitration
28 Legal proceedings.

Advantages

15.04 Harmonises the various Consultants' Appointments under an 'umbrella' contract.

It promotes mutual cooperation towards achieving quality of delivery.

Disadvantages

15.05 Professional indemnity insurers carefully scrutinise any agreement which contains 'best practice' and agreements to meet 'performance specification'. It is also difficult in practice to adopt a 'single fit' contract for all Construction team members since there are bound to be competing interests and differences in terms and conditions imposed by individual insurers.

16 Building contracts in Scotland*

16.01 The standard forms of building contract issued by the Joint Contracts Tribunal Limited are drafted with the law of England and Wales in mind. As the commentator on the JCT 80 contract in *Keating on Building Contracts* points out, where the works in question are to be carried out in Scotland, those forms are unlikely to be appropriate, and recourse should be had to the standard forms of building contract which are issued by the Scottish Building Contracts Committee. These make allowance for the different legal background in Scotland in the context of which the contract made between the parties will have to operate. At the time of writing, new Scottish forms are being drawn up to reflect the JCT's 2005 rewriting of the JCT forms. As these are not yet common currency, what follows relates to the more usually encountered 1999 form and its predecessors.

16.02 In framing its standard form contracts, the SBCC tries to keep as much of the material which appears in any given JCT contract in its Scottish counterpart as possible. In consequence, not only are most of the provisions of the Scottish Building Contract of 1999 common to that document and the 1998 JCT Standard Form of Building Contract, but authority drawn from English law on the parallel provisions of the co-relative JCT form is frequently cited and founded on in cases arising out of SBCC

---

*This section was written by Robert Howie.

ones. In this section it is proposed only to call attention to some of those areas of concern to the architect where the law of Scotland, as declared in its courts, has produced either results different from those obtaining in England in similar circumstances or differences in emphasis on matters which end in a common result.

16.03 The principal method which the SBCC has used to bring about the large measure of congruence between its forms and those of the JCT is the inclusion in the formal contract document, which takes the place of the Articles of Agreement in the JCT regime, of a provision to the effect that the contract shall be governed by the terms of the chosen JCT form as those stand amended by such of the JCT Amendments as the parties may have selected and by the provisions of the Scottish supplement appended to the contract as Appendix I thereof. The Abstract of Conditions normally features as Appendix II of the contract. It is by way of the formal contract document and the Scottish Supplement that the changes to the original JCT drafting of the Form chosen by the parties are made to reflect the Scottish element of the works. Of course, there is no rule of law which prevents the parties from making amendments of their own to the terms of the SBCC contract, and that is frequently done. The architect who is contemplating such alternations, should, however, consider whether in the context of Scots law, those changes will have the effect which he may know from experience they would have in England and Wales.

16.04 It is usual for the Form of Agreement to contain only three specifically Scottish provisions, although as the portion of the contract which is executed, it is in relation to this part that regard must be had to the requirements of Scots law regarding the execution of a formal self-proving contract. Those requirements vary depending on the status of the executing party, but will for the most part be found in the Requirements of Writing (Scotland) Act 1995. It is also in the Form of Agreement that there will be found the clause in which Scots law is chosen as the governing law of the contract, and the clause whereby disputes are referred to arbitration. The pre-printed SBCC Forms do not include any express choice of jurisdiction clause in relation to disputes which are litigated, presumably because the assumption is that disputes will be settled by arbitration; and that in those cases where arbitration is not provided for, the definition of 'court' for the purposes of the contract as meaning 'the Court of Session' is thought to have the effect of prorogating the jurisdiction of that court. It may be, however, that in cases where arbitration has been provided for but not utilised, Court proceedings can still be brought in sheriff court, or, indeed, in any court to the territorial jurisdiction of which defender is subject. There is, however, an implicit choice of jurisdiction in favour of the Court of Session in relation to disputes arising out of an arbitration relative to the contract, and, in light of the choice of Scots law as the governing law, there is an obvious practical convenience, not to say saving in cost, in suing, if needs be, on other matters in Scotland also.

16.05 The majority of the Scottish amendments are made in the Scottish Supplement which forms Appendix I. Some of these are merely matters of substitution of legal terminology (substituting 'assignation' for 'assignment', 'heritable' for 'real', etc.), but others are of more substantial import. The provisions regarding determination on insolvency are normally amended to reflect peculiarities of Scottish company and insolvency law, such as the ability to appoint a judicial factor on the estates of a Scottish registered limited liability company, and the effects of the separate legal personality from its members which is accorded a Scottish partnership. There are usually special provisions made about the purchase of off-site materials, which reflect differences between the common laws of property in England and Scotland and lengthy provisions about arbitration supplant those which are made for English arbitrations in the co-relative portions of the JCT forms.

16.06 It should not be assumed from this that all differences between English and Scottish law have been accounted for in the SBCC Forms: they have not. One major area of difficulty which arises in Scotland with the terms of a JCT form which are unamended by the counterpart SBCC Form concerns the trust fund sought to be created over the contractual retention monies by Clause 30.5 of the JCT 98 Contract. Whatever may be the position in England, these provisions are not in Scotland sufficient to create a trust over the retention monies in favour of the contractor on which he can rely in the event of the insolvency of the employer. The practical failure of these provisions from the point of view of the contractor was graphically illustrated by the decision in *Balfour Beatty-Ltd v Britannia Life Ltd 1997* SLT 10, a case decided in the context of very similar provisions in the SBCC Management and Works Contracts. In that case, the contract's provisions were judicially stigmatised as being 'wholly ineffective to achieve what may have been the intended purpose of the draftsman', because they did not serve to create a trust or other property right in specific assets of the management contractor. At best for the contractor, he can only make use of the clause to sue the employer for specific implement of the obligation to set up a trust in the retention monies (see *Fairclough Scotland Ltd v Jamaica Street Ltd,* 30 April 1992, unreported) – and that remedy is apt to be stultified if the employer becomes insolvent in the interim, or, pleading dispute about his right to set off monies, insists on putting the matter to arbitration or adjudication.

16.07 There are also other areas (of perhaps more immediate concern to the architect than the trust obligations of the employer in relation to retention monies) in which the Scottish courts have taken a different approach from that followed south of the border. A significant example arises in relation to the hierarchy provisions of the JCT Standard Form Building Contract, whereby any provisions in the bills of quantities inconsistent with those of the JCT standard form are subordinated to that form. Of late years, a practice appears lo have grown up in Scotland whereby the formal contract is not executed, but the contract is allowed to rest on the bills of quantities and the form of lender referring thereto, duly accepted, which incorporates the terms of the JCT form including the hierarchy clause. The bills will frequently amend the Conditions heavily, and, with a view to circumventing the hierarchy clause, will preface those amendments with a term to the effect that 'Notwithstanding the provisions of [the hierarchy clause] of the said Conditions, the amendments and modifications detailed hereunder shall apply…'

The perils of adopting this practice were recently highlighted in *Barry D. Trentham Ltd v McNeil* 1996 SLT 202, where that term was implicitly held to be ineffective to prevent the hierarchy clause from operating to strike down any inconsistent clause in the bills, albeit that it might be quite evident that all the special clauses of the contract drawn with the particular project in mind were to be found with bills. It is suggested that, in the light of the *Trentham* case, and the prior decision which it followed, it would be unwise for an architect who wished to amend the JCT or SBCC Forms to carry out that exercise in the contract bills: the better course would seem to be to secure the execution of a formal contract in amended terms, and to number among the amendments the necessary changes to the hierarchy clause itself.

16.08 Certification, too, is an area in which the Scottish courts have not always taken the same line as their English counterparts. As in England, the architect, when acting as certifier, is regarded as exercising a quasi-judicial office in which he should resist interference from his employer. He is expected to take care not to exceed his jurisdiction in that office, and to avoid issuing certificates which he has not been given competence by the parties' contract to issue (cf. *Ames Mining Ltd v The Scottish Coal Company Ltd,* 6 August 2003, unreported). If he does issue such certificates, they will be invalid. But on the controversial matter of the extent of the conclusive effect to be afforded an Architect's Final Certificate under the JCT Standard Form Contracts, the current leading decision in the Court of Session (*Belcher Food Products Ltd v Messrs Miller & Black* 1999 SLT 142) would seem to have taken a more restrictive view of the ambit within which the Final Certificate is conclusive than have the English cases. It would appear from that decision that, in Scotland at least, the Certificate will not operate as conclusive evidence as to the adequacy of workmanship or materials unless the contractual standard for such workmanship or materials has been stated in the contract to be the 'reasonable satisfaction of the Architect'. On the other hand, the Court of Session has made it clear that in cases where an adjudicator has determined a matter relevant to some task which an architect has to perform, or to a decision which he has to take in the course of his certifying functions, the architect cannot disagree with the adjudicator, but must rather give effect to his determination, albeit that, if new information has come to light since the date of the determination, the architect is entitled to make use of that information in updating the effects of the adjudicator's decision. If, therefore, an adjudicator has decided that a given sum is payable in respect of work in an interim certificate, the architect is bound by that decision until such time as it may be overridden by court action or arbitration. This holds true not only in relation to subsequent interim payment certificates, but in relation to the issue of the final certificate as well (*Castle Inns (Stirling) Ltd v Work Contracts Ltd* [2005] CSOH 178).

A further complication about final certificates is also highlighted by the same case. An adjudicator's award which is issued more after the final certificate becomes final under certain SBCC forms if it has not been challenged within 28 days of its issue. The result may be that, since a final certificate does not become conclusive for 60 days after its issue, a final certificate can in effect be amended by a subsequently issued adjudicator's decision which itself becomes final since that finality guarantees success to a challenger of the final certificate who alleges that it is erroneous at a date after that decision became final but before the final certificate had become conclusive.

16.09 It also behoves the architect lo pay close attention to the insurance provisions of the JCT contracts. In Clauses 22A, B and C of the 1998 Standard Form, provisions are made as to the allocation of responsibilities to insure the works and existing structures as between the employer and contractor. Over the past 10 years or so. the predecessors of these provisions have given rise to not a little litigation in Scotland, including two cases which reached the House of Lords. The net effect of that litigation is in certain circumstances to prevent the employer from suing the contractor or a sub-contractor for damage wrought by the latter either to the works themselves or to the building in which the works are taking place. In light of recent decisions in England concerning the liability of a project manager for failing to check that the appropriate insurances were in place, it is suggested that the employer's architect in Scotland who fails so to check is likely to be at risk of liability to his client if the application in the circumstances of the case in question of the above-mentioned House of Lords cases restricting the scope of the duty of care owed to the employer by the contractor or sub-contractor precludes that client from recovering his losses from the contractor or sub-contractor the fault of which had brought them about.

16.10 Time-bar is a further matter which is prone to give to difficulty, particularly when the client is English and used to dealing with a 6-year limitation period. It should be recalled that in Scotland the operative doctrine in the building contract context will be prescription rather than limitation, and more importantly, that prescription strikes after 5 years in breach of contract and implement of contract case, not 6. Complexities can attend the ascertainment of the date when the period of prescription commenced running, particularly in cases where – as in most JCT Forms – there is provision for certification of practical completion and the making good of defects. On such matters, it may be thought appropriate to seek legal advice in light of the circumstances which obtain in the individual case in question, but it is always necessary to be alive to the risk that valuable legal rights may be lost through prescription. It should be remembered that the ways in which prescription may be stopped from running are very limited (acts amounting to a 'relevant claim' or 'relevant acknowledgement' within the meaning of the Prescription and Limitation (Scotland) Act 1973 are called for) and that in the case of arbitration, particular pitfalls await the person who seeks to interrupt prescription by means of preliminary notice to arbitrate. A reference to adjudication, it is thought, is not a 'relevant claim'. The safest course is usually simply to sue in court, if needs be by way of recourse to the declarator *ad ante* procedure, for, saving one rather unlikely case, an action served on the person against whom the claim is asserted is always a 'relevant claim'.

16.11 The longest section of separate provision for Scotland in the SBCC contract is that which is concerned with adjudication and arbitration. As will be seen in the later chapter on Building Dispute Resolution in Scotland, the laws of England and Scotland on arbitration are very different, and accordingly, separate and detailed provisions have to be made for Scottish arbitrations.

20

Contractor and sub-contractor collateral warranties/third party rights

ANN MINOGUE

1 Architects and collateral warranties/ third party rights

1.01 Architects are likely to encounter collateral warranties or, more recently, third party rights in two circumstances. First, and most importantly, they themselves may be .asked to provide collateral warranties/third party rights, and second they may be expected to advise their clients – the employer under the building contract – on collateral warranties/third party rights to be given by contractors and sub-contractors either to the employer or to third parties such as funders, purchasers or tenants. Although in most cases employers will take direct legal advice on the provision of collateral warranties/third party rights to third parties, architects should still be aware of the nature of these collateral warranties/ third party rights in case advice is required. In the case of collateral warranties or third party rights required under standard documents, such as JCT forms, in favour of the employer, architects should satisfy themselves that the appropriate collateral warranties or third party rights are obtained from contractors or sub-contractors in favour of the employer. The detailed terms of architects' collateral warranties/third party rights are dealt with elsewhere in this book. This chapter will look at collateral warranties/third party rights generally, but will then concentrate on contractor/sub-contractor collateral warranties/third party rights.

2 What is a collateral warranty?

2.01 A collateral warranty is a form of contract which runs alongside, and is usually supplemental to, another contract. Usually a collateral warranty creates a contractual relationship between two parties where none would otherwise exist. It takes the form of a contract between the party to the underlying contract who is providing services or carrying out work and a third party who has an interest in the proper performance of that contract and, just like any contract, it must be signed by the Parties, most commonly as a deed. In this text, the person giving the collateral warranty will be called 'the warrantor' and the person to whom it is given 'the beneficiary'.

3 What are third party rights?

3.01 Third party rights are created under the underlying contract itself and in order to create them no separate form of contract is required. They now commonly appear, as an alternative to collateral warranties, in standard documents, including in particular the JCT 2005 suite. The use of third party rights was enabled by the Contracts (Rights of Third Parties) Act, 1999 which came fully into force in May 2000, and which radically affects the law in relation to privity of contract. The Act confers on a third party 'a right to enforce a term of the contract' where *either* the contract contains an express term to that effect *or* where the contract purports to confer a benefit on that third party. In both cases, the third party must be expressly identified in the contract by name, class or description, but need not be in existence at the time of the contract. The third party must, however, be capable of being ascertained with certainty. Accordingly, a general reference to 'purchasers of the building when completed' would be enforceable.

3.02 A 'right to enforce a term of the contract' in these circumstances means the right to all of the remedies which would have been available to a third party through the courts if it had been a party to the contract but subject to the terms of the contract including any relevant exclusions of liability or restrictions in the contract. In other words, contractual damages are recoverable but the parties can agree that recovery is excluded or capped.

3.0.3 More problematically, the Act also states that where a third party has a right to enforce a term of a contract, the parties may not without his consent 'rescind the contract, or vary it in such a way as to extinguish or alter his entitlement under that right' in certain circumstances. This can be excluded by agreement or by the courts or the arbitrator in defined circumstances.

3.04 The third party's rights will be subject to all defences and setoffs that would have been available to the contracting party had the third party been a party to the original contract unless the parties provide otherwise in the contract.

3.05 The effects of this legislation have been very far reaching indeed. There is no need for separate collateral warranties in favour of funders, purchasers and tenants. The relevant rights can be granted by a clause included in the original consultancy agreement or building contract. Those rights can be subject to exclusions and restrictions. In other words, the contractual damages which would otherwise be recoverable by the third party potentially include losses other than the cost of repair, but these can be subject to agreements that recovery is excluded or capped, that it is subject to 'net contribution clauses' and so on. Sub-contracts, too, can include a clause enabling the employer to pursue the sub-contractor directly.

3.06 The initial reaction of most of the contract producing bodies to the Act was to exclude any third party rights wholesale. This sweeping approach has more recently been superseded by a more careful and reflective use of the benefits that the Act has to offer. JCT Major Project Form published in 2005 is a case in point: while it excludes any third party rights generally, it sets out in a Third Party Rights Schedule specific rights to be vested in a funder or purchasers/tenants. The rights are triggered by a notice served by the employer on the contractor identifying the relevant party and the nature of its interest in the project. After triggering of the rights, the person identified in the employer's notice can pursue the contractor directly for breach of the provisions set out in the Third Party Rights Schedule. Other JCT forms provide for the alternative of collateral warranties or third party rights.

3.07 It is now increasingly accepted that third party rights are a simpler and more straightforward way of vesting rights in purchasers and tenants avoiding the extensive problems created by the need to secure the execution of collateral warranties by parties who may have finished their work or with whom the employer may be in dispute. Banks' and funders' lawyers are more dubious about the use of third party rights in place of collateral warranties because of the provision of 'step-in rights' where obligations and not just rights are imposed on the third party bank or funder in certain circumstances. Accordingly it is still common to see collateral warranties in their favour. For purchasers and tenants, both methods of granting them rights are in common use although the rights granted are essentially the same under both routes.

3.08 Because of this and to avoid repetition, the remainder of this chapter will focus on collateral warranties but the comments made apply equally to the same provisions as they appear in the Third Party Rights Schedules of the JCT standard forms.

4 Why have collateral warranties become so important?

4.01 The legal doctrine of privity of contract means that remedies for the improper performance of obligations under a contract are – subject to Contracts (Rights of Third Parties) Act 1999 – limited to the parties to that contract. For example, under the JCT 2005 Standard Building Contract SBC/XQ, if no collateral warranty is obtained and a sub-contractor is in breach of his sub-contract, the employer will not be able to sue him for breach of contract as the employer is not a party to the sub-contract. The employer would have to make his claim against the main contractor with whom he would have a contract and the main contractor would, in turn, claim against the defaulting sub-contractor. A particular problem arises where the sub-contractor's default does not place the main contractor in breach of the main contract: the clearest example is where a sub-contractor provides late or incorrect design information for work which does not constitute part of 'the Contractor's Designed Portion'. Even where this problem does not arise, if the contractor is insolvent, the employer will find himself unable to recover any of his losses from the insolvent main contractor and, without a collateral warranty, he cannot sue the sub-contractor for any breach of contract by him prior to the insolvency.

4.02 It was a desire to circumvent the legal problems that stem from the law of privity of contract that led to the development of the tort of negligence as set out in the famous case of *Donoghue v Stevenson* [1932] AC 562. That case established the 'neighbour' principle which obliges a party to take care to avoid acts which it can reasonably foresee are likely to injure its neighbour. 'Neighbours' were defined as being those so closely affected by a party's act that that party ought to have had them in contemplation when carrying out the act in question. 'Injury' initially meant physical harm but the courts came to extend it to financial loss. A duty of care in negligence is owed only to neighbours but there is no need for neighbours to be contractually linked to create a liability.

4.03 For many years the tort of negligence applied to cases of defective buildings, the leading case being *Anns v Merton London Borough Council* [1978] AC 728. Builders, architects and others involved in the construction process were held to owe fairly wide duties of care to all those who might reasonably be expected to

be affected by their negligent actions. This duty of care protected tenants and purchasers of developments. Therefore, parties who needed to be protected from negligent and defective building design or work were advised that they had some legal protection under the tort of negligence without needing any direct contractual link with the builders and designers.

4.04 The cases of *D & F Estates Ltd and Others v The Church Commissioners of England and Others* [1988] 49 BLR 1, *Murphy v Brentwood District Council* [1991] 1 AC 398 and other subsequent authorities dramatically altered the established legal position relating to defective buildings and negligence so that a builder would not be liable in tort to successive owners of a building (i.e. those with no contractual link to him) for any defects in the building itself. It was held that the cost of rectifying defects was economic loss and that this type of loss was not ordinarily recoverable in the tort of negligence. The builder would only be liable in tort if any defect caused personal injury or damage to other property (i.e. something other than the building). The principles governing liabilities in tort are discussed in more detail in Chapter 3.

4.05 The decisions in *D & F Estates* and *Murphy* left third parties legally exposed. As a result, collateral warranties became increasingly important as the only means of protection for third parties who were prevented from recovering losses suffered due to defective building work. It has now become common practice for employers, purchasers, tenants, funders, freeholders and others to require contractors, sub-contractors, and professional consultants with whom they do not have a contractual link to provide collateral warranties or, as noted above, third party rights to enable them to recover directly for any defects and other losses arising from their work.

4.06 Although more recent decisions of the House of Lords (*St Martins Property Corporation Ltd v Sir Robert McAlpine Ltd* [1994] AC 85) and of the Court of Appeal (*Darlington Borough Council v Wiltshier Northern Ltd* [1995] 1 WLR 68 and *Sir Alfred McAlpine Ltd v Panatown Ltd* [1998] 88 BLR 67) may enable contractual claims to be pursued on behalf of subsequent purchasers of a defective building, even though the purchaser has no contractual link with the contractor, the extent of the comfort afforded by these decisions is so imprecise that employers are usually still advised to ask for collateral warranties on behalf of purchasers, tenants and funders.

4.07 In addition, the courts have tried to avoid the draconian effects of the decisions in *D&F Estates* and *Murphy* by further developing the law of negligent misstatement under which professionals who give negligent advice can still be held liable for pure economic loss even to persons with whom they have no contract. The leading authority is *Hedley Byrne & Co v Heller and Partners*[1964] AC 465 and the doctrine has recently been extended in cases such as *Henderson v Merrett Syndicates Ltd* [1995] 2 AC 145. The precise ambit though of this exception too is uncertain and has not caused the torrent of demands for collateral warranties to ebb.

5 Who needs the benefit of collateral warranties?

Employers

5.01 As noted in paragraph 4.01 above, employers require collateral warranties from the contracting industry in their favour in two different circumstances, either:

● To supplement and reinforce their direct contractual rights. So, for example, the employer may seek collateral warranties from key sub-contractors and suppliers in respect of materials and workmanship supplied or carried out by them even though he also has contractual rights against the main contractor. The main advantage to the employer of obtaining collateral warranties in such circumstances is that if such workmanship or materials were to prove defective, proceedings could be brought directly against the party responsible in addition to the contractor. This will be particularly useful if the main contractor has become insolvent. It is suggested that this doubling-up of contractual protection should be discouraged except in exceptional cases. It results in an over-proliferation of paperwork and interferes with proper management of the work.

- Where, but for the collateral warranty, the employer may have no enforceable contractual right for the design and construction work. This is most commonly the case where specialist sub-contractors carry out design work in connection with the development, but the main contractor has no responsibility for such design (as is the case if JCT 2005 is used *without* Contractor's Designed Portion). Equally, an employer would also require collateral warranties if he uses management contracting to procure his development. Otherwise, he may find himself without any remedy since the management contractor's liability for works contractors' shortcomings is limited by the terms of the management contract.

As noted above, in the first case, it is really for the employer to decide whether he feels he needs this supplemental protection. In the second case, though, there is a much greater obligation on the architect to ensure that the correct collateral warranties are in place since, if they are not, the employer may well be left without any contractual remedy at all in respect of parts of the design of the development where the architect has agreed that such design will be carried out by the sub-contractor. SFA/99 excludes the architect's responsibility for such design and, in these circumstances, there must be a good argument that the architect has failed in his duties to the employer if he does not advise him that collateral warranties should be obtained or that the relevant element of design is properly described in the Contractor's Designed Portion.

Purchasers

5.02 Purchasers cannot generally sue vendors for defects in the development in the absence of express contractual undertakings from the vendor. A purchaser from an original employer would have no direct contractual link with those involved in the construction process unless the benefits of the construction contracts and the various consultancy agreements were assigned to him. Usually this will not be possible without the prior consent of the contractor or consultants. Sometimes, the building contract may be amended so that the contractor is obliged to consent to the assignment in advance of it. Purchasers from original developers were specially mentioned in *D & F Estates* and *Murphy* as having no rights in negligence against contractors for any defects arising in any building purchased. As a result, purchasers will often require collateral warranties to ensure that they are protected.

Tenants

5.03 A prospective tenant of a new development may require collateral warranties if the lease is to be granted on a full repairing basis, so that the landlord accepts no liability for defects in the building and the tenant becomes liable to carry out repairs at his own cost. With full repairing leases it is desirable that the tenant obtains collateral warranties from those involved in the construction process in order that he can recover, via a direct contractual link, repair costs from those responsible. Even where the landlord does accept some liability for defects in the building, tenants will usually also want a collateral warranty from the design and construction team in order to protect themselves against insolvency of the landlord developers.

Funders

5.04 Where a bank or institution provides finance for a development and takes a legal charge over the property to be developed, the funder will be concerned that on completion it is free of defects and is of a sufficient quality and value to provide adequate

security for the loan. Without a collateral warranty, a funder will have no direct contractual relationship with any of those involved in the design and construction of the development. A funder will usually want any collateral warranty to contain 'step-in' rights so that, should the employer/borrower default under the funding agreement, or act in such a way that would enable the contractor to terminate the building contract, the funder could 'step-in' and take over the completion of the development. It should be noted that although funders commonly require collateral warranties from sub-contractors including 'step-in' rights, it is hard to see that a funder could ever step into a sub-contract. His rights of 'step in' should be restricted to the contracts specifically entered into by the employer/borrower.

Other third parties

5.05 Collateral warranties may be required in a number of other circumstances. For instance, where development work is dependent on the consent of a neighbouring landowner, that neighbouring landowner may require a collateral warranty from those involved in the construction process to ensure that, should any damage occur to his property or should his business be disrupted as a result of the works, he would be able to recover from those responsible any costs incurred in repairing the damage. Collateral warranties may also be required where a developer lets a development to a tenant who carries out fitting-out works. In such circumstances the developer may require a collateral warranty from the tenant's designer and fit-out contractor to ensure such works are performed correctly.

6 Who should provide collateral warranties?

6.01 Exactly which contractor or sub-contractor should provide warranties depends upon the form of contractual procurement used.

JCT 2005 Standard Building Contract (and traditional forms of contracting)

6.02 Under traditional forms of contract – discussed comprehensively in Chapter 17 – the main contractor is fully responsible for his own and his sub-contractors, or suppliers, standard of workmanship and for the quality of all materials used but not for any sub-contractor's or supplier's design. The main contractor can, moreover, claim loss and expense for delay or errors in the design of sub-contractors unless that design is included in the Contractor's Designed Portion. 'Nomination' having disappeared from JCT forms, there are no JCT warranty forms to replace NSC/W (for nominated sub-contractors) and TNS/2 (for nominated suppliers). According, in circumstances where design is to be carried out by sub-contractors or suppliers but it cannot for some reason be included in the Contractor's Designed Portion it is recommended that the Architect refer the matter to the Employer and his advisers for guidance on the issue. The issues which will need to be addressed – drawing on the last version of NSC/W are briefly that:

- the sub-contractor warrants that he has exercised reasonable skill and care in the design of the sub-contract works, in the selection of the goods and materials to be used in the sub-contract works and in the satisfaction of any performance specification set out in the sub-contract. It is important to note that the warranty provided only extends to reasonable skill and care. It may also extend to suitability for required purpose which would, if the design formed part of a contract for the supply of goods and services and if the employer was relying on the skill and knowledge of the sub-contractor, be implied by the Supply of Goods and Services Act 1982;
- there is protection to the employer in respect of latent defects in workmanship after the final certificate has been issued under the main contract;

- the sub-contractors will be liable to the employer for any delay in issuing sub-contract design information to the architect; and any delay that may otherwise allow the main contractor to claim an extension of time under the main contract;
- that all disputes may be referred to adjudication and an appropriate procedure for disputes resolution is included.

Third parties may require warranties from the various design sub-contractors, as noted in Section 5 above.

JCT 2005 Design and Build Contract (and other design-and-build contracts)

6.03 Under design-and-build contracts, the contractor usually has the primary responsibility for both the design and construction of the works. It is common for contractors, however, to sublet the design of the works to independent firms of consultants. Employers and third parties may seek a warranty from the design consultants or indeed from sub-contractors in case, at a future date, defects arise in the works due to the design which cause losses that can not be recovered due to the contractor's liquidation, due to the inadequacy of the contractor's insurance cover, or due to a contractual cap on the contractor's liability. For the reasons outlined above, the proliferation of this doubling up of contractual protection by use of collateral warranties should be discouraged.

JCT Management Contract 2005 (and other forms of management contract)

6.04 In the JCT Management Building Contract, and in most other similar forms, the management contractor is liable for all the work carried out by the works contractors, including any design work. It provides, however, that the employer will have to pay the management contractor to remedy any default of the works contractors. This rule applies where the management contractor is unable to recover from a defaulting works contractor. This can obviously present problems to the employer should the management contractor be unable to recover or if the management contractor becomes insolvent. To deal with this problem a form of direct warranty agreement known as Management Works Contractor/Employer Agreement MCWC/E 2008 has been prepared for use with JCT Management Building Contract. This form imposes on the works contractors a duty to use all reasonable skill and care in the design of any part of the works he designs and in the selection of any materials or goods he may select. It now includes a copyright licence and an obligation to maintain professional indemnity insurance where required under the Works Contract. It also obliges the works contractor not to use materials or goods which do not confirm with British Standards or Codes of Practice or which contravene the guidelines set out in the Ove Arup *Good Practice in the Selection of Construction Materials* guide and to provide any design information to the management contractor on time. It does not, however, extend to delay by matters other than design so that the employer would have no direct claim against a works contractor in respect of simple delay in the carrying out of the work on site. It would be prudent to amend Form MC/E to protect the employer against *any* breach by the works contractor of his obligations. In addition, inevitably it will be usual for any third party with an interest in the development to seek collateral warranties from all the principal works contractors as well.

Construction management

6.05 In construction management contracts the employer engages a construction manager and also directly engages the contractors, usually known as 'trade contractors', who are actually to undertake the on-site works. As the construction manager will not ordinarily be liable for breaches of the trade contracts, the employer bears the risk of trade contractor insolvency and has no main contractor to sue for such breaches. It will therefore be usual for any third party with an interest in a development to seek collateral warranties from all the principal trade contractors as well as the construction manager.

7 Standard forms of collateral warranty

7.01 Initially collateral warranties in favour of third parties such as funders, purchasers and tenants tended to be tailor-made, usually to suit the requirements of particular employers. As they reallocate risk among the parties, they are often the subject of extensive negotiation. Non-standard warranties can vary greatly in scope and complexity with some drafted to be more favourable to beneficiaries and some to warrantors. They can also be known by a variety of names such as 'Duty of Care Agreement', or simply 'Warranty Agreement', and can be drafted as deeds or simple contract letter form agreements. As tailor-made warranties can be very diverse and negotiating them can lead to extensive argument before a development is begun, a number of standard forms have been drafted and are often used at least as a basis for these documents. The main standard form contractor and sub-contractor warranties are set out below.

Contractors' warranties

7.02 The JCT have produced warranties to be given by contractors to funders and purchasers/tenants. These warranties, CWa/F and CWa/P&T can be used with the Standard Building Contract, the Design and Build Contract and the Intermediate Building Contract. The warranties were first published in 1993 but a new edition was produced to sit alongside the 2005 suite of documents.

8 Key clauses of the JCT Standard Forms of Contractor Collateral Warranty

8.01 This section will comment on the Standard Forms of Contractor/Collateral Warranty, CWa/P&T and CWa/F, although comparative reference will also be made to consultants' warranties which are examined in more detail in Chapter 31. Because the terms of the contractors' warranties and the consultants' warranties do elide in a number of respects, much of what is said in relation to consultants' warranties is relevant to this Section too. Cross-reference should be made to Part 3 of Chapter 31.

The warranty itself

8.02 Most forms of warranty start by imposing a contractual obligation on the warrantor in favour of the beneficiary. Such a warranty in a contractor collateral warranty usually refers to the terms of the main contract. Clause 1 of MCWa/P&T states:

> 'The Contractor warrants as at and with effect from practical completion of the Works... that it has carried out the Works . . . in accordance with the Building Contract.'

This wording reflects the fact that such warranties are intended to be given or at least to be enforced *after* practical completion. Under this wording the contractor's liability under the warranty to the third party will be the same as its obligations under the main contract to the employer. The contractor's obligations under Standard Building Contract Design and Building Contract and IFC are similar in that the contractor has an absolute duty to complete the contract works in accordance with the contract and specification. This position contrasts with a consultant's obligations under consultancy appointments and warranties which are usually limited to a duty to exercise reasonable skill and care in the performance of his duties.

Economic and consequential loss

8.03 Under the law of negligence, losses which are deemed to be purely economic are generally not recoverable as noted in Section 4 above. Under contract law, however, such 'economic' loss can be recoverable. Therefore, if an employer suffers a loss of profit, a loss of rent revenue, or a diminution in value in his property due to a breach of contract by a contractor, he can claim such loss from the contractor in contract. Contractors have resisted the imposition of such all-embracing liability in collateral warranties. As a result of this, Clause 1.1 of CWa/P&T (but not CWa/F) contains two possible alternative drafting options which require amendment or deletion from the text of the printed form in order to select the option which is to apply. The options are as follows:

- To restrict the contractor's liability to reasonable costs of repair only and to exclude *all* other losses suffered or incurred by the beneficiary as a result of the contractor's breach of Clause 1. If this is to be adopted, then the Warranty Particulars in the main JCT Contract need to state that Clause 1.1.2 does *not* apply. Clause 1.2 then provides that the contractor is not liable for any losses incurred other than repair costs as referred to in Clause 1.1.1).
- To make the contractor liable for the costs of repair incurred by the beneficiary, and in addition, to cap his other liability for damages which would otherwise be recoverable by the beneficiary in accordance with common law principles including loss of profit, loss of rent revenue, etc., as outlined above to a maximum amount in respect of *each* breach of Clause 1. If this option is to be adopted, then the warranty particulars need to state that Clause 1.1.2 *does* apply and the amount of the cap needs to be stated

To make the contractor responsible for costs of repair and in addition to impose on him further unlimited liability for damages for breach of contract as outlined above, but without a cap. This option is not contemplated by the drafters of the JCT forms but is the preferred route for most beneficiaries. To achieve this the words from 'In the event of breach . . . ' in Clause 1.1 to the end of the Clause including both Clauses 1.1.1 and 1.1.2 should be deleted, as should clause 1.2.

Joint liability and contribution clauses

8.04 A further limitation on the beneficiary's right to claim damages from a contractor applies in the case where the contractor is not the only person responsible for the defect. CWa/P&T contains a net contribution clause which limits the liability of the warrantor to the proportion of the costs incurred by the beneficiary which it would be fair for him to pay having regard to his own and the other parties share of the blame. The relevant clause is Clause 1.3 which applies only where so stated in the Warranty Particulars and which states:

'The Contractor's liability to the Purchaser or Tenant under this Agreement shall be limited to the proportion of the Purchaser's or Tenant's losses which it would be just and equitable to require the Contractor to pay having regard to the extent of the Contractor's responsibility for the same, on the following assumptions, namely that:

1 the Consultant[s]referred to in the Warranty Particulars has or have provided contractual undertakings to the Purchaser or Tenant as regards the performance of his or their services in connection with the Works in accordance with the terms of his or their respective consultancy agreements and that there are no limitations on liability as between the Consultant and the Employer in the consultancy agreement[s];
2 the Sub-Contractor[s]referred to in the Warranty Particulars has or have provided contractual undertakings to the Purchaser or Tenant in respect of design of the Sub-Contract Works that he or they has/have carried out and for which there is no liability of the Contractor to the Employer under the Building Contract;

3 that the Consultant(s) and the Sub-Contractor(s) have paid to the Purchaser or Tenant such proportion of the Purchaser's or Tenant's losses which it would be just and equitable for them to pay having regard to the extent of their responsibility for the Purchaser's or Tenant's losses.'

This clause operates by 'assuming' that the consultants and sub-contractors have a legal liability to the beneficiary, even if in fact the beneficiary has not obtained collateral warranties from those other parties. The purpose of the clause is to entitle the court to calculate what percentage of the blame should be apportioned to those other parties. This is a calculation which the court is used to making under the Civil Liability (Contribution) Act 1978 where, for instance, two drivers negligently contribute to causing the same crash. Clause 1.3 is simply intended to cap the damages for which the contractor is liable, and it is a significant limitation on the value to a beneficiary of the CWa warranties.

Deleterious material clauses

8.05 Most forms of collateral warranty to funders, purchasers and tenants contain provisions related to excluded materials. Clause 2 of the CWa warranties contains such provisions whereby the contractor warrants absolutely that materials will not be used except in accordance with good practice guidelines:

'… it has not and will not use materials in the works other than in accordance with the guidelines contained in the edition of the publication "Good Practice in Selection of Construction Materials" (Ove Arup & Partners) current at the date of the building contract.'

The situation is different with consultants' collateral warranties as consultants only warrant in their appointments that they have exercised reasonable skill and care in the performance of their services and they therefore cannot offer an absolute warranty as to the use of materials. This approach is to be preferred to the previous practice of using extensive and out-dated lists of materials compiled by lawyers on a random and ill-informed basis.

Step-in rights

8.06 Where a warranty is to be provided to a funder or funding institution it is common for the warranty to contain step-in rights. Clauses 5 to 7 of CWa/F enable the funder to step into the employer's shoes should the employer behave in such a way as would enable the contractor to terminate the contract. This is most likely to occur if the employer encounters financial difficulties and is unable to pay the contractor. Step-in provisions such as these permit the fund actually to take on the duties, rights and responsibilities of the employer. Again, the effect of these provisions is elaborated in Part 3.

Insurance clauses

8.07 Contractors' warranties will not usually contain insurance clauses unless the contractor is to be responsible for some elements of the design of the works. Where such design obligations exist, they are often required to be backed by professional indemnity insurance. The relevant clause of the CWa warranties is Clause 5 in CWa/P&T and Clause 9 in CWa/F.

It is important to ensure that the insurance will be available up to the limit stated in the Warranty Particulars for any one claim rather than up to that limit for all claims unless the Warranty Particulars provide for an aggregate limit.

The insurance clauses contain provisions requiring the contractor to maintain the insurance for a certain period to be stipulated in the Warranty Particulars. This time limit should be at least as long as the contractor's liability under the warranty, which is either 6 years or 12 years – see Clause 8 of CWa/P&T.

The clauses state that insurance shall be maintained so long as it is available at commercially reasonable rates. This allows contractors to cease maintaining insurance if insurance premiums rise to an exorbitant level or if restrictions on level are imposed by insurers. However, the warranty also requires the contractor to notify the beneficiary if such insurance is no longer available.

Limitation

8.08 Most standard forms of warranty allow for the execution of a warranty as either a simple contract or as a deed. Where a warranty is signed as a simple contract consideration is required (see for example the consideration recital immediately before Clause 1 of the CWa warranties), and the limitation period for the warranty will run for 6 years from the date of any breach of the warranty. Where a warranty is executed as a deed, no consideration is required and the limitation period will run for 12 years from any breach. For this reason, beneficiaries tend to favour the execution of warranties as deeds, although the method of execution of the warranty should reflect that of the underlying contract to ensure that the warrantor's liability under the warranty lasts for a similar period as his liability under the contract. In addition to this cut-off period provided by the law on limitation, it is common to see clauses in warranties which limit the liability of the warrantor to a specific period of time, often calculated as a certain number of years following practical completion. For example, Clause 8 in CWa/P&T as noted above provides for a cut-off after 6 or 12 years to reflect whether a deed has been used or not.

The advantage of such a cause to a contractor is that it provides a fixed period under which the contractor will be liable and the contractor knows exactly when his liability under the warranty will end. As drafted, however, it does not affect his tortious liability.

Delay

8.09 If a contractor is in delay in completing the works under the building contract, the employer's remedy lies in liquidated and ascertained damages which may be deducted from monies due to the contractor in accordance with the provisions of the building contract. Plainly, the contractor does not want to create an alternative remedy for delay which might otherwise by-pass the provisions for liquidated and ascertained damages contained in the building contract by giving a collateral warranty which, under the terms of Clause 1, would give funders, purchasers and tenants a claim for unlimited damages for failure to complete the works in accordance with the building contract. For this reason, Clause 13 appears in CWa/F (Clause 9 in CWa/P&T) which states that:

'… the Contractor shall have no liability under this Agreement for delay under the Building Contract unless and until the funder serves notice pursuant to Clause 5 or Clause 6.4 (the "step-in" provisions). For the avoidance of doubt the Contractor shall not be required to pay liquidated and ascertained damage in respect of the period of delay where the same has been paid to or deducted by the Employer.'

This provision is acceptable to most funders, purchasers and tenants if properly advised.

Assignment

8.10 When developments are sold, or some other change of ownership takes place, it is common for the potential purchaser to request that any existing warranties are assigned to him. Under common law, the benefits of a contract can be assigned unless there is an express prohibition against assignment in the contract. Sometimes, the warrantor may require that assignments be permissible only with his consent, which shall not be unreasonably withheld. Alternatively the warrantor may only allow the assignment of the warranty a limited number of times, for example twice, or to purchasers or tenants of a specified part of the development. CWa/P&T and CWa/F contemplate assignment without consent, but only on two occasions. The client should be advised that, without some ability to assign the warranty at least once or twice, the marketability of a development may be adversely affected as potential future purchasers may be put off if they are unable to obtain the comfort of the relevant collateral warranties.

9 Key clauses of Third Party Rights Schedule in JCT Major Project Form, 2005 edition

9.01 As noted above, JCT Major Project Form (now JCT Major Project Construction Contract 2005) was the first time the JCT Suite of Documentation adopted Contracts (Rights of Third Parties) Act 1999 as the mechanism for conferring rights on funders, purchasers and tenants. The rights themselves are set out in the Third Party Rights Schedule and follow very closely the key clauses of CWa/F and CWa/P&T. They are largely replicated in other JCT Forms. Certain key differences are noted below.

Joint liability and contribution clauses

9.02 The MPCC is a design-and-build form of contract under which the contractor completes any further design required for the execution of the works. Accordingly, he has responsibility for *all* design going forward whether it be carried out by sub-consultants or sub-contractors to him. In these circumstances, a net contribution clause of the type discussed above is inappropriate and does not appear in the Third Party Rights Schedule.

Economic and consequential loss

9.03 As noted above, in respect of CWa/F there is no restriction on recoverable loss. However, the third party rights in favour of a purchaser or tenant contains the options noted above in respect of exclusions and caps on liability in addition to the costs of repair. The options are addressed in the Contract Particulars to the MPCC. It is vital that the Contract Particulars are properly completed since the fallback is a complete exclusion of losses other than the cost of repair.

Step-in under third party rights

9.04 Contracts (Rights of Third Parties) Act 1999 can only be used to confer on a third party *'a right'*. As noted in paragraph 3.02 above, it cannot be used to impose an obligation on a party who is not a party to the contract. Since the essence of the 'step-in' rights contained in collateral warranties is to impose on the funder the obligation to pay the contractor amounts due under the building contract after 'step-in', it has been suggested that third party rights cannot be used as the mechanism for creating enforceable 'step-in' provisions for funders. The MPCC overcomes this dilemma by making the grant of the rights by the contractor to the funder conditional upon the funder accepting liability for payment and performance of the employer's obligations in his notice. Unless the notice contains this assumption of responsibility, it is invalid and the funder is not able to exercise his step-in rights. A leading QC's opinion obtained by the JCT is clear that this mechanism is valid.

10 Sub-contractor collateral warranties

10.01 As part of the 2005 Suite of Documentation, the JCT have also published forms for the Sub-Contractor Collateral Warranty: for a funder (SCWa/F) – and for a purchaser or tenant – (SCWa/P&T). Again, these have been produced for use with Standard Building Contract, Design and Build Contract and Intermediate Building Contract.

The drafting broadly follows the forms of main contractor collateral warranty with similar provisions in relation to net contribution and caps on liability for costs other than the costs of repair under SCWa/P&T. Contrary to comments in paragraph 5.04 above, SCWa/F does include step-in rights for the funder if the main contractor's employment under the Building Contract is terminated. The employer is by passed by the step-in provisions.

10.02 Enabling clauses in relation to these sub-contractor collateral warranties are included in the JCT forms of main contract. Standard Building Contract at Clauses 7E provides for sub-contractor's warranties in favour of purchasers and tenants/funders and the employer respectively and simply requires the contractor to deliver the collateral warranties within 21 days from receipt of the employer's notice identifying the relevant sub-contractor, type of warranty and beneficiary. References are made to the standard form which is to be delivered subject only to amendments proposed by the sub-contractor and approved by the contractor and the employer approval not to be unreasonably withheld or delayed.

10.03 As hinted already, securing sub-contractors' collateral warranties present a huge logistical challenge on a major multi-let construction project. The costs entailed in obtaining such collateral warranties particularly after practical completion are huge and there are very few reported examples of such collateral warranties being relied on in practice.

21

The FIDIC contract

JEREMY GLOVER

1 Introduction

1.01 You might well ask what a chapter on the FIDIC form of contract is doing in a legal handbook for architects. Surely the FIDIC contract conditions apply to duties of engineers, not architects? The answer is quite simple: for international contractors, the most common form of contract is FIDIC, or at least a contract largely borrowed from the FIDIC form. Therefore, it is highly probable that if you are asked to advise on an appropriate form of contract for an international project, you will need to be aware of the FIDIC form; equally, if an architect is working abroad, perhaps administering the project, he may well find himself operating under some form of the FIDIC conditions.

1.02 The FIDIC organisation was founded in 1913 by France, Belgium and Switzerland. The UK did not join until 1949. The original FIDIC contract, or 'Red Book', was based on the detailed design being provided to the contractor by the employer. It therefore applied to civil engineering and infrastructure projects. This led to the development of the 'Yellow Book' for mechanical and electrical works, which had an emphasis on testing and commissioning and so was more suitable for the manufacture and installation of plant.

1.03 In 1995 a further contract was published (the 'Orange Book'). This was for use on projects procured on a design and build or turnkey basis, and dispensed with the engineer entirely, instead providing for an 'employer's representative'.

The new FIDIC forms 1999

1.04 In 1994 FIDIC established a task force to update its contract forms in the light of developments in the international construction industry. The key considerations included:

(i) The role of the engineer and in particular the requirement to act impartially in the circumstances of being employed and paid by the employer.
(ii) The desirability for the standardisation of the FIDIC forms.
(iii) The simplification of the FIDIC forms in light of the fact that the FIDIC conditions were in English but were often used by those whose language background was other than English.
(iv) The new contracts would be suitable for use in both common law and civil law jurisdictions.

1.05 This led to the publication of four new contracts in 1999:

(i) Conditions of Contract for Construction for Building and Engineering Works Designed by the Employer: The Construction Contract (the new 'Red Book');

(ii) Conditions of Contract for Plant and Design-Build for Electrical and Mechanical Plant and for Building and Engineering Works, Designed by the contractor: The Plant and Design/Build Contract (the new 'Yellow Book');
(iii) Conditions of Contract for EPC/Turnkey Projects: the EPC Turnkey Contract (the 'Silver Book');
(iv) A short form of contract (the 'Green Book').

1.06 Subsequently two other contract forms based on the 'Red Book' were published:

(i) The MDB version, the second version being published in March 2006. Essentially this is the 'Red Book' plus amendments from leading world banks and is for use on projects financed by those banks;
(ii) The 2007 Abu Dhabi Executive Affairs Authority General Conditions of Contract, introduced for construction of projects undertaken in Abu Dhabi on behalf of Public Entities.

1.07 In September 2008, FIDIC launched its new DBO (or Design-Build Operate) form of contract. The DBO form was a response to the call for a standard concession contract for the transport and water/waste sectors. The market was using the existing FIDIC 'Yellow Book' with operations and maintenance obligations tacked on. FIDIC recognised this unsatisfactory state of affairs and the need to tailor a form to meet the demand. Unsurprisingly, the new contract is known as the 'Gold Book'.

1.08 The FIDIC Forms also contain Guidance for the Preparation of Particular Conditions which include notes of the preparation of tender documents, and also highlights some of the key points which, if missed, could lead to difficulties during the project. For example, many major contracts are usually conducted by a joint venture (JV). If so, detailed requirements must be set out. These may include, parent company guarantees from each member of the JV and the appointment of a leader providing a single point of contact for the employer.

2 The content of the new FIDIC forms – the standard clauses

2.01 In keeping with the desire for standardisation, all of the contract forms include General Conditions together with guidance for the preparation of the Particular Conditions, and a Letter of Tender, Contract Agreement and Dispute Adjudication Agreements.

2.02 From a practical point of view, the key to reading and understanding the FIDIC form is to understand its structure. The FIDC form has 20 clauses which are perhaps best viewed as chapters covering the key project topics. Those clauses are as follows:

(i) Clause 1 – General provisions;
(ii) Clause 2 – The employer;
(iii) Clause 3 – The engineer or employer's representative;
(iv) Clause 4 – The contractor;
(v) Clause 5 – Design ('Silver Book', or Nominated sub-contractor ('Red Book')
(vi) Clause 6 – Staff and labour
(vii) Clause 7 – Plant, materials and workmanship
(viii) Clause 8 – Commencement, delays and suspension
(ix) Clause 9 – Tests on completion
(x) Clause 10 – Taking over
(xi) Clause 11 – Defects liability
(xii) Clause 12 – Tests after completion
(xiii) Clause 13 – Variations and adjustments
(xiv) Clause 14 – Contract price and payment
(xv) Clause 15 – Termination by employer
(xvi) Clause 16 – Suspension and termination by contractor
(xvii) Clause 17 – Risk and responsibility
(xviii) Clause 18 – Insurance
(xix) Clause 19 – *Force majeure*
(xx) Clause 20 – Claims, disputes and arbitration

2.03 In the 'Gold Book' there is a slightly different order, with the insurance clause having been moved to clause 19, while clause 17 has been renamed 'risk allocations' and the *force majeure* clause has been dropped and replaced with a new clause 18 headed 'exceptional risks'. This may well represent the way forward for any future amendment of the remaining four FIDIC contracts.

2.04 The most important clauses are discussed below.

2.05 Clause 2 addresses the role of the employer. Sub-clause 2.4 renders it mandatory upon the employer, following request from the contractor, to submit reasonable evidence of its financial arrangements and any material change to those arrangements. Failure to submit such evidence provides the contractor with the entitlement to suspend work, 'or reduce the rate of work', unless and until the contractor has received that reasonable evidence.

2.06 In addition, sub-clause 2.5 requires the employer to give notice and particulars to a contractor if it considers that it is entitled to any payment under any clause of the contract.

2.07 Clause 3 deals with the position of the engineer or employer's representative. This may be of particular interest to architects as they may often find themselves working under similar obligations and is dealt with in more detail below in Section 5.

2.08 Clause 4 is by far the longest sub-clause and covers the contractor's general obligations including, in the 'Red Book', the requirement that in respect of contractor designed works: 'it shall, when the works are completed, be fit for such purposes for which the part is intended as are specified in the Contract'. This is an absolute duty. In other words, the absence of negligence in the design, will not be a defence for the contractor.

2.09 In the 'Silver Book', clause 5 deals with design responsibility. Given the turnkey nature of the contract, the intention is to make the contractor responsible for the integration of the design and the construction of the works. Clause 5.1 notes that:

'The Contractor shall be responsible for the design of the works and for the accuracy of the Employer's Requirements (including design criteria and calculations)... Any data received by the Contractor, from the Employer or otherwise shall not relieve the Contractor from his responsibility for the design and execution of the works.'

2.10 Clause 4.21 provides details of the information required to be inserted by the contractor in the Progress Reports. The provision of this report is a condition of payment. Under clause 14.3, payment will be made only within 28 days of receipt of the application for payment *and* the supporting documents, one of which is the Progress Report.

2.11 While the importance of ensuring that the Progress Reports are accurate might seem obvious, His Honour Judge Wilcox, in the case of *Great Eastern Hotel Co. Ltd v John Laing Construction Ltd* 99 Con LR 45, highlighted some of the potential difficulties where that reporting is not accurate.

2.12 Under the terms of the particular contract, the construction manager was the only person on the project with access to all of the information and the various programmes. He was the only available person who could make an accurate report to the client at any one time, of both the current status of the project and the likely effects on both timing and costs.

2.13 It is only with knowledge of the exact status of the project on a regular basis that the employer can deal with problems that have arisen, and therefore anticipate potential problems that may arise, and make provisions to deal with these work fronts. As on any project, an employer will need accurate information of the likely completion date, and the costs, because this will affect his pre-commencement preparation and financing costs. Judge Wilcox concluded:

'Where a completion date was subject to change the competent Construction Manager had a clear obligation to accurately report any change from the original. Projected completion date, and the effect on costs.'

2.14 Clause 6 has particular importance in relation to personnel. The contractor must not only engage labour and staff, but must also make appropriate welfare arrangements for them.

2.15 Clause 8 makes provision for Commencement, Delay and Suspension. Sub-clause 8.3 sets out the manner in which the contractor should provide programmes showing how he proposes to execute the works.

2.16 Sub-clause 8.7 deals with delay or liquidated damages. To be able to levy such damages, the employer must make an application in accordance with sub-clause 2.5.

2.17 Clause 12 deals with measurement and evaluation. Measurement is a central feature of clause 12 and is the basis ultimately upon which payment to the contractor is calculated. Sometimes called a 'measure and value' type of contract, the arrangements in place in the FIDIC form proceed on the basis that the works are to be measured by the engineer. Those quantities and measured amounts of work are then to be paid for at the rates and prices in the contract, or else on the basis of adjusted rates or entirely new rates (if there is no basis for using or altering contract rates for the work).

2.18 Clause 13 addresses variations and incorporates adjustments for changes in legislation and in costs. However a variation is not binding provided the contractor notifies an inability to obtain the required goods. Equally, a variation is not binding in the case of contractor design if the proposed variation would have an adverse impact on safety or the achievement of specified performance criteria.

2.19 Clauses 15 and 16 deal with termination by the employer and suspension and termination by the contractor, while clause 17 deals with risk and responsibility. This includes at sub-clause 17.6 the exclusion of the liability of both contractor and employer: 'for loss of use of any works, loss of profit, loss of any contract or for any indirect or consequential loss or damage which may be suffered by the other party in connection with the contract'. This includes a cap on the liability of the contractor to the employer – something which was again new to the 1999 FIDIC form.

2.20 Clause 19 deals with *force majeure*. While most civil codes make provision for *force majeure*, at common law, '*force majeure*' is not a term of art and no provision will be implied in the absence of specific contractual provisions.

2.21 Finally, clause 20 deals with claims, disputes and arbitration. The way the FIDIC form operates when it comes to making claims merits further discussion.

3 Claims

How does the employer make a claim under the FIDIC form?

3.01 As stated above, sub-clause 2.5 of the FIDIC Conditions of Contract for Construction provides details as to how the employer is to make a claim. The key features of this sub-clause are:

(i) If the employer considers himself entitled to either any payment or an extension of the Defects Notification Period, he shall give notice and particulars to the contractor.

(ii) The notice relating to payment should be given as soon as practicable after the employer has become aware of the event or circumstance which gives rise to the claim.

(iii) The employer must also provide substantiation including the basis of the claim and details of the relief sought.

(iv) Once notice has been given, the engineer shall make a determination in accordance with sub-clause 3.5.

(v) The employer cannot make any deduction by way of set-off or any other claim unless it is in accordance with the engineer's determination.

3.02 The employer must give notice 'as soon as practicable' after becoming aware of a situation which might entitle him to payment. This is not a strict time limit although any notice relating to the extension of the Defects Notification Period must of course be made before the current end of that period. That said, as with any international contract, it should be remembered that the applicable law of the contract might have its own limitation rules which are different from those with which the reader is familiar and which might impose some kind of limit.

3.03 Sub-clause 2.5 is therefore in many ways a 'contractor-friendly' clause which is designed to prevent an employer from summarily withholding payment or unilaterally extending the Defects Notification Period. The final paragraph specifically confirms that the employer no longer has a general right of set-off and can set off sums only once the engineer has agreed or certified any amount owing to the contractor following a claim.

In what circumstances can a contractor make a claim?

3.04 A different set of rules apply to the contractor. Under clause 20.1, the contractor has a duty to notify the employer of an *entitlement* to additional time or money. The key features of sub-clause 20.1 are that:

(i) The contractor must give notice of time or money claims, as soon as practicable and not later than 28 days after the date on which the contractor became aware, or should have become aware, of the relevant event or circumstance.

(ii) Any claim to time or money will be lost if there is no notice within the specified time limit.

(iii) Supporting particulars should be served by the contractor and the contractor should also maintain such contemporary records as may be needed to substantiate claims.

3.05 The 28-day deadline does not necessarily start on the date of the claim event itself but on the date the contractor objectively should have become aware of the event. While it is relatively easy to identify the claim event in the case of a single event such as the receipt of an instruction, when, however, the claim event is a continuous event, such as unforeseeable weather over a certain period of time, it can become difficult to pinpoint the exact start of the 28-day period.

3.06 Sub-clause 20.1 is a time-bar clause or condition precedent which potentially provides the employer with a complete defence to any claim for time or money by the contractor not started within the required time-frame. In England and Wales, following the House of Lords case of *Bremer Handelsgesellschaft mbH v Vanden Avenne Izegem NV* [1978] 2 Lloyd's Rep, 113 such clauses are binding only if the language of the clause in question is clear. Here, sub-clause 20.1 expressly makes it clear that:

> 'If the contractor fails to give notice of a claim within such period of 28 days, the Time for Completion shall not be extended, the contractor shall not be entitled to additional payment, and the employer shall be discharged from all liability in connection with the claim.'

3.07 Further, the courts have recently confirmed their approval for condition precedents, provided that they fulfil the conditions laid out in the *Bremer case*. In the case of *Multiplex Construction v Honeywell Control Systems* [2007] EWHC 447 TCC Jackson J held that:

> 'contractual terms requiring a contractor to give prompt notice of delay serve a valuable purpose; such notice enables matters to be investigated while they are still current. Furthermore, such notice sometimes gives the employer the opportunity to withdraw instructions when the financial consequences become apparent.'

3.08 However, perhaps even FIDIC itself has recognised the potentially harsh consequences of the strict time limits within sub-clause 20.1. In the new 'Gold Book', there is a new sub-clause 20.1 (a) which gives the Dispute Board an element of discretion, noting:

> However, if the Contractor considers there are circumstances which justify the late submission, he may submit the details to the DAB for a ruling. If the DAB considers the circumstances are such that the late submission was acceptable, the DAB shall have the authority under this sub-clause to override the given 28-day limit and advise both the parties accordingly.

3.09 Accordingly, with the FIDIC form, as indeed with any construction contract:

(i) Parties should take care when concluding contracts to check any time-bar clauses governing claims they might make.

(ii) Parties should appreciate the risks they then run of not making a claim (even if to maintain goodwill) unless the other party agrees to relax the requirements or clearly waives them. This is perhaps especially the case where time-bar clauses, if cautiously operated, may generate a proliferation of claims.

(iii) Remember that the courts see the benefits of time-bar provisions and support their operation. A tribunal might bar an entire claim for what seems like a technical reason by which time it will usually be too late to make a new, compliant claim.

(iv) Indeed, even where the contract contains a clause such as sub-clause 20.1(a) of the 'Gold Book', potential claimants should not necessarily rely upon the other party already having the information they are required to provide.

4 The engineer's duties

4.01 Obviously, the engineer is not a party to the construction contract having a separate contract with the employer. However, there have been significant changes in the engineer's role as the FIDC form has developed. In the 1999 form, the express reference in the 1987 edition to the engineer's impartiality was replaced with the following:

> 'Whenever carrying out duties or exercising authority, specified in or implied by the Contract, the engineer shall be deemed to act for the employer.'

4.02 So, under the FIDIC form, the engineer essentially acts as agent for the employer and is expressly stated to be acting for the employer whenever he carries out his duties under the contract.

4.03 Sub-clause 3 provides a two-step process for the resolution of claims before the engineer. While the engineer is expressly the agent of the employer:

(i) under the first stage the engineer's duty is to 'endeavour to reach agreement' between the parties; if that fails, then
(ii) the engineer is obliged to make 'a fair determination'.

4.04 So what is a fair determination? In England and Wales, there has been considerable debate about the role of the engineer. Rix LJ, in the case of *Amec Civil Engineering Ltd v Secretary of State for Transport* [2005] CILL 2288 summarised the obligations of the engineer, or indeed the architect, in such circumstances. He said that the engineer or architect must:

(i) 'retain his independence in exercising [his skilled professional] judgment';
(ii) 'retain his independence in exercising [his skilled professional] Judgment';

(iii) 'act in a fair and unbiased manner' and 'reach his decisions fairly, holding the balance';
(iv) if he hears representations from one party, he must give a similar opportunity to the other party to answer what is alleged against him; and
(v) 'act fairly and impartially' where fairness is 'a broad and even elastic concept' and impartiality 'is not meant to be a narrow concept.'

5 Further information

5.01 It is not within the scope of this book, of course, to provide a full commentary of the FIDIC form. If you need further information about the FIDIC form, the FIDIC website – www.fidic.org – provides a valuable starting point and a generous amount of free information.

22

The Construction Act Payment Rules

MATTHEW NEEDHAM-LAING

'The Housing Grants Construction and Regeneration Act 1996 (and the Statutory Instrument made under it) constitutes a remarkable (and possibly unique) intervention in very carefully selected parts of the construction industry whereby the ordinary freedom of contract between commercial parties (without regard to bargaining power) to regulate their relationships has been overridden in a number of areas. . .'
(His Honour Judge Humphrey Lloyd QC in *Outwing Construction Ltd v H Randell & Son Ltd* [1999] 15 Const LJ vol 3)

1 Introduction

1.01 In this chapter we look at the provisions of the Housing Grants Construction and Regeneration Act 1996, referred to throughout this chapter as 'the HGCRA', together with the subordinate legislation that Parliament has passed pursuant to the HGCRA, in particular the Scheme for Construction Contracts (England and Wales) Regulations 1998 (SI 1998 No. 649), referred to throughout this chapter as 'the Scheme'. We also look at the local Democracy, Economic Development and Construction Act 2009 (refered to as the 'Construction Act 2009') which received royal assent on 12 November 2009.

1.02 Architects need to be aware of the practical effects of this legislation on contracts in the construction industry and take this into consideration when:

(a) negotiating their own terms of appointment with their clients;
(b) advising clients on the forms of building contract which may be used to employ the Contractor;
(c) acting as Contract Administrator during the course of the building works.

1.03 Architects need to appreciate the circumstances when the Scheme applies and be able to explain its impact to clients who may not be aware of the legislation. This is particularly so with professional appointments which have a tendency to be less formal in their formation; for instance, by exchange of letters rather than the more formal contract documentation which tends to be used to employ the Contractor.

1.04 The majority of drafting bodies involved in the drafting of standard forms of building contracts have ensured that their building contracts have been amended to incorporate the provisions of the HGCRA as have the professional bodies responsible for the various standard forms of appointment. The RIBA's Standard Form of Agreement for the appointment of an Architect S-Con-07-A published in 2007 has been drafted to comply with this legislation as was the earlier edition of the standard form SFA /99 which is still used by a number of architects. The other forms of appointment,

published by the Association of Consulting Architects, GC Works 5 and the BPF form of appointment also comply with the legislation as do all the JCT standard forms of construction contract 1998 and 2005 editions.

2 Background to the legislation

2.01 The construction industry has for years had a reputation for being plagued with disputes regarding payment not only between the employer and the contractor but particularly between the contractor and the sub-contractors and throughout the procurement chain. (See for example judicial comments in (Dawnays Ltd v FG Minter Ltd [1971] 2 All ER 1389 and more recently May LJ's judgement in Pegram Shopfitters Ltd v Tally Wiejl (UK) [2003]). The recession of the early 1990s brought into focus the problem of money not being passed down the contractual chain from the employer to the sub-contractors and suppliers via the contractor and there was considerable pressure from the industry bodies which represented sub-contractors that something should be done to rectify the situation. In July 1993 the Government announced that there would be a Joint Review of Procurement and Contractual arrangements in the construction industry chaired by Sir Michael Latham. In July 1994 Sir Michael Latham published his report titled 'Constructing the Team', which contained the results of his investigation into the construction industry and made a number of proposals for future contracts to remedy some of the abuses which Sir Michael had discovered were prevalent. Sir Michael felt that all parties should be encouraged to use standard forms of contract without amendment and that when any of the standard forms were used the following matters in relation to payment should be regarded as unfair and invalid:

(a) Any attempt to amend or delete the sections relating to terms and conditions of payment, including the right of interest on late payments.
(b) The exercise of any right of set-off, contra-charge or abatement without:
　(i) giving notice in advance.
　(ii) specifying the exact reason for the deduction.
(c) To seek to set-off in respect of any contract other than the one in progress.
(d) 'Pay when paid' conditions should be explicitly declared unfair and invalid.

2.02 Sir Michael made a number of other recommendations in his report, particularly in relation to adjudication, which are outside the scope of this chapter. He believed that in order to instil confidence within the construction industry, these central provisions should be underpinned by legislation. As a result, the then Conservative government passed the HGCRA, which imposed some of the recommendations made by Sir Michael in the form of rights which one party is free to exercise if he so wishes. The HGCRA achieves this by requiring the parties to expressly include within their contract, clauses which reflect the relevant recommendations, failing which the relevant paragraphs of the Scheme are automatically implied into the contract. This was a departure from earlier legislation, which sought to curtail freedom of contract between commercial parties by rendering certain terms in a contract unenforceable if they are unfair (for example, The Unfair Contract Terms Act 1997 and the Supply of Goods and Services Act 1982).

2.03 The HGCRA grants three important rights insofar as a party's' entitlement to payment is concerned:

(a) the right to payment by instalments for contracts lasting 45 days or more;
(b) the ability of a party to suspend performance if it has not been paid within a specified period;
(c) the outlawing of pay when paid clause, except in specific circumstances.

2.04 The HGCRA confers these rights upon the parties to a construction contract by permitting the parties to include them voluntarily in the contract with such other additions or refinements as they wish, provided those additions or refinements do not offend against the basic rights themselves. If the construction contract does not contain these rights then the payment provisions within the Scheme come into effect by being implied into the terms of the contract. The Scheme's provisions are therefore default provisions; it is always necessary to consider whether the construction contract complies with the HGCRA in order to determine whether the relevant provisions in the Scheme are to be incorporated into it. The payment provisions in this respect differ from the provisions in the Scheme relating to adjudication. If a construction contract does not comply with any one of the adjudication provisions in the HGCRA, then the Scheme's provisions are incorporated into the construction contract in total. On the other hand, if a construction contract does not comply with any of the rights relating to payment, then it is only the non-compliant provisions within the construction contract which are replaced by the relevant payment provisions within the Scheme, and not the Scheme's payment provisions in total.

3 To which contracts does the HGCRA apply?

3.01 Sections 104 to 107 of the HGCRA identify the requirements with which a 'construction contract' must comply before the payment provisions apply. Section 104(1) essentially defines a 'construction contract' as a contract to carry out 'construction operations' which in turn are defined in section 105(1). The two sections therefore need to be read together and in doing so it will be clear that it is only in exceptional circumstances that a contract for building or construction work will fall outside the ambit of the HGCRA. Section 104(2) extends the definition of a construction contract to include:

(a) architectural, design or surveying work in relation to construction operations; or
(b) the provision of advice on building, engineering, interior or exterior decoration or on the laying out of landscape in relation to construction operations.

3.02 It is clearly the intention of the HGCRA to grant the members of the design and professional, team the same rights to payment as those granted to contractors or sub-contractors by section 104(1).

3.03 It is not uncommon under some of the Government's framework agreements to require one member of the professional team to be appointed as lead consultant and that consultant in turn employs all the other consultants so there is one point of responsibility for the professional team or alternatively require the architect, to employ all of the members of the design team so that there is one point of responsibility for the design of the project. In these circumstances the architect must ensure that the sub-consultant's terms of appointment comply with the HGCRA, and when making payment to the sub-consultants the architect complies with all the relevant notice provisions. To maintain cash flow, the architect will need to ensure that the payment terms of its appointment with the employer operate in advance of those of its sub-consultants so if any deductions are made to its fees, these can be passed on to the appropriate sub-consultant without breaching the notice periods.

3.04 Architects are frequently appointed to design the complete building, right down to the interior furnishings which are to be installed within it. Any design or advice that the architect provides on matters such as the design of soft furnishings, letterheads, corporate logo, etc. do not fall within the definition of 'construction operations'. The statutory payment provisions will only apply to those parts of the appointment that relate to 'construction operations' and not to the parts of the appointment that fall outside that definition. This unsatisfactory situation, will only arise however where the parties have not entered into a formal contract which complies with the requirements of the HGCRA. The parties are perfectly entitled to agree contractually that the payment terms which are compliant with the HGCRA apply to the entirety of the services being provided whether or not they fall within the definition of 'construction operations'. It does, however, illustrate the importance of making sure that formal written appointments are in place either at the commencement of the commission or shortly thereafter.

3.05 The HGCRA only applies to contracts which have been entered into after 1 May 1998 (the date of commencement of the HGCRA) and then only where the construction operations are carried out in the United Kingdom.

3.06 It is the location of the construction operation which is important, consequently, the payment provisions would not apply to a construction contract which states that the law of the contract is English but the construction work is to be carried out in mainland Europe. The provisions of the HGCRA would, however, apply to a construction contract which specifies the law of the contract to be Dutch but the actual work is to be carried out in the UK, a not-uncommon situation with construction work at docks or harbours. It is also not uncommon for UK architects to be commissioned by foreign clients for buildings which are to be built abroad. The architectural and design work which is carried out in the UK under such a commission would not be covered by the HGCRA as architectural and design work does not come within the definition of 'construction operations' as the actual building work will be taking place abroad.

3.07 The final requirement a construction contract had to satisfy if the HGCRA was to apply is that the contract must be in writing (section 107(1)). However, when the Construction Act 2009 comes into force, the requirement for writing will disappear in respect of contracts mode thereafter. The definition of a contract in writing is similar to that contained in the 1996 Arbitration Act and extends beyond what would be regarded as an agreement in writing by most commercial people. The definition includes contracts made by exchange of letters or faxes (section 107(2)(b)) or where an oral agreement is evidenced in writing by one of the parties or by a third party (section 107(4)). One can foresee circumstances arising at an initial meeting between the client and his potential architect where the terms of an agreement are discussed and the discussion is recorded in the minutes of the meeting, either by the client or the architect, or perhaps by the client's project manager as a third party; under the HGCRA, this would be an agreement in writing.

3.08 Agreements in writing even extend to oral agreements which refer to terms which are in writing (section 107(3)). For example, in a situation where the client agrees orally with the architect that the architect's scope of work, the fees to be charged and the terms and conditions are to be those in the RIBA Standard Agreement (S-Con-07-A), then they have made an agreement in writing which would fall within the ambit of the HGCRA. It is worth noting that section 107(6) states that references in the HGCRA to anything being 'written' or 'in writing' include it being recorded by any means, therefore tape recordings and e-mails fall within the definition.

3.09 The Court of Appeal case *RJT Consulting Engineers Ltd v DM Engineering (Northern Ireland) Ltd* ((2002) 18 Const LJ No 5) has severally restricted the contracts which fall within the jurisdiction of the HGCRA. The facts of the case are typical of what can happen on a construction project. RJT Consulting ('RJT') was originally employed by the owner of a hotel to provide the outline design for mechanical and electrical work as part of the proposed refurbishment of the hotel. Once the main contract had been let RJT agreed with the sub-contractor DM Engineering ('DME') to complete the design of the mechanical and electrical works. A dispute arose between DME and RJT which DME referred to adjudication, however RJT argued that the contract was not evidenced in writing and consequently the adjudicator did not have jurisdiction to decide the dispute. The issue of whether the contract was or was not sufficiently evidenced in writing to grant the adjudicator jurisdiction eventually arrived at the Court of Appeal. The leading judgment was given by Ward LJ and it is instructive to recite in full his description of the written evidence relied upon by DME to support their submission that the contract was evidenced in writing:

'In my judgement, the learned judge was wrong to conclude as a matter of law that it was sufficient to give the jurisdiction to entertain an adjudication that there was evidence in writing capable of supporting merely the existence of an agreement, or its substance, being the parties to it, the nature of the work and the price.Even if that were all that was required, the documents relied on in this case are wholly insufficient. There were fee notes "for professional fees expended to date in connection with the Mechanical and Electrical Services on the project". Letters from the main contractor to the sub-contractor referred to the fact that the sub-contractor "engaged RJT Consulting to advise you on performance of your tender" but there is nothing to indicate what advice was to be given. On January 31, 2001 the sub-contractors wrote to the engineers saying, "As RJT Consulting Engineers have designed this project for DM Engineering (NI) Limited, can you provide us with your professional indemnity insurance..." There were drawing schedules prepared by RJT identifying the client as "D&M Engineers (NI) Limited". There were minutes of mechanical and electrical design meetings stating RJT/DM Engineers to review this along with the construction programme and confirm their proposals for "drawing production, approval, fabrication and commencement on site in each area." There were other minutes referring to the parties' connections with each other. All of this is evidence of the existence of the contract, some evidence of consideration and some indication that the nature of the work was design and advisory. But it is not evidence of the terms of the oral agreement that was made between the two gentlemen back in April 2000. It is certainly not evidence of the terms of the contract on which the respondents rely in the adjudication. . .'

3.10 Architects will recognise the documents described by Ward LJ as fairly typical of any project and they may even be aware of commissions they have received where the appointment documentation never progressed much beyond that in the RJT case. Even with, what must have been a considerable quantity of documentation and despite section 107(2) defining an agreement in writing in wide terms it was not sufficient evidence of the contract. What then is required to evidence an agreement in writing? In relation to the evidence necessary to come within the requirements to section 107, Ward LJ stated:

'what has to be evidenced in writing is literally, the J agreement, which means all of it, not part of it. A record of the agreement also suggests a complete agreement, not a partial one. The only exception to the generality of that construction is the instance falling within subsection 5 where the material or relevant parts alleged and not denied in written submissions in

the adjudication proceedings are sufficient. Unfortunately, I do not think subsection 5 can so dominate the interpretation of the section as a whole so as to limit what needs to be evidenced in writing simply to the material terms raised in the adjudication. It must be remembered that by virtue of section 107(1) the need for an agreement in writing is a precondition for the application of the other provisions of Part II of the Act, not just the jurisdiction threshold for a reference to adjudication.'

3.11 In short therefore, in respect of contracts made prior to such date as the Construction Act 2009 is brought into force, the whole of the terms and conditions of the agreement must be evidenced in writing, though they need not all be contained in a single document (*Alstom Signalling Ltd v Jarvis Facilities Ltd* [2004] EWHC 1285 TCC), it is sufficient that all the terms of the agreement are recorded by one or more of methods set out in section 107.

4 Contracts excluded from the payment provisions

4.01 Contracts specifically excluded from the ambit of the HGCRA are:

contracts of employment (section 104(3));
matters identified in section 105(2);
contracts with a residential occupier (section 106(1));
any other contract excluded by order of the Secretary of State.

4.02 Contracts of employment are contracts of service or apprenticeship between an employer and an individual employee. This would appear to be relatively straightforward. However, difficulties arise where self-employed architects or technicians are working in the architect's office; are they an employee or are they a sub-consultant? A detailed discussion as to the various tests the courts apply to determine the type of contract that exists between the employer and the employee are unfortunately beyond the scope of this chapter which can do no more than highlight some of the potential problems.

4.03 The matters specifically excluded from the definition of 'construction operations' primarily relate to drilling and mining of minerals, oil or natural gas, the nuclear processing, power generation or water supply and treatment industries, or the chemical, pharmaceuticals, oil, gas, steel or food and drink industries. Of more relevance to the architect, the section also excludes contracts for the manufacture or delivery to site of various building materials, plant and machinery or components for heating, ventilation, power supply, drainage, sanitation, water supply, fire protection or for security or communication systems where the contract does not include for those components to be installed in the building as well, i.e. supply only contracts. In addition, the section also excludes works which are of a wholly artistic nature.

4.04 A residential occupier is a person who is having construction works carried out on their house or flat which they occupy or intend to occupy. The definition does not extend to the construction work being carried out on a block of flats one of which is owned by the contracting party. As indicated above there is however nothing to prevent the architect agreeing with a client who is a residential occupier that payment terms which comply with the HGCRA should be incorporated into the appointment. If agreed then the terms would be contractually binding.

4.05 The list of construction contracts that have been excluded by the Secretary of State is extensive and reference should be made to the relevant statutory instruments (the Construction Contracts (England and Wales) Exclusion Order 1998 No. 648). However, it is worth noting that the following have been excluded:

(a) the power of highway authorities to adopt by agreement roads under section 38 of the Highways Act;
(b) the power of highway authorities to enter into agreement as to the execution of work under the Highways Act 1980

(c) planning agreements under section 106, which is an agreement imposing planning obligations on the land owner, and section 106A, which is a modificational discharge of planning obligations, or section 299A, relating to Crown planning obligations, of the Town and Country Planning Act 1990;

(d) agreements to adopt sewer, drainage or sewage disposal work under section 104 of the Water Industry Act 1991;

(e) construction contracts under the Private Finance Initiative;

(f) finance agreements such as contracts for insurance, etc;

(g) development agreements where the agreement includes a provision for the grant or disposal of a parcel of land upon which the principal construction operations are to take place.

5 The payment provisions in detail

5.01 Sections 109 to 113 of the HGCRA deal with the parties' right to payment in connection with a construction contract. In summary these rights are:

(a) the right for a party to be paid by stage payments throughout the duration of the contract where this is agreed between the parties or where the contract is estimated to be 45 days or more in duration;

(b) the right to be informed of the amount to be paid in any stage payment, and when that money is due for payment;

(c) the right to be given notice if it is intended that any payment be withheld;

(d) the right to suspend performance if payment is not made within the specified time

(e) making 'pay when paid' clauses ineffective except where a third party is insolvent.

5.02 The standard forms of appointment and the standard forms of construction contract include these rights within them but it is necessary to consider these provisions if:

(a) The contract has been further amended or

(b) The contract has been specially drafted for the project concerned or

(c) An informal agreement has been reached between the client and the contractor for example, an exchange of letters or reference to terms and conditions of contract within various written documents.

5.03 In these circumstances, it will be necessary to ascertain whether the terms and conditions of the contract comply with the provisions of the HGCRA and, if they do not, which part or parts of the Scheme applies/apply.

Payment by instalments

5.04 A party to a construction contract is entitled to payment by instalments only if the contract specifies that the duration of the work is to be 45 days or more or if it has been agreed by the parties, or if it is estimated, that the work will be of a greater duration. When calculating the duration of the work, Christmas Day, Good Friday or other bank holidays should not be included, but weekends are included within the 45-day period. The same method of calculation should be adopted when determining notice periods under the Scheme.

5.05 If the duration of the work exceeds the 45-day period then the HGCRA requires the construction contract to contain an adequate mechanism for determining what payments become due under the contract and when and provide for a final date for payment in relation to a sum when it becomes due. The parties are free to agree the amounts of the payments and the intervals at which, or the circumstances in which, they become due.

5.06 The issue of what might constitute an adequate mechanism was the subject of discussion in the case of *Alstrom Signalling Ltd v Jarvis Facilities Ltd* in which the parties had agreed that the applications for payment and payments in their sub-contract would be linked to the payment cycle in a separate main contract between Alstom Signalling Ltd ('Alstom') and Railtrack plc ('Railtrack'). In particular the final date for payment of a sum due under the

sub-contract between the parties was to be 7 days after the date of issue of the Railtrack certificate under the main contract. Jarvis Facilities Limited ('Jarvis') argued that by linking the final date for payment to the Railtrack certificate there was uncertainty in that it could be changed without reference to Jarvis. The Adjudicator agreed with Jarvis, stating 'the final date shall be a date that is embedded in the contract between the parties and is incapable of change absent consent of the contracting parties'. However, when the dispute came to court HHJ Humphrey Lloyd had no difficulty in deciding that the payment mechanism in the sub-contract did constitute an adequate mechanism for determining what payments become due under the sub-contract, stating:

> 'I find myself at a loss to understand why Schedule F does not comply with section 110 of the Act in terms of an adequate mechanism to determine when a payment was due for the purposes of section 110(1). The subcontract was made by reference to the main contract, both formally and financially Conventionally it seems that Alstom was to issue a certificate within 14 days of the receipt of an application (see for example, its letter of the 13 June 2003). Clause 2.6 said that payment would be made within seven days of the Railtrack certificate being issued in accordance with Annex Fl. There was therefore certainty as to the final date for payment – seven days of the Railtrack certificate. This satisfies section 110(1)(b). The fact that Railtrack, probably in breach of its contract with Alstom, might fail to issue its certificate in accordance with Annex Fl does not mean that for the purposes of section 110(1)(b) there is no final date. The final date remains seven days after the issue of the certificate. The fact that a date is set by reference to a future event does not render it any the less a final date.'

5.07 This decision appears to have caused some consternation and the draft bill amending the HGCRA proposes a specific provision to prevent the final date for payment being set by reference to a certificate issued under another contract. In reality HHJ Humphrey Lloyd's decision was not suggesting that a payment mechanism which depended on the vagaries of if and when a certifier under a separate contract issued a certificate was adequate. The dates when the certifier under a separate contract issued a certificate had to be certain and not subject to unilateral change. In the *Alstom* case the dates when Railtrack were to issue their certificate were set out in 'Schedule F' which formed part of the sub-contract and the pattern for issuing certificates could easily be projected beyond the last of a series of dates, stated in Schedule F, for the issue of the certificate as the parties had in fact projected the dates accordingly. As HJJ Humphrey Lloyd note: '. . .if Railtrack did not issue a certificate on time Alstom could hardly use it as a defence since clause 2.6 [of the sub-contract] is written on the assumption of due compliance. I therefore do not understand how it could be said that the date could be changed unilaterally'.

5.08 In summary therefore provided the event which identifies the due date and the final date for payment is readily recognisable then the contract complies with the requirement for an adequate mechanism for payment. The event could be a stage, milestone or completion, practical or substantial. It could be the result of action by a third party, such as a certificate under a superior contract or transaction, as is found in financing arrangements. This is particularly important for architects as their fees are frequently paid as a percentage of the total fee agreed, payment being due on completion of the Work Stages described within the RIBA standard form of appointment. No doubt both clients and architects are familiar, and comfortable, with this method of payment. However, architects should take care to identify in the contract by whom and at what point the work stage is completed to trigger the right to a periodic payment. The RIBA's Standard Agreement (S-Con-07-A) does generally provide sufficient detail as to when a work stage is completed by reference to the sub-mission to the Client of the relevant Work Stage report, the exceptions being Work Stages B (Design Brief), Work Stage H (Tender Action), Work Stage J (Mobilisation) and Work Stage L (Post practical completion). This is a definite improvement over the Services Supplement in SFA/99, where Work Stages C, D and E all refer to obtaining the client's approval before completion of the basic services contained within that work stage. The Small Works agreement (SW/99) has similar problems with its Schedule of Services, and therefore if architects persist in using these older forms of appointment they should be aware of these problems and the effect this may have on receiving payment.

It is also not uncommon for architects to be paid by a combination of periodic payments at completion of each work stage, up to work stage H, and thereafter to be paid on a monthly basis for work stages J, K and L. Again, the terms of appointment will need to be carefully drafted to ensure there is no confusion between the notice periods for the stage payments and those for the regular monthly payments. To prevent these problems the Architect should avoid attempts by the client to depart from the payment provisions contained in the S-Con-07-A or the SFA99, the SW99 (if they still use these forms).

5.09 Where the parties to a construction contract fail to agree the amount of any stage or periodic payments and/or the intervals or circumstances in which such payments become due under the contract, then paragraphs 2 to 4 of the Scheme apply. Paragraph 2 of the Scheme provides a method of calculating the total value of work carried out from the commencement of the contract up to the end of the relevant period and, essentially, consists of the value of work performed in accordance with the contract plus (if the contract so stipulates) payment for materials delivered to site for the purpose of the works plus (if the contract so stipulates) any other payments payable from the commencement of the contract to the end of the relevant period. Architects will be familiar with this method of arriving at the total value of work which has been carried out; the information that must be in the section 110(2) notice is not, however, the value of work actually carried out. This is discussed in greater detail below.

From this total aggregate value are deducted the sums which have previously been paid or are due for payment, to leave a balance which is payable for the relevant period in question. This method for identifying the amount due in any particular period is similar to the method adopted by the JCT forms of building contract.

5.10 Paragraph 2 of the Scheme must be read in conjunction with paragraph 12, which defines the value of work as 'an amount determined in accordance with the construction contract under which the work is performed or, where the contract contains no such provisions, the cost of any work performed in accordance with that contract together with an amount equal to an overhead or profit included in the contract price'. This enables a valuation to take place where there are no rates and prices in the contract or where the work has been varied.

5.11 The Scheme imposes, in paragraph 2(4), a maximum on the total amounts to be paid in any relevant period by stipulating that the amount 'shall not exceed the difference between the contract price and the aggregate of the instalments or stage periodic payments, which have become due'. This particular paragraph was the subject of some argument in the case of *Alstom Signalling Ltd v Jarvis Facilities Management Ltd* ([2004] EWHC 1285 (TCC)) in which Alstom had argued that paragraph 2(4) of the Scheme acted like a buffer, since the total amount of interim payments could not exceed the 'contract price', therefore if the contract price was going to be exceeded the interim payment provisions and particularly the requirement for a withholding notice could not operate. HHJ Humphrey Lloyd did not reject the suggestion that paragraph 2(4) operated buffer, but instead concentrated on the meaning of the term 'contract price' which is defined in the Scheme as 'the entire sum payable under the construction contract in respect of the work'.

5.12 After commenting on the poor drafting of the Scheme, HHJ Humphrey Lloyd decided that the 'entire sum' meant the final sum due under the contract, stating:

'In order to find out what is meant by the "entire sum" it is necessary to examine the construction contract, to ascertain the work done under it and then to determine what is payable for that work. The buffer may still apply, e.g. where interim payments prove to be overestimates or other mistaken assessments. It is probably directed to mundane situations where a contractor

or sub-contractor is paid generally on account what is asked for (e.g. by way of "drawings") which then get close to the total sum payable. It is aimed at over payments which are always difficult to recover.'

Dates for payment

5.13 The HGCRA identifies two dates which have less to do with payment and relate more to the service of the notices. The 'due date' starts the clock running on the timetable by which the paying party must serve their notice identifying the payment that is to be made to the receiving party for the relevant period (the section 110(2) notice). The section 110(2) notice which must be served within five days of a payment becoming due. The notice must state the amount of money that would be due, and the basis of its calculation, if the receiving party had carried out and complied in every way with the contract and there were no sums deducted by virtue of set-off or abatement from the payment to be made to the receiving party on this or any other construction contract. In effect, the notice identifies the value of work assuming it has been carried out correctly. The sum of money identified in the section 110(2) notice is not necessarily the sum actually due under the contract and nor does it necessarily mean the work to which the notice refers has been properly performed or completed.

5.14 There is no sanction imposed if the paying party fails to serve a section 110(2) notice.

5.15 The 'due date' also sets the clock running on the timetable for service by the paying party of a notice identifying any amounts it intends to withhold from the sum due and the grounds for doing so (the section 111(2) 'withholding notice'). The parties are free to agree the period of time within which this 'withholding notice' may be served, provided the date by which the notice is to be served is prior to the 'final payment'. If the paying party fails to serve the 'withholding notice' within the agreed time period, then section 111(1) prohibits the paying party from withholding payment after the final date for payment of any sum due under the contract.

5.16 The 'final date' crystallises the date when payment must be made and in the absence of a 'withholding notice', also triggers the receiving party's right to serve a notice of intention to suspend performance of the contract in the event of non-payment by the final date (the section 112 notice).

5.17 The parties are entitled to agree the timetable and periods when the due date and final date may occur after the relevant period for which payment is to be made. The parties are also entitled to agree the timetable for service of the various notices, with the exception of the section 110(2) notice, which must always be served not later than five days after the date on which a payment became due.

5.18 If the construction contract does not comply with these provisions of the HGCRA, then paragraphs 4 to 7 of the Scheme will apply. Paragraph 4 of the Scheme provides that the due date shall occur on the later of either:

(a) the expiry of 7 days following the relevant period; or
(b) the making of a claim in the form of a written notice specifying the amount of any payment or payments considered to be due, and the basis upon which they are calculated, by the receiving party.

5.19 The Scheme provides that the final date for payment is 17 days after the date the payment becomes due. The exception to this is the 'final payment', i.e. the balance of the contract price due after deduction of all instalment payments which have become due under the contract. The 'final payment' becomes due either 30 days following completion of the works or the making of a claim by the receiving party, whichever is the later.

5.20 An issue which has vexed academics, lawyers and the judiciary is whether a party who has failed to give a section 111(2) withholding notice within the agreed time period is still entitled to withhold payment in respect of a sum claimed on the basis that it is not due under the contract. This may appear to be a rather academic argument but as the majority of professional appointments and construction contracts provide for payment to be made at intervals on an interim basis, it is not uncommon for a paying party to dispute the sums claimed by the architect or contractor on the basis that the:

(a) work has not been done or is not completed or is incorrect;
(b) sum claimed includes contractual claims for additional payment which are not justified;
(c) work was not requested
(d) work has been incorrectly valued (more common in relation to contractor's claims but equally relevant where the architect is remunerated on an hourly charge).

5.21 All the above examples apply equally to architects fee claims as much as contractors claims and the issue of whether the paying party may raise argument as to why it is entitled to withhold payment in the absence of a section 111(2) withholding notice arise because section 110 does not identify the sum due under the contract but rather identifies a sum which hypothetically would have been due if everyone had performed as they should have and section 111 only prohibits a paying party from withholding payment after the final date for payment from a sum due under the contract. However if the sum claimed was never due under the contract then it follows that the sanction in section 111(1) is not applicable. The counter argument to this interpretation of the HGCRA is that it is contrary to the intended policy of ensuring prompt payment.

The Court of Appeal decision in *Rupert Morgan Building Services (LLC) Ltd v David Jervis, Herriet Jervis* ([2004] 1 WLR 1867) conveniently summarises the current approach to this problem in which Jacob LJ giving the leading judgment and the interpretation to be given to section 111(1) said:

'But the section [111] does not say that failure to serve a withholding notice creates an irrebuttable presumption that the sum is in the final analysis "properly payable. It merely says the paying party "may not withhold payment of a sum due". This throws one back to the contract to find the answer to how the sum is determined and when it is due."

The contract in question was a standard form published by the Architecture and Surveying Institute, clause 6.1 of which stated that "payments shall be made to the contractor only in accordance with architects certificates and Clause 6.33 stated that "the employer shall pay to the contractor the amount certified within 14 days of the date of the certificate, subject to any deductions and set-offs due under the contract.'

5.22 On the basis of the contractual terms contained in the Architecture and Surveying Institute standard form of contract Jacob LJ determined that '. . .it is not the actual work done which either defines the sum or when it is due. The sum [due] is the amount in the certificate'. He then proceeded to refer to the case of Clark Contracts Ltd v The Burrell Co (Construction Management Ltd (2002 SLT (Sh Ct) 103) in support of his conclusions.

5.23 The *Burrell* case concerned a Scottish edition of the JCT Standard Form of contract. The judge on the case had similarly determined that the sum stated in the architect's certificate was the sum due. The JCT Standard Form of contract used the contractual mechanism of the architect's certificate to identify the 'sum due' and while the architect's certificate was not conclusive evidence that the works for which the contractor sought payment were in accordance with the contract, this did not prevent the sum certified by the architect as being due under the contract, with the result that if the employer wished to withhold payment they were required to serve a withholding notice under section 111(2).

5.24 Both the *Rupert Morgan* case and the *Burrell* case deal with a situation where the contract contains a contractual mechanism for determining the payment of sums due under the contract by way of certificates issued by the architect. Not all construction

contracts contain such mechanisms – for example the JCT Design and Build Contract 2005 states:

'Subject to any notice given under clause 4.10.4 [withholding notice], the Employer shall no later than the final date for payment pay the Contractor the amount specified in the notice given under clause 4.10.3 [Section 110 notice] or, in the absence of a notice under clause 4.10.3, the amount due to the Contractor as determined in accordance with clause 4.8.'

5.25 Clause 4.8 of the contract being the method of calculating the value of the works properly carried either by reference to stage payments (Option A) or value of work properly carried out (Option B).

5.26 The important point to note being that the amount applied for by either the architect under the appointment or the contractor under design and build contract is not necessarily the sum that the Client is contractually required to pay in the absence of a withholding notice, unlike the JCT Standard Building Contract.

5.27 What then is the client/employer required to pay and what may the architect/contractor expect to receive in the absence of such a contractual mechanism? In an earlier Scottish case of *SL Timber Ltd v Carillion Construction Ltd* (2002 SLT 997) the judge, Lord Macfadyen, come to the view that the party applying for payment was not automatically entitled to be paid the sum it had applied for in the absence of a withholding notice:

'The more significant issue in the present case, in my opinion, is whether the defenders' failure to give a timeous notice under S 111 had the effect that there could be no dispute at all before the adjudicator as to whether the sums claimed by the pursuers were payable. The section provides that a party may not withhold payment after the final date for payment of a sum due under the contract unless he has given an effective notice of intention to withhold payment. In my opinion the words "sum due under the contract" cannot be equiparated with the words "sum claimed". . .

'. . . In my opinion, the absence of a timeous notice to withhold payment does not relieve the party making the claim of the ordinary burden of showing that he is entitled under the contract to receive the payment he claims. It remains incumbent on the claimant to demonstrate, if the point is disputed, that the sum claimed is contractually due. If he can do that, he is protected, by the absence of a S111 notice, from any attempt on the part of the other party to withhold all or part of the sum which is due. . .'

5.28 The differences in approach between the *Burrell* case and the *Carillion* case can be explained by the fact that in the *Carillion* case the contract had no architect or system of certificates, there was no contractual mechanism which identified the sum due under the contract. The contractor simply presented his bill which in itself did not make any sum due. If, however, the contractor, proved that the sum claimed represented work carried out, then the sum claimed became due. No withholding notice is necessary in respect of work which was not done as no payment could be due in respect of work not done.

Notice to withhold payment

5.29 The right to withhold payment from a party at common law arises by set-off or abatement. Set-off allows a paying party to deduct monies owed from sums due to the receiving party. The sums owed need not relate to the same contract but could relate to different contracts between the same parties. The test as to whether this is permissible is whether the sum to be set off is sufficiently closely connected with the sum to be paid that it would be unjust to allow the payment without taking into account the sum to be set off.

5.30 Abatement, on the other hand, is the withholding of money as the result of a breach of contract by a party which reduces the value of the work done by that party. The amount of money withheld must equate to the reduction of the value of the work done by that party on that contract. The most common form of abatement is for defective work.

5.31 The section 111 notice identifies the value of the work actually carried out in accordance with the contract by deducting the value of work not carried out or not carried out in accordance with the contract from the value of work that should have been carried out if the contract had been complied with as identified in the section 110(2) notice. This will seem to architects, quantity surveyors and contractors a rather unusual method of arriving at a valuation for the relevant period as they generally do not value work which was not in accordance with the contract, they only valued work that they believe is in accordance with it. The JCT standard forms still adopt this approach. (See, e.g., clause 4.16.1.1 of the JCT Standard Building Contract or clause 4.13.1.1 of the JCT Design and Build Contract.)

5.32 Section 111 prevents the paying party from exercising its right to set off or abate the sums due to the receiving party unless and until it has given a notice to the receiving party specifying the amount proposed to be withheld and the grounds for withholding payment. If there is more than one ground for deducting sums, then that notice must specify each ground and the amount to be deducted in relation to each ground. This notice must be given prior to the date for final payment; otherwise, the paying party may not withhold that payment after the final date. The parties are free to agree the prescribed period within which the notice may be given and the HGCRA anticipates that the notice to withhold payment may be combined with the notice which must be served under section 110(2).

5.33 If no agreement is reached between the parties as to the period when the section 111 notice may be given, then paragraph 10 of the Scheme applies. This stipulates that a notice shall be given not later than seven days before the final date for payment in the contract or, if there is no final date provided for in the contract, then in accordance with the provisions of the Scheme.

5.34 Both the HGCRA and the Scheme state what should be contained in the section 110 and section 111 notices but not the form that the notices should take. Neither the HGCRA nor the Scheme expressly state that the notices should be in writing, though because of the detailed information that they are required to contain the natural assumption might be to assume they should be written. However it is well established that interim and final certificates under a building contract which frequently contain detailed information as to amounts paid and sums owed need not be in writing unless the contract expressly requires them to be so (Hudson's Building and Engineering Contracts, 6.153).

5.35 Lord Hamilton in the Scottish case of *Strathmore Building Services Ltd v Greig (t/a Hestia Fireside Design)* ((2001) 17 Const LJ 72) decided that while sections 111 and 115 (Service of notices) of the HGCRA do not expressly stating that a section 111 notice (and by inference presumably a section 110 notice as well) must be in writing he considered the references in section 115 to 'any notice or other document' indicated that it was clearly intended such a notice should be in writing. No case law appears to have been cited by either party to support the contention that the withholding notice had to be in writing and it appears from the law report that the defendant conceded in argument that such a notice should be in writing.

5.36 The *Strathmore case* also consider whether a withholding notice which had been issued before an application for payment had been made could be effective. The judge rejected this stating:

'The purpose of section 111 is to provide a statutory mechanism on compliance with which, but only on compliance with which, a party otherwise due to make a payment may withhold such payment. It clearly, in my view, envisages a notice given under it being a considered response to the application for payment, in which response it is specified how much of the sum applied for it is proposed to withhold and the ground or grounds for

withholding any amount. Such a response cannot, in my view, effectively be made prior to the application itself being made. It may of course, be that the matter of withholding payment of any sum which might in future be applied for has previously been raised. In such circumstances a notice in writing given after receipt of the application but which referred to or incorporated some earlier written communication might suffice for the purpose – though I reserve my opinion on that matter'.

5.37 In summary, therefore, a paying party is generally not entitled to withhold payment from a sum due under the contract unless it serves a notice in writing after the date of receipt of the application for payment but before a date (which can be agreed between the parties) prior to the final date for payment or where the parties fail to agree such a date then paragraph 10 of the Scheme will apply and the notice must be served not later than 7 days prior to the final date for payment.

5.38 The exception to this rule is where a contract contains a contractual provision entitling the paying party the right to make no further payments in the event that the contract is determined. This exception would appear to contravene section 111 of the HGCRA, however, the House of Lords in the case of *Melville Dundas Ltd (In receivership) v George Wimpey UK Ltd* ([2007] 1 WLR 1136) decided that just such a contractual provision which entitled the employer to make no further payment on determination was valid, it cancelled out any existing right to payment and did not contravene section 111 of the HGCRA.

5.39 The relevant facts of the case illustrate the point. Melville Dundas entered into a JCT standard form of Building Contract with Contractor's Design (1998 edition) to construct a housing development for Wimp. On 2 May 2003 Melville Dundas applied for an interim payment of £396 630. The final date for payment was 16 May 2003 and Melville Dundas should have received payment on or before that date subject to any withholding notices served by Wimpey. In fact, Wimpey did not serve a withholding notice and neither did it make payment. Wimpey was therefore in breach of contract and would have had no defence to a claim for payment.

5.40 On a 22 May 2003 administrative receivers were appointed to Melville Dundas. The appointment of an administrative receiver falls within the contractual definition of insolvency and therefore this is the date Wimpey was first entitled to determine the contract and therefore the date of the insolvency event from which the 28 day period was calculated Wimpey in fact served its notice of determination on the 30 May 2003.

5.41 Clause 27.6.5.1 of the JCT standard form of Building Contract with Contractor's Design (1998 edition) states that in the event of the contractors employment being terminated the employer is not required to make any further payments to the contractor in respect of sums which became due and payable less that 28 days before the date of insolvency (as defined in the contract) or where the determination is for another valid reason then less than 28 days before the date of determination. In other words, the Contractor was still entitled to be paid sums which were due and payable and accrued 28 days or more before the date of insolvency or the date of the determination as the case may be. The JCT 2005 contracts all contain similar wording to the 1998 editions.

5.42 As a consequence of clause 27.6.5.1, Melville Dundas was not entitled to the £396630 as it became due and payable less than 28 days from the date of the insolvency event.

5.43 The *Melville Dundas* decision has been followed by the case of *Pierce Design International Ltd v Johnston* ([2007] EWHC 1691) which again concerned payment following termination under a JCT Standard Form of Building Contract (With Contractor's Design) 1998. The termination this time was became of the alleged failure of Pierce Design to proceed regularly and diligently with the work.

5.44 The *Pierce Design* case is interesting because the judge was invited by counsel for the defendant to limit the *Melville Dundas* decision to its facts i.e. that, clause 27.6.5.1 was valid only where there was an event of insolvency. In the absence of insolvency the clause should be struck down as it was contrary to section 111. The judge declined the invitation, stating:

> 'I am not attracted to an argument which seeks to suggest that, on the one set of facts, a clause in a standard form complies with the 1996 Act whilst, on another set of facts, it does not. That it seems to me to be a recipe for uncertainty and endless dispute. I consider a clause of this type either complies with the Act or it does not'

5.45 Clause 27.6.5.1 therefore complies with the HGCRA irrespective of the facts of the case.

5.46 The second issue in the *Pierce Design* case concerned the various interim payments which the defendant argued were no longer payable by virtue of clause 27.6.5.1. These payments were due at various dates during 2006 and therefore due and payable 28 days before the defendant served its notice to terminate the contract. The defendant's case was that clause 27.6.5.1 should be considered by reference to what is, or is not, reasonable at the time of the hearing rather than at the time the payments should have been made. This was particularly important for the defendant who at the time of the hearing had detailed cross claims.

5.47 Judge Coulson found that there were three tests each of which the contractor had to answer successfully in the affirmative in order to be entitled to payment pursuant to clause 27.6.5.1. These tests are:

(a) Were/are there amounts properly due to be paid by the employer to the contractor?
(b) Did the contractor's rights to those amounts accrue 28 days or more before the date when the right to determine arose?
(c) If so, has the employer 'unreasonably not paid' those amounts?

5.48 The first two tests were clearly satisfied on the facts, but in relation to the test of whether it was unreasonable not to pay, the judge considered that non-payment of sums properly due can only be justified where there is a withholding notice. If there was no withholding notice then the sums due were unreasonably not paid by the employer. The contractor having satisfied the three tests was entitled to payment.

5.49 It is important to distinguish between *Melville Dundas,* where the argument concerned sums which had become due within the 28 days prior to the termination of the contract, and the employer failed to serve a withholding notice but despite failing to serve the withholding notice the contractor was not entitled to payment, and the situation in *Pierce Design* where the sums became due long before the 28 day period referred to in clause 27.6.5.1. The difference in approach can be explained by the drafting of the clause itself, which starts on the premise that no further payments are payable following a termination until the works are completed and an account prepared. This was the situation in *Melville Dundas* and hence the question of reasonableness to withhold payment was irrelevant there simply was no obligation on the employer to make a payment. The clause then contains the exception allowing the contractor to be paid in respect of sums properly due to it and which right to be paid accrued 28 days prior to the termination and the payments have been unreasonably withheld by the employer, hence the three tests formulated by HHJ Coulsen in *Pierce Design.*

5.50 Of what relevance is the convoluted drafting of the JCT to architects, except in the administration of the self same JCT contracts? The *Melville Dundas* decision is in fact of considerable importance, because, it is not confined to insolvency but applies to any termination therefore, if an employer can in the event of a termination withhold payment irrespective of whether a withholding notice is issued, architects need to be vigilant that such clauses do not appear in their appointments, particularly as unlike the JCT, professional appointments frequently allow the employer to terminate the architects employment at will on very short notice.

6 The right to suspend performance for non-payment

6.01 This must be regarded as one of the most powerful sanctions given by a statute to a party attempting to recover money. Prior to the HGCRA, any suspension of performance by a party carried with it the potential risk of being regarded as repudiation of the contract, for which the suspending party could be liable for damages. The HGCRA now sets out a series of clear steps for notices which must be given to each of the parties to the contract before the right to suspend arises. If the notices are not served in compliance with the contract or if the contract does not comply with the provisions of the HGCRA, and the notices are not served in accordance with the relevant paragraphs of the Scheme, then each party must be aware of what the potential consequences may be. If a party has not received a sum due under the contract, in full, by the final date for payment, where no effective notice of withholding payment has been given, then that party has the right to suspend the performance of its obligations under the contract until payment has been made. The HGCRA stipulates that the right to suspend performance may not be exercised without first giving the party in default at least seven days' notice of the intention to suspend performance of the contract by the party owed the money to suspend performance of the contract. The notice must state the ground or grounds upon which it is intended to suspend the performance. The right to suspend performance ceases when the party in default makes payment in full of the amount due.

6.02 The HGCRA anticipates that the suspension of performance by one party will naturally affect the period within which, or the date by which, the contract should have been completed. The HGCRA therefore provides that when calculating the time period within which the contract should have been completed, or the date by which completion should be adjusted, a period of suspension of performance should be disregarded in computing the time for performance under the contract. In relation to architects, this right to extend the contractual time period by the equivalent period of suspension does not really protect the architect from the consequences of suspending work. If an architect suspends work for a week at a critical stage during the course of the building contract, then the knock-on consequences of that suspension may delay the building contract for a far longer period than the period of suspension. The HGCRA, however, only permits the period of suspension to be taken into account when calculating the time for performance of the architect's obligations under the architect's appointment and not the consequential delay that flows from the suspension.

6.03 A building contractor faces a similar dilemma when considering whether to suspend work for non-payment. The JCT have addressed this problem by incorporating a clause into its standard form of contract to the effect that to account for time for performance of the building contract will be extended to account for any delay that arises out of the suspension of performance of the contract. Architects may wish to include a similar express provision within their own terms of appointment, as the SFA/99 and SW/99 merely repeat the HGCRA.

7 'Pay when paid' clauses

7.01 The HGCRA renders ineffective any clause in a construction contract which makes receiving payment conditional upon the payer receiving payment from a third party. The exception to this is where the client becomes insolvent, then a 'pay when paid' clause in a contract would be effective. The HGCRA defines insolvency, but any architect experiencing the insolvency of their client should contact a solicitor who is a specialist in insolvency law.

7.02 The 'pay when paid' clause may have been rendered ineffective by the HGCRA but the author is aware of attempts in contracts to circumvent its effect by means of a 'pay when certified' clause. This type of clause leaves the party to whom money is owed in no better position than it would have been under a 'pay when paid' clause and architects need to be vigilant for 'pay when certified' clauses being introduced into their terms of appointment, particularly if they are working for a contractor on a design and build appointment where it may be attractive for the contractor's cash flow to link payment of sub-consultant's to the payment cycle under the building contract.

8 Interest on late payment of debts

8.01 The final matter to consider in relation to payment is the architect's entitlement to interest if payment is not made by the final date for payment. Interest can be claimed on late payment if there is an express term in the contract, or under the Late Payment of Commercial Debts (Interest) Act 1998. The RIBA form of appointment S-Con-07-A contains a clause that stipulates interest is to be paid at 5% over the Bank of England dealing rate current at the date the payment becomes overdue, in the event of a bill not being paid within 28 days.

8.02 If the appointment contains no express entitlement to interest on late payment of debts, then the architect will have to rely on the statutory provisions, which entitle him to claim interest on the outstanding debt from the final date for payment, either agreed by the parties or as determined under the Scheme. The rate of interest that can be claimed is set by the Secretary of State. Currently at 8% over the Bank of England dealing rate.

9 The Construction Act 2009

9.01 In March 2004 the Government announced a review of sections 104 to 117 of the HGRA. This review was chaired by Sir Michael Latham and was published in September 2004. Consultations on the proposed amendments to Part 2 of the HGCRA took place between March and June 2005 and this was followed by a second consultation in the summer of 2007 which set out detailed amendments to Part 2 of the HGCRA. A draft of the proposed Construction Contracts Bill was then published in July 2008 and consultations on the draft bill ended on the 12 September 2008. This draft Bill has since become incorporated into Part 8 of the Local Democracy, Economic Development and Construction Act. The Act received royal assent on 12 November 2009. It will not be brought into force for a number of months, and will not apply to contracts which have already been made when it is brought into force.

9.02 Part 8 of the Act consists of Sections 138 to 145. Sections 143 and 144 are specifically concerned with amending the existing payment provisions in the HGCRA. The Act will have a substantial effect on the current case law and existing standard forms of contract. In summary the amendments relevant to payment are as follows.

9.03 Section 139(1) of the Act removes the limitation that the HGCRA only applies to contracts in writing, by simple repealing section 107 thereby remedying the mischief created by *RJT Consulting* ((2002) 18 Const LJ No. 5). Contracts in writing, partly in writing and wholly oral contracts will be required to comply with the requirements of the HGCRA, failing which the Scheme will apply. Rather bizarrely, sub-section 2 then reintroduces the requirement that certain provisions in relation to adjudication must be in writing, but this is not relevant in relation to a discussion on payment provisions.

9.04 Section 142 of the Act inserts a new sub-section 110(1A) into section 110 of the HGRA to prevent periodic payments under a construction contract being conditional upon the performance of obligations (for example completion of work) under another contract or a third party's decision that these obligations have been performed under another contract. These provisions are intended to address the decision in *Alstom Signalling Ltd v Jarvis Facilities Ltd* ([2004] EWHC 1285 (TCC)) and the situation where payment to a sub-contractor is conditional upon the architect's certificate being issued to the main contractor under the main contract. However sub-section 110 (1C) excludes the application of sub-section 110(1A) where the contract is an agreement for carrying out construction operations by another person whether under sub-contract or otherwise and the obligations which are to be completed in order for a payment to become due are construction operations. The intention of sub-section 110(1C) is to prevent procurement methods such as management contracting being outlawed by sub-section 110(1A). The wording of sub-section 110(1C) therefore allows an employer to enter into an agreement with a management contractor to organise works contractors to carry out construction work with the management contractor's payments being conditional upon the Architect certifying the works contractor's work. The contract between the management contractor and the works contractor is not an agreement for works to be carried out by a third party and consequently sub-section 110(C) prevents the works contractor's payments being conditional upon the same Architect's certificate. It is difficult therefore to see how, in practical terms management contracting will continue to survive once these new provisions become law.

In addition sub-section 110(1D) outlaws the use of a payment mechanism where the payer (or a third party such as the architect) decides when payment becomes due. Such provisions could be used to delay the due date for payment and thus delay the operation of the other provisions in the HGCRA.

These provisions alone will render the payment provisions of the JCT Standard form of Building Contract 2005 as currently drafted and many of other contracts within the construction industry which rely upon certification to trigger payment to become illegal.

9.05 Section 143 rewrites the current section 110 regime for notices by repealing the existing section 110(2) and introducing new sections 110A and 110B. The new sections also introduce some new definitions as follows:

(a) 'payee' being a person to whom the payment is due;
(b) 'payer' being the person who is to make payment;
(c) 'specified person' which means a person specified in the construction contract or one 'determined in accordance with' terms in the contract. The guidance notes published with draft bill suggest that in practice, a 'specified person' is generally an architect or engineer, i.e. 'someone qualified to value construction work'; and
(d) 'payment due date' which means the date provided for by the contract as the date on which the payment is due, and merely provides a defined term for what is already referred to in the current section 110.

9.06 New section 110A(1) provides that a construction contract is to contain either:

(a) a provision which, in relation to every payment, requires the payer (or a 'specified person') to give the payee a 'payment notice'; or
(b) a provision requiring the payee to give the payer (or a 'specified person') a 'payment notice'.

9.07 In either case, the notice is to be given not later than five days after the payment due date. The proposed 'payment notice' equates to the certifying provisions and application for payment provisions contained in the standard forms of contract.

9.08 The existing section 110 notice requires the works to be valued on the basis that the payee has carried out his obligations under the contract and no set-off or abatement is permitted to be deducted from the valuation. (Section 110(2)). The new section 110A requires the sum notice to specify the considered to be due under the contract at the payment due date and the basis upon which that sum is calculated. The Act therefore reverts back to the tradition of valuing the work which is in accordance with the contract so that at least in respect of defective work it is not necessary to value it and then abatement the valuation in respect of the defects.

9.09 The valuation may result in the sum due to the payee being zero. However new section 110A(4) states that this is irrelevant which suggests that the payment notice under Section 110A(1) is mandatory. This is supported by the new section 110B which entitles the payee to give a payment notice specifying the amount it considers is due to it and the basis of that calculation in the event the payer or its specified person fails to do so. If a payee does give such a notice then the final date for payment is postponed by the equivalent number of days between the date when the payer or specified person should have given the payment notice and the date it was given by the payee (section 110B(3)).

9.10 Section 144 of the Act substitutes a new section 111 into the HGCRA and, in doing so, replaces the 'withholding notices'. The new section 111 now obliges the payer to pay the sum set out in the payment notice issued pursuant to section 110A or 110B as the case may be thus addressing the problem of *SL Timber v Carillion* and the need to prove a payment is due.

9.11 The guidance notes with the draft Bill state that the provision 'is intended to further facilitate "cash flow" by determining what is provisionally payable. What is properly and ultimately payable as a matter of the parties' contract is unaffected (see the decision of the Court of Appeal in *Rupert Morgan Building Services (LCC) Limited v Jervis* [2003] EWCA Civ 1563.'

9.12 New sections 111(3) and (4) allow the payer or specified person to issue a counter notice stating their intention to pay less than the sum specified in the payment notice issued under section 110(A) or 110(B) as the case may be. The counter notice can be served even if the section 110A payment notice was served by the payer or the specified person. This counter-notice is obviously the equivalent to the existing withholding notice but rather than stating the amount that is going to be withheld, it must state the amount the payer is proposing to pay and the basis upon which the sum is calculated. This may appear to be a fine distinction, but the sum stated in the section 111 notice becomes the sum which the payer must pay (section 111 (6)), and therefore to merely state the sum that is to be withheld and the reason why it is being withheld may not be sufficient for the notice to be valid.

9.13 The new section 111(5) must be read in conjunction with the new section 111(7) which together prescribe the timing when the counter notice may be served. The parties are free to agree in their contract the period of time when such notices are to be given before the final date for payment or, where there is no contractual provision, such number of days before the final date for payment as the relevant Scheme for Construction Contracts provides. Section 111(5)(b) has the effect of prohibiting the giving of such a counter-notice before the payee has actually given his payment notices either pursuant to section 110(A)(3) or section 110B. The intention of the new provision appears to be to address the issues raised in *Strathmore Building Services Ltd v Greig (t/a Hestia Fireside Design)* ((2001) 17 Const LJ 72) and *Pierce Design International Ltd v Johnston* ([2007] EWHC 1691) in relation to the timing of the service of these notices.

9.14 The new section 111(9) deals with the situation where a payment notice has been issued by the payer or specified person under section 110A(2) or a counter-notice has been issued under section 111(3) and these notices have been the subject of an adjudication. If the adjudicator decides that a sum which is greater than the sum specified in the notices should be paid, then such additional amount must be paid by the date which is the later of 7 days from the date of the adjudicator's decision or the date which, but for the notice, would have been the final date for payment. The assumption appears to be that the payer will have paid the amount in the notices irrespective of the dispute.

9.15 It is common for parties to ask an adjudicator to decide the sum due in respect of a certificate or application for payment, rather than ask what is due in addition to the sum certified. It is therefore possible for the adjudicator to decide a lesser sum than that certified but the new section 111(9) makes no provision for such a circumstance. If the adjudicator were to decide a lesser sum it would presumably be for the payer to issue a section 111(3) counter-notice at the next interim payment to recover the sum awarded by the adjudicator.

9.16 Section 111(10) codifies in statute the decision in *Melville Dundas Ltd (in receivership) and others v George Wimpey UK Ltd.* In the context of new section 111, it provides that the requirement to pay the 'notified sum' (section 111(1)) does not apply where the contract allows the payer to withhold moneys upon the payee's insolvency and the payee becomes insolvent after the expiry of the period for giving a counter-notice.

9.17 Section 145 of the Act amends the section 112 provisions of the HGCRA which entitle the party which has not received payment the right to stop working. The new Section 112 (1) now allows a party who has not been paid to suspend all work (as does the existing section 112) but alternatively if a party so wishes it may suspend some of its work or obligations. This may be useful for example where large items of plant are about to be delivered to the site and it would be costly for the contractor to cancel the order or find alternative storage if it were to suspend work completely.

9.18 A new sub-section 112(3A) is introduced to allow a party which has validly suspended work to recover its costs and expenses reasonably incurred as a result of the suspension. The ability of the contractor to recover loss and expense as a consequence of a suspension under Section 112 is already included in the JCT forms of contract and many of the other standard forms, but less commonly found in professional appointments. The addition of this statutory right should be welcomed by Architects for whom cash flow and profit margins are such that suspension of work for none payment has been a double edged sword.

9.19 Sub-Section 112(4) has also been amended, apparently to allow the party who has suspended work an extension of time not only for the period of the suspension but also any consequential delay, resulting from the suspension.

9.20 In summary, the Amendments to the HGCRA introduced by Part 8 of the Construction Act 2009 will, once it comes into force, achieve the following:

1. It will be applicable to all 'construction contracts' as currently defined whether they are in writing, partially in writing of wholly oral. Apart from the requirement of writing, all the current exclusions from the HGRCA, for example contracts with residential occupiers will continue to apply.
2. The contract must identify the 'payment due date'. The payment due date can be an actual date or day each month or it can be by reference to an event such as completion of an work stage or element of the works, but it cannot be identified by reference to a notice or certificate issued by the employer or the employer's Architect etc. or the performance of obligations under another contract or the decision by any person that obligations under another contract have been performed, except in the limited circumstances allowed by Section 110(1C). .
3. The contract must contain either a provision which requires the Employer or a 'specified person' (under a building contract this would usually be the Architect or contract administrator) to certify the sum due for payment to the contractor at the 'payment due date', or enable the contractor to make an application for payment. The same principles are applicable to a professional appointment and Architects would be wise to ensure that their appointments allow them to make the application for payment rather than being reliant upon the employer or its project manager certifying their fees.

4. Which ever procedure is adopted the certificate or application must be issued not later than 5 days after the 'payment due date'.

5. If the Employer or Architect/Contract administrator fails to issue a certificate then the contractor may make an application for payment at anytime after the date upon which the certificate should have been issued. The same principles are applicable to a professional appointment and Architects will be able to apply for payment in the event the employer fails to operate the terms of the appointment correctly.

6. The sum stated in any certificate or application for payment is the sum which must be paid on or before the 'final date for payment' unless the Employer or Architect/Contract Administrator issues a notice of intention to pay lesser amount, in which case they must specify the amount they propose to pay and the basis it is calculated on or before the prescribed period, which is either agreed between the parties or if not agreed then under the Scheme it is currently 7 days before the final date for payment.

7. If a party suspends performance for none payment then the contract must allow completion date to be extended to take account of all the consequential delay and not just the period of actual suspension.

8. If a party suspends performance for none payment then the Employer must pay the reasonable costs and expenses incurred by the Contractor or Architect (as the case maybe) as a consequence of the suspension.

In summarising the effect of the new legislation upon construction contracts I have tended to refer to terms which are used in construction contracts rather than professional appointments. The same principles apply to professional appointments even though the terminology used in professional appointments is different and procedures for applying for payment of fees usually less formal. Possibly the principal benefit for Architects is the removal of the need to have a contract in writing before the payment provisions apply. The Court of Appeal decision in *RJT Consulting Engineers Ltd v DM Engineering (Northern Ireland) Ltd* (2002) severely limited the benefit of the HGCRA in relation to professional appointments with their tendency to be less formal and less likely to be fully documented in writing.

Part D
Building dispute resolution

23

Litigation

ANTHONY SPEAIGHT QC

1 Methods of dispute resolution

1.01 It is in the nature of human life that from time to time there are disagreements. Sometimes such disputes can be sorted out by agreement. But if they cannot, the parties have to resort to some outside agency. In earlier times, and in more primitive societies, that agency tended to be the ruler – a feudal lord, a tribal chief, or possibly the king. In all modern societies the outside agency provided for dispute resolution takes the form of a court system.

1.02 Litigation is the process of dispute resolution before a court. In many spheres of activity, litigation is almost the invariable mode of dispute resolution. But in the construction world today it is not the only, nor even the most common, process. Most construction contracts contain an arbitration clause, by which the parties agree to be bound by the decision of a private dispute resolution mechanism: for many years, arbitration was the most common mode of determining construction disputes. Arbitration differs from litigation in that it takes place in private, and that the decision-maker, often an architect, is appointed by agreement of the parties. On the other hand, the actual nature of the proceedings is similar to litigation: the hearing is preceded by formal pleadings, and exchange of documents, and witnesses give evidence on oath. Arbitration is discussed in Chapter 24. Today, arbitration has been overtaken in popularity by adjudication, which is discussed in Chapter 25. Adjudication is similar to arbitration in that the decision-maker may well be an architect, but the procedures are far more summary and the decision is binding for only a temporary period. By legislation in 1996, a right to adjudication is now compulsory in almost all construction contracts. Such is the attraction of a quick decision that not only is adjudication today being used with great frequency, but it is relatively unusual for adjudicators' decisions to be challenged in subsequent litigation or arbitration. What is often the subject of court proceedings is the question whether an adjudicator's decision is enforceable: the grounds on which a successful challenge can be made are few, but parties anxious not to pay often try to make out an argument for non-enforcement. Of growing popularity, too, is mediation, which refers to consensual meetings by parties with a neutral facilitator: the success rate in achieving a settlement at mediations is very high. Mediation is described in Chapter 26. Nevertheless, litigation remains the fallback method of dispute resolution. The existence of litigation underpins the efficacy of the other modes.

2 Litigation in England and Wales

2.01 Construction litigation in England and Wales usually takes place in the Technology and Construction Court (the 'TCC'). The TCC is a specialist division of the High Court. There have traditionally been at any one time about a half a dozen permanent TCC judges who sit in London. In addition, there are some 20 Circuit Judges based in other major cities who sit as TCC judges when the need arises in their area. The modern TCC was created in 1998. Previously there had been a similar arrangement under which a number of judges had the less than meaningful designation of 'Official Referees'. The TCC is presided over by a High Court judge. The first appointee to this position was Mr Justice Dyson, who had been a distinguished construction practitioner at the Bar, and who has subsequently been promoted to even greater judicial distinction. The standing of the TCC has risen further in recent years, as result of initiatives introduced under the inspiration of Mr Justice Jackson, whose name was known to many architects as one of the co-authors of the most authoritatative legal textbook on professional negligence. In recent years the judicial make-up of the London court has developed from a situation in which only a few cases were heard by a High Court judge to a system in which several High Court judges are hearing TCC cases almost full time. The prestige of the TCC among English construction lawyers today is high.

2.02 All citizens have the right to conduct their own cases in court. But construction disputes are normally matters of such complexity that litigants in person are almost always at a real disadvantage to parties who are legally represented. In practice, almost all litigants in the TCC are represented. Unless a party is acting in person, the administrative aspects of litigation, such as issuing the claim form, must be undertaken by a member of a profession which has been approved to act as a 'litigator'. Only one profession has such approval – solicitors, that is members of the Law Society of England and Wales. The solicitor almost invariably instructs a barrister to act as advocate in the TCC. There is a corps of about 200 barristers who have specialist experience of construction work. They are members of the Technology and Construction Bar Association. In addition to their advocacy work, they often undertake advisory work, sometimes on the direct instruction of an architect.

2.03 An alternative venue for civil disputes is the county court. There are county courts in all towns of any size. An architect would be likely to use a county court if obliged to sue a client for unpaid fees. In such proceedings an architect might choose to act in person in relation to the administrative aspects. The court office will provide factual information as to the procedures. If, however, the response to the fees claim should be, as is sometimes the case, an allegation of professional negligence, then, of course, insurers should be notified, and a full legal team will certainly be required. An architect suing for fees might also act in person as the advocate at the hearing; alternatively, the architect might choose to instruct a barrister for the hearing. There are no longer any restrictions on who can instruct a barrister, and in some kinds of case there is a growing practice of lay clients instructing barristers directly, without the intervention of a solicitor.

2.04 Civil procedure has recently undergone major changes. The Civil Procedure Rules, which came into force in April 1999, implemented ideas proposed by Lord Woolf. These Rules apply to both the High Court and the county court. A significant feature of the new regime is encouragement of settlement. There are likely to be penalties in the payment of higher costs to be paid to the other side if parties unreasonably refuse to mediate, or decline to accept an offer in settlement, or fail to disclose sufficient information at an early stage. In fact, considerable exchange of information is expected to take place even before proceedings are commenced. The Pre-Action Protocol for Construction and Engineering Disputes requires not only the supply in correspondence of details of what parties will be saying but also an off-the-record meeting.

3 Litigation in Scotland[*]

3.01 The court system in Scotland has been described in paragraphs 3.01–3.05 of Chapter 5. Architects are more likely to be

[*]The section was written by Peter McCormack.

involved as parties or witnesses in civil actions in the Court of Session or the sheriff court. A party commencing an action (the 'pursuer') does so by serving a writ setting out his case (a 'summons' in the Court of Session or an 'initial writ' in the sheriff court) on the party being sued (the 'defender'). The parties have fixed times in which the defender lodges his answers ('defences') and they adjust their written cases in response to each other. A document called the 'closed record' (the latter word unusually having its emphasis on the second syllable!) is then printed which contains the final version of each party's written case. There may then be a legal debate between the parties as to the legal soundness of their cases, assuming that they are factually true, or as to the sufficiency of detail specified. Cases which can only be resolved by hearing evidence as to the facts come before a single judge or sheriff for a hearing known as a proof, when evidence is given by witnesses and speeches are then made on behalf of each party. At the end of a proof, the judge or sheriff usually does not give an immediate decision, but gives a later written decision. In the Court of Session only, some cases (mainly being simple personal injury actions) may be heard by a judge and jury of twelve (a 'jury trial') instead of by a judge alone. Since 1994 in the Court of Session there has been a special 'fast-track' procedure for Commercial Action, available to parties with business-related disputes.

24

Arbitration

MELANIE WILLEMS

1 What is arbitration?

1.01 Arbitration is a process whereby parties agree to refer an existing, or future, dispute to the determination of one or more independent persons (the arbitrator or the tribunal) in a judicial manner. The decision of the arbitrator is expressed in an award, which (subject to satisfying certain legal requirements relating to the manner in which the decision is made) will be binding on the parties and enforceable in law. English law recognises and supports the arbitral process by providing a statutory framework for arbitrations, set out in the Arbitration Act 1996 (the 'Act').

1.02 Arbitration is a consensual process. Unless the parties have agreed to refer their dispute to arbitration, there can be no arbitration. To explain this by an example, if a creditor claims that a debtor owes him money, unless the parties have agreed to resolve their disputes in a different way, the creditor can commence a court action (litigation) to recover the debt and the debtor cannot prevent him from commencing the proceedings. However, the creditor could not unilaterally refer the dispute to arbitration. Parties resolve their disputes by arbitration because that is what they have agreed to do.

1.03 As arbitration can exist only where there is an agreement between the parties, any arbitrator should comply with any procedure the parties have agreed for the arbitration. Giving the parties the possibility of procedural control, arbitration offers a flexible method of resolving disputes that fits the circumstances at hand. Further, the parties can choose the decision-maker for his or her particular skill or expertise relevant to the matter at hand.

2 The relevance of arbitration law to architects

2.01 Architects are almost bound to come across arbitration at some point during their professional careers for two principal reasons. First, the standard forms of agreements used in the construction industry (including the standard terms of engagement for architects) often provide that disputes will be determined by arbitration and not by the courts. Second, the construction industry is a fertile source of disputes. Indeed, the construction industry has developed its own model rules for arbitration, the Construction Industry Model Arbitration Rules ('CIMAR'), published by the Joint Contracts Tribunal.

2.02 An architect may also be required to give factual evidence during an arbitration arising out of a project in which he or she has been involved. Contractually, architects play an important role on projects and therefore also in any ensuing disputes. Under a number of construction contracts, architects certify works and issue certificates (including final certificates). Architects also commonly act as experts in arbitration proceedings. Finally, an architect may also be appointed as an arbitrator.

3 The purpose of this chapter

3.01 The purpose of this chapter is to provide architects with a summary of the legal framework for arbitrations and of the arbitral process. The chapter is not intended to be a manual on how to conduct an arbitration, nor is it a comprehensive reference work on the topic. There are many substantial books which fulfil these roles and interested readers should refer to the bibliography at the end of this book for more information.

3.02 This chapter also briefly mentions the importance of other methods for resolving disputes, such as adjudication and mediation, which have evolved as alternatives to both litigation and arbitration.

3.03 Because of the time and cost involved in resolving a detailed construction dispute formally by way of litigation or arbitration, the parties often attempt to resolve their dispute through such 'alternative' means of dispute resolution. Arbitration users sometimes complain that the procedure seems akin to litigation in court, with some procedural aspects appearing cumbersome and expensive (although, with the right arbitrator, arbitration can still offer an expeditious and efficient method of reaching a formal decision). Pressure therefore grew for alternatives to both litigation and arbitration. It has, of course, always been possible for parties to resolve their disputes by negotiation and agreement. However, negotiating a settlement to a dispute is often difficult, and so a number of techniques have evolved which are designed to help the parties to achieve a negotiated settlement of their disputes. These techniques have become known by the collective name of 'alternative dispute resolution' or 'ADR'. ADR is now widely recognised as a successful method of resolving disputes cheaply *and* quickly. A number of construction industry standard forms incorporate ADR into their dispute resolution clauses. ADR is likely to continue to be used increasingly in the construction industry, so it is important that architects are aware of the main ADR techniques.

3.04 Reference will be made to a number of standard forms and other documents, using the following abbreviations:

1 JCT 2005: the Joint Contracts Tribunal Standard Form of Building Contract, 2005 edition (as subsequently amended).
2 CA-S-07-A ('CA07'): RIBA Standard Agreement for the appointment of an Architect (2007).
3 CIMAR: the Construction Industry Model Arbitration Rules.

4 The Arbitration Act 1996

4.01 Arbitration in England and Wales has now been governed by the Arbitration Act 1996 (the 'Act') for more than a decade. It is generally thought amongst arbitration practitioners and users alike that the Act has introduced a welcome reform of the law relating to arbitration, which continues to be a popular alternative to litigation in the High Court. When the Act was first introduced, there was a feeling that arbitration in England was in danger of losing its way. In a number of arbitrations, the involvement of the High Court became necessary (sometimes because of 'tactical' applications to the court made by a recalcitrant party to the arbitration), increasing time and cost. Due to the state of the law prior to the Act, the courts did not universally recognise that an agreement to arbitrate between the parties should supersede the jurisdiction of the courts, which produced judicial decisions seen as interfering with or (at worst) frustrating the arbitral process. In many cases, awards by arbitrators were challenged and became the subject of scrutiny by the courts, despite one view that the courts are not meant to hear appeals from arbitrators, as arbitration is intended to produce a final decision.

4.02 The preamble to the Act states that its purpose is to 'restate and improve the law relating to arbitration . . . .' The Act has now firmly and formally adopted many concepts and principles found in arbitration laws internationally, inspired by the UNCITRAL Model Law for arbitration (published under the auspices of the UN Commission for International Trade Law). These principles include party autonomy (parties are free to decide the procedure for 'their' arbitration), the fact that arbitration takes precedence over litigation (so no court proceedings can be commenced if the parties have concluded an arbitration agreement in their contract) and limiting the grounds on which arbitral decisions can be challenged in the courts (which can be restricted to a serious procedural irregularity affecting the arbitral process). Under the Act, the role of the court is to be supportive of arbitration, and judicial practice has shown that most challenges arbitrator's decisions are dealt with robustly.

4.03 Much of the Act reflects the three overriding considerations set out in section 1:

'(a) The object of arbitration is to obtain the fair resolution of disputes by an impartial tribunal without unnecessary delay or expense;

(b) The parties should be free to agree how their disputes are resolved, subject only to such safeguards as are necessary in the public interest; and

(c) The court should not intervene in arbitrations save as expressly provided in the Act.'

4.04 The Act imposes a positive duty on any arbitral tribunal to ensure that these objectives are met. Section 33 provides that the Tribunal shall:

'(a) Act fairly and impartially as between the parties, giving each party a reasonable opportunity of putting his case and dealing with that of his opponent; and

(b) Adopt procedures suitable to the circumstances of the particular case, avoiding unnecessary delay or expense, so as to provide a fair means for the resolution of the matters falling to be determined.'

Arbitral tribunals are required to comply with this general duty in conducting the arbitral proceedings, in their decisions on matters of procedure and evidence, and indeed in the exercise of all other powers conferred by the Act. Arbitrators should have their obligations and duties under Section 33 at the forefront of their minds throughout an arbitration.

4.05 The Act has generally been welcomed as a substantial improvement to the law of arbitration. It sets out the law in a simple and logical manner which should make the law intelligible to all. In addition to governing the relationship between arbitrators and the courts, the Act also supplements any arbitration agreement (which can, in practice be very succinct, as short as simply referring to 'arbitration' in the contract) by offering a fall-back position as regards the most important procedural aspects of the arbitration. However, it is important to recall that this fall-back position can (often) be superseded by an agreement between the parties. To illustrate this function of the Act by way of an example, parties may not have spelt out in their contract how the arbitrator(s) should be appointed. If the parties have not agreed how this is to occur, the procedure set out in Sections 16 and 17 of the Act will apply. Arbitration proceedings that rely heavily on the Act to fill in the procedural blanks left unaddressed in the contract are sometimes referred to as 'ad hoc' arbitrations.

4.06 However, the Act only applies to arbitration agreements which are made or evidenced in writing (see later for comments on this requirement). The Act defines an 'arbitration agreement' as follows: 'an agreement to submit to arbitration present or future disputes (whether they are contractual or not' (sub-section 6(1)).

5 The importance of deciding whether a process is or is not 'arbitration'

5.01 The most important reason for distinguishing 'arbitration' from other decision-making or dispute-resolution processes is that if the process is arbitration, and in particular, if it is governed by the Act, the parties will be afforded a number of legal rights and remedies in respect of the process. Ultimately, the parties may seek to use the powers of the courts to enforce those rights or to obtain the remedies – subject, of course, to the role of the courts with regard to arbitration being supportive with any judicial review limited to what is deemed necessary in the public interest.

5.02 As one can imagine, there are a number of situations where a third party may be called on to resolve a contractual dispute between others. If the agreement in question expressly describes the process as 'arbitration' then it will be clear that the third party must act as an arbitrator and that, if he or she does, his or her decision (the award) will be enforceable in law. But even if the agreement does not expressly refer to arbitration, the courts might still consider the process to be an arbitration in substance. It is important in practice to be clear as to the capacity of any decision-maker that is appointed by the parties to a contract. For example, a third party may be charged with deciding an issue as an expert (the relevant clause may refer to the third party acting 'as an expert, but not as an arbitrator'). In contrast with arbitration, expert determination does not require the expert to follow a 'judicial process' (such as, for example, considering submissions from both parties instead of deciding purely on the basis of the decision-makers own expertise) and any expert is not automatically bound to adhere to the rules of natural justice (or 'due process'). Unless the expert has committed fraud, his or her decision will generally bind the parties even if it appears to be manifestly wrong.

5.03 Arbitration has the following characteristics which can be contrasted from other methods of resolving disputes:

1 There must be a valid agreement to arbitrate. In legal terms, an arbitration agreement must either form part of a valid, binding contract between the parties or it must amount to such a contract itself. In other words, the parties must have the relevant capacity (required by law) to make a contract, the terms of the contract must be sufficiently clear for it to be enforceable and there must be consideration, etc. All these issues are dealt with in respect of contracts generally elsewhere in this book. Arbitration agreements are considered in more detail later.

2 The decision made by the process will be a final and binding determination of the parties' legal rights, enforceable in law. This is to be contrasted with, for example, an agreement to engage in mediation (a form of ADR, a structured negotiations aided by an independent third party who does not, however, reach any decisions). In mediations, it is of the essence of the process that any view about the dispute expressed by the

Gentlemen – It was a very fine Oyster : the Court awards you a shell each

mediator will not be binding on the parties. Arbitration should also be contrasted with 'adjudication' which is governed by the Housing Grants Construction and Regeneration Act 1996 (see further paragraph 5.04 below).

3 The arbitrator is obliged to act impartially. He or she should be independent of the parties, even though he may be the nominee of one of them on a tribunal of three arbitrators.

4 The arbitrator is obliged to carry out his functions in a judicial manner, and in accordance with the rules of 'natural justice'. This feature distinguishes the arbitration process from various other dispute resolution processes which are to be found in commercial contracts, such as determination by an expert (see above). An expert can resolve a dispute by making his own enquiries or by using his own knowledge of the subject matter of the dispute. Apart from exceptional cases (commonly found in shipping and commodities arbitrations) an arbitrator cannot do this.

Architects are sometimes said to be acting in an arbitral or 'quasi arbitral' manner when considering and certifying applications for extensions of time and other claims under the building contracts, but that description is wrong. An architect who carries out such valuation and certification functions is not acting as an arbitrator. The architect in this context has a duty to act fairly but he does not have a duty to act judicially.

5 The arbitration tribunal must be appointed by the parties, or by a method to which they have consented (subject to the default appointed procedure in the Act). This emphasises the consensual nature of the process.

6 The parties to the arbitration process must be the same as the parties whose rights are being determined, and who will be bound by the arbitration award. In most construction industry arbitrations there will be little doubt that this requirement has been met, although it is of course important to ensure that the right corporate parties enter into any (sub)contracts containing the relevant arbitration agreement.

5.04 Statutory adjudication under the Housing Grants Construction and Regeneration Act 1996 is compulsory for most written construction contracts: the statute has the effect of writing a mandatory adjudication procedure (the 'Scheme') into each

construction contract that does not already contain acceptable adjudication provisions. The decision of any statutory adjudicator is 'interim but binding'. This means that the decision is binding on the parties until the dispute is finally determined by legal proceedings (commonly arbitration) or by agreement of the parties. The underlying principle in adjudication is sometimes referred to as 'pay first, argue later', and is intended to assist with cash flow on ongoing projects. Any more formal dispute resolution proceedings than adjudication are meant to be postponed until the end of the project – which (hopefully) will have been completed on the basis of the adjudicator's interim but binding determination.

5.05 Adjudications are meant to be completed within 28 or 42 days. They are sometimes described as 'rough justice' since the proceedings are fast moving and mistakes can be made. Adjudication proved extremely popular in the industry after its introduction, and came to be used to resolve a large number of complex disputes (perhaps more complex than had been envisaged by the legislative). The increasing popularity of adjudication has led to a fall in arbitrations, and also court litigation, in the construction industry. Some years ago now complaints were heard from judges in the construction courts that a significant amount of their business related to arguments over the enforcement of adjudicator's decisions, meant to be interim only. In recent years, there appear to have been the signs of a reversal of the trend in favour of adjudication.

6 The advantages and disadvantages of arbitration compared with litigation in court

6.01 Because arbitration is a consensual process, it follows that at some point, either when they are negotiating a contract, or later, after a dispute has arisen, the parties have chosen arbitration. A positive choice for arbitration instead of litigation is now necessary under the JCT 2005 Standard Form of Building Contract. The 'default' position under the JCT form is now in favour of litigation, and the parties will need to adopt arbitration instead by making appropriate amendemnts to the contract particulars (see Articles of Agreement 8 and 9). If parties do not opt for arbitration, disputes which cannot be resolved amicably must be determined by the courts.

Advantages

6.02 Arbitration has a number of potential advantages over court proceedings:

1 **The technical expertise of the arbitrator:** Arbitration enables the parties to choose their decision-maker. The parties may feel that they would prefer technical disputes to be decided by an arbitrator with the relevant technical expertise. This is, of course, a point of particular relevance in the construction industry where disputes about the construction process may often involve technical, architectural, engineering or quantity surveying/valuation issues. It should be noted that, notwithstanding any technical expertise the arbitrator may have, he or she should only decide the dispute in accordance with the evidence presented to him by the parties. It is often difficult to reach agreement after a dispute has arisen, so it is sensible to include a list of arbitrator candidates in the contract at the outset, before any falling out.

2 **Privacy:** Arbitration proceedings are private and confidential as between the parties. Proceedings in court are (in general) open to the public. The fact that a claim form has been issued by one party against another is a matter of public record. It is often important to parties that their 'dirty laundry' should not be aired in the public forum of the courts. It is for this reason that arbitration clauses are often found in partnership agreements (including architectural partnerships) where it is felt that public knowledge of a dispute between partners could be very damaging for the partnership business.

3 **Flexibility:** As noted above, the parties can have a great deal of control over the procedure, for example, by choosing their own arbitrator, fixing the venue for the hearing and setting the timetable for the dispute to be dealt with. It is an underlying principle of the Act that, subject to certain mandatory requirements, the parties are free to choose their own procedures for the resolution of their disputes. In litigation, the rules are determined by the court, in accordance with the Civil Procedure Rules. Disclosure of documents (which is explained later in this chapter) is an example of the difference. In litigation, standard disclosure of documents is nearly always required. In arbitration, disclosure is subject to the discretion of the tribunal.

4 **The ability to exclude appeals:** Parties are sometimes keen that, whatever the decision on a particular dispute may be, it should be final and binding in the sense that it is not subject to an appeal. It is not possible to agree to exclude rights of appeal from a decision of the courts but such agreements are possible with respect to arbitrations (see below): the parties can agree to be bound by an arbitration award even if the tribunal has made a mistake as to the law or the interpretation of the contract.

5 **The duty of tribunals to adopt procedures which are suitable to the circumstances of the case, avoiding unnecessary delay and expense:** In practice, this can mean that arbitration proceedings are quicker and more economical than equivalent proceedings in court.

6 **Powers of the tribunal:** The tribunal may be granted powers by the parties, or by the Act, which a judge does not have. For example, the Act gives an arbitrator a wider power to award interest on a compound basis, than is available to the court.

7 **Enforcement:** In cases involving foreign parties it can sometimes be easier to enforce the arbitration award in the foreign country than would be the case with a judgment of the courts. Many countries are parties to the New York Convention on the Recognition and Enforcement of Foreign Arbitral Awards (1958) (the 'New York Convention') and have agreed to recognise and enforce foreign arbitration awards, on reciprocal basis. While a judgment of the English courts will often be recognised and enforced in many countries, there are jurisdictions who recognise English arbitration awards but not English judgments.

Comparison with court process

6.03 All civil cases in the High Court and the county courts are governed by the Civil Procedure Rules (which came into force almost 10 years ago, in 1999). At the time, the Civil Procedure Rules were hailed as a welcome reform of civil and commercial litigation. These rules introduced a number of features aimed at streamlining the process of litigation, including the concept of a proactive judge whose task will be to manage the conduct of the case. They also include an 'overriding objective' which requires the parties and the courts to ensure that cases are handled justly. Parties are to be on an equal footing and expense is saved by dealing with the case in a manner which is proportionate to the amount of money involved, the importance of the case, the complexity of the issues and the parties' financial position. The overriding objective which applies to court proceedings is, perhaps, analogous to the general duty imposed on arbitral tribunals by section 33 of the Act.

6.04 Construction industry disputes of any reasonable size are generally referred to a specialist court of the High Court now called the Technology and Construction Court ('TCC'). In the major provincial centres, TCC business tends to be dealt with by designated judges, although there is no separate TCC in those centres. Judges in the TCC are experienced in dealing with construction industry disputes. They should be well aware of the terms of most of the standard forms of contract used by the industry and should quickly grasp the technical issues which arise. Traditionally, the TCC court has been at the forefront of adopting innovative procedures to reduce the delay and expense of litigation (even before the introduction of the reforms to the Civil Procedure Rules). Recent appointments to the bench have included some experienced and respected construction law practitioners with many years experience, and have helped to alleviate criticism regarding the quality of some judgments.

Disadvantages

6.05 One potential disadvantage of arbitration proceedings is the lack of an effective means to deal with disputes involving more than two parties. This area requires careful consideration as it can be of practical importance in the construction industry. Construction disputes may arise between the employer, architect, contractor and sub-contractor, all relating to the same subject-matter. For example, the employer wishes to recover damages arising from a defect which is partly caused by the architect's design and partly by the contractor's poor workmanship. Unless special provision is made in the arbitration agreements of all relevant (sub-) contracts, by which the various parties agree that all the separate disputes can be determined by the same arbitral tribunal, the disputes could be heard together. Even where such special provision is made, careful drafting is still required. Unless there are effective provisions of this nature written into the arbitration agreements, even if the same arbitrator is appointed to deal with the various disputes between the different parties, he or she does not have power to order the various arbitrations to be heard at the same time unless all the parties consent (see section 35 of the Act).

6.06 Where no provision is made for such multiparty disputes (or where the specific circumstances which have arisen have not been addressed), the party who is 'common' to both disputes (and therefore party to separate arbitrations) may consider that there is a risk of prejudice through inconsistent decisions reached by the various arbitration tribunals. For instance, a main contractor who is caught in the middle in this way may not have the certainty that any claim from the employer can be passed 'down the line' to the subcontractor on the same factual basis on which the employer relied against the main contractor. For that reason, section 35 of the Act allows parties to agree that (related) arbitral proceedings may be consolidated or heard together.

6.07 Examples of agreements which provided for multiparty disputes can be found in the JCT forms of main contract (see Conditions, Section 9.4.2 of the JCT Standard Form of Building

Contract 2005) and sub-contracts which provide for multiparty arbitration in certain circumstances. These standard forms seek to do this by reference to CIMAR, which both forms of contract adopt as the applicable rules for arbitrations arising out of those contracts. CIMAR provides detailed rules relating to the joinder of two arbitrations and the appointment of the tribunal. It is beyond the scope of this chapter to summarise the relevant rules, save as to say that similar provisions in prior editions of the JCT forms of contract were effective to allow one tribunal to hear arbitrations relating to the same works arising under a JCT main and subcontract (see *Trafalgar House v Railtrack* (1995) 75 BLR 55).

6.08 Another possible disadvantage with arbitration is that it may be less effective than litigation at dealing with the reluctant defendant. Defendants may raise a number of weak defences or counterclaims simply as a means of delaying the day when they have to pay their creditors. The courts provide procedures for dealing with defences which are obviously weak (such as applications to 'strike out' part of a case or to ask for early determination through summary judgment), in addition to providing a range of sanctions which can be used to prevent one of the parties from 'dragging its feet' during the litigation process. The equivalent arbitration procedures and sanctions are generally less effective, simply because the arbitral tribunal does not have the same powers of the court to impose immediate sanctions for procedural transgressions during the arbitration. However, while there may be less danger of a party's case being rejected if a time limit in an arbitration has been missed (as opposed to court, where that is the ultimate sanction), arbitrators can (and often do) mark their disapproval of a party's conduct in an award of legal costs at the end of proceedings. Arbitrators have a wide discretion when deciding whether to award a successful party a share of its legal costs (arguably wider than the discretion of the courts), and will consider unhelpful or obstructive conduct during the proceedings that may have led to increased costs. As regards further perceived disadvantages of arbitration, there is a view that means of enforcing an arbitral award are not as fast as the means of enforcing a court judgment.

6.09 Notwithstanding some of the drawbacks of arbitration, there is no doubt that arbitration can be used to great advantage. Where the arbitral tribunal makes sensible use of procedures appropriate to the particular circumstances of the case, some of which are explicitly provided in the established rules of arbitration (such as the short hearing procedure and documents only procedure permitted by CIMAR), the process can offer an efficient and economical way of resolving a dispute. Whatever the relative merits of arbitration when compared to litigation, a topic on which it is difficult to generalise in any event since much depends on the attitude of the parties and the decision-maker in question, it is clear that arbitration clauses will continue to be incorporated into construction industry standard forms.

7 The arbitration agreement

7.01 The Act applies only where the arbitration agreement is in writing. Section 5(2) of the Act provides that there is an agreement in writing:

1 If the agreement is made in writing (whether or not it is signed by the parties)
2 If the agreement is made by exchange of communications in writing or
3 If the agreement is evidenced in writing.

7.02 Also (by sub-section (3)), where parties agree otherwise than in writing by reference to terms which are in writing, they make an agreement in writing. So, for example, an oral agreement between an architect and employer which referred to the standard CA07 would satisfy the 'in writing' requirement of the Act, because the CA07 are written and contain an arbitration clause (although under the 2007 version of RIBA's appointment conditions, arbitration must be positively chosen under para 8 of the Model Letter). It is also possible (and indeed occurs frequently in the construction industry) for contracts to be formed not orally but by conduct: for example, if a subcontractor, having been sent the main contractor's proposed terms, starts work on site without referring to or objecting to the proposed contract terms, the subcontractor may be held to be bound by these terms and any arbitration clause they contain.

7.03 Because arbitration is a consensual process, the arbitration agreement is the very foundation of the process and can (or should) fulfil a number of important functions:

1 The agreement defines the types or categories of dispute that can be referred to arbitration. It therefore establishes, and limits, the scope of the jurisdiction of the arbitration tribunal. For example, Article A9 of CA07 provides that 'Any dispute or difference arising out of this Agreement may be referred to . . . arbitration'.
2 The agreement establishes the composition of the arbitration tribunal or the method by which the tribunal will be appointed. For example, Article B2.3 of CA07 assumes a sole arbitrator. It provides that 'the dispute or difference is referred to the arbitration and final decision of a person to be agreed between the parties' or, failing agreement within 14 days to a person nominated by an 'appointing body' (this could be the President of RIBA, but the parties will need to take a decision as to who appoints the arbitrator). The agreement should therefore state the number of arbitrators, their qualifications and how they will be appointed. Ideally, it may also contain a list of arbitrators that are acceptable to both parties, from which the tribunal can be selected once a dispute has arisen. If the agreement fails to deal with any of these matters, the Act provides default provisions to fill the gaps as noted above.
3 The agreement may prescribe the procedure or rules which the tribunal should follow. This may be done by setting out the procedure extensively (or specific procedural points) or, more usually, by reference to some other document which contains the procedure. For example, the JCT Standard Form of Building Contract 2005 incorporates CIMAR (Conditions, Section 9.3). Particularly in projects involving international parties, the arbitration rules of the court of arbitration of the International Chamber of Commerce ('ICC') or of the London Court of International Arbitration ('LCIA') are a popular choice.
4 The arbitration agreement may make other provisions in relation to the rules of law which the arbitration tribunal will apply. In English arbitration agreements which do not involve foreign parties, this provision is not usually necessary.

Each of these matters is considered below.

8 The jurisdiction of the arbitration tribunal

8.01 An award made by a tribunal which in fact does not have jurisdiction to determine the dispute is not enforceable and can be set aside. Confirming the jurisdiction of the arbitral tribunal is therefore an important starting point: as set out below in paragraph 8.02, where an arbitration agreement exists, the particular dispute must fall within the scope of disputes covered by that agreement, otherwise the tribunal will not have jurisdiction to determine that dispute. It is, of course, also open to the parties to agree, after the contract has been signed without an arbitration clause *and* after a dispute has arisen, that this particular dispute (only) should be resolved by arbitration. In all cases, the arbitral tribunal can, however, only determine disputes which are actually referred to it by the 'notice of arbitration' (the document which begins the arbitration process), or which the parties later agree should be determined by the tribunal.

8.02 It may be easy to determine whether there is actually an arbitration agreement (a matter of checking the contract conditions or other contractual documents), but what if the agreement which contains the arbitration clause never came into effect? For example, the parties work to a letter of intent which is never converted to a binding contract, or the contract is set aside because it is void, or is terminated as a result of one party's breach? It might be thought that in any of these circumstances there would be no arbitration agreement because the substantive agreement which contains the arbitration clause does not exist or is terminated. However, such a result is undesirable. It is logical to assume that parties who chose to refer any disputes under the contract to an arbitrator also wanted that arbitrator to decide whether or not the contract itself exists or is valid in the circumstances. Section 7 of the Act achieves this. It confirms the principle that the arbitration agreement is free-standing, and has its own existence quite apart from the underlying contract. The Act states that 'unless otherwise agreed by the parties, an arbitration agreement which forms or was intended to form part of another agreement (whether or not in writing) shall not be regarded as invalid, non existent or ineffective because that other agreement is invalid, or did not come into existence or has become ineffective and it shall for that purpose be treated as a distinct agreement'. The arbitration agreement is therefore separate from the substantive agreement in which it may be incorporated.

8.03 A further key question is whether the dispute in question falls within the scope of the arbitration agreement: did the parties intend for this particular dispute to go to the arbitrators? In most construction contracts which adopt one of the standard forms, there will be little doubt about this issue. The arbitration agreement in Article 8 (Articles of Agreement) of the JCT Standard Form of Building Contract 2005 applies to 'any dispute or difference between the Parties of any kind whatsoever arising out of or in connection with this Contract, whether before, during the progress or after the completion or abandonment of the Works' but subject to certain specified exceptions. It is hard to imagine any dispute between the employer and the contractor relating to the particular contract which might fall outside the scope of this arbitration clause (other than matters which fall within the specified exceptions). Referring to all disputes 'arising under', 'out of' or 'in connection with' the contract ensures that the arbitration agreement should be wide enough to cover claims in tort as well (such as, for example, allegations of misrepresentation or common law negligence).

8.04 While a dispute may fall within the scope of the arbitration clause, it is also necessary to consider whether there is any preliminary step to be completed before the dispute is capable of being referred to arbitration. For example, in the standard form civil engineering contract published by the ICE (7th edition: see clause 66A), a dispute must first be referred to the Engineer for his decision before it can be referred to arbitration. Care should be taken when considering such preliminary steps, or time limits, that are set out in arbitration agreements: they should be complied with (see further paragraph 8.07 below).

8.05 Most arbitration clauses amount to agreements to refer future disputes to arbitration (as opposed to agreements to refer a particular dispute to arbitration, which must be made after that dispute has arisen). The disputes actually referred to arbitration are (or should be) defined in the claimant's notice requesting arbitration. The notice of arbitration should describe the dispute referred to in clear terms (see further paragraph 8.03 above as to the question of whether the particular dispute is covered by the arbitration clause). Further, different disputes, not mentioned in the notice of arbitration (or even in existence at that time) must be referred to the tribunal either as agreed between the parties, or through service of further notices of arbitration. However, if new and different disputes arise after a first notice of arbitration, and additional notices require to be served, all the disputes will not necessarily be determined by the same arbitral tribunal, unless the rules permit this (CIMAR give the tribunal a discretion to allow additional disputes to be referred to the same tribunal, and the ICE Arbitration Procedure 2006 contains a rule allowing notices of further disputes or differences).

8.06 This is especially important where the claim may shortly become time barred by reason of the Limitation Act 1980, a 'time bar' being a procedural defence to a claim aimed at having claims determined

before the evidence becomes stale due to the passage of time. To avoid a 'time bar' defence, it is necessary to institute formal proceedings in respect of the claim within the relevant time limit (which may well be 6 years for breaches of contract), so a notice of arbitration will be required. A new claim, which is outside the scope of the original notice of arbitration, introduced by a party after the limitation period has expired, could be defeated by a Limitation Act defence.

8.07 The arbitration clause or the substantive contract may also include time limits by which claims must be notified or referred to arbitration. Failure to comply with these time limits can provide a complete defence to the claim. However, section 12 of the Act gives the court power to extend time in certain circumstances (described in more detail below). While time limits for the assertion of claims may seem procedural or technical in nature, such conditions precedent have been enforced by both arbitrators and the courts. They are matters that can affect the substantive rights of the parties. Arbitration notices served in disregard of time limits or other conditions precedent to arbitration are likely to have no effect.

9 Who decides where the tribunal has jurisdiction?

9.01 Who should decide if a party contends that the tribunal has no jurisdiction to determine the dispute, for example because there is no arbitration agreement? Strict logic might suggest that the tribunal cannot decide that question because, if there is no arbitration agreement, there is no validly appointed tribunal. However, in practice someone must decide this question and it seems sensible to trust the parties' arbitral tribunal to decide on its own jurisdiction and this is confirmed by the Act.

9.02 Section 30 of the Act provides that, unless otherwise agreed by the parties, the arbitral tribunal may rule on its own substantive jurisdiction, which will include questions such as (i) whether there is a valid arbitration agreement, (ii) whether the tribunal has been properly appointed (respecting any procedure agreed for the purpose between the parties, with no arbitrator suffering from a conflict of interest prevent him or her from taking up office) and (iii) what matters have been referred to arbitration in accordance with the arbitration agreement and the notice of arbitration. Any such ruling by the tribunal may then be challenged by proceedings in court, subject to the specific conditions attached to such a challenge by the Act. A party who wishes to object to the substantive jurisdiction of the tribunal must raise this objection not later than the time he takes the first step in the proceedings to contest the merits, otherwise he or she will be deemed to have accepted the tribunal's jurisdiction by participating in the proceedings before it.

9.03 Any objection during the course of the arbitration that the tribunal is exceeding its substantive jurisdiction must be made as soon as possible after the matter alleged to be beyond the tribunal's jurisdiction first comes to the party's knowledge. Under section 32 of the Act, the court may, on the application of a party, determine any question as to the substantive jurisdiction of the tribunal. However, applications to the court of this kind may only be made with the agreement of all other parties to the proceedings, or with the permission of the tribunal. Even then the court must be satisfied that the determination of the question to be put to it is likely to produce a substantial saving in costs and that the application has been made without delay and there is good reason why the matter should be decided by the court (and not the tribunal).

10 The composition of the arbitration tribunal

10.01 The second function of the arbitration agreement is to deal with the number of arbitrators and how they are to be appointed. It may also deal with other matters relating to the tribunal, such as their desired qualifications and (in international agreements) nationality of the arbitrators. Although highly desirable, it is not essential that the arbitration agreement deals with these matters. If it does not, the Act will provide the missing essential ingredients. As before, in the absence of agreement between the parties on the point, the Act provides the following:

1   Section 15 of the Act provides that arbitration means a sole arbitrator.
2   Section 16 of the Act sets out the procedure for appointing the arbitrator or arbitrators. If the tribunal is to consist of a sole arbitrator, the parties are jointly to appoint the arbitrator. If the tribunal is to consist of two arbitrators, each party is to appoint one arbitrator. In case of three arbitrators, each party is to appoint one arbitrator and those two arbitrators are to appoint a third arbitrator as the chairman of the tribunal.
3   Section 17 of the Act aims to offer a solution where the appointment process breaks down because a party does not cooperate. It provides that where each of two parties is to appoint an arbitrator and one party refuses or fails to do so, the other party, after giving notice to the party in default, may appoint his arbitrator as sole arbitrator. In the event of a failure of the procedure for the appointment of the arbitral tribunal and in the absence of agreement between the parties, any party may apply to the court to exercise its powers under section 18 of the Act. These include the power of the court to make any necessary appointments itself.

11 The number of arbitrators

11.01 While it is theoretically possible for an arbitration tribunal to be composed of any number of arbitrators, it is, however, very rare for there to be more than three. This is patently sensible for practical reasons, and importantly due to cost (since the parties need to bear the fees of the arbitrators). Under section 15(2) of the Act, unless otherwise agreed by the parties, an agreement that the number of arbitrators shall be two or any other even number shall be understood as requiring the appointment of an additional arbitrator as Chairman of the tribunal, which avoids the result being a 'draw'.

11.02 When three arbitrators are appointed, then the award of the majority of them will be binding unless the parties have expressed a contrary intention. Although some construction industry disputes (particularly international disputes) are dealt with by an arbitration tribunal of three arbitrators, it is most common to provide that disputes be resolved by a sole arbitrator. This is the provision which is found in CA/07 and also in the JCT Standard Form of Building Contract 2005. Two-member arbitral tribunals have not proven popular in the construction industry, though there are procedures (notably in the shipping industry) which involve two party-appointed arbitrators and an umpire who decides if the arbitrators cannot agree between themselves: section 21 of the Act is intended to deal with situation.

11.03 Although an arbitrator may have been appointed by only one of the parties, it is not that arbitrator's function to act as a 'champion' of or advocate for the party who appointed him or her. Any suggestion of a party-appointed arbitrator openly favouring the party that appointed him or her would cause doubts as to the regularity of the arbitral process, and could ultimately lead to any award being challenged. The party-appointed arbitrator must be independent of both parties and act impartially at all times. He or she must hear the evidence, listen to the argument, and then make the decision in the proper way.

12 The qualifications of arbitrators

12.01 In this context, the term 'qualification' may cover not only academic or other qualifications to act as an arbitrator, but also any other particular quality that the arbitration agreement specifies that the arbitrator should have. As regards the latter, the parties are free to specify what characteristics or experience the arbitrator shall have, though they should be mindful of the trap of specifying the perfect arbitrator – who may not be available to act when a real dispute arises.

12.02 It is not necessary for an arbitrator to have any particular formal qualification (to enable him or her to take up an appointment), but it is of course desirable that the arbitrator should have experience of acting as an arbitrator and, ideally, be familiar with the legal areas that may be relevant to disputes that are likely to arise under the contract in question. Arbitrators appointed in construction disputes are generally experienced legal practitioners, or have an engineering/surveying background (some hold both legal and technical industry qualifications).

12.03 Where the appointing body is one which maintains a list of arbitrators (such as the Chartered Institute of Arbitrators, or the RIBA or the RICS) it is likely that the appointed arbitrator will have such experience and, in the case of the Chartered Institute, the person nominated will almost certainly be a fellow of the Chartered Institute and have undertaken further practical training as an arbitrator.

13 Appointment of the tribunal in multi-party disputes

13.01 Multi-party disputes are a common feature of construction projects and efforts have been made in the standard forms of contracts to provide a mechanism for these disputes to be determined by the same tribunal. Where there is a multi-party arbitration, the arbitration agreement should make particular provision for the appointment of the tribunal. For example, the JCT 2005 forms of contract and the associated subcontract forms adopt the CIMAR provisions relating to the appointment of the tribunal.

14 Prescribing the arbitration procedure

14.01 'Party autonomy' is one of the underlying principles of the Act. This means that, subject to certain mandatory provisions, the parties are free to choose their own procedure. Typically, the procedure may be specified in the arbitration agreement (although as noted above, this is not always the case), often by adopting established rules of arbitration rather than setting out the procedure at length in the contract itself. If no procedure is referred to in the arbitration agreement or agreed separately by the parties (who in principle retain this freedom throughout the whole of the arbitration), then the arbitration tribunal is said to be 'master of its own procedure'. This is reflected in sub-section 34(1) of the Act which provides that 'it shall be for the tribunal to decide all procedural and evidential matters, subject to the right of the parties to agree any matter'. The arbitration clause in CA/07 (B2.3.1) specifies that CIMAR should apply to any significant claim.

14.02 Theoretically, leaving the procedure to be worked out by an experienced arbitrator should introduce the flexibility for the arbitrator to 'tailor' the procedure to deal with the particular dispute before him. Under the Act, the tribunal in any event has a positive duty to adopt appropriate procedures for the circumstances of the case (section 33). Most of the standard form agreements used in the construction industry specify the rules which will apply (such as CIMAR). These procedures present a range of options for the parties and for the tribunal, giving the parties the advantage of some certainty, and the tribunal the comfort that if it adopts an option envisaged by the prescribed rules then it is less likely that its decision will be attacked on the grounds of a serious procedural irregularity (under section 68 of the Act). Arbitration procedure is dealt with in a little more detail later in this chapter.

15 Other provisions which may be found in arbitration agreements

15.01 A number of other provisions may be included in arbitration agreements. For example, the arbitration clause is often part of a longer dispute-resolution provision, which may require the parties to exhaust other means of resolving their disputes before referring the dispute to arbitration (sometimes referred to as a 'stepped' or 'tiered' dispute resolution provision). The agreement may specify the manner in which the arbitration is to be commenced, for example how and where the arbitration notice is to be served. Also, the arbitration clause may state whether the arbitration tribunal is obliged to apply the law strictly, or is entitled to decide the dispute *ex aequo et bono* (meaning 'according to equity and good conscience') or in the light of usages and custom of the industry.

15.02 In arbitrations involving foreign parties, the agreement should refer to the applicable law, the language of the arbitration, and the place of arbitration. The latter issue is of practical importance. The law of the 'seat' of the arbitration governs the procedural aspects of the subsequent proceedings (for example, what powers the arbitrators have, how an award might be challenged). If the seat of the arbitration is not England and Wales, then the Act will not apply: the implications of adopting a seat other than England and Wales are beyond the scope of this chapter, and are treated fully in works relating to international arbitration.

16 How to commence arbitration proceedings

16.01 It is important to know how to commence arbitration proceedings. A mistake in the notice of arbitration, rendering it ineffective, may mean that a claim becomes time barred as a result of the expiration of a limitation period (see above). If the arbitration agreement does not specify how and when proceedings are deemed to be commenced then the provisions of section 14 of the Act will apply. The precise mechanism will depend on whether the arbitration agreement names a designated arbitrator or requires either the parties to appoint the arbitrator or a third party to do so. The underlying principle is that arbitral proceedings are commenced in respect of a matter when one party serves on the other party a notice in writing requiring him (or them) to submit that matter to the persons named, designated or to be appointed as arbitrator.

16.02 The form of notice need not be long or complex but it is important that it should identify the matters to be referred to arbitration in broad terms. It must also comply with the requirements of the arbitration agreement or section 14 of the Act, if the arbitration agreement is silent as to commencement. The arbitration notice should be served in accordance with the provisions of the arbitration agreement or, if there are no provisions, the method of service that is set out in section 76 of the Act. The notice may be served by any effective means. If a notice is served, addressed, prepaid and delivered by post to the addressee's last known principal residence or principal business address or, if a body corporate, to the registered or principal office, it will be treated as effectively served.

17 Arbitration procedure or rules

17.01 Once commenced, the arbitration will be conducted in accordance with the procedure or rules agreed between the parties, or failing agreement, as determined by the tribunal (being the 'master' of the procedure). In either case, as already noted, the tribunal must act fairly and impartially between parties, giving each party a reasonable opportunity to put his case and to deal with that of his opponent and adopting procedures which are appropriate for the circumstances of the case (section 33 of the Act). The objectives of the procedures in an arbitration can be summarised as follows:

1   First, to define the issues in the arbitration with sufficient precision so that each side can prepare the evidence and argument which it will rely on to prove its case (or disprove the other party's case). The procedure should also ensure that neither side can be taken by surprise by evidence or argument presented by its opponent.

2   Second, to make appropriate provision for the exchange of information and evidence relating to the matters in dispute.

3   Third, to make provision for the way in which the hearing itself will be conducted (if, indeed, a hearing is held).

17.02 Usually the specified rules will deal with these matters, while allowing the tribunal some discretion as to how they are applied. In most cases of any size, there will be a meeting with the tribunal at an early stage in the proceedings when the tribunal will make an 'order for directions' (setting out, step by step, how the tribunal and the parties will arrive at the final hearing of all the evidence if the case cannot be resolved before then). In substantial cases, these directions, and the need for further directions, are reviewed throughout. There is likely to be a further procedural hearing, which usually takes place much nearer to the trial date and serves as a check that the parties are indeed ready to go into the hearing (as they ought to be).

18 The general duty of the parties

18.01 Section 40 of the Act imposes a general duty on the parties to 'do all things necessary for the proper and expeditious conduct of the arbitral proceedings'. This includes complying without delay with the tribunal's directions and orders and also any step to obtain a decision of the court on a preliminary question of jurisdiction or law.

19 Definition of the issues

19.01 In most cases, the parties will be required to serve on each other a 'statement of case'. As the name suggests, this document sets out the nature of each side's case. The amount of information included in the statement of case will depend on the circumstances of the case. Sometimes, the statement will include full submissions of fact and law, supported by copies of the documents on which the party wishes to rely. The normal requirement is that the statements of case should set out, as concisely as possible, the material facts on which the party relies in support of its case. Generally, statements of case in arbitration are more readable than formal 'pleadings' in court. Good arbitration submissions tell the story convincingly without veering off into unsupported allegations, hyperbole, irrelevancies or repetition.

19.02 In large construction disputes, which can involve complex issues of fact and substantial quantities of documents, it may be necessary for the parties to serve schedules providing details of the factual matters which are in dispute (called 'Scott Schedules'). These large disputes call for all of the skills of the tribunal to devise procedures which will be appropriate and enable the arbitration to proceed to a speedy conclusion. An experienced arbitrator should not allow a complex claim for delay and disruption to turn into a re-staging of everything that happened on the project. Generally, in construction arbitrations the management of factual detail by all involved (experts, arbitrators, lawyers and witnesses) is one of the key challenges to be addressed.

20 The exchange of information and evidence

Disclosure of documents

20.01 In litigation, after the parties have exchanged their statements of case, each is required to disclose to the other documents in its possession, custody or control which either support that party's case, undermine that party's own case or support the case of the opposing party. Prior to the introduction of the Civil Procedure Rules, it was generally necessary to disclose documents that merely related to the issues, or documents that, once seen, might put the other side onto a 'trail of enquiry' towards other, more fruitful documents. However, concepts of relevance and the trail of enquiry have not had any place in English court procedure for some time now, and should have no place in arbitration either – especially since disclosure of documents is not a permanent fixture in arbitrations.

20.02 Disclosure of documents has never been mandatory in arbitration proceedings. However, there has been a (perhaps unwelcome) tendency for some arbitrators to copy the litigation procedures to the extent of requiring the parties to give disclosure of all their documents that fall within the test – but this approach is become less common nowadays. The more modern approach in arbitration is not to require the parties to produce more than the documents on which they rely, plus specific categories of documents which may be requested by the other party. Even then, the tribunal may decline to order a party to produce documents requested by the other party if the request is not reasonable. For instance, a reasonable request may relate to any internal minutes of a meeting at which it is known that the cause of an important defect was discussed. A potentially unreasonable request might be aimed at 'any and all' documents or correspondence passing between the main contractor and the sub-contractor concerning the piling works (this should be limited to dates or a time period, and the specific relevance of the piling works to the claims ought to be explained).

20.03 This modern approach is reflected in section 34(2)(d) of the Act which leaves it to the tribunal to decide 'whether any and if so which documents or classes of documents should be disclosed between and produced by the parties and at what stage'.

20.04 The manner in which documents are disclosed is also important. In litigation, parties are required to list all of the documents produced (which generally involves extracting them from files and listing them, chronologically). Arbitrators could impose a similar requirement but the more modern approach is to require the parties to identify the documents by more general categories, such as by file, or by simply providing relevant documents to the other side without any list.

20.05 Certain categories of documents, referred to as 'privileged documents' need not be disclosed. For most practical circumstances which architects are likely to come across, the only relevant categories of privilege are legal professional privilege and communications between the parties on a 'without prejudice' basis.

20.06 Documents covered by legal professional privilege are communications between clients and their qualified lawyers which come into existence for the purpose of *either* providing the client with legal advice *or* were prepared in contemplation of litigation or proceedings (and this includes arbitration claims). Documents produced by the lawyers, or at their request in order to collect or prepare evidence for the arbitration are also privileged.

20.07 It should be noted, however, that legal professional privilege only applies to confidential communications between clients and their qualified lawyers (and this includes in-house counsel) and to documents prepared by or at the request of qualified lawyers. There are a great number of construction industry arbitrations where lawyers are not involved but other consultants are engaged. Communications with such consultants and documents prepared by them will not be covered by legal professional privilege (see *New Victoria Hospital v Ryan* (Court of Appeal) 4 December 1992).

20.08 The long-running litigation against the Bank of England concerning the collapse of BCCI has produced some changes to the law of legal professional privilege (in particular the House of Lords in *Three Rivers District Council and others (Respondents) v Governor and Company of the Bank of England (Appellants)* [2004] UKHL 48). It is important to ensure that where legal advice is given, the 'client' is identified (in terms of a group of persons within an organisation that deal with the specific matter in issue) and that communications are kept between the 'client' and the lawyers. If documents are circulated widely, it may be that any privilege is lost.

20.9 Without prejudice communications are communications between the parties or their advisers, whether or not expressly marked 'without prejudice', which comprise negotiations to settle the dispute or part of the dispute and which are intended to be made on a 'without prejudice basis' (in other words, on the basis that they should not be referred to in the arbitration).

21 Evidence of fact and expert evidence

21.01 One of the main tasks of the tribunal is to establish the facts of the case. The way in which facts are proved will depend on the procedure adopted by the tribunal. As set out below, the Act allows a proactive arbitrator to take a much more 'inquisitorial' approach to the collection of evidence and the issues in dispute as one would expect from a judge in the TCC. However, legal proceedings in the common law tradition (and this includes arbitrations) will generally remain 'adversarial' in nature, with both parties advancing their case and the decision-maker picking the most convincing case, rather than taking the lead from the parties by establishing the facts and the law out of his or her own initiative.

21.02 Subject to any agreement between the parties, section 34(2) of the Act confers wide powers and a discretion to decide how the facts will be proved on the tribunal. For example, the tribunal can decide whether to apply the strict rules of evidence as to the admissibility, relevance or weight of any material (oral, written or other) on any matters of fact or opinion. The tribunal can also decide whether it should take the initiative in ascertaining the facts by making its own enquiries. The tribunal can decide whether and to what extent there should be oral or written evidence or submissions. Under section 37, the tribunal has the power to appoint experts or legal advisers to report to it and to the parties and to appoint assessors to assist it on technical matters.

21.02 In litigation, facts are proved by the evidence of witnesses which is normally given mainly in writing (in the form of a witness statement) and partly through oral examination, usually cross-examination. The witness statement sets out the witness's own story, while cross-examination is conducted by the opposing party's advocate with the aim of making the witness seem less credible and 'picking holes' in the testimony. In arbitration proceedings, the tribunal has the discretion to establish the facts on the basis of documents alone, possibly supplemented by written witness statements or by oral examination of all or some of the witnesses.

21.03 Because the tribunal is not bound by the strict rules of evidence which apply in court it can admit hearsay evidence and decide how much weight should be given to that evidence. It is also becoming increasingly common for arbitral tribunals to take an active part in examing the witnesses that appear before them. For instance, the arbitrator may have his or her own questions following a review of the written witness statement, and these questions may not necessarily coincide with those to be asked by the opposing party's advocate.

21.04 Construction disputes frequently raise important issues which turn on opinion evidence and not just evidence of fact. For example, if the tribunal has to decide whether an architect failed to use reasonable care and skill in designing a building it must first establish as a matter of fact how the building was actually designed. Whether that design was negligent is a matter of opinion. For that reason, most arbitration rules provide for the possibility of expert evidence being given on matters of opinion. Experts, although they appear on behalf of one party and will generally advance a position that assists that party (which party would otherwise not be relying on the expert in question), are meant to be independent and owe a duty to the tribunal rather than the party instructing them. Any architect who acts as expert witness should bear this duty of independence, and impartiality, in mind.

21.05 The collection and service of expert evidence is usually an expensive part of the arbitral process, with each party having its own expert and the tribunal having to assess and weigh the evidence of both experts to decide the dispute. For this reason, the tribunal is given the power to appoint experts to report to it and to the parties (section 37 of the Act). In those circumstances, the parties are given a reasonable opportunity to comment on any information, opinion or advice offered by any such expert.

21.06 Where the tribunal permits the parties to use their own experts, it is usually directed that the two experts meet with a view to narrowing and defining the issues in dispute. The duties of the expert are described below in the section referring to the architect as expert. It is not uncommon for the tribunal to interview both experts jointly at the hearing, to seek to explore the areas of difference that remain following discussions directly between the experts.

22 The arbitration hearing

22.01 A party may be represented in arbitration proceedings by a lawyer or any other person chosen by him.

22.02 The arbitration hearing is an expensive, and final, stage in the arbitration. Work in the period leading up to the hearing will be intensive. In large arbitrations, a practice developed of following the court procedure for the conduct of the hearings. Historically,

this would involve the claimant's representative opening the arbitration by explaining the whole of the case to the arbitrator and then taking the arbitrator through all of the relevant documents and correspondence. The claimant would then call his witnesses of fact and expert witnesses. Each witness would give their evidence in chief orally. The witness would then be cross-examined by the respondent's representative and might then be re-examined by the claimant's representative. The respondent's representative would present his case in a similar manner.

22.03 Today this 'traditional' approach is very rare. While the tribunal has a duty to allow each party a reasonable opportunity of putting his case and dealing with that of his opponent, it is quite consistent with that obligation to adopt procedures which curtail substantially the amount of oral presentation and argument at the hearing. Nowadays, tribunals increasingly require the parties to put in written submissions of law and take steps to reduce the length of the oral hearing. In short, the tribunal will read up on the case in advance and will use the time at the hearing to hear cross-examination of witnesses and experts, and also frequently to question the parties on the basis of what the cases that have been advanced so far.

22.04 Where there are significant factual disputes, it is more than likely that the tribunal will require the oral examination of witnesses, even though the witnesses will have served written witness statements. The sequence in which witnesses are called by

the parties is a matter for them and the tribunal. Most commonly the claimant calls all of its witnesses of fact and expert witnesses and then the respondent calls all of its witnesses. However, sometimes it is the case that the claimant will call all of his witnesses dealing with a particular topic (whether a factual topic or an issue of expert evidence) and the respondent will then call his witnesses dealing with that particular topic. The most appropriate procedure varies from case to case.

22.05 After the arbitrator has heard the evidence, the representatives of the parties will make their closing submissions. Again, it is common for these submissions to be put in writing and in more complex cases the arbitrator may order a short adjournment to give the parties the chance to prepare their submissions in the light of all the evidence which has been given and ask for those submissions to be delivered to him in writing. The arbitrator may then ask for a further short hearing to deal with any questions which he has on the written submissions.

23 The award

23.01 Having heard the evidence and submissions, the tribunal then renders its decision in the form of an award. The parties are also free to agree that the tribunal may make provisional awards, in advance of a final determination of the issues – a power the tribunal does not have in the absence of such an agreement. This additional power is often necessary where the tribunal wishes to make a provisional order for the payment of money or the disposal of property. In construction disputes, the arbitrators may be asked to order a sum due to a contractor on a provisional or interim basis, perhaps pending determination of entitlement or the carrying out of further work that affects the final valuation.

23.02 The parties are also free to agree the form of the final award but if there is no agreement the Act provides that the award should be in writing signed by all the arbitrators and shall contain the tribunal's reasons (unless it is an agreed award or the parties have agreed to dispense with reasons). The award is also required to state the seat (location) of the arbitration and the date when it is made.

23.03 Unless otherwise agreed by the parties, the tribunal may make more than one award at different times on different aspects of the matters to be determined. Typically this is done where the tribunal deals with issues of liability before considering the quantum of the claim. Establishing liability first is sometimes considered a sensible step to take because it allows the parties to reach a commercial agreement as to quantum without the need to hear expert evidence on this (such as the report of a quantity surveyor or other valuation expert).

23.04 The tribunal also has power to award simple or compound interest from such dates and at such rates and on such amounts as it considers just. The ability of the tribunal to award compound interest is wider than the equivalent power of the court.

23.05 The requirement to provide reasons as part of the award is to allow the court to consider any appeal. Accordingly, the arbitrator must state all his findings of fact (although he need not recite all the evidence which leads to the findings) and briefly state his reasoning on the issues of law. However, it should be recalled that the court will never review an arbitrator's findings of fact, and will only consider any potential error of law if the parties have not agreed to exclude the right to appeal on a point of law.

23.06 All awards, whether including reasons or not, should be certain (in the sense of being sufficiently clear and unambiguous), and final (unless clearly intended to be an interim award). If the reference to arbitration calls for an award in money terms, then the award should be in an appropriate form to allow it to be enforced as if it were a judgment of the High Court, i.e. it should specify precisely the sum of money found to be due, and which of the parties is to make the payment.

24 Costs

24.01 The costs of an arbitration will include the arbitrator's fees and expenses, the fees and expenses of any arbitral institution involved and finally the legal or other costs of the parties (including the professional fees of expert witnesses). Generally, the legal costs of the parties represent the largest item. The tribunal will deal with the allocation of costs in its award. In so doing, the tribunal has a wide discretion but there are general rules that are likely to apply. Subject to agreeing otherwise, the general principle is that 'costs should follow the event' (loser pays) – unless it appears to the tribunal that in the circumstances this would not be appropriate in relation to some, or all, of the costs. For example, the tribunal might take account that the claimant declined an offer to settle the claim for more than the amount of the eventual award. Or it may be that the claimant, while the overall winner, lost on a number of issues which took up substantial time at the hearing. As noted above, the tribunal is also likely to consider any relevant conduct by the parties that may have increased costs. For instance, a party that floods the arbitration with paper by disclosing a large amount of irrelevant documents may find that it has to pay a high proportion of the costs of the other party incurred in reviewing those documents.

24.02 While the parties are free to make their own agreement relating to the award of costs, they cannot agree *before* a dispute has arisen that one party is to pay the whole or part of the costs of the arbitration in any event (so irrespective of the outcome of the arbitration). This is intended to prevent the position where, through such an agreement, a party is dissuaded from commencing arbitration proceedings for fear of having to pay the other party's costs come what may. However, the parties may agree in advance that each party is to bear its own costs.

24.03 The parties can agree what costs will be recoverable and what fees will be paid to the arbitrator for his services. If the parties do not agree any of these matters then the provisions of the Act will apply.

24.04 The Act also gives the tribunal the power (again unless otherwise agreed by the parties) to direct that the recoverable costs of the arbitration, or of any part of the arbitral proceedings, shall be limited to a specified amount. This is a potentially important provision since it provides the tribunal with the means to ensure that the parties use the most economic and efficient procedures to bring their dispute to a point of determination.

25 The power of the tribunal in the case of a party's default

25.01 One advantage of litigation over arbitration is that the court is better able to deal with a party in default. This is not to suggest, however, that an arbitration tribunal is powerless to deal with a party's default. The parties have an explicit duty to comply without delay with the orders of the tribunal (see above) and can agree on the powers of the tribunal in case of a party's default. If there is no agreed provision then section 41 of the Act gives the tribunal power to dismiss a claim if there has been inordinate and inexcusable delay on the part of a claimant to pursue his claim (subject to the tribunal being satisfied on certain conditions). The Act also gives the tribunal power to continue the proceedings in the absence of a party in default and may make an award on the basis of the evidence before it. This is to deal with a defendant who fails to comply with the tribunal's directions or to participate in the proceedings. The tribunal's power to make peremptory orders is supplemented by the power of the court to enforce such orders (see later).

26 Arbitration procedures found in construction industry cases

26.01 There are two sets of rules commonly used in construction industry disputes because they are adopted in the standard building and civil engineering contract forms. CIMAR are adopted by the JCT contracts and the ICE Arbitration Procedure (England &Wales), 2006 edition (the 'ICE Procedure') by the ICE contract. Both sets of rules were issued after the Act was enacted and take advantage of its provisions. Both also deal expressly with many of the powers given to arbitrators and/or the courts by the Act. CIMAR actually sets out applicable sections of the Act in its rules.

26.02 Some features of CIMAR which are worth noting are:

1 The provisions relating to the joinder of separate arbitrations
2 The arbitrator is required to consider the form of procedure which is most appropriate for the dispute as soon as he is appointed. The rules offer three options:
   (i) a short hearing procedure;
   (ii) a documents only procedure;
   (iii) a full procedure with a hearing.
3 If there is no joint decision by the parties as to which procedure shall apply then the arbitrator shall direct which procedure is to be followed. The rules give guidance on this. They state that a short hearing is appropriate where the matters in dispute are to be determined principally by the arbitrator inspecting work, materials, machinery, etc. A documents only procedure is appropriate where the issues do not require oral evidence or because the sums in dispute do not warrant the cost of a hearing. Where neither of the previous two procedures is appropriate, the full procedure should be adopted 'subject to such modification as is appropriate to the particular matters in issue'.
4 The provisions relating to the award of costs, which flesh out the circumstances the arbitrator can take into account when making that decision.

26.03 In general, the ICE Procedure allows the arbitrator the flexibility to handle the case in the manner he considers to be appropriate, and is intended to take over some of the perceived advantages of adjudication (mainly the speedy resolution of disputes). The arbitrator may order the parties to define their cases by delivering 'short statements expressing their perception of the disputes or differences'. These statements should have sufficient detail of the issues to allow the arbitrator and the parties to discuss them at a preliminary meeting (rule 6.1). The arbitrator can however decide the form the statements should take (see further rule 8.1). Express provision is made for the arbitrator and the parties to consider whether and to what extent documents should be disclosed. Further powers to order disclosure of documents are set out in rule 8.3.

26.04 The ICE Procedure also includes two optional procedures which may be adopted when the parties so agree (the arbitrator may invite the parties to agree to these procedures but he cannot order them to do so):

1 There is provision for a 'short procedure' (for sums which do not exceed £50 000, or the where the parties agree): according to this procedure each side delivers to the other and to the arbitrator a file containing a statement as to orders or awards sought, reasons relied upon by the parties and copies of any documents relied upon. The other party then has 14 days to respond but counter-claims are not allowed – these require a new, separate reference. Thereafter, each party may comment on the other party's case within a futher 14-day period. The arbitrator will then make his or her award within a further period of 14 days. There is to be no hearing or cross-examination.
2 There is now also an 'expedited procedure' (for sums up to £250 000). Essentially, under this procedure the arbitrator will set a procedural timetable for a period not exceeding 100 days (which the parties by agreement, but not the arbitrator, may extend). This procedure will feature a sequential exchange of statements of case with specified periods (a defence to be served 21 days after the statement of case, followed by a reply within 14 days) and a formal hearing. The arbitrator is given a variety of express powers in relation to this hearing (which he or she may have under the Act in any event) – and may take the initiative as regards factual and legal matters, and questioning of witnesses.

3 There is a 'special procedure for experts': according to this procedure, parties submit a file containing a statement of factual findings sought, a report or statement from an expert and any other document relied upon by the parties. There is then a hearing for experts to express their views and be examined by the arbitrator. The rules provide that no costs of legal representation are allowed if this procedure is followed.

27 The role of the courts in arbitration proceedings

27.01 There is a limit to what can be achieved by a tribunal if a party refuses to comply with the arbitration agreement or with the tribunal's directions or award. Ultimately, resort must be made to the courts to enforce the process. The Act provides the necessary 'legal infrastructure' for arbitration by giving the court powers to support the process not only by enforcing decisions and awards of arbitral tribunals but also by providing a remedy if the arbitral tribunal ignores the fundamental requirements of arbitration. The powers of the court can be divided into the following general categories, as powers to:

1 enforce the arbitration agreement;
2 support of the arbitration process;
3 supervise the arbitration process;
4 decide points of law;
5 consider appeals and applications to set aside the award; and
6 enforce the award.

27.02 The general policy of the Act is that if the parties have agreed that their disputes should be resolved by arbitration then that agreement should be upheld. The objective of the court's powers is to ensure that the arbitration process runs smoothly and fairly. Even if the court intervenes in the arbitration process it is the arbitration tribunal, not the court, which resolves the substantive dispute.

28 Powers to enforce the arbitration agreement – 'staying' of court proceedings in favour of arbitration

28.01 If a party to an arbitration agreement commences proceedings in court in respect of a matter covered by the arbitration agreement then the Act gives the courts the power to hold that party to his agreement to arbitrate by ordering a 'stay' (which means a suspension) of the court proceedings. The effect of the stay will be that if the party who brought the court action still wishes to pursue his claim, it will only be able to do so by arbitration.

28.02 An application to stay court proceedings must be made before the applicant has taken any step in the proceedings to answer the substantive claim. If the applicant does take such a step he or she will waive his right to a stay.

28.03 Subject to that, section 9(4) of the Act provides that 'the court *shall* grant a stay unless satisfied that the arbitration agreement is null and void, inoperative or incapable of being performed' [emphasis added]. The use of mandatory words here means that the court has no discretion not to order a stay, unless the arbitration agreement itself is ineffective.

29 The court's powers exercisable in support of the arbitration process

29.01 A number of powers exercisable by the court have already been mentioned in this chapter, for example, in relation to the appointment of arbitrators. This power also extends to cases where an appointed arbitrator refuses to act, is incapable of acting, or dies; where an arbitration agreement provides for the appointment of an arbitrator by some third party and he refuses to make the appointment or does not make it within a reasonable time; and where two arbitrators are required to appoint a third party (or umpire) and do not appoint him.

29.02 Again as noted above, the court may also extend time limits for commencing arbitration proceedings under section 12 of the Act. This power is relevant where the terms of an arbitration agreement provide that any claim is to be barred unless the claimant takes some step to commence the proceedings within a specified time. It should however be emphasised that the circumstances in which the court will extend time are limited and it would be unwise to assume that an extension will be granted. The applicant should first exhaust any available arbitral process for obtaining an extension of time. The court must then be satisfied that the circumstances are such as were outside the reasonable contemplation of the parties when they agreed the provision in question, and that it would be just to extend the time, or that the conduct of one party makes it unjust to hold the other party to the strict terms of the provision in question.

29.03 The powers of the court in relation to arbitral proceedings are set out in sections 42–45 of the Act. Section 42 deals with the enforcement of peremptory orders of the tribunal, section 43 with securing the attendance of witnesses, section 44 with various powers exercisable in support of the arbitral proceedings and section 45 with determination of preliminary points of law. There are a number of common themes. First, with the exception of section 43, the court's powers are subject to any contrary agreement between the parties. That contrary agreement might be expressed in the arbitration rules which apply to the proceedings. Second, the powers of the court are in support of the arbitral proceedings, so generally the court will not exercise the power unless the applicant has exhausted any available arbitral process or the application is made with the consent of the tribunal.

29.04 The range of powers included in section 44 includes the taking and preservation of evidence, making orders relating to property which is the subject of the proceedings, the sale of any goods the subject of the proceedings and the granting of an interim injunction for the appointment of a receiver. The underlying rationale of the powers exercisable under section 44 is the recognition that a party may need to take prompt action to preserve its rights (for example by applying for an interim injunction) and it may be unable to secure those rights through arbitration for the simple reason that the arbitral tribunal has not been constituted.

29.05 The power of the court to determine a preliminary point of law under section 45 of the Act is to be distinguished from an appeal against the arbitrator's award (see later). Section 45 provides a means for the parties or the tribunal to obtain a ruling from the court on a point of law which substantially affects the rights of one or more of the parties. An application can only be made with the consent of all the parties or with the permission of the tribunal. Even then, the court must be satisfied that the determination of the question is likely to produce substantial savings in costs and that the application was made without delay.

30 Enforcement of arbitration awards

30.01 Arbitration awards may, with leave of the court, be enforced in the same manner as a judgment of the High Court (section 66 of the Act). Obtaining leave is almost always a pure formality unless the respondent can say that there was some severe defect in the arbitration process, such as problems with the arbitration tribunal's jurisdiction.

31 The court's powers to supervise the arbitration process

31.01 Although the underlying principle of the Act is to allow the arbitration process to take its own course, with the minimum of interference from the court, nonetheless the court is concerned to ensure that the arbitration is conducted in accordance with the basic standards of fairness and natural justice. The principal means by which the court exercises this supervisory role are through the power to remove an arbitrator or the power to set aside an award if there is a procedural irregularity.

31.02 Under section 23 of the Act, the court has power to remove an arbitrator on any of the following grounds:

'(a) that circumstances exist that give rise to justifiable doubts as to his impartiality;
(b) that he does not possess the qualifications required by the arbitration agreement;
(c) that he is physically or mentally incapable of conducting the proceedings or there are justifiable doubts as to his capacity to do so;
(d) that he has refused or failed –
(i) properly to conduct the proceedings; or
(ii) to use all reasonable despatch in conducting the proceedings or making an award, and that substantial injustice has been or will be caused to the applicant.'

31.03 The court has also power to set aside or vary an arbitration award where one of the parties applies on the basis that the tribunal lacked substantive jurisdiction (section 67).

31.04 Finally, the court can set aside, vary or remit an award back to the tribunal if there was a 'serious irregularity' affecting the tribunal, the proceedings or the award (section 68). A serious irregularity means an irregularity of a kind specified in the Act, which the court considers has caused or will cause substantial injustice to the applicant:

'(a) failure by the [arbitral] tribunal to comply with section 33 [under which it is obliged to act fairly and impartially and adopt procedures suitable to the circumstances of the particular case] . . .
(b) the tribunal exceeding its powers . . .
(c) failure by the tribunal to conduct the proceedings in accordance with the procedure agreed by the parties;
(d) failure by the tribunal to deal with all the issues that were put to it;
(e) any arbitral or other institution or person vested by the parties with powers in relation to the proceedings or the award exceeding its powers;
(f) uncertainty or ambiguity as to the effect of the award;
(g) the award being obtained by fraud or the award or the way in which it was procured being contrary to public policy;
(h) failure to comply with the requirements as to the form of the award; or
(i) any irregularity in the conduct of the proceedings or in the award which is admitted by the tribunal or by any arbitral or other institution or person vested by the parties with powers in relation to the proceedings or the award.'

31.05 The court's powers under sections 67 and 68 are subject to certain conditions, such as a time limit and the need to exhaust remedies available under the arbitral process. The right to make such a challenge can be lost (see section 73) by, for example, failing to make a timely and effective objection to the exercise of jurisdiction by the tribunal or to the offending conduct or action.

31.06 The issue of a serious irregularity is sometimes raised by the losing party wishing to challenge an arbitration award (especially if any right to appeal the award on a point of law has been excluded). However, section 68 was not intended, and does not in practice operate, as a backdoor through which arbitration awards may be challenged. As the court explained in *Petroships Pte Ltd v Petec Trading and Investment Corporation* [2001] Lloyd's Rep 348, section 68 reflects the internationally accepted view that the courts should be able to correct a serious disregard of due process in any arbitration. However, the provision should only come into play where something extraordinary has happened in the arbitration process, which is far removed from what could reasonably be expected of arbitrators. When looking for a substantial injustice to one of the parties (without which the courts will not interfere), it is not appropriate to ask what the outcome would have been had the matter been litigated rather than arbitrated. The parties, having chosen arbitration, should be held to that choice in all but the truly exceptional cases.

32 Appeals on points of law

32.01 A party's right to apply to set aside an award on the grounds of a serious irregularity cannot be excluded by agreement (although the right can be lost by conduct) but if the tribunal, having conducted the arbitration proceedings properly, reaches the wrong conclusion, it can be very difficult to challenge the award (as noted above). In contrast, the right to appeal to the courts on points of law can be excluded by agreement. Note, however, that neither the arbitration clause in the JCT Standard Form of Building Contract 2005 (Conditions, Section 9.7) nor CIMAR exclude the right to appeal on a point of law. If the right to appeal is not excluded, an appeal can only be made with the leave of the court, or the agreement between all parties. Leave of the court will be granted only if the court is satisfied:

'(a) that the determination of the question will substantially affect the rights of one or more of the parties,
(b) that the question is one which the tribunal was asked to determine,
(c) that, on the basis of the findings of fact in the award –
   (i) the decision of the tribunal on the question is obviously wrong, or
   (ii) the question is one of general public importance and the decision of the tribunal is at least open to serious doubt, and
(d) that, despite the agreement of the parties to resolve the matter by arbitration, it is just and proper in all the circumstances for the court to determine the question.'

(See section 69(3) of the Act.)

32.02 In practice, in a 'one-off' dispute (that is, a dispute which does not relate to a standard provision in a construction agreement), leave to appeal will usually only be granted in respect of a question of law if it is apparent to the judge that the arbitrator's award is obviously wrong. Even then, if the judge considers that it is possible that argument could persuade him that the arbitrator might be right, leave will often not be granted. In cases concerning the meaning of standard terms in contracts, the judge will be likely to take a less strict approach, but leave should not be given even in those cases, unless the judge considers that a strong prima facie case has been made out that the arbitrator was wrong in his construction of the contract. When the events to which the standard clause were applied in the particular arbitration were themselves 'one-off' events, the stricter criteria would, nevertheless, be applied.

32.03 Appeals from arbitration awards will therefore be infrequent. If an appeal is allowed, the court may confirm, vary, set aside, or remit the award for the reconsideration of the arbitrator, together with the court's opinion on the question of law which was the subject of the appeal.

32.04 It should be noted, however, that the JCT Standard Form of Building Contract 2005 (Conditions, Section 9.7) states that the parties agree that the High Court shall have jurisdiction over any appeal on a point of law. It is likely that this clause will be interpreted as an agreement between all the parties to the arbitration, with the effect that permission or leave of the court will not be required (see *Taylor Woodrow Civil Engineering Ltd v Hutchison IDH Development Ltd* (1998) Con LR 1). Since permission is very difficult to obtain, the effect of the provisions of the JCT Standard Form of Building Contract 2005 is to significantly increase the prospect of appealing on a point of law before the court.

33 The architect as arbitrator

33.01 As can be seen from the description of the law of arbitration set out in this chapter, the acceptance of the position of arbitrator is not something to be undertaken lightly. An architect who undertakes arbitrations should have a good working knowledge of the law and practice of arbitrations in addition to the law and practice of the construction industry. Furthermore, acting as an arbitrator can be time-consuming if the arbitration goes to a full hearing. After the hearing, the arbitrator must set aside sufficient time to write the award. This will involve reviewing all of the evidence and the submissions put to him during the proceedings.

33.02 When an arbitrator undertakes his appointment he is entitled to 'such reasonable fees as are appropriate in the circumstances' (section 64(1) of the Act) to be paid by the parties. If nothing is agreed between the arbitrator and the parties when he accepts his appointment then the arbitrator usually assesses what he considers to be a reasonable sum for his services and makes that sum, and the identity of the person who is liable to pay that sum, part of his award. Recovery of his or her fees is usually dealt with by notifying the parties that the arbitration award is available to be collected provided that fees are paid. This is usually a sufficient incentive for the claimant to pay the arbitrator's fees (whether or not the claimant is made liable for them by the award) so that the award may be obtained and the claimant can (if successful) proceed to enforce it.

33.03 However, statistically most arbitrations settle before the final award. In these circumstances the law probably is that the arbitrator is entitled to reasonable remuneration from the parties in respect of the work which has been carried out but that he or she is not entitled to payment (either as 'remuneration' or as 'damages' for lost opportunity) in respect of the fees which the arbitrator would have earned had there been a hearing and final award.

33.04 If there is a dispute between the arbitrator and the parties with regard to the level of remuneration then there are various ways for that to be determined by the court, depending on the circumstances of the case.

33.05 For these reasons, experienced arbitrators do not accept their appointment until the parties have accepted the arbitrator's terms of engagement. These terms usually provide that both parties are jointly and severally liable for the arbitrator's fees. It is common for arbitrators and parties to agree that there should be hourly remuneration rates for preparatory reading and interlocutory hearings and daily rates of remuneration for the hearing of the arbitration itself. It is also common for 'cancellation charges' to be stipulated by arbitrators to protect them from loss of revenue in the event that the arbitration is settled before the award is made. Arbitrators often also require some security on account of likely fees.

33.06 An arbitrator is generally not liable for actions taken in the capacity of arbitrator. Section 29(1) of the Act (which applies notwithstanding any contrary agreement between the parties) provides that an arbitrator is not liable for anything done (or omitted to be done) in the discharge (or purported discharge) of his or her functions as arbitrator unless the act or omission can be shown to have been in bad faith. The arbitrator's position is therefore different from that of judges who, when acting in their judicial capacity, are immune even where they have acted maliciously. The burden of proving bad faith on the part of an arbitrator lies on the person alleging it and would no doubt be a considerable burden to shift. In one case, the court held that bad faith covered malice in the sense of personal spite or desire to injure for improper reasons.

33.07 Section 24(4) of the Act provides that 'Where the court removes an arbitrator, it may make such order as it thinks fit with respect to his entitlement (if any) to fees or expenses, or the repayment of any fees or expenses already paid'. The Act does not deal explicitly with the position where an award has been set aside on the grounds of 'serious irregularity' caused by the arbitrator's failure to conduct the proceedings properly. Logic would suggest that the court would order an arbitrator to refund his fees if the circumstances were sufficiently serious.

33.08 Perhaps the best advice for an architect contemplating accepting an appointment as an arbitrator is to ensure that he is covered by appropriate professional indemnity insurance.

33.09 Architects who act as arbitrators may wish to have their own legal advice, if the dispute raises difficult issues of law. Section 37(1) of the Act provides that unless the parties agree otherwise, the arbitrator may appoint experts/legal advisers to report to him and to the parties and to attend the proceedings. However, the parties must be given a reasonable opportunity to comment on any information, opinion or advice offered.

33.10 It must, however, be the arbitrator, and not the legal adviser, who makes decisions and is seen to make decisions, even on points of law. He or she must not merely adopt the views put forward by the legal adviser without considering the matter himself.

33.11 The fees of the legal assessor are part of the fees of the arbitration and are recoverable by the arbitrator from the parties (see section 37(2) of the Act).

34 The architect as expert witness

34.01 Experienced architects may be requested to provide expert evidence in arbitration proceedings. The function of an expert witness is to state his professional opinion on the relevant issues in the arbitration. The opinion should be stated clearly, first in a written report, which is served prior to the hearing itself, and then orally at the hearing. Usually the expert will meet his opposite number before the hearing to identify common ground and define the issues on which they disagree.

34.02 An architect needs no special training to be an expert, since it is his expertise as an architect which is being called on. However, it is important to understand the nature of the role of the expert in the proceedings, since experts commonly believe that it is their task to advocate their party's case, to the extent of compromising their own opinion. Guidelines for expert witnesses in litigation and arbitration were given by the court in *National Justice Compania Naviera SA v The Prudential Assurance Company Ltd (the Ikarian Reefer)* [1993] 2 Lloyd's Reports 68 (QBD). The court advised that:

1 Expert evidence should be and should be seen to be independently produced by the expert witness, albeit that the expert is giving evidence on behalf of one of the parties and he should co-operate with the party's legal team in identifying the issues which he is to address and on the overall structure for his report.

2 The expert witness should present an objective unbiased opinion regarding matters which fall within his expertise.

3 An expert witness should never assume the role of advocate.

4 Any facts or assumptions upon which the expert witness's opinion is founded must be stated together with any material facts which could detract from his concluded opinion.

5 Any photographs, survey reports, plans and any other document upon which the expert witness has relied in his evidence must be provided to the other parties in the legal proceedings/arbitration at the same time as expert reports are exchanged.

6 If the expert witness does not have sufficient data available to him to form a properly researched conclusion, this fact must be revealed to the court/arbitrator together with an indication that the opinion is no more than provisional.

7 If any of the subject matter of the dispute falls outside the area of the expert witness's expertise, he is under a duty to inform the court/arbitrator in his report. Likewise, he should make it clear if, when under cross-examination, he is asked questions which are not within the area of his expertise.

8 Where the expert witness is unable to swear on oath that his report contains the truth, the whole truth, and nothing but the truth, this qualification must be stated in the report.

9 If an expert witness changes his mind with respect to a material issue of his evidence after reports have been exchanged, this change of view should immediately be communicated through the parties' representatives to the other side, and where appropriate to the court/arbitrator.

34.03 The Civil Procedure Rules governing court proceedings state that:

'(a) It is the duty of an expert to help the court on the matters within his expertise.

(b) This duty overrides any obligation to the person from whom he has received instructions or by whom he is paid.'

(See rule 35.3.)

34.04 The Civil Procedure Rules also require an expert to state the substance of all material instructions on the basis of which his report was written. This is a major change as previously communications between a party's lawyer and his expert were legally privileged. It is likely that arbitrators may follow the lead given by the courts by making it clear to experts appointed by the parties that they have a duty to the tribunal. They could also require the expert to summarise his instructions in his report.

25

Adjudication

DAVID FRIEDMAN QC

1 What is adjudication?

1.01 Adjudication is a procedure for obtaining a speedy and impartial decision on a construction dispute. The decision is not final but it is enforceable and binds the parties unless and until the dispute is finally resolved by litigation, arbitration or agreement.

1.02 Subject to limited exceptions, construction contracts, as defined by the Housing Grants, Construction and Regeneration Act 1996 (HGCRA), must give the parties to the contract the right to refer disputes to adjudication and must contain terms which HGCRA specifies. This right cannot be excluded by agreement and if a construction contract does not contain the required provisions then the adjudication provisions contained in the Scheme for Construction Contracts ('the Scheme') will apply (SI 1998 No. 649). If a construction contract does contain the required provisions it may also contain other provisions regulating the adjudication, provided those other provisions are not inconsistent with the provisions required by HGCRA.

1.03 Parties to contracts which are not covered by HGCRA may agree that their disputes shall be resolved by adjudication. In that event, subject to the precise terms agreed, the procedure will be the same as or similar to the procedure under HGCRA.

1.04 The three most important features of adjudication are (i) speed; (ii) the provisional nature of the decision; and (iii) the enforceability of the decision.

1.05 Speed The construction contract must provide a timetable designed to secure the appointment of an adjudicator within 7 days of a party giving notice of his intention to refer a dispute to adjudication. It must require the adjudicator to reach a decision within 28 days of referral. This period can be extended in only two situations: (i) the adjudicator can extend it by up to 14 days with the consent of the party who referred the dispute; (ii) after the reference, the parties can agree a longer period.

1.06 The provisional nature of the decision The decision may be overturned by a later decision of an arbitrator or the court. Thus the decisional is provisional.

1.07 Enforceability The decision is enforceable notwithstanding the fact that it is provisional. It is also likely to be enforceable notwithstanding the fact that it contains errors of fact or law and notwithstanding procedural irregularities.

1.08 Speed and the possibility of enforcement despite error have resulted in adjudication being referred to as a 'quick and dirty' procedure. As the Court of Appeal has said, the need to have the 'right' answer has been subordinated to the need to have an answer quickly: *Carillion Construction Ltd v Devonport* [2006]

BLR 15. Adjudication is nevertheless a popular procedure in the construction industry and parties often accept the adjudicator's decision and do not seek to challenge it by subsequent litigation or arbitration.

1.09 Adjudication is not the same as arbitration. In particular, arbitration is regulated by the Arbitration Act 1996; adjudication is not.

1.10 Adjudication is not the same as expert determination. In particular, the adjudicator is not, or is not necessarily, an expert; the procedure is different; and an expert's determination, unlike an adjudicator's decision, is final.

1.11 The Local Democracy, Economic Development and Construction Act 2009 (the Construction Act), which received its royal assent in November 2009, will modify HGCRA when it is brought into force. That is not expected to be for some months, and construction contracts entered into before it comes into force will not be affected by its amendments.

2 What is a construction contract?

2.01 Sections 104 and 105 of HGCRA make it impossible to give an answer to this question which is both short and accurate. Further information about these sections is given below but in broad terms: (i) a contract concerned with works of construction is likely to be a construction contract; and (ii) many contracts with professionals, including architects, are also construction contracts.

2.02 By virtue of section 104 of HGCRA a 'construction contract' is an agreement (a) for the carrying out of construction operations, (b) arranging for the carrying out of construction operations by others and (c) providing one's own or another's labour for the carrying out of construction operations. In addition, agreements relating to construction operations for architectural, design or surveying work and agreements for the provision of advice on building, engineering, interior or exterior decoration or the laying out of landscape are also construction contracts. Thus, contracts with construction professionals are construction contracts provided they relate to construction operations. Contracts of employment are not construction contracts.

2.03 Section 105(1) of HGCRA gives a list of 'construction operations'. Broadly speaking, the list includes all operations which an architect or a layman would consider to be construction operations. However, section 105(2) contains a long and complicated list of operations which are *not* to be considered as 'construction operations'. For the most part they are operations which are unlikely to concern architects, for example: (a) drilling for or extracting oil or natural gas; and (b) extracting minerals. However, architects should note that the following are *not* construction operations: (i) manufacturing or delivering to site various types of equipment and materials under a contract which does not provide for their installation; and (ii) various operations connected with sculptures, murals and other artistic works.

2.04 Architects concerned with the question whether a particular contract is or is not a construction contract will have to consider the detail in sections 104 and 105 before providing an answer.

3 Excluded construction contracts

3.01 The adjudication provisions in HGCRA do not currently apply to three categories of construction contracts: (i) construction contracts with residential occupiers; (ii) construction contracts which are not in writing; and (iii) contracts identified in the Construction Contracts (England and Wales) Exclusion Order 1998 (SI 1998 No. 648). When the Construction Act comes into force the HGCRA will apply to construction contracts which are not in writing and in addition to the power to exclude categories of contract there will be power to disapply particular parts of HGCRA to contracts which are not otherwise excluded from its operation.

3.02 Construction contracts with residential occupiers A construction contract with a residential occupier is a contract which principally relates to operations on a dwelling which one of the parties to the contract occupies, or intends to occupy, as his residence.

3.03 Construction contracts not in writing Section 107 of HGCRA currently specifies what amounts to an agreement in writing. Parts of section 107 are unsurprising. A written agreement need not be signed in order to amount to an agreement in writing. An agreement made by an exchange of written communications is in writing. An agreement is in writing if it is evidenced in writing (i.e. recorded by one of the parties or a third party with the authority of the parties). An agreement not in writing made by reference to terms which are in writing is an agreement in writing. Perhaps surprisingly, section 107(5) also provides, in effect, that an agreement which is not in writing shall be treated as being in writing if, in an adjudication, arbitration or legal proceedings, the existence of the agreement is alleged in written submissions by one party and the allegation is not denied by the other party. There has been debate about whether HGCRA applied to a written agreement which had been varied orally. It seems unlikely that it did: see *Treasure & Sons Ltd v Dawes* [2008] BLR 24. There may nevertheless have been a contractual obligation to adjudicate: see Section 5 below.

3.04 After the Construction Act comes into force HGCRA will apply to contracts which are not in writing but if the contract does not contain a number of specified written terms (see paragraph 4.01 below) the Scheme will apply.

3.05 The Exclusion Order At present a number of different contracts are excluded, for instance some contracts with the Highways Agency and with NHS Trusts; some contracts entered into under the private finance initiative; and finance and development agreements as defined. The position may change after the Construction Act comes into force: see paragraph 3.01 above. Architects concerned with the question whether a particular contract is or is not excluded, wholly or in part, will have to consider the details of any applicable Order.

3.06 HGCRA applies only to construction operations in England, Wales, Scotland or Northern Ireland and to contracts which were not made before 1 May 1998.

4 The terms required by HGCRA

4.01 To satisfy the requirements of section 108 of HGCRA a construction contract must: (i) enable a party to give notice at any time of his intention to refer a dispute to adjudication; (ii) provide a timetable with the object of securing the appointment of an adjudicator and the referral of the dispute to him within 7 days of such notice; (iii) require the adjudicator to reach a decision within 28 days or such longer period as is agreed by the parties after the reference; (iv) allow the adjudicator to extend the 28-day period by up to 14 days with the consent of the referring party; (v) impose a duty on the adjudicator to act impartially; (vi) enable the adjudicator to take the initiative in ascertaining the facts and the law; (vii) provide that the adjudicator's decision is binding until the dispute is finally determined by legal proceedings, arbitration or agreement; and (viii) provide that the adjudicator and his employees or agents shall not be liable for acts or omissions in the discharge or purported discharge of the adjudicator's functions unless the act or omission is in bad faith. After the Construction Act comes into force there must be written contractual terms fulfilling all the requirements mentioned and, in addition, there must be a written contractual term permitting the adjudicator to correct clerical or typographical errors in his decision. If the requirements of section 108 are not fulfilled the Scheme applies.

4.02 Contractual terms dealing with adjudication may be set out in the contract itself or may be incorporated into it by reference. Many organisations concerned with the construction industry have standard terms which regulate adjudications and which can be incorporated by reference. If there are contract terms which fully satisfy the requirements of section 108 and which are not in any respect inconsistent with it they will govern the adjudication. If the contract does not fully satisfy the requirements of section 108 or contains terms which are in any respect inconsistent with it the Scheme applies and replaces the contract terms in their entirety. All of the contract terms are void, not simply the term which contains the inconsistency: *Aveat Heating Ltd v Jerram Falkus Construction Ltd* [2007] EWHC 131 (TCC).

4.03 The fact that terms are in a standard form is no guarantee that they do satisfy the requirements of section 108. For instance, GC/Works adjudication provisions used to provide that the adjudicator's decision would be valid notwithstanding the fact that it was issued late. That was inconsistent with section 108. As a result, the GC/Works adjudication provisions failed in their entirety and adjudication was regulated by the Scheme: *Aveat Heating Ltd v Jerram Falkus Construction Ltd* [2007] EWHC 131 (TCC).

4.04 The risk of inconsistency with section 108 has resulted in some standard forms and some organisations concerned with adjudication using the Scheme provisions and not a bespoke set of rules; see, for instance, the JCT 2005 contracts and the TECBAR adjudication rules.

5 Contractual adjudications

5.01 Most standard form contracts include or incorporate terms providing for adjudication. Bespoke contracts may also do so. It follows that there may be a contractual obligation to adjudicate notwithstanding the fact that HGCRA does not apply, for instance because the contract was with a residential occupier or was not in writing: see *Treasure & Sons Ltd v Dawes* [2008] BLR 24.

6 Notice of adjudication

6.01 A construction contract must enable a party to give notice 'at any time' of his intention to refer a dispute to adjudication: section 108(2) of HGCRA. Such a notice is known as a 'notice of adjudication'. It must identify the dispute and, by doing so, defines it for the purpose of the adjudication. It thus establishes the limits of the adjudicator's jurisdiction and must be carefully drafted.

6.02 The notice can be given at any time. It can be given while the works are being carried out and adjudication can therefore be a useful tool to resolve disputes which would otherwise sour the working relationship of the parties or indeed bring the contract to a premature end. The notice can also be given after the works have been completed and even while litigation or arbitration is proceeding.

6.03 The possibility of 'ambush' should be noted. A claimant may spend considerable time preparing a case for adjudication. When he is fully prepared he serves the notice of adjudication. The tight timetable imposed by HGCRA then operates and limits the time available for the defendant to prepare an answer to the claim.

7 Is there a dispute?

7.01 There must be a dispute before a notice of adjudication can be validly given. A layman might think that it would be obvious whether or not there was a dispute but there have been a number of cases on this point and a number of different tests have been suggested. A useful, short answer to the question whether there is a dispute was given by HHJ Toulmin QC in *CIB v Birse* [2005] 1 WLR 2252: the test is whether, taking a common-sense approach, a dispute has crystallised. Whether a dispute has crystallised depends on the facts. A dispute may have crystallised although negotiations are still continuing. It may have crystallised simply because the defendant has failed to admit the claim: see *Halki Shipping Corp v Sopex Oils* [1998] 2 All ER 23 (an arbitration case). *Amec Civil Engineering v Secretary of State for Transport* [2005] 1 WLR 2339 contains a useful analysis of relevant principles.

7.02 There may be a dispute notwithstanding the fact that there is no valid defence, with the result that the claim is, in one sense, indisputable. On the other hand, there will not be a dispute if the claim has already been decided by an adjudicator (or arbitrator or court) and is for that reason indisputable.

8 Multiple disputes

8.01 Section 108(2) of HGCRA concerns the reference of 'a dispute' to adjudication and it has been held that in consequence a referring party can refer only a single dispute: *Fastrack Contractors Ltd v Morrison Construction Ltd* [2000] BLR 168. It is clear that this is the case when the Scheme applies because the Scheme contains a provision which would be unnecessary if there were a right to refer multiple disputes; i.e. the provision in paragraph 8(1) of the Scheme which provides that with the consent of the parties the adjudicator may adjudicate at one time on more than one dispute.

8.02 It follows that, absent consent, an adjudicator has no jurisdiction to deal with multiple disputes. Want of jurisdiction on this basis is not infrequently raised as a defence in enforcement proceedings.

8.03 In practice the inability to refer multiple disputes should not cause a problem. When the Scheme applies the adjudicator can deal with multiple disputes with consent. Further, there is nothing to stop a party giving a separate notice of adjudication in respect of separate disputes. Finally, and most important, a single dispute can properly raise a number of issues. For instance, in *David MaLean Housing Ltd v Swansea Housing Association Ltd* [2002] BLR 125 the dispute concerned what payment should be made as a result of a particular application for payment. That depended on a number of issues including the valuation of measured work, the valuation of variations, the valuation of provisional sums and direct loss and expense. 'The courts have adopted a robust approach to this point and have utilised what has been called a "benevolent interpretation of the notice" to conclude that whilst there may have been a number of issues in the adjudication in question, there was only one underlying dispute': *Michael John Construction Ltd v Golledge* [2006] EWHC 71 (TCC).

9 Does the dispute arise 'under' the contract?

9.01 The right provided by HGCRA is a right to refer disputes 'arising under the contract': section 108(1). Similar provisions in arbitration agreements are now given a wide meaning (see the decision of the House of Lords in *Premium Nafta Products Ltd v Fil Shipping Co. Ltd* [2007] UKHL 40) but it remains to be seen how section 108(1) will be interpreted. Some disputes which concern the contract may not arise under it; e.g. a dispute about whether the contract should be rectified.

10 Appointment of an adjudicator

10.01 Section 108(2) of HGCRA merely provides that the contract shall provide a timetable with the object of securing the appointment of an adjudicator and the referral of the dispute to him within 7 days of the notice of adjudication. The means of securing an appointment thus depend on the particular terms of the contract and, in default of any or sufficient terms, on the provision of the Scheme.

10.02 The contract may specify who is to be the adjudicator or it may identify a nominating body. If it does neither and the Scheme applies the referring party may ask any 'adjudicator nominating body' (i.e. any organisation which holds itself out as a body which will select an adjudicator) to make the appointment. Many organisations concerned with construction hold themselves out as adjudicator nominating bodies.

10.03 In practice the referring party will either have to request an adjudicator named in the contract to act or request a nominating body to make an appointment. The request should be accompanied by the notice of adjudication and should be made on the same day as the notice of adjudication.

10.04 The adjudicator has to act impartially. Thus, a person who is biased cannot be appointed but HGCRA does not require that the adjudicator be independent of the parties. In theory, an architect, engineer or quantity surveyor concerned with administration of the contract could be appointed. Such an appointment is undesirable and in practice is most unlikely to be made.

10.05 The person suggested as adjudicator should disclose any connection he has or has had with the parties to the dispute: see, for example, paragraph 4 of the Scheme. This enables the parties to object to the appointment and may result in the referring party having to restart the appointment process.

10.06 There is no appointment until the person suggested as adjudicator, whether identified in the contract or nominated by a nominating body, has agreed to act. The person first suggested may refuse or be unwilling to act. If that occurs the appointment process must be restarted. In practice the person suggested as adjudicator is unlikely to agree to act unless the referring party expressly agrees to pay his fees and expenses. He may require other terms to be agreed; e.g. that both parties, not just the referring party, expressly accept liability for his fees and expenses and/or terms concerning the conduct of the adjudication.

11 The referral notice

11.01 The timetable required by section 108(2) of HGCRA must have as one of its objects the referral of the dispute to the adjudicator within 7 days of the notice of adjudication. This requirement will be fleshed out by the terms of the contract or, in default of any or sufficient terms, by the Scheme.

11.02 In practice referral is by means of a document known as the 'referral notice'. The referral notice required by the Scheme must be accompanied by copies of, or relevant extracts from, the construction contract and such other documents as the referring party intends to rely upon. It must be served upon every other party to the dispute. It must be served within 7 days of the notice of adjudication.

11.03 The referral notice cannot go beyond the confines of the dispute identified in the notice of adjudication. It can and in practice it should give full details of the way the referring party puts its case in respect of that dispute. It must be carefully drafted. It may well be that the referring party will not be allowed to put in later documents to supplement the referral notice: see Section 12 which deals with procedure.

12 Procedure after the referral notice

12.01 By virtue of section 108(1) of HGCRA, the construction contract must enable the adjudicator to take the initiative in ascertaining the facts and law but, save for its requirements as to the time within which the adjudicator's decision has to be reached, it does not impose any further procedural requirements. However, the adjudicator's ability to take the initiative necessarily allows him to give directions for the conduct of the adjudication. His ability to give directions may also be expressed in the contract or in a set of procedural rules which the contract incorporates. It is expressed in regulation 13 of the Scheme.

12.02 The parties are entitled to make representations to the adjudicator about what directions should be given. Such representations will be in writing unless the adjudicator requires them to be made orally at an initial meeting to decide procedural matters.

12.03 In practice the adjudicator will usually give directions for the service of a written response to the referral notice. Because of the tight time constraints the response is likely to be required within a very short period. The next section deals further with the response.

12.04 The adjudicator's directions may, but will not necessarily, allow the submission of a reply by the referring party and/or the submission of other documents or arguments. The requirements of natural justice must be satisfied but, subject to that, the adjudicator has a full discretion as to how the dispute will be handled.

12.05 The adjudicator will have to decide whether there should be an oral hearing; if so, its date and length; and whether directions, and if so what directions, about evidence, including expert evidence, and legal submissions should be given. He may give directions about many other matters; e.g. about a view and about tests which he requires to be carried out.

13 The response to the referral notice

13.01 The response is the defendant's answer to the claim raised. It should answer the claim as fully as is reasonably possible. It too must be carefully drafted. Unless the adjudicator's directions require documents to be dealt with in some other way, all documents on which the defendant relies, in addition to those served with the referral notice, should be served with the response.

13.02 There are difficult legal distinctions between counterclaims (or cross-claims), set-offs and matters which abate (i.e. reduce) a claim. The distinctions can give rise to problems but a defendant's response in an adjudication should put forward all matters upon which the defendant relies to show that he is not obliged to pay what is claimed, whether in full or at all. In this context due account must be taken of the provisions in sections 109 to 113 of HGCRA, in particular the need for an effective withholding notice before a payment under a construction contract can be withheld: see section 111.

13.03 There may be jurisdictional challenges to the claim; for instance that HGCRA does not apply to the contract in question, that there is no dispute within the meaning of HGCRA or that for some reason the adjudicator has not been validly appointed. The party wishing to raise the challenge ('the challenger') has, in theory, a number of options.

13.04 The challenger can ignore the adjudication and raise the challenge in subsequent enforcement proceedings. This is not advisable. The challenge may fail and the challenger will have lost the ability to put forward a defence on the merits of the claim.

13.05 The challenger can seek a declaration from the court that the adjudicator has no jurisdiction. This may be appropriate in some cases but unless and until the declaration is granted the adjudication is likely to proceed and a defence on the merits can only be raised if the challenger participates in the adjudication. If he does participate in it he will be incurring costs both in the adjudication and in the court proceedings.

13.06 The challenger can ask the adjudicator to rule on the challenge and agree to be bound by his decision. That is not advisable. The adjudicator may not be a lawyer and even if he is will not necessarily come to the correct conclusion about the challenge.

13.07 The challenger can participate in the adjudication without raising the challenge. That is not advisable. There is a substantial risk that the challenger will be held to have waived the right to raise the challenge later.

13.08 The best course is for the challenger to raise the challenge, in addition to any defence on the merits, in the response. This may result in the adjudicator, if he considers a challenge well founded, declining to act further but it is important for the challenger to make it clear, preferably in the response itself, that he will maintain the challenge even if the adjudicator decides that it is not well founded and continues to act. This preserves the challenger's right to resist later enforcement proceedings on the ground that the adjudicator lacked jurisdiction.

14 Confidentiality

14.01 Adjudication, unlike arbitration, is not confidential although regulation 18 of the Scheme enables each party to require that information or documents which he provides shall be treated as confidential. If the Scheme does not apply the contract's adjudication terms may impose a more extensive confidentiality obligation.

14.02 Information or documents which are to be treated as confidential can nevertheless be considered in any court proceedings concerning the adjudication, for instance enforcement proceedings.

15 Resignation, revocation and abandonment

15.01 If the adjudicator cannot reach a fair decision within the time available to him under HGCRA he should ask the parties to agree to extend it. If they refuse he should resign: *Balfour Beatty v Lambeth BC* [2002] BLR 288. Continuing in such circumstances would be a breach of the rules of natural justice.

15.02 Whether an adjudicator is entitled or obliged to resign in other circumstances depends on the contractual terms which govern the adjudication. If the Scheme applies an adjudicator (a) is entitled to resign at any time provided he gives written notice to the parties (Scheme regulation 9(1)) and (b) is obliged to resign if the dispute referred to him is the same or substantially the same as a dispute previously referred to and decided by an adjudicator (Scheme regulation 9(2)).

15.03 When the Scheme applies the parties may at any time agree to revoke the appointment of the adjudicator. Further, it appears that the referring party is at any time entitled unilaterally to withdraw any claim in the adjudication or to discontinue the adjudication: *Midland Expressway Ltd v Carillion Construction Ltd* [2006] BLR 325.

15.04 The adjudicator's entitlement to fees and costs in the event of resignation, revocation or abandonment depends on the contractual terms governing the adjudication, including any additional terms agreed when the adjudicator was appointed.

15.05 In most circumstances there will be nothing to prevent a fresh adjudication being commenced after a resignation, revocation or abandonment.

16 The decision

16.01 HGCRA does not specify whether the decision should be in writing or whether reasons for it should be given but most contracts will include or incorporate rules dealing with these matters. The Scheme, for example, requires a written decision and entitles the parties to ask for reasons to be provided. In practice the adjudicator should always be asked to give reasons.

16.02 The decision must be made within 28 days of the referral notice; within 42 days if the referring party has agreed to an extension of up to 14 days requested by the adjudicator; or within any longer period which the parties have agreed: HGCRA section 108(2)(c) and (d). If the adjudicator fails to reach a decision within the relevant period the decision is probably a nullity: *Ritchie Brothers (PWC) Ltd v David Philip (Commercials) Ltd* [2005] SLT 341; *Cubitt Building Interiors Ltd v Fleetglade Ltd* [2006] EWHC 3413 (TCC). However, a decision reached within the relevant period may be valid even if it is not communicated to the parties until afterwards; but only if it is sent to the parties forthwith: *Cubitt Building Interiors Ltd v Fleetglade Ltd*, above.

16.03 The adjudicator is not entitled to exercise a lien and delay delivery of his decision pending payment of his fees: *Cubitt Building Interiors Ltd v Fleetglade Ltd*, above.

16.04 Currently, if the contract's adjudication provisions do not deal with the point expressly there will normally be an implied term which allows the adjudicator, of his own motion or at the invitation of one of the parties, to correct mistakes arising from accidental slips or omissions, provided he does so within a reasonable time of making his decision: *Bloor Construction (UK) Ltd v Bowmer* [2000] BLR 764. After the Construction Act comes into force such a term will be incorporated by the Scheme unless the contract itself contains a written provision allowing correction.

17 Fees and costs

17.01 Currently HGCRA does not deal with fees or costs. It follows that the adjudicator's ability to deal with these matters will depend on the terms of or incorporated in the contract including, if it applies, the terms of the Scheme. That will remain the case after the Construction Act comes into force but the Construction Act does deal with costs. It provides that a contractual provision relating to the costs of an adjudication will have no effect unless (a) it is in writing, is contained in the construction contract and empowers the adjudicator to allocate his fees and expenses between the parties or (b) it is made in writing after the giving of notice of intention to refer the dispute to adjudication.

17.02 In practice an adjudicator will always ensure that satisfactory terms with regard to his own fees and costs are in place before he accepts the appointment. If the contract does not cover this, as a minimum he will require the referring party to accept liability for his fees before agreeing to accept the appointment. In fact the contract may make the parties jointly and severally liable for his fees and/or may enable the adjudicator to apportion liability for them between the parties.

17.03 The adjudicator has no power to make any order as to the parties' respective costs of the adjudication unless the contract's adjudication terms include such a power.

18 Enforcement

18.01 If the losing party does not voluntarily honour the decision the successful party will need to enforce it. Proceedings in the Technology and Construction Court ('TCC') are the best and speediest method of enforcement. A claim form and an application for summary judgment have to be issued. The procedure in, and requirements of, Section 9 of the Technology and Construction Court Guide should be followed. They are designed to produce a judgment within 31 days of the issue of proceedings. The Pre-Action Protocol for Construction and Engineering Disputes does not apply to such enforcement proceedings and thus does not delay matters.

18.02 A winding-up petition is an alternative but, it is thought, a less satisfactory method of enforcement.

18.03 Attempts to prevent enforcement have been a growth industry since HGCRA came into force but '[o]ver the years, a sense of impatience can be felt, particularly in the Court of Appeal, with regard to attempts to prevent enforcement of adjudicators' decisions': per Akenhead J in *Cantillon Ltd v Urvasco Ltd* [2008] EWHC 282 (TCC). 'It should only be in rare circumstances that the courts will interfere with the decision of an adjudicator': per Chadwick L.J. in *Carillion Construction Ltd v Devonport Royal Dockyard Ltd* [2006] BLR 15.

18.04 Enforcement can be resisted on the ground that the adjudicator had no jurisdiction or exceeded his jurisdiction and on the ground that there was a breach of the rules of natural justice, both dealt with further below. There have been suggestions that it might be possible to challenge the validity of a decision on what are known as *Wednesbury* grounds, i.e. on the basis that the decision is so unreasonable that no reasonable adjudicator could have made it. This suggestion has not yet been fully considered by the courts but such authorities as there are suggest that it is not well founded: *London and Amsterdam Properties Ltd v Waterman Partnership Ltd* [2004] BLR 179 and *Carillion Construction Ltd v Devonport Royal Dockyard* [2005] BLR 310.

19 Ineffective defences to enforcement proceedings in the TCC

19.01 Enforcement cannot be resisted on the ground that the adjudicator (i) came to the wrong decision on the facts or made factual errors in his decision; (ii) made an error of law; or (iii) made a procedural error (*Bouygues (UK) Ltd v Dahl-Jensen (UK) Ltd* [2000] BLR 522) unless (see the next two sections) as a result the decision was outside the adjudicator's jurisdiction or was made in breach of the rules of natural justice. Mistakes by the adjudicator are unlikely to have this result.

19.02 It will not normally be possible to raise a counterclaim, cross-claim or set-off as a defence in enforcement proceedings but it may be possible to set-off an entitlement to liquidated damages if that entitlement follows logically from the adjudicator's decision or if the adjudicator's decision has not decided, either expressly or by implication, that there is such an entitlement: *Balfour Beatty Construction v Serco* [2004] EWHC 3336 (TCC).

19.03 A stay of execution is unlikely to be granted merely because the successful party is in financial difficulties and may be unable to repay money if the adjudicator's decision is reversed. It is likely to be granted if the successful party is or should be in liquidation.

20 Jurisdictional defences to enforcement proceedings

20.01 Jurisdiction depends first on whether the adjudication is statutory, under the HGCRA, or contractual; i.e. arising from contractual terms which enable an adjudication which is outside the ambit of the HGCRA. If it is statutory, the adjudicator will have jurisdiction only if there is a construction contract which (i) is within the definition in HGCRA; (ii) (until the Construction Act comes into force) is in writing; and (iii) is not excluded by HGCRA or any exclusion Order. Further, the adjudicator will have jurisdiction only if he has been validly appointed and if there is a dispute which arises under the contract. If the adjudication is contractual, jurisdictional limits will depend on the contract, not on the provisions of HGCRA. For instance, the contract may enable an adjudication involving a residential occupier or a contract which is not in writing within the meaning of the HGCRA.

20.02 The adjudication may also be outside the adjudicator's jurisdiction because (a) he did not decide it in time; (b) more than one dispute was referred to him; (c) the same dispute had been the subject of an earlier adjudication decision; (d) one or more of the parties to the adjudication was not in fact a contracting party; or (e) he decided a dispute which was not the dispute set out in the notice of adjudication.

20.03 It is possible that an error by the adjudicator will result in a decision outside his jurisdiction. That is not the case simply because the error results in a decision which gives an incorrect answer to the question which the adjudicator has to decide. It is the case if the error results in the adjudicator answering the wrong question: *Bouygues (UK) Ltd v Dahl-Jensen (UK) Ltd* [2000] BLR 522. In practice it may be difficult to decide whether the adjudicator has answered the right question, albeit incorrectly, or has answered the wrong question.

21 Natural justice defences to enforcement proceedings

21.01 In this context the relevant rules of natural justice are that (i) the tribunal should be unbiased; and (ii) a party should know the case it has to answer and have a fair opportunity to answer it. In adjudication there will also be a contractual duty to act impartially. Section 108(2) of HGCRA requires such a duty to be imposed on the adjudicator.

21.02 In theory, bias can be established in two ways: either (i) by proving that the adjudicator was actually biased; or (ii) by proving that the circumstances would lead a fair minded and informed observer to conclude that there was a real possibility that the adjudicator was biased: *Glencot Development and Design Co Ltd v Ben Barrett & Son (Contractors) Limited* [2001] BLR 207. Proof of either will rarely be possible but, for example, in *Glencot* the adjudicator was present during negotiations between the parties, acted as a mediator and had private communications with them. There was thus an arguable case of bias.

21.03 Complaints by the losing party to the effect that the adjudicator's decision is based on a point which he did not have a fair opportunity to answer or deal with are common. Such complaints arise more frequently in adjudication than in arbitrations because HGCRA subordinates the need to have the 'right' answer to the need to have an answer quickly: *Carillion Construction Ltd v Devonport* [2006] BLR 15. For that reason a breach of this rule of natural justice will only invalidate a decision if the adjudicator goes off 'on a frolic of his own' or the breach concerns a decisive or very important point: *Cantillon Ltd v Urvasco Ltd* [2008] EWHC 282 (TCC).

22 Severance

22.01 If lack of jurisdiction or breach of the rules of natural justice invalidate part but not all of the adjudicator's decision it is possible that the bad can be severed from the good and the good enforced: *Cantillon Ltd v Urvasco Ltd* [2008] EWHC 282 (TCC).

23 Getting a final answer

23.01 A party dissatisfied with the adjudicator's decision can commence legal proceedings or, if the contract contains an arbitration clause, an arbitration to obtain a final decision on the dispute. In some case the prospect of further proceedings leads to a settlement which modifies the decision. There is, however, no obligation on either party to take matters further and in practice the adjudicator's decision is often accepted and thus becomes the final decision on the dispute.

26

Mediation

CHRISTOPHER MIERS

'Mediation is not in law compulsory ... but alternative dispute resolution is at the heart of today's civil justice system . . .'
(Lightman J in his judgment in *Hurst v Leeming* [2002] EWHC 1051 (Ch))

1 Background

1.01 While mediation is said to have been founded in China and the Far East, modern mediation has its roots in the United States of America. Mediation in the US developed from the early twentieth century, and by the 1970s its potential for reducing court case loads was well recognised. In the UK, the use of mediation in the resolution of family disputes was developed from the late 1970s and early 1980s. By the early 1990s, court-annexed family mediations were well established (*Mediation: Principles, process, practice*, by L. Boulle and M. Nesic).

1.02 Prior to the late 1990s, proposing mediation was frequently mistaken for a sign of weakness in a party's case, and the opportunity to mediate was therefore overlooked. Following the Civil Justice Reforms initiated by Lord Woolf in England and Wales, which came into force in 1998, parties in dispute are now far more willing to mediate, including within the construction industry. In most construction disputes a genuine attempt to settle a dispute by mediation is now accepted as a sensible and necessary step, and is invariably encouraged by the UK courts. It is also the subject of an EU directive to encourage the use of mediation as a cost-effective and quicker alternative to civil litigation, for cross-border commercial disputes.

1.03 The increase in popularity of mediation has been matched by an increase in the number of trained mediators, and in the number of independent bodies who train and accredit mediators.

2 The principles

2.01 Mediation in the UK construction industry is a process of structured negotiation aided by a neutral third-party mediator. A mediator does not decide the dispute. Unlike in litigation, arbitration or adjudication, the resolution is a matter for the parties' own agreement.

2.02 The process is voluntary and consensual, although the mediation process may be incorporated into the dispute resolution procedures in a contract. A mediation can be undertaken at any time, including during the course of another dispute resolution process, such as litigation or arbitration, and where the dispute involves more than two parties. The parties enter into the mediation accepting that, however strong they believe their position to be in respect of the matters in dispute, they will benefit from being able to reach an agreed settlement on acceptable terms, without prolongation of the dispute.

2.03 There are two main forms of mediation: facilitative and evaluative. In facilitative mediation, the mediator assists the parties to reach agreement through a structured process without providing his own opinion on the merits of any party's case. In evaluative mediation, by contrast, the mediator may express a view on the merits of an element of the dispute. In each case the objective is to reach a binding agreement which settles either all or some of the matters in dispute. Most mediations in the UK are facilitative, and frequently the terms of the mediation agreement prevent the mediator from providing any opinion on the merits of the issues in dispute unless otherwise agreed beforehand by the parties.

3 Typical mediation process in construction disputes

Reaching agreement to mediate

3.01 The first step in the mediation process is reaching agreement between the disputing parties to attempt to settle the dispute by mediation. This in itself can take time and require persuasive negotiation, in particular where there are several parties to the dispute. The parties frequently have different views on the merits of mediation, and also on the optimum stage of the dispute for conducting a mediation.

3.02 Mediation is commonly included for in standard forms of contract, such as in the RIBA Standard Conditions of Appointment for an Architect S-Con-07, and in the JCT suite of contracts, as an optional first stage in attempting to resolve a dispute. JCT also publishes Practice Note 28, referring to mediation for a building contractor or sub-contractor dispute.

3.03 A 'mediation' procedure may sometimes also be incorporated into the contract as an ongoing dispute avoidance mechanism, whereby typically one or two mediators visit the site periodically to hold discussions with the parties to assist in preventing disputes arising.

3.04 If the dispute is in litigation, the court is likely to apply cost penalties to a party which does not participate or attempt to participate in some form of alternative dispute resolution (ADR) (e.g. *Dunnett v Railtrack plc (CA);* and *Leicester Circuits Ltd v Coates Brothers plc*) without good reason. This does not necessarily have to be mediation (*Corenso (UK) Ltd v The Burnden Group plc*). When considering whether a successful party should be deprived of its costs, the court will consider the circumstances of a refusal to mediate and is likely to take account of the nature of the dispute, the merits of the case, whether other settlement methods have been attempted, whether the costs of mediation would be disproportionately high, delay and the prospects of success (*Halsey v Milton Keynes NHS Trust and Steel v Joy and Halliday*

[2004] EWCA (Civ) 576). The potential of mediation to bring about settlement is well described by Mr Justice Lightman:

> 'the mediation process itself can and does often bring about a more sensible and more conciliatory attitude on the part of the parties than might otherwise be expected to prevail before the mediation, and may produce a recognition of the strengths and weaknesses by each party of this own case and that of his opponent, and a willingness to accept the give and take essential to a successful mediation. What appears to be incapable of mediation before the mediation process begins often proves capable of satisfactory resolution later.'
>
> (Lightman J in his judgment in *Hurst v Leeming* (above))

Selecting a mediator

3.05 Occasionally, where there is a mediation clause within a contract, a mediator may be named in advance. It is more common, however, to select a mediator at the time of the dispute and this gives the parties greater flexibility to determine any appropriate expertise which may be desirable in the mediator, depending on the nature of the dispute.

3.06 There are several professional and independent bodies with lists of experienced mediators, which can provide names of mediators on enquiry. These include: RIBA, CEDR, CIArb, RICS, CIOB and others which will have mediators familiar with construction disputes. One of these bodies may provide a selection of alternative names of mediators for the parties subsequently to agree if possible, or it may nominate a single mediator, depending on the parties' request. In some mediations a second, assistant or co-mediator, may also be requested. The National Mediation Helpline (www.nationalmediationhelpline.com) is also available, which is operated on behalf of the Ministry of Justice to put enquirers in contact with an accredited mediation provider. The Civil Mediation Council (www.civilmediation.org) is a further association of mediation providers.

3.07 Once selected, the mediator will usually require the parties to sign up to a mediation agreement. CEDR provides a Model Mediation Agreement which is available from its website (www.cedr.co.uk). A brief example mediation agreement is also attached to JCT Practice Note 28. In every case, the parties should enquire of the mediator whether there is a particular code of conduct or mediation procedure under which the mediator will be operating.

3.08 It is usual practice for the mediation agreement to require the parties to pay the mediator's fees in equal proportions.

Preparation for the mediation

3.09 Once appointed, the mediator will set out the procedure to be adopted, generally in discussion with the parties. This will usually include for each party to prepare and submit a case summary and a core bundle of relevant documents, each to be provided to the mediator and to the other party before the mediation. The mediator will also set a date for the mediation itself, and the duration of the mediation, taking into account the size and complexity of the dispute, by discussion with the parties. Typically, a mediation in respect of a small and/or straightforward dispute might be set down for half to 1 day, whereas a more complex and more substantial dispute may be set down for longer (as much as 5 days in the more extreme cases).

3.10 In addition to the documents provided to the mediator and to the other parties, a party may wish to prepare and take to the mediation additional documents which it intends to show only to the mediator in confidence.

3.11 Depending on the size and nature of the dispute, the parties will need to consider whether there is a need for legal representation, and expert evidence. It is not unusual for parties to be represented.

The mediation

3.12 Mediations tend to follow typical structures, although each mediation can be managed by the mediator in any manner to suit the particular nature of the dispute and the positions of the parties.

3.13 The mediation will usually take place in a neutral venue, although sometimes for reasons of costs one party will agree that the mediation can take place at the premises of the other party. For a two-party dispute, three rooms will usually be required: the main room for a round table meeting of the parties and the mediator together; and a separate break-out room for each party.

3.14 For each party, the mediation will usually be attended by: a senior member of staff from the party itself; a legal representative (if appropriate), such as a solicitor or barrister or both; and where appropriate one or more expert witnesses. In some cases on substantial claims, a member of the insurers and of the underwriters may also attend. It is important that each party attending has the authority to come to an agreement.

3.15 The mediator will usually structure the mediation to meet with the parties both together and separately. In a typical mediation, the mediation will commence with all parties gathered together, with each party invited to make a brief opening statement highlighting what they consider to be the principal issues. The benefit of this opening statement is not only to assist the other parties in understanding their position, but also to listen to the position of the other parties, and thereby gain a greater understanding of the obstacles to settlement. Depending upon the nature of the issues in dispute, and the potential for genuine dialogue in the wider group, the mediator may thereafter elect to speak to the parties separately, each in their own break-out room. In a multi-party case, typically, the mediator at this stage may choose to speak with all of the defendants together, without the claimant being present.

3.16 Through this next stage of the process, the mediator will work with the parties to establish the critical issues, to identify the obstacles to settlement, to assist each party in taking a realistic look at its own position, and to consider creatively the possible solutions to the dispute. The mediator will facilitate progressive negotiations between the parties.

3.17 During the course of separate meetings with the mediator, a party will frequently wish to disclose matters to the mediator which are confidential and not for repeating to the other parties. This is a normal part of the process, and the mediator will only divulge to another party details which he has been expressly authorised to divulge. Where the mediator considers it to be appropriate, he may call the parties back together into a group meeting, from time to time.

3.18 Mediators will not usually give advice to any party, nor will they comment on the likely outcome of the dispute if it were allowed to run to litigation or arbitration, unless the parties have agreed in advance that he should do so. An experienced mediator should, however, push each party to recognise weaknesses in their case, and to consider the strong points in the case of the other parties.

3.19 In considering and exploring offers for settlement, the mediator will assist a party in considering the alternatives to not achieving settlement, in terms of the escalating costs of continuing the dispute, the investment of time required by the party itself, the relatively long delay in otherwise achieving resolution of the dispute, and the lack of control of an outcome which is achieved other than by negotiation. In considering the acceptability of a sum being offered to settle the dispute, the mediator will also encourage a party to take account of the risk of proceeding, losing and paying the other parties costs. The courts have expressed the view that adopting an unreasonable position at a mediation is a matter which may lead to a party which succeeds at trial being deprived of its costs (*Earl of Malmesbury v Strutt & Parker* [2008] EWHC 424 (QB)). All these factors need to be taken into account when weighing up the acceptability of the best offer to settle which can be achieved through the mediation.

Agreement

3.20 If agreement is reached, parties can decide whether to set out the agreement in a written, signed document with the intention of it becoming a binding contractual agreement. This is a preferred option, in order to secure the agreement achieved before the parties leave the mediation. In certain cases parties wish to reflect on the agreement before finally signing up to a binding settlement, and it is not uncommon for parties to leave the mediation and thereafter to conclude a settlement agreement in the next few days. However, reaching a binding agreement at the end of the mediation is preferable, in order to avoid subsequent change in a party's position.

4 Mediation in practice

Advantages and disadvantages

4.01 In every dispute the opportunities for settling the dispute by ADR should be considered. The occasions when ADR may not be suitable will be the minority of instances.

The principal advantages of mediation are:

1 The opportunity for immediate settlement of the dispute.
2 A quick and relatively cheap way of settling the dispute.
3 The terms of any agreement remain within your control.
4 Hidden agenda items can be taken into account.
5 Gaining an early understanding of your opponent's case.
6 The mediation is confidential, unless the parties agree otherwise.
7 The mediation negotiations will focus only on the 'big issue' items.

Typical disadvantages of mediation are:

1 Achieving settlement generally requires compromise.
2 The parties must achieve a signed settlement agreement before the agreement will be enforceable.
3 A party may feel forced into a settlement which is below its reasonable expectation of the outcome of the case.
4 If the agreement is unsuccessful, some costs will have been wasted.

The importance of preparation

4.02 Good preparation is vital to enhance the likelihood of an outcome which you consider acceptable. Be on top of all of the facts,

and consider beforehand the various arguments that are likely to be raised. Undertake a realistic review of the weaknesses of your arguments and the areas of risk.

4.03 Settlement through mediation invariably involves a degree of compromise. A party going into a mediation needs to consider in detail beforehand, and to agree with other colleagues whose decision will be needed, on their worst acceptable settlement beyond which settlement will not be possible. Matters of costs already incurred and interest should be calculated in advance, to be considered in addition to the main sum in dispute, since a mediation settlement will normally be a single figure to sweep up all parts of a claim.

Selecting the right moment for mediation

4.04 The timing of the mediation relative to the progress of any ancillary formal dispute resolution process, such as litigation or arbitration, is likely to be relevant to the chances of the success of the mediation. Parties may naturally wish to mediate at the earliest possible date in order to reduce costs. However, generally, a certain amount of initial investigation needs to be carried out by each party, to ascertain the facts surrounding the issues in dispute, and possibly to obtain an initial expert opinion, before each party will be in a position to form a view as to the merits of their case. In the absence of a realistic view in particular in respect of the weaknesses of a party's own position, settlement of the dispute will be unlikely. An over-optimistic claimant is unlikely to be in a position to accept a settlement at a realistic level, and the claimant will therefore need to have time to follow through its own enquiry processes in the hands of its advisers and, where appropriate, experts, before being able to arrive at a realistic settlement proposition.

4.05 In construction disputes, for the purpose of initiating an action in court, each party is obliged by the Civil Procedure Rules to adhere to the Pre-Action Protocol for Construction and Engineering Disputes (this can be found on the Ministry of Justice website: www.justice.gov.uk). Adhering to the Pre-Action Protocol requires each party to conduct a substantial amount of work up front, in order to set out the details of the claim, and to consider in reasonable detail a response to the claim, following which the parties are required to attend a Pre-Action Meeting. The aim of the meeting is, amongst other matters, for the parties to consider whether, and if so how, the dispute might be resolved without recourse to litigation. In respect of each agreed issue or the dispute as a whole, the parties are obliged to consider whether some form of alternative dispute resolution procedure (Pre-Action Protocol for Construction and Engineering Disputes, paragraph 5.4) would be more suitable than litigation. The parties are therefore required to consider at the earliest reasonable stage the possibility of settling the dispute by means other than litigation.

27

Building dispute resolution in Scotland

ROBERT HOWIE

1 Arbitration in Scotland

1.01 It is common to find in building contracts in Scotland provisions for the arbitration of disputes which arise thereunder or in connection therewith. Indeed, an arbitration clause appears in the Scottish supplement to the JCT Standard Form Contract which is published by the Scottish Building Contract Committee. It is important to bear in mind that arbitration in Scotland proceeds upon a quite different basis from arbitration in England, and in consequence, there is usually little reliance placed on English authority when questions of Scottish arbitration law come before the courts. Whereas arbitration law in England is largely based on statute, as matters presently stand, the basis of domestic arbitration is almost exclusively the common law, statutory intervention being limited to the Arbitration (Scotland) Act 1894, the Articles of Regulation, 1695 and the third section of the Administration of Justice (Scotland) Act 1972. The English Arbitration Act 1996, like its statutory predecessors in 1950 and 1979, does not apply to domestic arbitration in Scotland.

1.02 However, in one important area, Parliament has intervened. Unlike the rest of the United Kingdom, Scotland has adopted the UNCITRAL model law for arbitration: it did so by the Law Reform (Miscellaneous Provisions) (Scotland) Act 1990, section 66. One might expect the practical importance of that adoption to be very limited in the context of Scottish construction contracts, for the UNCITRAL law applies only to 'international' commercial arbitrations, and in Scotland those may be expected to be uncommon. However, the definition accorded the word 'international' is a special one, the result of which is likely to render a dispute between a Scottish registered company and one registered in any other part of the United Kingdom, 'international', and thus subject to the provisions of the UNCITRAL model laws. But although this result is likely, it is not inevitable, and unfortunately satellite litigation can break out in the course of the arbitration as to whether or not the dispute is truly subject to the UNCITRAL model law. In *The Fennica case,* 6 July 2000, unreported, the Court of Session ordered an arbiter to hear a proof on contested averments of fact regarding the applicability of the Model Law to the arbitration in question after the arbiter had purported to decide that matter without hearing evidence. The proof lasted a week, and the satellite dispute delayed the main arbitration by 18 months! The architect, in considering whether or not to advise a client that he should seek to include in his contract an arbitration clause, ought therefore to give consideration to the question whether or not any dispute which may arise in relation to that contract will be 'international' within the meaning of the Law Reform (Miscellaneous Provisions) (Scotland) Act 1990, by which the UNCITRAL law is introduced. If any such dispute will be 'international', it is thought that it will be subject to the restrictions of the UNCITRAL Model Law, most notably those which restrict the ability of either party to seek a stated case for the opinion of the Court of Session on a point of law arising in the arbitration. Those restrictions, and therefore arbitration in a potential UNCITRAL case, may not always be thought to be of advantage: the case may throw up a dispute in which the client's rights may depend on legal issues, and the arbiter may not be legally qualified. At the outset, when it will not be known whether or not disputes will arise, still less what the issues in them may be, it may well be quite impossible to tell whether arbitration is likely to be advantageous to the architect's client. In such circumstances, the prudent course may be to exclude the arbitration clause from the parties' contract, leaving it to them to agree to arbitration themselves (if so desired) on individual disputes as those arise, and to tailor the selection of arbiter and his powers on a case-by-case basis as may be thought requisite to secure the resolution of the particular question or questions which have given rise to the dispute in hand.

1.03 It is not necessary for a building contract to contain an arbitration clause in order to allow the parties to adopt that mode of dispute resolution in relation to a given dispute if they both wish to do that. The existence or otherwise of an arbitration clause in a contract assumes importance when, at the time when a dispute arises the parties are not in agreement as to whether or not that dispute should be remitted to arbitration. If there is no arbitration clause incorporated into the contract, then because the basis of all jurisdiction in arbitration is consensual, the party opposed to arbitration can refuse to assent to it, and may effectively force his contradictor to litigate in order to secure a resolution of the dispute. But if, on the other hand, such a clause has been incorporated, the party insisting on arbitration can force his opponent to arbitrate as he had contracted to do, and, assuming that the obligation to arbitrate has not been waived, will be entitled to the sist (*anglice* stay) of any court proceedings about the dispute raised against him by the other party until the arbitration is completed or for some reason breaks down. This, of course, assumes that there exists a dispute between the parties, and that it falls within the ambit of the arbitration clause as properly construed. For it is a precondition of any arbitration that there is a dispute between the parties which may be arbitrated. It has been the practice of the court to decline to sist actions for arbitration (particularly where the demand for a sist is made in answer to a motion for summary decree in a court action designed to enforce one party's claims against the other) where the court is not persuaded that there exists a bona fide dispute between the parties, as opposed to a mere refusal by A to meet a claim made upon him by B. It is also necessary if a sist is to be secured, that the dispute in question should fall within the purview of the arbitration clause properly construed. Whether, in any given case, that requirement is met is a strictly legal question on which advice should be taken, but in the context of Clause 41 of the SBCC Agreement, it should rarely cause much difficulty, since that clause remits to arbitration any dispute arising under or in connection with the contract. Other clauses, however, particularly in bespoke contracts, may give rise to much greater difficulty.

1.04 Even where an arbitration clause appears in the contract, however, it is impossible to insist that a given dispute be arbitrated where either of the parties seeking so to insist has waived the right to do so or has become personally barred from so insisting, or the right so to insist has itself prescribed. The architect, if he should find himself involved with the initial stages of a dispute as agent for the employer, should therefore be alert to the danger of so acting – or failing to act – as to set up a plea of waiver or personal bar against his employer, a plea which may serve to prevent that employer from insisting that the dispute be arbitrated rather than publicly canvassed in court. Since both waiver and personal bar involve questions of fact, it is not possible to indicate in advance what conduct by the Architect may be found to raise such a plea. It is a matter in which the architect concerned about the problem should take advice in light of the circumstances of the case which faces him. Prescription of the right to arbitrate through the elapse of five years since the right came into existence without that right being exercised or being the subject of a relevant claim or acknowledgement for the purposes of the Prescription and Limitation (Scotland) Act 1973 is unlikely to be a matter which will arise as an issue of immediate practical importance for the architect, but it has been known to happen, and should not be overlooked. Moreover, extreme delays in proceeding with either arbitration or court action may allow the court to prevent the case from proceeding at all (*Tonner v Messrs Reiach & Hall* 2008 SC I – an architects' negligence case!). Again, this is a matter on which architect should take advice.

1.05 An issue which the architect is more likely to encounter, particularly in the context of the SBCC Standard Form Contracts, is the obverse of the prescription question: the prematurity of arbitration. It will be recalled that the Standard Form Building Contract contains provisions which preclude recourse to arbitration until the date of practical completion or alleged practical completion of the works. In the event that an arbitration has begun prior to that date, the party instigating it runs the risk of seeing his claim dismissed with an award of expenses being made against him unless his case has been brought in connection with one of the matters (the proper issue of certificates, etc.) excluded by the JCT Clause from the ambit of the general embargo on arbitration prior to practical completion. It should be borne in mind, however, that even if the right to arbitrate may be not lost through the passage of time, the underlying contractual rights about which the parties are in dispute may be being lost or rendered unprovable by that mechanism. It will be recalled that in varying regards conclusive effect is accorded the Final Certificate if proceedings in relation to those matters have not been begun before a date 60 days after the issue of the certificate in question. The architect should thus bear in mind that, even if the right to arbitration is not in danger of being prescribed, it may be that recourse to arbitration or court proceedings is required promptly if underlying rights are not to be destroyed by prescription or by conclusive evidence provisions in the contract.

1.06 Given that, as noticed above, the jurisdiction of an arbiter in Scotland derives from the contract of the parties, both the identity of the arbitral tribunal and the powers that are to be exercised by it are a matter for the consent of the parties. To combat the obvious problem that, once they are at odds over some dispute, the parties may fail to agree upon the identity of their arbiter, the SBCC Arbitration Clause follows the common practice of providing that, failing agreement between the parties on the matter within a specified time, either party may apply to a nominating body to appoint an arbiter. In practice, not many arbiters in construction disputes in Scotland are appointed in that way; at length, agreement, howsoever reluctant, usually prevails. The clause provides for different possible appointing bodies. When the terms of the clause are being considered at the outset, before the building contract

is entered into, it may be appropriate to consider which appointing body would be most likely to appoint an arbiter skilled in the resolution of the kind of dispute which is apt to arise in connection with that contract. In that regard, it should not be overlooked that although a dispute may at first sight appear to relate to one discipline, a more detailed consideration of it may disclose that the decisive issues will enter another discipline, and that in consequence a choice between competing areas of expertise of potential arbiters has to be made in deciding what category of person would make the best potential arbiter. The clause also gives rise to a practical problem to which the architect may wish to direct his client's attention at the contracting stage. Many arbiters appoint clerks to assist them, and usually both arbiter and clerk charge fees for their services. A number of arbiters proceed upon the footing of terms and conditions of appointment as arbiters, governing matters such as joint and several liability for fees and expenses and the size of those fees. Theoretically, fee scales in such terms and conditions form the terms of a separate ancillary contract between the arbiter and parties to which all consent. But in reality, where the arbiter is imposed on parties by the appointing authority and that arbiter presents terms which are unacceptable to a party (e.g. as regards the daily rate of remuneration), it would seem to be open to some doubt what that party can do to reject those terms if the arbiter is minded to insist on them. That result appears to follow from the unqualified and unconditional nature of the agreement embodied in the SBCC form to accept as arbiter such person as the appointing authority may specify. To avoid it, therefore, it may be desired to amend the standard form clause so as to render the agreement to accept the arbiter subject to prior agreement having been reached on the terms and conditions upon which he will act as such. The danger in such amendment is that, unless carefully drafted, it opens up the opportunity to frustrate – or at least delay – the arbitration process through dispute about ancillary questions such as the arbiter's fees.

1.07 There is in Scots law no objection in principle to the appointment of the architect himself as the arbiter, but although that practice was not uncommon in the nineteenth century, it is now viewed with some disfavour. Where the architect himself is appointed, he should be particularly scrupulous not to prejudge the issues which may be put to him for his decision (although he will not be assumed so to prejudge matters merely on account of his previous involvement in the case), and to apply the rules of natural justice in disposing of the dispute.

1.08 The powers available to the arbiter are also a matter to which some consideration should be given by an architect faced with the need to advise a client about either an arbitration clause in a contract or an executory Deed of Submission whereby an arbitration clause may be sought to be put into effect after a dispute has arisen. The latter instrument may be sought to be used by the opposing party to narrow down or alternatively to widen the powers accorded the arbiter in the original clause, and the architect should be on guard against any such amendment which might prejudice his client's interest. At the stage of framing the initial clause, similar care ought to be taken. At the outset, it will be impossible to tell what powers it might be tactically advantageous to the client for the arbiter to have, so the course of prudence – assuming that an arbitration clause is to be incorporated at all – is probably to seek to keep those powers wider, rather than narrower. The critical consideration is that, in the absence of special power accorded him by the parties in their contract of arbitration, an arbiter in Scotland has no power to assess or award damages, or to entertain a plea of compensation (*anglice* set-off). Given the frequency with which demands for damages are made in building contract cases, or claims made are met with assertions of the right to compensate under the Act of 1592 in respect of some cross-claim, the omission from the arbiter's arsenal of these powers is likely to prove improvident. In addition to these well-known problem areas, other potential difficulties may merit attention: the ability of the arbiter to award interest on damages from a date prior to decree, the general unavailability of caution for expenses, and the doubts which attend the ability to hear quasi-contractual claims or claims for rectification of the underlying building contract. The SBCC arbitration clause is drawn in broad terms so far as powers are concerned, but even in that case, certain powers are not accorded the arbiter, most notably the power to rectify the building contract in which the arbitration clause appears. The SBCC provisions on arbitration refer on to the Scottish Arbitration Code. This purports to give power to the architect to rectify the contract, 'to the extent permitted by law', but since the statute introducing rectification into Scots law allowed it to be undertaken only by 'the Court' it may well be that this provision of the Code has in fact no content. It is thought that where an unforeseen rectification problem arises in the course of an arbitration where special power anent rectification has not been given to the arbiter, the proper course is for the parties to take that question to the court for resolution, procedure in the arbitration being sisted pending that resolution (cf. *Bovis Construction (Scotland) Ltd v Glantre Engineering Ltd*, 27 July 1997, unreported).

1.09 The circumstances in which an arbiter's decision, actual or prospective, may be brought before the court are matters with which the architect is unlikely to be concerned, unless he himself is arbiter. In purely domestic arbitrations, it is open to a party to an arbitration to invite the arbiter, prior to issuing his decision on matter which involves questions of law, to state a case for the opinion of the Court of Session on such questions. In domestic arbitrations, that right has a statutory origin in section 3 of the Administration of Justice (Scotland) Act 1972. Prior to the coming into force of that section, the stated case procedure was available only in certain statutory arbitrations; in other cases, the arbiter's decision on the points of law was final. If the parties so desire, that finality may be maintained even today by the inclusion in their arbitration contract of a provision excluding for that arbitration the operation of section 3. It should be noted, however, that any such exclusion must appear in the original 'agreement to refer' and not merely in a later implementing deed of submission. If a case is to be stated, it must be stated before the arbiter issues his award on the matter in question. It is for this reason usual, where stated case procedure is available, to require the arbiter to issue his proposed findings in draft form prior to his issuing his award, so that, if it be thought appropriate, a stated case may be presented to the court within the period allowed by the third section. The detailed rules for the procedure to be followed in the stated case procedure are set out in Part 2 of Chapter 41 of the Rules of the Court of Session 1994, to which reference should be made. Whether or not to state a case is a matter for the arbiter's discretion, although where he refuses to state a case on a given question, he may be ordained by the Inner House of the Court of Session to do so under the procedure set out in Rule of Court 41.8. Where the application for a stated case is made before the facts of the dispute have been determined, the arbiter is empowered to defer consideration of the application until after that determination, and his exercise of that discretion will not be interfered with by the Court of Session under Rule of Court 41.8. As in other cases, however, that exercise is ultimately subject to judicial review in the Court of Session. Once a case has been presented to the court, it is unlikely that the arbiter will have any further concern with it until the court delivers its opinion. For the purposes of the arbitration in which it is given, that opinion is determinative of the legal issues with which it deals. No appeal from an opinion of the Court of Session under this procedure lies to the House of Lords and it is misconduct on the part of the arbiter for him not to follow it. In UNCITRAL cases, it is thought that the court can intervene only in the circumstances set out in the Schedule to the 1990 Act.

1.10 Once the arbiter has pronounced his final interlocutor, he is *functus officio* and has no further jurisdiction over the parties (cf. *Mowlem (Scotland) Ltd v Inverclyde Council,* 1 October 2003, unreported). His award is *res judicata* between them, but only as regards those matters which were in fact submitted to him and adjudicated upon. Matters not so submitted may be the subject of litigation, even if they might originally have been submitted to the arbiter. The arbiter's final interlocutor, however, like his other actings in the arbitration, is ultimately subject to the supervisory jurisdiction of the Court of Session by way of judicial review. Thus, his award may be challenged and, indeed, reduced, where the arbiter has exceeded the jurisdiction confided to him by the parties, failed to exhaust his jurisdiction, acted in breach of natural justice, breached the provisions of the 25th article of the Articles of Regulation 1695 (which are concerned with bribery, corruption and falsehood), been biased, or generally acted in a manner which is 'unreasonable' in the special sense in which that term is used in administrative law. His award is not subject to review, however, merely because a decision arrived at is wrong in law or based on erroneous findings in fact.

2 Adjudication in Scotland

2.01 The Housing Grants, Construction and Regeneration Act 1996 was passed by Parliament as an Act having application across the whole of the United Kingdom. Unsurprisingly, therefore, adjudication in Scotland shares much in common with adjudication in England and Wales: English cases are frequently cited in Scottish decisions on adjudication – indeed, there is scarcely a single Scottish case in which English authority is not cited – and occasionally, Scottish cases are relied upon in the English Courts *Homer Burgess Ltd v Chirex (Annan) Ltd* 2000 SLT 277 is probably the most frequently cited Scottish case, but *SL Timber Systems Ltd v Carillion Construction Ltd* 2002 SLT 997 and *Ballast plc v The Burrell Company (Construction Management) Ltd* 2001 SLT 1039 have also made appearances in the English cases. But although the court has sometimes sought to avoid differences arising between the Scots and English laws regarding adjudication (*Gillies Ramsay Diamond, Petitioner* 2003 SLT 162), particularly in the fields of enforcement and challenge of adjudicators' awards, there are some significant differences between the law concerning adjudication which obtains in Scotland and the English law with which many readers of this work will be more familiar. Though it may be tempting to him to pass over these as Scottish peculiarities with which he will have no concern, given the ease with which cases can acquire a cross-border dimension, some knowledge of the Scottish position may yet be of use to the English reader.

2.02 From the point of view of the architect, not the least of the significant features about adjudications in Scotland is their use as a mechanism for the recovery of professional fees, and the prosecution by that route of claims by employers for damages for breach of contract on the part of members of the professional team. It is understood that adjudications against members of the professional team are relatively more common in Scotland than they are in England, and where English professionals undertake work on Scottish building projects, this risk must be borne in mind. A contract whereunder an architect agrees to act as a contract administrator under a building contract has been held to be a 'construction contract' for the purposes of the 1996 Act (*Gillies Ramsay Diamond, Petitioner* 2003 SLT 162; upheld on appeal, 2004 SC 430), and it is thought that the same would hold true of a contract to act as a project manager for the construction or refurbishment of a building.

2.03 For an employer wishing to pursue a claim against his architect, there arc decided tactical attractions in proceeding by way of adjudication. Not infrequently, losses sustained by the employer have been contributed to through the actions of different members of the professional team as well as the contractor. Determination of the loss which is attributable to each may be far from easy. Where court proceedings to recoup these losses are raised, the ensuing action can become costly and time-consuming for the pursuing employer, given the likelihood that third party notices will be served by the defenders in order to bring the contractors and other professionals into the action either in order to prosecute claims for indemnity or relief against them or to contend that those others alone are liable to the Pursuer for his losses. Matters may become yet more complicated for the pursuer, for he may have to adopt such contentions for his own protection, and may face from some of those thus added to his action, defences alleging matters such as limitation of liability, the protection of a final certificate or the benefit of a 'net contribution' clause. All these problems the employer can avoid by adjudicating, since all the other claims among the other parties do not involve a dispute 'under the contract' between the employer and his architect, and so cannot fall within the jurisdiction of the adjudicator (section 108 of the 1996 Act; cf. *Barr Ltd v LAW Mining Ltd* 2003 SLT 488). He can recover all his losses from the architect (assuming the latter has no 'net contribution' clause in his contract) relying on the doctrine of joint and several liability (*Clydesdale Bank plc v Messrs MacLay Collier & Partners* [1998] SLT 1102), and leave it to the architect – or his underwriters – to sue the other parties in an effort to recoup the architect's losses. Lastly, in the event of his success in obtaining damages (particularly if he achieves a level of damages which, if not what he sought, he is prepared to rest content with), it is thought that the employer can effectively place upon the architect in any subsequent court action pursuant to section 108(3) of the 1996 Act, the burden of proving that he did not breach his contract with the employer in order to recover the monies paid out as damages in obedience to the adjudicator's award. Although the matter is not uncontroversial, it is thought that the Lord Ordinary's remark at first instance in *City Inn Ltd v Shepherd Construction Ltd* to the effect that an adjudicator's decision does not alter the burden of proof in a section 108(3) action applies only to the class of case (of which *City Inn* was an example) where the claimant in the adjudication seeks as pursuer in the court action to recover what he obtained at the hands of the adjudicator. (*City Inn Ltd v Shepherd Construction Ltd* 2002 SLT 781 at paragraph 59. This point was not challenged in the subsequent reclaiming motion (*anglice* appeal). See 2003 SLT 885.)

2.04 The law governing the actual operation of an adjudication is not dissimilar to that in England. In contrast to the position of an arbiter, an adjudicator in Scotland has been held to be able to award damages for breach of contract even though he has not been expressly empowered so to do (*Gillies Ramsay Diamond, Petitioners,* above). It is thought that, by parity of reasoning, an adjudicator ought to be able to entertain a plea of compensation under the Compensation Act 1592, even though an arbiter needs special power to do so. The entertaining of such a plea by the adjudicator in *Allied London & Scottish Properties plc v Riverbrae Construction Ltd* 2000 SLT 981 was not criticised in the subsequent litigation. It is thought, however, that he could not entertain a claim for rectification of the contract or its inducement by misrepresentation. Nor, in cases where damages are awarded, can he award interest from prior to the date of his decree in the absence of a special power so to do. The Interest on Damages (Scotland) Acts 1958 and 1971 which introduced the ability to award interest from before the date of decree in damages cases have not been extended to arbitrations or adjudications. In the normal case, he can allocate as between the parties responsibility for payment of his own fees and outlays, but without special power to that effect, he cannot award the parties their legal expenses. In those cases where such power is given and exercised, however, those expenses awarded are subject to taxation by the Auditor of Court in exactly the same way as expenses awarded by the court and it is only a taxed amount of expenses that the court will be willing to enforce in the context of an action to obtain payment of the sums awarded by the adjudicator (*Deko Scotland Ltd*, above). In Scotland, as well as in England, adjudicators are required to follow the rules of natural justice (*Ballast plc*, above), and they must decide the dispute according to the parties' legal entitlements rather than *ex aequo et bono*. The leading case on natural justice in adjudication in Scotland is now *Costain Ltd v Strathclyde Builders Ltd* 2004 SLT 102, a case which has given rise to some disquiet among adjudicators. The case contains an extended discussion of the place of natural justice in adjudications. In *Costain Ltd*, which was concerned with the failure of the adjudicator to disclose to the parties, and invite their comments on, legal advice received by him, the court held that as well as keeping free of bias, the adjudicator had a separate and additional overriding duty not, perhaps, always recognised in the English cases to hear both parties to the case on all material (including legal advice received by the adjudicator)

which might be relevant to the case in hand. In a case where that had not been done, it would be enough to justify the reduction of the adjudicator's decision that there was a possibility of injustice arising as a result of the breach: it was not necessary that actual prejudice be shown to have resulted. The adjudicator must also adhere to the statutory time limits for the reaching of his decision. This is now clearly the case in relation to adjudications under the statutory scheme (*Ritchie Brothers (PWC) Ltd v David Philp (Commercials Ltd* 2005 1 SC 384) and it is thought that, absent clear wording to the contrary in the contractual adjudication provisions, the same holds true for those adjudications to which the scheme does not apply. It is not clear whether the adjudicator's decision should also be issued within the statutory time limits, though there is authority for the view that it should be (*St Andrews Bay Development Ltd v HBG Management Ltd* 2003 SLT 740). The safe course for any architect sitting as an adjudicator is to obviate that kind of argument at the outset by issuing his decision to the parties within that number of days which they have conferred upon him for the delivery of his decision.

2.05 By contrast with those matters, however, the question of retention and the compensation of competing cross-claims is an area where Scots law is apt to part company from its southern neighbour. An exclusion in a Scottish contract of rights of 'set-off' has been held not to prevent the taking of a plea of retention in Scottish proceedings (*A v B* 2003 SLT 242), and the view has been expressed that, notwithstanding the prima facie restriction of the adjudicator's jurisdiction to single disputes, an arbiter to whom is referred a question such as 'to payment of what sum is the Claimant entitled?' must entertain such a plea of retention raised in defence of the claim, and all the disputed issues, such as late completion and damages (liquidated or otherwise) which may underpin it (*Construction Centre Group Ltd v Highland Council* 2002 SLT 1274). The same logic would seem to apply to pleas of compensation under the 1592 Act, though in that case, the pre-existing liquidation of the debts said to extinguish the sum claimed or part thereof is at least likely to make the entertaining of that plea a less daunting task for the adjudicator faced with the statutory time limit on the making of his decision.

2.06 The ability of the unsuccessful party in an adjudication to resist enforcement of the award on the grounds of retention or compensation of cross-claims has also given rise to some difficulty. A plea of retention cannot, it seems, be raised to suspend enforcement of an award – least if it could have been pleaded before the adjudicator and was not (*A v B,*) above – and it appears that the position in relation 'to compensation is similar (*Construction Centre Group Ltd v Highland Council* 2003 SLT 623). The position in relation to the compensation of debts, or rights to withhold which could not competently have been put before the adjudicator, because, for example, they arose in the period after the award was made, is unclear.

2.07 Probably the most important areas of difference between the laws in England and Scotland in relation to adjudication concern the questions of enforcement or challenge of awards. Such are the differences in this area that it can become an important question for the adviser of a client who has received a decision from an adjudicator whether he should seek to challenge or enforce that decision in England or in Scotland. Provided that the defender is subject to the jurisdiction of the Scottish courts (as many main contractors and employers will be) there is no necessary objection to the enforcement there of awards made by English adjudicators in respect of English building contacts. A clause prorogating the jurisdiction of an English court in relation to disputes under the contract may not in itself preclude enforcement in Scotland of the adjudicator's award meantime (See *Comsite Projects Ltd v Andritz AG* [2003] EWHC 958). Such enforcement actions have already been brought in Scotland, and, indeed, the oft-cited *Homer Burgess Ltd* is an early example. The main reason for seeking to enforce an English award in Scotland, it is thought, would be to allow a successful, but financially seriously straitened party faced with the prospect of cross-claims or a cross-action under section 108(3) of the 1996 Act at the instance of his opponent, to seek a court decree for the monies awarded him by the adjudicator which he could then enforce by diligence. Whereas in England the court has held that it will stay execution of the decree in circumstances of that class (See, for example, *Baldwin's Industrial Services plc v Barr Ltd* [2003] BLR 176), it has been held in the Outer House of the Court of Session that in Scotland there is no power so to do, and that the insolvency of the successful party is no ground for withholding an immediately enforceable decree for the sum awarded by the adjudicator (*SL Timber Systems Ltd*, above). By seeking to enforce his adjudicator's award in Scotland, therefore, the financially stricken sub-contractor – or perhaps its bankers – can secure the benefit of a perhaps fortunate adjudicator's award, and avoid those protections afforded by the English courts on which his opponent may hope, and expect, to be able to rely in avoiding the need to pay out *ad interim* to one likely to be unable to repay in the event of the payer's success in the cross-action.

2.08 By way of contrast, the second major difference between English and Scots law in this area relates to the challenge of awards made by adjudicators. In Scotland, it is not necessary for a party dissatisfied with an adjudicator's decision to wait for his opponent to attempt to enforce it and then defend the enforcement proceedings on whatever grounds may cause him to be so dissatisfied. For in Scotland, unlike England, the adjudicator's decisions arc subject to judicial review, and that method of challenge is not infrequently resorted to (*Allied London & Scottish Properties plc.* above and *Gillies Ramsay Diamond, Petitioner*, above are both judicial reviews). There is no time limit for the raising of such petitions, albeit that a degree of promptitude in raising any proposed review is expected. The availability of judicial review in Scotland as a mode of reviewing adjudication decisions has tended to cause a greater resort to administrative law cases as a source of precedent on review than has perhaps been the case in England. Thus, it has been stated that the decision of an adjudicator is subject to reduction in the event that it is 'Wednesbury unreasonable' (See *Ballast plc*, above), and it has been argued that reduction is similarly available if other elements of the classical Scottish touchstone of administrative law grounds of reduction set out in *Wordie Property Ltd v Secretary of State for Scotland* 1984 SLT 345 are not complied with. Likewise, the argument has been advanced that inadequacy of reasoning on the part of an adjudicator in his decision and note of reasons is in itself an error of law such as entitles the Court of Session to reduce his decision. In the reclaiming motion in *Gillies Ramsay Diamond, Petitioner*, the argument was advanced that, on the basis of House of Lords cases such as *O'Reilly v Mackman* [1983] 2 AC 287, there is no distinction

between *intra vires* and *ultra vires* errors of law in adjudication, so that the award should be reduced as would, say, a planning authority's decision letter be, if it were disfigured by errors of law about the merits of the case, even if it displayed none about jurisdictional matters. A decision to that effect would have run counter to those made by the Court of Appeal in *Bouygues Offshore (UK) Ltd v Dahl-Jensen (UK) Ltd* [2002] BLR 522 and *C & B Scene Concept Design Ltd v Isobars Ltd* [2002] 82 Con LR 154, as well as the Scottish rule about the review of arbiters' decisions noted in paragraph 1.10 above. The argument, however, was rejected, since *O'Reilly* and similar cases were concerned with English public law notions rather than contractually based jurisdictions such as adjudications, and for cases of the latter class, the Scottish rule in arbitration cases was the better guide, as well as the one more consonant with the policy of the adjudication provisions of the 1996 Act. Parliament had provided a mechanism for undoing the effects of adjudicators' errors in the shape of the section 108(3) action, and it was unnecessary to call into existence another (*Gilles Ramsay Diamond, Petitioner*, 2004 SC 430).While in England, the argument from *O'Reilly* may still be open, it was advanced in neither *Bouygues Offshore (UK) Ltd* nor *C & B Scene Concept Design Ltd*, and features in the pages of *Emden's Construction Law* in Scotland, it is now firmly excluded.

2.09 Recent years have seen an increase in the number of actions of the kind envisaged by section 108(3) of the1996 Act, in which parties dissatisfied with enforceable adjudicators' awards seek to re-litigate the issues argued over in the adjudication. It should be borne in mind that in Scotland, even if the adjudicator's decision is successfully overturned in such a case, neither his award insofar as it touches on the question of his fees and expenses, nor any interest which may have been attracted by his award before it was honoured will be repayable by the party who won the original adjudication. The same is true of any award of legal expenses which the adjudicator may have made (*Castle Inns (Stirling) Ltd, Petitioner v Clark Contracts Ltd* 2006 SCLR).

2.10 The private international law implications of such actions have not, it is fair to say, been fully worked out. The jurisdictional question has not really been canvassed, although decisions in relation to other classes of judicial review and private law matters may point the way forward (for example, *Bank of Scotland v Investment Management Regulatory Organization Ltd* 1989 SC 107) and the plea of *forum non conveniens* originally laid in *Homer Burgess Ltd* was departed from. The architect who conceives that he, or his client, may find himself in the cross-border 'debateable land' should therefore seek advice.

28

International arbitration

TONY DYMOND AND EMELITA ROBBINS

1 Introduction

1.01 The preceding Chapter 24 on arbitration sets out a summary of the legal framework and of the arbitral process for domestic arbitration in England and Wales; international arbitration is its closely related cousin. The purpose of this chapter on international arbitration is to give the reader an understanding of some of the common issues and where certain differences lie. It is not intended to be a practical guide as to how these matters should be dealt with since much will depend on the case in point and the relevant circumstances surrounding the matter, but some commentary is provided. The reader will find this chapter most useful if it is read after Chapter 24 to which it makes reference.

What makes an arbitration 'international'?

1.02 Essentially, international commercial arbitration is founded on the same judicial process as that of domestic arbitration, but distinguished in its widest sense by some element that transcends state boundaries, thereby making it 'international' and subject to other legal regimes. There is no defining criterion for what that international element might be. In England the law does not now distinguish between domestic and international arbitration, except when it comes to enforcement of foreign awards made in states which are signatories to the New York Convention. This is addressed later in this chapter. However, those states or arbitral institutions which do distinguish between domestic and international arbitrations generally do so by reference to:

- **the nature of the dispute**, e.g. if it involves international trade or the application of international law or the performance of the contract in a state other than that of the nation of the contracting parties; or
- **some factor connected to the parties**, e.g. their nationalities or their place of residence or business.

1.03 In France, for example, arbitration is treated as 'international' if it involves the 'interests of international trade', but in Switzerland it is the nationality of the parties that determines the matter. Under the Rules of Arbitration issued by the Court of Arbitration of the International Chamber of Commerce ('ICC Rules'), the question is decided by reference to the nature of the dispute. The question of whether an arbitration is 'international' therefore falls to be decided on a case-by-case basis, along with the issue of what legal regimes apply.

Legal regimes relevant in international arbitration

1.04 Typically there are four legal regimes that are relevant in international arbitration. The first is the substantive law of the contract, that is the system of law which governs the main contract, either chosen by the parties or determined by the arbitral tribunal.

The second is the arbitral law of the place of the arbitration, referred to as the 'seat' of the arbitration. The law of the seat usually governs issues such as the interpretation, recognition and enforcement of the arbitration agreement, interim measures, evidentiary issues and appeals of awards. Many states have adopted the United Nations Commission on International Trade Law ('UNCITRAL') Model Law (adopted by the UN General Assembly in 1976) in whole or in part, which provides for many of these issues. The third legal regime will be any arbitration rules drawn up or chosen by the parties to govern the arbitration or in default of agreement, determined by the tribunal at a preliminary hearing once the arbitration has begun. These may be rules imposed by an arbitral institution chosen by the parties to administer their arbitration. The law governing the recognition and enforcement of awards is the fourth legal regime. This will usually be the law of the place where a party is seeking to enforce an award. Each of these different legal regimes is considered in this chapter, with particular reference being given to those aspects most relevant to disputes arising out of international construction projects.

International construction arbitration

1.05 In international construction projects the use of arbitration as a means of dispute resolution has a historic background, with arbitration clauses incorporated into the most widely used standard forms of contract since their inception – the Conditions of Contract first published by the *Fédération Internationale des Ingénieurs-Conseils* ('FIDIC') in 1957. The motivation for the adoption of an arbitration clause into these early Conditions of Contract was the concern that a dispute in an international construction project might lead to parallel litigation in courts of different states, each declaring jurisdiction to determine the dispute, with the risk of expensive and inconsistent judgments.

1.06 The use of arbitration clauses in international construction projects is now widespread; in building contracts (whether or not based on FIDIC forms) and professional services contracts including those for the services of architects. International arbitration has maintained its appeal in international projects and is commonly found now at the conclusion of an escalating dispute resolution procedure which very often includes mandatory intermediate steps. The updated FIDIC forms include provision for a Dispute Adjudication Board (which investigates and recommends provisional decisions to resolve disputes) and an amicable dispute resolution stage, (such as mediation), followed by arbitration.

2 Factors relevant to the choice of international arbitration

2.01 The factors which militate in favour of the choice of arbitration to resolve domestic disputes are also relevant to international disputes. Many of these factors are listed in Chapter 24, such as the privacy of the proceedings; the technical expertise of the arbitrators (particularly relevant in construction arbitrations which can involve difficult technical issues and specialised forms of contract); and the flexibility the procedure affords the parties. For parties to an international arbitration, the flexibility and the control afforded to the parties to determine their own procedure may be of greater significance than to parties to domestic proceedings. This is because parties involved in an international project are often from distinct legal backgrounds and are unfamiliar with the different legal procedures known to the other party. Parties usually come from either a common law or civil law background; in which the role of the 'decision maker', the parties' legal representatives and the manner and method of proving or defending a case may be very different.

2.02 The most common reason given for the choice of international arbitration is by far the ease of enforcing an international arbitration award. The New York Convention on the Recognition and Enforcement of Foreign Arbitral Awards 1958 (the 'New York Convention') provides for the enforcement of 'international' or 'foreign' arbitration awards in most of the major countries of the world. There is no real global equivalent for the recognition and enforcement of domestic court judgments. The New York Convention has been important in facilitating the creation of international construction projects, including securing the provision of financial and economic measures requisite for such projects.

2.03 Another important factor is the opportunity international arbitration affords parties to contract out of a national court system and to refer a dispute to a neutral forum to which neither party has any connection. This can be particularly attractive to a party, if it is wary of referring a dispute to the national courts of their contracting counterparty or the place of performance of the contract, where the rule of law or independence of the judiciary is not well established.

2.04 An arbitrator's jurisdiction derives (at least in part) from the agreement between the contracting parties. This means that arbitration may not be well suited for dealing with multi-party disputes where these arise under separate contracts. This is very relevant in international construction and engineering projects, which may involve numerous parties with linked contractual relationships and where frequently an employer may take issue with more than one party, for example both the architect and contractor, in relation to the same dispute.

2.05 Multiple parties to a dispute may all agree to consolidate or hear together their related disputes. Alternatively the parties may confer a discretion upon an arbitrator to order a consolidation or hearing together of related disputes. The UK's Joint Contracts Tribunal ('JCT') has incorporated multi-party arbitration agreements into its standard forms, but no such provision has been made in the FIDIC Conditions of Contract. Provision for multiparty arbitration is included in many of the model arbitration clauses and arbitration rules which parties may choose from, including the ICC Rules and The London Court of International Arbitration ('LCIA') Arbitration Rules. Finally, the courts of the seat of the arbitration may have a jurisdiction to order a consolidation or hearing together of related disputes – for example, the Hong Kong courts have such a power, but only in relation to domestic disputes.

2.06 More generally, due consideration and recognition should always be given to the implications of the choice of seat, for it determines the supportive and supervisory role of the national courts and any mandatory laws that shall apply to any international arbitration. In Saudi Arabia, for example, the arbitral law provides that the tribunal must compose of men only, who must also be of Muslim faith. Failure to comply with this mandatory requirement of the seat could amount to a procedural ground on which the enforcement of an Award might be refused.

2.07 States vary in the support they give to the arbitral process and the extent to which they are prepared to interfere in that

process. This is reflected in the powers which the state confers on the tribunal itself and upon the courts to supervise that process and to make ancillary orders, e.g. for the production of documents, attendance of witnesses or injunctions.

3 The agreement to arbitrate

3.01 In international arbitration two types of arbitration agreements are commonly seen. The first is a basic arbitration clause in the main contract between the parties and tends to be relatively brief, because it provides for the resolution of future but as yet unknown disputes.

The second type sometimes called 'submission' agreements are discussed in section 3.10 below.

Institutional arbitration

3.02 In large international construction projects the parties very often sign up to an arbitration clause in the form of a model clause, recommended by one of the established arbitration institutions. The parties may make provision for an institution to administer the arbitration and for the arbitration rules of the institution to apply. This is known as an 'institutional arbitration'. The advantages of an institutional arbitration include the application of established international arbitration rules along with trained staff to appoint the tribunal, to ensure time limits are observed, to review the award and to assure the general smooth running of the arbitration.

3.03 The ICC recommends the following sample clause, where the parties have chosen the ICC Court of Arbitration to administer their international arbitration:

> 'All disputes arising out of or in connection with the present contract shall be finally settled under the Rules of Arbitration of the International Chamber of Commerce by one or more arbitrators appointed in accordance with the said Rules'.

This is a broad form clause and will encompass all types of disputes including claims for misrepresentation and non-contractual claims such as tort claims for professional negligence.

3.04 There are no international arbitration institutions which specialise in construction disputes, or specific international construction arbitration rules. Parties therefore use the established international institutions, such as the ICC, the LCIA, the China International Economic and Trade Arbitration Commission (CIETAC), the American Arbitration Association (AAA), the Singapore International Arbitration Centre (SIAC) and the Hong Kong International Arbitration Centre (HKIAC). The institutional arbitration rules of the ICC (which are widely used in international construction arbitrations) are referred to in greater detail in this chapter.

3.05 The ICC headquarters are in Paris, but an international arbitration under the ICC Rules may have arbitrators of any nationality, sitting in any place and using any language. The role played by the ICC Court of Arbitration is to ensure the proper application of the rules; it will appoint or confirm the appointment of arbitrators and in the absence of agreement between the parties fix the place of the arbitration. Some of the rules may be modified by the parties' agreement, but the ICC will refuse to administer arbitrations where the parties' agreement has modified rules that the ICC considers basic to the proper functioning of an ICC arbitration.

3.06 The ICC also administers the costs associated with the running of an international arbitration, which in an ICC arbitration can be significant (for a fuller explanation, see Section 8). Perhaps for this reason the use of UNCITRAL Arbitration Rules is gaining popularity in international construction circles. The UNCITRAL Arbitration Rules are a set of stand-alone arbitration rules which can be imported into an agreement to arbitrate to provide many of the same benefits of certainty over the procedure without reference to an arbitral institution or the associated expense. The UNCITRAL Arbitration Rules may be adapted by agreement between the parties and are sometimes used in conjunction with the International Bar Association's Rules on the Taking of Evidence in International Commercial Arbitration (the 'IBA Rules'). Since the major arbitral institutions amend their arbitration rules from time to time, parties may wish to include drafting to make it clear which version they are seeking to incorporate be this the version 'in force on the date of their agreement to arbitrate' or 'as modified and amended from time to time'.

Ad hoc arbitration

3.07 In principle, an ad hoc international arbitration operating without the supervision (and associated cost) of an institution tends to be cheaper than an institutional arbitration. The parties are free to draft a procedure entirely suited to their particular dispute, but the risk with this approach is that the success of the procedure is dependent on the willingness of the parties to cooperate in its drafting. The alternative is for the arbitration to proceed without a formal written procedure in accordance with directions made by the tribunal as and when required. In many ad hoc international construction arbitrations, parties chose to incorporate the UNCITRAL Arbitration Rules either as a whole or in part.

3.08 In ad hoc international arbitrations, in circumstances where the parties cannot agree on the choice of arbitrator(s), the parties are obliged to refer the decision to an appointing authority. Provision should be made for this possibility when the arbitration clause is drafted. The FIDIC forms suggest that where the UNCITRAL Arbitration Rules are used provision should be made to provide for the President of the FIDIC or a person appointed by the President to appoint the arbitral tribunal, when the parties cannot agree on its composition. Frequently, in the Royal Institute of British Architects (RIBA) contracts for architects' services this role is filled by the President of the RIBA, who is named as the appointer of the arbitrator. The RIBA's list of potential arbitrators includes individuals who are qualified as architects, engineers, quantity surveyors and some of these are additionally qualified as lawyers. The choice of appointing authority can be contentious and it is worth exploring with the proposed appointing authority how it makes its appointments and the identity of the individuals on its list.

3.09 There are a number of important clauses which should be included in an agreement to arbitrate:

(i) **The number of arbitrators and their method of selection.** In large international arbitrations, the custom is to appoint a three-person tribunal, but this may not always be necessary. The usual practice for the appointment of a tribunal is for each party to appoint or nominate one arbitrator and for the party appointed or nominated arbitrators to agree on the appointment of a third arbitrator to be the chair of the tribunal. In the absence of an express choice, the presumption under the ICC Rules is for a sole arbitrator, unless the value of the claim exceeds US$1.5 million, when the Court will consider whether the complexity of the dispute warrants the appointment of a three-person tribunal.

(ii) **The agreement to arbitrate should include the place or seat of the arbitration.** It should be noted that this does not mean that all arbitral proceedings have to take place there. The tribunal usually has discretion to hold proceedings at other venues.

(iii) **The arbitration agreement should designate the language of the proceedings.** Absent agreement of the parties, most arbitration rules provide the arbitrators with the power to decide the language of the arbitration.

Submission agreement

3.10 The other type of arbitration agreement commonly seen in international arbitrations, provides for the submission of an existing dispute to arbitration, and therefore usually sets out in much greater detail how the parties wish for the arbitration to proceed.

This is sometimes called a 'Submission Agreement'. It might include such details as the names of the arbitrators agreed upon, agreements reached regarding the procedure to be followed in the arbitration and the venue for the arbitration.

Pathological arbitration clauses

3.11 From time to time an agreement to arbitrate is so poorly drafted that it leads to a dispute over the correct interpretation or effectiveness of the clause. The dispute can result in the complete failure of the agreement to arbitrate or in the unenforceability of an arbitral award. Such defective clauses are known as 'pathological arbitration clauses'. The problems that arise include:

- equivocal drafting as to whether binding arbitration is intended or whether the parties are entitled to have recourse to national courts;
- conflicting or unclear procedures; and
- the inclusion of a reference to an arbitrator or arbitral institution that does not exist or refuses to act.

3.12 Most national courts will usually attempt to give meaning to the defective arbitration clause, in order to give effect to the intention of the parties to arbitrate their dispute. Where it is possible, a national court may discard the defective drafting if it is clear that the surviving clause represents the intention of the parties. The ICC encounters clauses from time to time which purport to provide for ICC arbitration but which fail in this purpose for lack of certainty. An example is a clause which refers an unresolved dispute between the parties 'to the International Chamber of Commerce'. Even if this clause is taken to be a broad reference to the ICC's Court of Arbitration, it fails because it is not clear what method of dispute resolution it is intended that the dispute be resolved by, e.g. conciliation or mediation or arbitration etc.

4 Procedure in international arbitration

4.01 The procedure for an international arbitration is derived from the procedural rules agreed by the parties, whether settled by the parties themselves or imposed by the application of institutional rules, or failing that procedural rules settled by the arbitral tribunal. In practice, the arbitral rules usually grant a tribunal a wide discretion to devise a procedure that the tribunal deems to be most appropriate for the dispute before it. Procedural requirements may also be imposed on the parties and/or the tribunal by the law of the seat of the arbitration. For example, a tribunal with its seat in England and Wales is required to act fairly, impartially and avoiding unnecessary delay or expense in accordance with section 33 of the Arbitration Act 1996.

Commencement date

4.02 The commencement date is of particular importance if a challenge to the claim is raised on the basis that it is time barred by the application of a limitation period arising under the substantive law of the contract. In ad hoc arbitration, the start date is either agreed by parties or determined in accordance with the law of the seat. An ICC arbitration is commenced on the date a Request for Arbitration is received by the Secretariat of the Court in accordance with Article 4 of the ICC Rules.

Appointment of the tribunal

4.03 If the dispute is to be referred to three arbitrators the usual practice is that each party may appoint one arbitrator or in the case of multiple claimants or multiple respondents they may appoint jointly. The party-appointed arbitrators agree upon the appointment of the third arbitrator. The practice varies slightly in an ICC arbitration. The ICC Court confirms the appointments of the party-nominated arbitrators and the court appoints the Chair of the tribunal unless the parties agree otherwise. All arbitrators are obliged to be independent of the parties and to act fairly and impartially in the conduct of the proceedings.

4.04 In an ICC arbitration the ICC Court Secretariat will transfer the case file to the tribunal once an advance on costs has been paid. The tribunal will then examine the Request for Arbitration and the Answer to determine what if any further clarifications are required before the 'Terms of Reference' for the arbitration are drawn up. This is a procedural feature particular to the ICC Rules. The Terms of Reference summarise each parties' claims and the relief sought, with sufficient detail to prevent either party from introducing a new claim later on in the proceedings which falls outside the Terms of Reference, unless it has been authorised by the tribunal. The Terms of Reference should also include a list of the issues in dispute, so as to enable the arbitral tribunal to ensure that all matters are considered in the arbitration and decided when it comes to drafting the award. Where the list of issues cannot be agreed by the parties, it is common for each party to submit separate lists to the tribunal.

4.05 After the appointment of the tribunal (and in the case of an ICC arbitration, after the agreement of the Terms of Reference) the parties come before the tribunal for a procedural meeting. At this meeting the tribunal will usually seek to establish a timetable for the arbitration, providing for such things as the preparation and exchange of witness statements, expert reports and disclosure. Subsequent procedural hearings may deal with issues that arise in the immediate run up to the main arbitration hearing, and the conduct of the arbitration hearing itself.

4.06 The procedure for the arbitration hearing will usually include written submissions exhibiting the evidence on which each party intends to rely (both documentary and in the form of witness statements). These submissions are usually presented consecutively, the claimant first, followed by the respondent and permission may be given for further 'reply' submissions. Provision is usually made for short oral openings; concise oral cross-examination of witnesses and short oral closings by both sides. Oral hearings tend to be very short by comparison with hearing before English courts and cross-examination is permitted but very limited. Some arbitral rules provide that consideration should be given to whether an oral hearing is necessary at all, but in most cases it will be important for arbitrators to hear directly from key witnesses and any experts to be able to judge their credibility and the weight to be given to their evidence.

4.07 Hearings are usually held in private and only the tribunal, the parties and their representatives are entitled to attend. After the conclusion of the hearing there may be further written submissions from the parties' legal representatives, following which the tribunal will draft its award.

4.08 The ICC Court of Arbitration reviews all international arbitration awards before they are published to the parties. This review is not on the merits of the decision, but so as to ensure that the tribunal has addressed all of the issues before it. This is thought to give greater international acceptability to the award than might be the case in an award issued by an ad hoc arbitral tribunal. This may be particularly useful in jurisdictions such as the People's Republic of China where enforcement of international awards has historically been not without difficulty.

5 Interim measures in international arbitrations

5.01 Interim measures in international arbitration are sometimes called 'provisional relief' or 'conservatory measures'. The range of measures sought can be wide reaching, relating to the preservation of evidence or party assets, or compelling a witness to attend a hearing and give evidence. A party may have recourse to the tribunal or to a national court to grant an interim measure.

5.02 The power of a tribunal to grant an interim measure will turn primarily upon the terms of the arbitration agreement and the law of the seat.

5.03 The ICC Rules provide: 'the Arbitral Tribunal may, at the request of a party, order any interim or conservatory measure it deems appropriate'.

5.04 There are similar provisions in the UNCITRAL Arbitration Rules and the LCIA Rules. The power conferred by the ICC Rules is wide ranging, it is not for example limited to measures which affect property or evidence which is the subject of the dispute. However the tribunal may only act once the case file has been provided to it by the ICC Court. There may be cause for a party to seek an interim measure before this, because it can take time to establish the arbitral tribunal and during that time vital evidence or assets could disappear, in which case a party will be obliged to apply to the national courts for the interim measure.

5.05 Typically an order will be sought to secure assets out of which an award may be satisfied when a recalcitrant debtor is deliberately dissipating assets to render itself eventually poor. Difficulties with this process can arise where the parties have chosen a neutral seat for the arbitration where the courts of that seat have no jurisdiction over the party (and their assets) against whom the interim measures are to be enforced. Necessarily then the parties will have to apply to a foreign court to render assistance to an arbitration with a seat elsewhere.

5.06 Most states permit their national courts to grant interim measures in support of an international arbitration. In practice a party may therefore have a choice as to whether an application for an interim measure is made to the tribunal or to the national courts. The appropriate course of action will depend in each case on the particular application, the relevant law and the relief sought and the ease of enforcement. If it is necessary for coercive action to be taken to deal with the issue the measure must usually be pursued through the national courts. In England, the court will only act with the permission of the tribunal (unless the matter is urgent) and only where the tribunal lacks jurisdiction or is unable to act effectively.

6 Evidence in international arbitration

6.01 Under most international arbitration rules the tribunal has a wide discretion to establish the facts of the case by any appropriate means, subject to any agreement by the parties and any mandatory laws of the seat.

Admissibility of evidence

6.02 There is very little authority on how a tribunal should address the admissibility of evidence in an international arbitration; the UNCITRAL Arbitration Rules, the ICC Rules of Arbitration and the LCIA Rules are silent on the matter. The consequence is that formal rules governing the admissibility of evidence tend not to apply in international arbitration and all evidence is accepted by the tribunal, with its weight and relevance assessed accordingly.

Disclosure

6.03 A party's expectation of the document production or disclosure process will depend on whether they are from a common or civil law background. A party from a civil law background is likely to object to the common law approach of producing all 'relevant' documents to an opponent's case, on the basis that it is costly and too onerous to apply. Parties who chose not to adopt institutional rules, or where such rules do not provide for discovery (as is the case with the UNCITRAL Arbitration Rules, the ICC Rules and the LCIA Rules), may incorporate the IBA Rules in whole or in part. The IBA Rules provide that the parties shall first submit to each other and the tribunal the documents on which each party intends to rely. After such an exchange, any party may submit a 'Request to Produce' to the arbitral tribunal, in which the requesting party is required to set out:

- documents or a narrow or specific requested category of documents that are reasonably believed to exist and to be in the possession of another party (and are not in the possession of the requesting party); and

- an explanation of how the documents requested are relevant and material to the outcome of the case.

The grounds set out in Article 3 of the IBA Rules are more restrictive than the comparative English Civil Procedure rules but far wider than any terms a European party would be familiar with. A party is entitled to object to a Request to Produce in accordance with limited grounds set out in the IBA Rules.

6.04 The current version of the IBA Rules is under review and it is anticipated that in any new version provision will be made for issues arising out of electronic disclosure. In recent years parties objecting to a Request to Produce have often cited the ground that the request placed an 'unreasonable burden' on them to produce, as a result of the overwhelming amount of electronic documentation falling into the category of documents requested. This is a consequence of the electronic revolution in document creation, and the use of email communication.

Factual witness evidence

6.05 Some civil law jurisdictions prevent a party-affiliated individual from giving evidence as a witness of fact; this is in sharp contrast to the common law practice which permits any person to present evidence including a party to the arbitration agreement. International arbitration practice generally follows the common law, though the tribunal may accord less weight to the evidence of a party-affiliated witness than to that of an independent witness. Generally, if a party submits a witness statement, the witness should be prepared to attend the arbitration and to give oral testimony, unless the parties have agreed otherwise or the arbitral tribunal has made such a direction. Sometimes a tribunal will exercise its discretion to refuse to hear a witness, if it determines that it is sufficiently well informed of the facts through other evidence that has already been admitted.

6.06 The IBA Rules provide that where a witness has submitted a statement but does not attend to provide oral testimony (without a valid reason), the arbitral tribunal may dismiss their evidence (Article 4(8)). There is no such express provision in the ICC Rules as to what happens when a witness fails to appear and it will be a matter for the tribunal to determine what, if any, weight should be given to the evidence contained in the statement.

6.07 The tribunal will usually provide the legal representatives of the parties with the opportunity to cross-examine the witnesses and it may put some questions directly to the witnesses itself.

Expert witnesses

6.08 The use of expert witnesses in international arbitration is not as common as in proceedings in the English courts, but in complex construction arbitrations the opinion of experts is often required because of the technical nature of the matters in dispute.

6.09 If a party wishes to call expert evidence and the request is acceded to by the tribunal, the other party will be given the same opportunity. Most tribunals will provide directions for experts of the same discipline to meet and to discuss any conflicting views in an attempt to narrow the issues in dispute, before each expert produces his report.

6.10 Most national laws and arbitration rules provide that the tribunal may appoint experts to assist it on specific or technical matters; in some cases such as under French law this is the case even if both parties object. The costs of such an appointment will generally form part of the overall costs of the arbitration, to be paid by the parties and not the tribunal. Therefore if a party objects, a tribunal is usually cautious to appoint. The tribunal will be aware that in practice the parties will be unlikely to allow the tribunal-appointed expert's evidence to stand unchallenged and will usually seek to adduce their own expert evidence. If such an appointment is made, Article 6 of the IBA Rules provides that the terms of reference for the tribunal-appointed expert should be closely defined after consultation with the parties and the parties should be afforded the opportunity to raise any objections to a tribunal-appointed expert's independence. In practice, the tribunal should also afford the parties an opportunity to put questions to the tribunal-appointed expert during the arbitration hearing.

Confrontation testimony

6.11 The simultaneous questioning of two or more witnesses on the same issues is increasingly being used as a technique. It is called 'confrontation testimony', 'witness conferencing' or, in one variant, 'hot tubbing'. It is popular where one or more issues have great importance to the tribunal reaching their final determination on the merits, such as the opinion from experts on the viability of a design. Confrontation testimony enables the tribunal to hear immediately where the witnesses are in agreement and where their accounts differ.

7 International arbitration awards – recognition, challenges and enforcement

7.01 At the conclusion of an international arbitration, the tribunal will publish its award which will generally be immediately final and binding. Typically the tribunal will require payment of all its fees and expenses before publication. The law of the seat may provide for certain limited rights of challenge or appeal. It is common for parties to an international dispute to contract out of the rights of appeal to the fullest extent possible under the law of the seat and many institutional rules including those of the ICC provide for this. If prior to the conclusion of the arbitration the parties reach a settlement, most international arbitration rules provide for the tribunal (if requested by both parties), to record the settlement in the form of an award which need not contain reasons.

7.02 The award, if not carried out voluntarily may be enforced by legal proceedings through the courts. There are a number of regional and international treaties and conventions which relate to the enforcement of awards, but the most important of these is the New York Convention which is recognised in over 140 countries. It requires the local courts of the contracting states to give effect to an agreement to arbitrate when seized of an action in a matter covered by an arbitration agreement by staying any court proceedings which are brought in breach of that agreement and also to recognise and enforce awards made in the territory of a state other than the state in which recognition and enforcement is sought, and to awards not considered as domestic in the state in which enforcement is sought. It has one principal formal requirement stipulated in Article II, that the arbitration agreement be in writing. Some states will only enforce awards made in other contracting states – another reason that care must be taken with the choice of the seat of the arbitration.

7.03 A party seeking recognition and enforcement of an award to which the New York Convention applies, is obliged to produce to the relevant court:

- the duly authenticated original award or a duly certified copy thereof; and
- the original agreement to arbitrate or a duly certified copy thereof.

Certified translations of the documentation are required if the official language of the country in which recognition and enforcement is sought is not the language of the documentation. The court will then usually grant recognition and enforcement of the award.

7.04 The New York Convention provides in Article 5, limited grounds on which a court may (it is discretionary) refuse enforcement:

Capacity	The parties to the agreement were under some incapacity, or the agreement to arbitrate is not valid under the law to which the parties have subjected it or the law of the seat where the award was made.
Notice	The party against whom the award is invoked was not given proper notice of the appointment of the arbitrators or of the proceedings or was otherwise unable to present his case.
Scope	The award deals with matters not within the scope of the agreement to arbitrate.
Procedure	The composition of the arbitral tribunal or its procedure was not in accordance with the agreement of the parties or absent such agreement not in accordance with the law of the seat.
Finality	The award has not yet become binding on the parties, or has been set aside or suspended, for example the ICC Court of Arbitration has yet to approve the award and issue it.
Arbitrability	The subject matter of the difference is not capable of settlement by arbitration under the law of the country where enforcement is sought.
Public Policy	Recognition or enforcement of the award would be contrary to the public policy of the country where enforcement is sought.

7.05 The grounds are relatively limited and largely concerned with procedural irregularities which must be proved by the applicant, except for the last two grounds which may only be raised by the national court charged with recognition and enforcement, of its own motion. The exact procedure to be followed and the way in which the New York Convention is interpreted is a matter for the national law and national courts of the country in which recognition and enforcement is sought.

7.06 Most states support the arbitral process and construe the bases for refusing enforcement fairly narrowly. In these states (among which the UK can be included) a refusal to recognise and enforce an award is very rare. Other signatory states have perhaps embraced the spirit of the convention less wholeheartedly and their courts construe the grounds more liberally (particularly the public policy ground) with the consequence that refusal to recognise or enforce an award is more common.

8 Costs in international arbitration

8.01 The law of costs in international arbitration is properly to be considered part of the law of the seat. In general, arbitral rules give the tribunal a broad discretion to make cost orders. Most rules are silent as to how that discretion should be exercised, though the LCIA rules provide that the cost award should in general reflect the parties' relative success and failure.

8.02 In practice, a losing party will often be ordered to pay the legal and other costs of the arbitration. These costs may include:

- a substantial proportion of the legal fees of the winning party;
- the fees and expenses of the arbitrators;
- the costs of any tribunal appointed experts; and
- any costs arising out of the administering of the arbitration by an institution.

These costs fall to be paid by the losing party in addition to their own legal costs and other expenses. Where there is no clear loser or where the winner has succeeded on only a part of its claim, a tribunal is likely to make some other order for the proportions in which the parties are to bear the costs. The tribunal will typically take into account any offers to settle made by the parties when making an award of costs on the basis that a party should not have to bear the costs of proceedings which ought not reasonably to have continued once the offer had been made.

8.03 The cost of an institutional arbitration may be significantly greater than the costs of conducting a similar arbitration on an ad hoc basis. Under the ICC Rules the charges made by the institution for administrative expenses, as well as the fees and expenses of any experts appointed by the arbitral tribunal and the arbitrators' fees, are given in terms of a fixed percentage of the sum in dispute on a sliding scale, so that the greater the sum in dispute the greater the overall fee but the smaller the percentage. The cost can be significant and is a reason given by international commercial parties for favouring the adoption of the UNCITRAL Rules of Arbitration, which provide many of the same benefits of certainty over the procedure without the added expenses of a supervising institution.

Part E

The architect in practice

29

Legal organisation of architects' offices

GRAHAM BROWN
SCOTTISH POSTSCRIPT BY GORDON GIBB

1 Managing an architectural business

1.01 Management is a creative activity, the exercise of which is about making and maintaining dynamic cultures within and by which the objectives of people as individuals, teams and organisations are achieved.

The manager of an architectural business is concerned with three types of relationship: between the owners of the business and their clients, between employer and employee, and between the owners of the business themselves. Other chapters deal with the first and second of these. This chapter deals with the third.

Responsible management of an architectural business is an essential pre-requisite for the successful management of architectural projects and is part of an architect's duty of care enshrined in the Architects Registration Board Code of Conduct.

Critical to the success of any business is its legal form and structure. The choice of the form of legal organisation is an important part of an architect's duty.

1.02 There are no formal restrictions in the professional codes governing the structures under which architects carry on their business. The Architects Act 1997 permits registered persons to practise as partnerships or companies, limited or unlimited, provided that the work of their practice, insofar as it relates to architecture, is under the control and management of a registered person. The RIBA Code of Professional Conduct states in its preface that 'A member is at liberty to engage in any activity, whether as proprietor, director, principal, partner, manager, superintendent, controller or salaried employee of, or consultant to, any body corporate or unincorporate, or in any other capacity provided that his conduct complies with the Principles of this Code and the Rules applying to his circumstances'.

1.03 While architects may choose to practise as sole traders, to form companies or to create larger amalgamations as group practices or consortia, many architects still practise in partnership. The main choice for architects setting up in business is usually between partnerships, limited liability partnerships and companies. A partnership provides the breadth of expertise a sole trader cannot provide without the formality of incorporating a registered company. (See Checklist 29.3 for an outline of the principal differences between partnerships and companies.)

2 Partnership

2.01 The law of partnership is governed by the Partnership Act 1890. (Section numbers in the text which follows are from the 1890 Act.) Unless otherwise specified in a partnership agreement, the provisions of the Partnership Act will apply. Partnership is defined in section 1 as 'the relation which subsists between persons carrying on a business in common with a view to profit'. 'Business' includes the practice of architecture. A single act, such as designing a house, may make a business and, if there is a series of such acts, a business will certainly be held to exist. A view to profit' requires only the intention to make a profit. The requirement of acting in common is important. It may be contrasted with barristers, who are in business with a view to profit but do not act in common: they merely share facilities. Unlike a company, a partnership has no legal personality. It is nothing more than the sum total of the individuals comprising it.

Formation of partnership

2.02 A partnership is a form of contract. Although many architects set up partnerships quite casually it is prudent to create the business formally and expressly by a deed of partnership executed under seal or written articles of partnership. The existence of a partnership can sometimes be inferred in law, however, from the behaviour of the individuals involved, even if no deed of partnership exists, and may exist even despite vigorous statements to the contrary.

Importance of clarity

2.03 Considerable importance may be attached to the existence of a partnership. For example, if two architects work together occasionally over several years and a case of negligence arises, both may be liable if a partnership exists even if only one of them has been negligent. If there is no partnership, however, one of them, if not personally involved in any negligence, will be safe from any claim. It can be vital to clients or suppliers of a practice to establish whether they are dealing with a partnership or one person. Architects are recommended on all occasions to clarify their relationship with each other in writing, particularly when working as group practices and consortia.

Sharing facilities and profits

2.04 If two or more architects do not intend to practise in partnership, but merely to share facilities, they must take great care to avoid the possibility of leading others into the assumption that they practise together as partners. Shared ownership of property, even if accompanied by sharing of net profits, is not normally on its own evidence of the existence of a partnership. Profit-sharing is, however, *prima facie* evidence of a partnership, but if it is just one piece of evidence among others it will be weighed with the other evidence. This is particularly important to architectural practices, since profit-sharing in the form of profit-related bonus payments is a common means of remunerating staff. Nevertheless, payment by profit-sharing will not of itself make an employee a partner in the business, nor will sharing in gross returns alone necessarily create a partnership. It is important to draft any contract of employment including any profit-sharing provision very carefully indeed. The relationship between the business and the outside world is important. Individuals can be 'held out' to the world as partners and the outside world will be entitled to treat them as partners. This can be done, for instance, by listing them as partners on the firm's notepaper.

Deed of partnership

2.05 Even though there are ways of determining whether a partnership exists, and the 1890 Act sets out terms which apply if partners have nothing written down, it is most important, if intending partners agree they are going into a business together, to set out the terms of their relationship in a deed of partnership since the terms expressed and implied by the Partnership Act can be draconian and unfair. The deed should cover the points outlined in Checklist 29.1.

Checklist 29.1 Items to be considered for a deed of partnership

Note: The terms of a partnership agreement, like any other contract, may be widely varied by mutual consent of the parties. Where no provision is made, those of the Partnership Act 1890 will apply. Figures in brackets refer to relevant clauses in that Act.

1 Name of firm
2 Place of business
3 Commencement date
4 Duration
5 Provision of capital
   (a) Amount
   (b) Proportion to be contributed by each partner
   (c) Distinctions between what is not partnership capital (a premium) and capital which is partnership property (contribution to working capital)
   (d) Capital should be expressed in money terms
   (e) Any special agreement for interest on capital (24(3), (4))
   (f) Valuation and repayments on death, etc. (42 and 43)
   (g) Rules for settlement for accounts after dissolution (44)
6 Property
   (a) What partners bring to the firm including contracts (20, 22, 24)
   (b) What belongs to firm as a whole (21)
   (c) What is co-owned but not partnership property
   (d) What is individually owned but used in the business (24)
7 Mutual rights and duties. If these are to be differentiated then they should be specified as holiday times, sabbaticals, work brought into the firm, etc.
8 Miscellaneous earnings. Whether or not income from lecturing, journalism, honoraria, etc. is to be paid into the firm.
9 Profits and losses. Basis for division among partners: if not equally then specified (24(1)). Any reservations such as about guaranteed minimum share of profits in any individual case.
10 Banking and accountants. Arrangements for signing cheques, presentation of audited accounts, etc.
11 Employment of *locum tenens*. Authority for, circumstances, and terms.
12 Constitution of firm. Provisions for changes (36).
13 Retirement at will. Age, fixed term or partnership for life, notice of retirement, etc. Arrangements for consultants and for payment during retirement. Repayment of capital and current accounts on death or retirement.
14 Dissolution. Any special circumstances (see Checklist 29.3).
15 Restrictions on practice. Any covenant restraining competition must be reasonable to interests of parties and public. Areas of operation.
16 Insurances. Various, including liability of surviving partners for dead partners' share in firm.
17 Arbitration. Method, number of arbitrators, etc.

Name of practice

2.06 In naming a firm, there are a number of considerations. Use of the words 'architect' or 'architects' is restricted by the Architects Act 1997 as amended. Only those persons who are on the Register of Architects maintained by the Architects Registration Board (ARB) are permitted to practise or carry on business under the name, style or title of 'architect', with the exception of 'landscape architects', 'naval architects' and 'golf course architects' who are outside the scope of the Act. It is important that any person wishing to use the words 'architect' or 'architects' in their practice title or name checks their acceptability first with ARB.

The provisions of the Business Names Act 1985 must be complied with if a partnership does not consist of the named partners. Certain names which are set out in statutory regulations or give the impression that the business is connected with HM Government or a local authority must gain the approval of the Secretary of State. The use in a firm's name of a retired, former or deceased partner may be permissible provided there is no intent to mislead; but caution is necessary to avoid the implication that such a person is still involved in the practice. The 1985 Act requires businesses to disclose certain information. The names and addresses of each partner must be prominently displayed at the business premises where the public have access. It is important to comply with the provisions of this Act. Failure to do so is a criminal offence or may render void contracts entered into by the practice. The Act requires that business documentation must contain the name of each partner. If there are more than 20 partners, however, the names of all partners can be omitted from business documents if they state the address of the principal place of business and also state that a full list of partners' names and relevant addresses may be inspected there.

Size of practice

2.07 There are still restrictions on the size of some partnerships. In the case of architects these have been removed by the Partnerships (Unrestricted Size) (No.4) Regulations 1992 so long as not less than three-quarters are registered under the Architects Act 1997.

Types of partner

2.08 The law is not concerned with distinctions between senior and junior partners. It is up to the partners to decide how to share profits, but they will be shared equally unless special provision is made. The Royal Institute of British Architects (RIBA) recommends strongly that all persons who are held out to be partners should be described as such without further distinction and, in particular, the term 'salaried partner' should be avoided. The purpose of this is to ensure that all persons described as partners share in the decision-making of the business and have access to appropriate information. Partners are fully responsible for the professional conduct of the practice and for keeping themselves properly informed about all partnership matters.

Associates

2.09 It is a common practice to recognise the status and contribution of senior staff qualified or not by describing them as 'associates'. The title 'associate' is not referred to in the Partnership Act and it has no meaning in law. If it is not intended that associates be partners and share in the liabilities of the partnership, it is unwise to use the term 'associate partner'. Its use may also contravene professional codes. If people are misled into thinking associates are partners, associates will find themselves liable as if they were partners, holding all the obligations without any rights or benefits.

Rights and liabilities of partners

2.10 Every partner has the following rights unless there is an agreement to the contrary:

1 To take full part in management of the business (section 24(5)).
2 To have an equal share in profits and capital of the business (section 24(1)).

3 To inspect the partnership books. These must be kept at the principal place of business of each firm (section 24(9)).

4 To dissolve the partnership at any time by giving notice to the other partners (section 26(1)).

5 By section 24(2) a firm must indemnify every partner in respect of payments made and personal liabilities incurred by them in acting as necessary or in the ordinary and proper conduct of the business of the firm.

6 Not to have new partners added without their consent (section 24(7)).

7 Not to have the fundamental nature of the partnership business altered without their consent. The consent of a majority of partners will suffice for changes in all other ordinary matters connected with the business.

8 Not to be expelled without express agreement (section 25).

Rights to which partners are not entitled

2.11 By section 24(4) there is no right to interest on capital subscribed by a partner, although by section 24(3) there is a right to interest on capital subscribed beyond that which was agreed to be subscribed.

2.12 By section 24(6) there is no right to remuneration for acting in the partnership business.

Liabilities

2.13 Under English law a partnership is a collection of individuals and not a corporate body. In addition to all their normal individual liabilities, each partner has added responsibilities as a member of a partnership.

2.14 Legal action may be taken against a partner jointly, or jointly and severally. By sections 9 and 10 of the Partnership Act every partner is personally liable jointly with all other partners for all debts and obligations incurred by the firm while he is a partner as well as jointly and severally for wrongs done by other partners acting in the ordinary course of the business of the firm or for wrongs done with the authority of co-partners. If a partnership is sued jointly, one or more partners may be sued at the same time. If an action is brought against a partnership jointly and severally, the partners may be sued singly or together. When judgment is given against one, further action may be brought against the others one by one or together until the full amount is paid. If only some of the partners are sued, they may apply to the courts to have their other partners enjoined as co-defendants.

2.15 The provisions of the Limitation Act 1980 and the Latent Damage Act 1986 apply to breaches of contract or of duty of care in tort.

2.16 Partners are not liable for the criminal actions of other partners unless they contributed to them or have knowledge of them. Architects may be liable, however, for breaches of their codes of professional conduct by fellow partners.

2.17 A partnership may indemnify one or more of its partners against the consequences of their liability. This device enables members of staff to share the management of a practice without outlaying capital to join the equity partnership.

2.18 A new partner entering a firm does not normally become liable for debts, obligations, or wrongs incurred or committed before their entry (section 17(1)). If a partner retires he will still be liable for debts or obligations incurred before his retirement (section 17(2)). If he dies, his estate will be liable for such debts or obligations. Moreover, a partner will continue to be treated as a member of the firm, attracting the usual liability, until notice of a change in the constitution of the partnership is advertised (section 36).

2.19 Every partner is an agent of the practice. Any action undertaken by any partner in carrying out the business of the practice will bind the practice unless it is outside their authority to act for the practice in that particular matter, and the person with whom they are dealing knows that they have no authority or does not believe them to be a partner (section 5).

2.20 Partners must render true accounts and full information on anything affecting the partnership or partners (section 28).

2.21 Partners are accountable to the partnership for any private profits they receive from any partnership transaction or from using partnership property, names, or connections (section 29(1)).

2.22 If a partner, while still a partner, competes with the practice without the consent of the other partners he must pay all profits made in consequence to the practice (section 30).

Relationship of partners one to another

2.23 A practice of any size may not discriminate against partners with regard to the provision of benefits, facilities or services or by expelling them or subjecting them to detriment under the Sex Discrimination Act 1975 as amended by the Sex Discrimination Act 1986. Practices may not discriminate in such matters on racial grounds under the Race Relations Act 1976 as amended by the Race Relations (Amendment) Act 2000. Discrimination against partners with disabilities for any reason related to their disabilities is not permitted under the Disability Discrimination Act 1995 as amended by the Disability Discrimination Act 2005.

Dissolution of partnerships

2.24 A partnership comes to an end in any of the following ways:

1 at the end of a fixed term, if it has been so set up;
2 at the end of a single specific commission, if it was set up for that commission alone;
3 on the death or bankruptcy of any partner, unless the partnership agreement makes provision for continuity of the partnership;
4 if any partner gives notice;
5 by mutual consent; or
6 by dissolution by the court.

2.25 Prior to the Finance Act 1985 there were tax benefits in cessation and re-formation of a partnership, but these have now been ended.

2.26 If a partner wishes to end the firm but is prevented by his fellow partners, application may be made to the court for dissolution on one of the grounds shown in Checklist 29.2.

Checklist 29.2: Grounds for dissolution of a partnership

Note: Figures in brackets refer to relevant clauses in the Partnership Act 1890.
1 By agreement of parties
  (a) Agreement per deed. End of fixed term or of single project.
  (b) By expiration, or notice (32). If for undefined time, any partner giving notice of intention (32(c)).
  (c) Illness. Special provisions in deed (to avoid need to apply to courts (35)).
Note: Expulsion. A majority of partners cannot expel unless express agreement in deed (25). There can be no implied consent to expel. Clarification required of arrangements in case partners fall out with each other.
2 By operation of law and courts
  (a) Subject to express agreement, partnership is dissolved as regards all by death or bankruptcy of any partner (33).
  (b) Any event making it unlawful to carry on the business of the practice such as if a partner is insane, incapable of carrying on their part of agreement, guilty of conduct prejudicial to the interests of the firm, wilfully and persistently breaches the partnership agreement or if their conduct is such that the other partners can no longer carry on business with them.
  (c) If the firm can only carry on at a loss.
  (d) If, in the opinion of the courts, it is just and equitable that the firm should be dissolved.

---

3 Limited liability partnerships

3.01 Introduced by the Limited Liability Partnership Act 2000, limited liability partnerships (LLPs) are essentially a hybrid between partnerships and limited liability companies. The Act is brief and is supplemented by the LLP Regulations 2001 which apply to LLPs certain provisions of a number of statutes including the Companies Act 2006 and the Insolvency Act 1986 as amended by the Insolvency Acts 1994 and 2000.

3.02 The intention of the Act is to give the benefits of limited liability while retaining other characteristics of a traditional partnership. An LLP is taxed in the same way as existing partnerships and the internal structure is similar to a partnership. Unlike a limited company, an LLP has no memorandum or articles of association relying instead upon an agreement, similar to a partnership agreement, designed to suit its members. An LLP is a separate legal entity. It is responsible for its assets and liabilities and the liability of its members are limited. But, as with companies, actions may be taken against individual members found to be negligent or fraudulent in their dealings.

LLPs are available to any 'two or more persons associated for carrying on a lawful business with a view to profit' by registration with Companies House.

3.03 A decision as to whether to adopt an LLP structure is likely to be made primarily in regard to its position on taxation. Key features of an LLP include:

1 It is a body corporate, that is a legal entity distinct from its members.
2 It can own property, employ people and enter into contracts. Debts incurred are debts of the LLP.
3 It is taxed as a partnership not as a company.
4 It has unlimited capacity, that is to say its activities are not restricted.
5 It has members but no directors or shareholders. It has no share capital and is not subject to company law regarding capital maintenance.
6 Its members have limited liability. It is liable for all its debts to the extent of its assets.
7 It has complete flexibility regarding its internal structure. It has no memorandum or articles of association and there are no requirements for board or general meetings or decision-making by resolution.
8 It is required to maintain accounting records, to prepare and deliver audited annual accounts and an annual return to Companies House. Exemptions from audit and full accounting apply as for companies.

Membership

3.04 Any natural or legal person such as a company may be members of an LLP. There are no shareholders, directors or secretary. All members are required to be registered as self-employed. Each member and the LLP itself are required to make annual self-assessment returns to HM Revenue and Customs. A minimum of two members are required of which two are designated members. If no members are identified as designated then all members are designated. Designated members have a statutory responsibility for certain tasks including signing the accounts, submitting the accounts to the Registrar, appointing and removing auditors, notifying the Registrar of membership changes, preparing, signing and submitting annual returns, and applying for striking off the register.

3.05 All members are agents of an LLP and as such are obliged to act in the interests of the LLP and to avoid conflicts of interest. The internal relationships between members are unregulated, leaving the matter to a separate and private agreement between members.

Agreement

3.06 There is no statutory requirement for LLPs to have a particular management structure including for the appointment of directors.

This should be formulated in a private LLP agreement unregistered with Companies House. Such agreement describing members' responsibilities should cover arrangements for management, decision making, capital contribution requirements, distribution of profits, membership changes, dispute resolution, liquidation, termination, and changes to the agreement. If an agreement is absent, the default provisions of the Regulations apply. These include that every member may take part in management, all members are entitled to share equally in the capital and profits, and no members are entitled to payment for their business or management actions.

Liability

3.07 An LLP is financially liable to the extent of its assets and members may risk losing the contributions they have made to these assets. In the event of liquidation, members are liable simply to make such contributions as they have agreed with the other members. Such arrangements should be included in the LLP agreement.

3.08 Members are liable for fraudulent or wrongful trading in the same way as are company directors and others under the Insolvency Acts.

3.09 Members are liable in tort for their negligent acts or omissions and the LLP will also be liable to the same extent.

4 Companies

4.01 Company law is enshrined in legislation. The Companies Act 2006 applies to all existing and new companies operating in the UK. The Act was implemented in stages up to and including 1 October 2009. Companies House provides full information on the Act and guidance on the changes it makes to previous legislation. Key changes relate to the formation of companies, the memorandum and articles, share capital, and directors' home addresses and include:

a) The objects of companies formed on or after 1 October 2009 are unrestricted unless restrictions are specifically inserted into their articles. Companies formed before that date can avoid future concerns that they are acting *ultra vires* by deleting all of their existing objects.
b) There are three new sets of Model Articles: for a public company limited by shares; a private company limited by shares; and a private company limited by guarantee. The relevant Model Articles apply to a new company unless its members choose to exclude or modify them.
c) Table A 1985 (and earlier versions) remain in force, so existing companies with Table A-based articles do not need to adopt new articles. They may, however, choose to update their articles by adopting some or all of the Model Articles.
d) Existing companies may remove the limit on allotting shares derived from pre-October authorised share capital.
e) Private limited companies with only one class of shares can give the directors unlimited power to allot new shares.
f) New terminology applies to the wording of shareholder resolutions authorising directors to allot shares, and to disapply pre-emption rights.
g) All directors should provide a service address (such as the company's registered office) to the company secretary. Those at serious risk of violence or intimidation can apply for an order to remove their residential address from post-2002 documents filed at Companies House and/or an order to prevent their home address being disclosed to a credit reference agency.

View of the professional organisations

4.02 Under its Code of Professional Conduct the RIBA may hold a member acting through a body corporate or unincorporate responsible for the acts of that body. This means that for the purposes of suspension or expulsion from the RIBA an architect who is a director of a company may be held personally liable for the acts of the company.

A separate legal persona

4.03 The most fundamental principle of company law is that a company is a distinct and separate entity in law from its members or directors. As a separate legal person a company can own and alienate property, sue and be sued, and enter into contracts in its own right. Although a company is owned by its shareholders and governed by its directors under the supervision of its shareholders, it is distinct in law from all of these. In relation to third parties it is the company which is usually liable, not the shareholders or directors. This is so, however large the percentage of shares or debentures held by one shareholder. A company may be liable in contract, tort, crime and for matters of property. Only in rare cases can directors or shareholders be held personally liable for debts and obligations of the company, for example, if they have been fraudulent or if directors allow the company to trade while it is insolvent.

Types of company

4.04 A company may be limited (by shares or guarantee) or unlimited. A company limited by shares is one in which the share-holders' liability to contribute to the company's assets is limited to the amount unpaid on their shares. A company limited by guarantee is one where the shareholders are liable as guarantors for an amount set out in its Memorandum in the event of the company being wound up. An unlimited company is subjected to the same rules as a limited company except that its shareholders are personally liable for all its debts and obligations in event of the company being wound up.

Formation of companies

4.05 Companies are formed by registration under the Companies Act. The following must be sent to Companies House:

1 A Memorandum of Association setting out the objects of the company. A company's objects are unrestricted unless restrictions are included in its Memorandum which should therefore be drafted carefully to comply with relevant professional codes. The Memorandum should contain provision for alteration as it can be changed only in certain circumstances as laid down by the Companies Act 2006.
2 Articles of Association containing the regulations of the company (subject to the Memorandum). All companies are required to adopt articles of assocation upon incorporation. Model articles prescribed under the Companies Act 2006 apply to companies who choose to adopt them and apply by default to companies formed under the Act but who do not register articles of their own with Companies House. The Articles may be altered by special resolution of a majority of voting company members.
3 A statement of initial nominal capital.
4 Particulars of the director(s) and secretary. All companies must have officers. This means at least one director for a private company, and at least two directors and a company secretary for a public limited company. A private limited company is not required to have a company secretary but it can choose to include in its articles a requirement to do so. Any change in the names and addresses of directors or secretary must be notified to Companies House. The Articles may require directors to have qualification shares. Anyone, even a corporation, may be a company director unless they are an undischarged bankrupt (though the court may give them leave to act) or are disqualified by the court under the Company Directors Disqualification Act 1986 or the Articles. The company may remove a director by ordinary resolution before the end of his term. Directors normally retire in rotation (one-third each year) but may resign by giving such notice as is required in the Articles. Directors are entitled only to such remuneration as is stated in the Articles. Companies may not loan to directors or connected persons except as provided under the Act.
5 Intended location of the registered office of the company.
6 The prescribed fee.

4.06 Companies House will issue a Certificate of Incorporation as evidence that the company is legally registered, and give the company a registered number. Without a Certificate of Incorporation a company does not exist in law and cannot do business.

Public and private companies

4.07 Companies, whether limited or unlimited, may be either public or private. A public company is the only sort of company permitted to offer its shares to the public. Only companies with a minimum authorised share capital of 50 000 in sterling or 65 600 in euros may be public limited companies. The Memorandum of Association must state that the company is a public company. An architect's practice will normally incorporate as a private company. The individuals (who would otherwise be partners) are likely to be directors and shareholders.

Profits

4.08 Profits are distributed among shareholders in accordance with the rights attached to their shares. Although there is a presumption that all shares confer equal rights and equal liabilities, this can be rebutted by a power in the company's Articles to issue different classes of shares. An example of a class of share is a preference share. Holders of preference shares will be entitled to dividends before ordinary shareholders. If there are insufficient funds, preference shareholders will be the only shareholders to receive dividends. Shares are also classed according to whether they have voting rights or not. In most architectural companies profits and dividends are small because directors are remunerated by salary under their service contracts with the company.

Name of company

4.09 Like partnerships, the name of a company is restricted by the Architects Act 1997 and the Business Names Act 1985. Limited companies must use the word 'Limited' after their name. It is an offence for public companies to choose names giving the impression that they are private companies, and vice versa. The use of a name similar to that of another company with the same type of business may constitute an actionable tort.

4.10 A company must state its corporate name on all business documents and on its seal. It must display this name legibly on the outside of its business premises. Other particulars including the place of registration, the registered number and the address of the registered office must be included on company business documents.

Size of company

4.11 A company may have an unlimited number of shareholders.

Rights and liabilities of shareholders

4.12 Shareholders holding shares with voting rights have the right to supervise the management of the company by voting in an annual general meeting, or in such extraordinary general meetings as may be called. Private companies are not required to hold an AGM unless they positively opt to do so. Decisions may be taken by written resolution.

4.13 Shareholders are paid dividends out of the profits of the company, in accordance with the rights belonging to their shares.

4.14 A partnership is bound by contracts made by one of its partners and is liable in tort for the acts or omissions of each partner. In contrast, shareholders cannot make contracts binding on a company, nor are they liable personally for debts or obligations of other shareholders. Shareholders are liable, however, for torts and obligations of a limited company to the amount unpaid on the nominal value of their shares. Frequently this is academic. Many small limited companies only have £100 worth of share capital split into smaller proportions still. If the company is unlimited, shareholders will be liable for the debts and obligations of the company in the event of its winding-up.

4.15 When a company is dissolved by winding-up, both present members and those who have been members in the 12 months preceding the winding-up are required to contribute towards the liability of the company but, for the reasons given above, this contribution is often nominal. Only in the case of a substantial unpaid up shareholding could it assume any significance and this is likely to be most unusual. The liabilities of past company members are not so wide-reaching as those of partners.

Rights and liabilities of directors

4.16 Under the Articles, directors are normally given the power to manage the company under the ultimate supervision of shareholders. They may delegate the management to a managing director.

4.17 Directors are not servants or agents of a company and can only bind it if some organ of the company has conferred appropriate authority upon them. Authority for this depends on the Articles or by special resolution of the shareholders. A director may be held to have had usual authority or to have been held out as having authority and this will bind the company. The third party need not be familiar with the Articles in either case. A managing director can normally be expected to have authority to bind the company.

4.18 The Companies Acts and the Insolvency Acts prescribe a large number of duties for directors. These include:

1   Directors must prepare and disclose company accounts in a specified form stating the financial position of the company. They must keep the books at the registered office of the company available for inspection by company officers at any time.
2   Directors must prepare an annual report reviewing the business of the company and recommending the amount of dividends to be paid.
3   The company must be audited annually if its turnover exceeds a specified amount or if at least 10% of its shareholders request an audit.
4   The report and accounts must be filed with Companies House at specified times to be available for inspection by the public.
5   The company may elect to hold an annual general meeting of shareholders in each calendar year but this may be dispensed with by resolution of the shareholders. Two persons can constitute a quorum. Extraordinary general meetings may be convened if there is some business the directors consider to be of special importance.
6   The company must keep a register of directors at its registered office disclosing certain information about directors and their interest in the shares or debentures of the company. Companies House must be informed of these particulars and any changes. A register of members containing similar information must also be kept by the company.
7   Directors have no right to remuneration except that specified in the Articles. Remuneration of directors is normally voted on by the shareholders at their general meetings.
8   Directors owe the company a fiduciary duty of loyalty and good faith. They are considered trustees of company assets under their control. They must account to the company for any profits they make by virtue of their position as directors and cannot use their powers as directors except to benefit the company. They must always devote themselves to promoting the company's interests and act in its best interest. Their duty of loyalty means they cannot enter into engagements where their personal interests might conflict with the company's interest and they must disclose their personal interests in such engagements to the shareholders. This duty can continue even after a director leaves the company.
9   Directors owe a duty to the company to exercise reasonable care in the conduct of the business. Such duties are not unduly onerous. Courts are reluctant to intervene in areas involving business judgement. In some circumstances directors will be expected to seek specialist advice and will be liable if they do not. Directors will not be liable for anything they have been authorised to do by shareholders. This duty is not owed to

Checklist 29.3: Differences between companies and partnerships

Partnerships	Companies
1 No separate legal personality (except in Scotland).	1 Separate legal personality from its shareholders.
2 Partners have unlimited liability.	2 Shareholders are liable only to the amount unpaid on their shares but may be liable on personal guarantees for some liabilities.
3 Partners' interests may be difficult to transfer subject to valuation agreement.	3 Interest of shareholders are their shares which can be easier to transfer subject to restrictions in Articles and to valuation agreement. Shares may be difficult to value.
4 May be difficult for a young architect to join a partnership since sufficient capital will need to have been accumulated to buy a share in the partnership or to take over a retiring partner's interest.	4 It is easier to join a company as it does not necessarily involve buying in.
5 Only promotion is to become a partner, so career prospects may be limited.	5 More kinds of promotion possible including to directorship through employment structure. In small companies this is a more theoretical than practical advantage.
6 Difficult for partners to resign and subject to agreement.	6 Easy for directors to resign but liability remains for up to 12 months.
7 Management through meetings of partners.	7 Management through Board of Directors supervised by shareholders, meeting annually.
8 Partners share profits equally unless there is an agreement to the contrary.	8 Company profits are divided according to rights attached to the shares. Employees are remunerated by salary, shareholders by dividends. These can be mixed and matched.
9 Can be formed informally by just starting up business with another person.	9 Must be registered to come into existence but company formation can be quick and cost less than £100.
10 No restrictions on powers of partners subject to agreement.	10 Company powers unrestricted subject to limitations imposed by Articles.
11 Each partner can bind the partnership.	11 No shareholder can bind the company but directors can.
12 Partnership details cannot be inspected by the public.	12 Matters filed with the Registrar of Companies are open to public inspection including Memorandum, Articles, details of directors, secretary, and registered office.
13 Accounts need not be publicised.	13 Accounts must be filed annually with the Registrar of Companies.
14 No audit required.	14 Annual audit may be required.
15 Partnership must make annual tax returns but partners are liable individually for declaring and paying their own tax.	15 Company liable for all declarations and payments of tax.
16 Less administration required.	16 More administration required.
17 Money can be borrowed in the names of the partners but partnership debtors cannot be used as security for loans.	17 May raise money subject to Articles by debentures, for example, or by fixed and floating charges over assets.
18 Death or departure of a partner can cause dissolution of the partnership unless otherwise agreed.	18 Transfer of shares will not end a company's existence.
19 Many ways to dissolve a partnership including instantly by agreement.	19 A company is dissolved only by liquidation in accordance with the Companies and Insolvency Acts or by winding-up.

shareholders, contractors or creditors (although a director may be liable to the creditor for fraudulent or wrongful trading). Since the duty is owed to the company, the company itself can sue directors who have been negligent or in breach of their fiduciary duties.

Dissolution

4.19 A company may be dissolved in two ways:

1 By winding-up under the Insolvency Acts. This may be voluntary or compulsory. Once a company has been wound up no judgment may be enforced against it.
2 By being struck off the Register under the Companies Act. This happens, for instance, if the company fails to file its annual accounts or returns. Companies may seek this form of dissolution themselves. They may do this to save the costs of a formal liquidation.

Companies versus partnerships

4.20 A list of the differences is set out in Checklist 29.3. The relative advantages and disadvantages will differ for individual businesses. Managers need to assess the business priorities when making a decision to form a company or a partnership. The size of the business may be relevant to the decision. Smaller businesses may find the paperwork and administration required for a company too arduous. Taxation is another factor in the decision. This is beyond the scope of this chapter. Managers should seek professional advice from an accountant or from a local tax office.

Service companies

4.21 Service companies are formed to provide services to a partnership. The company may employ staff and hold the premises. It will also normally provide things such as office equipment, stationery, cars and accountancy services to the practice. The advantages of a service company are related to the balance between income and corporation tax.

Group practices and consortia

4.22 Architects' businesses may come together to work in several forms of association, whether for a single project or on a more permanent basis. This chapter is not concerned with the operational and management factors for and behind the choice of form, but only with the legal issues. Further guidance is given in the RIBA Architect's Handbook of Practice Management. The creation of any association should be checked carefully with the professional indemnity insurers of each party.

Loose groups

4.23 These are associations in which practices or individuals pool their knowledge and experience. Such a group does not need to be registered, but some short constitution is desirable which clearly distinguishes it from a partnership. In company law a more formal 'Memorandum and Articles of Association' is necessary and is of far greater significance. It must set out the most important provisions of the company's constitution, including the activities which the company may carry out.

Group practices

4.24 Practices may group together for their mutual benefit and to give better service while each retains some independence:

1 Association. The degree of association may vary considerably from simply sharing office accommodation, facilities and expense, to a fully comprehensive system of mutual help. Beyond agreeing to a division of overhead expenses each practice retains their profits and their normal responsibility to their respective clients.

2 Coordinated groups. For large development projects it is not unusual for the work to be undertaken by two or more architectural practices with one of them appointed to coordinate the activities of the others. Practices are liable to the coordinating practice for torts committed in their areas of activity. The arrangement may be constructed under head and sub-consultancy agreements.

Single-project partnerships and group partnerships may be entered into on terms which are entirely a matter for individual agreements between the parties and are similar in law to any ordinary partnership.

Consortia

4.25 Consortia are little different in law from group practices. The term normally implies the association of practices with different professional skills acting as one in carrying out projects jointly yet retaining their separate identities and each with their own responsibility to the building owner. A consortium may be formed for the duration of a single project or on a more regular and permanent basis.

Difficulties

4.26 Any association of practices, whether permanent or temporary, must be very carefully planned. If practices are to merge completely, assets should be carefully assessed (including work in progress). Specific agreement is necessary on debts, including liabilities relating to previous contracts. These could be significant if a pre-merger project became the subject of a professional negligence claim.

4.27 If practices are to preserve their own identities and to continue to practise in their own right as well as together on common projects, the form of agreement becomes more critical and more complex. A new group or consortium, partnership or company should be created to contract with clients for common projects. Its agreement must resolve how far the assets of member practices are brought in, the extent of liabilities of the group, and the degree of independence retained by each member practice to carry on its own activities. A solicitor should always be consulted.

5 Premises and persons

5.01 Employers are obliged under the general duty of care to protect employees against personal injury in the course of their employment. They are obliged by statute to provide employees with healthy, safe and decent working conditions. For office workers these were originally set out in the Offices, Shops and Railway Premises Act 1963, but this is now subordinate to the Health and Safety at Work Act 1974 (HSW Act) together with regulations made under the two Acts. The HSW Act shifted the focus from premises to people. This chapter is concerned with its impact on an architect as employer, employee, or occupier of premises.

Accidents

5.02 Employers are required to notify the enforcing authority of accidents on the premises, subject to the requirements of the Reporting of Injuries, Diseases, and Dangerous Occurrences Regulations (RIDDOR), which cause the death, or the disablement for more than 3 days, of a person employed to work on the premises. A record must be kept of all accidents as they occur. In any case this is useful as a check against the possibility of persons making claims for accidents which did not happen on office premises.

Employees' right to information

5.03 Because the HSW Act is primarily for the benefit of employees, and because some employers are forgetful of their duties, the occupier is obliged to give employees information about the Act either by posting up an abstract in a sufficiently prominent place or by giving them an explanatory booklet.

Division of responsibility

5.04 One of the potentially confusing aspects of the HSW Act is the division of responsibility between owner and occupier, particularly in multi-occupied buildings. The employer, if not the occupier, is responsible for notifying the occupier of accidents to his employees and for notifying his own employees of the provisions of the Act.

Single occupation

5.05 An employer who occupies a whole building is responsible for ensuring that all provisions of the HSW Act are met.

Multi-occupation

5.06 When a building is in multi-occupation responsibility is divided. The owner is responsible for the fire risk assessment, fire alarms and signposting, and keeping free from obstruction all exits and means of escape in the building as a whole, cleaning, lighting and safety of the common parts, washing and sanitary facilities. Occupiers are responsible for the risk assessment and all other provisions of the HSW Act within the parts of the building they occupy.

Occupiers' Liability Acts 1957 and 1984

5.07 Occupiers owe a duty of care to all entrants on their premises. If the entrants are lawful visitors, reasonably practicable steps must be taken to make the premises safe for them and to protect them against all hazards, or give sufficient notice of them. Visiting workpeople such as window cleaners are responsible for their own safe working methods but if there are particular hazards in the area in which they will be working, then the employer, owner, or occupier has a duty to advise each visitor of those hazards. If it is foreseeable that persons unable to read warnings such as children or blind persons may be likely to get into hazardous areas, then protection must be adequate to keep them out. A duty of care is even owed to trespassers, although this duty is to take such care as is reasonable in all the circumstances of the case to see that they do not suffer injury on the premises by reason of the danger concerned. Sufficient warnings or discouragements will normally discharge the duty.

5.08 Responsibility for injury or damage arising from improper construction or maintenance, is not avoided by the transfer of the premises to another owner (Defective Premises Act 1972).

5.09 If a landlord has a repairing obligation to tenants, then the landlord has a responsibility to anyone who could be affected by the landlord's failure to keep the premises properly maintained.

Health and Safety at Work Act 1974

5.10 The Health and Safety of Work Act 1974 (HSW Act) is directed at people who work, whether employer, employee, or self-employed persons, and their responsibilities to each other and to third parties who may be affected by the work process or its results. Under the Act employers must maintain safe systems of work and keep plant and premises in safe condition. Adequate instruction, training, and supervision must be given for the purposes of safety. This may extend to guidance or instruction to employees visiting buildings or construction sites in the course of their employment particularly at times when the premises or site may be otherwise unoccupied. The RIBA provides detailed guidance on safety procedures with particular reference to safety on site. Unless fewer than five people are employed, an employer must prepare a written statement of the business's safety policies, organisation and arrangements and make this known and understood by all employees. Even if a written policy is not required, an employer is not entitled to disregard the Act.

5.11 Safety policy should deal with the safety responsibilities of all managers, inspection procedures, supervision, training, research and consultative arrangements regarding safety, fire drill procedure, reminders on keeping stairways and corridors free of obstructions, the marking and guarding of temporary hazards, use of machinery, accidents and first aid. Advice is obtainable from the Health and Safety Executive. However, employers should ensure that their safety policies are tailored specifically to meet the individual needs of their businesses. Anyone in a supervisory or managerial role will have specific health and safety responsibilities. While managers may delegate, they retain responsibility.

5.12 The employee in his turn has a duty to exercise reasonable care to himself and his fellow employees, to cooperate with his employer in carrying out statutory requirements and not to interfere with safety provisions. It is important for managers to remember that they are also employees.

5.13 A number of regulations are important to the office environment and organisation. Central to these are the Management of Health and Safety at Work Regulations 1999, containing the requirement, among other matters, that employers and the self-employed make and maintain a sufficient and suitable risk assessment for the purposes of identifying the measures required to be taken to comply with health and safety law. Equally important are the Workplace (Health, Safety and Welfare) Regulations 1992. More specific requirements are laid down in the Provision and Use of Work Equipment Regulations 1998, the Health and Safety (Display Screen Equipment) Regulations 1992, the Manual Handling Operations Regulations 1992 and the Personal Protective Equipment at Work Regulations 1992. The Health and Safety (First Aid) Regulations 1981 impose a duty upon employers to provide first aid equipment and facilities, to provide suitable persons with training in first aid, and to inform employees of the arrangements they have made. The British Safety Council Approved Code of Practice, Health and Safety (First Aid) Regulations 1981 is approved by the Health and Safety Commission to provide practical guidance in respect of the regulations. Although failure to comply with the Code's guidance is not in itself an offence, it is prudent to follow it. The Control of Substances Hazardous to Health Regulations 2002 (COSHH) impose a duty upon employers to ensure levels of hazardous substances do not harm employees or others who may be in contact with them. Hazardous substances used in the office include ammonia, solvents (for example correction fluid), adhesives, photocopy and laser printer toner, copier emissions, cleaning agents and dusts. The Electricity at Work Regulations 1989 require that electrical systems and equipment be maintained so far as is reasonably practical to prevent danger. Recommendations are provided on the frequency of formal inspection and electrical testing. The Health and Safety Executive publishes guidance enabling the obligations imposed by these, and other relevant regulations, to be met.

Enforcement

5.14 To ensure that the law on health and safety is respected, inspectors appointed by the enforcing authority have the power to enter premises to which the Act applies. They may inspect the premises, question anyone, or ask to see relevant certificates or notices. It is good practice to obtain evidence of their identity and authority before taking anyone round.

5.15 Inspectors have the power to make 'improvement' notices under which the offending practice must cease or the deficiency must be remedied within a certain period. They also have the power to issue a 'prohibition' notice under which the practice must cease or the premises must not be used until their requirements have been met. An appeal against a notice may be made to an industrial tribunal. Offences under the Health and Safety at Work Act are criminal offences, although breaches of the regulations

made there under can also result in civil liability. It is an offence to contravene requirements imposed by a notice. The offender may be liable to a fine even though damage has not been suffered. Although insurance may be taken out against the possibility of damages being awarded, insurance may not be used to protect against the results of criminal acts, such as fines or imprisonment under the Health and Safety (Offences) Act 2008.

Fire protection

5.16 The Regulatory Reform (Fire Safety) Order 2005 (FSO) is the most current and up-to-date legislation in respect of fire. The FSO has revoked all other fire regulations including the Fire Precautions (Workplace) Regulations 1997.

5.17 The FSO applies to most premises and covers most types of building, structure and open space. It requires any person who exercises some level of control in premises to take reasonable steps to reduce the risk from fire and ensure occupants can safely escape if a fire does occur.

5.18 The main requirements of the FSO are that the responsible person is to:

1 Carry out or nominate someone to carry out a fire risk assessment identifying the risks and hazards;
2 Consider who may be especially at risk;
3 Eliminate or reduce the risk from fire as far as is reasonably practical and provide general fire precautions to deal with any residual risk;
4 Take additional measures to ensure fire safety where flammable or explosive materials are used or stored;
5 Create a plan to deal with any emergency and, in most cases, document the findings; and
6 Review the findings as necessary.

5.19 Fire alarms must be tested at intervals and occupiers are required to take effective steps to ensure that all occupants are familiar with the means of escape and with the action to be taken in case of fire. Fire drills are the most effective way of doing this.

5.20 If any alterations are made to the premises the responsible person is required to review the fire risk assessment and take such measures as are reasonably necessary to reduce the risk from fire and ensure occupants can safely escape in the event of fire.

6 Insurance

6.01 A practice protects itself by insurance against financial risks. Some of these are ordinary risks such as fire, some are eventualities which a practice is not obliged to cover but which, as a good employer, it may wish to provide for, such as prolonged sickness of a member of staff. There are cases, however, when a practice is obliged by law to cover damage caused to other persons. Varieties of insurance which cover these risks follow.

Public liability

6.02 An owner or a lessee of premises, or someone carrying on a business in premises, may be legally liable for personal injury or damage to property of third parties caused by their negligence or that of their staff.

6.03 Since several people may be involved in a single incident and the level of damages may be very high, it is important for cover to be:

1 appropriate to status whether owner, lessee, or occupier;
2 extended to cover the actions of employers and employees, not just on the premises, but anywhere while on business;
3 extended to cover overseas if employers or employees are likely to be overseas on business.

Employers' liability

6.04 An employer is liable for personal injury caused to an employee in the course of employment by the employer's negligence or that of another member of staff, his agent or servant. It is important to arrange insurance to cover for injuries sustained:

1 during employment whether on or off the employer's premises;
2 overseas if employees are likely to be overseas on business.

Employers' Liability (Compulsory Insurance) Act 1969

6.05 Employers are required by statute to take out specific insurance to meet their obligations. The Employers' Liability (Compulsory Insurance) Act 1969 and the Employers' Liability (Compulsory Insurance) Regulations 1998 as amended require that every employer who carries on business in Great Britain shall maintain insurance under approved policies with authorised insurers against liability for bodily injury or disease sustained by employees and arising out of, and in the course of, their employment in that business. Cover must extend to an amount of £2m for any one occurrence. Employers' liability policies are contracts of indemnity. The premium is often based on the amount of wages paid by the insured to employees during the year of insurance. The size of the business is immaterial. The Act also provides for employees not ordinarily resident but who may be temporarily in Great Britain in the course of employment for a continuous period of not less than 14 days. Copies of the insurance certificate must be displayed at the place or places of business for the information of employees.

Motor vehicles

6.06 Third party insurance cover is a legal requirement under the Road Traffic Act 1988 as amended by the Road Traffic Act 1991 in respect of death or personal injury to third parties or damage to a third party's property. Cover may be invalidated if a car is used for purposes not covered by the policy. Cars owned and operated by a practice must therefore be covered for business use and cars owned by employees and used by them in their duties must be covered for occasional business use and travel to and from a place of work including for commuting.

6.07 If staff use their own cars on practice business their cover must be adequate, particularly in respect of fellow employees. Their policies should be checked to ensure that they include a third party indemnity in favour of the employer, otherwise if a claim results from an incident while the car is used on practice business, insurers may repudiate liability.

Professional indemnity

6.08 This is the insurance necessary to cover professional people for negligence. Such policies will normally only cover liabilities to third parties, not loss caused to a person's own business by reason of their negligence. Nor will they cover fraud.

6.09 Every architect in every form of practice is required by the Architects Registration Board to be covered by professional indemnity insurance. The scope of the policy, amount of the premium and other details are matters which must be worked out on an individual basis by the architect and an experienced insurance broker taking ARB's requirements into account.

6.10 In view of its importance, professional indemnity insurance is dealt with in a separate chapter.

7 Scottish postscript

Introduction

7.01 An individual architect in Scotland can operate either as a sole trader or, in certain circumstances, as a limited company.

Groups can operate as either limited companies, partnerships, limited partnerships or limited liability partnerships.

The Partnership Act 1890, the Business Names Act 1985 and the Limited Partnership Act 1907 apply equally to Scottish partnerships. The Offices, Shops and Railway Premises Act 1963 and the Health and Safety at Work Act 1974, as amended, apply in Scotland as in England.

The Architects Act 1997 (as amended) applies equally to Scotland and to England. Care needs to be taken in the naming the practice and in the correct use of singular/plural to ensure that the Act is complied with.

In many respects, the law in Scotland and England concurs in respect of the framework for establishment of an architectural practice. The essential differences are outlined below.

Sole traders on the business

7.02 The situation for architects practising as sole traders in Scotland is much the same as that in England, in relation to the setting up of the business. Business naming is governed by the Business Names Act 1985 relating to the disclosure of the proprietor's name on business documentation and at the place of business. The taxation position for sole traders, partnerships and companies is presently the same as exercised in England and Wales, although it could be subject to change as a result of the additional tax-raising powers of the Scottish Parliament, if they are implemented in the future.

Partnerships

7.03 As in England, it is inherent in the idea of partnership that association exists, and that business is carried out with a common view to profit. Within a partnership, the minimum number of partners is two. Although governed by the same statutes, there are fundamental differences between Scots and English law regarding the legal status of partnerships and their relationship with the partners themselves.

Firm naming

7.04 In Scotland, a collection of individuals or partners is called a 'firm'. The name of the business is the 'firm name'. The nature of the firm name is important in relation to legal proceedings in the Court of Session. If the firm name does not comprise the names of individuals, it is required in legal proceedings to add the names of all of the partners, up to a maximum of three. This does not apply if the name comprises the names of persons, no matter who they may be. This requirement also does not apply to actions in the sheriff courts (Sheriff Courts (Scotland) Acts 1907 and 1913, updated in 1939, 1971 and 2007). The Business Names Act 1985 requires the name of a firm to be registered unless it comprises only the true surnames of the partners without any additions other than their true first names or initials. If registered, the firm must display the registration certificate in a prominent place at the firm's principal place of business. Failure to do so is a criminal offence. The 1985 Act also demands the publication of the names of the persons or corporations using the business name. In partnership, the names of the partners and any former first names or surnames and nationality, if not British, of the partners must appear on all business letters, brochures and business cards.

The relationship between partners

7.05 The contract of partnership needs no special form. It may be oral, written or inferred by the nature of the relationship. As in any contract, the intention of the parties is relevant, inferred by law from the whole evidence. Every partner is an agent for the firm. His acts in the ordinary course of business and his signing the firm name binds the firm.

The relationship between partners is regulated by the partnership agreement. A partner who meets a firm debt has a right of relief against his co-partners and may call on them to contribute their contracted share to his loss. Terms in the contract of partnership, if verbal or poorly prepared, can be implied from the

Partnership Act, relating to the rights of sharing profits and the liability for losses, the right of access to the firm's books and to take part in its management.

Separate legal entity

7.06 In Scots law, the architectural practice or firm has a separate personality from its members. The partnership owns the funds of the partnership; the partners are not joint owners of the partnership funds. This is of importance relative to liability for debts and actions brought by and against the firm and its members and for diligences, ranking in bankruptcy and compensation. The tax position for a Scottish partnership is presently the same as that in England and Wales.

A partner is not directly liable for a debt owed by the practice. A debtor to a firm cannot plead compensation on a debt due by an individual partner, nor can a partner sued for a private debt plead compensation on a debt due to the firm. However, a partner suing for a private debt may be met with a plea of compensation on a debt due by the firm, while the firm sued may plead compensation on a debt due to a partner. The principle is that a partner is not a creditor in debts due to the firm but is a debtor in debts due by the firm.

A firm can sue and be sued. When suing, it does so either in its own name or in the names of all of the partners, indicating that it is for a firm debt. A firm may be either a debtor or creditor to any of its partners and consequently a partner may sue, or be sued by, the firm.

A firm is liable for the wrongful acts or omissions of its partners acting in the ordinary course of business (*Kirkintilloch Equitable Co-operative Society Ltd v Livingston and others* 1972 SLT 154). Further a firm, at common law, may be liable on the grounds that it received gratuitously the benefit of the wrongful act of a partner.

The extent of partners' liability

7.07 Every partner of a firm is jointly and severally liable for the debts of the firm. Further, the liability is unlimited, making him liable to his last penny to the firm's creditors if the firm does not meet its debts. Partners can be held liable only when the debt has been constituted against the firm. The creditor must sue the firm first. If the firm has been dissolved, all the partners within the jurisdiction must be sued together. The right of recovery of a debt is covered by the Prescription and Limitation (Scotland) Act 1973, as amended in 1984, under which the creditor has 5 years from the date of the loss or transaction to raise a competent action in court. The right of recovery under delictual liability for professional negligence or other wrongdoing is not so restricted.

Partnership property

7.08 Partnership property is all property originally brought into the partnership stock or acquired for the purposes and in the course of the firm's business. The partners must apply this property exclusively for the purposes of the partnership. If property has been bought with money belonging to the firm, it is deemed to have been bought on account of the firm. Property bought by partners individually, which may be loaned to the firm by agreement is not partnership property. Partnership property excludes land or buildings, which must be owned by one or more individuals or by trustees on behalf of the firm.

Retiring partners

7.09 A retiring partner of a firm remains liable for the debts or wrongful acts of the firm incurred or committed while he was a partner, irrespective of the fact that the other partners may have agreed to indemnify him against claims, unless the creditor in question is party to the arrangement. Any agreed limitation of liability in this regard will not restrict ongoing liability for professional negligence. It is of great importance to a retiring partner that all customers and clients are directly informed of the retirement or dissolution. Otherwise he may remain liable for the debts

or wrongful acts of the firm incurred or committed after his resignation (*Welsh and another v Knarston and others* 1973 SLT 66).

New partners

7.10 A new partner admitted to an existing firm does not automatically become liable to the creditors for anything done before he became a partner. This depends upon whether the whole assets are handed over to a new partnership and the business is continued, as before, in which case the liabilities are taken over with the assets and the new partner will be liable. If the new partner paid into the firm a sum as capital while the other partners contributing their share of the going business, the new partner will not share in the firm's previous liabilities.

Assignation

7.11 A partner may assign his interest in the partnership, but not to the point of making the assignee a partner, nor giving partnership rights. A partnership agreement may provide for a right to nominate a partner by inclusion within a will. However, a sole heir cannot become a partner without relevant provision in both the will and the partnership agreement (*Thomson v Thomson* 1962 SC (HL) 28).

Bankruptcy

7.12 In bankruptcy, the firm's creditors must rank before the partners against the firm's estate. The creditors of individual partners do not have a claim on the estate of the firm, although the creditors of the firm qualify for dividends from the estate of individual partners.

The process of divesting a bankrupt of his estate and property is sequestration, whereby the court will pass over the bankrupt's property to a trustee. He gathers in the assets and sells them; the net proceeds (after payment of administration expenses) being divided, as far as possible, amongst the creditors, according to their various priorities, in payment or part-payment of the debts due to them. Before sequestration an individual or firm may go through other stages in the process of inability to meet obligations (Bankruptcy (Scotland) Act 1985 section 7). 'Practical insolvency' is the first stage, being a present inability to meet debts due to insufficient liquidity. The second stage, or 'absolute insolvency', is when the individual or firm's liabilities exceed its assets. At this point, the firm is restricted to acting only in the interests of its creditors. Gifts cannot be made, nor can one creditor be favoured at the expense of others. Transactions, which have that effect, are referred to as 'fraudulent preferences' and may be reduced (overturned) at common law. The third stage is 'apparent insolvency', formerly known as 'notour bankruptcy', which is 'insolvency of a public or notorious nature'. This can be constituted by sequestration. Alternatively, apparent insolvency can be constituted by one of the following: voluntary disclosure to creditors that payment of debts in the normal course of business has ceased; insolvency concurring with a duly executed charge, the date of which has expired without payment being received by the creditor; the granting of a trust deed or a decree of adjudication, either for payment or in security; or by the equalisation of diligences.

Diligence is the legal process of attaching preper to force appearance in court or to allow the implementation of a judgment already pronounced. Diligence may be in the form of arrestment: attaching property in the hands of a third party; or poinding: the attachment of moveable property, the effect of which is to immobilise it. This may be followed by a judicially ordered sale for the benefit of the creditor.

A firm can be sequestrated without any of the partners themselves being sequestrated. If an individual is sequestrated he has the right to retain certain property. This is restricted to items of clothing for himself and his family and working tools or implements necessary to enable him to earn a living. Deliberate avoidance of the loss of assets in Bankruptcy through 'gratuitous alienations' (gifts) made by the insolvent person to trusted others or family can be challenged under the Act of 1985, section 34.

Termination

7.13 A partnership may terminate at the end of a fixed term, by rescission or by agreement, by notice of any of the partners, by death or bankruptcy of a partner, or by the court. When the partnership has been dissolved the general authority of the partners to bind the firm is ended other than to wind up the partnership affairs and complete transactions unfinished at the date of dissolution. At the winding up of the firm, all losses, including loss of capital, are paid out of profits with residual payments being made by or to the partners in proportion to the relationship stipulated in the partnership agreement.

Limited partnerships

7.14 Other than the differences noted above, in respect of the degree of limitation of liability achieved, the Limited Partnership Act 1907 applies in Scotland as it does in England, with the Act providing for registration of a limited partnership separately in Scotland. The Registrar will advise against the use of any name that is the same as the name of a limited company or another limited partnership already on the register. In addition, the names of limited partnerships are controlled by the Business Names Act 1985. Until a limited partnership is registered, it will be regarded as a general partnership with both the general and limited partners equally responsible for any debts and obligations incurred. The Act permits the creation of partnerships in which some partners may limit their liability for the firm's debts. There are two classes of partner within a limited partnership, being general and limited. General partners are fully liable as within a full partnership. Limited partners' liability can be restricted to the amount of their initial financial contribution to the partnership. Limited partners cannot take any part in the management of the firm without exposing themselves to full liability for the firm's debts.

Limited liability partnerships

7.15 The Limited Liability Partnership Act 2000 operates similarly in Scotland as in England and Wales. However, the Act provides that the incorporation document must state whether the registered office of the limited liability partnership is to be situated in England, Wales or in Scotland. At all times, a Scottish registered limited liability partnership must maintain its registered office in Scotland. In Scotland, in addition to the English provisions, a former member of a limited liability partnership or his trustee in bankruptcy or his permanent or interim trustee (within the meaning of the Bankruptcy (Scotland) Act 1985) may not interfere in the management or administration of any business or affairs of the limited liability partnership.

Companies

7.16 Although the Companies Act covers both countries, it is important to understand the effect of differing legal systems upon legal entities within England and Scotland.

Registered office

7.17 The Act refers to the requirement for stating the intended place of registered office. The exact address must be filed with the Registrar of Companies simultaneously with the Memorandum at the time of incorporation.

The registered office determines the nationality and domicile of the company, but not its residence. The shares of a company registered in Scotland are deemed to be located in Scotland, irrespective of the location of the share certificates. This has implications for capital transfer tax (death duties) in the event of the death of a shareholder.

The registered office may be changed at any time by a resolution of a board of directors, subject to notification to the Registrar of Companies. However, once established, the company cannot relocate its registered office to any part of the UK outside Scotland. As in England, the address of the registered office must be indicated on letterheads and other company forms and in the annual return. The principal office of the company need not be the registered office, and can be situated outside Scotland, and indeed outside the UK. Thus a 'Scottish' architectural practice can carry on its business almost wholly outside Scotland while still being subject to the jurisdiction of the Scottish courts.

Lien over shares

7.18 A company in Scotland has a common law right of retention or 'lien' over its shares whether fully or partly paid. This may be extended or restricted if so expressed in the articles of agreement. Articles will usually provide for a lien only to be exercisable over partly paid shares (*Bell's Trustee v Coatbridge Tinplate Co* (1886) 14 R (HL) 246). Unless the Articles provide otherwise, the company cannot sell shares subject to a lien in order to satisfy a debt owed to it.

Floating charges

7.19 The Companies (Floating Charges) (Scotland) Act 1961 makes exception to the rule that a lender can only acquire security over moveable property after delivery, and over heritable property through registration at the Register of Sasines. The floating charge gives the creditor a preferential right over the liquidator to recovery when the charge 'crystallises' on the winding-up of the company. It's possible that institutional credit for a limited company will be refused on the basis that the borrower's liability is unrealistically limited. To obtain such credit, personal guarantees are generally sought, with a liability being confirmed for a set sum to the lender by each director, usually on a 'joint and several' basis. A floating charge may be taken against personal property or the asset value of the company's work-in-progress at the time of winding-up. Any director unable to meet the obligations imposed as a result of personal guarantees on the winding-up of a company could be liable to sequestration.

Directors' liability

7.20 It is important to note that limitation of liability within a limited company does not restrict liability for negligence either as an officer of the firm or as an architect. Professional indemnity insurance should be held by the firm to cover errors or acts of professional negligence. There are also circumstances where a company director can be found liable to the company itself, in relation to the payment of dividends (*Flitcroft's Case* (1882) 21 Ch D 519). The Bankruptcy (Scotland) Act 1985, as amended in 1993, does not deal with the position of directors responsible for the payment of dividends. Dividends must only be paid out of company profits, not out of capital. A director who is responsible for an unlawful distribution could be liable to the company for breach of duty. Redress could be sought and the full amount of the dividend reimbursed to the company. However, this principle would only apply if the director knows the circumstances of the payment. An innocent director is not liable to repay a dividend that has been wrongfully paid.

30

Architects' contracts with clients

SARAH LUPTON

1 The appointment

1.01 An architect has many factors to take into account when considering an offer of an appointment and it is important that their implications are thoroughly understood before entering into a legal commitment to undertake the commission.

He must be satisfied that the client has the authority and resources to commission the work; he must appreciate the background to the proposal and understand its scope, at least in outline, and he must be aware of any other consultants who have been, or are likely to be, associated with the project.

The architect must be satisfied that he has the experience and competence to undertake the work; that the office has the necessary finance, staff, and other resources; and that the proposal will not conflict with any relevant codes of professional conduct, other commissions and commitments in the office, and the policy of the practice.

The preliminary negotiations between the parties often involve the exchange of business references, especially where the architect and the potential client are previously unknown to each other. On occasions, extensive enquiries about the client and the client's business may be necessary.

It is not unusual for architects to be invited to enter into collateral agreements with funding bodies or other third parties as a condition of the appointment; the possible implications of these agreements need to be considered by the architect and in particular it is important to ensure that any liabilities incurred are covered by the architect's professional indemnity insurance cover. Occasionally, clients ask the architect to enter into collateral agreements after the fees and terms of the appointment have been agreed but if this happens it is essential that the architect considers their conditions carefully, comparing them with those of the original appointment. If the proposed collateral agreements extend the services required or increase the architect's liabilities beyond those originally envisaged the terms of the appointment should be renegotiated.

1.02 Any appointment offered to an architect must be considered in relation to the requirements of the Architects Registration Board (ARB) Code of Conduct (Chapter 38), and also the codes of conduct of any other professional institutions of which the architect may be a member. The architect must be able to demonstrate that he has acted properly in obtaining the commission and is able to carry out the work in a suitable manner and in accordance with the appropriate codes and standards. An employer may not always be conscious of the constraints on the profession; the onus is on the architect to ensure that the employer is made aware of all the relevant matters.

The architect must consider his position in relation to any other architects who may have been involved in the same scheme. An employer is free to offer the commission to whomever he wishes, to obtain alternative schemes from different architects, and to make whatever arrangements for professional services he considers to be necessary. However, the architect is bound by the codes of professional conduct and must ensure that he has acted and continues to act properly and fairly in his dealings with other architects.

An architect who is approached by a potential client in connection with a project with which another architect has already been concerned has a duty to inform the first architect although the first architect has no power to prevent the second architect from proceeding with the work, provided that there is no breach of copyright. Apart from the professional obligation to advise the first architect, it is commercially prudent to do so.

1.03 The need to consider the position of other architects is particularly important in large, complex projects involving various consultant architects providing different but related services, especially when the arrangements for professional services change during the project. The scope of services and the relationships between consultant architects and executive architects can on occasion be the cause of misunderstanding and even difficulties in evolving and changing circumstances. The onus is on the project leader to ensure that the roles, relationships and responsibilities of everyone involved are clearly understood but it is particularly important that the architects are fully aware of the extent of their individual duties and liabilities.

1.04 Clients sometimes seek single all-in service appointments for the whole range of consultancy services required. The all-in services can be commissioned from an existing multi-disciplinary practice or from a single-discipline consultant who engages others as sub-consultants for any other specialist services that may be needed. Multi-disciplinary practices usually have their own well-established forms of agreement but in the case of the single-discipline consultant offering an all-in service care is needed in the drafting an agreed form of appointment. The standard conditions of services and remunerations of the various institutions still vary in detail although they are moving towards greater consistency and standardisation. The consultants concerned have to agree upon a unified approach to services, payment, conditions and liabilities before an offer can be made to a potential client. It is particularly important that the extent of the liabilities which may be incurred are considered in relation to the current professional indemnity insurance of the consultants concerned and any changes that may be needed in the extent of the cover. It is essential that the lead consultant offering the all-in service and therefore being totally liable to the client confirms his position with his own professional indemnity insurers before making the offer.

The architect often acts as the lead consultant in making an all-in service offer but occasionally the architect may act as a sub-consultant to a consultant from another discipline. Where the architect is required to act as a sub-consultant, or is appointing another architect as a sub-consultant, consideration should be given to the use of the sub-consultant agreement discussed below (paragraph 5.02).

2 Agreement of appointment

2.01 Although, in law, an oral agreement may be accepted as the basis of a contract of engagement between architect and employer, such an arrangement would not comply with the ARB and RIBA codes of conduct, and a formal procedure of appointment should always be adopted at the outset. Such a procedure creates a clearly identifiable legal basis for the commission and establishes a sound business approach to the relationship between the architect and the employer. The appointment may be made by either an exchange of letters or an exchange of a formal memorandum of agreement, in each case supported by appropriate supplementary material such as conditions of engagement.

An informal exchange of letters is frequently used but it is not recommended practice. Informal letters of appointment are liable to misinterpretation and misunderstanding and are often the source of difficulties and disagreements between the parties. In particular, they frequently neglect to cover matters required under the RIBA and ARB codes of conduct, for example to define clearly the services to be provided, or the provisions for termination. If the terms are to be agreed in a formal exchange of letters, then the parties should take legal advice, or refer to Roland Philips' *A Guide to Letter Contacts*.

2.02 Various institutions publish standard forms of agreement and their use is strongly recommended (see below). In particular the RIBA recommends to all members that its own forms are used wherever possible (2007 Code, Guidance Note 4). The format and content of these standard forms varies widely. The forms are generally self-explanatory but it is important that they are carefully read and fully understood by both the architect and the client before signing. With 'consumer' clients it is particularly important to discuss and agree all the terms of the standard form, as otherwise some of its terms may become void by operation of the Unfair Terms in Consumer Contracts Regulations 1999.

2.03 Where a standard form of agreement is not used, it is suggested that the following matters should be clearly identified in any exchange of letters between the parties:

1 The date of the agreement.
2 The name and address of the employer.
3 The name and address of the architect.
4 The title and address of the project.
5 The formal agreement to the appointment of the architect.
6 The basis of remuneration for the architect and the arrangements for payment.
7 The form and scope of services to be provided by the architect.
8 The allocation of responsibilities and any limitation of responsibilities.
9 The appointment procedure for a quantity surveyor, other consultants, and the clerk of works as appropriate.
10 The procedure to be followed in the event of the architect's incapacity.
11 The procedure for the termination of the agreement.
12 The procedure for resolving disputes between parties.
13 The name of an agreed adjudicator or the agreed nominator of an adjudicator.
14 The architects are subject to the disciplinary sanction of the ARB in relation to complaints of unacceptable professional conduct or serious professional incompetence.
15 Any additional matters required to be included by the applicable codes of conduct.

The basis of remuneration and the scope of services may be further defined in other documents to which reference should be made in the agreement.

When, as occasionally happens, employers wish to use their own forms of agreement, attention should be drawn to the merits of using one of the standard forms; they are more likely to be comprehensive; they represent the interests of the parties in an equitable manner, and are widely recognised in the industry. Where the client insists on the use of a non-standard form its terms and conditions should be compared with those of the nearest equivalent standard form; in the case of differences the form should be sent to the architect's professional indemnity insurers and impartial advice should be sought before entering into an agreement. It is particularly important that forms of agreement are compatible with the requirements of the Housing Grants, Construction and Regeneration Act 1996 and the ARB and RIBA Codes of Conduct (see Guidance Note 4 to the 2007 Code).

2.04 Where a commission arises out of a recognised competition, the competition conditions usually form the conditions of the appointment. Difficulties develop occasionally when the subsequent building is substantially different from that originally envisaged and where there has been a material change in the conditions. The subsequent appointment of consultants other than the original competition winners can be the cause of serious difficulties.

2.05 The form of appointment agreement should be signed by both parties, witnessed and dated, each keeping a copy. The onus is on the architect to explain the professional obligation to enter into a formal agreement before work commences; beginning work without a clear agreement of services and charges is not only commercially unwise it is also a breach of the codes which could result in disciplinary action. Failure to agree and confirm the services to be given and the charges to be made is also the most common source of dispute between architects and clients. The absence of clear and precise terms of appointment make it hard for a conciliator, an adjudicator, an arbitrator or the courts to resolve disputes in an equitable manner.

2.06 The authority of the architect is strictly limited to the terms of his appointment, that is, as shown in any form of agreement and conditions of engagement. It is in the interests of the employer, the architect, the quantity surveyor, and other independent consultants that these terms should be fully and clearly understood by everyone involved. It is not unusual for the form of services to be varied with changing circumstances during the work but it is essential that these changes are formally confirmed in amendments to the form of agreement.

2.07 The architect's contract of engagement is usually personal to himself or the partnership. He cannot delegate his duties completely, but he is under no obligation to carry out all the works personally or to go into every detail himself. The extent to which he may be prepared to delegate his duties to an assistant is a matter of competence, confidence, reliability, and experience of both the principal and the assistant. The architect is becoming increasingly dependent on the skill and labour of others within his office and elsewhere, but he remains responsible to his client within the terms of his appointment, and continues to be responsible for the acts and defaults of his subordinates. The subordinates in turn are responsible to their principal and could be held liable to their employers for results of their acts.

Where the business is conducted as an unlimited or a limited company, the relationships will depend upon the form of contract involved but the ethical responsibilities between the parties remain, and liability in tort continues regardless of the form of organisation.

3 Termination

3.01 Unless the appointment terms set out specific procedures (as is the case with the RIBA standard forms: see paragraph 5.01

below) the contract of engagement between the architect and his employer may be terminated by either party at reasonable notice. Reasons for the termination need not be stated, but in the event of dispute over outstanding fees or payments, the cause of the termination would be of importance to an adjudicator, an arbitrator or a court in determining a decision or an award.

In the event of the termination of the contract, any outstanding fees for work properly carried out become due to the architect, but it is unlikely that the employer could be held responsible for any loss of anticipated profits on work not yet carried out.

3.02 Difficulties sometimes arise in connection with the use of material prepared before the termination of the engagement took place. The standard forms of appointment usually define the rights of the parties in such circumstances. In the absence of any statement concerning the use of material following the termination of an engagement, it is generally assumed that if the work was substantially advanced at the time of termination it would be unreasonable for the employer not to be entitled to complete the project. It is usually accepted that the employer is entitled to a licence to use the drawings to complete the work effectively. The copyright, of course, remains with the architect unless some other agreement is made.

3.03 In the event of the death or the incapacity of the architect, it is usually held that the employer is entitled to the use of the drawings and other documents to complete the work, provided that payment has been made. Provision for the procedure to be adopted in such circumstances should be included in the standard form of agreement. The death of either party to a personal contract generally dissolves the contract, but it is usually possible, with agreement, for a third party to assume responsibility for the completion of the contract.

Agreements of appointments between companies and partnerships, rather than between individuals, avoid the occasional embarrassing technical difficulties and delays that occur in the transfer of responsibility to others in the event of the death or incapacity of an individual.

3.04 In the event of termination on the grounds of the bankruptcy or liquidation, the contract can be continued if both parties wish to do so and the receiver agrees, and provided that assurances about the payment of any fees and monies which may become due can be secured. The bankruptcy of the architect can pose problems of professional indemnity insurance and other matters and it is rare for arrangements to be made for an insolvent practitioner to continue in business other than under a voluntary administration arrangement.

3.05 The Scheme for Construction Contracts and the standard forms of appointment make provision for the suspension of work in the event of non-payment of fees. Non-payment of fees may be the architect's reason for wishing to terminate an appointment but before doing so it would be prudent for the architect to give formal notice of the intention to suspend work unless payment is made within a stated period and only then if payment is still not forthcoming to proceed with the termination.

4 Ownership

4.01 Ownership of drawings and other documents is often cause for concern. Correspondence and other documents exchanged between the architect and others in connection with the approval of plans, the running of the project, or the administration of the contract by the architect in his role as an agent technically belong to the employer provided that payment has been made, although in practice it is most unusual for all these documents to be automatically transferred to the employer. Other material, especially design material, prepared in the architect's professional capacity belongs to the architect, and this accounts for the greater part of the documentation prepared in the course of a project.

5 Standard Forms of Agreement for the Appointment of an Architect

5.01 The RIBA Standard Forms of Agreement for the Appointment of an Architect are the most widely used forms of appointment and are likely to remain so although others are available. The CIC has published a Consultants Contract, which is an extensive suite of documents intended for use on larger projects, for appointing all members of the project team. The New Engineering Contract (NEC), first published by the Institution of Civil Engineers in 1993 (now in a 2005 edition), includes a Professional Services Contract (PSC) for use in any consultancy appointment including that of an architect. The Joint Contracts Tribunal, publish a Consultancy Agreement (Public Sector) stated to be appropriate for use by Public Sector employers who are undertaking construction works and wish to engage a consultant (regardless of discipline) to carry out services in respect of such works'. It also publishes a version of its Homeowner/Occupier Contract which includes a form for appointment of a consultant. The Association of Consultant Architects (ACA) publishes a Standard Form of Agreement for the Appointment of an Architect (ACA SFA/08), which attracted press coverage as it followed criticisms made by the ACA of the 2007 RIBA forms as not being sufficiently protective of the architect. These criticisms were strongly defended by the RIBA, and the forms are currently in widespread use.

5.02 The RIBA Standard Agreements for the appointment of an architect have a long history in the course of which they have on occasion been subject to litigation and official comment. The use of the forms is not and cannot be mandatory and the parties to the contract of appointment are free to use whatever version or form of appointment they wish and to amend the forms to suit their particular requirements. However, the forms reflect the experience of consultants operating in all fields of activity and are consistent with current legislation. The current forms have been developed in consultation with other sectors of the industry and carefully balance the needs of the client and architect. An architect would have to have very good reasons not to recommend their use or to make significant amendments to them.

5.03 The Forms of Agreement introduced in 2007 provide a series of related appointment documents for use in various situations. Their scope and use are outlined clearly in the GN4 Annex 2007 of Guidance Note 4 to the RIBA Code of Professional Conduct. The forms replace the previous documents, i.e. the Standard Form of Agreement for the Appointment of an Architect SFA/99, the Conditions of Engagement for the Appointment of an Architect CE/99, Small Works Conditions SW/99, and other forms in the suite, for example the Form of Appointment as Planning Supervisor PS/99. These took into account the Unfair Terms in Consumer Contracts Regulations 1994, the Arbitration Act 1996, and the Housing Grants, Construction and Regeneration Act 1996. The new family of standard appointment documents additionally takes into account more recent legislation such as the Unfair Terms in Consumer Contracts Regulations 1999 and the Construction (Design and Management) Regulations 2007. The suite of documents comprises:

RIBA Standard Agreement 2007 (S-Con-07);
Contractor's Design Services (SS-CD-07);
RIBA Concise Agreement (C-Con-07);
RIBA Domestic Project Agreement (D-Con-07);
RIBA Agreement for the Appointment of a Sub-consultant (SubCon-07).

The forms are available in Architect or Consultant versions in printed and/or in on-line format. The Consultant versions would be particularly suitable for use with a multi-disciplinary consultant team so that all consultants are on the same contract terms. There are also additional Services schedules available (in electronic format only) as follows:

Access Management Services and client Guide-AM-07 (SS-AM-07);
CDM Co-ordinator's Services (SS-CDM-07);

Design Services for a Historic Building or Conservation Project and client Guide-HB-07 (SS-HB-07);
Schedule of Interior Design Services (SS-ID-07);
Initial Occupation and Post Occupation Evaluation and client Guide-L-07 (SS-L-07);
Master Planning Services (SS-MP-07);
Multi Disciplinary Services (SS-MD-07);
Project Management Services (SS-PM-07).

The following *draft* supplementary agreements are available (in electronic format only):

Third Party Rights Schedule (SA-TPR-07);
Warranty by a Sub-consultant (SA-SC-07);
Consultant Switch or Novation (SA-SN-07).

5.04 The RIBA Standard Agreement 2007 (S-Con-07-A) is the key document. (This replaces SFA/99, CE/99, PM/99 and PS/99.) It is suitable for use where the architect provides services for a fully designed building project of any size or complexity. It is sold as a pack of documentation (discussed below). These component parts are used together to form the agreement. In addition, by using parts of this pack, together with separate services schedules, the Standard Agreement can be tailored to cover a variety of professional roles and services. In this way the new suite of forms constitutes a flexible set of documents which cover the many different roles that the architect may be asked to fulfil.

For design build procurement, the architect may be appointed by the contractor using the RIBA Standard Conditions of Appointment (CA-S-07-A) along with the Contractor's Design Services (SS-CD-07) and the Schedule of Role Specifications (SS-RS-07). The architect may be appointed by the client using CA-S-07-A with the Schedules of Role Specifications and of Design Services, making it clear that the services are to prepare the employer's requirements. If novation or consultant switch to appointment by the contractor is contemplated, then provision for this should be made in the client appointment at the outset. This will require a supplementary tri-partite agreement between employer, contractor and architect, as well as a new appointment to the contractor. The RIBA do not publish a standard form of novation agreement, but do publish a set of draft clauses, Consultant Switch or Novation (SA-SN-07), which can form the basis for this agreement. Finalising the terms of this arrangement will usually require legal advice.

Where the architect is providing other services, for example acting as interior designer or CDM Co-ordinator, the RIBA Standard Conditions of Appointment (CA-S-07-A) may be used along with the appropriate Services Schedule as listed above.

For smaller projects there are two options, the RIBA Concise Agreement (C-Con-07) and the RIBA Domestic Project Agreement (D-Con-07). The former replaces SW/99 and is for use for a professional commission or construction project with simple contract terms, where the client is acting for business or commercial purposes. The Agreement comprises Concise Conditions of Appointment for a Small Project, Notes on use and completion, and a Model Letter.

For domestic projects the RIBA Domestic Project Agreement (D-Con-07). Replaces the equivalent 2005 edition, and comprises Conditions of Appointment for a Domestic Project, Services for a Small Project, Working with an architect for your home, Notes on use and completion, and a Model Letter. This form is not suitable where the client is acting in a commercial capacity, for example where a landlord is carrying out work to a rented flat.

RIBA Agreement for the Appointment of a Sub-consultant (SubCon-07) is devised for situations in which a consultant wishes, or is required by the client, to sub-contract part of his responsibility to another consultant who becomes a sub-consultant. It is not appropriate for use where the client wishes to make direct appointments with consultants. The client's consent to sub-contracting is required. The form can be used as printed regardless of the form of agreement between the client and the main consultant.

The terminology, format and conditions of the RIBA suite of documents are consistent but it is important that the architect should be sufficiently familiar with the differences in application and content of the forms in order to be able to advise clients on the selection of the form most appropriate to any given situation. It is particularly important that the architect is familiar with the conditions and is able to explain their meaning and application to a lay client.

All of the forms are available at RIBA bookshops and at www.ribabookshop.com

Plan of Work

5.05 As part of the development of the 2007 RIBA Agreements, revised versions of the Plan of Work were published, ensuring that the schedules of service and the Plan of Work are integrated. The Plan of Work is published in two formats: as an Outline Plan of Work 2007, which was approved by RIBA Council, and as an expanded version entitled *Plan of Work Multi-Disciplinary Services* by Roland Phillips and published in 2008. The latter is a guide to the Outline Plan, and which sets out the multi-disciplinary team's typical responsibilities and tasks in a series of tables. The current Plan of Work stages are as follows:

Plan of Work stages	
A	Appraisal;
B	Design Brief;
C	Concept;
D	Design Development;
F	Technical Design;
F	Production Information;
Fl	preparation of detailed information for construction;
F2	preparation of further information for construction required under the building contract;
G	Tender documentation;
H	Tender Action;
J	Mobilisation;
K	Construction to Practical Completion;
L	Post Practical Completion;
L1	administration of the building contact after practical completion;
L2	assisting building user during initial occupation period;
L3	review of project performance in use.

Standard Form of Agreement for the Appointment of an Architect

5.06 The Agreement for the Appointment of an Architect (S-Con-07-A) comprises:

Memorandum of Agreement (MA-S-07-A);
Model Letter of Appointment (ML-S-07);
Standard Conditions of Appointment (CA07-A);
Project Data (PD-S-07);
Fees and Expenses (SS-FE-07);
Schedule of Role Specifications (SS-RS-07);
Schedule of Design Services (SS-DS-07);
Notes on use and completion (Notes-S-07).

The Memorandum of Agreement (MA-S-07-A) make reference to (and therefore incorporates) the Standard Conditions of Appointment (CA-S-07-A). It requires insertion of the name of the client body, the firm of architects, and a representative of each, together with the 'roles' that the architect is to be appointed to (as defined in the Schedule of Role Specifications (SS-RS-07), for example as designer, design leader, lead consultant, and contract administrator). References to additional documents (such as Services Schedules) may be entered below the Standard Conditions of Appointment. The Memorandum allows for execution under hand or as a deed (where the law of England and Wales is applicable), and has a separate section for execution where the law of Scotland applies.

The Standard Conditions of Appointment (CA-S-07-A) are divided into two sections, A and B. Section A applies to all appointments, and covers the obligations and authority of the architect, the obligations and authority of the client, assignment and sub-contracting, payment, copyright and use of information, liabilities and insurance, suspension and termination, and dispute resolution. Sections B1 and B2 incorporate the requirements of the Housing Grants, Construction and Regeneration Act 1996, and are not required for projects not covered by that Act, for example where the client is undertaking work to their own house. Section B3 includes conditions applicable where the client is a Public Authority, i.e. to deal with freedom of information, and to prohibit corrupt gifts or payments.

Project Data (PD-S-07) requires insertion of the applicable law of the contract, and the effective date of the agreement. It also requires entries regarding the dispute resolution procedures selected, rules to be adopted, and the nominator of the adjudicator and arbitrator if appropriate (if no body is selected, the nominator/appointer is the RIBA). There are provisions for the limitation of the time during which action or proceedings may be opened and for the limitation of the amount of liability and the amount of professional indemnity insurance cover. The client's agreement or otherwise to the limitation of his rights is a matter of negotiation and agreement. The net contribution clause is referred to, unless stated otherwise in the Project Data this will apply.

The Project Data section also requires insertion of information about the project. The fullness of the description will depend upon how much is known at the time of execution of the Agreement, but an attempt must be made in order that the basis of the architect's services and fees can be demonstrated. It is likely that on many occasions only a brief statement can be made at the outset and further descriptions will have to be added as the nature of the work becomes clearer. The intention of the 'project description' is to ensure that there can be no misunderstanding about the nature of the work. In addition to as precise a description of the project as possible it could refer to such matters phasing or sectional completion, special submissions and negotiations; site information on ownership, boundaries, easements, covenants, planning consents, surveys and investigations, Health and Safety matters provided by the client; organisational and operational matters; accommodation, space and use requirements, cost limits, key dates and programme requirements. Where an initial brief already exists it should be attached to the agreement as an appendix.

Potential clients may wish to impose their own particular conditions, and there is opportunity for attaching these as an appendix to the Project Data. The implications of any non-standard conditions need to be carefully assessed. If a substantial extension to the liability or duties of the architect is likely to be incurred appropriate additional reimbursement should be negotiated. Extensions of liability outside those of an existing professional indemnity policy should be discussed with the architect's broker or insurers before acceptance. In the case of public bodies and others requiring the architect to undertake to maintain professional indemnity insurance for 6 years following completion of the works: the architect must insist that the undertaking is subject to the reasonable availability of insurance cover.

The Schedule of Role Specifications (SS-RS-07) and Schedule of Design Services (SS-DS-07) are of considerable importance and merit careful study. The Schedule of Role Specifications lists the roles that the architect could undertake, and entries are required to indicate which will be performed on project in questions, and over what work stages. Roles listed include not only architectural designer, contract administrator, lead designer and lead consultant (as was the case with SFA/99) but also project manager, cost consultant, civil and structural engineering designer, building services designer and CDM co-ordinator. This helps to ensure that a clear decision is made as to whether the architect will perform these roles, and if not that the client may need to

consider further appointments. A description of these roles is set out in the document. The Schedule of Design Services sets out in more detail the tasks the architect will perform as designer at each Work Stage, and also lists Other Services (for example, Party Wall matters). If any of these may be required this must be indicated, including the basis for charging fees (i.e. a time-charge or lump sum basis).

Under Fees and Expenses (SS-FE-07) the parties have to agree on the method for calculating the fees in relation to the services described in Schedule of Role Specifications (SS-RS-07) and Schedule of Design Services (SS-DS-07), and the percentages or lump sums involved. The document also covers hourly rates or other bases for different categories of staff or individuals; expenses and disbursements; mileage rates; and instalment payments (monthly or at end of each Work Stage).

Prospective clients frequently require an estimate of the anticipated total fees likely to be involved in projects. This is understandable but care is needed; difficulties often arise where fees have been forecast on the basis of a premature estimate of the likely total cost of the building work. If an estimate is made it is essential that the client is properly briefed on the nature of the estimate and its limitations. Similarly, difficulties can arise when a forecast of the likely duration of work is offered in the case of work to be charged on a time basis.

Where it is very difficult to assess the scope and extent of services required, it may be necessary to set up an appointment to cover the feasibility and preliminary stages of the project only, while the project brief is developed. This should nevertheless be a formal arrangement, albeit for a limited scope of services.

The client should be reminded that the architect's fees and charges and those of other consultants are net and do not include Value Added Tax (VAT) which is chargeable at the current rate regardless of the VAT status of the building work. Clients who are taxable persons under the Finance Act 1972 are able to recover such input tax from the Customs and Excise Department.

6 Speculative work and tendering for architects' services

6.01 The emergence of speculative work and competitive fee tendering has had a profound effect on the procedures of architects' negotiations with their clients and to some extent their relationships with clients. Speculative work in which the architect undertakes work at risk on the basis that payment will only be made in the event of the work proceeding is now widespread, especially in commercial and development work. Competitive fee-tendering has also become commonplace with official and quasi-official bodies being obliged to obtain competitive tenders for substantial projects, and with private clients becoming more aware of the possibilities of competitive fee-tendering.

6.02 The extent to which an architect is prepared to undertake speculative work must depend upon many factors such as the policy of the practice, the architect's knowledge of the potential client, the nature of the proposed project, the likelihood of its success, the architect's existing commitments, the capacity of the office now and in the foreseeable future, the possible income and profit from the commission if it proceeds, the extent of competition for the work and so on. But regardless of these conditions and the fact that the architect may not be paid initially, it is important that there should be a formal agreement between the architect and the client defining the extent of the service to be provided by the architect and the commitment of the client to the architect in the event of the project proceeding. In the event of the project proceeding it is usual for the architect to be reimbursed for the initial work undertaken at risk.

The cost of speculative work undertaken at risk by an architect may be substantial and it is important that the practice should budget for non-fee-earning speculative work, as part of its overheads, fixing a limit to the amount it does, and maintaining strict record of time and costs. Where teams of design and other consultants are involved in joint submissions on a speculative basis it is becoming usual for the costs to be shared.

6.03 Architects should be particularly wary of invitations to prepare design solutions in conjunction with competitive fee tenders often on the basis of scant information – only rarely would such an invitation be acceptable. Architects should also endeavour to discover details of others invited to submit fee tenders and refuse to participate in competitive fee bidding in which the number of tenderers or the form of competition is unreasonable.

As the range of possible sources of design and procurement routes widens it is understandable that clients should increasingly make detailed enquiries about services and charges before making formal appointments. The basis of comparison is often inadequate; architects should endeavour to ensure that clients fully appreciate the nature of the service being offered and do not make appointments on the basis of fee alone. Potential clients are often unaware of fundamental differences between, say, conventional design services and design by a contractor's organisation; more subtle differences in design services are certain to elude them unless they are carefully explained by the architect. The fee is determined by the service required and the cost of providing that service; unless this is known a fee quotation can be little more than a guess.

6.04 Dissatisfaction with the approach of some large commercial organisations seeking competitive fee bids led to the preparation and publication of the guidance note Guidance for Clients to Quality Based Selection as part of the RIBA-CIC series *Engaging an Architect*, published by RIBA Enterprises.

7 Appointments required by statute

7.01 On occasion the architect may be engaged to carry out duties required by statute; these duties may be specified in detail as part of the schedule of services or reference may be made to the relevant statute. It has to be recognised by both the client and the architect that statutory duties are non-negotiable; if for any reason the architect cannot or is not allowed to comply with the requirements of the legislation, the architect must withdraw, advising the client of the reasons for the termination of the appointment.

An appointment as a Construction (Design and Management) Regulations 2007 CDM Co-ordinator under the Health and Safety at Work etc. Act 1974 is probably the statutory appointment most frequently encountered. The duties are specified in detail in the regulations but payment arrangements and other matters have to be agreed between the parties. This appointment can be dealt with using the RIBA Standard Agreement together with the CDM Co-ordinator's Services (SS-CDM-07).

An appointment as a Surveyor under the Party Wall etc. Act 1996 is concerned with the carrying out of duties as specified in a disinterested and impartial manner regardless of the concerns of the parties. Again, the duties are specified in detail in the Act but payment arrangements and other matters have to be agreed between the consultant and the parties involved; if the parties cannot agree on the appointment the local authority will make the appointment, unless the local authority is a party in the dispute in which case the Secretary of State will make the appointment. There is no RIBA standard form to cover such appointments, which should not be dealt with under, for example RIBA Standard Agreement 2007 (S-Con-07), but should form a separate written agreement. Advising the client regarding Party Wall Matters (as opposed to the independent statutory function) is, however, covered as under Other Services in the Standard Agreement.

The most recent statutory duty is that of the adjudicator under Part 11 of the Housing Grants, Construction and Regeneration Act 1996 acting in the resolution of differences or disputes between the parties to a construction contract. The adjudicator is allowed considerable flexibility within the time scales of the Act in the carrying out of duties but generally adjudicator appointment agreements are tending to follow those of conventional appointments for arbitrators. Payment is usually on a time basis and it is now usual for the parties to agree an appropriate rate at the time of appointment. Various institutions publish standard terms of agreement for appointment of an adjudicator, for example the JCT and the CIC.

8 Scottish appointments[*]

8.01 The Architects Registration Board Code of Conduct, paragraph 11.1, stipulates that architects should not undertake professional work unless the terms of the contract have been recorded in writing. This is sound practice, as it reduces the scope for later disputes about the terms of the appointment. It is proper practice for appointments involving clients based in Scotland and services supplied or works located in Scotland to be in Scottish form. There are differences in substantive law, procedure, regulation and terminology which make this appropriate. While a simple exchange of letters is sufficient to form a written appointment in Scotland, the standard forms are to be preferred. It is desirable that contracts and appointments be formally executed in terms of the Requirements for Writing (Scotland) Act 1995. A clear decision should be taken at an early stage to proceed in this way, especially where one or more of the parties is or are accustomed to operating under non-Scottish conditions. The Royal Incorporation of Architects in Scotland (RIAS) publishes standard forms of appointment suitable for use in Scotland. These are in three versions: SCA/2000 (January 2008 Revision) which is applicable to the 'classic' architect to 'employer' client relationship where the architect can go on to be contract administrator; DBC/2000 (August 2008 Revision) which is suitable for the architect to 'employer' relationship where the 'employer' is to be and is the employer in a design build contract: and DBC/2000 (August 2008 Revision) which is suitable for the architect to 'contractor' relationship where the 'contractor' is to be or is the contractor in a design build contract. (The RIAS does not recommend the use of the so called 'novation' process in design and build, but recommends two separate appointments, the first with the 'employer', in JCT parlance, and the second and subsequent appointment with the 'contractor'. Where one architect is to enter into both appointments issues such as confidentiality and conflict of interest need to be addressed and, while both appointments will remain in place, the architect's performance under the appointments should be sequential and acting for both clients at the same time should be avoided.) A small projects version of the Scottish Conditions of Appointment is available. A subconsultant appointment is also now available (SCA/S-C/2007 (Sub-Consultant)). RIBA Agreement Packs are available for purchase in Scotland from RIAS, however not all forms are suitable for use in Scotland and a check should be made before purchase. Forms of appointment and advice are available from the RIAS Bookshops at 15 Rutland Square, Edinburgh EH1 2BE; Tel: 0131 229 7545; e-mail: bookshops@rias.org.uk.

[*]This section was written by Catherine Devaney.

31

Architects' collateral warranties

ANN MINOGUE

1 Architects and collateral warranties

1.01 Architects are likely to encounter collateral warranties in two circumstances. First, and most importantly, they themselves may be asked to provide collateral warranties and, second, they may be expected to advise their clients – the employer under the building contract – on collateral warranties to be given by contractors and sub-contractors either to the employer or to funders, purchasers or tenants.

1.02 This chapter is concerned with the first of these circumstances and looks in more detail at the forms of collateral warranties which an architect is likely to encounter. This chapter cannot review all the permutations which have been dreamt up by solicitors to funders, purchasers and tenants, on the one hand, and solicitors to consultants, on the other, over the last two decades. What it aims to do is to discuss the basic obligation to provide collateral warranties and then to look at the provisions of CoWa/P&T in detail followed by the 'step-in' rights conferred by CoWa/F. These two documents are the standard forms of collateral warranty published by the British Property Federation but agreed with The Association of Consulting Engineers, The Royal Incorporation of Architects in Scotland, The Royal Institute of British Architects and The Royal Institution of Chartered Surveyors. The JCT in 1992/1993 established a Working Party to look at both consultants' and contractors' collateral warranties but was not able to reach agreement on revisions which might be made to the existing standard forms of consultants' collateral warranties.

Inevitably, therefore, the parties to the original agreed BPF Standard Forms of Collateral Warranty have now divided into two camps: the Construction Industry Council published in 2003 new forms of collateral warranty – CIC/ConsWa/F and CIC/ConsWa/P&T – under its logo. The British Property Federation drafted a form of Consultancy Agreement in 2005 which adopts the provisions for Third Party Rights used in JCT Major Project Form 2003 – see Chapter 20 – but amended to reflect the different role of a consultant. At the same time, it produced new editions of its standard forms of collateral warranty – BPF CoWa/F and BPF CoWa/P&T, as before – amended to correspond with the changes included in its Consultancy Agreement. Inevitably, this proliferation of different forms of collateral warranty will do nothing to help increase standardisation in the construction industry. It seems inevitable that, instead, the property market, which had reached a degree of consensus on the appropriate provisions to include in collateral warranties, will now polarise and the length of this chapter in subsequent editions of this book will steadily increase.

1.03 In addition to the plethora of forms of collateral warranties, since the last edition of this book, there has been a plethora of new forms of consultancy agreement too – most notably the new

RIBA Standard Agreement for the appointment of an Architect (S-CON-07-A) and the CIC Consultants Contract CIC/Conscon 2006. These have both incorporated provisions for third party rights instead of or in addition to collateral warranties. The use of third party rights is addressed in paragraph 3 of Chapter 20.

1.04 For the purposes of this chapter, CIC/ConsWa/F and CIC/ConsWa/P&T will be used as a basis for explaining the usual terms of collateral warranties but reference will be made to those areas where the BPF Third Party Rights Schedule and the revised BPF collateral warranties differ from them.

2 The obligation to provide collateral warranties

2.01 There is obviously no general legal duty on anyone to agree the terms of or to enter into a collateral warranty in favour of a third party. If collateral warranties are required, then the employer would be well advised to ensure that there is a binding obligation imposed by the terms of his consultancy agreement with the architect to grant collateral warranties.

2.02 The first standard set of conditions of engagement to acknowledge the existence of collateral warranties was the Standard Form of Agreement for the Appointment of an Architect (SFA/92) produced by the Royal Institute of British Architects. The provisions included in SFA/92 were very antagonistic to collateral warranties. They were substantially revised in subsequent editions and A7.5.1 of CA-5-07-A Standard Conditions published by RIBA. In 2007 provides that:

'Where is it specified in the Project Data that the Architect will be required to enter into a collateral warranty or warranties in favour of Funders, Purchasers or Tenants and the terms of the warranty together with the names or categories of other parties who will sign such agreements are appended to this Agreement, the Architect enters into such agreement or agreements with a third party or parties within a reasonable period of being requested to do so by the Client, providing that all fees and other amounts have been paid.'

In other words, if everything is agreed in advance, collateral warranties will be given.

2.03 Interestingly, CA-5-07-A now incorporates Third Party Rights as an alternative to collateral warranties:

'A7.5.2   Where it is specified in the Project Data that a Third Party Rights Schedule in favour of Funders,

Purchasers or Tenants is applicable and appended to this Agreement the Client and Architect comply with the Supplementary Conditions set out in the appendix.'

Henceforward this chapter focusses on collateral warranties but the Third Party Rights will usually contain similar clauses to those outlined below see also section 3 of Chapter 20.

2.04 Of course, in practice, architects will often be faced with tailor-made consultancy agreements and these will endeavour to protect the client by imposing specific obligations on the architect in relation to the provision of collateral warranties or third party rights.

What the client needs to include where he anticipates that he may need to call for collateral warranties is a clause requiring the architect to give collateral warranties to parties precisely defined in accordance with a stipulated form of collateral warranty which should be attached to the consultancy agreement. If no form is stipulated and attached, the obligation is merely to enter into a form as agreed, and, again, the clause simply amounts to an 'agreement to agree' and is unenforceable by the client if the architect simply refuses to agree a draft.

2.05 The relevant provision must define the persons to whom collateral warranties are to be given. This is where the first difficulties in negotiation usually arise. In order to maintain maximum flexibility, the client will want collateral warranties in favour of:

- any person providing finance;
- any future purchaser of the project, or, where the project is capable of being divided into separate investment units, of any part of the project;
- any tenant of the project or of any part of the project;
- if the nature of the profit-sharing or other arrangements for the project requires it, freeholders or borough councils or other third parties who may have a loss if the project is negligently designed or constructed.

Architects should not accept these open-ended provisions which raise the prospect of their being required to enter into collateral warranties with, say, 60 shop tenants on a shopping centre or tenants of kiosks in the lobby of a major office development. It behoves both parties to look sensibly at the nature of the project and to arrive at an equitable solution – perhaps, to give collateral warranties to tenants of the anchor stores only in a shopping centre, or tenants who take more than a certain amount of lettable area in the case of a multi-tenanted office development.

2.07 Finally, there is much debate about the enforceability of a simple obligation to enter into a collateral warranty. Will the courts order specific performance of an obligation to enter into an agreement by making the architect sign it or will they suggest that damages for breach of the contractual obligation undertaken by the architect is an adequate remedy for the client so that the client must show that he has suffered a loss (presumably his loss of a funder, purchaser or tenant) because the architect has failed to comply with his contract? The latter is most widely held but opinions differ. In any event, applying to the courts, with all the costs and delays that entails, is not a satisfactory position for a client who has a tenant waiting to sign a lease with him provided a collateral warranty is forthcoming from the architect. It is for this reason that powers of attorney are frequently inserted by clients in tailor-made consultancy agreements in addition to the basic obligation to provide the collateral warranty. The power of attorney authorises the client to execute the collateral warranty on behalf of the architect if the architect, in breach of his contractual obligations, fails to execute it himself. Architects usually, and perhaps understandably, object to these provisions and yet they do no more than give the client rights to enforce an obligation in circumstances where the architect himself is in breach of contract.

2.08 The use of the Contracts (Rights of Third Parties) Act 1999 to obviate the need to sign a multitude of separate collateral warranty

documents is discussed in detail in Chapter 20. The Act will not, of course, prevent debates about the potential beneficiaries of third party rights and the issues discussed in paragraph 2.04 will continue. Nor will the Act obviate the need for debate about the terms of the third party rights to be granted and the issues discussed below will still arise. The Act does, however, provide a much simpler mechanism for delivery of the third party rights reducing the paper chase which exists at the moment. It also avoids arguments about the need for powers of attorney. . .

3 The terms of collateral warranties: CIC/ConsWa/P&T

Clause 1: The Warranty

'The Consultant warrants to the Purchaser/Tenant that it has exercised [and will continue to exercise] reasonable skill care and diligence in the performance of its services to the Client under the Appointment.'

3.01 Consultants generally warrant that they will exercise reasonable skill and care in the performance of their duties. Part II of the Supply of Goods and Services Act 1982 reflects this basic implied term. All the standard terms of engagement published by the relevant professional bodies provide for this or something similar. Consultants do not 'guarantee' results – they do not warrant that the results of their labours will be a building which is 'suitable' or which will comply with any particular performance specification or requirement. Hence, this basic warranty of reasonable skill care and diligence.

3.02 Arguably, if, under the terms of the consultancy agreement, the architect has assumed a higher duty of care – 'the skill, care and diligence reasonably to be expected of a properly qualified and competent consultant experienced in the provision of like services for projects of a similar size, scope and complexity to the Project' – then this duty of care might be reflected in the collateral warranty.

3.03 It should also be noted that the warranty relates to the 'Services' under the consultancy agreement. If, for example, the architect has been engaged to provide design services only and not inspection services, this formulation will relate the collateral warranty to the design services only. It is imperative, therefore, that any beneficiary of a collateral warranty also checks precisely the definition of services under the consultancy agreement.

Clause 2(a): The Exclusion of Economic and Consequential Loss

'... the Consultant shall be liable for the reasonable costs of repair, renewal and/or reinstatement of any part or parts of the Development to the extent that – the Purchaser/Tenant incurs such costs and/or – the Purchaser/the Tenant is or becomes liable either directly or by way of financial contribution for such costs. The Consultant shall not be liable for other losses incurred by the Purchaser/the Tenant.'

3.04 If this limitation on the basic warranty did *not* appear, then the architect would be liable to the purchaser/the tenant for damages for breach of contract assessed in accordance with the usual rules – broadly, contractual damages cover losses which are reasonably foreseeable at the date the contract was entered into as likely to arise as a result of the breach of it. In the case of the collateral warranty to a tenant, these would probably include cost of repair of defects caused by the consultant's negligence, additional professional fees, loss of profit, potentially business interruption and so on.

3.05 It is argued by the CIC that this is just too broad and the risks are unquantifiable. Accordingly, it accepts that the consultant must pick up the cost of repair as provided in Clause 2(a) but that all other losses should be excluded as the final sentence states. However, this is a position which architects may find difficult to sustain in practice under pressure from their clients. Clients, purchasers and tenants argue that designers and builders can anticipate the sort of business losses likely to be suffered by purchasers and tenants of the building and they would be liable for such losses if they had contracted with the owner/occupier in the usual way. Why should the architect escape this liability simply because he is working for a developer who is unlikely ever to go into occupation of the building? Accordingly, purchasers and tenants in particular would put a line through the whole of Clause 2(a). This leaves architects completely exposed to potential open-ended liability under the collateral warranty.

3.06 The British Property Federation argues that the drafting of Standard Collateral Warranties should anticipate the inevitable requirements of certain purchasers and tenants and, as with CWa/P&T should reflect various alternative provisions in relation to losses other than the cost of repair. The revised BPF Form of Collateral Warranty CoWa/P&T 2005 omits the final sentence of the drafting of Clause 2(a) in CIC/ConsWa/P&T and substitutes for it drafting which previously appeared in the BPF Guidance Notes as follows:

'The Consultant shall in addition be liable for other losses incurred by the Purchaser/the Tenant provided that the Purchaser/the Tenant has properly mitigated such losses and such additional liability of the Consultant shall not exceed [£•] in respect of each breach of the Consultant's warranty…'

This would seem to be a fair compromise and one which appears to be accepted, by a growing number of clients and, reluctantly, on smaller projects but not on large pre-lets by purchasers and tenants. The architect should note that he must have regard when fixing the limit to the fact that he also has unlimited liability for repair costs so the cap may be less than the actual amount of his professional indemnity cover. He should also check whether his professional indemnity cover contained any aggregate caps on liability for specified risks (e.g. pollution and contamination) which might cause him to revisit this cap.

Clause 2(b): 'The Contribution Clause'

'Without prejudice to any other exclusion or limitation of liability, damages, loss, expense or costs the Consultant's liability for such costs of the repair, renewal and/or reinstatement in question shall be further limited to that proportion thereof as it would be just and equitable to require the Consultant to pay having regard to the extent of the Consultant's responsibility for the same and on the assumptions that:

(i) all other consultants and advisers, contractors and sub-contractors involved in and the Development have provided contractual undertakings on terms no less onerous than those set out in Clause 1 to the Purchaser/Tenant in respect of the carrying out of their obligations in connection with the Development;

(ii) there are no exclusions of or limitations of liability nor joint insurance or co-insurance provisions between the Purchaser/Tenant and any other party referred to in this Clause 2 and any such other party who is responsible to any extent for such costs is contractually liable to the Purchaser/Tenant for the same;

(iii) all the parties referred to in this Clause 2 have paid to the Purchaser/Tenant such proportion of such costs which it would be just and equitable for them to pay having regard to the extent of their responsibility for the same.'

3.07 This revised drafting by the CIC is very wide indeed in relation to the potential parties from whom contribution can be assessed – '*all other consultants and advisors, contractor and sub-contractors*'. Of course, not all of these parties will also give

collateral warranties to any purchaser or tenant who will feel very exposed agreeing to such wording. The BPF restricts the relevant third parties to the project team as defined and the building contractor, these being the key players and the other parties from whom collateral warranties are likely to be sought by purchasers and tenants. It seems likely that this will be a future area of contention on collateral warranty wording though it has not been the case in the past.

3.08 The Civil Liability (Contribution) Act 1978 deals with contribution between people liable in respect of any damage in tort, for breach of contract or otherwise. Under the provisions of the Act, where two or more people have contributed to the same loss as a result of separately being in breach of contract, if one of them is sued for that loss, he can claim contribution from the others. Obviously, this right of contribution will be much more difficult if, say, the architect has given a collateral warranty but the contractor, who may have contributed to the loss, has not. Equally, if both the architect and the contractor have given collateral warranties, but the contractor is insolvent so that there is no recovery from him, then the architect is left with the full extent of the liability.

The effect of Clause 2(b) is to try to ensure that, if there is a latent defect in the building and the purchaser/the tenant wishes to sue, his recovery against, say, the architect is assessed on the assumption that the architect is only liable for his 'share' of the contribution to the loss even if the purchaser/the tenant is unable to recover from the contractor who may have also contributed to the loss either because the contractor has not given a collateral warranty at all or, having done so, is insolvent and so cannot meet his share.

3.09 Such clauses when they first appeared were resisted by purchasers and tenants who find it difficult to accept that they may be able to recover only 10% of their loss because of the contribution clause notwithstanding negligence by, say, the architect and breach of contract by the contractor. There is now an acceptance that in the context of the voluntary assumption of contractual responsibility inherent in the giving of a collateral warranty the principles of 'joint and several liability' under English law can operate unfairly, particularly in circumstances where one party's contribution to the loss is significantly more than another party's contribution but the first party cannot meet its share of responsibility. This is true in the case of, say, defective workmanship where the contractor may be held to be 80% or 90% culpable while the architect, who has also been negligent in failing to detect the defective workmanship in the course of his inspection duties, would usually bear only 20% to 10% of the share of the loss. If the contractor is not around, then obviously the architect must bear 100%. It is to be hoped that the relative consensus on the issue is not now de-railed by the plethora of forms.

3.10 There are, though, doubts as to the enforceability of the 'contribution clause'. In particular, there are elements of uncertainty in terms of the assumed nature and extent of the contractual undertakings which have been given by the other parties. In addition, there may be public policy issues involved in asking the courts to determine the potential liability by way of contribution of a party who is not involved in the proceedings, is not represented and does not have an opportunity to defend himself.

Clause 2(c): 'Defences of Liability'

'The Consultant shall be entitled in any action or proceedings by the Purchaser/the Tenant to rely on any limitation or exclusion in the Appointment and to raise the equivalent rights in defence of liability as it would have had against the Client under the Appointment.'

3.11 The purpose of this provision is to ensure that if, for example, the consultancy agreement contains a limitation on the architect's liability for negligence, that limitation is also imported into the collateral warranty and, hence, into the architect's relationship with the purchaser/the tenant. If it were not included, then there would be a strong argument that the purchaser/the tenant could sue the architect for an unlimited amount and, potentially, more than could be recovered from him by his client. It also allows the architect to argue, for example, that limitation periods for breach of the consultancy agreement have expired and, therefore, there is no claim against him by the purchaser/the tenant under the collateral warranty. The provision reinforces, should reinforcement be needed, the imperative that purchasers and tenants consider the terms of the consultancy agreement in order to determine the full extent of their rights under the collateral warranty.

3.12 But the provision is wider than this — if, for example, the architect's client requires him to produce a design detail in a certain way, perhaps against the advice of the architect, the architect will have a defence to any claim against him by the client. That defence will also be available, because of Clause 2(c), to the architect in any claim made against him by the purchaser/the tenant. Other 'rights in defence of liability' could arise through waivers, estoppels and so on.

3.13 In order to close the loop, the well-advised purchaser/tenant would ensure that he had included in his agreement with the client provisions prohibiting the client waiving, releasing or otherwise interfering with the architect in the performance of his duties so as to give rise to a 'defence of liability'. Although not watertight (since the circumstances in which the purchaser/the tenant is likely to sue the architect are circumstances where the developer is insolvent or cannot meet the liability in which case a claim for breach of contract against him is not much comfort), this does at least provide some protection to the purchaser or tenant who, hopefully, will not then find that his rights under the collateral warranty, when he comes to enforce them, are not worth anything.

Purchasers and tenants' solicitors sometimes try to include these prohibitions in the collateral warranty itself. This seems to be wrong in principle. The relationship between the client and his architect is covered by the consultancy agreement and the collateral warranty should not interfere with that relationship. If the purchaser/tenant wish to interfere in that relationship, they should do so in the agreement between themselves and the client.

Clause 2(d): 'Independent Enquiry'

'The obligations of the Consultant under or pursuant to this Agreement shall not be released or diminished by the appointment of any person by the Purchaser/the Tenant to carry out any independent enquiry into any relevant matter.'

3.14 This provision is designed to prevent a contribution claim by the architect arising from the involvement of an independent surveyor or even an in-house surveyor by the purchaser/the tenant in the development. In other words, as between the architect and the purchaser/the tenant the architect cannot argue that he is liable for less than the full amount of the damage suffered by the purchaser/the tenant (although he is not precluded from recovering a contribution from the purchaser/the tenant's independent surveyor if the latter too has been negligent).

Clause 3: 'Deleterious Materials'

3.15 Thankfully, the CIC has followed the approach adopted by the JCT in the CWa Forms and the consultant now warrants that he has exercised reasonable skill and care to see that materials are specified in accordance with the Guidelines contained in the addition of the publication *Good Practice in Selection of Construction Materials* (Ove Arup & Partners) current at the date of specification. This provision replaces the lengthy lists of materials which used to characterise consultancy agreements and collateral warranties, the death knell for which was sounded by the much-publicised attack by the Kirkforthan Brick Company Limited (the

only manufacturer of calcium silicate bricks in Scotland) on West Lothian District Council for '*reckless disparagement*' of its product. The only difficulty is that such lists were often used not just to forbid the use of specific products such as high alumina cement in structural elements but also to encourage environmentally friendly development by excluding also, for example, tropical hardwoods from non-renewable sources. Accordingly, these provisions may be expanded by more sophisticated clients to include reference to their standard environmental policies.

3.16 The Third Party Rights Schedule and the BPF Consultancy Agreement follow this approach as well. The latter requires also that the Consultant exercise reasonable skill, care and diligence to see that materials used in construction of those parts of the project to which the services relate will be in accordance with the *Good Practice Guide*. This is a point frequently raised by solicitors acting for purchasers and tenants.

Clause 4: Payment

'The Consultant acknowledges that the Client has paid all fees and expenses properly due and owing to the Consultant under the Appointment up to the date of this Agreement.'

3.17 The presence of this provision in the collateral warranty is, frankly, inexplicable. Given that a properly drafted consultancy agreement from the client's perspective (contrary to A7.5.1 of CA-5-07-A quoted in paragraph 2.02 above which is subject to fees being paid) would oblige the architect to enter into the collateral warranty when requested, it can only work against the architect who will also be obliged to give this acknowledgement even in circumstances where the basic statement is untrue. The truth is that the relationship between the client and architect is governed by the consultancy agreement and not by the collateral warranty which should not interfere in these issues. The CIC has marked the provision 'delete if not appropriate'. The BPF does not include it at all.

Clause 6: 'Copyright'

3.18 This provision obliges the architect to give the purchaser/the tenant a wide-ranging licence to copy and use those documents prepared by or on behalf of the architect for any purpose related to the premises — that is, those parts of the development which the purchaser/the tenant has bought or leased but not the whole. The licence extends to the copying and use of documents for an extension but not a right to reproduce the design for an extension. It should also be noted that, this provision refers to the licence being conditional upon:

'The Consultant having received payment of any fees properly due and owing as at the date of exercise by the licence.'

In other words, the architect can argue, in circumstances where entitlement is disputed under the consultancy agreement, that no copyright licence arises. This reflects the position of the architect under CA-S-07-A. It will not be acceptable to funders, purchasers and tenants and does not appear in BPF warranties.

Clause 7: 'Professional Indemnity Insurance'

3.19 While the architect should check that his professional indemnity insurance corresponds with the obligation set out in the collateral warranty at the date it is executed, this obligation is, after that, largely of academic interest because:

- The obligation is probably too uncertain to be enforceable since it is qualified by the following proviso: 'Provided always that such insurance is available at commercially reasonable rates.'
- There is no effective sanction for a breach by the architect of his obligation to maintain professional indemnity insurance.

Clause 8: 'Assignment'

3.20 Here, the CIC collateral warranty provides for two assignments to persons taking an assignment of the purchaser/tenant's 'whole' interest. Ownership of premises does not change frequently nor are leases often assigned, so this should meet most requirements of the purchasers or tenants although the assignment will not be valid if the property is divided up which may be a problem.

It should be remembered that an assignment does not create new rights. It extinguishes the assignor's rights and, from the date of the assignment, gives the assignee the rights which the assignor would otherwise have had. It does not mean that the assignee's limitation period starts again following an assignment of the collateral warranty. Similarly, it does not mean that the assignee can recover damages which would not have been recoverable by the assignor.

Equally, from the purchaser/tenant's point of view, if the architect has agreed to give him a collateral warranty in the first place because it is thought that the size of the interest which he is taking in the development warrants this degree of protection, and if that purchaser/tenant parts with his interest after occupying the building for, say, 2 years, then the new purchaser or tenant will still have losses if there are latent defects in the building caused by the architect's negligence. If he does not have the benefit of the collateral warranty, then he may have no redress whatsoever in respect of those losses.

Clause 10: 'Limitation'

'No action or proceedings for any breach of this Agreement shall be commenced against the Consultant after the expiry of —— years from the date of practical completion under the building contract.'

3.21 The CIC's guidance notes — assuming English law! — suggest that periods not exceeding 6 years should be inserted for consultancy agreements under hand and 12 years if the consultancy agreement is executed as a deed.

Even if such periods are included, there is a risk that Clause 10 will prevent claims being made against the architect by purchasers/tenants in circumstances where the client still has a valid claim against the architect for breach of the consultancy agreement and relevant limitation periods under the consultancy agreement have not expired. For example:

- If an act of negligence is committed by the architect during the defects liability period or, indeed, if negligent advice is given by the architect in relation to a defect which appears after the defects liability period has expired, Clause 10 may bar a claim even though limitation periods are still open under the consultancy agreement.
- If indemnities are included in the consultancy agreement, those can have the effect of extending limitation periods.
- If there is evidence of deliberate concealment on the part of the architect.

CIC/ConsWa/F

3.22 This contains, at Clauses 6, 7 and 8, provisions conferring on the funders 'step-in rights' entitling the funder to 'take over'

the appointment and to receive prior notice of termination of the appointment by the architect. They have limited application and they should only be included where such rights are properly covered under agreements between developers and their funders. The clauses warrant careful analysis.

- *Clause 6* This entitles the funder to serve notice on the architect upon termination of the finance agreement. In order to avoid an argument by the developer that the architect is in breach of his obligations under the appointment, it is important in such circumstances to ensure that the developer acknowledges that the architect is entitled to rely on notice given by the funder and, hence, the fact that the developer is a party to CIC/ConsWa/F even though he derives no benefit under it.
- *Clause 7* This requires the architect to give notice to the funder before terminating the appointment for breach by the developer. Again, it entitles the funder to serve notice on the architect requiring the architect to act for the funder in such circumstances. The developer should ensure in these circumstances that he has proper protection under the terms of his agreement with the funder against improper service of notice by the funder.
- *Clause 8* Finally, this requires the funder to accept liability for fees payable to the architect including fees outstanding at the date of service of any notice. This clause sometimes causes difficulties with funders but, of course, if a funder does not agree to meet outstanding fees, the architect will simply serve further notice on the funder in respect of breach of payment obligations under appointment. Clause 8 also provides that, if the funder nominates someone else to take over the appointment — perhaps, for example, another developer — it, the funder, will act as guarantor for the fees; in other words, the architect will not find himself in contract with a man of straw.

Another comment about these 'step-in rights' is that they can only appear as drafted in one collateral warranty on each project. If they are given to two or more different parties, the architect may be in an impossible position and may receive notices from two or more parties requiring him to contract with them. If step-in rights are to be given to more than one party, priority clauses must be included.

For comments on 'step-in' and third party rights, see Chapter 20.

4 Practical advice

4.01 An architect being asked to sign a consultancy agreement which contains an obligation to provide collateral warranties in a stipulated form or indeed being asked to sign the collateral warranty itself must clarify with his insurers their precise policy in relation to the issue of these documents. Most professional indemnity insurance policies will contain a specific endorsement about collateral warranties stipulating the numbers which may be given and the terms which are insured. If there is no special endorsement insurers must be questioned carefully about their position to ensure that, by entering into express contractual commitments with third parties, the architect is not allowing insurers to avoid liability or is not activating one of the policy exclusions.

It is prudent to have all warranties which contain any departure from forms accepted by insurers agreed with insurers.

32

Architects' liability

JAMES CROSS QC

1 Introduction

1.01 This chapter is principally about the liability of an architect to pay damages for professional negligence.

1.02 'Professional negligence' is a convenient shorthand for describing the liability of a professional – whether in contract or in tort – for breach of the obligation (or duty) to provide professional services with reasonable care and skill and diligence.

1.03 Professional negligence is a big topic, even when confined to architects. It should be appreciated, however, that it is nevertheless narrower in scope than the topic of the 'professional liability' of an architect, because an architect may be liable for the breach of obligations which are either different in character and content to the obligation of reasonable care and skill and diligence, or which are additional (sometimes more onerous) obligations which an architect must discharge. These other sources or forms of professional liability are discussed in this chapter in Section 2. Such other sources or forms of professional liability are important. Nevertheless, the vast majority of claims against architects are claims for professional negligence.

2 Other professional liability

(a) Introduction

2.01 The primary source of an architect's obligations vis-à-vis his employer client is, of course, the contract (or agreement of appointment) between the architect and the employer client (see Chapter 30). An architect may also owe contractual obligations to third parties as a result of the provision of collateral warranties (see Chapter 31). There is no substitute for examining the terms of each contract with care in order to identify and understand the obligations upon an architect in any particular case and, hence, what it is that an architect may be liable for. In theory, there are no restrictions upon the nature and content of the obligations which an architect can, or may agree to, assume and, hence, of the liabilities to which an architect may be subject. In practice, however, compliance with the ARB and RIBA Codes of Conduct leads to contracts being made substantially upon written standard forms of agreement of appointment – something which has done much to identify and define an architect's general and specific obligations both with clarity and consistency.

(b) Fitness for purpose etc.

2.02 An architect's professional obligations are rooted in the obligation to exercise reasonable care and skill. Like all professionals,

an architect does not ordinarily owe any stricter (or higher) obligation to achieve a particular result; to ensure, for example, that his design is fit for the purpose for which the architect knows it is intended to be used. In short, an architect's liability is usually dependent upon a finding of 'fault', in the sense of professional negligence. As Denning LJ stated in *Greaves & Co (Contractors) Ltd v Baynham Meikle & Partners* [1975] 1 WLR 1095:

> 'The law does not usually imply a warranty that [the professional man] will achieve the desired result, but only a term that he will use reasonable care and skill. The surgeon does not warrant that he will cure the patient. Nor does the solicitor warrant that he will win the case.'

And, as HHJ Humphrey Lloyd QC stated in *Payne v John Setchell Ltd* [2002] PNLR 7 to the same effect:

> 'A professional person ... does not normally undertake obligations of an absolute nature but only undertakes to exercise reasonable professional skill and care in performance of the relevant service or in the production of the product.'

2.03 In this important respect, an architect is ordinarily in a different (and more favourable) position to the building contractor whose obligations to his employer, as one who supplies work and materials as well as services, will often involve express or implied obligations relating to the quality and/or fitness for purpose of the contractor's workmanship and materials. Moreover, this general position so far as an architect is concerned tends to be reinforced by the standard forms of appointment of an architect (which serve to emphasise the central obligation of reasonable care owed by an architect); and by section 4 of the Supply of Goods and Services Act 1982 which provides for the implication, in certain circumstances, of fitness for purpose obligations into contracts for the sale of goods, but *not* – by contrast – into contracts for the supply of services (of which architects' appointments are examples).

2.04 Nevertheless, there may be circumstances in which an architect *does* owe stricter obligations either expressly or by implication. The case of *Greaves* itself (albeit involving structural engineers) provides an example. In that case the contractors undertook to build a factory complex and warehouse, supplying all necessary labour, materials and expertise to produce the finished product. The contractors engaged the defendants, consultant structural engineers, to design the warehouse. The building was to be constructed according to a newly introduced method of composite construction and was to be used for storing and moving oil drums loaded onto stacker trucks. Within a few months of completion the first floor began to crack: the floors were not designed with sufficient strength to withstand the vibration which was produced by the stacker trucks. The contractors claimed an indemnity from the engineers on the grounds that the engineers had warranted that their design would produce a building fit for its purpose. The Court of Appeal explained that the professional man is not usually under a duty to achieve a specified result, but they went on to compare the situation with that of a dentist who agrees to make a set of false teeth for a patient, in which case there is an implied warranty that they will fit his gums (*Samuels v Davies* [1943] KB 526). Denning LJ said:

> 'What then is the position when an architect or an engineer is employed to design a house or a bridge? Is he under an implied warranty that, if the work is carried out to his design, it will be reasonably fit for the purpose? Or is he only under a duty to use reasonable care and skill? In the present case . . . the evidence shows that both parties were of one mind on the matter. Their common intention was that the engineer should design a warehouse which would be fit for the purpose for which it was required. That common intention gives rise to a term implied in fact.'

He concluded:

> 'In the light of that evidence it seems to me that there was implied in fact a term that if the work was completed in accordance with the design it would be reasonably fit for the use of loaded stacker trucks. The engineers failed to make such a design and are therefore liable.'

2.05 Another example is provided by the decision in *Consultants Group International v John Worman Ltd* (1985) 9 ConLR 46 in which the claimants, providers of specialist architectural and consultancy services in connection with the refurbishment of an abattoir, were found to be under an express or implied contractual obligation to the defendant contractors (the architects' employers) to ensure that the works which they designed would be fit for purpose, namely in accordance with the relevant UK and EC standards and requirements for grant aid. Relevant factors in so deciding appear to have been that the claimant architects were, as the Court found, the 'prime movers in the project from start to finish' and the fact that the defendants had made it clear to the architects that they had no experience of abattoir work and would be dependent upon the architects' expertise and experience. More recently, in *Associated British Ports v Hydro Soil Services NV* [2006] EWHC 1187, the designers to whom the defendant design and build contractor sub-contracted the design of the strengthening works to a quay wall were found – upon a proper understanding of the design sub-contract – to owe the same obligation to the defendant in relation to fitness for purpose as that owed by the defendant to the claimant under the main design and build contract (i.e. that there was an express obligation upon the designers to provide a design for the strengthening works which was fit for purpose).

2.06 The three cases discussed in paragraphs 2.04 and 2.05 above were all cases in which the architect (or his equivalent) provided professional services only. In that context, the cases highlight the need either for express agreement in relation to the assumption of a fitness for purpose obligation or for facts which justify the implication of such an (absolute) obligation. They are the exception rather than the rule. For cases highlighting the rule, see *George Hawkins v Chrysler (UK) and Burne Associates* (1986) 38 BLR 36 (no basis for holding that the engineers who designed showers for installation at a foundry owed any stricter obligation in respect of the flooring on which the claimant slipped than the normal obligation of reasonable care and skill) and *Payne v John Setchell Ltd* [2002] PNLR 7 (issue of a certificate by an engineer that he was satisfied that the foundations of dwellings had been constructed in accordance with his design and were suitable for support of the dwellings was not a fitness for purpose warranty in respect of the foundations, only the expression of the defendant's professional opinion).

2.07 However, where, by contrast, the architect designs *and supplies* a product (or similar) pursuant to his professional appointment, it seems clear that different considerations arise and it is likely that the architect will owe a fitness for purpose obligation in respect of the product or article supplied. The fact of supply of the product or article is thought to be vital in this context: see *IBA v EMI and BICC Construction* (1980) 14 BLR 1.

(c) Honesty

2.08 It is no surprise that an architect owes fundamental obligations of honesty and integrity in his dealings with others in addition to obligations of competence. Honesty and integrity are, rightly, at the forefront of the conduct required of architects by RIBA.

2.09 There may, therefore, be circumstances in which an architect is liable for breach of his obligations of honesty and integrity. Vis-à-vis his employer client, any liability on the part of the architect for breach of such obligations is likely to be determined by reference to the principles of the law of agency (see, for example, in respect of an architect's liability in respect of bribes and secret commissions, the old case of *Tahrland v Rodier* (1866) 16 L.C. Rep. 473). Vis-à-vis third parties, any liability on the part of the architect (or vicarious liability of his principal) for breach of such obligations is likely to be in the tort of deceit: the making of a false statement of fact knowingly, or without an honest belief in its truth, or recklessly, careless whether it be true or false (*Derry v Peek* (1889) 14 App Cas 337). For a rare example of a case involving liability for fraudulent misrepresentation by an architect in inviting tenders: see *Pearson v Dublin Corporation* [1907] 1 AC 351.

2.10 There are many reasons why an architect's liability for breach of his obligations of honesty and integrity are likely to be rare. The ineffectiveness of professional indemnity insurance cover in respect of such liability also acts as a significant disincentive to the making of any allegation of fraud against an architect. Furthermore, there are, of course, significant evidential and other hurdles that properly need to be surmounted if such serious allegations are to be established. It should be noted, however, that there can be advantages to a claimant in alleging fraud. It may afford a remedy where there would otherwise be none (for example, vis-à-vis a contractor to whom – in the absence of any contractual relationship – an architect owes no duty of care in tort to safeguard the contractor from economic loss); it may enable damages to be recovered which could not otherwise be recovered (for example, contractual limitations on the amount of damages recoverable are likely to be of no effect in a case of fraud); it is likely to render any contributory negligence on the part of the claimant irrelevant; and it may enable a claimant to surmount a limitation defence which would otherwise bar a claim in contract or in tort or pursuant to statute.

(d) Agency

2.11 As the agent of his employer client, an architect will owe to his employer client (his principal) all the usual duties of an agent (see Chapter 2) and there may be circumstances in which, as a result, an architect owes fiduciary duties to his employer client. However, such fiduciary duties do not enlarge the scope of an architect's contractual (or tortious) duties (*Chesham Properties Ltd v Bucknall Austin Project Management Services Ltd* (1996) 82 BLR 92) and, in practice, the obligations of an architect as agent are most likely to be relevant in the context of the architect's authority (or not) to do things on his employer client's behalf and/or to bind his employer client vis-à-vis the contractor and others. Of course, most standard forms of building contract now seek to define the scope of an architect's authority in considerable detail with the result that cases involving breach of warranty of authority on the part of an architect (*Yonge v Toynbee* [1910] 1 KB 215) or personal liability as a result of entering into contracts with contractors without making it clear that the architect is acting only as agent for his principal (*Beigtheil and Young v Stewart* (1900) TLR 177 and *Sika Contracts v Gill and Closeglen Properties* (1978) 9 BLR 11) are now rare.

(e) Defective Premises Act 1972 ('DPA 1972')

2.12 Section 1(1) of the DPA 1972 provides:

'A person taking on work for the provision of a dwelling (whether the dwelling is provided by the erection or by the conversion or enlargement of a building) owes a duty –

(a) if the dwelling is provided to the order of any person, to that person; and

(b) without prejudice to paragraph (a) above, to every person who acquires an interest (whether legal or equitable) in the dwelling;

to see that the work which he takes on is done in a workmanlike or, as the case may be, professional manner, with proper materials and so that as regards that work the dwelling will be fit for habitation when completed.'

2.13 It is important to understand that the DPA 1972 gives rise to a separate right of action for breach of the statutory duty set out in Section 1(1). The DPA 1972 is an important piece of legislation. For reasons which have already been explained in Chapter 3, it is the more so (i) because since the decision of the House of Lords in *Murphy v Brentwood District Council* [1991] AC 398 there have been substantial restrictions on the ability of a claimant to recover damages for pure economic loss in tort (see further in Section 4 below) which do not affect a claim for damages for breach of the statutory duty set out in section 1(1); and (ii) because it has now been a very long time indeed since there was an 'approved scheme' for the purposes of section 2 of the DPA 1972, which significantly restricted the right of action for breach of the statutory duty set out in Section 1(1). (Until 31 March 1979 the main approved scheme was the 10-year NHBC scheme, but there has been no 'approved scheme' since then.)

2.14 The following points should be noted:

1 The statutory duty only applies in relation to an architect taking on work 'for or in connection with the provision of a dwelling', i.e. a building which is to be used as a home (a dwelling-house). It is not a duty owed by an architect taking on work in relation to the provision of commercial premises or premises used predominantly for commercial purposes: see *Catlin Estates Ltd v Carter Jonas (A Firm)* [2006] PNLR 15.

2 The DPA 1972 imposes a statutory obligation upon an architect in relation to work which an architect takes on for or in connection with the provision of a dwelling to ensure that he does that work in a 'professional manner' [i.e. with reasonable care and skill]. However, it is clear that a failure to exercise reasonable care and skill will not – of itself – give rise to a liability for breach of the statutory duty set out in section 1(1) of the DPA 1972 because the key obligation is that the architect should carry out his work in a manner which will result in the dwelling being fit for habitation when completed. A failure to carry out his work in a professional manner may result in the dwelling being defective when completed, but unless those defects render the dwelling unfit for habitation when completed there is no liability for breach of the statutory duty: see *Thompson v Clive Alexander & Partners* (1993) 59 BLR 77, following *Alexander v Mercouris* [1979] 1 WLR 1279, and itself followed in *Catlin Estates Ltd v Carter Jonas (A Firm)* (it was not enough for a claimant to prove that defects arose because of the architects' failure to carry out their work in a professional manner or to use proper materials because the duty imposed by section 1(1) was limited to the kind of defect in the work done and the materials used which made the dwelling unfit for habitation upon completion).

3 The statutory duty is owed in respect of both new construction and improvements.

4 The statutory duty applies as much to the failure to carry out work as the actual carrying out of work: *Andrews v Schooling* [1991] 1 WLR 783.

5 An architect who arranges for another to take on work for or in connection with the provision of a dwelling will be treated as having taken on the work himself if he does so in the course of

a business which consists of or includes providing or arranging for the provision of dwellings or installations in dwellings: DPA 1972, section 1(4).

6 Any term of an agreement which purports to exclude or restrict, or has the effect of excluding or restricting, the operation of any of the provisions of the DPA 1972, or any liability arising by virtue of any its provisions, is void: DPA 1972, section 6(3). An architect cannot therefore contract out of his DPA 1972 statutory duty or seek to restrict it.

7 The statutory duty is owed both to those who commission the work and to every other person who acquires an interest in the dwelling 'whether legal or equitable'. In practice, this means subsequent purchasers of the dwelling, mortgagees and tenants.

8 There are special rules affecting the time (the limitation period) within which claims for breach of the statutory duty set out in section 1(1) of the DPA 1972 must be made if they are not to be statute barred by the Limitation Act 1980. The effect of section 1(5) of the DPA 1972 is that the date on which the cause of action for breach of statutory duty accrues is 'when the dwelling was completed' and that any claim must be made within 6 years of that date. This is subject to the proviso that if, after completion of the dwelling, further work is done to rectify defects in the original work, any cause of action in respect of that further work does not accrue until such time as that 'further work was finished': see *Alderson v Beetham Organisation Ltd* [2003] 1 WLR 1686.

9 A claim for breach of the statutory duty set out in section 1(1) of the DPA 1972 is not 'an action for damages for negligence' within the meaning of section 14A of the Limitation Act 1980: *Payne v John Setchell Ltd* [2002] PNLR 7.

2.15 The balance of this chapter, substantially Sections 3 to 9 below, is concerned with the liability of an architect for professional negligence. The final section (Section 10) gives the Scots law perspective on the subject of this chapter.

3 Liability for professional negligence

Sources of the obligation of reasonable care and skill

(a) Contract

Express terms

3.01 Nowadays, the primary source of the architect's obligation to exercise reasonable care and skill is usually the *express* term to that effect either in the architect's contract of appointment with his employer/client or in the collateral warranty provided by an architect in favour of the beneficiary of a collateral warranty.

3.02 So far as contracts of appointment between the architect and his employer/client are concerned, any appointment upon

a RIBA Standard Form of Agreement is likely to oblige the architect, expressly, to 'exercise reasonable skill and care in conformity with the normal standards of the Architect's profession': see, for example, SFA/92 Clause 1.2.1; SFA/99 Clause 2.1 and SFA/2007 Clause A2.1.1 (S-Con-07) which adds obligation of reasonable diligence to that of reasonable skill and care.

3.03 So far as collateral warranties are concerned, the architect will ordinarily warrant expressly to the beneficiary that he has exercised, and will continue to exercise, 'reasonable skill, care and diligence' in the performance of his services to his employer client under his contract of appointment.

Implied terms
3.04 Section 13 of the Supply of Goods and Services Act 1982 provides that 'in a contract for the supply of a service where the supplier is acting in the course of a business, there is an implied term that the supplier will carry out the service with reasonable care and skill.' It follows that, in the absence of any standard form appointment or any express term requiring the exercise of reasonable care and skill, nevertheless there is an implied term to that effect in every contract (oral or written) whereby an architect is engaged to provide his professional services.

3.05 Section 14 of the Supply of Goods and Services Act 1982 provides that, where the time for the service to be carried out is not fixed by the contract or is left to be fixed in a manner agreed by the contract or determined by the course of dealing between the parties, 'there is an implied term that the supplier will carry out the service within a reasonable time'.

3.06 It is the implied term of reasonable care and skill (section 13) which is probably the more important of these two statutory provisions so far as architects are concerned, but for a case in which it was held that it was an implied term of the architect's appointment by the contractor under a design and build contract that the architect would provide his design drawings by particular dates (and not simply exercise reasonable care and skill to do so) so as to enable the contractor to comply with its contractual obligations – apparently without reference to section 14 of the 1982 Act, but in reliance on the parties' common intentions (as in the case of *Greaves*): see *CFW Architects (a firm) v Cowlin Construction Ltd* (2006) ConLR 116.

(b) Tort
Concurrent duty of care
3.07 Where there is a contract between the architect and his employer client it is very often unnecessary to seek to rely on any duty of care owed concurrently by the architect to his employer client in tort because of the express and/or implied contractual duty of care which is already part and parcel of the contractual relationship between them. The same is true of contracts between the architect and the beneficiary of a collateral warranty.

3.08 Nevertheless, suggestions that the existence of contractual duties of care should exclude the existence of any concurrent (or parallel) duty of care in tort were decisively rejected by the House of Lords in *Henderson v Merrett Syndicates Ltd* [1995] 2 AC 145. Essentially, a contractual relationship between the professional and his employer client was regarded as being a pre-eminent example of a proximate relationship involving an assumption of responsibility sufficient to make it fair, just and reasonable that a duty of care in tort should be owed by the professional to his employer client. It is now well established, therefore, that an architect owes a concurrent duty of care in tort to those whom he also owes contractual duties of care.

3.09 The significance of this conclusion is principally in the context of limitation of actions (the time which the law allows an employer client to bring a claim for professional negligence against his architect) because it allows a claimant to bring his claim in tort (in reliance on breach of the concurrent duty of care owed in tort within 6 years of the date of damage) in circumstances where his claim for breach of contract (in reliance on breach of the contractual

duty of care within 6 years of the date of breach) is already statute barred, and indeed may have become so without his knowledge. As Lord Goff said in *Henderson*:

> 'If concurrent liability in tort is not recognised, a claimant may find his claim barred at a time when he is unaware of its existence. This must moreover be a real possibility in the case of claims against professional men, such as solicitors or architects, since the consequences of their negligence may well not come to light until long after the lapse of six years from the date when the relevant breach of contract occurred. Moreover the benefits of the Latent Damage Act 1986, under which the time of the accrual of the cause of action may be postponed until after the [claimant] has the relevant knowledge, are limited to actions in tortious negligence.'

3.10 The scope of the concurrent duty of care in tort, in particular as to whether an employer client or similar – suing his architect only in tort because of, for example, limitation difficulties in respect of his claim in contract – may recover damages for pure economic loss in tort (damages which in many cases he could probably have recovered had his contractual claim still been 'alive') continues to be a matter of some debate and is discussed further in Section 4 below.

3.11 For present purposes, two things should be noted at this stage:

1 The contract out of which the concurrent duty of care in tort arises remains vitally important to a proper understanding of the scope of any concurrent duty of care in tort. It is often said that the concurrent duty of care in tort is 'co-terminous' or 'co-extensive' with the contractual obligation of reasonable care and skill. Such language recognises that the terms of the relevant contract limit or define the scope of the concurrent duty of care in tort and emphasises that the duty of care in tort is ordinarily no wider in scope than the relevant contractual obligation. So, for example, if there is no contractual obligation as a result of any breach of the contractual duty of care to pay damages in respect of particular losses (damages representing pure economic loss in tort, for example), there is no concurrent tortious obligation to do so: see *Greater Nottingham Co-operative Society Ltd v Cementation Piping & Foundations Ltd* [1989] QB 71.
2 A claimant faced with having to frame his claim for professional negligence against his architect in reliance on his claim in tort alone may find that the architect has defences available to him in tort which would not be available to him were the claim framed in contract as well, or instead. The most obvious example of this is in relation to the involvement of sub-consultants by architects or circumstances involving reasonable reliance by architects upon specialists (whether consultants, specialist sub-contractors or suppliers). In a contractual claim, such delegation of an architect's work to others, or reliance on specialists, will ordinarily not enable an architect to escape liability for services which the architect is himself contractually obliged to perform: see *Moresk Cleaners Ltd v Hicks* [1966] 2 Lloyd's Rep 338 (architect liable for design of reinforced concrete frame by structural engineer) and *Nye Saunders & Partners v Bristow* (1987) 37 BLR 92 (architect liable for cost estimate given by quantity surveyor). In a tortious claim, however, the engagement of competent specialists and reasonable reliance upon them in respect of particular work may enable an architect to escape liability in tort.

Duty of care to third parties
3.12 'Third parties', in this context, essentially means anyone with whom the architect does not have a contractual relationship. As the *source* of a duty of care in tort, the absence of a contractual relationship is of the very essence of the law of tort and the position is already well explained in Chapter 3, to which reference should be made. The principal debates in the context of the duty of care in tort owed to third parties are in relation to (i) identifying the third parties to whom a duty of care in tort is owed and (ii) more importantly, understanding the scope of the duty of care in tort which is owed. Each of those matters is discussed in more detail in Section 4 below.

(c) Statute

Supply of Goods and Services Act 1982

3.13 The relevant provisions of the Supply of Goods and Services Act 1982 have already been discussed above. The 1982 Act is a source of an architect's obligation of reasonable care and skill (and his obligation to provide his professional services within a reasonable time) only in the sense that it implies terms into an architect's contracts to that effect. The 1982 Act gives rise to no free-standing obligation of reasonable care and skill and no action for breach of statutory duty.

Construction (Design and Management) Regulations 2007

3.14 The Construction (Design and Management) Regulations 2007, and their predecessors the 1994 CDM Regulations, are the source of a number of important obligations and duties upon architects whether an architect is the 'designer' or 'CDM co-ordinator' within the meaning and/or for the purposes of the 2007 CDM Regulations. Those obligations are discussed in detail in Chapter 15 above. For present purposes, it suffices to observe that the CDM Regulations are not so much a source of an architect's obligation of reasonable care and skill as a 'spelling out' of the substantive content of that obligation so far as an architect's involvement in the design and management of construction projects is concerned. In short, it is likely that any breach of the duties and obligations imposed by the CDM Regulations will amount to professional negligence.

4 Scope of the obligation of reasonable care and skill

(a) Contract and concurrent duty of care in tort

Contract

4.01 The scope of the contractual obligation of reasonable care and skill in terms of the parties to whom that obligation is owed and the types of loss which may be recoverable for breach of that obligation is a matter which is, first and foremost, regulated and defined by the terms of the relevant contract.

4.02 Ordinarily, the obligation will obviously be owed to the party with whom the architect has entered into a contract. Ordinarily too, and subject to the application of general principles of causation and remoteness and mitigation of damage, the types of damage or loss for which the architect may be liable in damages for breach of his contractual obligation of reasonable care and skill vis-à-vis his employer client will embrace the following:

1 Damages in respect of personal injury sustained by his employer client, or in respect of the death of his employer client.
2 Damages in respect of (physical) damage to his employer client's property and in respect of financial losses sustained by the employer client in consequence of that damage, for example, the cost of repairing or replacing damaged property.
3 Damages in respect of any financial losses sustained by the employer client by reason of the architect's professional negligence, for example the costs involved in remedying or rectifying design or other defects in a building.

4.03 As a matter of terminology, financial loss in category 3 above is referred to in the language of the law of tort as 'pure economic loss' because it has no association – in the eyes of the law – with any damage to property. This concept is considered in more detail below, because its primary relevance is in the law of tort. For present purposes, however, it suffices to emphasise that there are no objections of principle to the recovery of pure economic loss in contract. Pure economic loss is routinely recovered in claims relying on breach of any contractual duty of care.

4.04 The following matters, however, should be noted as potentially affecting the scope of the contractual obligation of reasonable care and skill in terms of the parties to whom that obligation is owed and the losses which may be recoverable for breach of that obligation.

1 The effects of an assignment of an architect's appointment to another party; alternatively of a novation of an architect's appointment from, say, the building owner to the contractor on a design & build project. Assignment, alternatively novation, will always call for very careful consideration if the architect is not to find himself owing a contractual obligation of reasonable care and skill not only to a different party to his original employer client but also with, potentially, unintended consequences so far as an architect's liability for loss is concerned: see, for example, *Blyth & Blyth Ltd v Carillion Construction Ltd* (2001) 79 ConLR 142 in which, in reliance upon a novation agreement, the defendant contractors (the new client) – unsuccessfully, on the facts – sought to recover damages for their own losses sustained as a result of alleged professional negligence on the part of the claimant engineers in providing professional services for the original employer client (the provision of tender information) *before* the date of novation.
2 The potentially retrospective effect of an architect's appointment so as to impose obligations upon the architect in respect of professional services provided – as often happens – before the contract was made or formally concluded. Whether an architect's appointment expressly or impliedly has retrospective effect may be important: see *Consarc Design Ltd v Hutch Investments Ltd* [2002] PNLR 712.
3 The content of any contractual term of an architect's appointment seeking to limit the architect's professional negligence liability for loss and damage to a specified sum and/or to exclude the architect's liability for certain types of loss or damage. The effectiveness (enforceability) of such terms in circumstances where they are open to challenge under the Unfair Contract Terms Act 1977 (and they *are* open to challenge where the party with whom the architect contracts is a 'consumer' for the purposes of the 1977 Act (a householder is a 'consumer', for example) or where the contract is made upon the architect's written standard terms of business) depends upon whether the term satisfies the statutory requirement of reasonableness. For an example of a case involving an architect in which the statutory requirement of reasonableness *was* satisfied: see *Moores v Yakeley Associates Ltd* (1998) 62 ConLR 76 (a £250 000 limitation of liability in an architect's contract with his employer client was held to be reasonable on the facts – despite the architect having PI cover of £500 000 – having regard to such matters as the likely cost of the works (£250 000); the limitation being more than 10 times the amount of the architect's fees of £20 000; the involvement of solicitors on behalf of the employer client and their awareness of the relevant clause and their lack of objection to it; the employer client's means as compared to the architect's means; and the strength of the employer client's bargaining position as compared to the architect's). Net contribution clauses are also relevant in this context (albeit that they seek to limit the architect's liability in a different way) and they are discussed in more detail in Section 8 below.

Concurrent duty of care in tort

4.05 Many of the matters discussed above in paragraphs 4.01 to 4.04 are equally relevant to a consideration of the scope of any concurrent duty of care in tort. The principal unique debate so far as the scope of the concurrent duty of care in tort is concerned, however, is whether the duty extends to safeguarding the employer client from pure economic loss, or is limited – in the same way as the conventional duty of care in tort which is owed to third parties – to safeguarding the employer client from personal injury and damage to property only.

4.06 The debate is reflected in four first-instance decisions, three of which have determined that the concurrent duty of care in tort extends to the avoidance of pure economic loss (*Storey v Charles Church Developments Ltd* (1995) 73 ConLR 1; *Tesco Stores v*

Costain Construction Ltd [2003] EWHC 1487; and *Mirant-Asia Pacific Ltd v Ove Arup & Partners International Ltd* [2005] PNLR 10) and one of which has decided the matter the other way *(Payne v John Setchell Ltd* [2002] PNLR 7). The appellate courts have yet to consider the issue.

(b) Duty of care in tort to third parties

Personal injury

4.07 There is no doubt that an architect owes a duty of care in tort not to cause personal injury (or death) to those who might be foreseeably injured (or killed) as a result of his professional negligence: *Clay v A.J. Crump & Sons Ltd* [1964] 1 QB 533. In that case, an architect supervising demolition and rebuilding instructed the demolition contractor to leave a wall standing as a temporary measure which closed off one boundary to the site. He accepted the demolition contractor's word that the wall was safe, and, although he visited the site, he did not check for himself. Had he looked, he would have seen that the wall was tottering above a 6-foot trench cut under its foundations. The architect, together with the demolition contractor and the builder, was found liable when the wall collapsed and injured one of the builder's men.

4.08 Nevertheless, ordinarily, the safety of the contractor's employees is principally a matter for the contractor and it is not ordinarily (subject, nowadays, to the CDM Regulations) the architect's job to tell the contractor how to do its work or what safety precautions the contractor should take (especially with respect to temporary works). So, an architect was not negligent when he instructed a chase to be cut in a wall and, as a result of the builder choosing to do it without shoring the wall up, it fell and injured a workman: *Clayton v Woodman & Sons (Builders) Ltd* [1962] 1 WLR 585.

4.09 Where personal injury is suffered as a result of a design defect, again, it is thought to be uncontroversial that an architect owes a duty of care in tort to all those who may foreseeably be injured (or killed) as result of his professional negligence to take reasonable steps to avoid causing personal injury (or death): see, for example, *Eckersley v Binnie & Partners* (1988) 18 ConLR 1 (liability of engineer designers to claimants injured or killed in the Abbeystead explosion for failure properly to design for the risk of methane gas) and *Targett v Torfaen Borough Council* [1992] 3 AER 27 (liability of local authority designers to a council house tenant injured as a result of the failure to provide adequate lighting and a handrail).

Damage to 'other property' and consequential economic loss

4.10 It is also now tolerably well established that an architect owes a duty of care in tort not to cause physical damage to the property of anyone whose property might foreseeably be damaged as a result of his professional negligence. However, this principle is subject to two very significant qualifications:

1   The property involved must be what is referred to as 'other property', namely property which is different to the property in respect of which the architect is (or was) contractually engaged. This differentiation is vital because financial loss sustained as a result of physical damage to 'other property' is regarded as consequential economic loss which is generally recoverable in tort; whereas financial loss sustained as a result of defects in (or damage to) the property in respect of which the architect is (or was) engaged is – following *Murphy v Brentwood* – regarded as pure economic loss which is not generally recoverable in tort. In terms of its practical application, it can be seen too that the differentiation will be relevant particularly in the context of claims against architects in tort by subsequent owners and purchasers of property designed by an architect and/or whose construction has been inspected by an architect.
2   The existence (and scope) of any duty of care in respect of physical damage to 'other property' is very much affected by the question of whether the third party whose 'other property'

has been damaged (usually a subsequent owner or purchaser) had a reasonable opportunity to discover the relevant defect before it caused him damage.

'Other property'

4.11 Identifying what is, or what is not, damage to 'other property' will sometimes be straightforward: for example, properties adjoining, or in the vicinity of, a construction site which are damaged as a result of design defects in the permanent works or as a result of negligently 'supervised' construction operations on site will clearly be 'other property' in respect of which a duty of care in tort is owed. So, for example, in *Nitrigin Eireann Teoranta v Inco Alloys Ltd* [1992] 1 WLR 498, when a pipe supplied by specialist pipe-makers to a building owner cracked, the cost of repairs was irrecoverable economic loss because the defective pipe had not caused damage to anything other than itself. However, when the pipe cracked again a year later and caused an explosion which damaged surrounding plant, the cost of repairing the damaged plant was recoverable because the defective pipe had caused damage to 'other property'.

4.12 In other circumstances, the task of identifying what is, or what is not, damage to 'other property' may be difficult and contentious. It can be further complicated by reference (arguably unnecessary reference) to the pre-*Murphy v Brentwood* – and much-criticised – 'complex structure theory' (see further in Chapter 3 above). This will be particularly so, perhaps, in circumstances where an architect's design or 'supervision' role is limited to particular elements of a building only. The following are illustrations:

1   *Warner v Basildon Development Corporation* (1991) Const LJ 146 (negligent construction of foundations of a house by a builder which caused damage to parts of the superstructure of the house constructed by the same builder did not involve causing damage to 'other property'; therefore no recovery by subsequent purchasers of the house for diminution in value).
2   *Jacobs v Morton and Partners* [1995] 72 BLR 92 (engineer designers of piled raft foundations as part of a separate remedial scheme to repair cracking in an existing house were liable, when the remedial scheme failed, for the cost of demolition and rebuilding of the house on the basis that this involved damage to 'other property').
3   *Tesco Stores Ltd v Norman Hitchcox Partnership Ltd* (1997) 56 ConLR 42 (architect designers of shell works for a supermarket were not liable when fire spread in the supermarket as a result of inadequate compartmentation, for physical damage to the structure of the supermarket because in contrast to the damage caused to stock and equipment, this was not damage to 'other property').
4   *Tunnel Refineries Ltd v Bryan Donkin Co. Ltd* (1998) CILL 1392, (suppliers and manufacturers of a fan in a compressor were not liable in tort to the compressor owner/purchaser for the cost of replacing the compressors when the fan shattered so as to wreck the compressor on the basis that there was no damage to 'other property' as a matter of fact and degree).
5   *Bellefield Computer Services Ltd v E Turner & Sons Ltd* (2000) BLR 97 (negligent construction of an internal fire (compartment) wall in a dairy by a builder which meant that fire spread from a storage area so as to damage the rest of the dairy when it should not have done did not involve damage to 'other property' in circumstances where the whole dairy had been built by the same builder; therefore no recovery by subsequent purchasers of the cost of repairs to the fabric of the building itself beyond the storage area. However, there *was* recovery in respect of damage to the subsequent purchasers' plant, equipment, stock and other chattels in areas of the building beyond the storage area because such items were distinct items of 'other property').
6   *Payne v John Setchell Ltd* [2002] PNLR 7 (engineer designers of raft foundations to a pair of cottages built by the same builder were not liable to subsequent owners of the cottages for defects in the foundations on the basis that there was no damage to 'other property').

Reasonable opportunity discovery of defect

4.13 An important limitation upon the existence (and scope) of an architect's duty of care in tort to avoid causing damage to 'other property', particularly vis-à-vis subsequent owners and occupiers of property designed by an architect whose contents etc. ('other property') are damaged by reason of a design defect in the building, is the principle that an architect's liability is essentially confined to a liability in respect of damage to 'other property' caused by *latent* defects only – latent defects for these purposes being defects which could not reasonably have been discovered on reasonable inspection of the building by or on behalf of the subsequent owner or occupier. For cases illustrating this principle and its application see:

1 *Baxhall Securities Ltd v Sheard Walshaw Partnership* [2002] PNLR 564 (architect designers of an industrial warehouse were not liable to subsequent owners/occupiers of the warehouse whose electrical goods stored in the warehouse were damaged by flooding by reason of the negligent design of the rainwater drainage system because the relevant defect – the absence of adequate overflows – was one which ought reasonably to have been discovered by the claimants with the benefit of the skilled advice from a building surveyor which it was to be expected they would obtain).
2 *Sahib Foods Ltd v Paskin Kyriades Sands (A Firm)* (2003) Con LR 1 (architect designers of a food production factory were liable to their employer client (the occupiers, Sahib) for the spread of fire because of the negligent design decision to use combustible panels, but were not liable in tort to subsequent purchasers of the factory (the second claimants) because, on the facts, there was no evidence that the use of combustible panels was a defect which would not have been revealed by a pre-purchase survey/inspection).

4.14 More recently, however, the principle has been doubted: *Pearson Education Ltd v The Charter Partnership Ltd* (2007) BLR 324. In that case, the architect designers of a warehouse used for book storage were liable to subsequent occupiers of the warehouse for damage caused to their stock of books by flooding as a result of the negligent design of the rainwater drainage system because – despite there having been an earlier flood damaging the stock of a different occupier – the claimants 'neither knew nor should have known of the flood so that there was no reason why they should carry out any investigation of the adequacy of the rainwater systems'. In other words, on the facts, there was no question that the relevant defect should have been discovered. It was latent, so the subsequent occupiers were entitled to damages. Nevertheless, the principle absolving an architect in respect of damage caused by defects which should reasonably have been discovered was doubted by the Court of Appeal:

> 'if architect who has the primary responsibility for producing a safe design produces a defective design, it is not obviously fair, just and reasonable that he should be absolved from any liability in tort in respect of its consequences on the ground that another professional could reasonably be expected to discover his shortcoming . . . [I]t is not obvious why a failure of a person put at risk by a defective design, to take due care for his own safety or that of his property should break the chain of causation, rather than amount to contributory negligence'.

Pure economic loss

4.15 A general principle of professional negligence liability in tort, and it applies to architects as much as to any other profession, is that an architect is not liable in tort for pure economic loss. Putting matters another way, it is not within the scope of an architect's duty of care in tort to safeguard all those whom he may reasonably foresee will suffer loss if he is negligent from pure economic loss. He is liable to third parties in tort for causing personal injuries and damage to 'other property' as already explained and discussed above, but – ordinarily – the buck stops there.

4.16 In terms of its practical application to architects, the general principle means that an architect is not ordinarily liable in tort

(i) to subsequent owners and occupiers or similar in respect of the cost of repairing design (or other) defects in a building designed by him or (ii) to contractors with whom he has no contractual relationship in respect of, for example, negligent certification which causes contractors economic loss.

4.17 To any general principle there are, of course, exceptions. They have been discussed in Chapter 3. Much the most important of the exceptions to architects is the application of the *Hedley Byrne* principle – the essence of which requires a special relationship of proximity between the architect and any third party, a positive assumption of responsibility by the architect towards the third party to avoid causing him economic loss and reasonable reliance by the third party upon the architect, before a liability in tort for pure economic loss will be imposed.

4.18 So, on a 'normal' construction project it will usually be inimical to any *Hedley Byrne* liability of the architect in tort that the parties have chosen to formulate their contractual relationships in the way that they have because it will usually be inconsistent with the tortious duty alleged to be owed to the third party. This makes it unlikely that an architect who is not in a contractual relationship with someone involved with the project who claims to have suffered economic loss as a result of the architect's negligence will be liable to that party for such loss: see *Architype Projects Ltd v Dewhurst MacFarlane & Partners* (2003) 96 ConLR 35 (architect's claim against sub-consultant engineers on basis that the sub-consultants owed a duty of care in tort to the architect's employer client was struck out as having no reasonable prospect of success). It is similar considerations which, ordinarily, mean that an architect owes no duty of care in tort to a contractor to detect faults in the work carried out by the contractor so as to safeguard the contractor from economic loss, even though the architect clearly owes such a duty to his employer client: *Oldschool v Gleeson (Construction) Ltd* (1976) 4 BLR 103.

4.19 *Hedley Byrne* involved negligent statements and the provision of information and advice. It is clear in the light of *Henderson v Merrett* that the principle also applies to negligent conduct and the provision of negligent services, but – generally speaking – in the context of an architect's liability, English law has been resistant to imposing a liability for pure economic loss in the absence of some specific representation or intervention by the architect and/or in the absence of sound policy reasons why an architect should protect the position of parties with whom he has no contractual relationship in that way. Nevertheless, there may be circumstances, in which an architect will owe a *Hedley Byrne*-type duty of care in his communications and/or dealings with third parties to avoid causing them economic loss. The potential application of the *Hedley Byrne* principle so far as concerns subsequent purchasers and contractors, in particular, is discussed in paragraphs 4.20 and 4.21 respectively below.

Subsequent purchasers

4.20

1 *Machin v Adams* (1997) 84 BLR 79 (architect owed no duty of care to prospective purchasers of a property in respect of a letter which he provided to his employer client in which he made various statements relating to works of alteration and refurbishment being carried out at the property and the time which would be needed to complete them, including the statement that 'all works to date are to a satisfactory standard'. Even though the architect knew that this letter would probably be shown to the prospective purchaser, the works were ongoing and, on the facts, it was not reasonable that the purchaser should have proceeded without further enquiry).
2 *Lidl Properties v Clarke Bond Partnership* [1998] Env LR 622 (engineer owed a duty of care to a prospective purchaser of a supermarket in respect of statements made/advice given in an informal meeting about ground contamination and the likely costs of decontamination, but there was no liability on the facts because the engineer was not in breach of his duty and the claimant had not relied on the engineer's advice).

3 *Payne v John Setchell Ltd* [2002] PNLR 7 (engineer owed a duty of care to subsequent purchasers of the cottages in respect of his certificates/statements that the foundations were satisfactorily constructed because he intended that his certificates would be seen and relied upon, and was therefore liable to the subsequent purchasers for pure economic loss (diminution in value measured by cost of remedial works) in circumstances where the foundations were defective and his statement had not been made with reasonable care and skill).

4 *Offer-Hoar v Larkstore Ltd* [2006] PNLR 17 (geotechnical engineer owed no duty of care in tort to a subsequent owner in respect of a site investigation report because the use of the report by the subsequent owner was not reasonably foreseeable).

Contractors

4.21

1 *Townsend (Builders) Ltd v Cinema News and Property Management* (1958) 20 BLR 118 (architect's written statement to the contractor that he would serve all necessary notices required by building byelaws gave rise to liability to the contractor for damages when the notices were served late. This was pre-*Hedley Byrne*, but was a *Hedley Byrne*-type liability).

2 *Pacific Associates Inc v Baxter* [1990] 1 QB 993 (engineers not liable to contractors for economic loss caused by alleged negligent certification because there was a contractual structure in place whereby the contractor was entitled to challenge the engineer's decision in proceedings against the employer which made it inappropriate to impose a duty of care on the engineers. There was also a relevant disclaimer of personal liability on the part of the engineers for their acts and omissions in carrying out their duties under the building contract). Ordinarily, an architect owes no *Hedley Byrne* duty of care in tort to a contractor in and about his administration of the building contract as the agent of his employer client to avoid causing the contractor economic loss. Obviously, deliberate misapplication by an architect of the provisions of the building contract when issuing certificates is a very different matter: see *Lubenham Fidelities Investment Co. Ltd v South Pembrokeshire DC* (1986) 6 ConLR 85.

3 Before any building contract is entered into, however, the position may be different: *J Jarvis & Sons Ltd v Castle Wharf Developments Ltd* [2001] EWCA Civ 19 (no reason in principle why the professional agent of the employer under a building contract could not be liable to a contractor for negligent misstatements made by the agent to the contractor to induce him to tender, but there was no reliance and no liability on the facts).

5 Breach of the obligation of reasonable care and skill: pre-construction work stages

Appraisal and feasibility

Site investigation and surveys

5.01 Appraising the site and the construction project which is proposed essentially requires the architect to take reasonable steps to investigate the site with a view to satisfying himself, and so advising his employer client, as to the feasibility and buildability of the contemplated scheme on the particular site involved. Commonly, such steps will involve:

1 Considering the need for ground investigation of the site and advising his employer client on the appointment of specialist consultants/contractors to carry out any necessary investigation. Not to carry out any investigation at all of made ground, for example, or to advise as to the need for specialist investigation in such circumstances, is likely to be negligent: *see Eames London Estates Ltd v North Hertfordshire DC* (1980) 259 EG 491 (industrial building constructed on made ground,

architect designer of the foundations made no examination of the ground and so took no steps to satisfy himself as to the bearing capacity of the ground). However where an architect recognises the risk and recommends the appointment of an appropriate specialist to deal with the matter, the architect will ordinarily be entitled to rely on that specialist to carry out – or organise the carrying-out by others of – whatever ground investigation is needed (and to rely on such ground information as is produced): see *Industry Commercial Properties v South Bedfordshire DC* [1985] 1 All ER 787 (structural engineers engaged, on architect's recommendation, to design foundations to warehouse failed to see to it that a proper site investigation was carried out; architect entitled to rely on engineers).

2 Ensuring that significant assumptions made about ground conditions for the purposes of design are verified by appropriate ground investigation: *Ove Arup & Partners International Ltd v Mirant Asia Pacific Construction (Hong Kong) Ltd (No. 2)* (2006) BLR 187 (engineer designers of foundations were negligent in making assumptions about bearing capacity which need to be verified by site investigation).

3 Visiting the site himself for the purposes of obtaining accurate (above ground) site information by taking measurements and so forth himself, or checking measurements and dimensional information provided by others: see *Columbus Co Ltd v Clowes* [1903] 1 KB 244 (site was bigger than assumed for design purposes by the architect in reliance on information provided by someone with no authority to provide it) and *Cardy v Taylor* (1994) 38 ConLR (site was smaller than assumed for design purposes by the architect and the building had to be redesigned).

4 Visiting the site himself for the purposes of making other relevant observations and generally considering the effect of observable site features in terms of their consequences and implications for the contemplated project: see *Dalgleish v Bromley Corporation* (1953) 161 EG 738 (site on a steep slope making the expense of the contemplated project uneconomic); *Armitage v Palmer* (1959) 173 EG 91 (proposed position of building on the site potentially interfering with easement enjoyed by neighbouring owners); *Acrecrest Ltd v WS Hattrell & Partners* (1979) 252 EG 1107 (insufficient regard paid by architects to the effect of the removal of trees on the site).

Cost estimates

5.02 The preparation and provision of cost estimates by an architect, and the ongoing need to consider revisions to cost estimates and to provide up-to-date cost information as a project progresses, are among the key services which an architect commonly provides. Cost estimates must be produced with reasonable care and skill. Ordinarily that means:

1 Liability to an employer client for a negligent cost estimate cannot be avoided by delegating the task to a quantity surveyor: *Nye Saunders & Partners v Bristow* (1987) 37 BLR 92 (estimate of £238 000, which was within the client's budget of £250 000, was based on current costs, rather than on an estimate of what the likely outturn cost (£440 000) was going to be over the life of the project).

2 A cost estimate ordinarily needs to be a forecast of the likely out-turn cost of the project: *Nye Saunders*. An architect therefore needs to be careful to identify factors which are foreseeably likely to affect that anticipated final cost of construction.

3 A cost estimate needs to be reasonably accurate when objectively assessed by reference to the information which ought to have been taken into account at the time the estimate was produced. However, the fact that the final out-turn cost is in excess of a cost estimate, perhaps massively so, is not evidence of negligence in itself: *Copthorne Hotel (Newcastle) Ltd v Arup Associates* (1996) 58 ConLR 105.

Planning and building control

5.03 An architect must ordinarily obtain both planning permission and building regulation consent. An architect is expected to have a good working knowledge of planning and building control requirements accordingly, and this may extend to having some knowledge of relevant planning law in certain circumstances where an architect holds himself out as being able to advise on the planning aspects of a project and does not advise his employer client to seek legal advice on the matter: see *B L Holdings Ltd v Robert J. Wood & Partners* (1979) 10 BLR 48 (reversed, on the facts, on appeal).

Design

Generally

5.04 In the absence of any fitness for purpose obligation (as to which see Section 2 above), the design obligation is one of reasonable care and skill. Whether or not that obligation has been complied with in any particular case will inevitably depend on the facts of the case and the view of those facts taken by the court, assisted (almost always) by the evidence of independent experts (usually architects themselves) as to the objective standard(s) which the particular architect in question ought to have attained. This is true of any complaint of professional negligence on the part of an architect (i.e. it is applicable in *all* situations covered by Sections 5 and 6 of this chapter), but is perhaps most commonly encountered in practice in the context of the architect's paradigm responsibility for design.

5.05 The standard demanded by an architect's obligation of reasonable care and skill is the reasonable care and skill of the ordinarily competent architect. An architect is not required to have an extraordinary degree of skill or the highest professional attainments. However, 'he must bring to the task he undertakes the competence and skill that is usual among architects practising their profession. And he must use due care': see the Australian decision of *Voli v Inglewood Shire Council* [1963] ALR 657. In *Eckersley v Binnie & Partners* (1988) 18 ConLR 1, Bingham LJ's observations regarding the standard to be attained by engineers are equally applicable to architects:

> 'a professional man should command the corpus of knowledge which forms part of the professional equipment of the ordinary member of his profession. He should not lag behind other ordinarily assiduous and intelligent members of his profession in knowledge of new advances, discoveries and developments in his field. He should be alert to the hazards and risks inherent in any professional task he undertakes to the extent that other ordinarily competent members of the profession would be alert. He must bring to any professional task he undertakes no less expertise, skill and care than other ordinarily competent members would bring but need bring no more. The standard is that of the reasonable average. The law does not require of a professional man that he be a paragon combining the qualities of polymath and prophet'.

British Standards and Codes of Practice

5.06 Bearing in mind the function of codes of practice and British Standards, a design which does not comply with relevant guidance is likely to require justification and explanation if it is not be found to be a negligent design: see the New Zealand decision of *Bevan Investments Ltd v Blackball and Struthers (No. 2)* [1973] 2 NZLR 45. However, in the same way that non-compliance with relevant guidance will not automatically lead to a finding of negligence, so rigid adherence to the relevant guidance will not automatically save an architect from a finding of negligence either, particularly – perhaps – where the design is a novel one: *Holland Hannen and Cubitts (Northern) Ltd v Welsh Health Technical Services Organisation* (1985) 35 BLR 1.

Choice of materials

5.07 Design includes the choice and specification of materials. The decision to use new materials or to use a proprietary product or system will require the making of appropriate enquiries

by an architect to ensure its suitability for the job in question: see *Richard Roberts & Holdings Ltd v Douglas Smith Stimson Partnership* (1988) 46 BLR 50 (negligent investigation by architects of specialist linings for effluent tanks) and *Michael Hyde & Associated Ltd v J D Williams & Co Ltd* [2001] PNLR 233 (negligent acceptance by architects of assurances regarding risk of discoloration of stored textiles with selected heating system).

Buildability

5.08 An architect must ordinarily consider the buildability of his design. An architect is entitled to expect certain standards of skills and experience on the part of those who will build the design and, on certain projects, may be entitled to expect very high standards of skill and experience, as in the British Library case (*Department of National Heritage v Steensen Varming Mulcahy* (1998) ConLR 33). Nevertheless, an architect's design must give rise to realistic expectations of buildability: *George Fischer Holding Ltd v Multi Design Consultants Ltd* (1998) 61 ConLR 85 (design of roof requiring perfect construction of the end lap joints if it was not to let in water was unrealistic in its expectations of workmanship).

Tender action

Tender documentation

5.09 RIBA Standard Forms of Agreement commonly require an architect to prepare and collate tender documents in sufficient detail to enable a tender or tenders to be obtained. They also commonly require an architect to consider with the employer client the responsibilities of the parties and the authority and duties of the architect under the building contract. This process will often involve the architect in preparing contract documents (including relevant specifications and contract drawings) and will often involve advising his employer client as to the choice of building contract and the way in which it should be completed.

5.10 So far as the preparation of contract documents is concerned, the principal objectives to be achieved are that they should contain a comprehensive description of all the work which is necessary for the satisfactory completion of the project and that, so far as possible, there is internal consistency between the various contract documents (for example between architectural drawings and specifications and any Bills of Quantities). Where the architect is the lead consultant, these responsibilities call for wider co-ordination and liaison.

5.11 So far as the choice of building contract is concerned, there are numerous standard forms of building contract (many of them very complex) available and an architect is required to exercise reasonable care and skill when advising his employer client as to which form to use. He also needs to be careful when advising as to the choices to be made regarding the incorporation (or not) of particular terms and conditions into the building contract, for example, in respect of the insurance of the works. The exercise of reasonable care and skill in such circumstances may well involve the architect in recommending to his employer client that he should take legal or other appropriate professional advice.

5.12 More generally, an architect may be called upon to make strategic choices and/or to give advice (and probably at a much earlier stage in many cases) as to the procurement route which his employer client should take on a particular project. He will need to exercise reasonable care and skill when doing so (which will include ensuring that the employer client is involved with the choices to be made and the various alternatives available so that any decisions are taken on a properly informed basis) and, moreover, he will need to keep his recommendations under review as circumstances change: see *Plymouth & South West Co-operative Society Ltd v Architecture, Structure & Management Ltd* (2006) 108 ConLR 77 (architects were negligent in proceeding with their original recommended approach to construction works when they should have realised that that approach would result in a costs overrun).

Appointment of contractor

5.13 RIBA Standard Forms of Agreement anticipate that no building contract should generally be awarded unless competitive tenders have first been invited and refer to the following as services commonly provided by an architect: consideration with the employer client of a list of tenderers, the invitation of tenders and the appraisal of tenders when they are received and consideration with the employer client of the appointment of a contractor. This process commonly requires choices to be made between competing tenders and tenderers and, ultimately, may require the architect to make a recommendation to his employer client as to which contractor should be appointed/selected to carry out the work. All of this calls for the exercise of reasonable care and skill by the architect, the demands of which may embrace the following when seeking to discharge obligations to the employer client as to the appointment of a contractor:

1   Being careful not to make positive recommendations about a contractor which are not justified: *Pratt v George Hill & Associates* (1987) 38 BLR 25 (negligent written statement by architect that contractor was 'very reliable' when, in fact, the contractor was anything but reliable).

2   Taking reasonable steps to check as to the skill and relevant experience of the contractor and, in an appropriate case, as to the experience and relevant capabilities of a nominated subcontractor: *Equitable Debenture Assets Corp Ltd v William Moss Group Ltd* (1984) 2 ConLR 26.

3   Taking reasonable steps in an appropriate case to check on the financial standing of the contractor: *Partridge v Morris* [1995] CILL 1095 (architect negligent because he failed to obtain or consider a bank reference or a trade credit reference, or failed to make appropriate enquiries of other architects, to carry out a company search or to obtain a copy of the contractor's accounts). Such steps may also include ensuring that suitable insurance arrangements are put in place by the contractor: *Pozzolanic Lytag Ltd v Brian Hobson Associates* (1999) BLR 267.

4   Taking reasonable steps to check the tender for errors: *Tyrer v District Auditor of Monmouthshire* (1973) 230 EG 973.

6   Breach of the obligation of reasonable care and skill: construction work stages

Periodic inspection (and supervision)

6.01 RIBA Standard Forms of Agreement refer to 'periodic inspection', not 'supervision'. Periodic inspection is generally regarded as being less onerous than supervision. The following summary of the relevant principles relating to an architect's obligation of periodic inspection is drawn largely from the judgment of HHJ Peter Coulson QC in *Ian McGlinn v Waltham Forest Contractors Ltd* (2007) 111 ConLR 1. The Judge also referred, with approval, to relevant passages (see now in the 6th edition, paragraphs 9-236 to 9-253) of *Jackson & Powell on Professional Liability*.

1   The frequency and duration of inspections should be tailored to the nature of the works going on at site from time to time: see *Corfield v Grant* (1992) 29 ConLR 58. It is not enough for the architect religiously to carry out an inspection of the work either before or after the fortnightly or monthly site meetings, and not otherwise. The dates of such site meetings may well have been arranged some time in advance, without any reference to the particular elements of work being progressed on site at the time. Moreover, if inspections are confined to the fortnightly or monthly site meetings, the contractor will know that, at all other times, his work will effectively remain safe from inspection.

2   Depending on the importance of the particular element or stage of the works, the inspecting professional can instruct the contractor not to cover up the relevant elements of the work until they have been inspected: see *Florida Hotels Pty Ltd v Mayo* [1965] 113 CLR. 588. In most cases, however, the need for such an instruction is unlikely to arise because, if the architect is carrying out inspections which are tailored to the nature of

the works proceeding on site at any particular time, he will have timed his inspections in such a manner as to avoid affecting the progress of those works.

3   The mere fact that defective work is carried out and covered up between inspections will not, therefore, automatically amount to a defence to an alleged failure on the part of the architect to carry out proper inspections; that will depend on a variety of matters, including the architect's reasonable contemplation of what was being carried out on site at the time, the importance of the element of work in question, and the confidence which the architect may have in the contractor's overall competence: see *Sutcliffe v Chippendale & Edmondson (A Firm)* (1971) 18 BLR 149.

4   If the element of the work is important because it is going to be repeated throughout one significant part of the building, such as the construction of a proprietary product or the achievement of a particular standard of finish to one element of the work common to every room, then the architect should ensure that he has seen that element of the work in the early course of construction/assembly so as to form a view as to the contractor's ability to carry out that particular task: see *George Fischer Holdings Ltd v Multi Design Consultants Ltd* (1998) 61 Con LR 85.

5   However, even then, reasonable examination of the works does not require the architect to go into every matter in detail; indeed, it is almost inevitable that some defects will escape his notice: see *East Ham Corporation v Bernard Sunley & Sons Ltd* [1966] AC 406. Nevertheless, where he does notice defective workmanship and draw it to the contractor's attention, the architect is obliged to monitor progress to ensure that either the defect is rectified or the value of the defective work is deducted from the contractor's account: *Ian McGlinn v Waltham Forest Contractors Ltd*.

6   It can sometimes be the case that an employer with a claim for bad workmanship against a contractor makes the same claim automatically against the architect, on the assumption that, if there is a defect, then the architect must have been negligent or in breach of contract for missing the defect during construction. However, that is a misconceived approach. The architect does not guarantee that his inspection will reveal or prevent all defective work: see *Consarc Design Ltd v Hutch Investments Ltd* [2002] PNLR 712. It is not appropriate to judge an architect's performance by the result achieved.

6.02 To this summary, it can be added that the engagement of a Clerk of Works will not ordinarily diminish the architect's obligation of periodic inspection as summarised above, although the traditional demarcation is that a Clerk of Works will be attentive to matters of detail, whilst an architect's concern will be upon more important matters: see *Kensington, Chelsea and Westminster AHA v Wettern Composites Ltd* [1985] 1 AER 346. Nevertheless, the involvement of a Clerk of Works by the architect's employer client (and the architect's own confidence (or not) in the Clerk of Works) will be relevant matters wherever the essential complaint is one of bad workmanship by the contractor; not least in the context of the issues discussed in Section 8 below, because an architect will not usually be liable for negligence and/or breach of contract on the part of the Clerk of Works.

Duty to review own design

6.03 An architect with obligations of periodic inspection (or supervision) is required to review his own design as necessary until the completion of construction. 'The architect is under a continuing duty to check that his design will work in practice and to correct any errors which may emerge': *Brickfield Properties Ltd v Newton* [1971] 1 WLR 862. However, the obligation to review is generally regarded as being reactive (i.e. as requiring a trigger such as the discovery of defect which calls the design into question) rather than proactive (i.e. as something which an architect, having completed his design work, must do as a matter of course): see *New Islington and Hackney Housing Association Ltd v Pollard Thomas & Edwards Ltd* [2001] PNLR 515 (the duty to review only arises 'where something occurs to put the architect on notice that, as a reasonably competent architect, he ought to review the design'). Moreover, it will be rare for the duty to review to extend beyond practical completion, but not impossible: see *London Borough of Merton v Lowe* (1981) 18 BLR 130 (discovery of cracks in ceiling after practical completion triggered duty to review design before issue of final certificate) and *University of Glasgow v Whitfield* (1988) 42 BLR 66 (continuing problems with water ingress at practical completion triggered an obligation to review on the rather special facts of that case in circumstances where no final certificate had ever been issued and the architect was called back to look at the problem of water ingress 3 years after practical completion).

6.04 The line between reviewing a design and reporting on one's own mistakes can sometimes be a thin one, but an architect is ordinarily under no duty of self-accusation: *Chesham Properties Ltd v Bucknall Austin Project Management Services Ltd* (1996) 82 BLR 92 (no duty upon an architect to advise, warn or inform of own actual or potential deficiencies in performance).

6.05 The duty to review discussed here is, of course, distinct from the architect's quite separate obligation in the construction work stages of a project to review design information provided to him by contractors or specialists.

Contract administration

Interim certificates and valuations

6.06 There is obviously a link between an architect's inspection obligations and his obligations when issuing interim certificates. As HHJ Stabb QC explained in *Sutcliffe v Chippendale & Edmondson (A Firm)* (1971) 18 BLR 149:

'the issuing of certificates is a continuing process, leaving each time a limited amount of work to be inspected and I should have though that more than a glance around was to be expected. Furthermore, since everyone agreed that the quality of work was always the responsibility of the architect and never that of the quantity surveyor and since work properly executed is the work for which a progress payment is being recommended, I think that the architect is duty bound to notify the quantity surveyor in advance of any work which he, the architect, classifies as not properly executed, so as to give the quantity surveyor the opportunity of excluding it'.

In short, not only must an architect act fairly when carrying out his certification obligation, he must also take reasonable care to ensure that his interim valuations of the work on the basis of which payment will be made to the contractor are reasonable and justified by the work done at the time, both in terms of quality and amount.

Final certificates

6.07 It is clear that, as with interim certificates, an architect may also be liable for negligence in issuing a final certificate: *Sutcliffe v Thackrah* [1974] AC 727. Moreover, the consequences of such negligence may be particularly serious if the final certificate is of the 'conclusive evidence' variety so far as the contractor's materials and workmanship are concerned because then the final certificate may (dependent upon the wording of the building contract) have the effect of preventing the employer from establishing liability on the part of the contractor (as in the much criticised decision in *Crown Estates Commissioners v John Mowlem & Co Ltd* (1994) 70 BLR 1) and of absolving the contractor from his liability to contribute to the architect pursuant to the 1978 Act (see Section 8 below).

Other certificates and notices

6.08 All certification obligations upon an architect call for the exercise of reasonable care and skill in addition to the obligation to act fairly as between employer and contractor: see, for example, *George Fischer Holdings Ltd v Multi Design Consultants Ltd* (1998) 61 Con LR 85 (negligent issue of certificate of practical completion). Similarly, an architect needs to be careful when

deciding whether or not to issue, for example, a notice stating that the contractor has failed to proceed regularly and diligently with the works; and needs to be careful to ensure that his own approach as to the way in which such notice provisions should operate is one which a reasonably competent architect would take: *West Faulkner Associates v London Borough of Newham* (1992) 71 BLR 1 (architect failed to issue a notice when he should have done because he took a negligent approach to the meaning of the relevant clause).

Extensions of time

6.09 In *John Barker Construction Ltd v London Portman Hotel Ltd* (1996) 83 BLR 35 the judge was critical of the architect in that case for 'making an impressionistic, rather than a calculated, assessment of the time which he thought was reasonable for the various items individually and overall'. However, an impressionistic assessment only is not necessarily negligent and there is little support for the view that anything approaching a full retrospective delay analysis to demonstrate the effects of delay must be carried out before an architect can properly certify an extension of time. An architect is required to act fairly, lawfully, rationally and logically when considering an extension of time; but what logical analysis is actually required in any particular case will depend on many different factors and is very much dependent on the quality of the information available to enable the assessment to be made. The proper approach to be taken by an architect to the assessment of extensions of time was considered at length by HHJ Seymour QC in *Royal Brompton Hospital NHS Trust v Hammond & Others (No. 7)* (2000) 76 ConLR 148. In that case, having referred to the number of established ways in which the effects of delay might be assessed and some of the difficulties involved in making that assessment, it was emphasised:

'that the duty of a professional man, generally stated, is not to be right, but to be careful . . . [T]he fact that he is in the event proved to be wrong is not, in itself, any evidence that he has been negligent. His conduct has to be judged having regard to the information available to him, or which ought to have been available to him, at the time he gave his advice or made his decision or did whatever else it is that he did'.

So, an approach to assessment of extensions of time which 'did not depend upon any sort of scientific evaluation of any particular type of material, but simply upon impression formed on the basis of previous experience' was not negligent on the facts. Indeed, '. . . in practical terms the burden shouldered by a claimant who contends that an architect or a project manager has been negligent in granting, or being involved in the grant of, an extension of time for completion of works governed by a contract in the Standard form is a heavy one: unless the case is very obvious it is most unlikely to succeed'.

Instructions and information

6.10 Cooperation between employer and contractor is vital to satisfactory progress in the construction stages of a project and, as the employer's agent, the architect is often at the sharp end of ensuring the smooth running of the project. Issuing instructions as and when required, and within a reasonable time of the need to issue an instruction arising, is part and parcel of this aspect of an architect's job; so too is the provision of accurate drawings and other information to the contractor in the course of the work in a regular and orderly manner. It is no surprise that an architect needs to do all these things on behalf of his employer with reasonable care and skill: see *London Borough of Merton v Leach (Stanley Hugh) Ltd* (1985) 32 BLR 51.

7 Damages

Measure of damages

7.01 The general principles upon which damages for breach of contract and/or negligence in tort are ordinarily assessed have already been discussed in Chapters 2 and 3 above. The fundamental principle so far as an architect's liability is concerned is that a claimant is entitled to be put into the position, so far as an award of money can do so, in which he would have been had the architect not been negligent.

Types of loss

7.02 Applying the fundamental principle in any particular case can lead to an architect being liable for a variety of losses. Commonly however the losses will fall into one or more of the three categories discussed below.

Cost of repairs

7.03 The costs of correcting the consequences of an architect's negligent errors are at the forefront of the majority of professional negligence claims against architects. This is true of claims in respect of building defects which are alleged to be the product of an architect's negligence (the cost of putting the defects right (rectification costs)); it is also true of claims in respect of damage to 'other property' alleged to have been caused by an architect's negligence (the cost of repairing or replacing damaged property (reinstatement costs)).

7.04 The following are the key points:

1 It must always be fair and reasonable to incur (or to have incurred) the cost of repairs before an architect will be liable for the cost of repairs. It very often will be fair and reasonable to insist on rectification/reinstatement. However, cost of repairs must always be a reasonable and proportionate way of remedying the relevant defect or damage: see *Ruxley Electronics and Construction Ltd v Forsyth* [1996] 1 AC 344 (claimant not entitled to cost of completely rebuilding a 6 ft deep swimming pool which should have been constructed to a depth of 7 feet 6 inches because, on the facts, demolition and reconstruction of the swimming pool was out of all proportion to the benefit to be gained).

2 Where it is not fair and reasonable to rebuild, a sum in respect of diminution in value will usually be the appropriate alternative or, rarely, a sum in respect of loss of amenity. In some cases involving residual blight, it may be appropriate for a claimant to recover damages in respect of diminution in value in addition to cost of repairs: see *George Fischer Holdings Ltd v Multi Design Consultants Ltd* (1998) 61 Con LR 85.

3 Where cost of repairs have not already been incurred, a claimant's intentions as to whether or not he may (or will) actually carry out the work of repair and/or the use to which he may (or will) put any award of damages in respect of cost of repairs may be relevant to the question of whether an award of cost of repairs is fair and reasonable: see *Ruxley* and *McGlinn v Waltham Forest Contractors Ltd* (2007) 111 ConLR.

4 Where the only way of rectifying defects or repairing damages is by building to a higher standard than that originally designed for, it has been said that a claimant may recover for the full cost of building to that higher standard without giving credit for any betterment. However, if building to a competent design in the first place would have cost the claimant more than the cost of building the defective design which was actually built, it is arguable that credit should be given for this.

5 Where, by contrast, the claimant *chooses* to build to a higher standard, the claimant cannot properly recover for the increased costs involved in building to that higher standard: see *Ministry of Defence v Scott Wilson Kirkpatrick* (2000) BLR 20.

6 A claimant who carries out remedial work in reliance on professional expert advice will probably be regarded as having acted reasonably, but that will not automatically mean that the cost of those works are recoverable from the architect: see *Board, of Governors of the Hospitals for Sick Children v McLaughlin and Harvey plc* (1987) 19 ConLR 25 and compare with *Ministry of Defence v Scott Wilson Kirkpatrick.*

7 A claimant who delays in carrying out repairs because he is financially (or otherwise) unable to do so before he is the recipient of an award of damages will not usually be successfully criticised for failing to mitigate his loss; and will have his cost of repairs assessed at the later date of trial rather than the earlier (and conventional) date of breach: see *Dodd Properties (Kent) Ltd v Canterbury City Council* [1980] 1 WLR 433 and *Alcoa Minerals of Jamaica Inc v Herbert Broderick* [2002] 1 AC 371.

8 Losses which are consequential upon the cost of repairs are, in principle, recoverable by a claimant. Professional fees are an obvious example, as are the costs of alternative accommodation or alternative premises where repairs reasonably require the subject premises to be vacated for the duration of the repairs.

Wasted expenditure

7.05 Where an architect's negligence causes a building project to be abandoned (for example, as a result of a negligent under-estimate of out-turn costs as in *Nye Saunders v Bristow*), the wasted costs incurred in progressing the project to that stage will be the principal claim, subject to the duty of mitigation and giving credit for the value of any development carried out.

Overpayments/additional expenditure

7.06 Where an architect's negligence causes overpayments to have been made to the contractor, such overpayments are recoverable in principle, particularly – for example – if the contractor has become insolvent. Similarly, where an architect's failure to design properly leads to the need to expend additional sums, this additional expenditure too may be recoverable in an appropriate case: see *Turner Page Music Ltd v Torres Design Associates Ltd* [1997] CILL 1263.

Causation, foreseeability and mitigation

Causation

7.07 For any loss to be recoverable from an architect, it must have been caused by the architect's professional negligence. This is often straightforward, but in a case where the complaint is one of negligent advice to his employer client or to a third party it will usually be necessary for the employer client or the third party to prove what they would have done (and, in particular, that they would have acted differently) had the correct advice been given: see *Hill Samuel Bank v Frederick Brand Partnership* (1993) 45 ConLR 141 (defective panels recommended by an architect would still have been chosen by the claimant even if the architect had properly investigated the suitability of the panels).

Foreseeability

7.08 For any loss to be recoverable from an architect it, or – more pertinently – its type, must be reasonably foreseeable: see *Balfour Beatty Construction (Scotland) Ltd v Scottish Power plc* (1994) 71 BLR 20 (wastage of concrete and site resources was a foreseeable consequence of the interruption of electricity supply: the demolition and reconstruction of an aqueduct was not). However, once the type of loss is reasonably foreseeable, the architect will ordinarily be liable for the full consequences of damage of that type: *Acrecrest Ltd v W.S. Hattrell & Partners* (1979) 252 EG 1107 (slight damage by heave as a result of tree removal reasonably foreseeable: architects liable for inadequate foundations to prevent damage by heave which was far greater than could have been anticipated).

Mitigation

7.09 A claimant must always take reasonable steps to mitigate his loss. He cannot recover for loss which he either ought to have avoided as a result of taking mitigating action or which he has in fact avoided as a result of taking mitigating action.

8 Sharing liability for professional negligence with others

8.01 Leaving aside the claims which an architect may be able to make in contract (or in tort) against a sub-consultant (or similar) for damages amounting to an indemnity in respect of such liability as the architect may have to his employer client as a result of breaches of obligations owed by the sub-consultant directly to the architect, there are two main routes by which an architect may be able to share his liability for professional negligence with others, namely:

1   by reducing the amount of his liability to the claimant by reason of contributory negligence on the part of the claimant, which involves the application of the Law Reform (Contributory Negligence) Act 1945; and/or
2   by claiming a contribution (or indemnity) towards his liability to the claimant from others who are also liable to the claimant in respect of the same damage for which the architect is liable, which involves the application of the Civil Liability (Contribution) Act 1978.

Law Reform (Contributory Negligence) Act 1945 ('the 1945 Act')

8.02 Contributory negligence is a defence to negligence claims in tort. It is also a defence to claims in contract where the architect's liability in contract is the same as his liability in tort: *Forskirings-aktieselskapet Vesta v Butcher* [1989] AC 852.

8.03 Whether the defence of contributory negligence is successful will always depend on the facts and upon consideration as to whether the claimant contributed to his own loss by failing to take reasonable care of his own person or property. The concept of 'responsibility' for the purposes of section 1(1) of the 1945 Act, includes the concepts both of causative potency and blameworthiness (or culpability); and the overriding criterion is that any reduction of the claimant's damages must be 'just and equitable'. In that regard it will always be relevant to consider the extent to which the damage caused by the architect's negligence was within the very scope of the risk which it was his obligation to guard against; but even where wholly within the risk (fire spread because of inadequate fire spread design, for example), the extent to which the claimant himself was responsible for the damage remains a relevant consideration (for example, where his contributory negligence caused the fire in the first place): see *Pride Valley Foods Ltd v Hall & Partners (Contract Management) Ltd* (2001) 76 Con LR 1 (claimant's damages reduced by 50% for its contributory negligence in failing to take reasonable steps to prevent a fire starting in the factory which then spread out of control because of the use of panels which the defendants failed to warn the claimant were highly combustible) and *Sahib Foods Ltd v Paskin Kyriades Sands* (2003) 93 ConLR 1 (claimant's damages reduced by 50% for its contributory negligence both in relation to the outbreak of the fire (which was nothing to do with the defendant) and the spread of fire (for which the defendant was largely to blame)).

Civil Liability (Contribution) Act 1978 ('the 1978 Act')

8.04 The 1978 Act is a very important piece of legislation. The need for rights of contribution has its origins in the long-standing rule that where a claimant suffers the same damage as a result of breaches of contract and/or negligence on the part of a number of different parties (the single loss (cost of repair) suffered as a result of poor workmanship by a contractor which should have been picked up on inspection by an architect being a paradigm example), the claimant is at liberty to recover compensation in full against only one of the 'guilty' parties if that is what he chooses to do, because each party with a common liability to the claimant for the same damage is separately liable to the claimant for the whole of the damage or harm suffered by the claimant. It was the common

law's long-standing failure to permit or provide for contribution between concurrent wrongdoers in that situation which is the fundamental injustice (the unjust enrichment of the non-contributing wrongdoer at the expense of the other) that the 1978 Act (and its predecessor, the 1935 Act) was intended to address.

8.05 Most discussions of the 1978 Act require a working terminology to identify the various parties involved. This Section is no exception. Unfortunately, there is no unanimity in either cases or textbooks as to the terminology which should be used. The terminology used in this Section therefore adopts the terminology used by the House of Lords in *Royal Brompton Hospital NHS Trust v Hammond* [2002] 1 WLR 1397 whereby:

A   means the person who has suffered damage and who is the person with a claim. **A** is usually the claimant.
B   means the person against whom **A** makes his claim: the person who is alleged to be liable to **A** in respect of the damage suffered by **A**. **B** is usually the Defendant and, for the purposes of this discussion, is the architect.
C   means the person from whom **B** seeks contribution (or indemnity) in respect of his (**B**'s) liability to **A**. **C** is usually either a co-defendant with **B** or a Third Party jointed by **B** into the proceedings for the purposes of claiming a contribution (or indemnity). For the purposes of this discussion, **C** (and, of course, there may be more than one **C**) is likely to be the contractor and/or another construction professional.

The right to contribution

8.06 The key provisions are section 1(1) of the 1978 Act as 'supplemented' by section 1(6) and section 6(1).

'1 Entitlement to contribution

(1) Subject to the following provisions of this section, any person liable in respect of any damage suffered by another person may recover contribution from any other person liable in respect of the same damage (whether jointly with him or otherwise). . .

(6) References in this section to a person's liability in respect of any damage are references to any such liability which has been or could be established in an action brought against him in England and Wales by or on behalf of the person who suffered the damage; but it is immaterial whether any issue arising in any such action was or would be determined (in accordance with the rules of private international law) by reference to the law of a country outside England and Wales.'

. . . 6 Interpretation

(1) A person is liable in respect of any damage for the purposes of this Act if the person who suffered it (or anyone representing his estate or dependants) is entitled to recover compensation from him in respect of that damage (whatever the legal basis of his liability, whether tort, breach of contract, breach of trust or otherwise).'

8.07 'liable': 'The 1978 Act is drafted on the basis that the word "liability" is used potentially in the widest possible sense': *R A Lister & Co Ltd v E G Thomson (Shipping) Ltd (No. 2)* [1987] 3 All ER 1032. It embraces a liability of B to A, and C to A, whatever the legal basis of the liability (whether in tort, breach of contract, breach of trust or otherwise) and it embraces any liability which could be established by A in an action brought against either B or C in England and Wales. It includes a liability under the DPA 1972: *McKenzie v Potts* (1997) 50 ConLR 40.

8.08 'damage': does *not* mean 'damages'. The fact that the damages recoverable by A from B or C may be different, does not mean that B and C's liability is not a common liability in respect of the same damage: see *Eastgate Group Ltd v Lindsay Morgan Group Inc* [2002] 1 WLR 642. 'Damage' means 'the harm suffered by the "another person" [i.e. A], to use the phrase in section 1(1), for which that person is entitled to recover compensation': *Birse Construction*

Ltd v Haiste Ltd [1996] 1 WLR 675 (a passage approved by the House of Lords in *Royal Brompton Hospital NHS Trust v Hammond* [2002] 1 WLR 1397).

8.09 'any person liable [i.e. B] in respect of any damage suffered by another person [i.e. A]':

1   It does not matter that B has ceased to be liable in respect of the damage suffered by A since the time when the damage occurred – for example as a result of compromising the claim or as a result of the fact that the limitation period has since expired against him – provided that 'he was so liable immediately before he made or was ordered or agreed to make the payment in respect of which the contribution is sought': 1978 Act, section 1(2). In short, B's liability to A does not need to be a continuing or present liability at the time the contribution claim is made.

2   Where B has reached a bona fide settlement with A, there is no need for B to prove his own liability to A in order to be able to claim contribution from C, provided that 'he would have been liable assuming that the factual basis of the claim against him could be established': 1978 Act, section 1(4). So, B does not need to prove the facts which A alleged against him. However, he *does* have to show that A's claim against him was good in law: *Dubai Aluminium Co Ltd v Salaam* [2003] 2 AC 366. He must also show that the settlement was reasonable, for example that heads of loss claimed against him were recoverable from him in law: *J Sainsbury plc v Broadway Malyan (a firm)* [1999] PNLR 286 (architects' settlement with building owner was unreasonable because it had made no allowance for the building owner's contributory negligence and it had assumed that the fire brigade would have been able to control the fire when there was only a chance (no more than 35%) that they would have done so).

8.10 'may recover contribution from any other person liable …' [i.e. C]: It does not matter that C has ceased to be liable in respect of the damage suffered by A since the time when the damage occurred, 'unless he ceased to be liable by virtue of the expiry of a period of limitation or prescription which extinguished the right on which the claim against him in respect of the damage was based': 1978 Act, section 1(3). So B is not prevented from claiming contribution from C if, by the time the contribution claim is made (which is very often the position), the relevant limitation period applicable to A's claim against C (or C's liability to A) has expired, because the ordinary effect of a limitation defence is that it only bars the remedy, and does not extinguish the right on which the claim is based. It follows that the proviso is of narrow scope. Moreover, the expiry of the 15-year long-stop provided for by section 14B of the Limitation Act 1980 does not extinguish the right to bring a claim in negligence; it only bars the remedy: *Financial Services Compensation Scheme Ltd v Larnell (Insurances) Ltd* [2006] PNLR 13.

8.11 '. . . in respect of the same damage'

1   These are the most important words in the 1978 Act and were the focus of the decision of the House of Lords in the architect's case of *Royal Brompton Hospital NHS Trust v Hammond* [2002] 1 WLR 1397.

2   Lord Bingham stated:

'It is. . . a constant theme of the law of contribution from the beginning that B's claim to share with others his liability to A rests upon the fact that they (whether equally with B or not) are subject to a common liability to A. I find nothing in section 6(1)(c) of the 1935 Act or in section 1(1) of the 1978 Act, or in the reports which preceded those Acts, which in any way weakens that requirement. Indeed both sections, by using the words "in respect of the same damage", emphasise the need for one loss to be apportioned among those liable.'

3   The need for a shared or common liability of B and C to A emphasises that the sufferer of the damage 'inflicted' by B and

C must be the same person as the person who is entitled to recover the compensation for that damage.

4   The right to contribution arises not only in respect of a common liability of B and C for the same damage, but also in respect of a common liability of B and C for *part of the same damage*. Lord Bingham framed the relevant questions to be asked as follows:

'When any claim for contribution falls to be decided the following questions in my opinion arise. (1) What damage has A suffered? (2) Is B liable to A in respect of that damage? (3) Is C also liable to A in respect of that damage or some of it? ... I do not think it matters greatly whether, in phrasing these questions, one speaks (as the 1978 Act does) of "damage" or of "loss" or "harm", provided it is borne in mind that "damage" does not mean "damages" ... and that B's right to contribution by C depends on the damage, loss or harm for which B is liable to A corresponding (even if in part only) with the damage, loss or harm for which C is liable to A. This seems to me to accord with the underlying equity of the situation: it is obviously fair that C contributes to B a fair share of what both B and C owe in law to A, but obviously unfair that C should contribute to B any share of what B may owe in law to A but C does not.'

5   So, in *Royal Brompton Hospital* itself, the nature of the damage suffered by a hospital by reason of an architect's breaches, namely the weakening or impairment of its prospects of success as against the main contractor was quite different to the damage suffered by the hospital by reason of the main contractor's breaches, namely wrongful delay in practical completion. Indeed, a claim against an architect for wrongful certification is in respect of damage done to a building owner's relations with the contractor and is not the same damage as the damage suffered by the building owner as a result of negligence by the architect in failing to prevent defective work. As Lord Bingham stated:

'It would seem to me clear that any liability the Employer [Hospital] might prove against the Contractor would be based on the Contractor's delay in performing the contract and the disruption caused by the delay, and the Employer's damage would be the increased cost it incurred, the sums it overpaid and the liquidated damages to which it was entitled. Its claim against the Architect, based on negligent advice and certification, would not lead to the same damage because it could not be suggested that the Architect's negligence had led to any delay in performing the contract'.

6   A claim by an employer against a contractor for negligent site investigation services and a claim by the employer against insurance brokers for failure to insure against the contingency were not claims for 'the same damage' entitling the insurance brokers to claim a contribution against the contractor: see the *Royal Brompton Hospital* case in holding that *Hurstwood Developments Ltd v Motor and General & Andersley & Co Insurance Services Ltd* [2001] EWCA Civ 1785 was 'wrongly decided'.

Restrictions on the right to contribution

8.12 C must have a substantive liability to A: *Co-operative Retail Services v Taylor Young Partnership Ltd* [2002] 1 WLR 1419.

1   In the CRS case, C (Wimpey) was employed by A (the Co-op) to build it a new HQ which burned down shortly before practical completion. Under the joint insurance arrangements under the relevant JCT Contract, Wimpey and the Co-op were co-insureds in respect of the risk of fire. The Co-op alleged that the fire was the result of negligence on the part of the professional team: the architect (Taylor Young) and the M&E engineer (Hall) – collectively 'B' in the terminology of this section. The professional team (B) sought a contribution from Wimpey, alleging that Wimpey's negligence or breach of contract had also caused or contributed to the fire. The professional team's claim for contribution failed. It failed on a number of inter-related grounds, but the essence of the argument which was at the forefront of the reasoning in the House of Lords was that

Wimpey was simply never liable to the Co-op either in negligence or in contract for the fire damage sustained by the Co-op because the effect of the contractual arrangements for joint insurance was to eliminate (by agreement between A and C) 'the ordinary rules for the payment of compensation for negligence and for breach of contract' as between Wimpey and the Co-op.

2 In *Oxford University Fixed Assets Ltd v Architects Design Partnership* (1999) 64 ConLR 12 the architect's claim for contribution against the contractor also failed – this time because the effect of the issue of a final certificate by the architect was that the contractor's liability to the claimant simply could not be established because the claimant employer's claim against the contractor was barred by the issue of that certificate.

8.13 The requirement to pay 'compensation'. Not only must C be liable to A, but C's liability to A must be to pay 'compensation' to A. This too was very important in the *CRS* case and arguably provided a distinct reason why the professional team's contribution claim against the contractor failed. In the *CRS* case, because of the contract agreed between Wimpey and the Co-op, Wimpey's only liability to the Co-op in respect of the fire was to reinstate the property (the Works) damaged by the fire using the insurance proceeds to do so. This was not a liability to pay compensation and, for that reason, could not give rise to rights of contribution. Lord Rodger dealt with the matter succinctly:

'Under section 1(1) of the [Act] a person who is liable in respect of damage can recover contribution from any other person who is liable in respect of the same damage. It follows that the appellants can recover contribution from Wimpey in respect of the fire damage to the works only if Wimpey were "liable in respect of" the fire damage. Section 6(1) provides that a person is liable in respect of any damage if the person who suffered it "is entitled to compensation from him in respect of that damage". So the appellants can recover a contribution from Wimpey only if CRS were "entitled to recover compensation from [them] in respect of" the fire damage to the works.

On no conceivable construction of section 6(1) can it be said that a person who is liable to restore damaged work is a person from whom the employer is "entitled to recover compensation" in respect of the fire damage to the works.'

Lord Hope's views were similar:

'The employer has no claim for compensation against the contractor. All he can do is insist that the contractor must proceed with due diligence to carry out the reinstatement work and must authorise the release to him of the insurance monies. The contractor has no claim for compensation against the employer. All he can do is insist that the employer must use the insurance monies for payment of the cost of carrying out the reinstatement work . . . The ordinary rules for the payment of compensation for negligence and for breach of contract have been eliminated.'

8.14 Contractual limitation or exclusion clauses. One of the reasons why the *CRS* case is important is because it serves as an important reminder that the 1978 Act essentially respects contractual arrangements between the parties which are in place at the time damage is sustained by A. It seems clear, that subject to satisfying the requirements of reasonableness under the Unfair Contract Terms Act 1977 where appropriate, such limitations or exclusions are effective in terms of placing an upper limit on C's liability to contribute to B. In a professional negligence context, this is of very considerable importance where a professional seeks – by contract – to limit his liability to A to a specific sum, as in *Moores v Yakeley Associates Ltd* (1998) 62 ConLR 76 (discussed in Section 4 above) or, perhaps more usually, to the amount of his professional indemnity insurance cover. (And see section 2(3) of the 1978 Act in this context.)

8.15 Another limitation (or control) mechanism is a net contribution clause, sometimes called a 'proportional liability clause', sometimes also called an 'equitable contribution clause'. A net

contribution clause essentially seeks to do 'what it says on the tin' which – so far as the liability of **B** and/or **C** to **A** is concerned – is to limit the professional's liability to **A** to a proportional or proportionate liability only; in other words to a liability which effectively seeks to render any claim by **B** against **C** for contribution otiose because – if the clause does its job properly – **B**'s maximum liability to **A** reflects **B**'s fair and reasonable contribution to the damage, no more and no less. In other words, such a clause seeks to be an express contractual modification of the usual consequences of joint and several liability. The following points should be borne in mind:

1 Contractual regulation (or indeed exclusion) of rights of contribution is expressly contemplated by Section 7 of the 1978 Act.

2 Net contribution clauses are, of course, commonplace in many standard form contracts used in the construction and engineering industry. The standard forms of appointment (or of collateral warranty) of an architect or an engineer published by RIBA or ACE provide examples. Among other things, such clauses are relied on by consultants, and more especially by their professional indemnity insurers, to seek to shift the risk of the effects of insolvency of other liable parties away from the consultant and on to the employer.

3 To date, net contribution clauses have not been the subject of any decided cases in the English (or Welsh) Courts. They have, however, been the subject of two recent Scottish decisions: *Glasgow Airport Limited v Messrs Kirkman & Bradford* [2007] CSOH 52 and *Langstane Housing Association Limited v Riverside Construction Limited (& Others)* [2009] CSOH 52; (2009) 124 ConLR 211.

4 In the *Glasgow Airport* case there was no argument that a net contribution clause was effective; it being accepted by both parties that it was. (The argument was as to the proper construction of the clause.)

5 The decision of the Court of Session in *Langstane* is altogether more interesting. Its focus was the net contribution clause – Clause B8.2 – in the ACE Conditions of Engagement, B(1). The Court of Session considered two issues of particular relevance: (i) whether the net contribution clause was a term of the contract which '*purports to exclude or restrict liability for breach of duty arising in the course of any business*' within the meaning and/or for the purposes of Section 16(1) of the Unfair Contract Terms Act 1977 (NB. Section 16 is in Part II of UCTA which applies to Scotland only); and (ii) whether, if it was, it was fair and reasonable to incorporate the term in the contract. In relation to the first issue, Lord Glennie agreed with the engineers' argument that the net contribution clause did not seek to exclude or restrict liability for the engineers' breach of duty: 'it simply sought to ensure that the [engineers] were only held liable for the consequence of their own breach of duty and were not held liable, by the doctrine of joint and several liability, for the breaches of duty by other contractors and consultants'. Lord Glennie felt that there was considerable force in this argument, stated that 'the point is incapable of further elaboration' and decided, accordingly, that UCTA did not apply so as to impose a 'fair and reasonable' test in the case before him. In relation to the second issue, Lord Glennie was clear that – even if he was wrong in relation to the first issue – nevertheless the net contribution clause was fair and reasonable on the particular facts of the case.

'It is a relevant matter that the clause is part of a body of conditions drafted by a professional body and is widely used within the profession and in the industry. Albeit that they have attracted controversy, this has not stopped them being used. The [claimants] themselves have shown a willingness to contract on the basis of the ACE Conditions. Further, and perhaps of greatest importance, it is open to the [claimants], who choose their contractors and consultants, to ensure that proper insurance is in place in the event that one or more of them is in breach of contract or duty. If proper insurance is in place, then it should be possible in the event of insolvency of the contractor or consultant to go against the insurer. I see nothing unfair or unreasonable in the client taking the risk that he has adequately covered himself against the possible insolvency of those whom he himself has appointed'.

6 In the writer's view, it is likely to be safer to assume that, in England and Wales, net contribution clauses must satisfy the statutory requirement of (UCTA) reasonableness if they are to be an effective contractual regulation of rights of contribution in place of the 1978 Act in a business liability context.

Assessment of the amount of contribution

8.16 Apportionment is pre-eminently a question of fact in each case and reported cases on apportionment are first and foremost examples only of how responsibility or liability may be split in any particular case. Extracting any general principles from cases on apportionment is difficult. Nevertheless:

1 The question of apportionment between B and C under the 1978 Act should be considered separately from the assessment of contributory negligence as between A on the one hand, and B and C on the other: *Fitzgerald v Lane* [1989] AC 328.
2 The concept of 'responsibility', for the purposes of section 2(1), includes the concepts both of causative potency and blameworthiness (or culpability): *Madden v Quirk* [1989] 1 WLR 702. However, the overriding criterion is that apportionment must be 'just and equitable' , and this allows the court to have regard to other matters, including breaches of duty or conduct which are non-causative: see *Re-Source America International Ltd v Platt Site Services and Barkin Construction Ltd* [2004] EWCA (Civ) 665 followed in *Brian Walker Partnership PLC v HOK International Ltd* [2006] PNLR 5. So, as Lord Nicholls remarked in the *Dubai Aluminium* case:

> 'if one of three defendants equally responsible is insolvent, the court will have regard to this fact when directing contribution between the two solvent defendants. The court will do so, even though insolvency has nothing to do with responsibility'.

8.17 For apportionment examples, see *Equitable Debenture Assets Corp Ltd v William Moss Group Ltd* (1984) 2 ConLR 1 (liability for defective design of curtain wall was apportioned 75% to the specialist design sub-contractors and 25% to the architects; liability for bad workmanship to the parapet walling was apportioned 80% to the specialist sub-contractors, 15% to the main contractors and 5% to the architects) and *Oxford University Press v John Stedman Design Group* (1990) 34 ConLR 1 (liability for three different defects in a warehouse floor – cracking, surface crazing and edge breakdown – were apportionedas between the architect and the contractors respectively, on the basis of 60:40 (cracking); 50:50 (surface crazing) and 0:100 (edge breakdown).

Special time limit for claiming contribution

8.18 There is a special limitation period for contribution claims: 2 years from the date on which the right (B's right) to contribution accrued: section 10(1).

8.19 In circumstances where B is held liable in respect of damage to A either by a judgment given in any civil proceedings or an award in any arbitration the right to contribution accrues on the date of the judgment or award as the case may be: 1978 Act, section 10(3). This means a judgment or award which ascertains the quantum, and not merely the existence, of the relevant liability: *Aer Lingus PLC v Gildacroft Ltd* [2006] 1 WLR 1173.

8.20 In circumstances where B 'makes or agrees to make any payment to one or more persons in compensation' for the damage, the right to contribution accrues on 'the earliest date on which the amount to be paid by him is agreed between him (or his representative) and the person (or each of the persons, as the case may be) to whom the payment is to be made': 1978 Act, section 10(4). Time runs from the date of the agreement, not from the date of the formal consent order: *Knight v Rochdale Healthcare NHS Trust* [2004] 1 WLR 371.

9 When liability for professional negligence is barred by lapse of time

9.01 The Limitation Act 1980 imposes time limits within which litigation or arbitration must be commenced if the relevant claim is not to be statute barred.

9.02 Time limits for claims under the DPA 1972 and for claims for contribution under the 1978 Act have already been discussed above.

9.03 So far as claims for professional negligence are concerned, the relevant time limits vary according to whether the claim is made in reliance upon a contractual duty of care or a tortuous duty of care. Reference should be made to Chapters 2 and 3 above respectively for a fuller understanding of the limitation periods affecting claims in contract and in tort. The following is a brief summary only.

(a) Contract

9.04 For professional negligence claims in contract, the relevant limitation period is ordinarily 6 years from date of breach. Where the contract has been entered into as a deed or under seal (which is now common for architect appointments on large building projects) the relevant limitation period is 12 years from date of breach.

(b) Tort

9.05 For professional negligence claims in tort in respect of personal injury, the primary limitation period claims is ordinarily 3 years either from the date when personal injury was caused or 3 years after the 'date of knowledge' (Limitation Act 1980, section 14), if later. This time limit may also be disapplied by the courts in certain circumstances.

9.06 For professional negligence claims in tort in respect of physical damage to property or where the harm suffered is in the form of pure economic loss, the primary limitation period is ordinarily 6 years from the date of damage/harm or, if later, 3 years from the date when the claimant first knows about the damage and certain material facts about it: Limitation Act 1980, section 14A (as inserted by the Latent Damage Act 1986). However, this is all subject to a long-stop provision which prevents an action for damages for professional negligence in tort being brought after the expiry of 15 years after the act or omission which is alleged to be negligent and to which the damage suffered is alleged to be attributable: Limitation Act 1980, section 14B.

10 Liability in Scots law[*]

10.01 In substance, Scots law in relation to the liability of an architect to pay damages in compensation is much the same as the law of England and Wales. Liability may arise from breach of contract at common law, from delict (fault and negligence) at common law and from breach of statutory duty.

10.02 The test for professional negligence is whether the architect has failed to exhibit the standard of skill and care to be expected of an architect of *ordinary* competence at the material time. Failing to exhibit the highest degree of skill and care is not professional negligence. Failing to follow normal practice does not of itself constitute professional negligence. Only if performance falls below the lower end of the scale of acceptable competence is the architect liable. The standard of ordinary competence and whether performance has fallen below the standard are issues of fact to be established by the evidence of witnesses skilled in the profession. The rules for assessing damages are broadly similar.

[*]This section was written by Angus Stewart QC.

10.03 A possible area of difference from English law is in the question of third-party rights of recovery in delict at common law, for example when a subsequent purchaser who had nothing to do with the original commission sues the architect for design faults. While *Murphy v Brentwood District Council* has clearly limited rights of recovery in England (paragraph 2.13 above), an alternative approach, suggested by certain Commonwealth decisions, might be seen as persuasive in Scotland. The common law of Scotland already recognises that contracts may confer enforceable contractual rights on third parties, although the doctrine has yet to be exploited in the construction context (cf. *Strathford East Kilbride Ltd v HLM Design Ltd* [1997] SCLR 877). As in England contractual warranties are in use. Another area of possible difference relates to the effect of final certificates. In *Belcher Food Products Ltd v Miller and Black and Others* [1999] SLT 142, Lord Gill reserved his opinion as to whether a JCT final certificate excluded the client's right of action against the contractor for faulty work and materials (see paragraph 6.07 above). The following legislation does not extend to Scotland: Defective Premises Act 1972, Civil Liability (Contribution) Act 1978 and Latent Damage Act 1986.

10.04 Scotland has its own scheme of time limits for suing (limitation) and extinction of claims by lapse of time (prescription). Most of the law on this subject likely to be encountered in practice is contained in the Prescription and Limitation (Scotland) Act 1973 (as amended). Subject to a number of qualifications and to the dispensing power of the court in appropriate cases, actions for, or which include a claim for compensation for personal injuries have to be brought within 3 years of the injury. Other claims for compensation have to be brought within 5 years of the damage and the court has no dispensing power. In the case of concealed damage, time starts to run only when the damage is discovered or becomes discoverable (cf. paragraphs 9.01 to 9.06 above). Architects have to keep in mind time limits for legal claims when advising clients on the action to be taken in relation to building defects, or they will risk exposing themselves to liability. Remember: 5 years for building defects! The Scottish courts have an inherent power to terminate court proceedings which have been subject to inexcusable delay: *Tonner v Messrs Reiach & Hall, Architects,* 2007 SLT 1183.

33

Architects' professional indemnity insurance

JAMES LEABEATER

1 Why be insured?

In case of claims

1.01 If architects make mistakes they can cause their clients to suffer financial loss which is many times larger than the fees the architects received for the particular project. On larger projects, architects can be liable for millions of pounds in damages. If an architect practises in a limited company, a large claim can cause the company to become insolvent, thereby leaving the client without full compensation. If architects are practising as a partnership, the partners will each be personally liable for the full amount of the claim, which could potentially lead to partners being made bankrupt. Suitable professional indemnity insurance will, subject to the limits of cover, protect the company or partnership against the financial impact of the claim.

Professional rules

1.02 Guidance Note 5 of the Architects' Code of Professional Conduct (see Chapter 38) provides that architects should not undertake professional work without adequate and appropriate professional indemnity insurance cover. It lays down the minimum cover required, by reference to the gross fee income of the particular practice.

Required by clients

1.03 Since architects can cause substantial losses, clients will often require architects to provide proof of adequate insurance cover. Standard form agreements often require cover for the same reason: for example, Clause 7.4 of the Standard Conditions of Appointment (see Chapter 30) requires the architect to maintain insurance in the amount stated in the appendix to the agreement, which will be the subject of negotiation between the architect and client.

For these and other reasons, architects need professional indemnity insurance, and they need to know the basic principles of how it works.

2 Some basic insurance principles

2.01 The subject-matter of an insurance policy may be the property owned by the insured, which he wishes to insure (e.g. the contract works), or it may be liability on the part of a person or company to third parties (e.g. the liability of the architect to the client). In this chapter, we are concerned with the latter.

The broker

2.02 The insured arranges insurance through a broker. The broker is usually the agent of the insured, not the insurer, although he will have connections with different insurers.

The proposal

2.03 The insured will have to complete a proposal form. On the basis of that proposal form (and what the broker tells him) the insurer will offer to write the risk for a certain premium, subject to the terms of the proposed policy. There may be a process of negotiation about the terms of cover. The architect may then choose to accept the insurer's offer and there will come into existence a binding contract of insurance.

The insured will generally have to warrant that the facts stated on the proposal form are true. If they are not, the insurer may have the right to avoid liability. This is discussed further below.

Disclosure of material facts

2.04 As a matter of law, the parties to an insurance contract owe each other a duty of good faith. This is specific to insurance contracts, and arises principally because the insurer has to rely upon the insured and the broker for information about the risk. As part of the duty of good faith, the insured must disclose to the insurer every fact which is material before the risk is written. A fact is material if it would influence the judgment of a prudent insurer in fixing the premium or other terms, or determining whether he will take the risk.

If the insured fails to disclose a material fact, and if the non-disclosure of the material fact induced the insurer to enter into the contract on the relevant terms, then the insurer will be entitled to treat the insurance contract as avoided, so that he is not bound to indemnify under the contract, and (unless the failure to disclose was fraudulent) the insured recovers the premium he has paid. The insurer is allowed to avoid the contract even though the non-disclosure was innocent.

Only if there has been a significant loss do insurers usually carry out investigations into the insured whereby they discover grounds for avoidance. In such cases the remedy of the avoidance can be ruinous for the insured. It is therefore very important for the insured to make sure that he has disclosed all material facts accurately. If necessary, he should take advice from the broker on what to disclose.

The policy may contain a term that insurer agrees not to avoid the policy if the insured can establish that the failure to disclose was innocent.

2.05 The proposal form will set out a number of questions which must be answered accurately and fully. However, the insured must disclose all material facts even if they are not covered by any matters in the proposal form. In particular, he must disclose any claims made against him, and any negligent work carried out. More generally, he must disclose:

1   Facts indicating that the subject matter of the insurance is exposed to more than the ordinary degree of risk or that the liability of the insurer is greater than he would have expected it to be.
2   Facts indicating that the insured has some special motive: for example, that he has greatly over insured.
3   Facts showing that there is a moral hazard, suggesting that the insured is not a fit person to be insured: for example, that he has been convicted or suspected of fraud.
4   Facts which are to the insured's knowledge material or regarded by insurers as material.

2.06 The insured in general need not disclose:

1   Facts which are already known to the insurer or which it might reasonably be presumed to know.
2   Facts which the insurer could have discovered by making some enquiries.
3   Facts where the insurer has waived further information.
4   Facts tending to lessen the risk.

Terms of insurance policies

2.07 A further idiosyncrasy of insurance contracts is that the terms are classified differently. In other contracts, breach of a condition will give the innocent party the right to treat the contract as being at an end, while breach of a warranty will give rise to a claim for damages only. Under insurance contracts, the position is different.

1   A warranty must be exactly complied with, and if it is not so complied with, the insurer is discharged from all liability from the date of breach of the warranty.
2   Other terms may be 'conditions precedent'. Unless the insured complies with the condition precedent, insurers will (depending upon the particular clause) have no liability under the policy, or have no liability for a particular claim.
3   Otherwise, breach of a condition may give rise to a right on the part of insurer to reject a claim and/or a right to damages caused by the breach.

Whatever the correct description of the term of the contract, the insured must comply strictly with it or he may jeopardise the effectiveness of cover under the policy.

3 Professional indemnity insurance policies

3.01 There is no one standard architects' professional indemnity policy. Careful reference must be made to the actual terms of the particular policy to see what it covers and what it does not cover. Insurance contracts are interpreted by giving effect to the usual meaning of the language used. In the case of ambiguity, the court will favour the interpretation which is against the person who drafted it: almost always the insurer.

3.02 The purpose of a professional indemnity policy is to indemnify the insured in respect of claims made against or notified to him within the period of the policy for breach of professional duty. The policy will generally indemnify the insured against sums which he becomes legally liable to pay by way of compensation for breach of professional duty (in tort or contract) as a result of a court order, arbitration award or settlement. Architects would be well advised to ensure that the particular policy responds to sums which are awarded by adjudicators (see Chapter 25).

Limits of indemnity

3.03 The insured will be liable for a certain sum by way of excess or deductible in respect of each and every claim, although there may be a clause which allows related claims to be treated as one claim for the purposes of the deductible.

3.04 The insured must be careful to select an appropriate level of cover, depending on the value of the projects on which he works. It may, for example, be a limit of £5m for each and every claim, including the claimant's legal costs. Other ways of limiting cover are to provide that there is an aggregate limit of (say) £5m in respect of all claims made in the year, or in respect of a series of claims which are linked in a defined way (e.g. they arise out of the same originating cause).

3.05 The policy is likely to cover the insured's own legal costs in addition to sums payable to the third party. Whether such costs are included within the limit of indemnity or not depends upon the wording of the particular policy. If payment to the third party is greater than insurers' limit of indemnity, then insurers' liability to pay costs may be scaled down by the proportion which the level of indemnity bears to the total amount payable to the third party.

Claims made

3.06 Professional indemnity policies are usually 'claims made' policies: they respond to claims made against or notified to the insured within the period of the policy, not claims arising out of a breach of duty within the policy period. Partners should ensure that the firm's policies continue to cover them against claims in retirement, and sole practitioners should obtain 'run-off' cover to protect them through retirement.

3.07 The policy will require the insured to inform insurers of claims made as soon as possible. It will probably require the insured to inform insurers of any circumstance or event which is likely to result in a claim. Failure to do so may mean that insurers do not have to pay. The importance of timely notification of claims to insurers cannot be overstated. Disputes about whether or not the insured has notified insurers of a claim or a circumstance likely to give rise to claim are common. Confrontational correspondence may be sent or difficult meetings held; the employer may blame the contractor for delays and the contractor may in turn blame the architect for late provision of design. The architect will have to consider whether the correspondence amounts to a notification of a claim or a circumstance likely to give rise to a claim; and, if he has already notified insurers of a claim or circumstance in relation to the project, whether he should notify insurers of a further claim or circumstance. It is prudent to notify insurers of each relevant document or conversation until insurers say otherwise; if in doubt, seek advice from a broker or solicitor.

3.08 An insurer will not generally be liable for claims which the insured knew about before the policy was agreed. They should be covered by the previous year's policy. The insured should therefore ensure that all claims or circumstances likely to give rise to a claim have been notified to insurers before the end of each policy year. This is always important, but particularly so when the architect is changing insurers.

3.09 If the insured makes a fraudulent claim on the policy, then the insured is not permitted to recover at all in respect of that claim, even if the claim or part of it could have been made honestly. This rule arises from the duty of good faith. It may be reinforced by a term in the policy.

Control of the claim and subrogation

3.10 The insurer will be entitled to take control of the claim once it has been notified to it. The insured may not admit liability for any breach of duty or compensation without the insurer's consent. The insured will have to give all such assistance to insurer as is necessary for it to handle any claim. However, in the event of a dispute between the insured and insurer, the policy will probably provide that the insured need not contest any legal proceedings unless an independent lawyer (often a Queen's Counsel) has advised that such proceedings may be contested with the probability of success.

3.11 If the claim against the insured is successful, and the insurer indemnifies the insured for the loss, the insurer will be subrogated to the insured's position in respect of any possible claims against third parties (e.g. the building contractor) in respect of the loss. The insured may be required to allow the insurer to use his name to bring proceedings against such third parties. The policy will, however, generally provide that the insurer will not exercise rights of subrogation against employees of the insured, unless there was dishonest, criminal or malicious conduct on the part of the particular employee.

Exclusions

3.12 The insured should read the exclusions to cover with care. The following are common exclusions:

1 An excess or deductible (see paragraph 3.03 above).
2 Claims arising out of participation in a consortium or joint venture.
3 Claims arising out of any circumstance or event which has or should have been disclosed by the insured on the proposal form or renewal form (see paragraph 3.08 above).
4 Claims caused by a dishonest, fraudulent, criminal or malicious act or omission on the part of any partner, director or principal of the insured. Such conduct on the part of employees, on the other hand, if it leads to liability to third parties, will generally be covered by the policy.
5 Claims made out of performance warranties, collateral warranties, penalty clauses or liquidated damages clauses unless the liability would have existed in the absence of such clauses. This is because such warranties or clauses generally extend the usual liability of the architect. They impose guarantees in respect of work done, whereas usually the architect is only liable in the event he has failed to exercise reasonable care and skill.
6 Claims arising out of a survey or valuation report carried out by the insured, unless it was earned out by a qualified architect or surveyor and a disclaimer as specified by the insurer was included in the terms of appointment. The disclaimer normally tries to exclude liability for woodwork and parts of the structure which are covered up, and high alumina cement.
7 The policy may only cover work done in the United Kingdom.

Fees recovery extension

3.13 It may be possible for the insured to extend the policy to protect the insured against costs which are necessarily incurred in recovering or attempting to recover professional fees.

4 Risk management

4.01 Architects can take steps to minimise the likelihood of claims being made against them. This is largely a matter of common sense, but the following list may be helpful.

1 Consider the terms of your appointment carefully. Make sure its terms are clearly agreed, and that fee provisions and the scope of services are expressly stated.
2 Do not take on work which is beyond the capability of the person or the capacity of the team doing it.
3 Have a system set up to check drawings and other work before it is sent out.
4 Make sure that everyone knows when deadlines fall. Do not agree to take on projects with unrealistic deadlines.
5 Have a proper document management system.
6 Make sure you know and comply with contractual formalities. Many disputes arise when there are no proper records of variations to the works, or additional instructions. The fact that the project is proceeding amicably at the beginning does not mean it will stay that way until the end. Everyone will benefit from a clear record of the scope, cost and time implications of work done.
7 Consider any third party guarantee, collateral warranty or duty of care deed very carefully, and check that it will be covered by the policy. If necessary, take legal advice.
8 Make sure any consultants or contractors have written terms of appointment and insurance.
9 Make sure that all projects are properly supervised.
10 If project is going wrong, ensure that you keep good records of what is happening.

34

Copyright

CLIVE THORNE

1 Copyright

1.01 UK copyright law is contained in the Copyright, Designs and Patents Act 1988 ('the Act') and the subsidiary legislation made under that Act. Copyright exists only in works which come within one of the categories prescribed as being capable of having copyright protection. These are as follows:

1 literary work;
2 dramatic work;
3 musical work;
4 artistic work (including a work of architecture being a building or a model for a building);
5 sound recordings;
6 films;
7 broadcasts (including electronic transmissions);
8 typographical arrangements of published editions.

The Act describes all these copyright categories as 'works'.

Material which does not fall within one of the categories will have no copyright protection; it will not be copyright material.

1.02 Copyright subsists for defined periods which differ according to the category of work.

Following the amendment of the Act by the Duration of Copyright and Rights in Performance Regulations 1995 (SI 1995 No. 3297) which came into force on 1 January 1996, the duration of copyright in each category of work can be summarised as follows:

1 Literary, dramatic, musical and artistic works – which includes architectural works: 70 years from the end of the calendar year in which the author died.
2 Sound recordings: 50 years from the end of the year in which they were made or, if released before the end of that period, 50 years from the end of the calendar year in which released.
3 Films: 70 years from the end of the calendar year in which the last of the principal director, the author of the screenplay, the author of the dialogue or the composer of the specially created music dies, or if there is no one within this designated list, 50 years from the end of the year in which they were made.
4 Broadcasts and cable programmes: 50 years from the end of the calendar year in which the broadcast was made or the cable programme included in a cable programme service.
5 Typographical arrangements: 25 years from the end of the calendar year in which the edition was first published.

1.03 If a work is entitled to copyright protection, the right vested in the copyright owner is that of preventing others from doing certain specified acts, called 'the restricted acts' (paragraph 2.02).

The restricted acts are specified by the Act in relation to each category of work and differ for each category.

Acts done in relation to a copyright work which are not one of the restricted acts specified for that type of work do not infringe.

1.04 Performing restricted acts without the consent of the copyright owner may not constitute breach of copyright if they fall withing certain exceptions:

1 fair dealing (e.g. for purposes of non-commercial research, private study, criticism, or review);
2 use of less than a substantial part of a work;
3 use for certain educational purposes;
4 use for certain library and archival purposes;
5 use in parliamentary and judicial proceedings and certain other public administration functions;
6 incidental inclusion of a work.

There are other exceptions, differing according to the types of works or subject matters (for example, see paragraphs 6.01 and 6.02).

1.05 In most cases the author of a work is its first owner. But there are special rules which can override this general provision (see paragraph 5 below).

1.06 There is no copyright in ideas – only in the manner of their expression.

1.07 To acquire copyright protection, works must be recorded in a material form.

1.08 Literary, dramatic, musical and artistic works must be original (i.e. have involved the use of independent skill and labour by the author).

1.09 The work does not have to be published, nor does it have to be registered, for it to have copyright protection.

1.10 The author of the work must be a 'qualified person': a citizen or resident of the UK or of one of the countries which is a signatory to the Berne Copyright Convention or the Universal Copyright Convention (UCC). Alternatively, the work must have been made or published in a qualifying country, which for most purposes (although there are important exceptions for sound recordings, films, broadcasts and cable programmes) are the same countries. There are no significant countries which are not parties to one or the other of these conventions. China signed both Conventions in 1992.

The nature of copyright

1.11

'Copyright is a right given to or derived from works, and is not a right in novelty of ideas. It is based on the right of an author, artist or composer to prevent another person copying an original work, whether it be a book, picture or tune, which he himself has created. There is nothing in the notion of copyright to prevent a second person from producing an identical result (and himself enjoying a copyright in that work) provided it is arrived at by an independent process.'

(Gregory Committee on Copyright Law (1952))

'A writer writes an article about the making of bread. He puts words on paper. He is not entitled to a monopoly in the writing of articles about the making of bread, but the law has long recognized that he has an interest not merely in the manuscript, the words on paper which he produces, but in the skill and labour involved in the choice of words and the exact way in which he expresses his ideas by the words he chooses. If the author sells copies of his article then again a purchaser of a copy can make such use of that copy as he pleases. He can read it or sell it second-hand, if he can find anyone who will buy it. If a reader of the original article is stimulated into writing another article about bread the original author has no reason to complain. It has long been recognized that only the original author ought to have the right to reproduce the original article and sell the copies thus reproduced. If other people were free to do this they would be making a profit out of the skill and labour of the original author. It is for this reason that the law has long given to authors, for a specified term, certain exclusive rights in relation to so-called literary works. Such rights were recognized at common law at least as early as the fifteenth century.'

(Whitford Committee on Copyright and Design Law (1977))
upon whose recommendations the Copyright, Designs and Patents Act 1988 is largely based.

These two quotations contain as clear an exposé of the nature of copyright as can be found anywhere.

As the word itself implies, 'copyright' is literally a right to prevent other people copying an original work. It should be noted that it must be an original *work*, not an original idea.

The sources of copyright law

1.12 UK copyright law is now contained in the Copyright, Designs and Patents Act 1988 ('the Act'), as amended. There are a significant number of rules and regulations contained in statutory instruments made under the Act or under powers contained in the European Communities Act 1972 to bring into effect the UK's obligations under European Community directives. In addition, certain orders in council extend the provisions of the Act to works originating outside the UK.

The UK is party to a number of international conventions dealing with reciprocal international copyright recognition. The most important are the Berne Copyright Convention and the Universal Copyright Convention.

More recently, the WTO TRIPS Agreement consolidates many of the provisions to both Berne and the UCC.

There is a body of case law contained in the law reports consisting of judgments in copyright cases. Decisions on earlier legislation, the Copyright Acts of 1911 and 1956, are sometimes still relevant.

The history of copyright law

1.13 Copyright effectively came into existence with the invention of printing. The foundations of copyright were in the granting of licences by the Crown to printers giving them the right to print (i.e. copy) against the payment of fees to the Crown. In 1662 the Licensing Act was passed, which prohibited the printing of any book which was not licensed and registered at the Stationers Company.

The first Copyright Act was passed in 1709. This Act gave protection for printed works for only 21 years from the date of printing and unprinted works for 14 years. Again, books had to be registered at the Stationers Company.

The Copyright Act 1842 was the next important piece of legislation relating to copyright. Although it accorded copyright protection only to literary works, it laid down as the period of copyright the life of the author plus 7 years after his death, or 42 years from the date of publication, whichever should be the longer.

Architects' plans, provided they had artistic quality, first became entitled to copyright protection as artistic works under the Fine Arts Copyright Act 1862.

The Copyright Act 1911 repealed all previous copyright legislation. This Act extended copyright protection to 'architectural works of art', with the result that, as the courts held in *Meikle v Maufe* [1941] 3 All ER 144, buildings and the plans upon which they were based were entitled to copyright protection. Plans and sketches were protected as 'literary works' and drawings as 'artistic works'. The Copyright Act 1911 was repealed by the Copyright Act 1956. Protection for works of architecture under the 1956 Act was similar to that accorded by the 1911 Act. The 1988 Act repealed the 1956 Act. It came into force on 1 August 1989.

Database right

1.14 Following the implementation of an EC Council Directive on the legal protection of databases, the Copyright Rights in Databases Regulations 1997 (SI 1997. No. 3032) which came into force on 1 January 1998 created a new 'database right' which gives a certain degree of protection where there has been a 'substantial investment in obtaining, verifying or presenting the contents of the database'. A database is defined as a 'collection of independent works, data or other materials arranged in a systematic or methodical way and individually accessible by electronic or other means'. In addition, a new class of literary work, qualifying for copyright protection, has been created for databases but the originality test is stricter than for other works.

The database right can subsist whether or not the database or its contents is a copyright work. The general rule is that the right subsists for 15 years from the end of the calender year in which the database was completed and the maker of the database will be the first owner of the database right.

If a database qualifies for protection, the owner can prevent third parties extracting or re-utilising all or a substantial part of the contents of the database without consent.

2 Protection under the Copyright, Designs and Patents Act 1988

2.01 Works of architecture are included in the definition of 'artistic works' for copyright purposes. Section 4 of the Act defines an 'artistic work':

'S.4 (1) In this Part "artistic work" means –
    (a) a graphic work, photograph, sculpture or collage, irrespective of artistic quality,
    (b) a work of architecture being a building or a model for a building, or
    (c) a work of artistic craftsmanship.

(2) In this part – "building" includes any fixed structure, and a part of a building or fixed structure; "graphic work" includes
    (a) any painting, drawing, diagram, map, chart or plan, and
    (b) any engraving, etching, lithograph, woodcut or similar work;

"photograph" means a recording of light or other radiation on any medium on which an image is produced or from which an image may by any means be produced, and which is not part of a film; "sculpture" includes a cast or model made for purposes of sculpture.'

Works of architecture include both buildings and models for buildings. The plans, sketches, and drawings upon which works of architecture are based are also artistic works which have their own separate copyright. So also do the notes prepared by the architect, but these are protected not as artistic works but as literary works.

There is no definition of 'fixed structure', although a decision under the 1956 Act held that a garden, in that case a somewhat elaborately laid-out garden, was a 'structure' and therefore a work of architecture.

A 'drawing' is not defined by the Act. The definitions of 'artistic work' and 'literary work' are wide so that they cover all the typical output of an architect's office: design sketches, blueprints, descriptive diagrams, working drawings, final drawings, artistic presentations, notes, both alphabetical and numerical and reports.

Restricted acts

2.02 As referred to in paragraph 1.03 above, there are separate restricted acts specified in the Act in relation to each category of work. The restricted acts applicable to works of architecture are the same as those applicable to artistic works, although there are certain special exceptions (paragraph 6) from these restricted acts in relation to works of architecture. The acts restricted by the copyright in an artistic work include either directly or indirectly:

1   copying the whole or a substantial part of the work;
2   issuing copies of the work to the public;
3   renting or hiring the work.

Secondary infringement arises in relation to possessing or dealing with, or providing the means for making the work, when the alleged infringer knows, or has reason to believe the work is an infringing copy.

Originality and artistic content

2.03 The copyright in an artistic work (for example, a building, model, architectural drawing or plan) is not necessarily dependent on any aesthetic appeal nor requires any artistic character.

The test for originality is a low one, as was demonstrated in *Walter v Lane* [1900] AC 539, a case which it was held that a reporter was entitled to copyright in his verbatim report of a public speech. The work must originate from the author instead of merely being copied from another work. One of the leading cases on originality is *Interlego AG v Tyco Industries Inc* [1989] AC 217 in which it was held that skill, labour and judgment merely in the process of copying cannot confer originality so as to give copyright protection to the copy. This is despite the fact that mere copying of an artistic work may in fact require considerable skill. That case involved copyright in design drawings for toy bricks. The drawings were amended with small emendations. There was insufficient skill and labour in making the emendations to establish 'originality'.

In *University of London Press Ltd v University Tutorial Press Ltd*, which concerned the copying of examination papers, the court held that 'the word "original" does not in this connection mean that the work must be the expression of original or inventive thought . . . but that it should originate from the author'.

2.04 For architectural works, the inclusion of some distinctive design detail will make the architect's task of proving infringement much easier. In *Stovin-Bradford v Volpoint Properties Ltd* [1971] Ch 1007 the courts were influenced by the fact that although many details of the architect's drawings were not reproduced in the constructed buildings, 'a distinctive diamond-shaped feature which gave a pleasing appearance to the whole' was reproduced. In *Meikle v Maufe* (above) the judge dismissed them as not being of artistic merit.

2.05 Some distinctive design feature may also be important when it could otherwise be proved that the person sued was without any knowledge of the claimant's prior design, and that he produced identical solutions because of a similarity in circumstances.

Duration of copyright

2.06 The protection of copyright in an artistic work extends for the lifetime of the artist/author and a further period of 70 years from the end of the calendar year in which he died. In the case of architectural works, this period is not affected by the fact that the work was not published during the architect's lifetime.

In the case of joint works, the 70 years runs from the end of the calendar year in which the last of the joint authors dies. A joint work is one in which the work is produced by the collaboration of two or more authors in which the contribution of each author is not distinct from that of the other author or authors. Thus if a building is designed by two architects, but one is exclusively responsible only for the design of the doors and windows, so that it is possible to distinguish between the contributions of the two architects it will not be a joint work.

3 Qualification

3.01 In order to qualify for copyright protection in the UK, the qualification requirements of the Act must be satisfied as regards either the author or the country in which the work was first published.

3.02 As regards authors, in the case of unpublished works, copyright will subsist only if the author was a 'qualifying person' at the time when the work was made, or, if it was being made over a period, for a substantial part of that period. In the case of a published work, the author must be a 'qualifying person' qualified at the time when the work was published, or immediately before his death (if earlier).

3.03 For copyright purposes, the expression 'qualified person' refers to any British citizen, British Dependent Territories citizen, a British National (overseas), a British Overseas citizen, a British subject, or a British protected person within the meaning of the British Nationality Act 1981, or a person domiciled or resident in the UK or in another country to which the Act extends or is applied, or a body incorporated under the laws of the UK or such another country. The countries to which the Act extends or has been applied are the signatories to the Berne Copyright Convention and the Universal Copyright Convention, which includes all the major and most of the developing countries in the world.

The provision relating to corporations is not important to architects because a corporation cannot be the author of an artistic work.

3.04 As regards the country of publication, the work must have been published first in either the UK or another country to which the Act extends or has been applied, i.e. Berne Convention or UCC countries.

Publication in one country shall not be regarded as other than first publication by reason of the simultaneous publication elsewhere. Publication elsewhere within 30 days shall be regarded as simultaneous.

3.05 The Act now provides that the territorial waters of the UK shall be treated as part of the UK for copyright purposes. In addition, oil rigs and other structures which are present on the UK continental shelf for purposes directly connected with the exploration of the sea bed or the exploration of their natural resources and UK aircraft and ships are subject to UK copyright law as if they were in the UK.

4 Publication

4.01 The meaning of the word 'publication' is important as it is relevant to qualification for copyright protection and the duration of copyright. 'Publication' is defined in the Act as meaning the issue of copies to the public. In the case of literary, dramatic, musical and artistic works it includes making the work available to the public by means of an electronic retrieval system.

There is a special provision in relation to architectural works. In the case of works of architecture in the form of a building or an artistic work incorporated in a building, construction of the building shall be treated as equivalent to publication of the work.

4.02 The issue to the public of copies of a graphic work representing, or of photographs of, a work of architecture in the form of a building, or a model for a building, does not constitute publication for the purposes of the Act. Nor does the exhibition, issuing to the public of copies of a film including the work, or the broadcasting of an artistic work constitute publication. Thus, the inclusion of a model of a building in a public exhibition such as the Royal Academy Summer Exhibition, would not amount to publication, nor would the inclusion of photographs of the model in a book.

5 Ownership

5.01 Subject to the exception for employees set out in the following paragraph, ownership of artistic copyright in drawings usually resides with the architect who actually drew the plan, drawing, sketch, or diagram. As a chose in action it passes to its owner's personal representatives after his death. If a builder constructs the building without reference to any plans he will be the author and owner of the work of architecture.

Employees

5.02 There is, however, an important exception to this provision: the copyright in architects' drawings, buildings, or models produced by an employee in the course of his employment automatically vests in his employer, whether the latter is an architect in partnership, a limited company, or a public authority. The copyright in work created by employees in their personal time and not in the course of employment vests in them (*Thomas Scott v Universal Components Ltd* [2002] Ch D 31/10/02). An employer can discourage employees from accepting private commissions by providing in the contract of employment – that the copyright in the employee's work, whether produced in the course of employment or not, will vest in the employer. Section 178 of the Act provides that the words 'employed', 'employee', 'employer' and 'employment' refer to employment under a 'contract of service or apprenticeship'. Frequently, architects employ independent architects and artists to carry out parts of the drawing; increasingly persons who would appear to be employees are for a variety of reasons (not unconnected with tax and Social Security payments) engaged as self-employed sub-contractors. Such persons are rarely employed under 'a contract of service' as distinct from 'a contract for services'. Employer architects would be well advised to make it an express term of a sub-contractor's appointment that copyright should vest in the employing architect.

The old provisions regarding Crown copyright have been changed in the 1988 Act. The position now is that where a work is made by an officer or servant of the Crown in the course of his duties, the Crown will be the first owner of the copyright in the work.

Partners

5.03 A partner of a firm is not an 'employee' of the partnership and hence will own the legal title to a work created by him. However, if the work in question is created in the ordinary course of the partnership business and for the purposes of the partnership, the copyright in the work will be considered as a partnership asset. The legal title remains with the partner who created the work until a written assignment is executed, but the other partners have a right to apply the copyright to benefit the partnership. For the avoidance of doubt, the partnership deed (Chapter 29) should set out what happens as regards ownership of copyright.

Ownership of drawings

5.04 Ownership of copyright in drawings should be distinguished from ownership of the physical paper upon which they are drawn. Generally upon payment of the architect's fees the client is entitled to possession of all the drawings prepared at his expense. In the absence of agreement to the contrary, copyright remains with the architect who also has a lien on (right to withhold) the drawings until his fees are paid. If all copyright is assigned to the client he may make such use of it as he wishes. Architects should note that even if they have assigned the copyright, by virtue of the provisions of section 64 of the Act, they may reproduce in a subsequent work part of their own original design provided that they do not repeat or imitate the main design. This provision enables architects to repeat standard details which would otherwise pass to the client upon prior assignment of copyright.

Joint ownership

5.05 A work of joint authorship is one which results from the collaboration of two or more authors where it is not possible to distinguish the contribution of those authors. There is no requirement for the authors to have a joint intention to create the work (*Robert James Beckingham v Robert Hodgens & Others* [2003] EWCA Civ 143). The general rule, in a situation of joint authorship, is that the joint authors will be the joint owners of the copyright in the work. The first instance decision of *Robin Ray v Classic FM plc* [1998] FSR 622 suggests that joint authors will always hold copyright as tenants in common in equal shares (i.e. hold district severable shares that can be assigned or passed by will). However, the consensus of opinion suggests this decision is wrong and that there may be situations where joint authors will hold title as joint tenants (i.e. where one owner's share will pass automatically to the joint owner on death).

6 Exceptions to infringement of architects' copyright

Photographs, graphic works

6.01 Frequently, photographs of buildings designed by architects appear as part of advertisements by the contractors who constructed the buildings. As a matter of courtesy, the contractor usually makes some acknowledgment of the design, but he is not required to do so. By section 62 of the Act, the copyright in a work of architecture is not infringed by making a graphic work representing it, making a photograph or film of it, or broadcasting or including a visual representation of it in a cable programme service. Copies of such graphic works, photographs and films can be issued to the public without infringing the copyright in the building and models of it. Making a graphic work in this sense refers to a perspective or even detailed survey of the building as built: it would remain an infringement to copy the drawing or plan from which the building was constructed.

Reconstruction

6.02 Section 65 provides that where copyright exists in a building, anything done for the purposes of reconstructing a building does not infringe copyright. There will be no infringement of the drawings or plans in accordance with which the building was, by or with the licence of the copyright owner, constructed if subsequent reconstruction of the building or part thereof is carried out by reference to original drawings or plans. This point is of particular importance in connection with the now-established 'implied licence' considered in paragraphs 8.05–8.12 below.

Fair dealing

6.03 A general defence to any alleged infringement of copyright in an artistic work is 'fair dealing' for the purpose of criticism or review, provided that there is sufficient acknowledgment. As reproduction by photograph is the most likely method of illustrating a review and as a photograph of a building is specifically exempt from infringement, this defence of 'fair dealing' would appear to be needed only in the case of drawings of buildings. A sufficient acknowledgment is an acknowledgment identifying the building by its name and location, which also identifies the name of the architect who designed it. The name of the copyright owner need not be given if he has previously required that no acknowledgment of his name should be made.

Fair dealing with an artistic work for the purposes of research for a non-commercial purpose, with a sufficient acknowledgment, is also a defence to an alleged copyright infringement. However, there are limits on how, and how many copies may be made.

6.04 Special exceptions are contained in the Act for copying for educational purposes and copying by libraries and archives and by public administration. These provisions are too detailed to be included here, and if necessary they should be specifically referred to or professional advice should be obtained.

7 Infringement

7.01 To prove infringement, a claimant must show that:

1 copyright subsists in his work;
2 the copyright is vested in him;
3 the alleged infringement reproduces a substantial part of his work in material particulars;
4 the alleged infringement was copied from his work.

7.02 No action for infringement of copyright can succeed if the person who is claimed to have infringed had no knowledge of the existence of the work of the owner. Copyright restricts the right to copy, which presupposes some knowledge of the original by the copier. Ignorance of the fact that the work copied was the copyright owner's is not, however, a defence. It is in the nature of architects' copyright that the person allegedly infringing must have had access directly or indirectly to the drawings. Infringement can therefore take three forms, as detailed below.

7.03 What is a 'substantial part' in a 'qualitative' rather than a 'quantitative' test?

Copying in the form of drawings

7.04 It is rare for drawings to be copied in every detail, and many would-be infringers of an architect's copyright consider that if details are altered, infringement is avoided. This is not so, and section 16 of the Act makes it clear that references to reproduction include reproduction of a 'substantial part'. The word 'substantial' refers to quality rather than to quantity. Reference has already been made to the distinctive diamond-shaped detail in the *Stovin-Bradford* case. It does not matter that the size of the copy may have been increased or reduced or that only a small detail of an original drawing has been copied.

Copying the drawing in the form of a building

7.05 Two-dimensional plans can be 'copied' three-dimensionally in the form of a building which reproduces the plans. The leading case on this form of infringement is *Chabot v Davies* [1936] 3 All ER 221. Mr Chabot, who was not an architect but 'a designer and fixer of shop fronts and the like', prepared a drawing for the defendant, who 'was just about to open what is known as a fish and chip shop'. Mr Chabot was able to show that the contractor had actually been handed his drawing by the defendant and had made a tracing from it. The defendant argued that a plan cannot be reproduced by a shop front but only by something in the nature of another plan. The judge held, however, that 'reproduce . . . in any material form whatsoever' must include reproduction of a drawing by the construction of an actual building based on that drawing.

In *Cala Homes (South) Ltd v Alfred McAlpine East Ltd* [1995] FSR 818 the defendant had allegedly copied floor plans. Hence it

was difficult to see whether there had in fact been infringement. However, it was held that if it is possible to show copying whether by recreating the floor plan by measurement of the building or by reference to the plans which the defendant used to construct the building, then infringement may be established as the plans have been reproduced in a 'material form'.

Infringement by copying a building by another building

7.06 The leading case is *Meikle v Maufe* [1941] 3 All ER 144. In 1912 Heal & Son Ltd employed Smith & Brewer as architects for the building of premises on the northern part of the present site of Heal's store in Tottenham Court Road. At that time there were vague discussions about a future extension on the southern part of the site, but because of difficulties over land acquisition nothing could be done. In 1935 Heal's employed Maufe as their architect for the extension of the building. Meikle was by this time the successor in title to Smith & Brewer's copyright, and he claimed that both the extension as erected and the plans for its erection infringed the original copyright. Maufe admitted that he thought it necessary to reproduce in the southern section of the facade the features which appeared in the original northern section. His object was 'to make the new look like the old throughout nearly the whole of the Tottenham Court Road frontage'. The layout of the interiors was also substantially reproduced. The defendants put forward three arguments:

1 There could not be a separate copyright in a building as distinct from copyright in the plans on which it was based.
2 If there was a separate copyright in a building it would belong to the building contractor.
3 It was an implied term of Smith & Brewer's original engagement that Heal's should have the right to reproduce the design of the original in the extension.

7.07 The first argument failed following *Chabot v Davies*. The second argument failed because copyright protection in a building is limited to the original character or design, and in the making of such character or design the contractor plays no part. The third argument failed in this particular case as the Copyright Act 1911, under which this case was tried, provided that copyright remained with its original author, unless he had agreed to pass the right to another. Heal's contended that Smith & Brewer had impliedly consented to the reproduction of their design because they had known of the possibility of extension. The judge having heard the facts concerning the discussion about land acquisition held that he could not reasonably imply such a term in this case.

Copying a building in the form of drawings

7.08 As mentioned in paragraph 6.01, copyright in a work of architecture is not infringed by making a graphic work representing it, making a photograph or file of it, or broadcasting or including a visual representation of it in a cable programme service. In addition, once a building is erected, it is not an infringement of copyright to create and use drawings of the building to repair or reconstruct the building (see paragraph 6.02).

8 Licences

Express licence

8.01 Paragraph 6.01 of the Conditions of Engagement which appear in the RIBA Standard Form of Agreement for the Appointment of an Architect (SFA/99) states that copyright in all documents and drawings prepared by the architect remains the property of the architect. Section 91 of the Act permits prior assignment of future copyright so that client and architect can agree at the beginning of an engagement to vary the Conditions of Engagement so that the copyright which will come into existence during the commission will vest in the client.

8.02 Paragraph 6.02 of the Conditions of Engagement modifies paragraph 6.01, to give the client a licence to use the architect's design in certain circumstances.

Paragraph 6.01 entitles the client to copy and use the architect's design (including drawings, documents and bespoke software) for purposes related to the project provided that:

(a) the entitlement applies only to the site or part of the site to which the design relates; and
(b) any fees due to the architect have been paid (NOTE: if the client is in default of payment, the architect can suspend further use of the licence on giving 7 days' notice to the client).

This entitlement applies to the operation, maintenance, repair, reinstatement, alteration, extension, promotion, leasing and sale of the works but excludes the reproduction of the architect's design for any part of any extension of the project or for any other project.

Sub-paragraph 6.2.2 provides that if permitted use occurs after the date of the last service performed under the agreement and prior to practical completion of the construction of the project the client shall:

(a) obtain the architect's consent if the architect has not completed detailed proposals. The architect's consent must not be unreasonably withheld; and/or
(b) pay a reasonable licence fee if none is agreed.

Finally, sub-paragraph 6.2.1 provides that the architect shall not be liable for the consequences of any use of any information or designs prepared by the architect except for the purposes for which they were provided.

8.03 Copyright may also be expressly assigned to the client at some later stage, but it is usual to grant a licence authorising use of copyright subject to conditions rather than an outright assignment of all the architect's rights. An increasing number of public and commercial clients make it a condition of the architect's appointment that all copyright shall vest in the client.

The architect should not consent to this without careful thought. Following *Meikle v Maufe* it would seem reasonable that a client should not be prevented from extending a building and incorporating distinctive design features of the original building so that the two together should form one architectural unit. If the time between the original building and the extension were 23 years, as in that case, it would be restrictive to make use of copyright to force the client into employing the original architect or his successor in title. Less scrupulous clients could, however, make use of an architect's design for a small and inexpensive original building with the undisclosed intention of greatly extending the building using the same design but at no extra cost in terms of architects' fees.

8.04 So far as drawings are concerned, it must be remembered that they are the subject of copyright 'irrespective of artistic quality' so that a prior express assignment of copyright to the client could theoretically grant him copyright in respect of even the most simple standard detail contained in the drawings (but see paragraph 5.04).

Implied licence

8.05 While the RIBA Architect's Appointment contains an express licence of the architect's copyright, situations may arise where the RIBA Architect's Appointment does not form part of the contract between the architect and the client or where the terms of the RIBA Architect's Appointment do not cover particular circumstances. Problems may then arise as to what rights the client has to use the architect's drawings. As long ago as 1938, the RIBA took counsel's opinion on the theory that an architect impliedly licenses his client to make use of the architect's drawings for the purposes of construction even when the client does not employ the architect to supervise the building contract. Such an implied consent can be understood when from the beginning of the engagement the client made it clear that all he required of the architect was drawings; for if the client received the drawings

and paid for them, they would be valueless unless he could use them for the purpose of construction. The courts would not allow an architect to use his copyright to prevent construction in such circumstances. Counsel advised further that even if it had originally been assumed that the architect would perform the full service and supervise construction but the client subsequently decided that he did not require supervision, an implied licence to use the copyright in the drawings would arise in the client's favour when working drawings had been completed. Counsel did not then believe that an implied licence could arise at an earlier stage, but since 1938 the extent of architects' work and its stages have increased greatly. Cumulatively detailed drawings required for outline planning consent, detailed planning consent, and Building Regulations consent all create different stages, and an implied licence can now arise earlier than was contemplated in 1938.

8.06 Before any term can be implied into a contract, the courts must consider what the parties would have decided if they had considered the question at the time they negotiated other terms of the engagement. The courts are reluctant to imply a term unless it is necessary to give efficacy to the intention of the parties. Application of these rules to an architect's engagement would suggest that it is reasonable to infer that the architect impliedly consents to the client making use of his drawings for the purpose for which they were intended. If, therefore, the nature of the engagement is not full RIBA service but, for example, obtaining outline planning permission and no more, the architect impliedly consents to the client making use of his copyright to apply for such permission. Again, if an architect is instructed to prepare drawings of a proposed alteration for submission to the client's landlord, the client may use the drawings to obtain a consent under the terms of his lease but not for any other purpose, and certainly not for the purpose of instructing a contractor to carry out the alteration work.

8.07 The whole question of implied licence has been considered by the Court of Appeal in the cases of *Blair* and *Stovin-Bradford*, both of which have been fully reported. The facts in these cases are set out in paragraphs 8.08 and 8.09 below. In addition, reference should be made to *Robin Ray v Classic FM plc*, mentioned earlier at paragraph 5.05, which reviewed the authorities relating to implied copyright licences in consultancy agreements.

Blair v Osborne & Tompkins

8.08 Blair was asked by his clients whether it would be possible to obtain planning consent for development at the end of his clients' garden. Having made enquiries, Blair advised that it should be possible to obtain consent for erection of two semi-detached houses. The clients instructed Blair to proceed to detailed planning consent stage and agreed to pay on the RIBA scale. The application was successful, and Blair sent the planning consent to his clients, with his account for £70 for 'taking instructions, making survey, preparing scheme and obtaining full planning consent'. As was well known to the architect, the clients did not at that stage know whether they were going to develop the land or sell it.

They paid Blair's account, which he acknowledged, adding 'wishing you all the best on this project', but did not employ him to do any further work because they sold the plot to a contractor/developer. They also handed over Blair's drawings to the contractor, who used his own surveyors to add the detail necessary to obtain Building Regulations consent, and this consent having been obtained the contractor erected the houses. When the architect discovered that his plans were being used he claimed that this was an infringement of his copyright. The Master of the Rolls pointed out that although the RIBA Conditions of Engagement stated that copyright remained with the architect, it was open to him to give a licence for the drawings to be used for a particular site. The judge was influenced by the provision in the RIBA Conditions which entitled both architect and client to terminate the engagement 'upon reasonable notice'. To his Lordship it seemed inconceivable that upon the architect withdrawing he could stop any use of the plans on the ground of infringement of copyright. It seemed equally inconceivable that he could stop their use at an earlier stage when he had done his work up to a particular point and had been paid according to the RIBA scale. Widgery LJ approved the defendant's submission that the implied licence was 'to use whatever plans had been prepared at the appropriate stage for all purposes for which they would normally be used, namely, all purposes connected with the erection of the building to which they related'. If this was not right 'the architect' could hold a client to ransom and that would be quite inconsistent with the term that the engagement could be 'put an end to at any time'. In the writer's opinion this was an unfortunate decision and went much further than was required.

Stovin-Bradford v Volpoint Properties Ltd and Another

8.09 The defendant companies, which had their own drawing office, acquired an old factory which they considered had considerable development potential, and applied for planning consent for the erection of seven large warehouses. Permission was refused, and the defendants approached Stovin-Bradford, whose work they had previously admired, explaining that they needed a plan and drawing that 'showed something which was more attractive-looking than the existing building'. What they wanted was 'a pretty picture', but because they had their own drawing office, they did not need the full services of an architect. It was accepted by the court that although the then Conditions of Engagement were not incorporated into their contract, both architect and defendants were fully aware that they existed. It was also accepted that both parties were concerned only with obtaining planning permission. As the trial judge held, the agreement reached between the parties was very simple and amounted to this: 'that Stovin-Bradford would suggest architectural improvements to the defendant's existing plan for the modification and extension of the existing building for the purpose of trying to obtain planning permission and that he would receive for this plan the sum of 100 guineas and his out-of-pocket expenses.' The drawing was produced showing an 'effect quite striking to the eye: a unification of two original structures into one with, in particular, a diamond feature in the left hand building caused by the arrangement of the roof line and the windows placed in the top part of the old portal frame building'. The plan was passed to the defendants, who made certain amendments and obtained planning permission. Stovin-Bradford had presented his account for the agreed 'nominal' 100 guineas, headed it 'Statement no. 1' and confirmed that the payment was 'for preparing sketch plans and design drawings in sufficient detail to obtain or apply for planning permission'. With commendable foresight, at the foot of the bill was typed a note saying: 'The copyright of the design remains with the architect and may not be reproduced in any form without his prior written consent'. The defendants proceeded to erect the buildings, and although many details were changed, the result incorporated the particular features of the Stovin-Bradford design to which the trial judge drew notice. At first instance, the trial judge held that there was an infringement and awarded £500 damages as the amount which would have been reasonably chargeable for a licence to make use of the copyright.

8.10 The Court of Appeal judgment in the *Blair* case having been published shortly afterwards, the defendants appealed on the ground that the *Blair* case was decisive authority for the view that whenever an architect prepared plans for obtaining planning permission, the client could use them for the building as he liked without further payment. This time Lord Denning, the Master of the Rolls, referred to the stages of normal service in the RIBA Conditions (now replaced by Architect's Appointment), which he defined as being: (1) plans up to an application for outline planning permission; (2) plans up to an application for detailed planning permission; (3) working drawings and specification for contractor to tender; (4) all an architect's work to completion of the building. (The author has often thought that this would be the most sensible division of the RIBA stages of normal service, but in fact the stages were not so defined in the then existing

Conditions – though the stages in the current Architect's Appointment roughly correspond to this division including, for example, appraisal, strategic briefing, outline proposals, detailed proposals, tender documentation and construction to practical completion.) Again the judges referred to the provision for termination upon reasonable notice and commented that the scale charges for 'partial services' seemed to be so fixed that they contained an in-built compensation for the use of designs and drawings right through to completion of the work. Lord Denning pointed out that in the Blair case charges had been in accordance with the RIBA scale, i.e. 1/6 of the full fee. But in this case the architect had charged on 'agreed nominal fee' basis, and his fee was far less than the percentage fee (which would have been, at 1/6, some £900). The Court of Appeal confirmed that there was an infringement, that an implied licence had not arisen, and that damages of £500 were reasonable.

Conclusions

8.11 From these two decisions it would appear that charging by the RIBA scales for partial services (whether originally contemplated or brought about by a termination) will give rise to an implied licence, while charging a nominal fee will not. If the agreement between the parties is silent it is usually the case that some form of licence will be implied but the extent of that licence will depend on the facts. The RIBA Architect's Appointment provides that the client will have an express licence to use the drawings only for the specific purpose for which they were prepared, and in particular that the preparation of drawings for obtaining planning permission does not carry with it the right to use them for construction of the building without the architect's express consent (which ought not to be unreasonably withheld).

8.12 The implied licence probably includes a right to modify the plans, although the law is not settled on this point (*Hunter v Fitzroy Robinson* [1978] FSR 167). If the Architect's Appointment does not apply, the probability is that the implied licence will not be revocable by the architect even if his fees have not been paid.

Alterations to architect's drawings and works of architecture

8.13 If the client alters the plans or the completed building, the probability is that he will not thereby be in breach of the architect's copyright (*Hunter v Fitzroy Robinson*). However, the client may not 'sell or hire' buildings or plans as the unaltered work of the architect (see Section 11 below dealing with moral rights).

9 Remedies for infringement

Injunction

9.01 An injunction can be obtained to prevent the construction of a building that would infringe the copyright in another building, even if that building is part-built. Section 17 of the 1956 Act provided that no injunction could be granted after the construction of a building had started, nor could an injunction be granted to require the building (so far as it has been constructed) to be demolished. This provision was repealed by the 1988 Act and is not re-enacted in any form.

However, there is a general principle of law that an injunction will not be granted if damages are an adequate relief. It is probable that a court would, in most cases, apply this rule in the case of an injunction to prevent the construction of a building when the construction has substantially commenced. The decision of the court will depend upon all the facts and circumstances of the case.

Damages account of profits

9.02 Damages are available to compensate the claimant for the loss in value of the copyright resulting from the infringing action. An alternative claim to damages is an account of profits. The claimant asks for the profits that the defendant has made by the unauthorised exploitation of the copyright. In *Chabot v Davies* the court held that the measure of damages for infringement of the designer's copyright was the amount which he might reasonably have charged for granting a licence to make use of his copyright. In *Meikle v Maufe* the court rejected an argument that the architect might reasonably claim the profit which he would have made if he had been employed to carry out the work which infringed his copyright: 'Such profits do not provide either a mathematical measure for damages or a basis upon which to estimate damages. Copyright is not the sickle which reaps an architect's profit.'

Graham J in the *Stovin-Bradford* case confirmed the licence fee basis of the two earlier cases and awarded £500 against the claimant's request for £1000 and the defendant's suggestion of between £10 and £20. Although this point has not been decided with reference to architect's copyright, it would appear that on general principles, exemplary damages could be awarded in addition to the licence fee where the breach was particularly flagrant.

In the case of *Potton Ltd v Yorkelose Ltd* [1990] 17 FSR the defendants admitted that they had constructed 14 houses, in infringement of the claimants' copyright, on a style of house named 'Grandsen'. The defendants' houses were substantial reproductions of the claimants' Grandsen drawings and they had copied the drawings for obtaining outline planning permission and detailed planning permission. It was held that the claimants were entitled to the profits realised on the sale of the houses, apportioned to include profits attributable to (i) the purchase, landscaping and sale of the land on which the houses were built; (ii) any increase in value of the houses during the interval between the completion of the houses and their sale; and (iii) the advertising, marketing and selling of the houses.

In the case of *Charles Church Development plc v Cronin* [1990] 17 FSR the defendants admitted that they had had a house built based on plans which were the copyright of the claimant. The distinction between this case and *Potton Ltd v Yorkelose Ltd* is that in the former case the houses were built for sale and had been sold, whereas in this case the house had not been sold and the claimants had obtained an injunction to prevent its sale. In the former case the claimant sued for an account of profits. In the latter case the claim was for compensatory damages for the loss caused by the infringement. The judge held that the measure of damages was a fair fee for a licence to use the drawings, based on what an architect would have charged for the preparation of drawings. The architect's fee should be calculated on the basis that the architect would have provided the whole of the basic services – in that case 8.5% of the building costs.

Secondary losses, such as payment discounts and overdraft requirements relating to cash flow problems, caused by an infringement are too remote to merit compensation (*Claydon Architectural Metalwork Ltd v DJ Higgins & Sons Ltd* [1997] Ch D 16/1/97).

9.03 The court can award additional damages under section 97(2) of the Act in cases of flagrant infringement of copyright. In *Cala Homes v McAlpine* Laddie J said that when considering whether to award additional damages, the court must look at all the circumstances of the case: 'Although the court must have regard to the flagrancy of the infringement and the benefit accruing to the defendant, there is no requirement that both or indeed either of these features be present. It is possible to envisage cases where the infringer has gained no benefit from his infringement save for the satisfaction of spite fulfilled. In such a case, if infringement was flagrant it appears that the court might award additional damages.' Laddie J acknowledged that these damages could be 'of a punitive nature.'

More recently, the High Court in *Nottinghamshire Healthcare National Health Service Trust v News Group Newspapers Ltd* [2002] EWHC 109 held that additional damages can be awarded under section 97 of the Act in a case of deliberate or reckless infringement. However, additional damages will not be awarded if a successful claimant seeks an account of profits (*Redrow Homes Ltd v Bett Brothers Plc* [1998] HL 22/1/98).

10 Industrial designs

10.01 The law on this subject is complicated involving both UK and European rights. It is not proposed to deal with this matter at length, but merely to warn architects, who may be commissioned to design articles or components capable of mass reproduction, to seek professional advice before entering into any agreement commissioning the design of such articles or components or assigning or licensing the rights therein.

Moreover, any architect who does design such articles or components should seek professional advice as to what steps should be taken to protect them. Industrial design falls mid-way between copyright (not registrable in the UK), which is concerned with 'artistic quality', and patents, which must be registered and are not concerned with artistic quality but with function and method of manufacture. The law on industrial designs was considerably changed by the 1988 Act. The present law is thus contained in the Registered Designs Act 1949 (as amended by the 1988 Act and the Registered Designs Regulations 2001 and 2003) and the 1988 Act.

Registered designs

10.02 A design of any industrial (or handicraft, which includes sculpture) item, part of an item or its ornamentation resulting from features of lines, contours, colours, shape, textures and materials, provided it is new and has individual character, may be registered at the Patent Office under the provisions of the Registered Design Act 1949, as amended by the Registered Designs Regulations 2001 and 2003.

Protection can now be granted to designs irrespective of artistic merit and in the case of European Registered Design for the dimensional designs. Protection is not granted for features of a design that are (inter alia) not new or of individual character, are dictated by their technical function, consist of features which must be reproduced so as to permit the product to fit or connect to another ('must-fit') or conflict with an earlier design application or registration.

It is the design not the article bearing the design that is protected. Therefore, although a registered owner must specify the products to which the design will be applied or incorporated this does not limit the scope of protection, although the monopoly will be in the UK only. Advice on qualification for design registration and protection should be sought from solicitors or patent agents practising in the field of registered design.

10.03 Copyright is a negative right entitling the owner to restrain copying of the work provided the reproduction is not independently evolved. Registration of design is positive and grants to the registered owner the exclusive right to use the design, thereby entitling the owner to restrain reproduction of the design in the UK, regardless of independent creation. For this reason a registration is valid only if the design (or a variation that is wholly insignificant) has not previously been used, published or exhibited anywhere in the world. The proviso (among other express exceptions) is that the earlier design should reasonably have become known in the normal course of business to persons working in the European Economic Area and specialising in the sector concerned.

10.04 Registered design protection lasts for 5 years, on payment of fees, and is renewable up to 25 years. The owner of the registered design would normally be the original author, and therefore the copyright owner as well, but frequently manufacturers who commission a component insist upon the design being registered in their names.

10.05 A design is taken to have been used industrially for the purpose of the Registered Designs Act if it is applied to more than 50 articles.

Design right

10.06 The Act largely abolished copyright protection for most industrial designs although copyright will subsist in the design document in addition strengthened the registered design system, introduced a new unregistered right called 'design right'. 'Design' means the design of any aspect of the shape or configuration (whether internal or external) of the whole or part of an article.

The design must be original in the copyright sense and also in the sense that it is not commonplace in the relevant design field. Originality in the copyright sense has already been considered in detail but in addition the design itself must not be commonplace. One of the leading cases in this area is *Ocular Sciences Ltd v Aspect Vision Care Ltd* [1997] RPC 289 which decided that the word 'commonplace' requires an objective assessment and is likely to cover 'any design which is trite, trivial, common-or-garden, hackneyed or of the type which would excite no peculiar attention in those in the relevant art'. The general rule (*Farmers Build Ltd v Carier Bulk Materials Handling Ltd* [1999] RPC 461 (CA)) to determine if a particular design is commonplace is whether, from the perspective of the ultimate consumer, at the time of creation the features of design are reproduced in the design of similar articles. The closer the similarity in features the more likely the design in question is 'commonplace'.

It should be noted that design right does not subsist in a method or principle of construction, nor does it subsist in surface decoration. Moreover, it does not subsist in features of shape or configuration of an article which enables the article to be connected to, or placed in, around or against, another article so that either article may perform its function; nor must it be dependent upon the appearance of another article of which the article is intended by the designer to be an integral part. This means that designs of spare parts are normally excluded from design right protection. Because design right subsists additionally to and does not replace artistic copyright, the exclusions from design right protection do not remove artistic copyright protection from, for example, surface decoration.

Design right does not subsist unless and until the design has been recorded in a design document or an article has been made to the design.

Design right expires 15 years from the end of the calendar year in which the design was first recorded in a design document or an article was made to the design. Alternatively, if articles made to the design are made available for sale or hire within 5 years from the end of that calendar year, the design right will expire 10 years from the end of the calendar year in which that first occurred. In the last 5 years of design right protection licences for the exploitation of the design must be granted (licences of right) if requested.

To qualify for design right protection the requirements set out in sections 217 to 221 of the Act must be met: these are too detailed to be set out here but have similarity to the qualification requirements described in section 3 above. However, the differences are such that reference must be made to the actual sections.

10.07 As for copyright protection, design right enables the owner to prevent unauthorised copying and other infringements. The test for infringement of design right was differentiated from the copyright test in *Woolley Jewellers Ltd v A& A Jewellery Ltd* [2002] EWCA Civ. 1119: 'There is a difference between an enquiry into whether the item copied forms a substantial part of the copyright work and an inquiry into whether the whole design containing the element copied is substantially the same design as that which enjoys design right protection.' Arden LJ went on to conclude that: 'It may not be enough to copy a part or even a substantial part. Regard has to be had to the overall design which enjoys design right.'

The provisions of the Act ensure that a claimant cannot succeed in both copyright and design right infringement claims in respect of the same acts of infringement.

Community designs

10.08 The Community Design Regulation came into force on 6 March 2002. It created the following additional European Community-wide protection for UK designs:

(a) Registered Community Designs – registration of qualifying designs entitles the owner to a monopoly against use of that design throughout the EU for a maximum of 25 years from filing. The registration process is equivalent to the UK system and can be organised via the UK Patent Office or direct with the Office of Harmonization in the Internal Market in Alicante;

(b) Unregistered Community Designs – qualifying designs automatically receive EU wide protection against copying lasting 3 years from the first public disclosure of the design in the EU.

The rules relating to the qualification for both unregistered and registered Community designs are equivalent to the rules for UK registered designs, as outlined in paragraphs 10.02 to 10.05 above. This differentiates the protection granted by virtue of the UK unregistered design right with the rights granted by the Community unregistered design right (see paragraph 10.06 above).

11 Moral rights

11.01 Moral rights of authors have existed in all continental European legal systems for many years, but the 1988 Act introduced them to UK law for the first time.

11.02 There are four basic categories of moral rights contained in the Act:

1 the right to be identified as author;
2 the right to object to derogatory treatment of work;
3 false attribution of work;
4 the right of privacy of certain photographs and films.

11.03 Under section 77(4)(c) of the Act the author of a work of architecture in the form of a building or a model for a building, has the right to be identified whenever copies of a graphic work representing it, or of a photograph of it, are issued to the public.

Section 77(5) also provides that the author of a work of architecture in the form of a building also has the right to be identified on the building as constructed, or, where more than one building is constructed to the design, on the first to be constructed.

The right must be asserted by the author on any assignment of copyright in the work or by instrument in writing signed by the author. In the case of the public exhibition as an artistic work (for example, the inclusion of a model of a building in an exhibition), the right can be asserted by identifying the author on the original or copy of the work, or on a frame, mount or other thing to which the work is attached. If the author grants a licence to make copies of the work, then the right can be asserted for exhibitions by providing in the licence that the author must be identified on copies which are publicly exhibited.

There are certain exceptions to the right of which the most important is that it does not apply to works originally vested in the author's employer (see paragraph 5.02).

11.04 The author of a literary, dramatic, musical or artistic work has the right to object to his work being subjected to derogatory treatment. 'Treatment' means any addition to, deletion from or alteration to or adaptation of the work. The treatment is derogatory if it amounts to distortion or mutilation of the work or is otherwise prejudicial to the honour or reputation of the author.

The right in an artistic work is infringed by the commercial publication or exhibition in public of a derogatory treatment of the work, or a broadcast or the inclusion in a cable programme service of a visual image of a derogatory treatment of the work.

In the case of a work of architecture in the form of a model of a building the right is infringed by issuing copies of a graphic work representing, or of a photograph of, a derogatory treatment of the work.

However, and most importantly, the right is not infringed in the case of a work of architecture in the form of a building. But if a building is the subject of derogatory treatment, the architect is entitled to have his identification on the building as its architect removed.

In the case of works which vested originally in the author's employer, the right does not apply.

11.05 In the case of a literary, dramatic, musical or artistic work, a person has the right not to have its authorship falsely attributed to him. Thus an architect can prevent a building which he has not designed being attributed to him as its architect.

11.06 The right to privacy of certain films and photographs applies only to films and photographs commissioned for private and domestic purposes and accordingly is hardly relevant here.

11.07 The rights to be identified as an author of a work and to object to derogatory treatment of a work subsist as long as copyright subsists in the work. The right to prevent false attribution continues to subsist until 20 years after a person's death.

11.08 Moral rights can be waived by an instrument in writing signed by the person entitled to the right. However, moral rights may not be assigned to a third party although they pass on death as part of the author's estate and can be disposed of by his will.

12 Law of copyright in Scotland

12.01 There is no difference between the law of copyright in Scotland and England and the Copyright, Designs and Patents Act 1988 applies equally to both countries with the exception of sections 287 and 292 (which deal with Patents County Courts) and Schedule 6 (which makes specific provisions for the Hospital for Sick Children), all of which apply only to England. The power to legislate on intellectual property in Scotland is reserved to the UK Parliament in terms of the Scotland Act 1998.

35

Architects and the law of employment

RUTH DOWNING

1 Introduction

In approaching the task of revising this chapter for the last edition, from the original work of Sir Patrick Elias I noted that in its original form and layout it reflected a time when the concept of 'employment law' meant as much the law governing the relations of large trades unions and employers as the, then nascent concepts of redundancy and unfair dismissal and the newly created industrial tribunals. I noted also that in the original form, equal importance had been given to the law on collective labour relations as to individual rights. The common law governing individual rights were similarly holding their own against the statutory creations of unfair dismissal and sex and race discrimination. Passing references were made to the (potential) effect of European legislation on domestic law!. If for no reason other than that European Directives have been the major factor in the increase in employment legislation, substantial additions to the chapter were plainly necessary. The chapter was for example silent on matters of great significance such as the Disability Discrimination Act 1995 which plainly called for inclusion. There has been no let up in the volume and scope of changes which have been brought, principally to reflect the European influence, and this revision seeks to include a summary of those changes. Age discrimination is now in force, there have been amendments to the Disability Discrimination Act to name but two issues which needed to be added.

Conscious that this chapter serves to inform architects of the basic law which affects them as employers within their own practices and should serve to inform them of the necessity of seeking expert advice I have still endeavoured to maintain something of the original format, whilst alerting the reader to the enormously wider protection enjoyed by their employees.

2 Sources and institutions

2.01 Although the law of employment is a mixture of the rules developed by the common law (see Chapter 1) and those laid down by Parliament, the latter is now by far the predominant source. The domestic legislation is now further fuelled by the requirement to fulfil our obligations to Europe on social policies and matters of equality, and the effect of these Directives will be seen in the rights created by the Act of Parliament or Regulations.

2.02 The basic division which can still be drawn is between individual employment law, which is concerned with the relations between employer and employee, and the collective labour relations law, which regulates the relationship between employers and trade unions (TUs).

2.03 The basic relationship between the employer and the individual worker is defined by the contract of employment. This is the starting point for determining the rights and liabilities of parties. But as we shall see below, the last 30 years have seen the emergence of a whole range of statutory rights relating to such matters as unfair dismissal, redundancy, and maternity rights. Furthermore, it is a fundamental principle that, save in certain very exceptional cases, it is not open to the parties to contract out of these rights. They provide what is sometimes called *a floor of rights*, below which the rights of employees cannot sink. Although these rights originated in different statutes, they were first consolidated in 1978 and are now to be found in the Employment Rights Act 1996, together with the Employment Relations Act 1999, the Employment Act 2002 and those parts of the anti-discrimination laws which relate specifically to the workplace.

2.04 It will probably be widely known that the enforcement of the individual rights of unfair dismissal and discrimination are enforced in the employment tribunal (originally the *industrial* tribunal) the composition of which is a legally qualified chairman (now accorded the title of 'employment judge') and two lay wing members. These are nominated by the TUC and the CBI. The aim of the tribunal was always to discourage legal representation by the absence of a costs regime and by the informality of the system. The original idea was rather to see the representation of the applicant by the TU representatives and the employer by a member of the personnel staff. That is not the present situation and although many applicants and respondents do present their own cases, the complexity of the law as it has developed and the potential value of the claims, both in monetary and publicity terms, has made the presence of lawyers by far the norm.

2.05 Two further points about these tribunal hearings are worth noting. First, in most cases which go to the tribunals (notably unfair dismissals and those where discrimination is alleged) a conciliation officer seeks to bring about a settlement of the case before it is heard by the tribunal. These officers are employed by the Advisory, Conciliation and Arbitration Service (ACAS), and, like the tribunals themselves, they are to be found throughout the country. They have no power to compel anyone to discuss the case with them. But it is often advisable to do so, because a settlement can save both publicity and the costs of the action.

The second point to note about the tribunals system is that there is an appeal from the industrial tribunal, but only on a point of law, to the Employment Appeal Tribunal (EAT). Findings of fact in the Employment Tribunal cannot be interfered with by the EAT unless they are clearly perverse or cannot on any view be justified by the evidence. The EAT is technically a branch of the High Court (see Chapter 1) but is differently constituted, consisting of a judge and two others with experience in industrial relations, rather than a single judge alone accompanied by two wing members. Appeals from the EAT then go to the Court of Appeal, and any final appeal is to the House of Lords.

2.06 As has been noted, the Employment Tribunals are constituted to administer rights created by Parliament and imposed upon the relationship of employer/employee. These rights are quite separate from those rights which are created by the parties themselves and enshrined in their contract. Until 1994 an employee who wished to bring a contractual claim, for instance for wrongful dismissal, was obliged to take that type of claim to a court – either the High Court or a county court. In 1994 tribunals were empowered to hear claims in contract for damages arising from breach of the contract of employment, or failure to pay sums due under the contract. There is a limit of £25 000 on what the tribunal can award on such a contractual claim. Claims can only be brought on the termination of the contract. The tribunal has no power to hear cases based upon a claim for damages for personal injuries sustained in the course of employment.

Collective labour relations law

2.07 The law regulating collective labour relations is still significantly the law of the jungle, being a power relationship. However, the law does regulate this relationship in various ways. First, it sets limits to the industrial sanctions which can lawfully be used by the parties. This area of the law is highly complex, and it is not considered further in this chapter. Second, the state provides conciliation and arbitration services (ACAS) to help promote the peaceful settlement of disputes. Finally, various rights are given to recognised trade unions, i.e. those which have been recognised by employers, and also to the officials and members of recognised trade unions (see Section 5).

3 The contract of employment

3.01 Every worker has a contract with his employer. But a distinction is drawn in law between employees and independent contractors. The former are integrated into the organisation of the business, and work under what is termed a contract *of service*. In contrast, the latter perform a specific function and are usually in business on their own account – e.g. the plumber or window cleaner – and work under a contract *for services*. In borderline cases the distinction is often very difficult to draw. Also, the description which the parties choose to place on their status is not decisive, though it will be a factor to consider in a marginal case. The main importance of the distinction in the field of employment law is that only employees working under a contract of service are eligible to benefit from most of the statutory rights, e.g. unfair dismissal, redundancy, and maternity. In addition, an employer may be vicariously liable for the torts committed by his employees, but only rarely for those of independent contractors (see Chapter 3).

3.02 The test of whether an individual is indeed an employee has gone through various fashions, e.g. the 'control test', the 'organisational test'. A continuing theme through all such tests has been the requirement that an employee renders the service *personally*, i.e. no substitute can be sent along by a true employee to perform the work required.

  Of the various tests which the courts have applied over the years to try and establish this critical identity, one which has stood the test of time is that set out in *Ready Mixed Concrete (South East) Ltd v Minister of Pensions* [1968] 2 QB 497. It posed three questions

1 Did the worker undertake to provide his own work and skill in return for remuneration?
2 Was there a sufficient degree of control to enable the worker fairly to be called an employee?
3 Were there any other factors inconsistent with the existence of a contract of employment?

This has come to be termed the 'multiple test'. The emphasis on different aspects of the three part test have perhaps shifted over the years and a more recent addition to the tests has been the concept of mutuality of obligation. This looks at the irreducible requirement of the employer to provide work and the corresponding personal obligation of the employee to perform it. All aspects continue to be useful tools to answer the critical question. A helpful point may be to remember that policy certainly suggests that an individual who *could* be a servant *should* be one unless there is some good reason for holding otherwise.

  That maxim has not, however, been very evident in the handling of the issue of agency workers or 'temps'. Three possible scenarios exist: that the agency workers supplied to the end client is employed by the placement agency; that they are employed by the end client; or that they are employed by neither. The cogent reasons why the worker should be found to be someone's employee were reflected in a series of decisions starting with *Montgomery v Johnson Underwood Ltd* [2001] IRLR 269 where the EAT held that the long-term nature of Ms Montgomery's relationship with her agency established the relationship of employee/employer between them. The Court of Appeal reversed this and like decisions on the ground that there was no *control* at all present in the relationship, while noting the obvious need to afford agency workers some protection.

  The possibility that the worker would enjoy protection by being the employee of the end user was the subject of *Brook Street Bureau v Dacas* [2004] IRLR 358. Six years work for the same local authority raised, in the Court of Appeal's mind at least, the possibility of an implied contract of employment. The matter was next considered and guidance given by the EAT in *James v LB of Greenwich* [2006] IRLR 168 where a restrictive approach was adopted. The key question was whether it was *necessary* in any particular case to find an employment contract. The Court of Appeal giving its judgement in this case at [2008] IRLR 302 and indeed in other similarly decided has underlined the point that such a contract will only be regarded as being necessary if the relationship can *only* be explained in this way. That will not depend upon length of service or integration into the client's workforce, and it is likely only to arise if the agency relationship is thought to be a sham or the worker and client have plainly negotiated and agreed on terms and conditions direct.

  Thus the practical result for companies who use employment agencies to supply staff is that bona fide arrangements with such agencies for the supply of staff, however long that arrangement goes on, is unlikely to fix them with employment obligations vis-à-vis those workers.

3.03 The National Minimum Wage Act 1998 has introduced a further concept; that of a 'worker'. The term is also used in a number of regulations granting social rights. It is far wider than that of employee and will effectively cover many of those persons who hitherto fell short of the definition while bearing the description and characteristics of independent contractor rather uneasily.

Creating the contract: control of recruitment

3.04 The basic principle is that the contract of employment is a voluntary agreement. This means that the employer can choose both with whom he will contract and the terms on which he is willing to contract. However, statute law has curbed this freedom in a number of ways. In relation to recruitment the employer can chose to employ whomsoever he likes, provided he does not refuse to recruit a person on grounds of their sex, sexual orientation, marital status, pregnancy, race, colour, ethnic or national origins, nationality, religion, age, disability or TU membership or activities. In addition the recruitment must not be offered on terms which may amount to indirect discrimination on any of the above grounds. Thus setting an upper age limit for applicants, even before the coming into force of the law on age discrimination would nearly always be to the detriment of a considerably larger proportion of women than men because more women than men are likely to be later starters in the employment field and thus less able to comply with an age requirement or the experience which went with it, and accordingly indirectly discriminatory.

The interview

3.05 An employee being interviewed is under no obligation gratuitously to disclose details of his past. However, he must not misrepresent it, save that in certain exceptional cases he may lawfully be able to deny that he has committed any criminal offences if his convictions are 'spent convictions' within the meaning of the Rehabilitation of Offenders Act 1974. Whether or not a conviction is spent depends upon the nature of the offence and the period since the conviction. Note that subsequent enactments to ensure the protection of vulnerable groups such as children and the requirements for many contractors to undergo criminal record bureau checks before being accepted for contracts where they will have contact with children has removed the blanket nature of the ROA. It is therefore no longer possible to say with any certainty that a candidate for employment can rely upon its provisions and employers will need to check in any given situation whether they are not only permitted but obliged to seek such information.

The terms of contract

3.06 The basic position, consistent with the notion of freedom of contract, is that it is up to the parties to agree to the terms which will bind them. Exceptionally, terms of the agreement may be struck out as being contrary to public policy, e.g. a term in unreasonable restraint of trade (see paragraph 4.32). But generally the parties will be held to their bargain. From an employer's point of view it is sensible for all the important terms of the contract to be committed to paper and for the job to be conditional on their acceptance. This may eliminate later confusion and disagreements.

3.07 However, in the sphere of employment law the contract is not always expressly stipulated in this way. A number of points need to be noted. First, in many situations there is no real bargaining between individuals at all. The terms of employment may have been agreed between the employer and a recognised trade union negotiating collective agreements, and variations in those terms occur as the collective agreements are amended from time to time. Then the collective agreement operates as the source of the terms of the individual contract of employment. Second, once a contract of employment is agreed, the employer has a statutory obligation to provide the employee with a written statement of the particulars of his contract, and he must do this within 2 months of the employee commencing employment. Third, even where terms are expressly agreed between the parties to the contract and contained in the written particulars, they will rarely cover all the matters that will arise in the course of the employment relationship. So the express terms will have to be supplemented by implied terms. These implied terms may be usefully divided into two categories. Some will arise because of the particular relationship between the employer and the employee, and will often depend upon the customs and practices of a particular firm. For example, it may have become the practice for overtime to be worked in certain circumstances, or for employees to be more flexible in the range of tasks they perform than their specific job obligations would suggest. Once practices of this kind become reasonable, well known, and certain, they will become contractual duties. Other implied terms depend not so much on the particular employment relationship but are imposed as an incident of the general relationship between employers and employees. The judges have said that certain duties will be implied into all employment relationships, e.g. a duty on the employee not to disclose confidential information to third parties, to take reasonable care in the exercise of his duties, and to show good faith in his dealings with the employer. Likewise there are some implied duties imposed on the employer, e.g. a duty to treat the employee with respect, to take reasonable care for his health and safety, and not to act in such a way as to undermine the trust and confidence on which the contract of employment is based. This last implied term has proved of particular importance in the field of constructive dismissal (see Section 4, paragraph 4.05 below).

Equal Pay Act 1970

3.08 Although equal pay is plainly an equal opportunity issue, (see Section below) it fits into the scheme of considering the contract of employment because the legal framework is contractual, i.e. it works by importing into every contract of an equality clause. The Equal Pay Act 1970, came into force at the end of 1975. Strictly it is a misnomer, for it covers not merely pay but also all contractual terms and conditions of employment. Broadly it states that if a woman is employed on like work with a man (and this involves looking at what they actually do, and not what they might be required to do under their contracts) or on work which is rated as equivalent on a job evaluation scheme, then she is entitled to have the same terms and conditions applied to her as apply to him. An equality clause automatically becomes part of her contract of employment, except that it will not operate where there are differences which stem from 'a material factor that is not the difference of sex'. That difference must be objectively justifiable and what amounts to objective is that it should be 'reasonably necessary'. It must also be 'significant and relevant'. It was noted in *Cadman v HSE* [2004] IRLR 971 that there is a significant difference between what is 'reasonably necessary' and 'necessary'. The latter would require an employer to show that it was the only course open to him whereas the 'reasonably' imports a degree of choice among a range of possible options which may all justify a pay differential. If the 'material factor' cannot be justified then it ceases to be a '*material factor*'.

3.09 However, if the woman is not employed on like work, she cannot complain under the Act because she considers that the differential between the respective rates of pay is too great. Indeed, in one case a woman who was a leader of a group of adventure playground workers was paid less than one of the men in the group. But the EAT held that since her job was more responsible than the man's, this meant that it was not like work, and consequently she could not claim the same pay (*Waddington v Leicester Council for Voluntary Services* [1977] 2 All ER 633)!

3.10 The original legislation has been amended on several occasions, principally to reflect the need to bring the Act into line with the European Directive on equal pay. Thus the time limit for enforcing a claim was extended in 2003, so that a finding in a claimant's favour can result in an award of arrears of 6 years. If the employer has concealed facts material to the claim the 6-year period will run only from the date of discovery of the relevant facts. In amending regulations in 2004 the tribunals were granted the power to decide the question of 'equal value' by themselves without the need to commission an independent expert report. Finally, the concept of indirect discrimination has been imported into equal pay so that where pay is determined by the application of an apparently neutral criterion or practice which in fact disadvantages a substantially higher proportion of women, unless that practice can be justified objectively by factors unrelated to sex, then the pay will be unlawful.

Statement of the main terms of the contract

3.11 The sources of the contract of employment are so diverse that Parliament in 1963 thought it desirable that the employer should give to the employee a written statement of the principal terms. The position is now governed by the sections 1 to 7 of the Employment Relations Act 1996 and provides a comprehensive code. In particular there are certain details which must be provided in a 'principal statement' and then some which may be added later in the supplementary statements. It was hitherto the law that the obligation could be fulfilled by referring the employee to other documents to ascertain these details. There is now a very limited power for the employer to refer the employee on in this way but he can do so for matters such as sick pay and pension. What the first and principal statement must contain are details of: pay, intervals at which payment will be made and hours of work. Thereafter he may give additional statements regarding grievance and disciplinary procedures, and holidays. Any changes in the terms must be notified in writing within a month of the changes happening.

3.12 However, if the employer does in fact draw up a proper written contract, this will be binding upon the employee, provided he accepts it as such. If the contract contains all the information that would have to be put in the written particulars, the latter can be dispensed with.

4 Equal opportunities

4.01 Anti-discrimination law, or what hereafter will be termed generically as 'Equal Opportunities' now plays such a far-reaching part in not just the recruitment of staff but their daily relations within the workplace and their evolving rights that it is necessary that the issue has accorded its own section. It must also be observed that it is the issues of sex, race and disability that now form such a huge part of the work of the employment tribunals that employers should be aware of the complexities of the issue. Just as the acts govern the recruitment or dismissal of staff they create and protect ongoing rights to the treatment at work, both in the promotion and the advancement of staff but also in the relations between staff and management. Claims under all these legislation can be brought during the currency of employment and the potentially destructive effect of litigation between parties who continue to work together on a daily basis during and after the hearing of such claims can readily be imagined. Compensation for all types of discrimination is uncapped and the tribunals have now recorded their first multi-million pounds awards. As an illustration of the way in which the legislation affects every stage of the employment from recruitment through to termination the Disability Discrimination Act serves as a useful illustration.

Disability Discrimination Act 1995

4.02 Many practices will be aware of the legislation from the professional involvement in the designing and adaptation of premises. From the employment lawyers' point of view it is perhaps best to bear in mind that the tribunals are rarely troubled by claims that there is no wheelchair access or that the doors are too narrow. Indeed, many of the claims made involve applicants whose disability is not physical in origin; see for example, the leading case on the definition of disability *Goodwin v The Patent Office* [1999] IRLR 4, where the applicant was a paranoid schizophrenic. A significant number of claims involve stress-related illnesses such as depression, and statistics on the initial years of the Act reveal that back and neck problems are the most common disabilities relied upon thus far.

4.03 A person is disabled within the meaning of the Disability Discrimination Act (DDA) if they have a physical or mental impairment which has a substantial and long-term adverse effect on their ability to carry out normal day-to-day activities. The first matter of note is that the seemingly easy phrase 'normal day-to-day activities' is itself defined by the statute. In Schedule 1 to the Act it makes clear that the impairment will only be taken to affect this ability if it affects one of a list of eight faculties; e.g., mobility, visual senses, cognitive powers, physical strength and dexterity, and the perception of physical danger. Thus it is a two-stage process: does this man's impairment, e.g. loss of an eye, affect his ability to perform the day-to-day activities (e.g. reading). That is an impairment, but is it substantial? Or at least more than trivial? Guidance notes appended to the DDA give examples which will fall on each side of the line and reward attention if attempting to decide if someone is indeed disabled. An inability to climb stairs would be a disability of mobility, but not if the same person could not travel in comfort in a car for more than 2 hours. An inability to carry a tray of food would be a disability but not if the only problem was not being able to carry heavy luggage. Note also that the concept of the day-to-day activities excludes the ability to do any particular job, i.e. it is not relevant that the blind man cannot type at the same speed as a sighted man. It is also not relevant whether the disability impacts on particular hobbies or sports. Note also that

some statutory presumptions of disability have been grafted onto the original Act. Since December 2005 a person with cancer, multiple sclerosis or HIV is deemed to be disabled whether or not they otherwise fulfil the statutory criteria or matters such as the length of time that the disability has or will last or more pertinently the effect on normal day-to-day activities.

4.04 There are essentially three ways in which a person can be discriminated against on the ground of their disbility, as now set out amended section 3A DDA 1995.

1 Direct discrimination (section 3A(5)) – this is less favourable treatment on the ground of that person's disability. The test for that less favourable treatment is by reference to how the employer would treat a person not having that particular disability but whose other relevant circumstances, including abilities, are the same as, or not materially different from, those of the disabled person.
2 Discrimination taking the form of less favourable treatment for a disability-related reason (section 3A(1) and (5)).
3 Discrimination taking the form of a failure to comply with a duty to make reasonable adjustments imposed on him with regards the disabled person (section 3A(2)).

The differences between the way in which an employee makes out their claim and the defences which relate to the three heads are briefly set out here. It is however another branch of equal opportunities legislation that continues to develop and to become more complex.

Direct discrimination

It is unlawful to give less favourable treatment to a person on grounds of their disability if the employer would not treat another person who did not have the disability but whose circumstances were not materially different to those of the disabled person. Since the comparison can be with a real or hypothetical comparator it is more difficult for an employee to make out this type of discrimination as this illustration shows. *High Quality Life Styles Ltd v Watts* [2006] IRLR 850 concerned an HIV-positive care worker who was dismissed from his job working with adults with learning difficulties when he revealed his medical condition. Since those in his care exhibited behaviour which included biting and scratching, any injury to him of this nature laid his charges open to a risk of infection by him. Held not discrimination because any employee who had an attribute with the potential to pass on a similarly serious and harmful infection or other injury would also have been refused employment. It is not open to an employer to seek to justify direct discrimination so that if the comparison argument fails there is no further defence available.

There is also important new law in this field, in the form of 'associative discrimination', that is where the less favourable treatment is experienced not by the disabled person but some connected person. In *Coleman v Attridge Law* [2008] IRLR 722 the complainant was the mother of, and principal carer for, a severely disabled child. Difficulties over her need for time off work led her to accept redundancy but then to claim unfair (constructive) dismissal. The ECJ has now held that this was indeed discrimination on grounds of a person's disability (just that the disabled person was not the same as the person suffering the less favourable treatment). In doing so it echoes the situation in race discrimination where, for example, a white person is refused entry to a club because he is with a black person who is barred on the ground of his colour, which has been accepted law for many years. However, the ECJ did not go as far as saying that there should be positive discrimination in favour of such a class of people, so that no obligations to make reasonable adjustments will arise. Note that the effects of this judgment are likely to be applicable to age discrimination as well.

Disability-related reason

An example of such discrimination might be where the employee is refused employment not because he is wheelchair bound per se but because the employer believes that it will obstruct the office unreasonably.

The House of Lords has recently affirmed the view that this form of discrimination, also depends on a comparative approach, ending a controversy that has existed since the decision in *Clark v TDG Ltd t/a Novacold* [1999] IRLR 318. After that decision the *causal* test was held to be the correct one i.e. the only question was whether the employee had been treated less favourably by reason of his disability. Thus to take a not uncommon example, if a disabled person required extensive periods off work to attend treatment and was dismissed as a result it was not open to the employer to argue that he would have dismissed an able bodied person who required a like amount of time off for a reason unconnected to any disability. However, in *LB of Lewisham v Malcolm* [2008] IRLR 700 (a case about housing but accepted as being equally applicable to employment law), the House of Lords has reverted to a *comparative* test. Thus the correct question is whether the employer would have treated a person with a disability the same as one without in like circumstances. In *Malcolm* a schizophrenic tenant had illegally sublet his tenancy, blaming his actions upon his mental condition. It was accepted that any tenant who sublet in this way would have been evicted. Accepting, as the tribunal did, that Mr Malcolm would not have acted as he did except for his mental condition would under the *causal* test have been sufficient to give him the protection of the DDA. Under the *comparative* test, no such protection will now exist.

A defence of justification is available to a finding of disability-related discrimination (but not if the less favourable treatment arises in the course of direct discrimination). The justification must be both 'material to the circumstances of the particular case and substantial'. The concept of justification is familiar in equal opportunity legislation but whereas it is usually prefaced by the need to be 'objectively' justified, no such qualification is required here. Rather it is sufficient that it falls within a band of what a reasonable employer would do. Thus there is much less opportunity for the tribunal to interfere with the employer's justification of his conduct.

Failure to make reasonable adjustments

The obligation to take positive steps to make it possible for a disabled person to overcome their disabilities is a cornerstone of the legislation. The importance of that has been underlined by the recent amendment of the DDA which removes the employer's right under section 5(2)(b) to argue that he had a good reason for not making adjustments. The only defence now available in this respect is by the amended section 3A(6). If the discrimination is disability-related and the tribunal has found that a duty to make reasonable adjustments had arisen then the employer can only justify a failure to do so under section 3A(6) if he can show that the treatment would have been justified *even if* he had complied with the obligation to make reasonable adjustments under section 4A(l).

Thus an employer who refuses employment to a secretary with arthritic wrists because she fails the typing speed test but who did not provide to her an adapted keyboard (i.e. a reasonable adjustment) on which to take the test, can justify his refusal to employ her only if he can also show that the provision of such a keyboard would have made no difference, i.e. because she would still not have been able to achieve the required speed.

Sex discrimination

4.05 The scope of sex and race discrimination legislation covers not merely recruitment to employment but also promotion and any other non-contractual aspects of employment. For example, if the employer gives certain benefits, e.g. cheap loans or mortgages, or training opportunities, he cannot grant these on a discriminatory basis. The general comments on recruitment made above hold good. Recruitment cannot be refused because of the sex of the candidate. Conditions that impact more on women may be indirectly discriminatory; examples would be the requirement to work full time, to work in the office all the time, etc.

4.06 Exceptionally, sex discrimination is permitted where it is a genuine occupational qualification, for example on the grounds of physiology or decency. The most relevant permissible discrimination for architects is where a job is given in the UK, but it requires duties to be performed in a country whose laws and customs are such that a woman could not effectively carry out the task. Even then, it must be necessary for the employer to discriminate for this reason. So if he already employs a sufficient number of male architects to cater adequately for that particular foreign connection, this exception will not apply. Advertisements for job vacancies also need careful drafting to avoid any suggestion of unlawful discrimination.

4.07 Those who consider they have been discriminated against may complain to an employment tribunal. If the complaint is successful, the tribunal may award a declaration of the rights of the parties, an order requiring the employer to take such action as is necessary to obviate the adverse effects of the discrimination, or compensation which may include compensation for injured feelings. It is only the legal employer who is normally liable, even though the discriminatory acts are in fact done by a subordinate member of staff. The employer is however deemed to be liable for such actions unless he can show that he has taken all reasonably practical steps to eliminate the discrimination, e.g. has a clear policy and monitors it, then he is entitled to a statutory defence and will escape liability. In that case, the particular members of staff who actually committed the acts of discrimination will be personally liable. This is one reason why, although only the employer can discriminate against an employee other named memebers of staff are joined as respondents.

4.08 For many women sex discrimination in the workplace has been synonymous with *harassment*, or the inappropriate and unwelcome attention of male colleagues. Strangely, the SDA as originally drafted contained no mention of harassment as a form of discrimination. The only means of complaining was to show that the treatment meted out by an amorous colleague would not have been shown to a male employee and thus the less favourable treatment was done on the ground of sex. This has now been obviated by the amending section 4A of the SDA which contains a definition of harassment as 'unwanted conduct which has the effect of violating that person's dignity, or creating an intimidating, hostile, degrading, humiliating or offensive environment for her'. The conduct can be verbal or physical and the section creates two distinct forms of harassment, sexual (section 4A(ii) and non-sexual section 4A(i)). It is therefore no defence for the harasser to say that his conduct is sexually neutral; it is sufficient if it creates the environment as set out in the section.

Since the scheme of the SDA was based on the complainant's ability to show a difference of treatment based on sex and not sexual orientation, the SDA did not as originally drafted protect gay people who were treated differently, harassed or abused by reason of that sexual identity. The House of Lords decision in 2003 on a long running and high profile case about the position of gay servicemen was that the Act did not protect such claimants and that a change to the legislation would be necessary to effect any such change. The situation was changed with the Employers Equality (Sexual Orientation) Regulations 2002 which has since December 2003 made such discrimination unlawful.

Race Relations Act 1976

4.09 It is also unlawful, under the Race Relations Act 1976, to discriminate on grounds of race, colour, ethnic or national origins, or nationality in respect of the terms of employment. As with sex discrimination, there is no upper limit on the compensation which may be awarded.

It was long the case that the Race Relations Act (RRA) did not protect against discrimination on the grounds of religion. The *Employer Equality (Religion or Belief) Regulations 2003*, which came into force in December 2003, now make it unlawful to discriminate on grounds relating to the religious persuasion or belief of employees. There is however an exemption under regulation 7 (3) if a particular religious belief is a 'genuine and determining occupational requirement' or the employer has 'an ethos' based upon a particular religion or belief which means that being of that particular religion or belief is a genuine occupational requirement. Plainly, being a member of the Church of England is a requirement for employment as a vicar but the exception is limited so that a local education authority was held to be wrong to refuse to employ a non-Roman Catholic teacher to appointment in an authority maintained RC school because an education authority cannot have a particular religious ethos, albeit that the school plainly did.

Age discrimination

4.10 Discrimination on the ground of age has been unlawful since October 2006. In common with the now familiar structure of equal opportunities legislation this encompasses direct, indirect, instructions to discriminate, harassment and victimisation. Direct discrimination occurs when a person is treated less favourably on grounds of age. Uniquely in the equal opportunities legislation it is possible to justify treatment done *directly* on the ground of age, provided such treatment is 'objectively and reasonably justified by a legitimate aim including legitimate employment policy, labour market and vocational training objectives, and if the means of achieving the aim are appropriate and necessary'. Since justification necessarily legitimises proven discrimination the reasons for it must be cogent. Guidance is given in Article 6 of the Framework Directive, although no illustrative examples are given in the Age regulations themselves. The objectives include the fixing of maximum age recruitment based on the training requirements of the post or the needs for a reasonable period of employment before retirement. Conversely, the fixing of minimum conditions of age, professional experience or seniority in service for access to employment are also potentially justifiable criteria. However the whole issue is subject to a 'long-stop', namely that where the applicant's age is already greater than the prospective employers' normal retirement age, or if he has none, the age of 65 or if within 6 months of application he would reach that normal retirement age or 65, then the employer does not discriminate in refusing the applicant employment.

Maternity, parental and family-related rights

4.11 All employees are now entitled to a 26-week period of Ordinary Maternity Leave (OML). In addition those who have 26 weeks employment at a date before the 15th week before the Expected Week of Childbirth (EWC) is entitled to another 26 weeks Additional Maternity Leave (AML). All terms and conditions, apart from the obligation to pay salary, remain in force. The employee is also entitled to Statuary Maternity Pay for the duration of their respective leave. It is paid at the rate of 90% of the employee's wages, subject to the current maximum of £123 per week. A detailed consideration of the benefits' position is outside the scope of this work.

Proper notification must be given of the intention to take maternity leave and to return. In the former case it must be in writing, given no later than the 15th week before the EWC and request the starting date of the leave, which must not be earlier than 11 weeks before the EWC. The employer should then respond, within 28 days, giving the date for the ending of the leave and the return to work. Changes to that must also be notified. Exercise of the right to return notice must also be given in writing.

The timings are important, the rights new and extended, and the potential for suspicion and misunderstanding between employer and employee rife. It is imperative that guidance is taken before dealing with these rights. A failure to permit a return to work is automatically unfair and special rules apply to the situation when a redundancy arises in the absence of the employee. The matter is one which requires expert assistance to avoid problems,

particularly if health problems delay the employee's ability to return to work on the originally appointed day.

3.12 New rights to reflect the government's commitment to 'family-friendly policies' should also be noted. Two new Regulations and an amendment to the ERA 1996 have introduced the right to time off work to assist with children and dependants. The *Paternity and Adoption Leave Regulations 2002* give a right to 2 weeks leave to the father of a child, which includes the partner of the mother or any person which will have responsibility for the child's upbringing. Same sex couples enjoy the same rights; 26 weeks employment is the prerequisite for the leave. The adoptive parents of a child have the similar right in respect of a newly placed child. An adoption that regularises the position of an existing child, e.g. where the natural mother and new partner adopt her child is not covered.

The *Maternity and Parental Leave Regulations 1999* also create rights in respect of older children, up to the age of 5 years (or 18 years if the child is disabled). The employee must have worked for 1 year to acquire the rights and may claim a maximum of 13 weeks leave in respect of any one child (i.e. 26 weeks for twins) and 18 weeks if the child is disabled. The request must be made 21 days in advance of the time to be taken and it is unpaid (unless the employer wishes to implement more advantageous rights). Refusal of rights can lead to a complaint to the employment tribunal. For the emergencies that family life throws up and which cannot be anticipated 21 days in advance Section 57(A) ERA 1996 has created the right for unpaid dependants' leave. This is intended to deal with illness, injury or death or less dramatically if existing arrangements for care have fallen through. The time limit for the leave is unspecified, simply what is *reasonable*. A *dependant* is widely defined as somebody in the same household, but does not include lodgers, tenants, au pairs, etc.

Finally, as noted above the early cases law on indirect discrimination centred on the requirement for full-time working which frequently impacted on mothers. The social trend towards job shares, home working, etc. is now underpinned by the *Flexible Working (Eligibility, etc.) Regulation 2002*, the *Flexible Working (Procedural Requirements) Regulations 2002* and the *Part Time Workers (Prevention of Less Favourable Treatment) Regulations 2000*. The former enable an employee with 26 weeks service and a child aged under 6 years (18 years if disabled) to request (not require) that hours be altered to accommodate them. One request per annum is permitted. The latter Regulation regularises the position of part-time workers who must enjoy the same rights on a pro rata basis as full-time workers.

Protected disclosure – 'Whistleblowers'

4.13 Since recent cases on the treatment of compensation to those dismissed or treated less favourably because they have made *protected disclosures* have stressed that such action is a form of discrimination it falls naturally to refer briefly to it in this section. The statutory definition of what amounts to a *qualifying* disclosure is set out in section 47 ERA 1996 and the circumstances in which an employee must make it in order for it to become *protected* are set out in section 48K ERA 1996. In essence an employee who believes that his employer, has done something which might amount to a criminal act or a breach of a legal obligation, or something which will cause a health and safety risk is entitled to bring those to his employer's attention, and ultimately to the wider world, without being dismissed or otherwise penalised as a result. Dismissal is automatically unfair and compensation uncapped. ('Disclosure' is something of a misnomer since the employee will often be telling the employer what he already knows, because he is perpetrating the act, but there is no need for it to be a revelation.) The employee must however have a reasonable belief that his fears are true, but if he is ultimately proved wrong he is still protected. Conversely since the disclosure must also be made in good faith, if it is made out of malice or a dislike of the subject then however true the allegation is, the employee will not be protected. The scheme of the proetection leans heavily towards disclosure to the employer in the first instance, and to certain designated bodies. For example a charity worker can make a disclosure direct to the Charity Commissioners without needing to fulfil any of the additional requirements referred to in the Act. If the employee wishes to disclose the information beyond these boundaries then requirements such as the gravity of the issues involved, the failure of the employer to respond to initial disclosure and genuine fears for reprisals if the information is not shared externally, will justify wider disclosure, for example to the media, be protected. Any disclosure for personal gain will lose its protected status.

Victimisation

4.14 Reference has been made in the preceding paragraphs to the protection afforded under the equal opportunities legislation including a right not to be victimised and all the acts and regulations include clauses designed to protect those who seek to assert their rights from being penalised for doing so. The term *victimisation* carries a technical meaning in that the employee must be able first to point to the doing of a 'protected act' which triggers, or is alleged to have triggered the objectionable behaviour. The bringing of a claim in a tribunal is the obvious example but the various Acts also give protection to those who indicate their intention to do so or take preliminary steps towards enforcing their rights. Once a person can show that he has done a protected act then any actions taken against him do not require proof that they were done on grounds of the attribute e.g. disability, sex, that first led him to complain. A straight causal link between the protected act and the objectionable behaviour is sufficient.

5 Dismissal

Wrongful dismissal at common law

5.01 The most significant intervention of statute law in the area of individual rights has been in relation to dismissal. At common law, provided the employer terminates the contract in accordance with its terms, the employee will have no redress. Generally this means that the employer must give the employee that notice to which he is entitled under his contract of employment. The relevant period of notice will often be specified in the contract, but if it is not, then it will be a reasonable period. However, statute law now lays down a minimum period of notice which must be given, whatever the contract says, and that minimum period depends upon how long the employee was employed. Currently the minimum is 1 week's notice for employment of up to 2 years, and 1 week for each year of employment up to 12 years, i.e. if 2 years' employment, 2 weeks' notice; 6 years' employment, 6 weeks' notice etc. up to a maximum of 12 years. The contract may stipulate more than this, but any provision for notice of less than the minimum will not be applied. Note that this is the notice that the employer must give to the employee. It does not operate the other way. An employee with over 1 month's service must give 1 week's notice, but that is the only minimum requirement. The contract might specify a longer period which will apply if it is longer than the statutory minimum. A claim also arises when the employee believes that the conduct of his employer has been so bad that it repudiates the contract. The employee may therefore accept that repudiatory conduct and resign.

5.02 If the employer dismisses with no notice or with inadequate notice, then this is termed a 'wrongful dismissal', and the employee will have a remedy in the ordinary courts or in the employment tribunal for breach of contract. Because a claim for wrongful dismissal is a contractual claim, the employer is entitled to any of the defences available to any other defendant to such a claim. So, for example, if the employee has committed an act of gross misconduct, then the employer may rely on that misconduct as constituting a repudiation of the contract, and may lawfully

consider himself discharged from his obligations under it, including his obligation to give notice (see paragraph 4.05). But the courts and the employment tribunals do not readily find that misconduct is gross. Such conduct might include dishonesty or physical violence.

Unfair dismissal

5.03 The common law, then, sees a man's job essentially in contractual terms. Provided the contract is complied with, the employee has no grounds of complaint. This means that the reason for a dismissal can rarely be questioned at common law. As long as the employer has given the required notice, it matters not whether it is because the employee is dishonest, or smokes cigarettes, or has blond hair. Managerial prerogative is left untouched. But overlaid on the contractual relationship is a set of statutory obligations which are unique to the contract of employment and which require the employer to have a fair reason for the dismissal, and to be acting reasonably in relying upon it. The basic law of unfair dismissal can be considered under the following heads.

Eligibility

5.04 The employee must be eligible to make his complaint to the tribunal. He must have one year's continuous employment, except when dismissal is alleged to be for one of a number of a specified category of reasons e.g. for making a protected disclosure, for asserting a statutory right, on grounds of sex, race or other forms of discrimination. Until October 2006 an employee who had reached the *normal retiring age* for his job, was ineligible to claim, thus effectively making retirement a fair reason for dismissal. The considerable number of cases on the definition of just what *was* a normal retirement age have all been rendered obsolete by the need to conform with the age discrimination legislation. The position is now governed by sections 98ZA–ZF ERA 1996 which require the employer to justify objectively a retiring age of less than 65.

An employee who ordinarily works outside the UK are also ineligible to claim. However, if his 'base' is in this country then he will be eligible. This includes employees who work in an 'enclave', e.g. an RAF base abroad or someone whose work abroad is for the benefit of a UK-based employer, such as foreign correspondent for a newspaper.

Dismissal

5.05 The employee must show that he has been dismissed. Sometimes what in form appears to be a resignation will in law constitute a dismissal (known as constructive dismissal). For example, if the employer unilaterally reduces the wages or alters the hours of work or otherwise acts in breach of contract, the employee may resign and claim that his resignation was merely a response to an act by his employer which was tantamount to a dismissal (though the dismissal is not inevitably unfair). In order to claim constructive dismissal, the act complained of must constitute a breach of contract, although an act on the part of the employer which involves destroying the trust and confidence in the employment relationship will constitute a breach of the implied term mentioned in paragraph 4.02 above, and entitle the employee to leave and claim that he has been dismissed. For instance, such conduct as falsely and without justification accusing an employee of theft, failing to support a supervisor, upbraiding a supervisor in the presence of his subordinates, and a director using intemperate language and criticising his personal secretary in front of a third party have all been held to amount to conduct which justifies the employee leaving and claiming that he has been dismissed. Cases on constructive dismissal illustrate the important distinction between wrongful and unfair dismissal. Because constructive dismissal requires a breach of contract on the part of the employer, it is automatically wrongful. But it is not necessarily unfair because the test for fairness is a different one. Similarly, a refusal to renew a fixed-term contract will amount to a dismissal. That dismissal cannot be wrongful because a contract which comes to an end by the effluxion of time will not have been ended by any form of breach, but it may nevertheless be unfair if the decision not to renew is unreasonable (see below).

The EAT has recently made a controversial decision in this area by holding that the conduct complained of, if it is to justify the employee resigning, must be judged by whether if fall outside the band of reasonable responses from the employer. The previous held view was that what amounted to conduct sufficient to justify an employee resigning was to be judged objectively. The decision in *Abbey National plc v Farebrother* [2007] IRLR 320 brings the test for constructive dismissal into line with that for 'ordinary' dismissal, by adopting the same test for the fairness of a dismissal. The rational of the most recent decision: *Claridge v Daler Rowney Ltd* [2008] IRLR 672 stresses that it is unacceptable to have two different tests for the two different types of dismissal, and that the conduct complained of by the employee should satisfy this test if it is to justify resignation.

A fair reason

5.06 Once a dismissal is established, the employer must show that he has a fair reason for the dismissal. Some reasons for dismissal are, by statute, automatically unfair. These include dismissals for reasons connected with maternity, trade union membership and the assertion by the employee of health and safety or other statutory rights or for *whistle blowing* activities that is the making of a *protected disclosure*. Similarly, a number of reasons are specifically stated to be potentially fair – misconduct, capability, redundancy, the fact that a statutory provision prohibits a person from working, and any other substantial reason.

Capability covers both inherent incompetence and incapability arising from ill health. The latter may include a prolonged absence or perhaps a series of short, intermittent absences. Some other substantial reason is a residual category covering a potentially wide range of reasons. Perhaps the most important is that it may justify dismissals where the employer takes steps to protect his business interests. For example, an employer who was concerned about his employees leaving and setting up in competition decided to require them to enter into a restraint of trade agreement (see paragraph 3.35). Some employees refused to sign the agreement and were dismissed. Again, employees who are dismissed because they refuse to accept new hours of work introduced by the employer may well be found to have been fairly dismissed if the changes had been made in order to improve efficiency. A refusal to accept new arrangements is now a common basis for such dismissal.

The employer must be acting reasonably

5.07 But it is not enough simply for the employer to have a fair reason. The law requires that 'the determination of the question whether the dismissal is fair or unfair ... depends on whether in the circumstances (including the size and administrative resources of the employer's undertaking) the employer acted reasonably or unreasonably in treating [the reason] as a sufficient reason for dismissing the employee' which 'shall be determined in accordance with equity and the substantial merits of the case' (ERA 1996, section 98(4)).

Many factors may have to be considered in determining this question. The length of service of the employee, the need for the employer to act consistently, the size and resources of the company or firm will all be relevant factors. For example, a small firm cannot as readily accommodate the lengthy illness of an employee as a large organisation.

Procedural factors are as important in these cases. ACAS has produced a code of practice on disciplinary matters – Disciplinary Practice and Procedures in Employment. Like other codes, it is not directly legally binding but should be taken into account in any legal proceedings before a tribunal, since it is open for a tribunal to find a dismissal for a fair reason nevertheless unfair, if it was not effected in accordance with good procedural practice.

5.08 The code emphasises the need for warnings, a chance to state a case, and a right of appeal. That in simple terms covers the huge canon of reported cases on unfair dismissal. Most employers will have a disciplinary code which envisages a system by which errant employees receive an ascending scale of warnings; informal oral, formal oral and then, first, second and final written. That procedure will also contain the power to dismiss for gross misconduct. Gross misconduct will cover the obvious transgressions such as dishonesty, drunkenness or gross insubordination. The employer can also write into the procedure acts which are peculiarly important to his business. Similarly, an act of negligence of such magnitude that the employer cannot afford a repeat may justify immediate dismissal.

5.09 Once an employer thinks that the employee may have committed an act of misconduct that may lead to dismissal it is imperative that he engages in a proper and fair system for the determination of the guilt of the employee and to consider the appropriate response. Since the case of *British Home Stores v Burchell* [1978] IRLR 379 a three-fold test has been the orthodox approach. It must be established that the employer believed in the guilt of the employee. Then the employer must show that he had reasonable grounds upon which to sustain that belief. Finally the employer must show that at the time at which he formed that belief on those grounds he must have carried out as much investigation into the matter as was reasonable in all the circumstances. The form of the investigation is not laid down nor for any hearing that takes place. In particular there is no requirement that the hearing should be quasi-judicial with cross examination of witnesses. So long as the employee has a clear understanding of the charge and an opportunity to state his case before an impartial panel, then the procedure is likely to be fair. An appeal procedure is also required and any deficiencies in the first hearing can be cured by a proper opportunity to state a case at the appeal.

5.10 When the last edition of this chapter was written the statutory grievance and statutory disciplinary procedures enacted by the Employment Act 2002 were barely in force. At the time of writing their total repeal has been accomplished by the Employment Act 2008. Happily, therefore, it is not now necessary to try and condense and summarise the practical effect of the huge explosion of highly technical litigation which somewhat surprisingly resulted from their introduction. This was the more so as they introduced a seemingly straightforward and no doubt well intentioned concept that no employee could start a tribunal claim unless they had first gone through their employers internal grievance procedure, and that an employer who dismissed an employee without first going through a disciplinary process would have, without more, done so unfairly. The penalty for the latter was a requirement for the tribunal to increase any award of compensation by a minimum of 10%, with a potential 50% increase. The employee's failure to complete the grievance procedure before starting a tribunal claim could be met by a corresponding compensation.

The repeal of the statutory procedures has been replaced, by an amendment to TULR(C)A 1992 which will state that, where an employer is found to have breached an applicable Code of Practice which relates to disciplinary resolution the tribunal will have power to increase any award of compensation by up to 25%. An employee may suffer a corresponding reduction of up to 25% if he breaches any applicable Code on grievance resolution in his bringing of a claim.

As was observed in the earlier edition the statutory procedures would not represent any radical departure from the sort of procedure most reasonable employers already had in place. A clear statement of the basis for disciplinary action, an opportunity to hear and respond to the allegation and a form of appeal remain essential but hardly novel forms of procedure. With the reversion to the link to the Codes of Practise good employers will not notice much difference. A lasting legacy will however be that employees will have to go through some form of internal process to alert their employers to their potential claim to a tribunal. Hitherto, i.e. before the EA 2002, an employee could institute a claim for discrimination without even a preliminary warning to his employer, let alone an opportunity to resolve the matter internally.

The EA 2008 also provides for claims to be determined without a hearing – i.e. on paper!

5.11 It was also necessary in the last edition to avert to the effect the EA 2002 was to have on what had until then been a fundamental tenet of unfair dismissal law. Following the decision in *Polkey v Dayton Services Ltd* [1988] IRLR 142 it was not open to an employer to argue that although a dismissal was unfair, usually because of the lack of a fair procedure, subsequent events would have rendered that dismissal fair, or rather would have shown that there would have been no difference to the outcome. The employee was entitled to a finding of unfair dismissal although any subsequent award of compensation would reflect the realities of the situation. Thus a failure to go through a proper investigation into alleged dishonesty by an employee would make the dismissal unfair, but if the investigation would have shown that the employee had indeed stolen money and that investigation would have taken about 3 weeks then his losses would be limited to that period.

That position was reversed by section 98A ERA 1996. Thus a finding that the employer had failed procedurally longer rendered the dismissal unfair if he could show that he would still have dismissed even if he had followed the procedure. That too has been repealed by the new Employment Act 2008 and brings a return to *Polkey*.

5.12 Although the ACAS Code and the preceding remarks have been related to the matters of misconduct and redundancy, it will be appreciated that all situations where dismissal may follow require the employer to be fully apprised of the facts and capable of rational justification. Thus the employee whose ability to perform the job, i.e. his capability, is in question must be told of his employer's concerns. He must be given an opportunity to improve, having been given a clear statement of what it is which is inadequate in his performance. If the employer concludes that he cannot or will not make the grade then and there, for example, no alternative jobs within the business, given the nature and size of his undertaking then substantively and procedurally the employer is likely to be able to In substi resist any challenge that he has failed unfairly to discharge his statutory obligations.

5.13 One important point to note about the tribunal hearing is that it is not open to the tribunal to find a dismissal unfair merely because it disagrees with the employer. It must not substitute its own judgement for that of the employer. For example, in a disciplinary case a tribunal might conclude that it would probably have given a further, final warning before dismissing. But that does not necessarily make the dismissal unfair. It is often perfectly possible for there to be a number of reasonable responses to a particular situation. One employer might dismiss, another might give a final warning, yet both may be acting within the range of reasonable responses to particular conduct. Provided the tribunal finds the employer's response to be within this range of reasonable responses, it should not find the dismissal to be unfair.

Remedies

5.14 There are three remedies envisaged: reinstatement, which means the employee being given the old job back and treated in all respects as though he had never been dismissed; re-engagement, which may involve being taken back in a different job, or perhaps in the same job but without back-pay, or on slightly different terms; and finally compensation. A tribunal must consider the three remedies in the order just given. In deciding whether to order reinstatement or re-engagement, the tribunal must consider three factors: (1) whether the employee wants his job back – if not, the tribunal must go straight on to consider compensation; (2) whether it is practicable to take the employee back – and in regard to a small firm it is likely that a tribunal will find that it is

not because of personality conflicts involved; and (3) whether the employee has caused or contributed to his own dismissal – if he has, at least to any significant degree, he is unlikely to be awarded his job back.

5.14 Usually employees do not want reinstatement or re-engagement, so the tribunal simply assesses compensation. However, even if reinstatement or re-engagement is ordered, the employer is not finally compelled to obey the order, though he will have to pay additional compensation if he refuses to do so. The usual compensation is made up of two elements. One is the basic award, which is calculated in essentially the same way as a redundancy payment (see paragraph 4.21). The other is the compensatory award, which is designed to take account of the actual loss suffered by the employee following from the dismissal. This will depend on such factors as when he is likely to obtain new employment, and what he will then earn. The amount will be reduced if the employee has caused or contributed to his own dismissal, the tribunal deciding what reduction would be just and equitable in all the circumstances, e.g. the tribunal may find that the employee is 50% to blame and reduce his compensation by half. The maximum compensatory award is now £66 200. The amounts are reviewed and increased in February each year. The size of the maximum award, vastly increased in recent years permits of quite detailed assessment on both loss of earnings and pension.

Redundancy

5.16 Redundancy has already been referred to in the context of potentially fair reasons for dismissal and the *Polkey* principle. It merits a discrete section because the termination of employment by reason of redundancy remains a feature of the working life of many employees. It has an importance independent of claims before the tribunal and raises a number of legal implications for the employer. First it is necessary to identify what, in law, amounts to a redundancy.

5.17 The three main situations in which a redundancy arises are (1) where the employer closes down altogether; (2) where the employer moves the place of work (though it should be noted that the place of work is where the employee can be required to work under his contract and not where he normally works, e.g. if the contract stipulates that he can be required to work anywhere in Great Britain and the firm moves from London to Glasgow, but his job is still available in Glasgow, this is not a redundancy); and (3) where the need for employees to do a particular kind of work has ceased or diminished. It is this final category which has caused and continues to cause considerable difficulties. Note first that there may be a constant amount of *work* but that the employer may require a smaller number of employees to perform it. Controversy raged over the question whether if the work which had diminished was that work which the employee was contractually engaged to perform, or merely work which he had come to perform as a matter of fact? This controversy came to be known as the '*function* test' as against the *contract* test. The significance of the dispute was that an employee with a contractual job description of say, driver, but who had come effectively to operate as a warehouseman, would be redundant if the employer decided to dispense with some warehousemen if the functional test was applied, but not if the contractual test was. Thus if selected for dismissal and unhappy with the situation he could complain that he was not redundant (contractual test) and that his dismissal was not for redundancy and unfair. Conversely, the employer could argue that functionally he was now a warehouseman and that the need for them had diminished. The controversy is said to have been finally determined by the House of Lords in *Murray v Foyle Meats Ltd* [1999] ICR 827, where the then Lord Chancellor Lord Irving, declared that the two tests both 'missed the point', stressing that the key word was 'attributable' and that there was no reason why a dismissal should not be attributable to a diminution in the employer's need for employees inspective of the terms of his contract or the function which he performed.

Note also that a dismissal may look like a redundancy situation but the dismissal may be for reasons of business efficiency. It is yet a further example within employment law of a deceptively simple concept containing traps for the unwary and needing expert assistance.

Establishing a redundancy claim

5.18 It is important to note that two sorts of redundancy claims may come to a tribunal. The first is where an employee believes that he has been made redundant and is refused a redundancy payment by his former employer. Secondly, and much more commonly the employee accepts that his dismissal is by reason of redundancy but claims that the dismissal is unfair by reason of inadequate warning or consultation or that he has been unfairly selected from a group of potential candidates.

Eligibility

5.19 He must be eligible to present the claim. In order to do this he must have 1 year's employment over the age of 18, be below 65, and normally work in Great Britain. Exceptionally, although he normally works abroad, he will be entitled to claim if he is in Great Britain at the employer's request at the time of dismissal. The qualifying period of employment was reduced from 2 years to 1 year with effect from 1 June 1999.

Offers of alternative employment

5.20 The detailed requirements of warning, consultation and selection are beyond the scope of this work. A procedure must be devised which addresses the employees right to notice of the impending redundancy and that the selection of the retained employees is an objective and transparent system which will withstand scrutiny. A key concept in the redundancy process is also the offer of alternative employment. This is important for two reasons: first from the employee's point of view he is entitled to the opportunity to stay with business albeit in a different capacity. Secondly the employee's entitlement to a statutory redundancy payment will be compromised if he unreasonably refuses an offer of suitable alternative employment. The job is unlikely to be considered suitable if it means a significant loss of status or pay. Whether any refusal is reasonable will depend upon the employee's personal circumstances. However, the employee does have a trial period of up to four weeks to decide whether a job is suitable, and within that period he is working without prejudice to his redundancy claim. But, of course, if he refuses the job after the trial period, it will still be open to the employer to claim that it was suitable employment and has been unreasonably refused.

Amount

5.21 The employee's compensation depends on his age, wages at the time he was dismissed, and years of service. Broadly speaking it is ½ a week's pay for a complete year of service between the ages of 18 and 22, 1 week's pay for each year of service between 24 and 41, and 1½ weeks' pay for each complete year of service between 41 and 65. The maximum number of years that can be taken into account is 20. The week's pay is calculated from the gross figure, but is subject to a maximum (at present) of £350 per week. So the most that can be recovered under the statute is for someone with 20 years' service, all over the age of 41, who on dismissal was earning at least £330 per week gross. He will receive £350 × 1½ × 20 = £10 500 Of course, employers may voluntarily pay more than the law requires, or they may be bound to pay more than the law requires by a term in the contract of employment.

5.22 Employees in their 64th year when they are dismissed have their redundancy payment reduced by 1/12 for each month of their 64th year, so that by the time they reach 65 their redundancy payment has reduced to nil. Of course this makes good sense: employees who retire do not get redundancy payments.

The redundancy fund, which used to help employers meet redundancy payments, has been abolished.

Consultation with recognised trade unions and the D of E

5.23 In addition to the consultation which the employee must engage in with the individual employees who are selected for redundancy there also exists, in certain circumstances an obligation to consult with recognised TU representatives. Although essentially a *collective labour relations* issue, it is important that the employer proposing any large-scale redundancies, i.e. more than 20 employees, deals with this issue as well as the individual staff issues. When an employer is *proposing* to make redundant more than 20 employees he must consult at least 30 days before the first dismissal is likely to take place, and if over 100 employees are affected then the period is 90 days. The two periods laid down are the *minimum* acceptable times and consultation should start '*in good time*' and in any event within these timescales. A failure to follow the procedure and to enter into proper consultations designed to avoid if possible any redundancies, to reduce the number of any such dismissals and to mitigate the effect of dismissals can lead to the making of a *protective award*. This is a sum of money which can be a maximum of 90 days pay and will paid in addition to any redundancy pay due to the employees. The Court of Appeal held in *Susie Radin Ltd v GMB* [2004] ICR 893 that the purpose of the proptective award is punitive and thus need bear no relation to the actual harm done or any loss occcasioned by the failure to consult properly. Further, 90 days is effectively the starting point for the calculation of the award. The potential penalty is large and, by definition, if payable by a firm which is facing large-scale redundancies, an unwelcome addition to their financial difficulties. Any practice anticipating such an exercise should seek expert advice and be prepared to enter into genuine consultation and discussion with TU or other works representatives, however academic an exercise this may appear.

Transfer of undertakings

5.24 Transfer of undertakings is included under the general heading of redundancy although it is important to note that the purpose of the Transfer of Undertakings (Protection of Employment) Regulations 2006 (replacing the original 1981 regulations) has as its purpose the preservation of employment rather than the ending of it. The Regulations first enacted a fundamental change to the common law principal that any attempt by an employer to transfer the contract of employment to another employer would simply bring the employment to an end. Rather, they act to preserve the full terms and conditions of the original employment while transferring the obligations to the new employer and if the employee is dismissed as a result of the transfer to make that dismissal automatically unfair.

The 2006 Regulations repeat substantially the 1981 version save for two important areas. The first is to extend the meaning of what amounts to a relevant transfer. The transfer of an 'economic entity which retains its identity' reflects the original concept of a business transfer as recognised by the 1981 Regulations. The definition now also covers 'a service provision change', that is where activities carried out by one party are contracted out to another. It equates to the now familiar concept of 'outsourcing' or contracting out of services together with re-tendering of contracted out services or the reversion to in-sourcing.

The other matter of central importance to the regulations is to clarify the extent of protection afforded to employees when a relevant transfer takes place. Regulation 4 now makes clear that the Regulations apply to any employee (provided that they are assigned to the undertaking or part of it to be transferred) who was employed immediately before the transfer or 'would have been so employed if they had not been dismissed'. Thus pre-emptive dismissals will not prevent the protection being engaged and making any such dismissal automatically unfair, as will those which coincide more immediately with the transfer. The dismissal will, however, not be automatically unfair if it is for an 'economic, technical or organisational reason' (ETO) what amounts to an

ETO is not easy to define, and the regulations do not attempt to do so. Even if an ETO can be identified the dismissal will only be fair if it also satisfies the basic requirement of section 98 ERA 1996, that is reasonableness in all the circumstances, both procedurally and substantively.

Fixed-term contracts

5.25 Special rules apply to fixed-term contracts. First, if a fixed-term contract is not renewed, this in law amounts to a dismissal. But it is not necessarily unfair. In particular, if the employee is taken on for a fixed period and knows in advance that his contract is likely to be temporary and will not be renewed when the fixed term expires, a refusal to renew the contract is likely to be justified. The employer will still have to show that he is acting reasonably in not renewing the contract, but that should not be too difficult in most situations.

5.26 Second, where a fixed-term contract is for a year or more, an employee may sign away his rights to unfair dismissal, i.e. he may agree in writing that he will not claim for unfair dismissal if his contract is not renewed once the fixed term ends. This is one of the exceptional cases where an agreement to sign away statutory rights is binding. But such an agreement is not binding as regards dismissals which take effect during the fixed term. It applies only to the dismissal arising from the non-renewal of the fixed term. Similarly, rights to redundancy may also be signed away, but curiously only where the fixed term is for two years or more.

5.27 This leaves the crucial question: What is a fixed-term contract? The answer is one with an ascertainable date of termination (though it is still fixed term even if the parties can terminate it earlier by giving notice). So if the contract is to last for a particular task, and it is impossible to predict how long the job will last, this is not a fixed-term contract. When it comes to an end, it terminates because the task is completed. But this in law will not constitute a dismissal. Consequently, even if the employer is acting unreasonably in not continuing to employ the employee, the latter will have no claim for unfair dismissal.

Reference

5.28 An employer is under no legal duty to provide a reference. If he does so, there are certain legal pitfalls he must take care to avoid. If the statement is untrue, it may be libellous and he could be liable in defamation. However, he will be able to rely upon the defence of qualified privilege, which means that he will not be liable unless it can be shown that the statement was inspired by malice, i.e. was deliberately false and intended to injure the employee. See also below that as the protection from discriminaiton extends beyond the end of employment a reference which is less favourable on grounds of the sex, race etc of the subject will lay the author open to a further claim.

5.29 An employer who hires an employee on the basis of an untrue reference may bring a legal action against the employer issuing the reference. If it is deliberately false, the liability will be for deceit. If it is negligently written, e.g. claims are made which he could have discovered were false with some inquiries, liability will probably exist for negligence mis-statement under the doctrine of *Hedley Byrne v Heller* [1964] AC 465.

5.30 Certainly the employer owes a duty to his former employee not to prepare a reference negligently. In *Spring v Guardian Assurance Plc* [1994] 3 WLR 354, an insurance salesman successfully sued his former employers. They had negligently provided a reference to prospective new employers who, relying on the negligent reference, had declined to employ him. Finally, if the employer dismisses an employee for misconduct or incompetence, but then proceeds to write him a glowing reference, he may find difficulty in convincing the tribunal that the reason for which he was dismissed was, in fact, the true reason.

Duties on former employees

5.31 Once the contract is terminated, this does not mean that there are no further duties imposed on the former employee. In particular, the employee is not free to divulge confidential information or trade secrets to rivals. However, he can use his own individual skill and experience, e.g. organisational ability, even though that was gained as a result of working for the former employer. But the distinction between the knowledge which can and cannot be imparted is vague.

The House of Lords has recently made clear that the ending of employment does not signal an end to the potential liability for acts of discrimination by the ex-employer. See *Rhys Harper v Relaxion Group* [2003] IRLR 484 a joint appeal in three cases on the RRA, SDA and DDA, respectively. In each case acts perpetrated after termination laid the employer open to claims. The acts might include the refusal to investigate complaints, or to do so satisfactorily, to provide a reference which was adverse or to consider reinstatement.

Restricting competition: restraint of trade

5.32 In addition, the employee may be prevented from setting up in competition with his former employer. But this will be so only if he entered into an express clause in his contract of employment which prohibited such competition. Even then, such clauses will be binding only if they are reasonable and not contrary to the public interest. They must not be drawn wider than is necessary to protect the employer's interests; otherwise they will be considered to be in unreasonable restraint of trade and therefore void. Reasonable restrictions might prevent an architect from soliciting the clients of his former employer, and they may even encompass restrictions on the employee's right to compete within a certain area for a particular time. But if the area is drawn too widely, or the duration too long, the clause will be void and unenforceable.

6 Collective labour relations law

6.01 As mentioned above, the main provisions in the area of collective labour relations law are concerned with giving certain rights to unions and their officials. However, these are in practice given only to recognised trade unions, i.e. those with which the employer is willing to negotiate.

There is once again a mechanism by which a TU can seek to enforce recognition. Since June 2000, Section 70A, TULRCA has provided a means by which the workforce can be balloted to seek views on recognition. A 40% majority in favour is required. The ballot is seen as something of a last resort with the involvement of CAC as the primary means by which some accommodation between employer and employee might be accomplished. Detailed provisions are set out in the Act but essentially the method can only be used by one union, if another has already secured rights of recognition there is no scope for the two unions battling it out by way of a ballot. If unsuccessful, a TU cannot apply again to re-start the process within 1 year. Importantly, the power does not apply to small businesses with under 21 employees. If successful the rights conferred by the recognition are limited to the negotiation over pay, holidays and hours of work.

The consequences of recognition

6.02 Once a union is recognised by an employer, the following consequences follow.

Disclosure of information

6.03 The unions have a right to receive information from the employer without which they would be impeded in collective bargaining and which it is good industrial relations practice to disclose. However, there is a wide range or exceptions, e.g. information received in confidence, or information which would damage the employer's undertakings (such as how tender prices are calculated). Some guidance can be given by the Code of Practice on Disclosure of Information produced by ACAS. It should be emphasised, though, that no information need be divulged until the recognised union asks for it.

Consultation over redundancies

6.04 As soon as the decision to make redundance has crystallised, the employer should consult with any appropriate employee representatives among the group from which the redundancy or redundancies are to be made. This consultation may be with trade union officials or employees' representatives elected for that purpose, whichever the employer chooses. The representatives may make representations upon these proposals, and the employer must in turn reply to their points, though he is not obliged to accept them.

As noted above, in the case of collective redundancies this consultation is required if it proposed to make 20 or more employees redundant within 90 days. But this period will not apply if there are special circumstances making it impossible for him to comply with it, e.g. a sudden and unforeseen loss of work. In the case of these collective redundancies, it is necessary to notify the Department of Employment.

Reasonable time off for union officials and members

6.05 Union officials have a right to reasonable time off with pay for industrial relations activities involving the employer, e.g. negotiating, handling grievances, and attending training courses connected with these matters. What is reasonable will depend upon such factors as the size of the firm, the job of the employee, and the number of other officials. Some guidance can be found in the ACAS Code of Practice on Time Off.

6.06 Union members also have a right to reasonable time off, but without pay, for trade union matters, e.g. attending union conferences. Again the ACAS Code of Practice gives some guidance, though its principal message is that it is for employers and unions themselves to negotiate what is reasonable in all circumstances.

Health and safety representatives

6.07 Recognised unions are entitled to appoint safety representatives, who have an important role to play in helping to maintain health and safety standards. This is further discussed in paragraph 6.03.

Dismissal for union membership or non-membership

6.08 Under the Trade Union and Labour Relations (Consolidation) Act 1992 it is automatically unfair to dismiss an employee because he does not belong to a particular trade union, or because he has been refused membership of any particular trade union. The closed shop – and the complicated law relating to it – are now both things of the past.

6.09 The other side of the coin is the same. It is also automatically unfair to dismiss an employee because he does belong to a union.

7 Health and safety

7.01 The health and safety of employees is governed primarily by the Health and Safety at Work Act (HSWA) 1974. This Act now receives considerable underpinning from the six sets of regulations introduced after 1992 under the umbrella of the Management of Health and Safety at Work Regulation (now amended as the 1995 Regs). They are The Workplace (Health, Safety and Welfare) Regulations 1992 (now amended as the 1995 Regs), the Provision and Use of Work Equipment Regulations 1992 (now 1995), the Personal Protective Equipment Regulations 1992, The Manual Handling Regulations 1992 and the Health and Safety (Display Screens Equipment) Regulations 1992.

These the regulations concentrate on aspects of work, as can be seen from their titles, e.g. manual handling, protective equipment and computers, applying the regulatory scheme across all workplaces and all trades. That represents a building upon the scheme of the HSWA, with its focus on the prevention of accidents but more significantly a final departure from the old legislative scheme where the protection enjoyed had been specific to workplaces, e.g. the Factories Acts or the Offices, Shops and Railway Premises Act, to specific trades, e.g. the Woodworking Regulations or even to the use of particular substances, e.g. lead or asbestos. Now the obligation e.g. to make sure that the access to premises are safe will apply across all workplaces, trades, etc.

The Health and Safety at Work Act 1974

7.02 Under the old Acts the only persons protected were those who were employed by the owner or occupier of the factory or workplace. The HSWA extended that protection by placing duties upon employers, the self-employed and persons otherwise in control of premises. (Duties are also owed by the designers, manufacturers, importers and suppliers of articles for use at work.) The duties are owed not just to employees but to any person who may be affected by work activities requiring that the employer do all that is *reasonably practicable* to ensure the health, safety and welfare of his employees. The Act also cast upon employees duties to take reasonable care for their own safety, to cooperate with employers so as to permit them to comply with their obligations and not to interfere with anything provided in pursuance of these statutory obligations. The 1992 (and amended 1995 versions) Regulations give protection to employed and self-employed but also cast upon all those categories of people the corresponding duty to observe the requirements of the regulations.

The protection is greater also in that the duty of the employer is now less to the 'reasonably practicable' standard and more likely to be that what is provided shall be to *suitable and sufficient* level. That is almost certainly a higher level of care.

However, the key feature of the *six pack* of Regulations and the major invention is that of the *risk assessment*. Although that was foreshadowed by the HSWA 1974 with clear policies on accident prevention the risk assessment will remain the real legacy of the new statutory framework. The concentration is now firmly on prevention by a focussed assessment of what could go wrong and how it can be avoided.

Safety representatives and committees

7.03 Where the employer recognises a trade union, that union is entitled to appoint safety representatives, who must then be consulted by the employer on health and safety matters. In addition, the safety representatives have a right to formally inspect at least once every 3 months those parts of the premises for which they are responsible; to investigate any reportable accidents, i.e. those that result in the employee being absent for 3 days or more; and to examine any documents relating to health and safety, save those for which there are specific exemptions, e.g. personal medical records. Furthermore, provided at least two safety representatives request this, the employer must set up a safety committee within 3 months of the request. This committee may keep under review health and safety policies and performance. The 1992 Regulations introduced extended rights on consultation with safety representatives e.g. on any matter which might substantially affect the health and safety of workers.

Enforcement of the legislation

7.04 The powers of inspectors are quite wide, appointed under the HSWA. They can enter premises uninvited at any reasonable time, require the production of records or documents which the law requires to be kept, and oblige persons to answer questions. They may prosecute in the criminal courts if they find the laws infringed. But, in addition, they can now take effective action without the need to have recourse to the courts. They may issue 'improvement' or 'prohibition' orders. The former oblige the employer to bring his place or premises up to scratch within a certain specified period. The latter actually compel him to stop using the place or premises until the necessary improvements have been made. But prohibition orders can be issued only if the inspector considers that there is a risk of serious personal injury. The employer can appeal to an industrial tribunal against these orders. An appeal suspends the operation of an improvement order until the appeal is heard, but a prohibition order continues in force pending the appeal unless the employer obtains permission to the contrary from a tribunal. Breach of either order is automatically a criminal offence. Indeed, individual managers who are knowingly parties to a breach of the prohibition order may even be sent to prison.

Reporting accidents

7.05 Every employer should keep a record of accidents at the workplace. In addition, some accidents may have to be reported to the enforcing authorities. These include fatalities and accidents involving serious personal injury, including those resulting in hospital in-patient treatment. These accidents have to be reported to the authorities by the quickest practicable means, and a written report must be sent within seven days. For other accidents, involving absences from work of three days or more, notification to the authorities is not necessary provided the employer has reasonable grounds to believe that the employee will claim industrial injury benefit. In this case the relevant information will, in any event, be sent to the Department of Works and Pensions and they will transfer it to the enforcing authorities.

Compensation for accidents at work

7.06 The legislation discussed above is designed to prevent accidents. Indeed the HSWA specifically states that it does not create any civil liability as does the Management of Health and Safety at Work Regulations. The remaining five of the six regulations *do* create such liability for breach of statutory duty and some commentators on the legislation take the view that any breach of the regulations will be relevant to establishing a breach of the common law duties, i.e. that the employer has been negligent e.g. in *not* carrying out a statutory risk assessment.

An employee seeking damages for injuries suffered at work can frame his care in one of the following four ways:

1 Every employer owes a common law duty to take reasonable care to ensure the safety of his employees. More specifically this requires that he should provide safe plant and appliances, adopt safe systems of work, and employ competent employees. If an accident occurs because of a breach of this duty, the employer will be liable.
2 Breaches of the Regulations will be the basis of a claim for breach of statutory duty and because of their specific and wide coverage there will be regulations apt to cover most occurences and accidents.
3 The employer may be liable under the Occupiers Liability Act 1957. This imposes a duty of care on occupiers of premises to all those lawfully entering his premises. The standard of the duty is to take all reasonable practicable steps to make the premises safe. A claim under this Act may be made by someone not employed by the occupier.

4 Where a person, whether a worker or a third party, is injured as a result of the negligence of an employee acting in the course of his employment, the employer will be vicariously liable for the injury caused. Even if he is not personally liable under items 1–3, he may still be held responsible.

Finally note that injury to an employee can be caused not just by tripping over a loose carpet or lifting a heavy weight. The law on *stress at work* continues to develop, albeit that the Court of Appeal has restricted the scope of such litigation somewhat. An employer who is alerted to the employees inability to cope with the demands of a job, or who complains of the oppressive behaviour of managers ignores such warnings at his peril. A prudent employer in the 21st century should be alive to the greater subtleties of his obligations and the need to look to employees mental as well as physical well-being.

8 Employment law in Scotland*

8.01 Employment legislation is UK based and applies to Scotland as to England and Wales. As in England, an employer is required to observe the terms of the Employment Rights Act 1996 (with amendments thereto effected by such primary legislation as the Public Interest Disclosure Act 1988 – whistle-blowing and such secondary legislation as the Maternity and Paternal Leave, etc. Regulations 1999), the Sex Discrimination Act 1975, the Race Relations Act 1976, the Equal Pay Act 1970, the Disability Discrimination Act 1995 and the National Minimum Wage Act 1998. The employer is also obliged to obtemper most employment law/anti-discriminatory statutory instruments e.g. as from 1 and 2 December 2003, respectively, the Employment Equality (Sexual Orientation) Regulations 2003 and Employment Equality (Religion or Belief) Regulations 2003 took effect. The Employment Equality (Age) Regulations 2006 came into effect on 1 October 2006.

Any judicial forum also has to have due regard to the substantive and procedural rights of Employers and Employees in terms of the Human Rights Act 1998.

The common law principles derived from Scots law are very similar to their English counterparts although, in actions raised in Scotland based on the common law of contract and the potential breach thereof in an employment context, Scottish Courts, in spite of the occasional judgment of the Outer House of the Court of Session to the contrary, are markedly less likely to grant an interdict i.e. a specific order prohibiting a course of action on the employer's part (e.g. disciplinary action or dismissal). The lead cases or restraint of trade are the same in England, Wales and Scotland. However, as there is a slightly different view in Scotland as to the construction of contracts and the severability of clauses, when orders restricting competition are granted or refused there can be differences in individual cases. A separate system of Employment Tribunals operates in Scotland with appeals initially to the Employment Appeal Tribunal (both bodies being governed by their own Regulations). Appeals lie thereafter to the Inner House of the Court of Session and then to the House of Lords. As a result of the separate appellate structure, occasionally the interpretation of substantive law can be different until matters are finally resolved by the supreme appellate forum.

*This section was written by Jim Murphie.

36

International work by architects

RICHARD DYTON

1 Introduction

1.01 Any international work undertaken by architects is subject to legal complications over and above those in Britain because of the different legal and insurance systems involved. However, increasingly, architects are able to work in a European and, indeed, world market and, providing appropriate legal advice is taken, the opportunities available outweigh the perceived complications.

1.02 In the following paragraphs brief summaries are given of the legal and insurance requirements of countries in which British architects find themselves involved. There are also references to the very different attitudes and cultures in those other countries which may require an increased sensitivity by British architects.

The European Union

Right of establishment and freedom to provide services – the Architects Directive 85/384 EEC

1.03 Three of the fundamental principles underlying the Treaty of Rome are the free movement of workers, the freedom to set up business in any member state and the freedom to provide services in a member state, other than that in which the provider of these services is based. In order to ensure that those principles are met so far as architects are concerned the Community has adopted Directive 85/384 EEC which has been implemented into UK law by the Architects' Qualifications (EEC Recognition) Order 1987 (SI 1987 No. 1824, as amended by SI 1988 No. 2241 and SI 2002 No. 2842).

Mutual recognition of architectural qualifications

1.04 The Directive allows architects with appropriate UK qualifications to practise anywhere in the EC and architects from other member states to have the equivalent right to practise in this country. The Directive sets out in detail what are the minimum qualifications required for such mutual recognition and how these are to be proved.

Right of establishment and freedom to provide services

1.05 The Directive similarly lays down rules for the mutual recognition of an architect's rights to set up in practice in a host member state or to provide architectural services in another member state.

The fundamental principle contained in the Directive is that there must be no discrimination against other EC nationals which would make it more difficult for them to establish themselves or provide services in the host state than it would be for nationals of that state.

1.06 Similar provision has been made for the mutual recognition within the Community of those employed in the construction industry by the following measures:

1 **The Certificates of Experience Directive 64/77/EC** This directive aims to ensure that experience of doing a particular job in one member state is recognised in other member states. Certificates are issued by the competent authority, in the state where the experience is gained so that a registration body in any other member state can recognise the holder as a suitably experienced person. In some European countries a period of experience and/or training is required before a person can set up as an independent plumber or electrician.

2 **First General Directive on Professional Qualifications 89/48/EC** This directive, which has been implemented in the UK by the European Communities (Recognition of Professional Qualifications) Regulations 1991 (SI 1991 No. 824), deals with the general system for recognising professional education and training in regulated professions for which university courses lasting at least 3 years is required. Courses for engineers, surveyors and other construction industry professionals lasting 3 years or more are covered by this directive.

3 **Second General Directive on Professional Qualifications 92/51/EC** This directive complements Directive 89/48/EC by extending the regime provided by that directive to qualifications obtained on completion of such education and training over a shorter period, whether at secondary level (possibly complemented by professional training and experience), postsecondary level, or even merely through professional experience. It has been implemented in the UK by the European Commissions (Recognition of professional qualifications) (Second General System) Regulations 1996 (SI 2374 No. 1996).

It applies to any national of a member state who wishes to pursue a 'regulated' profession in a host member state, whether in a self-employed capacity or as an employed person, other than a profession covered by a specific directive establishing arrangements for mutual recognition of professional qualifications (e.g. the Architects Directive), or an activity covered by certain specific directives principally concerned with introducing mutual recognition of technical skills based on experience in another member state and listed in an annex to the Directive. The Directive will only apply in cases where Directive 89/48/EEC is inapplicable, i.e. where the training required in the host state is less than 3 years' higher education at university level.

Belgium

1.07 Architects are divided into three categories: principals, civil servants and salaried architects. The architect, despite being required to supervise the building work, acts only as adviser to the client and not generally as agent. He provides designs, costings and quantities, technical drawings and supervision. Contractors and architects in Belgium are jointly responsible for major defects in buildings for a period of ten years. Following changes in the law in 1985, professional indemnity insurance is obligatory for Belgian architects and insurance companies have established a technical inspectorate to reduce the risk of major defects. Approval of a building by the technical inspectorate is usually accepted by insurance companies as evidence of satisfactory construction. The contractual liability of the architect is 10 years following the completion of the building, but in tort the normal period of limitation is 30 years. However, with regard to latent minor defects which do not fulfil the statutory 'sufficiently serious' criterion, a client may bring a claim in contract up to 30 years from handover, provided the claim is made promptly on discovery.

Denmark

1.08 It is not necessary to hold a licence to practise architecture in Denmark. It is possible to register with the Danish Professional Body, 'the DAL', if the architect has the qualifications listed in Council Directive 85/384/EEC on the mutual recognition of diplomas and certificates. The contractual limitation period for claims against the architect is 20 years. However, in principle, under the standard contract conditions, architects' liability may extend for only 5 years from handover of the building (although in private construction projects this condition may be excluded). The Danish Building Defect Fund is an independent statutory institution which aims both to prevent the occurrence of building faults and to ensure the repair of defects in buildings covered by the Fund (for a period of 20 years). A one-off premium, equivalent to 1% of the building cost, is paid by the building owner to the fund. Half of this sum is used to cover the cost of an inspection which is carried out just before the end of the 5-year period following handover. If any defects are discovered, the fund has recourse against any consultant found to be liable, including the architect under his professional indemnity policy, within this 5-year post-handover period. The remainder of the premium is used to cover the repair of any defects discovered after the 5-year inspection, for up to 20 years.

France

1.09 In France the architect's profession has traditionally been regarded as artistic rather than technical. By contrast, engineers are highly trained technically and tend to perform the type of technical duties undertaken in Britain by an architect. The architects and engineers in France are assumed to be jointly responsible with the contractor for the completed development. In the event of a claim arising from a defect in the building, all the parties are normally joined in the action and responsibilities will be apportioned between them. Any contractor or designer can be held responsible for 100% of the cost of repair while investigations are carried out into the cause of the defect. Under France's Civil Code the contractual period of liability in France for claims against architects is 2 years from 'Réception' (approximately equivalent to Practical Completion) for minor repairs and 10 years for structural defects. Liability is strict in that any claim against the architect does not need to prove negligence – merely that a building is not fit for its purpose. In addition, full economic and consequential losses are recoverable both in contract and in tort. Insurance is compulsory for anyone who could be liable under the Civil Code and 'decennial' liability insurance is taken out by the employer, although any claims paid by the insurance company may be pursued against the architect since subrogation rights are rarely waived. The importance of buying the correct insurance policy should not be underestimated.

Germany

1.10 The German construction industry is the largest in Europe. Architects and engineers supervise the construction of a project and the architect's responsibility does not, therefore, end with the design. There is more management and administration work in their job than is the case in many of the other EU member countries. Demarcation between engineers and architects is less clear

cut than in Britain. Both professionals have 4 to 6 years of technical training before an additional 2 years of training for each gives them their qualification to practice. For contractual claims the limitation period for an architect is 30 years, but in tort it is 3 years. The standard German architect's appointment document (the HOAC) sets a statutory minimum fee scale, although clients have devised numerous ways to circumvent the statutory minimum fees. The liability for the architect is, like France, 'strict' in that negligence does not have to be proved, although this is normally only the case for claims of rectification of design or fee disputes. If damages are claimed, then there is a greater onus of proof upon the client. Some loss of profit is normally recoverable but not to the extent of full consequential losses as in France.

Ireland

1.11 There are no obstacles to British architects wishing to practise in Ireland as British architectural qualifications are recognised there. The duties of an architect in Ireland are similar to those existing in Britain, so that his terms of engagement will exclude him from liability in respect of work or advice provided by other professional advisers but will make him liable for errors, patent or latent, in the design for which he is responsible. Whereas in England and Wales the position of an architect's liability in negligence towards third parties has been restricted by recent case law, this is not so for Ireland, where anyone affected by the careless act of another, whose interests that other person ought reasonably to have taken into account, would be entitled to recover compensation for negligence unless there was some public policy reason why this should not be permitted.

Italy

1.12 The roles of the architect and engineer overlap considerably. Clients may appoint an architect or an engineer to a project, or alternatively a director of works who takes responsibility not only for the design, but also manages and supervises the construction. Design-and-build contracts have been particularly popular in Italy. As in France, the contractual limitation period for actions against architects is 10 years. Professional indemnity insurance is not obligatory and is rarely taken out by consultants. Unusually, the construction industry in Italy is not prone to extensive litigation which is largely due to the cost and length of judicial procedures. A recent European Court of Justice decision ordered Italy to relax its laws restricting architects qualified in other EU countries from working in Italy. Italy had failed to properly implement the European directive that relates to the mutual recognition of architectural qualifications. The requirements it put in place in relation to the documents that a non-Italian architect had to provide were too onerous. Furthermore, Italy was in breach of the general European principle of freedom to provide services because it prevented people who were trying to exercise that freedom from establishing a permanent base in Italy. A court decision like this is very expensive for a member state. The fines imposed are hefty and daily fines can be imposed until the member state amends its legislation appropriately. This decision should improve the ease with which architects can set up a practice in Italy.

Netherlands

1.13 In order to use the title 'architect' in the Netherlands, it is necessary to first be enlisted in the legal register (which is called the SBA). A British qualified architect can register because their qualifications are recognised in the Netherlands by virtue of the European directive mentioned above. Liability in contract extends for 10 years from major defects. However, one important difference in the Netherlands is that the damages awarded to a plaintiff may only amount to half the designer's fees and it is possible to opt out of liability altogether as part of the contract of engagement. Given the nature of the soil in the Netherlands, demolition and piling contractors normally have direct contracts with the employer. For the same reason, many contracts will have an engineering element.

Portugal

1.14 The qualifications of British architects will be recognised in Portugal. Prior to commencing practising, it is necessary to register with the official Portuguese registration authority, the Ordem dos Arquitectos (OA). Networking is common in Portuguese business and so a contract with a local architect will be useful. The role of an architect in Portugal is unfortunately ill defined, but a significant difference is that, for contractors, statutory liability extends only for 5 years for private works and 2 years for state works after the commissioning of a building if the contract is silent on the point. Since 1991, professional indemnity insurance is obligatory for 'designers' (including architects) involved in private construction works, such insurance being to provide cover for a 5-year post-construction liability period.

Spain

1.15 The Spanish economy suffered a slump during the mid-1990s, following the Seville Expo and the Barcelona Olympics, but recovered towards the end of the decade. Every building project in Spain must be designed and supervised by a registered architect who is responsible for the aesthetics of the building. He undertakes to design and supervise the building, provide project documentation and prepare sub-contracts for other professionals. Spain's legal system imposes onerous legal responsibility on the design architect. It is the individual architect, rather than the firm that he works for, who is liable for the designs he prepares. For this reason, all architects in Spain carry extensive liability insurance. Architects' registration is maintained by the 17 colleges of architects, one for each autonomous community. The 'Collegio' has considerable power since each architect must be a member, the level of fees is set by the college and it also provides building permit approval. A separate 'technical architect' is responsible for supervising the technical aspects of the building and his role covers much of the work which would be carried out in the UK by a quantity surveyor. Claims against architects must be made within 10 years of the commencement of the project but this is extended to 15 years where there has been a breach of contract.

Rest of the World

China

1.16 Most noticeably, the culture affecting the industry is, not surprisingly, entirely different. For example, if the client decides to redesign at any stage in the works, then there is no cost implication for the client. A commonly used form of building contract where British architects or engineers are involved in China is the FIDIC form (see Chapter 21 for more detail). However, the concept of an independent consultant acting fairly between the parties is not a widely recognised concept in China. There has been much greater scope for work in China, for two reasons. First, in the form of massive works in the run-up to the 2008 Olympic Games, which China hosted, and secondly, following China's full membership of the World Trade Organization (WTO) in November 2002. In the lead-up to the Olympic Games, 40 new sporting venues needed to be created, together with improvements to airports, roads, other transport infrastructure and telecommunications. Joining the WTO has removed many of the obstacles that previously existed for foreign architects wishing to work in China. Foreign architects can now take majority shareholdings in local joint ventures and in 3 to 5 years' time will be able to set up wholly owned Chinese subsidiaries. Generally speaking, the potential for work is good and is assisted by the Chinese view that a project is more prestigious if a foreign architect was involved in its design.

Malaysia

1.17 Like many of the other South-east Asian countries, Malaysia is experiencing a rapidly growing construction industry. No person can practise as an architect unless he is registered with the Board of Architects. Under the Malaysian Architect Act, no person other than a registered architect shall be entitled to recover in any

court any charge, fee or remuneration for any professional service rendered as an architect in Malaysia. Therefore, foreign architects not registered with the Board of Architects who provide architectural services in Malaysia cannot sue the defaulting employer for payment in Malaysia. A registered architect in Malaysia is only entitled to be paid in accordance with the scale of fees set by the Board of Architects. Foreign architects can secure temporary registration if resident and possessing special expertise or forming the foreign component of a joint venture. Often the best way to proceed in Malaysia is by way of an unincorporated joint venture.

Hong Kong

1.18 Hong Kong became a Special Administrative Region of China on 1 July 1997 and English cases are still persuasive (but not binding) authorities. Law from other Commonwealth countries is also used to decide the rights and obligations of the parties. Australian cases, in particular, can prove useful as authorities, for example, in relation to the interpretation of 'pay when paid' clauses. Again, cultural differences play a significant role in the legal system and the importance of 'saving face' means that many disputes are referred to arbitration rather than litigation in order to maintain privacy. Consequently, the procedure for arbitration is particularly well established and the prominence of the Hong Kong International Arbitration Centre is an example of its importance. Whilst arbitration procedure is similar to that in the UK, it is regulated by the Hong Kong Arbitration Ordinance and the UNCITRAL United Nations model law on arbitration and procedure is often used. Architects who wish to practise in Hong Kong face a relatively straightforward procedure. To practise in Hong Kong, no permit from the Chinese government is required. However, before one can practise as an architect in Hong Kong, he must satisfy the requirements set out in the Architect Registration Ordinance such as being a member of Hong Kong Institute of Architects (HKIA) and to satisfy the Architect's Registration Board that he has one year's relevant professional experience in Hong Kong before the date of the application for registration. The contract with the employer by an architect can be made in any form or simply on the standard conditions of engagement set out in the form of Agreement between Client and Architect and Scale of Professional Charges prepared by the HKIA. In Hong Kong, the scope of works normally performed by an architect may fall into two different categories, i.e. pre-contractual and post-contractual duties. The most important of the pre-contractual duties is design. The post-contractual duties are certification, supervision and carrying out of inspections, compliance with laws and the general administration of the building contract for the employer.

USA

1.19 Apart from Europe, one potential, but as yet largely unrealised, market for British architects is the USA. Whereas in the UK the client usually engages the architect by an appointment separate from those of other consultants, in the USA it is far more common for the architect to be appointed by the client and then for the architect to sub-contract to other consultants the performance of the engineering and mechanical services. Thus the architect will assume vicarious liability for the actions of the consultants employed by him, something which the British architect is best advised to avoid.

In contrast to the UK position, there is much wider use of standard forms produced by the American Institute of Architects (AIA). The AIA produce a whole series of agreements from the 'Owner and Architect Agreement' to the main form of building contract, together with sub-contracts. These are widely accepted within the USA, although there may be slight amendments from state to state.

In the USA architects must be licensed and individual states and territories regulate entry into, and practice of, the professions within their jurisdiction. State statutes and regulations are based on the principle that practice by one who is not of proven technical and professional competence endangers the 'public's health, safety and welfare'. Licensing laws and regulations often restrict the use of the title 'architect', as well as outlining qualifications and procedures for registration as an architect, addressing any issues of reciprocity of registration with other states and defining the unlawful practice of architecture.

In a similar way, and unlike the UK, each state has its own Building Codes and these are the primary regulatory instruments for the design of buildings and structures on the site. Since local jurisdictions are authorised to adopt and enforce building regulations, Building Codes vary among states and even among cities within the same state. There are an estimated 13 000 Building Codes in the United States. The codes cover, *inter alia*, specific design and construction requirements, permissible construction types, and egress requirements. Once a Building Code has been adopted by a jurisdiction it becomes a document that holds the force of law. Violation of building codes and regulations is viewed seriously and may lead to the architect being held legally liable or his licence being revoked. Some jurisdictions allow for construction to be stopped for non-compliance and continued non-compliance may lead to a fine or a prison sentence. It is, therefore, important for an architect to establish which building codes are in force in the jurisdiction where he is working.

Another important contrast with the UK is that there are no quantity surveyors in the USA. The architect is therefore responsible for the preparation of the contract documents for approval by the client. However, as mentioned above, the standard forms produced by the AIA usually do not require modification since they are widely accepted.

It is the contractor's responsibility to quantify and estimate once the architect has produced plans and specifications. Once again, the AIA produces a guide to tendering or 'bidding' which the client and architect can use to determine to whom the contract is let. The architect's role in producing designs and plans is not greatly different from that in the UK although in the USA 'shop drawings' are produced and a contractor is given somewhat greater scope to decide how to implement those plans.

On the question of liability in general architects tend to be sued slightly more in the USA than in the UK. This may be partly because the nature of US society is more litigious and partly because up to approximately 20% of all claims against the architect are personal injury claims. This latter characteristic is because building workers tend to sue the architect as a way of increasing the amount of compensation received for physical injury (the state-run basis being a no-fault compensation scheme, known as 'Workers' Compensation Insurance'). By accepting the state-run compensation, the worker cannot pursue his employer and may look to the architect to top up his damages.

The law relating to breach of contract and negligence varies from jurisdiction to jurisdiction and the periods of time in which claims can be made against an architect are not always clear. The length of time within which an action for negligence can be brought may be as short as 4 years. For actions for breach of contract the period may be only 1 year. In some jurisdictions, time limits are not specified and the time periods themselves may start to run at different times. It is a rapidly changing area of law and, therefore, it is important that the architect seeks legal advice as to the limitation rules that apply in the particular jurisdiction in which he is working.

In relation to insurance, there are general differences between the UK and the USA. Usually, in the latter, there is only one annual aggregate of liability cover whereas in the UK it is usual for each and every claim to be covered (although this may contain a limit in aggregate and other conditions). Also, in the USA there are specific areas of exclusion from cover such as a claim relating to asbestos or pollution. UK insurers will not automatically extend cover for a UK architect to work in the USA and it may be necessary to obtain additional insurance in the USA itself.

United Arab Emirates

1.20 Despite the fact that Abu Dhabi, the capital city of the UAE, is known as 'the Manhattan of the Gulf' and Dubai was, until recently, the fastest-growing commercial centre in the region, there is almost no regulation of architects or their work. Foreign architectural firms seeking a licence to work in the country are required

to have a local sponsor and to submit fully attested professional qualification certificates, for all professional disciplines to the local government office responsible for issuing the licence. This is repeated each year when the trade licence is renewed. In Dubai they are required to also belong to the local Society of Engineers. Clients generally rely on the terms of their contract with the architect and professional indemnity cover is almost always required: some government institutions have been known to require that the insurance be provided through local insurance companies. The limitation period for contractual claims against the architect, if specified in the contract, is commonly 10 years but the limitation period for tortious claims is 3 years from the date the claimant becomes aware of the harmful act. In any event, no tortious claim can be brought after 15 years from the date on which the harmful act occurred. It is also worth noting that under UAE law contractual and tortious claims cannot be brought at the same time.

Japan

1.21 Construction firms deal with about 40% of all building design in Japan via design-and-build-style packages. Independent architectural firms of varying sizes carry out the remaining 60% of building design. In the average Japanese firm, architectural staff spend two-thirds of their time carrying out building design work and the remaining third of their time carrying out construction supervision. Sometimes these roles overlap, notably when design development continues after construction has commenced.

Contracts in Japan are interpreted in accordance with the doctrine of good faith and fair dealing. The literal meaning of a contract will not be applied if it is not in the interests of fairness to do so. Contracts are, therefore, inexact and adaptable. This is a concept that will seem alien to British architects who rely on contracts to set out their obligations in detail.

Liability for work carried out is usually shared by the design and construction teams on a project. Liability may also be shared with third parties such as insurers. An architect is only likely to be asked to assume individual responsibility for any performance failure where there is no confidence in his proposed approach to a design. After a project has been completed, the architect will usually make at least one follow-up visit to the site a year later to check that there have not been any problems post completion.

In Japan the cost of negligence/liability is more predictable because the courts tend to award smaller amounts. As a result, there is less incentive to litigate and litigation is, as a result, less frequent. It is currently rare for Japanese architects to have liability insurance which suggests that potential awards for liability are considered to be so small that the risk does not justify the expense of buying insurance premiums. However, the number of architects who carry insurance is now increasing because the number of actions against architects is also increasing. It is still the case that litigation is discouraged by the Japanese legal system as it is expensive and time consuming but as it becomes more common, more architects will invest in insurance premiums.

General remarks

1.22 The larger firms of architects in the UK have already been active in seeking appointments abroad and their type of involvement will depend very much upon the role their client gives them. They may be appointed directly by the client as the main architect for the project; they may combine with a local firm of architects and form a kind of joint venture; they may establish a local office in that particular country governed by local laws; or they may simply have an advisory role either to the client or as the job architect in an otherwise uninvolved position. The Architects' Directive which was implemented in the UK in 1987 enabled British architects to practise in any other member country of the EU without restriction. In theory this sounds very simple but in practice there are still some restrictions, as, for example, in Germany where foreign architects who wish to practise there must satisfy the qualification requirements to show adequate knowledge of German regulations and the language. The European Commission has struggled to force member states to implement the legislation properly. It has brought infringement proceedings against Greece and Spain and also forced Belgium and Italy to amend their legislation to give the Directive proper effect. As the harmonisation process continues, the obstacles to British architects working within the European Union shall, likewise, diminish.

1.23 Although these introductory paragraphs have concentrated mainly upon Europe, the Far East and the USA, the object of this chapter is to give architects a brief glimpse of some of the legal pitfalls in working abroad together with the areas where architects will need to seek specialist legal advice in relation to their employment worldwide.

The next section deals with the problem of conflicts between different jurisdictions and some examples of the different approaches used to deal with these problems.

2 Conflicts of laws

2.01 The legal problems which the architect encounters when working overseas always involve issues of jurisdiction and proper law: do the courts of the country in which the building is constructed have jurisdiction over him and which law will be applied to resolve a dispute arising from the design and construction of the building? In particular, it is important for the architect to know whether the terms of his appointment will be recognised in another country; whether he will be able to enforce his rights against a foreign party in a foreign jurisdiction; what law will govern the performance of the architect's services; and whether the architect's insurance will cover him for work done overseas.

Jurisdiction and proper law

2.02 It is of the utmost importance that the architect gives early consideration, before the employer has retained other consultants, the Contractor or sub-contractors, to the question of jurisdiction and proper law. Even if the employer has in mind certain contractors/consultants, the architect should attempt to influence the employer in relation to the type of appointment, building contract or sub-contract to be used so that its terms are familiar to the architect and so that the jurisdiction and proper law clauses throughout the contract documents are consistent.

Clearly, the choice of jurisdiction to establish where and in which type of forum disputes will be heard is an important consideration and, in such a clause, thought should be given to such matters as which law is to be applied, convenience, reliability of the different courts, speed, costs, the location of assets, and whether the resulting judgment will travel. In some cases, the parties may prefer to contract out of the court system and have their disputes resolved privately, by arbitration. There may, however, be local law restrictions on contracting out of the jurisdiction of the courts. Where the parties are prepared to litigate, it is possible to provide for exclusive jurisdiction clauses or alternatively, non-exclusive clauses which will allow the parties a choice of forum. In circumstances where there are restrictions on the parties' rights to choose jurisdiction, jurisdiction may be reserved to the local courts. For example, local statutes may prohibit choice of jurisdiction clauses in certain types of contract, or a party may have a constitutional right to be sued in the courts of his state. Furthermore, there may be treaty obligations which regulate the choice of jurisdiction, or there may be relevant matters of local public policy. This underlines the importance of taking legal advice beforehand so that the position can be confirmed.

There should also be a 'proper' or 'governing' law clause which specifies the substantive law of the contract which will govern the 'parties' legal rights and obligations under the contract. This may be included in the jurisdiction clause but, more usually, is dealt with in a separate clause. Without such provision the courts will reach their own view on what the substantive law should be, which creates uncertainty in any dispute resolution process. When there is no express choice, the English courts (following the 1980 Rome Convention on the Law Applicable to Contractual Obligations) usually apply a choice of the law of the legal system with the closest

connection to the case. For example, if asked to adjudicate on a dispute between two French parties with the subject-matter in France, the court would apply French law on the basis that this implements the reasonable and legitimate expectations of the parties to a transaction. Although this is the principle adopted by the English courts, it is far better to provide expressly in the contract for the proper law. This is because, first, local courts in another jurisdiction may adopt different principles and, secondly, it does not leave the parties' intentions open and uncertain to be decided by the court. Most countries with established legal systems will apply the law chosen expressly by the parties to the contract.

Brussels Convention

2.03 The above analysis helps to answer the question, whether the terms of the architect's appointment can be made subject to a familiar jurisdiction and law despite the fact that he is working in a foreign jurisdiction and being subject to foreign laws, provided that care is taken in the drafting of the jurisdiction clause. There is, however, an important qualification to these comments, brought about by the implementation of EC Regulation 44/2001 (the 'Brussels Regulation'). This came into force on 1 March 2002, superseding the Brussels Convention of 1968. Currently, the Brussels Regulation covers jurisdiction and enforcement issues in 26 of the 27 European Union states (France, Germany, Italy, Belgium, the Netherlands, Luxembourg, Ireland, the UK, Greece, Spain, Portugal, Sweden, Austria, Bulgaria, Cyprus, the Czech Republic, Estonia, Hungary, Latvia, Lithuania, Malta, Poland, Romania, Slovakia, Slovenia and Finland). While Denmark is not subject to the Brussels Regulation, a separate agreement between it and the EU which came into effect on 1 July 2007 effectively extends the Regulation's application to cover Denmark.

The principles also extend to other countries, such as Norway under the Lugano Convention. Under the Brussels Regulation and Lugano Convention the general rule is that persons domiciled in a particular member country must be sued in that country. Domicile is a complex concept but can be loosely equated to residence combined with a 'substantial connection' with a chosen country. For corporations domicile is associated with 'seat'. Article 23 of the Brussels Regulation, however, provides that where parties agree to settle disputes under the jurisdiction of the court in a particular member country, 'that court, or those courts, shall have exclusive jurisdiction'. This overrides any local law prohibiting jurisdiction clauses but it is important that the formalities are complied with in order to give effect to Article 23. These are that the agreement confirming jurisdiction shall be in writing or evidenced in writing or in a form which accords with practices which the parties have established between themselves unless it relates to a matter involving international trade or commerce, where other rules apply. In addition, there is a strict requirement of evidence of consent by all the relevant parties.

The question of the architect suing for his fees in the context of the rules of the Brussels Regulation where there is no Article 23 jurisdiction clause in the contract has been considered by the European Court of Justice in *Hassan Shenavai v Klaus Kreischer* (although this case considered the virtually identical Article 17 of the Brussels Convention, which Article 23 replaced). Here a German architect was suing a German national residing in the Netherlands for his fees. According to the Brussels Convention (as then was) the general criterion for determining jurisdiction is the domicile of the defendant. However, the Court applied one of the exceptions to the Domicile rule namely that in matters relating to a contract, the defendant may also be sued in 'the courts for the place of performance of the obligation in question'. The principal obligation in question, when the proceedings were for the recovery of architects' fees, was held to be the specific contractual obligation for the defendant to pay the fee, in the Netherlands, rather than the contractual relationship as a whole. In this case the place of performance was not the place of the architect's practice nor the site of the planned building but the place where the fee was to be treated as being paid. This was held to be the residence of the client in the Netherlands. Whether that position would apply if the proper law of the contract were English is doubtful. The architect could have safeguarded himself in that case by including in the contract a jurisdiction clause providing for the courts of his choice to have

jurisdiction. Although this is a relatively old case it is still good law and was reinforced by the more recent case (2009) of *Commercial Marine Piling Ltd v Pierse Contracting Ltd*.

The facts of the Scottish case *Bitwise Ltd v CPS Broadcast Products BV* (2002) were distinguished from the *Hassan Shenavai* case. The Scottish court followed the reasoning in the earlier case by reiterating that, in order to rely on a particular performance obligation under a contract as being indicative of the jurisdiction that applied to the contract, that obligation should also form part of the basis of the claim.

2.04 Where there appears to be a conflict between, for example, the obligations of the architect as described in the appointment governed by English law, and the obligations of the architect as described in the building contract (governed by another law), the appropriate law to be applied would be determined by the particular court having jurisdiction under its domestic conflict of law principles. Thus, for example, if the dispute were to be settled in an English court, that court would be obliged to enquire with which legal system the overall transaction had its closest and most real connection. This would determine the 'proper law' of the contract and the judges would consider a variety of circumstances, such as the nature of the contract, the customs of business, the place where the contract was made or was to be performed, the language and form of the contract, in order to determine which legal system should apply.

2.05 The second question which concerns an architect, once he has gone through the trauma and expense of pursuing, defending or counterclaiming in a dispute against a party from another jurisdiction, is whether he would be able to enforce his successful judgment against that party. Outside the European Union, where the Brussels Regulation does not apply, the ease and likelihood of recognition of foreign judgments depends on whether there is an applicable treaty between the particular countries concerned, which provides for reciprocal enforcement of judgments. If such a treaty exists then, subject to various formalities, the court of one country will enforce the other country's judgment against the defendant's assets in that jurisdiction provided, normally, that the judgment is for money only. Where no mutual recognition treaty exists between the country of judgment and the desired country of execution, the process has to be started afresh in that country although in many jurisdictions the existence of a foreign judgment in relation to the same issues will operate as proof of a debt which permits a more expedited process. This matter should be dealt with by professional advisers when entering into the appointment.

For enforcement within the European Union and EFTA countries, the Brussels Regulation and the Lugano Convention are not limited to money judgments nor to final judgments. The court in which enforcement is sought has very limited powers to investigate the jurisdiction of the court which gave the judgment. In other words, it is much easier to enforce a judgment in a country within the European Union than outside it. Enforcement may only be refused on the grounds of public policy, lack of notice of proceedings, the irreconcilability of the judgment given in a dispute between the same parties in the state in which recognition is sought, irreconcilability with an earlier judgment given in a non-contracting state involving the same cause of action and between the same parties (subject to the judgment satisfying certain conditions) and certain cases involving preliminary questions as to status. The foreign European court may not question the findings of fact on which the original court based its judgment, nor can a judgment be reviewed as to its substance.

Insurance

2.06 The third question which the architect should always consider in relation to overseas work is the extent to which his insurance will cover him for breaches of duty in the particular country in which he is working. No general answer can be given to this, nor can any statement be guaranteed in the future, since insurers will take different views in relation to various countries and at different times. For example, the type of insurance available on any project carried out in France would be the decennial project insurance towards which all the construction team pay premiums. This would cover the architect for breaches of duty for up to 10 years although it may not relieve the architect altogether because there may be subrogation rights to the insurers. However, architects who wish to practise in the USA may (due, perhaps, to the increased prevalence of claims brought against the architect there) have to seek separate professional indemnity insurance with local insurers since many UK-based insurers will not extend their cover to claims arising in the USA. In any event, before undertaking any overseas work the architect should check with his professional indemnity insurers whether or not he will be covered or can obtain cover from them in respect of that work.

Contractual duties

2.07 The standard of performance which local law may impose on architects clearly depends exclusively on the law at any particular time in the country concerned, and this can only be determined through personal experience of the architect of work in the jurisdiction and by legal advice. As between the parties who are bound contractually, the architect's duties will normally be defined in the contract documents. If the local law provides that duties are owed by the architect to third parties in tort, or indeed to parties with whom he is already in contract, the standard and scope of such duties can only be determined by reference to local lawyers. The architect will normally have to ensure that there is compliance with the local building regulations, etc., although it will first be necessary to check the architect's role under the building contract to determine if it is simply to check or to ensure compliance.

Copyright

2.08 One important aspect of international work that should be considered by architects is the protection of their copyright in relation to the designs, plans and drawings which they have prepared for the overseas work. Although it may be possible to include provision in the appointment for protection of copyright vis-à-vis the client, the drawings may be used by a number of parties who may be tempted to infringe the copyright of the architect and use the designs elsewhere, without permission. The position in the majority of developed countries roughly approximates to the provisions of the Berne Convention drawn up in 1886 with the most recent revisions in Paris in 1979. The UK has acceded to these provisions in the Copyright Act 1988 as amended by the Copyright etc. and Trade Marks (Offences and Enforcement) Act 2002. The Berne Convention gives protection for a minimum of the life of the author, and a post-mortem period of 50 years (although among EU member states this period has now been increased to 70 years) and requires countries bound by it to abandon any rules of deposit or registration as a condition of copyright protection. The Berne Convention also provides for the protection of the author's moral rights, which protects the author's right to have the work attributed to his name and the right to object to derogatory treatment of the work (once the moral right has been asserted). Any country can sign up to the Berne Convention and clearly, if the architect is dealing in a country which is a signatory to the Berne Convention he is fully protected. In other countries there may be a lesser form of protection, as under the Universal Copyright Convention (UCC), which gives protection for the life of the author plus 25 years and provides for any condition of registration or deposit to be satisfied when copies bear the symbol '©' accompanied by the name of the copyright owner and the year of first publication of the document. The USA has ratified the Berne Convention, as have a large number of non-EU countries, recent examples being Democratic People's Republic of Korea (2003), the Federated States of Micronesia (2003), Vietnam (2004), Samoa (2006) and Yemen (2008). As of April 2008, there were 163 signatories to the Berne Convention; a full list of those countries that have ratified

the Convention is located at. www.wipo.org/treaties/ib/berne/index.html. Where a country is a signatory of both the Berne Convention and the UCC, the Berne Convention takes precedence. Some countries belong only to the lesser of the two Conventions, i.e. the UCC. In a number of developing countries no international treaty obligations subsist whatsoever and the architect will have to rely on local copyright law, if any. Local legal advice should be sought as to the means of protecting copyright and to comply with those local laws.

Commercial considerations

2.09 Finally, the architect should consider practical commercial matters, such as failure of the employer to pay fees, the country's available resource of hard currency, and exchange rate fluctuations, taking advice from persons experienced in international work who may be able to recommend suitable insurance to cover these risks, together with ECGD cover and political credit risk insurance and possibly a performance bond. In addition, if the advice of local lawyers is to be obtained, this might best be channelled through British lawyers since many foreign lawyers, such as those in Germany, are not obliged to advise on the most cost-efficient procedure in any situation.

3 The future

3.01 As can be seen in other chapters in this book, the liability of architects is not clear-cut and is a point of constant discussion and negotiation, particularly in relation to the architect's appointment and the problems encountered by architects striving to stay within the terms of their insurance cover. In the UK this is due to the change of direction in the law relating to architects' duties. Clearly, when there is such uncertainty in our own country, that confusion can only be compounded when dealing with other jurisdictions, some based on the common law system (which is the basis of our own system) and some based on civil law systems as in many of the European countries.

3.02 The scope for work within Europe was given a substantial fillip by the enlargement from the European Community of 12 States in 1995 to the European Union of 27 States by 2007. This growth represents a dramatic increase of opportunity in Europe for UK architects. Already UK architects have appreciated the significance of the German construction industry, which, in the eastern part of Germany grew significantly in the early 1990s. Opportunities in the newer member states are particularly available to the medium or larger sized UK firms because these firms should be able firstly, to analyse effectively the advertisements (including OJEU Notices) for work opportunities abroad and, secondly, to establish the necessary local link to enable compliance with local legislation. Those UK architects who most readily adapt to the changing legislation of Europe will eventually reap the rewards in terms of a much greater client base and work experience.

3.03 Elsewhere, architectural practices are increasingly looking towards the high growth economies of Asia, Thailand, Malaysia, Hong Kong and the Middle East. The main problems experienced in these locations are cultural and financial rather than legal. Increasing experience will, in time, overcome such difficulties and established firms will see the progression into China as the next step. In the USA, UK architects continue to be in demand for their particular style and, although by far the biggest problem is obtaining professional indemnity insurance, careful risk allocation in the appointment documentation increasingly enables UK insurers to extend cover for work in these territories.

37

Architects' registration

SARAH LUPTON

1 The nature of professionalism in architecture

1.01 The concept of a professional person and an institutional profession has been continually evolving since the eighteenth century. Numerous studies of the subject have been made; one of the most concise appeared in 1970 as the report of the Monopolies Commission (Part 1: *The Report* A report on the general effect on the public interest of certain restrictive practices so far as they prevail in relation to the supply of professional services (Cmnd 4463). Part 2: *The Appendices* (Cmnd 4463–1)). Appendix 5 of the Report provides a range of definitions and descriptions which vary considerably but there is a general acceptance that a professional person is one who offers competence and integrity of service based upon a skilled intellectual technique and an agreed code of conduct.

1.02 The early history and development of the architectural profession in Britain are analysed in Barrington Kaye, *The Development of the Architectural Profession in Britain.* In a parallel study, *Architect and Patron*, Frank Jenkins, analysed the development of professional relations between architects and their clients prior to the beginning of the 1960s.

1.03 The place of professionalism and the role of the professional person in a rapidly changing society has been questioned frequently, not only by society in general but also by the members of the professions. The concerns of society are reflected in the Government's questioning of the role of the Architects Registration Council of the United Kingdom in the late 1980s and subsequent legislation, leading to the establishment of the Architect's Registration Board with its lay majority. There is a trend towards increased regulation of many professions (see, for example, concerns raised in the reports resulting from the Shipman Inquiry, or the Nursing and Midwifery Council special report of 2008), but architects are the only profession within the construction industry that has a protected title, and is subject to statutory regulation. The concerns of the architectural profession in this period of change, are reflected in the radical changes in its codes, the periodic reviews that it undertakes of the professions, and the ongoing debate on the status and role of the profession, as can be seen in the architectural press.

2 Architects' registration

2.01 In 1899 the first Architects' Registration Bill attempted to restrict the practice of architecture to those who were formally qualified; it was rejected, as were several others that followed. In 1931 the Architects (Registration) Act did not achieve the full intentions of its sponsors. It provided for the setting up of a register of architects but in merely protecting the use of title 'architect' it did not prevent others from carrying on the practice of architecture in the way that the sponsors hoped. This remains the position in the United Kingdom; it is an offence for anyone other than those on the register to use the title 'architect' but anyone may design buildings, carry out project administration, and undertake all the tasks usually done by architects. The Architects (Registration) Act 1931 and the amending Acts of 1938 and 1969 provided for the setting up, maintenance, and annual publication of a Register of Architects; the maintenance of proper standards of professional conduct; and the provision of limited financial assistance for some students. The registration body was funded by the annual registration fee of those on the register.

2.02 In the 1980s many of the professions found themselves under criticism; there was an increasing concern for consumer rights; and the role of the professional bodies as the protectors of the public interest was questioned. In the case of the architectural profession the whole basis of its statutory position under the Architects (Registration) Acts 1931 onwards was questioned; other professions in the construction industry asked why architects alone enjoyed protection of title and architects themselves questioned the value of protection of title when the function and activity were open to anyone wishing to offer their services. The Royal Institute of British Architects and other bodies also questioned the role and need for a statutory registration body. The RIBA Council, originally in favour of the dissolution of the Registration Council and the transfer of its powers to the RIBA, reversed its policy and campaigned for its retention. The Government undertook an extensive consultative exercise.

2.03 In parallel with these discussions, Sir Michael Latham was conducting a Government-sponsored review of procurement and contractual arrangements in the construction industry and in July 1994 his final report, *Constructing the Team*, appeared. Its executive summary covered a wide range of radical recommendations some of which were to receive official support, although not as many as Latham had hoped. As there was little opportunity in the crowded parliamentary programme to introduce a Construction Bill the Government took advantage of a largely non-contentious Bill on housing grants to adopt its preferred recommendations from the Latham Report, as Part II of the Housing Grants, Construction and Regeneration Act 1996. Also, having made its decision on registration following the receipt of the Warne Report on the future of registration it added a Part III to the same Act. Subsequently, Part III of the Housing Grants, Construction and Regeneration Act 1996 was repealed in the Architects Act 1997.

2.04 The Architects Act 1997 also repealed the Architects (Registration) Act 1931, the Architects Registration Act 1938, the Architects' Qualifications (EEC Recognition) Order 1987, and the Architects' Qualifications (EC Recognition) Order 1988. The provisions of the Act are significantly different in principle and detail from those of the 1931 and 1938 legislation. In place of the large former Architects Registration Council, which consisted almost exclusively of architects, there is now a small Architects Registration Board (ARB) consisting of seven members elected by persons on the register and eight persons appointed by the Privy Council in consultation with the Secretary of State. As the Act specifically makes registered persons ineligible from being appointed persons, there must always be a lay majority on the Board.

2.05 In addition to the Board, the Act makes provision for a Statutory Professional Conduct Committee which is responsible for disciplinary matters. The make-up of the Professional Conduct Committee is interesting – it comprises:

- four elected members of the Board;
- three appointed members of the Board;
- three persons nominated by the President of the Law Society; and
- six persons appointed by the Board, including three persons registered in Part 1 of the Register of whom the address of at least one in the Register is in Scotland.

3 Eligibility for registration

3.01 Persons are eligible for registration if they hold such qualifications and have gained such experience as the ARB may prescribe or if they have an equivalent standard of competence. For UK registration this normally means that they must pass recognised Parts 1, 2 and 3 qualifications. (A list of all the Part 1, Part 2 and Part 3 qualifications is available on the ARB website (www.arb.org.uk) or from the ARB.) In addition, applicants for registration are required to complete a minimum period of 2 years' structured and recorded architectural experience in a range of activities.

The Board's General Rule 13 states that the 2 years' practical training experience should be working under the direct supervision of an architect registered in the EU, and 12 months must be undertaken in the UK, under the direct supervision of a UK-registered person; 12 months must be undertaken after completion of a 5-year course of study and award of a Part 2 qualification. These requirements can be varied by the Board, acting within guidelines published by the Board from time to time.

3.02 Under the Architects Act 1997, the ARB has the statutory responsibility for prescribing those qualifications which lead to entry onto the UK Register of Architects.

New Prescription Procedures came into place in September 2003, alongside ARB's new assessment criteria which form the basis upon which ARB makes decisions regarding prescription. Schools of architecture, and other institutions that award architectural qualifications, must apply for and obtain the decision of the ARB as to whether those qualifications will be recognised as a prescribed qualification.

In addition to the ARB prescription of qualifications, the RIBA operates a validation procedure. This is a peer review process that 'monitors schools of architecture's compliance with internationally recognised minimum standards in architectural education and encourages excellence and diversity in student achievement'. Visiting Boards, composed of experienced practising architects, academics and lay persons, visit schools of architecture to assess standard of courses for exemption from the RIBA's Examinations in

Architecture. Although these visits had been in the past run jointly with the ARB, under the current Prescription Procedures the ARB need no longer participate in visits to Schools of Architecture. Nevertheless the two institutions continue to work closely in the development and monitoring of criteria for assessment and validation of courses. For example, the criteria used by the ARB to prescribe qualifications and the RIBA to validate qualifications are jointly held. These are currently under review, but the intention is that the new criteria will similarly be agreed and applied by both institutions.

3.03 The Recognition of Professional Qualifications Directive (2005/36/EC), which covers the architectural profession, requires that 'a Member State which makes access to or pursuit of a regulated profession in its territory contingent upon possession of specific professional qualifications (referred to hereinafter as the host Member State) shall recognise professional qualifications obtained in one or more other Member States . . . and which allow the holder of the said qualifications to pursue the same profession there, for access to and pursuit of that professional' (Article 1). The requirements of this Directive (which supersedes the Architects Directive (85/384/EEC)) have recently been implemented through the European Communities (Recognition of Professional Qualifications) Regulations 2007, and the Architects (Recognition of European Qualifications) Regulations 2008. The effect of this is to introduce significant changes to the Architects Act.

Under the new system, an EU applicant who is eligible to practise, or is lawfully established, as an architect in his home state, and who holds a qualification which is specifically listed in the Directive, and is a national of an EEA country, (or a 'Directive Rights National' i.e. someone with an enforceable Community right), would usually be eligible to register on 'Part 1' of the Register. 'Part 2' of the Register is reserved for visiting EEA architects who may provide temporary or occasional services only in the UK. EU applicants who do not meet all the requirements for automatic recognition should contact the ARB regarding their eligibility.

In the case of overseas applicants for registration other than EEA nationals the Board requires them to sit the ARB's prescribed examination, which provides recognition that candidates have achieved a standard of attainment that the Board views as comparable to prescribed qualifications at Parts 1 and 2 levels. Overseas persons wishing to undertake further academic and professional work in the UK would be prudent to check their position with regard to registration before embarking on a course.

3.04 An application fee and an annual retention fee are payable for registration, these being set annually by the Board.

3.05 It is an offence to become registered or attempt to become registered by making false or fraudulent representations or declarations, the penalty for which is a fine not exceeding level 3 on the standard scale. It is also an offence for an unregistered person to practise or carry on a business under a title containing the word 'architect', the penalty for which is a fine not exceeding level 4 on the standard scale.

3.06 A person's name may be removed from the register, if the Professional Conduct Committee makes an erasure or suspension order; or if that person fails to pay the annual retention fee.

3.07 Disciplinary Orders may be made by the Professional Conduct Committee in the event of a registered person being found guilty of unacceptable professional conduct, or serious professional incompetence, or a criminal offence relevant to the fitness of the person to practise as an architect. Unacceptable professional conduct and serious professional incompetence are assessed taking into account the Architects Code: Standards of Professional Conduct and Practice and the context of the particular circumstances of the case.

38

Professional conduct of architects

SARAH LUPTON AND PETER ANDERSON

1 Codes of professional conduct

1.01 An agreed and enforceable code of professional conduct is an essential part of any recognised profession. It is the profession's demonstration of its commitment to the service it offers and the standards that it upholds. Codes are devised in the interests of the clients of the profession and less directly in the interests of its members through the maintenance of the status of the profession in the eyes of society. The integrity of purpose of the codes and the impartiality of their enforcement is crucial to the public's perception of the profession. The requirements of codes change and evolve in response to changing circumstances and attitudes and emerging economic, political and social pressures. They have to reflect the attitudes of the membership of the profession and the consequences of legislation and litigation but, above all, the explicit and implicit expectations of an increasingly sophisticated clientele.

1.02 Architects in the United Kingdom are subject to the Code of Conduct of the Architects Registration Board (ARB). In addition those architects who choose to join other professional bodies such as the Royal Institute of British Architects (RIBA) or the Royal Incorporation of Architects in Scotland (RIAS) become subject to their codes. Until 1998 and the advent of the ARB the codes of the Architects Registration Council (ARC) and the codes of the institutions covered similar ground. While this remains the case – indeed, from 2003 the RIAS Code is now in full alignment with that of the ARB – there remain significant differences between the ARB and RIBA Codes.

1.03 The codes have both positive and negative aspects; there are essential actions that are specifically required and there are also actions which are specifically prohibited. The codes must not be regarded as a mere technical formality; they have a direct effect on practice and the ways in which an architect works. A lack of knowledge of the detailed requirements of the codes is not acceptable as a defence in the case of an alleged misdemeanour or breach of the codes; in some circumstances it could even be held to compound the offence. Lay clients are not expected to be familiar with the requirements of the codes but architects are required to inform their clients that architects are subject to the disciplinary sanction of the ARB. It is essential that architects have available copies of all the current relevant codes of conduct for immediate reference.

1.04 The ARB Code of Conduct is primarily concerned with the protection of the interests of the public and relations between architects and their clients. The codes of the institutions are not incompatible with the ARB Code and reflect many of the same concerns.

1.05 Failure to comply with the ARB Code could result in the removal of the person's name from the register, terminating the person's right to practise under the title 'architect' and possibly leading to the loss of livelihood. Failure to comply with the requirements of the code of a particular institution may lead to the suspension or loss of membership but provided that the person is not in breach of the ARB Code the right to practise under the title 'architect' remains and the business may continue. There are 'unattached' architects who are eligible for institutional membership but do not take up membership, and there are a few properly qualified individuals who do not apply for registration. The extent to which a person feels that it is necessary to take up and retain the right to the title or to continue institutional membership has to be a matter for the commercial and professional judgement of the individual. There are no statutory requirements for the employment of architects in the marketplace and clients may use whomsoever they wish to prepare designs, or inspect building works. Should clients pursue such action, neither the ARB nor the professional institutions have any power to address matters of complaint.

1.06 Where allegations of improper conduct also concern matters covered by the ARB Code the institutions usually delay disciplinary proceedings until the ARB's findings are known in order to avoid unnecessary expense and inconvenience for the parties. Where an allegation of a breach of one of the codes relates to court proceedings it is usual for all disciplinary proceedings to be delayed until after the court's decision but it should be noted that disciplinary proceedings are not conditional on the court's decision.

2 ARB Code of Conduct

2.01 The full title of the ARB code of conduct is *The Architects Code: Standards of Professional Conduct and Practice* (the Code). It can be viewed and downloaded from the ARB web site at www.arb.org.uk and is published in hard copy. The Code has recently been revised by the ARB (which involved a public consultation) and at the time of writing it is intended that the new version, discussed below, will be effective from January 2010. The Code comprises a statement of twelve Standards with which architects are expected to comply, an introduction, a six-page explanation of the twelve Standards and a two-page Guidance Note. All parts of the Code are inter-related and have to be read together. In addition to the Code the Board also publishes General Rules, Investigations Rules and Professional Conduct Committee Rules.

   A breach of the Code can result in the ARB Professional Conduct Committee issuing a disciplinary order reprimanding the architect; or fining the architect; or suspending the architect's registration for a period of up to two years; or erasing the architect's name from the register.

The Code begins by setting out the standards as follows:

"As an architect you are expected to:

1. Be honest and act with integrity
2. Be competent
3. Promote your services honestly and responsibly
4. Manage your business competently
5. Consider the wider impact of your work
6. Carry out your work faithfully and conscientiously
7. Be trustworthy and to look after your clients' money properly
8. Have appropriate insurance arrangements
9. Maintain the reputation of architects
10. Deal with disputes or complaints appropriately
11. Co-operate with regulatory requirements and investigations
12. Have respect for others"

The Introduction

2.02 The overriding obligation of the Code is that the architect is expected to act competently and with integrity in carrying out professional work. The Introduction comments that the fact that a course of conduct is not specifically referred to in the Code does not mean that it cannot form the basis of disciplinary proceedings: architects are expected to have regard to the spirit of the Code as much as its express terms. Conversely, it comments that not every shortcoming on the part of an architect will necessarily give rise to disciplinary proceedings (minor transgressions of the Code are not likely to prompt action unless they form part of a pattern of unacceptable professional conduct or serious professional incompetence).

Disciplinary orders may be made if an architect is convicted of a criminal offence which is relevant to the person's fitness to practise as an architect. In addition, a disciplinary order may be made against an architect if, after considering the case, the Professional Conduct Committee is satisfied the architect is guilty of unacceptable professional conduct and/or serious professional incompetence.

The Standards

2.03 The twelve Standards have to be read in conjunction with the Introduction and the Guidance Notes. Each of the Standards is helpfully amplified and illustrated by brief notes on some applications of the Standard to which they refer. Most of the Standards concern self-evident aspects of sound business and good practice but some are less obvious but equally important; practising architects must be aware of all twelve Standards and must understand their full implications.

The importance of the Standards must not be under-estimated; the consequences of an architect's failure to understand or apply the principles of the Standards can be serious. In the following commentary the numbers in parentheses refer to the sub-clauses of the Standards.

Standard 1: Honesty and Integrity

2.04 In its stringent requirements Standard 1 of the Code embodies many of the traditional principles of professional codes of conduct especially in context of relationships between architects and their clients and other affected parties. It is stated to underpin the Code, and will be taken to be required in any consideration of an architect's conduct under any of the other standards (1.1).

Architects are prohibited from making a statement which is contrary to their professional opinion or which they know to be misleading, or unfair to others, or otherwise discreditable to the profession (1.2).

Architects are required to disclose in writing to a prospective client or employer any financial or personal business interest which would or could raise a conflict of interest and doubts about their integrity if not so declared. Where the situation cannot be satisfactorily resolved and the parties concerned have not given their informed consent architects are required to withdraw from the situation (1.3). Developing complexity in funding arrangements, joint venture initiatives, partnering, and non-traditional procurement procedures increases the possibilities of conflicts of interest arising, especially where circumstances change during the project.

Where an architect has received any inducement for the introduction or referral of work, this should be disclosed to the client or prospective client at the outset (1.4).

Standard 2: Competence

2.05 Architects are expected to be competent to carry out any professional work that they undertake (2.1). It is fundamentally important that architects have regard to this standard, and do not take on commissions, however attractive, that they do not have the expertise to deliver. Where work is done by others working under the direction of the architect the architect is responsible for ensuring that they have the necessary competence to carry out the work and are properly supervised (2.1). Architects should have arrangements in place for the conduct of their business in the event of their death, incapacity, absence from or inability to work (2.2). This is clearly of particular relevance for sole practitioners, but even in larger practices architects must arrange for the smooth handover of projects in their absence.

Architects are expected to ensure that the necessary communication skills and local knowledge are available to them (2.3). This would be particularly relevant to UK registered architects who are undertaking work outside the UK (as the Code still applies to them) and to those registered architects who qualified outside the UK.

Architects are required to keep their knowledge and skills in areas relevant to their professional work up to date. This Standard reflects the policy of most professions which now require their members to undertake continuing professional development work. Failure to maintain professional competence could count against an architect in the event of that competence having to be investigated (2.4).

Standard 3: Honest promotion of your services

2.06 Architects are expected to promote their professional services in a truthful and responsible manner (3.1) This allows architects to advertise their services provided that it is not done in a manner that is untruthful or misleading and complies with the codes applying to advertising, including those of the Advertising Standards Authority (3.2).

The business style of the practice must not be misleading. (3.3) Difficulties can arise when partnerships are dissolved, businesses are restructured, and where former partners or staff setting up new practices wish to take credit for their previous work. Ideally these matters should be covered in termination agreements but where this has not happened care must be taken to ensure that any statements made are factually correct and capable of objective justification (3.1).

Principals in a practice are expected to ensure that all architectural work is under the control and management of one or more architects, and that their names are made known to clients and any relevant third party (3.4). Clients must be notified promptly of any change in the architect responsible for the work.

Standard 4: Competent management of your business

2.07 Architects are expected to have effective systems in place to ensure that their practices are run professionally and that projects are regularly monitored and reviewed (4.1). This would include ensuring that appropriate and effective internal procedures are in place. Architects should also ensure that they are able to provide adequate professional, financial and technical resources when entering into a contract and throughout its duration and that there are sufficient suitably qualified and supervised staff to enable the delivery of an effective and efficient client service (4.2). Although no prudent architect would knowingly take on work without the necessary competence and resources being available difficulties can arise in at least three ways. First, the nature of the work may not be fully apparent at the start of the project; second, the needs of the project and the nature of the work may vary during the project; and third, the circumstances of the architect's practice may change drastically during the work. It is important that the situation is continually monitored and essential that the client is immediately advised of anything that might prevent the architect from fulfilling the obligations under the Standard.

Architects are required to ensure that adequate security is in place to safeguard records for their clients (including electronic records), taking full account of data protection legislation, and that clients' confidential information is safeguarded (4.3). The safeguarding of confidential electronic information may in some cases require secure back-up storage.

Architects are prohibited from undertaking professional work unless the terms of the contract have been recorded in writing. The standard requires that terms should specify the identity of the parties, the scope of the work, the fee or method of calculating it, the allocation and any limitation of responsibilities, the provisions for suspension or termination of the appointment, a statement that they have adequate and appropriate insurance cover as specified by the Board, their complaints handling procedure and any special provisions for dispute resolution (4.4). Apart from being requirements of the Code these procedures represent good practice and are obviously in the best interests of both the client and the architect. A large proportion of disputes and complaints to the ARB arise from inadequate, informal or non-existent terms of appointment, leaving the client uncertain as to the service they can expect from their architect. Any agreed variations to the written agreement should be recorded in writing (4.5) and it should be made clear to the client the extent to which any of the architectural services are being subcontracted (4.7).

Architects are expected to ensure that their client agreements record their position under the Code, ie that they are registered with the Architects Registration Board and are subject to the Code; and that the client can refer a complaint to the Board where it appears the standards in the Code have not been met (4.6)

At the end of the contract the architect is required to return to the client on request all the papers, plans and other property to which the client is legally entitled (4.8). Normally this material includes all the drawings and other documents used in the works but not the material used by the architect in the development of the design. It may be pertinent to note that although the client is entitled to the drawings and other documents on the final payment of fees and charges the copyright in the design remains with the architect, unless otherwise specifically agreed.

Standard 5: Considering the wider impact of your work

2.08 The possible implications of this Standard are extremely wide-ranging although the guidance note only refers to the need to take into account the environmental impact of professional activities (5.1).

Standard 6: You should carry out your professional work faithfully and conscientiously and with due regard to relevant technical and professional standards

2.09 The overriding concern of practising architects must be to ensure that work is carried out with due skill, care and diligence and without undue delay, and so far as it is practicable within the time scale and cost limits agreed with the client (6.1 and 6.2). The requirement reflects the standard applied by the courts in their consideration of allegations of professional negligence. Architects are expected to keep the client informed of the progress of work undertaken on their behalf and of any issue which may significantly affect its quality or cost (6.3). Another key source of

disputes and complaints to the ARB is the fact that the client felt that they were not fully updated on progress, and architects should always ensure that adequate reporting systems are in place.

Architects, when acting between parties or giving advice, are required to exercise impartial and independent professional judgment to the best of their ability and understanding (6.4).

Architects offering or taking part in the offering of a service which combines consulting services with contracting services must make it clear to all parties in writing that their advice will no longer be impartial (6.4).

Standard 7: Trustworthiness and safeguarding clients' money

2.10 Generally architects should avoid situations in which they are required to hold monies belonging to the client, but where it is necessary to do so the requirements of the Standard should be followed in every detail, and before doing so an architect invited to manage the client's monies would be wise to take impartial advice.

A careful record of all transactions must be kept with the monies being held in an interest-bearing account separate from any account held by the practice or the architect concerned (7.1, 7.2).

The designated 'client account' must be protected with the bank being instructed in writing that the account may not be combined with other accounts or set-off against other claims (7.3).

Withdrawals may only be made from a client account on the client's instructions or on behalf of the client (7.4).

Unless otherwise agreed any interest earned has to be paid to the client (7.5).

Standard 8: Insurance arrangements

2.11 An architect is expected to have 'adequate and appropriate' insurance cover. The insurance policy must cover work undertaken by employees (8.1). The cover should be adequate to meet a claim and architects are required to maintain a minimum level, including run-off cover, in accordance with the Board's guidance.

The Standard draws attention to the need for insurance to cover work outside the architect's main professional practice (8.2). It is important that practitioners obtain confirmation from their insurers that any extensions in the services provided are covered by their insurance policies.

The requirement that employed architects should ensure that professional indemnity insurance cover or other appropriate cover is provided by their employer could pose problems in practice but the Code takes a practical view and the requirement is qualified by the phrase 'so far as possible' (8.3). There is no mention of the possible consequences of an employer's default on insurance cover.

If required architects must provide evidence to demonstrate compliance with this Standard (8.4).

Standard 9: Maintaining the reputation of architects

2.12 Architects should ensure that their professional finances are managed responsibly (9.1), and are expected to conduct themselves in a way which does not bring either themselves or the profession into disrepute (9.2). An architect is required to report to the Registrar within 28 days if they are convicted of a criminal offence; are made the subject of an order of disqualification from acting as a company director; are made the subject of a bankruptcy order; are director of a company which is wound up, make an accommodation with creditors or fail to pay a judgement debt (9.2). It should be noted that not all such instances would result in any action being taken by the ARB or the PCC, as in times of recession even with prudent management a firm may nevertheless get into financial difficulties. The standard is aimed primarily at irresponsible and willful conduct.

Architects are also required to inform the Board of any serious breach of the Code by another architect which may come to their notice (9.3). The Standard's requirement that an architect must draw attention to the apparent misconduct of fellow practitioners provoked some critical comments when it first appeared, but is a common feature of the codes of professionals generally and has been retained in this version. The standard is qualified by the phrase 'in appropriate circumstances' and architects are required to consult with the Board if in any doubt.

The Standard accepts that an architect appointed as an arbitrator, adjudicator, mediator, conciliator or expert witness and in receipt of privileged information may have duties which take precedence over any requirements to report breaches of the Code to the Board (9.4).

Apart from such situations or those concerned with the settlement of a dispute an architect may not enter into an agreement which would prevent any party from reporting an apparent breach of the Code to the Board (9.5). An architect is required to use their best endeavours to cooperate and assist with any investigation by the Board (9.6).

Standard 10: Deal with disputes or complaints appropriately

2.13 The requirements of the Standard are rigorous; they lay down strict time limits for dealing with complaints. The provisions of the Standard represent good practice and reflect those already included in a number of Quality Assurance Schemes.

Architects are expected to have a written procedure for prompt and courteous handling of complaints and provide this to clients. This should include the name of the architect who will respond to complaints (10.1). As far as practicable the client should be sent an acknowledgement of the complaint within ten days and the complaint should be dealt with within thirty days of the receipt of the complaint (10.2). At every stage complaints have to be handled promptly, courteously and sympathetically.

Wherever it is thought to be appropriate the Standard encourages the use of alternative dispute resolution procedures such as mediation or conciliation (10.3).

Standard 11: Co-operation with regulatory requirements and investigations

2.14 Architects are expected to co-operate fully and promptly with the Board, within any specified timescale, if asked to provide information which it needs to carry out its statutory duties, including evidence of compliance with the Standards. This requirement is broadly expressed and would cover such matters as evidence of compliance with insurance or CPD requirements set by the Board (11.1). Architects are required to notify the Board promptly and in writing of any changes in their details held on the Register. Under the Act, architects who do not tell the Board of a change of address may be removed from the Register (11.2).

Standard 12: Respect for others

2.15 This standard is new with the 2010 code, but a version of this is found in most if not all other professional codes. It requires architects to treat everyone fairly and in line with the law, and not to discriminate because of disability, age, gender, sexual orientation, ethnicity, or any other inappropriate consideration.

3 RIBA Code of Professional Conduct

3.01 The latest version of the RIBA Code of Professional Conduct and Standard of Professional Performance came into effect in January 2005. This replaced the previous version which had been published in April 1997, which in turn had replaced the 1981 version. The 1981 Code was of particular significance, in that the changes reversed much of the Institute's long-established stance on professionalism. They removed the restrictions on carrying on

the business of trading in land or buildings, or as property developers, auctioneers, estate agents or contractors, subcontractors, manufacturers or suppliers in or to the construction industry; permitted members to negotiate fees with potential clients and abandoned the mandatory minimum fee system; removed the ban on practising in the form of a limited liability company and extended the permitted means by which an architect might bring himself to the notice of potential clients.

The 1997 version introduced the Standard of Professional Performance as part of its Code of Professional Conduct, whereby the RIBA predated the use of standards in the Code of Conduct published by the Architects Registration Board in August 1997. Both Codes took into account the requirements of the Architects Act 1997.

In July 2003 RIBA Council agreed to a complete redrafting of its Code of Professional Conduct. The Code review coincided with a notification from the Office of Fair Trading that it considered undertakings 3.1 and 3.3 of the RIBA Code of Professional Conduct to be contrary to the Competitions Act 1998, following which the RIBA Council agreed that the two undertakings should be suspended. A small task group was set up to undertake the review and the result was approved by the RIBA Council in September 2004. The RIBA Code of Professional Conduct was published in January 2005. It can be downloaded from the RIBA website at www.architecture.com and is also published in hard copy.

3.02 The 2005 RIBA Code of Professional Conduct and Standard of Professional Performance comprises an introduction, a statement of the Royal Institute's values, three principles of professional conduct, brief notes which explain how the principles can be upheld, and a series of nine Guidance Notes which are published separately. The RIBA web site explains that the Guidance Notes are intended 'to provide both advice and information on best practice and to act as a support and aide to members in their professional work. They distinguish between conduct and practice which is obligatory and that which is only advisable or preferable. This distinction will be taken into account when a formal complaint of professional misconduct is made against a member.'

The 2005 Code is much shorter than the previous Code, and the use of the separate Guidance Notes means that these can be updated in the light of changing circumstances. As stated on the web site: 'the focus of the 2005 code is the consumer, and society at large. It is more outward-looking than its predecessor and states the standards of professional ethics and behaviour expected of chartered architects in the early twenty-first century more clearly and concisely.' Inevitably the RIBA Code of Professional Performance has much in common with the ARB Code of Conduct although there are some differences. In particular, the RIBA Code's provisions covering the behaviour of members to each other has no equivalent in the ARB Code. Members of the RIBA who are registered architects are subject to both and need to be aware of the substance of each of the codes.

Values

3.03 The Values are stated as follows.

'Honesty, integrity and competency, as we concern for others and for the environment, are the foundations of the Royal Institute's three principles of professional conduct set out below. All members of the Royal Institute are required to comply'.

Principles

3.04 The Code has three principles based on integrity, competence and relationships with others. Each of these is supported by outline guidance notes, which explain how each of these three principles may be upheld, and by more detailed guidance and information in a separate series of nine guidance notes, three for each principle. The guidance notes can also be downloaded from the RIBA web site.

Principle 1: Integrity. Members shall act with honesty and integrity at all times

This principle is supported by the following guidance:

1.1 The Royal Institute expects its Members to act with impartiality, responsibility and truthfulness at all times in their professional and business activities.

1.2 Members should not allow themselves to be improperly influenced either by their own, or others', self-interest.

1.3 Members should not be a party to any statement which they know to be untrue, misleading, unfair to others or contrary to their own professional knowledge.

1.4 Members should avoid conflicts of interest. If a conflict arises, they should declare it to those parties affected and either remove its cause, or withdraw from that situation.

1.5 Members should respect confidentiality and the privacy of others.

1.6 Members should not offer or take bribes in connection with their professional work.

The principle is also supported by three separate Guidance Notes, namely Guidance Note 1: Integrity, Conflicts of Interest, Confidentiality and Privacy, Corruption and Bribery, Guidance Note 2: Competition, and Guidance Note 3: Advertising.

Guidance Note 1 expands on Principle 1, explaining 'Members are expected to act with integrity in all their professional and business activities. This means acting with honesty, fairness and impartiality at all times and not allowing oneself to be improperly influenced either by self-interest or the interests of others' (1.1). This may appear to be self-evident but as practice and construction becomes more complicated the need to emphasise its importance becomes greater. For example, Guidance Note 1 makes it clear that members should not undertake an independent certifying role if connected with the contracting party. If members find themselves in situations inconsistent with their professional obligations they are advised to remove themselves from it and if necessary resign from the commission.

The requirement not to make a statement written or otherwise which is contrary to his knowledge or professional opinion or which he knows to be misleading was first covered in the 1997 version of the code. The new code also advises members not to be party to statements which they know to be 'untrue, misleading, unfair to others, or contrary to their own professional knowledge' and clarifies the obligation by explaining the 'be party to' means not only making such a statement, but also 'acquiescing to its being made by others' (Guidance Note 1).

Conflicts of interest should be declared to the client or employer, and 'if the conflict is unacceptable or cannot be resolved, the member should withdraw from the engagement or resign from the employments' (Guidance Note 1).

Under the 1981 Code there had been a prohibition on simultaneous practice as an independent consultant and involvement as a principal of business trading in land or buildings, property development, auctioneering, estate agency, contracting, manufacturing, or materials supply unless the firm is clearly distinct from the architectural practice. This has been dropped from the code, instead the emphasis is on transparency, with Guidance Note 1 advising 'Members involved in any other business activity which might impact, even indirectly, on their practice of architecture, must declare that involvement to the client or employer before any contract is finalised.' The note does not require this to be in writing, but this would be sensible.

Members are advised to 'adhere to any reasonable contractual provisions regarding confidentiality', to comply with the legal rights of privacy and with the prevailing data protection legislation (Guidance Note 1). This replaces the stronger prohibition not to disclose confidential information or to use it for his own benefit or that of others without the written consent of the parties concerned is slightly wider in scope than Standard 11.6 of the ARB Code.

The requirement not to offer or take bribes in connection with professional work is of long-standing duration. The prohibition on any gifts or inducements has been relaxed somewhat, with Guidance Note 1 stating that the exchange of small gifts and advantages in the normal course of business (such as promotional gifts or corporate hospitality) is not prohibited so long as the value to the recipient is not such that it exerts an improper influence over them. The Note does not specifically prohibit a member from allowing his name to be used in the advertising of any service or product associated with the construction industry, however members should proceed with utmost care as clearly a conflict of interest could develop.

Guidance Note 2: Competition contains advice regarding obtaining work, both in relation to design competitions, and in competitively tendering for work. In both cases it refers to further guidance, namely the RIBA–CIC publication Guidance for Clients on Quality based selection, and to the RIBA Competitions Office.

Guidance Note 3 contains detailed advice about advertising. In particular it emphasises that in advertising members should not imply expertise or resources beyond those which can be provided, or seek to unfairly discredit competitors. The Note states that all marketing and promotional material should:

- be legal, decent, honest and truthful;
- be prepared with a sense of responsibility to consumers, to society generally and to the environment and natural resources;
- respect the principles of fair competition (see Guidance Note 2 on competition); and should not:
- imply expertise or resources beyond those which can be provided;
- unfairly discredit competitors either directly or by implication;
- encourage or condone unacceptable behaviours.

The Note gives guidance on the form of business names, and the use of the term Chartered Architect and the RIBA crest and affix (note that the only Chartered Members who may use the affix without being registered are the fully retired and those in other non-practising types of occupation, for any other non-registered member the use of 'RIBA' would constitute a breach of section 20 of the Architects Act 1997). The note also explains which practices may define themselves as an 'RIBA Chartered Practice'. (In 2007, the Privy Council extended the right to use the 'chartered' status to practices which qualify under the RIBA's Chartered Practice Scheme.)

Principle 2: Competence. In the performance of their work Members shall act competently, conscientiously and responsibly. Members must be able to provide the knowledge, the ability and the financial and technical resources appropriate for their work

This principle is supported by the following guidance:

2.1 Members are expected to apply high standards of skill, knowledge and care in all their work. They must also apply their informed and impartial judgment in reaching any decisions, which may require members having to balance differing and sometimes opposing demands (for example, the stakeholders' interests with the community's and the project's capital costs with its overall performance).

2.2 Members should realistically appraise their ability to undertake and achieve any proposed work. They should also make their clients aware of the likelihood of achieving the client's requirements and aspirations. If members feel they are unable to comply with this, they should not quote for, or accept, the work.

2.3 Members should ensure that their terms of appointment, the scope of their work and the essential project requirements are clear and recorded in writing. They should explain to their clients the implications of any conditions of engagement and how their fees are to be calculated and charged. Members should maintain appropriate records throughout their engagement.

2.4 Members should keep their clients informed of the progress of a project and of the key decisions made on the client's behalf.

2.5 Members are expected to use their best endeavours to meet the client's agreed time, cost and quality requirements for the project.

The principle is also supported by three separate Guidance Notes, namely Guidance Note 4: Appointments, Guidance Note 5: Insurance, and Guidance Note 6: CPD.

The guidance given under 2.2 above is particularly important in practice. It is essential that architects undertake a thorough appraisal of their ability to carry out any proposed commission before accepting it. This includes having the necessary competence and that the practice is adequately resourced (something that may particularly be an issue in times of economic recession). This is underlined in Guidance Note 4. Just as important, and frequently a cause for complaints regarding architects, members are required to make it clear to the client the likelihood of achieving the client's requirements and aspirations. Failure to point out an unrealistic expectations would be a breach of the Code.

Guidance Note 4 reflects the ARB Code requirements regarding the need for a written appointment (4.1 and 4.2) 4.2 sets out what should be covered, which includes a clear statement of the client's requirements, the role of others who are to undertake services, the method of calculation of remuneration, and the provision for termination and dispute resolution. Unlike the ARB Code, the RIBA guidance refers to standard forms of appointment published by the RIBA. Although there is no absolute requirement to use these forms, members are 'encouraged' to do so wherever possible (a useful outline of the 2007 editions is included as GN4 Annex 2007). The Guidance Note requires that the terms are provided to the client at the outset of the project.

Guidance Note 4 also reminds members that if they are registered architects they are obliged under the terms of the ARB's Code to hold professional indemnity insurance and states 'members practising as a principal of an RIBA Registered Practice are also required by the Royal Institute to hold appropriate professional indemnity insurance'. Guidance Note 5 expands on the requirements for insurance, and gives helpful advice as to the key terms and provisions within an adequate PII insurance policy.

The Code does not attempt to define or explain the 'high standards of skill, knowledge and care' which members are expected to apply in all their work. Instead, it refers to Guidance Note 5, which sets out the CPD requirements for members. Under the RIBA's CPD scheme, all chartered members who are practising are required to:

- carry out a minimum of 35 hours of CPD annually;
- achieve a minimum of 100 points each year, of which 50% should be structured CPD wherever possible;

- complete an annual professional development plan; and
- keep records of CPD undertaken.

Principle 3: Relationships. Members shall respect the relevant rights and interests of others

This principle is supported by the following guidance:

3.1 Members should respect the beliefs and opinions of other people, recognise social diversity and treat everyone fairly. They should also have a proper concern and due regard for the effect that their work may have on its users and the local community.

3.2 Members should be aware of the environmental impact of their work.

3.3 Members are expected to comply with good employment practice and the RIBA Employment Policy, in their capacity as an employer or an employee.

3.4 Where members are engaged in any form of competition to win work or awards, they should act fairly and honestly with potential clients and competitors. Any competition process in which they are participating must be known to be reasonable, transparent and impartial. If members find this not to be the case, they should endeavour to rectify the competition process or withdraw.

3.5 Members are expected to have in place (or have access to) effective procedures for dealing promptly and appropriately with disputes or complaints.

The principle is also supported by three separate Guidance Notes, namely Guidance Note 7: Relationships, Guidance Note 8: Employment and Equal Opportunities and Guidance Note 9: Complaints and Dispute Resolution, as well as being supported by Guidance Notes 1 and 2 cited above.

Principle 3 differs in scope from the requirements in that it covers not only relationships with clients, employees, and society at large, but also relations with other members of the RIBA. The undertakings of Principle 3 include many of the matters covered in former versions of the Code. Guidance Note 7 reinforces and expands on some of the advice in Guidance Note 2. For example it states that 'members should neither maliciously nor unfairly seek to damage another member's reputation or practice'. There is also guidance regarding supplanting another architect, e.g. 'Members should not deliberately approach another architect's client in a conscious attempt to take over an active project' and the steps that should be taken when approached to replace another architect. The code does not prevent an architect from undertaking work in situations where another architect has or had an engagement with the same client but the architect is advised to notify the other architect. The undertaking is devised in the interests of both architects but it is often misunderstood. A member engaged to give an opinion on the work of another architect must do so fairly and objectively, based on their own knowledge and experience, and should refrain from personal criticism. Members are required to report to the RIBA any alleged breach of code of which he may become aware and assist the Royal Institute in its investigation, except 'where prevented by law or the courts' (such as an agreed settlement which precludes any further action). The former undertaking that required members to respect and maintain confidentiality in relation to matters involving alleged or proven breaches of the Code has been dropped, as there could be circumstances whereby the same breach ought to be reported to the ARB under its Code.

Members are required to report any disqualification from acting as a Director, and are warned that any criminal conviction which relates in any way to a member's practice of architecture may be regarded as sufficient grounds for automatic expulsion from membership. Although 7.11 of the Guidance does not require the conviction to be reported, it might be sensible to do this, and to note that it may in any event be reported under 7.10 above.

Guidance Note 8 covers employment, and may be particularly relevant in periods of recession. Unlawful discrimination is prohibited, and members are required to comply with all employment law. The Note refers to the RIBA Employment Policy, adopted in 2004. In particular, with regard to students, employer are required to 'have due regard for the employee's general training and education in accordance with the objectives of the RIBA's Professional Experience and Development Record Scheme (PEDR)', and are required to provide them with a written contract (the RIBA publishes a model form), to provide them with a mentor, and with a reasonable breadth of experience, and to permit them time to attend courses.

Guidance Note 5 deals with dispute resolution and complaints, to support the requirement that 'Members are expected to have in place (or have access to) effective procedures for dealing promptly and appropriately with disputes or complaints'. If the complaint cannot be resolved internally, members, attention is drawn to the Royal Institute's various independent Alternative Dispute Resolution (ADR) services, which include mediation, adjudication and arbitration, and an Annex to the Note gives a brief outline of these processes.

4 Statement of Professional Conduct of the Royal Incorporation of Architects in Scotland (RIAS)

4.01 The Architects Act 1997 applies throughout the United Kingdom and as elsewhere an architect practising in Scotland is subject to its Code. In addition the architect members of the Royal Incorporation of Architects and architect members of the Royal Institute of British Architects are subject to their respective codes. Many architects belong to both bodies and as such are subject to requirements of all three codes.

4.02 The existence of a separate RIAS Code stems from the Incorporation's Charter of 1922 and consequent By-laws, which call for a Declaration to be made by all who join. This statement of principle is the basis against which any alleged complaint is judged. The RIAS Council has authority to publish intimations illustrating good practice behaviour and which, in the breach, require investigation and possible disciplinary sanctions. These comprise, as with RIBA: reprimand, suspension and expulsion. The Charter authorises the by-laws. The most recent version of the by-laws is dated 22 January 2004. Any member joining RIAS signs a Declaration that they will not conduct themselves 'in a manner which in the opinion of the Special Committee of the Disciplinary Panel is derogatory to his or her professional character or engaging in any occupation which in the opinion of the Special Committee of the Disciplinary Panel is inconsistent with the profession of an architect'.

4.03 It is a prerequisite of membership of RIAS that applicants demonstrate their registration with ARB. For this reason the first intimation of every Statement of Professional Conduct, published since 1982, has been to bind active architect members explicitly to the code requirements of the registration body.

Prior to the 1997 Act, the 1931 Act which governed the activity of the Architects Registration Council of the United Kingdom (ARCUK), made it difficult and cumbersome for ARCUK to deal with complaints. For this reason the RIAS published additional intimations which enabled it to address complaints effectively and efficiently in Scotland, the numbers increasing during the later 1980s and into the 1990s as consumerism advanced.

4.04 However, the possibilities of one complaint being subject to three separate sets of investigations under three distinct codes (RIAS, RIBA and ARB) was considered to be extremely undesirable. As soon as a clear and robust code emerged from ARB with its second edition in September 1999, it became possible to start to address revisions to the RIAS Code, and in particular the intimations.

At the same time arrangements were put in place to refer all serious complaints directly to ARB in recognition of its statutory role and powers.

4.05 The 1993 RIAS Statement included 16 intimations, one of which incorporated a six-point set of Client Account Rules. The intimations dealt with a range of issues including carrying Professional Indemnity Insurance and undertaking Continuing Professional Development, having proper forms of agreement in place for appointments with an architect in control. The code had attempted to deal with competitive fee-tendering by referral to set procedures, and included reference to advertising, and promotion.

Reviewing the ARB Code made clear that the majority of the intimations could be swept away, as they could now be dealt with by ARB, and slight differences between Codes would cause confusion.

4.06 The January 2000 RIAS Statement therefore only included two intimations, the second of which regulated behaviour between RIAS members and 'employees, employers, professional colleagues and business associates'. This required members to notify another member if they had been invited or instructed to proceed with work on a project that another member had been engaged with.

Secondly, it required members not to attempt to supplant another member.

And thirdly, it required – subject to a member's right and obligations under the ARB Code – that members having any matter of complaint or protest against another member, to notify the Secretary of the Incorporation, and make no other protest.

4.07 After a further year, it became clear that ARB was not specifically concerned under its code with the specifics of the obligations related to continuing professional development. The Incorporation therefore approved a further adjustment to its Statement in February 2001 clarifying members' obligations as individuals and as employers, and emphasising the need to record their activity.

4.08 By the summer of 2003, however, it became clear that with new forms of procurement (including on-line fee bidding) and further interest by the Office of Fair Trading in any code aspects that could inhibit competition (i.e. the curb on attempting to supplant), the supplementary intimations were no longer appropriate.

From June 2003, therefore, the RIAS Code incorporates merely the ARB Code under Intimation 1.

4.09 RIAS Council, in agreeing this step, approved plans for continuing to issue wise counsel to members on matters of behaviour, via its other organs of communication, and dealing with matters of dispute or complaint (particularly between members) through conciliation, via a panel of members with appropriate experience.

4.10 The sanction of RIAS disciplinary procedures remain in place, however, to deal with behaviour about which ARB would have no interest, as it has no consumer-related aspects, but which could be seen to be damaging the Incorporation and thus in breach of the Declaration.

4.11 At the same time, RIAS staff continue to handle a wide range of complaints from third parties – most often clients – giving advice and assistance where possible to indicate ways in which difficulties can be overcome. For any serious complaints, complainants are referred to ARB.

4.12 The RIAS Charter and by-laws have been subject also to substantial revision during 2001–2003 as a result of the realignment of roles vis-à-vis RIBA, post the devolution settlement of 1999. The greater clarity between the respective roles of ARB, RIBA and RIAS is welcome, and is reflected in the current simplicity of the RIAS Statement of Professional Conduct.

4.13 The Statement of Professional Conduct:
A member shall be bound by the Declaration signed upon election and in particular of the responsibility for upholding the repute of the Royal Incorporation as a professional body and of fellow members as individuals. Actions inconsistent with the Declaration shall be held to constitute unprofessional conduct and as such will be dealt with by Council in accordance with by-law 16.1.

The Declaration:

'I declare that I have read the Charter and by-laws of the said Incorporation and the by-laws of my chapter, and will be governed and bound thereby, and will submit myself to every part thereof and to any alterations thereof which may hereafter be made until I have ceased to be a member: and that by every lawful means in my power I will advance the interests and objects of the said Incorporation.'

4.14 By-law 18 clearly sets out the current position – by-law 18 clarifying the role of RIAS vis-à-vis ARB:

18 Discipline

18.1 The Council shall put in place formal procedures for handling of complaints.

18.2 Any Member contravening the Declaration signed by the Member or conducting himself or herself in a manner which in the opinion of the Special Committee of the Disciplinary Panel is derogatory to his or her professional character or engaging in any occupation which in the opinion of the Special Committee of the Disciplinary Panel is inconsistent with the profession of an architect shall following investigation and disciplinary procedures as approved by the Council from time to time be liable to reprimand, suspension or expulsion.

18.3 Where a complaint against a member is considered and determined by the Architects Registration Board or any successor to it, the Council shall be entitled to accept, adopt and apply the findings of the Architects Registration Board both in relation to the merits of the complaint and any penalty imposed as being the appropriate disposal of a complaint involving a breach of by-law 18.2 without holding any further enquiry or proceedings provided always that the Council shall have before it a copy certified by the Clerk or other authorised official of the Architects Registration Board of their findings. The Council shall not however be obliged if it so resolves to adopt and apply the determination of the Architects Registration Board.

4.15 As can be seen from the wording of by-law 18.2, where a complaint is submitted to RIAS it is in practice considered in the first place by the Secretary (or Chief Executive, if such is appointed), who, on a direction from the President, remits the complaint to an Investigation Committee. The Investigation Committee carries out preliminary work to identify whether there is a case to answer. It submits a report to the Council of RIAS who then determine whether or not to act on any recommendation to establish the Special Committee of the Disciplinary Panel referred to in by-law 18.2.

4.16 If such a Special Committee of the Disciplinary Panel is set up (members of the Disciplinary Panel are appointed for periods from time to time and do not require to be members of the Council of RIAS), then the RIAS Legal Adviser is instructed to prosecute before that Committee the case made against the member. A formal written complaint is formulated and then served on the respondent member who has the opportunity to submit written answers. Thereafter a formal hearing is convened. The RIAS Legal Adviser has the responsibility to present the evidence which can be cross-examined by the respondent or any representative of the respondent. The respondent can then present any evidence that is considered relevant and necessary. The Special Committee of the Disciplinary Panel appoints an independent lawyer, typically a QC of the Scots Bar, to act as its adviser for the conduct of the proceedings.

At the conclusion of the proceedings, the Special Committee advises RIAS and the respondent of its opinion and submits a report to RIAS Council. RIAS Council then consider the opinion of the Special Committee and any recommendation it may have made in relation to penalty. Again, the independent legal adviser would be present at the meeting of RIAS Council for this limited purpose and RIAS Council would then decide on any penalty to be imposed.

Bibliography

General construction law

Duncan Wallace, I. (1994) *Hudson's Building and Engineering Contracts* (11th edn) (1st Supplement 2003) Sweet & Maxwell, London

Furst, S. and Ramsey, V. (eds) (2006) *Keating on Construction Contracts* (8th edn) Sweet & Maxwell, London

Lloyd, H. and Bartlett, A. (eds) (2002) *Emden's Construction Law* (9th edn) (looseleaf) Lexis Nexis Butterworths, London

Marsden, S. and Makepeace, P. (2003) *Construction and Engineering Law: A Guide for Project Managers,* Butterworths Tolley, London

Uff, J. (2009) *Construction Law* (10th edn) Sweet & Maxwell, London

Wilmot-Smith, R. (2006) *Construction Contracts: Law and Practice,* Oxford University Press, Oxford

General liability: contract and tort

Beale, H. (2008) *Chitty on Contracts* (30th edn) Sweet & Maxwell, London

Buckley, R. (2005) *The Law of Negligence* (4th edn) Lexis Nexis Butterworths, London

Cooke, J. (2009) *Law of Tort* (9th edn) Pearson Education, Harlow

Dugdale, A. (ed) (2005) *Clerk and Lindsell on Torts* (19th edn) Sweet & Maxwell, London

Furmston, M. (2006) *Cheshire Fifoot and Furmston's Law of Contract* (15th edn) Oxford University Press, Oxford

Lewison, K. (2007) *The Interpretation of Contracts* (4th edn) Sweet & Maxwell, London

Murphy, J. (2007) *Street on Torts* (12th edn) Oxford University Press, Oxford

Murray, R. (2008) *Contract Law – The Fundamentals* Sweet & Maxwell, London

Rogers, W. (2006) *Winfield and Jolowicz on Tort* (17th edn) Sweet & Maxwell, London

Treitel, G. (2007) *The Law of Contract* (12th edn) Sweet & Maxwell, London

Wood, S. Walton, C. Cooper, R. and Percy, R. (2006) *Charlesworth and Percy on Negligence* (11th edn) Sweet & Maxwell, London

Construction contract law

Adriaanse, J. (2007) *Construction Contract Law* (2nd edn) Palgrave Macmillan, Basingstoke

Baker, E. and Champion, R. (2008) *Tendering and Procurement in Construction Case in Point* RICS Books, London

Barnes, P. (2006) *The JCT 05 Standard Building Sub-Contracts* Blackwell Publishing, Oxford

Chappell, D. (2006) *Construction Contracts: Questions and Answers* Taylor and Francis, London

Chappell, D. (2007) *Understanding JCT Standard Building Contracts* (8th edn) Taylor and Francis, London

Davidson, J. (2006) *JCT 2005 What's new?* RICS Books, London

Huse, J. (2002) *Understanding and Negotiating Turnkey and EPC Contracts* (2nd edn) Sweet & Maxwell, London

Jones, D. Savage, D. and Westgate, R. (2003) *Partnering and Collaborative Working: Legal and Industry Practice* LLP Professional Publishing, London

Lupton, S. (2007) *Which Contract?* RIBA Publications, London

Murdoch, J. and Hughes, W. (2007) *Construction Contracts: Law and Management* (4th edn) Taylor and Francis, London

Ndekugri, I. and Rycroft, M. (2009) *The JCT 05 Standard Building Contract Law and Administration* Butterworth Heinemann, Oxford

Roe, S. and Jenkins, J. (2003) *Partnering and Alliancing in Construction Projects* Sweet & Maxwell, London

Williamson, A. (2006) *Keating on JCT Contracts* Sweet & Maxwell, London

Construction contract administration and claims

Birkby, G. Ponte, A. and Alderson, F. (2008) *Good Practice Guide: Extensions of Time* RIBA Publishing, London

Carnell, N. (2005) *Causation and Delay in Construction Disputes* (2nd edn) Blackwell Publishing, Oxford

Chappell, D. (2006) *Contractual Correspondence for Architects and Project Managers* (4th edn) Wiley Blackwell, Oxford

Constable, A. and Lamont, C. (2007) *Construction Claims Case in Point* RICS Books, London

Davison, R. and Mullen, J. (2008) *Evaluating Contract Claims* (2nd edn) Wiley-Blackwell, Oxford

Eggleston, B. (2008) *Liquidated Damages and Extensions of Time* (3rd edn) Wiley-Blackwell, Oxford

Jamieson, N. (2009) *Good Practice Guide: Inspecting Works* RIBA Publishing, London

Keane, P. and Caletka, A. (2008) *Delay Analysis in Construction Contracts* Wiley-Blackwell, Oxford

Lamont, C. and Scott Holland, G. (2007) *Contract Administration Case in Point* RICS Books, London

Pickavance, K. (2005) *Delay and Disruption in Construction Contracts* (3rd edn) Informa Legal, London

Dispute Resolution

Baker, E. and Lavers, A. (2005) *Expert Witness Case in Point* RICS Books, London

Chern, C. (2007) *Chern on Dispute Boards* Blackwell Publishing, Oxford

Coulson, P. (2008) *Construction Adjudication* Oxford University Press, Oxford.

Davis, M. and Akenhead, R. (2006) *The Technology and Construction Court* Oxford University Press, Oxford.

Harris, B. Planterose, R. and Tecks, J. (2007) *The Arbitration Act 1996 A Commentary* (4th edn) Blackwell Science, Oxford

Jenkins, J. and Stebbings, S. (2006) *International Construction Arbitration Law* Kluwer Law International

Kendall, J. Freedman, C and Farrell, J. (2008) *Expert Determination* (4th edn) Sweet & Maxwell, London

Mackie, K. Miles, D. Marsh, W and Allen, T. (2007) *The ADR Practice Guide: Commercial Dispute Resolution* (3rd edn) Tottel Publishing, Hayward's Heath

Merkin, R. and Flannery, L. (2008) *Arbitration Act 1996* (4th edn) Informa Publishing, London

Mills, R. (2005) *Construction Adjudication Case In Point* RICS Books, London

Morgan, D. (2008) *Dispute Avoidance* RIBA Publishing, London

Richbell, D. (2008) *Mediation of Construction Disputes* Blackwell Publishing, Oxford

Sutton, D. Gill, J. and Gearing, M. (2007) *Russell on Arbitration* (23rd edn) Sweet & Maxwell, London

Tackaberry, J. and Marriott, A. (eds) (2003) *Bernstein's Handbook of Arbitration and Dispute Resolution Practice* (4th edn) Sweet & Maxwell, London

Professional and construction liability

Barrett, K. (2008) *Defective Construction Work* Wiley-Blackwell, Oxford

Cornes, D. and Winward, R. (2002) *Winward Fearon on Collateral Warranties* (2nd edn) Wiley-Blackwell, Oxford

Lamont, C. and Constable, A. (2006) *Building Defects Case in Point* RICS Books, London

Patten, B. (2003) *Professional Negligence in Construction* Taylor & Francis, London

Patterson, F. (2005) *Professional Indemnity Insurance Explained* RIBA Publications, London

Powell, J. Stewart, R. and Jackson, R. (2008) *Jackson and Powell on Professional Liability* (6th edn) Sweet & Maxwell, London

Partnership and Company Law

Banks, R. (2002) *Lindley and Banks on Partnership* (18th edn) (2nd Supplement 2007) Sweet & Maxwell, London

Blackett-Ord, M. (2007) *Partnership Law* (3rd edn) Tottel Publishing, Hayward's Heath

Davies, P. (2008) *Gower and Davies Principles of Modern Company Law* (8th edn) Sweet & Maxwell, London

Keenan, D. (2006) *Smith and Keenan's Law for Business* (13th edn) Pearson Education, Harlow

Mayson, S. French, D. and Ryan, C. (2009) *Mayson, French and Ryan on Company Law* (26th edn) Oxford University Press, Oxford

Morse, G. (2006) *Partnership Law* (6th edn) Oxford University Press, Oxford

Walmsley, K. (2009) *Butterworths Company Law Handbook* (23rd edn) LexisNexis, London

Employment Law

Bell, A. (2006) *Employment Law* (2nd edn) Sweet & Maxwell, London

Bowers, J. (2009) *A Practical Approach to Employment Law* (8th edn) Oxford University Press, Oxford

Deakin, S. and Morris, G. (2009) *Labour Law* (5th edn) Hart Publishing, Oxford

Leighton, P. and Proctor, G. (2006) *Effective Recruitment: A Practical Guide* (2nd edn) Thorogood, London

Pitt, G. (2009) *Employment Law* (7th edn) Sweet & Maxwell, London

Ryley, M. and Goodwyn, E. (2008) *Employment Law for the Construction Industry* (2nd edn) Thomas Telford, London

Copyright and Intellectual Property

Britta, M. and Gage, L. (2005) *Design Law: Protecting and Exploiting Rights* Law Society Publishing, London

Cornish, W. and Llewellyn, D. (2007) *Intellectual Property: Patents, Copyrights, Trademarks and Allied Rights* (6th edn) Sweet & Maxwell, London

Garnett, K. Davies, G. and Harbottle, G. (2005) *Copinger and Skone James on Copyright* (15th edn) (3rd Supplement 2009) Sweet & Maxwell, London

Hart, T. Fazzani, L. and Clark, S. (2009) *Intellectual Property Law* (5th edn) Palgrave Macmillan Law, Basingstoke

Torremans, P. (2008) *Holyoak and Torremans Intellectual Property Law* (5th edn) Oxford University Press, Oxford

Property Law and Obligations relating to land

Aldridge, T. (2009) *Boundaries, Wall and Fences* (10th edn) Sweet & Maxwell, London

Chynoweth, P. (2007) *The Party Wall Casebook* (2nd edn) Blackwell Publishing, Oxford

Garner, S. and Frith, A. (2008) *A Practical Approach to Landlord and Tenant* (5th edn) Oxford University Press, Oxford

Gaunt, J. and Morgan, J. (2008) *Gale on the Law of Easements* (18th edn) Sweet & Maxwell, London

Gray, K. and Gray, S. (2008) *Elements of Land Law* (5th edn) Oxford University Press, Oxford

Hannaford, S. and Stephens, J. (2004) *Party Walls Case in Point* RICS Books, London

Hannaford, S. Stephens, J. and O'Hagan, R. (2008) *Rights to Light: Case in Point* RICS Books, London

Harpum, C. Bridge, S. and Dixon, M. (2008) *Megarry & Wade: The Law of Real Property* (7th edn) Sweet & Maxwell, London

Isaac, N. and Walsh, M. (2008) *Easements and other Rights Case in Point* RICS Books, London

Mynors, C. (2002) *The Law of Trees and Forestry* Sweet & Maxwell, London

Powell, D. (2009) *Boundary Disputes and How to Resolve Them* (4th edn) RICS Books, London

Sara, C. (2007) *Boundaries and Easements* (4th edn) Sweet & Maxwell, London

Planning and other Regulatory Law

Coren, P. and Collins, J. (2006) *Good Practice Guide: Negotiating the Planning Maze* RIBA Publishing, London

Duxbury, R. (2009) *Telling & Duxbury's Planning Law and Procedure* (14th edn) Oxford University Press, Oxford

Griffiths, O. (2007) *Understanding the CDM Regulations* Taylor & Francis, London

Joyce, R. (2007) *CDM Regulations 2007 Explained* Thomas Telford, London

Moore, V. (2008) *A Practical Approach to Planning Law* (10th edn) Oxford University Press, Oxford

Mynors, C. (2006) *Listed Buildings, Conservation Areas and Monuments* (4th edn) Sweet & Maxwell, London

Polley, S. (2008) *Understanding the Building Regulations* (4th edn) Spon Press, London

Tricker, R. (2007) *Building Regulations in Brief* (5th edn) Butterworth Heinemann, Oxford

European and EU Law

Bovis, C. (2008) *EU Public Procurement Law* Edward Elgar Publishing, Cheltenham

Craig, P. and de Burca, G. (2007) *EU Law Text, Cases and Materials* (4th edn) Oxford University Press, Oxford

Davies, K. (2006) *Understanding EU Law* (3rd edn) Routledge-Cavendish, London

Kaczorowska, A. (2008) *European Union Law* Routledge-Cavendish, London

Kramer, L. (2006) *EU Environmental Law* (6th edn) Sweet & Maxwell, London

Musker, D. (2002) *Community Design Law: Principles and Practice* Sweet & Maxwell, London

Twigg-Flesner, C. (2008) *The Europeanisation of Contract Law* Routledge-Cavendish, London

Scots Law

Anderson, R. (2000) *A Practical Guide to Adjudication in Construction* W. Green, Edinburgh

Davidson, F. (2000) *Arbitration in Scotland* W. Green, Edinburgh

Davidson, F. and MacGregor, L. (2008) *Commercial Law in Scotland* (2nd edn) W. Green, Edinburgh

Gibb, A. (2009) *Contract Law Basics* W. Green, Edinburgh

Macaulay, M. and Ramsey, L. (2002) *Construction and Procurement Law* W. Green, Edinburgh

Stewart, W. (2004) *Delict* (4th edn) W. Green, Edinburgh

Walker, D. (2002) *Prescription and Limitation of Actions* (6th edn) W. Green, Edinburgh

Table of Statutes and Statutory Instruments

Table of Cases

391

Table of Legislation

European Legislation

International legislation

Index

lost modern grant doctrine, easements, 36
Low Carbon Building Standards Strategy for Scotland (Sullivan Report), 115–117
Lugano Convention, conflicts of laws, 370

mains, construction of, 64, 71
Malaysia, international work by architects, 367
management contracting
  advantages, 222
  and collateral warranties, 230
  disadvantages, 223
  procurement options, 174
manager burdens (Scotland), 52
material, rights of, 211–212
maternity, parental and family-related rights, 356
measurement contracts, procurement options, 174
mechanical ventilation and air conditioning (Scottish Regulations), 108
mediation
  agreement, 279
  background, 277
  Model Agreement, 278
  National Mediation Helpline, 278
  practical points, 279
  preparation for mediator, 278
  principles, 277
  reaching agreement to mediate, 277–278
  selection of best time for, 279
  selection of mediator, 278
  structures, 278–279
  typical process, 277–279
'mere puffs', and misrepresentation, 15
metering, 108
metropolitan districts, England, 57
minor works, JCT Documents, 219
misrepresentation
  damages for, 16
  negligent mis-statement, law of, 16
  reliance, 15–16
  remedies for, 16
  and representation, 15
  statement of existing fact, 15
missives, sale of land and buildings (Scotland), 51
mitigation, liability of architect, 330
moral rights, 349–350
mortgages, 32, 40
Mosaic Law of King Hammurbai of Persia, 91
moveable property (Scotland), 49
MSPs (Members of Scottish Parliament), 43, 44

National House Builders' Council (NHBC), 51
national parks, Scotland, 70
National Planning Framework (Scotland), 133, 135
National Planning Policy Guidelines (NPPG), Scotland, 133
National Register of Access Consultants, 83
Natural England, 61
natural justice
  arbitration, 257
  defences, enforcement proceedings, 276
  inability to reach fair decision, 274
natural lighting, Building (Scottish Regulations), 105
NEC3 Professional Services Contract (June 2005), 175
  acceptance, 210
  additional conditions of contract (Option Z), 210
  adjudication (England and Wales), 213
  changes in law (Option X2), 209
  collateral warranty agreement (Option x8), 210
  compensation events, 211
  Concise Conditions of Appointment for an Architect, 209, 213–214
  consultant's obligations, 210
  and Contracts (Rights of Third Parties) Act 1999, 210
  core clauses, 210
  defects, correcting, 211
  delayed damages (Option X7), 209–210
  Domestic Project Agreement for the Appointment of an Architect (D-CON-07-A), 214
  Framework Contract for appointment of service suppliers, 209
  indemnity, 212
  instructions to stop/not to start work, 211
  insurance cover, 212
  interpretation of law, 210
  liability, 212, 215
  limitation of liability (Option X18), 210
  material, rights of, 211–212
  Memorandum of Agreement, 213
  Model Letter (ML-C-07), 214
  Option Clauses, 211
  parties' main responsibilities, 210–211

payment, 211, 214–215
publicity, 212
quality, 211
set-off rights, lack of, 215
SFA/99 (Standard Form of Architect's appointment) compared with, 209, 210, 212–213, 214
Standard Conditions of Appointment of an Architect, 214–215
suspension and determination, 213
termination, 213
  consultant's data, 212
  contract data, 212
  by employer (Option X11), 210
  Standard Form of Agreement for the Appointment of an Architect (SFA/99) (RIBA), 212–213
third party agreements, 213
time issues, 211
transfer of rights (Option X9), 210
nee vi, nee clam, nec precario (long use by claimant over right over land), 36, 37
negative burdens, Scotland, 51
negligence
  breach of duty, 22–23
  and collateral warranties, 228
  and contract law, 22
  definition of 'neighbours', 228
  duty of care in, 21–22, 228
  foreseeability of harm, 21, 23
  legal duty to take care, 21–22
  liability for negligent conduct, 24
  negligent mis-statement, law of, 16, 24
  and nuisance, 27
  professional, *see* professional negligence
  Scots law, 47
  'three-stage test', 22
  'two-stage test', 21, 22
negotiated procedure, public works contract awards, 144, 146
'neighbour' principle, duty of care, 21, 29
Netherlands, international work by architects, 366
New Engineering Contract (NEC)
  Professional Services Contract, 309
  standard forms of contract, *see* NEC3 Professional Services Contract (June 2005)
noise, 66, 107
Nominated Sub-contracts/Nominated Subcontract Conditions, JCT Documents, 217
non-natural user, concept, 28
Northern Ireland
  common law, 3
  Northern Ireland Assembly, 6
Notice of Irregularity, England and Wales, 80
Notice of Objection, England and Wales, 80
notour bankruptcy, 305
nuisance, 26–28
  and easements, 34
  Scots land law, 53
nursing homes, Scotland, 72

obiter dicta (things said by the way), 4
offer and revocation of, 11, 12
Office of Public Sector Information, 44
Official Certificate of Search, 33
'officious bystander' test, terms of contract, 13
open procedure, public works contract awards, 144, 146
Ordem dos Arquitectos (OA), Portuguese registration authority, 367
Ordinary Maternity Leave (OML), 356
Ordnance Survey maps, 34, 35
Outer House, Court of Session (Scotland), 46, 363
overpayments/additional expenditure, 330
overriding objective, Civil Procedure Rules, 258
ownership of land
  Crown, 5, 49
  pro indiviso, 50
  Scots law
    abolition of feudal tenure, 49–50, 52
    divided ownership, 50–51
    freehold or leasehold non-existent, 50
    shared ownership, 50

parishes, rural, 57
Parliament
  European, 140, 141
  Scottish, 6, 43–44
  United Kingdom, 4, 44
Partner Authority Scheme (PAS), 78
partnerships
  assignation, 305
  associates, 296
  bankruptcy, 305

clarity, importance of, 295
versus companies, 301
  see also companies
copyright, 344
deed of partnership, 296
defined, 295
dissolution of, 298
formation, 295
'holding out' to be partners, 296
liability, 297–298, 305
limited, 306
limited liability, 298–299, 306
name of practice, 296, 304
new partners, 305
property, 305
relationship of partners one to another, 298, 304–305
retiring partners, 305
rights of partners, 296–297
rights to which partners not entitled, 297
in Scotland, 46–47, 304–306
separate legal entity (Scotland), 305
sequestration, 305
sharing facilities and profits, 295–296
size of practice, 296
termination, 306
types of partner, 296
party walls, 155–159
  award, 156
  boundary structures, Scotland, 158–159
  building owner's rights, 157–158
  common interest doctrine, 158
  definitions, 155
  fence walls, 155
  Foundation Notice, 155
  legal presumption, 35
  Line of Junction Notice, 155
  notices, 155–156
  party structures/Party Structure Notices, 155
  Party Wall etc Act 1996, 155, 158
  Schedule of Condition, 156, 157
  surveyors, 156
payment provisions
  advance payments code, private streets, 65
  collateral warranties, 316
  Housing Grants Construction and Regeneration Act 1996 (HGCRA)
    contracts excluded from payment provisions, 241–242
    dates for payment, 243–244
    instalment payments, 242–243
    notice to withhold payment, 244–246
    'pay when paid' clauses, 242, 246–247
    right to suspend performance for non-payment, 246
  JCT Standard Form of Building Contract (2005 edition)
    certificates, 198–200, 207
    changes to payment regime, 199–200
    contract sum and adjustments, 195
    fluctuations, 200–202
    Gross Valuation and interim certificates, 200
    interim certificates, 199
    loss and expense, 201
    NEC3 Professional Services Contract (June 2005), 211, 214–215
    non-payment of certificates, 207
    off-site materials, valuation, 200
    retention, 200
  late payment of debts, interest on, 247
  standard forms of building contract, 218, 222
pedestrian protective barriers, safety requirements, Building (Scotland) Regulations 2004, 106
performance of contract, partial, right to sue and remedies, 16
permissive waste, 38
personal injury
  compensation for accidents at work, 363
  duty of care in tort, 324
  liability of contractors, 204–205
personal right, defined, 49
pet shops, statutory authorities, 67
petroleum, statutory authorities, 67
photographs
  definitions, 342
  exceptions to copyright infringement, 344
  and moral rights, 350
pipes, ducts and vessels, insulation under Scottish Regulations, 107
plaintiffs, 9
planning advice notes (PANs), Scotland, 133